Ireland

Fionn Davenport

James Bainbridge, Amanda Canning, Tom Downs, Catherine Le Nevez,
Ryan Ver Berkmoes, Neil Wilson

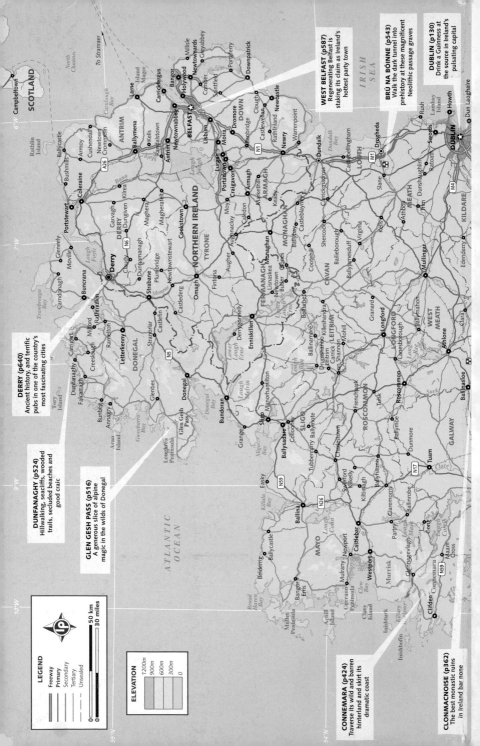

DERRY (p640)
Ancient history, and terrific pubs in one of the country's most fascinating cities

DUNFANAGHY (p524)
Hillwalking, seacliffs, wooded trails, secluded beaches and good craic

GLEN GESH PASS (p516)
A generous slice of alpine magic in the wilds of Donegal

CONNEMARA (p424)
Traverse its wild and barren hinterland and skirt its dramatic coast

CLONMACNOISE (p362)
The best monastic ruins in Ireland bar none

WEST BELFAST (p587)
Regenerating Belfast is staking its claim as Ireland's hottest party town

BRÚ NA BÓINNE (p543)
Walk the dark tunnel into prehistory at these magnificent Neolithic passage graves

DUBLIN (p130)
Drink a Guinness at the source in Ireland's pulsating capital

LEGEND

Freeway
Primary
Secondary
Tertiary
Unsealed

0   50 km
0   30 miles

ELEVATION

1200m
900m
600m
300m
0

SCOTLAND

NORTHERN IRELAND

ATLANTIC OCEAN

IRISH SEA

North Channel

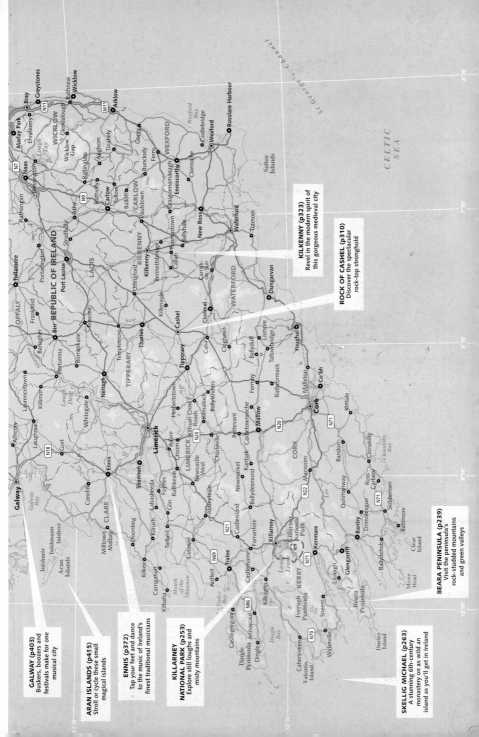

GALWAY (p403)
Buskers, boozers and festivals make for one musical city

ARAN ISLANDS (p415)
Stroll or cycle these small magical islands

ENNIS (p372)
Tap your feet and dance to the music of Ireland's finest traditional musicians

KILLARNEY NATIONAL PARK (p253)
Explore still loughs and misty mountains

SKELLIG MICHAEL (p263)
A stunning 6th-century monastery on as wild an island as you'll get in Ireland

BEARA PENINSULA (p239)
Visit the peninsula's rock-studded mountains and green valleys

ROCK OF CASHEL (p310)
Discover the spectacular rock-top stronghold

KILKENNY (p323)
Revel in the modern spirit of this gorgeous medieval city

On the Road

FIONN DAVENPORT Coordinating Author
Taken in front of City Hall (p96), illustrating two important points: when the summer sun shines, shorts and short sleeves make a mockery of Dublin's rainy reputation and cycling is by far the best way to get around the city, especially if you're a travel writer on a deadline.

JAMES BAINBRIDGE This was snapped on the rocks at Derrynane National Historic Park (p265), while walking off lunch at the Blind Piper (p266). Later we descended to the beach, where an old man said my kagool-wrapped friend looked like Tom Crean. 'Who's he?' asked my friend. 'Google him,' came the canny old Kerryman's reply.

AMANDA CANNING I'd taken the coastal path out to Charles Fort (p218), nibbling wild garlic along the way. The views across the sparkling water back to Kinsale and out to the Atlantic were simply stunning. Coming back I stumbled across the wonderful Harbour Bar (p223) and a glorious day turned into a memorable night.

TOM DOWNS A woman in Sligo shared with me her observation that 'In Ireland, Americans like to take pictures of sheep'. I decided to take the concept a notch further and shoot a self portrait – with sheep. This was in County Donegal, in a field I walked through to reach St Colmcille's birthplace (p529).

RYAN VER BERKMOES St Patrick's Day in Limerick, does it get any more Irish than that? Well it does, because it was pissing down rain to boot – or on my boots. I took shelter in this pub and took solace in this pint. Even though the state of Irish beer is deplorable, (the Guinness is getting colder, milder and more quaffable; what pub has something other than bland international brews like Heineken and Budweiser along with the toothless Smithwicks and a flavour-free stout?), on this day with these people it was the best pint ever.

CATHERINE LE NEVEZ Galway promises to be brilliant craic but potentially disastrous for my research schedule when I'm invited to the pub over the road from where I'm staying for a 'quick pint'… which later goes on to see the pub's regulars pouring their own behind the bar. Ah, sure; when in Rome…

NEIL WILSON Exploring off the beaten track is one of the best bits of researching a Lonely Planet guide. As Robert Byron wrote, 'The supreme moments of travel are born of beauty and strangeness in equal parts', and Cuilcagh Mountain (p483), on the border between Counties Fermanagh and Cavan, is both strange and beautiful – an otherworldly plateau of fractured gritstone rising above a sea of blanket bog. One of the most interesting hikes I've ever done.

For author bios see p734

Ireland Highlights

With the depth of its compelling history, the jaw-dropping beauty of its landscapes, and the warmth of its people – and its pubs – Ireland is a small country packed tight with unforgettable experiences. Here's what our authors, staff and travellers love most about it – share your Irish highlights at lonelyplanet.com/bluelist.

OLIVER STREWE

1 DUBLIN PUBS

Immerse yourself in the history, heritage and hedonism of Dublin, the city that carries itself like the capital it is but feels like a friendly provincial town, no more so than in any of its 1000-odd pubs (p130).

Fionn Davenport, author and Dubliner

INISHMÓR (GALWAY)

We spent a long weekend in winter on the three rugged little islands sitting off the west coast. On the first morning on Inishmór (p417), we cycled up and down farm lanes lined with dry-stone walls and wandered around the ruins, then the weather turned to shite so we ran for the pub and spent the afternoon drinking Guinness, eating pies and counting Aran jumpers.

Liz Heynes, Lonely Planet, Melbourne

2

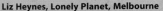

IRELAND'S BEST COASTAL WALK (DERRY & ANTRIM)

Put on your walking boots, shoulder your rucksack and set off along one of Ireland's finest coastal walks, stretching for 16km between the swaying rope bridge of Carrick-a-Rede (p664) and the grand geological flourish of the Giant's Causeway (p662).

Neil Wilson, author

3

GLENDALOUGH (WICKLOW)

Glendalough (p152) is basically a beautiful valley with two huge lakes, an old monastic sight, and an amazing opportunity for hiking, but the scenery is the real reason to go. In the spring, both the drive there (which is through Wicklow) and the actual place itself are breathtaking.

Pengy, Thorn Tree member

RICHARD CUMMINS

BALTIMORE (CORK)

A more romantic place than Baltimore (p229) I can't imagine. It also has one of the finest pubs in all of Ireland: to sit on the square outside Bushe's Bar (p230) with a crab sandwich and a Guinness, watching the activity in the harbour and in Roaring Water Bay with the islands and mountains in the background...getting the picure?

tony_b, Thorn Tree member

LEFT:GARETH MCCORMACK

RICHARD CUMMINS

KINSALE (CORK)

This charming harbour town (p218) is known for its culinary delights, and rightfully so! Stroll along the quay, take in a picnic near the lighthouse and sample some of Ireland's finest foods.

marally, Bluelist contributor

TRADITIONAL MUSIC

Whether it's the haunting refrain of an old Gaelic ode or the rousing heights of a modern-day jig, Irish music stands out for its creativity, enjoyability and sheer pervasiveness. From tiny rural pubs where a few codgers give an impromptu session with little more than a couple of spoons to Dublin's heaving music venues, where the inheritors of U2's mantle jam every night, music is a major part of Irish life for locals and visitors alike. And, it goes well with beer!

Ryan Ver Berkmoes, author

7

DOUG MCKINLAY

SLIEVE LEAGUE (DONEGAL)

Remote and rugged, Slieve League (p514) are the highest sea cliffs in all of Europe (600m plus). It's a perfect cycle from Donegal town, with great little ocean road detours. You can hike (carefully) to the top or just take in the view from a parking lot, midway up.

Steve Slattery, Lonely Planet, Melbourne

8

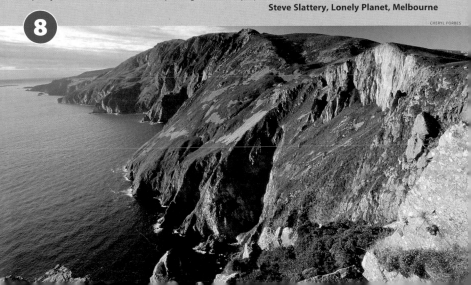

CHERYL FORBES

CONNEMARA (GALWAY)

Cruise or ramble this otherworldly region of shimmering charcoal grey and green hills above reef-fringed lakes. The stretch along Lough Inagh to Kylemore Abbey inspires. Set off from atmospheric Mallmore House (p431) in Clifden to hike the coastal Sky Road (p431).

ROXY123, Bluelist contributor

9

RICHARD CUMMINS

DINGLE PENINSULA (KERRY)

I once hitched from London to Dingle (p285) for a freezing cold New Years party at Dick Mack's pub (p289). The people I met were a wonderful, crazy lot, loaded with local history and lore. The best tip I would offer is get off the main road. I was taken in and fed ales and steak, went with a horse doctor to ancient stables, was shown ruined towers, battle grounds and fairy mounds. I had my genealogy corrected more than once and met sheepdogs and poets and girls with terrible teeth.

Dan Austin, Lonely Planet, Melbourne

GUINNESS IS GOOD FOR YOU

ITS AN ILLUSION

⑩ CYCLING IRELAND

RICHARD CUMMINS

You lock your titanium bike to a post outside the pub, in all the latest gear to combat wind/rain/chills, wearing your helmet, reflective vest, and sunglasses...as you chat with a 70-year-old gentleman wearing tweeds and a bowler, who just finished his afternoon of drinking pints, and is now picking up his equally old – and unlocked – pink bicycle.

Jennipoo_McFluffer, Bluelist contributor

⑫ HOOK PENINSULA (WEXFORD)

A curvy promontory shooting out of Ireland's south coast, the Hook Peninsula (p176) has been a first port of call for everyone from the Anglo–Normans to tourists arriving at Rosslare Europort ferry terminal. Ruins peek from its hedges like clues in some cloak-and-dagger tale, and the local folk happily explain its romantic history of shipwrecks and ghost bands in the dunes. Two prime places to get the low-down are the visitor centre at Europe's oldest working lighthouse (p177) and Hotel Naomh Seosamh (p177), the headquarters of the Irish Federation of Leprechaun Hunters.

James Bainbridge, author

MARTIN MOOS

13 WEST BELFAST

Learn about Northern Ireland's troubled history as you tour the political murals and peace lines of West Belfast in the back of a black taxi (p593), leavened with a touch of black humour from the wise-cracking driver.

Neil Wilson, author

DOUG MCKINLAY

14 BEARA PENINSULA (CORK)

There's a truly magical air about the Beara Peninsula (p239). It'd take a brittle soul to not be awed by its dramatic, snarling coastline; hidden valleys traced with stone walls and bright yellow gorse; colourful villages swooping down to the ocean; and remote islands bobbing in the Atlantic. The final surprise is that so few people seem to have discovered the secret.

Amanda Canning, author

Contents

Contents

Regional Map Contents

County Donegal p504

Counties Derry & Antrim pp640-41

Counties Fermanagh & Tyrone pp678-9

Belfast pp578-9

Counties Down & Armagh pp612-13

Counties Mayo & Sligo p442 & p464

Central North pp476-7

Counties Meath & Louth p542

Dublin p78

County Galway pp404-5

Central South p340

County Wicklow p147

County Clare pp368-9

Counties Limerick & Tipperary p299 & p308

County Kilkenny p324

County Kerry p247

County Cork pp200-01

Counties Wexford & Waterford p167 & p184

Destination Ireland

After 10 years of the same government, the Republic went to the polls on 24 May 2007 with the whole country expecting change. The outgoing Taoiseach, Bertie Ahern, couldn't quite escape the whiff of scandal surrounding his private finances and his party, Fianna Fáil, was under constant attack by the opposition for having squandered the opportunities presented them by the single greatest period of economic growth in history, with a slew of short-sighted decisions and broken promises. On 25 May, Ireland awoke to discover that despite what every poll had told them, the country wasn't quite ready for a whole new change of direction and had voted to put Bertie and his team back into power for another five years.

Who could blame them? On the surface, Ireland has never had it so good. The world's favourite poster-child for untrammelled economic development has become a marvel of dynamic entrepreneurialism, a forward-thinking paragon of modernity that is not about to take a break any time soon.

These are, unquestionably, exciting times, with the country virtually unrecognisable from the Ireland of 20 years ago, when high unemployment and a battered economy meant that emigration was a fact of life for someone in almost every family, and opportunities were slices of luck that really couldn't be trusted. But no country can change completely in such a short space of time – not even Ireland, which has undergone the kind of socioeconomic transformation Stalin would have dreamt about when concocting his five-year plans. Ireland has changed all right, but in so doing the country has developed two distinct personalities that will become evident as you make your way around.

You won't be able to avoid the much-trumpeted child of the Celtic Tiger, the architect of the New Ireland, a land of motorways and multiculturalism planned and developed in between double-decaf lattes and time-outs at the latest spa offering thermal mud treatment. With 60% of the population under 40, the memories of uncertain Ireland before the Celtic Tiger are fast receding in the face of the unfettered optimism brought on by these prosperous times. These Celtic cubs are overseeing the grand transformation of the country from rural backwater to the envy of Europe, with world-class hotels, dining from all corners of the globe and a range of services designed to get the most out of the country's natural bounty, which is pretty spectacular.

Ireland's *other* personality is a little more traditional, and if the regular polls of departing tourists are to be believed, still holds the key to Ireland's draw as a tourist destination. At the heart of it all is the often breathtaking scenery, still gorgeous enough to make your jaw drop despite the best efforts of developers to scar some of the most beautiful bits with roundabouts, brutal suburbs and summer bungalows. From the lonely, windlashed wilderness of Donegal to the postcard landscapes of West Cork, Ireland is one of the world's most beautiful countries, and worth every effort you make to explore it. The sometimes overwhelming popularity of the scenic superstars like Connemara and Kerry has seen the emergence of quieter idylls as the preferred destination of the discerning traveller, who has discovered the beauty of the lakes of Roscommon, the villages of Waterford and the rarely visited counties like Westmeath. Here you can come into contact with a more genuine Ireland, the kind removed from the slick machinery of the tourist trail.

The slow grind that resulted in the end of violence in Northern Ireland has meant that the province can finally go about showing to a much wider audience that it is just as beautiful and interesting as the rest of the island. In 2007, Lonely Planet's Blue List put it in the world's top 10 destinations to visit for good reason – the province has always had plenty to see, but it was tough to appreciate the likes of South Armagh's rural scenery when it was known as 'Bandit Country' due to the high level of IRA activity.

Ireland is a complex, often contradictory country, and those contradictions are evident everywhere you go, from the thatched rural pub advertising wi-fi connection and imported Australian wines to the group of Polish-born schoolkids chatting away to each other in Irish. No sooner do you make an assumption about the place than something will confound you completely, leaving you none the wiser than before you began. But don't worry, you're in good company: most of the Irish are as confused about it as you are.

All of this confusion hardly fits the traditional, timeworn view of a nation of friendly people made happy by the conviviality of a drink among friends, but the Irish have always mocked those fanciful notions kept alive by many a wishy-washy tourist brochure and the likes of *The Quiet Man*. Of course the Irish love a drink, but they know that they also have huge problems with the stuff, and the country is tackling the issue on a national level.

Yet for all of the problems thrown up by any modern society – and Ireland has plenty of them on its plate – the fact remains that the Irish warmth and welcome is the real deal, and millions of visitors testify to the sheer ease with which they made friends here. Someone *will* stop and help you find your way when you're standing on a corner gawking at a map; you *will* strike up a conversation if you're sitting alone in a pub; and there *is* a very good chance that if you're stuck somewhere a local will volunteer a lift to wherever you need to go. The Irish love complaining about their country – about the crappy weather, the horrible traffic, the unplanned construction, the venal corruption – and will swear to you that you're the luckiest person on earth because you don't have to live here, but they only do it because this is the greatest country on the planet. Make sense? Well, it does here.

Getting Started

Compact, relatively homogenous and *theoretically* crossed by car in less than four hours, Ireland doesn't pose any major challenges to the visitor other than the ones set by the often inclement weather; the horrendous traffic that can make getting through a two-dog town a 45-minute struggle against road rage; and the high price of pretty much everything, which will require an elastic budget. Otherwise, Ireland is a doddle.

WHEN TO GO

The Irish weather works on the 'four seasons in a day' principle, which basically means that you can't predict a thing when it comes to the behaviour of the sky. Some basic assumptions, however, can be made.

In summer, from June to August, the days are reasonably warm and – most importantly – very long: at the height of summer you won't need to turn on lights until after 10pm. It is also peak tourist season, which means there are far more people just about everywhere but the most remote corners of the island, and prices are at their highest. Not surprisingly, most of the yearly festivals occur during these times so as to take advantage of the crowds and the more favourable weather.

See Climate Charts (p703) for more information.

Spring (March to May) and autumn (September to November) make good alternatives, although the country's ever-growing popularity as a tourist destination can often blur the lines between mid- and high-season tourism. Still, you have a better chance of some peace and quiet, and the weather can be surprisingly better in April and September than in mid-July – again, it's all part of the uncertainty principle. Spring festivities include the ever-popular St Patrick's Festival.

Although temperatures will barely venture below freezing, winter (December to February) can be brutal, but huge parts of the country – the west and northwest in particular – are at their savage and beautiful best in the cold winter light. Crowds are at their thinnest, but many of the country's tourist attractions and services close down in October and don't reopen until Easter, which paradoxically leaves visitors with a more convincing taste of how Ireland is experienced by most of the Irish: it's cold, grey and dark by 5pm, but there's always a pub to escape into when the rain starts sheeting down.

COSTS & MONEY

There are no two ways about it: Ireland is an expensive destination by any standards. The country is obsessed with what they call 'rip-off culture', which

---

DON'T LEAVE HOME WITHOUT...

Ireland won't test your survival skills unless you're the worse for wear in the middle of nowhere, but there are a few essentials you won't want to leave behind:

- Good walking shoes
- Raincoat
- UK/Ireland electrical adapter
- A finely honed sense of humour
- A hollow leg
- Decent Irish-themed playlists for your iPod – see p59 for our recommendations.

hurts locals as much as visitors. The sting is felt most everywhere, but visitors will feel it most when it comes to bed and board.

In Dublin, the bare minimum to survive is about €50 a day: €20 to €25 for a hostel and €20 for sustenance, which leaves enough for a pint. Outside the capital things are a little better, but not much: if you're in a tourist hot zone it'll be reflected in the prices, which are only marginally better than in Dublin. If your purse strings are a little more relaxed, you can get a decent bed for around €80 in the capital, €60 outside of it. For €120 you can sleep pretty luxuriously most anywhere except those *very* special places.

No matter where you are, eating out is expensive. For less than €10, don't expect much more than soup and what comes in between two slices of bread. Very ordinary meals will cost €20 or more; the better restaurants won't blink twice when charging €35 for the fish in a fancy sauce.

Car rental is also costly in Ireland. Be sure to check your car-insurance policy back home before accepting the exorbitant insurance policies offered at car-rental agencies. If your credit card usually covers car-rental insurance, confirm that the policy applies in Ireland.

TRAVELLING SUSTAINABLY

Ireland's 40 shades of green don't, it seems, include the all-important eco-green, at least according to the European Environment Agency, which rates Ireland's carbon footprint as 5.0 global hectares per person, more than double the global average.

Everyone has a car, which results in longer traffic lines and a stressed-out infrastructure; everyone has plenty of money, which means that city break travel is increasingly ubiquitous – statistics show that the Irish take an average of three foreign holidays a year; and the Minister for Tourism announced in 2007 that the aim is to double the number of foreign tourists visiting Ireland to 10 million by the year 2012. Considering that domestic tourism accounts for another six million yearly visits and that hotels, restaurants and a host of facilities are constantly being built, upgraded and developed to deal with these massive numbers (for such a small country anyway), sustainable travel has become a core issue if Ireland is to continue attracting visitors with its mix of great scenic beauty, distinctive heritage and wonderful culture.

As so many visits to Ireland begin in Dublin, you could start your trip by dropping into **Cultivate** (☎ 01-674 5773; www.cultivate.ie; 15-19 West Essex St) in Temple Bar, Ireland's only sustainability-focused living and learning centre. The centre has an eco-shop, lots of information stands, and hosts workshops and classes on everything from composting to green building.

Throughout this book we have endeavoured to highlight any accommodation or project that puts green issues at the forefront of their planning; for more, see the Environment chapter (p74); the 'Eco Kind of Green' itinerary (p29); our Top 10 Green Projects (p24); and our Greendex (p759).

Offsetting

Paying someone else to offset your greenhouse gas emissions isn't the perfect solution to the major issue of global warming, but it is a step in the right direction. The most popular offsetting programme involves tree-planting, but there are other schemes such as methane collection and combustion. **Carbon Neutral Ireland** (www.carbonneutralireland.ie) can help you calculate your emissions and advise you how to offset them.

Planning

Create an itinerary that allows you to explore and experience the best of Ireland while maintaining some level of eco-responsibility. Your aim should

HOW MUCH?

Irish Times €1.60

1km taxi fare €1.45

Cinema ticket €8.50

Admission to Gaelic football match €12-15

Aran sweater €50+

GREEN WEBSITES

Check out the following online resources for in-depth info on how to travel in Ireland without being an environmental bully or leaving too deep a carbon footprint:

- **www.cultivate.ie** Sustainable living centre in Dublin's Temple Bar
- **www.sustourism.ie** All-Ireland project committed to building a sustainable tourist infrastructure
- **www.greenbox.ie** An integrated 'green zone' that includes Fermanagh, Leitrim, West Cavan, North Sligo, South Donegal and North West Monaghan
- **www.enfo.ie** Ireland's public information service on environmental matters, including sustainable development
- **www.thevillage.ie** Ireland's first eco-friendly and sustainable urban plan is an extension of the village of Cloughjordan, County Tipperary

be to benefit locally owned business and any venture that preserves the local culture.

This means choosing locally owned accommodation over the big, multinational chain hotels (see below for our selection of green-friendly accommodation); restaurants that make an effort to use local produce; and activities that benefit the local community rather than exploit it. A good example is golf, where you should endeavour to play the older established courses rather than the newer mega-resorts designed to draw in wealthy players with a mix of US-style course design and on-course houses that are nothing more than a huge drain on local resources. Throughout this book we have endeavoured to keep all of these considerations uppermost in our thinking.

Sustainable Tourism Ireland (www.sustourism.ie) is a handy starting point with a list of enterprises from B&Bs to urban planning projects that put eco-responsibility and sustainability to the fore.

Fly Less

There are numerous boat services serving Ireland from Britain and France and often some return fares don't cost that much more than one-way fares, not to mention the plethora of special offers designed to challenge the cheap flight hegemony. Boats arrive in Dublin, Belfast, Larne and Wexford; for more details, see the Transport chapter (p719).

TOP 10 GREEN SLEEPS

- **Anna's House B&B** Strangford Lough, County Down; p620
- **Benwiskin Centre** Ballintrillick, County Sligo; p474
- **Coosan Cottage Eco Guesthouse** Athlone, County Westmeath; p501
- **Corcreggan Mill Cottage Hostel** Dunfanaghy, County Donegal; p525
- **Jampa Ling Buddhist Centre** Bawnboy, County Cavan; p483
- **Omagh Independent Hostel** Omagh, County Tyrone; p689
- **Otto's Creative Cooking** near Bandon, County Cork; p222
- **Phoenix Vegetarian Restaurant & Accommodation** Mt Caherconcee, County Kerry; p293
- **Rocky View Farmhouse** Fanore, County Clare; p395
- **Shiplake Mountain Hostel** Dunmanway, County Cork; p237

Use Less Plastic

The Republic placed a levy of 15c on all plastic bags at the point of sale in 2002, and it has proved remarkably effective, reducing the use of these noxious carriers by up to 40%. Northern Ireland introduced a 5p levy in July 2007. We urge you to use as few plastic bags as possible; most shops sell cloth bags that can be stashed away when not in use.

Stay Longer

An extended visit, as opposed to the rush-in, rush-out limitations of city-break travel, is preferable because it allows for 'slow travel' – the kind of exploratory travel that allows you to take your time and get to know a place without needing to rush (and find the fastest form of transport) to get you around. The ideal is a bike tour – throughout the book we have included details of rental agencies. Some organisations also run bike tours; see p720.

TRAVEL LITERATURE

Travel in Ireland seems to inspire writers, some of whom seem obsessed with using Guinness as a metaphor for Irish life. As irritating as that is to the Irish and anyone else with an aversion to bad metaphors, some manage the job with cleverness and humour.

Ireland – In a Glass of Its Own by Peter Biddlecombe is a hilarious trip around Ireland, based on the premise that the 32 counties can be said to represent the constituent parts of a pint of the black stuff.

Pint-Sized Ireland by Evan McHugh is the story of the ultimate Aussie pilgrimage, a journey the length and breadth of Ireland to find the perfect pint. The entertaining means do justify the ridiculous ends.

McCarthy's Bar has sold millions of copies thanks to the colourful account of author Pete McCarthy's attempt to rediscover Ireland by having a pint in every pub that bears his name. His follow-up, *The Road to McCarthy*, is a look at the Irish diaspora.

Silver Linings by Martin Fletcher is a compelling portrait of Northern Ireland at odds with its bruised and tarnished image as a war-scarred region. Northerners on both sides of the divide are friendly, funny and as welcoming as anyone else on the island.

Endurance by Dermot Somers is a brilliant and fascinating collection of stories of heroic and historic travels in Ireland, from the mythic legends of old to the dawn of modern Ireland.

A Secret Map of Ireland is Rosita Boland's brilliantly insightful tale of her travels across the 32 counties, uncovering stories, myths and fascinating details about the counties, towns and villages she comes across.

The Oxford Illustrated Literary Guide to Great Britain and Ireland traces the movements of famous writers who have immortalised various towns and villages in Ireland.

The Height of Nonsense by Paul Clements is a fascinating story of Irish quirks, eccentrics and oddities, travelling the GMRs (Great Mountain Roads) in search of the truth about druids, banshees, highwaymen and loose women.

'Travel in Ireland seems to inspire writers, some of whom seem obsessed with using Guinness as a metaphor for Irish life'

INTERNET RESOURCES

The internet has become an indispensable planning tool for travellers. Ireland is well wired, so there's a lot of useful information available online. Here are a few sites to get you started.

Blather (www.blather.net) This wry webzine dishes out healthy portions of irreverent commentary on all things Irish. It's a savvy way to get up-to-date on current events and attitudes.

TOP 10

Dublin ○   Sea

REPUBLIC OF
IRELAND   Wales

Must-See Irish Movies

Predeparture planning is always more fun if it includes a few flicks to get you in the mood. The follow-ing films are available on video or DVD. For more information about Irish cinema and TV, see p57.

1 *Bloody Sunday* (2002) Director: Paul Greengrass

2 *The Dead* (1987) Director: John Huston

3 *My Left Foot* (1989) Director: Jim Sheridan

4 *The Crying Game* (1992) Director: Neil Jordan

5 *The Quiet Man* (1952) Director: John Ford

6 *Inside I'm Dancing* (2004) Director: Damien O'Donnell

7 *Cal* (1984) Director: Pat O'Connor

8 *Adam & Paul* (2004) Director: Lenny Abrahamson

9 *The Magdalene Sisters* (2002) Director: Peter Mullan

10 *Michael Collins* (1996) Director: Neil Jordan

Top Irish Fiction

Getting stuck into some fiction is the best way to gain insight into Irish issues and culture, for there's no greater truth in Ireland than the story that's been made up. Here are the essentials to kick-start a lifelong passion; for more information see p55.

1 *Dubliners* (1914) James Joyce

2 *The Book of Evidence* (1989) John Banville

3 *The Butcher Boy* (1992) Patrick McCabe

4 *Paddy Clarke Ha Ha Ha* (1993) Roddy Doyle

5 *The Third Policeman* (1967) Flann O'Brien

6 *The Ballroom of Romance & Other Stories* (1972) William Trevor

7 *Amongst Women* (1990) John McGahern

8 *All Summer* (2003) Claire Kilroy

9 *Facing White* (2007) Various Authors

10 *Angela's Ashes* (1996) Frank McCourt

Top Green Projects

There's nothing more satisfying than helping, participating in, visiting…or just being aware of projects that are working to protect the very environment that drew you here in the first place.

1 **Ecos Environmental Centre** (Ballymena, County Antrim, p674) A visitor centre dedicated to alternative energy sources and sustainable technology.

2 **Copper Coast GeoPark** (Tramore, County Waterford, p192) Anglo–Irish enclave with the dubious distinction of being the only village in Ireland without a pub.

3 **Cuilcagh Mountain Park** (County Ferman-agh, p689) One of Europe's largest blanket bogs now supporting a regeneration project.

4 **Jampa Ling Buddhist Centre** (Bawnboy, County Roscommon, p483) Galupa Bud-dhism, philosophy and meditation.

5 **T Bay** (Tramore, County Waterford, p192) Ireland's biggest surf school runs eco-walks around one of Europe's largest inter-tidal lagoons.

6 **The Village** (Cloughjordan, County Tip-perary, p74) Sustainable community on a 67-acre lot adjoining Cloughjordan village.

7 **Rockfield Ecological Estate** (Mullingar, County Westmeath, p499) An inspiring insight into sustainable living, as well as traditional Irish culture and crafts.

8 **Coosan Cottage Eco-Guesthouse** (Athlone, County Westmeath, p501) Eco-friendly guest cottage, utilising wind-generated electricity and sawdust-pellet heating.

9 **Brigit's Garden** (Oughterard, County Gal-way, p427) A nonprofit garden with mean-dering trails through four seasonal gardens.

10 **Bog of Allen Nature Centre** (Robertstown, County Kildare, p344) Institution run by the Irish Peatland Conservation Council tracing the history of bogs and peat production.

Entertainment Ireland (www.entertainmentireland.ie) Countrywide listings for clubs, theatres, festivals, cinemas, museums and much more. It's well worth consulting this site as you plan your next move in Ireland.

Fáilte Ireland (www.ireland.ie) The Republic's tourist board information site has heaps of practical info. It features a huge accommodation database with photos.

Fine Gael (www.ripoff.ie) Not the website of the actual political party, but an antigovernment website sponsored by the main opposition party, whose aim is to win favour by appearing along-side the poor consumer; we don't buy it, but it does tell it like it is in relation to prices.

Irish Election (www.irishelection.com) The best of Irish political blogging, this is a great site to familiarise yourself with the issues dominating the Irish scene.

Lonely Planet (www.lonelyplanet.com) Comprehensive travel information and advice.

Mongrel (www.mongrel.ie) Irreverent and hilarious, this is alternative Ireland's look at every-thing, from Americana to wedding videos.

Northern Ireland Tourism (www.discovernorthernireland.com) Northern Ireland's official tourism information site is particularly strong on activities and accommodation.

Itineraries
CLASSIC ROUTES

GO WEST!
One Week/Mayo to West Cork

Begin at the excavated **Céide Fields** (p457) in Mayo. Wind your way round the coast, stopping at some of Ireland's wildest beaches, to the pretty village of **Pollatomish** (p457). Head to the pub-packed heritage town of **Westport** (p446) continue past **Croagh Patrick** (p449) and through **Leenane** (p436) – situated on Ireland's only fjord – to **Connemara National Park** (p434). Take the beautiful coastal route, passing **Kylemore Abbey** (p433) and Clifden's scenic **Sky Road** (p431) through pretty **Roundstone** (p429), or the stunning wilderness of the inland route through Maam Cross to **Galway** (p403). Move on to the fishing villages of **Kinvara** (p437) and **Ballyvaughan** (p396) in the heart of the **Burren** (p388) and visit the ancient **Aillwee Caves** (p397). Explore the **Dingle Peninsula** (p284) before following the **Ring of Kerry** (p258), ending in **Killarney National Park** (p253). Continue down the **Beara Peninsula** (p239) to the Italianate **Garinish Island** (p240), with its exotic flowers. Follow the coast to **Cork** (p200) through Castletownshend and the fishing village of **Union Hall** (p227).

This tourist trail takes you past some of Ireland's most famous attractions and spectacular countryside. It's only about 300km so you could manage it in two days but what's the point? You won't be disappointed on this route.

THE LONG WAY ROUND   Three Weeks/Starting & Ending in Dublin

Start your loop just north of Dublin at the **Casino at Marino** (p111), not a place to cash your chips but a 19th-century Italianate trompe l'oeil mansion. Continue north to the mind-blowing Neolithic necropolis at **Brú Na Bóinne** (p543), built before the Great Pyramids were even a twinkle in Pharaoh's eye. Continue north to **Mellifont Abbey** (p563), Ireland's first Cistercian abbey, and on to the pretty village of **Carlingford** (p574) on the lough, with its 16th-century buildings. Work your way through the Mourne Mountains – hiking to the top of **Slieve Donard** (p628) – to the **Ards Peninsula** (p616) and **Strangford Lough** (p620). Take a Black Taxi tour in **Belfast** (p576) before moving northwest to the World Heritage site of **Giant's Causeway** (p662), best enjoyed at sunset. Continue around the stunning coastline of north Donegal, stopping at stunning **Killyhoey Beach** (p525), to beautiful **Glenveagh National Park** (p530). Head south through the monastic ruins of **Glencolumbcille** (p515) and into lively **Sligo** (p463), where you can climb the Stone Age passage grave, **Carrowkeel** (p470), with panoramic views of Lough Arrow. For the west coast as far as Cork, follow the Into the West route (opposite). From Cork, head east to **Fota Wildlife Park** (p213) for a picnic and then on to **Dungarvan Castle** (p193), with its unusual 12th-century shell. Drive around the picturesque **Hook Peninsula** (p176), stopping for ice cream in the seaside town of **Dunmore East** (p190). Spot the unusual varieties of geese in the famous **Wexford Wildfowl Reserve** (p173) before moving on to County Wicklow and **Wicklow Mountains National Park** (p147). Now settle into a well-deserved pint of Guinness at the **Long Hall** (p131), back in Dublin.

A loop to give you a real feel for Ireland's savage and spectacular coastline, as well as the heart of its long history. Four days will see you complete the 750km that make the full circle, but little else; best done in a couple of weeks.

TIP TO TOE
Two Weeks/Derry to Wexford

Begin by walking the city walls of **Derry** (p640) and exploring its fascinating history. Delve deeper at one of Ireland's best museums, the **Ulster American Folk Park** (p690), which reproduces a typical 19th-century Ulster village at the time of mass emigration to America. Just south of here the town of **Omagh** (p689), site of one of the worst single atrocities in the North's history (a car bomb), acts as a stark reminder of the region's tragic political history. From here, head south to **Castle Coole** (p682), a National Trust–restored 18th-century mansion, before spending an afternoon boating or fishing on **Lough Erne** (p682). For more watery pastimes you can't beat **County Cavan** (p478), which has a lake for every day of the year. Hire a boat in Mountnugent and fish on **Lough Sheelin** (p482) before moving on to **Tullynally Castle's** (p499) Chinese and Tibetan garden in Westmeath. The **Seven Wonders of Fore** (p499), Westmeath's answer to the Seven Wonders of the World, while less awe inspiring, will keep you entertained for an hour or two before a wander around the splendid **Belvedere House** (p496), overlooking Lough Ennell, with its multimedia exhibition. Place a bet at **Kilbeggan Races** (p498) emboldened by a tipple of fine whiskey at **Locke's Distillery** (p498). Hike up the beautiful **Slieve Bloom Mountains** (p356) for the best view of the midlands, before moving south to the delightful village of **Inistioge** (p335) in County Kilkenny, with its quaint village square and rambling estate, Woodstock Park. In County Wexford have a picnic in the **John F Kennedy Arboretum** (p181) before a visit to the tranquil Cistercian **Tintern Abbey** (p177).

This north–south 400km route covers it all: from Ulster's fine architecture and heritage, through the midlands and its abundance of lakes, to the beautiful country-side of the sunny southeast. You will enjoy this selection of different tastes.

ROADS LESS TRAVELLED

AN ECO KIND OF GREEN
One Week/Dublin to Tramore

Get all the support info you'll need at **Cultivate** (p21) in Dublin, Ireland's only sustainable living information centre. You'll have to get out of the capital sharpish, but your first stop should be the **Rockfield Ecological Estate** (p499) in Rathowen, where you'll get inspiring insights into sustainable living, as well as traditional Irish culture and crafts. If you need some eco–R&R, stop by the **Jampa Ling Buddhist Centre** (p483) before bedding down at the ecofriendly **Coosan Cottage Eco Guesthouse** (p501) in Athlone. Head west to Connemara and **Brigit's Garden** (p427), before turning southward to West Cork, where organic local produce is almost a way of life. A great overnight option is the **Shiplake Mountain Hostel** (p237), where you sleep in old wooden caravans, shower using fresh spring water and breakfast on the hostel's own duck eggs before walking the local hills. Proof that eco-credentials aren't just earned roughing it is in the superb **Ballymaloe cookery school** (p216), home to Ireland's most famous chef Darina Allen (see also p273) and the place to learn the basics of Irish cooking. Moving east along the rugged coastline, stop at the **Copper Coast GeoPark** (p192), centred on Annestown. This attractive Anglo–Irish enclave has a good surf beach and the dubious distinction of being the only village in Ireland without a pub! Your final stop is the cheap 'n' cheerful beach resort of Tramore, which has become an unlikely haven for New-Age Californians, one of whom runs **T-Bay** (p192), Ireland's biggest surf school and a nonprofit organisation that is trying to promote eco-awareness through surfing and guided walks.

Ireland's eco-credentials are only just being established, but here is a selection over 500km to prove that travelling sustainably can still bring you the best the country has to offer, from the surprisingly rich midlands through the rugged west to the scenic south.

BEST OF THE ISLANDS

Three Weeks/Tory to West Cork

Ireland's outlying islands are many and varied, and offer the visitor an insight into a traditional lifestyle rarely seen in the Western world. Start at the barren and remote **Tory** (p521), off Bloody Foreland in Donegal, a Gaeltacht (Irish-speaking) area with a school of primitive painters and a wonderful spot for bird-watching. Joined to the mainland by a bridge, **Achill** (p452), in County Mayo, with its deserted Famine village and dramatic cliffs, is Ireland's largest offshore island and is renowned for its water sports. **Inishturk** (p451), just south of Achill, with fewer than 100 inhabitants, gets very little tourist traffic despite its sheltered sandy beaches. Off the coast of Galway, the three Aran Islands are probably Ireland's most visited. The largest, **Inishmór** (p417), has some fine archaeological remains, including the magical fort of Dún Aengus. The middle island, **Inishmaan** (p421), favourite of the writer JM Synge, is a pleasure to walk around with its stone walls and tiny fields. The smallest and least visited, **Inisheer** (p422), best accessed from Doolin in County Clare, has some wonderful wild walks. Some very special islands to visit are Europe's most westerly. On the **Blasket Islands** (p294), off Kerry, uninhabited since 1953, you can spot puffins, seals and porpoises. **Skellig Michael** (p263), off Caherciveen in Kerry, a Unesco World Heritage site and home to a 7th-century monastery, is a breathtaking, truly spiritual place and a highlight of any trip to Ireland. Ornithologists and orators alike will enjoy **Clear Island** (p230), also called Cape Clear Island, off the western coast of Cork, famous for its Manx shearwater and its lively Storytelling Festival in September.

If you're one to appreciate the cultural experience and simple pleasures of island life, you won't want to hurry this trail. Take three weeks if you can spare it and properly experience the unique differences of Ireland's islands. Otherwise try to get in at least a day trip.

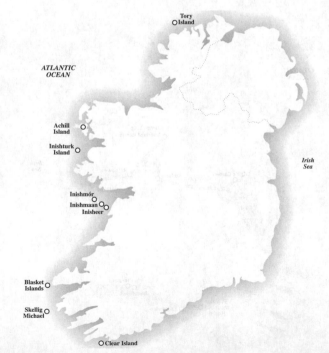

TAILORED TRIPS

ADRENALINE ADVENTURES

Thrill seekers should kick off their action and adventure tour of the west coast of Ireland with a **rock-climbing** (p266) session on the cliffs of the Iveragh Peninsula in County Kerry. The next day, travel north along the coast to the windy world of Rough Point on the lovely Dingle Peninsula. There, you can take flight with some white-knuckle **kitesurfing** (p290). Stay firmly on the water next and build your biceps even more with some **sea kayaking** (p381) at the small town of Kilrush in County Clare.

Cross the wilderness of Connemara by **mountain bike** (p432 and p433) and head for Glassillaun Beach, County Galway. There, go **scuba diving** (p434) in some of the country's clearest waters and see colourful marine life brought north by the Gulf Stream. Down the road in Leenane, scramble down on foot to Killary Harbour to sail its sheltered waters in a **catamaran** (p436). Then test your physical strength and endurance nearby on a **cross-country assault course** (p450) at beautiful Delphi, located next to Ireland's only fjord, before heading north to **surf** (p471) the waves on world-class, near-perfect 10ft tubes at Bundoran, County Donegal.

CELTIC SITES & CHRISTIAN RUINS

Begin at the stunning Neolithic tombs of **Newgrange** (p543) and **Knowth** (p544) in County Meath in the heart of Brú na Bóinne (the Boyne Palace), where the legendary Irish hero Cúchulainn was conceived. Nearby, stand at the top of the celebrated **Hill of Tara** (p549), a site of immense folkloric significance and seat of the high kings of Ireland until the 11th century. Across the plain is the **Hill of Slane** (p546), where St Patrick lit a fire in 433 to proclaim Christianity throughout the land. Venture west to **Kells** (p555) on the road travelled by Queen Medb herself in the Irish Stone Age epic, the *Táin Bó Cúailnge*, pausing to explore the monastic ruins and high crosses before continuing to County Roscommon. Just outside Tulsk village is **Cruachan Aí** (p488), the most important Celtic site in Europe, with 60 scattered megalithic tombs and burial sites. Head south to **Clonmacnoise Abbey** (p362), the 6th-century monastic site in County Offaly. Continue south through the heart of the country to the impressive monastic site that sits atop the craggy **Rock of Cashel** (p310) in County Tipperary. Turn east and head through County Kilkenny, stopping at the Cistercian **Jerpoint Abbey** (p334) at the pretty village of Thomastown. From here, travel northeast to Wicklow and magnificent **Glendalough** (p152), where the substantial remains of a monastic settlement linger by two lakes – it's as atmospheric a site as you'll ever find.

CHILDREN ON BOARD

For fun both historical and zoological, Ireland has a lot to offer. Step back in time with a multimedia tour of medieval Kerry at the **Kerry County Museum** (p278) in Tralee. Recharge your batteries on the Tralee and Dingle light **steam railway** (p278) and chug around Tralee Bay on a trip back in time. About 1km away from here, you can watch wheat being milled at Blennerville in Ireland's largest working **windmill** (p278), built in 1800. Still in County Kerry,

you can zip on down the peninsula to Dingle to see turtles, stingrays and exotic fish up close in the **Dingle Oceanworld** (p286) aquarium. Popular features here are the touch pool, walk-through tunnel, shark tank and Amazon jungle section, complete with piranhas. Pursuing the theme of watery adventures, catch a boat into the bay to see the famously friendly **Fungie the dolphin** (p286) at play; the attention-loving bottlenose shows up most days. The next day make your way to Killarney and take a relaxing tour in the town's beloved horse-drawn **jaunting cars** (p253). From here, head east to the wonderful, fence-free **Fota Wildlife Park** (p213) in Carrigtwohill, East Cork, where you'll see more than 90 species of exotic and endangered wildlife like cheetahs, macaques and oryxes.

THE SOUTHERN PANTRY

There are great restaurants and shops all over Ireland, but this mini-tour focuses on Ireland's largest county because it is just brimming with gourmet eateries and specialist food stores. Start in West Cork, where gourmet cuisine is taken for granted: in Clonakilty, **Twomey's** (p223) is where you can buy the best black pudding for which the town is famous. Cork is renowned for its cheeses, and in **Durrus** (p235) you can visit the local cheesemakers before making a pitstop at the superb **Good Things Café and Cookery School** (p235). Back east and south of Cork City, Kinsale is just full of top nosh, including the **Fishy Fishy Café** (p221), which is only open during the day. Southeast of Cork City, Cobh is home to the **Belvelly Smokehouse** (p215) where you can taste, learn and buy all kinds of smoked fish. All of this eating will build up a thirst, and you can quench it at the **Franciscan Well Brewery** (p209) in Cork City, where you can also stock up at the daily **English Market** (p207). From here, continue east to Midleton and the **Farmgate Restaurant** (p215), one of Ireland's very best. The farmers market is better than the one in Cork City, but it's only a weekly affair. Finally, don't forget the world-famous **Ballymaloe House** (p216), just south of Midleton.

History

VENI, VIDI, VICI

If there is one historical theme most Irish have an opinion about, it is being conquered, and it matters not a jot that to many the facts are a little hazy. 'Eight hundred years' has long been the rallying call of Irish nationalists, these years being roughly the period of time dear old Britannia ruled the Irish roost. And while Ireland's fractious relationship with its sister island across the Irish Sea casts an overwhelming shadow over Ireland's history of conquest and domination, it's not just the English that conquered and even when they did, their relationship with their new subjects was fraught with complexities and contradictions rather than being the simple narrative of conquest and rebellion that some nationalists would have us believe.

The island has been the subject of a series of conquests since the 8th century BC, when the fearsome Celtic warrior tribes began making steady attacks on the island – the last of these tribes, commonly known as the Gaels (which in the local language came to mean 'foreigner'), came ashore in the 3rd century BC and proceeded to divide the island into at least five kingdoms. They also set about creating the basics of what we now term 'Irish' culture: they devised a sophisticated code of law called the Brehon Law that remained in use until the early 17th century and their swirling, mazelike design style, evident on artefacts nearly 2000 years old, is considered the epitome of Irish design.

Yet the Celts weren't 'Irish' in any nationalistic sense. The kingdoms were constantly at war with each other, and even though they all nominally paid allegiance to a high king who sat at Tara, in County Meath, their support was fraught and fluid, given when it suited and withdrawn just as quickly when it didn't. It was this lack of unity that allowed the Vikings to make such easy forays into Ireland, targeting the rich monastic settlements that had grown up as a result of the steady Christianisation of the Celts beginning in the end of the 4th century AD. Even the Battle of Clontarf (1014), taught to every Irish schoolkid as the ultimate showdown between the native 'Irish' lead by the High King Brian Ború and the Viking invaders, wasn't quite as straightforward as that: fighting alongside the Vikings was the king of Leinster, Máelmorda mac Murchada, who was looking to use the Vikings in a bid to oust Ború and take the throne for himself (both mac Murchada and Ború lost their lives, but Ború's armies won the day). Like the Celts before them, the Vikings eventually settled, giving up the rape-rob-and-run policy in favour of integration and assimilation: by intermarrying with the Celtic tribes they introduced red hair and freckles to the Irish gene pool.

The '800 years' of English rule in Ireland nominally began in 1169, when an army of English barons (actually Cambro-Norman, being a mix of Welsh and

For a concise, 10-minute read on who the Celts were see www.ibiblio.org/gaelic/celts.html.

The Course of Irish History by TW Moody and FX Martin is a hefty volume by two Trinity College professors who trace much of Ireland's history to its land and its proximity to England.

TIMELINE

10,000–8000 BC	4500 BC	700–300 BC
After the last Ice Age ends, humans arrive in Ireland during the Mesolithic Era, originally crossing a land bridge between Scotland and Ireland. Few archaeological traces remain of this group.	The first Neolithic farmers arrive in Ireland by boat from as far afield as the Iberian peninsula, bringing cattle, sheep, and crops, marking the beginnings of a settled agricultural economy.	Iron technology gradually replaces bronze. The Celtic culture and language arrives, ushering in 1000 years of cultural and political dominance.

Norman nobles) landed in Wexford and quickly captured the two Hiberno-Viking ports of Wexford and Waterford. But their arrival was not nearly as neat as veni, vidi, vici (I came, I saw, I conquered). The Norman invasion of Ireland was originally a tactical alliance between the barons – led by Richard Fitz-Gilbert de Clare, earl of Pembroke (1130–1176; aka Strongbow) – and Dermot MacMurrough (d 1171; Diarmait mac Murchada), the king of Leinster (yes, only this one was ironically a direct descendant of Brian Ború), who had been ousted from his throne by an alliance of Irish chieftains spurred on by the High King himself, Turlough O'Connor (1088–1156; Tairrdelbach mac Ruaidri Ua Conchobair). In return for help in defeating his enemies (and capturing the crown of the high king for himself) MacMurrough promised Strongbow the hand in marriage of his daughter Aoife as well as the kingdom of Leinster, and Strongbow duly obliged by capturing Dublin in 1171 and then marrying Aoife the very next day. MacMurrough's plans all went a little awry, though, and he was hardly to guess on his deathbed later that year that he'd determined the course of the next 800 years and cemented his place at the top of the list of great Irish traitors.

In truth, while MacMurrough may have provided the catalyst for the Norman invasion, Henry II had been plotting to get his hands on Ireland since 1155, when the English Pope Adrian IV issued him the Bull Laudabiliter, granting him the right to bring rebel Christian missionaries in Ireland to heel. Armed with the blessing of the pope and uneasy about Strongbow's growing power and independence of mind, Henry sent a huge naval force in 1171, landed at Waterford and declared it a royal city. He assumed a semblance of control, but the Norman lords continued to do pretty much as they pleased. Barons such as de Courcy and de Lacy set up independent power bases.

Although the gradual assimilation of the Anglo-Norman nobles and their hirelings into Irish society – which provoked the oft-quoted phrase *Hiberniores Hibernis ipsis,* or 'more Irish than the Irish themselves' – can easily be viewed as a form of internal conquest, as their feudal control over the land and the people who worked that land became near total, it wasn't until 1534 that the English crown, occupied by Henry VIII, saw fit to once more send armies across the water. Henry's actions, however, were entirely motivated by his break with the Catholic Church over the pope's failure to grant him dispensation to divorce: the Anglo-Irish were a little iffy about Henry's decision to go it alone and Silken Thomas' abortive uprising gave Henry the excuse he needed to cement his absolute authority in Ireland. Within seven years, Henry had confiscated the lands of the most rebellious lords, eliminated the power of the Irish church and had himself declared King of Ireland.

Elizabeth I further consolidated English power in Ireland, establishing jurisdiction in Connaught and Munster, despite rebellions by the local ruling families. Ulster remained the last outpost of the Irish chiefs. Hugh O'Neill,

The expression 'beyond the Pale' came into use when the Pale was the English-controlled part of Ireland. To the British elite, the rest of Ireland was considered uncivilised.

300 BC–AD 800	AD 431–32	550–800
Ireland is divided into five provinces: Leinster, Meath, Connaught, Ulster and Munster. Meath later merges with Leinster.	According to medieval chronicles, Pope Celestine I sends Bishop Palladius to Ireland to minister to those 'already believing in Christ'; St Patrick arrives the following year to continue the mission.	The flowering of early monasticism in Ireland. The great monastic teachers begin exporting their knowledge across Europe, ushering in Ireland's 'Golden Age'.

earl of Tyrone, led the last serious assault on English power in Ireland for centuries. O'Neill – who supposedly ordered lead from England to re-roof his castle, but instead used it for bullets – instigated open conflict with the English, and so began the Nine Years' War (1594–1603). He proved a courageous and crafty foe, and the English forces met with little success against him in the first seven years of fighting.

The Battle of Kinsale, in 1601, spelled the end for O'Neill and for Ulster. Although O'Neill survived the battle, his power was broken and he surrendered to the English crown. In 1607, O'Neill and 90 other Ulster chiefs sailed to Europe, leaving Ireland forever. This was known as the Flight of the Earls, and it left Ulster open to English rule.

With the native chiefs gone, Elizabeth and her successor, James I, could pursue their policy of Plantation with impunity, and while confiscations took place all over the country, Ulster was most affected because of its wealthy farmlands and as punishment for being home to the primary fomenters of rebellion. It is here that Ulster's often tragic fate was first begun. The Plantations also marked the final collapse of the Gaelic social and political superstructure and the total conquest of Ireland by the English.

Oliver Cromwell's invasion following the Irish rebellion of 1641 – an attempted coup d'état by the Irish Catholic gentry driven by fears that the anti-Royalist Protestant forces were about to invade – served to re-establish total English rule, but it also ushered in the most punitive period of social legislation in Irish history. The main intended effect of the Penal Laws was to facilitate the dispossession of the landed Catholic population. In 1641 Catholics had owned 60% of land in Ireland and by 1776 Catholic land ownership in Ireland stood at only 5%. Six hundred years after Strongbow first landed in Wexford, the conquest of Ireland was complete.

THE SLOW BIRTH OF A NATION

The signing of the Anglo-Irish Treaty in 1921 saw the end of the War of Independence and the establishment of an Irish state – albeit a truncated one, due to the terms of the treaty that allowed six Ulster counties to remain part of the United Kingdom – for the first time in history. In the immediate aftermath of WWI, which was ostensibly fought to protect the rights of small nations, the new Irish state was but the logical and expected result of an 800-year struggle by the Irish to free themselves from the yoke of foreign rule.

Yet the concept of the Irish nation is, in historical terms, a relatively recent one, owing much of its ideological impetus to the republican fervour that gripped Europe in the aftermath of the French Revolution. Although the English crown had held Ireland in its grip since the end of the 12th century, the subjugated inhabitants of the island did develop a general identity borne out of common misfortune but were united in little else.

Cromwell: An Honourable Enemy by Tom Reilly advances the unpopular view that perhaps the destruction of Cromwell's campaign is grossly exaggerated. You're no doubt familiar with the common view; here's the contrary position. (Yes, Reilly is Irish.)

For articles exploring the Irish struggle, check out http://larkspirit.com.

795–841	1014	1166
Vikings begin to plunder Irish monasteries; their raping and pillaging urges sated, they establish settlements throughout the country, including Dublin, and soon turn it into a centre of economic power.	The Battle of Clontarf takes place on Good Friday (April 23) between the forces of the High King, Brian Boru, and the forces led by the King of Leinster, Máelmorda macMurchada.	King of Leinster, Dermot Mac-Murrough, is ousted; he escapes to England where he pleads with Henry II for help. Henry directs him toward a host of barons led by Richard FitzGilbert de Clare, aka Strongbow.

Paradoxically, it was the privileged few that led the majority of rebellions against the English crown, beginning in the 1590s with the Nine Years' War and Hugh O'Neill's failed rebellion against Elizabeth I, considered to be the first quasi-nationalist rebellion against English rule.

The next significant movement came in the wake of the Irish rebellion of 1641, when a group of Gaelic and Anglo-Norman Catholic lords set up a de facto independent Irish state known as the Confederation of Kilkenny (after its capital) that had nominal control over two-thirds of the island (the area outside the so-called Pale, roughly the extent of Leinster and the limit of direct English rule). They demanded autonomy for the Irish parliament and full rights for Catholics, including an end to the Plantations, all the while reasserting their loyalty to the English crown, thereby pitting themselves squarely against Cromwell's parliamentary forces. It all came to a bloody and ignominious end with Cromwell's Irish campaign of 1649–53: not only was the Confederation destroyed, but all of the lands previously owned by the Old Irish gentry were permanently dispossessed.

Another attempt to resist the British in the spirit of the Confederation of Kilkenny was the Jacobite Rebellion of the late 17th century, where Irish Catholic monarchists rallied behind James II after his deposition in the Glorious Revolution. James' defeat at the Battle of the Boyne ensured the complete victory of the English Protestant Ascendancy. The punitive conditions of the Penal Laws and the consciousness of defeat and dispossession served to create a powerful religious and ethnic identity – Gaelic and Roman Catholic – that would eventually become the basis of Irish nationalism.

In the interim, however, with Roman Catholics rendered utterly powerless, the seeds of rebellion against autocracy were planted by a handful of liberal Protestants inspired by the ideologies of the Enlightenment and the unrest provoked by the American War of Independence and then the French Revolution.

The first of these liberal leaders was a young Dublin Protestant, Theobald Wolfe Tone (1763–98), who was the most prominent leader of a Belfast organisation called the United Irishmen. They had high ideals of bringing together men of all creeds to reform and reduce Britain's power in Ireland, but their attempts to gain power through straightforward politics proved fruitless, and they went underground, committed to bringing change by any means. The tragic failure of the French to land an army of succour in 1796 left the organisation exposed to retribution and the men met their bloody end in the Battle of Vinegar Hill in 1798.

The Act of Union, passed in 1801, was the British government's vain attempt to put an end to any aspirations toward Irish independence, but the nationalist genie was well out of the bottle and two distinct forms of nationalist expression began to develop. The first was a breed of radical republicanism, which advocated use of force to found a secular, egalitarian Irish republic;

In 1870, after the Great Famine and ongoing emigration, more than one-third of all native-born Irish lived outside of Ireland.

For the Cause of Liberty: A Thousand Years of Ireland's Heroes by Terry Golway vividly describes the struggles of Irish Nationalism.

1169	1172	1350–1530
Henry's Welsh and Norman barons land in Wexford and capture Waterford and Wexford with MacMurrough's help. Although no one knows it at the time, this is the beginning of an 800-year occupation by Britain.	King Henry II invades Ireland, using the 1155 Bull Laudabiliter issued to him by Pope Adrian IV to claim sovereignty, forcing the Cambro-Norman warlords and some of the Gaelic Irish kings to accept him as their overlord.	The Anglo-Norman barons establish power bases independent of the English crown. Over the following two centuries, English control gradually recedes to an area around Dublin known as 'the Pale'.

the second was a more moderate movement, which advocated nonviolent and legal action to force the government into granting concessions.

The most important moderate was a Kerry-born Catholic called Daniel O'Connell (1775–1847). In 1823 O'Connell founded the Catholic Association with the aim of achieving political equality for Catholics. The association soon became a vehicle for peaceful mass protest and action: in the 1826 general election it supported Protestant candidates who favoured Catholic emancipation. Two years later, O'Connell himself went one better and successfully stood for a seat in County Clare. Being a Catholic, he couldn't actually take his seat, so the British government was in a quandary. To staunch the possibility of an uprising, the government passed the 1829 Act of Catholic Emancipation, allowing some well-off Catholics voting rights and the right to be elected as MPs.

The Great Hunger by Cecil Woodham-Smith is the classic study of the Great Famine of 1845-51.

O'Connell continued to pursue his reform campaign, turning his attention toward the repeal of the Act of Union. His main weapon was the monster rally, which attracted hundreds of thousands of people eager to hear the 'Liberator' (as he was now known) speak. But O'Connell was unwilling to go outside the law, and when the government ordered the cancellation of one of his rallies, he meekly stood down and thereby gave up his most potent weapon of resistance.

O'Connell's failure to defy the British was seen as a terrible capitulation as the country was in the midst of the Potato Famine, and the lack of urgency on the part of the authorities in dealing with the crisis served to bolster the ambitions of the more radical wing of the nationalist movement, led in the 1840s by the Young Irelanders, who attempted a failed rebellion in 1848, and later by the Fenians, architects of yet another uprising in 1867. The Irish may have been bitterly angry at the treatment meted out by the British, but they weren't quite ready to take up arms en masse against them.

Instead, the nationalist cause found itself driven by arguably the most important feature of the Irish struggle against foreign rule: land ownership. Championed by the extraordinary Charles Stewart Parnell (1846–91), the Land League initiated widespread agitation for reduced rents and improved working conditions. The conflict heated up and there was violence on both sides. Parnell instigated the strategy of 'boycotting' tenants, agents and landlords who didn't adhere to the Land League's aims: these people were treated like lepers by the local population. The Land War, as it became known, lasted from 1879 to 1882 and was momentous. For the first time, tenants were defying their landlords en masse. The Land Act of 1881 improved life immeasurably for tenants, creating fair rents and the possibility of tenants owning their land.

The other element of his two-pronged assault on the British was at Westminster where, as leader of the Irish Parliamentary Party (IPP) he led the fight for Home Rule, a limited form of autonomy for Ireland. Parliamentary

1366	1534–41	1585
The English crown enacts the Statutes of Kilkenny, outlawing intermarriage, the Irish language and other Irish customs to stop the Anglo-Normans from assimilating too much with the Irish. It doesn't work.	Henry VIII declares war on the property of the Irish church, as part of his break with the Catholic Church. In 1541 he arranges for the Irish parliament to declare him King of Ireland.	Potatoes from South America are introduced to Ireland, where they eventually become a staple on nearly every table in the country.

THE GREAT FAMINE

As a result of the Great Famine of 1845–51, a staggering three million people died or were forced to emigrate from Ireland. This great tragedy is all the more inconceivable given that the scale of suffering was attributable to selfishness as much as natural causes. Potatoes were the staple food of a rapidly growing, desperately poor population, and when a blight hit the crop, prices soared. The repressive Penal Laws ensured that farmers, already crippled with high rents, could ill afford the little subsistence potatoes provided. Inevitably, most tenants fell into arrears with little or no concession given by mostly indifferent landlords, and were evicted or sent to the dire conditions of the workhouses.

Shamefully, during this time there were abundant harvests of wheat and dairy produce – the country was producing more than enough grain to feed the entire population and it's said that more cattle were sold abroad than there were people on the island. But while millions of its citizens were starving, Ireland was forced to export its food to Britain and overseas.

The Poor Laws in place at the height of the Famine deemed landlords responsible for the maintenance of their poor and encouraged many to 'remove' tenants from their estates by paying their way to America. Many Irish were sent unwittingly to their deaths on board the notorious 'coffin ships'. British Prime Minister Sir Robert Peel made well-intentioned but inadequate gestures at famine relief, and some – but far too few – landlords did their best for their tenants.

Mass emigration continued to reduce the population during the next 100 years and huge numbers of Irish emigrants who found their way abroad, particularly to the USA, carried with them a lasting bitterness.

mathematics meant that the Liberal Party, led by William Gladstone, was reliant on the members of the IPP to maintain a majority over the Conservatives and Parnell pressed home his advantage by forcing Gladstone to introduce a series of Home Rule bills – in 1886 and 1892 – which passed the Commons but were defeated in the House of Lords. Parnell's ascendency, however, came to a sudden end in 1890 when he was embroiled in a divorce scandal – not acceptable to prurient Irish society. The 'uncrowned king of Ireland' was no longer welcome. Parnell's health deteriorated rapidly and he died less than a year later.

The term 'boycott' comes from Charles C Boycott, a County Mayo land agent who was, yes, boycotted by Parnell's Land League in 1880.

As the 20th century dawned, Ireland was overwhelmingly committed to achieving Home Rule. A new Liberal government under Prime Minister Asquith had removed the House of Lords' power to veto bills and began to put another Home-Rule-for-Ireland bill through Parliament. The bill was passed (but not enacted) in 1912 against strident Unionist opposition, epitomised by the mass rallies organised by the recently founded Protestant vigilante group, the Ulster Volunteer Force (UVF).

The outbreak of WWI in July 1914 merely delayed Irish ambitions as a majority of the Irish Volunteers – founded by academic Eoin MacNeill as a nationalist answer to the UVF – heeded the call to arms and enlisted in the

1594	1601	1607
Hugh O'Neill, earl of Tyrone, orders lead from England to re-roof his castle, but instead uses it for bullets – instigating open conflict with the English in what would eventually be termed the Nine Years' War.	The Battle of Kinsale is fought between Elizabeth's armies and the combined rebel forces led by Hugh O'Neill. O'Neill surrenders and the back of the Irish rebellion against the crown is broken.	O'Neill and 90 other Ulster chiefs sail to Europe, leaving Ireland forever. This is known as the Flight of the Earls, and it leaves Ulster open to English rule and the policy of Plantation.

British army. It was felt that just as England had promised Home Rule to Ireland, so the Irish owed it to England to help her in her hour of need.

A few, however, did not. Two small groups – a section of the Irish Volunteers under Pádraig Pearse and the Irish Citizens' Army led by James Connolly – conspired in a rebellion that took the country by surprise. A depleted Volunteer group marched into Dublin on Easter Monday 1916, and took over a number of key positions in the city, claiming the General Post Office on O'Connell St as headquarters. From its steps, Pearse read out to passers-by a declaration that Ireland was now a republic and that his band was the provisional government. Less than a week of fighting ensued before the rebels surrendered to the superior British forces. The rebels weren't popular and had to be protected from angry Dubliners as they were marched to jail.

The Easter Rising would probably have had little impact on the Irish situation had the British not made martyrs of the rebel leaders. Of the 77 given death sentences, 15 were executed, including the injured Connolly, who was shot while strapped to a chair. This brought about a sea change in public attitudes, and support for the republicans rose dramatically.

By the end of the war, Home Rule was far too little, far too late. In the 1918 general election, the republicans stood under the banner of Sinn Féin and won a large majority of the Irish seats. Ignoring London's Parliament, where technically they were supposed to sit, the newly elected Sinn Féin deputies – many of them veterans of the 1916 Easter Rising – declared Ireland independent and formed the first Dáil Éireann (Irish assembly or lower house), which sat in Dublin's Mansion House under the leadership of Eamon de Valera. The Irish Volunteers became the Irish Republican Army (IRA) and the Dáil authorised it to wage war on British troops in Ireland.

A lot more blood would soon seep into Irish soil, but the Civil War would lead – inevitably – to independence and freedom, albeit costly, for the country was partitioned and six Ulster provinces were allowed remain part of the UK, sowing the seeds of division and bloodshed that tormented the provinces half a century later.

The events leading up to the Anglo-Irish War and their effect on ordinary people are movingly and powerfully related in JG Farrell's novel *Troubles*, first published in 1970.

A MATTER OF FAITH

In 2007, a joint survey by a Catholic and a Protestant organisation revealed that only 52% of young people knew the names of the four Evangelists…and that only 38% knew that there were four of them (Matthew, Mark, Luke and John, just so you know). Only 10% knew that the Immaculate Conception referred to Mary and less than half could name the Father, Son and the Holy Spirit (or Ghost) as the three persons of the Trinity.

A sharp decline in religious practice is a Europe-wide phenomenon, particularly among Christians, but Ireland is a special case, for religion is a central feature of Irish history and the centuries-old fight for identity and independence has been intimately intertwined with the struggle for

1641	1649–53	1688–1690
The English Civil Wars have severe repercussions. The native Irish and Anglo-Norman Catholics support Charles I against the Protestant parliamentarians in the hope of restoring Catholic power in Ireland.	Cromwell lays waste throughout Ireland after the Irish support Charles I in the English Civil Wars; this includes the mass slaughtering of Catholic Irish and the confiscation of two million hectares of land.	Following the deposition of King James II, James' Catholic army fights William's Protestant forces, resulting in William's victory at the Battle of the Boyne, 12 July 1690.

recognition and supremacy between the Roman Catholic and Protestant churches. There are few European countries where religion has played such a key role and continues to exert huge influence – not least in the fact that the island remains roughly divided along religious lines – to the point that for many outside observers Ireland is somewhat akin to a Christian Middle East, a complex and confusing muddle that lends itself to oversimplified generalisations by those who don't have two lifetimes to figure it all out. Like us, for instance, in this short essay.

The relative ease with which the first Christian missionaries in the 5th and 6th centuries AD converted the local pagan tribes and their strong tradition of druidism was in part due to the clever fusing of traditional pagan rituals with the new Christian teaching, which created an exciting hybrid known as Celtic, or Insular Christianity – the presence on some early Christian churches of such decorative elements as Sheila-na-Gigs, a lewd female fertility symbol, is but one example.

Irish Christian scholars excelled in the study of Latin and Greek learning and Christian theology in the monasteries that flourished at, among other places, Clonmacnoise in County Offaly, Glendalough in County Wicklow and Lismore in County Waterford. It was the golden age, and the arts of manuscript illumination, metalworking and sculpture flourished, producing such treasures as the Book of Kells, ornate jewellery, and the many carved stone crosses that dot the island 'of saints and scholars'.

The nature of Christianity in Ireland was one of marked independence from Rome, especially in the areas of monastic rule and penitential practice, which emphasised private confession to a priest followed by penances levied by the priest in reparation – which is the spirit and letter of the practice of confession that exists to this day. The Irish were also exporting these teachings abroad, setting up monasteries across Europe such as the ones in Luxeuil in France and Bobbio in Italy, both founded by St Columbanus (AD 543–615).

To gain some insight into the mind of Michael Collins, read *In His Own Words*, a collection of Collins' writings and speeches.

The Golden Age ended with the invasion of Ireland by Henry II in 1170, for which Henry had the blessing of Pope Adrian IV and his papal laudabiliter, a document that granted the English king dominion over Ireland under the overlordship of the pope. Ireland's monastic independence was unacceptable in the new political climate brought on by the Gregorian reform movement of 1050–80, which sought to consolidate the ultimate authority of the papacy in all ecclesiastical, moral and social matters at the expense of the widespread monastic network. The influence of the major Irish monasteries began to wane in favour of the Norman bishops who oversaw the construction of the great cathedrals, most notably in Armagh and Dublin.

The second and more damaging reform of the Irish church occurred in the middle of the 16th century, and once again an English monarch was at the

1695	1795	1798
Penal laws (aka the 'popery code') prohibit Catholics from owning a horse, marrying outside of their religion, building churches out of anything but wood, and from buying or inheriting property.	Concerned at the attempts of the Society of United Irishmen to secure equal rights for non-Establishment Protestants and Catholics, a group of Protestants create an organisation – the Orange Institution.	The flogging and killings of potential rebels sparks a rising led by the United Irishmen and their leader, Wolfe Tone. Wolfe Tone is captured and taken to Dublin, where he commits suicide.

heart of it. The break with the Roman Catholic Church that followed Henry VIII's inability to secure papal blessing for his divorce of Catherine of Aragon in 1534 saw the establishment in Ireland (as in England) of a new Protestant church, with Henry as its supreme head. The Irish, however, were not ready to change their allegiances and remained largely loyal to Rome, which set off the religious wars that would dominate Irish affairs for the next 200 years and cast a huge shadow over the country that has not quite faded yet.

Henry was concerned that his new-found enemies on the continent would use Ireland as a base from which to invade England, so he decided to bring Ireland fully under his control, a policy that was continued by his daughter Elizabeth I. Their combined failure to convert Ireland to the new religion resulted in the crown ordering the pacification of the country by whatever methods possible, but the resultant brutality merely served to solidify Irish resentment and their commitment to Roman Catholicism.

The resistance had its most glorious moment in the Nine Years' War (1594–1603), when a combined alliance of Irish chieftains led by Hugh O'Neill fought the English armies to a standstill before eventually surrendering in 1603. The 'flight of the earls' in 1607, which saw O'Neill and his allies leave Ireland forever, marked the end of organised Irish rebellion and the full implementation of the policy of Plantation, whereby the confiscated lands of Catholic nobles were redistributed to 'planted' settlers of exclusively Protestant stock. This policy was most effective in Ulster, which was seen by the English as the hotbed of Irish resistance to English rule.

Neil Jordan's motion picture *Michael Collins*, starring Liam Neeson as the revolutionary, depicts the Easter Rising, the founding of the Free State and Collins' violent demise.

Alongside the policy of Plantation, the English also passed a series of Penal Laws in Ireland, which had the effect of almost totally disenfranchising all Catholics and, later, Presbyterians. The Jacobite Wars of the late 17th century, which pitted the Catholic James II against his son-in-law, the Protestant William of Orange, saw the Irish take sides along strictly religious lines: the disenfranchised Catholic majority supported James while the recently planted Protestant landowning minority lent their considerable support to William. It was William who won the day, and 12 July 1690 – when James was defeated at the Battle of the Boyne – has been celebrated ever since by Ulster Protestants with marches throughout the province.

Until the Catholic Emancipation Act of 1829, Irish Roman Catholics were almost totally impeded from worshipping freely. Clerics and bishops couldn't preach, with only lay priests allowed to operate, so long as they were registered with the government. The construction of churches was heavily regulated, and when allowed, they could only be built in barely durable wood. The most effective of the anti-Catholic laws, however, was the Popery Act of 1703, which sought to 'prevent the further growth of Popery' by requiring that all Catholics divide their lands equally among their sons, in effect diminishing Catholic land holdings. When the emancipation act was passed,

1801	1828–29	1845–51
The Act of Union unites Ireland politically with Britain. The Irish Parliament votes itself out of existence following a campaign of bribery. Around 100 Members of Parliament move to the House of Commons in London.	Daniel O'Connell exploits a loophole in the law to win a seat in Parliament but is unable to take it because he is Catholic. The prime minister passes the Catholic Emancipation Act giving limited rights to Catholics.	A mould ravages the potato harvest. The British government adopts a laissez faire attitue, resulting in the deaths of between 500,000 and one million, and the emigration of up to two million others.

it only granted limited rights to Catholics who owned a set area of land; the apartheid that preceded it ensured that they were few in number.

Hardly surprising then that the Catholic Church was heavily involved in the struggle for Irish freedom, although the traditionally conservative church was careful to only lend its support to lawful means of protest, such as Daniel O'Connell's Repeal Movement and, later, Parnell's Home Rule fight. When Parnell became embroiled in the divorce scandal in 1890, the church condemned him with all its might, thereby ending his career. It also condemned any rebel notion that smacked of illegality or socialism – the Easter Rising was roundly denounced from the pulpit for its bloodletting and its vaguely leftist proclamation.

If the Roman Catholic Church was shackled for much of the English occupation, it more than made up for it when the Free State came into being in 1922. The church's overwhelmingly conservative influence on the new state was felt everywhere, not least in the state's schools and hospitals and over virtually every aspect of social policy. Divorce, contraception, abortion and all manner of 'scurrilous literature' were obvious no-nos, but the church even managed to say no to a variety of welfare plans that would, for instance, provide government assistance to young mothers in need.

The Free State, and the Republic of Ireland that followed it in 1948, was 96% Catholic. Although 7.5% of the Free State population in 1922 was Protestant, their numbers had halved by the 1960s, with a disproportionately high rate of emigration among Protestants who felt threatened or unwelcome in the new Catholic state. The Catholic Church compounded the matter by emphasising the 1907 Ne Temere decree, which insisted that the children of mixed marriage be raised as Catholic under penalty of excommunication.

The dramatic decline in the influence of the church over the last two decades is primarily the result of global trends and greater prosperity in Ireland, but the devastating revelations of clerical abuse of boys and girls in the care of the Church over the last half century have defined an almost vitriolic reaction against the Church, particularly among the younger generation. The Church's reluctance to confront its own responsibilities in these shocking scandals, which include knowing about paedophiliac priests and consequently shuffling them from parish to parish, has heightened a sense of deep betrayal among many of the faithful.

The Irish in America by Michael Coffey takes up the history of the Famine where many histories leave off: the turbulent experiences of Irish immigrants in the USA.

A STATE APART: NORTHERN IRELAND

On 8 May 2007, the Northern Ireland Assembly, the devolved legislature of the province, finally meets again for the first time since October 2002. The First Minister, the Rev Ian Paisley, smiles, shakes hands and poses for photos with the Deputy First Minister, Martin McGuinness.

This is no straightforward meeting. Even if you've only kept one lazy eye on Irish affairs these last 30 years, you'll know that the sight of a Loyalist

1879–82	1912	1916
The Land War, led by the Land League, sees tenant farmers defying their landlords en masse to force the passing of the Land Act in 1881, which allows for fair rent, fixity of tenure and free sale.	Sir Edward Carson, a Dublin lawyer, forms the Ulster Volunteer Force (UVF) to create organised resistance against the passing of the Home Rule Bill, which would grant limited autonomy to Ireland.	The Easter Rising: a group of republicans take Dublin's General Post Office and announce the formation of an Irish Republic. After less than a week of fighting, the rebels surrender to the superior British forces.

firebrand like Paisley – who has a history of deep-rooted, often vicious enmity toward Irish nationalism and republicanism – and an ex-IRA commander like McGuinness shaking hands is nothing short of highly improbable. Needless to say, this historic agreement is the culmination of a painstakingly long road of domination, fighting, negotiation, concession and political posturing that began…

Well, it began in the 16th century, with the first Plantations of Ireland by the English crown, whereby the confiscated lands of the Gaelic and Hiberno-Norman gentry were awarded to English and Scottish settlers of good Protestant stock. The policy was most effective in Ulster, where the newly arrived Protestants were given an extra leg-up by the Penal Laws, which successfully reduced the now landless Catholic population to second-class citizens with little or no rights. Interestingly, from 1707 the Penal Laws also applied to Presbyterians (of which Paisley is one, albeit the founder of his own Free Presbyterian Church), who were considered not much better than Catholics.

Ireland Since the Famine by FSL Lyons is a standard history for all students of modern Ireland.

But let us fast-forward to 1921, when the notion of independent Ireland moved from aspiration to actuality. The Anglo-Irish Treaty resolved the thorny issue of Ulster's Protestant majority – represented by an armed and defiant Ulster Volunteer Force – by roughly partitioning the country and establishing a Boundary Commission that would decide on the final frontiers between north and south. A series of inflammatory press leaks meant that the findings of the commission – basically redividing the frontier so as to include more nationalists in the Free State – were never instituted and to this day Northern Ireland's borders are as they were in 1921.

On 22 June 1921 the Northern Ireland parliament came into being, with James Craig as the first prime minister. His Ulster Unionist Party (UUP) was to rule the new state until 1972, with the minority Catholic population (roughly 40%) stripped of any real power or representative strength by a parliament that favoured the Unionists through economic subsidy, bias in housing allocations and gerrymandering: Derry's electoral boundaries were redrawn so as to guarantee a Protestant council, even though the city was two-thirds Catholic. To keep everyone in line, the overwhelmingly Protestant Royal Ulster Constabulary and their militia, the B-Specials, made no effort to mask their blatantly sectarian bias. To all intents and purposes, Northern Ireland was an apartheid state.

The first challenge to the Unionist hegemony came with the long-dormant IRA's border campaign in the 1950s, but it was quickly quashed and its leaders imprisoned. A decade later, however, the authorities met with a far more defiant foe, in the shape of the Civil Rights Movement, founded in 1967 and heavily influenced by its US counterpart as it sought to redress the blatant sectarianism in Derry. In October 1968 a mainly Catholic march in Derry was violently broken up by the RUC amid rumours that the IRA

1919–21	1921	1921–22
Irish War of Independence, aka the Black and Tan War on account of British irregulars wearing mixed police (black) and army khaki uniforms, begins in January 1919.	Two years and 1400 casualties later, the war ends in a truce on 11 July 1921 that leads to peace talks. After negotiations in London, the Irish delegation signs the Anglo-Irish Treaty on 6 December.	The treaty gives 26 counties of Ireland independence and allows six largely Protestant Ulster counties the choice of opting out. The Irish Free State is founded in 1922.

had provided 'security' for the marchers. Nobody knew it at the time, but the Troubles had begun.

In January 1969 another civil rights movement, called People's Democracy, organised a march from Belfast to Derry. As the marchers neared their destination they were attacked by a Protestant mob. The police first stood to one side and then compounded the problem with a sweep through the predominantly Catholic Bogside district. Further marches, protests and violence followed, and far from keeping the two sides apart, the police were clearly part of the problem. In August British troops went to Derry and then Belfast to maintain law and order. The British army was initially welcomed in some Catholic quarters, but soon it too came to be seen as a tool of the Protestant majority. Overreaction by the army actually fuelled recruitment into the long-dormant IRA. IRA numbers especially increased after Bloody Sunday (30 January 1972), when British troops killed 13 civilians in Derry.

Northern Ireland's Parliament was abolished in 1972, although substantial progress had been made towards civil rights. A new power-sharing arrangement, worked out in the 1973 Sunningdale Agreement, was killed stone dead by the massive and overwhelmingly Protestant Ulster Workers' Strike of 1974.

While continuing to target people in Northern Ireland, the IRA moved its campaign of bombing to mainland Britain. Its activities were increasingly condemned by citizens and parties on all sides of the political spectrum. Meanwhile, Loyalist paramilitaries began a sectarian murder campaign against Catholics. Passions reached fever pitch in 1981 when republican prisoners in the North went on a hunger strike, demanding the right to be recognised as political prisoners. Ten of them fasted to death, the best known being an elected MP, Bobby Sands.

The waters were further muddied by an incredible variety of parties splintering into subgroups with different agendas. The IRA had split into 'official' and 'provisional' wings, from which sprang more extreme republican organisations such as the Irish National Liberation Army (INLA). Myriad Protestant, Loyalist paramilitary organisations sprang up in opposition to the IRA, and violence was typically met with violence.

In the 1990s external circumstances started to alter the picture. Membership of the EU, economic progress in Ireland and the declining importance of the Catholic Church in the South started to reduce differences between the North and South. Also, American interest added an international dimension to the situation.

A series of negotiated statements between the Unionists, nationalists and the British and Irish governments eventually resulted in the historic Good Friday Agreement of 1998. The new assembly, led by First Minister David Trimble of the UUP and Deputy First Minister Seamus Mallon of the nationalist Social Democratic and Liberal Party (SDLP) was beset by sectarian

Brendan O'Brien's popular *A Pocket History of the IRA* summarises a lot of complex history in a mere 150 pages, but it's a good introduction.

1922–23	1932	1948
Unwilling to accept the terms of the treaty, forces led by Éamon de Valera take up arms against their former comrades, led by Michael Collins. A brief but bloody civil war ensures, resulting in the death of Collins.	After 10 years in the political wilderness, de Valera leads his Fianna Fáil party into government and goes about weakening the ties between the Free State and Britain.	Fianna Fáil loses the 1948 general election to Fine Gael in coalition with the new republican Clann an Poblachta. The new government declares the Free State to be a republic at last.

divisions from the outset, which resulted in no less than four suspensions, the last from October 2002 until May 2007.

During this period, the politics of Northern Ireland polarised dramatically, resulting in the falling away of the more moderate UUP and the emergence of the hardline Democratic Unionist Party (DUP), led by Ian Paisley; and, on the nationalist side, the emergence of the IRA's political wing, Sinn Féin, as the main torch-bearer of nationalist aspirations, under the leadership of Gerry Adams and Martin McGuinness.

The hardening of political opinion was almost inevitable. While both sides were eager to maintain an end to the violence, neither side wanted to be accused of having a soft underbelly, especially if both sides' aspirations could not, despite what was promised, be realised by purely political means. Consequently, the DUP and Sinn Féin dug their heels in, with the main sticking points being decommissioning of IRA weapons and the identity and composition of the new police force ushered in to replace the RUC. Paisley and the Unionists made increasingly difficult demands of the decommissioning bodies (photographic evidence, Unionist witnesses etc) as they blatantly refused to accept anything less than an open and complete surrender of the IRA, while Sinn Féin refused to join the police board that monitored the affairs of the Police Service of Northern Ireland (PSNI), effectively refusing to change their policy of total noncooperation with the security forces. In the background, now inactive members of the paramilitary groups on both sides were revealed to be involved in all kinds of murky dealings such as drug dealing and turf wars – the most spectacular moment of all came in December 2004 when a £26.5m bank robbery saw the finger of blame pointed directly at republicans.

But Tony Blair and Bertie Ahern were not about to see their political legacy ruined by northern stubbornness. They continued to turn the screws on both sides, urging them to continue negotiating just as everyone else had begun to despair of ever seeing a resolution. In an effective bit of strong-arming, they set a deadline for resolution and made vague threats to both sides about the consequences of not meeting the deadline. But in a typically Irish bit of face-saving, the Unionists balked at the deadline of 26 March, 2007 and, in a deal agreed with Sinn Féin, announced that they would take their seats in the assembly on 8 May. It was a classic case of 'we'll do it, but we'll do it our way'.

SHOULD I STAY OR SHOULD I GO?

The poignant image of starving emigrants, forced to leave the land of their birth for far-flung fields because to stay would be to die, is one of Irish history's more emotional issues, especially as emigration has played a singularly important role in the country's social, economic and political life. A whole century's worth of sad songs intone the emigrant's plight and places the

A History of Ireland by Mike Cronin summarises all of Ireland's history in less than 300 pages. It's an easy read, but doesn't offer much in the way of analysis.

1949	1969	1972
Ireland leaves the British Commonwealth, and in so doing the South cuts its final links to the North.	Marches by the Northern Ireland Civil Rights Association are disrupted by Loyalist attacks and police action, resulting in rioting. It culminates in the 'Battle of the Bogside' and is the beginning of the Troubles.	The Republic (and Northern Ireland) become members of the EEC. On Bloody Sunday, 13 civilians are killed by British troops; Westminster suspends the Stormont government and introduces direct rule.

AMERICAN CONNECTIONS

Today, more than 40 million Americans have Irish ancestry, a legacy of successive waves of emigration spurred by events from the Potato Famine of the 1840s to the Depression of the 1930s. Many of the legendary figures of American history, from Davy Crockett to John Steinbeck, and 16 out of the 42 US presidents to date are of Irish descent.

Here's a list of places covered in this guide that have links to past US presidents or deal with the experience of Irish emigrants to the USA:

■ Andrew Jackson Centre (p673), County Antrim

■ Arthur Cottage (p675), County Antrim

■ Dunbrody Heritage Ship (p180), County Wexford

■ Grant Ancestral Homestead (p693), County Tyrone

■ Kennedy Homestead (p181), County Wexford

■ Queenstown Story Heritage Centre (p214), County Cork

■ Ulster American Folk Park (p690), County Tyrone

blame for it squarely at someone else's door, namely the Anglo-Irish lords and the English.

Yet the issue is not nearly as straightforward as that. Ireland's emigrant patterns have followed two basic models: the 'push' model, where people left because they were evicted, faced poverty or religious persecution; and the 'pull' model, where emigrants were attracted to foreign lands by the promise of a significantly better life – 600-acre plots in the US Midwest for next-to-nothing were quite an enticing prospect in the mid-19th-century.

The tragic image of the Irish emigrant was born as a result of the Great Famine of 1845–51, the watershed of Irish emigration. But the Irish had been leaving Ireland long before then, primarily as a result of the collapse of cereal-crop and linen prices (Ireland's two most important exports) in the post-Napoleonic era after 1815. It is estimated that between one and 1.5 million people emigrated in the years leading up to 1845. Nevertheless, the severe crisis provoked by the repeated failures of potato harvests led to a dramatic increase in the numbers leaving Ireland: it is estimated that 1.25 million left the country between 1845 and 1851, with the majority departing from the west of the country – a population loss from which that part of Ireland has never fully recovered. In 1841, the population of the Ireland was 6.5 million (excluding 1.6 million living in what eventually became Northern Ireland); 20 years later, it had fallen to 4.4 million.

The deep-rooted scar caused by the Famine and its socioeconomic aftermath has given rise to the enduring myth that entire families were forced to

1974	1981	1993
The Sunningdale Agreement results in a new Northern Ireland Assembly. Unionists oppose the agreement and the Ulster Workers' Council calls a strike that paralyses the province and brings an end to the Assembly.	Ten Republican prisoners die as the result of a hunger strike. The first hunger striker to die, Bobby Sands is elected to Parliament on an Anti-H-Block ticket. Over 100,000 people attend Sands' funeral.	Downing Street Declaration is signed by British PM John Major and Irish PM Albert Reynolds. It states that Britain has no 'selfish, strategic or economic interest in Northern Ireland'.

emigrate, conjuring up the emotive idea of the old, sickly parents huddled together on the ship. Statistics show that in the main it was young people who left. Indeed, going abroad to seek one's fortune became a rite of passage for many Irish right up to the 1980s. Parents and older relatives generally stayed behind, and the remittances sent home by their emigrant sons and daughters (£1.4 million yearly in 1851) became an important supplement to income.

What is certain, however, is that emigration was to prove a major drain of Irish resources for more than a century thereafter. Between 1871 and 1961, the average annual net emigration from Ireland consistently exceeded the natural increase in the Irish population, which shrank from about 4.4 million in 1861 (excluding the 1.3 million living in what eventually became Northern Ireland) to 2.8 million in 1961. Ireland's lagging economic development meant that emigration was especially acute during the so-called Age of Mass Migration (1871–1926), when all manner of Europeans were emigrating to the new worlds in their millions, and in the post-WWII era (1951–61), when the European economies were in recession.

Although the Irish population began growing again in the 1960s – the lack of contraception or abortion, coupled with a major push on the part of the authorities to encourage a high birth rate, was especially helpful – net migration remained negative (departures exceeding arrivals) until the 1990s except for a brief flurry in the 1970s. An estimated 3 million Irish citizens currently live abroad, of whom 1.2 million were born in Ireland. The majority live in the US and the UK.

The turning point came in 1996, when Ireland officially became a country of net immigration – the last EU nation to do so. Rapid economic growth and an unprecedented demand for labour not only saw unemployment tumble from 15.9% in 1993 to a historic low of 4.2% in 2005 but the number of arrivals grow from about 18,000 in 1987 to more than 68,000 per annum in 2002. The growth in Irish immigration has been driven increasingly by non-Irish migrants, with more than half of all non-Irish arriving in Ireland since 2000 having been born outside the EU. According to the 2006 census, 10% of the population is now foreign born. The dramatic shift in Ireland's migration is best understood when compared to the rest of Europe, for in one short decade the country went from being the only EU member with negative net migration to having the second-highest migration rate after Luxembourg. For 150 years Ireland was a country to escape from; nowadays, people can't get into it fast enough.

Not quite. A surprising fact, hidden among the statistics that show Ireland as a country of immigration, is that the Republic is still at the top of the European emigration charts, losing a higher percentage of its native born than any other country in Europe – roughly about 25,000 a year. These numbers, however, have been largely offset by the phenomenon

Many films depict events related to the Troubles, including *Bloody Sunday* (2002), *The Boxer* (1997; starring Daniel Day-Lewis) and *In the Name of the Father* (1994; also starring Day-Lewis).

mid–1990s	**1994**	**1998**
Low corporate tax, restraint in government spending, transfer payments from the EU and a low-cost labour market result in the 'Celtic Tiger' boom, transforming Ireland into one of Europe's wealthiest countries.	Sinn Féin leader, Gerry Adams, announces a 'cessation of violence' on behalf of the IRA on 31 August. In October, the Combined Loyalist Military Command also announces a ceasefire.	On 10 April, 1negotiations culminate in the Good Friday Agreement, under which the new Northern Ireland Assembly is given full legislative and executive authority.

of the 'returning Irish', who account for roughly the same on a yearly basis.

Economics are unquestionably an important underlying factor for all emigration and immigration, but in Ireland, societal mores that impinge on the freedoms it allows its citizens is another key driver. Ireland's relative poverty undoubtedly resulted in millions seeking opportunities elsewhere, but in recent times the restrictive attitudes of Irish society – particular in the post-WWII era, when conservative mores dictated that the baby-boomer generation would not have the same rights and freedoms as found elsewhere – pushed many young people to make new lives abroad. Although Irish society has changed dramatically in the last 20 years, rural emigration – to Dublin and beyond – remains a fact of life in Ireland.

Nevertheless, a buoyant and prosperous economy with bountiful employment, coupled with an increasingly liberalised society richly flavoured by multicultural influences, has set Ireland on a path it has never been on before. The overwhelming hopelessness of Irish poverty and the suffocating stranglehold of the conservative Church on the nation's morality are very much a thing of the past, and while important questions about the future of the country and its population remain unanswered and subject to a host of widely divergent predictions, it is clear that this small, relatively young nation has finally come of age.

A History of Ulster by Jonathon Bardon is a serious and far-reaching attempt to come to grips with Northern Ireland's saga.

1998	2005	2007
The 'Real IRA' detonate a bomb in Omagh, killing 29 people and injuring 200. It is the worst single atrocity in the history of the Troubles, but public outrage and swift action by politicians prevent a Loyalist backlash.	The IRA issues a statement, ordering its units not to engage in 'any other activities' apart from assisting 'the development of purely political and democratic programmes through exclusively peaceful means'.	The NI Assembly resumes after a five-year break when talks between Unionists and Republicans remain in stalemate. They resolve their primary issues.

The Culture

THE NATIONAL PSYCHE

The Irish are justifiably renowned for their easy-going, affable nature. They're famous for being warm and friendly, which is just another way of saying that the Irish love a bit of a chat, whether it be with friends or strangers. They will entertain with their humour, alarm you with their willingness to get stuck in to a good debate and will cut you down with their razor-sharp wit. Slagging – the Irish version of teasing – is an art form, which may seem caustic to unfamiliar ears but is quickly revealed as intrinsic element of how the Irish relate to one another; it is commonly assumed that the mettle of friendship is proven by how well you can take a joke rather than the payment of a cheap compliment.

The Irish aren't big on talking themselves up; self-deprecation is a much-admired art form in Ireland, but it is generally accepted that the more you talk yourself down, the higher your reality is likely to be. The other trait the Irish have is begrudgery – although it's something only recognised by them and generally kept within the wider family. It's kind of amusing, though, to note that someone like Bono is subject to more intense criticism in Ireland than anywhere else in the world.

Beneath all of the garrulous sociability and self-deprecating twaddle lurks a dark secret, which is that, at heart, the Irish are low on self-esteem. They're therefore very suspicious of praise and tend not to believe anything nice that's said about them. The Irish wallow in false modesty like a sport.

This goes some way toward explaining the peculiar relationship Ireland has with alcohol. The country regularly tops the list of the world's biggest binge drinkers, and while there is an increasing awareness of and alarm at the devastation caused by alcohol to Irish society (especially young people), drinking remains the country's most popular social pastime with no sign of letting up; spend a weekend night walking around any town in the country and you'll get a first-hand feel of the influence and effect of the booze.

Some experts put Ireland's binge-drinking antics down to the dramatic rise in the country's economic fortunes. Whatever the truth of it, there is no denying that the Celtic Tiger has transformed Irish society in ways no one could foresee, with this generation of under-30s utterly unaware of life before the untrammelled possibilities of the current age, when unemployment, emigration and a cap on ambition were basic facts of life.

Prosperity has served the country well, and while a huge question mark still remains over the equitable distribution of the wealth accrued during the last decade, there is no doubt that the island has seen some dramatic shifts in traditional attitudes. Not so long ago, Roman Catholicism was a central pillar of everyday life in Ireland; today, the Church's grip on society has slackened to the point that a recent survey revealed that one-third of Irish youth didn't know where Jesus was born or what was celebrated at Easter.

LIFESTYLE

The Irish may like to grumble – about work, the weather, the government and those feckin' eejits on reality TV shows – but if pressed will tell you that they live in the best country on earth. There's loads *wrong* with the place, but isn't it the same way everywhere else?

Traditional Ireland – of the large family, closely linked to church and community – is quickly disappearing as the increased urbanisation of Ireland continues to break up the social fabric of community interdependence

The most popular names in Ireland are Jack and Emma.

that was a necessary element of relative poverty. Contemporary Ireland is therefore not altogether different from any other European country, and you have to travel further to the margins of the country – the islands and the isolated rural communities – to find an older version of society.

Ireland has long been a pretty homogenous country, but the arrival of thousands of immigrants from all over the world – 10% of the population is non-Irish – has challenged the mores of racial tolerance and integration. To a large extent it has been successful, although if you scratch beneath the surface, racial tensions can be exposed. So long as the new arrivals take on the jobs that many Irish wouldn't bother doing anymore, everything is relatively hunky dory; it's when the second generation of immigrants begin competing for the middle class jobs that Ireland's tolerant credentials will truly be tested.

The average number of children per family has fallen to 1.4, the lowest in Irish history.

POPULATION

The total population of Ireland is around 5.9 million: 4.2 million in the Republic and 1.7 million in Northern Ireland. There has been a steady increase in population since 1961, but the figures have a way to go before they reach their pre-Famine levels: before the tragedy of 1841–51 the population was in excess of eight million. Death and emigration reduced the population to around five million, and emigration continued at a high level for the next 100 years.

Although the effects of emigration have been tempered by a slow-down in the rate and an increase in the rate of immigrant arrivals – 10% of the population is now foreign-born – Ireland still loses proportionally more of its native children to emigration than any other European country; in 2005 more than 20,500 left the country to seek their fortunes elsewhere.

Dublin is the largest city and the capital of the Republic, with around 1.2 million people (about 40% of the population) living within commuting distance of the city centre. The Republic's next largest cities are Cork, Galway and Limerick. Ireland's population is predominantly young: 41% is aged under 25 and in fact Ireland has the highest population of 15- to 24-year-olds and second highest of under 15-year-olds in Europe.

GAY-FRIENDLY IRELAND

The best things that ever happened to gay Ireland were the taming of the dictating church and the enactment of protective legislation against any kind of sexual discrimination. According to Brian Merriman, the Artistic Director of the International Dublin Gay Theatre Festival, the collapse of church authority and the shocking revelations of priestly abuse, coupled with the liberalisation of the divorce law, helped Ireland come to terms with its own sexual and social honesty:

'Ireland is no longer talking about 'them' when referring to anyone who is vaguely unconventional; they're talking about 'us', and that every family has the potential to be different,' he says with great conviction, 'it's not just 'them' who have the gay in the closet. They're everywhere!'

But it's not all good. There is a huge difference still between attitudes in urban and rural Ireland, he says, and while legislation and liberalisation have been very important, there is still a legacy of internalised homophobia.

'Our enemies are no longer as clearly visible, so it's hard to know sometimes who exactly thinks what.'

He believes, however, that gays and lesbians need to be more visible in Irish society, if only to continue the struggle for parity of esteem and respect. Merriman says that 'the fight will not stop until the constitutional ban on gays getting married is lifted and that there are no second-class citizens in 21st century Ireland.'

In Northern Ireland, Belfast is the principal city, with a population of around 277,000. It has the youngest population in the UK, with 25% aged under 16.

These figures (and population counts throughout the book) are based on the last census of 2002.

Females outnumber males in Dublin by 20,000.

SPORT

Ireland, by and large, is a nation of sports enthusiasts. Whether it's shouting the team on from the sideline or from a bar stool, the Irish have always taken their sport seriously.

Gaelic Football & Hurling

Gaelic games are at the core of Irishness; they are enmeshed in the fabric of Irish life and hold a unique place in the heart of its culture. Their resurgence towards the end of the 19th century was entwined with the whole Gaelic revival and the march towards Irish independence. The beating heart of Gaelic sports is the Gaelic Athletic Association (GAA), set up in 1884, 'for the preservation and cultivation of National pastimes'. The GAA is still responsible for fostering these amateur games and it warms our hearts to see that after all this time – and amid the onslaught of globalisation and the general commercialisation of sport – they are still far and away the most popular sports in Ireland.

Gaelic games are fast, furious and not for the faint-hearted. Challenges are fierce, and contact between players is extremely aggressive. Both games are played by two teams of 15 players whose aim is to get the ball through what resembles a rugby goal: two long vertical posts joined by a horizontal bar, below which is a soccer-style goal, protected by a goalkeeper. Goals (below the crossbar) are worth three points, whereas a ball placed over the bar between the posts is worth one point. Scores are shown thus: 1–12, meaning one goal and 12 points, giving a total of 15 points.

Gaelic football is played with a round, soccer-size ball, and players are allowed to kick it or hand-pass it, like Aussie Rules. Hurling, which is

---

AN IMMIGRANT TALE

Zaituna Aieiken is a 29-year-old Uyghur born in East Turkistan but raised in Kazakhstan, who arrived in Ireland in 2004. She settled first in Carrick-on-Suir, County Waterford before moving to Dublin six months later, where she began studying Health Care with a view toward beginning a new career as a Care Assistant; for now, though, she pays the rent as a domestic cleaner.

Her take on the importance of the pub in Irish society is surprising: 'If you want to find a good job in Ireland,' she says, 'you need to drink in an Irish pub, because that's where all the best opportunities come up!'

The pub is also the best place to hook up with members of the opposite sex, although she has little faith in Irish men's commitment to long-term relationships, especially with foreigners. 'Irish guys only want to have fun,' she says with a smile.

Although she feels quite welcome and has never been a victim of racism, she thinks that the older generation are kinder and friendlier than young people, who tend to be a little more intolerant and impatient with foreigners who are struggling to assimilate.

She has plenty of Irish acquaintances, but she socialises mostly within the so-called Russian community, made up mostly of non-Russian citizens of the former USSR, where she feels completely accepted as a Muslim woman.

'During Ramadan my Russian Orthodox friends come for sundown meals, and during Easter I go to their houses to celebrate. Everyone is the same and we all enjoy each other's company.' A great lesson indeed.

considered by far the more beautiful game, is played with a flat ashen stick or bat known as a hurley or *camán*. The small leather ball, called a *slíothar*, is hit or carried on the hurley; hand-passing is also allowed. Both games are played over 70 action-filled minutes.

Both sports are county-based games. The dream of every club player is to represent his county, with the hope of perhaps playing in an All-Ireland final in September at Croke Park in Dublin, the climax of a knockout championship that is played first at a provincial and then interprovincial level.

You can find out more about the history and rules of Gaelic sports on the Gaelic Athletic Association website at www.gaa.ie.

Rugby & Football

Rugby and football (soccer) enjoy considerable support all over the country, particularly around Dublin; football is very popular in Northern Ireland.

Although traditionally the preserve of Ireland's middle classes, rugby captures the mood of the whole island in February and March during the annual Six Nations Championships, because the Irish team is drawn from both sides of the border and is supported by both nationalists and unionists. In recognition of this, the Irish national anthem is no longer played at internationals, replaced by the slightly dodgy but thoroughly inoffensive *Ireland's Call*, a song written especially for the purpose. See p110 and www.irishrugby.ie for more details.

There is huge support in Ireland for the 'world game', although fans are much more enthusiastic about the likes of Manchester United, Liverpool and the two Glasgow clubs (Rangers and Celtic) than the struggling pros and part-timers that make up the **National League** (www.fai.ie) in the Republic, and the **Irish League** (www.irishfa.com) in Northern Ireland. It's just too difficult for domestic teams to compete with the multimillionaire glitz and glamour of the English Premiership, which has always drawn off the cream of Irish talent. The current crop of local lads playing in England include Robbie Keane (Spurs), Damien Duff (Newcastle), Aiden McGeady (Celtic) and David Healy (Leeds).

At an international level, the Republic and Northern Ireland field separate teams; in 2007 Northern Ireland was on its best run of form for years thanks to the inspirational manager Lawrie Sanchez (who then left to take over at English premiership team Fulham) while the Republic wasn't doing much of anything. International matches are played at Croke Park, Dublin (until 2009 at least) and **Windsor Park** (☎ 9024 4198; off Lisburn Rd), Belfast.

Horse Racing & Greyhound Racing

A passion for horse racing is deeply entrenched in Irish life and comes without the snobbery of its English counterpart. If you fancy a flutter on the gee-gees you can watch racing from around Ireland and England on the TV in bookmakers shops every day. No money ever seems to change hands in the betting, however, and every Irish punter will tell you they 'broke even'.

Ireland has a reputation for producing world-class horses for racing and other equestrian events like showjumping, also very popular albeit in a much less egalitarian kind of way. Major annual races include the Irish Grand National (Fairyhouse, April), Irish Derby (the Curragh, June) and Irish Leger (the Curragh, September). For more information on events contact **Horse Racing Ireland** (☎ 045-842 800; www.hri.ie; Thoroughbred County House, Kill, Co Kildare).

Traditionally the poor-man's punt, greyhound racing ('the dogs'), has been smartened up in recent years and partly turned into a corporate outing. It offers a cheaper, more accessible and more local alternative to horse racing. There are 20 tracks across the country, administered by the **Irish Greyhound Board** (☎ 061-316 788; www.igb.ie; 104 Henry St, Limerick).

Golf

Golf is enormously popular in Ireland and there are many fine golf courses. The annual Irish Open takes place in June or July and the Irish Women's Open in September. For details of venues, contact the **Golfing Union of Ireland** (☎ 01-269 4111; www.gui.ie; 81 Eglinton Rd, Donnybrook, Dublin 4). Ireland's best include Darren Clarke, Paul McGinley and, of course, 2007 Open champion winner Padraig Harrington – the first Irish player to win a major since Fred Daly in 1947. Keep an eye out for teen sensation Rory McIlroy, who completed an Irish double in 2007 when he won the Silver Medal at the Open for best amateur.

Cycling

Cycling is a popular spectator sport and major annual events include the gruelling **FBD Insurance Rás** (www.fbdinsuranceras.com), formerly known as the Milk Rás; an eight-day stage race held in May which sometimes approaches 1120km (700 miles) in length, and the Tour of Ulster, a three-day stage race held at the end of April. For more information on events see www.irishcycling.com.

Athletics

Athletics is popular and the Republic has produced a few international stars, particularly in middle- and long-distance events. Cork athlete Sonia O'Sullivan consistently leads in women's long-distance track events worldwide, and Catherina McKiernan is one of the world's top marathon runners. In Ireland, the main athletic meets are held at Morton Stadium, Dublin. The **Belfast Marathon** (www.belfastcitymarathon.com) on the first Monday in May and the **Dublin Marathon** (www.dublincitymarathon.ie) is run on the last Monday in October.

> Visit www.medialive .ie for everything you wanted to know about Irish media but were afraid to ask.

Boxing

Boxing has traditionally had a strong working-class following. Irish boxers have often won Olympic medals or world championships. Barry McGuigan and Steve Collins, both now retired, were world champions in their day; the best of the current crop is Dublin boxer Bernard Dunne, who, at the time of writing, was the European Super Bantamweight champion.

Road Bowling

The object of this sport is to throw a cast-iron ball along a public road (normally one with little traffic) for a designated distance, usually 1km or 2km. The person who does it in the least number of throws is the winner. The main centres are Cork and Armagh and competitions take place throughout the year, attracting considerable crowds. The sport has been taken up in various countries around the world, including the USA, Germany and the Netherlands, and a world championship competition has been set up (see www.irishroadbowling.ie).

Handball

Handball is another Irish sport with ancient origins and, like Gaelic football and hurling, is governed by the GAA. It is different from Olympic handball in that it is played by two individuals or two pairs who use their hands to strike a ball against a forecourt wall, rather like squash.

MEDIA
Newspapers

Five national dailies, six national Sundays, stacks of Irish editions of British publications, hundreds of magazines, more than a dozen radio stations, four terrestrial TV stations and more digital channels than you could shake the remote control at…Ireland just doesn't run out of subjects to discuss.

The dominant local player is Independent News & Media, owned by Ireland's primo businessman, Tony O'Reilly. Its newspapers – the *Irish Independent, Sunday Independent* and *Evening Herald* – are by far the biggest sellers in each market.

The massive overspill of British media here, particularly in relation to the saturated Sunday market, is the biggest challenge facing the Irish media. Rupert Murdoch's News International recognised the importance of the Irish market early, established an office in Dublin and set about an assault of the newspaper racks with its main titles, the *Irish Sun, News of the World* and *Sunday Times*. Every UK tabloid paper now has an Irish edition, leading to accusations by media speculators that Irish culture is being coarsened by the widespread availability of even more tasteless tabloid tat. The traditions of the UK tabloids, who have built circulation on the back of celebrity buy-ups and salacious stories about sex and crime, have inevitably been exported and are beginning to have an influence on the editorial position of the Irish titles, particularly on Sunday.

What this means, of course, is that local papers lacking Murdoch's mammoth resources will struggle even more than they already do; the country's best newspaper, the *Irish Times*, nearly went under in 2002 and is constantly worried about circulation. All of this goes a way toward explaining how all the English newspapers cost less than a euro, whilst the three Irish national dailies all cost €1.60.

In the north the three main papers are the *Belfast Telegraph*, with the highest circulation, followed by the pro-Unionist *Newsletter* – Europe's oldest surviving newspaper having begun publication in 1737 – and the equally popular pro-Nationalist *Irish News*.

TV & Radio

Yeats is Dead, edited by Joseph O'Connor and penned by 15 Irish authors from populist Marian Keyes to heavyweight Anthony Cronin and plenty in between, is a screwball comedic caper about a petty criminal who gets his hands on Joyce's last manuscript.

Irish TV is small fry, it always has been. It lacks the funding and the audience available to behemoths like the BBC. But – and this is a huge but – compared to that of most other European countries it is actually good. However, the national broadcaster, RTE, gets its fair share of abuse for being narrow-minded, conservative, boring, short-sighted and way behind the times – and that's just for turning down the chance to produce the enormously successful comedy drama series *Father Ted* (a gentle and hilarious poke at conservative Ireland, which was then commissioned by Britain's Channel 4).

There are four terrestrial TV channels in Ireland. RTE's strength is in its widespread sports coverage and news and current affairs programming – it's thorough, insightful and often hard-hitting. Programmes like *Today Tonight, Questions and Answers* and *Prime Time* are as good, or better, as anything you'll see elsewhere in the world; the reporting treats the audience like mature responsible adults who don't need issues dumbed down or simplified. But let's not forget the Angelus, Ireland's very own call to prayer: 18 sombre hits of a church bell heard at 6pm on RTE1 (and at noon on radio). Undoubtedly out of step with a fast-paced and secular society, it is a daily reminder of the state-encouraged piety of not so long ago.

The purely commercial TV3 has a lightweight programming philosophy, with second-string US fluff to compliment its diet of reality TV shows and celebrity nonsense. The Irish-language station TG4 has the most diverse and challenging output, combining great movies (in English) with an interesting selection of dramas and documentaries *as gaeilge* (but with English subtitles). The main British TV stations – BBC, ITV and Channel 4 – are also available in most Irish homes, through cable.

The big players in the digital TV business are the homegrown NTL and the behemoth that is Sky, who continue to make solid progress in bringing the multichannel revolution into Irish homes.

In the radio market RTE is also the dominant player, with three stations: Radio 1 & 2 and Lyric FM. However, it's position is being challenged by a combination of independent national stations (Today FM and Newstalk 106-108) and a plethora of local and regional stations.

RELIGION

About 3.7 million residents in the Republic call themselves Roman Catholic, followed by 3% Protestant, 0.5% Muslim and the rest an assortment of other beliefs including none at all. In the North the breakdown is about 60% Protestant and 40% Catholic. Most Irish Protestants are members of the Church of Ireland, an offshoot of the Church of England, and the Presbyterian and Methodist Churches.

Statistics don't tell the whole story though, and the influence of the Catholic Church has waned dramatically in the last decade. Most young people see the church as irrelevant and out-of-step with the major social issues of the day, including divorce, contraception, abortion, homosexuality and cohabitation. The terrible revelations of widespread abuse of children by parish priests, and the untidy efforts of the church authorities to sweep the truth under the carpet, have provoked a seething rage among many Irish at the church's gross insensitivity to the care of their flock, while many older believers feel an acute sense of betrayal that has led them to question a lifetime's devotion to their local parishes.

And then there's money: increased prosperity means that the Irish have become used to being rewarded in *this* life, and so many have replaced God with mammon as a focus of worship. But old habits die hard, and Sunday Mass is still a feature of the weekly calendar, especially in rural communities. Oddly enough, the primates of both the Roman Catholic Church (Archbishop Sean Brady) and the Church of Ireland (Archbishop Robert Eames) sit in Armagh, Northern Ireland, the traditional religious capital of St Patrick. The country's religious history clearly overrides its current divisions.

ARTS
Literature

Of all their national traits, characteristics and cultural expressions it's perhaps the way the Irish speak and write that best distinguishes them. Their love of language and their great oral tradition have contributed to Ireland's legacy of world-renowned writers and storytellers. And all this in a language imposed on them by a foreign invader; the Irish responded to this act of cultural piracy by mastering a magnificent hybrid: English in every respect but flavoured and enriched by the rhythms, pronunciation patterns and grammatical peculiarities of Irish.

Before there was anything like modern literature there was the Ulaid (Ulster) Cycle, Ireland's version of the Homeric epic, written down from oral tradition between the 8th and 12th centuries. The chief story is the *Táin Bó Cúailnge* (Cattle Raid of Cooley), about a battle between Queen Maeve of Connaught and Cúchulainn, the principal hero of Irish mythology. Cúchulainn appears in the work of Irish writers right up to the present day, from Samuel Beckett to Frank McCourt.

Zip forward 1000 years, past the genius of Jonathan Swift (1667–1745) and his *Gulliver's Travels;* stopping to acknowledge acclaimed dramatist Oscar Wilde (1854–1900); *Dracula* creator Bram Stoker (1847–1912) – the name of the count may have come from the Irish *droch fhola* (bad blood);

Circle of Friends by the queen of Irish popular fiction, Maeve Binchy, ably captures the often hilarious peculiarities of the lives of two hapless country girls in the 1940s who come to Dublin in search of romance.

The Booker Prize-winning novel *The Sea* by John Banville is an engrossing meditation on mortality, grief, death, childhood and memory.

and the literary giant that was James Joyce (1882–1941), whose name and books elicit enormous pride in Ireland but we've yet to meet five people who have read all of *Ulysses*!

The majority of Joyce's literary output came when he had left Ireland for the artistic hotbed that was Paris, which was also true for another great experimenter of language and style, Samuel Beckett (1906–89). Influenced by the Italian poet Dante and French philosopher Descartes, his work centres on fundamental existential questions about the human condition and the nature of self. He is probably best known for his play *Waiting for Godot* but his unassailable reputation is based on a series of stark novels and plays.

Of the dozens of 20th century Irish authors to have achieved published renown, some names to look out for include playwright and novelist Brendan Behan (1923–64), who weaved tragedy, wit and a turbulent life into his best work, including *Borstal Boy*, *The Quare Fellow* and *The Hostage*. Inevitably, Behan died young of alcoholism.

Belfast-born CS Lewis (1898–1963) died a year earlier, but he left us *The Chronicles of Narnia*, a series of allegorical children's stories (one made into a 2005 film). Other Northern writers have, not surprisingly, featured the Troubles in their work: Bernard McLaverty's *Cal* (also made into a film) and his more recent *The Anatomy School* are both wonderful.

Contemporary writers are plentiful, including superstar Roddy Doyle (1958–), author of the Barrytown trilogy *The Commitments*, *The Snapper* and *The Van* as well as a host of more serious books; the Booker-prize winning John Banville (1945–), who nabbed the prestigious award with *The Sea*; and the wonderful Colm Tóibín (1955–), whose *The Master* (2004), about Henry James, won the Los Angeles Times' Novel of the Year award.

Ireland has produced its fair share of female writers. The 'come here and I'll tell you a story' style of Maeve Binchy (1940–) has seen her outsell many of the greats of Irish literature, including Beckett and Behan, and her long list of bestsellers includes *Light a Penny Candle* (1982) and *Circle of Friends* (1990); both have been made into successful films.

Nuala O'Faolain, former opinion columnist for the *Irish Times*, 'accidentally' wrote an autobiography when a small publisher asked her to write an introduction to a collection of her columns. Her irreverent, humorous and touching prose struck a chord with readers and the essay was re-published as *Are You Somebody?* (1996), followed by *Almost There – the Onward Journey of a Dublin Woman* (2003), which both became international bestsellers.

Ireland can boast four winners of the Nobel Prize for Literature: George Bernard Shaw in 1925, WB Yeats in 1938, Samuel Beckett in 1969 and Seamus Heaney in 1995. The prestigious annual IMPAC awards, administered by Dublin City Public Libraries, accept nominations from public libraries around the world for works of high literary merit and offer a €100,000 award to the winning novelist. Previous winners have included David Malouf (Australian) and Nicola Barker (English).

Poetry

WB Yeats (1865–1939) was both playwright and poet, but it's his poetry that has the greatest appeal. His *Love Poems*, edited by Norman Jeffares, makes a suitable introduction for anyone new to his writing.

Pádraig Pearse (1879–1916) used the Irish language as his medium and was one of the leaders of the 1916 Easter Rising. *Mise Éire* typifies his style and passion.

Patrick Kavanagh (1905–67), one of Ireland's most respected poets, was born in Inniskeen, County Monaghan. *The Great Hunger* and *Tarry Flynn* evoke the atmosphere and often grim reality of life for the poor farming

---

The adventure only begins when youngster Tony accidentally bumps off his girlfriend and tries to bury the evidence in Robert Quinn's stylish and accomplished debut thriller *Dead Bodies* (2003).

Patrick McCabe's *The Butcher Boy* is a brilliant, gruesome tragicomedy about an orphaned Monaghan boy's descent into madness, by one of Ireland's most imaginative authors. It has received several awards and was made into a successful film.

John McGahern's simple, economical prose *Amongst Women* centres on well drawn, complex yet familiar characters, in this case a west-of-Ireland family in the social aftermath of the War of Independence.

community. You'll find a bronze statue of him in Dublin, sitting beside his beloved Grand Canal (see p340).

Seamus Heaney (1939–) won the Whitbread Book of the Year to add to his accolades for *The Spirit Level*. His translation of the 8th-century Anglo-Saxon epic *Beowulf* has been widely praised. Some of his poems reflect the hope, disappointment and disillusionment of the peace process.

Paul Durcan (1944–) boldly tackles awkward issues such as the oppressive nature of Catholicism and Republican activity in his trademark unconventional style.

Cork-born Irish-language poet Louis de Paor has twice won Ireland's prestigious Sean O'Riordan Prize with collections of his poetry. Tom Paulin (1949–) writes memorable poetry about the North (try *The Strange Museum*) as does Ciaran Carson (1948–). Many of Paula Meehan's (1955–) magical, evocative poems speak of cherished relationships.

For a taste of modern Irish poetry try *Contemporary Irish Poetry* edited by Fallon and Mahon. *A Rage for Order*, edited by Frank Ormsby, is a vibrant collection of the poetry of the North.

Cinema

Ireland's film-making tradition is pretty poor, largely because the British cinema industry drained much of its talent and creative energies and the Irish government pleaded poverty any time a film-maker came looking for some development cash. The last decade has seen a change in the Irish government's attitudes, but what has long been true is that the country has contributed more than its fair share of glorious moments to the silver screen, as well as a disproportionate number of its biggest stars.

Hot on the heels of such luminaries as Gabriel Byrne *(Miller's Crossing, The Usual Suspects)*, Stephen Rea *(The Crying Game, The End of the Affair)* and the Oscar-winning Liam Neeson (for *Schindler's List*), Daniel Day-Lewis and Brenda Fricker (both for *My Left Foot*), are the late-arriving but always excellent Brendan Gleeson, who has had supporting roles in literally dozen of films; the very handsome Cillian Murphy *(Breakfast on Pluto, The Wind That Shakes the Barley* among several others) and the bad-boy Brando-wannabe himself, Colin Farrell, whose work has been, well, less than…anybody see *Alexander*? Northern Ireland's James Nesbitt has become almost ubiquitous on British TV after achieving fame in the series *Cold Feet* and *Murphy's Law*, and made the transition to the big screen in 2005 with a small part in Woody Allen's *Match Point*.

The re-establishment of the Irish Film Board in 1993 was part of the government's two-pronged effort to stimulate the local film industry. Big international productions *(Braveheart, Saving Private Ryan* etc) were tempted here with generous tax incentives in order to spread expertise among Irish crews, while money was pumped into the local film industry – with mixed critical results.

Ireland has been working hard to cast off its 'Oirland' identity – that sappy we're-poor-but-happy version so loved by Hollywood's plastic Paddys – but the local film industry is under phenomenal pressure to come up with the goods. And in film, the 'goods' means a commercial success. Exit the creative space to make really insightful films about a host of Irish subjects, enter the themed film designed to make a commercial splash in Britain and the US. Favourite themes include Mad 'n' Quirky – *The Butcher Boy, Disco Pigs* and *Breakfast on Pluto*; Smart-arse Gangsters – *I Went Down* and *Intermission*; and Cutesy Formulaic Love Story – *When Brendan Met Trudy*. Never mind the Irish Welles or Fellini, where's the local equivalent of Loach, Leigh or Winterbottom?

The Pulitzer Prize-winning *Angela's Ashes* by Frank McCourt tells the relentlessly bleak autobiographical story of the author's poverty-stricken Limerick childhood in the Depression of the 1930s, and has been made into a major film by Alan Parker.

In June 2006, Colm Tóibín became the first Irish author to win the prestigious IMPAC prize for his novel *The Master*, about Henry James.

John Crowley's pacey, well-scripted drama *Intermission* (2003) follows a host of eccentric characters in pursuit of love, starring Colin Farrell, Colm Meaney and Ger Ryan.

Well, say the film board, they're called Jim Sheridan (*In the Name of the Father, My Left Foot*) and Neil Jordan. The latter is undoubtedly Ireland's greatest director: *The Company of Wolves, Mona Lisa, The Crying Game* and *Michael Collins* are but four examples of his rich film biography.

New directors include the impossibly young-but-well-connected Kristen Sheridan (1977–), daughter of Jim and director of *Disco Pigs*. Another bright talent is Damien O'Donnell, who debuted with *East is East* (1999) and went from strength to strength with *Heartlands* (2002) and the outstanding Irish film of 2004, *Inside I'm Dancing*. That same year saw the release of *Adam & Paul*, written by Mark O'Halloran and directed by Lenny Abrahamson, a half-decent portrayal of two Dublin junkies and their quixotic quest for a fix. It was a roaring success at the Irish box office.

See p706 to find out when film festivals are held throughout the year.

Music
TRADITIONAL & FOLK

Irish music (known here as traditional music, or just trad) has retained a vibrancy not found in other traditional European forms, which have lost out to the overbearing influence of pop music. This is probably because, although Irish music has retained many of its traditional aspects, it has itself influenced many forms of music, most notably US country and western – a fusion of Mississippi Delta blues and Irish traditional tunes that, combined with other influences like Gospel, is at the root of rock and roll. Other reasons for its current success include the willingness of its exponents to update the way it's played (in ensembles rather than the customary *céilidh* – communal dance – bands), the habit of pub sessions (introduced by returning migrants) and the economic good times that encouraged the Irish to celebrate their culture rather than trying to replicate international trends. And then, of course, there's *Riverdance*, which made Irish dancing sexy and became a worldwide phenomenon, despite the fact that most aficionados of traditional music are seriously underwhelmed by its musical worth. Good stage show, crap music.

Traditionally, music was performed as a background to dancing, and while this has been true ever since Celtic times, the many thousands of tunes that fill up the repertoire aren't nearly as ancient as that; most aren't much older than a couple of hundred years. Because much of Irish music is handed down orally and aurally, there are myriads of variations in the way a single tune is played, depending on the time and place of its playing. The blind itinerant harpist Turlough O'Carolan (1680–1738) wrote more than 200 tunes – it's difficult to know how many versions their repeated learning has spawned.

For most, traditional music is intimately associated with the pub session, but records show that the very first pub session was held in 1947…in London, featuring emigrant Irish musicians who wouldn't have been allowed to play in pubs at home. But this all changed soon thereafter, thanks to the folk explosion in the US and the superlative efforts of Seán O'Riada (1931–71), the single most influential figure in the traditional renaissance. In 1961 he formed Ceoltóirí Chualann, a band featuring a fiddle, flute, accordion, bodhrán and uilleann pipes, and began to perform music to listen to rather than for dancing. When his band performed at the Gaiety Theatre in Dublin, it gave a whole new credibility to traditional music. Members of the band went on to form the Chieftains, who still play an important role in bringing Irish music to an international audience.

With added vocals come bands such as the Dubliners with their notorious drinking songs; the Wolfe Tones, who've been described as 'the rabble end of the rebel song tradition'; and the Fureys. Younger groups such as Clannad,

John Boorman's film *The General* (1998) about Dublin's most notorious crime boss is both horrific and uneasily funny in its portrayal of the mindless brutality and childlike humour of Martin Cahill.

Paddy Breathnach's hilarious road movie *I Went Down* (1998) follows the capers of two unlikely petty criminals sent on a mission by a low-rent loan shark.

Jim Sheridan's authentic drama *The Boxer* (1998) is a film about a former IRA member's emergence and readjustment from a Belfast prison, to discover everyone, including his girlfriend, has moved on.

Altan, Dervish and Nomos espouse a quieter, more mystical style of singing, while Kíla and the Afro-Celt Foundation stretches the boundaries by combining traditional music with reggae, Eastern and New-Age influences.

Christy Moore is the most prominent of the contemporary singer-songwriters playing in a broadly traditional idiom. He has been performing since the 1960s, and although a pivotal member of the influential bands Planxty and Moving Hearts, he's probably best known for his solo albums.

See p706 for details on when traditional music festivals are held.

POPULAR MUSIC

It may have begun with the showbands, who toured the country in the 1960s playing Top 40 hits, but it really took off with Van Morrison, whose blues-infused genius really put Irish music on the map. On his heels came Phil Lynott and Thin Lizzy, who made their breakthrough with *Jailbreak* (1975). Other great 1970s rockers included Horslips, who played an infectious trad-infused style known as Celtic rock; the Undertones, whose biggest hit, *Teenage Kicks*, was John Peel's favourite song of all time; Stiff Little Fingers, aka SLF, who to our minds are as good a punk band as any that ever was; and the Boomtown Rats, fronted by Bob 'fuck off, I'm trying to save the world' Geldof.

Just as the Rats were celebrating the virtues of sex, drugs and rock and roll, a young drummer pinned a note on his school notice board looking for fellow pupils who were interested in forming a band. By late 1976 Larry Mullen had his band, and it took them four years to release their first album. When they did, *Boy* (1980) stood out from the rest for Bono's impassioned vocals, Edge's unique guitar style and Adam's I-just-learnt-the-bass strumming. Behind them, Larry used his years of military-style drumming to keep a steady beat.

U2 went on to produce a string of brilliant albums before becoming the world's biggest rock act in the aftermath of the truly wonderful *The Joshua Tree* (1987). They've remained supernovas in the pop firmament through thick and thicker; their last album, *U218* (2006), was a long-awaited singles collection that barely does justice to their high-quality output. And, just to show that even in their mid-40s the band hadn't quite put on the shawl of sad old rockers, in 2007 they were back in the recording studio working on material for a new album.

Of all the Irish acts that followed in U2's wake during the 1980s and early 1990s, a few managed to comfortably avoid being tarred with 'the next U2' burden. London-based Irish rabble-rousers The Pogues played a compelling blend of punk and Irish folk, made all the better by the singular figure of Shane McGowan, whose empathetic and lucid song-writing talent was eventually overshadowed by his chronic alcoholism. Still, McGowan is credited with writing Ireland's favourite song, *A Fairytale of New York*, sung with emotional fervour by everyone around Christmas. Sinead O'Connor thrived

The haunting and beautiful novel *The Story of Lucy Gault* by William Trevor, dubbed the Irish Chekhov, tells of a young girl who, believed by her family to be dead, is brought up by a caretaker at the end of the Ascendancy years.

Reading In the Dark by Seamus Deane is thoughtful prose (the Guardian Fiction Prize winner) and recounts a young boy's struggles to unravel the truth of his own history growing up in the Troubles of Belfast.

Hot Press (www.hotpress .com) is a fortnightly magazine featuring local and international music interviews and listings.

TOP TRAD ALBUMS

- *The Quiet Glen* (Tommy Peoples)
- *Paddy Keenan* (Paddy Keenan)
- *Compendium: The Best of Patrick Street* (Various)
- *The Chieftains 6: Bonaparte's Retreat* (The Chieftains)
- *Old Hag You Have Killed Me* (The Bothy Band)

THE EUROVISION SONG CONTEST

Ireland has the dubious honour of being the most successful country ever to participate in the cheese-fest that is the Eurovision Song Contest, which has been held yearly since 1956. The first success came in 1970, when a fresh-faced, 16-year-old from Derry called Dana sang 'All Kinds of Everything'; 10 years later, Johnny Logan took home the big prize with 'What's Another Year?' and then did it again in 1987 with 'Hold Me Now'. Ireland won the competition three times in a row from 1992-94 and again in 1996. As the winner gets to host it the following year, the joke in Ireland was that the rest of Europe was voting for them so as to leave them footing the hosting bill. Seven titles and four second-places wasn't bad, but Ireland hasn't won it in over 10 years and in 2007 came dead last for the first time: only Albania gave it *cinq points*, leaving the media to gnash their teeth and wonder where it all went wrong.

---

by acting like a U2 antidote – whatever they were into she was not – and by having a damn fine voice; the raw emotion on *The Lion and the Cobra* (1987) makes it a great offering. And then there was My Bloody Valentine, the pioneers of late 1980s guitar-distorted shoegazer rock: their 1991 album *Loveless* is one of the best Irish albums of all time.

The 1990s were largely dominated by DJs, dance music and a whole new spin on an old notion, the boy band. Behind Ireland's most successful groups (Boyzone and Westlife) is the Svengali of Saccharine, impresario Louie Walsh, whose musical sensibilities seem mired in '60s showband schmaltz. Commercially mega-successful but utterly without musical merit, the boy band (and girl band) phenomenon was a compelling reminder that in the world of pop, millions of people *can* be wrong, and we have long since believed that former Boyzone frontman Ronan Keating does indeed say it best when he *says nothing at all*.

Foggy Notions is a visually striking, subversive magazine catering to eclectic music tastes.

Non–boy band stand-out acts include Paddy Casey (listen to his multi-platinum album *Living*; his new album, *Addicted to Company*, was released in late 2007), Damien Rice (he followed up his multi-million selling *O* with the disappointing *9*) and a pair of new arrivals, the supremely talented Fionn Regan (his debut *The End of History* has impressed everyone) and the Belfast-born Duke Special, whose left-of-centre *Songs from the Deep Forest* has also earned plenty of critical acclaim. Other performers to look out for are Julie Feeney – her debut, *13 Songs*, scooped the top prize at the 2006 Choice Music Prize, Ireland's answer to Britain's Mercury Award – and soul-folk-rockers the Frames, who have a phenomenally loyal following earned over more than 15 years of releasing albums and touring.

After years of techno and finger-picked acoustic guitar tracks, the amped-up rock band has finally made a comeback. Bell X1 (their best albums are *Music in Mouth* and *Flock*), Cork-based Republic of Loose (2006's *Aaagh* was a big local hit) and the blockbuster sound of Snow Patrol – who had international success with *Final Straw* (2003) and *Eyes Open* (2006) – are but three of a whole host of bands looking to make some noise.

Other successful debut albums of recent years include *Future Kings of Spain* by the indie rock band of the same name, and the also-eponymous *Hal*, a feast of cheerful and melodic pop that's guaranteed to put a smile on anyone's face. London-based baroque pop act the Divine Comedy, fronted by Derry-born composer and lyricist Neil Hannon, blends jazz, classical and pop influences with tongue-in-cheek lyrics. Their 2006 album *Victory for the Comic Muse* topped the poll at the 2007 Choice Music Prize and proved that there was still room in these over-earnest times for a bit of irony.

See p706 for details on when music festivals are held.

OUR 10 BEST IRISH ALBUMS

- *Loveless* (My Bloody Valentine) – utterly intoxicating indie classic that just piles on the layers of sound and melody.
- *Boy* (U2) – best debut album of all time? We think so.
- *The End of History* (Fionn Regan) – too early to say if it's a classic, but it's bloody good.
- *Live & Dangerous* (Thin Lizzy) – released in 1978, it remains one of the greatest live albums ever recorded.
- *I Do Not Want What I Haven't Got* (Sinead O'Connor) – try listening to the Prince-penned 'Nothing Compares to U' and not feel her pain.
- *St Dominic's Preview* (Van Morrison) – everyone knows *Astral Weeks*, but this 1972 album is every bit as good.
- *O* (Damien Rice) – with millions of record sales, we're not going to argue with its merit.
- *Inflammable Material* (Stiff Little Fingers) – forget the Sex Pistols; this album about the life in the Troubles gets our vote for best punk album ever.
- *The Book of Invasion* (Horslips) – this totally catchy album is Celtic rock at its best.
- *13 Songs* (Julie Feeney) – Choice Prize winner in 2006 for her excellent debut.

Architecture

Ireland is packed with prehistoric graves, ruined monasteries, crumbling fortresses and many other solid reminders of its long, often dramatic, history. The principal surviving structures from Stone Age times are the graves and monuments people built for the dead, usually grouped under the heading of megalithic (great stone) tombs. Among the most easily recognisable megalithic tombs are dolmens, massive three-legged structures rather like giant stone stools, most of which are 4000 to 5000 years old. Good examples are the Poulnabrone Dolmen (p397) in the Burren and Browne's Hill Dolmen (p352) near Carlow town.

Passage graves such as Newgrange and Knowth (p544) in Meath are huge mounds with narrow stone-walled passages leading to burial chambers. These chambers are enriched with spiral and chevron symbols and have an opening through which the rising sun penetrates on the winter or summer solstice, thus acting as a giant celestial calendar.

The Irish names for forts – *dun, rath, caiseal/cashel* and *caher* – have ended up in the names of countless towns and villages. The Irish countryside is peppered with the remains of over 30,000 of them. The earliest known examples date from the Bronze Age, most commonly the ring fort, with circular earth-and-stone banks, topped by a wooden palisade fence to keep out intruders, and surrounded on the outside by a moatlike ditch. Outside Clonakilty in County Cork, the ring fort at Lisnagun (Lios na gCon) has been reconstructed to give some idea of its original appearance (see p224).

Some forts were constructed entirely of stone; the Iron Age fort of Dún Aengus (p418; the largest of the Aran Islands) on Inishmór is a superb example.

After Christianity arrived in Ireland in the 5th century, the first monasteries were built. The early stone churches were often very simple, some roofed with timber, such as the 6th-century Teampall Bheanáin (Church of St Benen) on Inishmór of the Aran Islands, or built completely of stone, such as the 8th-century Gallarus Oratory (p296) on the Dingle Peninsula. Early hermitages include the small beehive huts and buildings on the summit of Skellig Michael (p263) off County Kerry.

As the monasteries grew in size and stature, so did the architecture. The 12th-century cathedral (p153) at Glendalough and the 10th- to 15th-century cathedral (p364) at Clonmacnoise are good examples, although they're tiny compared with European medieval cathedrals.

Round towers have become symbols of Ireland. These tall, stone, needle-like structures were built largely as lookout posts and refuges in the event of Viking attacks in the late 9th or early 10th centuries. Of the 120 thought to have originally existed, around 20 survive intact; the best examples can be seen at Cashel (p311), Glendalough (p153) and Devenish Island (p683).

With the Normans' arrival in Ireland in 1169, came the Gothic style of architecture, characterised by tall vaulted windows and soaring V-shaped arches. Fine examples of this can be seen in the 1172 Christ Church Cathedral in Dublin (see p100) and the 13th-century St Canice's Cathedral in Kilkenny (see p327).

Racy London-based
Edna O'Brien bases her
sensationalist 1997 novel
Down by the River on the
controversial true story
of a 14-year-old Dublin
girl who was raped and
went to England for an
abortion.

Authentic, traditional Irish thatched cottages were built of limestone or clay to suit the elements, but weren't durable and have become rare, the tradition dying out around the middle of the 20th century.

In Georgian times, Dublin became one of the architectural glories of Europe, with simple, beautifully built Georgian terraces of red brick, with delicate glass fanlights over large, elegant, curved doorways. From the 1960s Dublin's Georgian heritage suffered badly but you can still see fine examples around Merrion Square (p99).

The Anglo-Irish Ascendancy built country houses such as the 1722 Castletown House (p343) near Celbridge, the 1741 Russborough House (p157) near Blessington and Castle Coole (p682), which are all excellent examples of the Palladian style, with their regularity and classical correctness. Prolific German architect Richard Cassels (also known as Richard Castle) came to Ireland in 1728 and designed many landmark buildings including Powerscourt House (p148) in County Wicklow and Leinster House (p97; home to Dáil Éireann, the Irish government) in Dublin.

Ireland has little modern architecture of note. For much of the 20th century the pace of change was slow, and it wasn't until the construction of Dublin's Busáras Station in the 1950s that modernity began to really express itself. It was designed by Michael Scott, who was to have an influence on architects in Ireland for the next two decades. The poorly regulated building boom of the 1960s and 1970s, however, paid little attention to the country's architectural heritage and destroyed more than it created. From that period Paul Koralek's 1967 brutalist-style Berkeley Library in Trinity College, Dublin, has been hailed as Ireland's best example of modern architecture.

Since the 1980s more care has been given to architectural heritage and context, the best example of which has been the redevelopment of Dublin's previously near-derelict Temple Bar area (p94). Ireland's recent boom at the turn of the last century spawned a huge growth of building work around Dublin of mixed quality. Some good examples in the Docklands area include the imposing Financial Services Centre and Custom House Square; further downriver in the Grand Canal Docks, the centrepiece of the whole area will be a 2000-seat Performing Arts Centre designed by the world's hottest architect, Daniel Libeskind.

Probably the most controversial piece of modern architecture to be unveiled in recent years has been the Monument of Light (p104; re-christened simply The Spire) on Dublin's O'Connell St. At seven times the height of the GPO (120m in total), the brushed steel hollow cone was always going to face opposition, but since its unveiling in spring 2003, the awe-inspiring structure and beautifully reflective surface have won over all but a few hardened cynics.

Visual Arts

Ireland's painting doesn't receive the kind of recognition that its literature and music do. Nevertheless, painting in Ireland has a long tradition dating back to the illuminated manuscripts of the early Christian period, most notably the Book of Kells.

The National Gallery (p96) has an extensive Irish School collection, much of it chronicling the people and pursuits of the Anglo-Irish aristocracy.

Like other European artists of the 18th century, Roderic O'Conor featured portraits and landscapes in his work. His post-impressionist style stood out for its vivid use of colour and sturdy brush strokes. James Malton captured 18th-century Dublin in a series of line drawings and paintings.

In the 19th century there was still no hint of Ireland's political and social problems in the work of its major artists. The most prominent landscape painter was James Arthur O'Connor, while Belfast-born Sir John Lavery became one of London's most celebrated portrait artists.

Just as WB Yeats played a seminal role in the Celtic literary revival, his younger brother, Jack Butler Yeats (1871–1957), inspired an artistic surge of creativity in the early 20th century, taking Celtic mythology and Irish life as his subjects. (Their father, John Butler Yeats, had also been a noted portrait painter.) William John Leech (1881–1961) was fascinated by changing light, an affection reflected in his expressionistic landscapes and flower paintings. Born to English parents in Dublin, Francis Bacon (1909–92) emerged as one of the most powerful figurative artists of the 20th century with his violent depictions of distorted human bodies.

The stained-glass work of Harry Clarke (1889–1931) is also worth a mention in the canon of modern Irish art: heavily influenced by contemporary styles including Art Nouveau and Symbolism, Clarke's work was primarily for church windows (see p381 and p487).

The pioneering work of Irish cubist painter Mainie Jellett (1897–1944) and her friend, modernist stained-glass artist Evie Hone (1894–1955), had an influence on later modernists Barrie Cooke (1931–) and Camille Souter (1929–). Together with Louis Le Brocquy (1916–), Jellett and Hone set up the Irish Exhibition of Living Art in 1943 to foster the work of nonacademic artists. Estella Solomons (1882–1968) trained under William Orpen and Walter Osborne in Dublin and was a noted portrait and landscape painter. The rural idyll of the west of Ireland was also a theme of Paul Henry's (1876–1958) landscapes. In the 1950s and 1960s, a school of naïve artists including James Dixon appeared on Tory Island, off Donegal.

Contemporary artists to watch out for include Nick Miller, New York-based Sean Scully and Fionnuala Ní Chíosain.

Experimental photographer Clare Langan's work has gained international recognition with her trademark ethereal images of elemental landscapes.

Murals have been an important way of documenting Ireland's more recent political history. Powerful political murals (p589) can be seen in West Belfast and Derry (see the boxed text, p646).

The Irish countryside is peppered with the remains of over 30,000 forts.

Double Drink Story by Caitlin Thomas (nee MacNamara), who subjugated her impulse to write under the weight of husband Dylan's celebrity and her own addictions, is an eloquent, self-deprecating account of their debaucherous life, love-hate relationship and the burden of creativity, making a brilliant literary memoir.

Theatre

Dublin and Belfast are the main centres, but most sizable towns, such as Cork, Derry, Donegal, Limerick and Galway, have their own theatres. Ireland has a theatrical history almost as long as its literary one. Dublin's first theatre was founded in Werburgh St in 1637, although it was closed only four years later by the Puritans. Another theatre, named the Smock Alley Playhouse or Theatre Royal, opened in 1661 and continued to stage plays for more than a century. The literary revival of the late 19th century resulted in the establishment of Dublin's Abbey Theatre (p137), now Ireland's national theatre. Its role is to present works by historical greats such as WB Yeats, George Bernard Shaw (1856–1950), JM Synge (1871–1909) and Sean O'Casey (1880–1964), as well as to promote modern Irish dramatists. Also in Dublin, the Gate Theatre (p137) produces classics and comedies, while the Gaiety and Olympia Theatres (p138) present a range of productions, as does the Grand Opera House (p583) in Belfast. Dublin's Project Arts Centre (p138) offers a more experimental programme.

One of the most outstanding playwrights of the last two decades is Frank McGuinness (1956–), who has had a prolific output since the 1970s. His plays, such as *The Carthaginians*, explore the consequences of 1972's Bloody Sunday on the people of Derry. Young London-Irish playwright Martin McDonagh (1971–) uses the darker side of a romantic rural Irish idyll as his inspiration. Among his work, *The Leenane Trilogy* has been performed by Britain's National Theatre and on Broadway, where he has won a number of Tony Awards. *Dancing at Lughnasa* by Brian Friel (1929–) was a great success on Broadway and in London and has been made into a film.

Other talented young playwrights to watch out for include Dubliner Conor McPherson (whose acclaimed play *The Weir* was commissioned by the Royal Court).

The work of playwright and poet Damian Gorman (1962–) has received considerable praise. *Broken Nails,* his first play, received four Ulster Theatre awards. Mark O'Rowe (who also wrote the film script *Intermission*) received commendable reviews for his graphically violent and controversial play *Crestfall* in 2003 at the Gate.

See p706 for details on when various arts and theatre festivals are held.

Dance

The most important form of dance in Ireland is traditional Irish dancing, performed communally at céilidhs, often in an impromptu format and always accompanied by a traditional Irish band. Dances include the hornpipe, jig and reel. Irish dancing has received international attention and success through shows such as *Riverdance* and its offshoots, and while this glamorised style of dance is only loosely based on traditional dancing, it has popularised the real art and given a new lease of life to the moribund Irish dancing schools around the country.

Ireland doesn't have a national dance school, but there are a number of schools and companies around the country teaching and performing ballet and modern dance. The Dance Theatre of Ireland and the Irish Modern Dance Theatre are based in Dublin, while the Firkin Crane Centre in Cork is Ireland's only venue devoted solely to dance.

See p706 for information on when dance festivals are held.

Food & Drink

Generations of travellers who visited these shores during bleaker times typically mused that Irish food is great until it's cooked. They advised getting drunk before eating, or complained that a meal was more a flavourless penance rather than a pleasurable repast. Those days are long gone; visitors are now coming to Ireland *for* the food, rather than in spite of it.

A culinary renaissance has taken place, and the Irish are now enjoying the fine cuisine that they have long deserved. The island has always been blessed with a wealth of staples and specialities, with meat, seafood and dairy produce the envy of the world. At the twilight of the 20th century a new wave of cooks began producing what is sometimes promoted as 'New Irish Cuisine'.

In truth, the new cuisine is more a confident return to the traditional practice of combining simple cooking techniques with the finest local ingredients. Many of the new chefs merely strive to offer their patrons the sort of meals that have always been taken for granted on well-run Irish farms. Whatever you want to call it, it has aroused the nation's taste buds (p270).

But gastronomes have more than rediscovered traditions to thank. The Irish diners of today – generally a more affluent and worldly bunch than their forebears – have become more discerning and adventurous. To meet their demands, restaurants are continually springing up on city streets and in old country homes with menus spruced up with all sorts of international touches. Luckily, excellent food isn't reserved for urbanites and the rich – there's a real appreciation for quality food all over the country, which means you'll find creative dishes in the smallest café in the remotest part of the island.

Of course, you can still find leathery meat, shrivelled fish and overcooked vegetables, if that's what you're looking for. But why punish yourself, when hearty fare that will make your palate sing is so readily available?

STAPLES & SPECIALITIES
Potatoes
It's a wonder the Irish retain their good humour amid the perpetual potato-baiting they endure. But, despite the stereotyping, and however much we'd like to disprove it, potatoes are still paramount here and you'll see lots of them on your travels. The mashed potato dishes colcannon and champ (with cabbage and spring onion respectively) are two of the tastiest recipes in the country.

Meat & Seafood
Irish meals are usually meat-based, with beef, lamb and pork common options. Seafood, long neglected, is finding a place on the table in Irish homes. It's widely available in restaurants and is often excellent, especially in the west. Oysters, trout and salmon are delicious, particularly if they're direct from the sea or a river rather than a fish farm. The famous Dublin Bay Prawn isn't actually a prawn, but a lobster. At its best, the Dublin Bay Prawn is superlative, but it's priced accordingly. If you're going to splurge, do so here – but make sure you choose live Dublin Bay Prawns because once these fellas die, they quickly lose their flavour.

Bread
The most famous Irish bread, and one of the signature tastes of Ireland, is soda bread. Irish flour is soft and doesn't take well to yeast as a

Visit www.ravensgard.org/prdunham/irishfood.html for a highly readable and complete history of Irish cuisine, with fascinating chapters such as 'The Most Widely Used Cooking Methods in Pre-Potato Ireland' and 'Collecting of Blood for Pudding Making'.

The renowned Georgina Campbell guides (www.ireland-guide.com) are annual publications with over 900 recommendations for munching, supping and snoozing on the Emerald Isle.

Over 10,000 oysters are consumed each year at the exuberant Galway Oyster International Festival (www.galwayoysterfest.com; p409).

TOP FIVE IRISH CHEESES

■ Ardrahan – Flavoursome farmhouse creation with a rich, nutty taste

■ Corleggy – Subtle, pasteurised goats cheese from County Cavan (p481)

■ Durrus – Fine-food fans will fall for this creamy, fruity cheese (p236)

■ Cashel blue – Creamy blue cheese from Tipperary

■ Cooleeney – Award-winning Camembert-style cheese

If you want to know your natural-rind goats cheese from your semi-soft washed-rind cows cheese, you'll find enlightenment, and a complete list of Irish cheesemakers, at www .irishcheese.ie.

raising agent, so Irish bakers of the 19th century leavened their bread with bicarbonate of soda. Combined with buttermilk, it makes a superbly light-textured and tasty bread, and is often on the breakfast menus at B&Bs.

The Fry

Perhaps the most feared Irish speciality is the fry – the heart attack on a plate that is the second part of so many B&B deals. In spite of the hysterical health fears, the fry is still one of the most common traditional meals in the country. Who can say no to a plate of fried bacon, sausages, black pudding, white pudding, eggs and tomatoes? For the famous Ulster fry, common throughout the North, simply add fadge (potato bread).

DRINKS
Nonalcoholic Drinks
TEA

The Irish drink more tea, per capita, than any other nation in the world and you'll be offered a cup as soon as you cross the threshold of any Irish home. It's a leveller and an icebreaker, and an appreciation for 'at least a cup in your hand' is your passport to conviviality here. Preferred blends are very strong, and nothing like the namby-pamby versions that pass for Irish breakfast tea elsewhere.

Visit www.foodisland .com, a site run by state food board Bord Bia, for recipes, a short culinary history of Ireland and links to producers of Irish food, from whom you can purchase that prized truckle of farmhouse cheese or whiskey-flavoured fruit cake.

RED LEMONADE

This product, basically a regular glass of lemonade with colouring, has been produced in Ireland since the end of the 19th century and is still made to virtually the same recipe today. Always more popular in the Republic than the North, it's a favourite for adults and children alike. It's commonly used as a mixer with brandy and whiskey.

Alcoholic Drinks

Drinking in Ireland is no mere social activity: it's the foundation on which Irish culture is built. Along with its wonderful drinks, this fact helps to explain why through centuries of poverty and oppression the Irish always retained their reputation for unrivalled hospitality and good humour.

The Book of Guinness Advertising by Jim Davies. My Goodness! A collection of Guinness' finest posters from the 1920s to the end of the 20th century.

STOUT

Of all Ireland's drinks, the 'black stuff' is the most celebrated. While Guinness has become synonymous with stout the world over, few outside Ireland realise that there are two other major producers competing for the favour of the Irish drinker: Murphy's and Beamish & Crawford, both based in Cork city. More exciting still is the recent re-emergence of independent Irish brewers (Guinness, Murphy's and Beamish & Crawford are no longer Irish-owned) – turn to p275 to whet your appetite.

OTHER IRISH BEERS

Beamish Red Ale This traditional-style red ale, brewed in Cork city by Beamish & Crawford (p205), is sweet and palatable.

Caffrey's Irish Ale One of the most exciting additions to Ireland's beer map, this creamy ale has only been around since 1994. It's a robust cross between a stout and an ale, brewed in County Antrim.

Kaliber This nonalcoholic lager was made popular by famous Irish athlete Eamon O'Coughlan. Even in the name of research we couldn't be bothered trying it but it seems to have some credibility among the more clean-living publicans.

McCardles Traditional Ale This wholesome, dark, nutty ale is hard to come by, but worthy of an exploration.

Smithwicks Smithwicks is a lovely, refreshing full scoop with a charming history. It's brewed in Kilkenny (see p329), on the site of the 14th-century St Francis Abbey in what is Ireland's oldest working brewery.

Guinness Is Guinness: The Colourful Story of a Black and White Brand by Mark Griffiths delves into the origins and eventual worldwide dispersion of the great stout. Guinness devotees will find it colourful and insightful.

WHISKEY

While whiskey shares only equal billing with stout as the national drink of Ireland, in the home it is paramount. At last count, there were almost 100 different types of Irish whiskey, brewed by only three distilleries – Jameson's, Bushmills and Cooley's. A visit to Ireland reveals a depth of excellence that will make the connoisseur's palate spin, while winning over many new friends to what the Irish call *uisce beatha* (the 'water of life').

IRISH COFFEE

Stories about the origin of Irish coffee abound but the most common one credits Joe Sheridan, a barman at Shannon airport, with the creation in the 1940s. All travellers arriving in Ireland from the USA would stop over in Shannon for an hour or two before heading on to their final destination. Landing in the bracing cold, shivering passengers used to approach Sheridan looking for an alcoholic drink and something that might heat them up. He hit upon the winning blend of Irish whiskey and piping hot coffee, topped with rich cream. It was just the trick then, and still is today.

Established in 1608, Bushmills in County Antrim is the world's oldest legal distillery (see p661). By the time of Bushmills' official opening, whiskey was already exceedingly popular among the common people of Ireland.

POITÍN

Making *poitín* (illicit whiskey), has a folkloric respect in Ireland. Those responsible came to be regarded as heroes of the people, rather than outlaws of the land as the authorities tried to brand them. In tourist and duty-free

---

A SNIFTER OF WHISKEY HISTORY

Nobody really knows whether whiskey was first made in Scotland or Ireland, but for the purpose of this book we'll just go along with the Irish version of the story. Whiskey has been made here since the 10th century, when monks brought the art of distillation back from their ecclesiastical jaunts to the Middle East. In Arabia, the technique had been used to distil perfume from flowers, but the monks evidently saw a very different use for it. As the legend maintains, they soon developed a method of distilling whiskey from barley. The monks then fiercely protected their secret for several centuries.

Incidentally, Irish monks did have a solid reputation as hard drinkers. Monastic protocol limited monks to a mere gallon (5L) of ale a day. Another rule insisted that they be able to chant the Psalms clearly, so we might reasonably assume the monks managed to build up a sturdy tolerance in order to walk this fine line.

Had the monks not been so secretive, their claim to being the inventors of whiskey might not be disputed today. The Scots make an equally valid, if much later claim, dating to the 15th century. By the way, Scotch whisky is not only spelled differently, it is distilled twice rather than the three times preferred by the Irish. American Bourbon is distilled but once.

shops you'll see a commercial brand of *poitín* which is strictly a gimmick for tourists. Don't bother; it's just an inferior spirit with little to credit it. There are still *poitín* makers plying their trade in the quieter corners of Ireland. It is not uncommon in Donegal, the *poitín* capital, for deals to be sealed or favours repaid with a drop of the 'cratur'. In the quiet, desolate, peaty bogs of Connemara a plume of smoke rising into the sky may not just be a warming fire. Or in West Cork, one of the most fiercely patriotic and traditional pockets of Ireland, a friend of a friend may know something about it.

WHERE TO EAT & DRINK

It's easy to eat well in the cities and you'll be able to find any kind of cuisine your taste buds desire, from Irish seafood to foreign fusion. Along the west coast, you'll be spoilt for choice when it comes to seafood and local produce.

If you ask a local for 'somewhere to eat', you'll probably be directed to his or her favourite pub because, outside the cities, the best place for a feed, particularly lunch, *is* often the pub. Virtually every drinking house will offer the simple fare of soup, potatoes, vegetables, steaks and chicken. Some extend themselves and have separate dining rooms where you can get fresh soda breads, and hearty meals like shepherd's pie, casseroles and seafood dishes.

For breakfast, you're most likely to be eating at your accommodation, as most lodgings in Ireland offer B&B.

Standard restaurant hours in Ireland are from noon to around 10.30pm with many places closed one day of the week, usually Monday, or sometimes Sunday.

VEGETARIANS & VEGANS

Oh boy, you're a long way from home now. Ireland provides so few vegetarian options that your convictions might be tested. In the cities and bigger towns there will be enough dedicated eateries to keep your spirits up, but once you head out into rural Ireland you enter the vegetarian's wilderness. Take heart, though, as modern restaurants are opening up in old country homes throughout Ireland, and many of them have surprisingly sophisticated menus.

We trust vegans have brought packed lunches; Ireland really won't be your cup of black tea. Save yourself time and heartache and buy the most up-to-date restaurant guide as soon as your plane touches down. And get used to the incredulous question, 'What, you don't eat any dairy produce!?!'

EATING WITH KIDS

You can bring *na páiste* (the children) to just about any Irish eatery, including the pub. However, after 7pm, the kids are banished from most boozers and the smarter restaurants. You will sometimes see children's menus but normally small portions of the adult fare will do. For more information on travelling with children, see p702.

HABITS & CUSTOMS
How the Irish Eat

The Irish have hefty appetites and eat almost 150% of the recommended daily calorie intake according to the EU. This probably has as much to do with their penchant for snacks as the size of their meals (which *are* big).

When Ireland was predominantly agricultural, breakfast was a leisurely and communal meal shared with family and workers around midmorning, a few hours after rising. As with most of the developed world, it's now a fairly rushed and bleary-eyed affair involving toast and cereals. The traditional fry is a weekend indulgence, while the contracted version of bacon and eggs is still

The Bridgestone guides (www.bestofbridgestone.com) by John and Sally McKenna are a well-respected series of Irish food guides written by a husband-and-wife team. Books include the *Vegetarian Guide to Ireland*, *Food Lover's Guide to Northern Ireland*, and the annual *100 Best Restaurants*.

Café Paradiso Cookbook and *Paradiso Seasons* are creative and modern vegetarian cookbooks with ne'er a brown lentil stew in sight; from the eponymous Cork restaurant (p208).

popular whenever time allows. The day's first cup of tea comes with breakfast and most people will admit to not being themselves until they've had it.

Elevenses is the next pit stop and involves tea and snacks to tide over appetites until the next main meal. Afternoon tea takes the same form and serves the same function, also breaking up the afternoon.

Lunch is traditionally the biggest meal of the day, which is probably a throwback to farming Ireland, when the workers would return home ravenous after a morning's work. However, the timing of the main meal today is one of the most visible rural/urban divides. Outside the cities, lunch is still usually the most substantial meal every day of the week, while the workers in urban areas have succumbed to the nine-to-five drudgery and usually eat lunch on the run. However, on weekends, everybody has dinner midafternoon, usually around 4pm on Saturday and before 2pm Sunday. They might call it 'lunch' but don't be deceived – it's the most substantial meal of the week.

'Supper' is increasingly becoming the main meal for urbanites, and it takes place as soon as the last working parent gets home.

Etiquette

Conviviality is the most important condiment at the Irish table. Meal times are about taking the load off your feet, relaxing and enjoying the company of your fellow diners. There is very little prescribed or restrictive etiquette. In fact, the only behaviour likely to cause offence could be your own haughtiness. The Irish will happily dismiss any faux pas but if they think you have ideas above your station, they're quick to bring you back down to earth.

COOKING COURSES

Cooking has regained its sex appeal in Ireland and plenty of schools are finding their classes increasingly popular. The teaching is usually relaxed and sociable, and takes place in beautiful settings; a stint at one of these cookery schools could quite easily be the highlight of your trip:

Ballymaloe (p216; ☎ 464 6785; www.cookingisfun.ie; Ballycotton, Co Cork) From half-day sessions to 12-week certificate courses. Classes are held in an old apple-storage house, and there are cottages in the grounds for overnight students.

Belle Isle School of Cookery (p682; ☎ 6638 7231; www.irish-cookery-school.com; Enniskillen, Co Fermanagh) A range of cookery and wine courses lasting from one day to four weeks. Luxurious accommodation in Belle Isle Castle and its estate cottages.

Berry Lodge (p385; ☎ 708 7022; www.berrylodge.com; Annagh, Co Clare) Offering in-depth instruction, often over more than one day. Packages including classes, accommodation and meals are available.

Castle Leslie (p486; ☎ 88109; www.castleleslie.com; Glaslough, Co Monaghan) Offering a programme of year-round courses with master chef Noel McMeel. Themed courses cover everything from 'Irish cooking by seasons' to 'death by chocolate' and 'food and erotica'.

Fiacri Country House Restaurant (p320; ☎ 43017; www.fiacrihouse.com; Roscrea, Co Tipperary) Course are run year-round, from one day to five weeks.

Ghan House (p575; ☎ 937 3682; www.ghanhouse.com; Carlingford, Co Louth) Offers hands-on cooking classes and cooking demonstrations. Accommodation is also available.

Good Things Café (p235; ☎ 61426; www.thegoodthingscafe.com; Durrus, Co Cork) Runs cookery courses year-round, including a two-day 'miracle' programme for beginners.

Pangur Ban (p434; ☎ 41243; www.pangurban.com; Connemara, Co Galway) Two-day weekend courses, covering specific themes such as 'bread and cakes'.

MARKETS

There are few better ways to eat well in Ireland than to fill your shopping basket with local, seasonal produce at a farmers' market. The markets have

Slowfood Ireland (www .slowfoodireland.com) is an organisation committed to local and artisan food production. It runs various sociable events through the country, from bangers 'n' mash parties to cheese and wine evenings.

The Ballymaloe series of cookbooks by various members of Ireland's first family of cooking, the Allens, have an extraordinary reputation in Ireland and abroad. The emphasis is on using top-quality ingredients simply and with love.

seen a real resurgence in recent years and most Irish towns now host one at
least once a week. Check out www.irelandmarkets.com for a definitive list.

EAT YOUR WORDS
Food Glossary

bacon and cabbage – slices of boiled bacon or gammon with boiled cabbage on the side served
with boiled potatoes

barm brack – spicy, cakelike bread, traditionally served at Halloween with a ring hidden inside
(be careful not to choke on it!)

blaa – soft and floury bread roll

black and white pudding – black pudding is traditionally made from pig's blood, pork skin
and seasonings, shaped like a big sausage and cut into discs and fried; white pudding is the same
without the blood

boxty – potato pancake, becoming rarer on menus

carrigeen – seaweed dish

champ – Northern Irish dish of potatoes mashed with spring onions (scallions)

coddle – Dublin dish of semi-thick stew made with sausages, bacon, onions and potatoes

colcannon – mashed potato, cabbage and onion fried in butter and milk

crubeens – dish of pigs' trotters from Cork

drisheen – another Cork dish of intestines stuffed with sheep or pigs' blood and bitter tansey,
boiled in milk

dulse – dried seaweed that's sold salted and ready to eat, mainly found in Ballycastle, County
Antrim

fadge – Northern Irish potato bread

farl – general name for triangular baking

Guinness cake – popular fruitcake flavoured with Guinness

Irish stew – quintessential stew of mutton (preferably lamb), potatoes and onions, flavoured
with parsley and thyme and simmered slowly

potato bread – thin bread made out of spuds

soda bread – wonderful bread, white or brown, sweet or savoury, made from very soft Irish flour
and buttermilk

yellowman – hard, chewy toffee made in County Antrim

The *Avoca Café Cookbooks*,
by Hugo Arnold, contain
hearty, wholesome
recipes from the family-
run Avoca Handweaver
restaurants originally
based in Wicklow (see
p139) and now with 10
establishments across the
Republic.

Environment

THE LAND

It is clear, from the literature, songs and paintings of Ireland, that the Irish landscape exerts a powerful sway on the people who have lived in it. The Irish who left, especially, have always spread this notion that the old sod was something worth pining for, and visitors still anticipate experiencing this land's subtle influence on perception and mood. Once you've travelled the country, you can't help but agree that the vibrant greenness of gentle hills, the fearsome violence of jagged coasts and the sombre light of so many cloudy days is an integral part of experiencing Ireland.

The entire island stretches a mere 486km north to south, and 275km east to west, so Ireland's impressive topographical variety may come as a surprise. The countryside does indeed have an abundance of the expected greenery. Grass grows nearly everywhere in Ireland, but there are notable exceptions, particularly around the dramatic coasts.

Massive rocky outcrops like the Burren (p388), in County Clare, are for the most part inhospitable to grass, and although even there the green stuff does sprout up in enough patches for sheep and goats to graze on, these vast, otherworldly landscapes are mostly grey and bleak. Nearby, the dramatic Cliffs of Moher (p388) are a sheer drop into the thundering surf below. Similarly, there is no preparing for the extraordinary hexagonal stone columns of the Giant's Causeway (p662) in County Antrim, or the rugged drop of County Donegal's Slieve League (p514), Europe's highest sea cliffs. Sand dunes buffer many of the more gentle stretches of coast.

The boglands, which once covered one-fifth of the island, are more of a whiskey hue than green – that's the brown of heather and sphagnum moss, which cover uncut bogs. Travellers will likely encounter a bog in County Kildare's Bog of Allen (p344) or while driving through much of the western counties – much of the Mayo coast is covered by bog, and huge swaths also cover Donegal. The rural farms of the west coast have a rugged, hard-earned look to them, due mostly to the rock that lies so close to the surface. Much of this rock has been dug up, to create tillable soil, and converted into stone walls that divide tiny paddocks. The Aran Islands (p415) stand out for their spectacular networks of stone walls.

Smaller islands dot the shores of Ireland, many of them barren rock piles supporting unique ecosystems – Skellig Michael (p263) is a breathtakingly jagged island just off the Kerry coast. The west of Ireland is also the country's most mountainous area. Much of the west coast is a bulwark of cliffs, hills and mountains. The highest mountains are in the southwest; the tallest mountain in Ireland is Carrantuohil (1039m) in County Kerry's Macgillycuddy's Reeks (p255).

But topography in Ireland always leads back to the green. The Irish frequently lament the loss of their woodlands, much of which were cleared by the British (during the reign of Elizabeth I) to build ships for the Royal Navy. Little of the island's once plentiful oak forests survive today, and much of what you'll see is the result of relatively recent planting. Instead, the countryside is largely comprised of green fields divided by hedgerows and stone walls. Use of this land is divided between cultivated fields and pasture for cattle and sheep.

Of the nine counties that originally comprised the province of Ulster, six are now part of Northern Ireland while three are part of the Republic.

In 1821, the body of an Iron-Age man was found in a bog in Galway with his cape, shoes and beard still intact.

WILDLIFE

Ireland's flora and fauna is, by and large, shy and subtle, but as in any island environment, travellers who set out on foot will discover an Ireland that is resplendent with interesting species.

Animals

The illustrated pocket guide *The Animals of Ireland* by Gordon D'Arcy is a handy, inexpensive introduction.

Apart from the fox and badger, which tend to shy away from humans and are rarely seen, the wild mammals of Ireland are mostly of the ankle-high 'critter' category, such a rabbits, hedgehogs and shrews. Hikers often spot the Irish hare, or at least glimpse the blazing-fast blur of one running away. Red deer roam the hillsides in many of the wilder parts of the country, particularly the Wicklow Mountains, and in Killarney National Park, which holds the country's largest herd.

For most visitors, the most commonly sighted mammals are those inhabiting the sea and waterways. The otter, rarely seen elsewhere in Europe, is thriving in Ireland. Seals are a common sight in rivers and along the shore, as are dolphins, which follow the warm waters of the Gulf Stream towards Ireland. Some colonise the coast of Ireland year-round, frequently swimming into the bays and inlets off the western coast.

Many travellers visit Ireland specifically for the birding. Ireland's westerly location on the fringe of Europe makes it an ideal stopover point for birds migrating from North America and the Arctic. In autumn, the southern counties become a temporary home to the American waders (mainly sandpipers and plovers) and warblers. Migrants from Africa, such as shearwaters, petrels and auks, begin to arrive in spring in the southwestern counties.

See the excellent Birds of Ireland News Service website at www.bird sireland.com/pages /birding_in_ireland.html.

The reasonably rare corncrake, which migrates from Africa, can be found in the western counties, in Donegal and around the Shannon Callows, and on islands such as Inishbofin in Galway. In late spring and early summer, the rugged coastlines, particularly cliff areas and islands, become a haven for breeding seabirds, mainly gannet, kittiwake, Manx shearwater, fulmar, cormorant and heron. Puffins, resembling penguins with their tuxedo colour scheme, nest in large colonies on coastal cliffs.

The lakes and low-lying wetlands attract large numbers of Arctic and northern European waterfowl and waders such as whooper swans, lapwing, barnacle geese, white-fronted geese and golden plover. The important Wexford Wildfowl Reserve (p173) holds half the world's population of Greenland white-fronted geese, and little tern breed on the beach there, protected by the dunes. Also found during the winter are teal, redshank and curlew. The main migration periods are April to May and September to October.

Irish Birds by David Cabot is a pocket guide describing birds and their habitats, and outlines the best places for serious bird-watching.

The magnificent peregrine falcon has been making something of a recovery and can be found nesting on cliffs in Wicklow and elsewhere. In 2001, 46 golden eagle chicks from Scotland were released into Glenveagh National Park in Donegal in an effort to reintroduce the species. By 2005, several pairs began breeding, but none has successfully hatched an egg yet. This may well change in the next year or two, as the birds fully mature sexually. Some of the eagles have expanded their range well beyond the park – frequent sightings have been reported in Counties Mayo and Antrim.

Plants

Although Ireland is sparsely wooded, the range of surviving plant species is larger here than in many other European countries, thanks in part to the comparatively late arrival of agriculture.

There are remnants of the original oak forest in Killarney National Park and in southern Wicklow near Shillelagh. Far more common are pine plantations, which are growing steadily. Hedgerows, planted to divide fields

CONNEMARA PONIES

Ireland's best-known native animal is the Connemara pony – the largest of the pony breeds. The Connemara's ancestors, possibly introduced to Ireland by the Celts, developed the sturdiness and agility for which they are known while roaming the wilds of Connemara. According to legend, the breed also inherited some Spanish blood from the Spanish Armada's stallions, who swam ashore from the wreckage of 1588 to mate with local mares.

The compact and powerful Connemara pony was highly valued by farmers, who tamed wild mares and used them to plough fields and haul rock from the fields. Breeding did not become selective until 1923, when the Connemara Pony Breeders' Society was founded by a group based in Clifden. The Connemara pony, it seems, had been weakened by life in the stables and by indiscriminate breeding. Since then, it has been developed and refined, transforming the old work horse into a show horse. Connemara ponies are known for their gentle disposition and are great riding horses – adults and children alike can mount them.

and delineate land boundaries throughout Ireland, actually host many of the native plant species that once thrived in the oak forests – it's an intriguing example of nature adapting and reasserting itself. The Burren in County Clare is home to a remarkable mixture of Mediterranean, alpine and arctic species.

The bogs of Ireland are home to a unique flora adapted to wet, acidic, nutrient-poor conditions and whose survival is threatened by the depletion of bogs for energy use. Sphagnum moss is the key bog plant and is joined by plants such as bog rosemary, bog cotton, black-beaked sedge (whose spindly stem grows up to 30cm high) and various types of heather and lichen. Carnivorous plants also thrive, such as the sundew, whose sticky tentacles trap insects, and bladderwort whose tiny explosive bladders trap aquatic animals in bog pools.

For information on parks, gardens, monuments and inland waterways see www.heritageireland.ie.

NATIONAL PARKS

Ireland has six national parks: the Burren (p388), Connemara (p424), Glenveagh (p530), Killarney (p253), Wicklow Mountains (p148) and Ballycroy National Park (p456). These have been developed to protect, preserve and make accessible areas of significant natural heritage. The newest park, Ballycroy National Park, was not fully up and running at the time of research, but likely will be during the lifetime of this edition. The other parks are all open year-round and have information offices.

Forests & Forest Parks

Coillte Teoranta (Irish Forestry Board; ☎ 01-661 5666; www.coillte.ie; Leeson La, Dublin) administers about 3500 sq km of forested land, which includes designated picnic areas and 12 forest parks. This constitutes about 70 percent of the Republic's forest land. These parks open year-round and have a range of wildlife and habitats. Some also have chalets and/or caravan parks, shops, cafés and play areas for children.

Look for *Reading the Irish Landscape* by Frank Mitchell and Michael Ryan for info on Ireland's geology, archaeology, urban growth, agriculture and afforestation.

National Nature Reserves

There are 66 state-owned and 10 privately owned National Nature Reserves (NNRs) in the Republic, represented by Dúchas (the government department in charge of parks, monuments and gardens). In Northern Ireland there are over 40 NNRs, which are leased or owned by the Department of the Environment. These reserves are defined as areas of importance for their special flora, fauna or geology and include the Giant's Causeway (p662) and Glenariff (p671) in Antrim, and North Strangford Lough (p620) in County Down. More information is available from the **Environment & Heritage Service** (☎ 028-9054 6533; www.ehsni.gov.uk).

The Greenbox (www
.greenbox.ie) offers a
range of eco-friendly
activities and tours in
northwest Ireland.

ENVIRONMENTAL ISSUES

Ireland does not rate among the world's biggest offenders when it comes to polluting the environment, but the country's recent economic growth has led to an increase in industry and consumerism, which in turn generate more pollution and waste. While the population density is among Europe's lowest, the population is rising. More people are settling in new suburban developments, especially in Counties Meath and Killarny, which are both within commuting distance of Dublin. As more people drive cars and fly in planes, Ireland grows more dependent on nonrenewable sources of energy. The amount of waste has risen substantially since the early 1990s.

Surprisingly, water quality has been a problem for communities deriving their tap water from Lough Corrib, in the west. In March 2007, Galway City, Tuam and Headford were put on Boil Notice, due to the presence of Cryptosporidium in the water. Human and animal waste was assumed to be the cause. The problem was quickly resolved, but served as notice that economic progress can have averse affects on quality of life.

CLIMATE CHANGE & OTHER LOOMING CONCERNS

It remains to be seen what's in store for Ireland as the earth's oceans and atmosphere warm up, but scientists have offered a long list of likely scenarios. The gentlest of forecasts has the weather of Northern Ireland resembling the current conditions in County Cork, while Cork turns into Ireland's version of the Côte d'Azure.

By mid-century, winter temperatures are expected to rise by 1°C on average, while rainfall is predicted to increase, especially in the already wet northwest. Flooding may pose more of a problem in the Shannon River Basin. Summer temperatures may rise by as much as 2.5°C on average, while rainfall is likely to drop significantly during these months. Seasonal drought may become a problem, wildfires may be a growing concern, and due to new irrigation costs the potato may cease to be a viable cash crop in much of Ireland.

The rise in sea level will have a direct effect on Ireland's coasts. Gently sloped beaches along the west coast will disappear as higher waves erode sand and tides extend further inland. Already, climatologists are advising against development within 100m of flat coastlines. Many cities, including Dublin, Cork, Limerick and Galway, will be at increased risk of inundation in the event of storm surges unless seawalls are built.

The impact on biodiversity is a huge question mark, since it is difficult to estimate how well various plant and animal species will adapt to climate change and related side effects. Heath and peatlands, of which Ireland has a large proportion, are considered sensitive to extended periods of dryness. Ireland is currently at the southern extent of the range of salmon, which may stay further north (and be difficult to farm) if the island's streams warm too much for their breeding. New bird species may migrate to Ireland as their habitats elsewhere change or shrink, which will likely have a dramatic effect on delicate ecosystems.

One hotly debated question is the effect of global warming on the North Atlantic Drift, also known as the Gulf Stream, which carries warm waters north from the Gulf of Mexico and the west coast of Africa. Some scientists argue the Gulf Stream is already losing strength, and may stop circulating altogether within the next few decades. If that happens, Arctic waters may exert a greater influence on Ireland, dramatically cooling things off – at least until global warming brings up the temperature of the Arctic region. In that scenario, Ireland can forget about a Mediterranean climate – Scandinavian would be more like it. The weakening of the Gulf Stream is not universally accepted, and its possible effects are questioned. But, needless to say, folks will be talking a lot about the weather in the near future.

At the same time, concern for the environment is growing and the government has taken some measures to offset the damage that thriving economies can cause. Recycling programmes do much to reduce the amount of rubbish generated from consumer packaging. In 2002 the much-publicised plastic bag tax, dubbed the 'plastax', resulted in a 90% drop in bag waste. In 2005, a group called Sustainable Projects Ireland Ltd purchased a 67-acre lot next to the village of Cloughjordan, in North Tipperary, and announced plans to develop the site as a sustainable community. **The Village** (www.thevillage.ie) project will involve efficient water service, orientation of homes to maximise exposure to the sun, and an emphasis on wooded walkways over motorways. Meanwhile, the Republic has established 35 wind farms in an effort to reduce the country's reliance on fossil fuels.

While these are positive signs, they don't really put Ireland at the vanguard of the environmental movement. Polls seem to indicate the Irish are slightly less concerned about the environment than are the citizens of most other European countries, and the country is a long way from meeting its Kyoto Protocol requirement for reduced emissions. The government isn't pushing the environmental agenda much beyond ratifying EU agreements, although it must be said these have established fairly ambitious goals for reduced air pollution and tighter management of water quality.

The annual number of tourists in Ireland far exceeds the number of residents (by a ratio of about 1.5 to one), so travellers can have a huge impact on the local environment. Tourism is frequently cited as potentially beneficial to the environment – that is, responsible visitor spending can help stimulate eco-friendly sectors of the economy. Eco-tourism is not really burgeoning in a formalised way, although an organisation called The Greenbox has established standards for eco-tourism on the island and promotes tour companies that comply to these standards. The rising popularity of outdoor activities such as diving, surfing and fishing create economic incentives for maintaining the cleanliness of Ireland's coasts and inland waters, but increased activity in these environments can be harmful if not managed carefully.

Ireland's comprehensive and efficient bus network makes it easy to avoid the use of a car, and the country is well suited to cycling and walking holidays. Many hotels, guesthouses and hostels tout green credentials, and organic ingredients are frequently promoted on restaurant menus. It's not difficult for travellers to minimise their imprint while in Ireland. See p21 for more information on travelling sustainably.

To see a growing list of low-impact holiday options in Ireland (and elsewhere), visit www .responsibletravel.com.

Dublin

Western Europe's most intimate capital is a city bursting with confidence, which is hardly surprising considering that the last two decades have seen Dublin transformed from delightful backwater struggling to get by into a decadent metropolis that puts no limits on its ambitions. Heritage and hedonism live side by side in Dublin, reflected in the elegance of its Georgian architecture and the garrulous sociability of its citizens, both of which lend character and charm to a city that already has plenty in reserve.

The good times have been good for so long that most Dubliners take them for granted and a whole generation has grown up knowing nothing but the kind of easy prosperity that keeps fancy labels in the wardrobe and golf clubs in the boot of the car. They take it as given that Dublin is a multicultural melting pot where Russians shop for tinned caviar, Nigerian teenagers discuss the merits of hair extensions and Koreans hawk phone cards from their cars. They are confident in the knowledge that their city is so hip that travellers from all over the world can't wait to get here and indulge in the many pleasures it has to offer.

Because pleasure is something Dublin knows all about – from its music, art and literature to the legendary nightlife that has inspired those same musicians, artists and writers, Dublin knows how to have fun and does it with deadly seriousness. As you'll soon find out.

HIGHLIGHTS

- **Antiquated Scholars** Strolling the cobbled grounds of Elizabethan Trinity College (p90)

- **Book-Bound Serenity** Ancient books, bibles and other printed wonders from the world over in the Chester Beatty Library (p95)

- **Choice Addresses** Georgian gems surrounding the landscaped Merrion Square (p99) and St Stephen's Green (p98)

- **History Lesson** The past up close and personal at Kilmainham Jail (p103)

- **Mine's a Guinness** A pint or five in one of Dublin's many pubs and clubs (p130)

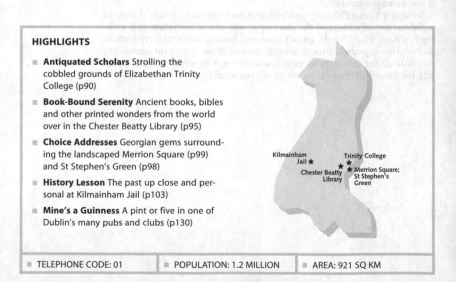

Kilmainham Jail ★
Chester Beatty Library
Trinity College ★
★ Merrion Square; St Stephen's Green

■ TELEPHONE CODE: 01　　　■ POPULATION: 1.2 MILLION　　　■ AREA: 921 SQ KM

HISTORY

Dublin celebrated its official millennium in 1988, but there were settlements here long before AD 988. The first early-Celtic habitation, around 500 BC, was at a ford over the River Liffey, giving rise to the city's Irish name, Baile Átha Cliath (Town of the Hurdle Ford).

The Celts went about their merry way for 1000 years or so, but it wasn't until the Vikings showed up that Dublin was urbanised in any significant way. By the 9th century, raids from the north had become a fact of Irish life, and some of the fierce Danes chose to stay rather than simply rape, pillage and depart. They intermarried with the Irish and established a vigorous trading port at the point where the River Poddle joined the Liffey in a *dubh linn* (black pool). Today there's little trace of the Poddle, which has been channelled underground and flows under St Patrick's Cathedral to dribble into the Liffey by the Capel St (Grattan) Bridge.

Fast-forward another 1000 years, past the arrival of the Normans in the 12th century and the slow process of subjugating Ireland to Anglo-Norman (then British) rule, a process in which Dublin generally played the role of bandleader. Stop at the beginning of the 18th century, when the squalid city packed with poor Catholics hardly reflected the imperial pretensions of its Anglophile burghers. The great and the good – aka the Protestant Ascendancy – wanted big improvements, and they set about transforming what was in essence still a medieval town into a modern, Anglo-Irish metropolis. Roads were widened, landscaped squares laid out and new town houses were built, all in a proto-Palladian style that soon become known as Georgian (after the kings then on the English throne). For a time, Dublin was the second-largest city in the British Empire and all was very, very good – unless you were part of the poor, mostly Catholic masses living in the city's ever developing slums. For them, things stayed pretty much as they had always been.

The Georgian boom came to a sudden and dramatic halt after the Act of Union in 1801, when Ireland was formally united with Britain and its separate parliament closed down. Dublin went from being the belle at the Imperial ball to the annoying cousin who just wouldn't take the hint, and it slid quickly into economic turmoil and social unrest. During the Potato Famine, the city's population was swollen by the arrival of tens of thousands of starving refugees from the west, who joined the ranks of an already downtrodden working class. As Dublin entered the 20th century, it was a dispirited place plagued by poverty, disease and more social problems than anyone cared to mention. It's hardly surprising that the majority of Dublin's citizenry were pissed off and eager for change.

The first fusillade of change came during the Easter Rising of 1916, which caused considerable damage to the city centre. At first, Dubliners weren't too enamoured of the rebels, who caused more chaos and disruption than most locals were willing to put up with, but they soon changed their tune when the leaders were callously executed: Dubliners are natural defenders of the defenceless underdog.

As the whole country lurched radically towards full-scale war with Britain, Dublin was, surprisingly, not part of the main theatre of events. In fact, although there was an increased military presence, the odd shooting in the capital and the blowing up of some notable buildings – such as the Custom House in 1921 – it was business as usual for much of the War of Independence. People went to work and socialised in pretty much the same way as when there wasn't a war.

A year later, Ireland – minus its northern bit – was independent, but it then tumbled into the Civil War, which led to the burning out of more notable buildings, this time the Four Courts in 1922. Ironically the war among the Irish was more brutal than the struggle for independence – O'Connell St became sniper row and the violence left deep scars that are only today beginning to disappear.

When the new state finally started doing business, Dublin was an exhausted capital. Despite slow and steady improvements, the city – like the rest of Ireland – continued to be plagued by rising unemployment, high emigration rates and a general stagnation that hung about the place like an impenetrable cloud. Dubliners made the most of the little they had, but times were tough. Then, in the 1960s, a silver lining appeared in the shape of an economic boom: Dublin went suburban and began the outward expansion that continues unabated today.

A boom ain't a miracle, however, and Dublin trudged along for another couple of decades with pretty much the same age-old problems (high unemployment, emigration) and some

DUBLIN

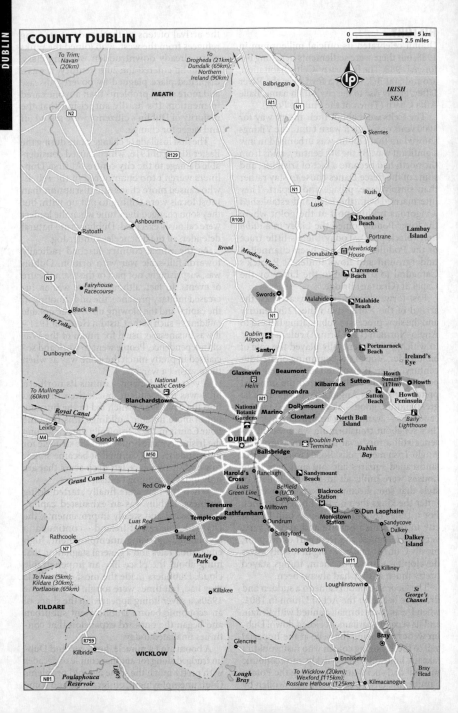

DUBLIN IN...

Two Days

Kick-start your day with a mean brunch at **Gruel** (p124) on Dame St, a stone's throw from **Trinity College** (p90), where the walking tour includes entry to the **Book of Kells** (p93). Ramble through atmospheric **George's St Arcade** (p139) to Grafton St to catch the buskers and splurge on Dublin's most exclusive shopping street. Round it off with a cocktail, dinner and outdoor movie on the terrace at **Eden** (p127), one of Dublin's trendiest restaurants, located in **Temple Bar** (p94), before falling into bed at the **Irish Landmark Trust** (p119), which you and six friends have made your home. The next day marvel at the art of the **Chester Beatty Library** (p95) before strolling up to the **Guinness Storehouse** (p102) for a tour that ends with a glass of 'plain' in the Gravity Bar, which has stunning 360-degree views of the city.

Four Days

Follow the two-day itinerary, then wander around the historic **Glasnevin Cemetery** (p110) before moseying into the peaceful **National Botanic Gardens** (p110). Back in town, browse the **designer shops** (p139) in Temple Bar and grab a bite at **Diep Noodle Bar** (p130), then take the **Dublin Literary Pub Crawl** (p115). The following day take the Dublin Area Rapid Transport (DART) along the coast to the pretty village of **Dalkey** (p142). Gather your strength with a fine meal at **L'Gueuleton** (p126) before a gig at **Vicar Street** (p137).

---

new ones (drug addiction, gangland criminality) before everything began to change and a terrible beauty known as the Celtic Tiger was born. Fifteen years later, Dublin is a place transformed, a capital in more than name and a city that has finally taken its rightful place as one of the most vibrant in Europe.

ORIENTATION

Greater Dublin sprawls around the arc of Dublin Bay, bounded to the north by the hills at Howth and to the south by the Dalkey headland. Small and compact, the city centre has a clear focus and is a walker's delight. It is split in two by the unremarkable River Liffey, which traditionally marks a psychological and social break between the affluent southside and the poorer northside.

South of the river, over O'Connell Bridge, is the Temple Bar area and the expanse of Trinity College. Nassau St, along the southern edge of the campus, and pedestrianised Grafton St are the main shopping streets. At the southern end of Grafton St is St Stephen's Green. About 2km west, beside the river, is Heuston Station, one of the city's two main train stations.

North of the Liffey are O'Connell St and, just off it, Henry St, the major shopping thoroughfares. Most of the northside's B&Bs are on Gardiner St, which becomes rather rundown as it continues north. At the northern end of O'Connell St is Parnell Sq. The main

bus station, Busáras, and the other main train station, Connolly Station, are near the southern end of Gardiner St.

The postcodes for central Dublin are Dublin 1 (immediately north of the river) and Dublin 2 (immediately south). The Dublin 4 postcode, covering the swanky neighbourhoods of Ballsbridge, Donnybrook and Sandymount, is synonymous with affluence and is often used as a descriptive term. A handy tip is to remember that even numbers apply to the southside and odd ones to the north.

See p140 for information on transport to/from the airport and train stations.

INFORMATION
Bookshops

Cathach Books (Map p86; ☎ 671 8676; www.rare books.ie; 10 Duke St) A rich and remarkable collection of secondhand Irish-interest books, including 1st editions.
Connolly Books (Map p84; ☎ 670 8707; 43 East Essex St) Left-wing bookshop beloved of Marxists and radicals.
Dubray Books (Map p86; ☎ 677 5568; 36 Grafton St) Excellent local shop with a good Irish-interest section.
Dublin Writers Museum (Map pp82-3; ☎ 872 2077; 18 North Parnell Sq)
Eason (Map p84; ☎ 873 3811; 40 Lower O'Connell St) One of the biggest magazine stockists in Ireland.
Eason – Hanna's (Map p86; ☎ 677 1255; 27-29 Nassau St) Academic tomes, bestsellers and stationery.

(Continued on page 88)

DUBLIN (pp82-3)

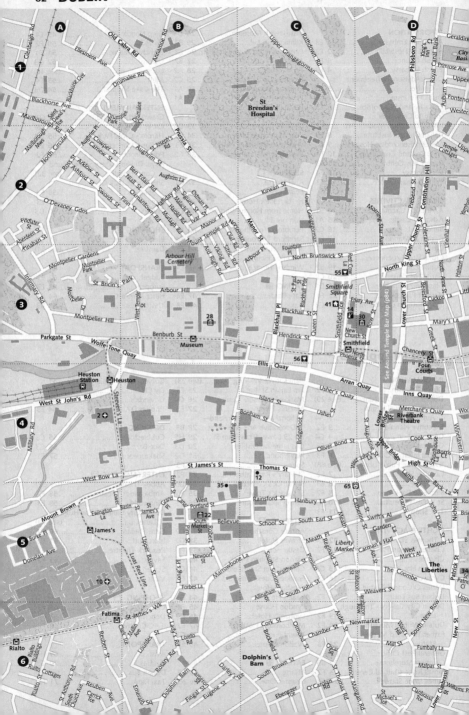

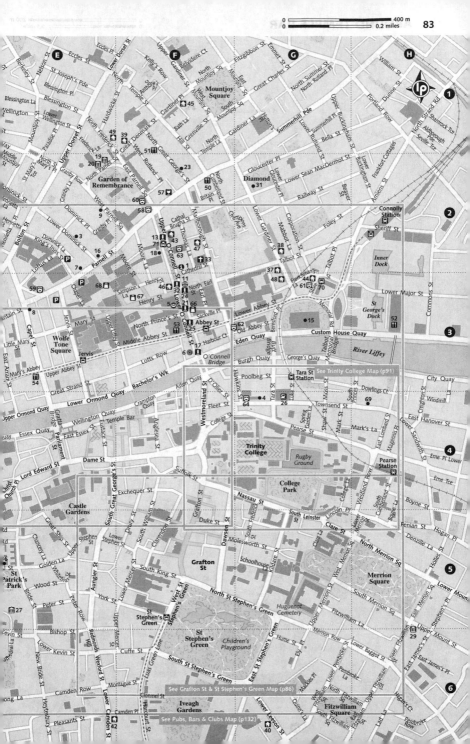

0 ————————— 200 m
0 ————————— 0.1 mile

INFORMATION

American Express.....................(see 4)
An Post...1 E3
Connolly Books............................ 2 D3
Cultivate......................................3 C3
Dublin Tourism Centre...............4 E3
Eason...5 E1
First Rate.....................................6 F3
Internet Exchange...................(see 80)
O'Connell's Pharmacy...............7 F1
Talk Shop....................................8 D3
Thomas Cook..............................9 F3
USIT...10 F2
Waterstone's...........................(see 82)
Well Woman Clinic...................11 E2

SIGHTS & ACTIVITIES

1916 Easter Rising Walk...........12 E4
An Taisce...................................13 B4
Ark...14 D3
Bank of Ireland.........................15 F3
Chester Beatty Library..............16 C4
Christ Church Cathedral...........17 B4
City Hall....................................18 C4
Cycle-Logical............................19 E2
Dublin Castle............................20 D4
Dublin Musical Pub Crawl.......(see 49)
Dvblinia.....................................21 B4
Four Courts...............................22 A3
Gallery of Photography............23 D3
Gray Line Dublin Tour.............(see 4)
Grayline Tours..........................24 E2
Harrisons...................................25 F2
Municipal Buildings.................26 C4
National Photographic Archives.27 D3
Ormond Quay Hotel.................28 C2
Pat Liddy Walking Tours...........(see 4)

Record Tower............................29 D4
Square Wheel Cycleworks........30 D3
St Audoen's Catholic Church....31 A4
St Audoen's Church of Ireland..32 A4
St Michan's Church...................33 A2
St Werburgh's Church...............34 C4
Stock Exchange.........................35 E3
Sunlight Chambers....................36 C3
Temple Bar Information Centre..37 D3
Wild Wicklow Tour..................(see 4)

SLEEPING 🏠

Abbey Court Hostel...................38 E2
Ashfield House..........................39 F2
Barnacles Temple Bar House.....40 D3
Clarence Hotel..........................41 C3
Dublin Citi Hotel.......................42 E3
Irish Landmark Trust.................43 D3
Jurys Inn Christ Church.............44 B4
Kinlay House.............................45 C4
Litton Lane Hostel....................46 E2
Morgan Hotel............................47 E2
Morrison Hotel..........................48 D2
Oliver St John Gogarty's Penthouse
   Apartments.............................49 E3
Paramount Hotel.......................50 C3
Westin Dublin...........................51 F3

EATING 🍴

Ar Vicoletto.............................. 52 D3
Avoca Handweavers.............(see 79)
Bar Italia................................... 53 C3
Bar Italia................................... 54 D2
Bottega Toffoli.......................... 55 C4
Chameleon................................56 E3
Eden...57 D3
Enoteca Delle Langhe................58 D2

Epicurean Food Hall..................59 E2
Gruel..60 D3
La Taverna di Bacco..............(see 58)
Larder..61 C3
Leo Burdock's............................62 C4
Mermaid Café...........................63 D3
Monty's of Kathmandu.............64 D3
Odessa.......................................65 D4
Queen of Tarts..........................66 C3
Silk Road Café.......................(see 16)
Soup Dragon.............................67 C2
Toscana......................................68 C3
Winding Stair............................69 D2

ENTERTAINMENT 🎭

Ark...(see 14)
Bank of Ireland Arts Centre......70 E3
Boilerhouse Sauna....................71 D3
Irish Film Institute....................72 D3
Olympia Theatre........................73 D3
Project Arts Centre....................74 D3
Temple Bar Music Centre.........75 D3
Tivoli Theatre............................76 A4

SHOPPING 🛍

5 Scarlett Row...........................77 C3
Arnott's......................................78 E1
Avoca Handweavers..................79 F4
Claddagh Records.....................80 D3
DesignYard................................81 C3
Jervis St Centre.........................82 D1
Meeting House Square Market..83 D3
Smock..84 C3
Urban Outfitters........................85 E3

TRANSPORT

Iarnród Éireann Travel Centre...86 F1

(Continued from page 79)

Greene's Bookshop (Map p86; ☎ 676 2554; www.greenesbookshop.com; 16 Clare St) What all secondhand bookshops should be – packed with dusty tomes.

Hodges Figgis (Map p86; ☎ 677 4754; 56-58 Dawson St) Widest selection of titles in Dublin.

Hughes & Hughes Dublin Airport (Map p78; ☎ 814 4034); St Stephen's Green (Map p86; ☎ 478 3060; St Stephen's Green Shopping Centre) Magazines, bestsellers and new titles.

Irish Museum of Modern Art (IMMA; Map p80; ☎ 612 9900; Royal Hospital Kilmainham) Contemporary-art and Irish-interest books.

Library Book Shop (Map p91; ☎ 608 1171; Trinity College) Irish-interest books, including ones on the *Book of Kells*.

Murder Ink (Map p86; ☎ 677 7570; 15 Dawson St) Mystery titles.

National Gallery (Map p86; ☎ 678 5450; Merrion Sq West) Traditional-art and Irish-interest books.

Sinn Féin Bookshop (Map pp82-3; ☎ 872 7096; 44 West Parnell Sq)

Stokes Books (Map p86; ☎ 671 3584; 19 George's St Arcade) Irish historical books, old and new.

Waterstone's Dawson St (Map p86; ☎ 679 1415; 7 Dawson St); Jervis St Centre (Map p84; ☎ 878 1311; Jervis St)

Cultural Centres

Alliance Française (Map p86; ☎ 676 1732; 1 Kildare St)

British Council (Map p80; ☎ 676 4088; Newmount House, 22-24 Lower Mount St)

Goethe Institute (Map p86; ☎ 661 1155; 37 North Merrion Sq)

Instituto Cervantes (Map p80; ☎ 668 2024; 58 Northumberland Rd)

Italian Cultural Institute (Map p80; ☎ 676 6662; 11 Fitzwilliam Sq)

Emergency

For national emergency numbers, see the inside front cover.

Confidential Line Freefone (☎ 1800 666 111) Garda confidential line to report crime.

Drugs Advisory & Treatment Centre (Map pp82-3; ☎ 677 1122; Trinity Ct, 30-31 Pearse St)

Rape Crisis Centre (Map pp82-30; ☎ 1800 778 888, 661 4911; 70 Lower Leeson St)

Samaritans (☎ 1850 609 090, 872 7700) For people who are depressed or suicidal.

Internet Access

Global Internet Café Basement (Map pp82-3; ☎ 878 0295; 8 O'Connell St Lower; per hr €5; ☯ 8am-11pm Mon-Fri, from 9am Sat, from 10am Sun)

Internet Exchange (Map p84; ☎ 670 3000; 3 Cecilia St; per hr €5; ☯ 8am-2am Mon-Fri, 10am-midnight Sat & Sun)

Internet Resources

Balcony TV (www.balconytv.com) Interviews and music from a balcony in central Dublin. **Discover Ireland** (www.ireland.ie) Official website of Discover Ireland, the public face of the Irish Tourist Board.

Dublin Tourism (www.visitdublin.com) Official website of Dublin Tourism.

Dubliner (www.thedubliner.ie) Gossip, features and other Dublin-related titbits.

Nixers.com (www.nixers.ie) A good place to check if you're looking for casual work over the summer.

Laundry

Laundry facilities can be found quite easily in the city centre, with prices starting at about €7.50 a load; ask at your accommodation for the nearest one. Alternatively most hostels, B&Bs and hotels will provide the service. In hostels, prices start at around €6 and it is generally self-service.

All-American Laundrette (Map p86; ☎ 677 2779; Wicklow Ct, South Great George's St)

Laundry Shop (Map pp82-3; ☎ 872 3541; 191 Parnell St)

Left Luggage

Left-luggage facilities are available at all transport centres, including the airport.

Busáras (Map pp82-3; ☎ 703 2434; locker per 24hr €4-9; ☯ 7am-10.30pm) Main bus station north of the Liffey.

Connolly Station (Map pp82-3; ☎ 703 2363; bag per 24hr €2.50; ☯ 7am-10pm Mon-Sat, 8am-10pm Sun) The main train station on the northside.

Dublin Airport (Map p78; ☎ 814 4633; Greencaps Left Luggage & Porterage, Dublin airport; per bag per 24hr €4.50-12; ☯ 7am-10pm Mon-Sat, from 8am Sun)

Libraries

Dublin Corporation (Map p86; ☎ 661 9000; Cumberland House, Fenian St; ☯ 9.30am-5pm Mon-Fri) For information on public libraries.

ILAC Centre Public Library (Map pp82-3; ☎ 873 4333; ILAC Centre, Henry St; ☯ 10am-8pm Mon-Thu, to 5pm Sat) One of the city's largest public libraries.

Media

Besides the national dailies (see p694), there are a number of Dublin-specific publications and media outlets.

NEWSPAPERS & MAGAZINES

Dublin Event Guide (free) Fortnightly coverage of all things entertainment throughout the city.

Dubliner (€3.99) Monthly magazine that mixes city-related offerings with interviews and features.

Evening Herald (€1) Evening tabloid with thorough entertainment listings and a terrific flat-finder section.

In Dublin (free) A monthly ad rag.

Mongrel (free) Excellent and irreverent magazine with features and interviews.

RADIO

Phantom 105.2 Alternative music, from mod to metal.

Spin 103.8 Chart music and chat for 18 to 24 year olds.

Medical Services

Should you experience an immediate health problem, contact the casualty section of the nearest public hospital; in an emergency, call an ambulance (☎ 999). There are no 24-hour pharmacies in Dublin; the latest openings are until 10pm.

Baggot St Hospital (Map p80; ☎ 668 1577; 18 Upper Baggot St; ⏰ 7.30am-4.30pm Mon-Fri) Southside city centre.

City Pharmacy (Map p84; ☎ 670 4523; 14 Dame St; ⏰ 9am-10pm)

Dental Hospital (Map p86; ☎ 612 7200; 20 Lincoln Pl; ⏰ 8am for pre-booked appointments) If you need to get those choppers looked at; if you don't have an appointment, head in after noon.

Doctors on Call (☎ 453 9333; ⏰ 24hr) Request a doctor to come out to your accommodation at any time.

Eastern Regional Health Authority (Map pp82-3; ☎ 679 0700, 1800 520 520; www.erha.ie; Dr Steevens' Hospital, Steevens' Lane; ⏰ 9.30am-5.30pm Mon-Fri) Central health authority with Choice of Doctor Scheme, which can advise you on a suitable GP from 9am to 5pm Monday to Friday. Information services for those with physical and mental disabilities.

Grafton Medical Centre (Map p86; ☎ 671 2122; www.graftonmedical.ie; 34 Grafton St; ⏰ 8.30am-6.30pm Mon-Thu, to 6pm Fri) One-stop shop with male and female doctors, physiotherapists and a tropical medicine bureau.

Mater Misericordiae Hospital (Map p80; ☎ 830 1122; Eccles St) Northside city centre, off Lower Dorset St.

O'Connell's Pharmacy Grafton St (Map p86; ☎ 679 0467; 21 Grafton St; ⏰ 9am-10pm); O'Connell St (Map p84; ☎ 873 0427; 55-56 O'Connell St; ⏰ 9am-10pm)

St James' Hospital (Map pp82-3; ☎ 453 7941; James St) Southside.

Well Woman Centre Lower Liffey St (Map p84; ☎ 661 0083; 35 Lower Liffey St; ⏰ 9.30am-7.30pm Mon & Thu-Fri, 8am-7.30pm Tue-Wed, 10am-4pm Sat & 1-4pm Sun); Pembroke Rd (Map p80; ☎ 660 9860; 67 Pembroke Rd; ⏰ 10am-7.30pm Mon-Wed, 8am-7.30pm Thu, 10am-4pm Sat) For female health issues. Supplies contraceptives, including the morning-after pill (€52).

Money

There are currency-exchange counters at Dublin airport in the baggage-collection area, and on the arrival and departure floors. The counters are open 5.30am to 11pm.

There are numerous banks around the city centre with exchange facilities, open during regular bank hours.

American Express (Amex; Map p84; ☎ 605 7709; Dublin Tourism Centre, St Andrew's Church, 2 Suffolk St; ⏰ 9am-5pm Mon-Sat)

First Rate (Map p84; ☎ 671 3233; 1 Westmoreland St; ⏰ 8am-9pm Mon-Fri, 9am-9pm Sat, 10am-9pm Sun Jun-Sep, 9am-6pm Oct-May)

Thomas Cook (Map p84; ☎ 677 1721, 677 1307; 118 Grafton St; ⏰ 9am-5.30pm Mon, Tue, Fri & Sat, 10am-5.30pm Wed, 9am-7pm Thu)

Post

An Post (Map p84; ☎ 705 8206; St Andrew's St)

General Post Office (Map pp82-3; ☎ 705 7000; O'Connell St; ⏰ 8am-8pm Mon-Sat) Dublin's famed general post office has a free poste restante service, a philatelic counter and a bank of telephones.

Telephone

Talk Shop (⏰ 9am-11pm); Temple Lane (Map p84; ☎ 672 7212; The Granary, 20 Temple Lane); Upper O'Connell St (Map pp82-3; ☎ 872 0200; 5 Upper O'Connell St) For cheap international phone calls.

Tourist Information

No tourist information offices in Dublin provide any information over the phone – they're exclusively walk-in services.

All telephone bookings and reservations are operated by Gulliver, a computerised information and reservation service that is available at all walk-in offices or from anywhere in the world. It provides up-to-date information on events, attractions and transport, and can also book accommodation. You can book via www.visitdublin.com or www.gulliver.ie, or via telephone: in Ireland call ☎ 1800 668 668; from Britain call ☎ 00800 6686 6866; from the rest of the world call ☎ 353-669 792083.

Dublin Tourism (www.visitdublin.com); Dublin Airport (arrivals hall; ☺ 8am-10pm); Dun Laoghaire (Dun Laoghaire ferry terminal; ☺ 10am-1pm & 2-6pm Mon-Sat); O'Connell St (Map pp82-3; 14 Upper O'Connell St; ☺ 9am-5pm Mon-Sat); Wilton Tce (Map p80; Wilton Tce; ☺ 9.30am-noon & 12.30-5pm Mon-Fri)

Dublin Tourism Centre (Map p84; ☎ 605 7700; www.visitdublin.com; St Andrew's Church, 2 Suffolk St; ☺ 9am-7pm Mon-Sat, 10.30am-3pm Sun Jul & Aug, 9am-5.30pm Mon-Sat Sep-Jun) Dublin's main tourist office. There is a booking fee of €4.50 for serviced accommodation or €7.50 for self-catering accommodation, and a 10% deposit which is refunded through your hotel bill.

Fáilte Ireland head office (Map p80; ☎ 1850 230 330; www.ireland.ie; Wilton Tce; ☺ 9am-5.15pm Mon-Fri)

Travel Agencies

American Express (Amex; Map p84; ☎ 605 7709; Dublin Tourism Centre, St Andrew's Church, 2 Suffolk St; ☺ 9am-5pm Mon-Sat)

Thomas Cook (Map p84; ☎ 677 1721, 677 1307; 118 Grafton St; ☺ 9am-5.30pm Mon, Tue, Fri & Sat, 10am-5.30pm Wed, 9am-7pm Thu)

USIT (Map p84; ☎ 602 1904; www.usit.ie; 19 Aston Quay; ☺ 9.30am-6.30pm Mon-Wed & Fri, 9.30am-8pm Thu, 9.30am-5pm Sat) Travel agency of the Union of Students in Ireland.

DANGERS & ANNOYANCES

Petty crime of the bag-snatching, pickpocketing and car-break-in variety is a low- to mid-level irritant. Hired and foreign-registered cars are favoured targets – they seem to have a smash-*my*-window sign splayed across their bonnets. Take sensible precautions; supervised car parks for overnight parking aren't a bad idea. Remember also that insurance policies often don't cover losses from cars.

The area north of Gardiner St, O'Connell St and Mountjoy Sq is not especially salubrious, and is afflicted with drug addiction, crime and occasional violence. Phoenix Park is a no-

> **THE DUBLIN PASS**
>
> If you're planning some heavy-duty sightseeing, you'll save a packet by investing in the **Dublin Pass** (adult/child 1 day €31/17, 2 days €49/29, 3 days €59/34, 6 days €89/44). Not only do you gain free entry into 30 attractions, but you can skip whatever queue there is by presenting your card. The card is available from any of the Dublin Tourism offices (left).

go area after dark; camping there is not just illegal, but also an invitation to trouble.

The problem of sloppy drunkenness after closing hours is another potential hassle. Where there are pubs and clubs there are worse-for-wear revellers looking to get home and/or get laid, and sometimes the frustrations of getting neither can result in a trip to the casualty department of the nearest hospital – hospitals are clogged to bursting with drink-related cases throughout the weekend.

SIGHTS
Trinity College & Around

Dublin's oldest and most beautiful university stretches its leafy self across much of the south city centre's most valuable real estate. Just south of Trinity College is Grafton St, Dublin's most elegant shopping street, which runs up to the main entrance to St Stephen's Green. Surrounding and beyond Dublin's most popular green lung is the capital's exquisite Georgian heritage, a collection of galleries, museums, and private and public buildings as handsome as any you'll see in Europe. Back at Trinity College, take a few steps northwest of the main entrance to find yourself in Temple Bar, where bacchanalia and bohemia scrap it out for supremacy. When the sun sets, Bacchus is king.

TRINITY COLLEGE

On a summer's evening, when the bustling crowds have gone for the day, there's hardly a more delightful place in Dublin than the grounds of Ireland's most prestigious **university** (Map p91; ☎ 896 1000, walking tours ☎ 896 1827; tour incl Long Room €10; ☺ tours every 40min 10.15am-3.40pm Mon-Sat, 10.15am-3pm Sun mid-May–Sep), a masterpiece of architecture and landscaping beautifully preserved in Georgian aspic. Not only is it Dublin's most attractive bit of historical real estate, but it's also home to one of the world's

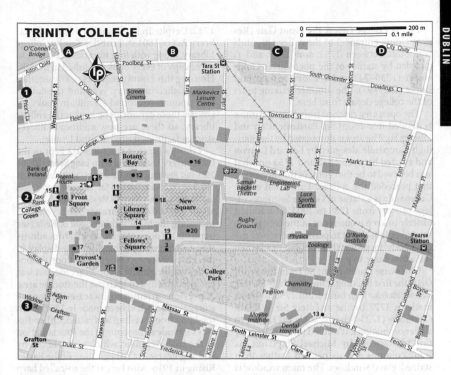

TRINITY COLLEGE

INFORMATION		Dublin Experience................(see 2)		Printing House..........................**16** B2
Library Bookshop.....................(see 14)		Edmund Burke Statue............**8** A2		Provost's House.......................**17** A2
		Exam Hall...............................**9** A2		Rubrics Building......................**18** B2
SIGHTS & ACTIVITIES		Front Gate.............................**10** A2		Sphere within Sphere.............**19** B2
1937 Reading Room...................**1** A2		George Salmon Statue..........**11** A2		Victorian Museum
Arts & Social Science Building........**2** B3		Graduates' Memorial		Building................................**20** B2
Berkeley Library........................**3** B2		Building................................**12** B2		
Campanile................................**4** A2		Lincoln Place Gate..................**13** C3		**SLEEPING**
Chapel....................................**5** A2		Long Room.........................(see 14)		Accommodations Office..........**21** A2
Dining Hall..............................**6** A2		Old Library............................**14** B2		
Douglas Hyde Gallery of Modern		Oliver Goldsmith		**ENTERTAINMENT**
Art.......................................**7** A3		Statue..................................**15** A2		Players' Theatre......................**22** C2

most famous – and most beautiful – books,
the gloriously illuminated *Book of Kells*. There
is no charge to wander the gardens on your
own between 8am and 10pm.

Officially, the university's name is the University of Dublin, but Trinity is its sole college.
Its charter was granted by Elizabeth I in 1592 –
on grounds confiscated from an Augustinian
priory which was dissolved in 1537 – with the
hope that young Dubliners would desist from
skipping across to Continental Europe for
their education and becoming 'infected with
popery'. The 16-hectare site is now in the centre of the city, but when it was founded it was
described as 'near Dublin' and was bordered

on two sides by the estuary of the Liffey. Nothing now remains of the original Elizabethan
college, which was replaced in the Georgian
building frenzy of the 18th century. The most
significant change, however, is the student
population: the university was exclusively
Protestant until 1793, but today most of its
15,000-odd students are Catholic (although
until 1970 they were forbidden from attending
by their own church on pain of excommunication). All of this would surely have horri-
fied Archbishop Ussher, one of the college's
founders, whose greatest scientific feat was the
precise dating of the act of creation to 4004
BC. Nice work, Mr Ussher.

Facing College Green, the Front Gate (Regent House entrance) to the college grounds was built between 1752 and 1759 and is guarded by statues of the poet Oliver Goldsmith (1730–74) and the orator Edmund Burke (1729–97). The summer walking tours of the college depart from here.

The open area reached from Regent House is divided into Front Sq, Parliament Sq and Library Sq. The area is dominated by the 30m-high Campanile, designed by Edward Lanyon and erected between 1852 and 1853 on what was believed to be the centre of the monastery that preceded the college. To the left of the Campanile is a statue of George Salmon, college provost from 1888 to 1904, who fought bitterly to keep women out of the college. He carried out his threat to permit them 'over my dead body' by promptly dropping dead when the worst came to pass.

Clockwise round Front Sq from the Front Gate, the first building is the **chapel** (☎ 896 1260; Front Sq; admission free), built from 1798 to plans made in 1777 by the architect Sir William Chambers (1723–96) and, since 1972, open to all denominations. It's noted for its extremely fine plasterwork by Michael Stapleton, its Ionic columns and its painted (rather than stained-glass) windows. The main window is dedicated to Archbishop Ussher.

Next to the chapel is the **dining hall** (Parliament Sq; ☺ students only), originally designed in 1743 by Richard Cassels (aka Castle) but dismantled 15 years later because of problems caused by inadequate foundations. The replacement was completed in 1761 and may have retained some elements of the original design. It was extensively restored after a fire in 1984.

The 1892 **Graduates' Memorial Building** (Botany Bay; ☺ closed to public) forms the northern side of Library Sq. Behind it are tennis courts in the open area known as Botany Bay. The legend behind this name is that the unruly students housed around the square were suitable candidates for the British penal colony at Botany Bay in Australia.

At the eastern side of Library Sq, the red-brick **Rubrics Building** dates from around 1690, making it the oldest building in the college. It was extensively altered in an 1894 restoration and then underwent major structural modifications in the 1970s.

To the south of the square is the **Old Library** (☎ 896 2320; Library Sq), built in a rather severe style by Thomas Burgh between 1712 and 1732. Despite Ireland's independence, the Library Act of 1801 still entitles Trinity College Library, along with four libraries in Britain, to a free copy of every book published in the UK. Housing this bounty requires nearly another 1km of shelving every year and the collection amounts to around 4.5 million books. Of course, these cannot all be kept at the college library, so there are now additional library storage facilities dotted around Dublin.

Trinity's greatest treasures are kept in the Old Library's stunning 65m **Long Room** (☎ 896 2320; East Pavilion, Library Colonnades; adult/student/child €8/7/free; ☺ 9.30am-5pm Mon-Sat year-round, noon-4.30pm Sun Oct-Apr, 9.30am-4.30pm Sun May-Sep), which houses about 250,000 of the library's oldest volumes, including the breathtaking *Book of Kells* (see opposite). Your entry ticket includes admission to temporary exhibitions on display in the East Pavilion. The ground-floor Colonnades was originally an open arcade, but was enclosed in 1892 to increase the storage area. A previous attempt to increase the room's storage capacity had been made in 1853, when the Long Room ceiling was raised. Other displays include a rare copy of the Proclamation of the Irish Republic, which was read out by Pádraig Pearse at the beginning of the Easter Rising in 1916. Also here is the so-called harp of Brian Ború, which was definitely not in use when the army of this early Irish hero defeated the Danes at the Battle of Clontarf in 1014. It does, however, date from around 1400, making it one of the oldest harps in Ireland.

Continuing clockwise around the Campanile there's the **1937 Reading Room** and the **Exam Hall** (Public Theatre), which dates from 1779 to 1791. Like the chapel it was the work of William Chambers and also has plasterwork by Michael Stapleton. The Exam Hall has an oak chandelier rescued from the Houses of Parliament (now the Bank of Ireland) across College Green and an organ said to have been salvaged from a Spanish ship in 1702, though evidence indicates otherwise.

Behind the Exam Hall is the 1760 **Provost's House**, a very fine Georgian house where the provost (college head) still resides. The house and its adjacent garden are not open to the public.

To one side of the Old Library is Paul Koralek's 1967 **Berkeley Library** (Fellows' Sq; ☺ closed to public). This solid, square brutalist-style building has been hailed as the best example of modern architecture in Ireland, though it has to be admitted the competition isn't great. It's fronted by Arnaldo Pomodoro's 1982–83 sculpture **Sphere within Sphere**.

George Berkeley was born in Kilkenny in 1685, studied at Trinity when he was only 15 years old and went on to a distinguished career in many fields, particularly in philosophy. His influence spread to the new colonies in North America where, among other things, he helped to found the University of Pennsylvania. Berkeley in California, and its namesake university, are named after him.

South of the Old Library is the 1978 **Arts & Social Science Building**, which backs on to Nassau St and forms the alternative entrance to the college. Like the Berkeley Library, it was designed by Paul Koralek; it also houses the **Douglas Hyde Gallery of Modern Art** (☎ 896 1116; www.douglashydegallery.ie; admission free; 🕑 11am-6pm Mon-Wed & Fri, 11am-7pm Thu, 11am-4.45pm Sat).

After the *Book of Kells*, the college's biggest tourist attraction is the **Dublin Experience** (☎ 896 1688; Arts & Social Science Bldg; adult/student €5/4, incl Book of Kells €11/9; 🕑 10am-5pm mid-May–Sep). It's a 45-minute multimedia introduction to the city which is vaguely satisfying if it's too wet to actually walk around the subject itself. Shows take place at the back of the Arts & Social Science Building.

Behind the Rubrics Building, at the eastern end of Library Sq, is New Sq. The highly ornate **Victorian Museum Building** (☎ 896 1477; New Sq; admission free; 🕑 by prior arrangement), built from 1853 to 1857, has the skeletons of two enormous giant Irish deer just inside the entrance, and the Geological Museum upstairs.

The 1734 **Printing House**, designed by Richard Cassels to resemble a Doric temple, and now used for the microelectronics and electrical engineering departments, is on the northern side of New Sq.

At the eastern end of the college grounds are the rugby ground and College Park, where cricket is played. There are a number of science buildings here also. The **Lincoln Place Gate** at this end is usually open and makes a good entrance or exit from the college, especially if you're on a bicycle.

BANK OF IRELAND
The imposing **Bank of Ireland** (Map p84; ☎ 671 1488; College Green; admission free; 🕑 10am-4pm Mon-Wed & Fri, 10am-5pm Thu), directly opposite Trinity College, was originally built in 1729 to house the Irish Parliament. When the Parliament voted itself out of existence by the Act of Union in 1801, it became a building without a role. It was sold in 1803 with instructions that the

---

THE PAGE OF KELLS

More than half a million visitors stop in each year to see Trinity's top show-stopper, the world-famous *Book of Kells*. This illuminated manuscript, dating from around AD 800 and thus one of the oldest books in the world, was probably produced by monks at St Colmcille's Monastery on the remote island of Iona, off the western coast of Scotland. Repeated looting by marauding Vikings forced the monks to flee to the temporary safety of Kells, county Meath, in AD 806, along with their masterpiece. Around 850 years later, the book was brought to the college for safekeeping and has remained here since.

The *Book of Kells* contains the four Gospels of the New Testament, written in Latin, as well as prefaces, summaries and other text. If it were merely words, the *Book of Kells* would simply be a very old book – it's the extensive and amazingly complex illustrations that make it so wonderful. The superbly decorated opening initials are only part of the story, for the book has smaller illustrations between the lines.

And here the problems begin. Of the 680 pages, only two are on display – one showing an illumination, the other showing text – which has led to it being dubbed the *page* of Kells. No getting around that one, though: you can hardly expect the right to thumb through a priceless treasure at random. No, the real problem is its immense popularity, which makes viewing it a rather unsatisfactory pleasure. Punters are herded through the specially constructed viewing room at near lightning pace, making for a there-you-see-it, there-you-don't kind of experience.

To really appreciate the book, you can get your own reproduction copy for a mere €22,000. Failing that, the library bookshop stocks a plethora of souvenirs and other memorabilia, including Otto Simm's excellent *Exploring the Book of Kells* (€10.95), a thorough guide with attractive colour plates, and a popular DVD-ROM showing all 800 pages for €29.95.

interior be altered to prevent its being used as a debating chamber in the future; consequently, the large central House of Commons was remodelled, but the smaller chamber of the House of Lords survived. After independence the Irish government chose to make Leinster House the new parliamentary building and ignored the possibility of restoring this fine building to its original use.

Inside, the banking mall occupies what was once the House of Commons, but it offers little indication of its former role. The Irish House of Lords is a much more interesting place, with Irish-oak woodwork, a late-18th-century Dublin-crystal chandelier, tapestries and a 10kg silver-gilt mace.

Éamon MacThomás, a Dublin historian and author, runs **tours** (admission free; ☒ 10.30am, 11.30am & 1.45pm Tue) of the House of Lords, which also include an informal talk as much about Ireland, and life in general, as the building itself.

TEMPLE BAR

Dublin's top tourist precinct (Map p84) is a maze of cobbled streets sandwiched between Dame St and the Liffey, running from Trinity College to Christ Church Cathedral. In Temple Bar you can browse for vintage clothes, check out the latest art installations, get your nipples pierced and nibble on Mongolian barbecue. In good weather you can watch outdoor movies in one square or join in a pulsating drum circle in another: it's all part of Dublin's very own cultural quarter, now one of Europe's best-known entertainment districts.

In spite of the odd bit of culture, the moniker is a little bogus and the area has lost much of its authenticity in its overbearing efforts to sell the unquantifiable thing that is the 'Dublin Experience'. During the day and on weekday nights Temple Bar does have something of a bohemian bent about it – if you ignore the crappy tourist shops and dreadful restaurants serving bland, overpriced food – but at weekends, when the party really gets going, it all gets very sloppy. The huge, characterless bars crank up the sounds and throw their doors open to the tens of thousands of punters looking to drink and score like the end of the world is nigh. By 3am, the only culture on display is in the pools of vomit and urine that give the whole area the aroma of a sewer – welcome to Temple Barf.

Temple Bar Information Centre (Map p84; ☎ 677 2255; www.templebar.ie, www.visit-templebar.ie; 12 East Essex St; ☒ 9am-5.30pm Mon-Fri) publishes the *Tascq* cultural guide to Temple Bar, which gives information on attractions and restaurants in the area. It's available from the information centre or at businesses around Temple Bar. It's best to check the websites for details of events, particularly the Diversions festival (p116).

Meeting House Square (Map p84) is one of the real success stories of Temple Bar. On one side is the excellent **Gallery of Photography** (Map p84; ☎ 671 4653; admission free; ☒ 11am-6pm Mon-Sat), hosting temporary exhibitions of contemporary local and international photographers. Staying with the photography theme, the other side of the square is home to the **National Photographic Archive** (Map p84; ☎ 671 0073; admission free; ☒ 11am-6pm Mon-Sat, 2-6pm Sun), a magnificent resource for anyone interested in a photographic history of Ireland.

At the western end of Temple Bar, in the shadow of Christ Church Cathedral, is **Fishamble Street** (Map p84), the oldest street in Dublin. It dates back to Viking times – not that you'd know that to see it now.

On Parliament St, which runs south from the river to the City Hall and Dublin Castle, the **Sunlight Chambers** (Map p84) beside the river has a beautiful frieze around its façade. Sunlight was a brand of soap manufactured by the Lever Brothers, who were responsible for the late-19th-century building. The frieze shows the Lever Brothers' view of the world: men make clothes dirty, women wash them!

Buildings on interesting **Eustace Street** (Map p84) include the 1715 Presbyterian Meeting House, now the **Ark** (Map p84; ☎ 670 7788; www.ark .ie; 11A Eustace St), an excellent children's cultural centre. The Dublin branch of the Society of United Irishmen, who sought Parliamentary reform and equality for Catholics, was first convened in 1791 in the Eagle Tavern, now the **Friends Meeting House** (Map p84; Eustace St). This should not be confused with the other Eagle Tavern, which is on Cork St.

Merchant's Arch leads to the **Ha'penny Bridge** (Map p84), named after the ha'penny toll once needed to cross. The **Stock Exchange** (Map p84) is on Anglesea St, in a building dating from 1878.

DUBLIN CASTLE

The centre of British power in Ireland for the guts of 800 years, **Dublin Castle** (Map p84; ☎ 645

HANDEL WITH CARE

In 1742 the nearly broke GF Handel conducted the very first performance of his epic work *Messiah* in the since demolished Dublin Music Hall, on the city's oldest street, Fishamble St. Dean Swift – author of *Gulliver's Travels* and dean of St Patrick's Cathedral – had suggested his own and Christ Church's choirs participate, but revoked his invitation, vowing to 'punish such vicars for their rebellion, disobedience and perfidy'. The concert went ahead nonetheless, and the celebrated work is performed at the original spot in Dublin annually – now a hotel that bears the composer's name.

8813; www.dublincastle.ie; Cork Hill; adult/student/child €4.50/3.50/2; 10am-4.45pm Mon-Fri, 2-4.45pm Sat & Sun) was originally built on the orders of King John in 1204, but it's more higgledy-piggledy palace than castle. Only the Record Tower, completed in 1258, survives from the original Norman construction. Parts of the castle's foundations remain and a visit to the excavations is the most interesting part of the castle tour. The moats, which are now completely covered by more modern developments, were once filled by the River Poddle. The castle is also home to one of Dublin's best museums, the Chester Beatty Library (below).

The castle, which tops Cork Hill, behind the City Hall, is still used for government business, and tours (every 20 minutes) are often tailored around meetings and conferences or are sometimes cancelled altogether, so it's wise to phone beforehand.

CHESTER BEATTY LIBRARY

The world-famous **Chester Beatty Library** (Map p84; 407 0750; www.cbl.ie; Dublin Castle, Cork Hill; admission free; 10am-5pm Mon-Fri, 11am-5pm Sat, 1-5pm Sun year-round, closed Mon Oct-Apr) houses the collection of mining engineer Sir Alfred Chester Beatty (1875–1968), bequeathed to the Irish State on his death. The breathtaking collection is spread over two floors and includes more than 20,000 manuscripts, rare books, miniature paintings, clay tablets, costumes and other objects. The library runs tours at 1pm Wednesday, and 3pm and 4pm Sunday.

The **Artistic Traditions Gallery** on the 1st floor begins with memorabilia from Beatty's life, before embarking on an exploration of the art of Mughal India, Persia, the Ottoman empire, Japan and China. Here you'll find intricately designed little medicine boxes and perhaps the finest collection of Chinese jade books in the world. The illuminated European texts are also worth examining.

The **Sacred Traditions Gallery** on the 2nd floor gives a fascinating insight into the major rituals and rites of passage of the major world religions – Judaism, Christianity, Islam, Buddhism and Hinduism. There are audiovisual explorations of the lives of Christ and the Buddha, as well as the Muslim pilgrimage to Mecca.

Head for the collection of Qurans from the 9th to the 19th centuries, considered to be among the best illuminated Islamic texts. You'll also find ancient Egyptian papyrus texts (including Egyptian love poems from around 1100 BC), scrolls and exquisite artwork from Burma, Indonesia and Tibet – as well as the second-oldest biblical fragment ever found (after the Dead Sea Scrolls).

The comprehensive **Reference Library** (by appointment only), complete with a finely lacquered ceiling that Beatty himself had installed in his own London home, is a great resource for artists or students.

The library regularly holds specialist workshops, exhibitions and talks on everything from origami to calligraphy, and admission is free. It's easy to escape from the rigours of Western life on the serene rooftop **Japanese garden** or at the Silk Road Cafe (p126) on the ground floor, which serves delicious Middle Eastern cuisine.

BEDFORD & RECORD TOWERS

Directly across the Upper Yard from the main entrance to the castle is the **Bedford Tower** (Map p84; Dublin Castle, Cork Hill). In 1907 the collection known as the Irish Crown Jewels was stolen from the tower and never recovered.

The entranceway to the castle yard, beside the Bedford Tower, is topped by a statue of Justice that has always been a subject of mirth. She faces the castle and has her back to the city – seen as a sure indicator of how much justice the average Irish citizen could expect from the British. The scales of justice also had a distinct tendency to fill with rain and tilt in one direction or the other, rather than assuming the approved level position. Eventually a hole was drilled in the bottom of each pan so the rainwater could drain out.

The chunky medieval **Record Tower** (Map p84), between the lower yard and Castle Gardens, is not just the oldest bit of the whole place (built in the 13th century), but it's the last remaining medieval tower in Dublin. Today it is home to the small **Garda Museum** (☎ 666 9998; admission free; 9.30am-4.30pm Mon-Fri, weekends by prior arrangement only), which tells the story of the various Irish police forces, beginning with the Royal Irish Constabulary, founded by order of Robert Peel in 1816.

CITY HALL

Fronting Dublin Castle on Lord Edward St, **City Hall** (Map p84; ☎ 222 2204; www.dublincity.ie; Cork Hill; adult/student/child €4/2/2; 10am-5.15pm Mon-Sat, 2-5pm Sun) was built by Thomas Cooley between 1769 and 1779 as the Royal Exchange, and later became the offices of the Dublin Corporation (now known as the Dublin City Council). It stands on the site of the Lucas Coffee House and the Eagle Tavern, in which Dublin's infamous Hell Fire Club was established in 1735. Founded by Richard Parsons, earl of Rosse, it was one of a number of gentlemen's clubs in Dublin where less-than-gentlemanly conduct took place. It gained a reputation for debauchery and black magic, but there's no evidence that such things took place.

The Story of the Capital is a multimedia exhibition in the basement, tracing the history of Dublin from its earliest beginnings.

The 1781 **Municipal Buildings**, just west of the City Hall, were built by Thomas Ivory (1720–86), who was also responsible for Bedford Tower (p95) in Dublin Castle.

NATIONAL MUSEUM OF IRELAND – ARCHAEOLOGY & HISTORY

Designed by Sir Thomas Newenham Deane and completed in 1890, the star attraction of this branch of the **National Museum of Ireland** (Map p86; ☎ 677 7444; www.museum.ie; Kildare St; admission by donation; 10am-5pm Tue-Sat, 2-5pm Sun) is the Treasury, home to the finest collection of Bronze Age and Iron Age gold artefacts in the world, and the world's most complete collection of medieval Celtic metalwork.

The centrepieces of the Treasury's unique collection are Ireland's most famous crafted artefacts, the **Ardagh Chalice** and the **Tara Brooch**. Measuring 17.8cm high and 24.2cm in diameter, the 12th-century Ardagh Chalice is made of gold, silver, bronze, brass, copper and lead. Put simply, this is the finest example of Celtic art ever found. The equally renowned Tara Brooch was crafted around AD 700, primarily in white bronze but with traces of gold, silver, glass, copper, enamel and wire beading, and was used as a clasp for a cloak.

The Treasury includes many other stunning pieces, many of which are grouped together in 'hoards', after the manner in which they were found, usually by a farmer digging up a field or a bog. Be sure not to miss the Broighter and Mooghaun hoards.

An upstairs exhibition illustrates Dublin's Viking era, with items from the excavations at Wood Quay – the area between Christ Church Cathedral and the river, where Dublin City Council plonked its new headquarters. Other exhibits focus on the 1916 Easter Rising, and the independence struggle between 1900 and 1921. Frequent short-term exhibitions are also held.

NATIONAL GALLERY

A magnificent Caravaggio and a breathtaking collection of works by Jack B Yeats – William Butler's kid brother – are the main reasons to visit the **National Gallery** (Map p86; ☎ 661 5133; www.nationalgallery.ie; West Merrion Sq; admission free; 9.30am-5.30pm Mon-Wed, Fri & Sat, 9.30am-8.30pm Thu, noon-5.30pm Sun), but not the only ones. Its excellent collection is strong in Irish art, but there are also high-quality collections of every major European school of painting. There are free tours at 3pm Saturday, and 2pm, 3pm and 4pm Sunday.

The gallery has four wings: the original Dargan Wing, the Milltown Rooms, the North Wing and the spectacular new Millennium Wing. On the ground floor of the Dargan Wing (named after railway magnate and art-lover William Dargan, whose statue graces the front lawn) is the imposing Shaw Room (named after writer George Bernard, another great benefactor; his bronze statue keeps Dargan company outside), lined with full-length portraits and illuminated by a series of spectacular Waterford crystal chandeliers. Upstairs, a series of rooms is dedicated to the early and high Italian Renaissance, 16th-century northern Italian art, and 17th- and 18th-century Italian art. Fra Angelico, Titian and Tintoretto are among the artists represented, but the highlight is undoubtedly Caravaggio's *The Taking of Christ* (1602), which lay for over 60 years in a Jesuit house in Leeson St and was accidentally discovered by chief curator Sergio Benedetti.

The central Milltown Rooms were added between 1899 and 1903 to hold Russborough House's art collection, which was presented to the gallery in 1902. The ground floor displays the gallery's fine Irish collection, plus a smaller British collection, with works by Reynolds, Hogarth, Gainsborough, Landseer and Turner. Absolutely unmissable is the **Yeats Collection** at the back of the gallery, displaying more than 30 works by Irish impressionist Jack B Yeats (1871–1957), Ireland's most important 20th-century painter.

Upstairs are works from Germany, the Netherlands and Spain. There are rooms full of works by Rembrandt and his circle, and by the Spanish artists of Seville. The Spanish collection also features works by El Greco, Goya and Picasso.

The North Wing was added only between 1964 and 1968, but has already undergone extensive refurbishment. It houses works by British and European artists.

The impressive new Millennium Wing, with its light-filled modern design, can also be entered from Nassau St. It houses a small collection of 20th-century Irish art, high-profile visiting collections (for which there is a charge to visit), an art reference library, a lecture theatre, a good bookshop and Fitzer's Café.

LEINSTER HOUSE

Dublin's grandest Georgian home, built by Richard Cassels between 1745 and 1748 for the very grand James Fitzgerald, earl of Kildare, is now the seat of both houses of the Oireachtas na Éireann (Irish Parliament) – the Dáil (Lower House) and Seanad (Upper House). Originally called Kildare House, it was changed to **Leinster House** (Map p86; ☎ 618 3000, tour information 618 3271; www.irlgov.ie/oireachtas; Kildare St; admission free; ⊙ observation gallery 2.30-8.30pm Tue, 10.30am-8.30pm Wed, 10.30am-5.30pm Thu Nov-May) after the earl assumed the title of Duke of Leinster in 1766.

Leinster House's Kildare St frontage was designed by Richard Cassels to look like a town house, whereas the Merrion Sq frontage was made to look like a country house. Hard to imagine it now, but when Cassels built the house it was in the wild expanses south of the Liffey, far from the genteel northern neighbourhoods where Dublin's aristocracy lived. Never short of confidence, the earl dismissed his critics, declaring, 'Where I go, society will follow' There's no doubt about it: Jimmy Fitz had a nose for real estate.

The Dublin Society, later named the Royal Dublin Society, bought the building in 1814 but moved out in stages between 1922 and 1925, when the first government of independent Ireland decided to establish Parliament here. The obelisk in front of the building is dedicated to Arthur Griffith, Michael Collins and Kevin O'Higgins – the architects of independent Ireland.

The Seanad meets in the north-wing saloon, while the Dáil meets in a less interesting room, originally a lecture theatre, which was added to the original building in 1897. When Parliament is sitting, visitors are admitted to an observation gallery. You'll get an entry ticket from the Kildare St entrance on production of some identification. Bags can't be taken in, or notes or photographs taken. Prearranged guided tours (free) are available weekdays when parliament is in session.

NATURAL HISTORY MUSEUM

Very dusty, a little creepy and utterly compelling, the **Natural History Museum** (Map p86; ☎ 677 7444; www.museum.ie; Merrion St; admission free; ⊙ 10am-5pm Tue-Sat, 2-5pm Sun) has scarcely changed since 1857, when Scottish explorer Dr David Livingstone delivered the opening lecture. In the face of the city's newer hi-tech museums, its Victorian charm has been beautifully preserved, making the 'dead zoo' one of Dublin's more interesting museums. The huge and well-organised collection numbers about two million items, of which about 10,000 are on display. That moth-eaten look often afflicting neglected stuffed-animal collections has been kept at bay, and children are likely to find the museum fascinating.

On the ground floor, the collection of skeletons, stuffed animals and the like covers the full range of Irish fauna. It includes three skeletons of the Irish giant deer, which became extinct about 10,000 years ago. On the 1st and 2nd floors are fauna from around the world.

GOVERNMENT BUILDINGS

On Upper Merrion St, the domed **Government Buildings** (Map p86; ☎ 662 4888; www.taoiseach.gov.ie; Upper Merrion St; admission free; ⊙ tours 10.30am-3.30pm Sat) were opened for business in 1911. Architecturally, they are a rather heavy-handed Edwardian interpretation of the Georgian style. Each free 40-minute tour takes about 15 people, so you may have to wait a while for a big enough group to assemble. Tours can't be booked in advance, but if you go in on Saturday morning you can put your name down for one later in the day. You get to see the office of the taoiseach (prime minister), the cabinet room, the ceremonial staircase with a stunning stained-glass window designed by Evie Hone (1894–1955) for the 1939 New York Trade Fair, and innumerable fine examples of modern Irish arts and crafts. Tickets for the tours are available from the ticket office of the **National Gallery** (Map p86; ☎ 661 5133; www.national gallery.ie; West Merrion Sq; ⏰ 9.30am-5.30pm Mon-Wed, Fri & Sat, 9.30am-8.30pm Thu, noon-5.30pm Sun).

NATIONAL LIBRARY
Flanking the Kildare St entrance to Leinster House is the **National Library** (Map p86; ☎ 603 0200; www.nli.ie; Kildare St; admission free; ⏰ 10am-9pm Mon-Wed, 10am-5pm Thu & Fri, 10am-1pm Sat), which was built between 1884 and 1890 by Sir Thomas Newenham Deane and his son Sir Thomas Manly Deane, at the same time and to a similar design as the National Museum. Leinster House, the library and museum were all part of the Royal Dublin Society (formed in 1731), which aimed to improve conditions for poor people and to promote the arts and sciences. The library's extensive collection has many valuable early manuscripts, 1st editions, maps and other items; its reading room featured in James Joyce's *Ulysses*. Temporary displays are often held in the entrance area.

On the 2nd floor is the **Genealogical Office** (Map p86; ☎ 603 0200; 2nd fl, National Library, Kildare St; ⏰ 10am-4.30pm Mon-Fri, 10am-12.30pm Sat), where you can obtain information on how best to trace your Irish roots. A genealogist can do the trace for you (at a fee dependent on research) or simply point you in the right direction (for free).

ST STEPHEN'S GREEN & AROUND
While enjoying the nine gorgeous, landscaped hectares of Dublin's most popular square, consider that once upon a time **St Stephen's Green** (Map p86; admission free; ⏰ dawn-dusk) was an open common used for public whippings, beatings and hangings. Activities in the green have quietened since then and are generally confined to the lunch-time-picnic-and-stroll variety. Still, on a summer's day it is the favourite retreat of office workers, lovers and visitors alike, who come to breathe a little fresh air, feed the ducks and cuddle on the grass.

Although a stone wall was erected in the 17th century when Dublin Corporation sold off the surrounding land to property developers, railings and locked gates were only added in 1814 when an annual fee of one guinea was charged to use the green – a great way to keep the poor out. In 1877 Arthur Edward Guinness pushed an act through Parliament that opened the green to the public once again. He also paid for the green's lakes and ponds, which were added in 1880.

The fine Georgian buildings around the square date mainly from Dublin's mid- to late-18th-century Georgian prime. At that time the northern side was known as the Beaux Walk and it's still a pretty fancy stretch of real estate; drop in for tea at the imposing 1867 **Shelbourne hotel** (p120) and you'll see what we mean. Just beyond the hotel is a small **Huguenot cemetery** (Map p86) dating from 1693, when many French Huguenots fled here from persecution under Louis XIV.

The main entrance to the green is through **Fusiliers' Arch** (Map p86) at the northwestern corner. Modelled on the Arch of Titus in Rome, the arch commemorates the 212 soldiers of the Royal Dublin Fusiliers who died in the Boer War (1899–1902).

Across the road from the western side of the green are the 1863 **Unitarian Church** (Map p86; ⏰ for worship 7am-5pm) and the **Royal College of Surgeons** (Map p86), with a fine façade. During the 1916 Easter Rising, the building was occupied by the colourful Countess Markievicz (1868–1927), an Irish nationalist married to a supposed Polish count. The columns still bear bullet marks.

On the southern side of the green is **Newman House** (Map p86; ☎ 716 7422; 85-86 St Stephen's Green; adult/child €5/4; ⏰ tours noon, 2pm, 3pm & 4pm Tue-Fri Jun-Aug), now part of University College Dublin. These two buildings have some of the finest plasterwork in the city. The Catholic University of Ireland, predecessor of University College Dublin, acquired No 85 in 1865, then passed it to the Jesuits. Some of the plasterwork was too detailed for Jesuit tastes, however, so cover-ups were prescribed. On the ceiling of the upstairs saloon, previously naked female figures were clothed in what can best be described as furry swimsuits. One survived the restoration process.

Attached to Newman University Church is the **Newman Chapel**, built between 1854 and 1856 with a colourful neo-Byzantine interior that attracted a great deal of criticism at the time. Today it's one of the most fashionable churches in Dublin for weddings.

One of Dublin's most beautiful parks is the landscaped **Iveagh Gardens** (admission free; ☺ dawn-dusk year-round), directly behind Newman House and reached via Clonmel St, just off Harcourt St. The imposing walls give the impression that they are private gardens, but they are one of the nicest places to relax on a summer's day or before a show in the National Concert Hall.

MERRION SQUARE

St Stephen's Green may win the popularity contest, but tranquil **Merrion Square** (Map p86; admission free; ☺ dawn-dusk) is our choice for favourite city park. Surrounding the well-kept lawns and beautifully tended flower beds are some of Dublin's most exceptional Georgian frontages, with fine doors, peacock fanlights, ornate door knockers and foot scrapers (used by gentlemen to scrape mud from their boots before venturing indoors).

Despite the air of affluent calm, life around here hasn't always been a well-pruned bed of roses. During the Famine, the lawns of the square teemed with destitute rural refugees who lived off the soup kitchen organised here. The British embassy was located at 39 Merrion Sq East until 1972, when it was burnt out in protest against the killing of 13 innocent civilians on Bloody Sunday in Derry.

That same side of Merrion Sq once continued into Lower Fitzwilliam St in the longest unbroken series of Georgian houses anywhere in Europe, but in 1961 the Electricity Supply Board (ESB), in a myopic crime against history and aesthetics, knocked down 26 of the houses in order to build an office block that is now one of the city's worst eyesores.

Just to prove that it is mindful of Dublin's priceless architectural heritage, the ESB had the decency to preserve one fine old Georgian house, **No 29 Lower Fitzwilliam St** (Map pp82-3; ☎ 702 6165; www.esb.ie/education; 29 Lower Fitzwilliam St; adult/student/child €5/2.50/free; ☺ 10am-5pm Tue-Sat, 1-5pm Sun, closed 2 weeks before Christmas) at the southeastern corner of Merrion Sq. It has been restored to give a good impression of genteel home life in Dublin between 1790 and 1820. A short film on its history is followed by a 30-minute guided tour in groups of up to nine.

OSCAR WILDE HOUSE

In 1855 the surgeon Sir William Wilde and the poet Lady 'Speranza' Wilde moved with their one-year-old son Oscar to 1 North Merrion Sq, the first Georgian residence constructed on the square (1762). They stayed here until 1878 and it is likely that Oscar's literary genius was first stimulated by the creative atmosphere of the house, where Lady Wilde hosted the city's most famous (and best frequented) literary salon.

Today it is owned by the American College Dublin, which has converted part of the house into a **museum** (Map p86; ☎ 662 0281; www.amcd .ie/oscarwildehouse/about/html; 1 North Merrion Sq; admission €5; ☺ tours 10.15am & 11.15am Mon, Wed & Thu) devoted to Oscar Wilde.

Enthusiasts should visit the **Oscar Wilde statue** at the northwestern corner of the square, as it is adorned with the witty one-liners for which Oscar Wilde became famous.

The Liberties & Kilmainham

At the top of a small hill, just west of Dublin Castle, is the most impressive monument of medieval Dublin, Christ Church Cathedral. It stood firmly inside the city walls, unlike that other great place of worship, St Patrick's, which lay just outside of them. Beneath both

---

LITERARY ADDRESSES

Merrion Sq has long been the favoured address of Dublin's affluent intelligentsia. Oscar Wilde (1854–1900) spent much of his youth at 1 North Merrion Sq. WB Yeats (1865–1939) lived at 52 East Merrion Sq and later, between 1922 and 1928, at 82 South Merrion Sq. George (AE) Russell (1867–1935), the 'poet, mystic, painter and cooperator', worked at No 84. Daniel O'Connell (1775–1847) was a resident of No 58 in his later years. The Austrian Erwin Schrödinger (1887–1961), co-winner of the 1933 Nobel Prize for physics, lived at No 65 between 1940 and 1956. Dublin also seems to attract writers of horror stories: Joseph Sheridan Le Fanu (1814–73), who penned the vampire classic Carmilla, was a resident of No 70.

of them, to the west, is the Liberties, Dublin's oldest surviving neighbourhood. The western end of the Liberties has a curious aroma in the air: it is the smell of roasting hops, used in the production of Guinness – Dublin's black gold and, for many visitors, the epitome of all things Irish. Further along James St is Kilmainham, home to the old prison that was central to the struggle for Irish independence (and a city highlight) and an ancient soldiers' hospital, now the country's most important modern art museum.

CHRIST CHURCH CATHEDRAL

The mother of all of Dublin's churches is **Christ Church Cathedral** (Church of the Holy Trinity; Map p84; ☎ 677 8099; www.cccdub.ie; Christ Church Pl; adult/student €5/2.50; ☺ 9.45am-5pm Mon-Fri, 10am-5pm Sat & Sun), just south of the river and west of Temple Bar. It was founded in 1030 on what was then the southern edge of Dublin's Viking settlement. It was later smack in the middle of medieval Dublin: Dublin Castle, the Tholsel (Town Hall; demolished in 1809) and the original Four Courts (demolished in 1796) were all close by. Nearby, on Back Lane, is the only remaining guildhall in Dublin. The 1706 Tailors Hall was due for demolition in the 1960s, but survived to become the office of An Taisce (National Trust for Ireland; Map p84).

The original wooden church in this spot wasn't really a keeper, so the Normans rebuilt the lot in stone from 1172, mostly under the impetus of Richard de Clare, earl of Pembroke (better known as Strongbow), the Anglo-Norman noble who invaded Ireland in 1170.

Throughout much of its history, Christ Church vied for supremacy with nearby St Patrick's Cathedral but, like its neighbour, it fell on hard times in the 18th and 19th centuries – earlier, the nave had been used as a market and the crypt had housed taverns – and was virtually derelict by the time restoration took place. Today, both Church of Ireland cathedrals are outsiders in a largely Catholic nation.

From the southeastern entrance to the churchyard you walk past ruins of the chapter house, which dates from 1230. The entrance to the cathedral is at the southwestern corner and as you enter you face the northern wall. This survived the collapse of its southern counterpart but has also suffered from subsiding foundations.

The southern aisle has a monument to the legendary Strongbow. The armoured figure on the tomb is unlikely to be Strongbow (it's more probably the earl of Drogheda), but his internal organs may have been buried here. A popular legend relates that the half figure beside the tomb is Strongbow's son, who was cut in two by his father when his bravery in battle was suspect.

The southern transept contains the superb baroque tomb of the 19th earl of Kildare (died 1734). His grandson, Lord Edward Fitzgerald, was a member of the United Irishmen and died in the abortive 1798 Rising.

An entrance just by the southern transept descends to the unusually large arched crypt, which dates back to the original Viking church. Curiosities in the crypt include a glass display case housing a mummified cat chasing a mummified mouse, which were trapped inside an organ pipe in the 1860s! From the main entrance, a bridge, part of the 1871–78 restoration, leads to Dvblinia (below).

DVBLINIA

Inside the old Synod Hall attached to Christ Church Cathedral, **Dvblinia** (Map p84; ☎ 679 4611; www.dublinia.ie; adult/student/child €6/5/3.50; ☺ 10am-5pm Apr-Sep, 11am-4pm Mon-Sat & 10am-4.30pm Sun Oct-Mar) is a kitschy and lively attempt to bring medieval Dublin to life. Models, streetscapes and somewhat old-fashioned interactive displays do a fairly decent job of it, at least for kids. The model of a medieval quayside and a cobbler's shop are both excellent, as is the scale model of the medieval city. The Viking World is a similar recreation of 9th and 10th-century Dublin. Finally, you can climb neighbouring St Michael's Tower for views over the city to the Dublin Hills.

Your ticket gets you into Christ Church Cathedral free (via the link bridge).

ST PATRICK'S CATHEDRAL

It was at this **cathedral** (Map pp82-3; ☎ 475 4817; www.stpatrickscathedral.ie; St Patrick's Close; adult/senior/student/child €5/4/4/free/; ☺ 9am-6pm Mon-Sat, 9-11am, 12.45-3pm & 4.15-6pm Sun Mar-Oct, 9am-6pm Mon-Fri, 9am-5pm Sat, 10-11am & 12.45-3pm Sun Nov-Feb), reputedly, that St Paddy himself dunked the Irish heathens into the waters of a well, so the that bears his name stands on one of the earliest Christian sites in the city and a pretty sacred piece of turf. Although there's been a church here since the 5th century, the present building dates from 1190 or 1225 (opinions differ) and it has been altered several times, most notably in 1864 when the flying buttresses were added, thanks to the neo-Gothic craze that swept the nation. St Patrick's Park, the expanse of green beside the cathedral, was a crowded slum until it was cleared and its residents evicted in the early 20th century.

Like Christ Church Cathedral, the building has suffered a rather dramatic history of storm and fire damage. Oliver Cromwell, during his 1649 visit to Ireland, converted St Patrick's to a stable for his army's horses, an indignity to which he also subjected numerous other Irish churches. Jonathan Swift was the dean of the cathedral from 1713 to 1745, but prior to its restoration it was very neglected.

Entering the cathedral from the southwestern porch you come almost immediately, on your right, to the graves of Swift and his long-time companion Esther Johnson, aka Stella. On the wall nearby are Swift's own Latin epitaphs to the two of them, and a bust of Swift.

The huge, dusty Boyle Monument to the left was erected in 1632 by Richard Boyle, earl of Cork, and is decorated with numerous painted figures of members of his family. The figure in the centre on the bottom level is of the earl's five-year-old son Robert Boyle (1627–91), who grew up to become a noted scientist. His contributions to physics include Boyle's Law, which relates the pressure and volume of gases.

The cathedral's choir school dates back to 1432, and the choir took part in the first performance of Handel's *Messiah* in 1742. You can hear the choir sing matins at 9.40am and evensong at 5.35pm Monday to Friday (except Wednesday evening) during the school year. The carols performed around Christmas are a real treat; call ☎ 453 9472 for details of how to obtain a hard-to-get ticket.

To get to the cathedral, take bus 50, 50A or 56A from Aston Quay, or bus 54 or 54A from Burgh Quay.

MARSH'S LIBRARY
One of the city's most beautiful open secrets is **Marsh's Library** (Map pp82-3; ☎ 454 3511; www .marshlibrary.ie; St Patrick's Close; adult/child/student €2.50/ free/1.50; ☺ 10am-1pm & 2-5pm Mon & Wed-Fri, 10.30am-1pm Sat), a barely visited antique library with a look and atmosphere that has hardly changed

since it opened its doors to awkward scholars in 1707. It's just around the corner from St Patrick's Cathedral.

Crammed into its elaborately carved oak bookcases are over 25,000 books dating from the 16th to early 18th centuries, as well as maps, numerous manuscripts and a collection of incunabula (books printed before 1500). One of the oldest and finest tomes in the collection is a volume of Cicero's *Letters to His Friends* printed in Milan in 1472.

The building was commissioned by Archbishop Narcissus March (1638–1713) and designed by Sir William Robinson, the creator of the Royal Hospital Kilmainham (now the Irish Museum of Modern Art; p103); today it is one of the only 18th-century buildings in Dublin still used for the purpose for which it was built. In short, it's a bloody gorgeous place and you'd be mad not to visit.

ST WERBURGH'S CHURCH
Of undoubtedly ancient but imprecise origin, **St Werburgh's** (Map p84; ☎ 478 3710; Werburgh St; admission by donation; ☺ 10am-4pm Mon-Fri) has undergone numerous face-lifts: in 1662, 1715 and, with some elegance, in 1759 after a fire in 1754. The church's tall spire was dismantled after Robert Emmet's uprising in 1803 for fear that rebels might use it as a vantage point for snipers. The church is closely linked with the history of uprisings against British rule; interred in the vault is Lord Edward Fitzgerald, a member of the United Irishmen, the group that led the 1798 Rising. In what was a frequent theme of Irish rebellions, compatriots gave him away and he died as a result of the wounds he received during his capture. Ironically, his captor Major Henry Sirr is buried in the adjacent graveyard. In the porch you will notice two fire pumps that date from the time when Dublin's fire department was composed of church volunteers.

You will need to phone or visit the caretaker at 8 Castle St to see inside.

ST AUDOEN'S CHURCHES
St Audoen, the 7th-century bishop of Rouen and patron saint of Normandy, must have had a few friends in Dublin to have two churches named after him. Both are just west of Christ Church Cathedral. The more interesting of the two is the smaller **Church of Ireland** (Map p84; ☎ 677 0088; Cornmarket, High St; admission free; ☺ 9.30am-4.45pm Jun-Sep), the only surviving

DUBLIN

G-FORCE GUINNESS

Ireland's new 9000-strong Nigerian community were dismayed to taste the 4.5% Irish Guinness, a limp and 'watery' version compared to the potent (and sweeter) 7.5% version at home. Nigeria is Guinness' third-largest market (after Ireland and Britain) and the increased alcohol volume in its beer harks back to the 18th century when beer was fortified to survive the ship's long journey to Africa. Guinness duly responded to the Nigerians' complaint and now produces the Dublin Guinness Foreign Extra to satisfy the Nigerian palate.

medieval parish church still in use in Dublin. It was built between 1181 and 1212, though recent excavations unearthed a 9th-century burial slab, suggesting that it was built on top of an even older church. Its tower and door date from the 12th century, and the aisle from the 15th century, but the church today is mainly a 19th-century restoration.

As part of the tour, you can explore the ruins, as well as the present church and the visitor centre in **St Anne's Chapel**, which houses a number of tombstones of leading members of Dublin society from the 16th to the 18th centuries. At the top of the chapel is the tower, which houses the three oldest bells in Ireland, dating from 1423. Although the church's exhibits are hardly spectacular, the building itself is very beautiful and a genuine slice of medieval Dublin.

The church is entered from the north through an arch off High St. Part of the old city wall, this arch was built in 1240 and is the only surviving reminder of the city gates.

Joined onto the older Protestant St Audoen's is the newer and larger **St Audoen's Catholic Church** (Cornmarket, High St; admission free; ⊙ 9.30am-5.30pm Jun-Sep, 10am-4.30pm Oct-May), a large church whose claim to local fame is Father 'Flash' Kavanagh, who used to read Mass at high speed so that his large congregation could head off to more absorbing Sunday pursuits, such as football.

GUINNESS STOREHOUSE

Dublin's number one attraction by a stroll is this beer-lover's Disneyland, a multimedia bells-and-whistles homage to the country's most famous export and the city's most en-

during symbol. The **Guinness Storehouse** (Map pp82-3; ☎ 408 4800; www.guinness-storehouse.com; St James's Gate Brewery; adult/child/student under 18yr/student over 18yr/senior €14/5/7.50/9.50/9.50; ⊙ 9.30am-5pm), the only part of the massive, 26-hectare St James's Gate Brewery open to the public, is a suitable cathedral in which to worship the black gold; shaped like a giant pint of Guinness, it rises seven impressive storeys high around a stunning central atrium. At the top is the head, represented by the Gravity Bar, with a panoramic view of Dublin.

The Gravity Bar is also the best place to get an idea of how big the brewery actually is. From the time Arthur Guinness founded the St James's Gate Brewery in 1759, the operation has expanded down to the Liffey and across both sides of the street; at one point, it had its own railroad and there was a giant gate stretching across James St, hence the brewery's proper name. At its apogee in the 1930s, it employed over 5000 workers, making it the largest employer in the city. Increased automation has reduced the workforce to around 600, but it still produces 2.5 million pints of stout *every day*.

You'll get to drink one of those pints at the end of your tour, but not before you have walked through the extravaganza that is the Guinness floor show, spread across 1.6 hectares and involving an array of audiovisual, interactive displays that cover pretty much all aspects of the brewery's history and the brewing process. It's slick and sophisticated, but you can't ignore the man behind the curtain: the extensive exhibit on the company's incredibly successful history of advertising is a reminder that for all the talk of mysticism and magic, it's all really about marketing and manipulation.

It's all a moot point, however, when you have that pint in your hand and you're surveying all below you from the vertiginous heights of the Gravity Bar. This is the best pint of Guinness you'll ever drink, the cognoscenti like to claim, but just make sure you've got good friends and conversation to enjoy it with: after all, isn't that the whole point?

Around the corner at **No 1 Thomas St** (Map pp82-3; ⊙ closed to public) a plaque marks the house where Arthur Guinness (1725–1803) lived. In a yard across the road stands **St Patrick's Tower** (Map pp82-3; ⊙ closed to public), Europe's tallest smock windmill (with a revolving top), which was built around 1757.

To get to the Storehouse, take bus 21A, 78 or 78A from Fleet St, or the Luas Green Line to James's Gate.

IRISH MUSEUM OF MODERN ART

Ireland's most important collection of modern and contemporary Irish art is housed in the elegant, airy expanse of the Royal Hospital at Kilmainham, which in 1991 became the **Irish Museum of Modern Art** (IMMA; Map p80; ☎ 612 9900; www.imma.ie; Military Rd; admission free; ☺ 10am-5.30pm Tue-Sat, noon-5.30pm Sun). Catch bus 24, 79 or 90 from Aston Quay.

The Royal Hospital Kilmainham was designed by William Robinson (who also designed Marsh's Library; see p101), and was built between 1680 and 1687 as a home for retired soldiers. It fulfilled this role until 1928, after which it languished for nearly 50 years until a 1980s restoration. At the time of its construction, it was one of the finest buildings in Ireland and there were mutterings that it was altogether too good a place for its residents.

The gallery's 4000-strong collection includes works by artists such as Picasso, Miró and Vasarely, as well as works by more contemporary artists, including Gilbert and George, Gillian Wearing and Damien Hirst. The gallery displays ever-changing shows from its own works, and hosts regular touring exhibitions.

Modern Irish art is always on display, and Irish and international artists live and work on site in the **converted coach houses** behind the south wing. The **New Galleries**, in the restored Deputy Master's House, should also not be missed. There are free guided tours (2.30pm Wednesday, Friday and Sunday) of the museum's exhibits throughout the year, but we strongly recommend the free seasonal heritage tours (hourly from 11am to 4pm Tuesday to Saturday, and from 1pm to 4pm Sunday) of the building itself, which run from July to September.

KILMAINHAM JAIL

If you have *any* desire to understand Irish history – especially the juicy bits about resistance to English rule – then a visit to **Kilmainham Jail** (Map p80; ☎ 453 5984; www.heritageireland.com; Inchicore Rd; adult/student/child €5.50/2.10/2.10; ☺ 9.30am-5pm Apr-Oct, 9.30am-4pm Mon-Sat, 10am-4pm Sun Nov-Mar) is an absolute must. This threatening grey building, built between 1792 and 1795, has played a role

in virtually every act of Ireland's painful path to independence.

The uprisings of 1798, 1803, 1848, 1867 and 1916 ended with the leaders' confinement here. Robert Emmet, Thomas Francis Meagher, Charles Stewart Parnell and the 1916 Easter Rising leaders were all visitors, but it was the executions in 1916 that most deeply etched the jail's name into the Irish consciousness. Of the 15 executions that took place between 3 May and 12 May after the rising, 14 were conducted here. As a finale, prisoners from the Civil War were held here from 1922. The jail closed in 1924.

An excellent audiovisual introduction to the building is followed by a thought-provoking tour through the eerie prison, the largest unoccupied building of its kind in Europe. Incongruously sitting outside in the yard is the *Asgard*, the ship that successfully ran the British blockade to deliver arms to nationalist forces in 1914. The tour finishes in the gloomy yard where the 1916 executions took place.

To get here, catch bus 23, 51, 51A, 78 or 79 from Aston Quay.

WAR MEMORIAL GARDENS

By our reckoning, the most beautiful patch of landscaped greenery in Dublin is the **War Memorial Gardens** (Map p80; ☎ 677 0236; www .heritageireland.ie; South Circular Rd, Islandbridge; admission free; ☺ 8am-twilight Mon-Fri, from 10am Sat & Sun), if only because they're as tranquil a spot as any you'll find in the city. Designed by Sir Edwin Lutyens, they commemorate the 49,400 Irish soldiers who died during WWI; their names are inscribed in the two huge granite bookrooms that stand at one end. A beautiful spot and a bit of history to boot.

Take bus 25, 25A, 26, 68 or 69 from the city centre to get here.

O'Connell Street & Around

After decades of playing second fiddle to Grafton St and the other byways of the southside, the northside's grandest thoroughfare is finally getting its mojo back and can once again declare itself Dublin's finest avenue. Lining and surrounding it are a bunch of fabulous buildings, fascinating museums and a fair few of the city's cultural hot spots too – just a handful of reasons to cross O'Connell Bridge and take on the northside.

O'CONNELL STREET STATUARY

Although overshadowed by the Spire, O'Connell St is lined with statues of Irish history's good and great. The big daddy of them all is the 'Liberator' himself **Daniel O'Connell** (Map pp82–3), whose massive bronze bulk soars high above the street at the bridge end. The four winged figures at his feet represent O'Connell's supposed virtues: patriotism, courage, fidelity and eloquence.

O'Connell is rivalled for drama by the spread-armed figure of trade-union leader **Jim Larkin** (1876–1947; Map pp82–3), just outside the general post office; you can almost hear the eloquent tirade.

Looking on with a bemused air from the corner of pedestrianised North Earl St is a small statue of **James Joyce** (Map pp82–3), who wagsters like to refer to as 'the Prick with the Stick'. Joyce would have loved the vulgar rhyme.

Further north is the statue of **Father Theobald Mathew** (1790–1856; Map pp82–3), the 'Apostle of Temperance' – a hopeless role in Ireland. This quixotic task, however, also resulted in a Liffey bridge bearing his name. The northern end of the street is completed by the imposing statue of **Charles Stewart Parnell** (1846–91; Map pp82–3), Home Rule advocate and victim of Irish morality.

O'CONNELL STREET

It's amazing what a few hundred million euros and a new vision will do to a street plagued by years of neglect, a criminally blind development policy and a history as a hothouse of street trouble. It's difficult to fathom why O'Connell St (Map pp82–3), once so proud and elegant, could have been so humbled that the street's top draw was an amusement arcade. One-armed bandits and poker machines on the street that was the main stage for the Easter Rising in 1916? How could it all go so wrong?

It's a far cry from the 18th-century days of empire, when as Drogheda St (after Viscount Henry Moore, earl of Drogheda) it cut a swath through a city brimming with Georgian optimism. It became O'Connell St in 1924, but only after spending a few decades as Sackville St – a tribute to a lord lieutenant of Ireland. Whatever its name, it was always an imposing street, at least until the fast-food joints and the crappy shops started invading the retail spaces along it. Thankfully, Dublin Corporation is committed to a thorough reappraisal of the street's appearance: a lot done, more to do.

The first project was the impressive **Spire** (the Monument of Light; Map pp82–3), which graced the spot once occupied by Admiral Nelson (who disappeared in explosive fashion in 1966). Soaring 120m into the sky, it is, apparently, the world's tallest sculpture, although that hardly impresses the locals, who refer to it as the 'biggest needle around', in reference to the drug blight of the north inner city. Other (ongoing) projects have seen the widening of the pavements and the limiting of traffic, although the street will truly be grand when the plethora of fast-food joints are given the elbow.

GENERAL POST OFFICE

Talk about going postal. The **GPO building** (Map pp82–3; ☎ 705 7000; www.anpost.ie; O'Connell St; ⏰ 8am-8pm Mon-Sat) will forever be linked to the dramatic and tragic events of Easter Week 1916, when Pádraig Pearse, James Connolly and the other leaders of the Easter Rising read their proclamation from the front steps and made the building their headquarters. The building – a neoclassical masterpiece designed by Francis Johnston in 1818 – was burnt out in the subsequent siege, but that wasn't the end of it. There was bitter fighting in and around the building during the Civil War of 1922; you can still see the pockmarks of the struggle in the Doric columns. Since its re-opening in 1929 it has lived through quieter times, but its central role in the history of independent Ireland has made it a prime site for everything from official parades to personal protests.

CUSTOM HOUSE

James Gandon (1743–1823) announced his arrival on the Dublin scene with the stunning, glistening white building that is the **Custom House** (Map pp82–3), one of the city's finest Georgian monuments. It was constructed between 1781 and 1791, in spite of opposition from city merchants and dockers at the original Custom House, upriver in Temple Bar.

In 1921, during the independence struggle, the Custom House was set alight and completely gutted in a fire that burned for five days. The interior was later extensively redesigned, and a further major renovation took place between 1986 and 1988.

The best complete view of a building that stretches 114m along the Liffey is obtained from across the river, though a close-up inspection of its many fine details is also worthwhile. The building is topped by a copper dome with four clocks. On top stands a 5m-high statue of Hope.

Beneath the dome is the **Custom House Visitor Centre** (Map pp82-3; ☎ 888 2538; Custom House Quay; admission €1.30; ⏰ 10am-12.30pm Mon-Fri, 2-5.30pm Sat & Sun mid-Mar–Oct, closed Sat Nov–mid-Mar), which features a small museum on Gandon himself, as well as information on the history of the building.

ST MARY'S PRO-CATHEDRAL
Dublin's most important **Catholic church** (Map pp82-3; ☎ 874 5441; Marlborough St; admission free; ⏰ 8am-6.30pm) is not quite the showcase you might expect. For one, it's in a cramped street rather than on its intended spot on O'Connell St, where the GPO is now located: the city's Protestants had a fit and insisted that it be built on a less conspicuous side street. And less conspicuous it certainly was, unless you were looking for purveyors of the world's oldest profession. Then you were smack in the middle of Monto – as Marlborough St was then known – the busiest red-light district in Europe, thanks to the British army stationed here. After independence and the departure of the British, Monto became plain old Marlborough St and the only enduring evidence is in the writings of James Joyce, who referred to the area where he lost his virginity as 'Nighttown'.

The area mightn't be the hot spot it used to be, but at least you won't be distracted while admiring the six Doric columns of the cathedral, built between 1816 and 1825 and modelled on the Temple of Theseus in Athens. The best time to visit is Sunday at 11am for the Latin Mass sung by the Palestrina Choir, the very choir in which Count John McCormack, Ireland's greatest singing export (sorry Bono), began his career in 1904.

Finally, a word about the term 'pro' in the title. It roughly means 'unofficial cathedral', due to the fact that church leaders saw this building as an interim cathedral that would do until funds were found to build a much grander one. Which has never happened, leaving this most Catholic of cities with two incredible-but-underused Protestant cathedrals and one fairly ordinary Catholic one. Irony one, piety nil.

DUBLIN CITY GALLERY – THE HUGH LANE
The splendid **Hugh Lane Gallery** (Map pp82-3; ☎ 874 1903; www.hughlane.ie; 22 North Parnell Sq; suggested donation €2; ⏰ 9.30am-6pm Tue-Thu, 9.30am-5pm Fri & Sat, 11am-5pm Sun), housed in the wonderful 18th-century Charlemont House, is looking better than ever thanks to a fantastic face-lift which has seen the unveiling of a new €13 million modernist extension that more than doubles the gallery's capacity. The new building, based in the old National Ballroom, spans three floors and includes 13 bright galleries showing works from the 1950s onwards, a specialist bookshop and chic restaurant in the basement.

The gallery's remit neatly spans the gap between the old masters of the National Gallery (p96) and the contemporary works exhibited in the Irish Museum of Modern Art (p103).

All the big names of French impressionism and early-20th-century Irish art are here. Sculptures by Rodin and Degas, and paintings by Corot, Courbet, Manet and Monet sit alongside works by Irish greats Jack B Yeats, William Leech and Nathaniel Hone.

The gallery's **Francis Bacon Studio** was painstakingly moved, in all its shambolic mess, from 7 Reece Mews, London, where the Dublin-born artist lived for 31 years. Bacon, who claimed that chaos suggested art to him and famously hated Ireland, would no doubt have found it amusing that a team of conservators spent years cataloguing scraps of newspaper, horse whips, old socks, dirty rags, jars of pickle and mouse droppings, to reverently reassemble it all in Dublin.

The gallery was founded in 1908 by wealthy art dealer Sir Hugh Lane, who died on the *Lusitania* in 1915 when the ship was torpedoed by a German U-boat. Following his death, a bitter row erupted between the National Gallery in London and the Hugh Lane Gallery over the jewels of his collection; even now, after years of wrangling, half the works are displayed in Dublin and half in London on a rotating basis, but for the time being the Hugh Lane will hold

DUBLIN

on to its most prized possession, Renoir's *Les Parapluies.*

DUBLIN WRITERS MUSEUM

A collection of memorabilia, ephemera and other stuff that's associated with the rich literary heritage of Dublin makes the **Dublin Writers Museum** (Map pp82–3; ☎ 872 2077; www .writersmuseum.com; 18 North Parnell Sq; adult/child/student €7/4.40/5.95; ⏰ 10am-5pm Mon-Sat Sep-May, to 6pm Jun-Aug, 11am-5pm Sun year-round) a compelling visit for anyone interested in the city's scribblers. Unfortunately, the museum draws the line in the 1970s, so there's nothing on the new generation of pen merchants. However, if you're interested in the letters, photographs, 1st editions and other bits and bobs of Beckett, Behan and the like, you won't be disappointed.

The museum also has a bookshop and restaurant, Chapter One (p129). Admission includes taped guides with readings from relevant texts in English and other languages. If you plan to visit the James Joyce Museum (p143) and the Shaw Birthplace (p112), bear in mind that a combined ticket (adult/student/child €12/10/7.40) is cheaper than three separate ones.

While the museum concerns itself primarily with dead authors, next door at No 19, the Irish Writers' Centre provides a meeting and working place for their living successors.

JAMES JOYCE CULTURAL CENTRE

Denis Maginni, the exuberant, flamboyant dance instructor immortalised by James Joyce in *Ulysses,* taught in this **house** (Map pp82–3; ☎ 878 8547; www.jamesjoyce.ie; 35 North Great George's St; adult/child/student €5/free/4; ⏰ 10am-5pm Tue-Sat). In 1982 Senator David Norris, a renowned Joycean scholar and leading gay-rights activist, bought the run-down house and restored it before opening it as a centre for the study of Joyce and his books.

Visitors can see the room where Maginni taught, and a collection of pictures that include the 17 different Dublin homes occupied by the nomadic Joyce family, and the real individuals fictionalised in the books. Some of the fine plaster ceilings are restored originals, others careful reproductions of Michael Stapleton's designs. For information on James Joyce–related walking tours departing from the centre, see p115.

Smithfield & Phoenix Park

For nearly a decade the Smithfield area has been like an urban debutante, full of promise – it *will* take over from Temple Bar as the city's hipster district, and it *will* spearhead the northside's cultural renaissance. Yet it remains very much a work in progress, and while the sexy new square and brand new buildings have undoubtedly made an impact, the real reason to visit is – ironically – to explore the remaining traces of old Dublin. Further west, however, is Dublin's grandest public park, home of the president and the zoo; on the way is one of the city's best museums.

SMITHFIELD

Earmarked in the mid-1990s for major residential and cultural development, Smithfield (Map pp82–3), bordered to the east by Church St, to the west by Blackhall Pl, to the north by North King St and to the south by Arran Quay, has progressed in fits and starts but has not quite evolved into the promised cultural quarter. At the centre of the development is the old hay, straw, cattle and horse marketplace, Smithfield Market, which has now been replaced by a new open civic space. The flagship of the Historic Area Rejuvenation Project (HARP), whose brief is to restore the northwest inner city, the space features a pedestrianised square bordered on one side by 26m-high gas-lighter masts, each with a 2m-high flame. The old cobblestones were removed, cleaned up and put back, along with new granite slabs that manage to give the whole square a modern feel without sacrificing its traditional beauty.

Bordering the eastern side of the square is the Old Jameson Distillery. In keeping with the area's traditional past, the old fruit and vegetable market still plies a healthy wholesale trade on the square's western side.

CHIMNEY

As part of the ongoing development of the Smithfield area, a distillery chimney, built by Jameson in 1895, has been converted into Dublin's first and only 360-degree **observation tower** (Map pp82–3; ☎ 817 3800; Smithfield Village; adult/child/student/family €5/3.50/3.50/10; ⏰ 10am-5pm Mon-Sat, 11am-5.30pm Sun). A glass lift shuttles visitors to the top where, behind the safety of glass, you can see the entire city, the sea and the mountains to the south. On a clear day, it makes for some nice photo opportunities.

NATIONAL MUSEUM OF IRELAND – DECORATIVE ARTS & HISTORY

So much for the austere life of a soldier. Until it was decommissioned over a decade ago, Collins Barracks, built in 1704 on the orders of Queen Anne, was the largest military barracks in the world. In 1997 the early neoclassical grey stone building on the Liffey's northern bank was given a sparkling, modern makeover and now houses the decorative-arts-and-history collection of the **National Museum of Ireland** (Map pp82–3; ☎ 677 7444; www.museum.ie; Benburb St; admission free; ⏰ 10am–5pm Tue–Sat, 2–5pm Sun). The exhibits are good, but the building is stunning: at its heart is the huge central square surrounded by arcaded colonnades and blocks linked by walking bridges. While wandering about the plaza, imagine it holding up to six regiments in formation. The whole shebang is the work of Thomas Burgh (1670–1730), who also designed the Old Library (p92) in Trinity College and St Michan's Church (p108).

Inside the imposing exterior lies a treasure trove of artefacts ranging from silver, ceramics and glassware to weaponry, furniture and folk-life displays. Some of the best pieces are gathered in the exhibition *Curator's Choice*, a collection of 25 objects hand-picked by different curators, displayed with an account of why they were chosen.

The museum itself offers a glimpse at Ireland's social, economic and military history over the last millennium. It's a big ask – too big, say its critics – but well-designed displays, interactive multimedia and a dizzying array of disparate artefacts make for an interesting and valiant effort. On the 1st floor is the museum's Irish silver collection, one of the largest collections of silver in the world; on the 2nd floor you'll find Irish period furniture and scientific instruments; while the 3rd floor has simple and sturdy Irish country furniture.

Lovers of modern furniture and design will enjoy the exhibition on iconic Irish designer Eileen Gray (1878–1976), which is a museum highlight. Gray was one of the most influential designers of the 20th century, and the exhibition documents her life and work, and shows examples and models of her most famous pieces. The fascinating *Way We Wore* exhibit displays Irish clothing and jewellery from the past 250 years. An intriguing socio-cultural study, it highlights the role of jewellery and clothing in bestowing messages of mourning, love and identity.

A new exhibition chronicling Ireland's **Easter 1916 Rising** is on the ground floor. Visceral memorabilia such as first-hand accounts of the violence of the Black and Tans and of post-Rising hunger strikes, the handwritten death certificates of the republican prisoners and their postcards from Holloway prison bring to life this poignant period of Irish history.

OLD JAMESON DISTILLERY

Smithfield's biggest draw is the **Old Jameson Distillery** (Map pp82–3; ☎ 807 2355; www.jameson.ie; Bow St; adult/child/student €10/6/8; ⏰ tours every 35min 10am–5.30pm), a huge museum devoted to *uisce beatha* (the water of life). To its more serious devotees, that is precisely what whiskey is, although they may be put off by the slickness of the museum, which shepherds visitors through a compulsory tour of the re-created factory and into the ubiquitous gift shop.

On the way, however, there's plenty to discover. Beginning with a short film, the tour runs through the whole process of distilling, from grain to bottle. There are plenty of interesting titbits, such as what makes a single malt, where whiskey gets its colour and bouquet, and what the difference is between Irish whiskey and Scotch (other than the spelling, which prompted one Scot to comment that the Irish thought of everything: they even put an 'e' into whisky).

Then it's straight to the bar for a drop of the subject matter; eager drinkers can volunteer for the tasting tour, where you get to sample whiskies from all over the world and learn about their differences. Finally, you head to the almighty shop. If you're buying whiskey, go for the stuff you can't buy at home, such as the excellent Red Breast or the super exclusive Midleton, a very limited reserve that is appropriately expensive.

FOUR COURTS

Appellants quake and the accused may shiver, but visitors are only likely to be amazed by James Gandon's imposing **Four Courts** (Map p84; ☎ 872 5555; Inn's Quay; admission free), Ireland's uppermost courts of law. Gandon's Georgian masterpiece is a mammoth structure incorporating a 130m-long façade and a collection of statuary. The Corinthian-columned central block, connected to flanking wings with enclosed quadrangles, was begun in 1786 and not completed until 1802.

The original four courts (Exchequer, Common Pleas, King's Bench and Chancery) all branch off the central rotunda.

The Four Courts played a brief role in the 1916 Easter Rising without suffering damage, but the events of 1922 were not so kind. When anti-Treaty forces seized the building and refused to leave, it was shelled from across the river. As the occupiers retreated, the building was set on fire and many irreplaceable early records were burned – an event that sparked off the Civil War. The building wasn't restored until 1932.

Visitors are allowed to wander through the building, but not to enter courts or other restricted areas. In the lobby of the central rotunda you'll see bewigged barristers conferring, and police officers handcuffed to their charges.

ST MICHAN'S CHURCH

The macabre remains of the ancient dead are the attraction at **St Michan's Church** (Map p84; ☎ 872 4154; Lower Church St; adult/child/student €3.50/2.50/3; ◷ 10am-12.45pm & 2-4.45pm Mon-Fri, 10am-12.45pm Sat May-Oct, 12.30-3.30pm Mon-Fri Nov-Apr), near the Four Courts, founded by the Danes in 1095 and named after one of their saints. Incredibly, it was the *only* church on the north side of the Liffey until 1686. The original church has largely disappeared beneath several additions, most dating from the 17th century (except for the battlement tower, which dates from the 15th century). It was considerably restored in the early 19th century and again after the Civil War, during which it had been damaged.

The very unchurchlike interior – it looks a bit like a courtroom – contains an organ from 1724 that Handel may have played for the first performance of his *Messiah*. A skull on the floor on one side of the altar is said to represent Oliver Cromwell. On the opposite side, a penitent's chair was where 'open and notoriously naughty livers' did public penance.

The big draw is the tour of the subterranean crypt, where you'll see bodies between 400 and 800 years old, preserved not by mummification but by the constant dry atmosphere. Tours are organised on an ad hoc basis depending on how many people there are. Catch bus 134 or the Luas Red Line to Smithfield from the city centre to get here.

PHOENIX PARK

Measuring 709 glorious hectares, **Phoenix Park** (Map p80; admission free) is Europe's largest city park and a green lung that is more than double the size of New York's Central Park (a paltry 337 hectares), and larger than all of London's major parks put together. Here you'll find gardens and lakes; pitches for all kinds of British sports from soccer to cricket to polo (the dry original one, with horses); the second-oldest zoo in Europe; a castle and visitor centre; the headquarters of the Garda Síochána (police); the Ordnance Survey offices; and the homes of both the president of Ireland and the US ambassador, who live in two exquisite residences more or less opposite each other. There's even a herd of some 500 fallow deer.

The deer were first introduced by Lord Ormond in 1662, when lands once owned by the Knights of Jerusalem were turned into a royal hunting ground. In 1745 the viceroy Lord Chesterfield threw it open to the public and it has remained so ever since. (The name 'Phoenix' has nothing to do with the mythical bird; it is a corruption of the Irish *fionn uisce*, meaning 'clear water'.)

In 1882 the park played a crucial role in Irish history, when Lord Cavendish, the British chief secretary for Ireland, and his assistant were murdered outside what is now the Irish president's residence by an obscure nationalist group called the Invincibles. Lord Cavendish's home is now called Deerfield and is used as the official residence of the US ambassador.

Near the Parkgate St entrance to the park is the 63m-high **Wellington Monument**. This took from 1817 to 1861 to build, mainly because the Duke of Wellington fell from public favour during its construction. Nearby is the **People's Garden**, dating from 1864, and the **bandstand** in the Hollow.

Established in 1830, the 12-hectare **Dublin Zoo** (Map p80; ☎ 677 1425; www.dublinzoo.ie; Phoenix Park; adult/child/family €14/9.50/40; ◷ 9.30am-6pm Mon-Sat, 10.30am-6pm Sun Mar-Sep, 9.30am-dusk Mon-Fri, 9.30am-dusk Sat, 10.30am-dusk Sun Oct-Feb) is one of the oldest in the world, but is mainly of interest to children. It used to be a run-down zoo where depressed animals used to depress visitors, but a substantial face-lift has made it a much more pleasant place for animals to live and for you to stroll around.

The large Victorian building behind the zoo, on the edge of the park, is the Garda Siochana Headquarters. It was designed by

Benjamin Woodward in the 19th century. His work also includes the Old Library in Trinity College (p92).

In the centre of the park, the **Papal Cross** marks the site where Pope John Paul II preached to 1.25 million people in 1979. The **Phoenix Monument**, erected by Lord Chesterfield in 1747, looks very un-phoenix-like and is often referred to as the Eagle Monument. The southern part of the park is a 200-acre stretch (about 81 hectares) known as the Fifteen Acres (don't ask, nobody knows) which is given over to a large number of football pitches – winter Sunday mornings are the time to come and watch. To the west, the rural-looking **Glen Pond** corner of the park is extremely attractive.

Back towards the Parkgate entrance is **Magazine Fort** on Thomas' Hill. Built at snail's pace between 1734 and 1801, the fort has served as an occasional arms depot for the British and, later, the Irish armies. It was a target during the 1916 Easter Rising and again in 1940, when the IRA made off with the entire ammunitions reserve of the Irish army (they retrieved it after a few weeks).

The residence of the Irish president, **Áras an Uachtaráin** (Map p80; ☎ 617 1000; Phoenix Park; admission free; ⏰ guided tours hourly 10.30am-4.30pm Sat) was built in 1751 and enlarged in 1782, then again in 1816, this time by noted Irish architect Francis Johnston, who added the Ionic portico. From 1782 to 1922 it was the residence of the British viceroys or lord lieutenants. After independence it became the home of Ireland's governor general until Ireland cut ties with the British Crown and created the office of president in 1937.

Tickets for the tour can be collected from the **Phoenix Park Visitor Centre** (☎ 677 0095; adult/ concession/family €2.75/1.25/7; ⏰ 10am-6pm Apr-Sep, 10am-5pm Oct, 10am-5pm Mon-Sat Nov & Dec, 10am-5pm Sat & Sun Jan-Mar), the converted former stables of the papal nunciate, now devoted to the park's history and ecology over the last 3500 years. Next door is the restored four-storey **Ashtown Castle**, a 17th-century tower house 'discovered' inside the 18th-century nuncio's mansion when the latter was demolished in 1986 due to dry rot. You can only visit the castle on a guided tour from the visitor centre.

Take bus 10 from O'Connell St, or bus 25 or 26 from Middle Abbey St to get to Dublin's beloved playground.

Beyond the Royal Canal

These days it makes for a lovely walk, but when 'Long' John Binns put his money into the construction of the Royal Canal (Map p80) from 1790, it was an exercise in misplaced optimism and self-flagellating revenge. The usefulness of such waterways was already on the wane, and he only invested in the project because when he was a board member of the Grand Canal a colleague mocked his day job as a shoemaker. Sure enough, the canal was a massive bust; Binns lost a pile of money and became a figure of fun.

Binns' catastrophe is the stroller's good fortune and the towpath alongside the canal is perfect for a walk through the heart of the city. You can join it beside Newcomen Bridge at North Strand Rd, just north of Connolly Station, and follow it to the suburb of Clonsilla and beyond, more than 10km away. The walk is particularly pleasant beyond Binns Bridge in Drumcondra. At the top of Blessington St a large pond, used when the canal also supplied drinking water to the city, attracts water birds.

Beyond the Royal Canal lie the suburbs and an authentic slice of north city life. There are also some beautiful gardens, the country's biggest stadium, a historic cemetery and one of the most interesting buildings in all of Dublin.

CROKE PARK

It's a magnificent stadium – if you're impressed by them – that is Ireland's largest and the fourth-largest in Europe, but **Croke Park** (Map p80; ☎ 819 2323; Clonliffe Rd) is about much more than 82,000-plus sporting butts on plastic seats. No, Croker – as it's lovingly known in Dublin – is the fabulous fortress that protects the sanctity and spirit of Gaelic games in Ireland, as well as the administrative HQ of the Gaelic Athletic Association (GAA), the body that governs them. Sound a little hyperbolic? Well, the GAA considers itself not just the governing body of a bunch of Irish games, but the stout defender of a cultural identity that is ingrained in Ireland's sense of self (see When History Really Matters, p110). To get an idea of just how important the GAA is in Ireland, a visit to the **Croke Park Experience** (☎ 855 8176; www .gaa.ie; New Stand, Croke Park, Clonliffe Rd; adult/child/student museum €5.50/3.50/4, museum & tour €9.50/6/7; ⏰ 9.30am-5pm Mon-Sat, noon-5pm Sun Apr-Oct, 10am-5pm Tue-Sat, noon-4pm Sun Nov-Mar) is a must, though it will

WHEN HISTORY REALLY MATTERS

At 5.31pm on 24 February 2007, history was made. It happened at Croke Park, when the band struck the first notes of 'God Save the Queen'. The English rugby team stood proudly to attention, and the 82,000 in the crowd applauded respectfully before settling down to a long-anticipated Six Nations match between Ireland and 'the old enemy'.

A quarter of a century ago, the above paragraph would have seemed the stuff of heretical fantasy, a perverse dream that would – could – never, ever come true. Before that date in February, the last official representatives of Britain to set foot inside Croke Park did so on 1 November 1920, when soldiers opened fire on the crowd in retaliation for the earlier killing of 14 British agents; 14 people, including a player and two young boys, died. In the intervening 76 years, the Republic of Ireland came into being and the Gaelic Athletic Association (GAA) admirably went about the task of establishing itself as the premier sporting and cultural association in the country, with a wide-ranging influence that included a ban on all 'foreign' (read: English) games in its holiest cathedral, Croke Park.

The Irish did play football and rugby – quite successfully in recent decades – but they did so away from GAA-controlled pitches, with internationals played at Lansdowne Road, owned by the Irish Rugby Football Union (IRFU). But Lansdowne Road began a long-overdue reconstruction in 2007, leaving the rugby crowd and the Football Association of Ireland (FAI) with a major dilemma: with no alternative stadium in Ireland to stage internationals, they were confronting the possibility of staging home games in – gasp – Britain!

The GAA had refused to even talk about it for a couple of years, but in April 2005 they voted, by the slenderest of margins, to allow temporary use of Croke Park to their rival associations. And so 24 February 2007 came, and with it history of the most momentous kind. Eighty minutes later, another bit of history: Ireland had won, 43–13, by the biggest margin ever.

A neat and fitting end to a powerful bit of history. But in the interests of (often) boring accuracy, it must be mentioned that the English were not the first team to play an English game at Croke Park: two weeks earlier, the French earned that particular honour with a hard-fought win over a spirited Irish side who were overawed by the sense of occasion. But it was the English that really mattered. As always.

help if you're any kind of sporting enthusiast. The twice-daily tours (except match days) of the impressive stadium are excellent.

To get to Croke Park, catch bus 3, 11, 11A, 16, 16A or 123 from O'Connell St.

NATIONAL BOTANIC GARDENS

Founded in 1795, the 19.5-hectare **National Botanic Gardens** (Map p78; ☎ 837 7596; Botanic Rd, Glasnevin; admission free; ☒ 9am-6pm Mon-Sat, 11am-6pm Sun Apr-Oct, 10am-4.30pm Mon-Sat, 11am-4.30pm Sun Nov-Mar) are directly north of the centre, flanked to the north by the River Tolka.

In the gardens is a series of curvilinear glasshouses dating from 1843 to 1869. The glasshouses were created by Richard Turner, who was also responsible for the glasshouse at Belfast Botanic Gardens and the Palm House in London's Kew Gardens. Within these Victorian masterpieces you will find the latest in botanical technology, including a series of computer-controlled climates reproducing environments of different parts of

the world. Among the pioneering botanical work conducted here was the first attempt to raise orchids from seed, back in 1844; pampas grass and the giant lily were also first grown in Europe in these gardens.

To get here, catch bus 13, 13A or 19 from O'Connell St, or bus 34 or 34A from Middle Abbey St.

GLASNEVIN CEMETERY

Ireland's largest and most historically important burial site is **Prospect Cemetery** (Map p80; ☎ 830 1133; www.glasnevin-cemetery.ie; Finglas Rd; admission free; ☒ 24hr, tours 2.30pm Wed & Fri), better known simply as Glasnevin Cemetery, after the north Dublin suburb it lies in – and an easy walk from the National Botanic Gardens. It was established in 1832 as a burial ground for Catholics, who were increasingly prohibited from conducting burials in the city's Protestant cemeteries. Not surprisingly, the cemetery's monuments and memorials have staunchly patriotic overtones, with numerous high crosses, shamrocks, harps and other Irish symbols. The cemetery is mentioned in *Ulysses* and there are several clues for Joyce enthusiasts to follow.

The most interesting parts of the cemetery are at the southeastern Prospect Sq end. The single most imposing memorial is the colossal monument to Cardinal Mc-Cabe (1837–1921), archbishop of Dublin and primate of Ireland, while a modern replica of a round tower acts as a handy landmark for locating the tomb of Daniel O'Connell, who died in 1847 and was reinterred here in 1869 when the tower was completed. Charles Stewart Parnell's tomb is topped with a huge granite rock. Other notable people buried here include Sir Roger Casement, who was executed for treason by the British in 1916 and whose remains weren't returned to Ireland until 1964; the republican leader Michael Collins, who died in the Civil War; the docker and trade unionist Jim Larkin, a prime force in the 1913 general strike; and the poet Gerard Manley Hopkins.

There's also a poignant 'class' memorial to the men who have starved themselves to death for the cause of Irish freedom over the century, including 10 men from the 1981 H Block hunger strikes.

The watchtowers in the cemetery were once used to keep watch for body snatchers.

To get to the cemetry, take bus 40, 40A or 40B from Parnell St.

CASINO AT MARINO

It's not the roulette-wheel kind of casino, but the original Italian kind, the one that means 'house of pleasure' or 'summer home', and this particular **casino** (Map p80; ☎ 833 1618; Malahide Rd; adult/concession/family €2.90/1.30/7.50; ☯ 10am-5pm May & Oct, 10am-6pm Jun-Sep, noon-4pm Sat & Sun Feb, Mar, Nov & Dec, noon-5pm Sat & Sun Apr) is one of the most enchanting constructions in all of Ireland. Entrance is by guided tour only; the last tour is 45 minutes before closing.

It was built in the mid-18th century for the Earl of Charlemont, who returned from his grand tour of Europe with more art than he could store in his own home, Marino House, which was on the same grounds but was demolished in the 1920s. He also came home with a big love of the Palladian style – hence the architecture of this wonderful folly.

The exterior of the building, with a huge entrance doorway, and 12 Tuscan columns forming a templelike façade, creates the expectation that its interior will be a simple single open space. But instead it is an extravagant convoluted maze: flights of fancy include chimneys for the central heating that are disguised as roof urns, downpipes hidden in columns, carved draperies, ornate fireplaces, beautiful parquet floors constructed of rare woods, and a spacious wine cellar. A variety of statuary adorns the outside but it's the amusing fakes that are most enjoyable. The towering front door is a sham – a much smaller panel opens to reveal the secret interior. The windows have blacked-out panels to hide the fact that the interior is a complex of rooms, not a single chamber.

To get to the casino, take bus 20A, 20B, 27, 27B, 42, 42C or 123 from the city centre, or travel on the Dublin Area Rapid Transport (DART) to Clontarf road.

Beyond the Grand Canal

The more attractive of Dublin's two canals is the Grand Canal (Map p80), built to connect Dublin with the River Shannon. It makes a graceful 6km loop around the south city centre and has a lovely path running alongside it which is perfect for a pleasant walk or cycle. At its eastern end the canal forms a harbour connected with the Liffey at Ringsend, through locks that were built in 1796. The large Grand Canal Dock, flanked by Hanover and Charlotte Quays, is now used by windsurfers and canoeists and is the site of a major new development, including Dublin's first real skyscraper, which will be home to U2's purpose-designed recording studios.

At the northwestern corner of the dock is Misery Hill, once the site for the public execution of criminals. It was once the practice to bring the corpses of those already hung at Gallows Hill, near Upper Baggot St, to this spot, to be strung up for public display for anything from six to 12 months.

The loveliest stretch of the canal is just southwest, between Mount St Bridge and Baggot St. The grassy, tree-lined banks were a favourite haunt of the poet Patrick Kavanagh, whose difficult love affair with the city is echoed in the hauntingly beautiful 'On Raglan Road', later put to music by Van Morrison. Another Kavanagh poem requested that he be commemorated by 'a canal bank seat for passers-by', and his friends obliged with a seat beside the lock on the southern side of the canal. A little further along on the northern side you can sit down beside Kavanagh himself, cast in bronze, comfortably lounging on a bench and watching his beloved canal.

If you absolutely must know about the construction and operation of Ireland's canals, then catch the DART to Grand Canal Dock for a visit to the **Waterways Visitor Centre** (Map p80; ☎ 677 7510; www.waterwaysireland.org; Grand Canal Quay; adult/student/child €2.50/1.20/1.20; ☷ 9.30am-5.30pm Jun-Sep, 12.30-5pm Wed-Sun Oct & May) on the Grand Canal Basin. Otherwise, admiring the 'Box on the Docks' – as this modern building is nicknamed – is plenty good enough for the average enthusiast of artificial waterways.

Just southeast of the city centre, beyond the canal, is **Ballsbridge** (Map p78), the epitome of posh Dublin and home to most of the embassies and a batch of luxurious B&Bs. The main attractions around it are the Royal Dublin Society Showground and the **Lansdowne Road rugby stadium** (Map p80), which was undergoing renovation at the time of writing, though **Herbert Park** (Map p80) is also a favourite spot for sport, walking or just sitting around.

ROYAL DUBLIN SOCIETY SHOWGROUND

The **Royal Dublin Society Showground** (RDS Showground; Map p80; ☎ 668 9878; Merrion Rd, Ballsbridge), about 15 minutes from the city centre by bus 7 from Trinity College, is used for various exhibitions throughout the year. The society was founded in 1731 and has had its headquarters in a number of well-known Dublin buildings, including Leinster House (p97) from 1814 to 1925. The society was involved in the foundation of the National Museum (p96 and p107), National Library (p98), National Gallery (p96) and National Botanic Gardens (p110). The most important annual event at the showground is the August **Dublin Horse Show** (☎ tickets 668 0866), which includes an international showjumping contest. Ask at the tourist office or consult a listings magazine for other events.

SHAW BIRTHPLACE

OK, so it's technically on the city side of the canal, but only just. Noted playwright George Bernard Shaw was born and lived until the age of 10 in what is now home to a **museum** (Map p80; ☎ 475 0854; 33 Synge St; adult/child/student €7/4.40/5.95; ☷ 10am-1pm & 2-5pm Mon-Sat year-round, plus 11am-1pm

& 2-5pm Sun Easter-Oct) dedicated to him and the times he grew up in. The museum has an audio presentation of Shaw's life, re-creating a Victorian household.

Note that it's possible to buy a combination ticket (adult/student/child €12/10/7.40) that also gives you access to the Dublin Writers' Museum and James Joyce Museum in Sandycove.

To get to the museum, take bus 16, 19 or 122 from Trinity College.

IRISH-JEWISH MUSEUM

Just around the corner from the Shaw House is the **Irish-Jewish Museum** (Map p80; ☎ 453 1797; 4 Walworth Rd; admission free; ☷ 11am-3.30pm Tue, Thu & Sun May-Sep, 10.30am-2.30pm Sun only Oct-Apr). Located in an old synagogue, the museum was opened in 1985 by the then Israeli president, Chaim Herzog, who was actually born in Belfast. Dublin's small but culturally important Jewish population is remembered through photographs, paintings, certificates, books and other memorabilia.

ACTIVITIES
Beaches & Swimming

Dublin is hardly the sort of place to work on your suntan, and even a hot Irish summer day is unlikely to raise the water temperature much above freezing. However, there are some pleasant beaches. Many Joyce fans feel compelled to take a dip in **Forty Foot Pool** at Sandycove (p143). Sandy beaches to the north of Dublin include **Sutton** (11km), **Portmarnock** (11km), **Malahide** (11km), **Claremount** (14km) and **Donabate** (21km). Although the beach at **Sandymount** is nothing special, it is only 5km southeast of central Dublin. Take No 3 from Fleet St.

The **National Aquatic Centre** (Map p78; ☎ 646 4300; www.nac.ie; Snugborough Rd, Blanchardstown; adult/child & student €12/10; ☷ 2-10pm Mon-Fri, 9am-8pm Sat & Sun), built to accommodate the Special Olympics World Summer Games held in Dublin in 2003, is the largest indoor water park. Besides its Olympic-size competition pool, it has water rollercoasters, wave and surf machines, a leisure pool and all types of flumes. It's a great day out for the family but on weekends be prepared to join the line of shivering children queuing for slides. Take bus 38A from Hawkins St to Snugborough Rd.

There is a dearth of quality pools in the city centre – most are small, crowded and not very hygienic. An excellent exception is the **Markievicz Leisure Centre** (Map pp82-3; ☎ 672 9121; cnr Tara & Townsend Sts; adult/child €5.50/2.80; ☺ 7am-8.45pm Mon-Fri, 9am-5.45pm Sat, 10am-3.45pm Sun), which has a 25m pool, a workout room and a sauna. For the admission price you can swim pretty much as long as you like; children are only allowed at off-peak times (ie any time except for 7am to 9am, noon to 2pm and 5pm to 7pm Monday to Friday).

Cycling

Dublin is compact and flat, making it a cinch to get around by bike. Rust red cycle lanes throughout the city make it easier than ever, but traffic congestion, motorised maniacs and roadworks can make for a treacherous obstacle course. Nonetheless, with your wits about you, it's the fastest way to get about the increasingly congested centre.

Bike theft is a major problem, so be sure to park on busier streets, preferably at one of the myriad U-shaped parking bars. Overnight street parking is dodgy; most hostels and hotels offer secure bicycle-parking areas.

Irish Cycling Safaris (☎ 260 0749; www.cyclingsafaris .com; University College Dublin, Belfield; tour €590; ☺ end Apr-early Oct) organises eight highly recommended themed week-long tours of the countryside. Each group cycles at its own pace, with a guide following in a backup vehicle. The price also includes bike hire, and hotel and B&B accommodation.

Recommended bike shops:

Cycle-Logical (Map p84; ☎ 872 4635; 3 Bachelor's Walk) A shop for serious enthusiasts, with top-quality gear and info on cycling events throughout the country. It does not do repairs.

Square Wheel Cycleworks (Map p84; ☎ 679 0838; South Temple Lane) Quick, friendly and excellent for repairs.

Bike hire has become increasingly more difficult to find because of crippling insurance costs. Typical hire costs for a mountain bike are between €10 and €25 a day or up to €100 per week. Raleigh Rent-a-Bike agencies can be found through the following businesses:

Cycleways (Map pp82-3; ☎ 873 4748; www .cycleways.com; 185-186 Parnell St) Dublin's best bike shop, with expert staff who pepper their patter with all the technical lingo. Top-notch rentals.

Eurotrek (☎ 456 8847; www.raleigh.ie)

MacDonalds Cycles (Map p86; ☎ 475 2586; 38 Wexford St) Friendly and helpful, great for the amateur enthusiast.

WALKING TOUR

Dubliners of old would assure their 'bitter halves' that they were 'going to see a man about a dog' before beating a retreat to the nearest watering hole. Visiting barflies need no excuse to enjoy the social and cultural education – ahem – of a tour of Dublin's finest, most charming and most hard-core bars.

Start in the excellent **Anseo** (**1**; p132) on Camden St, which pulls a seriously hip and unpretentious crowd on the strength of its fabulous DJs. Head deep into the city centre and stop at Dublin's smallest pub, the **Dawson Lounge** (**2**; p131), for an appropriately diminutive tipple, before sinking a pint of plain in the snug at South Anne St's **Kehoe's** (**3**; p131), one of the city centre's most atmospheric bars. Discuss the merits of that unwritten master-

---

WALK FACTS

Start Camden St
Finish Ormond Quay
Distance 2.5km
Duration One hour to two days!

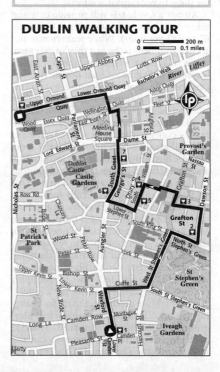

DUBLIN WALKING TOUR

piece with a clutch of frustrated writers and artists in **Grogan's Castle Lounge** (4; p131) on Castle Market, a traditional haunt that admirably refuses to modernise. Just around the corner on South William St is the supertrendy **South William** (5; p133), where homemade pies, good music and the cool brigade mix to great effect; if it's more conversation you require, make your way to the **Long Hall** (6; p131), where the vicissitudes of life are discussed in a sombre Victorian setting. Shake that booty down the road at the **Globe** (7; p133). Cross the Liffey and make a beeline for Ormond Quay and **Sin É** (8; p133), a small bar with a big reputation for top-class music and a terrific night out. If you've followed the tour correctly, it's unlikely that you'd now be referring to this guide. How many fingers?

DUBLIN FOR CHILDREN

Sometimes holidaying with small children requires the organisation of an army boot camp, boundless energy and patience, bottomless pockets and a sense of humour, so it really helps when the facilities and goodwill are there to back up your efforts.

All but a few hotels will provide cots and many have baby-sitting on request (normally €7 to €10 per hour). While waiters may not act like your baby is the first they've ever seen, you'll still find a warm reception for junior travellers in Dublin, at least during the day. Frustratingly, many city-centre restaurants are unwilling to accommodate diners under 12, especially babies, after 6pm. You'll need to check before making a booking. Most restaurants – even exclusive ones – have highchairs and will gladly heat bottles and baby food, but so-called kiddie menus lack imagination and rarely stretch further than the ubiquitous chicken nuggets or sausages with chips. That said, places catering specifically for families who want to eat more nutritious food are cropping up all the time, and the pizza chain Milano has resourcefully added free weekend childcare facilities to its Dublin restaurants.

Travellers will find that nappy-changing facilities and city-centre playgrounds are remarkably few and far between. Shopping centres and department stores (or a hotel if you're stuck) are good places to try for changing nappies. There's a reasonabley sized playground on Gardiner St (Map pp82–3) and in St Stephen's Green (p98), where you can also feed the ducks. The Iveagh Gardens (p99)

doesn't have a playground but has a waterfall and small maze, and is a lovely quiet space to relax while your children play.

The **Ark** (Map p84; www.ark.ie; 11A Eustace St) is a children's cultural centre that organises plays, exhibitions and workshops for four to 14 year olds. You really need to book in advance for events.

Lambert Puppet Theatre (☎ 280 0974; www.lambert puppettheatre.com; Clifton Lane, Monkstown) stages puppet shows for the over-threes in Monkstown, 10km south of Dublin.

The National Museum (p96 and p107), Natural History Museum (p97) and the Irish Museum of Modern Art (p103) run fun, educational programmes for children at weekends. A nice spot for a picnic is **Newbridge House** (Map p78; ☎ 843 6534; Donabate; adult/child €3.50/2; 🕙 10am-5pm Tue-Sat, 2-6pm Sun Apr-Sep, 2-5pm Sat & Sun Oct-Mar), with its large traditional farm, which has cows, pigs and chickens, a large park and an adventure playground. It's northeast of Swords at Donabate, 19km from the centre. You can get here on the Suburban Rail service (€2.40, 30 minutes), which departs hourly from either Connolly or Pearse Station in the city centre.

The *Irish Times* runs a column on things to do with kids in its Wednesday edition.

If your hotel doesn't have a baby-sitting service, you could try a couple of agencies that provide professional nannies. It's up to you to negotiate a fee with the nanny, but €13 per hour is the average, plus taxi fare if the nanny isn't driving. You'll need to sign a form beforehand, which the agency will fax to your hotel.

Recommended agencies:
Belgrave Agency (☎ 280 9341; 55 Mulgrave St, Dun Laoghaire; fee per hr €18)
Executive Nannies (☎ 873 1273; 43 Lower Dominick St; fee per hr €20)

TOURS

Dublin is an easy city to see on foot, so a guided walking tour is an ideal way to double up on a bit of culture and exercise. For longer tours or a cushier ride, there are numerous themed citywide bus tours, and several companies do day trips further afield.

Bus Tours

City Sightseeing (Map pp82-3; www.citysightseeing .co.uk; Dublin Tourism, 14 Upper O'Connell St; adult/ child/family €16/7/38; 🕙 every 8-15min 9am-6pm) City

Sightseeing's time-tested hop-on, hop-off open-top tours. Tours take 1½ hours.

Dublin Bus Tours (www.dublinbus.ie; tours €14-25; ☾ tours daily) O'Connell St (Map pp82-3; ☎ 872 0000; 59 Upper O'Connell St); Suffolk St (Map p84; Dublin Tourism Centre, St Andrew's Church, 2 Suffolk St) It offers a variety of tours, including Dublin City Tour, Ghost Bus Tour, Coast and Castles Tour, and South Coast and Gardens Tour.

Grayline Dublin Tour (☎ 872 9010; www .irishcitytours.com; adult/child/student/senior/family €15/6/12.50/12.50/36; ☾ every 15min 9.30am-5pm, to 5.30pm Jul & Aug) Bachelor's Walk (Map p84; 33 Bachelor's Walk); Suffolk St (Map p84; Dublin Tourism Centre, St Andrew's Church, 2 Suffolk St) Another hop-on, hop-off tour (1½ hours) of the city's primary attractions.

Wild Wicklow Tour (Map p84; ☎ 280 1899; www .discoverdublin.ie; Dublin Tourism Centre, St Andrew's Church, 2 Suffolk St; adult/child €28/25; ☾ 9.10am) Award winning and lots of fun, this top 8½-hour tour leaves from Dublin Tourism Centre and does a quick city tour before heading down the coast to Avoca Handweavers, Glendalough and the Sally Gap.

Walking Tours

1916 Easter Rising Walk (Map p84; ☎ 676 2493; www.1916rising.com; International Bar, 23 Wicklow St; adult/child €12/free; ☾ 11.30am Mon-Sat, 1pm Sun Mar-Oct) A recommended two-hour tour run by graduates of Trinity College that takes in parts of Dublin that were directly involved in the Easter Rising. It leaves from the International Bar.

Dublin Footsteps Walking Tours (Map p86; ☎ 496 0641; Bewley's Bldg, Grafton St; adult €9; ☾ 10.30am Mon, Wed, Fri & Sat Jun-Sep) Departing from Bewley's on Grafton St, these excellent two-hour tours weave Georgian, literary and architectural Dublin into a fascinating walk.

Dublin Literary Pub Crawl (Map p86; ☎ 454 0228; www.dublinpubcrawl.com; Duke, 9 Duke St; adult/ student €12/10; ☾ 7.30pm Mon-Sat, noon & 7.30pm Sun Apr-Nov, 7.30pm Thu-Sun Dec-Mar) An award-winning 2½-hour walk-and-performance tour led by two actors around pubs with literary connections. There's plenty of drink taken, which makes it all the more popular; get to the Duke pub by 7pm to reserve a spot.

Dublin Musical Pub Crawl (Map p84; ☎ 478 0193; www.discoverdublin.com; Oliver St John Gogartys, 58-59 Fleet St; adult/student €12/10; ☾ 7.30pm Apr-Oct, 7.30pm Thu-Sat Nov-Mar) The story of Irish traditional music and its influence on contemporary styles is explained and demonstrated by two expert musicians in a number of Temple Bar pubs. Tours meet upstairs at Oliver St John Gogartys and take 2½ hours.

James Joyce Walking Tour (Map pp82-3; ☎ 878 8547; James Joyce Cultural Centre, 35 North Great George's St; adult/student €10/9; ☾ 2pm Tue, Thu & Sat) Excellent 1¼-hour walking tours of northside attractions associated with James Joyce, departing from James Joyce Cultural Centre.

Pat Liddy Walking Tours (Map p84; ☎ 831 1109; www.walkingtours.ie; Dublin Tourism Centre, St Andrew's Church, 2 Suffolk St; adult/child/student €12/5/10) Award-winning themed tours of the city by well-known Dublin historian Pat Liddy, including Viking & Medieval Dublin (10.30am Tuesday, Thursday and Sunday, and 2.30pm Saturday), the Historic Northside (10.30am Wednesday and Friday), and Georgian and Victorian Splendours (10.30am Monday and 2.30pm Friday). All tours depart from the Dublin Tourism Centre.

Boat Tours

Viking Splash Tours (☎ 707 6000; www.vikingsplash .ie; adult/child/family from €20/10/60; ☾ 9am-5.30pm Mar-Oct, 10am-4pm Tue-Sun Nov, 10am-4pm Wed-Sun Feb) Patrick St (Map pp82-3; 64-65 Patrick St); St Stephen's Green (Map p86; North St Stephen's Green) It's hard not to feel a little cheesy with a plastic Viking helmet on your head, but the punters get a real kick out of these amphibious 1¼-hour tours that end up in the Grand Canal Dock.

Carriage Tours

You can pick up a horse and carriage with a driver-commentator at the junction of Grafton St and St Stephen's Green (Map p86). Half-hour tours cost up to €60 and the carriages can take four or five people. Tours of different lengths can be negotiated with the drivers.

FESTIVALS & EVENTS

It wasn't so long ago that a few trucks dressed up as floats, stilt walkers and a flat-bed lorry loaded with peat briquettes were all you'd expect of Dublin's St Patrick's Day Parade. If you wanted a bit of festive glamour, New York's famous parade was the place to go. But then came the economic boom and the realisation that the event was a tourist bonanza waiting to happen. Now 17 March is just part of St Patrick's *Festival*, a four-day extravaganza of activities ranging from street theatre to fireworks, all fuelled by lots and lots of booze.

And therein lies the secret to Dubliners' love of festive events: sure, *officially* it's all about celebrating the city's rich cultural heritage, but really it's an excuse to go a little bit mad.

DUBLIN

DUBLIN WITH A DIFFERENCE

Check out the antique incunabula – so old they're not even called books – at Marsh's Library (p101), one of Dublin's least-visited museums, or root around for rare original manuscripts and antique maps in cramped Cathach Books (p79). Break out of the book mode with some comedy in the intimate International Bar (p137) at 9.30pm on Wednesday nights (admission €9). Take a thrillseeker's safari in a speedboat around Dublin bay and its islands from Malahide to Dalkey with **Sea Safaris** (☎ 806 1626; www.seasafari.ie; Malahide Marina; per hr €25), or don your best Edwardian garb and join in the fun on 16 June as the city celebrates Bloomsday (opposite).

The following list is by no means exhaustive; for more details check out the website run by **Dublin Tourism** (www.visitdublin.com). For information on special events in Ireland as a whole, see p706.

Temple Bar Trad Festival (☎ 677 2397; www .templebartrad.com) Traditional music festival in the bars of the cultural quarter over the last weekend in January.

Jameson Dublin International Film Festival (☎ 872 1122; www.dubliniff.com) Local flicks, arty international films and advance releases of mainstream movies make up the menu of the city's film festival, which runs over two weeks in late February.

St Patrick's Festival (☎ 676 3205; www.stpatricks festival.ie) The mother of all festivals; hundreds of thousands gather to 'honour' St Patrick over four days around 17 March on city streets and in venues.

Heineken Green Energy Festival (☎ 1890 925 100; www.mcd.ie) Four-day rock and indie music festival based outside Dublin Castle and in adjacent venues in May.

Convergence Festival (☎ 674 6415; www .sustainable.ie; 15-19 Essex St) Ten-day green festival in late June on sustainable living, with a diverse programme of workshops, exhibitions and children's activities.

Diversions (☎ 677 2255; www.temple-bar.ie) Free outdoor music, children's and film events at weekends from June to September in Temple Bar's Meeting House Sq.

Dun Laoghaire Festival of World Cultures (☎ 271 9555; www.festivalofworldcultures.com) Colourful multicultural music, art and theatre festival on the last weekend of August.

Oxegen (www.mcd.ie) Two-day gig in mid-July at Punchestown Racecourse with heavyweight headline acts.

Liffey Swim (☎ 833 2434) Five hundred lunatics swim 2.5km from Rory O'More Bridge to the Custom House in late July – one can't but admire their steel will.

Dublin Theatre Festival (☎ 677 8439; www .dublintheatrefestival.com) Well-established international theatre festival over a fortnight in late September.

Dublin Fringe Festival (☎ 872 9016; www.fringefest .com) Comedy and alternative fringe theatre from late September to early October.

SLEEPING

Dublin is one of Europe's more expensive cities to sleep in and, unfortunately, until you reach the upper price brackets, you're not always getting great value for money. Dublin's tourism boom also means that in high season, from around May to September, getting the room you want at a reasonable price can be a challenge. Always book ahead unless you're happy to stay out in the sticks and grapple with a two-hour traffic-choked journey into town. On the upside though, new hotels are springing up all the time, thanks in part to the city's licensing laws that allow canny business folk to obtain a lucrative bar licence if a requisite number of rooms are attached.

The addition of the Luas tram line in 2004 has made the suburban hotels more accessible, so if you can't find central accommodation (the obvious choice for the short-term visitor) a suburban hotel is an option worth considering. Not surprisingly, accommodation south of the Liffey is pricier than that on the northside. While some good deals can be found on the northside, most bargains are in less than salubrious areas around Gardiner and Dorset Sts.

With prices, it's not just quality that counts, but position: for instance, a large-roomed comfortable B&B in the northside suburbs may cost you as little as €50 per person, while the owners of a small, mediocre guesthouse within walking distance of Stephen's Green won't balk at asking €100 for the box room. A quality guesthouse or midrange hotel can cost anything from €80 to €200, while the city's top accommodation doesn't get interested for less than €200. At the other end of the scale there are the ubiquitous hostels, the bedrock of cheap accommodation; the standards have uniformly gone up but so have the prices, and a bed will cost anything from €18 to as much as €34. (Note that hostel rates don't include breakfast; exceptions are noted.)

And then the good news. Many hotels have a weekend or B&B rate that can save you as

BLOOMSDAY

It's 16 June. There's a bunch of weirdos wandering around the city dressed in Edwardian gear talking nonsense in dramatic tones. They're not mad – at least not clinically – they're only Bloomsdayers committed to commemorating James Joyce's epic *Ulysses*, which anyone familiar with the book will tell you (and that doesn't necessarily mean that they've *read* the bloody thing) takes place over the course of one day. What they mightn't be able to tell you is that Leopold Bloom's latter-day odyssey takes place on 16 June 1904 because it was on that day that Joyce first 'stepped out' with Nora Barnacle, the woman he had met six days earlier and with whom he would spend the rest of his life. (When James' father heard about this new love he commented that with a name like that she would surely stick to him.)

Although Ireland treated Joyce like a literary pornographer while he was alive, the country (and especially Dublin) can't get enough of him today. Bloomsday is a slightly gimmicky and touristy phenomenon that appeals almost exclusively to Joyce fanatics and tourists, but it's plenty of fun and a great way to lay the groundwork for actually reading what could be the second-hardest book written in the 20th century (the hardest, of course, being Joyce's follow-up blockbuster *Finnegan's Wake*, the greatest book *never* to be read).

In general, events are designed to follow Bloom's progress around town, and in recent years festivities have expanded to continue over four days around 16 June. On Bloomsday proper you can kick things off with breakfast at the James Joyce Cultural Centre (p106), where the 'inner organs of beast and fowl' come accompanied by celebratory readings.

In the morning, guided tours of Joycean sites usually leave from the general post office (p104) and the James Joyce Cultural Centre. Lunch-time activity focuses on **Davy Byrne's** (Map p132 Duke St), Joyce's 'moral pub', where Bloom paused to dine on a glass of Burgundy and a slice of Gorgonzola. Street entertainers are likely to keep you amused through the afternoon as you take guided walks and watch animated readings from *Ulysses* and Joyce's other books; there's a reading at **Ormond Quay Hotel** (Map p84; Ormond Quay) at 4pm and **Harrisons** (Map p84; Westmoreland St) later in the day.

Events also take place in the days leading up to and following Bloomsday. The best source of information about what's on in any particular year is likely to be the James Joyce Cultural Centre or the free *Dublin Event Guide*, close to the date.

---

much as 40% on the rack rate; others offer similar discounts for midweek stays. There are also great savings if you book online (see Booking Services, p118). These rates are generally available year-round, but are tougher to find during the high season.

Trinity College & Around

You can't get more central than the relatively small patch of real estate just south of the Liffey, which has a good mix of options ranging from backpacker hostels to the fanciest hotels. Bear in mind that the location comes with a price.

BUDGET

Ashfield House (Map p84; ☎ 679 7734; www.ashfieldhouse.ie; 19-20 D'Olier St; dm/s/d from €13/58/102; 🖳) A stone's throw from Temple Bar and O'Connell Bridge, this modern hostel in a converted church has a selection of tidy four- and six-bed rooms, one large dorm

and 25 en-suite private rooms. It is more like a small hotel but without the price tag. A continental-style breakfast is included – a rare beast indeed for hostels. Maximum stay is six nights.

Avalon House (Map p86; ☎ 475 0001; www.avalonhouse.ie; 55 Aungier St; dm/s/d €18/32/64; 🖳) Before there was tourism, this hostel in a gorgeous Victorian building catered to the thin trickle of adventurers who landed in Dublin. They flood in these days – book ahead – but Avalon still takes good care of them, whether they are young backpackers or families. The lounges are great for hanging out and there's free wi-fi.

Barnacles Temple Bar House (Map p84; ☎ 671 6277; www.barnacles.ie; 19 Lower Temple Lane; dm/d from €18.50/40; 🖳) Bright, spacious and set in the heart of Temple Bar, this hostel is immaculately clean, and has nicely laid-out en-suite dorms and doubles with in-room storage. Because of its location, rooms are quieter

DUBLIN

BOOKING SERVICES

If you arrive without accommodation, staff at Dublin Tourism's walk-in booking offices will find you a room for €4 plus a 10% deposit.

If you want to book a hotel from elsewhere in Ireland or abroad, the easiest way is to go through Gulliver Info Res, Dublin Tourism's computerised reservations service, via their website www.visitdublin.com, or book directly yourself from the accommodation's own website. See p89 for a list of Dublin Tourism offices and Gulliver contact numbers.

Internet bookings made in advance are your best bet for deals on accommodation. These are just a handful of services that will get you a room at a competitive rate:

All Dublin Hotels (www.all-dublin-hotels.com)
Dublin City Centre Hotels (http://dublin.city-centre-hotels.com)
Dublin Hotels (www.dublinhotels.com)
Go Ireland (www.goireland.com)
Hostel Dublin (www.hosteldublin.com)
Under 99 (www.under99.com)

See p695 for more options, or try www.lonelyplanet.com/accommodation.

---

towards the back. Top facilities, a comfy lounge, and linen and towels are provided.

Kinlay House (Map p84; ☎ 679 6644; www.kinlay house.ie; 2-12 Lord Edward St; dm/d from €19/34; ☐) A former boarding house for boys, this busy hostel has some massive, 24-bed mixed dorms, as well as smaller rooms. Not for the faint hearted – the hostel has a reputation for being a bit of a party spot.

MIDRANGE

Grafton House (Map p86; ☎ 679 2041; www .graftonguesthouse.com; 26-27 South Great George's St; s/d from €55/110) Run by those hip folks down at the Globe bar (p133), this heritage-building hotel has 17 en-suite rooms that have been whipped into bright and funky shape. Expect contemporary fittings, stylish walnut furniture, retro wallpaper and all mod must-haves, including data ports and veggie breakfasts, at a fine price.

Dublin Citi Hotel (Map p84; ☎ 679 4455; www.dublin citihotel.com; 46-49 Dame St; s/d Sun-Thu from €79/89, Fri-Sat €120/159) An unusual turreted 19th-century building is home to this cheap and cheerful hotel. Rooms aren't huge but are simply furnished and have fresh white duvets. Prices are reasonable considering it's only a stagger (literally) from Temple Bar. Hic.

Albany House (Map pp82-3; ☎ 475 1092; www .albanyhousedublin.com; 84 Harcourt St; s/d from €80/140) We don't mind that this city-centre gem is a little dog-eared in places because it feels like a genuine Georgian Dublin home. Albany House is spread over three houses and still has its origi-

nal features and incredible plasterwork intact. Opt for bright, tastefully furnished modern rooms, or bigger original rooms complete with antique furniture. Excellent value.

Drury Court Hotel (Map p86; ☎ 475 1988; www.drury courthotel.com; 28-30 Lower Stephen St; s/d from €85/130; ☐) Centrally located with rooms primarily aimed at the business traveller, the Drury Court is a good choice if you're not looking to be inspired by your surroundings, but still fancy a good night's kip in comfort.

Mercer Hotel (Map p86; ☎ 478 2179; www.mercer hotel.ie; Lower Mercer St; s/d from €99/160) A fairly plain frontage hides a pretty decent hotel; largish rooms are dressed in antiques, giving the whole place an elegant, classic look. There is a dizzying array of room deals available; the off-peak rates are sensational.

Central Hotel (Map p86; ☎ 679 7302; www.central hotel.ie; 1-5 Exchequer St; s/d from €100/135) The rooms are a little snug for the grand Edwardian-style décor, but it's still a classy joint – no more so than in the wonderful 1st-floor Library Bar, all leather armchairs and sofas, and nothing short of one of the finest spots for an afternoon drink in the whole city. Location-wise, the name says it all.

our pick Number 31 (Map p80; ☎ 676 5011; www .number31.ie; 31 Leeson Close; s/d/t from €120/175/230) This place could be a set from the film *The Ice Storm*. The former home of modernist architect Sam Stephenson (of Central Bank fame) still feels like a real 1960s home, with its sunken sitting room, leather sofas, mirrored bar and Perspex lamps. Its 21 bedrooms are

---

TOP FIVE SLEEPS

■ Best B&B – Grafton House (opposite)

■ Best boutique hotel – Number 31 (opposite)

■ Best budget sleep – Isaacs Hostel (p121)

■ Best luxury hotel – Merrion (p120)

■ Best view – Clarence Hotel (p120)

---

split between the chichi coach house and the more gracious Georgian house, where rooms are individually furnished with French antiques and big beds. Gourmet breakfasts are served in the conservatory. Children under 10 are not permitted.

Paramount Hotel (Map p84; ☎ 417 9900; www .paramounthotel.ie; cnr Parliament St & Essex Gate; s/d €120/240) Behind the Victorian façade, the Paramount's lobby is a faithful re-creation of a 1930s hotel, complete with dark-wood floors, leather chesterfield couches and heavy velvet drapes. The 70-odd rooms don't quite bring *The Maltese Falcon* to mind, but they're handsomely furnished and very comfortable.

Morgan Hotel (Map p84; ☎ 679 3939; www.the morgan.com; 10 Fleet St; r from €140; 🖳) Designer cool can often be designer cold, but the hypertrendy Morgan falls on the right side of the line – but only just. The look is all-cream contemporary (nothing too exceptional), but the facilities are top rate. Aromatherapy treatments and massages are extra, as is breakfast (€18).

Trinity Lodge (Map p86; ☎ 617 0900; www .trinitylodge.com; 12 South Frederick St; s/d from €140/180) Martin Sheen's grin greets you on entering this cosy, award-winning guesthouse. Not that he's ditched movies for hospitality: he just enjoyed his stay (and full Irish breakfast, presumably) at this classically refurbished Georgian pad so much that he let them take a mugshot. Room 2 has a lovely bay window.

La Stampa (Map p86; ☎ 677 4444; www.lastampa .ie; 35 Dawson St; r weekday/weekend €160/200; 🖳) La Stampa is an atmospheric little hotel on trendy Dawson St, with 29 Asian-influenced white rooms decorated with rattan furniture and exotic velvet throws. It has just added an Ayurvedic spa, but to fully benefit from your restorative treatments ask for a top-floor bedroom away from the revelling at SamSara bar (p133), located below.

Irish Landmark Trust (Map p84; ☎ 670 4733; www .irishlandmark.com; 25 Eustace St; 2/3 nights from €620/820) This fabulous heritage 18th-century house has been gloriously restored to the highest standard by the Irish Landmark Trust. You can have this unique house, which sleeps up to seven in its double, twin and triple bedrooms, for two or more nights all to yourself – single nights, alas, are not available. Furnished with tasteful antiques, and authentic furniture and fittings (including a grand piano in the drawing room), this kind of period rental accommodation is unique and utterly special.

TOP END

Westin Dublin (Map p84; ☎ 645 1000; www.westin .com; Westmoreland St; s/d from €184/300; 🅿 🖳) The Westin began life as an Allied Irish Bank, and now uses the old bank vaults and marble counters in its basement Mint Bar. The hotel rooms exude classic American grandeur, with an understated style that includes separate shower and bath, laptop-sized safe and Westin's trademark Heavenly Bed, which has 10 luxurious layers to envelop you. Ask to take a look at the beautiful banqueting hall, in the former banking area, with its exquisite ceiling and gold-leaf plasterwork. Breakfast will set you back €25.

Browne's Townhouse (Map p86; ☎ 638 3939; www.brownesdublin.com; 22 North St Stephen's Green; s/d from €195/250; 🖳) This is an exquisite Georgian building in a perfect location. Above a reputable restaurant are 11 superb, individually styled bedrooms, each the height of comfort and elegance. It's a little bit of

---

UNIVERSITY ACCOMMODATION

From mid-June to late September, you can stay in accommodation provided by the city's universities. Be sure to book well in advance.

Trinity College (Map p91; ☎ 608 1177; www.tcd.ie; Accommodations Office, Trinity College; s/d from €35/70; 🖳) Comfortable rooms ranging from basic to en suite in one of the most atmospheric settings in Dublin.

Mercer Court (Map p86; ☎ 478 2179; reservations@mercercourt.ie; Lower Mercer St; r from €99; 🖳) Owned and run by the Royal College of Surgeons, Mercer Court has modern rooms that are up to hotel standard.

HOME AWAY FROM HOME

Self-catering apartments are a good option for visitors staying a few days, for groups of friends, or families with kids. Apartments range from one-room studios to two-bed flats with lounge areas, and include bathrooms and kitchenettes. A decent two-bedroom apartment will cost about €100 to €150 per night. Good, central places include the following:

Clarion Stephen's Hall (Map pp82-3; ☎ 638 1111; www.premierapartmentsdublin.com; 14-17 Lower Leeson St) Deluxe studios and suites, with in-room safe, fax, modem facilities and CD player.

Home From Home Apartments (Map p80; ☎ 678 1100; www.yourhomefromhome.com; The Moorings, Fitzwilliam Quay) Deluxe one- to three-bedroom apartments in the southside city centre.

Latchfords (Map p86; ☎ 676 0784; www.latchfords.ie; 99-100 Lower Baggot St) Studios and two-bedroom flats in a Georgian town house.

Oliver St John Gogarty's Penthouse Apartments (Map p84; ☎ 671 1822; www.gogartys.ie; 18-21 Anglesea St) Perched high atop the pub of the same name (p132), these one- to three-bedroom places have views of Temple Bar.

18th-century elegance updated to suit the needs of the 21st.

Westbury Hotel (Map p86; ☎ 679 1122; www .jurysdoyle.com; Grafton St; s/d/ste from €210/245/750; P ☐) Visiting celebs looking for some quiet time have long favoured the West-bury's elegant suites, where they can watch TV from the Jacuzzi before retiring to a four-poster bed. Mere mortals tend to make do with the standard rooms, which are comfortable enough but lack the sophisticated grandeur promised by the luxurious public spaces.

Shelbourne (Map p86; ☎ 676 6471; www.the shelbourne.ie; 27 North St Stephen's Green; r from €255; P ☐) Two years and many millions later, a sorely missed old friend has returned and the city's most iconic hotel is once again the best address in town. The rooms have all been given a thorough going over, the public spaces have rediscovered their grandeur, and afternoon tea in the Lord Mayor's Lounge is still one of the best experiences in town.

Clarence Hotel (Map p84; ☎ 407 0800; www.the clarence.ie; 6-8 Wellington Quay; r €350-380, ste €720-2600; ☐) Dublin's coolest hotel is synonymous with its rock-star owners, Bono and the Edge, so it's hardly surprising that it is used to dealing with celebrity heavyweights. The 50-odd rooms aren't short on style, but they lack that grandeur you would expect from a top hotel; a top-to-bottom refurb is on the cards, though, so it may be closed by the time you get here.

Merrion (Map p86; ☎ 603 0600; www.merrionhotel .com; Upper Merrion St; r from €470; P ☐ ☎) This is a resplendent five-star hotel set in a ter-

race of beautifully restored Georgian town houses. Try to get a room in the old house (which has the largest private art collection in the city) rather than the newer wing to sample the hotel's truly elegant comforts. Located opposite government buildings, its marble corridors are patronised by visiting dignitaries and the odd celeb. Even if you don't stay, come for the superb afternoon tea (€32), with endless cups of tea served out of silver pots near a raging fire.

The Liberties & Kilmainham

There is not that much on offer in this part of town, but the following exception is pretty convenient.

Jurys Inn Christchurch (Map p84; ☎ 454 0000; www.jurysinns.com; Christchurch Pl; r from €97) A chain hotel that's so generic you may wake up not knowing if you're in Detroit or Darmstadt, let alone Dublin, but it's the perfect choice if you a) wish to remain anonymous, b) don't want to be troubled by personal service, or c) get a fantastic deal online and just want a place to sleep it off.

O'Connell Street & Around

There are a few elegant hotels around O'Connell St, but the real draw round these parts is just to the east on Gardiner St, Dublin's B&B row. Caveat emptor, however: as well as some excellent B&Bs, there are some bad choices; here we only include ones we feel are the former. The further north you go, the dodgier the neighbourhood gets – that heady inner-city mix of drugs and crime – so stay alert, especially past Mountjoy Sq on Upper Gardiner St.

BUDGET

Marlborough Hostel (Map pp82-3; ☎ 874 7629; www
.marlboroughhostel.com; 81-82 Marlborough St; dm/d from
€13/58; 🖳) Next to the Pro-Cathedral, this
well-located hostel has 76 beds and adequate
facilities. High Georgian ceilings make up
for small rooms, but the slightly run-down
showers in the basement are a bit of a trek
from the dorms.

Isaacs Hostel (Map pp82-3; ☎ 855 6215; www.isaacs
.ie; 2-5 Frenchman's Lane; dm/d from €14/62; 🖳) Located
in a 200-year-old wine vault, this popular,
grungy hostel with loads of character is the
place to head if you want one of the cheapest
beds in town – without sacrificing the basics of health and hygiene. The lounge area is
where it all happens, from summer BBQs to
live music, and the easygoing staff are on hand
24/7 for advice and help. Global nomads will
feel right at home.

Litton Lane Hostel (Map p84; ☎ 872 8389; www
.irish-hostel.com; 2-4 Litton Lane; dm/d from €15/70) True
to its origins as a dog-eared recording stu-
dio (once patronised by Van Morrison), this
friendly hostel could do with a lick of paint
but retains a certain grungy charm. Dorms
are mixed, and so are the showers, which all
kind of lends new meaning to its motto 'Don't
Sleep Around; Sleep with Us'.

Abbey Court Hostel (Map p84; ☎ 878 0700; www
.abbey-court.com; 29 Bachelor's Walk; dm/d €22/88; 🖳)
Spread over two buildings on the Liffey quays,
this large, well-run hostel has 33 clean dorms
with good storage. En-suite doubles are in the
newer building, where a light breakfast is also
provided in the café Juice.

MIDRANGE & TOP END

Anchor Guesthouse (Map pp82-3; ☎ 878 6913; www
.anchorguesthouse.com; 49 Lower Gardiner St; s/d from
€55/75) Most B&Bs round these parts offer
pretty much the same sorts of things: TVs,
tea- and coffee-making facilities, a half-
decent shower and clean linen. The Anchor
does all of that, but it has an elegance you
won't find in many of the other B&Bs along
this stretch. This lovely Georgian guesthouse,
with its delicious wholesome breakfasts,
comes highly recommended by readers.
They're dead right.

Lyndon House (Map pp82-3; ☎ 878 6950; 26 Gardiner
Pl; s/d from €60/100) There are seven simple en-
suite rooms and two small standard rooms
in this modestly furnished but very friendly
Georgian house.

Townhouse (Map pp82-3; ☎ 878 8808; www
.townhouseofdublin.com; 47-48 Lower Gardiner St; s/d/tr
from €70/115/132) The ghostly writing of Irish-
Japanese author Lafcadio Hearn may have
influenced the Gothic-style interior of his
former home. A dark-walled, gilt-framed
foyer with a jingling chandelier leads into
82 individually designed, comfy rooms.
Some rooms in the new wing at the back are
larger with balconies overlooking the small
Japanese garden.

Castle Hotel (Map pp82-3; ☎ 874 6949; www.castle
-hotel.ie; 3-4 Great Denmark St; s/d/tr from €75/115/145)
In business since 1809, the Castle may be
slightly rough around the edges but it's one
of the most pleasant hotels this side of the
Liffey. The fabulous *palazzo*-style grand
staircase leads to the 50-odd bedrooms,
whose furnishings are traditional and a tad
antiquated but perfectly good; check out
the original Georgian cornicing around the
high ceilings.

Walton's Hotel (Map pp82-3; ☎ 878 3131; www
.waltons-hotel.ie; 2-5 North Frederick St; s/d/tr €80/120/160)
Better known for its legendary musical in-
strument shop next door, this friendly hotel
was opened by the Walton family in an effort
to preserve the traditional Georgian heritage
of the building. With the help of the Castle Hotel it's done just that. The 43 rooms
are clean and spacious: with a superb location overlooking Findlater's Church and the
Rotunda Hospital, Walton's is an excellent
choice. Children under 12 stay for free.

Lynham's Hotel (Map pp82-3; ☎ 888 0886;
www.lynams-hotel.com; 63-64 O'Connell St; s/d/tr from
€85/130/170) A midrange hotel smack in the
middle of O'Connell St is almost too good
to be true. Now that Dublin's premier street
is halfway back to its glorious best, Lynham's becomes a rare gem indeed – a smart,
friendly hotel with 42 pleasant rooms decorated in country-style pine furniture. Room
41 is a lovely dormer triple with an additional camp bed – handy for groups who
want to share. Ask for discounts midweek.

Browns Hotel (Map pp82-3; ☎ 855 0034; www
.dublin-hotel.net; 80-90 Lower Gardiner St; s/d €89/115) The
22 rooms fill up pretty quickly at this small
hotel, whose popularity is cemented by neat
and tidy rooms replete with modern furnishings. Book early.

Gresham Hotel (Map pp82-3; ☎ 874 6881; www
.gresham-hotels.com; Upper O'Connell St; r €200, ste €450-
2500; 🖳) A city landmark and one of Dublin's

oldest hotels, the Gresham shed its traditional granny's parlour look with a major overhaul some years ago. Despite its brighter, smarter, modern appearance and a fabulous open-plan foyer, its loyal clientele – elderly groups on shopping breaks to the capital and well-heeled Americans – has stuck firmly. Rooms are spacious and well serviced, though the décor is a little brash.

Smithfield & Phoenix Park

It's still an area in development, but Smithfield – especially along the quays – is a good spot to stay as it's close to all the action.

Comfort Inn Smithfield (Map pp82-3; ☎ 485 0900; www.comfortinndublincity.com; Smithfield Village; r €130-150) This modern hotel, with big bedrooms and plenty of earth tones to soften the contemporary edges, is your best bet in this part of town. We loved the floor-to-ceiling windows – great for checking out what's going on below in the square.

Morrison Hotel (Map p84; ☎ 887 2400; www.morrisonhotel.ie; Lower Ormond Quay; r €285-580, ste €1400; 🖵) The Morrison recently upped the ante in the 'hip hotel' stakes with the addition of 48 new bedrooms in the adjoining former printworks. Fashion designer John Rocha's loosely Oriental style is still evident in the Zen-like furnishings, but extras such as Apple Mac plasma screens, iPod docking stations and Aveda goodies clinch it for us. For a few quid extra, nab a far superior studio den in the new wing; there's a balcony and enough space to throw a party.

Beyond the Royal Canal

The Royal Canal winds its way through the leafy suburb of Drumcondra, about 3km east of Upper O'Connell St along Dorset St. There are B&Bs aplenty here, most of which are in late-Victorian or Edwardian beauties that are generally extremely well kept and comfortable. As they're on the airport road, they tend to be full virtually all year, so advance booking is recommended. Buses 3, 11, 11A, 16 and 36A from Trinity College and O'Connell St all stop along the Drumcondra Rd.

Charleville Lodge (☎ 838 6633; www.charlevillelodge.ie; 268-272 North Circular Rd, Phibsboro; s/d from €45/64; Ⓟ) Made up of a terraced row of houses that is the height of 19th-century Victorian elegance and luxury, Charleville is a great option just outside the city centre. The owners love old stuff (the house is full of gorgeous antiques) but are

far from old and stuffy and give proper credence to the old cliché of a 'home away from home'. Take Bus 10 from O'Connell St.

Griffith House (☎ 837 5030; www.griffithhouse.com; 125 Griffith Ave; s €50, d with/without bathroom €80/70) This elegant house, on a beautiful, tree-lined avenue, has four double rooms, three of them with en suite. Each room is tastefully appointed, with large, comfortable beds and nice furniture.

Tinode House (☎ 837 2277; www.tinodehouse.com; 170 Upper Drumcondra Rd; s/d €54/78) This comfortable Edwardian town house has four elegant bedrooms. A familial welcome and excellent breakfast are part of the package.

Beyond the Grand Canal

The south city suburb of Ballsbridge is full of quality hotels and guesthouses that generally offer more for your euro than the city centre. Bus 5, 7, 7A, 8, 18 or 45 will get you there in about 10 minutes, or it's a 30-minute walk. Also worth checking out is the increasingly gentrified suburb of Ranelagh, accessible from the city centre via the Luas, the light-rail system.

MIDRANGE

Sandford Townhouse (Map p80; ☎ 412 6880; 52 Sandford Rd, Ranelagh; s/d €50/70; Ⓟ) An elegant Victorian home with three large and comfortable rooms, the town house is within a short walking distance of the Luas, making it a convenient hop to and from the city centre.

Waterloo House (Map p80; ☎ 660 1888; www.waterloohouse.ie; 8-10 Waterloo Rd, Ballsbridge; s/d €65/118; Ⓟ) A short walk from St Stephen's Green, this lovely guesthouse is spread over two ivy-clad Georgian houses off Baggot St. Rooms are tastefully decorated with high-quality furnishings in authentic Farrow & Ball Georgian colours, and all have cable TV and kettles. Home-cooked breakfast is served in the conservatory or in the garden on sunny days.

Ariel House (Map p80; ☎ 668 5512; www.ariel-house.net; 52 Lansdowne Rd, Ballsbridge; r from €99; Ⓟ) Somewhere between a boutique hotel and a luxury B&B, this highly rated Victorian-era property has 28 en-suite rooms, all individually decorated in period furniture, which lends the place an air of genuine luxury. A far better choice than most hotels.

Pembroke Townhouse (Map p80; ☎ 660 0277; www.pembroketownhouse.ie; 90 Pembroke Rd, Ballsbridge; s €90-

165, d €100-210; (P)) This superluxurious town house is a perfect example of what happens when traditional and modern combine to great effect. A classical Georgian house has been transformed into a superb boutique hotel, with each room carefully crafted and appointed to reflect the best of contemporary design and style, right down to the modern art on the walls and the handy lift to the upper floors. May we borrow your designer?

Schoolhouse Hotel (Map p80; ☎ 667 5014; www .schoolhousehotel.com; 2-8 Northumberland Rd, Ballsbridge; s/d from €169/199; (P)) This is a real beauty: a converted Victorian schoolhouse that is now a superb boutique hotel with 31 exquisite rooms, each named after an Irish writer, and stocked with luxury toiletries and all sorts of modern amenities. A place ahead of its – ahem – class.

TOP END

Herbert Park Hotel (Map p80; ☎ 667 2200; www .herbertparkhotel.ie; Merrion Rd, Ballsbridge; s/d from €230/270; (P)(🖳)) This upmarket hotel, southeast of the city centre, caters mainly to business travellers. Its décor is firmly traditional, while rooms are kitted out to the highest standard and offer every modern amenity. Check the website for special offers – at the time of writing, rooms were selling for less than half the quoted rate.

Four Seasons (Map p80; ☎ 665 4000; www.fourseasons .com; Simmonscourt Rd, Ballsbridge; r from €295; (P)(🖳)(🐾)) The muscular, no-holds-barred style of American corporate innkeeping is in full force at this huge hotel that has sought to raise the hospitality bar. Its OTT mix of styles – anyone for faux Victorian Georgian with a bit of baroque thrown in for good measure? – has its critics, but there's no denying the sheer quality of the place. The spa is superb, and the lit basement pool a treat. For many, this is the best hotel in town. We're suckers for a slightly more demure luxury, so we'll stick it in the top three. It is in the grounds of the Royal Dublin Society Showground.

EATING

A couple of decades ago, eating out was the sole preserve of the idle rich, the business lunch and the very special occasion. Which was kind of handy, as there were literally only a handful of decent restaurants to choose from. These days, Dublin has more restaurants than

it knows what to do with and a population that has made fashion out of food to the point that, for many, you aren't what you eat but *where* you eat. You can still eat French (and Irish) *haute cuisine* any night of the week, but you'll also find Nepalese, Brazilian and pretty much everything in between.

Restaurateurs have finally twigged that not every meal has to be a once-a-year splurge and that wallet-friendly menus mean more turnover. They're happy and we're happy. Cropping up all over Dublin are mid-priced restaurants that offer very good food at competitive prices and keep crimes against the palate to a minimum.

The most concentrated restaurant area is Temple Bar, but apart from a handful of good places, the bulk of eateries offer bland, unimaginative fodder and cheap set menus for tourists. Better food and service can usually be found on either side of Grafton St, while the top-end restaurants are clustered around Merrion Sq and Fitzwilliam Sq. Fast-food chains dominate the northside, though some fine cafés and eateries are finally appearing there too. The area around Parnell St, in particular, is worth checking out for the spate of new exotic restaurants – a reflection of the increasingly diverse ethnic communities that have settled in the area.

Ireland has excellent beef, pork, seafood, dairy foods and winter vegetables, and many good restaurants now source their ingredients locally from organic and artisan producers.

For many restaurants, particularly those in the centre, it's worth booking for Friday or Saturday nights to ensure a table.

Trinity College & Around

If you spent your whole time in this area you would eat pretty well; the south city centre is the hub of the best the city has to offer.

BUDGET

Listons (Map p80; ☎ 405 4779; 25 Camden St; lunch €3-8; ⏰ 8.30am-7.30pm Mon-Thu, to 6.30pm Fri, 10am-6pm Sat) Lunchtime queues out the door testify that Listons is undoubtedly the best deli in Dublin. Its sandwiches with delicious fillings, roasted vegetable quiches, rosemary potato cakes and sublime salads will have you coming back again and again. The only problem is there's too much to choose from. On fine days it's great to retreat to the

DUBLIN

solitude of the nearby Iveagh Gardens with your gourmet picnic.

Lemon (Map p86; pancakes from €3.75; 9am-7pm Mon-Sat, 10am-6pm Sun) South William St (672 9044; 66 South William St); Dawson St (672 8898; 61 Dawson St) Dublin's first (and best) pancake joint is staffed by a terrific bunch who like their music loud and their pancakes good: proper paper-thin sweet and savoury crepes smothered, stuffed and sprinkled with a variety of toppings, fillings and sauces. There's a second branch on nearby Dawson St.

Queen of Tarts (Map p84; 670 7499; Lord Edward St; goods from €4; 7am-6pm) Pocket-sized Queen of Tarts is the mother of all bakery-cafés with its mouth-watering array of savoury tarts and filled focaccias, fruit crumbles and wicked pastries. It's perfect for breakfast or lunch – if it's full you can take-away to the quiet Chester Beatty garden across the road.

Cake Café (Map p80; 633 4477; Pleasant Pl; mains €4-8; 10am-6pm) Dublin's best-kept pastry secret is this great little café in a tough-to-find lane just off Camden St. The easiest way in is through Daintree stationery shop (61 Camden St); through the back of the Daintree is the self-contained yard, which in good weather is the best spot to enjoy a coffee and a homemade cake.

our pick **Gruel** (Map p84; 670 7119; 68a Dame St; breakfast €4, lunch €4.50-8, brunch €5-12, dinner mains €9-15; 7am-9.30pm Mon-Fri, 10.30am-10.30pm Sat & Sun) For its ever growing list of devotees, Gruel is the best dish in town, whether it's for the superfilling, tasty lunchtime roast-in-a-roll – a rotating list of slow-roasted organic meats stuffed into a bap and flavoured with homemade relishes – or the exceptional evening menu, where pasta, fish and chicken are given an exotic once-over. Go, queue and share elbow space with the table behind you: it's worth the effort. It doesn't accept bookings.

Simon's Place (Map p86; 679 7821; George's St Arcade, South Great George's St; mains from €4.50; 9am-5.30pm Mon-Sat) Simon hasn't had to change the menu of doorstep sandwiches and wholesome vegetarian soups since he first opened shop two decades ago – and why should he? His grub is as heartening and legendary as he is. It's a great place to sip a coffee and watch life go by in the old-fashioned arcade.

Larder (Map p84; 633 3581; 8 Parliament St; mains €6; 8am-6pm) This new caff has a positively organic vibe to it, what with its wholesome porridge breakfasts, gourmet sandwiches such

---

TOP FIVE BITES

- Best budget eats – Gruel (left)
- Best brunch – Odessa (p127)
- Best sandwich to go – Bottega Toffoli (below)
- Best lunch – L'Gueuleton (p126)
- Best splurge – Town Bar & Grill (p128)

---

as *serrano* ham, gruyere and rocket, and speciality Suki teas (try the China gunpowder). It's confident about its food – we like the fact that it lists suppliers – and so are we.

Honest to Goodness (Map p86; 677 5373; George's St Arcade; mains €6; 9am-6pm Mon-Sat, noon-4pm Sun) A devastating fire kept this wonderful café under wraps for much of 2007, but it finally reopened and went back about the business of dispensing wholesome sandwiches, imaginative breakfasts and homemade soups and smoothies. Add to that delicious home-baked goodies and Fairtrade coffee, all at rock-bottom prices…niiice.

Fallon & Byrne (Map p86; 472 1000; Exchequer St; deli mains €6-9, brasserie mains €17-28; deli 9am-8pm Mon-Sat, 11am-6pm Sun, brasserie noon-4.30pm & 6.30-10.30pm Mon-Wed, to 11.30pm Thu-Sat, 11am-4pm Sun) The much anticipated opening of an upmarket food hall, wine cellar and restaurant in the style of New York's Dean & Deluca caused a great stir among Dublin's food cognoscenti mid-2006. The queues for the delicious deli counter are constant, while the chic buzzy brasserie upstairs hasn't failed to impress either, with long red banquettes, a diverse menu of creamy fish pie, beef carpaccio and roast turbot, and excellent service.

Bar Italia (Map p84; 679 5128; 4 Essex Quay; lunch €7-10; 8am-6pm Mon-Fri, 9am-6pm Sat, noon-6pm Sun) One of a new generation of eateries that's showing the more established Italian restaurants how the Old Country *really* eats, Bar Italia is a favourite with the lunchtime crowd, who come for the ever changing pasta dishes, homemade risottos and excellent Palombini coffee.

Bottega Toffoli (Map p84; 633 4022; 34 Castle St; sandwiches & salads €8-11; 10am-6pm Tue-Sat) Tucked away in the city centre (to the point that you would never find it unless you actually looked for it) is this superb Italian café, home of one of the best sandwiches you'll eat in town:

VEGGIE BUDGET BITES

Blazing Salads (Map p86; ☎ 671 9552; 42 Drury St; mains €3.50-8.50; ☼ 10am-6pm Mon-Sat, to 8pm Thu) Organic breads (many suitable for special diets), Californian-style salads, smoothies and pizza slices can all be taken away from this delicious vegetarian deli.

Fresh (Map p86; ☎ 671 9552; top fl, Powerscourt Townhouse Shopping Centre, 59 South William St; lunch €5-9; ☼ 9.30am-6pm Mon-Sat, 10am-5pm Sun) This long-standing vegetarian restaurant serves a variety of salads and filling hot daily specials. Many dishes are dairy- and gluten-free without compromising on taste. The baked potato topped with organic cheese (€5.50) comes with two salads and is a hearty meal in itself.

Cornucopia (Map p86; ☎ 677 7583; 19 Wicklow St; mains from €6; ☼ 9am-7pm Mon-Wed & Fri-Sat, to 9pm Thu) For those escaping the Irish cholesterol habit, Cornucopia is a popular wholefood café turning out healthy goodies. There's even a hot vegetarian breakfast as an alternative to muesli.

Govinda's (Map p86; ☎ 475 0309; 4 Aungier St; mains €6-11; ☼ noon-9pm) Authentic beans-and-pulses vegetarian place run by the Hare Krishna, now with branches on both sides of the river (at 83 Middle Abbey St; also open noon to 9pm). The cheap, wholesome mix of salads and Indian-influenced hot daily specials are filling and tasty.

---

beautifully cut prosciutto, baby tomatoes and rocket salad drizzled with imported olive oil, all on homemade *piadina* bread that is just too good to be true.

Dunne & Crescenzi (Map p86; ☎ 677 3815; 14 South Frederick St; mains €9; ☼ 9am-7pm Mon & Tue, to 10pm Wed-Sat) This exceptional Italian eatery delights its regulars with a basic menu of rustic pleasures: *panini*, a single pasta dish and a superb plate of mixed antipastos drizzled in olive oil. The shelves are stacked with wine, the coffee is perfect and the desserts are sinfully good.

MIDRANGE

Good World (Map p86; ☎ 677 2580; 18 South Great George's St; dim sum €4-6, mains €8-22; ☼ 12.30pm-2.30am) A hands-down winner of our best-Chinese-restaurant competition, the Good World has two menus, but to really get the most of this terrific spot, steer well clear of the Western menu and its unimaginative dishes. With listings in two languages, the Chinese menu is packed with dishes and delicacies that keep us coming back for more.

La Maison des Gourmets (Map p86; ☎ 672 7258; 15 Castle Market; mains €5-15; ☼ 8am-7pm Mon-Sat, to 9pm Thu) The city's Francophiles all seem to amass at this tiny French café above a bakery – and for good reason. The menu is small, but the salads, *tartines* (open sandwiches) with daily-special toppings such as roast aubergine and pesto, and plates of charcuterie are divine. It also has a fine range of pastries, baked goodies and herbal teas. You can get a traditional country breakfast of meats, cheeses and warm crusty bread for €12.

Market Bar (Map p86; ☎ 677 4835; Fade St; mains €7-14; ☼ noon-11pm) This one-time sausage factory, now a fashionable watering hole (p133), also has a super kitchen knocking out Spanish tapas and other Iberian-influenced bites. Dishes come in half and full portions, so you can mix and match your dishes and not pig out. Proof that the carvery lunch isn't the height of pub dining.

Avoca Handweavers (Map p84; ☎ 677 4215; 11-13 Suffolk St; mains €8-15) This airy 1st-floor café was one of Dublin's best-kept secrets (because of an absence of any obvious signs) until it was discovered by the Ladies who Lunch. If you can battle your way past the designer shopping bags to a table, you'll relish the simply delicious rustic delights of organic shepherd's pie, roast lamb with couscous, and sumptuous salads. There's also a take-away salad bar and hot counter in the basement. For more information on the handicrafts, see p139.

Juice (Map p86; ☎ 475 7856; 73 South Great George's St; mains €8-16; ☼ noon-10pm Mon-Thu, noon-11pm Fri & Sat, 10am-10pm Sun) A creative vegetarian restaurant, Juice puts an imaginative, California-type spin on all kinds of dishes. The real treat is the selection of fruit smoothies, a delicious and healthy alternative to soft drinks.

Café Bardeli (Map p86; www.cafebardeli.ie; mains €9-13; ☼ 7am-11pm) Grafton St (☎ 672 7720; Bewley's Bldg, Grafton St); South Great George's St (☎ 677 1646; 12-13 South Great George's St) With three branches in the city – including a spectacular one in Dublin's most beloved café, Bewley's of Grafton St – the folks behind Bardeli have hit the nail firmly on the head: great crispy pizzas with imaginative toppings such as spicy lamb and tzatziki, fresh homemade pastas, and salads such as broccoli, feta and chickpea that you'll dream about for days. All in a buzzing atmosphere at prices that won't break the bank. No reservations, so prepare to wait on a busy night. See also p129.

Village (Map p86; ☎ 475 8555; 26 Wexford St; mains €10-15; ☯ noon-8.30pm Mon-Fri & Sun) Forget plain old pub grub: even an accomplished chef would be proud of the menu at Village (p133), one of Dublin's most popular pub venues. How about pan-fried *piri-piri* (chilli) perch with vegetable ratatouille (€14)? A great choice for lunch or early dinner.

Pizza Milano (Map p86; ☎ 670 7744; 38 Dawson St; mains €10-18; ☯ noon-11pm) Pizzas are pretty good in this large but stylish pizza emporium, but what we really like are the free on-site child minders on Sunday between noon and 4.30pm; they'll entertain your little ones while you eat.

Bistro (Map p86; ☎ 671 5430; 4-5 Castle Market; mains €10-19; ☯ noon-10pm) The real draw at this place in summer is its outdoor seating, set on a lively pedestrianised strip behind the George's St Arcade. An excellent menu of fish, pasta and meat specials, a well-stocked wine cellar and efficient service make this the warm-weather choice for alfresco dining.

Peploe's (Map p86; ☎ 676 3144; 16 North St Stephen's Green; mains €10-20; ☯ noon-11pm Mon-Sat) Lots of air kissing and comparing of shopping-bag contents take place at this sophisticated and sumptuous wine bar at one of the fanciest addresses in town. A highly ambitious menu complements the superb wine list.

Yamamori (Map p86; ☎ 475 5001; 71 South Great George's St; mains €10-28; ☯ 12.30pm-11pm) This popular Asian restaurant with long communal tables serves filling noodle- and rice-based staples, as well as sushi. Children are well catered for and service is smart, which is handy for a pre-cinema bite.

Silk Road Cafe (Map p84; ☎ 407 0770; Chester Beatty Library, Dublin Castle; mains around €11; ☯ 11am-4pm Mon-Fri) Museum cafés don't often make you salivate, but this vaguely Middle Eastern–North African–Mediterranean gem is the exception. The menu is about two-thirds veggie, with Greek moussaka and spinach lasagne house specialities complementing the deep-fried chickpeas and hummus starters. For dessert, there's Lebanese baklava and coconut *kataïfi* (angel-hair pastry), or you could opt for the

juiciest dates this side of Tyre. All dishes are halal and kosher.

Clarendon Café Bar (Map p86; ☎ 679 2909; Clarendon St; mains €11-17; ☯ noon-8pm Mon-Sat, to 6pm Sun) The Stokes brothers (of Bang fame; see opposite) have given pub food a go and come up trumps at this place, spread across three stylishly designed floors. The only difference between here and a proper restaurant is that the wait staff won't flinch when you order lager to go with your meal.

Wagamama (Map p86; ☎ 478 2152; South King St; mains €11-18; ☯ 11am-11pm) Production-line rice and noodle dishes served pronto at canteen-style tables mightn't seem like the most inviting way to dine, but boy this food is good. The basement it's served in is surprisingly light and airy – for a place with absolutely no natural light.

El Bahia (Map p86; ☎ 677 0213; 1st fl, 37 Wicklow St; mains €11-20; ☯ 6-11pm Mon-Sat) Dark and sultry, the intimate atmosphere at El Bahia, reputedly Ireland's only Moroccan restaurant, is like that of a desert harem. The food is equally exotic with a range of daily *tagines* (stews), couscous and *bastillas* (pastry stuffed with chicken or fish) to tempt you. The sweet Moroccan coffee brewed with five warming spices is delicious.

Chameleon (Map p84; ☎ 671 0362; 1 Lower Fownes St; mains €12-20; ☯ 6-11pm Tue-Sat, to 10pm Sun) Friendly, characterful and draped in exotic fabrics, Chameleon serves up oodles of noodles and Indonesian classics, including satay, *gado gado* (veggies with peanut sauce), nasi goreng and *mee goreng* (spicy fried noodles). If you can't decide, try the rijsttafel – it's a selection of several dishes and rice.

Toscana (Map p84; ☎ 670 9785; www.toscana.ie; 3 Cork Hill; mains €12-24) A pleasant trattoria decorated in the style of the 'old country,' Toscana serves up Italian classics and adds a few Irish touches – how about following a killer plate of penne with Baileys cheesecake?

L'Gueuleton (Map p86; ☎ 675 3708; 1 Fade St; mains €12-25; ☯ noon-3pm & 6-11.30pm Mon-Sat) Dubliners have a devil of a time pronouncing the name (which means 'the Gluttonous Feast' in French) and have had their patience tested with the no-reservations, get-in-line-and-wait policy, but they just can't get enough of the restaurant's take on French rustic cuisine, which makes twisted tongues and sore feet a small price to pay. The steak is sensational, but the Toulouse sausages with *choucroute* (sauerkraut) and Lyonnaise potatoes is a timely reminder that when it comes to the pleasures of the palate, the French really know what they're doing.

Locks (Map p80; ☎ 454 3391; 1 Windsor Tce; mains €16-20; ⊙ noon-4pm & 6-10pm Mon-Sat) When chef Troy Maguire left the immensely popular L'Gueuleton (opposite) in early 2007 to team up with ex-Bang manager Kelvin Rynhardt to take over one of the steady stalwarts of the Dublin dining scene, the bar was suddenly set very, very high. Would Locks shake off its old-town dust? Could Maguire re-create the informal-but-superb French campagnard cooking that made his former kitchen such a huge hit? Would Locks be as cool as Bang used to be? And would the prices stay this side of decent? Thankfully, yes on all counts, and while it's still early days, Locks promises to be one of the most sought-after tables in town for years to come.

Ar Vicoletto (Map p84; ☎ 670 8662; 5 Crow St; mains €12-25; ⊙ noon-10pm) When it's good, it's very, very good, with superb Italian dishes washed down with splendid local reds in a convivial atmosphere. But it can be a little inconsistent and sometimes quite disappointing. Still, it's worth the risk.

Aya (Map p86; ☎ 677 1544; Clarendon St; mains €12-28; ⊙ 11.30am-11pm) Attached to the Brown Thomas department store, Aya is the best Japanese restaurant in town – which frankly isn't saying much, considering the paltry competition. There's a revolving sushi bar where you can eat your fill for €25 every night (except Thursday and Saturday), between 5pm and 9pm (maximum 55 minutes), or else you can go á la carte from the extensive menu.

Saba (Map p86; ☎ 679 2000; www.sabadublin.com; 26-28 Clarendon St; mains €12-28; ⊙ noon-11pm) Southeast Asian cuisine hits Dublin with a stylish bang at this supercool eatery that seeks to impress with its extensive menu and contemporary décor. Both are good without being exceptional, but it's packed every night so what the hell do we know?

Monty's of Kathmandu (Map p84; ☎ 670 4911; 28 Eustace St; mains €13-21; ⊙ 12.30-2.30pm & 6-11.30pm Mon-Sat, 6-11pm Sun) The trade of award-winning Monty's is built on people who keep returning for typical Nepalese dishes such as *gorkhali* (chicken cooked in chilli, yoghurt and ginger) or *kachila* (raw marinated meat). The Shiva beer complements these hearty, spicy dishes. Ethnic food doesn't get much better than this.

Odessa (Map p84; ☎ 670 7634; 13 Dame Ct; mains €13-25) Odessa's lounge atmosphere, with comfy sofas and retro standard lamps, attract the city's hipsters, who flock here for homemade burgers, steaks or daily fish specials. You may not escape the sofa after you've quaffed a few of Odessa's renowned cocktails while playing a game of backgammon. Weekend brunch is *extremely* popular: you have been warned.

Jaipur (Map p86; ☎ 677 0999; www.jaipur.ie; 41 South Great George's St; mains €17-20; ⊙ noon-10pm) Critics rave about the subtle and varied flavours produced by Jaipur's kitchen, which is down to its refusal to skimp on even the smallest dash of spice. What you get here is as close to the real deal as you'd get anywhere outside of Delhi.

TOP END

Eden (Map p84; ☎ 670 5372; Meeting House Sq; mains €15-25; ⊙ noon-2.30pm & 6-10.30pm Mon-Fri, noon-3pm & 6-11pm Sat & Sun) Eden is the epitome of Temple Bar chic with its trendy wait staff, minimalist surroundings, high ceiling, hanging plants and terrace onto Meeting House Sq. But the food is the real star: Eleanor Walsh's unfussy modern Irish cuisine uses organic seasonal produce, complemented by a carefully chosen wine list. Seating on the gas-heated terrace is at a premium on summer evenings, when classic films are projected onto the nearby Gallery of Photography.

Bang (Map p86; ☎ 676 0898; www.bangrestaurant.com; 11 Merrion Row; mains €15-28; ⊙ 12.30-3pm & 6.30-10.30pm Mon-Sat) The hip and handsome Stoke twins have brought a touch of Denmark to Dublin in appropriately stylish surrounds – and have created a favourite with the 30-somethings who have a little cash to burn. The modern European grub – carefully created by chef Lorcan Cribbin (ex-Ivy in London, don't you know) – is sharp, tasty and very much in demand. Thai baked sea bass, medallions of beef and melt-in-your-mouth roast scallops are just a random selection. Reservations are a must, even for lunch.

Ely Wine Bar (www.elywinebar.ie; mains €15-29; ⊙ noon-3pm & 6-10pm Mon-Fri, 1-4pm & 6-10pm Sat) Ely Wine Bar (Map p86; ☎ 676 8986; 22 Ely Pl); Ely CHQ (Map pp82-3; ☎ 672 0010; Custom House Quay); Ely HQ (Map p80; ☎ 633 9986; Hanover Quay) Scrummy homemade burgers, bangers and mash, and wild smoked salmon salad are some of the meals you'll find in this basement restaurant. Dishes are prepared with organic and free-range produce from the owner's family farm in county Clare, so you can rest assured of the quality. There's a large wine list to choose from, with over 70 sold by the glass. There are now two new branches on both sides of the Liffey down near the docklands: Ely CHQ, on the northside in an atmospheric old tobacco warehouse; and the spectacular Ely HQ, on the Grand Canal Docks.

Town Bar & Grill (Map p86; ☎ 662 4724; 21 Kildare St; mains €18-28; ☷ noon-11pm Mon-Sat, to 10pm Sun) On any given night, you're likely to share this low-ceilinged basement dining room with a selection of Ireland's most affluent and influential people, who conduct their oh-so-important affairs barely above a murmur. But the slight stuffiness of the place is swept aside by the simply mouth-watering food, which ranges from lamb's liver to slow-rotated rabbit or sweet pepper–stuffed lamb. One of the best in town.

Dax (Map p80; ☎ 676 1494; 23 Upper Pembroke St; mains €18-30; ☷ noon-2.15pm & 6-11pm Tue-Fri, 6-11pm Sat) Olivier Meisonnave, convivial ex–maître d' of Thornton's, has stepped out with Irish chef Pól ÓhÉannraich to open this posh-rustic restaurant named after his home town, north of Biarritz. In a bright basement, serious foodies can sate their palate on sea bass with celeriac purée, pork wrapped in *serrano* ham, and truffle risotto.

Balzac (Map p86; ☎ 677 8611; 35 Dawson St; mains €18-30; ☷ 6-11pm) It's official: Paul Flynn is one of the best chefs in Ireland. He made his name with the simply stunning Tannery Restaurant (p194) in Dungarvan, county Waterford, and his first Dublin venture will only serve to cement his growing reputation. The elegant old-world dining room is a fitting setting for the superb cuisine – how about oysters mignonette followed by champagne and truffle risotto?

Mermaid Café (Map p84; ☎ 670 8236; 22 Dame St; mains €18-31; ☷ 12.30-2.30pm & 6-11pm Mon-Sat, 12.30-3pm & 6-9pm Sun) The Mermaid is an American-style bistro with natural wood furniture and abstract canvases on its panelled walls. It caters mainly to a hip gourmand crowd, who appreciate the inventive ingredient-led organic food such as monkfish with buttered red chard or braised lamb shank with apricot couscous. Its informal atmosphere, pure food and friendly staff make it difficult to get a table without notice.

Thornton's (Map p86; ☎ 478 7000; Fitzwilliam Hotel; midweek 2-/3-course lunch €30/40, dinner mains €45; ☷ 12.30-2pm & 7-10pm Tue-Sat) Kevin Thornton lost one of his two Michelin stars in 2006, but he defiantly believes that his eatery is as good as any in town – and he has every reason to do so. His mouth-watering interpretation of new French cuisine is superb and the service is faultless, if a little too formal in this ubertrendy room overlooking St Stephen's Green. Want to watch a grown-up squirm? Ask for ketchup.

Restaurant Patrick Guilbaud (Map p86; ☎ 676 4192; 21 Upper Merrion St; 2-/3-course set lunch €33/45, dinner mains about €35; ☷ 12.30-2.30pm & 7.30-10.30pm Tue-Sat) With two Michelin stars on its résumé, this elegant restaurant is one of the best in Ireland, and head chef Guillaume Lebrun does his best to ensure that it stays that way. Next door to the Merrion Hotel, Guilbaud has French *haute cuisine* that is beautifully executed and served in delectable surroundings. The lunch menu is a steal, at least in this stratosphere.

The Liberties & Kilmainham

Fast-food outlets and greasy-spoon diners still dominate the food map in this part of the city, but there's one spot that rises out of the boiling oil and batter-in-a-bucket and takes its place among the legends.

Leo Burdock's (Map p84; ☎ 454 0306; 2 Werburgh St; cod & chips €8.50; ☷ noon-midnight Mon-Sat, 4pm-midnight Sun) You will often hear that you haven't eaten in Dublin until you've queued in the cold for a cod and chips wrapped in paper from the city's most famous chipper. Total codswallop, of course, but there's something about sitting on the street, balancing the bag on your lap and trying to eat the chips quickly before they go cold and horrible that smacks of Dublin in a bygone age. It's nice to revisit the past, especially if you don't have to get stuck there.

O'Connell Street & Around

The capital's premier street is still playing catch-up with the southside, but it's getting closer. Ignore the unfortunate plethora of fast-food joints that still plague O'Connell St itself, and seek out our selection of quality eateries that more than make the grade.

BUDGET

Epicurean Food Hall (Map p84; Lower Liffey St; lunch €3-12; ☷ 9.30am-5.30pm Mon-Sat) Need to refuel and rest the bag-laden arms? Then this busy arcade with 20-odd food stalls is just the ticket. Quality is hit and miss, but you won't go wrong with a hot bagel with the works from Itsabagel or a finger-licking kebab from Istanbul House, rounded off with an espresso from the excellent El Corte.

Soup Dragon (Map p84; ☎ 872 3277; 168 Capel St; soups €4.50-9.50; ☼ 8am-5.30pm Mon-Fri, 11am-5pm Sat) Eat in or take away one of 12 tasty varieties of homemade soups, including shepherd's pie or spicy vegetable gumbo. Bowls come in three different sizes, and prices include fresh bread and a piece of fruit. Kick start your day (or afternoon) with a healthy all-day breakfast selection: try fresh smoothies (€3.75), poached eggs in bagels (€3.20), or generous bowls of yoghurt, fruit and muesli (€4).

Cobalt Café & Gallery (Map pp82-3; ☎ 873 0313; 16 North Great George's St; mains €5-9; ☼ 10am-4.30pm Mon-Fri) This gorgeous, elegant café in a bright and airy Georgian drawing room is a must if you're in the hood. Almost opposite the James Joyce Cultural Centre, Cobalt has a simple menu, but you can enjoy hearty soups by a roaring fire in winter, or fresh sandwiches in the garden on warmer days.

Football-mad developer Mick Wallace has managed to single-handedly create a thriving new Italian quarter, with cafés and eateries popping up all over Quartier Bloom, the new lane from Ormond Quay to Great Strand St.

La Taverna di Bacco (Map p84; ☎ 873 0040; 24 Lower Ormond Quay; mains €8-9; ☼ 12.30-10.30pm Mon-Sat, from 5pm Sun)and **Enoteca Delle Langhe** (Map p84; ☎ 888 0834; Bloom's Lane; ☼ noon-11pm), a few doors up, serve simple pastas, antipasti and Italian cheeses, along with the delicious produce of Wallace's own vineyard and others in Piemonte.

MIDRANGE

Alilang (Map pp82-3; ☎ 874 6766; 102 Parnell St; mains €7-15; ☼ noon-2.30pm & 5.30-11.30pm Mon-Thu, noon-2.30pm & 5.30pm-midnight Fri, 12.30pm-midnight Sat & Sun) With elements of Chinese, Japanese and Thai cuisine, this Korean restaurant on diverse Parnell St has plenty to whet appetites. Tasty dishes such as *padun* (seafood pancake), cod and tofu hotpot, or barbecued meats cooked at your table DIY style, with gas burner, skillet and spicy marinade, make the food a talking point. Although the bright and shiny décor may not be conducive to romantic first dates,

the atmosphere at Ailang is strangely inviting. Steer clear of the dull wine list in favour of Ailang's own Hite beer.

Bar Italia (Map p84; ☎ 874 1000; 28 Lower Ormond Quay; mains €9-16; ☼ 10.30am-11pm Mon-Sat, 1-9pm Sun) The slightly fancier younger brother of the immensely successful café just across the Liffey (see p124) is bigger and just as good; it's as if they were using the same kitchen.

TOP END

Winding Stair (Map p84; ☎ 873 3292; 40 Lower Ormond Quay; mains €15-26; ☼ noon-4pm & 6-10pm Tue-Sat, from 1pm Sun) There was much tearing of hair and gnashing of teeth when this Dublin institution closed in 2005. Thankfully it reopened in 2006 with the same simple décor and warm atmosphere, but with the addition of an excellent wine list and a wonderful Irish menu – creamy fish pie, bacon and organic cabbage, steamed mussels, and Irish farmyard cheeses – all prepared with much TLC.

Chapter One (Map pp82-3; ☎ 873 2266; 18-19 North Parnell Sq; mains €23-30; ☼ lunch Tue-Fri, dinner Tue-Sat) Savour classic French cuisine such as foie gras, duck *confit* or rabbit cassoulet to the tinkle of the grand piano in the lovely vaulted basement of the Dublin Writers Museum (p106). This place is one of the city's top 10 restaurants. Try to arrive before 7pm for the three-course pre-theatre special (€34).

Rhodes D7 (Map pp82-3; ☎ 804 4441; Mary's Abbey; mains €23-30; ☼ noon-10pm Tue-Sat, to 4pm Sun & Mon) Is Ireland ready for a truly British restaurant? Londoner and celebrity chef Gary Rhodes thinks so, opening this big, brash northside eatery. While you won't spot the Tintin-haired one sweating it out in the kitchen, he did devise the menu, and his British staples – including cheddar rarebit, roast cod with lobster champ – have been given an Irish twist.

Beyond the Grand Canal

The fancy suburbs of the south city centre have long been home to a handful of terrific restaurants, but the leading light these days is Ranelagh, which has undergone a mini revolution in recent years. Located only 10 minutes or so away from town by Luas, it is a convenient destination when town is packed to overflowing.

Café Bardeli (Map p80; ☎ 496 1886; 62 Ranelagh Rd; mains €9-15; ☼ 12.30-11pm Mon-Sat, to 10pm Sun) If it ain't broke, do it again: Café Bardeli hit Ranelagh in 2004 with the same no-fuss menu that made its big sister such a roaring success on South Great George's St (see p125) and just hasn't looked back.

Diep Noodle Bar (Map p80; ☎ 497 6550; 19 Ranelagh Rd; mains €9-17; ☼ 2.30-11.30pm) Top-notch Thai and Vietnamese dishes such as *pad thai* (Thai fried noodles), red-snapper vermicelli or seafood rice noodles come to your table at lightning speed in this funky place. Décor is sparse, modern and clean. It's packed at weekends but you'll get a table early or late without a booking.

French Paradox (Map p80; ☎ 660 4068; 53 Shelbourne Rd; mains €10-18; ☼ noon-3pm & 6-9.30pm Mon-Thu, noon-9.30pm Fri-Sat) This bright and airy wine bar, set over an excellent wine shop of the same name, serves fine authentic French dishes such as cassoulet, a variety of foie gras, cheese and charcuterie plates, and large green salads. All are there to complement the main attraction: a dazzling array of fine wines, mostly French (unsurprisingly), sold by the bottle, glass or even 6.25cL taste! A little slice of Paris in Dublin 4.

Mint (Map p80; ☎ 497 8655; 47 Ranelagh Rd; mains around €16; ☼ noon-3pm & 6-10pm Tue-Sun) The people at Mint are ambitious. Chef Oliver Dunne crossed the water from Gordon Ramsay's Pied à Terre in London and his diverse menu has Michelin aspirant written all over it, the small room is sleek and low lit, the service formal but friendly. Expect exceptional classics such as veal on foie gras and mushroom risotto, and duck *confit*.

DRINKING

When they talk of Dublin being a great party town, what they're really saying is that it's a great drinking town. Which it most certainly is, and there's a pretty good chance that it's one of the main reasons you came in the first place. The pub remains the alpha and omega of all social life – a meeting point for friends and strangers alike, and where Dubliners are at their friendly and convivial best (and, it must be said, sometimes their drunken and belligerent worst!).

There are pubs for every taste and sensibility, although traditional haunts populated by flat-capped pensioners bursting with insightful anecdotes are disappearing under a modern wave of designer bars and themed locales that wouldn't seem out of place in any other city in the world. All the while, of course, the Irish-pub theme is being ex-

TOP FIVE PUBS

- Best for a decent pint and a chat – Grogan's Castle Lounge (opposite)
- Best for beats and beatniks – Anseo (p132)
- Best for fiddles and *bodhráns* – Cobblestone (opposite)
- Best for getting jiggy with it – Village (p133)
- Best to see and be seen – South William (p133)

ported throughout the world like a McPub; if the trend continues, Dublin may be the last place to come to if you're looking for a spit-and-sawdust boozer.

Dublin's infamous party zone is Temple Bar, where giant bars pump out booze and chart music to a thirsty, animated throng of revellers – Ireland's own 'Ibiza in the rain'. It's not so bad for a midweek drink, but come the weekend it's strictly for tourists and visitors with T-shirts advertising themselves as part of a hen or stag group. More discerning party animals favour the strip of supersized bars on Dawson St and – more recently – the bars along Wexford and Camden Sts, southwest of St Stephen's Green. But don't worry: you can't go too far in the city centre without finding a pub with a bit of life in it.

Last orders are at 11.30pm Monday to Thursday, 12.30am Friday and Saturday and 11pm on Sunday, with 30 minutes' drinking-up time each night. However, many central pubs have licenses to serve until 1.30am, 2.30am and – for those with a superspecial 'theatre licence' – until 3am.

Traditional Pubs

Dublin still has some good, old-style, traditional establishments.

Flowing Tide (Map p132; ☎ 874 0842; 9 Lower Abbey St) Directly opposite the Abbey Theatre, this place attracts a great mix of theatregoers and northside locals. It's loud, full of chat and a great place to drink.

Patrick Conway's (Map p132; ☎ 873 2687; 70 Parnell St) Although it's slightly out of the way, this place is a true gem of a pub. It has been operating since 1745, and no doubt new fathers have been stopping in here for a celebratory pint since the day the Rotunda Maternity Hospital opened across the road in 1757.

Palace Bar (Map p132; ☎ 677 9290; 21 Fleet St) With its mirrors and wooden niches, Palace Bar is often said to be the perfect example of an old Dublin pub. It's within Temple Bar and is popular with journalists from the nearby *Irish Times*.

Dawson Lounge (Map p132; ☎ 677 5909; 25 Dawson St) To see the smallest bar in Dublin, go through a small doorway, down a narrow flight of steps and into two tiny rooms that always seem to be filled with a couple of bedraggled drunks who look like they're hiding. Psst, here's a secret: a certain sunglassed lead singer of a certain ginormous Irish band is said to love unwinding in here from time to time.

John Mulligan's (Map p132; ☎ 677 5582; 8 Poolbeg St) Outside the eastern boundary of Temple Bar, John Mulligan's is another pub that has scarcely changed over the years. It featured as the local in the film *My Left Foot* and is also popular with journalists from the nearby newspaper offices. Mulligan's was established in 1782 and has long been reputed to have the best Guinness in Ireland, as well as a wonderfully varied collection of regulars.

Stag's Head (Map p132; ☎ 679 3701; 1 Dame Ct) At the intersection of Dame Ct and Dame Lane, just off Dame St, the Stag's Head was built in 1770 and remodelled in 1895. It's sufficiently picturesque to have featured in a postage-stamp series depicting Irish pubs.

Long Hall (Map p132; ☎ 475 1590; 51 South Great George's St) Luxuriating in full Victorian splendour, this is one of the city's most beautiful and best-loved pubs. Check out the elegant chandeliers and the ornate carvings in the woodwork behind the bar. The bartenders are experts at their craft – an increasingly rare experience in Dublin these days.

Kehoe's (Map p132; ☎ 677 8312; 9 South Anne St) This is one of the most atmospheric pubs in the city centre and a real favourite with all kinds of Dubliners. It has a beautiful Victorian bar, a wonderful snug, and plenty of other little nooks and crannies. Upstairs, drinks are served in what was once the publican's living room. And it looks it!

Neary's (Map p132; ☎ 677 8596; 1 Chatham St) A showy Victorian-era pub with a fine frontage, Neary's is popular with actors from the nearby Gaiety Theatre. The upstairs bar is one of the only spots in the city centre where you stand a chance of getting a seat on a Friday or Saturday night.

Grogan's Castle Lounge (Map p132; ☎ 677 9320; 15 South William St) A city-centre institution, Grogan's has long been a favourite haunt of Dublin's writers and painters, as well as others from the bohemian, alternative set. An odd quirk of the pub is that drinks are marginally cheaper in the stone-floor bar than in the carpeted lounge, even though they are served by the same bar!

James Toner's (Map p132; ☎ 676 3090; 139 Lower Baggot St) With its stone floor, Toner's is almost a country pub in the heart of the city, and the shelves and drawers are reminders that it once doubled as a grocery store. Not that its suit-wearing business crowd would ever have shopped here…

Hartigan's (Map p132; ☎ 676 2280; 100 Lower Leeson St) This is about as spartan a bar as you'll find in the city, and it's the daytime home to some serious drinkers, who appreciate the quiet, no-frills surroundings. In the evening it's popular with students from the medical faculty of University College Dublin.

Sackville Lounge (Map p132; Sackville Pl) This tiny one-room, wood-panelled 19th-century bar is discreetly located just off O'Connell St, which perhaps explains why it's so popular with actors, theatregoers and anyone who appreciates a nice pint in a gorgeous old-style bar.

Live-Music Pubs

The following places are excellent venues for catching some traditional Irish and contemporary music.

Sean O'Casey's (Map p132; ☎ 874 8675; 105 Marlborough St) This place has a weekly menu of live rock and some Irish traditional music sessions.

Hughes' Bar (Map p132; ☎ 872 6540; 19 Chancery St) Directly behind the Four Courts, this bar has nightly, if impromptu, sessions that often result in a closed door – that is, they go on long past official closing time. The pub is also a popular lunchtime spot with barristers working nearby.

Cobblestone (Map pp82-3; ☎ 872 1799; North King St) This pub is on the main square in Smithfield, an old northside marketplace. There's a great atmosphere in the cosy upstairs bar, where the nightly music sessions – both traditional and up-and-coming folk and singer-songwriter acts – are superb.

Oliver St John Gogarty's (Map p132; ☎ 671 1822; 58-59 Fleet St) There's live traditional music nightly at this busy Temple Bar pub, catering to a mostly tourist crowd.

International Bar (Map p132; ☎ 677 9250; 23 Wicklow St) The International has live jazz and blues most nights.

Bruxelles (Map p132; ☎ 677 5362; 7-8 Harry St) This place has weekly live rock music, perhaps the only link the now trendy pub has to its heavy-metal past.

O'Donoghue's (Map p132; ☎ 661 4303; 15 Merrion Row) The most famous traditional music bar in Dublin, O'Donoghue's is where world-famous folk group the Dubliners started off in the 1960s. On summer evenings a young, international crowd spills out into the courtyard beside the pub.

Mother Redcaps (Map p132; ☎ 453 8306; Back Lane) A legendary spit-on-the-floor, no-frills folk-music venue, which reopened after a few year's respite. It's above a pub of the same name.

Bars

The following modern bars are Dublin's current hot spots.

Anseo (Map p132; ☎ 475 1321; 28 Lower Camden St) Unpretentious, unaffected and incredibly popular, this cosy alternative bar is a favourite with those who live by the credo that to try too hard is far worse than not trying at all. Wearing cool like a loose garment,

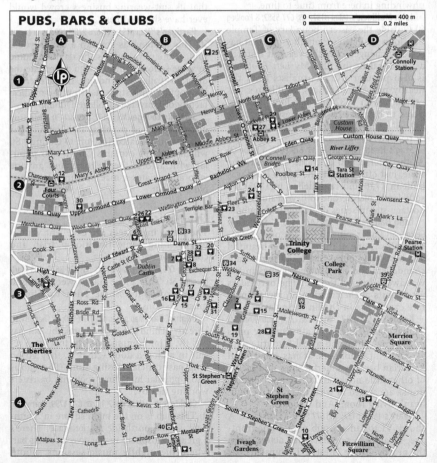

PUBS, BARS & CLUBS

the punters thrive on the mix of chat and terrific music.

Dice Bar (Map pp82-3; ☎ 674 6710; 79 Queen St) Co-owned by singer Huey from band Fun Lovin' Criminals, the Dice Bar looks like something you'd find on New York's Lower East Side. Its black-and-red-painted interior, dripping candles and distressed seating, combined with rocking DJs most nights, make this place a magnet for Dublin's beatnik crowds.

No 4 Dame Lane (Map p132; ☎ 679 0291; 4 Dame Lane) This stylish bar across two floors is popular with clubby kids and professionals alike. They come for the modern ambience and the DJ-led entertainment, which is mellow midweek, but loud and dancy weekends.

Market Bar (Map p132; ☎ 677 4835; Fade St) This fashionable watering hole is run by the same guys as the Globe (below), around the corner. Little would you know this beautiful airy Victorian space was a sausage factory in a former life.

Globe (Map p132; ☎ 671 1220; 11 South Great George's St) One of Dublin's first proper café-bars, the Globe, with its wooden floors and plain brick walls, is as much a daytime haunt for a good latte as it is a supercool night-time watering hole. Nightly DJs, a relaxed atmosphere and friendly staff keep the place buzzing with a mix of hip young locals and clued-in visitors.

Hogan's (Map p132; ☎ 677 5904; 35 South Great George's St) Hogan's is a gigantic boozer spread across two floors. A popular hang-out for young professionals, it gets very full at the weekend with folks eager to take advantage of its late licence.

Octagon Bar (Map p132; ☎ 670 9000; Clarence Hotel, 6-8 Wellington Quay) Temple Bar's most chic watering hole is where you'll find Dublin's celebrities and their hangers-on. Drinks are more expensive than elsewhere – a flute of *bellini*

(peach and champagne) will set you back €13, but judging by the clientele who have passed the bouncer's strict entry test, this is hardly a concern.

Porterhouse (Map p132; ☎ 679 8847; 16-18 Parliament St) Dublin's first microbrewery is our favourite Temple Bar watering hole. Especially popular with foreign residents and visitors, the Porterhouse sells only its own stouts and beers – and they're all excellent.

SamSara (Map p132; ☎ 671 7723; 35-36 Dawson St) This huge Middle Eastern–themed drinking emporium packs young office types and pre-clubbers in at weekends, when the bar runs late.

Shakespeare (Map pp82-3; ☎ 878 8650; 160 Parnell St) A wonderful hybrid of traditional pub and new cosmopolitanism, this Korean-owned bar makes unlikely but successful bedfellows of a decent pint and karaoke fun.

South William (Map p132; ☎ 679 3701; South William St) Dublin's newest and coolest bar has it all behind its huge glass frontage: top-class music, great DJs, a downstairs club, and probably the best pub grub in Dublin, with delicious pies created by Troy Maguire from Lock's.

Sin É (Map p132; ☎ 878 7009; 14-15 Upper Ormond Quay) This excellent quayside bar is proof that the most important quality for any pub is ambience. There's no real décor to speak of, but this place buzzes almost nightly with a terrific mix of students and professionals, the hip and the uncool. It helps that the DJs are all uniformly excellent.

Village (Map p132; ☎ 475 8555; www.thevillagevenue .com; 26 Wexford St) Packed to overflowing every weekend, this large modern bar is where the lovely lads and gorgeous gals show off their plumage in a fun-time courting ritual that has the rest of them queuing up at the door to join in. There are excellent DJs nightly;

the nightclub bit of the venue (right) opens Thursday through Saturday.

ENTERTAINMENT

Dublin's status as an entertainment capital has been hyped out of all reality by tourist authorities and other interested parties. Fact is – for its diminutive size – it's *pretty* good, with a range of options to satisfy nearly all desires, from theatre to dog racing and most distractions in between.

For entertainment information, pick up a copy of the *Event Guide,* a bimonthly freebie available at many locations, including bars, cafés and hostels; the weekly music-review *Hot Press;* or the fortnightly freebie *In Dublin.* Friday's *Irish Times* has a pull-out entertainment section called the *Ticket,* which has comprehensive listings of clubs and gigs.

Cinemas

Ireland boasts the highest attendances in Europe of young cinemagoers. Consequently it's best to book in advance by credit card, or be prepared to queue for up to half an hour for tickets at night-time screenings. Dublin's cinemas are more heavily concentrated on the northern side of the Liffey. Admission prices are generally €6 for afternoon shows, rising to around €8 in the evening.

Irish Film Institute (Map p84; ☎ 679 5744; 6 Eustace St) The multiscreen cinema shows classics and art-house films. The complex also has a bar, a café and a bookshop. Weekly membership (€2) is required for some uncertified films, which can only be screened as part of a 'club'.

Savoy (Map pp82-3; ☎ 874 6000; Upper O'Connell St; ☽ from 2pm) A traditional four-screen first-run cinema, Savoy has late-night shows on weekends.

Screen (Map pp82-3; ☎ 671 4988; 2 Townsend St; ☽ from 2pm) Between Trinity College and O'Connell Bridge, the Screen shows new independent and smaller commercial films on its three screens.

Cineworld (Map pp82-3; ☎ 872 8400; Parnell Centre, Parnell St; ☽ rom10am) This multiscreen cinema is where you'll get all the mainstream releases.

Nightclubs

A decade-long roller-coaster ride has left Dublin's clubland a little dizzy. From crap to brilliant and then to…well, less than brilliant, clubs have had a rude awakening in the last few years. These days, clubs have to tackle restrictive opening hours, late-night bars offering a free version of the same, and the continuing squeeze of the musical mainstream: Dublin's population may be increasingly multicultural, but they're a largely conservative bunch whose tastes range from charty stuff to a bit of alternative rock, and from R&B to commercially flavoured dance music. Still, the reputation as a party town persists, which is down to the punters themselves, for Dubliners really know how to have a good time.

The seemingly endless list of what's on is constantly changing, so check out the listings in the *Event Guide* and *In Dublin;* the listings here are by no means exhaustive. Most clubs open just after pubs close (11.30pm to midnight) and close at 2.30am or 3am. Admission to most costs between €5 and €8 Sunday to Thursday, rising to as much as €15 or €20 on Friday and Saturday. For gay and lesbian clubs, see p136.

Tripod (Map p80; ☎ 478 0025; www.pod.ie; 35 Harcourt St; admission €5-20; ☽ Mon-Sat) Launched in late 2006 on the site of former club PoD in the atmospheric old Harcourt Street station, Tripod now integrates three venues (geddit?): a state-of-the-art 1300-capacity live rock and pop venue, a smaller dance club and the intimate live venue Crawdaddy (opposite).

Village (Map p132; ☎ 475 8555; 26 Wexford St; www.thevillagevenue.com; admission €8-10; ☽ Thu-Sat) When the live music ends (see p133), the club kicks off, taking 600-odd groovers through a consistent mix of new and old tunes, dance-floor classics and whatever else will shake that booty. A great venue, an eager crowd and an overall top night out.

Underground@Kennedy's (Map p132; ☎ 661 1124; 31-32 Westland Row; ☽ 11.30pm-2.30am Fri & Sat) Beneath this busy pub is a suitably sweaty, darkened room that plays regular host to some top-class local and international DJs playing a variety of styles from house to hip-hop.

Lillie's Bordello (Map p132; ☎ 679 9204; www.lilliesbordello.ie; Adam Ct; admission €10-20; ☽ 11pm-3am) Lillie's is strictly for big hairs, wannabes and visiting rock stars. Don't think you'll get to rub shoulders with celebs though, as they'll be whisked out of view and into the VIP room in a flash. As you might expect, the music is mostly safe and commercial.

Renard's (Map p132; ☎ 677 5876; www.renards.ie; South Frederick St; admission free-€10; ☽ 10.30pm-2.30am) Run by Colin Farrell's godfather, this is the actor's (and other celebs') favourite den of iniquity when in town. Renard's is an intimate club with a strict door policy when busy; music is mainly house, with soul, funk and jazz making the odd appearance.

Rogue (Map p132; ☎ 675 3971; 64 Dame St; admission €8-12; ☒ 11.30pm-3am Mon-Sat) A relative newcomer on the block, Rogue is an intimate two-floored venue that's home to the Bodytonic crew, who decamped from now defunct Wax. Expect to hear melodic and deep house and techno at the excellent Discotonic on Saturday nights.

Hub (Map p132; ☎ 670 7655; 11 Eustace St; admission €6-15) Arctic Monkeys, We are Scientists and comedian Jimmy Carr have all graced the decks at the legendary rock-indie-electronic night Trashed on Tuesdays, hosted by Trev Radiator. Otherwise it's a mixed bag of indie hits and drinks promos for all and sundry.

Rí Rá (Map p132; ☎ 677 4835; Dame Ct; admission €5-11; ☒ Mon-Sat) This long-established club changed hands in 2007, but the new owners are bent on continuing the long-standing commitment to music without frenetic beats – for now, at least. The emphasis has long been on funky stuff, from soul to hip-hop, but there's plenty of rock thrown in and Monday's '80s-fest Strictly Handbag is now in its 16th year. Upstairs, the Globe bar (p133) converts into a chilled-out drink and chat area.

Live Music

Bookings can be made either directly at the venues or through **HMV** (Map p86; ☎ 679 5334; 65 Grafton St) or **Ticketmaster** (☎ 0818 719 300, 456 9569; www.ticketmaster.ie), but they charge between 9% and 12.5% service charge *per ticket*, not per booking, on credit-card bookings.

CLASSICAL MUSIC & OPERA VENUES

Classical music concerts and opera take place in a number of city-centre venues. There are also occasional performances in churches; check the press for details.

National Concert Hall (Map p80; ☎ 417 0000; www.nch.ie; Earlsfort Tce) Ireland's premier orchestral hall hosts a variety of concerts year-round, including a series of lunchtime concerts from 1.05pm to 2pm on Tuesday, June to August.

Gaiety Theatre (Map p86; ☎ 677 1717; www.gaietytheatre.com; South King St) This popular Dublin theatre hosts a programme of classical concerts and opera.

Bank of Ireland Arts Centre (Map p84; ☎ 671 1488; Foster Pl) The arts centre hosts a free, regular midweek lunchtime recital beginning at 1.15pm, as well as an occasional evening programme of concerts. Call for details.

Helix (Map p78; ☎ 700 7000; www.thehelix.ie; Collins Ave, Glasnevin) Based in Dublin City University, the Helix hosts, among other things, an impressive array of international operatic and classical recitals and performances. To get here, take bus 11, 13, 13A or 19A from O'Connell St.

Dublin City Gallery – the Hugh Lane (Map pp82-3; ☎ 874 1903; www.hughlane.ie; Charlemont House, Parnell Sq) At noon on Sunday, from September to June, the art gallery hosts up to 30 concerts of contemporary classical music.

Royal Dublin Society Showground Concert Hall (Map p80; ☎ 668 0866; www.rds.ie; Ballsbridge) The huge hall of the RDS Showground hosts a rich programme of classical music and opera throughout the year.

ROCK & POP VENUES

Ambassador Theatre (Map pp82-3; ☎ 1890 925 100; O'Connell St) The Ambassador started life as a theatre and then became a cinema. Not much has changed inside, making it a cool retro place to see visiting and local rock acts perform.

Crawdaddy (Map p80; ☎ 478 0225; www.pod.ie; 35A Harcourt St) Named after the London club where the Stones launched their professional careers in 1963, Crawdaddy is an intimate bar-venue that specialises in putting on rootsy performers – from African drum bands to avant-garde jazz artists and flamenco guitarists. It is attached to the nightclub Tripod (opposite).

Gaiety Theatre (Map p86; ☎ 677 1717; www.gaietytheatre.com; South King St; ☒ to 4am) This old Victorian theatre is an atmospheric place to come and listen to late-night jazz, rock or blues on the weekend.

Isaac Butt (Map pp82-3; ☎ 855 5884; Store St) Local garage, rock, metal and indie bands sweat it out most nights in this grungy venue opposite Busáras.

Olympia Theatre (Map p84; ☎ 677 7744; Dame St) This pleasantly tatty place features everything from disco to country on Friday night; Midnight at the Olympia runs from midnight to 2am on Friday.

Point Depot (Map p80; ☎ 836 3633; East Link Bridge, North Wall Quay) This is Dublin's premier indoor venue for rock and pop acts, and artists such as Diana Ross, Prince and Jamiroquai have all played here. Originally constructed as a

DUBLIN

GAY & LESBIAN DUBLIN

Dublin's not a bad place to be gay. Most people in the city centre wouldn't bat an eyelid at cross-dressing or public displays of affection between same-sex couples, but discretion is advised in the suburbs.

Information

Gay & Lesbian Garda Liaison Officer (☎ 666 9000) If you do encounter any sort of trouble or harassment on the streets, don't hesitate to call.

Gay Community News (www.gcn.ie) A useful nationwide news- and issues-based monthly paper. The new glossy *Q-Life* and *Free!* are entertainment guides that can be found in Temple Bar businesses and the Irish Film Institute on Eustace St.

Gay Switchboard Dublin (☎ 872 1055; www.gayswitchboard.ie) A friendly and useful voluntary service that provides information ranging from where to find accommodation to legal issues.

Outhouse (Map pp82-3; ☎ 873 4932; www.outhouse.ie; 105 Capel St) Top gay, lesbian and bisexual resource centre. Great stop-off point to see what's on, check notice boards and meet people. It publishes the free *Ireland's Pink Pages*, a directory of gay-centric services, which is also accessible on the website. If you do encounter any sort of trouble or harassment on the streets, don't hesitate to call the Outhouse.

Sexual Assault Unit (Map pp82-3; ☎ 666 6000) Call or visit the Pearse St Garda station.

Festivals & Events

Pride (www.dublinpride.org) A week-long festival of theatre, performance, music, readings and – inevitably – a high-energy, colourful parade through the city centre for the city's queers, dykes, bis and fetishists.

Lesbian & Gay Film Festival (☎ 670 6377; www.irishculture.net/filmfestival) An international film and documentary festival held at the Irish Film Institute in August.

Sleeping

Frankies Guesthouse (Map pp82-3; ☎ 478 3087; www.frankiesguesthouse.com; 8 Camden Pl; s €40-60, d €90-110) Although most of the city's hotels wouldn't think twice about checking in same-sex couples, the same cannot be said of many of the city's B&Bs. One central option is this comfortable, exclusively gay and lesbian B&B with pleasant rooms equipped with TV, and tea and coffee facilities.

Drinking

Dragon (Map p132; ☎ 478 1590; 64-65 South Great George's St) The latest addition to Dublin's scene, this big disco-bar with colourful Asian décor, comfy booths and small dance floor attracts young pre-George revellers.

George (Map p132; ☎ 478 2983; 89 South Great George's St) You can't miss the bright purple George, Temple Bar's only overtly gay bar, which has a reputation for becoming ever more wild and wacky as the night progresses. At 6.30pm on Sunday it is packed for an enormously popular bingo night, while Thursday night is the Missing Link game show hosted by Annie Balls.

Front Lounge (Map p132; ☎ 670 4112; 33 Parliament St) A lavish lounge attracting a mixed upmarket clientele. Drag queen Panti runs the cabaret and karaoke night, Casting Couch, on Tuesday.

Entertainment

There are plenty of clubs that run gay and lesbian nights. The scene is constantly changing, however, and while the nights listed are pretty steady, we recommend that you call ahead to confirm that they're still on. Check www.gay-ireland.com for other entertainment venues.

Boilerhouse Sauna (Map p84; ☎ 677 3130; 12 Crane Lane; admission €20; ◷ 1pm-6am Sun-Thu, 24hr Fri & Sat) This is a popular late-night destination for people looking to sweat it out after partying at George (see above), just around the corner. It's big and very clean, and is reputed to be the best-run of Dublin's saunas.

Rí Rá (Map p132; ☎ 677 4835; Dame Ct) Strictly Handbag is a long-running Monday night at one of Dublin's friendlier clubs. It's not exclusively gay, but it is popular with the gay community.

rail terminus in 1878, it has a capacity of around 6000.

Sugar Club (Map p80; ☎ 678 7188; 8 Lower Leeson St) There's live jazz, cabaret and soul music at weekends in this comfortable new theatre-style venue on the corner of St Stephen's Green.

Temple Bar Music Centre (Map p84; ☎ 670 0533; Curved St) The centre hosts all kinds of gigs, from Irish traditional to drum and bass, for a non-image-conscious crowd.

Vicar Street (Map pp82-3; ☎ 454 5533; www.vicar street.com; 58-59 Thomas St) Smaller performances take place at this intimate venue, near Christ Church Cathedral. It has a capacity of 1000 spread between table-serviced group seating downstairs and a theatre-style balcony. It has a varied programme of performers, with a strong emphasis on folk and jazz.

Village (Map p86; ☎ 475 8555; www.thevillage venue.com; 26 Wexford St) An attractive midsize venue that is a popular stop for acts on the way up and down, the Village has gigs virtually every night of the week, featuring a diverse range of rock bands and solo performers. It is also a good showcase for local singer-songwriters.

Whelan's (Map p86; ☎ 478 0766; www.whelanslive .com; 25 Wexford St;) Whelan's is such an institution with Irish singer-songwriters and other lo-fi performers that the press often refer to them as the 'Whelan's clique'. They include the likes of Glen Hansard & The Frames, Paddy Casey, Mark Geary, Damien Rice and Mundy.

Sport
Croke Park Stadium (Map p80; ☎ 836 3222; www .gaa.ie; Clonliffe Rd) Hurling and Gaelic football games are held from February to November at this stadium, north of the Royal Canal in Drumcondra. From late 2006 until the redevelopment of the Lansdowne Road stadium is completed, rugby and football internationals are played here too. Catch bus 19 or 19A to get here. For more on the stadium, see When History Really Matters, p110.

Harold's Cross Park (Map p80; ☎ 497 1081; 151 Harold's Cross Rd; adult/child €7/2; ☼ 6.30-10.30pm Mon, Tue & Fri) Greyhound racing takes place near Rathmines in this newly revamped venue. Take bus 16 or 16A from the city centre.

Leopardstown Race Course (Map p78; ☎ 289 3607; Foxrock) The Irish love of horse racing can be observed about 10km south of the city centre in Foxrock. Special buses depart from the

city centre on race days; call the racecourse for details.

Shelbourne Park Greyhound Stadium (Map p80; ☎ 668 3502, on race nights ☎ 202 6601; Bridge Town Rd, Ringsend; adult/child €8/4; ☼ 6.30-10.30pm Wed, Thu & Sat) A top-class dog track with terrific vantage points from the glassed-in restaurant, where you can eat, bet and watch without leaving your seat. Take bus 3 from D'Olier St.

Theatre
Dublin's theatre scene is small but busy. Bookings can usually be made by quoting a credit-card number over the phone, and the tickets can then be collected just before the performance.

Abbey Theatre (Map pp82-3; ☎ 878 7222; www .abbeytheatre.ie; Lower Abbey St) The famous Abbey Theatre, near the river, is Ireland's national theatre. It puts on new Irish works, as well as revivals of classic Irish plays by writers such as WB Yeats, JM Synge, Sean O'Casey, Brendan Behan and Samuel Beckett. Tickets for evening performances cost up to €25, except on Monday, when they are cheaper. The smaller and less expensive Peacock Theatre (Map pp82-3; ☎ 878 7222) is part of the same complex.

Ark (Map p84; ☎ 670 7788; 11A Eustace St) A 150-seater venue that stages shows for kids aged between five and 13.

Gaiety Theatre (Map p86; ☎ 677 1717; www.gaiety theatre.com; South King St) Opened in 1871, this theatre is used for modern plays, TV shows, musical comedies and revues.

Gate Theatre (Map pp82-3; ☎ 874 4045; www .gatetheatre.ie; 1 Cavendish Row) To the north of the Liffey, the Gate Theatre specialises in international classics and older Irish works with a touch of comedy by playwrights such as Oscar Wilde, George Bernard Shaw and Oliver Goldsmith, although newer plays are sometimes staged too. Prices vary according to what's on, but they're usually around €20.

Helix (Map p78; ☎ 700 7000; www.thehelix.ie; Collins Ave, Glasnevin) The Helix, Dublin City University's new theatre venue, has already established its reputation as a serious theatre with its mix of accessible and challenging productions. To get here, take bus 11, 13, 13A or 19A from O'Connell St.

International Bar (Map p86; ☎ 677 9250; 23 Wicklow St) This is one of several pubs that host theatrical performances; it also hosts comedy on Wednesday evening at 9.30pm (admission €9).

Olympia Theatre (Map p84; ☎ 677 7744; 72 Dame St) This theatre specialises in light plays and, at Christmastime, pantomimes.

Players' Theatre (Map p91; ☎ 677 2941, ext 1239; Regent House, Trinity College) The Trinity College Players' Theatre hosts student productions throughout the academic year, as well as the most prestigious plays from the Dublin Theatre Festival in October.

Project Arts Centre (Map p84; ☎ 1850 260 027; www.project.ie; 39 East Essex St) This centre puts on excellent productions of experimental plays by up-and-coming Irish and foreign writers.

Tivoli Theatre (Map p84; ☎ 454 4472; 135-136 Francis St) Experimental and less commercial performances take place here.

SHOPPING

Dubliners only recently acquired the kind of disposable income required for retail therapy, but a Saturday stroll would make you think that they're making up for lost time and that the shops were in danger of running out of goods. Weekends are the worst: the main shopping districts are chock-a-block with gaggles of teenagers, pram-pushing families, serious consumer couples, tourists and the odd elderly lady bravely making her way through the chaos.

Unless you enjoy the hustle and bustle, save your shopping for weekdays – the earlier the better.

British and US chains dominate the high street and major shopping centres but there are also numerous small, independent shops selling high-quality, locally made goods. Irish designer clothing and streetwear, handmade jewellery, unusual homewares and crafts, and cheeses to die for are readily available if you know where to look.

While souvenir hunters can still buy toy sheep, Guinness magnets and shamrock tea towels, a new breed of craft shop offers one-off or limited-edition crafts and art. Traditional Irish products such as crystal and knitwear remain popular choices, and you can increasingly find innovative modern takes on the classics.

Grafton St is the city's most prestigious shopping thoroughfare, but it's largely the domain of the British-style high-street shop, as is busy Henry St, just off O'Connell St. In the warren of streets between Grafton St and South Great George's St, you'll find a plethora of Irish-owned fashion outlets, jewellers and secondhand stores. Francis St in the Liberties is great for antiques and art.

Citizens of non-EU countries can reclaim the VAT (value-added tax) paid on purchases made at stores displaying a cash-back sticker; ask for details.

Most department stores and shopping centres are open from 9am to 6pm Monday to Saturday (open to 8pm Thursday) and noon to 6pm Sunday.

Department Stores & Shopping Centres

Powerscourt Townhouse Shopping Centre (Map p86; ☎ 679 4144; 59 South William St) The wonderful Powerscourt Townhouse Shopping Centre, just to the west of Grafton St, is a big, modern shopping centre in a fine old building. There are some decent restaurants on all its floors, and the Irish Design Centre sells the work of up-and-coming Irish fashion designers.

Arnott's (Map p84; ☎ 805 0400; 12 Henry St) Occupying a huge block with entrances on Henry, Liffey and Abbey Sts, this formerly mediocre department store has been completely overhauled and is now probably Dublin's best. It stocks virtually everything you could possibly want to buy, from garden furniture to high fashion, and everything is relatively affordable.

Brown Thomas (Map p86; ☎ 605 6666; 92 Grafton St) This is Dublin's most expensive department store, suitably stocked to cater for the city's more moneyed shoppers. You'll find every top label represented here.

Dundrum Town Centre (Map p78; ☎ 299 1700; Sandyford Rd, Dundrum; ☼ 9am-9pm Mon-Fri, 8.30am-7pm Sat, 10am-7pm Sun) Modern Ireland's grandest cathedral is this huge shopping and entertainment complex in the southern suburb of Dundrum. Over 100 retail outlets are represented. To get here, take the Luas to Ballaly, or catch bus 17, 44C, 48A or 75 from the city centre.

St Stephen's Green Shopping Centre (Map p86; ☎ 478 0888; St Stephen's Green) Inside this flash shopping centre you will discover a diverse mixture of chain stores and individual shops.

Jervis St Centre (Map p84; ☎ 878 1323; Jervis St) Just north of the Capel St Bridge, this is an ultramodern mall with dozens of outlets.

DUBLIN MARKETS

Blackberry Fair (Map p80; Lower Rathmines Rd; ☻ 10am-5pm Sat-Sun) You'll have to rummage through a lot of junk to find a gem in this charmingly run-down weekend market that stocks furniture, records and a few clothes stalls. It's cheap though.

Blackrock Market (Main St, Blackrock; ☻ 11am-5.30pm Sat & Sun) This long-running market, in an old merchant house and yard in the seaside village of Blackrock, south of Dublin, has all manner of stalls selling everything from New Age crystals to futons.

George's St Arcade (Map p86; George's St Arcade; ☻ 9am-6pm Mon-Sat, 10am-6pm Sun) This excellent covered market between South Great George's and Drury Sts has some great secondhand clothes shops, and stalls selling Mediterranean food, jewellery and records.

Meeting House Square Market (Map p84; Meeting House Sq; ☻ 8am-5pm Sat) This open-air food market in Temple Bar takes place every Saturday, but get here early for the best pickings and to avoid the huge crowds. With a multitude of stalls selling top organic produce from around the country, you can also buy diverse snacks such as sushi, waffles, tapas, oysters and handmade cheeses.

Clery's & Co (Map pp82-3; ☎ 878 6000; O'Connell St) This graceful shop is a Dublin classic. Recently restored to its elegant best, it caters to the more conservative Dublin shopper.

Debenham's (Map pp82-3; ☎ 873 0044; Henry St) This UK giant hit these shores in 2006; it's bold and glass-fronted on the outside and holds street-smart fashion labels such as Zara, Warehouse and G-Star on the inside, as well as the obligatory homewares and electrical sections.

ILAC Centre (Map pp82-3; ☎ 704 1460) Off Henry St near O'Connell St, the ILAC Centre is a little dilapidated but has some interesting outlets with goods at affordable prices.

Clothing

Temple Bar and the area around Grafton St are the best places for all kinds of designer gear, both new and secondhand.

Costume (Map p86; ☎ 679 5200; 10 Castle Market) From casuals to sparkly full-length dresses, Costume specialises in stylish contemporary women's wear from young European designers. Its own Costume label sits alongside pieces by Temperley, Anna Sui, newcomer Jonathan Saunders and Irish label Leighlee.

Smock (Map p84; ☎ 613 9000; Smock Alley Ct, West Essex St) This tiny designer shop on the edge of Temple Bar sells cutting-edge international women's wear from classy 'investment labels' Easton Pearson, Veronique Branquinho and AF Vandevorft, as well as a small range of interesting jewellery and lingerie.

5 Scarlet Row (Map p84; ☎ 672 9534; 5 Scarlet Row) Beautiful, modern, exclusive, minimalist. If that's what you're after, try the creations of

Eley Kishimoto, Zero, Irish designer Sharon Wauchob and mens' wear label Unis at 5 Scarlet Row. Co-owner Eileen Shields worked with Donna Karan in New York before returning to found her own gorgeous shoe label, which retails here.

BT2 (Map p86; ☎ 679 5666; 88 Grafton St) This is Brown Thomas' young and funky offshoot, with high-end casuals for men and women and a juice bar upstairs overlooking Grafton St. Brands include DKNY, Custom, Diesel, Ted Baker and Tommy Hilfiger.

Jenny Vander (Map p86; ☎ 677 0406; 50 Drury St) A visit to Jenny Vander is like walking into an exotic 1940s boudoir. The selection of antique clothing, hats and jewellery is pretty wild, although you won't find many bargains.

Urban Outfitters (Map p86; ☎ 670 6202; 4 Cecilia St) Its loyal clientele think it's the funkiest shop in town, and they're not far wrong, with the latest styles complemented by the coolest gift items and even a trendy record store.

Irish Crafts & Souvenirs

Avoca Handweavers (Map p84; ☎ 677 4215; 11-13 Suffolk St) This contemporary craft shop is a treasure trove of interesting Irish and foreign products. The colourful shop is chock-a-block with woollen knits, ceramics, handcrafted gadgets and a wonderful toy selection – and not a tweed cap in sight.

Claddagh Records (Map p84; ☎ 677 0262; 2 Cecilia St) This shop sells a wide range of Irish traditional and folk music.

DesignYard (Map p84; ☎ 474 1011; Cow's Lane) A high-end craft-as-art shop where everything you see – be it glass, batik, sculpture, painting – is one-off and handmade in Ireland. It also showcases contemporary jewellery from young international designers.

Kilkenny Shop (Map p86; ☎ 677 7066; 6 Nassau St) This shop has a wonderful selection of finely made Irish crafts, featuring clothing, glassware, pottery, jewellery, crystal and silver from some of Ireland's best designers.

GETTING THERE & AWAY
Air
Dublin Airport (Map p78; ☎ 814 1111; www.dublinairport.com), 13km north of the centre, is Ireland's major international gateway airport, with direct flights from Europe, North America and Asia. For information on who flies in and out of here, see p716 and p720.

Boat
Dublin has two ferry ports: the **Dun Laoghaire ferry terminal** (☎ 280 1905; Dun Laoghaire), 13km southeast of the city, serves Holyhead in Wales and can be reached by DART to Dun Laoghaire, or bus 7, 7A or 8 from Burgh Quay or bus 46A from Trinity College; and the **Dublin Port terminal** (Map p78; ☎ 855 2222; Alexandra Rd), 3km northeast of the city centre, serves Holyhead, Mostyn and Liverpool.

Buses from Busáras are timed to coincide with arrivals and departures: for the 9.45am ferry departure from Dublin Port, buses leave Busáras at 8.30am. For the 9.45pm departure, buses depart from Busáras at 8.30pm. For the 1am sailing to Liverpool, the bus departs from Busáras at 11.45pm. All bus trips cost €2.

See p719 for details of ferry journeys.

Bus
Busáras (Map pp82-3; ☎ 836 6111; www.buseireann.ie; Store St) is just north of the river behind Custom House.

For information on fares, frequencies and durations to various destinations in the Republic and Northern Ireland, see p721.

Car & Motorcycle
A number of hire companies have desks at the airport, and other operators are based close to the airport and deliver cars for airport collection. Listed are some of the main hire companies in Dublin:

Avis (www.avis.com) City (Map pp82-3; ☎ 605 7500; 1 East Hanover St); Dublin Airport (☎ 844 5204)

Budget (www.budgetcarrental.ie) City (Map p80; ☎ 837 9802; 151 Lower Drumcondra Rd); Dublin Airport (☎ 844 5150)

Dan Dooley Car Hire (www.dan-dooley.ie) City (Map p86; ☎ 677 2723; 42-43 Westland Row); Dublin Airport (☎ 844 5156)

Europcar (www.europcar.com) City (Map p80; ☎ 614 2800; Baggot St Bridge); Dublin Airport (☎ 844 4179)

Hertz (www.hertz.com) City (Map p80; ☎ 660 2255; 149 Upper Leeson St); Dublin Airport (☎ 844 5466)

Sixt Rent-a-Car (www.icr.ie) City (☎ 862 2715; Old Airport Rd, Santry); Dublin Airport (☎ 844 4199)

Thrifty (www.thrifty.ie) City (Map p80; ☎ 1800 515 800; 125 Herberton Bridge, just off South Circular Rd); Dublin Airport (☎ 840 0800)

Train
For general train information, contact **Iarnród Éireann Travel Centre** (Map p84; ☎ 836 6222; www.irishrail.ie; 35 Lower Abbey St; ◴ 9am-5pm Mon-Fri, 9am-1pm Sat). **Connolly Station** (Map pp82-3; ☎ 836 3333), just north of the Liffey and the city centre, is the station for Belfast, Derry, Sligo and other northern destinations. **Heuston Station** (Map pp82-3; ☎ 836 5421), just south of the Liffey and well west of the centre, is the station for Cork, Galway, Killarney, Limerick, Wexford, Waterford and other destinations west, south and southwest of Dublin. See p725 for more information.

GETTING AROUND
To/From the Airport
There is no train service to/from the airport, but there are bus and taxi options.

BUS
Aircoach (☎ 844 7118; www.aircoach.ie; one way/return €7/12) Private coach service with two routes from the airport to 18 destinations throughout the city, including the main streets of the city centre. Coaches run every 10 to 15 minutes between 6am and midnight, then hourly from midnight until 6am.

Airlink Express Coach (☎ 872 0000, 873 4222; www.dublinbus.ie; adult/child €5/2) Bus 747 runs every 10 to 20 minutes from 5.45am to 11.30pm between the airport, central bus station (Busáras) and Dublin Bus office on Upper O'Connell St; bus 748 runs every 15 to 30 minutes from 6.50am to 10.05pm between the airport, and Heuston and Connolly Stations.

Dublin Bus (☎ 872 0000; www.dublinbus.ie; 59 Upper O'Connell St; adult/child €2/0.75) A number of buses serve the airport from various points in Dublin, including buses 16A (Rathfarnham), 746 (Dun Laoghaire) and 230 (Portmarnock); all cross the city centre on their way to the airport.

TAXI

There is a taxi rank directly outside the arrivals concourse. A taxi should cost about €20 from the airport to the city centre, including a supplementary charge of €2.50 (not applied going to the airport). Make sure the meter is switched on.

Car & Motorcycle

Traffic in Dublin is a nightmare and parking is an expensive headache. There are no free spots to park anywhere in the city centre during business hours (7am to 7pm Monday to Saturday), but there are plenty of parking meters, 'pay and display' spots (€2.50 to €4.80 per hour), and over a dozen sheltered and supervised car parks (around €5 per hour).

Clamping of illegally parked cars is thoroughly enforced, with a €80 charge for removal. Parking is free after 7pm Monday to Saturday and all day Sunday in all metered spots and on single yellow lines.

Car theft and break-ins are a problem, and the police advise visitors to park in a supervised car park. Cars with foreign number plates are prime targets; never leave your valuables behind. When you are booking accommodation, check on parking facilities.

Public Transport

BUS

The office of **Dublin Bus** (Map pp82-3; ☎ 872 0000; www.dublinbus.ie; 59 Upper O'Connell St; ☺ 9am-5.30pm Mon-Fri, 9am-2pm Sat) has free single-route timetables of all its services.

Buses run from around 6am (some start at 5.30am) to 11.30pm. Fares are calculated according to stages: one to three stages costs €1, four to seven stages €1.40, eight to 13 stages €1.60, and 14 to 23 stages €1.90. You must tender exact change for tickets when boarding buses; anything more and you

will be given a receipt for reimbursement, which is only possible at the Dublin Bus main office.

LUAS

The **Luas** (www.luas.ie; ☺ 5.30am-12.30am Mon-Fri, from 6.30am Sat, 7am-11.30pm Sun) light-rail system has two lines: the Green Line (trains every five to 15 minutes), which connects St Stephen's Green with Sandyford in south Dublin via Ranelagh and Dundrum; and the Red Line (trains every 20 minutes), which runs from Lower Abbey St to Tallaght via the north quays and Heuston Station. There are ticket machines at every stop or you can buy tickets from newsagencies throughout the city centre; a typical short-hop fare will cost you €1.70.

NITELINK

These late-night buses run from the College St, Westmoreland St and D'Olier St triangle, covering most of Dublin's suburbs. Buses leave at 12.30am and 2am Monday to Wednesday, and every 20 minutes between 12.30am and 3.30am Thursday to Saturday. Tickets start at €4.

TRAIN

The **Dublin Area Rapid Transport** (DART; ☎ 836 6222; www.irishrail.ie) provides quick train access to the coast as far north as Howth (about 30 minutes) and as far south as Greystones in county Wicklow. Pearse Station (Map p86) is convenient for central Dublin south of the Liffey, and Connolly Station for north of the Liffey. There are services every 10 to 20 minutes, sometimes even more frequently, from around 6.30am to midnight Monday to Saturday. Services are less frequent on Sunday. Dublin to Dun Laoghaire takes about 15 to 20 minutes. A one-way DART ticket

---

FARE-SAVER PASSES:

- **Adult Short Hop** (€8.80) Valid for unlimited one-day travel on Dublin Bus, DART and suburban rail travel, but not Nitelink or Airlink.

- **Bus/Luas Pass** (adult/child €6.50/3.10) One day unlimited travel on both bus and Luas.

- **Family Bus & Rail Short Hop** (€13.50) Valid for travel for one day for a family of two adults and two children aged under 16 on all bus and rail services except for Nitelink, Airlink, ferry services and tours.

- **Rambler Pass** (1/2/5/7 days €6/11/17.30/21) Valid for unlimited travel on all Dublin Bus and Airlink services, but not Nitelink.

from Dublin to Dun Laoghaire or Howth costs €2.20; to Bray it's €2.50.

There are also suburban rail services north as far as Dundalk, inland to Mullingar and south past Bray to Arklow.

Some DART passes:

Adult Weekly Inner Rail Pass (€23) Valid on all DART and suburban train services between Bray to the south and Rush and Lusk to the north.

All Day Ticket (€7.20) One-day unlimited travel on DART and suburban rail services.

Taxi

All taxi fares begin with a flagfall fare of €3.80, followed by €1.50 per kilometre thereafter from 8am to 10pm. In addition there are a number of extra charges – €1 for each extra passenger and €2 for telephone bookings; there is no charge for luggage.

Taxis can be hailed on the street and found at taxi ranks around the city, including O'Connell St, College Green in front of Trinity College and St Stephen's Green at the end of Grafton St. There are numerous taxi companies that will dispatch taxis by radio. Some options:

City Cabs (☎ 872 2688)
National Radio Cabs (☎ 677 2222)

Phone the **Garda Carriage Office** (☎ 475 5888) if you have any complaints about taxis or queries regarding lost property.

AROUND DUBLIN

At the first sight of the sun – or any kind of tolerable weather – Dubliners like to get out of the city, and for many the destination is one of the small seaside villages that surround the capital. To the north are the lovely villages of Howth and Malahide, slowly and reluctantly being sucked into the Dublin conglomeration, while to the south is Dalkey, which has long since given up the fight but has managed to retain that village vibe.

DALKEY

South of Dun Laoghaire is Dalkey (Deilginis), which has the remains of a number of old castles. On Castle St, the main street, two 16th-century castles face each other: **Archibold's Castle** and **Goat Castle**. Next to the latter is the ancient **St Begnet's Church**, dating from the 9th century. **Bulloch Castle**, overlooking Bullock Harbour, north of town, was built by the monks of St Mary's Abbey in Dublin in the 12th century.

Goat Castle and St Begnet's Church have recently been converted into the **Dalkey Castle & Heritage Centre** (☎ 285 8366; www.dalkeycastle .com; Castle St; adult/child/student €6/4/5; ⏰ 9.30am-5pm Mon-Fri, 11am-5pm Sat & Sun). Models, displays and exhibitions form a pretty interesting history of Dalkey and give an insight into the area during medieval times.

Dalkey has several holy wells, including **St Begnet's Holy Well**, next to the ruins of another church dedicated to St Begnet on the 9-hectare **Dalkey Island**, a few hundred metres offshore from Coliemore Harbour. Reputed to cure rheumatism, the well is a popular destination for tourists and the faithful alike. To get here, you can hire a boat with a small outboard engine in Coliemore Harbour. To get one, simply show up (you can't book them in advance); they cost around €25 per hour.

To the south there are good views from the small park at Sorrento Point and from Killiney Hill. **Dalkey Quarry** is a popular site for rock climbers, and originally provided most of the granite for the gigantic piers at Dun Laoghaire Harbour. A number of rocky **swimming pools** are found along the Dalkey coast.

Queen's (☎ 285 4569; 12 Castle St; lunch €8-10; ⏰ noon-4pm & 5-7.30pm Mon-Fri, noon-4pm Sat & Sun) is a Dalkey institution offering a great pub lunch of meat and fish dishes.

The Dalkey branch of **Jaipur** (☎ 285 0552; 23 Castle St; mains €15-20; ⏰ noon-11pm), an excellent city-centre Indian restaurant (see p127), does more of the same here.

OK, so it's not strictly Dalkey, but all self-respecting crustacean-lovers should make the 1km trip to **Caviston's Seafood Restaurant** (☎ 280 9245; Glasthule Rd, Sandycove; mains €14-28; ⏰ noon-6pm Tue-Sat) for a meal to remember. Local fish and seafood are cooked simply with imaginative ingredients that enhance rather than overpower their flavour.

Dalkey is on the DART suburban train line or, for a slower journey, you can catch bus 8 from Burgh Quay in Dublin. Both cost €2.

HOWTH

The pretty fishing village of Howth (Binn Éadair), built on steep steps that run down to the waterfront, is a popular excursion from Dublin and has developed as a residential suburb of the city. The most desirable properties are on the hill above the village, located on a bulbous head that juts into the northern edge of Dublin Bay. The views from the top are magnificent. Although the harbour's role as a shipping port has long gone, Howth is a major fishing centre and yachting harbour.

Howth is only 15km from central Dublin and easily reached by DART or by simply following the Clontarf Rd out around the northern bay shoreline. En route you pass Clontarf, site of the pivotal clash between Celtic and Viking forces at the Battle of Clontarf in 1014. Further along is North Bull Island, a wildlife sanctuary where many migratory birds pause in winter.

History

Howth's name (which rhymes with 'both') has Viking origins and comes from the Danish word *hoved* (head). Howth Harbour was built from 1807 and was at that time the main Dublin harbour for the packet boats from England. Howth Rd was built to ensure rapid transfer of incoming mail and dispatches from the harbour to the city. The replacement of sailing packets with steam packets in 1818 reduced the transit time from Holyhead to seven hours, but Howth's period of importance was short – by 1813 the harbour was already showing signs of silting up, and it was superseded by Dun Laoghaire in 1833. The most famous arrival to Howth was King George IV, who visited Ireland in 1821 and

is chiefly remembered because he staggered off the boat in a highly inebriated state. He did manage to leave his footprint at the point where he stepped ashore on the West Pier.

In 1914 Robert Erskine Childers' yacht, *Asgard*, brought a cargo of 900 rifles into the port to arm the nationalists. During the Civil War, Childers was court-martialled by his former comrades and executed by firing squad for illegal possession of a revolver. The *Asgard* is now on display at Kilmainham Jail (p103) in Dublin.

Sights

AROUND THE PENINSULA

Most of the town backs onto the extensive grounds of **Howth Castle**, built in 1564 but much changed over the years, most recently in 1910 when Sir Edwin Lutyens gave it a modernist make-over. Today the castle is divided into four very posh and private residences. The original estate was acquired in 1177 by the Norman noble Sir Almeric Tristram, who changed his surname to St Lawrence after winning a battle at the behest (or so he believed) of his favourite saint. The family has owned the land ever since, though the unbroken chain of male succession came to an end in 1909.

On the grounds are the ruins of the 16th-century **Corr Castle** and an ancient dolmen (tomb chamber or portal tomb made of vertical stones topped by a huge capstone) known as **Aideen's Grave**. Legend has it that Aideen

DETOUR: SANDYCOVE & JAMES JOYCE MUSEUM

About 1km north of Dalkey is Sandycove, with a pretty little beach and the **Martello tower** – built by British forces to keep an eye out for a Napoleonic invasion – which now houses the **James Joyce Museum** (☎ 280 9265; Sandycove; adult/child/student €7/4.20/6; ☑ 10am-1pm & 2-5pm Mon-Sat, 2-6pm Sun Apr-Oct, by arrangement only Nov-Mar). This is where the action begins in James Joyce's epic novel *Ulysses*. The museum was opened in 1962 by Sylvia Beach – the Paris-based publisher who first dared to put *Ulysses* into print – and has photographs, letters, documents, various editions of Joyce's work and two death masks of Joyce on display. A combined ticket for the James Joyce Museum, the Shaw Birthplace and the Writers Museum is adult/student/child €12/10/7.40.

Below the Martello tower is the **Forty Foot Pool**, an open-air sea-water bathing pool that took its name from the Fortieth Foot, an army regiment that was stationed at the tower until the regiment was disbanded in 1904. At the close of the first chapter of *Ulysses*, Buck Mulligan heads off to the Forty Foot Pool for a morning swim. A morning wake-up here is still a local tradition, winter or summer. In fact, a winter dip isn't much braver than a summer one since the water temperature varies by only about 5°C. Basically, it's always bloody cold.

Pressure from female bathers eventually opened this public stretch of water, originally nudist and for men only, to both sexes despite strong opposition from the 'forty foot gentlemen'. They eventually compromised with the ruling that a Togs Must Be Worn sign would now apply after 9am. Prior to that time nudity prevails and swimmers are still predominantly male.

died of a broken heart after her husband was killed at the Battle of Gavra near Tara in AD 184, but the legend is rubbish because the dolmen is at least 300 years older than that.

The **castle gardens** (admission free; 🕑 24hr) are worth visiting, as they're noted for their rhododendrons (which bloom in May and June), azaleas and a long, 10m-high beech hedge planted in 1710.

Also within the grounds are the ruins of **St Mary's Abbey** (Abbey St, Howth Castle; admission free), originally founded in 1042 by the Viking King Sitric, who also founded the original church on the site of Christ Church Cathedral. The abbey was amalgamated with the monastery on Ireland's Eye (right) in 1235. Some parts of the ruins date from that time, but most are from the 15th and 16th centuries. The tomb of Christopher St Lawrence (Lord Howth), in the southeastern corner, dates from around 1470. See the caretaker or read instructions on the gate for opening times.

A more recent addition is the rather ramshackle **National Transport Museum** (☎ 832 0427; www.nationaltransportmuseum.org; Howth Castle; adult/child/student €3.50/2/2; 🕑 10am-5pm Mon-Sat Jun-Aug, 2-5pm Sat, Sun & bank holidays Sep-May), which has a range of exhibits, including double-decker buses, a bakery van, fire engines and trams – most notably a Hill of Howth electric tram that operated from 1901 to 1959. To reach the museum, go through the castle gates and turn right just before the castle.

The allure of history and public transport aside, most visitors set foot in the demesne armed with golf clubs, as here you'll find **Deer Park Golf Course** (☎ 832 2624; Howth Castle; 18 holes Mon-Fri €17.50, Sat & Sun €25, club rental €16; 🕑 8am-dusk Mon-Fri, 6.30am-dusk Sat & Sun), a public facility attached to a hotel. An 18-hole course, two nine-hole courses and a par-3 course, all with splendid views of Dublin Bay and the surrounding countryside – once described by HG Wells as the best view west of Naples – are the big draw.

Howth is essentially a very large hill surrounded by cliffs, and **Howth Summit** (171m) has excellent views across Dublin Bay right down to Wicklow. From the Summit you can walk to the top of the Ben of Howth, which has a cairn said to mark a 2000-year-old Celtic **royal grave**. The 1814 **Baily Lighthouse** at the southeastern corner is on the site of an old stone fort and can be reached by a dramatic cliff-top walk. There was an earlier hilltop beacon here in 1670.

IRELAND'S EYE

A short distance offshore from Howth is Ireland's Eye (Map p78), a rocky sea-bird sanctuary with the ruins of a 6th-century monastery. There's a Martello tower at the northwestern end of the island, where boats from Howth land, while a spectacularly sheer rock face plummets into the sea at the eastern end. As well as the sea birds overhead, you can see young birds on the ground during the nesting season. Seals can also be spotted around the island.

Doyle & Sons (☎ 831 4200; return €12) takes boats out to the island from the East Pier of Howth Harbour during the summer, usually on weekend afternoons. Don't wear shorts if you're planning to visit the monastery ruins because they're surrounded by a thicket of stinging nettles. And bring your rubbish back with you – far too many island visitors don't.

Further north from Ireland's Eye is **Lambay Island**, an important sea-bird sanctuary that cannot be visited.

Sleeping & Eating

Wright's Findlater (☎ 832 4488; www.wrightsfindlater howth.com; Harbour Rd; mains €10-21) A modern all-in restaurant, bar and lounge, Wright's Findlater's has an Asian-influenced restaurant, Lemongrass, on the 1st floor, above a stylish bar that does terrific grub with an emphasis on fish.

Abbey Tavern (☎ 839 0307; www.abbeytavern.ie; Abbey St; mains €22-26, 3-course dinner €38) This atmospheric 16th-century tavern serves better-than-average pub grub, with an emphasis on seafood and meat. There's a bar menu all day.

King Sitric (☎ 832 5235; www.kingsitric.ie; East Pier; mains €35-48, 5-course dinner €55; 🕑 lunch & dinner Mon-Fri, dinner only Sat) Howth's most famous restaurant, praised for its superb seafood and prize-winning wine list, has added eight marvellous rooms (€145 to €205) to its premises right on the port. Each is named after a lighthouse, and all are extremely well decorated, with wonderful views of the port.

If you want to buy food and prepare it yourself, Howth has fine seafood that you can buy fresh from the string of shops on West Pier.

Getting There & Away

The easiest and quickest way to get to Howth from Dublin is on the DART, which whisks you there in just over 20 minutes for a fare of €2. For the same fare, buses 31 and 31A from Lower Abbey St in the city centre run as far as the Summit, 5km to the southeast of Howth.

MALAHIDE

Malahide (Mullach Ide) was once a small village with its own harbour, a long way from the urban jungle of Dublin. The only thing protecting it from the northwards expansion of Dublin's suburbs is Malahide Demesne, 101 well-tended hectares of parkland dominated by a castle once owned by the powerful Talbot family. The handsome village remains relatively intact, but the once quiet marina has been massively developed and is now a bustling centre with a pleasant promenade and plenty of restaurants and shops. A great way to Dublin from the sea is by boarding a speedboat run by **Sea Safaris** (☎ 806 1626; www .seasafari.ie; Malahide Marina; per hr €25) and going for an hour-long trip around Dublin Bay.

Sights

MALAHIDE CASTLE

Despite the vicissitudes of Irish history, the Talbot family managed to keep **Malahide Castle** (☎ 846 2184; www.malahidecastle.com; adult/child/student/ family €7/4.40/6/20, incl Fry Model Railway €12/7.50/10/34; ◯ 10am-5pm Mon-Sat, 11am-6pm Sun Apr-Oct, 11am-5pm Sat & Sun Nov-Mar) under its control from 1185 to 1976, apart from when Cromwell was around (1649–60). It's now owned by Dublin County Council. The castle is the usual hotchpotch of additions and renovations; the oldest part is a three-storey 12th-century tower house. The

façade is flanked by circular towers that were tacked on in 1765.

The castle is packed with furniture and paintings. Highlights are a 16th-century oak room with decorative carvings, and the medieval Great Hall, which has family portraits, a minstrel's gallery and a painting of the Battle of the Boyne. Puck, the Talbot family ghost, is said to have last appeared in 1975.

The **parkland** (admission free; ◯ 10am-9pm Apr-Oct, 10am-5pm Nov-Mar) around the castle is a good place for a picnic.

FRY MODEL RAILWAY

Ireland's biggest **model railway** (☎ 846 3779; Malahide Castle; adult/child/student/family €7/4.40/6/20; ◯ 10am-1pm & 2-5pm Mon-Sat, 2-6pm Sun Apr-Sep, 2-5pm Sat, Sun & holidays Oct-Mar) is 240 sq metres, and authentically displays much of Ireland's rail and public transport system, including the DART line and Irish Sea ferry services, in O-gauge (32mm track width). A separate room features model trains and other memorabilia. Unfortunately the operators suffer from the overseriousness of some grown men with complicated toys; rather than let you simply look and admire, they herd you into the control room in groups for demonstrations.

Getting There & Away

Malahide is 13km north of Dublin. Bus 42 (€2) from Talbot St takes around 45 minutes. The DART stops in Malahide (€2.35), but be sure to get on the right train (it's marked at the front of the train) as the line splits at Howth Junction.

County Wicklow

COUNTY WICKLOW

Wild and often wonderful Wicklow (Cill Mhantáin) is Dublin's favourite playground – its rich and varied landscapes the preferred getaway for many a busy urbanite, many of whom are so taken by the county's beauty that they now reside within its postal districts.

Yet the 'Garden of Ireland' – as the county is known – has been successful in fending off the worst ravages of the urban expansion, mostly because so much of the county remains defiantly opposed to the planners' bulldozers. Strict planning regulations aside, there's little to be done about the county's most imposing natural feature, a gorse-and-bracken mountain spine that is as wildly beautiful as it is impenetrable to the planners who want to lay out yet another housing estate.

Here, history and geology work together to great effect and preserve one of Ireland's most stunning landscapes, replete with dramatic glacial valleys, soaring mountain passes and some of the country's most important archaeological treasures – from breathtaking early-Christian sites to the elegant country homes of the wealthiest of Ireland's 18th-century nobility.

Linking much of Wicklow's attractions is the 132km-long Wicklow Way, the country's foremost walking trail and – if you've got the legs for it – still the best and most satisfying way to explore the county. From the suburbs of southern Dublin to the rolling fields of County Carlow, the Way leads walkers along disused military supply lines, old bog roads and nature trails over the eastern flanks of the mountains.

HIGHLIGHTS

- **Monastic Magic** Evocative ruins and marvellous slopes and forests of gorgeous Glendalough (p152)
- **Body & Mind** Treat the body, and the mind will surely follow at Macreddin, home of Brook Lodge and Wells Spa (p164)
- **The Hills are Alive** Ireland's most popular hiking trail, the Wicklow Way (p155)
- **The Art Iis Hot** Art and atmosphere of magnificent Russborough House (p157)
- **The Glory of the Garden** Gorgeous Italianate gardens and the impressive waterfall at Powerscourt Estate (p148)

★ Russborough House   ★ Powerscourt Estate

★ Glendalough

★ Wicklow Way

Macreddin ★

■ POPULATION: 114,700	■ AREA: 2025 SQ KM

NATIONAL PARKS

Wicklow Mountains National Park covers more than 20,000 hectares of mountainous blanket bogs and woodland. Eventually, virtually all of the higher ground stretching the length of the mountains will fall under the protection of the national park, which will cover more than 30,000 hectares.

Within the boundaries of the protected area are two nature reserves, owned and managed by the Heritage Service, and legally protected by the Wildlife Act. The larger reserve, west of the Glendalough Visitor Centre, conserves the extensive heath and bog of the Glendalough Valley plus the Upper Lake and valley slopes on either side. The second, Glendalough Wood Nature Reserve, conserves oak woods stretching from the Upper Lake as far as the Rathdrum road to the east.

Most of Ireland's native mammal species can be found within the confines of the park. Large herds of deer roam on the open hill areas, though these were introduced in the 20th century after the native red-deer population became extinct during the first half of the 18th century. The uplands are the preserve of foxes, badgers and hares. Red squirrels are usually found in the pine woodlands – look out for them around the Upper Lake.

The bird population of the park is plentiful. Birds of prey abound, the most common being peregrine falcons, marlins, kestrels, hawks and sparrowhawks. Hen harriers are a

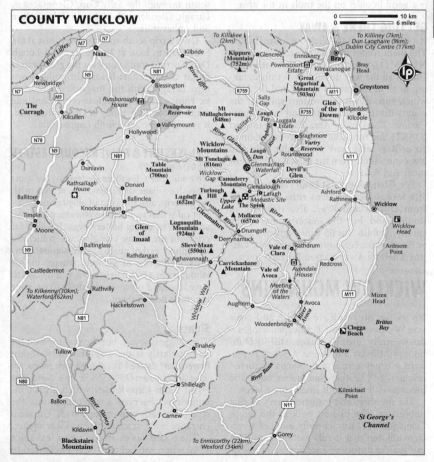

rarer sight, though they too live in the park. Moorland birds found in the area include meadow pipits and skylarks. Less common birds such as whinchats, ring ouzels and dippers can be spotted, as can red grouse, whose numbers are quickly disappearing in other parts of Ireland. For information, call in or contact the **National Park Information Point** (☎ 0404-45425; www.wicklownationalpark .ie; Bolger's Cottage, Miners' Rd, Upper Lake, Glendalough; ⊙ 10am-6pm May-Sep, 10am-dusk Sat & Sun Oct-Apr), off the Green Rd that runs by the Upper Lake, about 2km from the Glendalough Visitor Centre. There's usually someone on hand to help, but if you find it closed the staff may be out running guided walks. *Exploring the Glendalough Valley* (Heritage Service; €1.80) is a good booklet on the trails in the area.

GETTING THERE & AWAY

It's a cinch to get to Wicklow from Dublin. The main routes through the county are the N11 (M11), which runs north–south from Dublin all the way through to Wexford, taking in all of the coastal towns; and the N81, which runs down the western spine of the county through Blessington and into County Carlow. The Dublin Area Rapid Transport (DART) line runs southward from Dublin as far as Bray, and there are regular train and bus connections from the capital to Wicklow town and Arklow.

For Glendalough, **St Kevin's Bus** (☎ 01-281 8119; www.glendaloughbus.com) runs twice daily from Dublin and Bray, also stopping in Roundwood. For the western parts of the county, Dublin Bus 65 runs regularly as far as Blessington. For more details, see the Getting There & Away section for each town.

WICKLOW MOUNTAINS

No sooner do you leave Dublin and cross into Wicklow than the landscape changes – dramatically. From Killakee, still in Dublin, the Military Rd begins a 30km southward journey across vast sweeps of gorse-, bracken- and heather-clad moors, bogs, and mountains dotted with small corrie lakes.

The numbers and statistics aren't all that impressive. The highest peak in the range, Lugnaquilla (924m), is really more of a very large hill, but that hardly matters here. This vast granite intrusion, a welling-up of hot igneous rock that solidified some 400 million years ago, was shaped during the Ice Ages into the schist-capped mountains visible today. The peaks are marvellously desolate and as raw as only nature can be. Between the mountains are a number of deep glacial valleys, most notably Glenmacnass, Glenmalure and Glendalough, while corrie lakes such as Lough Bray Upper and Lower, gouged out by ice at the head of the glaciers, complete the wild topography.

Beginning on Dublin's southern fringes, the narrow Military Rd winds its way through the most remote parts of the mountains, offering some extraordinary views of the surrounding countryside. The best place to join it is at Glencree (from Enniskerry). It then runs south through the Sally Gap, Glenmacnass, Laragh, Glendalough and on to Glenmalure and Aghavannagh.

On the trip south you can divert east at the Sally Gap to look at Lough Tay and Lough Dan. Further south you pass the great waterfall at Glenmacnass before dropping down into Laragh, with the magnificent monastic ruins of Glendalough nearby. Continue south through the valley of Glenmalure and, if you're fit enough, climb Lugnaquilla.

ENNISKERRY & POWERSCOURT ESTATE

☎ 01 / pop 2800

On a summer's day there are few lovelier spots than the village of Enniskerry, replete with art galleries and the kind of all-organic gourmet cafés that would have you arrested if you admitted to eating battery eggs. It's all a far cry from the village's origins, when Richard Wingfield, earl of nearby Powerscourt, commissioned a row of terraced cottages for his labourers in 1760. These days, you'd want to have laboured pretty successfully to get your hands on one of them.

Sights

The village is lovely, but the main reason for its popularity is the magnificent 64-sq-km **Powerscourt Estate** (☎ 204 6000; www.powerscourt .ie; adult/child/student €7.50/4.50/6.50; ⊙ 9.30am-5.30pm Feb-Oct, 9.30am-4.30pm Nov-Jan), which gives contemporary observers a true insight into the style of the 18th-century super-rich. The main entrance is 500m south of the village square.

The estate has existed more or less since 1300 when the LePoer (later anglicised to

Power) family built themselves a castle here. The property changed Anglo-Norman hands a few times before coming into the possession of Richard Wingfield, newly appointed Marshall of Ireland, in 1603 – his descendants were to live here for the next 350 years. In 1731 the Georgian wunderkind Richard Cassels (or Castle) was given the job of building a Palladian-style mansion around the core of the old castle. He finished the job in 1743, but an extra storey was added in 1787 and other alterations were made in the 19th century.

The Wingfields left during the 1950s, after which the house had a massive restoration. Then, on the eve of its opening to the public in 1974, a fire gutted the whole building. The estate was eventually bought by the Slazenger sporting-goods family who have overseen a second restoration, as well as the addition of two golf courses, a café, a huge garden centre and a bunch of cutesy little retail outlets as well as a small exhibition on the house's history.

Basically, it's all intended to draw in the punters and wring as many euros out of their pockets as possible in order to finish the huge restoration job and make the estate a kind of profitable wonderland. If you can deal with the crowds (summer weekends are the worst) or, better still, avoid the worst of them and visit midweek, you're in for a real treat. Easily the biggest drawcards of the whole pile are the simply magnificent 20-hectare formal gardens and the breathtaking views that accompany them.

Originally laid out in the 1740s, the gardens were redesigned in the 19th century by Daniel Robinson, who had as much fondness for the booze as he did for horticultural pursuits. Perhaps this influenced his largely informal style, which resulted in a magnificent blend of landscaped gardens, sweeping terraces, statuary, ornamental lakes, secret hollows, rambling walks and walled enclosures replete with more than 200 types of trees and shrubs, all beneath the stunning natural backdrop of the Great Sugarloaf Mountain to the southeast. Tickets come with a map laying out 40-minute and hour-long tours of the gardens. Don't miss the exquisite Japanese Gardens or the Pepperpot Tower, modelled on a three-inch actual pepperpot owned by Lady Wingfield. Our own favourite, however, is the animal cemetery, final resting place of the Wingfield pets and even some of their favourite milking cows. Some of the epitaphs are astonishingly personal.

A 7km walk to a separate part of the estate takes you to the 130m **Powerscourt Waterfall** (☎ 204 6000; adult/child/student €5/3.50/4.50; ☯ 9.30am-7pm May-Aug, 10.30am-5.30pm Mar-Apr & Sep-Oct, to 4.30pm Nov-Jan). It's the highest waterfall in Britain and Ireland, and is most impressive after heavy rain. You can also get to the falls by road, following the signs from the estate. A nature trail has been laid out around the base of the waterfall, taking you past giant redwoods, ancient oaks, beech, birch and rowan trees. There are plenty of birds in the vicinity, including the chaffinch, cuckoo, chiffchaff, raven and willow warbler.

Activities

One of the best health spas around is **Powerscourt Springs Health Farm** (☎ 276 1000; Coolakay; day programme €255), the perfect spot for a bit of pampering. The full-day treatment includes a three-course lunch, use of all of the facilities and a full body treatment.

Tours

All tours that take in Powerscourt start in Dublin.

Bus Éireann (☎ 836 6111; www.buseireann.ie; Busáras; adult/child/student €28.80/18/25.20; ☯ 10am mid-Mar–Oct) A whole-day tour that takes in Powerscourt and Glendalough (all admissions included), departing from Busáras.

Dublin Bus Tours (☎ 872 0000; www.dublinbus.ie; 59 Upper O'Connell St; adult/child €25/12; ☯ 11am) A visit to Powerscourt is included in the four-hour South Coast & Gardens tour, which takes in the stretch of coastline between Dun Laoghaire and Killiney before turning inland to Wicklow and on to Enniskerry. Admission to the gardens is included.

Grayline Tours (☎ 872 9010; www.irishcitytours.com; Gresham Hotel, O'Connell St; adult/child €38/19; ☯ 10am Sun) Incorporating Wicklow's big hits – Powerscourt, Glendalough and the lakes and a stop at Avoca, then takes in Dun Laoghaire and Dalkey (includes admission to Glendalough visitor centre and Powerscourt, but not coffee).

Sleeping

Summerhill House Hotel (☎ 286 7928; www.summerhill househotel.com; s/d from €80/100; ℗) A truly superb country mansion about 700m south of town just off the N11 is the best place around to lay your head, on soft cotton pillows surrounded by delicate antiques and pastoral views in oils. Everything about the place – including the top-notch breakfast – is memorable.

Coolakay House (☎ 286 2423; www.coolakayhouse .com; Waterfall Rd, Coolakay; s/d €45/80; ℗) A modern working farm about 3km south of Enniskerry (it is signposted along the road), this is a great option for walkers along the Wicklow Way. The four bedrooms are all very comfortable and have terrific views, but the real draw is the restaurant, which does a roaring trade in snacks and full meals (mains around €11).

The nearest youth hostel is in Glencree, 10km west of here.

Eating

Powerscourt Terrace Café (☎ 204 6070; Powerscourt House; mains €8-13; ⏲ 10am-5pm) The folks at Avoca Handweavers (p161) have applied all their know-how and turned what could have easily been just another run-of-the-mill tourist-attraction café into something of a gourmet experience. A slice of quiche on the terrace, overlooking the gardens in the shadow of the Great Sugarloaf? Yes please.

Emilia's Ristorante (☎ 276 1834; the Square; mains €13-21; ⏲ 5-10.45pm Mon-Sat, noon-9.30pm Sun) A lovely 1st-floor restaurant to satisfy even the most ardent craving for thin-crust pizzas. Emilia's does everything else just right too, from the organic soups to the perfect steaks down to the gorgeous meringue desserts.

Poppies Country Cooking (☎ 282 8869; the Square; mains around €9; ⏲ 8.30am-6pm) If the service wasn't so slow and the organisation so frustratingly haphazard, this pokey little café on the main square would be one of the best spots in Wicklow. The food – when you finally get a chance to eat it – is sensational: wholesome salads, filling sandwiches on doorstop-cut bread and award-winning ice cream will leave you plenty satisfied.

Johnnie Fox (☎ 295 5647; Glencullen; Hungry Fisherman's seafood platter €31; ⏲ noon-10pm) Busloads of tourists fill the place nightly throughout the summer, mostly for the knees-up, faux-Irish floorshow of music and dancing, but there's nothing contrived about the seafood, which is so damn good we'd happily sit through yet another chorus of *Danny Boy* and even consider joining in the jig. The pub is 3km northwest of Enniskerry in Glencullen.

Getting There & Away

Enniskerry is 18km south of Dublin, just 3km west of the M11 along the R117. **Dublin Bus** (☎ 872 0000, 873 4222) service 44 (€2.10, every 20 minutes) takes about 1¼ hours to get to Enniskerry from Hawkins St in Dublin. Alternatively, you can take the DART train to Bray

(€2.50) and catch bus 185 (€1.40, hourly) from the station, which takes an extra 40 minutes.

Getting to Powerscourt House under your own steam is not a problem (it's 500m from the town), but getting to the waterfall is tricky. **Alpine Coaches** (☎ 286 2547) runs a shuttle service between the DART station in Bray, the waterfall (€5.50 return) and the house (€4). Shuttles leave Bray at 11.05am (11.30am July and August), 12.30pm, 1.30pm (and 3.30pm September to June) Monday to Saturday, and 11am, noon and 1pm Sunday. The last departure from Powerscourt House is at 5.30pm.

GLENCREE
☎ 01

Just south of the County Dublin border and 10km west of Enniskerry is Glencree, a leafy hamlet set into the side of the valley of the same name, which opens east to give a magnificent view down to Great Sugarloaf Mountain and the sea.

The valley floor is home to the Glencree Oak Project, an ambitious plan to reforest part of Glencree with the native oak vegetation, mostly broadleaf trees, that once covered most of the country but now covers only 1% of Ireland's landmass.

The village, such as it is, has a tiny shop and a hostel but no pub. There's a poignant **German cemetery** dedicated to 134 servicemen who died in Ireland during WWI and WWII. Just south of the village, the former military barracks are now a retreat house and reconciliation centre for people of different religions from the Republic and the North.

There's a beautiful 18th-century farmhouse, **Knockree Hostel** (☎ 286 4036; www.anoige. ie; Knockree, Enniskerry), with wonderful views over Glencree. At the time of writing, it was being renovated and will hopefully reopen sometime in 2008 as a five-star hostel.

TOP FIVE EATS IN WICKLOW

- Roundwood Inn (opposite)
- Rathsallagh House (p158)
- Tinakilly Country House & Restaurant (p163)
- Grangecon Café (p158)
- Marc Michel (p162)

SALLY GAP

One of the two main east–west passes across the Wicklow Mountains, the Sally Gap is surrounded by some spectacular countryside. From the turn-off on the lower road (R755) between Roundwood and Kilmacanogue near Bray, the narrow road (R759) passes above the dark and dramatic Lough Tay, whose scree slopes slide into **Luggala** (Fancy Mountain). This almost fairy-tale estate is owned by one Garech de Brún, member of the Guinness family and founder of Claddagh Records, a leading producer of Irish traditional and folk music. The small River Cloghoge links Lough Tay with Lough Dan just to the south. It then heads up to the Sally Gap crossroads, where it cuts across the Military Rd and heads northwest for Kilbride and the N81, following the young River Liffey, still only a stream.

ROUNDWOOD

☎ 01 / pop 440

Reputed to be Ireland's highest village, Roundwood hardly towers above the world at 238m, but it is a handy and popular stop for walkers along the Wicklow Way, which runs past the town about 3km to the west. The long main street leads south to Glendalough and southern Wicklow. Turn-offs lead to Ashford to the east and the southern shore of Lough Dan to the west. Unfortunately, almost all Lough Dan's southern shoreline is private property and you can't get to the lake on this side.

The town has shops and a post office, but not a bank or an ATM. The nearest ATM is at the petrol station in Kilmacanogue, at the junction of the M11 and the R755.

Activities

Guided or self-guided tour options up to eight days in Wicklow (and plenty of other spots in Ireland) are available with **Footfalls Walking Holidays** (☎ 0404-45152; www.walkinghiking ireland.com; Trooperstown, Roundwood). An eight-day trek through the Wicklow Mountains complete with bed and board will cost €999.

Sleeping & Eating

Roundwood Caravan & Camping Park (☎ 281 8163; www.dublinwicklowcamping.com; camp sites €8; ☺ Apr-Sep) Top-notch facilities, including a kitchen, dining area and TV lounge, make this one of the best camp sites in all of Wicklow. It is about 500m south of the village and is served by the daily St Kevin's Bus service between Dublin and Glendalough.

Tochar House (☎ 281 8247; dm/s/d €22/41/80) In the middle of Main St, the house has newly renovated rooms where a liberal use of pine wood lends plenty of light. The dorm (which is extremely popular with walkers and cyclists) has a bathroom, shower, and tea and coffee facilities, but is not available to single travellers, only to groups of two or more. It is directly behind the pub, so there's plenty of noise at weekends.

Ballinacor House (☎ 281 8168; ballinacor@eircom .net; s/d €36/65; ☺ May-Sep) Highly recommended is this supercomfortable house about 2km south of town on the road to Laragh, which is popular with walkers and has some commanding views over the lovely countryside. The owners are friendly and have been known to give lifts into Laragh to guests.

Roundwood Inn (☎ 281 8107; Main St; mains €16-32, bar food €10-16; ☺ bar noon-9pm, restaurant 7.30-9.30pm Fri & Sat, 1-3pm Sun) This 17th-century German-owned house has a gorgeous bar with a snug and open fire, in front of which you can sample bar food with a difference: on the menu are dishes such as Hungarian goulash and Irish stew with a German twist. The more-formal restaurant is the best in town, and has earned deserved praise for its hearty, delicious cuisine. The menu favours meat dishes, including season game, Wicklow rack of lamb, and a particularly good roast suckling pig. Reservations are required.

Getting There & Away

St Kevin's Bus (☎ 281 8119; www.glendaloughbus.com) passes through Roundwood on its twice-daily jaunt between Dublin and Glendalough (one way/return €8/12, 1¼ hours).

GLENMACNASS

Desolate and utterly deserted, the Glenmacnass Valley, a stretch of wild bogland between the Sally Gap crossroads and Laragh, is one of the most beautiful parts of the mountains, although the sense of isolation is quite dramatic.

The highest mountain to the west is Mt Mullaghcleevaun (848m), and River Glenmacnass flows south and tumbles over the edge of the mountain plateau in a great foaming cascade. There's a car park near the top of the waterfall. Be careful when walking on rocks near **Glenmacnass Waterfall** as a few people have slipped to their deaths. There are fine walks up Mt Mullaghcleevaun or in the hills to the east of the car park.

WICKLOW GAP

Between Mt Tonelagee (816m) to the north and Table Mountain (700m) to the southwest, the Wicklow Gap is the second major pass over the mountains. The eastern end of the road begins just to the north of Glendalough and climbs through some lovely scenery northwestwards up along the Glendassan Valley. It passes the remains of some old lead and zinc workings before meeting a side road that leads south and up Turlough Hill, the location of Ireland's only pumped storage power station. You can walk up the hill for a look over the Upper Lake.

GLENDALOUGH

☎ 0404 / pop 280

If you're looking for the epitome of rugged and romantic Ireland, you won't do much better than Glendalough (Gleann dá Loch, 'Valley of the Two Lakes'), truly one of Ireland's most beautiful corners and a highlight of any trip along the eastern seaboard.

The substantial remains of this important monastic settlement are certainly impressive, but the real draw is the splendid setting, two dark and mysterious lakes tucked into a deep valley covered in forest. It is, despite its immense popularity, a deeply tranquil and spiritual place, and you will have little difficulty in understanding why those solitude-seeking monks came here in the first place.

History

In AD 498 a young monk named Kevin arrived in the valley and decided that it would be a good spot for a bit of silent meditation. He set up house in what had been a Bronze Age tomb on the southern side of the Upper Lake. For the next seven years he slept on stones, wore animal skins, maintained a near-starvation diet and – according to the legend – made friends with the birds and animals. Word eventually spread of Kevin's natural lifestyle, and he began attracting disciples who were seemingly unaware of the irony that they were flocking to hang out with a hermit who wanted to live as far away from other people as possible.

Kevin's preferred isolation notwithstanding, a settlement quickly grew and by the 9th century Glendalough rivalled Clonmacnoise (p362) as Ireland's premier monastic city: thousands of students studied and lived in a thriving community that was spread over a considerable area. Inevitably, Glendalough's success made it a key target of Viking raiders, who sacked the monastery at least four times between 775 and 1071. The final blow came in 1398, when English forces from Dublin almost completely destroyed it. Efforts were made to rebuild and some life lingered on here as late as the 17th century, when, under renewed repression, the monastery finally died.

Orientation & Information

At the valley entrance, before the Glendalough Hotel, is **Glendalough Visitor Centre** (☎ 45325; adult/child & student €5.30/2.10; ☉ 9.30am-6pm mid-Mar–Oct, 9.30am-5pm Nov–mid-Mar). It has a high-quality 17-minute audiovisual presentation called *Ireland of the Monasteries*, which does exactly what it says on the tin.

Coming from Laragh you first see the visitor centre, then the Glendalough Hotel, which is beside the entrance to the main group of ruins and the round tower. The Lower Lake is a small dark lake to the west, while further west up the valley is the much bigger and more impressive Upper Lake, with a large car park and more ruins nearby. Be sure to visit the Upper Lake and take one of the surrounding walks.

A model in the visitor centre should help you fix where everything is in relation to everything else.

Sights
UPPER LAKE

The original site of St Kevin's settlement, **Teampall na Skellig** is at the base of the cliffs towering over the southern side of the Upper Lake and accessible only by boat; unfortunately, there's no boat service to the site and you'll have to settle for looking at it across the lake. The terraced shelf has the reconstructed ruins of a church and early graveyard. Rough wattle huts once stood on the raised ground nearby. Scattered around are some early grave slabs and simple stone crosses.

Just east of here and 10m above the lake waters is the 2m-deep artificial cave called **St Kevin's Bed**, said to be where Kevin lived. The earliest human habitation of the cave was long before St Kevin's era – there's evidence that people lived in the valley for thousands of years before the monks arrived. In the green area just south of the car park is a large circular wall thought to be the remains of an early Christian *caher* (stone fort).

Follow the lakeshore path southwest of the car park until you come to the considerable remains of **Reefert Church** above the tiny River Poulanass. It's a small, plain, 11th-century Romanesque nave-and-chancel church with some reassembled arches and walls. Traditionally, Reefert (literally 'Royal Burial Place') was the burial site of the chiefs of the local O'Toole family. The surrounding graveyard contains a number of rough stone crosses and slabs, most made of shiny mica schist.

Climb the steps at the back of the churchyard and follow the path to the west and you'll find, at the top of a rise overlooking the lake, the scant remains of **St Kevin's Cell**, a small beehive hut.

LOWER LAKE

While the Upper Lake has the best scenery, the most fascinating buildings lie in the lower part of the valley east of the Lower Lake,

huddled together in the heart of the ancient monastic site.

Just round the bend from the Glendalough Hotel is the stone arch of the **monastery gatehouse**, the only surviving example of a monastic entranceway in the country. Just inside the entrance is a large slab with an incised cross.

Beyond that lies a **graveyard**, which is still in use. The 10th-century **round tower** is 33m tall and 16m in circumference at the base. The upper storeys and conical roof were reconstructed in 1876. Near the tower, to the southeast, is the **Cathedral of St Peter and St Paul** with a 10th-century nave. The chancel and sacristy date from the 12th century.

At the centre of the graveyard to the south of the round tower is the **Priest's House**. This odd building dates from 1170 but has been heavily reconstructed. It may have been the location of shrines of St Kevin. Later, during penal times, it became a burial site for local priests – hence the name. The 10th-century **St Mary's Church**, 140m southwest of the round tower, probably originally stood outside the walls of the monastery and belonged to local nuns. It has a lovely western doorway. A little

COUNTY WICKLOW

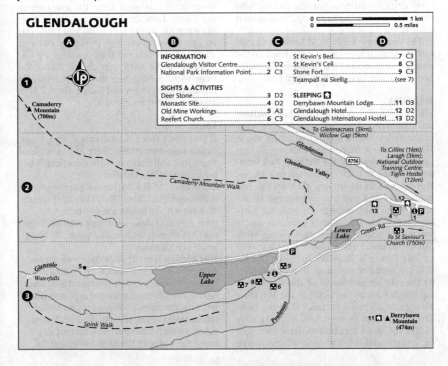

GLENDALOUGH

0 — 1 km
0 — 0.5 miles

INFORMATION
Glendalough Visitor Centre............1 D2
National Park Information Point......2 C3

SIGHTS & ACTIVITIES
Deer Stone.........................3 D2
Monastic Site......................4 D2
Old Mine Workings..................5 A3
Reefert Church.....................6 C3

St Kevin's Bed........................7 C3
St Kevin's Cell.......................8 C3
Stone Fort............................9 C3
Teampall na Skellig..............(see 7)

SLEEPING
Derrybawn Mountain Lodge..........11 D3
Glendalough Hotel.................12 D2
Glendalough International Hostel...13 D2

COUNTY WICKLOW

to the east are the scant remains of **St Kieran's Church**, the smallest at Glendalough.

Glendalough's trademark is **St Kevin's Kitchen** or Church at the southern edge of the enclosure. This church, with a miniature round towerlike belfry, protruding sacristy and steep stone roof, is a masterpiece. How it came to be known as a kitchen is a mystery as there's no indication that it was anything other than a church. The oldest parts of the building date from the 11th century – the structure has been remodelled since but it's still a classic early Irish church.

At the junction with Green Rd as you cross the river just south of these two churches is the **Deer Stone** in the middle of a group of rocks. Legend claims that when St Kevin needed milk for two orphaned babies, a doe stood here waiting to be milked. The stone is actually a *bullaun* (a stone used as a mortar for grinding medicines or food). Many such stones are thought to be prehistoric, and they were widely regarded as having supernatural properties: women who bathed their faces with water from the hollow were supposed to keep their looks forever. The early churchmen brought the stones into their monasteries, perhaps hoping to inherit some of their powers.

The road east leads to **St Saviour's Church**, with its detailed Romanesque carvings. To the west, a nice woodland trail leads up the valley past the Lower Lake to the Upper Lake.

Activities

The Glendalough Valley is all about **walking** and clambering. There are nine marked ways in the valley, the longest of which is about 10km, or about four hours walking. Before you set off, drop by the **National Park Information Point** (☎ 45425; ⏳ 10am-6pm daily May-Sep, 10am-dusk Sat & Sun Oct-Apr) and pick up the relevant leaflet and trail map (all around €0.50) or, if you're solo, arrange for walking partners. It also has a number of excellent guides for sale – you won't go far wrong with David Herman's *Hillwalker's Wicklow* (€6) or Joss Lynam's *Easy Walks Near Dublin* (€10). A word of warning: don't be fooled by the relative gentleness of the surrounding countryside or the fact that the Wicklow Mountains are really no taller than big hills. The weather can be merciless, so make sure to take the usual precautions, have the right equipment and tell someone where you're

going and when you should be back. For Mountain Rescue call ☎ 999.

The easiest and most popular walk is the gentle hike along the northern shore of the Upper Lake to the lead and zinc **mine workings**, which date from 1800. The better route is along the lakeshore rather than on the road (which runs 30m in from the shore), a distance of about 2.5km, one way, from the Glendalough Visitor Centre. Continue on up the head of the valley if you wish.

Alternatively, you can walk up the **Spink** (from the Irish for 'pointed hill'; 380m), the steep ridge with vertical cliffs running along the southern flanks of the Upper Lake. You can go part of the way and turn back, or complete a circuit of the Upper Lake by following the top of the cliff, eventually coming down by the mine workings and going back along the northern shore. The circuit is about 6km long and takes about three hours – if you feel like going on, check out the boxed text, opposite.

The third option is a hike up **Camaderry Mountain** (700m), hidden behind the hills that flank the northern side of the valley. The walk starts on the road just 50m back towards Glendalough from the entrance to the Upper Lake car park. Head straight up the steep hill to the north and you come out on open mountains with sweeping views in all directions. You can then continue up Camaderry to the northwest or just follow the ridge west looking over the Upper Lake. To the top of Camaderry and back is about 7.5km and takes about four hours.

Tours

If you don't fancy discovering Glendalough under your own steam, there are a couple of tours that will make it fairly effortless. They both depart from Dublin.

Bus Éireann (☎ 01-836 6111; www.buseireann.ie; Busáras; adult/child/student €28.80/18/25.20; ⏳ departs 10am mid-Mar–Oct) Includes admission to the visitor centre and a visit to Powerscourt Estate in this whole-day tour which returns to Dublin at about 5.45pm. The guides are good but impersonal.

Wild Wicklow Tour (☎ 01-280 1899; www.discover dublin.ie; adult/student & child €28/25; ⏳ departs 9.10am year-round) Award-winning tours of Glendalough, Avoca and the Sally Gap that never fail to generate rave reviews for atmosphere and all-round fun, but so much craic has made a casualty of informative depth. The first pick-up is at the Dublin Tourism office, but there are a variety of pick-up points throughout Dublin; check the point nearest you when booking. The tour returns to Dublin about 5.30pm.

Sleeping

BUDGET

Glendalough International Hostel (☎ 45342; www.anoige.ie; the Lodge; dm Jun-Oct €23, Nov-May €19) Conveniently, this modern hostel is near the round tower, set amid the deeply wooded glacial area that makes up the Glendalough Valley.

MIDRANGE

Most B&Bs are in or around Laragh, a village 3km east of Glendalough, or on the way there from Glendalough.

WALK: THE WICKLOW WAY – GLENDALOUGH TO AUGHRIM

The Wicklow Way is one of Ireland's most popular long-distance walks because of its remarkable scenery and its relatively fluid and accessible starting and finishing points – there are plenty of half- and full-day options along the way.

This section is 40km long and takes you through some of the more remote parts of the Wicklow Mountains and down into the southeastern foothills. There's relatively little road walking but the greater part of the day is through conifer plantations. The walk should take between 7½ and eight hours, with an ascent of 1035m.

From the **National Park Information Point** on the southern side of the Upper Lake, turn left and ascend beside Lugduff Brook and **Pollanass Waterfall**. Veer left when you meet a forest track, then left again at a junction and cross two bridges. The Way leads northeast for about 600m then, from a tight right bend, heads almost directly southwards (via a series of clearly marked junctions), up through the conifer plantations, across Lugduff Brook again and beside a tributary, to open ground on the saddle between **Mullacor** (657m) and **Lugduff** (1¾ hours from Glendalough). From here on a good day, massive Lugnaquilla sprawls across the view to the southwest; in the opposite direction is Camaderry's long ridge above Glendalough, framed against the bulk of Tonelagee. Follow the raised boardwalk down, contour above a plantation and drop into it where a steep muddy and rocky path descends to a forest road; turn left.

If you're planning to stay at Glenmalure Youth Hostel (see p157), rather than go all the way down to the crossroads in Glenmalure, follow the Way from the left turn for about 1km southwards. At an oblique junction where the Way turns southeast, bear left in a westerly direction and descend steeply to the road in Glenmalure. The hostel is about 2km northwest.

To continue straight on along the Way from the left turn, follow forest roads south then southeast for 1.6km to a wide zigzag above open ground, then contour the steep slope, swing northeast and drop down to a minor road beside two bridges. Continue down to an intersection and Glenmalure; it's about 1¼ hours from the saddle.

The Way presses straight on (south) through the crossroads for 500m, across the Avonbeg River and past silent **Drumgoff Barracks**, built in 1803 but long-since derelict, then right along a forest track. Keep left past a ruined cottage and start to gain height in two fairly long reaches; go through two left turns then it's down and across a stream. About 800m further on, turn right along a path to start the long ascent almost to the top of **Slieve Maan** (550m) via four track junctions, maintaining a southwesterly to south-southwesterly direction. Back on a forest track, the Way turns left (southeast) close to unforested ground to the west. With a few more convoluted turns, you're out of the trees and on a path between the plantation and the road (mapped as the Military Rd). The Way eventually meets the latter beside a small tributary of the Aghavannagh River (two hours from Glenmalure).

Walk down the road for about 250m, then turn off left along a forest track, shortly bearing left to gain height steadily on a wide path over **Carrickashane Mountain** (508m). Descend steeply to a wide forest road and continue down for about 1km. Bear right to reach a minor road and turn right. Leave the road 500m further on and drop down to another road – Iron Bridge is just to the right (an hour from Military Rd).

Walk 150m up to a road and turn left; follow this road down the valley of the Ow River for 7.5km to a junction – Aughrim is to the left, another 500m. Buses along the Dublin to Wexford line stop here.

Glendale (☎ 45410; www.glendale-glendalough.com; Laragh East; s/d €36/60, cottage per week €250-600; ℗) This is an immaculately modern and tidy B&B with large, comfortable rooms. Also available are five modern self-catering cottages that sleep six. Every cottage has all the mod cons, from TV and video to a fully equipped kitchen complete with microwave, dishwasher and washer-dryer. The owners will also drop you off in Glendalough if you don't fancy the walk.

ourpick Glendalough Cillíns (☎ 45140, for bookings 45777; St Kevin's Parish Church, Glendalough; r €45) In an effort to recreate something of the contemplative spirit of Kevin's early years in the valley, St Kevin's Parish Church rents out six *cillíns* (hermitages), for folks looking to take time out from the bustle of daily life and reflect on more spiritual matters. In keeping with more modern needs, however, there are a few more facilities than were present in Kevin's cave. Each hermitage is a bungalow consisting of a bedroom, a bathroom, a small kitchen area and an open fire supplemented by a storage heating facility. The whole venture is managed by the local parish, and while there is a strong spiritual emphasis here, it is not necessarily a Catholic one. Visitors of all denominations and creeds are welcome, so long as their intentions are reflective and meditative; backpackers looking for a cheap place to bed down are not. The hermitages are in a field next to St Kevin's Parish Church, about 1km east of Glendalough on the R756 to Laragh.

Laragh Mountain View Lodge (☎ 45282; fax 45204; Glenmacnass; s/d €50/80; ℗) It praises itself as 'heaven on earth', which it isn't, but it does have great views. The house itself is a modern bungalow with comfortable, tidy rooms, but what makes this place worth checking out is the location: the middle of gorgeous nowhere. It's about 3km north of Laragh, on the R115 to Glenmacnass.

Derrybawn Mountain Lodge (☎ 45644; derrybawnlodge@eircom.net; Derrybawn, Laragh; s/d €50/90; ℗) Beautifully positioned on Derrybawn Mountain (474m) is this handsome lodge with eight comfortable rooms and some pretty spectacular views of the surrounding countryside. The owners are both members of the local Mountain Rescue, so there are plenty of insider tips to be had on where and how to hike. It's about 4km south of Laragh.

Glendalough River House (☎ 45577; www.glendaloughriverhouse.com; Laragh; s/d €58/82; ℗) This 200-year-old restored farmhouse, on the river at the beginning of the Green Rd pedestrian path to Glendalough from Laragh, is an absolute delight. The bedrooms are large and well-appointed, while the breakfast will load you up with all the energy you'll need for a hike in the surrounding hills. You can also have the farmhouse all to yourself by taking it on a self-catering basis.

TOP END

Glendalough Hotel (☎ 45135; www.glendaloughhotel .com; s/d €120/190; ℗) There's no mistaking Glendalough's best hotel, conveniently located next door to the visitor centre. There is no shortage of takers for its 44 fairly luxurious bedrooms.

Eating

Laragh's the place for a bit of grub, as there's only one sit-down spot in Glendalough.

During summer, villagers put out signs and serve tea and scones on the village green.

Wicklow Heather Restaurant (☎ 45157; Main St, Laragh; mains €12-18; ☯ noon-8.30pm) This is the best place for anything substantial. The trout (farmed locally) is excellent.

Glendalough Hotel (☎ 45135; 3-course lunch €19, bar mains around €10; ☯ noon-6pm) The hotel's enormous restaurant serves a very good lunch of unsurprising dishes, usually involving some chicken, beef and fish. The bar menu – burgers, sandwiches, sausages and the like – is also quite filling.

Getting There & Away

St Kevin's Bus (☎ 281 8119; www.glendaloughbus.com) departs from outside the Mansion House on Dawson St in Dublin at 11.30am and 6pm Monday to Saturday, and 11.30am and 7pm Sunday (one way/return €11/18, 1½ hours). It also stops at the Town Hall in Bray. Departures from Glendalough are at 7.15am and 4.30pm Monday to Saturday. During the week in July and August the later bus runs at 5.30pm, and there is an additional service at 9.45am.

GLENMALURE

As you go deeper into the mountains southwest of Glendalough near the southern end of the Military Rd, everything gets a bit wilder and more remote. Beneath the western slopes of Wicklow's highest peak, Lugnaquilla, is Glenmalure, a dark and sombre blind valley flanked by scree slopes of loose boulders.

After coming over the mountains into Glenmalure you turn northwest at the Drumgoff bridge. From there it's about 6km up the road beside the River Avonbeg to a car park where trails lead off in various directions.

Glenmalure figures prominently in the national tale of resistance against the British. The valley was a clan stronghold, and in 1580 the redoubtable chieftain Fiach Mac Hugh O'Byrne (1544–97) and his band of merry men actually managed to defeat an army of 1000 English soldiers; the battle cost the lives of 800 men and drove Queen Elizabeth into an apoplectic rage. In 1597 the English avenged the disaster when they captured O'Byrne and impaled his head on the gates of Dublin Castle.

Sights & Activities

Near Drumgoff is Dwyer's or **Cullen's Rock**, which commemorates both the Glenmalure battle and Michael Dwyer, a 1798 Rising rebel who holed up here. Men were hanged from the rock during the Rising.

You can walk up Lugnaquilla Mountain or head up the blind Fraughan Rock Glen east of the car park. Alternatively, you can go straight up Glenmalure Valley passing the small, seasonal An Óige Glenmalure Hostel, after which the trail divides – heading northeast, the trail takes you over the hills to Glendalough, while going northwest brings you into the Glen of Imaal (p159).

The head of Glenmalure and parts of the neighbouring Glen of Imaal are off-limits. It's military land, well posted with warning signs.

Sleeping

Glenmalure Hostel (☎ 01-830 4555; www.anoige.ie; Greenane; dm €15; ☷ Jun-Aug, Fri & Sat only Sep-May) No phone, no electricity (lighting is by gas), just a rustic two-storey cottage with 19 beds and running water. This place has a couple of heavyweight literary links: it was once owned by WB Yeats' femme fatale, Maud Gonne, and was also the setting for JM Synge's play, *Shadow of a Gunman*. It's an isolated place, but it is beautifully situated beneath Lugnaquilla.

Glenmalure Log Cabin (☎ 01-269 6979; www .glenmalure.com; 11 Glenmalure Pines, Greenane; 2 nights €220-290, 3 nights €350-500) In the heart of Glenmalure, this modern, Scandinavian-style lodge has two en-suite rooms, a fully

equipped kitchen, a living room kitted out with all kinds of electronic amusements, including your very own DVD library. Hopefully, though, you'll spend much of your time here enjoying the panorama from the sun deck. There's a two-night minimum stay, except for July and August when it's seven days.

Birchdale House (☎ 0404 46061; tmoylan@ wicklowcoco.ie; Greenane; s/d €38/65) and **Woodside** (☎ 0404 43605; www.woodsideglenmalure.com; Greenane; s/d €40/70) are two comfortable, modern homes in Greenane, towards the southern end of the valley.

WESTERN WICKLOW

As you go west through the county, the landscape gets less rugged and more rural, especially towards the borders of Kildare and Carlow. The wild terrain gives way to rich pastures: east of Blessington the countryside is dotted with private stud farms where some of the world's most expensive horses are trained in jealously guarded secrecy.

The main attraction in this part of Wicklow is the magnificent Palladian pile at Russborough House, just outside Blessington, but if it's more wild scenery you're after, you'll find it around Kilbride and the upper reaches of the River Liffey, as well as further south in the Glen of Imaal.

BLESSINGTON

☎ 045 / pop 3147

There's little to see in Blessington; it's basically made up of a long row of pubs, shops and 17th- and 18th-century town houses. It's the main town in the area, and as such makes a decent exploring base. Just outside Blessington is the Poulaphouca Reservoir, created in 1940 to drive the turbines of the local power station to the east of town and to supply Dublin with water.

The **tourist office** (☎ 865 850; Blessington Craft Centre, Main St; ☷ 10am-5pm Mon-Fri) is across the road from the Downshire House Hotel.

Sights

Magnificent **Russborough House** (☎ 865 239; Blessington; adult/child/student €6.50/3.50/5; ☷ 10am-5pm Mon-Sat May-Sep, 10.30am-5.30pm Sun & bank holidays Apr & Oct, closed rest of year) is one of Ireland's finest stately homes, a Palladian pleasure palace built for

Joseph Leeson (1705–83), later the first Earl of Milltown and, later still, Lord Russborough. It was built between 1741 and 1751 to the design of Richard Cassels, who was at the height of his fame as an architect. Poor old Richard didn't live to see it finished, but the job was well executed by Francis Bindon. Now, let's get down to the juicy bits.

The house has always attracted unwelcome attention, beginning in 1798 when Irish forces took hold of the place during the Rising; they were soon turfed out by the British army who got so used to the comforts of the place that they didn't leave until 1801, and then only after a raging Lord Russborough challenged their commander, Lord Tyrawley, to a duel 'with blunderbusses and slugs in a sawpit'. Miaow.

The house remained in the Leeson family until 1931. In 1952 it was sold to Sir Alfred Beit, the eponymous nephew of the co-founder of the de Beers diamond-mining company. Uncle Alfred was an obsessive art collector, and when he died his impressive haul – which includes works by Velázquez, Vermeer, Goya and Rubens – was passed on to his nephew, who brought it to Russborough House. The collection was to attract the interest of more than just art-lovers.

In 1974 the IRA decided to get into the art business by robbing 16 of the paintings. They were eventually all recovered, but 10 years later the notorious Dublin criminal Martin Cahill (aka the General) masterminded another robbery, this time for Loyalist paramilitaries. On this occasion, however, only some of the works were recovered and of those several were damaged beyond repair – a good thief does not a gentle curator make. In 1988 Beit got the picture and decided to hand over the most valuable of the paintings to the National Gallery; in return for the gift, the gallery agreed to lend other paintings to the collection as temporary exhibits. The sorry story didn't conclude there. In 2001 two thieves took the direct approach and drove a jeep through the front doors, making off with two paintings worth nearly €4 million, including a Gainsborough that had been stolen, and recovered, twice before. And then, to add abuse to the insult already added to injury, the house was broken into again in 2002, with the thieves taking five more paintings, including two by Rubens. Incredibly, however, both hauls were quickly recovered.

The admission price includes a 45-minute tour of the house and all the important paintings, which, given the history, is a monumental exercise in staying positive. Whatever you do, make no sudden moves. You can take an additional 30-minute **tour** (adult/child €4/ free; 2.15pm Mon-Sat, hourly on Sun) of the bedrooms upstairs, which contain more silver and furniture.

Activities

Rathsallagh Golf Club (403 316; green fees hotel guest/ visitor €65/80) is known – somewhat optimistically – as 'Augusta without the Azelias', but it is still one of the best parkland courses in Ireland, stretching over 6.5km amid mature trees, small lakes and shallow streams.

Sleeping & Eating

Haylands House (865 183; haylands@eircom.net; Dublin Rd; s/d €45/70; P) We highly recommend this comfortable B&B for its lovely rooms (all with en suite), warm welcome and excellent breakfast. It's only 500m out of town on the main Dublin road. As it's popular, book early if you can.

ourpick Rathsallagh House & Country Club (403 112; www.rathsallaghhousehotel.com; Dunlavin; s/d from €135/185) About 20km south of Blessington, this fabulous country manor, converted from Queen Anne stables in 1798, is more than just a fancy hotel. Luxury is par for the course here, from the splendidly appointed rooms to the exquisite country-house dining (the food here is some of the best you'll eat anywhere in Ireland; five-course meals are €65) and the marvellous golf course that surrounds the estate. Even the breakfast is extraordinary: it has won the National Breakfast Award three times. (Is there anything Irish tourism doesn't have an award for?)

Grangecon Café (857 892; Tullow Rd; mains €9-16; 10am-5pm Tue-Sat) Salads, home-baked dishes and a full menu of Irish cheeses are the staples at this tiny, terrific café in a converted schoolhouse. Everything here – from the pasta to the delicious apple juice – has a wholesome flavour and many of the ingredients are organic. A short but solid menu will leave you satisfied and encouraged about the future of Irish dining.

Getting There & Away

Blessington is 35km southwest of Dublin on the N81. There are regular daily services by

Dublin Bus (☎ 01-872 0000, 873 4222); catch bus 65 from Eden Quay in Dublin (€3.60, 1½ hours, every 1½ hours). **Bus Éireann** (☎ 01-836 6111) operates express bus 005 to and from Waterford, with stops in Blessington two or three times daily; from Dublin it's pick-up only, and from Waterford drop-off only.

GLEN OF IMAAL

About 7km southeast of Donard, the lovely Glen of Imaal is about the only scenery of consequence on the western flanks of the Wicklow Mountains. It's named after Mal, brother of the 2nd-century king of Ireland, Cathal Mór. Unfortunately, the glen's northeastern slopes are mostly cordoned off as an army firing range and for manoeuvres. Look out for red danger signs.

The area's most famous son was Michael Dwyer, who led rebel forces during the 1798 Rising and held out for five years in the local hills and glens. On the southeastern side of the glen at Derrynamuck is a small whitewashed, thatched cottage where Dwyer and three friends were surrounded by 100 English soldiers. One of Dwyer's companions, Samuel McAllister, ran out the front, drawing fire and meeting his death, while Dwyer escaped into the night. He was eventually deported in 1803 and jailed on Norfolk Island, off the eastern coast of Australia. He became chief constable of Liverpool, near Sydney, before he died in 1825. The cottage is now a small **folk museum** (☎ 0404-45325; Derrynamuck; admission free; ☼ 2-6pm mid-Jun–Sep) located on the Knockanarrigan–Rathdangan road.

THE COAST

Mountains and other inland marvels dominate Wicklow's impressive scenery, but the coastline has some very pretty spots between the largely unassuming towns and small coastal resorts. Most attractive of all are the fine beaches of Brittas Bay, a wide lazy arc of coastline between Wicklow and Arklow. Running alongside it is the N11 (M11) from Dublin to Wexford, a busy road that cuts through a great glacial rift, the **Glen of the Downs**, carved out of an Ice Age lake by floodwaters. There's a forest walk up to a ruined teahouse on top of the ridge to the east. If you're looking for quieter and more scenic coastal byways, we recommend the

coastal route through Greystones, Kilcoole and then along country lanes to Rathnew.

BRAY

☎ 01 / pop 26,200

You'd be hard pressed to find traces of the glorious seaside resort once described as the 'Irish Brighton', but the sleepy dormitory town of Bray is a fairly pleasant spot, and you could do far worse than spend an afternoon strolling up and down the promenade or messing about on the beach. Its proximity to Dublin on the DART line means that there's no reason to overnight here, but you'll have to resist the late-night temptations of one of our favourite bars in Ireland. There's also a great scenic walk from here south to Greystones.

Information

The **tourist office** (☎ 286 7128, 286 6796; ☼ 9.30am-1pm & 2-5pm Mon-Sat Jun-Sep, 2-4.30pm Oct-May) is in the courthouse (built in 1841) beside the Royal Hotel at the bottom of Main St.

Sights

Top of the pretty small heap is the **heritage centre** (☎ 286 7128; Old Courthouse; adult/student €4/2; ☼ 9am-5pm Mon-Fri, 10am-3pm Sat) above the tourist office, where you can explore Bray's 1000-year history and examine the lengths to which engineer William Dargan (1799–1867) went to bring the railroad to Bray. Your kids will hate you for it.

You can make it up to them at the **National Sealife Centre** (☎ 286 6939; www.sealifeeurope.com; Strand Rd; adult/child €10.50/7; ☼ 11am-5pm Mon-Sat, 10am-5pm Sun). The British-run aquarium has a fairly big selection of tanks stocked with 70 different sea and freshwater species.

About 3km south of Bray on the Greystones road are **Killruddery House & Gardens** (☎ 286 3405; www.killruddery.com; Killruddery; house & gardens adult/child €10/3, gardens only €6/2; ☼ 1-5pm May, Jun & Sep). A stunning mansion in the Elizabethan Revival style, Killruddery has been home to the Brabazon family (earls of Meath) since 1618 and has one of the oldest gardens in Ireland. The house, designed by trendy 19th-century architects Richard Morrisson and his son William in 1820, was *reduced* to its present-day huge proportions by the 14th earl in 1953; he was obviously looking for something a little more bijou. The house is impressive, but the prize-winner here is the magnificent orangery, built in 1852 and chock-full of statuary and

COUNTY WICKLOW

COUNTY WICKLOW

plant life. If you like fancy glasshouses, this is the one for you.

Activities

One of the most beautiful **coastal walks** in Wicklow stretches from the southern end of Bray's promenade over Bray Head and down to the tiny commuter town of Greystones, 7km further south. The path is pretty smooth and easy to follow, but you can make a detour and clamber up **Bray Head** (240m) through the pine trees all the way to the large cross, erected in 1950. The head is full of old smuggling caves and railway tunnels, including one that's 1.5km long. From the top, there are fine views of the Great Sugarloaf Mountain. Back on the coastal path, you approach Greystones via a narrow footbridge over the railway, after which the path narrows until you hit the lovely harbour in Greystones. Here you should relax in **Byrne's** (Greystones Pier), better known as Dan's, which serves a gorgeous pint.

Festivals

The **Bray Jazz Festival** (www.brayjazz.com) brings some pretty decent players to the seaside town over the May Bank Holiday – the first weekend of the month.

Eating

There are a couple of half-decent spots for a bite of lunch in Bray; one in particular has a lovely seafront setting.

Betelnut Café (☎ 272 4030; Mermaid Art Centre, Main St; snacks €3-7; ⌚ 8am-6pm Mon-Fri, 10am-6pm Sat, noon-6pm Sun, late on show nights) A decent café in an arts centre? Rather than reflect on Bray's lack of choice, head to this really good spot for a lunchtime nibble or a pre-theatre bite; sandwiches and salads are freshly prepared and the coffee is done just right.

Barracuda (☎ 276 5686; Strand Rd; mains €16-25; ⌚ noon-9pm) When you've had your fill of live sea creatures in the National Sealife Centre, head upstairs to this minimalist, metal-and-mirrors restaurant and see what happens to Nemo when a really good chef gets his hands on him…or not. For your newly found love of the sea and all its inhabitants, there's always a good steak.

Drinking & Entertainment

Harbour Bar (☎ 286 2274; Seapoint Rd) A strong contender for Ireland's best pub, here you can enjoy an excellent pint of Guinness in a quiet atmosphere of conviviality. There is a separate lounge with velvet curtains, assorted paintings and cosy couches. Sundays see the gay and lesbian community chill to some terrific DJs.

Clancy's Bar (☎ 286 3191; Quinnsboro Rd) A real spit-and-sawdust kind of place with a clientele as old as the wood in the bar; it's perfect for a quiet pint and a chat.

Porter House (☎ 286 0668; Strand Rd) The Bray branch of one of Temple Bar's most popular pubs, this equally popular watering hole does a roaring trade in beers from around the world as well as its own selection of intoxicating brews. It's all a little too cheesy for our tastes.

Mermaid Art Centre (☎ 272 4030; Main St; admission free; ⌚ 10am-6pm Mon-Sat) An art gallery, theatre and cinema. The theatre puts on excellent gigs and modern, experimental-style plays, while the cinema shows art-house movies almost exclusively. Call to check prices. The art gallery has constantly changing exhibitions featuring the latest Irish and European works.

Getting There & Away

BUS

With the **Dublin Bus** (☎ 872 0000) service, buses 45 (from Hawkins St) and 84 (from Burgh Quay) serve Bray (one way €2.30, one hour).

St Kevin's Bus (☎ 281 8119; www.glendaloughbus .com) to Dublin departs from Bray Town Hall (€2.50, 50 minutes) at 8am and 5pm Monday to Friday, 10.30am and 5pm Saturday, 10.30am and 6.30pm Sunday. From Dublin, buses depart from in front of the Mansion House on Dawson St.

TRAIN

Bray train station (☎ 236 3333) is 500m east of Main St just before the seafront. The DART (one way €3, 30 minutes) runs into Dublin and further north to Howth every five minutes at peak times and every 20 or 30 minutes at quiet times.

The station is also on the main line from Dublin to Wexford and Rosslare Harbour, with up to five trains daily in each direction Monday to Saturday, and four on Sunday.

KILMACANOGUE & THE GREAT SUGARLOAF

☎ 01 / pop 850

At 503m, it's not even Wicklow's highest mountain, but the Great Sugarloaf is one of the most distinctive peaks in Ireland, its conical tip visible for many miles around.

The mountain towers over the small village of Kilmacanogue, on the N11 about 4km south of Bray, which would barely merit a passing nod were it not for the presence of the mother of all Irish craft shops just across the road from the village.

Avoca Handweavers (☎ 286 7466; www.avoca.ie; Main St) is one hell of an operation, with seven branches nationwide and an even more widespread reputation for adding elegance and style to traditional rural handicrafts. Operational HQ is in a 19th-century arboretum, and its showroom will leave you in no doubt as to the company's incredible success.

Shopping for pashminas and placemats can put a fierce hunger on you, and there's no better place to satisfy it than at the shop's splendid **restaurant** (mains €11-16; ☼ 9.30am-5.30pm), which puts a premium on sourcing the very best ingredients for its dishes. It is best known for its beef-and-Guinness casserole, but vegetarians are very well catered for as well. Many of the recipes are available in the two volumes of the *Avoca Cookbook*, both on sale for €25.

Bus Éireann (☎ 836 6111) operates bus 133 from Dublin to Wicklow town and Arklow, with stops in Kilmacanogue (one way/return €3.20/5.10, 30 minutes, 10 daily).

GREYSTONES TO WICKLOW

The resort of Greystones, 8km south of Bray, was once a charming fishing village, and the seafront around the little harbour is idyllic. In summer, the bay is dotted with dinghies and windsurfers. Sadly, the surrounding countryside is vanishing beneath housing developments.

Sights

Horticulturalists from around the world can be found salivating and muttering in approval as they walk around the 8-hectare **Mt Usher Gardens** (☎ 0404-40116; www.mountushergardens.ie; adult/child/student €7/3/6; ☼ 10.30am-6pm mid-Apr–Oct), just outside the unremarkable town of Ashford, about 10km south of Greystones on the N11. OK, not really, but the gardens are pretty special, with trees, shrubs and herbaceous plants from around the world laid out in Robinsonian style – ie according to the naturalist principles of famous Irish gardener William Robinson (1838–1935) – rather than the formalist style of preceding gardens.

Sleeping

Hunter's Hotel (☎ 40106; www.hunters.ie; Newrath Bridge, Rathnew; s/d from €100/170; ℗) This exquisite property just outside Rathnew on the R761 is an absolute find, with 16 stunning rooms, each decorated with unerringly good taste. The house, one of Ireland's oldest coaching inns, is surrounded by an award-winning garden that is part of the Wicklow Gardens Festival (see the boxed text, p163).

Eating

Hungry Monk (☎ 287 5759; Church Rd; mains €13-23; ☼ 7-11pm Wed-Sat, 12.30-9pm Sun) An excellent 1st-floor restaurant on Greystones' main street. The blackboard specials are the real treat, with dishes like suckling pig with prune and apricot stuffing to complement the fixed menu's classic choices – fresh seafood, Wicklow rack of lamb, bangers 'n' mash and so forth. This is one of the better

---

WALK: THE GREAT SUGARLOAF

Before you attack the 7km, moderately difficult walk to the summit, we recommend that you get the *Wicklow Trail Sheet No 4* (€1.50) from the tourist office in Bray.

Start your walk by taking the small road opposite **St Mochonog's Church** (named after the missionary who administered the last rites to St Kevin). Ignore the left turn and continue round the bend until you get to a small bridge on your right. To your right, you'll see the expanse of the **Rocky Valley** below, a defile eroded by water escaping from a glacial lake that developed during the last Ice Age about 10,000 years ago. Continue on the path until you reach a fork: the lower road to the right continues round the mountain, while the left turn will take you up to the summit. As you reach the top, the track starts to drop; turn left and scramble up the rocky gully to the top. Return by the same path and continue southwards until you reach a large grassy area. Cross it, keeping to your left until you reach a gate. With the fence on your right, go downhill until you reach a path of grass and stones. This path takes you around the southern side of the mountain, where you will eventually pass a small wood on your right. Immediately afterwards you will see, on your left, a sports pitch known as the Quill. Beyond it is Kilmacanogue.

WICKLOW GARDENS FESTIVAL

More than 40 private and public gardens participate in the yearly **Wicklow Gardens Festival** (☎ 20070; www.wicklow.ie), which runs from the beginning of May roughly through to the middle of August. The obvious advantage for green thumbs and other garden enthusiasts is access to beautiful gardens that would ordinarily be closed to the public. Some of the larger gardens are open throughout the festival, while other smaller ones only open at specific times; call or check the website for details of entrants, openings and special events, including all manner of horticultural courses.

---

places to get a bite along the whole of the Wicklow coast.

our pick **Organic Life/Marc Michel** (☎ 201 1882; Tinna Parc, Kilpedder; mains around €16; ☒ 10am-5pm, restaurant noon-4pm) Our favourite spot in all of Wicklow is this superb organic restaurant attached to the Organic Life shop in the town of Kilpedder, about 2km south of the Greystones turnoff on the N11. All of the vegetables are grown in the fields surrounding you, while the beef served in the superb burger is bought from a local cattle rancher. The only pity is that it's only open for lunch.

Getting There & Away

Bus Éireann (☎ 836 6111) operates bus 133 from Dublin to Wicklow Town and Arklow with stops outside Ashford House (one way/return €5.50/7.90, one hour, 10 daily).

WICKLOW TOWN

☎ 0404 / pop 7031

Bustling Wicklow town has a fine harbour and a commanding position on the crescent curve of the wide bay, which stretches north for about 12km and includes a long pebble beach that makes for a fine walk. Besides one top-notch attraction, there's not much to keep the visitor but it is a decent exploring base. The **tourist office** (☎ 69117; www.wicklow.ie; Fitzwilliam Sq; ☒ 9.30am-6pm Jun-Sep, 9am-1pm & 2-5pm Oct-May, closed Sun) is in the heart of town.

Sights

WICKLOW'S HISTORIC GAOL

Wicklow's infamous **gaol** (☎ 61599; www.wicklows historicgaol.com; Kilmantin Hill; adult/child/student incl

tour €6.80/3.95/4.90; ☒ 10am-6pm, last admission 5pm), opened in 1702 to deal with prisoners sentenced under the repressive Penal Laws, was renowned throughout Ireland for the brutality of its keepers and the harsh conditions suffered by its inmates. The smells, vicious beatings, shocking food and disease-ridden air have long since gone, but adults and children alike can experience a sanitised version of what the prison was like – and stimulate the secret sadist buried deep within – in the highly entertaining tour of the prison, now one of Wicklow's most popular tourist attractions. Actors play the roles of the various gaolers and prisoners, adding to the sense of drama already heightened by the various exhibits on show, including a life-size treadmill that prisoners would have to turn for hours on end as punishment, and the gruesome dungeon.

On the 2nd floor is a model of the HMS *Hercules*, a convict ship that was used to transport convicts to New South Wales under the captaincy of the psychotic Luckyn Betts: six months under his iron rule and most began to see death as a form of mercy. The top floor is devoted to the stories of the prisoners once they arrived in Australia. Tours are every 10 minutes except between 1pm and 2pm.

OTHER SIGHTS

The few remaining fragments of the **Black Castle** are on the shore at the southern end of town, with pleasant views up and down the coast. The castle was built in 1169 by the Fitzgeralds from Wales after they were granted land in the area by the Anglo-Norman conqueror, Strongbow. It used to be linked to the mainland by a drawbridge, and rumour has it that an escape tunnel ran from the sea cave underneath up into the town. At low tide you can swim or snorkel into the cave.

The walk south of town along the cliffs to **Wicklow Head** offers great views of the Wicklow Mountains. A string of **beaches** – Silver Strand, Brittas Bay and Maheramore – start 16km south of Wicklow. With high dunes, safe bathing and powdery sand, the beaches attract droves of Dubliners in good weather.

Festivals

The long-established **Wicklow Regatta Festival** (☎ 68354) is held every year for 10 days between July and August. The extensive programme of events and activities includes swimming,

rowing, sailing and raft races, singing competitions, concerts and the Festival Queen Ball.

Sleeping & Eating

Town lodgings aren't anything unusual, but
there are a couple of places within a few kilometres of Wicklow that are pretty special. If
you're looking for something central for a
night's stay, there's a clutch of B&Bs in and
around Dunbur Hill and a few more uphill
along St Patrick's Rd.

Grand Hotel (☎ 67337; www.grandhotel.ie; Abbey
St; s/d from €85/125; **P**) Wicklow town's best accommodation is this mock-Tudor hotel that is
quite a bit short of 'grand', but it's a handsome,
comfortable place nonetheless. The rooms are
immaculate, and the smallish size of the place
assures a personalised, friendly service.

Wicklow Bay Hostel (☎ 69213, 61174; www.wicklow
bayhostel.com; Marine House; dm €15; **P**) This large,
bright-yellow hostel overlooking the harbour
is a long-standing favourite with backpackers, who appreciate the spotless dorms,
friendly buzz and two enormous kitchens.

Bakery Restaurant (☎ 66770; Church St; mains €18-
32; �an 6-10pm Mon-Sat, 11.30am-3.30pm & 6-10pm Sun) A
mouth-watering menu that changes monthly
offers all kinds of good dishes – from rich
game meats to interesting vegetarian options.
This is perhaps the best restaurant in town.

Getting There & Around

Bus Éireann (☎ 01-836 6111) runs bus 133, serving Wicklow town from Dublin (€7, 1½
hours, 10 daily); Wicklow town is also served
by express bus 2 running between Dublin
(one hour, 12 daily) and Rosslare Harbour.

Iarnród Éireann (Irish Rail; ☎ 01-836 6222) serves
Wicklow town from Dublin on the main
Dublin to Rosslare Harbour line (one way/
return €12.50/15.50, one hour, five daily).
The station is a 10-minute walk north of
the town centre.

Wicklow Cabs (☎ 66888; Main St) usually sends
a few cabs to meet the evening trains from
Dublin. The fare to anywhere in town should
be no more than €5.

SOUTHERN WICKLOW

RATHDRUM
☎ 0404 / pop 2123

The quiet village of Rathdrum at the foot of
the Vale of Clara comprises little more than
a few old houses and shops, but in the late
19th century it had a healthy flannel industry and a poorhouse. It's not what's in the
town that's of interest to visitors, however,
but what's just outside it.

The small **tourist office** (☎ 46262; 29 Main St;
�an 9am-5.30pm Mon-Fri) has leaflets and information on the town and surrounding area,
including the Wicklow Way.

Sights

> Woe be to the man by whom the scan-
> dal cometh…It would be better for
> him that a millstone were tied about
> his neck and that he were cast into the
> depth of the sea rather than he should
> scandalise one of these, my least lit-
> tle ones.
>
> James Joyce, *A Portrait of the Artist*
> *as a Young Man*

Joyce's fictional dinner-table argument wasn't
about a murderer or any such criminal, but
about Charles Stewart Parnell (1846–91), the
'uncrowned king of Ireland' and unquestionably one of the key figures in the Irish
independence movement. **Avondale House**, a
marvellous 209-hectare estate, dominated by
a fine Palladian **mansion** (☎ 46111; adult/student &
child €5/4.50; �an 11am-6pm May-Aug, Tue-Sun only Mar, Apr,

DETOUR: TINAKILLY COUNTRY HOUSE & RESTAURANT

Wicklow has no shortage of fine country homes converted into luxury manor hotels, but **Tinakilly
Country House & Restaurant** (☎ 69274; www.tinakilly.ie; Rathnew; s/d from €169/334), a magnificent
Victorian Italianate house just outside Rathnew (about 5km west of Wicklow town) stands out for
sheer elegance. The guest rooms are divided between the period rooms in the west wing, decked
out in original antiques, four-poster and half-tester canopy beds; and the shockingly sumptuous
suites in the east wing, which have gorgeous views of either the richly colourful garden or the
Irish Sea, albeit somewhere in the distance. And then there's the restaurant, which takes country-
house cuisine to a whole new level of sophistication. A five-course dinner costs €55.

Sep & Oct, by appointment only rest of year), designed by James Wyatt in 1779, was his birthplace and Irish headquarters. Of the house's many highlights, the most impressive are the stunning vermilion-coloured library (Parnell's favourite room) and beautiful dining room.

From 1880 to 1890, Avondale was synonymous with the fight for Home Rule, which was brilliantly led by Parnell until 1890 when a member of his own Irish Parliamentary Party, Captain William O'Shea, sued his wife Kitty for divorce and named Parnell as co-respondent. Parnell's affair with Kitty scandalised this 'priest-ridden' nation, and the ultraconservative clergy declared that Parnell was 'unfit to lead' – despite the fact that as soon as the divorce was granted the two lovers were quickly married. Parnell resigned as leader of the party and withdrew in despair to Avondale, where he died the following year.

Surrounding the house are 200 hectares of forest and parkland, where the first silvicultural experiments by the Irish Forestry Service (Coillte) were conceived, after the purchase of the house by the state in 1904. These plots, about half a hectare in size, are still visible today, flanking what many consider to be the best of Avondale's many walking trails, the Great Ride. You can visit the park during daylight hours year-round.

Sleeping

Old Presbytery Hostel (☎ 46930; www.hostels-ireland .com; the Fairgreen, Rathdrum; dm/d €15/40; **P**) A modern, centrally located IHH hostel that looks more like campus accommodation. There is a mix of large, comfy dorms and well-appointed en-suite doubles as well as family rooms. A laundry and a TV room round off the facilities. You can also camp in the grounds.

our pick **Brook Lodge & Wells Spa** (☎ 0402-36444; www.brooklodge.com; Macreddin; r/ste from €260/330; **P**) The favourite chill-out spot for Dublin's high-flyers is this luxurious country house about 3km west of Rathdrum in the village of Macreddin. The 39 standard rooms set a pretty high tone, with four-poster and sleigh beds dressed in crisp Frette linen, but the suites sing an altogether more harmonious tune, each a minimalist marvel that wouldn't seem out of place in a New York boutique hotel – massive beds, flat-screen plasma TVs, top-of-the-range sound system and every other style sundry. The accommodation is pure luxury, but it's the outstanding spa that keeps guests

coming back for more. Mud and flotation chambers, Finnish and aroma baths, Hammam massages and a full-range of Decléor and Carita treatments make this one of the top spas in the country. Your credit card will never have nestled in softer hands.

Getting There & Away

Bus Éireann (☎ 836 6111) service 133 goes to Rathdrum from Dublin (one way/return €8/10.20, 1¾ hours, 10 daily) on its way to Arklow.

Iarnród Éireann (☎ 01-836 6222) serves Rathdrum from Dublin on the main Dublin to Rosslare Harbour line (one way/return €13.50/16.50, 1¼ hours, five daily).

VALE OF AVOCA

In summer, tour buses and other interested parties clog the road through the scenic Vale of Avoca on their way to the renowned mills in the eponymous village. En route, tourists ooh and aah at the gorgeous scenery of the darkly wooded valley which begins where the Rivers Avonbeg and Avonmore come together to form the River Avoca. This is a lovely spot suitably named the **Meeting of the Waters**, made famous by Thomas Moore's 1808 poem of the same name.

The Meeting of the Waters is marked by a pub called the **Meetings** (☎ 0402-35226; www .themeetingsavoca.com; s/d €40/65; ⏰ noon-9pm), which serves food (mains €10 to €19) and has music on weekends year-round. There are *céilidhs* (traditional music and dancing sessions) between 4pm and 6pm Sunday, April to October. There's also a guesthouse attached (known as Robin's Nest) with decent, clean rooms. Buses to Avoca from Dublin stop at the Meetings, or you can walk from Avoca, 3km south of here.

Avoca

☎ 0402 / pop 570

The tiny village of Avoca (Abhóca) still trades on its setting for the now-defunct BBC TV series *Ballykissangel*, but the main reason to visit is to amble about – and hopefully spend loads of money in – the superstar of all Irish cottage industries, **Avoca Handweavers** (☎ 35105; www.avoca.ie; Old Mill, Main St; ⏰ 9.30am-6pm), housed in Ireland's oldest working mill.

It's been turning out linens, wools and other fabrics since 1723, and all of Avoca's much-admired line is produced here. You are free to wander in and out of the weaving sheds.

Just in case you might want some local info, the **tourist office** (☎ 35022; Old Courthouse; ✆ 10am-5pm Mon-Sat) is in the library.

SLEEPING

River Valley Park (☎ 41647; fax 41677; camp sites €14) This well-equipped camp site is about 1km south of the village of Redcross, 7km northeast of Avoca on the R754 country road.

Koliba (☎ /fax 32737; www.koliba.com; Beech Rd; s/d €48.50/69; ✆ Apr-Oct) A thoroughly modern bungalow with comfortable, well-appointed rooms (all with en suite). LKoliba is 3km out of Avoca on the Arklow road.

Sheepwalk House & Cottages (☎ 35189; www.sheepwalk.com; Arklow Rd; s/d €55/90, cottages per week €275-659) Built in 1727 for the Earl of Wicklow, this is our favourite place to stay in Avoca (although it's 2km out of town). The main house is splendid, with beautifully appointed rooms, while the converted outbuildings – complete with beamed ceilings, fireplaces and flagstone floors – are a wonderful option for groups of four or six.

GETTING THERE & AWAY

Bus Éireann (☎ 836 6111) operates bus 133 from Dublin, which serves Avoca via Bray, Wicklow and Rathdrum on its way to Arklow (one way/return €8.80/12.20, two hours, 10 daily).

ARKLOW

☎ 0402 / pop 9955
Wicklow's biggest and busiest town is a thriving commercial centre built around what was once an important local port. Although this may not inspire you to change route and come here, chances are if you're in this part of the county you'll probably end up here anyway. There's a local belief that the town is included in Ptolemy's 2nd-century map of Europe, but what is absolutely verifiable is that Sir Francis Chichester's prize-winning transatlantic yacht *Gypsy Moth III* (now in Greenwich, England) was built here.

The town's seafaring past is explored in the small **maritime museum** (☎ 32868; St Mary's Rd; admission €3.50; ✆ 10am-1pm & 2-5pm Mon-Sat May-Sep), which features a model of the *Titanic*, some salvaged items from the *Lusitania* and

an extraordinary model of a ship made from 10,000 matchsticks.

For all other info, there's the **tourist office** (☎ 32484; www.arklow.ie; ✆ 9.30am-1pm Mon-Sat Jun-Sep) in the Coach House.

There is a white, sandy beach, but it lies between the docks and a gravel plant; you're better off heading 10km north to **Brittas Bay** or 7km south to the more sheltered **Clogga Beach**.

Sleeping & Eating

Plattenstown House (☎ /fax 37822; Coolgreany Rd; s/d €40/65; P) This gorgeous traditional farmhouse set in 50 acres of land about 5km south of town. Family antiques throughout this elegant 19th-century home, great views of the lovingly tended gardens and comfortable, well-appointed rooms make this place a terrific choice in the area.

Otherwise, there's a fairly broad range of decent B&Bs, each offering comfortable rooms and a well-cooked breakfast. Try **Valentia House** (☎ 39200; www.geocities.com/valentiahouse; Coolgreany Rd; s/d €45/90; P) or **Pinebrook** (☎ 31527; www.pinebrook.net; Ticknock Close, Briggs La; s/d €42/78; P).

Kitty's of Arklow (☎ 31669; Main St; lunch €9-17, dinner €23-26; ✆ noon-5pm & 6-10.30pm) An Arklow institution, Kitty's serves a great version of the usual bar food choices during the day – from beef burgers to fillets of plaice – while the evening menu tackles some exciting seafood dishes and an impressive range of meat dishes. It's not new cuisine, but it's a fine take on the classics.

Getting There & Away

Bus Éireann (☎ 836 6111) operates bus 133 from Dublin, which serves Avoca via Bray, Wicklow and Rathdrum on its way to Arklow (one way/return €10/12.50, 2¼ hours, 10 daily); Arklow is also served by express bus 2 between Dublin and Rosslare Harbour (1½ hours, 12 daily). All buses stop outside the Chocolate Shop.

Iarnród Éireann (☎ 01-836 6222) serves Arklow from Dublin (one way/return €13.20/16.50, 1¼ hours, five daily) on the Arrow suburban line as well as by Intercity train to Rosslare Harbour – the price is the same no matter which train you take.

Counties Wexford & Waterford

Ireland's sunny southeast cosies up to the Gulf Stream, making it the country's warmest, driest area. Nonetheless, the tourist trail mostly bypasses Counties Wexford and Waterford, which is, of course, great news for anyone with a few days to spare and a love of quiet roads with sea views. The largely coastal counties are lined with sandy seaside spots, from Kilmore Quay, a fishing village of thatched, whitewashed cottages, to Tramore, where the 5km beach is overlooked by the Holy Cross Church and the Big Dipper.

If you've fallen for the coast by the time you reach the estuary dividing the two counties, there's a handy short cut on a car ferry. Otherwise, follow the River Barrow to New Ross, where you can board a 'coffin ship' and put yourself in the flapping shoes of hapless Famine émigrés.

East of the estuary, gazing across at Tramore's more refined neighbour, Dunmore East, is the extraordinary Hook Peninsula. Its history of marauding Vikings, lighthouse-keeping monks, a shipwrecked Norman, and shadowy knights' sects arrived from the Crusades, has long attracted grail hunters and conspiracy theorists. Visitors will find themselves drawn, trancelike, down the flat, lonely promontory towards the oldest working lighthouse in the world.

Inland, the magical history tour continues at Enniscorthy and Vinegar Hill. The National 1798 Rebellion Centre narrates the bloody year when county Wexford's 'pikemen' and 'croppies' fought 23 battles against the English. Elegant Lismore has a more aristocratic past, while prehistoric remains hide among the heather in the Nire Valley and Comeragh Mountains.

HIGHLIGHTS

- **Coastal Crusade** Knights Templar relics on the Hook Peninsula (p178)
- **Eco-fun** Tramore and the Copper Coast GeoPark (p192)
- **Nestle in the Nire** Hilly northern County Waterford's hideaways (p198) for all budgets
- **Vikings and Gadgets** Bright lights and booty at the Waterford Museum of Treasures (p185)
- **Humble Homestead** The Kennedy dynasty's backwoods beginnings near New Ross (p181)
- **Horror Story** Poignant Vinegar Hill and the National 1798 Rebellion Centre in Enniscorthy (p181)

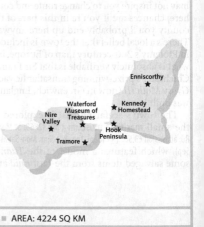

- POPULATION: 218,142
- AREA: 4224 SQ KM

COUNTY WEXFORD

pop 131,750

Invaders and privateers have always had a magnetic attraction to County Wexford, lured by its sexily navigable rivers and fertile land…oh baby. The Vikings founded Ireland's first major towns on the wide, easy-flowing River Slaney, which cuts a swathe through the middle of the county. These days, the hordes descend on Wexford's fine beaches to build more innocent sand castles.

Wexford town is pleasant enough but only retains a few traces of its Viking past. To feast on big dollops of history, visit Enniscorthy's National 1798 Rebellion Centre and the site of the insurgents' last stand, Vinegar Hill, or put yourself in the shoes of Famine emigrants by boarding the Dunbrody Heritage Ship at New Ross.

Wrecks litter the sea off the Hook Peninsula, which also has some fascinating history on land. Everyone from the Norman settlers to the Knights Templar passed through the flat, haunting promontory, which tapers towards one of the world's oldest lighthouses. A great way to unwrap this landscape would be to cycle, pausing in pretty waterfront villages like Duncannon and Kilmore Quay to sample catches from the surrounding waves. The area is at the southwest end of the 221km Wexford Coastal Walk

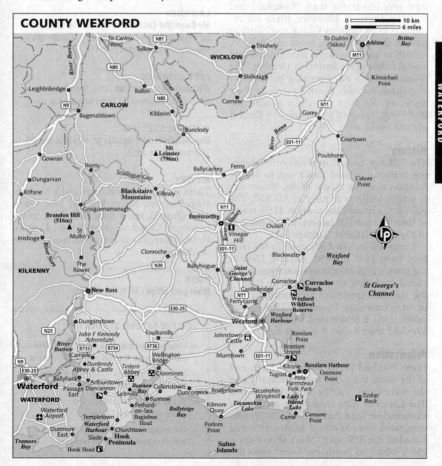

COUNTY WEXFORD

0 ——— 10 km
0 ——— 6 miles

(Slí Charman), which starts at Kilmichael Point on the County Wicklow border.

Keep your ears open for remnants of a dialect called Yola, sometimes called 'Forth and Bargy', which still survives in southeastern County Wexford. Yola stands for 'ye olde language' and is a mixture of old French, English, Irish, Welsh and Flemish. Examples of the language are *kyne* (cow), *hime* (home), *hachee* (bad-tempered) and *stouk* (a truculent woman).

WEXFORD TOWN
☎ 05391 / pop 8860

On the surface, Wexford (Loch Garman) seems an unremarkable provincial centre, a sleepy port town where the silted estuary now sees less traffic than Waterford and Rosslare Harbour. However, there are reminders of its glorious Viking and Norman past in the meandering lanes off Main St, as well as some medieval monuments and a world-class opera festival in October. The townsfolk are a more retiring bunch than elsewhere, but this doesn't preclude their crowding the pubs and clubs around the Bull Ring. Wexford's proximity to Dublin attracts weekenders.

History

The Vikings named it Waesfjord (meaning 'harbour of mud flats') and its handy location near the mouth of the Slaney encouraged landings as early as AD 850. The Normans captured the town in 1169; traces of their fort can still be seen in the grounds of the Irish National Heritage Park.

Cromwell included Wexford in his Irish tour from 1649 to 1650. Around 1500 of the town's 2000 inhabitants were put to the sword, including all the Franciscan friars – the standard treatment for towns that refused to capitulate. During the 1798 Rising, rebels made a determined, bloody stand in Wexford town before they were defeated.

Orientation

From Wexford Bridge at the northern end of the town, the quays lead southeast along the waterfront, via the small kink called The Crescent. This is home to a statue of Commodore John Barry (1745–1803), who emigrated from Wexford to America and founded the US navy. Most shops are a block inland on North and South Main St.

Information

BOOKSHOPS

Readers' Paradise (☎ 24400; 2 Slaney St; ☽ 9.30am-6pm Mon-Sat) A good spot for Irish-interest second-hand paperbacks.
Wexford Book Centre (☎ 23543; 5 South Main St; ☽ 9am-6pm Mon-Thu & Sat, 9am-7pm Fri, 1-5pm Sun) Has books on Irish topics plus a limited selection of foreign newspapers and magazines.

INTERNET ACCESS

Office 1 (☎ 21884; 74 North Main St; per hr €3; ☽ 9am-9pm Mon-Sat, 11am-8pm Sun)
Tangiers (☎ 46404; 19 Trimmers La; per hr €3.50; ☽ 9am-10pm Mon-Sat, 2-7pm Sun)

LAUNDRY

My Beautiful Laundrette (☎ /fax 24317; St Peters Sq; ☽ 9.30am-1pm & 2-5pm Mon-Fri, 9.30am-1pm Sat) Self-service wash and dry €15 to €17.

LEFT LUGGAGE

O'Hanrahan Station (☎ 22522; Redmond Pl) Has left-luggage facilities for €2.50 per item per day.

MEDICAL SERVICES

Wexford General Hospital (☎ 42233) On the N25, 2.5km west of the centre.

MONEY

There is an Allied Irish Bank and a National Irish Bank on North Main St near Common Quay St, and a Bank of Ireland on the corner of Common Quay St and Custom House Quay. The tourist office has a bureau de change.

POST

Main post office (☎ 45314; Anne St)

SOUTHEASTERN STROLLS

- Wexford Coastal Walk (p167) – 221km along a coast littered with 1000 wrecks
- Mt Leinster (p183) – views of five counties from its 796m summit
- St Declan's Way (p195) – 94km pilgrim route via Lismore Castle
- Comeragh Mountains (p198) – glacial moraine and Stone Age remains

WEXFORD

0   200 m
0   0.1 mile

To Ferrycarrig Lodge (2km);
Irish National Heritage Park (3.5km);
Enniscorthy (20km)

To Ferryback Camping &
Caravan Park (600m);
Wexford Wildfowl
Reserve (5km); Curracloe
(13km); Dublin (135km)

To N25; Wexford General
Hospital (2.5km);
Clonard House (3km);
Waterford (61km)

To Wexford Golf Club (2km);
Hook Head (40km);
Duntannon (40km)

To N25; Johnstown
Castle & Gardens (7km);
Rosslare Strand (12km);
Rosslare Harbour (20km)

SIGHTS & ACTIVITIES
Bull Ring	12 B3
County Wexford Tourism	(see 12)
Franciscan Friary	13 B3
Lone Pikeman Statue	(see 12)
Selskar Abbey	14 A2
St Iberius' Church	15 B3
Westgate	16 A2

SLEEPING
Auburn Terrace	17 A1
Blue Door	18 B2
Kirwan House	19 B3
McDonald's	20 C4
McMenamin's Townhouse	21 A2
Talbot Hotel	22 D4
White's of Wexford	23 B2

EATING
Café Gusto	24 C4
Cappuccino's	25 B3
Dunne's Stores	26 B2
Greenacres Food Hall	27 B2
Heavens Above	28 C4
La Riva	29 C3
Vine	30 B2
Yard	31 B2

DRINKING
Centenary Stores	32 B2
Sky & the Ground	(see 28)
Thomas Moore Tavern	33 B3

ENTERTAINMENT
Cineplex	34 A1
Theatre Royal	35 B3
Wexford Arts Centre	36 B3
Wexford Festival Opera	37 B3
Wexford Festival Opera Box Office	38 B3

TRANSPORT
Ardcavan Coach Company Bus Stop	39 C3
Bus Station	40 B1
Mace (Bus Tickets)	41 B1
Wexford Cabs	42 B2

INFORMATION
Allied Irish Bank	1 B3
Bank of Ireland	2 B2
County Wexford Tourism	3 A2
Main Post Office	4 B3
My Beautiful Laundrette	5 B4
National Irish Bank	6 B3
Office 1	7 B2
Readers' Paradise	8 B2
Tangiers	9 B2
Tourist Office	10 C3
Wexford Book Centre	11 B3

COUNTIES WEXFORD & WATERFORD

TOILETS

There are public toilets near the statue of
Commodore Barry.

TOURIST INFORMATION

Tourist office (☎ 23111; Crescent Quay; ☼ 9.15am-
1pm & 2-5pm Mon-Fri Nov-Mar, 9am-1pm & 2-6pm
Mon-Sat Apr-Oct)
County Wexford Tourism office (☎ 52900; www
.wexfordtourism.com; 8A Westgate; ☼ 9am-1pm &
2-5pm Mon-Fri)

Sights

Originally a beach where provisions were
boated into the city, the **Bull Ring** became a
centre for bull baiting in medieval times: the
town's butchers gained their guild charter

by providing a bull each year for the sport.
The **Lone Pikeman statue** commemorates the
participants in the 1798 Rising, who used
the place as an open-air armaments factory.
There's usually a Friday **market** beside the Bull
Ring from 9am.

The only survivor of the six original town
gates is the 14th-century **Westgate**, beside
the defunct Westgate Heritage Centre at
the northern end of town. It was originally
a tollgate, and the recesses used by the toll
collectors are still intact, as is the lockup
used to incarcerate 'runagates' – those who
tried to avoid paying. Some stretches of the
town wall are also in good nick, including a particularly well-preserved section
near Cornmarket.

After Henry II murdered his friend Thomas á Becket, he did penance for the bloody deed at **Selskar Abbey**, founded by Alexander de la Roche in 1190. Strongbow's sister Bascilla is supposed to have married one of Henry II's lieutenants in the abbey. Its present ruinous state is a result of Cromwell's visit in 1649. The ruins are entered by a staircase next to the old Westgate Heritage Centre on Westgate.

South of the Bull Ring, **St Iberius' Church** (☎ 40652; North Main St; ☷ 10am-5pm Mon-Sat) was built in 1760 on the site of several previous churches (including one reputed to have been founded before St Patrick came to Ireland). Oscar Wilde's forebears were rectors here. The Renaissance-style frontage is worth a look, but the real treat is the Georgian interior with its finely crafted altar rails and set of 18th-century monuments in the gallery. Phone ahead to organise a guided tour (donations appreciated).

In 1649 Cromwell's forces made a bonfire of the original 13th-century **Fransiscan Friary**, so most of the present building is from the 19th century. Only two original walls remain. Some parts, such as the tabernacle, are very modern, creating an appealing architectural incongruity. The friary (☎ 22758; cnr Francis & School Sts; ☷ 10am-6.30pm) houses a relic and wax effigy of St Adjutor, a boy martyr slain by his own father in ancient Rome.

Activities

Wexford Golf Club (☎ 42238; Mulgannon; 18 holes weekdays/weekends €30/35; ☷ 8am-dusk Mon-Sat, members only 7am-2pm Sun) is well signposted off the R733, about 2km southwest of town. Even hackers will appreciate the views of Wexford and the harbour.

Tours

Guided one-hour **walking tours** (☎ 087-614 0790; adult/concession/family €4/3.50/10) leave at 10.30am and 2.30pm Monday to Saturday year-round from outside the office of County Wexford Tourism on Westgate.

Festivals & Events

The **Wexford Festival Opera** (☎ 22400, box office ☎ 22144; www.wexfordopera.com; 49 North Main St), an 18-day extravaganza normally held at the **Theatre Royal** in October, began in 1951 and has grown to be the country's premier opera event. Rarely performed operas and shows are staged for packed audiences, and fringe

VIKING RIVER PATHS

Although little remains of Viking Wexford, the *keysers* (meaning 'roads to the quays') still exist. These tiny arteries, just one packhorse wide, fall at right angles to the river and were of vast importance. The lifeblood of the city ran through them: honey, wheat and malt were taken from Wexford's warehouses to the waterside, and whale oil, wool and fish came from the harbour into town.

The main road was Keysers Lane, which led from Keysergate in the old city walls to the Viking ship pool (now the semicircular Crescent). The gradual silting up of the harbour left the *keysers* as an interesting historical footnote…and a modern traffic nightmare.

street theatre, poetry readings and exhibitions give the town a fiesta atmosphere. Many local bars even run their own amateur song competitions. Booking is essential and should be done at least three months in advance; the programme usually comes out in June.

Sleeping

Accommodation for October, when the Wexford Festival Opera takes place, is often booked out months in advance.

BUDGET

Ferrybank Camping & Caravan Park (☎ 44378; www .wexfordcorp.ie; Ferrybank; camp sites €10; ☷ Easter-Sep) Right across the river from the centre, council-run Ferrybank is in a windy location but has fantastic views of town. Facilities include a heated pool next door, laundry facilities and a children's play area.

Kirwan House (☎ 21208; kirwanhostel@eircom.net; 3 Mary St; dm/s/tw/q €22/38/52/44) This basic hostel, popular with both workers and backpackers, is okay once you get used to its shadowy interior and eccentric atmosphere. Dorms have en-suite bathrooms, and there's a dishevelled garden at the back of the old Georgian building.

MIDRANGE

Decent midrange accommodation is fairly sparse in the city centre.

Blue Door (☎ 21047; http://indigo.ie/~bluedoor; 18 Lower George St; s/d from €45/80) The breakfasts are a plus at this 200-year-old town house, with smoked salmon and vegetarian alternatives. Recently renovated, it's central but quiet, and floor-to-ceiling windows make the bedrooms bright and airy.

McDonald's (☎ 23457; 114 South Main St; s/d €50/80) Located above a pub, out of earshot of the nightly entertainment, McDonald's offers comfortable rooms off institutional corridors.

our pick Clonard House (☎ /fax 43141; www.clonard house.com; Clonard Great; s/d €50/85; ✤ mid-Apr–Oct; P) A diamond find, this is like being invited to stay the night at a stately home. The Georgian farmhouse has grand reception rooms and a suspended staircase leading to bedrooms overlooking gardens, farmyard or rolling countryside; some have four-poster beds. It's off the N25 3km west of town.

Auburn Terrace (☎ 52750; Auburn Rd; s/d €55/90; P) This friendly B&B in a late-Victorian town house is sensitively decorated with period colours and furniture.

Ferrycarrig Lodge (☎ 42605; www.wexford-accommodation.com; Ferrycarrig Rd; s/d €60/80; ✤ closed Jan; P) The spacious Ferrycarrig is in a wonderful position on the River Slaney, 2km north of town and a 10-minute walk from the Irish National Heritage Park. Rooms are attractively decorated with white ceilings and colourful walls; some have balconies.

McMenamin's Townhouse (☎ /fax 46442; www .wexford-bedandbreakfast.com; 6 Glena Tce, Spawell Rd; s/d €60/90; P) This award-winning B&B has moved to opposite County Hall. Rooms are furnished with Victorian antiques including canopied beds. You get well looked after; the breakfast menu features homemade breads and jams, kippers, and kidneys with sherry.

TOP END

White's of Wexford (☎ 22311; www.whitesofwexford .ie; Abbey St; s/d €100/150; P) With its bars, restaurants, swimming pool, leisure club and spa, White's is a contemporary colossus. The 157 rooms are all metal right angles, plasma and glass, gazing across the river to Curracloe Beach or down at the courtyard that's used as an ice rink during winter.

Talbot Hotel (☎ 22566; www.talbotwexford.ie; Trinity St; s/d €110/180; P) This huge quayside hotel has big, stylish bedrooms, many with river views. There's a classy bar and grill with vaulted ceilings and fancy woodwork, a bright modern restaurant and a pool, steam room, sauna and gym in a converted grain mill.

Eating

Café Gusto (☎ 24336; 106 South Main St; snacks & mains €4-9; ✤ 9am-3pm Mon-Wed, 9am-5pm Thu-Sat) This bright little café is good for a 'big' breakfast or New York bagel, and lunches such as burgers, *goujons* (strips of fish or meat coated in breadcrumbs and deep-fried) and salads.

Cappuccino's (☎ 23669; 25 North Main St; breakfast €5-8; ✤ 8am-6pm Mon-Sat, 10am-6.30pm Sun) From the full Irish to bagels, *paninis*, wraps and naan, the imaginatively named Cappuccino's is perfect for breakfast or a snack. Wexford's teens come here to tuck into desserts and the many hot drinks.

Vine (☎ 22388; 109 North Main St; mains €16-20; ✤ 6-10pm) The open kitchen serves fragrant Thai dishes in this 1st-floor restaurant, a land of fairy lights, mirrors and metal flowers.

Yard (☎ 44083; 3 Lower George St; mains €17-25; ✤ 8.30am-10pm) The latest venture from Centenary Stores' owner is a cool, intimate restaurant with low lighting, dark furniture, Air on the stereo and candles on the tables, alongside contemporary European cuisine.

Heavens Above (☎ 24877; 112-113 South Main St; mains €18-25; ✤ 5-10pm Mon-Sat, 4-9pm Sun) For those wanting an eat-out treat without too much formality, the atmosphere is just right at this dark-wood-and-candles restaurant above the Sky & the Ground. The large portions will appeal to fans of fine meat, seafood and vegetarian dishes.

our pick La Riva (☎ 24330; warrengillen@dol.ie; Henrietta St; mains €18-28; ✤ 6-11pm Mon-Sat) At this 1st-floor bistro, entered via a staircase lined with rave newspaper reviews, the beautifully presented Irish-Mediterranean dishes are prepared from organic, locally sourced ingredients. Admire the creamy soups, fancy sauces and the glittering views of the night-time quay.

For self-caterers, there's a **Dunne's Stores** (Slaney St; ✤ 8am-12am), or you could put together a gourmet picnic at **Greenacres Food Hall** (☎ 22975; 7 Selskar St; ✤ 9.30am-6pm Mon-Sat), which has a great selection of cheese, meats, olives and wine.

Drinking

Centenary Stores (☎ 24424; thecstores@eircom.net; Charlotte St) One of Wexford's livelier spots, this former warehouse is a pleasing mix of old and new, with friezes on the ceiling above the plasma screens in the bar. Its Guinness is the best in the vicinity, and the nightclub is full even on Sundays. More civilised are the Sunday lunchtime trad music sessions.

Thomas Moore Tavern (☎ 24348; Cornmarket) A low-beamed institution that's popular for a quiet chat, followed by a sing-along after 9.30pm. Given how many people pile in for the renowned sessions, you'll find it hard not to make new friends.

Sky & the Ground (☎ 21273; 112-113 South Main St) This top-quality watering hole is a Wexford favourite. Its decoration is pure old-man's-pub, with enamel signage and a roaring fire, but it attracts a youthful clientele. It has trad sessions on weeknights, and attached Café Paradiso serves tapas and other snacks.

Entertainment

Theatre Royal (☎ 22144; High St) The Royal stages drama and opera by local and touring companies. At the time of writing, it was closed for reconstruction, with a swish new complex due in 2008.

Wexford Arts Centre (☎ 23764; www.wexfordartscentre.ie; Cornmarket) In an 18th-century market hall, this centre caters for exhibitions, theatre, dance and music, and screens arts films at 8pm on a Tuesday (€7).

Cineplex (☎ 21490; Redmond Rd; adult/child €8/5) This multiscreen cinema is located near the train station.

Getting There & Away

The N25 leads southeast from the quays and Trinity St to Rosslare Harbour. For Duncannon or Hook Head, turn west either at The Crescent along Harpers Lane or from Paul Quay along King St Lower.

BUS

Bus Éireann (☎ 22522) buses leave from O'Hanrahan train station on Redmond Place and travel to Rosslare Harbour (€4, 30 minutes, at least nine daily), Waterford (€11.50, one hour, six daily Monday to Saturday, three Sunday) and Dublin (€12, three hours, at least nine daily), normally via Enniscorthy (€5.10, 25 minutes). Tickets are available from nearby newsagency **Mace** (Redmond Pl).

Ardcavan Coach Company (☎ 22561; The Crescent) runs a bus to/from Dublin (€10, 2½ hours), leaving Dublin at 6pm Monday to Saturday, and Wexford at 8am Monday to Saturday, and 8pm Sunday (also 6pm September to April).

TRAIN

O'Hanrahan Station (☎ 22522; Redmond Pl) is at the northern end of town. Wexford is on the Dublin (€18.50, 2½ hours) to Rosslare (€4, 25 minutes) Europort line (via Enniscorthy and Wicklow), serviced by three trains daily in each direction.

Getting Around

Most newsagencies sell parking discs (per hour €1.20).

For a 24-hour taxi service, call **Wexford Cabs** (☎ 23123; 3 Charlotte St) or **AA Cabs** (☎ 40222). Most fares around the centre are €5.

AROUND WEXFORD TOWN
☎ 05391

Irish National Heritage Park

The excellent **Irish National Heritage Park** (☎ 20733; Ferrycarrig; adult/child under 13/child 13-16/family €7.50/3.75/4.25/19; 🕐 9.30am-6.30pm Apr-Sep, 9.30am-5.30pm Oct-Mar) successfully squashes 9000 years of Irish history (up to the Normans) into one outdoor theme park.

Take a deep breath and plunge in, past a recreated Neolithic farmstead, stone circle, ring fort, monastery, *crannóg* (lake settlement), Viking shipyard, Norman castle and more. Sound effects and smoking fires add to the realism, as do the frequent 1½-hour guided tours, in which knowledgeable costumed actors really bring the place to life.

The park is about 3.5km northwest of Wexford town on the N11. A taxi from Wexford town costs about €7.

Johnstown Castle & Gardens

Parading peacocks guard this splendid 19th-century castellated house, the former home of the once-mighty Fitzgerald and Esmonde families.

The empty castle overlooks a small lake and is surrounded by 20 hectares of wooded **gardens** (car & passengers May-Sep €5; 🕐 9am-5.30pm). The outbuildings house the **Irish Agricultural Museum** (☎ 71247; adult/child €6/4; 🕐 9am-12.30pm & 1.30-5pm Mon-Fri, 2-5pm Sat & Sun Apr, May, Sep & Oct, closed Sat & Sun Nov-Mar, 9am-5pm Mon-Fri, 11am-5pm Sat & Sun Jun-Aug; 👌). It has collections of farm machinery and Irish country furniture, a horse-drawn caravan and a small Famine exhibition. There's a pleasant 15-minute walk around the lake.

The castle is 7km southwest of Wexford town en route to Murntown.

Wexford Wildfowl Reserve

The Slobs may not sound impressive (the name derives from the Irish *slab*, meaning 'mud, mire or a soft-fleshed person'), but this swathe of low-lying land reclaimed from the sea is bird heaven. It's home to a third of the world's population of Greenland white-fronted geese – some 10,000 birds in total.

Wexford Wildfowl Reserve (☎ 23129; North Slob; admission free, guided tours on request; ☯ 9am-6pm mid-Apr–Sep, 10am-5pm Oct–mid-Apr), which protects the birds' feeding grounds, has an observation tower, assorted hides and a visitor centre with detailed exhibits. Winter is a good time to spot the brent goose from Arctic Canada, and throughout the year you'll see numerous species of wader and wildfowl.

The reserve is over the bridge from Wexford on the Dublin road. Head north for 3km, before taking the signposted right turn just before the Mazda garage. The visitor centre is another 2km along the lane.

Curracloe Beach

Over 11km long, Curracloe is one of a string of deserted beaches that line the coast north of Wexford town. The high-octane opening scenes of the Normandy landing in *Saving Private Ryan* (1997) were filmed here. Many of the birds found at the Wexford Wildfowl Reserve can also be seen here in the **Raven Nature Reserve**. It's 13km northeast of Wexford off the Dublin road. If you're discreet you can pitch a tent in the sheltered dunes.

Hotel Curracloe (☎ 37308; www.hotelcurracloe.com; s/d €45/80) is a small family-run hotel with a staid, but snug, interior and traditional sessions on Friday, Saturday and Sunday nights. It's a 30-minute walk from the beach.

ROSSLARE STRAND

☎ 05391

Rosslare (Ros Láir) town is rather soulless but opens onto a glorious Blue Flag beach. In summer, the beach is the habitat of hordes of ice cream–powered children. In winter, the empty sands billow at the feet of the occasional solitary walker.

The long shallow bay is perfect for windsurfing. Windsurf, kayak, sailing and surf hire and tuition are available at **Rosslare Watersports Centre** (☎ 32032; ☯ 10am-6pm Jul & Aug). **Rosslare Golf Links** (☎ 32203; green fee weekdays/weekends €50/70) runs along the beach road. There are gentle walks towards Rosslare Point, 7km north.

TOP BLUE FLAG WEXFORD BEACHES

- Curracloe (left) – 11 sandy kilometres of film set
- Duncannon (p178) – gradually sloping beach ideal for paddlers
- Rosslare (left) – sand-and-stone strand, between Wexford town and Rosslare Harbour

---

Sleeping & Eating

Doyle's (☎ 32182; doylesbandb.rosslare@ireland.com; Orchard Park House, Tagoat; s/d €45/75) A homely farmhouse with electric blankets and long corridors lined with paintings of rosy pastoral scenes. It's on the R736 from Rosslare Strand to Tagoat.

Killiane Castle (☎ 58885; www.killianecastle.com; Drinagh; s/d €65/100) Northeast of the N25 en route to Wexford, this farmhouse B&B is in a 17th-century house. It's an ugly building, but attached is a 13th-century castle and the leafy grounds offer a golf range, tennis, croquet and nature trails.

Kelly's Resort Hotel (☎ 32114; www.kellys.ie; s/d incl meals €149/298; ℗) Kelly's is a Wexford institution and a massive hit with families. Everything, but everything, is on offer: tennis, golf, crazy golf, snooker, table tennis, badminton, yoga, croquet…and the SeaSpa, where you can pamper yourself silly with a range of treatments as wide as the sea outside. There are two good restaurants, and a café for snacks. Most accommodation is sold as packages: for example, a double room for three nights over a Bank Holiday weekend costs €930, including all meals.

Apart from **Le Marine** (☎ 32114; mains €18-25; ☯ noon-10pm), the wonderful Gallic bistro-bar at Kelly's, Rosslare is short on restaurants. The beachfront **Le Colosseo** (☎ 73975; Strand Rd) was changing hands at the time of research, rumoured to be reopening as a Chinese restaurant.

Getting There & Away

The daily 9.40am bus to Dublin (€14.50, 3½ hours) stops in Wexford (€4, 30 minutes). Monday to Saturday, there is a bus to Rosslare Harbour (20 minutes) at 6.20pm.

On the main Dublin–Wexford–Rosslare Europort line, three trains per day in each direction call at Rosslare Strand (from

Dublin €23.50, three hours; from Wexford €9.50, 20 minutes; from Rosslare Europort €9.50, 10 minutes). There is one train daily Monday to Saturday in each direction between Rosslare Strand and Waterford (€18, 1¼ hours).

ROSSLARE HARBOUR
☎ 05391 / pop 1050

Rosslare Harbour is a busy port with connections to Wales and France from the monolithic Europort ferry terminal. It's not particularly pretty or pedestrian friendly, but if you're waiting for a ferry, or have just arrived and are too green to go on, there's plenty of accommodation and restaurants.

Orientation & Information
The ferry port is the main focus of the town, where you will also find Rosslare Europort train station. A road leading uphill from the harbour becomes the N25 and takes you to the B&Bs and hotels. Further along this road are Kilrane and Tagoat, where there are more sleeping and eating options. There's a **Bank of Ireland** (St Martin's Rd) with an ATM and bureau de change, just off the N25.

Sights
This twee but interesting-all-the-same **Yola Farmstead folk park** (☎ 32610; Tagoat; adult/child/family €6/4.50/15; ☼ 10am-6pm, last admission at 5pm May-Oct, 10am-4.30pm Mon-Fri Mar, Apr & Nov) is a good place to come with the little 'uns. It's a reconstructed 18th-century village with thatched cottages, a working windmill and a tiny church, all intended to give visitors an impression of what life was like in rural Ireland (minus the hopeless poverty and the smells). There are hens, sheep, deer, rabbits, pigs and exotic birds for small kids to marvel at, and a genealogy centre. The park is just outside Tagoat, on the N25.

Sleeping & Eating
There are plenty of B&Bs on St Martin's Rd.

St Martin's B&B (☎ /fax 33133; www.saintmartins rosslare.com; St Martin's Rd; s/d €50/70; P) This purpose-built B&B has beautifully decorated, homey rooms. No 7 has a four-poster bed and there's a conservatory with books on Ireland to help you plan your trip (or the next one). John, the owner, is an opencast mine of local information, and early breakfasts are available for ferry-catchers.

Harbour View Hotel (☎ 61450; www.harbourview hotel.ie; s/d €80/130) The sprightly rooms still tell of their renovation and the service melts away the Europort's hulking presence. Its Seasons Restaurant (mains €12 to €23, open from 5.30pm to 9.30pm) is the best place to eat in town, with a large Chinese selection. Bar food (€8.50 to €18) is served from noon.

Leaving town on the N25, the first pub in Ireland (geographically speaking) is **The Kilrane Inn** (☎ 33661; Kilrane; bar food €4-12, mains €10-22; ☼ noon-3pm & 5-9pm), a pleasant pub with a bright, modern restaurant attached. Its owners, the O'Donoghue brothers, still can't agree on whether Chelsea or Liverpool is the better team.

Morgan's Café (☎ 31358; Tagoat; €4-8; ☼ 5-10pm Wed-Sun) is an excellent fish-and-chip shop.

Getting There & Away

BOAT
Stena Line Express (☎ 33115; www.stenaline.ie; ☼ May-Sep) sails between Rosslare Harbour and Fishguard in Wales (adult €30, motorbike and driver €67, car and driver €117 to €222, two hours, two sailings per day). Check-in is about one hour before sailing. Stena Line also runs its Superferry (adult €30, motorbike and driver €52, car and driver €92 to €182, 3½ hours, two sailings per day) year-round.

Irish Ferries (☎ 33158; www.irishferries.com) sails to Pembroke in Wales (3¾ hours, twice daily). Single fares start at €29 for a foot passenger, €49 for a motorbike and driver, €89 for a car and driver. Between April and December there are ferries to Cherbourg, France (19½ hours, up to three a week) and, between April and September, less frequent sailings to Roscoff, France (18 hours). Single fares are from €56 for a foot passenger, €90 for a motorbike and driver, and €99 for a car and driver.

For more information see p719.

BUS
Buses and trains depart from the Rosslare Europort station, which you'll find at the ferry terminal.

Bus Éireann (☎ 22522) has services to lots of Irish towns and cities, including Dublin (€15, three hours, 13 daily Monday to Saturday, 11 Sunday), Wexford (€12, 30 minutes, 13 daily Monday to Saturday, 11 Sunday) and Cork (€19.50, four hours, five daily Monday to Saturday, three Sunday) via Waterford (€13.50, 1½ hours).

CAR
Budget (☎ 33318), **Hertz** (☎ 33238) and **Europcar Murrays** (☎ 33634) are in the ferry terminal.

TRAIN
Three trains daily in each direction operate on the Rosslare Europort–Rosslare Strand–Wexford–Dublin route (to Rosslare Strand €4.50, 10 minutes; to Wexford €4.50, 25 minutes; to Dublin €18.50, three hours). Trains on the Rosslare Europort–Limerick route stop in Waterford (€9, 1¼ hours, two daily Monday to Saturday). For more information call ☎ 33114.

SOUTH OF ROSSLARE HARBOUR
☎ 05391
About 9km south of Rosslare Harbour is Carnsore Point, home to the east coast's first wind farm. Ireland's first four nuclear power stations would be here had not cost (and protests) aborted the scheme.

The village of **Carne** has a few pretty, white-washed, thatched cottages and a fine beach.

Locals and visitors alike pack the **Lobster Pot** (☎ 31110; Carne; lunch €6-12, dinner mains €20-27; ☿ restaurant noon-9pm Tue-Sat, 12.30-7.30pm Sun Feb-Dec) in summer, but it's worth the squeeze to get at the superfresh seafood in this gorgeous pub/restaurant. The chowder is one of the best on this planet.

Heading back up the road takes you past Lady's Island Lake containing **Our Lady's Island**, site of an early Augustinian priory and still a centre of devotion. Fervent pilgrims used to crawl round the island; people still walk it barefooted. Look out for the stump of the Norman tower, which tilts more than the Leaning Tower of Pisa. You can drive out to the castle on the island and walk a 2km circuit taking in Our Lady's shrine, though the route is often waterlogged.

On the lake's eastern shore is **Castle View Heights** (☎ 31140), which has a restaurant, craft shop and minigolf.

There's a well-equipped camp site, **St Margaret's Beach Caravan & Camping Park** (☎ 31169; stmarg@eircom.net; St Margaret's Beach; camp sites €16; ☿ mid-Mar–mid-Oct), 500m from the beach.

There's no public transport to this area.

KILMORE QUAY
☎ 05391 / pop 400
Straight out of a postcard, peaceful Kilmore Quay is a small, working fishing village noted for its quaint thatched cottages, lobsters and great restaurants. The harbour is the jumping-off point for Ireland's largest bird sanctuary, the Saltee Islands (see p176), which are clearly visible out to sea.

Mussel in on the four-day **Seafood Festival** (☎ 29918) in early July for music, dancing and, of course, plenty of tastings of the goodies landed in the port.

Sights & Activities
In the harbour aboard a lightship with its original furniture and fittings, the **Maritime Museum** (☎ 21572; adult/child €4/2; ☿ noon-6pm daily Jun-Aug, noon-6pm Sat & Sun Sep-May) explains the history of the town's lifeboat.

To charter a boat for sea angling, contact **John Devereaux** (☎ 29637), **Eammon Hayes** (☎ 29723) or **Leslie Bates** (☎ 29806).

Sailing Ireland (☎ 39163; Sallystown, Murrintown) offers lessons (from €60 per person) and half-day cruises (from €200 per boat).

Sandy beaches stretch northwest and northeast from Forlorn Point (Crossfarnoge). There are some signposted **walking trails** behind the peaceful dunes, circled by serenading skylarks. Look out for **St Patrick's Bridge causeway**, which stretches towards Little Saltee. A Dutch trawler ran aground there in 2006.

Wrecks like the SS *Isolde* and *Ardmore*, both dating back to the 1940s, and extraordinary marine life should keep divers occupied. Contact **Pier House Dive Centre** (☎ 29703; http://homepage.eircom.net/~pierhousedivecentre) to hire gear, arrange a dive or refill air tanks.

Sleeping & Eating
Mill Road Farm (☎ 29633; www.millroadfarm.com; R739; s/d €40/70; ☿ closed late Dec; P) About 2km northeast of Kilmore Quay on the R739, this farmhouse on a working dairy farm offers simple, tastefully decorated rooms and breakfasts featuring homemade bread and free-range eggs.

Quay House (☎ 29988; www.kilmorequay.net; s €40-45, d €80-90; P ▢) This whitewashed guesthouse in the telegraph office has country-pine floors, rosy red bedspreads and a sociable lounge. Out back is an annex with cheaper rooms and facilities for fishermen.

Wooden House (☎ 48879; www.thewoodenhouse.ie; s/d €85/120; mains €13-18) Traditionally a great place for a sandwich, a pint and live music (Thursday to Sunday), the friendly Wooden House has added some stylish bedrooms with sea views and skylights.

PRINCE OF THE SALTEES

The Saltees were bought in 1943 by Michael Neale, who immediately proclaimed himself 'Prince of the Saltees'. Something of a strange one, he erected a throne and obelisk in his own honour on Great Saltee, and had a full-blown coronation ceremony there in 1956. Although the College of Arms in London refuted Neale's claim to blue blood, he won a small victory when Wexford County Council began addressing letters to 'Prince Michael Neale'.

The prince broadcast his intention to turn Great Saltee into a second Monte Carlo, but was distracted by a war right on his doorstep. In an escalation of hostilities, he released two ferrets, then a dozen foxes, then 46 cats onto the island to kill the rabbits that he hated so.

Prince Michael died in 1998, but before his death decreed: 'All people, young and old, are welcome to come, see and enjoy the Islands, and leave them as they found them for the unborn generations to come, see and enjoy'.

COUNTIES WEXFORD & WATERFORD

Hotel Saltees (☎ 29601; www.hotelsaltees.ie; s/d €90/140) The new owners have done some spring-cleaning, hanging painterly canvases to create a contemporary feel and installing a Sri Lankan chef in the restaurant. Accommodation is in plain motel-style rooms.

Kehoe's (☎ 29830; mains €7-20) An inviting old pub decorated with nautical equipment, ideal for a dram or a taste of one of the many seafood dishes. There is live music at weekends.

Silver Fox Seafood Restaurant (☎ 29888; mains €15-30; ☺ noon-9.30pm Jun-Aug, 5-9.30pm Mon-Sat, 12.30-2.30pm & 5-9.30pm Sun Sep-May) The QE2's former head chef has replaced founder Nicky Cullen, who decamped to the deli opposite. The room itself is slightly lacking in character, but the food ranges from prawns, plaice, platters, and lobster from the tank to fishfree options such as guinea fowl and wok-fried egg noodles.

Getting There & Away

Public transport is limited. **Bus Éireann** (☎ 22522) service 383 runs to/from Wexford on Wednesday and Saturday (€3, 45 minutes, two services in each direction). The **Viking Shuttle Bus** (☎ 21053) covers the same route more regularly; for times, ask at the post office.

SALTEE ISLANDS

Once the haunt of privateers, smugglers and 'dyvars pyrates', the Saltees now have a peaceful existence as one of Europe's most important bird sanctuaries. Over 375 recorded species make their home here, 4km offshore from Kilmore Quay, principally the gannet, guillemot, cormorant, kittiwake, puffin, aux, and the Manx shearwater. The best time to visit is the spring and early-summer nesting

season. The birds leave once the chicks can fly, and by early August it's eerily quiet.

The two islands, 90-hectare Great Saltee and 40-hectare Little Saltee, feature some of the oldest rocks in Europe, dating back over 2000 million years, and were inhabited as long ago as 3500 to 2000 BC. From the 13th century until the dissolution of the monasteries, they were the property of Tintern Abbey, after which various owners were granted the land.

Two of the Wexford rebel leaders, Bagenal Harvey and John Colclough, hid here after the failed 1798 Rising. The men were betrayed by a paid informer, tracked down in a six-hour manhunt, taken to Wexford, hanged, and their heads stuck on spikes.

To book a crossing to the Saltees try local boatmen such as **Declan Bates** (☎ 053-29684, 087-252 9736).

Boats travel from Kilmore Quay harbour roughly every hour in summer, between about 10.30am and 3pm. Actually docking on the islands depends on the wind direction: the operators will know the night before whether a landing is possible or not. It's a 30-minute crossing and the return fare is €22 per person (half-price for children) if the boat is full, €120 if you're the only one on the boat.

For more information read *Saltees: Islands of Birds and Legends* by Richard Roche and Oscar Merne (O'Brien Press).

HOOK PENINSULA & AROUND
☎ 051

The long, tapering finger of the Hook Peninsula is an undiscovered joy. There are no blockbustingly major visitor attractions, but around every other bend is a quiet beach, a crumbling fortress, a stately abbey or a seafood restaurant. In good weather, it's a fine journey out to Hook Head, then back along the western side to Duncannon.

Cromwell's statement that Waterford town would fall 'by Hook or by Crooke' referred to the two possible landing points from which to take the area: here or at Crooke in County Waterford.

Duncormick to Wellington Bridge

Signposted as the Bannow Drive, and covered by a free leaflet, the promontory east of the Hook Peninsula is littered with Norman ruins. The invaders founded a town at **Bannow**, yet nothing of it remains other than a ruined church. Enthusiastic historians, eyeing the uneven ground in front of the church and the shifting sands of the estuary, speak of the 'buried city of Bannow'. The headland to the southeast, surmounted by the 19th-century **Martello tower**, is **Baginbun Head**, where the Normans first landed (1169) for their conquest of Ireland.

Bannow Bay is a wildfowl sanctuary, rich in birdlife such as brent geese, redshank, wigeon and teal, and a top cultivation site for Irish oysters. The remains of medieval village **Clonmines**, which fell into decline when its estuary silted up, are southwest of Wellington Bridge. The ruins are on private land, but you get a good view of them just south of the bridge as you head north into town. The redbrick chimney in a roadside paddock on the other side of the bridge is an old **silver mine**. It was in operation from the 1530s to 1851, and supplied the Irish mint.

Tintern Abbey

On the way to Fethard-on-Sea is an early 13th-century Cistercian abbey in 100 acres of woodland. William Marshal, earl of Pembroke, founded **Tintern Abbey** (☎ 562 650; Saltmills; adult/child incl guided tour €2/1; ☒ 10am-6pm mid-Jun–Sep, 10am-5pm Oct, last admission 45 min before closing) after he nearly perished at sea and swore to establish a church if he ever made it to Ireland. It was named after the Welsh abbey his first monks came from. Make time for the **Tintern Trails**, short woodland and coastal tracks around the abbey estate. A free walking map is available from the visitor centre or the tourist office in Fethard-on-Sea.

To get there, follow the signed left turn-off the R733 or R734.

Fethard-on-Sea

pop 330

Continuing south towards the Head, you'll come across Fethard, the largest village in the area. It's home to the scant ruins of 9th-century church **St Mogue's** and a 15th-century **castle** (too unstable to walk inside), which belonged to the bishop of Ferns. There's a small but helpful **tourist office** (☎ /fax 397 502; www.thehook-wexford.com; Main St; ☒ 9.30am-5.30pm Mon-Fri) opposite the castle.

Hotel Naomh Seosamh (☎ 397 129; aobrien@eircom. net; Main St; s/d €30/60; [P]) has a small-town feel and comfortable rooms and a bar where you'll get some chat. As its fire engine–red porch suggests, it used to be the police barracks. Impress landlord Arthur with your investigations of the Hook and he'll give you a leprechaun-hunting certificate.

About 1km north of town, the quiet little **Ocean Island Camping & Caravan Park** (☎ 397 148; camp sites €24; ☒ Apr-Sep) has a shop, a playground, and laundry and games rooms.

The Village (☎ 397 116; snacks & meals €2-8; ☒ 5-9pm Mon-Wed, 4-10pm Thu & Fri, 3-10pm Sat & Sun) is a takeaway selling fish and chips, sizzlin' chicken tenders and all the usual fare.

Hook Head

The journey from Fethard to **Hook Head** takes in a hypnotic stretch of horizon and sea, with few houses between the flat, open fields on the narrowing peninsula. There are views across Waterford Harbour and, on a clear day, as far as the Comeragh and Galtee Mountains.

About 5km northeast of the lighthouse, ghostly **Loftus Hall**, built by the Marquis of Ely in the 1870s, gazes across the estuary at Dunmore East. The English-owned Loftus estate once covered much of the peninsula.

About 3km further on, turning left at a small roundabout brings you to the village of **Slade**, where the most activity is in the swirl of seagulls above the ruined castle and harbour.

Further south, dramatic Hook Head is crowned by Europe's, and possibly the world's, oldest working **lighthouse** (☎ 397 055; adult/child €5.50/3; ☒ 9.30am-5.30pm Mar-Oct, 9.30am-5.30pm Sat & Sun Nov-Feb), staffed until 1996. It's said that monks lit a beacon on the head from the 5th century and that the first Viking invaders were so happy to have a guiding light that they left them alone. In the early 13th century William Marshal erected a solider beacon, which has remained largely unchanged. Traces of the lighthouse keepers' lives remain inside the black-and-white-striped tower. Access is by half-hour guided tour. The visitor centre has a decent restaurant and tourist information section, which stocks guides including local historian Billy Colfer's informative *The Hook Peninsula*.

There are brilliant, blustery **walks** on both sides of the head, a haunting place in the evening. Be careful of the freak waves and numerous blowholes on the western side of the peninsula. The rocks around the lighthouse are Carboniferous limestone, rich in **fossils**. If you search carefully, you may find 350-million-year-old shells and tiny disc-like pieces of crinoids, a type of starfish. A good place to hunt is Patrick's Bay, across the peninsula from Loftus Hall. Hook Head visitor centre has a free map of the area's nine accessible beaches. At low tide, there is a good walk between Grange and Carnivan beaches, past caves, rock pools and Baginbun Head (p177).

The head is a good vantage point for **birdwatching**: over 200 species have been recorded passing through. You might even get lucky and see dolphins or **whales** in the estuary, particularly between December and February.

The area is also a favourite for **diving**. The best sites are out from the inlet under the lighthouse or from the rocks at the southwestern corner of the head. Underwater scenery is pleasant, with lots of caves, crevasses and gullies, and it's a maximum of 15m deep. If it's too rough, try Churchtown, 1km north of the point on the western side of the peninsula. The rocks south of Slade Harbour are a popular area. The nearest hire shop is in Kilmore Quay (p175).

Duncannon & Around

Driving from Hook Head towards Duncannon, you'll come across the ruins of a fortified **medieval church** opposite the Templar's Inn. In 1172, Henry II granted land hereabouts to the Knights Templar; they made nearby Templetown their HQ and built various churches. The 13th-century structure they built here was later added to by the Knights Hospitaller and the Loftus estate. On the ground to the left of the church, a stone slab bears a Templar seal: a lamb and crucifix.

There's something fantastically pleasing about the small holiday resort of Duncannon: the sandy beach, fine views of Waterford Harbour, pleasant eating-and-drinking options and laid-back air all work a calming alchemy on your brain. In July, sculptors transform the beach into a surrealist canvas at the **Duncannon International Sand Sculpting Festival** (☎ 087-205 8491; www.visitduncannon.com/sand_festival.htm).

To the west of the village is star-shaped **Duncannon Fort** (☎ 389 454; duncannonfort@hotmail .com; adult/child €5/3; ❧ 9.30am-5.30pm Jun–mid-Sep), used as a set for *The Count of Monte Cristo* starring Richard Harris and Guy Pearce. It was built in 1588 to stave off a feared attack by the Spanish Armada, and later used by the Irish army as a WWI training base. There's a small maritime museum and a café. A military re-enactment weekend takes place here over the June bank holiday.

About 4km northwest of Duncannon is pretty **Ballyhack**, from where a ferry sails to Passage East in County Waterford (see the boxed text, p191). It's dominated by 15th-century **Ballyhack Castle** (☎ 389 468; adult/child €1.50/75c; ❧ 10am-6pm mid-Jun–mid-Sep, last admission 45 min before closing), a Knights Hospitallers tower house, containing a small exhibition on the Crusades.

SLEEPING & EATING
The Moorings (☎ 389 242; Duncannon; s €35-40, d €70-80) In a line of cottages with twee names, the Moorings ticks the friendliness and value-for-money boxes. Large bathrooms and sofas abound, and angling can be arranged.

Glendine Country House (☎ 389 500; www.glendine house.com; Arthurstown; s €75-85, d €110-130) Run by the Crosbie family in a creeper-covered former dower house, this guesthouse is homely rather than stately. Bay windows overlook the estuary and grounds populated by deer, cattle and sheep. Rooms range from crisp modern affairs to those stacked with period furniture. Organic fare and home-baked treats such as cream teas are on offer.

Dunbrody Country House Hotel & Restaurant (☎ 389 600; www.dunbrodyhouse.com; Arthurstown; with breakfast & dinner from s €160-225, d €270-400, restaurant meal €48-60) Kevin Dundon's (see boxed text, opposite) hotel and restaurant in an 1830s Georgian manor are not a typical country-house set-up. Rooms are period-decorated but the emphasis is on a relaxation rather than history, with touches such as a food smoker (principally used for salmon, which is on sale), and a dinky bar in the grounds. Local produce informs the seasonal menu in the gourmet restaurant, which, at the time of research, was set to be joined by an oyster bar. If that's not enough for one weekend, Dunbrody's 300 acres also contain a spa and cookery school.

Templar's Inn (☎ 397 162; Templetown; dishes €11-22; 🕓 12.30-9pm Mar-Oct, noon-8pm Thu-Sun Nov-Mar) This roadside pub looks like a wayfarers' tavern, but it's a great place to settle in for a steak or seafood and a read of the information on the area's Knights Templar connections. Outdoor seats look over fields and the medieval church.

Sqigl Restaurant & Roche's Bar (☎ 389 188; sqigl restaurant@eircom.net; Quay Rd, Duncannon; mains €10-25; 🕓 bar food 10.30am-10pm, restaurant 7-10pm Wed-Sat Feb-Easter, Tue-Sun Easter-Dec) Local produce is the mainstay of this fabulous restaurant, where dishes range from pan-seared sea bass to spring lamb. The same kitchen serves the beautifully decorated pub next door, where there are trad sessions on Friday, Saturday and, during summer, midweek.

Dunbrody Abbey

Dunbrody Abbey is a beautiful 12th-century ruin on the western side of Hook Head, beside the R733 about 9km north of Duncannon, southwest of the village of Campile. The **Dunbrody Abbey Visitor Centre** (☎ 388 603; www.dunbrodyabbey.com; adult/child €2/1; 🕓 10am-6pm May–mid-Sep), as well as allowing entry to the Cistercian abbey, contains the ruins of **Dunbrody Castle** (adult/child €4/2), a craft shop and

museum with a huge doll's house, pitch and putt, and a yew-hedge **maze**. Entrance to the latter two attractions is included in the castle admission fee.

Getting There & Away

BUS

West Coast Wexford Rural Transport (☎ 389 410; Ramsgrange Centre, New Ross) is bravely attempting to connect the Hook with the outside world. A service links Wellington Bridge and New Ross on Tuesday; Fethard, Duncannon, Arthurstown, Ballyhack and New Ross on Tuesday and Thursday, continuing to Waterford on Saturday; Wellington Bridge, Saltmills (near Tintern Abbey), Fethard, Duncannon, Arthurstown, Ballyhack and Wexford on Wednesday; Wellington Bridge, New Ross and Waterford on Friday; and Wellington Bridge and Wexford on Saturday. Return fares are €5 to €8; €3 for students and under-16s, free for under-fives.

On Monday and Thursday, **Bus Éireann** (☎ 05391-22522) service 370 runs between Waterford, New Ross, Duncannon, Templetown, Fethard, Wellington Bridge and Wexford. The entire journey takes 2¾ hours. The same bus links Waterford, New Ross and Duncannon from Monday to Saturday (departing in the evening), and Waterford, New Ross, Wellington Bridge and Wexford on Wednesday and Saturday. In all cases there is one service in each direction.

IRELAND'S FAVOURITE STRAWBERRIES

Chef Kevin Dundon is regularly seen in the *Irish Independent*, on RTÉ One's *The Afternoon Show* and trying to outdance fellow celebs on *Jigs 'n' Reels*. Formerly the executive chef at Dublin's Shelbourne Hotel, he has won recognition for his truth-to-materials approach. 'A lot of chefs can cook sophisticated food, but very few can cook simple food. There's very little room for error, you have to find the best ingredients and be spot on', he says.

Dundon moved to Dunbrody House 10 years ago and his recipe book, *Full On Irish*, is peppered with reveries about Wexford produce. Given its miles of coastline, the county is a prime patch for seafood such as Kilmore Quay scallops, Baginbun Bay cockles and mussels, wild salmon from Waterford estuary, and swordfish, tuna and sea bass landed at Duncannon.

The area is most famous for its strawberries, which are sold at roadside stalls throughout the county during summer. Dundon combines them with goats cheese (from Blackwater in eastern Wexford) in a salad. Another renowned local crop is the British Queen potato, which prospers on Hook Head, a success Dundon puts down to the Gulf Stream.

'We're two months ahead of the rest of Ireland in terms of weather, so we get the first crop of potatoes', he says. 'The soil is sandy, which is ideal for potato growing. British Queens are very floury, and that's unique to Ireland. When you cook them, their skins split and they wink up at you'.

FERRY

If you're travelling on to Waterford, it's well worth taking the Ballyhack–Passage East car ferry (see the boxed text, p191), which saves you a detour via New Ross.

NEW ROSS

☎ 051 / pop 4680

The big attraction at New Ross (Rhos Mhic Triúin), 34km west of Wexford town, is the opportunity to board a 19th-century Famine ship. The town, which developed as a 12th-century Norman port on the River Barrow, also advertises itself as the 'Norman gateway to the Barrow Valley'. It's not especially pretty, but the eastern bank has some intriguing steep, narrow streets and St Mary's Church.

A group of rebels tried to seize New Ross during the 1798 Rising. They were repelled by the defending garrison, leaving 3000 dead and much of the place in ruins.

The **tourist office** (☎ 421 857; The Quay; ✹ 10am-6.30pm Apr-Sep, 10am-5pm Oct-Mar) is inside the Dunbrody Visitor Centre, where there's also a small café. Surf the net at **Solaak Inventures** (☎ 420 807; 5 The Quay; per hr €4; ✹ 10am-11pm Mon-Sat, 1pm-12am Sun).

Sights & Activities

You can board the **Dunbrody Heritage Ship** (☎ 425 239; www.dunbrody.com; adult/child €7/4; ✹ 10am-6pm Apr-Sep, 10am-5pm Oct-Mar), a full-scale reconstruction of an 1845 sailing ship, and learn about the poor souls forced to board 'coffin ships' to the US during the Famine. Their sorrowful, sometimes-inspiring stories are brought to life by actors. Entrance is by a 40-minute tour, including a 10-minute film detailing the history of the original three-masted barque and the construction of the new one. There's a database of Irish emigration to America from 1845 to 1875, containing over two million records.

The two- to three-hour cruise on the **Galley River Cruising Restaurant** (☎ 421 723; www.rivercruises.ie; North Quay; cruise & lunch/dinner €25/40; ✹ 12pm, 3pm & 7pm May-Oct) drifts slowly up the River Barrow, through rolling fields and peaceful farmlands. You can just enjoy the ride over a cup of tea (€12 to €17) or enhance it with a quality meal.

The roofless ruin on Church Lane is **St Mary's Abbey**, one of the largest medieval churches in Ireland. It was founded by Isabella of Leinster and her husband, William,

in the 13th century. Ask at the tourist office for access.

Sleeping & Eating

MacMurrough Farm Hostel (☎ 421 383; www.macmurrough.com; MacMurrough; dm €14-16, d €34-40; ✹ Mar-Oct; ℗) Brian and Jenny's farm hostel is in a beautiful hilltop location up a track 3.5km northeast of town (phone for directions). Inside the whitewashed outhouse, the stove-warmed common room and en-suite dorms with their cheery duvets have a rural charm. There is also an equally quaint two-person self-catering accommodation (per night/week €60/350) in the old stables.

Riversdale House (☎ 422 515; www.wexford-bnb .com; Lower William St; s/d €50/80; ✹ Mar-Nov; ℗) The only town-centre B&B, uphill from the Quay, has been going 25 years. Friendly, energetic owner Ann is a former National Housewife of the Year and cookery teacher. Paintings by the family and china from Ann's travels decorate the pink rooms, and there's a conservatory opening onto tranquil gardens.

Brandon House Hotel (☎ 421 703; www.brandonhousehotel.ie; New Ross; s/d €125/190; ℗ 🖳) The Brandon, 2km south of New Ross, on a hill with river views, is not as classy or individualistic as nearby Duncannon's country-house hotels, but has some winning elements: open log fires, extensive gardens, a library bar and rooms big enough for a small family. There's a deluxe health-and-leisure club, featuring the full Jacuzzi-pool-gym-sauna-treatment spa complement.

Sid's Diner (☎ 421 973; Marsh Meadows; mains €6-12; ✹ 7am-7pm Mon-Sat) Sid's, 1.5km south of the centre, is a truly eclectic experience: stodgy classics served in an American diner–style café by Renault-branded staff (it's next to the showroom).

Upper Deck Café (☎ /fax 425 391; 8 Mary St; sandwiches €4-7, mains €6-10; ✹ 9am-5.30pm Mon-Sat) This first-floor café adds a modern twist to the whole-food formula, with paper shamrock chains adorning the ceiling. Grab a quick sandwich, or pig out on hot-counter specials.

Getting There & Away

Bus Éireann (☎ 05391-22522) buses depart from Dunbrody Inn on the Quay and travel to Waterford (€4.50, 30 minutes, 11 daily Monday to Saturday, seven Sunday), Dublin (€10.50, three hours, four daily), Rosslare Harbour (€10.50, one hour, four daily Monday to

Saturday, three Sunday) and Wexford (€5.50, 40 minutes, four daily Monday to Friday, three Saturday).

AROUND NEW ROSS

☎ 051

About 7km south of New Ross, the **Kennedy Homestead** (☎ 388 264; www.kennedyhomestead.com; Dunganstown; adult/child/family €5/2.50/14; ☼ 10am-5pm Jul & Aug, 11.30am-4.30pm Mon-Fri May, Jun & Sep, by appointment rest of the year) was the birthplace of Patrick Kennedy, great grandfather of John F Kennedy, who left Ireland for the USA in 1848. When JFK visited the farm in 1963 and hugged the current owner's grandmother, it was his first public display of affection according to his sister Jean. Jean later unveiled the plaque here. The outhouses have been turned into a museum that establishes the context of Kennedy's visit and examines the Irish-American dynasty's history on both sides of the Atlantic.

Containing 4500 species of trees and shrubs in 252 hectares of woodlands and gardens, the **John F Kennedy Arboretum** (☎ 388 171; jfkarboretum@opw.ie; New Ross; adult/child €3/1.50; ☼ 10am-8pm May-Aug, 10am-6.30pm Apr & Sep, 10am-5pm Oct-Mar, last admission 45 min before closing) is the promised land for families on a sunny day. The park, 2km southeast of the Kennedy Homestead, was funded by prominent Irish-Americans as a memorial to JFK. There's a small visitor centre, tearooms and a picnic area.

Slieve Coillte (270m), opposite the park entrance, has a viewing point from where you can see the arboretum and six counties on a clear day.

ENNISCORTHY

☎ 05392 / pop 3240

A quiet market town, Enniscorthy (Inis Coirthaidh) has a warren of steep streets descending from Pugin's cathedral to the Norman castle and the River Slaney. For the Irish, Enniscorthy is forever linked to some of the fiercest fighting of the 1798 Rising, when rebels captured the town and set up camp at Vinegar Hill. A visitor centre tells the story brilliantly.

Information

The local **tourist office** (☎ 34699; Mill Park Rd; ☼ 9.30am-5pm Mon-Fri, 11am-5pm Sat & Sun Easter-Sep, 9.30am-4pm Mon-Fri Oct-Easter), inside the National 1798 Rebellion Centre, has free leaflets containing maps of the town and area.

One-hour **guided walks** (€5) of the town can be booked for a minimum of five people at **Castle Hill Crafts & Tours** (☎ 36800; Castle Hill).

At the bottom of Castle Hill, on and around Abbey Sq, are the main post office and two banks. **Internet Cafe' Plus** (☎ 43676; 2 Templeshannon; per hr €2; ☼ 10am-10pm Mon-Fri, noon-10pm Sat & Sun) overlooks Enniscorthy Bridge.

Sights

It's worth visiting the excellent **National 1798 Rebellion Centre** (☎ 37198; 98com@iol.ie; Mill Park Rd; adult/child €6/3.50; ☼ 9.30am-5pm Mon-Fri, 11am-5pm Sat & Sun Easter-Sep, 9.30am-4pm Mon-Fri Oct-Easter) before climbing Vinegar Hill. It examines events such as the French and American revolutions that sparked Wexford's abortive uprising against British rule in Ireland, before chronicling the bloody struggle itself and its consequences. The engaging interactive displays include a chessboard with pieces representing key figures in the Rising, and a multiscreen recreation of the finale atop a virtual Vinegar Hill. From Abbey Sq walk out of town along Mill Park Rd, then take the first right after the school.

The Normans left the village the stout, four-towered **Enniscorthy castle**. Queen Elizabeth I awarded its lease to the poet Edmund Spenser for the flattering things he said about her in his epic *The Faerie Queene*. Rather ungratefully, he sold it on to a local landlord.

Like everything else in these parts, the castle was attacked by Cromwell in 1649. During the 1798 Rising rebels used the building as a prison.

The **Wexford County Museum** inside the castle was closed at the time of research, with some doubt over whether it would reopen. The dusty museum is much loved for its hotchpotch of exhibits, such as a jaunting car and battered ships' figureheads.

Restored to its original glory (check out the star-spangled roof), the Roman Catholic **St Aidan's Cathedral** (1846) was designed by Augustus Pugin, the architect behind the Houses of Parliament in London.

Every Irish schoolchild knows the name of **Vinegar Hill**, associated with one of the most bloodthirsty battles of the 1798 Rebellion and a turning point in the struggle.

After capturing Enniscorthy, a group of rebels set up camp around the windmill on

COUNTIES WEXFORD & WATERFORD

Vinegar Hill. A month later, English troops attacked and forced the rebels to retreat, massacring hundreds of women and children in the 'follow-up' operation.

At the top of the hill there's a memorial to the uprising, and panoramic views of Enniscorthy and the surrounding hills. To get there, follow the brown sign from Templeshannon on the eastern side of the river. It takes about 45 minutes to walk there.

Activities

Eighteen-hole **Enniscorthy Golf Club** (☎ 37600; New Ross Rd; green fee weekday/weekend €30/40) is 2.5km southwest of town.

Fishing is possible at the trout lakes at nearby **Rainbow Farm** (☎ 40707; Kellystown, Adamstown), or on the sea through **Danny's Bait & Tackle** (☎ 43571; St Senan's Rd).

Festivals & Events

Enniscorthy holds its **Strawberry Fair** (☎ 33540) in late June/early July, when pubs extend their hours, and strawberries and cream are laid on heavily.

Sleeping

Murphy's (☎ 37837; murphysguesthouse@gmail.com; 9 Main St; s from €40-45, d €60-70; P) This B&B used to be above a pub; now it's above a clothes shop. Although it has lost most of its character, it's a comfortable central option with a (microscopic) car park.

Old Bridge House (☎ 34222; obhouse@indigo.ie; Slaney Pl; s/d €40/70) The Redmonds' guesthouse is the perfect antidote to big-hotel blandness and B&B tweeness. The gangly building overlooking the Slaney is packed with pot plants, prints and intriguing items.

Treacy's Hotel (☎ 37798; www.treacyshotel.com; Templeshannon; s/d €95/150) The rooms resemble something you might find off a motorway, but the hotel scores with two bars, a nightclub and a Thai restaurant. There's entertainment such as Irish dancing and guests can use the leisure centre opposite for free.

Monart (☎ 38999; www.monart.ie; The Still; s/d/tr €185/290/435) An adults-only spa resort, hidden in woodland 2km west of Enniscorthy, with rooms surrounding a pond. Modern touches such as a glass walkway have been added to the main house without lessening its stately grandeur. Treatments on offer range from hydrotherapy to dry flotation.

Eating

Baked Potato (☎ 34085; Rafter St; snacks & meals €5.50-8.50; ⏰ 8am-6pm Mon-Sat) One of a cluster of café/'s doing a brisk trade in homemade cakes, pies, sandwiches, and daily specials.

De Olde Bridge (☎ 38624; 2 Templeshannon; snacks €2.50-4, meals €6-11.50; ⏰ 8am-4pm Mon-Sat, 9am-4pm Sun) This café is the place for cheap, old-fashioned stomach-stokers, like lasagna, lamb cutlets or the full Irish.

The Bailey (☎ 30353; Barrack St; mains €13-27; ⏰ 10am-10pm) Leather armchairs lurk between Jurassic pot plants in this converted grain store. Dishes range from pub grub with a twist to more interesting options like Cajun salmon steak.

Galo Chargrill Restaurant (☎ 38077; 19 Main St; mains €18-28; ⏰ noon-3pm & 5.30-10pm Tue-Sun) Locals love this Portugese restaurant, but it didn't make us spill our Portugese beer with delight. It has a Mediterranean feel and the food on offer includes fish pie and skewered chicken and meat dishes.

There's a **farmers market** (☎ 087-411 4481; Abbey Sq; ⏰ 9am-2pm Sat) that sells local and organic veg, bacon, cheese, bread, fish and fruit.

Drinking & Entertainment

Pubs in Enniscorthy are split between no-frills traditional bars and flash hang-outs.

Antique Tavern (☎ 33428; 14 Slaney St) Travellers beware: this tiny riverside hostelry is closed to rogues including 'bandits, footpads, thimblemen, three-card tricksters, and persons of no fixed abode'.

The Bailey (☎ 30353; Barrack St) This riverside bar has a venue staging local and national music and comedy.

Slaney Plaza Cinema (☎ 37060; www.slaneyplaza .net; Templeshannon; adult/child €8/5.50) Screens mainstream and art-house films.

Shopping

The Enniscorthy area has been recognised as a centre of pottery since the 17th century. One of the oldest potteries is **Carley's Bridge Potteries** (☎ 33512; fax 34360; ⏰ 9am-12.45pm & 2-5.30pm Mon-Fri), on the road to New Ross. The free *Slaney Tourism* leaflet, available at the tourist office, features a pottery trail.

Getting There & Away
BUS

Bus Éireann (☎ 05391-22522) stops on the Shannon Quay on the eastern bank of the river,

COUNTIES WEXFORD & WATERFORD

outside the **Bus Stop Shop** (☎ 33291; ☽ 9am-10pm) where you can buy tickets. There are nine daily buses to Dublin (€10.50, 2½ hours), and eight to Rosslare Harbour (€8.20, one hour) via Wexford (€5.10, 25 minutes).

TRAIN
The **train station** (☎ 33488) is on the eastern bank of the river. The one line serves Dublin (€18.50, 2¼ hours), Wexford (€5, 25 minutes) and Rosslare Europort (€8, 45 minutes) three times daily.

FERNS
☎ 05393 / pop 950
This sleepy village was once the powerhouse of the kings of Leinster, in particular Dermot MacMurrough (1110–71), whose name is forever associated with bringing the Normans to Ireland (see p34). The Normans left behind a cathedral and a doughty castle, later smashed to pieces by Cromwell.

Ferns Castle (☎ 66411; ☽ 10am-6pm mid-Jun–mid-Sep, last admission 45 min before closing) was built around 1220. A couple of walls and part of the moat survive; you can climb to the top of the one complete tower. Parliamentarians destroyed the castle and executed most of the local population in 1649. The ruins are thought to stand on the site of Dermot MacMurrough's old fortress. In the visitor centre are a café and a tapestry depicting local history.

At the eastern end of the main street is **St Edan's Cathedral**, built in early Gothic style in 1817. Its **graveyard** contains a ruined high cross, said to mark the resting place of Dermot MacMurrough.

Behind the cathedral are two medieval ruins: the Norman-built **Ferns Cathedral** and, with an unusual square-based round tower, **St Mary's Abbey**. Dermot MacMurrough founded it in 1158, inviting Augustinian monks to run a monastery here. An early Christian settlement founded here by St M'Aodóg in 600 was destroyed by the Vikings.

Further out of town is **St Peter's Church**, built from stones taken magpie-like from Ferns Cathedral and St Mary's Abbey.

As you only need an hour or so to take in the sights of Ferns, bigger Enniscorthy, about 12km southwest, is a more obvious base for accommodation. However, B&B **Coolbawn** (☎ 66452; s/d €60/80), near Ferns Cas-

tle, is more pleasant and better value than most of its competitors in Enniscorthy.

Bus Éireann (☎ 05391-22522) has nine daily buses from Ferns to Dublin (2¼ hours), eight to Rosslare Harbour (1¼ hours) via Enniscorthy (15 minutes) and Wexford (40 minutes), and three to Waterford (one hour) Monday to Saturday (one on Sunday).

MT LEINSTER
The highest peak in the Blackstairs is Mt Leinster (796m), which has magnificent views of Counties Waterford, Carlow, Kilkenny and Wicklow from the top.

The car park at the foot of the mountain is signposted from Bunclody, 16km northwest of Ferns. From there, it's a steep 1½-hour-return walk. Coming from the Kilkenny side of the mountains, follow the South Leinster Scenic Drive signs from Borris. The last few kilometres are on narrow, exposed roads with steep fall-offs.

Mt Leinster is home to some of Ireland's best hang-gliding: contact the **Irish Hang Gliding & Paragliding Association** (http://ihpa.ie).

For guided walks in the Blackstairs Mountains, contact **Brian Gilsenan** (☎ 05393-77828). Ordnance Survey's Discovery map number 68 covers the area.

COUNTY WATERFORD

pop 108,000
It sometimes feels as though the Celtic Tiger, that formidable emblem of Irish progress and modernisation, suddenly felt less formidable and wandered off for a cat-nap when he reached County Waterford. The quiet county is a warren of untouristy hideaways, mostly along a coast that stretches from Waterford Harbour to the Cork border. It is starting to market itself, but this is good news for families. Fáilte Ireland has produced a *Cool for Kids* brochure covering the area, and there are even plans to mark family-friendly venues with 'smiley face' signs.

The attractive sandy coastline has seaside resorts to suit everyone. There's genteel Dunmore East, and historic Ardmore's golden beaches and cliff-top walks. There's also Tramore, famous for years as a candy-floss-and-chips resort, which has added eco-activities to its more obvious tourist attractions. At the other end of the Copper Coast GeoPark's 25km of strata, you can get views of it all from unspoilt Helvick Head, at the tip of a Gaeltacht (Irish-speaking) headland with its own road signs, heritage and culture.

The rejuvenated county town of Waterford is split between pedestrian plazas soundtracked by buskers and, around the oldest building in Ireland, medieval lanes and Georgian architecture.

In the seemingly unchartered north, the Nire Valley feels like a lost world, concealed by the Comeragh and Monavullagh Mountains. Its easy air, friendly folk and beautiful rolling hills are worth exploring: walks are enlivened by Neolithic stone circles, barrows and standing stones.

The tranquil River Blackwater runs through the county, gathering up the little towns of Cappoquin and lovely Lismore on its banks. The latter is home to a pre-Raphaelite window by Edward Burne-Jones (the only one in Ireland) and more history than a person knows what to do with.

WATERFORD TOWN

☎ 051 / pop 45,750

Ireland's oldest city, Waterford (Port Láirge), is first and foremost a busy port. Some parts of the city still feel almost medieval though, with narrow alleyways leading off many of the larger streets. Reginald's Tower marks the city's Viking heart and there are some attractive Georgian homes and warehouses. Ireland's flashiest museum, on the quays, uses state-of-the-art computer wizardry to get Waterford's history across; continue the sensory stimulation with a tour round the Waterford Crystal factory.

Although that seedy port-town feel is still evident in places, the city has received a face-lift in recent years. Pedestrianised streets and public artworks have improved the centre, and it's now a more attractive place to wander.

History

In the 8th century Vikings settled at Port Láirge, which they renamed Vadrafjord and turned into a booming trading post. To consolidate their presence there, they adopted a ferocity that made Waterford the

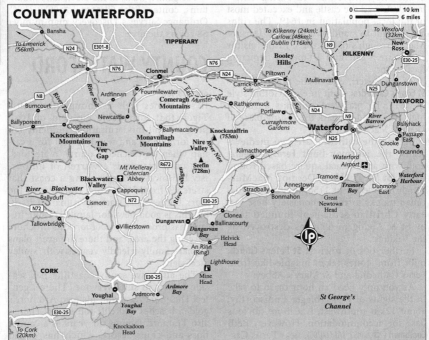

COUNTY WATERFORD

most powerful and feared settlement in the country. Local tribes paid a tribute known as *Airgead Sróine* (nose money): defaulters had their noses cut off!

Acknowledging Waterford's strategic importance, the newly arrived Anglo-Normans attacked the town, defeating a combined Irish-Viking army and hurling 70 prominent citizens to their deaths off Baginbun Head. Strongbow finished the takeover in 1170 with 200 soldiers and 1000 archers, and married local chief Dermot MacMurrough's daughter.

In 1210 King John extended the original Viking city walls and Waterford became Ireland's most powerful city. In the 15th century it resisted the forces of two pretenders to the English Crown, Lambert Simnel and Perkin Warbeck, thus earning the motto *Urbs intacta manet Waterfordia* (Waterford city remains unconquered).

The luck didn't last: the city defied Cromwell in 1649, but in 1650 his forces returned and Waterford surrendered. The town escaped the customary slaughter but its Catholics were either exiled to the west or shipped as slaves to the Caribbean, and the population declined.

Orientation

Waterford lies on the tidal reach of the River Suir, 16km from the coast. The main shopping street runs directly south from the Suir, beginning as Barronstrand St and passing through John Roberts Sq before becoming Broad St, Michael St and John St, which intersects with Parnell St; this then runs northeast back up to the quay-lined river, becoming The Mall on the way. Most of the sights and shops lie within this triangle.

Information

BOOKSHOPS

Waterford Book Centre (☎ 873 823; 25 John Roberts Sq; ☉ 9am-6pm Mon-Thu & Sat, 9am-9pm Fri, 1-5pm Sun) An excellent store with three floors of books, some foreign papers and magazines, and a café.

INTERNET ACCESS

Waffle House (☎ 086-050 8196; 31 Patrick St; per 30/60min €1/2; ☉ 8.30am-8pm)
Waterford e-Centre (☎ 878 448; 10 O'Connell St; per 30/60min €2.80/4.50; ☉ 9.30am-9pm Mon-Thu, 9.30am-8pm Fri, 9.30am-6pm Sat, 11am-6pm Sun)

LAUNDRY

Snow White Laundrette (☎ 858 905; Mayor's Walk; ☉ 9.15am-1.30pm & 2.30-6pm Mon-Sat)

LEFT LUGGAGE

Plunkett train station (☎ 873 401) Leave luggage for €2.50 per item per 24 hours.

MEDICAL SERVICES

Waterford Regional Hospital (☎ 848 000; Dunmore Rd) A little out of town. Follow the quays east and watch out for the signs.

MONEY

There's a branch of the **Allied Irish Bank** (☎ 874 824; Meagher Quay) by the clock tower, and ATMs throughout the town.

POST

The main post office is on Parade Quay in the city centre. There are also branches on O'Connell St and High St, open Monday to Saturday (half-day Thursday).

TOILETS

You'll find toilets in the bus station, nearby on Merchant's Quay, and near the clock tower.

TOURIST INFORMATION

Waterford city tourist office (☎ 875 823; www .southeastireland.com; Merchants Quay; ☉ 9am-6pm Mon-Sat May-Sep, 9.15am-5pm Mon-Sat Oct-Apr, 11am-5pm Sun Jul-Aug) This large office is the best source of info and help in Counties Waterford and Wexford.
Waterford Crystal tourist office (☎ 358 397; Cork Rd; ☉ 9am-5pm Jan-Mar & Oct, 9am-6pm Apr-Sep, closed Nov & Dec)

Sights & Activities

Waterford Museum of Treasures (☎ 304 500; www .waterfordtreasures.com; Hanover St; adult/child €4/2; ☉ 9.30am-6pm Apr, May & Sep, 9.30am-9pm Jun-Aug, 10am-5pm Oct-Mar) is one of Ireland's widest-ranging and most hi-tech museums. It's a dazzling, intriguing, provoking, and at times plain bewildering maze of metal, glass and state-of-the-art audiovisual displays.

The fun begins on the 3rd floor, from where (plugged into an audioguide) you follow the exhibitions as they wend their way through history. A highlight is the 'Viking longship', a rocking ride narrated by Waterford's Nordic forebears, who call themselves 'children of the raven' but sound more like comedic Scotsmen. You can also attend the marriage

WATERFORD

0 — 200 m
0 — 0.1 mile

INFORMATION
Allied Irish Bank..................................1 C4
Main Post Office..................................2 C4
Snow White Laundrette.......................3 B5
Tourist Office.......................................4 B4
Waffle House..5 B5
Waterford Book Centre.......................6 B4
Waterford e-Centre.............................7 B4

SIGHTS & ACTIVITIES
Beach Tower...8 B4
Bishop's Palace....................................9 C5
Christ Church Cathedral.....................10 C5
City Hall..11 D5
Clock Tower..12 C4
French Church.....................................13 C5
Galley River Cruising Restaurant
    Pick-up Point.............................(see 42)
Half Moon Tower................................14 B5
Holy Trinity Cathedral........................15 C4
Reginald's Tower.................................16 D5

Rice Chapel...17 B6
Theatre Royal......................................18 C5
Waterford Heritage Survey..................19 B4
Waterford Museum of Treasures....(see 4)

SLEEPING
Avondale...20 C5
Brown's Townhouse............................21 C6
Granville Hotel....................................22 B4
Mayor's Walk House...........................23 B5
Portree Guesthouse............................24 A4
Rice Guesthouse.................................25 B6
Tower Hotel..26 D5

EATING
47 The Bistro......................................27 B5
Bodéga!..28 C5
Café Lucia...29 C5
Haricot's Wholefood Restaurant.........30 B4
Paddy Gonzales...................................31 C4

Saturday market.................................32 B4
Wine Vault..33 C5

DRINKING
Geoff's..34 B5
Katty Barry's.......................................35 D5
T&H Doolan's.....................................36 B4

ENTERTAINMENT
Forum...37 A4
Garter Lane Arts Centre......................38 B4
Kazbar...(see 28)
Ruby's...39 C6
Waterford Cineplex............................40 B5

TRANSPORT
Altitude (Bicycle Hire).........................41 A5
Bus Éireann Station............................42 A4
Euro Lines....................................(see 42)
Suirway..(see 42)

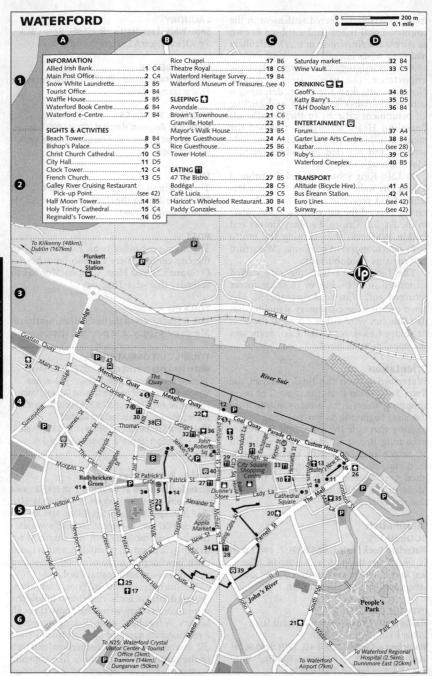

of Strongbow and local princess Aoife, who promises to teach her Anglo-Norman lord how the Irish feast.

Though they can feel a little lost under the weight of 21st-century technology, there are some beautiful 'real' exhibits. Golden Viking brooches, jewel-encrusted Norman crosses, the magnificent 1372 Great Charter Roll and 18th-century church silver are among the booty from a thousand years of history.

The oldest complete building in Ireland and the first to use mortar, 12th-century **Reginald's Tower** (☎ 304 220; The Quay; adult/child €2/1; ☒ 9.30am-6pm Jun-Aug, 9.30am-5pm Sep-May) is an outstanding example of medieval defences, and was the city's key fortification. The Normans built its 3m- to 4m-thick walls on the site of a Viking wooden tower. English-appointed local officials stayed in this 'safe house', as did many royal visitors.

Over the years, the building served as an arsenal, a prison and a mint. The exhibits relating to the latter role are interesting: medieval silver coins, a wooden 'tally stick' with notches indicating the amount owed, a 12th-century piggy bank (smashed) and a coin balance used to determine weight and bullion value. Architectural oddities include the toilet that drained halfway up the building.

On the top floor are audiovisual presentations about Waterford's defences; it's probably enough to watch just one. Behind the tower, a section of the **old wall** is incorporated into the Bowery bar. The two arches were sally ports, to let boats 'sally forth' into the inlet.

The pride of every middle-class living room, Waterford Crystal has become one of the world's most famous luxury brands. The **Waterford Crystal visitor centre** (☎ 332 500; www.waterfordvisitorcentre.com; Cork Rd), complete with restaurant and tourist office, is 2km south of the centre. You can lurk in the **shop** (☒ 8.30am-6pm Mar-Oct, 9am-5pm Nov-Feb), but we recommend the one-hour **factory tour** (adult/child €9.50/6.50; ☒ 8.30am-4pm Mar-Oct, 9am-3.15pm Mon-Fri Nov-Feb). The transformation of glowing-hot balls of glass into diamond-cut crystal is near miraculous, and the guides have real insider knowledge of the factory's workings. In summer buy tickets in advance from the tourist office to avoid queues.

The first Waterford glass factory was established at the western end of the riverside quays in 1783, but closed 68 years later because of punitive taxes imposed by the British. Revived last century, the business now employs 700 people, among them highly skilled glass-blowers, cutters and engravers. The glass is a heavy-lead crystal made from red lead, silica sand and potash.

Bus 3C runs there from opposite the Clock Tower every 15 minutes (€1.50).

CHURCHES

Christ Church Cathedral (☎ 858 958; Cathedral Sq; ☒ 10am-6pm Mon-Sat) is Europe's only neoclassical Georgian cathedral. Designed by local architect John Roberts, it was built on the site of an 11th-century Viking church, also the site where the 12th-century marriage of Strongbow and Aoife took place. The highlight is the 15th-century **tomb of James Rice**, seven times lord mayor of Waterford: sculpted worms and frogs crawl out of the statue of his decaying body. A guided tour is available (€4).

Also a **concert venue** with wonderful acoustics, its broad programme of performances features everything from choirs to pop quartets.

The sumptuous interior of the Catholic **Holy Trinity Cathedral** (☎ 875 166; Barronstrand St) boasts a carved-oak baroque pulpit, painted pillars with Corinthian capitals and 10 Waterford Crystal chandeliers. It was built between 1792 and 1796 by John Roberts, who, unusually, also designed the Protestant Christ Church Cathedral.

The elegant ruin of the **French Church** is on Greyfriars St, announced by a statue of Luke Wadding, the Waterford-born Franciscan friar who persuaded the Pope to negotiate with Charles I on behalf of Irish Catholics. Hugh Purcell gave the church to the Franciscans in 1240, asking them in return to pray for him once a day. The church became a hospital after the dissolution of the monasteries, and was then occupied by French Huguenot refugees between 1693 and 1815. John Roberts is buried here. Ask the staff at Reginald's Tower to let you in.

Edmund Ignatius Rice, founder of the Christian Brothers, established his first school at Mt Sion on Barrack St, where the **Rice Chapel** is a delightful combination of red brick and stained glass. Rice's tomb takes pride of place, awaiting the likely canonisation of its occupant.

OTHER BUILDINGS

The Mall, a wide 18th-century street built on reclaimed land, was once a tidal inlet. From the river end, its stateliest buildings are John Roberts' **City Hall** (1788) and **Theatre Royal**, arguably Ireland's most intact 18th-century theatre, and Richard Cassels' austere **Bishop's Palace** (1741), now the city engineering offices.

Crumbling fragments of the old city wall include **Half Moon Tower**, and **Beach Tower** at the top of Jenkin's Lane (both are just off Patrick St).

GENEALOGICAL CENTRE

If you have ancestors from the county, **Waterford Heritage Survey** (☎ 876 123; Jenkin's La; ✆ 9am-1pm & 2-5pm Mon-Thu, 9am-2pm Fri) may have the details you need to complete the family tree.

Tours

A must-do for any visitor to Waterford is Jack Burtchaell's **guided walking tour** (☎ 873 711, 851 043; tour €5; ✆ 11.45am & 1.45pm). Jack is blessed with the 'gift of the gab', and brings every nook and cranny of Waterford alive, effortlessly squeezing 1000 years of history into one hour. Be warned, audience participation is expected! Tours leave from outside the Waterford Museum of Treasures, picking up walkers from the Granville Hotel en route.

Two-hour **cruises** along the Suir and Barrow, leaving Merchants Quay at 3pm, are run by **Galley River Cruising Restaurant** (☎ 421 723; www.rivercruises.ie; North Quay, New Ross; cruise €10; ✆ May-Oct). Dunmore East–based Sea Safari (p190) picks up from Meagher Quay.

SUPER SAVERS

The **Waterford City Pass** (€11.70) gets you into the 'Big Three' attractions: the Waterford Museum of Treasures, Reginald's Tower and a guided tour of the Waterford Crystal Visitor Centre, saving you €4 on the individual admission prices. Pick it up from the tourist offices or any of the three attractions.

Alternatively there's the **Southeast Explorer** scheme. Buy entry to Waterford's museum or crystal centre, Lismore Heritage Centre, Dunbrody Famine Ship, Hook Lighthouse or the National Irish Heritage Park, and you'll get 25% off admissions to the other five attractions.

Festivals & Events

Waterford's **International Light Opera Festival** (☎ 874 402; The Mall) takes place in the last fortnight in September. It's cheaper and more easily accessible than the more famous Wexford Festival Opera but booking is still advisable.

Sleeping

Waterford is bereft of budget accommodation, but frequent buses to Tramore allow you to base yourself at one of the budget options there.

MIDRANGE

Mayor's Walk House (☎ 855 427; mayorswalkbandb@eircom.net; 12 Mayor's Walk; s/d €28/50) This respectable B&B is in a tall, thin building. The landing bathrooms are shared, but the large (if dated) rooms have their own washbasins.

Avondale (☎ 852 267; www.staywithus.net; 2 Parnell St; s/d/tr from €45/60/70) Red-carpeted Avondale has a homey feel, with six pleasant, old-fashioned rooms. Ask for a room at the back as the road can be noisy. Breakfast is not supplied.

Portree Guesthouse (☎ 874 574; www.portreeguesthouse.ie; Mary St; s/d €45/80; [P]) Behind the Portree's drab grey exterior are fine Georgian innards and a smashing B&B run by helpful proprietors. It's on a quiet street: a bonus in noisy Waterford.

Rice Guesthouse (☎ 371 606; www.riceguesthouse.com; 35-36 Barrack St; s/d/tr €55/100/120) Above a pub popular with locals of all generations, this purpose-built guesthouse has 21 rooms. It's a five-minute walk from the centre.

our pick **Brown's Townhouse** (☎ 870 594; www.brownstownhouse.com; 29 South Pde; d €120; [🖵]) This lovely Victorian town house, near the People's Park, has snug beds in comfy rooms. Guests sit sociably round one table at breakfast, and can choose pancakes and other alternatives to the full Irish.

TOP END

Granville Hotel (☎ 305 555; www.granville-hotel.ie; Meagher Quay; s/d from €80/95; [P]) The floodlit 18th-century building overlooking the river is the Granville, one of Ireland's oldest hotels. Public rooms and bedrooms maintain a touch of Georgian elegance. The hotel's had its share of famous guests: Charles Stuart Parnell gave a speech from a 1st-floor window.

Tower Hotel (☎ 862 300; www.towerhotelwaterford.com; the Mall; s/d from €99/162) The rooms are a little anonymous but bright and modern. Overall, the marina-side hotel is good value, with a leisure centre and a stylish bar-restaurant overlooking the water.

Eating

BUDGET & MIDRANGE

Crepes and cheeses are available alongside craft-work at the weekly Saturday **market** (George's St; ☿ 9am-3pm).

Café Lucia (☎ 854 023; 2 Arundel La; mains €6.50-9.50; ☿ 9.30am-5pm Mon-Sat) You may have to wait for one of the colourful seats in this deservedly popular place, which dishes out homemade soups, fresh juices, salads, *paninis*, wraps and Thai fish cakes.

Haricot's Wholefood Restaurant (☎ 841 299; 11 O'Connell St; mains €8-10; ☿ 9am-8pm) With local art-work on the walls and Billie Holiday on the stereo, this a great place to tuck into the newspaper, along with dishes such as fish chowder, beef stew and vegan casserole.

47 The Bistro (☎ 844 774; 47 Patrick St; mains €10-15; ☿ 11.30am-9.30pm Mon-Sat, noon-9pm Sun) A popular restaurant with curvy contemporary décor, serving sizzling stir-fries, stodgy classics such as Irish stew and pasta, and delicious desserts. Book ahead to get a table.

Paddy Gonzales (☎ 856 856; 50 High St; mains €13-18; ☿ 10am-10pm) This pub, which looks more like an American diner with its seating booths, is overpriced but a good option if you're travelling with children. It offers breakfasts, a carvery and, Wednesday to Saturday nights, Mexican food.

TOP END

ourpick Wine Vault (☎ 853 444; www.waterfordwinevault.com; High St; mains €16-26; ☿ 12.30-2.30pm & 5.30-10.30pm Mon-Sat) One of a cluster of quality eateries, this beautiful little restaurant is on two

floors of an Elizabethan town house, with one floor housing the wine cellar. The food is a treat, ranging from starters like rabbit sausages and West Cork mussels to calamari and onwards.

Bodéga! (☎ 844 177; 54 John St; dinner mains €16-27; ☿ noon-5pm Mon-Fri & 5.30-10pm Mon-Wed, 5.30-10.30pm Thu, 5.30pm-12.30am Fri & Sat) The décor is all Spanish cantina, but the French chef's menu is straight out of his homeland. The ever-changing menu, altered according to what's freshest, features wonderful dishes such as *moules frites* (mussels with fries) and Toulouse sausage, and there's a late-opening wine bar.

Drinking

The nightlife relies heavily on the students at the Waterford Institute of Technology, many of whom disappear home at weekends.

T&H Doolan's (☎ 841 504; 32 George's St) A licensed establishment for over 300 years, historic Doolan's is a popular place to watch sport on the box and live bands with names like the Shamrocks and the Dead Beats.

Geoff's (☎ 874 787; 9 John St; mains €4-8; ☿ food served noon-8.30pm Mon-Sat) This cavernous pub with creaky wooden floors and rock music pumping from the speakers packs in a lively student crowd.

Katty Barry's (☎ 855 095; Mall La) Don't be discouraged by the plain exterior and side-street location; this small, friendly place serves a smooth Guinness.

Entertainment

Clubs and slick bars are concentrated around the Apple Market area. The best are Ruby's, where cover bands play for free, and Kazbar, both on John St.

Garter Lane Arts Centre (☎ 855 038; boxoffice@garterlane.ie; O'Connell St) This is a much complimented theatre in an 18th-century building, staging art-house films, exhibitions, music, dance and plays.

Theatre Royal (☎ 874 402; the Mall) Stages theatre, musicals and dance.

Forum (☎ 871 111; www.forumwaterford.com; The Glen) The mighty Forum hosts everything from gay club nights to the Irish kick-box-ing championships. Its venues include the Gallery Theatre.

Waterford Cineplex (☎ 843 399; Patrick St) This five-screen complex shows mainstream films for €8/5 per adult/child.

Getting There & Away

AIR

Waterford Airport (☎ 875 589; www.flywaterford.com; ⏰ 8am-8.30pm Mon-Sat, 9am-8.30pm Sun) is 7km south of the city at Killowen. **AerArann** (☎ in the UK 0800 587 2324, in the Republic 0818 210 210; www.aerarann.com) flies daily to London's Luton airport, six days a week to Birmingham and Manchester, and twice a week to Lorient, France. Prices to the UK start at €40 one way, excluding taxes. **Slattery Sun** (☎ 066-718 6230; www.slatterys.com) flies to France, Portugal and Spain.

BUS

The **Bus Éireann** (☎ 879 000) station is on the waterfront at Merchant's Quay. There are plenty of buses daily to Tramore (€2.50, 30 minutes), Dublin (€11.50, three hours) via Enniscorthy or Carlow, Wexford (€12, 1½ hours), Killarney (€21.50, 4¼ hours) via Cork (€16.50, 2¼ hours), and Dungarvan (€9.70, 50 minutes).

Euro Lines (☎ 879 000) runs daily buses to London (€40, 13 hours) at 7pm with stops including Cardiff and Bristol, and to Tralee (€40, 5¼ hours) at 8.30am. Stops include Dungarvan, Cork and Killarney.

Suirway (☎ office 382 209, 24hr timetable 382 422; www.suirway.com) buses depart to Dunmore East (€3.20, 30 minutes, six daily Monday to Saturday) and Passage East (€3, 30 minutes, three daily Monday to Saturday) from next to the Bus Éireann station. Look for the red-and-white buses.

TRAIN

Plunkett train station (☎ 873 401) is on the northern side of the river. Trains run to Dublin (€28, 2¾ hours, four to six daily) via Kilkenny (€12.50, 45 minutes), and Limerick (€21.50, 2¾ hours, three daily Monday to Saturday).

TOP THREE WATERFORD BEACHES

- Counsellor's Beach (right) – one of several sandy beaches at Dunmore East

- Clonea Strand (p193) – this popular 3km beach near Dungarvon has lifeguards in July and August

- Bunmahon (p192) – rare species of plants grow among the dunes at Bunmahon on the Copper Coast

---

Getting Around

There is no bus service to the airport. A **taxi** (☎ 393 940) will cost around €17.

Disc parking (per hour €1.20) operates in the centre and there are paid car parks along the quays and at The Glen, just west of the centre.

There are taxi ranks at Plunkett train station and at the top of Barronstrand St.

Altitude (☎ 870 356; altitude@indigo.ie; 22 Ballybricken; ⏰ 9.30am-6pm Mon-Fri & 9.30am-5.30pm Sat) hires bicycles for €15 per day.

DUNMORE EAST

☎ 051 / pop 1550

Strung out along a coastline of red sandstone cliffs and discreet coves, Dunmore East (Dún Mór) is a special spot. The views across to Hook Head lighthouse in County Wexford are magnificent; the main street is lined with thatched cottages; and the working harbour is overlooked by an unusual **Doric lighthouse** (1825) and cliffs full of screaming kittiwakes.

Dunmore's most popular beaches are the south-facing **Counsellor's Beach**, among the cliffs, and **Ladies Cove** in the village. They can get busy with day-trippers from Waterford, 20km northwest.

In the 19th century, the town was a station for the steam packets that carried mail between England and the south of Ireland.

Sea Safari (☎ 086-813 1437; adult/child €30/20; ⏰ noon, 1.30pm & 3pm Easter-Sep), run by the vivacious winner of RTÉ reality TV show *Cabin Fever*, offers one-hour trips in a high-powered 10m 'rib' around caves, shipwrecks, fishermen and seals.

Dunmore East Adventure Centre (☎ 383 783; www.dunmoreadventure.com) hires out equipment for windsurfing, canoeing, surfing and snorkelling. Two-hour tasters to week-long activity packages are available in these sports and others, including archery and rock climbing.

If you fancy shark fishing or exploring wrecks off the coast contact **Dunmore East Angling Charters** (☎ 383 397).

There are great views of town from the 18-hole **golf course** (☎ 383 151; week/weekend €25/35).

Sleeping

Brookside (☎ 383 893; alanpriest@eircom.net; Ballymabin; s/d €50/70; ⏰ Apr-Oct; P) A friendly, English-run B&B with a modern feel to the en-suite rooms.

Avon Lodge (☎ 385 775; www.avonlodgebandb
.com; Lower Dunmore East; s/d €55/76; ☺ Apr-Oct; **P**)
Tour guide, musician and driving instructor
Richie's attractive B&B is in a great location
near the sea.

Strand Inn (☎ 383 174; www.thestrandinn.com; Ladies Cove; s €55-70, d €85-120) The sizeable rooms
are bright affairs with white dressers and,
beyond their flowery curtains, views across
the waves.

Haven Hotel (☎ 383 150; s €55-75, d €110-150;
☺ restaurant 6pm-9pm, Mar-Oct) Built in the 1860s
as a summer house for the Malcolmson family, whose coat of arms can still be seen on
the fireplaces, the Haven is an elegant retreat
with wood-panelled bathrooms and, in two
rooms, four-poster beds.

Eating & Drinking

Bay Café (☎ 383 900; Dock Rd; mains €3-7; ☺ 9am-
6pm) A friendly café with harbour views so
good there's a whale-watching guide stuck
to the window.

Haven Hotel (☎ 383 150; mains €10.50-19.50; bar food
€5.50-14.50; ☺ restaurant 6-9pm, 12.30-2.15pm Sun, bar food
12.30-2.15pm Mon-Fri Mar-Oct) Local produce underpins everything from the Sunday carvery in
the restaurant to baguettes in the funky bar.

Strand Inn (☎ 383 174; www.thestrandinn.com; Ladies
Cove; mains €22.50-29; ☺ 12.30-4.30pm & 6.30-10pm Feb-
Dec) This recommended fish restaurant at the
water's edge has a French feel. Steaks and
duck are on offer but the real temptation is
in dishes such as pan-fried black sole, Hake
Dijonnaise and Bouillabaisse.

There are Tuesday night trad sessions at
Power's Bar (☎ 383 318; Dock Rd), which is nicknamed 'the Butcher's'.

Getting There & Away

Suirway runs buses here from Waterford
(see opposite page for details).

TRAMORE
☎ 051 / pop 9200

Amusement arcades, sand castles and candy
floss – hurray, hurray, hurray! Tramore's
fairground and fast-food outlets along the
seafront are terrifically tacky, contrasting with
the sober town, which leads up a steep hillside
to the Holy Cross Church (1860).

Tramore ('big beach' in Irish) is the busiest
of County Waterford's seaside resorts, with
a delightful 5km beach and 30m-high sand
dunes at the eastern end. A premier surfing
spot, it is being developed as an eco-tourism
destination by local activities companies,
which aim to curb the damage inflicted by
the beach-going hordes.

The **tourist office** (☎ 381 572; www.tramore.net;
Railway Sq; ☺ 10am-6pm Mon-Sat Jun-Aug), in the old
train station, has an excellent free brochure
detailing six walks around town; another covers the Dolmen Drive, a 35km route taking in
megalithic tombs and **standing stones**.

Sights

Tramore Bay is hemmed in by **Great Newtown
Head** to the southwest and **Brownstown Head** to
the southeast. Their 20m-high concrete pillars
were erected by Lloyds of London in 1816
after a shipping tragedy: 363 lives were lost
when the *Seahorse* mistook Tramore Bay for
Waterford Harbour and was wrecked.

The **Metal Man**, a huge 18th-century sailor
made from iron, stands at Great Newtown
Head. In white breeches and blue jacket, he
points dramatically seawards as a warning
to approaching ships. Legend has it that if
a girl hops around the base of the statue
three times on one leg, she will be married
within a year.

There are good views of the heads from **Guil-
lamene Cove**, where a sign dating back over 60
years decrees that the beach is for 'men only'.

COUNTIES WEXFORD &
WATERFORD

A SNEAKY SHORTCUT

If you're travelling between Counties Waterford and Wexford, cut out a long detour around Waterford Harbour and the River Bannow by taking the **car ferry** (☎ 382 480; http://homepage.eircom.net
/~passferry; ☺ 7am-10pm Mon-Sat & 9.30am-10pm Sun Apr-Sep, 7am-8pm Mon-Sat & 9.30am-8pm Oct-Mar).

The boat runs between Passage East, about 11km east of Waterford town, and Ballyhack in
County Wexford. Both are pretty little fishing villages with thatched cottages and neat harbours,
and the five-minute crossing is a short burst of pleasure.

There's a continuous service throughout the day. Tickets for pedestrians cost €1.50/2 single/
return, for cyclists €2/3, for cars €8/11. Return tickets are valid for an unlimited time.

Suirway (opposite) runs three buses daily Monday to Saturday to Passage East from Waterford.

The cliff-top 19th-century **Coast Guard Station** (☎ 393 833; Love La; ⊙ 9am-4.30pm Mon-Fri) houses a community arts centre.

Activities

The excellent nonprofit **T-Bay** (☎ 391 297; www .surftbay.com; The Beach; ⊙ 9am-8pm May-Aug, 10am-5.30pm Sep-Apr) is not only Ireland's biggest surf school, but runs eco-walks around the Back Strand, one of Europe's largest intertidal lagoons. Surfing lessons cost from €45 to €65, depending on whether you have group or private lessons; equipment hire is €15 to €25.

West of Tramore is the rugged coastline of the **Copper Coast GeoPark** (☎ 396 686; www .coppercoastgeopark.com), which takes its name from the 19th-century copper mines outside Bunmahon. Nestling among the area's scalloped coves and beaches are geological formations dating back 460 million years, including quartz blocks, fossils, and former volcanoes. One-hour guided walks are available in July and August, or pick up a map from the park office. The park is centred on Annestown, an attractive Anglo–Irish enclave with a good surfing beach and the dubious distinction of being the only village in Ireland without a pub.

To explore caves, coves and cliffs in sea kayaks, contact friendly Mick O'Meara at **Sea Paddling** (☎ 358 995; www.seapaddling.com; half/full day from €45/75). The company covers the local area from the Copper Coast to the Saltee Islands.

Sprawling water park **Splashworld** (☎ 390 176; www.splashworld.ie; Railway Sq; adult/child €10/7.50) boasts roaring rapids, splash slides, pirate ships and the like, and 'balmy temperatures all year round'. It's open for about three hours a day during the week, and six at weekends.

The first European horse-race meeting of the year takes place on January 1 at **Tramore Racecourse** (☎ 381 425; www.tramore-racecourse.com; Graun Hill), one of many events throughout the year.

The town has a pony trekking and riding centre, **Lake Tour Stable** (☎ 381 958).

Sleeping

Newtown Caravan & Camping Park (☎ 381 979; www.newtowncove.com; Dungarvan Coast Rd; camp sites €23; ⊙ Easter-Sep) About 2km out of town, this family-run affair is the best local camp site.

Fitzmaurice's Caravan & Camping Park (☎ 381 979; www.newtowncove.com; Riverstown; camp sites €26; ⊙ Easter-Sep) This park at the western entrance

to town, 300m from the beach, has laundry facilities, a shop, and views of Hook Head.

Beach Haven House B&B & Hostel (☎ 390 208; www.beachhavenhouse.com; Waterford Rd; B&B s/d from €35/70, hostel dm/d €20/50; P) Life's a beach at Avery and Niamh's shipshape establishment. The Californian couple will show you how to embrace Tramore's candyfloss cheesiness. The B&B has eight light, modern cream-coloured rooms, with skylights and seashell decorations, and the surprisingly civilised hostel has seven plain but spotless rooms and dorms. Bike rental is available.

Cliff House (☎ 381 497; www.cliffhouse.ie; Cliff Rd; s €55-60, d €80-90; ⊙ Mar-Oct; P) This spotless modern B&B has a thoughtful breakfast selection and stunning cliff-top views. Two rooms have their own balconies on the seaward side; if you don't get one, you can still gaze out of the conservatory. It's a long walk to the centre of town, but there's a shortcut along the cliffside Doneraile Walk.

O'Shea's Hotel (☎ 381 246; www.osheas-hotel.com; Strand St; s €65, d €130-140) The rooms are not as classy as the black-and-white exterior suggests, but the family-run hotel near the beach is a good choice if you're suffering from B&B fatigue.

Eating

Tramore possibly has more fast food per square metre than anywhere else on the planet, but there are some gourmet options for those who don't like chips.

The Vic Café (☎ 386 144; 1 Lower Main St; lunch €10-12; ⊙ 9am-4.30pm Mon-Wed, 9am-8.30pm Thu & Sun, 9am-9.30pm Fri, 9am-10pm Sat) With tribal art and abstract canvases on the walls, the Vic is a popular spot for reading the paper or discussing the latest show at the community arts centre. The menu mixes traditional dishes and those with a modern, Thai twist.

The Pine Room (☎ 381 683; Turkey Rd; mains €13-22; ⊙ 6-9.45pm) Tramore's best restaurant is found inside a Georgian house with seascapes decorating the walls and a rustic feel. The emphasis is on meat, with some great chicken dishes on the menu as well as a vegetarian dish of the day.

Esquire (☎ 381 324; Little Market St; mains €15-22; ⊙ bar food noon-7pm, restaurant noon-4pm & 6-9.30pm) Located behind the post office, this gastropub with the feel of a smugglers' haunt serves locally caught fish in slurpcious portions, as well as traditional meaty dishes like duck, lamb and veal, and a veggie option.

Getting There & Away

Bus Éireann (☎ 879 000) runs frequent buses daily between Waterford and Tramore (€2.50, 30 minutes). The bus stop is outside the tourist office near Splashworld.

DUNGARVAN

☎ 058 / pop 7800

Nestling beneath the Monavullagh and Comeragh hills, market town Dungarvan (Dún Garbhán) has a picturesque waterfront ringing the bay where the River Colligan meets the sea. Overlooking the bay are the ruins of a castle and an Augustinian abbey.

St Garvan founded a monastery here in the 7th century, but most of the centre dates from the early 19th century when the duke of Devonshire rebuilt the streets around Grattan Sq. Modern Dungarvan is the administrative centre of Waterford.

Dungarvan has some great restaurants and makes a convenient base for exploring western County Waterford, the Ring Peninsula and the mountainous north.

Orientation & Information

Dungarvan's main shopping area is Grattan Sq, to the southwest of the river. Main St (also called O'Connell St) runs along the square's southern edge and turns into Parnell or Lower Main St, which leads to the harbour.

The **tourist office** (☎ 41741; info@dungarvantourism .com; TF Meagher St; ☻ 9.30am-5pm Mon-Fri year round, plus 10am-5pm Sat May-Sep) is next to the post office.

Most of the banks are on Grattan Sq. Internet access is available at **Sip & Surf** (☎ 48658; Davitt's Quay; per hr €5; ☻ 8.30am-8pm Mon-Fri, 10.30am-5.30pm Sat, 2-6pm Sun) and for free at the **library** (☎ 41231; The Quay).

Sights & Activities

Dungarvan's colourful 18th-century **Davitt's Quay** is the best bit of town; grab a pint and watch the boats sail in.

A major renovation project is returning **Dungarvan Castle** (☎ 48144; admission free; ☻ 10am-6pm Jun-Sep, last admission 45 min before closing) to its former Norman glory. Once inhabited by King John's constable Thomas Fitz Anthony, the oldest part of the complex is the unusual 12th-century shell keep, built to defend the mouth of the river. The 18th-

century British army barracks house a visitor centre with various exhibits. Admission is by guided tour.

Waterford County Museum (☎ 45960; www .dungarvanmuseum.org; St Augustine St; admission free; ☻ 9am-5pm Mon-Fri, 2-5pm Sat Jun-Sep) is small but nicely presented and worth a visit. It covers the town's maritime history (with relics from shipwrecks), Famine history, local personalities and various other titbits, all displayed in a former wine store.

The solitary **St Augustine's Church** on the eastern side of the bridge overlooks Dungarvan Harbour. It was built in 1832 and once had a thatched roof. There are features incorporated from the original 13th-century abbey, including a well-preserved tower and nave. The abbey was destroyed during the Cromwellian occupation of the town.

The **Old Market House Arts Centre** (☎ 48944; Lower Main St; admission free; ☻ 11am-5pm Tue-Sat) hosts regularly changing local exhibitions.

Near Dungarvan, back towards Tramore, is **Clonea Strand**, a beautiful patch of pristine beach.

Festivals & Events

Over the early May bank-holiday weekend, 17 Dungarvan pubs and two hotels play host to the **Féile na nDéise**, a lively traditional music and dance festival that attracts around 200 musicians. For more information phone ☎ 086-252 3729.

Sleeping

The Whitehouse (☎ 41951; Youghal Rd; s/d €35/60; P) Willie and Olive White, parents of the local musician Ollie, run a friendly budget B&B with a conservatory, 10 minutes' walk from the centre.

Casey's Townhouse (☎ 44912; 8 Emmet Tce; s/d €40/60) There's a real sense of house-pride in this tranquil B&B in an early-1900s town house. Breakfasts are huge and delicious, with a scrambled-egg-and-smoked-salmon escape from the Irish fry-up.

Mountain View House (☎ /fax 42588; www.mountain viewhse.com; O'Connell St; s €55-70, d €90-100; P ⌨) This beautiful Georgian house, built in 1815 and set in walled grounds, has great high-ceilinged rooms and views of the Comeragh Mountains. Internet costs €5 per 30 minutes. Walk for five minutes down O'Connell St from Gratton Sq; it's signposted on the left before the technical college.

Tannery Townhouse (☎ 45420; www.tannery.ie; Church St; s/d from €60/100; ⏱ Feb-Dec; 🅿 🖳) The Tannery Restaurant has applied all its taste and talent to this boutique guesthouse, which feels incongruously chichi with its stripy carpets. Behind their pink-and-grey doors, the seven velvety rooms have plasma tellies and broadband. Fridges in the rooms are stacked with juices, fruit and pastries so guests can eat a continental breakfast in peace.

Lawlor's Hotel (☎ 41122; www.lawlorshotel.com; Meagher St; s/d from €90/150) Praised by William Makepeace Thackeray in 1843 as a 'very neat and comfortable inn', Lawlor's is today a pleasantly worn and old-fashioned hotel with surprisingly modern bedrooms, some with harbour views.

Eating

Shamrock Restaurant (☎ 42242; O'Connell St; snacks & mains €4-15; ⏱ 8.30am-9pm Mon-Sat) An unpretentious café where the local workforce sits at lines of wooden tables, quietly tucking into the full Irish made with local produce.

Interlude (☎ 45898; Davitt's Quay; lunch €5.50-20; ⏱ 11am-7pm Tue-Wed, 11am-9.30pm Thu-Sat, 10.30am-5.30pm Sun) For a light lunch, look no further than this funky cafe, full of weird knobbly furniture. Indie music gives the place a contemporary vibe, and there's a wide range of cakes, sweets and snackettes.

Mill Restaurant (☎ 45488; Davitt's Quay; mains €16-28; ⏱ 5-9.45pm Wed-Sat, 5-9pm Sun) From the moment you walk in the door, you feel at ease: staff are patient with kids, the place is smart but relaxed, and it's clear everyone's having a good time. Seafood and steak are the specialities, but there's a hotch-potch of dishes from around the world, including pizzas.

Tannery Restaurant (☎ 45420; www.tannery.ie; 10 Quay St; mains €18-29; ⏱ 12.30-2.30pm Tue-Fri & Sun, 6.30-9.30pm Tue-Sat, 6.30-9pm Sun Jul & Aug) An old leather tannery has been miraculously transformed into one of Ireland's most innovative restaurants. Top chef Paul Flynn creates seasonally changing dishes (described as 'modern Irish food with a continental twist'), like whole baked hake, wild-rabbit lasagna with lemon, sage and hazelnut butter, and roast lump of lamb with feta cheese and mint. Everything is served so beautifully that it's almost – almost – a shame to eat it.

Entertainment

Moorings (☎ 41461; Davitt's Quay) A laid-back quayside bar with a heated beer garden and palm trees. During summer, there are music sessions on Tuesday, Thursday and Sunday, and DJs on Saturday. Its intimate and fresh-as-you-like seafood restaurant (mains €16 to €23, open from 6pm to 9.15pm daily Easter to October, 6pm to 9.15pm Friday and Saturday November to Easter) is also worth a visit. There is bar food (€11.50 to €17) such as smoked salmon tagliatelle, and six rooms upstairs (single/double €50/€80).

SGC Cinema (☎ 45796; shopping centre; adult/child €8/5.50) Shows Hollywood films.

Getting There & Away

Bus Éireann (☎ 051-879 000) buses pick up and drop off on Davitt's Quay on the way to and from Waterford (€9, one hour, 11 daily), Cork (€13, 1½ hours, 13 daily) and Dublin (€13.50, 3¾ hours, three Sunday only).

RING PENINSULA

☎ 058 / pop 380

Rugged and unspoiled, An Rinn (meaning 'the headland') is one of Ireland's most famous Gaeltacht areas. The drive to Helvick Head takes you to the end of the peninsula, with views of the Comeragh Mountains, Dungarvan Bay, and the Copper Coast drifting away to the northeast.

Follow signs to An Rinn then Cé Heilbhic, passing Ballynagaul ('village of strangers'; it was founded by fishermen from elsewhere).

At the small working harbour in Helvick Head is a **monument** to the crew of *Erin's Hope*. They brought guns from New York in 1867, intending to start a Fenian uprising, but were arrested when they landed here. Sitting on rocks right over the water below, the intriguing house with round towers and a walled garden was on the market for €3 million at the time of research.

Coláiste na Rinne (☎ 46128; www.anrinn.com), the prestigious 100-year-old Irish-language college just off the Helvick Head road, runs summer language courses for 10- to 19-year-olds.

Ex-Waterford Crystal worker Eamonn Terry returned home to set up his own workshop, **Criostal na Rinne** (☎ 46174; ⏱ 9am-6pm Mon-Fri), where you can buy glassy items or have them inscribed.

Sleeping & Eating

Ocean View (☎ 46400; Ringville; s/d €35/70) A modern B&B with sweeping mountain views from the en-suite rooms.

Seaview (☎ 41583; www.seaviewdungarvan.com; Pulla; s €45, d €60-90) On the back road from Ringville to the N25 and the Drum Hills is this bright guesthouse with views of Dungarvon and the Comeragh Mountains from its conservatory.

An Linn Bhuidhe (☎ 46854; Ringville; mains €8-10; ☺ 10am-3pm Mon-Sat, 11am-4pm Sun) A sunny, popular café serving wholesome tucker like all-day breakfast, garlic mushrooms, lasagna, quiche, and leak and potato soup with a big dollop of cream.

The Old Storyteller (An Seanachaí; ☎ 46755; Pulla; mains €11-29, bar food €11.50-19.50; ☺ 12.30-9pm) This restored 19th-century pub with a thatched roof and a cheeky mural on the wall has a carvery lunch every day. There is live music from Thursday to Sunday during summer.

There's a small supermarket in Ringville.

Getting There & Around

Bus Éireann (☎ 051-879 000) stops in Ringville en route to Ardmore (30 minutes) and Waterford (€10, 1¼ hours) via Dungarvon. The buses stop once daily in July and August; Friday and Saturday only in other months.

Pubs, accommodation and shops are scattered along the peninsula; you really need a car or bicycle to get around.

ARDMORE

☎ 024 / pop 415

The bare bones of a seaside village overlooking the strand, Ardmore may look pretty but insignificant, but it's claimed that St Declan set up shop here between 350 and 420. This brought Christianity to southeast Ireland long before St Patrick arrived from Britain to convert the heathens. Above the popular resort are a finely preserved 12th-century **round tower** and some cobweb-banishing cliff walks.

Sights & Activities

Guides to the local area are available at **Ardmore Pottery** (☎ 94152; ☺ 10am-6pm May-Sep, 10am-6pm Sat & Sun Oct-Apr).

In a striking position on a hill above town, the ruins of **St Declan's Church** stand on the site of St Declan's original monastery alongside a cone-roofed, 29m-high, 12th-century **round tower**, one of the best examples of these structures in Ireland.

On the outer western gable wall of the 13th-century church, weathered 9th-century carvings set in unusual arched panels show the Archangel Michael weighing souls, the adoration of the Magi, Adam and Eve, and a clear depiction of the judgment of Solomon. Inside the church are two Ogham stones featuring the earliest form of writing in Ireland, one with the longest such inscription in the country.

Local lore tells that St Declan was buried in the 8th-century Oratory (Beannachán), which was re-roofed and modernised in 1716. Inside is an empty pit beneath a missing flagstone, the result of centuries of relic collecting.

The site was leased to Sir Walter Raleigh in 1591 after the dissolution of the monasteries. In 1642, the building was occupied by Royalist troops, 117 of whom were hanged here.

Pilgrims once washed in **St Declan's Well**, located in front of the ruins of Dysert Church, behind the new hotel development above Ardmore Pottery. A 5km **cliff walk** leads from the well. On the one-hour round trip you'll pass the wreck of a crane ship that was blown ashore in 1987 on its way from Liverpool to Malta.

At the southern end of the beach is **St Declan's Stone**, different geologically to other rocks in the area. It was perhaps brought by glacier from the Comeragh Mountains, but according to legend, St Declan's bell, which he is often pictured with in his hand, drifted across the sea from Wales on the stone after his servant forgot to pack it. He decreed that wherever the stone came to rest would be the place of his resurrection.

The 94km **St Declan's Way** mostly traces an old pilgrimage route from Ardmore to the Rock of Cashel (County Tipperary). Catholic pilgrims walk along it on St Declan's Day (24 July). For more information on the walk, ask at Ardmore Pottery or the tourist office in Lismore, which the trail passes through.

Sleeping & Eating

Duncrone (☎ 94860; www.duncronebandb.com; Ardo; s/d €45/65; P) Out in the open on the hill above town, Duncrone's rooms are all pale blues, greens and oranges. The Dunne family is a friendly bunch and breakfast can be made to order.

The Olde Forge (☎ 94750; Main St; mains €13-21.50; ☺ 9am-11pm Jun-Aug, 9.30am-4pm Mon-Thu, 9.30am-9pm Fri-Sun Sep-May) A friendly café with a chessboard floor, black-and-white local photographs on the wall, a good choice of sandwiches, cakes and scones, and a small selection of meat dishes.

White Horses (☎ 94040; Main St; lunch mains €8-13, dinner mains €13-24; 🕒 11am-4pm & 6-11pm Tue-Sun May-Sep, 6-10pm Fri, 11am-4pm & 6-11pm Sat, noon-4pm Sun Oct-Dec & mid-Feb–Apr) This smashing bistro serves nourishing standards, like fresh seafood chowder, or fried brie with tomato chutney, on plates handmade in the village. Staff are great, and will serve kids half portions from the adult menu if they fancy something more adventurous than burgers.

There is a small **supermarket** attached to the post office.

Getting There & Away

There are two buses daily Monday to Friday (three Saturday, one Sunday) from Cork (€11.10, 1¾ hours) to Ardmore. In July and August there are two buses daily Monday to Saturday to Waterford (€12, two hours) via Ringville and Dungarvan; on Friday and Saturday only in other months. Buses stop outside O'Reilly's pub on Main St.

CAPPOQUIN & AROUND
☎ 058 / pop 740

The small market town of Cappoquin is overlooked by the rounded, heathery Knockmealdown Mountains. To the west lies the picturesque Blackwater Valley, where traces of the earliest Irish peoples have been discovered.

The **Dromana Drive** to Cappoquin from Villierstown (An Baile Nua), 6km south, traces the River Blackwater through the Dromana Forest. At the bridge over the River Finisk is a remarkable **Hindu-Gothic gate**, inspired by the Brighton Pavilion in England and unique to Ireland.

There's excellent coarse and game fishing locally, with salmon-fishing permits available from **Titelines** (☎ 54152) tackle shop in the main street.

Mt Melleray Cistercian Abbey (☎ 54404; 🕒 noon-5pm Tue-Sun), 6km north of town in the Knockmealdown foothills (signposted from Cappoquin), is a fully functioning monastery with 28 Trappist monks. The abbey was founded in 1832 by 64 monks who were expelled from a monastery near Melleray in Brittany, France. There are tearooms and a heritage centre.

Turn right off the road to Mt Melleray for the forest walks and picnic spots at **Glenshelane Park**.

Cappoquin House & Gardens (☎ 54004; adult/child €10/free; 🕒 9am-1pm Mon-Sat Apr-Jul) is a Georgian mansion (built 1779) and gardens overlooking the River Blackwater. It's the private residence of the Keane family who've lived here for 200 years. The entrance to the house is just north of the centre of Cappoquin; look for a set of huge black iron gates.

While the rooms at **Richmond House** (☎ 54278; www.richmondhouse.net; N72; s €95-140, d €150-240; dinner menu €35-54; 🕒 restaurant 6-9pm Tue-Thu, 7-9pm Fri-Mon) are forgettable for a country-house hotel (and there's little difference between standard and superior), the restaurant is excellent. Meals are heavy on local produce such as Helvick salmon and there's great vegetarian choice.

Barron's Bakery (☎ 54045; the Square) uses the same Scotch Brick Ovens it has used since 1887. Sandwiches and a mouth-watering selection of cakes and buns are available in its café.

Getting There & Away

Bus Éireann (☎ 051-879 000) services stop in Cappoquin en route to Lismore and Dungarvan (€5, 20 minutes) on Monday, Thursday and Saturday. There is a Sunday bus to Dublin (4¼ hours) at 3.55pm. On Friday there are buses to Waterford (€12, one hour) at 5.50pm and Cork (1½ hours) at 9.40am. Cork is also served on Sunday at 6.10pm except in July and August. Buses stop outside Morrissey's pub.

LISMORE
☎ 058 / pop 790

County Waterford's 'heritage town', a quiet place on the River Blackwater overshadowed by an elegant 19th-century castle, is, quite rightly, steeped in its own history. Over the centuries, statesmen and luminaries have streamed through Lismore, the location of a great monastic university founded by St Cartach, or Carthage, in the 7th century. King Alfred of Wessex attended the university; Henry II visited the papal legate Bishop Christian O'Conairche here in 1171; even Fred Astaire dropped by when his sister Adele married into the Cavendish family, which owns the castle. Older locals can't agree whether or not Astaire tap-danced down Main St after closing time.

Lismore once had over 20 churches, but 9th- and 10th-century Viking raids decimated the town. Most of its existing buildings date from the early 19th century. Between doses of history, you can picnic in the **Millennium Gardens**, beside the castle car park, or take a 20-minute riverside stroll along **Lady Louisa's Walk** to the cathedral with its Edward Burne-Jones window.

Information

The helpful **tourist office** (☎ 54975; lismore heritage@eircom.net; Main St; ☷ 9.30am-5.30pm Mon-Fri, 10am-5.30pm Sat, noon-5.30pm Sun May-Oct, 9.30am-5.30pm Mon-Fri Nov-Apr) can be found inside the Lismore Heritage Centre. Guided tours of town take place at 11am and 3pm daily in July and August. Alternatively, the informative *Lismore Walking Tour Guide* (€3) describes all the local sights.

Sights

'One of the neatest and prettiest edifices I have seen', commented William Thackeray in 1842 about the striking **St Carthage's cathedral** (1679). And that was before the addition of the Edward Burne-Jones **stained-glass window**, which features all the Pre-Raphaelite hallmarks: an effeminate knight and a pensive maiden against a sensuous background of deep-blue velvet and intertwining flowers. Justice, with sword and scales, and Humility, holding a lamb, honour Francis Currey, who helped to relieve the suffering of the poor during the Famine.

The cathedral also contains some noteworthy **tombs**, including the elaborately carved MacGrath family crypt dating from 1557. A tour leaflet (€2), aimed at kids but fun for all, leads you round the building's oddities and wonders, including the fossils in the pulpit!

From the Cappoquin road there are stunning glimpses of the riverside **Lismore Castle**, which is closed to day-trippers but available for groups to hire from €4000 per night. You can visit the three hectares of **gardens** (☎ 54424; www.lismorecastle.com; adult/child €7/3.50; ☷ 1.45pm-4.45pm Apr-Oct, from 11am Jun-Aug), thought to be the oldest in Ireland, divided into the walled Jacobean upper garden and less formal lower garden. There are brilliant herbaceous borders, magnolias and camellias, and a splendid yew walk where Edmund Spenser is said to have written *The Faerie Queen*. The contemporary sculptures dotting the gardens have been joined by a contemporary **art gallery** (☎ 54061; www.lismore

castlearts.ie; ☷ May-Oct) in the west wing of the castle.

The original castle was erected by Prince John, Lord of Ireland, in 1185. After a stint as the local bishop's residence, it was presented to Sir Walter Raleigh in 1589 along with 200 sq km of the surrounding countryside. He later sold it to the earl of Cork, Richard Boyle, whose son Robert, known as the 'father of modern chemistry' for devising Boyle's Law, was born here.

Most of the current castle was constructed in the early 19th century. During its rebuilding, workmen discovered the 15th-century *Book of Lismore* and 12th-century Lismore Crozier, both in the National Museum in Dublin. The book not only documents Irish saints' lives, but also has an account of Marco Polo's voyages. The castle is owned by Peregrine Cavendish, 12th Duke of Devonshire, who also owns Chatsworth in Derbyshire, England.

In the old courthouse is the **Lismore Heritage Centre** (☎ 54975; www.discoverlismore.com; Main St; adult/child €4.50/4; ☷ 9.30am-5.30pm Mon-Fri, 10am-5.30pm Sat, noon-5.30pm Sun May-Oct, 9.30am-5.30pm Mon-Fri Nov-Apr). The fascinating interpretive centre, which features an audiovisual presentation, takes you from the arrival of St Carthage in AD 636 to the present day, via the discovery of the *Book of Lismore* behind a wall in the castle in 1814 and John F Kennedy's visit in 1947.

Sleeping & Eating

Pine Tree House (☎ 53282; www.pinetreehouselismore .com; s/d from €40/70) The formidable Daphne Power's rooms are more pleasant than the modern exterior suggests, and there's a dog the size of a horse to play with. It's past Blackwater Community School at the southwest end of town.

Northgrove (☎ 54325; www.lismorebedandbreakfast .com; Tourtane; s €40-55, d €65-80; ☐) In a quiet location off the N72 to Cork, pleasant Northgrove's rooms are named after flowers and the walls are decorated with Van Gogh's great lost Irish series.

Ballyrafter House Hotel (☎ 54002; www.waterford hotel.com; s/d €95/170; lunch €28, dinner €44; ☷ Mar-Oct; Ⓟ) Log fires and home cooking make this country-house hotel a cosy place to stay. The simple bedrooms overlook stately gardens complete with peacocks. There are good views of the castle from the restaurant, where you can sample local salmon, honey and cheeses.

Foley's (☎ 53671; Main St; mains €10-24; ⊙ 9am-9pm) This pub serves a good selection of steak, fish and homemade burgers, with extra temptations such as cheese sauces, in relaxing surrounds with peacock wallpaper, leather-backed benches and an open fire.

Getting There & Away

There are **Bus Éireann** (☎ 051-879 000) services in both directions between Lismore and Dungarvan (€5.10, 30 minutes) via Cappoquin on Monday, Thursday and Saturday, and a Sunday bus to Dublin (4½ hours) at 3.45pm. On Friday there are buses to Waterford (€12, 1¼ hours) at 5.40pm and Cork (1¼ hours) at 9.50am. Cork is also served on Sunday at 6.20pm except in July and August. Buses stop outside O'Dowd's on West St.

NORTHERN COUNTY WATERFORD

Some of the most scenic parts of County Waterford are in the north around Ballymacarbry and in the Nire Valley, which runs between the Comeragh and Monavullagh Mountains. While not as rugged as the west of Ireland, with which it shares the same 370-million-year-old red sandstone, this mountain scenery has a stark beauty of its own and doesn't attract much tourist traffic. It's also a great area to catch traditional music and dancing, whether in pubs like Melody's Nire View or around kitchen tables.

Sights & Activities

Lord and Lady Waterford dwell at **Curraghmore Gardens** (☎ 051-387 102; fax 051-387 481; Portlaw; admission by guided tour €4; ⊙ 2-5pm Thu Easter–mid-Oct), 14km northwest of Waterford town. The 2500-acre estate has belonged to the family since the 12th century. By prior appointment, the fine Georgian **house** (admission €6; ⊙ 9am-1pm Mon-Fri), containing some superior plaster work, is open to visitors. Lord Waterford normally conducts the tours.

It's a superb area for walkers, with rolling hills and woodland stuffed with megalithic remains. The Comeragh Mountains, where there are ridges to trace and loughs to circle, are named after their many *coums* (valleys, often of glacial origin). Coumshingaun and Coum Iarthair – next to Crotty's Lough, and named after an outlaw who lay low in a cave there – are some of Ireland's finest *coums*.

Stop for a pint and *panini* in **Melody's Nire View** (☎ 052-36169; Ballymacarbry), where the genial folk have free leaflets on local walks and activities.

Otherwise make sure you're around for the **Autumn Walking Festival** (☎ 052-36239), which takes place on the second weekend in October, with guided walks for all and traditional music in the pubs.

The **East Munster Way** walking trail (p699) covers some 70km between Carrick-on-Suir in County Tipperary and the northern slopes of the Knockmealdown Mountains. Access is at Fourmilewater, about 10km northwest of Ballymacarbry.

From March to September, the Rivers Nire and Suir are great for **fishing**. Permits can be arranged through Hanora's Cottage (see below) or the **fly-fishing centre** (☎ 052-36752; Clonanav), which also has a school and guesthouse.

Sleeping

Powers the Pot (☎ 052-23085; www.powersthepot.net; Harney's Cross; camp sites €14; ⊙ May-Sep) An intimate little camping ground run by archaeology and hiking buff Niall. Gaelic steak and other filling meals (€10 to €15) are served in the smashing thatched bar, which has great acoustics for musicians to jam around the peat fire. It's in the hills 9km southeast of Clonmel, signposted from the road to Rathgormuck, and also accessible from Ballymacarbry (head towards Hanora's Cottage, turn left over the bridge and it's signposted).

Hanora's Cottage (☎ 052-36134; www.hanoras cottage.com; Nire Valley, Ballymacarbry; s €120-170, d €170-250) This 19th-century ancestral home next to Nire Church houses one of the best B&Bs in the country. The beautifully restored rooms have hot tubs, and there's a spa in the conservatory with mountain views. The adults-only cottage also has an excellent gourmet restaurant (meal €48, 7pm to 9pm Monday to Saturday) and offers walkers unbeatable packed lunches. Take the road east out of Ballymacarbry, opposite Melody's; it's about 5km further on.

Getting There & Away

Bus Éireann (☎ 051-879 000) runs Tuesday services from Ballymacarbry to Dungarvan (45 minutes, 3pm) and Clonmel, Tipperary (one hour, 9.43am). There are also two buses between Clonmel and Ballymacarbry on Friday afternoon. A taxi from Clonmel to Ballymacarbry costs €28. For Curraghmore Gardens, regular buses between Waterford and Carrick-on-Suir, Tipperary, stop in Fiddown, 5km north of Portlaw.

County Cork

Flung out on the far-western reaches of Ireland, Cork comes very close indeed to the misty-eyed vision of the country many visitors hold in their imagination.

Follow the country's three bony-fingered peninsulas out into the Atlantic and you'll find an epic, wind-lashed coastline riddled with vibrant seaside villages, their harbours bustling with fishing boats bringing home the day's catch.

Meander east and you're swept along by half a millennium of struggle and turbulence, the tide of history leaving an enduring mark on the towns of the south coast. Away from all this potentially overwhelming drama, the gentler, rolling hills of the north ooze a more sedate charm.

And, of course, there's Cork city, nonchalantly pushing Dublin out the way as it swaggers into the 21st century. If you want cocktail bars, modern-art galleries and avant-garde theatre, they're all here.

What will stay most with you, though, in both city and countryside, is that stomping live-music session in a creaky old pub, that meal of the finest, freshest Irish produce, and the steady humour of a population fiercely proud of its past and confident of its future.

HIGHLIGHTS

- **City Spectacular** Buzzing Cork city, with its great selection of restaurants (p207), pubs (p209), music (p210) and theatres (p209)
- **I Want to be Alone...** The stunning coastal road around the Beara Peninsula (p239)
- **Taste of the West** Some of the best food to be had along Cork's southern coast, from Kinsale (p218) to Clonakilty (p223)
- **Gougane Barra Magic** Unexpected splendour in inland Cork, with mountainous forests and a glacial lake (p231)
- **Ahoy There!** Unspoilt fishing villages, including Union Hall (p227), Glandore (p227), Castletownshend (p227), Castletownbere (p242) and Baltimore (p229)

Beara Peninsula ★ · Gougane Barra Forest Park ★ · Cork ★ · Kinsale ★ · Castletownbere ★ · Glandore ★ · Clonakilty ★ · Union Hall ★★ · Baltimore ★ · Castletownshend ★

■ POPULATION: 481,000   ■ AREA: 7508 SQ KM

COUNTY CORK

CORK CITY

☎ 021 / pop 119,000

Cork buzzes with the energy of a city that's certain of its place in Ireland. Indeed, so confident is the former 'Rebel City' that locals only half-jokingly refer to it as the 'People's Republic of Cork'. The city has long been dismissive of Dublin and with a burgeoning arts, music and restaurant scene, it's now getting a cultural reputation to rival the capital's.

The River Lee flows around the centre, an island packed with grand Georgian parades, cramped 17th-century alleys and modern masterpieces such as the opera house. The flurry of urban renewal that began with the city's stint in 2005 as European Capital of Culture continues apace, with new buildings, bars and arts centres springing up all over town. The best of the city is still happily traditional though – snug pubs with live music sessions most of the week, excellent local produce in an ever-expanding list of restaurants and a genuinely proud welcome from the locals.

HISTORY

Cork has a long and bruising history, inextricably linked with Ireland's struggle for nationhood.

The story begins in the 7th century, when St Finbarre founded a monastery on a

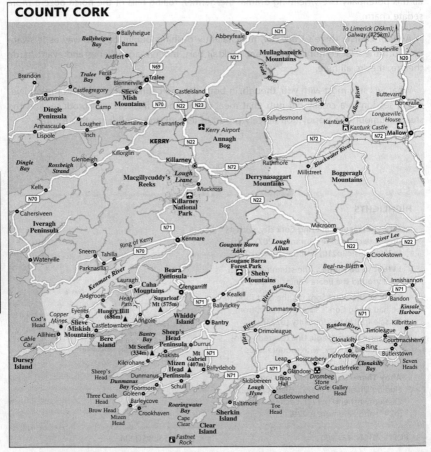

COUNTY CORK

corcach (marshy place). By the 12th century the settlement had become the chief city of the Kingdom of South Munster, having survived raids and sporadic settlement by Norsemen. Irish rule was short-lived, and by 1185 Cork was under English rule. Thereafter it changed hands regularly during the relentless struggle between Irish and Crown forces. It survived Cromwellian assault only to fall to that merciless champion of Protestantism, William of Orange.

During the 18th century Cork prospered, with butter, beef, beer and whiskey exported round the world from its port. A mere century later famine devastated both county and city, and robbed Cork of millions of its inhabitants by death or emigration.

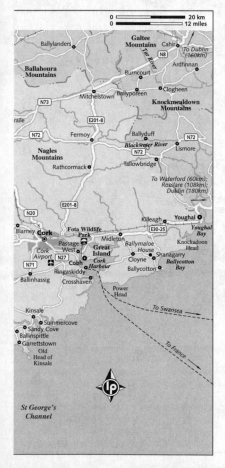

The 'Rebel City's' deep-seated Irishness ensured that it played a key role in Ireland's struggle for independence. Mayor Thomas MacCurtain was killed by the Black and Tans in 1920. His successor, Terence Mac-Swiney, died in London's Brixton prison after a hunger strike. The British were at their most brutally repressive in Cork – much of the centre, including St Patrick's St, the City Hall and the Public Library, was burned down. Cork was also a regional focus of Ireland's self-destructive Civil War in 1922–23.

ORIENTATION

The city centre lies on an island in the River Lee, which is crisscrossed by bridges. St Patrick's St runs from St Patrick's Bridge on the North Channel of the Lee, through the city's main shopping and commercial area, to the Georgian Grand Pde that leads to the river's South Channel. North and south of St Patrick's St lie the city's most entertaining quarters: webs of narrow streets crammed with pubs, cafés, restaurants and shops.

Across St Patrick's Bridge is an equally bustling area, focused around MacCurtain St, with its own spread of pubs, restaurants and shops. East of MacCurtain St, you'll find Kent Train Station and budget B&Bs. West of Bridge St is Shandon, which has a village atmosphere, especially in the narrow lanes around its hilltop churches.

From midway down Grand Pde, Washington St leads southwest to the university.

INFORMATION
Bookshops

Connolly's Bookshop (☎ 427 5366; Rory Gallagher Pl, Paul St) Great chat and masses of secondhand books.

Liam Ruiséal Teo (☎ 427 0981; 49-50 Oliver Plunkett St) New and secondhand books, including plenty on Cork.

Mainly Murder (☎ 427 2413; 2A Paul St) Crime novels galore.

Vibes & Scribes (☎ 450 5370; 3 Bridge St; ☒ 10am-6.30pm Mon-Sat, 12.30-6.30pm Sun) Four floors of books, CDs and DVDs. Also on Lavitt's Quay.

Waterstone's (☎ 427 6522; 69 St Patrick's St; ☒ 9am-7pm Mon-Thu & Sat, 9am-8pm Fri, noon-6pm Sun) Has the best travel section in the southwest.

Emergency

Mercy University Hospital (☎ 427 1971; www.muh .ie; Grenville Pl)

COUNTY CORK

CORK

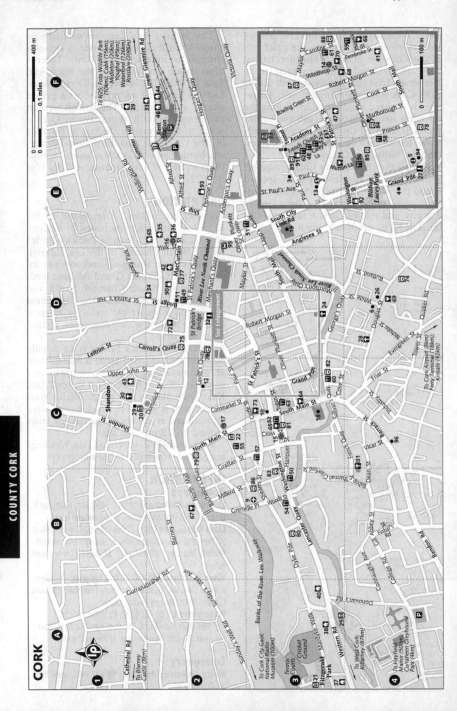

Internet Access

Webworkhouse.com (☎ 427 3090; www
.webworkhouse.com; 8A Winthrop St; per hr
€1.50-3; ☻ 24hr) Plus low-cost international
phone calls.

Wired to the World (☎ 453 0383; www.wired
totheworld.ie; 28 North Main St; per hr €1; ☻ 9am-
midnight Mon-Sat, 10am-midnight Sun) Also at Thompson
House on MacCurtain St, and Washington St.

Left Luggage

There's no left-luggage facility at the train
station.

Cork Bus Station (☎ 450 8188; cnr Merchant's Quay &
Parnell Pl; per item for 24hr €2.70; ☻ 7.45am-midnight
Mon-Fri, 9am-6pm Sat year-round & Sun in summer)

Libraries

Cork City Library (☎ 492 4900; www.corkcitylibrary.ie;
57-61 Grand Pde; ☻ 10am-5.30pm Mon-Sat)

Money

The banks on St Patrick's St have ATMs
and currency exchange. There are bureaux
de change in the tourist office and at the
bus station.

Post

Main post office (☎ 485 1042; Oliver Plunkett St;
☻ 9am-5.30pm Mon-Sat)

Tourist Information

Cork City Tourist Office (☎ 425 5100;
www.corkkerry.ie; Grand Pde; ☻ 9am-6pm Mon-Sat,
10am-5pm Sun Jul-Aug, 9.15am-5pm Mon-Fri & 9.30am-
4.30pm Sat Sep-Jun) Souvenir shop and information desk
with plenty of brochures and books about the city and
county. Stena Line Ferries (see p719) has a desk here.

DANGERS & ANNOYANCES

Cork cherishes its reputation as being a less
hard-skinned place than Dublin, but watch

COUNTY CORK

out for ugly scenes around central pubs and clubs late at night.

SIGHTS
Cork City Gaol

Faint-hearted souls may find **Cork City Gaol** (☎ 430 5022; www.corkcitygaol.com; Convent Ave; adult/child €7/3.50; ☼ 9.30am-6pm Mar-Oct, 10am-5pm Nov-Feb, last admission 1hr before closing) a little grim, but it's certainly a highly unusual and worthwhile attraction. An audio-tour guides you around the restored cells, which feature models of suffering prisoners and sadistic-looking guards. It's very moving, bringing home the harshness of the 19th-century penal system. The most common crime was that of poverty; many of the inmates were sentenced to hard labour for stealing loaves of bread.

The prison closed in 1923, reopening in 1927 as a radio station. The change of use is reflected in the upstairs **National Radio Museum** (adult/child €6/3.50; ☼ 9.30am-6pm Mar-Oct, 10am-5pm Nov-Feb) where, alongside collections of beautiful old radios, you can hear the story of Guglielmo Marconi's conquest of the airwaves.

To get there, walk from the city centre, or take bus 8 from the bus station to the University College Cork (UCC); walk north across Fitzgerald Park, over Mardyke Bridge, along the River Lee Walkway and follow the signs up the hill.

Crawford Municipal Art Gallery

Cork's public **gallery** (☎ 490 7855; www.crawfordartgallery.com; Emmet Pl; admission free; ☼ 10am-5pm Mon-Sat) houses a small but excellent permanent collection, featuring works by Irish artists such as Jack Yeats and Seán Keating. Look out for Keating's *Men of the South* (1921), a fine piece of historical romanticism depicting members of the North Cork Batallion of the IRA.

The Sculpture Galleries contain snow-white plaster casts of Roman and Greek statues, given to King George IV by the pope in 1822. George didn't like the present and stuck the sculptures in the cellar until someone suggested that Cork might appreciate them.

The downstairs exhibition hall hosts superior temporary displays, and there's a stylish café (see p208).

St Finbarre's Cathedral

Spiky spires, gurning gargoyles and rich sculpture make up the exterior of Cork's Protestant **cathedral** (☎ 496 3387; http://cathedral.cork.anglican.org; Bishop St; adult/child €3/1.50; ☼ 10am-5.30pm Mon-Sat & 12.30pm-7.30pm Sun Apr-Sep, 10am-12.45pm & 2-5pm Oct-Mar), an attention-grabbing mixture of French Gothic and medieval whimsy. Local legend says that the golden angel on the eastern side will blow its horn when the apocalypse is due to start…

The grandeur continues inside, with marble floor mosaics, a colourful chancel ceiling and a huge pulpit and bishop's throne. Quirky items on display include a cannonball blasted into an earlier medieval spire during the Siege of Cork (1690).

Most of the ostentation is the result of a competition, held in 1863, to choose an architect for the building. William Burges was the hands-down winner, and once victory was assured he promptly redrew all his plans – with an extra choir bay and taller towers – and his £15,000 budget went out the window. Luckily, the bishop understood such perfectionism and spent the rest of his life fundraising for the project.

The cathedral sits at an aloof distance south of the centre, on the spot where Cork's patron saint, Finbarre, founded his monastery in the 7th century.

Lewis Glucksman Gallery

The **Glucksman** (☎ 490 2760; www.glucksman.org; University College Cork; admission free; ☼ 10am-5pm Tue, Wed, Fri & Sat, 10am-8pm Thu, noon-5pm Sun), a startling limestone, steel and timber construction, is a visible symbol of Corkonian optimism. Opened in 2004 to great excitement, the €12-million building has three huge display areas, which host ever-changing art exhibitions and installations. If you're in town, don't miss the free fortnightly curatorial tours; the website has details. Its situation in the grounds of the UCC means that it's always buzzing with people coming to attend lectures, view the artwork or procrastinate in the basement café (see p207).

Cork Public Museum

Located in a pleasant Georgian house in Fitzgerald Park, this **museum** (☎ 427 0679; www.corkcitycouncil.ie/amenities; Fitzgerald Park; admission free; ☼ 11am-1pm & 2.15-5pm Mon-Fri, 11am-1pm & 2.15-4pm Sat year-round, 3-5pm Sun Apr-Sep) recounts Cork's history from the Stone Age right up to local football legend Roy Keane, with a diverse collection of local artefacts. There's a café next door.

Take bus 8 to the main gates of the UCC and follow the signs.

Beamish & Crawford Brewery

This famous **brewery** (☎ 491 1100; www.beamish.ie; South Main St; guided tour adult/concession €7/5; ⏰ 10.30am & noon Tue & Thu May-Sep, 11am Thu Oct-Apr) is the oldest porter brewery in Ireland. Enjoyable tours end in the bar, where you can pour your own pint. It's fronted by the Counting House, a building that takes first prize for eye-blinding architectural awfulness (mock Tudor, crow-stepped gables, classical pediment *and* pebbledash).

Shandon

Throw a few galleries, antique shops and cafés among the colourful lanes and squares and **Shandon** could easily emerge as Cork's 'Latin Quarter'. Perched on a hillside overlooking the city centre, it's a great spot for the views alone.

Shandon is dominated by **St Anne's Church** (☎ 450 5906; www.shandonbells.org; John Redmond St; ⏰ 9.30am-4.30pm Mon-Sat), aka the 'Four-Faced Liar', so-called as each of the tower's four clocks used to tell a different time. Wannabe campanologists can ring the **bells** (adult/child €6/3.90) on the 1st floor of the 18th-century Italianate tower and continue up to the top for 360-degree views of the city.

Cork had the largest butter market in the world during the 1860s, exporting butter as far as India, South America and Australia. The Butter Exchange was in Shandon and you can still spot dairy motifs throughout the area: look out for the cow above the **Shandon Craft Centre** (O'Connell Sq), now housing souvenir shops and the **Butter Market Café** (☎ 430 2303; ⏰ 7.30am-2.30pm Mon-Sat). The **Cork Butter Museum** (☎ 430 0600; www.corkbutter.museum; O'Connell Sq; adult/child €3/2.50; ⏰ 10am-5pm Mar-Jun & Sep-Oct, 10am-6pm Jul-Aug, by arrangement Nov-Feb) reveals the historical importance of the industry to the whole country with a 25-minute video, buttermaking artefacts and history panels.

Other Sights

It's worth popping into the **Cork Vision Centre** (☎ 427 9925; www.corkvisioncentre.com; St Peter's Church, North Main St; admission free; ⏰ 10am-5pm Tue-Sat) to view the frequently changing art exhibitions,

many of them featuring local artists and photographers. Also on display is a scale model of the city centre.

One of Cork's most famous figures was Father Theobald Mathew, the 'Apostle of Temperance', who went on a short-lived crusade against alcohol in the 1830s and 1840s – a quarter of a million people took the 'pledge', and whiskey production halved. The **Holy Trinity Church** (Fr Mathew Quay) was designed by the Pain brothers in 1834 in his honour, and the Father Mathew Bingo Hall around the corner also celebrates his memory. Mathew's **statue** stands on St Patrick's St.

Red Abbey Tower (Red Abbey St), the only medieval building left in Cork, is all that remains of a 14th-century Augustinian priory. Its location is fairly anonymous, but a bit of imagination will help create a stirring sense of antiquity.

On Grand Pde, near the tourist office, is the ornate **Nationalist Monument**, erected in memory of the Irish patriots who died during the 1798 and 1867 Risings.

TOURS

Arrangements Unlimited (☎ 429 3873; www .arrangements.ie) Organises walking tours on request.
Bus Éireann (☎ 450 8188; www.buseireann.ie; adult/ child €9.90/6.30; ⏰ departs 10.30am daily Easter-Sep) Three-hour open-top bus tour of Cork and Blarney Castle, from the bus station.
Cork City Tour (☎ 430 9090; adult/child €13/5; ⏰ 9.30am-5pm Apr-Oct) Hop-on-hop-off open-top bus linking the city's main areas of interest.
Cork Historic Walking Tours (☎ 085-100 7300; www.walkcork.ie; adult/child €10/5; ⏰ Mon-Fri Apr-Sep) Runs four 90-minute tours from the tourist office.
Haunted History Tour (☎ 430 5022; corkgaol@indigo .ie; tour €15; ⏰ 8pm Thu-Sat) Ghostly tour around Cork City Gaol.

FESTIVALS & EVENTS

Book well in advance, particularly for the October jazz and film festivals. Programmes for both are available from the **Cork Opera House** (☎ 427 0022; www.corkoperahouse.ie; Emmet Pl).
Cork Pride (www.corkpride.com) Week-long gay-pride celebrations in May/June.
Corona Cork Film Festival (www.corkfilmfest.org) Eclectic week-long programme of international films held in October.
Eigse Literary Festival (Tigh Litríochta; ☎ 431 2955; www.munsterlit.ie; 84 Douglas St) Writing workshops, readings and exhibitions in February. Details available from the Munster Literature Centre.

COUNTY CORK

Guinness Jazz Festival (www.corkjazzfestival.com) All-star line-up in venues across town held, in October.

International Choral Festival (www.corkchoral.ie) From late April to early May in the City Hall and other venues.

Slow Food Ireland (www.slowfoodireland.com) Promotes and supports local artisan producers, with cheese tastings and other events throughout the year.

SLEEPING
Budget
Sheila's Hostel (☎ 450 5562; www.sheilashostel.ie; 4 Belgrave Pl, Wellington Rd; 8-/4-bed dm €15/18, d €52; P 🖳) Sheila's heaves with young travellers, and it's no wonder with the continual improvements made to the place. A cinema room with free daily films has been added to the facilities, which include a sauna, free internet access, a pool room and barbecue. Staff can arrange bicycle and car hire. Breakfast is €3 extra.

Kinlay House Shandon (☎ 450 8966; www.kinlayhousecork.ie; Bob & Joan's Walk; dm €16-20, s/d €45/49, r with bathroom €52; 🖳 🕭) This labyrinthine hostel is in a quiet spot near St Anne's Church in Shandon. The décor has seen better days but the place has a fun, laid-back atmosphere. Guests can use the next-door gym at a discount.

Cork International Hostel (☎ 454 3289; www.anoige.ie; 1 & 2 Redclyffe, Western Rd; 10-/6-/4-bed dm €16/18/20, d €44; P 🖳) Housed in a fine red-brick building near the university, this An Óige hostel has bright dorms and cheerful staff who do a great job coping with the constant stream of guests. The drawback is the 2km walk (or bus 8 ride) to the centre, along a busy road. Breakfast is €4.50 extra.

Brú Bar & Hostel (☎ 455 9667; www.bruhostel.com; 57 MacCurtain St; 6-/4-bed dm €17.50/22.50, tr €50; P 🖳 🕭) Run by helpful Kiwi managers, this buzzing hostel has its own internet café, with free Web access for guests, and a fantastic bar popular with backpackers and locals alike. The dorms (with bathroom) are on the small side but are pristinely maintained and smartly decorated – ask for one on the upper floors to avoid noise from the bar.

Near the train station are a handful of basic but clean B&Bs, including **Tara House** (☎ 450 0294; 52 Lower Glanmire Rd; s/d €45/70) and the neighbouring **Oaklands** (☎ 450 0578; s/d €45/70). You'll get a friendly welcome across the road at **Aaran House Tourist Hostel** (☎ 455 1566; dm €14, d €38), not least from Reilly the dog.

Midrange
Western Rd has the biggest choice of B&Bs.

Emerson House (☎ 450 3647; www.emersonhousecork.com; 2 Clarence Tce, North Summer Hill; r from €40; P) Near the top of busy Summer Hill is this gay and lesbian B&B tucked away on a quiet terrace. The accommodation, in a Georgian house retaining many original features, is comfortably elegant, and host Cyril is a mine of information on the area.

Victoria Hotel (☎ 427 8788; www.thevictoriahotel.com; Patrick St; r €40-90 per person) You can't get better value for such a central location than this historic hotel, making it popular with large groups. Cheerful staff proudly tell you that Charles Stuart Parnell once stayed here, as did Stephen Daedalus in James Joyce's *A Portrait of the Artist* (his dad had drisheen for breakfast). It's been updated since then, with a new entrance on St Patrick's St and large, freshly decorated rooms.

Auburn House (☎ 450 8555; www.auburnguesthouse.com; 3 Garfield Tce, Wellington Rd; s/d €45/75, with bathroom €58/80; P) There's a warm family welcome at this neat B&B, which has smallish but impeccably kept rooms brightened by window boxes. Try to bag one of the back rooms, which have sweeping views over the city. Veggies will relish the meat-free sausages for breakfast.

Acorn House (☎ /fax 450 2474; www.acornhouse-cork.com; 14 St Patrick's Hill; s €52-65, d €90-110) A handsome, high-ceilinged, part-Georgian house, this listed building has attractive rooms painted in mellow yellows and soothing greens. Antiques such as washstands and ewers give a personal touch, and the house has the advantage of being on a quiet street yet close to the city centre.

[our pick] **Garnish House** (☎ 427 5111; www.garnish.ie; Western Rd; s €60-80, d €90-140; P 🕭) 'Will you be wanting a cup of tea now?' is the greeting you'll receive when you arrive on the doorstep of this large B&B near the centre. And then out comes the tea. And the scones. And the chocolate cake. And the soda bread. And more tea. And so the hospitality goes on, with every attention lavished upon you until you leave. You could stay for a month and still not get through the breakfast menu, though we'd recommend you stop trying once you get to the porridge with cream, honey and whiskey. To top it all off, rooms are smartly decorated with comfortable beds and crisp linens.

Crawford House (☎ 427 9000; www.crawfordguesthouse.com; Western Rd; s €75-85, d €110-120; P)

Another top-notch B&B, Crawford House has spacious rooms with king-size beds, gracious furnishings and some bodacious Jacuzzis to splash around in. The standard is that of a contemporary hotel, the atmosphere that of a family home.

Top End

Isaac's Hotel (☎ 450 0011; www.isaacs.ie; 48 MacCurtain St; s/d €110/135, 2-bed apt €160; **P** **▣**) The interior doesn't quite match the grand façade but you can expect charming service, large rooms and comfy beds at this old hotel in a Victorian furniture warehouse. The hotel's Greene's Restaurant, serving international cuisine, is set against a floodlit rocky waterfall, a startling sight in a city venue.

Imperial Hotel (☎ 427 4040; www.flynhotels.com; South Mall; s/d standard €135/175, superior €175/215; **P** **&**) Fast approaching her bicentenary, the Imperial knows how to age gracefully. A large-scale refurbishment has seamlessly merged the hotel's opulent period detail with flash contemporary touches, such as an Aveda spa, and DVD players in the superior rooms. Throw in two top restaurants, a food hall and a double-storeyed pub and you need a damn good reason to step foot outside at all.

Hayfield Manor (☎ 484 9500; www.hayfieldmanor .ie; Perrott Ave, College Rd; s/d €180/220; **P** **▣** **&**) Roll out the red carpet and pour yourself a sherry for *you have arrived*. A mile from the city centre but with all the ambience of a country house, Hayfield combines the luxury and facilities of a big hotel with the informality and welcome of a small one. If you're not rolling around the beautiful bedrooms (choose from traditional or contemporary styling), take afternoon tea in the library or have a facial at the Beautique.

EATING
Budget

Café Gusto (☎ 425 4446; www.cafegusto.com; 3 Washington St; dishes €4-5; ☯ 7.45am-6pm) Wraps, salads and pittas and a commitment to the finest fillings are the order of the day at this simple café. Gusto's assertion that it makes the best coffee in Cork is no idle claim either. You can sit in at high counter tops or take away, and there's a second branch at Lapps Quay.

Triskel Café (☎ 427 4644; www.triskelart.com; Tobin St; lunch €5-8; ☯ 8.30am-5pm Mon-Sat, also on performance nights) Attached to the Triskel Arts Centre, this cool, confident café is often quiet during the day, when you can scoff veggie lasagne, salads, *panini* and the finest carrot cake known to mankind peacefully. Wine is by the glass, or go for a healthy smoothie.

Café Glucksman (☎ 490 1848; www.glucksman.org; Lewis Glucksman Gallery, University College Cork; dishes €8-11; ☯ 10am-5pm Mon-Sat & noon-4pm Sun) The café at the Lewis Glucksman Gallery has panoramic views of the university grounds outside its picture windows and is all stark modernity within. The food is modern European in approach, so expect dishes such as poached salmon in lemon-butter or tagliatelle with blue cheese on the menu.

Quay Co-op (☎ 431 7026; www.quaycoop.com; 24 Sullivan's Quay; mains €8-11; ☯ 9am-9pm Mon-Sat) Flying a cheerful flag for alternative Cork, this favourite offers a range of self-service veggie options, all organic, including big breakfasts, rib-sticking soups and casseroles. The menu changes daily. It also caters for gluten-, dairy- and wheat-free needs, and is amazingly child-friendly. You can track down most of Cork's alternative organisations and events on the noticeboard downstairs.

Farmgate Café (☎ 427 8134; English Market; lunch €4-13, dinner €18-30; ☯ 8.30am-10pm Mon-Sat) An unmissable Cork experience at the heart of the English Market, the Farmgate, like its sister restaurant in Midleton (see p215), has mastered the magic art of producing delicious food without fuss or faddism. We defy you to find fresher food in Cork; the Farmgate sources all its ingredients, from rock oysters to the lamb for an Irish stew, from the market. Its location, perched on a balcony above the stalls, makes for great people-watching too.

SELF CATERING

our pick **English Market** (☯ 9am-5.30pm Mon-Sat) Cork picnickers are a fortunate bunch. The wonderful market is a self-caterer's paradise with so many tasty delicacies to choose from it's hard to show restraint. The emphasis is on local produce, with cheeses, ham, buttered eggs, sausages, bread and smoked salmon on offer, but there are some imports such as olives and wine too. If you have cooking facilities, the fresh-fish sellers will tell you exactly what to buy and how to cook it. Otherwise, perch at stall-side counters or take your lunch to Bishop Lucey Park, a popular alfresco eating spot.

Quay Co-op Organic & Wholefood Shop (Sullivan's Quay; ☯ 9am-6.15pm Mon-Sat) This is an excellent

COUNTY CORK

place for self-caterers; you'll find it next door to Quay Co-op.

Midrange

Boqueria (☎ 455 9049; www.boqueriasixbridgest.com; 6 Bridge St; breakfast €3-8, tapas €4-15; breakfast ☽ 8.30am-noon, tapas noon-late Mon-Sat & 5pm-late Sun) This tapas bar is a shining addition to Cork's wonderful eateries. In addition to the usual onion-garlic-tomato combinations, the chefs use local creations such as sourdough, Gubbeen cheese, and salmon to create tasty Irishified tapas. It's a dusky, intimate spot, favoured by couples in the evenings, and at lunch by friends seeking a civilised glass of wine.

Café de la Paix (☎ 427 9556; 16 Washington St; www .cafedelapaixcork.com; lunch €4-10, dinner €10-14; ☽ 8am-11.30pm Mon-Thu, 8am-12.30am Fri, 10am-12.30am Sat & noon-11pm Sun) An unassuming red exterior hides this chilled-out wine bar backing on to the River Lee. Picture windows make the most of the view from the simple white interior and there's a fabulous riverside deck outside. Global favourites grace the menu, from Thai curries to daily pasta specials, and the food scores highly both on flavour and presentation. It's tapas only after 10pm.

Currans (☎ 422 3950; www.curranscork.com; 5 Adelaide St; mains €10-23; ☽ noon-10pm Sun-Wed, noon-11pm Thu-Sat) A retirement home for Cork's unwanted fixtures and fittings, Currans' interior is entirely made up of artefacts salvaged from the city's demolished buildings. The wood panelling comes from the GPO, the radiators from Linville Hospital, even the lift is reclaimed from the tax office. The menu is a similar hotch-potch of reliable favourites – pizzas, burgers, seafood and steaks – and there's a delightful rooftop terrace if you ever tire of the interior.

Scoozi's (☎ 427 5077; 3-4 Winthrop Ave; lunch €9-12, mains €12-15; ☽ 9am-11pm Mon-Sat, noon-10pm Sun) There's lots of exposed brickwork and burnished wood inside this hugely popular café-restaurant, tucked down a lane between Winthrop and Caroline Sts. Snug alcoves add intimacy as the fast and friendly young staff dish up breakfasts, pizzas, pastas, grills and a fair selection of wine. It's a great place for families too.

Crawford Gallery Café (☎ 427 4415; www.crawford artgallery.com; Emmet Pl; mains €13-14, set menu €25; ☽ 10am-4.30pm Mon-Sat) An elegant blue dining room and exquisite seasonal and locally produced food make for high-class gallery grazing

---

> ### EATING IN THE HUGUENOT QUARTER
>
> The pedestrianised streets north of St Patrick's St throng with cafés and restaurants, and the place hops day and night. There's a plethora of options – all have outside tables and many serve late so the best advice is go for a wander and find somewhere that suits your mood and budget. Among our favourites are the New World cuisine at **Amicus Café & Restaurant** (☎ 427 6455; 14a French Church St), Spanish-Mexican fare at **Café Mexicana** (☎ 427 6433; www.cafemexicana.net; 1 Carey's Lane) and the global menu at **Strasbourg Goose** (☎ 427 9534; 17-18 French Church St).

---

at the Crawford. It's also a quality place for a spot of eavesdropping.

Isaac's Restaurant (☎ 450 3805; 48A MacCurtain St; lunch €13-23, dinner €16-23; ☽ 12.30-2.30pm & 6.30-10.30pm) Housed in an 18th-century warehouse, Isaac's captures a nostalgic Parisian-café atmosphere to go with its lively menu. Daily specials might include penne with Gubbeen chorizo or crab cake with chilli mayonnaise, and there are always good veggie options.

Top End

Fenn's Quay (☎ 427 9527; www.fennsquay.ie; 5 Sheares St; lunch €5-20, dinner €18-28; ☽ 10am-late Mon-Sat) You could spend all day at this exceptionally comfortable place, starting with scones fresh out of the oven for breakfast and ending with fish straight from the English Market (p207) for dinner. The simple interior – whitewashed walls and wooden furniture – is matched by a straightforward food philosophy: quality local produce cooked with care and attention. Before 7.30pm, a two-course dinner will set you back €22.50.

Café Paradiso (☎ 427 7939; www.cafeparadiso.ie; 16 Lancaster Quay; lunch €12-16, dinner €24-25; ☽ noon-3pm & 6.30-10.30pm Tue-Sat) At arguably the best vegetarian restaurant in Ireland, the inventive dishes will seduce even the most committed carnivore. The charming staff promote happy interaction and there's a Mediterranean ambience in the animated dining room. Creativity maintains the standard of dishes and the wine list reflects a real passion for the vine. For post-pudding paradise, slither upstairs to one of three stylish double rooms (€160), reserved exclusively for diners.

Jacques Restaurant (☎ 427 7387; http://jacques restaurant.ie; 9 Phoenix St; mains €22-27; ♥ 6-10pm Mon-Sat) With more than 25 years in the business, Jacqueline and Eithne Barry have built up a terrific network of local suppliers to help them realise their culinary ambitions – the freshest Cork food cooked simply. The menu, served in an elegant dining room, is dictated by what's available and in season – if it's on, the roast duck with apricot stuffing is a particular pleasure. A two-course menu is available from 6pm to 7pm for €21.90.

Ivory Tower (☎ 427 4665; www.seamusoconnell.com; Exchange Bldgs, 35 Princes St; mains €28-35; ♥ 6.30-10pm Wed-Sat) Hiding behind an unpromisingly shabby entrance is this delightfully eclectic place done up like a granny's parlour – albeit a granny whose tastes run to upright pianos, safari hats and moon-and-star motifs. The menu is equally intriguing – chef Seamus O'Connell's 'missions' to Japan having influenced the accomplished cuisine – and few concessions are made to the timid (the speciality is blackened shark with banana ketchup). A five-course menu is available at €60; a three-course menu is served between 6.30pm and 8pm for €30.

DRINKING

Cork's pub life is cracking, easily rivalling that of Dublin in quality. Drink Guinness at your peril, or Murphy's and Beamish, which are brewed locally. Cork also has its very own brewpub, the Franciscan Well Brewery.

An Spailpín Fánac (☎ 427 7949; South Main St) 'The Wandering Labourer' really hangs on to its character, with exposed brickwork, stone-flagged floors, snug corners and open fires. There are good trad sessions every night bar Saturday.

our pick Sin É (☎ 450 2266; Coburg St) You could easily while away an entire day at this great old place over the Lee North Channel. There are no frills or fuss here – just a comfy, sociable pub long on atmosphere and short on pretension. Hunker down in the dark downstairs or swivel in the barber's chair in the brighter upstairs room. There's music most nights, much of it traditional but with the odd surprise.

Mutton Lane Inn (☎ 427 3471; Mutton Lane) Tucked down the tiniest of laneways off St Patrick's St, this inviting pub lit by candles and fairy lights is one of Cork's most intimate drinking holes. It also has one of the best beer selections in the city. It's miniscule and much-admired so

try to get in early to bag the snug, or join the smokers perched on beer kegs outside.

Long Valley (☎ 427 2144; Winthrop St) A Cork institution that dates from the mid-19th century and is still going strong, the Long Valley has a landscape that fits its name. The upstairs Hayloft is usually quieter if the main bar is busy.

Franciscan Well Brewery (☎ 421 0130; www.franciscan wellbrewery.com; 14 North Mall) The copper vats gleaming behind the bar give the game away: the Franciscan Well brews its own beer. And very good it is too, whether you're after stout, ale, lager or wheat beer. The best place to enjoy it is in the enormous beer garden at the back. The pub holds regular beer festivals with other small Irish breweries – check the website for details.

Hi-B (☎ 427 2758; 108 Oliver Plunkett St) Up a dingy flight of stairs, tiny Hi-B is one of Cork's most idiosyncratic pubs, in no small part thanks to landlord Brian O'Connell. If you've never been thrown out of a pub and think you've missed out, try getting out your mobile here. Or ordering a soft drink. Or looking at Brian in a 'funny' way. There's jazz on the piano on Wednesday nights to add to the entertainment.

Crane Lane Theatre (☎ 427 8487; Phoenix St) Newly opened Crane Lane is fast becoming a city institution, thanks to its courtyard beer garden, theatrical décor and regular live-music sessions. It also does a good line in specialty tipples – Swedish wild berry cider, anyone?

Pubs are Cork's best asset but if you hanker after a cocktail, there's a booming bar scene:

Chambers (☎ 422 2860; Washington St; ♥ late Thu-Sun) A haberdasher swallowed a copy of *Elle Decoration*, and Chambers was born.

Suas (☎ 427 8973; www.suasbar.com; 4-5 South Main St; ♥ late Fri-Sat) Fantastic rooftop location high above Main St; the entrance is by Wagamama's.

ENTERTAINMENT

For listings pick up a copy of **WhazOn?** (www .whazon.com), available from the tourist office and some B&Bs and shops.

Theatre

Cork's cultural life is as fine as any in Ireland and attracts numerous internationally renowned performers.

Cork Opera House (☎ 427 4308; www.corkopera house.ie; Emmet Pl; box office ♥ 9am-8.30pm, to 5.30pm non-performance nights) This leading venue has been entertaining the city for more than 150

COUNTY CORK

years with everything from opera and ballet to stand-up and puppet shows. Performances are as varied as *Carmen*, Nanci Griffith, and the musical *I, Keano*.

Everyman Palace Theatre (☎ 450 1673; www.everymanpalace.com; 15 MacCurtain St; tickets from €12; box office ⏰ 10am-7.30pm Mon-Sat, to 6pm non-performance nights) Acclaimed musical and dramatic productions are the main bill of fare here, but there's also the occasional high-quality opera, rock band, storyteller and comedian.

Granary (☎ 490 4275; www.granary.ie; Dyke Pde; tickets around €12) Contemporary and experimental works are staged at the Granary by the University College Cork drama group and visiting companies. Look out for any related workshops, symposiums and installations.

Cork Arts Theatre (☎ 450 5624; www.corkartstheatre.com; Camden Court, Carrolls Quay; tickets €10-20) Newly rebuilt, this excellent theatre shows thought-provoking drama and runs workshops for new writers and kids.

Triskel Arts Centre (☎ 472 2022; www.triskelart.com; Tobin St; tickets around €15) Expect a varied programme of live music, installation art, photography and theatre at this intimate venue. There's also a great café, Triskel Café (p207).

Cinemas

Gate Multiplex (☎ 427 9595; North Main St; tickets adult/child €8/5.50) Multiscreen cinema showing mainstream films.

Kino (☎ 427 1571; www.kinocinema.net; Washington St; tickets €8, matinee €5.50) Shows art-house flicks.

Live Music

Cork overflows with tunes. As well as the pubs mentioned earlier (p209), the following places

are either dedicated music venues or bars known particularly for their live events. These are just the tip of the iceberg – refer to *WhazOn* or Plugd Records (opposite) and www.corkgigs.com for more. Buy tickets at the venues themselves or from Plugd.

An Cruiscín Lán (☎ 484 0941; www.cruiscin.com; Douglas St) Trad bands and world, blues and pop musicians all play at this acclaimed bar south of the river.

Fred Zeppelins (☎ 427 3500; www.fredzeps.com; 8 Parliament St) There's a hard edge to this dark den of a bar, popular with goths, rockers and anyone who feels uncomfortable leaving the house without a packet of Rizlas. There are regular gigs upstairs and DJs downstairs.

Savoy (☎ 425 1419; www.savoycork.com; St Patrick's St) The Savoy sweeps the spectrum from singer-songwriters and rock bands to tribute bands and regular club nights. Recent gigs have seen the Lemonheads and the Levellers strut the stage.

Half Moon Theatre (☎ 427 0022; www.halfmoontheatre.ie; Emmet Place) One of Cork's best venues for live music, comedy and drama. Saturday night sees Lobby Live, featuring an ever-interesting line-up of local and international bands. Music joins the dots between blues, folk, trad, rock and alternative.

Nightclubs

Cork's club life really does rival Dublin's, in quantity if not in quality. Most clubs go all guns blazing for pissed students and 20-somethings on the pull. If this is your bag, **Redz** (17 Liberty St), **Qube** (74 Oliver Plunkett St) and **Vibes** (Paul St) will keep you happy.

Entry ranges from free to €15 and most of these places open until 2am on Friday and Saturday.

Scotts (☎ 422 2779; www.scotts.ie; Caroline St; ⏰ Fri-Sat) This deluxe venue, all dark wood and moody lighting, has a fine restaurant downstairs and an upstairs club that features mainstream floor-fillers for well-groomed over-20s.

Havana Browns (☎ 427 1969; www.havana-browns.com; Hanover St; ⏰ nightly) One of Cork's most popular clubs, Havana Browns has three bars, a VIP room, an outdoor terrace and a fine line in neon and amber back-lighting. The music doesn't stray far from MTV's current playlist.

our pick Liquid Lounge (☎ 427 6097; www.liquidlounge.ie; 29 Marlborough St; ⏰ Wed-Sat) If you're

---

GONE TO THE DOGS

If you tire of the pubs, the live music and the theatre, there's always the dogs. Greyhound-racing is big news in Ireland, particularly with families, and **Curraheen Greyhound Park** (☎ 454 3095; www.igb.ie; Curraheen Park; adult/child €10/5; ⏰ Wed, Thu & Sat from 6.45pm) is one of the country's swankiest stadiums. There are 10 races a night, and a restaurant, bar and live music to keep you entertained in between. Curraheen is 5.5km from the centre; to get there, take bus 8. A free bus drops you back between 10.30pm and 12.30am.

more interested in good music than get-ting laid, Liquid Lounge is here to save you. There are regular gigs on Saturday nights, featuring bands signed to Irish labels, and DJ sets cover anything from Arcade Fire and the Yeah Yeah Yeahs to Kraftwerk and De La Soul. There's a top roof terrace to boot.

SHOPPING

As well as the full range of national and in-ternational stores, there are some excellent specialist outlets in Cork. The little streets north of St Patrick's St, packed with smaller boutiques, are the most interesting.

O'Connaill (☎ 437 3407; 16B French Church St) Don't leave Cork without sampling the Chocolatier's Hot Chocolate (€3.30) at the tiny counter at O'Connaill confectioners. The foolhardy can stagger away with 2.5kg slabs of chocolate but there are subtler concoctions on offer, with wafer-thin slivers of cocoa flavoured with exotic flourishes such as coffee beans or chilli.

Living Tradition (☎ 450 2564; 40 MacCurtain St; ✆ 10am-6pm Mon-Sat) Head here for traditional and world-music CDs, instruments, publica-tions and gig info.

Plugd Records (☎ 427 6300; 4 Washington St) A terrific music shop that stocks everything from techno to nu-jazz beats. You can buy tickets for gigs and pick up the very latest info on the club scene.

Union Chandlery (☎ 455 4334; 4-5 Penrose's Quay) Camping and trekking gear, wetsuits, sail-ing equipment and guides are on sale, and there's an information board on sporting activities around the county.

GETTING THERE & AWAY

Air

Cork airport (☎ 431 3131; www.cork-airport.com) is 8km south of the city on the N27. Fa-cilities include ATMs and car-hire desks (p212). Airlines servicing the airport in-clude bmibaby, Malev Hungarian Airlines, Ryanair and Wizz. There are direct flights within Europe only; other overseas flights go via Dublin.

See p212 for information on getting into town.

Boat

Brittany Ferries (☎ 427 7801; www.brittany-ferries .com; 42 Grand Pde) sail to Roscoff (France) at 4pm every Saturday from the end of March to October. The crossing takes 15 hours and you have to book accommodation (reclin-ing seat/2-/4-berth cabin €10/125/155). The best fares are available online. Some sam-ple high-season fares (not including ac-commodation) are: car and two passengers €430; motorcycle and driver €147; and foot passenger €92.

Bus

Bus Éireann (☎ 450 8188; www.buseireann.ie) oper-ates from the bus station on the corner of Merchant's Quay and Parnell Pl. You can get to most places in Ireland from Cork, in-cluding Dublin (€9.50 single, 4¼ hours, six daily), Killarney (€13.50 single, one hour 40 minutes, 14 daily), Waterford (€14.90, 2¾ hours, 14 daily) and Kilkenny (€14.90 single, three hours, three daily).

GAY & LESBIAN CORK

Cork Pride (www.corkpride.com) Week-long festival every May/June with events throughout the city.

Flux! (☎ 450 5405; www.fluxcork.com; 56 MacCurtain St; ✆ from 2pm daily, to 2am Fri & Sat) Sleek new bar scene with DJs at the weekend.

Grub café-bar (☎ 427 8470; www.gayprojectcork.com; 8 South Main St; ✆ 11am-10pm Mon-Fri, 11am-7pm Sat-Sun) Housed at the same premises as the Other Place.

Instinct (www.instinctbarcork.com; Sullivan's Quay; ✆ 9pm-late Fri-Sat) Lively club with DJs, Kylie parties, salsa lessons and quiz nights.

L.Inc (☎ 480 8600; www.linc.ie; 11A White St; ✆ office 11am-3pm Mon-Fri, drop-in times noon-3pm Tue & 8-10pm Thu) Excellent resource centre for lesbians and bisexual women.

Loafers (☎ 431 1612; www.loafersbar.com; 26 Douglas St) Cork's oldest and most laid-back gay bar.

Other Place (☎ 427 8470; www.gayprojectcork.com; 8 South Main St) Hosts the Southern Gay Health Project (www.gayhealthproject.com) and has a bookstore, a café-bar and a nightclub, which operates from 10pm to late Friday to Sunday. Check the nightclub's website at www.theotherplaceclub.com for details.

www.gaycork.com What's-on listings and directory.

COUNTY CORK

Car

The following companies have desks at the airport. In our experience, Budget has the best rates.

Alamo/National (☎ 431 8623; www.carhire.ie)
Avis (☎ 432 7460; www.avis.ie)
Budget (☎ 431 4000; www.budget.ie)
Hertz (☎ 496 5849; www.hertz.ie)
Sixt (☎ 4318644; www.e-sixt.ie)
Thrifty (☎ 434 8488; www.thrifty.ie)

Train

Kent Train Station (☎ 450 4777) is north of the River Lee on Lower Glanmire Rd. Bus 5 runs into the centre (€1.30) and a taxi costs from €7 to €8.

Routes include Dublin (€68, three hours, 16 daily), Limerick (€22.50, 1½ hours, nine daily), Tralee (€29.50, 2¼ hours, nine daily), Killarney (€22.50, 1½ hours, nine daily).

The train journey to Waterford is long and circuitous: better to take the bus.

GETTING AROUND
To/From the Airport

A taxi into town costs €13 to €18. Bus 226 runs between the airport and the bus station, and into the city centre (€3.80). Journey time for both is 30 minutes.

To/From the Ferry Terminal

The ferry terminal is at Ringaskiddy, 15 minutes by car southeast of the city centre along the N28. Taxis cost €25 to €30. Bus Éireann runs a fairly frequent service from the bus station to link up with sailings (adult/child €4.60/2.90, 50 minutes).

Bicycle

You can rent bikes and glean cycling tips from affable Aidan and Robbie at **Rothar Cycles** (☎ 431 3133; www.rotharcycletours.com; 55 Barrack St; per day/week €25/80). They offer a one-way pick-up service from other towns for €30 (with a €100 refundable deposit) and run frequent summer cycling tours.

Bus

Most places are within easy walking distance of the centre. A single bus ticket costs €1.30.

Car

Streetside parking requires scratch-card parking discs (€1.80 per hour) obtained from the tourist office and some newsagencies. Be

warned – the traffic wardens are ferociously efficient and the cost of retrieving your vehicle hefty. There are about 10 signposted car parks around the central area, with charges of €1.30 per hour, and €3 overnight.

Cork has a Park & Ride system to help tackle city-centre congestion; it's €5 for a return bus fare into the centre, from 7.30am to 7.30pm Monday to Saturday. The car park is on the southern approach from Kinsale; the drop-off point is Lapp's Quay.

Taxi

For taxi hire, try **Cork Taxi Co-op** (☎ 427 2222) or **Shandon Cabs** (☎ 450 2255).

AROUND CORK CITY

BLARNEY CASTLE

One of the most popular tourist stops in Ireland is **Blarney Castle** (☎ 021-438 5252; www.blarneycastle.ie; Blarney; adult/child €8/2.50; ☺ 9am-7pm Mon-Sat & 9.30am-5.30pm Sun Jun-Aug, 9am-6pm or sundown Mon-Sat & 9.30am-5pm or sundown Sun Oct-Apr, 9am-6.30pm Mon-Sat & 9.30am-5.30pm Sun May & Sep, last admission 30min before closing). Crowds flock here to kiss the **Blarney Stone**, said to grant the gift of the gab.

The way is not easy for those seeking eloquence. The stone is perched at the top of the 15th-century castle, reached by a steep climb up slippery spiral staircases. On the battlements, you bend backwards over a long, long drop (with safety grill and attendant to prevent messy accidents) to kiss the stone; as your shirt rides up, coach loads of onlookers stare up your nose. Once you're upright, don't forget to admire the stunning views before descending.

The custom of kissing the stone is a relatively modern one, but Blarney's association with smooth talking goes back a long time. Queen Elizabeth I is said to have invented the term 'to talk blarney' out of exasperation with Lord Blarney's ability to talk endlessly without ever actually agreeing to her demands.

Be warned: quiet Blarney moments don't exist in the race for the stone. Your best bet is to leave the kissing until late when the crowds start to drift off. If it all gets too much, vanish into the **Rock Close**, part of the wonderful gardens, which includes

COUNTY CORK

A SNEAKY SHORTCUT: PASSAGE WEST

If you're travelling between east and west Cork, avoid Cork city centre by using the **Ferry Link** (☎ 021-481 1223; pedestrian/car €1/4.50; ☽ 7am-12.15am). The crossing connects Glenbrook and Carrigaloe (near Cobh) and takes five minutes. Bikes travel free.

---

a fairy glade, a witch's kitchen and a set of wishing steps.

Blarney is 8km northwest of Cork and buses run frequently from Cork bus station (€2.70, 30 minutes).

FOTA

Fota Wildlife Park (☎ 021-481 2678; www.fotawildlife.ie; Carrigtwohill; adult/child/under-2s €12.50/8/free; ☽ 10am-4.30pm Mon-Sat & 11am-4.30pm Sun mid-Mar–Oct, 10am-3pm Mon-Sat & 11am-3pm Sun Nov–mid-Mar, last admission 1hr before closing) is a terrific place, where animals roam without a cage or fence in sight. Kangaroos bound past, monkeys and gibbons leap and scream on wooded islands, and capybaras root around in the bushes. New to the park is the Cheetah Run – at 4pm daily the cats are made to chase their dinner as it whizzes along a wire at 104 km/h in front of them.

A tour train runs a circuit round the park every 15 minutes in high season (one way/return €1/2), but the 2km circular walk offers a more close-up experience. There are duck-feeding opportunities, a playground and café en route.

From the wildlife park, you can take a stroll down to the Regency-style **Fota House** (☎ 021-481 5543; www.fotahouse.com; Carrigtwohill; adult/child €5.50/2.20; ☽ 10am-5pm Mon-Sat & 11am-5pm Sun Apr-Oct, 11am-4pm daily Nov-Mar, last admission 30min before closing). The interior contains a fine kitchen and ornate plasterwork ceilings. The lack of 18th- and 19th-century furnishings is compensated for by info boards and interactive displays bringing the rooms to life.

Attached to the house is the 150-year-old **arboretum**, which has a Victorian fernery, magnolia walk and some beautiful trees including giant redwoods and a Chinese ghost tree.

Fota is 10km east of Cork. The hourly Cork to Fota train (€3.85 return, 13 minutes) goes on to Cobh. There's a car park (€3) shared by the park and the house.

COBH

☎ 021 / pop 6800

In the wake of the Famine, 2.5 million people emigrated from the port of Cobh (pronounced cove) – go on a grey day, and the sense of loss is still almost palpable. When the sun shines and the crowds flock in, though, you'll see another side to this hilly little town. The spectacular cathedral looks down over brightly coloured houses, the wide seaside promenade and the glittering estuary, and Cobh seems to shake off its sad past.

Cobh has become a popular stopover for visiting cruise liners whose clientele are whisked off in coaches to tourist hot spots.

History

For many years Cobh was the port of Cork and has always had a strong connection with Atlantic crossings. In 1838 the *Sirius*, the first steamship to cross the Atlantic, sailed from Cobh. The *Titanic* made its last stop here before its fateful journey in 1912, and when the *Lusitania* was torpedoed off the coast of Kinsale in 1915, it was here that many of the survivors were brought and the dead buried. Cobh was also the last glimpse of Ireland for the people who emigrated during the Famine.

In 1849 Cobh was renamed Queenstown after Queen Victoria paid a visit. The name lasted until Irish independence in 1921 when, unsurprisingly, the local council reverted to the Irish Cobh.

The world's first yacht club, the Royal Cork Yacht Club, was founded here in 1720, but now operates from Crosshaven on the other side of Cork Harbour.

Orientation

Cobh is on Great Island, which fills much of Cork Harbour, and is joined to the mainland by a causeway. It faces Haulbowline Island (once the base of the Irish Naval Service) and the greener Spike Island (which houses a prison). The waterfront comprises the broad Westbourne Pl and West Beach, from where steep streets climb inland. There's a delightful waterside park with a bandstand and playground next to the tourist office.

Information

The Old Yacht Club contains a **tourist office** (☎ 481 3301; www.cobhharbourchamber.ie; ☽ 9.30am-5.30pm Mon-Fri, 1-5pm Sat-Sun) and arts centre.

Sights

COBH, THE QUEENSTOWN STORY

Part of Cobh train station has been cleverly converted into an unmissable **heritage centre** (☎ 481 3591; www.cobhheritage.com; Cobh Heritage Centre; adult/child €6.60/3.30; ☒ 9.30am-6pm May-Oct & 10am-5pm Nov-Apr, last admission 1hr before closing; ☒), which is a cut above many other 'interpretative centres'. It contains a fascinating series of exhibitions about Ireland's mass emigrations in the wake of the Famine, when some families became so desperate to leave they boarded leaky vessels that became known as 'coffin ships'. There's also some shocking stuff on the fate of convicts, shipped to Australia in transport 'so airless that candles could not burn'. The era of the great liners is re-created, including the tragedies of the *Titanic* and *Lusitania*, both intimately connected to Cobh.

For people trying to trace ancestors there's a genealogy centre attached. For those more interested in a bun and a cup of tea, there's an adjoining café (see right).

ST COLMAN'S CATHEDRAL

Standing dramatically above Cobh on a hillside terrace, the massive French Gothic **St Colman's Cathedral** (☎ 481 3222; Cathedral Pl; admission by donation) is out of all proportion to the unassuming town. Its most exceptional feature is the 47-bell carillon, the largest in Ireland, with a range of four octaves. The biggest bell weighs a stonking 3440kg – about as much as a full-grown elephant! You can hear carillon recitals at 4.30pm on Sundays between May and September.

The cathedral, designed by Pugin, was begun in 1868 but not completed until 1915. Much of the funding was raised by nostalgic Irish communities in Australia and the USA.

COBH MUSEUM

A small **museum** (☎ 481 4240; www.cobhmuseum .com; High Rd; adult/child €2/1; ☒ 11am-1pm Mon-Sat & 2-5.30pm daily Apr-Oct) is housed in the 19th-century Scottish Presbyterian church overlooking the train station. There are model ships, paintings, photographs and curious artefacts tracing Cobh's history.

Tours

Marine Transport Services (☎ 481 1485; www.mts .ie) One-hour boat tours (adult/child €5.50/3.50) four times daily June to September.

Titanic Trail (☎ 481 5211; www.titanic-trail.com; adult/child €9.50/4.75; ☒ 11am year-round & 2pm May & Jun-Aug) Michael Martin's 1¼-hour guided walk leaves from the Commodore Hotel on Westbourne Pl, with a free sampling of stout at the end. Contact Michael for details of his ghoulish Ghost Walk (€15).

Sleeping

Westbourne House (☎ 481 1391; 12 Westbourne Pl; s/d €25/50) The friendly owner of this historical house (an old shipping agent's) provides good value beyond the reasonable price. Lavish it ain't, but the rooms are big and sunny and the many yachting pictures go with those harbour views.

Commodore Hotel (☎ 481 1277; www.commodore hotel.ie; Westbourne Pl; s/d €57/96) Frequent promotional deals add to the attraction of this classic seaside hotel. Soaring chandeliered hallways lead to newly renovated rooms (it's worth paying an extra €15 for one with a sea view) and the whole place exudes a pleasant retro vibe.

Amberleigh (☎ 481 4069; www.amberleigh.ie; West End Terrace; s/d €60/90; ⓟ) You'll receive a warm welcome at this beautiful Victorian house perched on a hill overlooking the harbour. There are just four guest rooms, all of them enormous with high ceilings and fresh white décor. There's also a guest lounge, with a crackling fire on chilly evenings.

Knockeven House (☎ 481 1778; www.knockeven house.com; Rushbrooke; s/d €75/120; ⓟ) Knockeven is a splendid, relaxed Victorian house, 1.5km north of Cobh. Huge bedrooms are done out with period furniture and overlook a magnificent garden full of magnolias and camellias. Breakfasts are great too – homemade breads and fresh fruit – and are served in the sumptuous dining room.

Eating & Drinking

There's a **farmers market** on the seafront every Friday from 10am to 1pm.

Queenstown Restaurant (☎ 481 3591; lunch €4-7; ☒ 10am-5pm) Coffee, tea and tasty lunches, including salads and lasagne, are served up in Cobh's Old Railway Station. You eat on the platform surrounded by trunks, timetables and a nostalgic longing for the age of steam.

Jacob's Ladder (☎ 481 5566; www.watersedgehotel .ie; lunch €6-14, dinner €18-28; ☒ 11.30am-9pm) This upbeat restaurant at the Water's Edge Hotel has a great view over the harbour. It's fairly pricey and has a wide range of meat, poultry and excellent fish dishes, all done with some creativity.

Kelly's (☎ 481 1994; Westbourne Pl) Sunny Kelly's is filled with sociable punters day and night. The pub's two rooms are decked out with pew-style seating, chunky wooden furniture, a wood-burning stove and, curiously, a stag's head. It's also a great spot to watch televised sport.

Getting There & Away
Cobh is 15km southeast of Cork, off the main N25 Cork–Rosslare road. Hourly trains connect Cobh with Cork (€5.25 return, 24 minutes).

Getting Around
All of Cobh's sites are within walking distance. If you need a cab try the **Cobh Taxi Owners Association** (☎ 086-815 8631).

MIDLETON & AROUND
☎ 021 / pop 3900
Most visitors sweep through the Midleton area on their way to the Old Midleton Distillery but it's worth a bit more of your time. Rather ambitiously named the 'Irish Riviera' by the tourist board, it's nonetheless full of pretty villages, craggy coastline and some heavenly rural hotels. Midleton itself is a pleasant and bustling market town though with plenty of accommodation in the surrounding area, there's no real reason to stay here.

The **tourist office** (☎ 461 3702; www.eastcork tourism.com; 9.30am-1pm & 2-5.15pm Mon-Sat May-Sep) is by the entrance gate to the distillery.

Sights
The big attraction in town is the former Jameson **Old Midleton Distillery** (☎ 461 3594; www .jamesonwhiskey.com; adult/concession €9.75/6; 9am-6pm). Coach-loads pour in to tour the restored 200-year-old building and purchase bottles from the gift shop. Jameson's delicious 12-year distillery reserve is available nowhere in the world except here.

You visit as part of one-hour **guided tours** (10am-5pm Mar-Oct, at 11.30am, 2.30pm & 4pm Nov-Feb). They start with a film and continue with a walk that reveals the whole whiskey-making process. The tour ends in the bar, where everyone gets a free snifter, and luckier volunteers get to taste assorted Irish whiskys, Scotch and bourbon.

SMOKIN'

Two kilometres out of town on the N25 towards Fota, the effervescent Frank Hederman runs **Belvelly** (☎ 481 1089; www .frankhederman.com), the oldest natural smokehouse in Ireland – and indeed the only one. Seafood and cheese are smoked here, but the speciality is fish, in particular salmon. In a traditional process that takes 24 hours from start to finish, the fish is filleted and cured before being hung in the tiny smokehouse to smoke over beechwood chips. No trip to Cork is complete without a visit to an artisan food producer, and Frank is more than happy to show you around – phone or email to arrange.

Sleeping & Eating
Midleton Farmers Market is one of Cork's best markets, with tons of local produce on offer and producers happy to chat. It's on every Saturday morning behind the courthouse on Main St.

our pick **Farmgate Restaurant** (☎ 463 2771; the Coolbawn; coffee & snacks 9am-5.30pm, lunch 12.30-4pm Mon-Sat, dinner 6.45-9.30pm Thu-Sat) The original and sister establishment to Cork's Farmgate Café (p207), the Midleton restaurant offers the same superb blend of traditional and modern Irish in its approach to cooking. In the front is a shop selling local produce, including organic fruit and vegetables, cheeses and preserves. Behind is the farmhouse-style café-restaurant, where you'll eat as well as anywhere in Ireland.

Bayview Hotel (☎ 464 6746; www.thebayview hotel.com; Ballycotton; s/d €127/190; P) The cliff-top Bayview is all about the ocean with terrific vistas from its lounges, restaurant and swish bedrooms (for the best views, ask for a 3rd-floor room with a balcony). There's nowt to do here but drink in that view, laze on the terrace, meander along the cliffs or enjoy a pint in the village – the Blackbird does a good pull of the black stuff.

Getting There & Away
Midleton is 20km east of Cork. There are buses every 30 minutes from Monday to Saturday (hourly on Sunday) from Cork bus station (€5, 25 minutes). There are no buses between Cobh and Midleton, and you'll need a car to explore the surrounding area.

COUNTY CORK

YOUGHAL

☎ 024 / pop 6400

The ancient walled seaport of Youghal (Eochaill; pronounced yawl), at the mouth of the River Blackwater, has history coming out of its ears and really makes the most of it.

The town was a hotbed of rebellion against the English in the 16th century, and Oliver Cromwell wintered here in 1649 as he sought to drum up support for his war in England and quell insurgence from the pesky Irish. Youghal was granted to Sir Walter Raleigh during the Elizabethan Plantation of Munster, and he spent brief spells living here in his house, Myrtle Grove.

Orientation & Information

The Clock Gate at the southern end of North Main St is Youghal's major landmark.

Youghal Visitor Centre (☎ 20170; www.eastcork tourism.com; Market Sq; ☯ 9am-5.30pm Mon-Fri, 10am-5pm Sat & Sun), housed in an attractive old market house on the waterfront, contains a small **heritage centre** that will help you get to grips with all that history. Pick up the free leaflet *Youghal Town Trail*, or the excellent booklet *Youghal: Historic Walled Port* (€4.50) to learn more.

Guided tours (adult/child €6/3) lasting 1½ hours, leave the visitor centre at 10.30am Monday to Friday during July and August (on request at other times).

Sights & Activities

Youghal has two Blue Flag **beaches** (clean, safe beaches given the EU Blue Flag award), ideal for building sandcastles and swimming.

Claycastle (2km) and Front Strand (1km) are both within walking distance of town, off the N25. Claycastle has wheelchair access and summer lifeguards.

Whale of a Time (☎ 086-328 3256; www.whaleoofa time.ie) runs sea and river cruises (adult/child €20/15), including whale-watching trips.

Dinky **Fox's Lane Folk Museum** (☎ 20170, 291 145; www.tyntescastle.com/fox; North Cross Lane; adult/child €4/2; ☯ 10am-1pm & 2-6pm Tue-Sat Jul-Aug) contains more than 600 household gadgets dating from 1850 to 1950, and a Victorian kitchen.

Walking Tour

Youghal's history is best understood through its landmarks. Heading through town from south to north, this tour details the more prominent sights.

The curious **Clock Gate** was built in 1777, and served as a clock tower and jail concurrently: several prisoners taken in the 1798 Rising were hung from its windows.

The beautifully proportioned brick **Red House**, on North Main St, was designed in 1706 by the Dutch architect Leuventhen, and features some Dutch Renaissance details. A few doors further up the street are six **almshouses** built by Englishman Richard Boyle, who bought Raleigh's Irish estates and became the first earl of Cork in 1616 in recognition of his work in creating 'a very excellent Colony'. The almshouses were given to ex-soldiers, along with an annual pension of £5.

Across the road is 15th-century **Tynte's Castle** (http://tyntescastle.com), which originally had a defensive riverfront position. When the River

---

DETOUR: THE BALLYMALOE EXPERIENCE

Drawing up at wisteria-clad **Ballymaloe House** (☎ 465 2531; www.ballymaloe.ie; Shanagarry; s/d from €165/260; P ⓰), you know you've arrived somewhere special. The Allen family has been running this superb hotel and restaurant in the old family home for more than 40 years now and the place just keeps getting better. The rooms have been individually decorated in period furnishings and are a pleasing mass of different shapes and sizes. The Grey Room, with its double-aspect windows, is our favourite. Guests can enjoy the garden, tennis court, swimming pool, shop, minigolf and public rooms. And don't forget the celebrated restaurant, its menu drawn up daily to reflect the availability of local produce. The hotel also runs wine and gardening weekends – check the website for details.

A few kilometres down the road on the R628, the Allen's **cookery school** (☎ 464 6785; www .cookingisfun.ie) sits on 100 acres of land. Lessons, from half-day sessions (€50 to €105) to 12-week certificate courses (around €9000), take place in the old apple-storage house, and the teaching style is relaxed and encouraging. There are pretty cottages in the grounds for overnight students.

Blackwater silted up and changed course in the 17th and 18th centuries, the castle was left high and dry.

Built in 1220, **St Mary's Collegiate Church** incorporates elements of an earlier Danish church dating back to the 11th century. Inside there's a monument to Richard Boyle, portrayed with his wife and 16 kids. The Earl of Desmond and his troops, rebelling against English rule, demolished the chancel roof in the 16th century; and Cromwell is believed to have given a funerary speech inside for a fallen general in 1650. The churchyard is bounded by a fine stretch of the 13th-century **town wall** and one of the remaining turrets.

Beside the church, **Myrtle Grove** is the former home of Sir Walter Raleigh. Local tradition claims that he smoked the first cigarette and planted the first potatoes here, but historians (the spoilsports) tend to disagree. His **gardens**, on the other side of St Mary's, have recently been restored and are open to the public.

Sleeping

Clonvilla Caravan & Camping Park (☎ 98288; clonvilla@hotmail.com; Clonpriest; camp sites €20; ⊗ Mar-Oct) Facilities are basic at this small site 4km out of town, but it's quiet enough.

Roseville (☎ 92571; www.rosevillebb.com; New Catherine St; s €45-50, d €61-70; ⊗ mid-Jan–mid-Dec; P) In the heart of Youghal, shiny red Roseville with its own walled garden has the mood of a country house. The rooms won't win any style awards but you'll sleep well on big comfy beds and be assured of a cheery welcome from landlady Phyllis.

Avonmore House (☎ 92617; www.avonmoreyoughal .com; South Abbey; s/d €50/70) This grand Georgian house near the clock tower swims in history. Built in 1752 on the site of a Franciscan abbey destroyed by Cromwellian troops, Avonmore belonged to the earls of Cork before passing into private hands in 1826. Things are a lot less turbulent these days – expect bright, plain rooms and friendly hosts.

Ballymakeigh (☎ 249 5184; www.ballymakeighhouse .com; Killeagh; s/d €75/130) Down a winding lane, past the cows and banks lined with bluebells in spring, Ballymakeigh is farmhouse lodging at its best. There are six simple, stylish bedrooms, a working farm to explore and a tennis court for the active. Landlady Margaret Browne is a former TV chef, so don't

miss out on her five-course dinners (€45). Ballymakeigh is 12km west of Youghal, near the village of Killeagh.

Aherne's (☎ 92424; www.ahernes.net; 163 North Main St; s/d €150/240; P &) This charming four-star place has individually decorated rooms furnished with antiques. There's a great sense of style and comfort and, best of all, you get a fabulous breakfast in the restaurant (see below).

Eating

Aherne's Seafood Bar & Restaurant (☎ 92424; 163 North Main St; bar food €12-38, dinner €24-38; ⊗ bar food noon-10pm, dinner 6.30-9.30pm) If you're serious about seafood the only place to eat in Youghal is Aherne's, an award-winning restaurant justifiably famous for its terrific menu. If the restaurant is too formal, sample fishy delights in the cosy bar – the salmon and potato gratin is the very definition of comfort food.

Priory (☎ 92574; www.thepriory.ie; 56 North Main St; ⊗ 9.30am-6pm Tue-Fri, 10am-5pm Sat, 11am-2pm Sun, extended opening hours in summer) This delightful sandwich bar and deli specialises in Irish and artisanal produce. The ciabattas (from €3.55) are named after famous chefs; our favourite is the Allen, stuffed with Irish ham, Cashel blue and Ballymaloe relish. You can perch on tall stools inside, or have a hamper made up to take to the beach. At the time of writing, there were plans to open a restaurant too.

Drinking & Entertainment

Dancing Thru the Ages (☎ 92571; www.dancing thrutheages.com; Mall Arts Centre; adult/child €20/15; ⊗ 8.30pm Wed & Thu Jul-Aug) Irish dancing is given a contemporary twist by dancers and musicians who clearly enjoy the frenetic shows as much as the audience does. Tickets are available at the Mall Arts Centre or the Youghal Visitor Centre.

For an end-of-day pint and traditional live music, nowhere beats **Treacy's** (aka the Nook; 20 North Main St), Youghal's oldest boozer.

Getting There & Around

Bus Éireann (☎ 450 8188; www.buseireann.ie) run frequent services to Cork (€8.80, 50 minutes, 14 daily) and Waterford (€13, 1½ hours, 11 daily).

Streetside disc parking costs €0.60 per hour, but some of the car parks are free.

COUNTY CORK

WESTERN CORK

KINSALE

☎ 021 / pop 4100

Kinsale (Cionn tSáile) bursts with life and colour. Narrow winding streets, tiny houses and bobbing fishing boats and yachts give it a seductive picture-postcard feel. Its sheltered bay is guarded by a huge and startling fort, just outside the town at Summercove.

Blessed by media visits from personalities such as Keith Floyd and Rick Stein, Kinsale has been labelled the gourmet centre of Ireland and, for such a small place, it certainly contains far more than its fair share of international-standard restaurants.

Kinsale also attracts arty types and there are lots of crafty galleries and shops for treats and trinkets.

History

In September 1601 a Spanish fleet anchored at Kinsale was besieged by the English. An Irish army from the north, which had appealed to the Spanish king to help it against the English, marched the length of the country to liberate the ships, but was defeated in battle outside the town on Christmas Eve. For the Catholics, the immediate consequence was that they were banned from Kinsale; it would be another 100 years before they were allowed back in. Historians now cite 1601 as the beginning of the end of Gaelic Ireland.

After 1601 the town developed as a shipbuilding port. In the early 18th century, Alexander Selkirk left Kinsale Harbour on a voyage that left him stranded on a desert island, providing Daniel Defoe with the idea for *Robinson Crusoe*.

Orientation

Most of Kinsale's hotels and restaurants are situated near the harbour and within easy walking distance of the town centre, but there are a couple of restaurants out at Scilly, a peninsula to the southeast. A path continues from there to Summercove and Charles Fort.

Information

There's a post office and an Allied Irish Bank with ATM on Pearse St. Toilets are next to the tourist office. For online information, check out www.kinsale.ie.

Bookstór (☎ 477 4946; www.bookstor.ie; 1 Newman's Mall) Has all you need for a good read.

Elasnik Web Café (☎ 477 7356; Market Sq; per 30/60min €2.50/5; ☒ 10am-10pm) Free coffee thrown in with the hourly rate.

Market Street Drycleaning & Laundrette (☎ 477 2875; Market St; ☒ 9am-6pm Mon-Fri)

Tourist office (☎ 477 2234; kinsaletio@eircom.net; cnr Pier Rd & Emmet Pl; ☒ 9.30am-1pm & 2.15-5.30pm Mon-Sat Mar-Oct, daily Jul-Aug) Opening hours are flexible, especially in the quieter months. Has a free map detailing walks in and around Kinsale.

Sights

A sweet little **museum** (☎ 477 7930; Market Sq; adult/concession €2.50/1.50; ☒ 10am-5pm Mon-Sat, 2-5pm Sun) is based in the 17th-century courthouse that was used for the inquest into the sinking of the *Lusitania* in 1915. The museum contains information on the disaster, as well as curiosities as diverse as Michael Collins' hurley stick and shoes belonging to the eight-foot-tall Kinsale Giant.

In Summercove, 3km east of Kinsale, stand the huge ruins of 17th-century **Charles Fort** (☎ 477 2263; adult/child €3.70/1.30; ☒ 10am-6pm mid-Mar-Oct, 10am-5pm Nov–mid-Mar, last admission 45min before closing). This is one of the best-preserved 17th-century star-shaped forts in Europe, and is worth a visit for its spectacular views alone. It was built in the 1670s to guard Kinsale Harbour and remained in use until 1921, when much of the fort was destroyed as the British withdrew. Most of the ruins you see inside date from the 18th and 19th centuries. The best way to get here is to walk – follow the signs around the bay from Scilly.

An early-16th-century **tower house** (☎ 477 4855; www.winegeese.ie; Cork St; adult/child €2.90/1.20; ☒ 10am-6pm Tue-Sun Easter-end Oct, last admission 45min before closing) was occupied by the Spanish in 1601. Since then it has served as a custom house, as a prison for French and American captives and as a workhouse during the Famine. There are lively exhibits detailing its history and a small **wine museum** relating the story of the Irish wine trade.

St Multose is the patron saint of Kinsale, and the Church of Ireland **church** (rectory ☎ 477 2220; Church St) is one of Ireland's oldest, built around 1190 by the Normans on the site of a 6th-century church. Not much of the interior

KINSALE

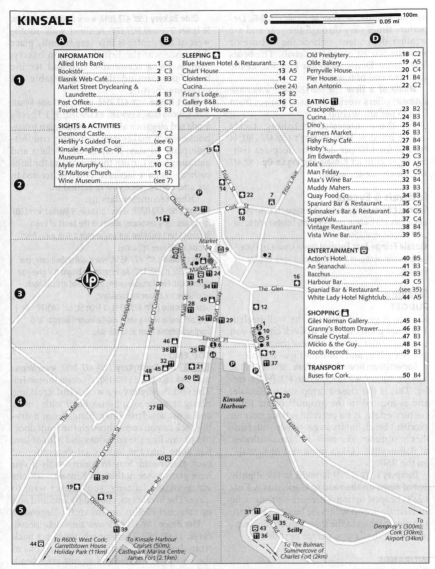

0   100m
0   0.05 mi

INFORMATION
Allied Irish Bank.................................1 C3
Bookstór..2 C3
Elasnik Web Café..............................3 B3
Market Street Drycleaning &
  Laundrette.......................................4 B3
Post Office...5 C3
Tourist Office....................................6 B3

SIGHTS & ACTIVITIES
Desmond Castle................................7 C2
Herlihy's Guided Tour................(see 6)
Kinsale Angling Co-op.......................8 C3
Museum...9 C3
Mylie Murphy's...............................10 C3
St Multose Church...........................11 B2
Wine Museum.............................(see 7)

SLEEPING
Blue Haven Hotel & Restaurant......12 C3
Chart House.....................................13 A5
Cloisters..14 C2
Cucina..(see 24)
Friar's Lodge...................................15 B2
Gallery B&B....................................16 C3
Old Bank House..............................17 C4

Old Presbytery................................18 C2
Olde Bakery....................................19 A5
Perryville House..............................20 C4
Pier House.......................................21 B4
San Antonio....................................22 C2

EATING
Crackpots.......................................23 B2
Cucina...24 B3
Dino's..25 B4
Farmers Market...............................26 B3
Fishy Fishy Café..............................27 B3
Hoby's...28 B3
Jim Edwards....................................29 C3
Jola's...30 A5
Man Friday......................................31 C5
Max's Wine Bar...............................32 B3
Muddy Mahers.................................33 B3
Quay Food Co..................................34 B3
Spaniard Bar & Restaurant..............35 C5
Spinnaker's Bar & Restaurant..........36 C5
SuperValu..37 C4
Vintage Restaurant.........................38 B4
Vista Wine Bar................................39 B5

ENTERTAINMENT
Acton's Hotel..................................40 B5
An Seanachai..................................41 B3
Bacchus...42 B3
Harbour Bar.....................................43 C5
Spaniad Bar & Restaurant........(see 35)
White Lady Hotel Nightclub............44 A5

SHOPPING
Giles Norman Gallery......................45 B4
Granny's Bottom Drawer.................46 B3
Kinsale Crystal.................................47 B3
Mickio & the Guy............................48 B4
Roots Records.................................49 B3

TRANSPORT
Buses for Cork.................................50 B4

COUNTY CORK

is original but the exterior is preserved beautifully. The graveyard has some interesting large family tombs, and several victims of the *Lusitania* sinking are also buried there. Inside, a flat stone carved with a round-handed figure was traditionally rubbed by fishermen's wives to bring their husbands home safe from the sea.

Activities

An entertaining stroll through the town's history, **Herlihy's Guided Tour** (☎ 477 2873; adult/child €7/1; ⏰ 11.15am daily plus 9.15am summer) leaves from the tourist office.

For sailings to Charles Fort, James Cove and up the Bandon River you can phone **Kinsale Harbour Cruises** (☎ 477 8946, 086-250 5456;

www.kinsaleharbourcruises.com; adult/child €12.50/6). Departure times vary through the year and are weather dependent – check the website or with the tourist office for details. The boats leave from Denis Quay on Pier Rd, at the southern end of town.

Whale of a Time (☎ 087-120 3463; www.whaleofatime.ie) offers weekend coastal cruises from €20/15 per adult/child.

For those interested in fishing, tackle can be hired at **Mylie Murphy's** (☎ 477 2703; 14 Pearse St) for €10 per day. For deep-sea fishing trips, contact **Kinsale Angling Co-Op** (☎ 477 4946; www.kinsale-angling.com).

Festivals & Events

Gourmet Festival (www.kinsalerestaurants.com) Tastings, meals and harbour cruises in early October add to the town's foodie reputation.

Kinsale Fringe Jazz Festival (www.kinsale.ie) Chilled-out entertainment over the late-October bank-holiday weekend.

Sleeping

BUDGET

Kinsale is geared towards the well-heeled. There are good bus links to Cork city, so you might consider staying in one of the city's hostels (see p206) and commuting to Kinsale.

Garrettstown House Holiday Park (☎ /fax 477 8156; www.garrettstownhouse.com; camp sites €13; ✆ Apr–mid-Sep) This is the closest camp site to Kinsale, and is located in the grounds of an 18th-century estate. It's a peaceful setting near an excellent beach but it can get rowdy with families in summer. The park is 1.3km southwest of Ballinspittle (11km southwest of Kinsale) on the R600.

Dempsey's (☎ 772 124; Eastern Rd; dm €15) Slightly out of town on the road to Cork, this is Kinsale's cheapest option. There are separate male and female dorms with wide bunks, a kitchen, and picnic tables in the front garden. Buy supplies from the Texaco garage next door.

MIDRANGE

Cloisters (☎ 470 0680; www.cloisterskinsale.com; Friar St; s €70, d €80-90) Little touches make the difference at this delightful B&B near Desmond Castle. A smiling welcome and chocolates await your arrival and the orthopaedic mattresses are so comfy only the cooked breakfasts will tempt you out of bed. Room 5, with its striking black and white scheme, is our top choice though all the rooms have smart décor.

Olde Bakery (☎ 477 3012; www.theoldebakery.com; 56 Lower O'Connell St; r €80) A short walk southwest of the centre is this very friendly place that once was the British garrison bakery. Rooms are a reasonable size and terrific breakfasts around the kitchen table get everyone chatting.

Chart House (☎ 477 4568; www.charthouse-kinsale.com; 6 Dennis Quay; s €80-130, d €120-170; **P**) There's a relaxed elegance about this Georgian townhouse which makes it an incredibly comfortable place to stay. Drapes, chandeliers and antique pieces furnish the rooms and the large bathrooms have Jacuzzis. You'll be treated to tea and coffee once you're settled in.

Other recommendations:

Cucina (☎ 470 0707; www.cucina.ie; 9 Market St; r €80) Fresh, neutrally decorated rooms in the heart of town. Breakfast isn't included but you're only a skip away from Cucina's café (see opposite).

Gallery B&B (☎ 477 4558; www.gallerybnb.com; the Glen; s €55, d €90-110) An exterior so bright it'll give you concussion. Comfortable rooms inside and artistic hosts who serve ice cream for breakfast.

San Antonio (☎ 477 2341; 1 Friar St; s/d €40/70; **P**) Fine old house with a cosy, old-fashioned interior and landlord Jimmie is an absolute star.

TOP END

ourpick **Old Presbytery** (☎ 477 2027; www.oldpres.com; Cork St; s €90, d €100-160; ✆ closed Jan–mid-Feb) The Old Presbytery is a wonderful, creaking, tilting treasure of a house filled with curios and antiques. Irish linen hangs from a drying rack as you come through the front door, old prams line the corridors and a lot of love has gone into the individual decoration of each guestroom. Stay in room 6 only if you have plans to see nothing of Kinsale – with its sunroom and balcony, you'll never want to leave. The breakfasts, cooked by landlord and former chef Phillip, are the stuff of legend.

Pier House (☎ 477 4475; www.pierhousekinsale.com; Pier Rd; r €120-140) This superb B&B, set back from the road in a sheltered garden, is one of the best places in Ireland to rest your feet. Pristine rooms, decorated with shell-and-driftwood sculptures, have black-granite bathrooms attached with power showers, underfloor heating and special non-misting mirrors! Four of the rooms also have balconies and sea views. The whole place is wonderfully decorated and equipped, with bold artworks, modern furniture, a hot tub, sauna and barbecue.

Old Bank House (☎ 477 4075; www.oldbankhouse kinsale.com; 11 Pearse St; standard r €120-170, deluxe €160-230) Georgian elegance and style give a timeless quality to this top-of-the-range hotel. Beautiful *objets d'art* and paintings grace the walls, and the luxurious public rooms add a country-house ambience. The owners are lovely, and breakfasts, with homemade breads and jams, are superb.

Perryville House (☎ 477 2731; www.perryvillehouse .com; Long Quay; s €150, d €200-380; P) It's top to bottom grandeur at family-run Perryville, whether you're pulling up outside its imposing wrought-iron-clad façade or taking afternoon tea in the drawing room. There are nice touches throughout, with fresh flowers, antiques and dressing gowns in all the rooms. The more expensive suites have king-sized four-poster beds, sea views and the biggest bathrooms we've ever seen. Cooked breakfast is extra (€12).

Also recommended:

Blue Haven Hotel & Restaurant (☎ 477 2209; www .bluehavenkinsale.com; 3 Pearse St; €140-230) Boutique hotel with lavishly comfortable rooms and incredibly accommodating service. Off-season deals make it a real winner.

Friar's Lodge (☎ 477 7384; www.friars-lodge.com; Friar St; r from €150) A guestbook full of praise attests to the bliss to be had here, from the decanter of sherry waiting in reception to warm squishy rooms.

Eating

Kinsale fully deserves its billing as the gourmet capital of the west and you can eat wonderfully on every budget. The town's busy fleet of fishing vessels ensures that the town's restaurants have a particularly high reputation for seafood. There's a weekly **farmers market** (9.30am-1.30pm Tue) in front of Jim Edwards' restaurant.

BUDGET

Cucina (☎ 470 0707; www.cucina.ie; 9 Market St; meals €4-14; ☯ 9am-5pm Mon-Sat, last orders 4pm) To a laidback soundtrack of electro-lounge, welcoming Cucina serves up healthy wraps, salads and soups in a bright, Mediterranean-feel dining room. An inventive brunch menu is served until 11.30am.

Vista Wine Bar (☎ 470 6866; Shearwater, Pier Rd; lunch €4-14, tapas €5-9) This shiny modern bar has spectacular views over the marina, and voyeurs will enjoy spying on the sun-kissed sailors pottering about on their boats beneath the balcony. Come for quiches and the baking at lunch, tapas in the evening (from 6pm) and wine and coffee any time of day.

Dino's (☎ 477 4561; Pier Rd; mains €9-12; ☯ 8am-10.30pm) This nautically themed chipper and family restaurant is Kinsale's most convenient cheap fuel stop. Besides fish and chips, Dino's does breakfasts (€6.50) and an all-day four-courser (€21.95).

Spaniard Bar & Restaurant (☎ 477 2436; www .thespaniard.ie; Scilly) This is a good old seafarers bar on Scilly, with low ceilings and a peat fire, so why not crack some crab claws or settle for a sandwich at the bar. Meals at the bar are between €6 and €17.50 (with prices for most dishes around €10). There's a pricier restaurant upstairs; mains are between €17.50 and €22. Wednesday is trad music night and there are other impromptu sessions throughout the year.

Muddy Mahers (☎ 477 4602; www.muddymaher.com; 1 Main St; mains €10-22; ☯ noon-3pm & 6-9.30pm Mon-Fri, noon-9.30pm Sat & Sun) The big bar meals here are good and tasty. The menu includes plenty of meat dishes, veggie options, a great ocean chowder (€6), an even better fish pie (€10.50) and well-filled sandwiches, including the Holy Cow! steak special (€9).

Kinsale has a **SuperValu** (Pearse St; ☯ 8.30am-9pm Mon-Sat, 10am-9pm Sun) and the tremendous **Quay Food Co** (☎ 477 4000; www.quayfood.com; Market Quay; sandwiches €3.75; ☯ 9am-6pm Apr-Sep, 9.30am-5.30pm Mon-Sat) for local produce and little luxuries.

MIDRANGE

our pick Fishy Fishy Cafe (☎ 470 0415; Crowley's Quay; mains €13-33; ☯ noon-4pm Mon-Fri, noon-4.30pm Sat & Sun) Fishy Fishy was voted Seafood Restaurant of the Year 2007 by the Georgina Campbell food guides. The setting is beautifully understated, with stark white walls splashed with bright artwork and a terrific decked terrace at the front. All the fish is caught locally, from the fried haddock in Kinsale beer to the best oak-smoked salmon we've ever tasted. Plump for the Fishy Fishy Pie (€19.50), chock-full of salmon and seafood, if you want to try a little bit of everything.

Jim Edwards (☎ 477 2541; www.jimedwardskinsale .com; Market Quay; bar meals €7-19, restaurant meals €15-30; ☯ bar 12.30-10pm, restaurant 6-10pm) Like many places in Kinsale, this much-frequented eatery has bar food of a restaurant standard. A steady Irish touch is nicely frothed with European influences. In the bar you may need to fight for

COUNTY CORK

attention amid the clamour, but once served you'll want to stay all night. The restaurant specialises in steaks and fish, and does an excellent seafood platter for €29.90.

Bulman (☎ 477 2131; www.thebulman.com; Summercove; mains €16-21; ☺ 12.30-9.30pm) This is seaside eating at its best. The Bulman is an escape from central Kinsale to an unspoilt harbourside venue where salty informality is a style in its own right. Seafood excels here, with chowder or salmon cakes for lunch and dinners that add adventurous New World touches to sea bream and tiger prawns, among many choices.

Also recommended:

Crackpots (☎ 477 2847; crackpots@iol.ie; Cork St; mains €17-26; ☺ from 6pm Wed-Sat) A 'ceramic restaurant' serving an international menu on crockery made in the on-site pottery. A three-course set menu is available between 6pm and 7pm for €25.

Spinnakers Bar & Restaurant (☎ 477 2098; www .kinsalerestaurants.com; Scilly; mains €14-25) A bright, jaunty pub on the water, serving local seafood, fish and steak.

TOP END

Vintage Restaurant (☎ 477 2502; www.vintagerestaurant .ie; 50 Main St; mains €18-24; ☺ 6-10pm Tue-Sun, closed Jan) The décor may be a little fusty these days but the Vintage is one of the reasons that Kinsale deserves its gourmet label, with prices that are truly justifiable. Unbeatable dishes range from oyster starters to mains of lobster in brandy or sea bass in white port crème; fish that demand a magic touch – and get it.

Hoby's (☎ 477 2200; 5 Main St; mains €18-25; ☺ 6-10.30pm) More excellent Irish-European cuisine is served at this swish place. Subtle colours, thoughtful seating, candlelight and friendly service make you feel that it's all just for you. A three-course set menu is available for €27.50.

our pick Jola's (☎ 477 3322 www.jolasrestaurant .com; 18-19 Lower O'Connell St; lunch €6-10, dinner €20-25; ☺ noon-3.30pm & 6pm-late, café open all day) With its double-height ceilings, exposed brick walls, stunning chandelier and warm brown tones, Jola's brings a dash of metropolitan style to Kinsale. The food is equally adept, confidently marrying Eastern European and Irish cuisine. The blinis are our favourite but nothing on the menu will disappoint you, from the veal with horseradish mash to the lamb shank with *boczek* (Polish pork belly). A three-course set menu costs €25.95 between 6pm and 7pm.

Man Friday (☎ 477 2260; www.man-friday.net; cnr River & High Rds, Scilly; mains €21-30; ☺ 6.30-10.15pm) Out of town, at relaxing Scilly, this 30-year-old restaurant has outdoor seating with views across the harbour to Kinsale. Book if you want a terrace table on balmy evenings. While excellent fish dishes are the norm, there are also great steak, lamb, duck and vegetarian options.

Max's Wine Bar (☎ 477 2443; 48 Main St) This local favourite was closed for renovation at the time of writing, but should be open by the time you're in town. Expect Irish-French crossover in both surroundings and cuisine.

DETOUR: KINSALE & CLONAKILTY

Along the coastal road between Kinsale and Clonakilty are three magnificent restaurants. If you're remotely interested in good Irish food, plan to make a detour.

Dillons (☎ 023-46390; Timoleague; mains €18-24, no credit cards; ☺ Thu-Sun dinner) Bright, inviting Dillons serves interesting variations on Irish staples in its bistro-style dining room. The emphasis is on meat (for example, Skeaglianore duck breast or roast quail) but there are interesting fish and veggie options too, such as tomato and goat's cheese bread pudding. No credit cards accepted.

Casino House (☎ 023-49944; Kilbrittain; mains €19-27; ☺ Thu-Mon dinner, closed Jan–mid-Mar) A bright, simply decorated farmhouse overlooking a sparkling bay is the perfect setting for the modern Irish cuisine of Casino House. Local produce is used in every dish; depending on the season, you might expect to see Ummera salmon, Ballydehob duck or Kilbrittain lamb on the menu.

Otto's Creative Cooking (☎ 023-40461; www.ottoscreativecatering.com; Dunworley, near Butlerstown, near Bandon; ☺ lunch Sun, dinner Wed-Sat, closed Jan & Feb) You have to book at this remote spot at a stunning location near Butlerstown. There's plenty of choice on the set menus, with all the produce locally sourced and much of it organic and coming from Otto's itself. A four-course lunch is available for €35, a five-course dinner for €55. Why not make a night of it and stay in one of the individually decorated guestrooms (€110/130 for a single/double) reserved for diners?

COUNTY CORK

Drinking & Entertainment

our pick **Harbour Bar** (☎ 477 2528; Scilly; ⏱ from 6pm) Romping home in Kinsale's 'most unusual bar' stakes, this is a little gem of a place. It's so much like being in someone's front room that you forget you're in a bar at all. Landlord Tim presides over the battered old sofas and small brick bar, shares stories and keeps the fire stoked in the hearth. Wonderfully bonkers.

Spaniard Bar & Restaurant (☎ 477 2436; www .thespaniard.ie; Scilly) There are stomping trad sessions in the lounge bar every night except Tuesday and Thursday.

Acton's Hotel (☎ 477 2135; www.actonshotelkinsale .com; Pier Rd) Stages a terrific Sunday lunchtime jazz session in its Waterfront bar, featuring the famous Cork City Jazz Band.

An Seanachai (☎ 477 7077; 6 Market St) This cavernous barnlike pub has trad music sessions every night Friday to Monday.

Bacchus (☎ 477 2382; www.bacchuskinsale.com; Main St; ⏱ 11pm-2.30am Thu-Sat) This nightclub has a breezy, youngish crowd at weekends, with live bands on Fridays.

Shopping

Giles Norman Gallery (☎ 477 4373; 45 Main St) There's a big selection of evocative black-and-white imagery of Ireland here, from a master of the genre. Prints start at €30/45 (unframed/ framed).

Granny's Bottom Drawer (☎ 477 4839; 53 Main St) A great range of exquisite Irish linen, damask and vintage-style homeware is sold at this cheerful shop.

Kinsale Crystal (☎ 477 4493; Market St) Sells exquisite work by an ex-Waterford craftsman who stands by the traditional 'deepcutting, high-angle style'. A wine glass will set you back €60, while large pieces are in the hundreds.

Mickio & the Guy (☎ 470 0921; www.mickioandthe guy.ie; 38 Main St) Traditional toys and cool clobber keep kids happy and stylish at this classy emporium.

Roots Records (☎ 477 4963; www.rootsrecords.ie; 1 Short Quay) This useful music shop has absolutely everything from trad to reggae.

Getting There & Away

Bus Éireann (☎ 450 8188) services connect Kinsale with Cork (€5.90, 50 minutes, 14 daily Monday to Friday, 11 Saturday and five Sunday). The bus stops at the Esso garage on Pier Rd, near the tourist office.

Getting Around

You can hire bikes from **Mylie Murphy's** (☎ 477 2703; 14 Pearse St; per day €10). For a taxi call **Kinsale Cabs** (☎ 477 2642).

CLONAKILTY

☎ 023 / pop 4150

Cheerful, brightly coloured Clonakilty is a bustling market town that knows how to look after its visitors. You'll find smart B&Bs, top restaurants and cosy pubs alive with great music.

Clonakilty is famous for two important Cork products. Firstly, it was the birthplace of Michael Collins (see boxed text, p224), a matter of extreme pride to the community; a statue of the Big Fella stands on the corner of Emmet Sq. Secondly, it's the source of the best black pudding in Ireland. It features on many local restaurant menus and you can buy varieties based on 19th-century recipes from **Edward Twomey** (☎ 33733; www.clonakiltyblack pudding.ie; 16 Pearse St; puddings from €2.50).

History

Clonakilty received its first charter in 1292 but was re-founded in the early 17th century by Richard Boyle, the first earl of Cork. He settled it with 100 English families and planned a Protestant town from which Catholics would be excluded. His plan ultimately failed: Clonakilty is now very Irish and very Catholic – the Presbyterian chapel has been turned into a post office.

From the mid-18th to mid-19th centuries more than 10,000 people worked in the town's linen industry. The fire station stands on the site of the old linen market.

Orientation

Roads converge on Asna Sq, dominated by a monument commemorating the 1798 Rising. Also in the square is the Kilty Stone, a piece of the original castle that gave Clonakilty (Clogh na Kylte, meaning 'castle of the woods') its name.

Information

The **Allied Irish Bank** (cnr Pearse & Bridge Sts) has an ATM. The post office is in the old Presbyterian chapel on Bridge St.

There are public toilets on the corner of Connolly and Kent Sts.

Fast.Net (☎ 34545; 32 Pearse St; per hr €5; ⏱ 9am-6pm Mon-Fri, 10am-5pm Sat) Internet access.

MICHAEL COLLINS – THE 'BIG FELLA'

County Cork, and especially the Clonakilty area, has a deeply cherished association with Michael Collins, the 'Big Fella', commander-in-chief of the army of the Irish Free State, which won independence from Britain in 1922.

Collins was born on a small farm at Woodfield near Clonakilty as the youngest of eight children, and went to school in the town. He lived and worked in London from 1906 to 1916, returning to Ireland to take part in the Easter Rising after which he became a key figure in Irish Nationalism. He revolutionised the way the Irish rebels fought, organising them into guerrilla-style 'flying columns', and was the main negotiator of the 1921 Anglo–Irish Treaty that led to the Irish Free State. The mixed reaction to the treaty, with many thinking Ireland had made too many concessions to the British, plunged the country into a brutal civil war.

On a tour of western Cork, Michael Collins was ambushed and killed by antitreaty forces on 22 August 1922 at Beal-na-Bláth, near Macroom. Each year, a commemorative service is held on the anniversary of the killing. To visit the site, follow the N22 west from Cork for about 20km, then take the left turn (R590) to Crookstown. From there turn right onto the R585 to Beal-na-Bláth. The ambush site is on the left after 4km.

A useful map and leaflet *In Search of Michael Collins* (€4) is available at the Clonakilty tourist office, outlining places in the district associated with him. A visit to the **Michael Collins Centre** (☎ 023-46107; www.michaelcollinscentre.com; adult/child 10-16 €5/3; ☻ 10.30am-5pm Mon-Fri, 11am-2pm Sat mid-Jun–Sep) is an excellent way to make sense of his life and that period of Ireland's history. A tour reveals photos, letters and a reconstruction of the 1920s country lane where Collins was killed, complete with armoured vehicle. The centre also runs car tours of the crucial locations in Collins' life (€70, 3½ hours). It's signposted off the R600 between Timoleague and Clonakilty.

The **Clonakilty Museum** (Western Rd; admission €3; ☻ Jun-Sep) has some more memorabilia, including Collins' weapons and uniform. The museum is run on a voluntary basis: contact the tourist office for exact opening hours.

Kerr's Bookshop (☎ 34342; www.kerr.ie; 18 Ashe St) Sells fiction and guidebooks.

Library (Old Mill Library; ☎ 34275; Kent St; ☻ 10am-6pm Tue-Sat) For a €2.50 membership you can use the computers for free.

Tourist office (☎ 33226; info@corkkerrytourism.ie; Ashe St; ☻ 9.30am-5.30pm Mon-Sat Sep-Jun, 9am-7pm Mon-Sat & 10am-5pm Sun Jul-Aug) Has a good, free map.

Wash Basket (☎ 34821; Spiller's Lane; ☻ 9am-6pm Mon-Sat) Has a same-day laundry service (€8-10).

Sights & Activities

Of the more than 30,000 ring forts scattered across Ireland, **Lisnagun** (Lios na gCon; ☎ 32565; www .liosnagcon.com; adult/child €5/3; ☻ noon-4pm) is the only one that's been reconstructed on its original site. Complete with souterrain and central thatched hut, it gives a vivid impression of life in a 10th-century farmstead. To get there, take the turning on the roundabout at the end of Strand Rd, signposted to Bay View House B&B. Follow the road uphill to the T-junction, turn right, then continue for about 800m before turning right again (signposted).

Nostalgia buffs and kids will love **West Cork Model Railway Village** (☎ 33224; www.modelvillage.ie; Inchydoney Rd; adult/child €7/4.25; ☻ 11am-5pm Sep-Jun, 10am-5pm Jul-Aug). It features a working replica of the West Cork Railway as it was during WWII, and superb miniature models of the main towns in western Cork c 1940. A **road train** (adult/child incl admission to Railway Village €11/6.25; ☻ daily summer, weekends winter) leaves from the Railway Village on a 20-minute commentated circuit of Clonakilty.

The bay is good for **swimming**, albeit in a bracing sort of way. The sandy Blue Flag **beach** at Inchydoney Island, 4km from town, is good too, but watch out for the dangerous riptide; when lifeguards are on duty a red flag indicates danger. The **West Cork Surf School** (☎ 086-869 5396; www.westcorksurfing.com) is based there, should you fancy a ride on the waves. A two-hour lesson will set you back €35.

Sleeping

The town's hostel had shut at the time of writing; check with the tourist office to see if another has opened in its place.

COUNTY CORK

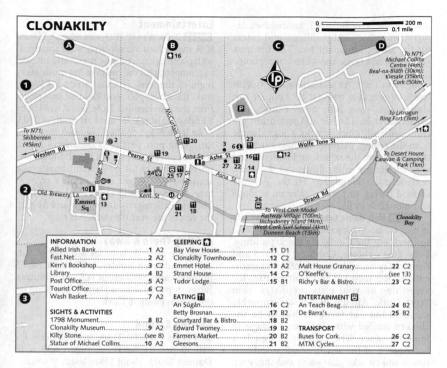

Desert House Caravan & Camping Park (☎ 33331; deserthouse@eircom.net; Coast Rd; camp site €10, r per person €35; ☯ Easter & May-Sep) This attractive park, 1.5km southeast of town on the road to Ring, is on a dairy farm overlooking the bay. B&B rooms inside are an orgy of patterned carpets and floral wallpaper.

Tudor Lodge (☎ 33046; www.tudorlodgecork.com; McCurtain Hill; s €40-45, d €60-70) Very much *not* a Tudor Lodge, this modern family home sits pleasantly above it all a short walk from the town centre. Standards are kept up to scratch in impeccably smart, peaceful rooms.

Bay View House (☎ 33539; www.bayviewclonakilty .com; Old Timoleague Rd; s €40-70, d €80) This frothy pink house offers immaculate B&B standards, a genial welcome and great breakfasts. Rooms 5 and 6, and the cosy landing lounge, offer fantastic views over the fields that slope down to Clonakilty Bay. There's also a 'garden suite', with private conservatory.

Strand House (☎ 34719; www.ansugan.com; Sand Quay; s/d €45/70) There are few frills at this B&B but you do get a relaxed atmosphere and enormous rooms in a great location a couple of doors down from An Súgán restaurant.

Clonakilty Townhouse (☎ 35533; www.clonakilty townhouse.com; Wolfe Tone St; s/d €60/110; ♿) There's a buzzing atmosphere at this large purpose-built B&B in the centre of town. Spic-and-span rooms are simply decorated, with snow-white duvets and sparkling bathrooms, and the service is unfailingly friendly.

Emmet Hotel (☎ 33394; www.emmethotel.com; Emmet Sq; s/d €65/120) This lovely Georgian accommodation option on the square happily mixes period charm and old-world service with the perks of a modern hotel. Rooms are large and simple, with a relaxing ambience, and O'Keeffe's Restaurant serves up tasty Irish food made from organic and local ingredients.

Eating

Self-caterers should pay a visit to the twice-weekly **farmers market** (McCurtain Hill; ☯ 10am-2pm Thu & Sat).

Betty Brosnan (☎ 34011; 58 Pearse St; meals €4-13; ☯ 9am-5pm Mon, Tue, Thu-Sat, 9am-2.30pm Wed) A prime place for affordable yet satisfying snacks, this busy café offers lots of breakfast choices (including a 14-inch cooked

Irish for the 'very hungry'), sandwiches, lasagne, smoothies and puddings, and caters for the gluten-intolerant too. The upstairs gallery displays black-and-white travel photography.

An Súgán (☎ 33719; www.ansugan.com; 41 Wolfe Tone St; bar meals €4-30, mains €13-25) Another top choice, this snug little oasis exudes idiosyncratic style. The bar and restaurant are crammed with knick-knacks – jugs dangle from the ceiling, patrons' business cards are stuffed beneath the rafters, and lanterns and even ancient fire extinguishers dot the walls. Seafood is the thing here – try the 'Atlantic seafood basket' of prawns, salmon, scallops and monkfish in filo pastry.

ourpick Malt House Granary (☎ 34355; 30 Ashe St; mains €18-25; ☽ 5-10pm Mon-Sat) You'll be able to check out the Clonakilty black pudding, Boile goat's cheese, Gubbeen chorizo and Bantry Bay mussels among other ingredients on the menu at the Malt House, for everything on your plate originates from West Cork. All the dishes are superbly executed but our favourite has to be the chicken stuffed with Gubbeen sausage in Jameson sauce. The interior design is a hotchpotch of the stylish (dark wood furniture and chunky glassware) and the, erm, not (what's with this fairy pouring water into oyster shells?) but such quirks make us love it even more.

Gleesons (☎ 21834; www.gleesons.ie; 3-4 Connolly St; dinner €19-29; ☽ 6.30-9.30pm Mon-Fri, 6-10pm Sat) Considered by many to be Clonakilty's best restaurant, Gleesons gets one rave review after another. The surrounds are nicely understated, with wood and a slate décor, and the international menu is simple but perfectly prepared, using organic, fair-trade and local seasonal food. The seafood is particularly tasty but for something that'll really stick to your ribs, how about fillet of Irish beef with wild mushrooms? For €35 you can indulge in the three-course set menu.

Also recommended:

Courtyard Bar & Bistro (☎ 35802; 3-4 Harte's Courtyard; mains €4-9) Huge sandwiches, quiches and burgers served all day. There's also a lovely riverside terrace.

Richy's Bar & Bistro (☎ 21852; www.richysbarand bistro.com; Wolfe Tone St; lunch €8-16, dinner €14-30) And now for something completely different – a modern bistro serving 'West Cork fusion' (eg sushi with black pudding).

Entertainment

ourpick De Barra's (☎ 33381; www.debarra.ie; 55 Pearse St) A marvellous atmosphere, walls splattered with photos, press cuttings, masks and musical instruments, plus the cream of live music every night of the week (starting around 9.30pm) make this a busy pub. Noel Redding, bass player from the Jimi Hendrix Experience, used to be a Friday-night regular until his death in 2003.

An Teach Beag (☎ 33883; 5 Recorder's Alley) This intriguing pub, part of O'Donovan's Hotel, is not as old as it looks, but has all the atmosphere necessary for good traditional music sessions. You might even catch a *scríocht* (a session by storytellers and poets) in full flow. There's music nightly during July and August; the rest of the year it's weekends only.

Getting There & Away

There are eight daily buses Monday to Saturday, and seven Sunday, to Cork (€6.80, 65 minutes) and Skibbereen (€7, 40 minutes). Buses stop across from Harte's Spar shop on the bypass going to Cork.

Getting Around

MTM Cycles (☎ 33584; 33 Ashe St) hires bikes for €10/50 per day/week. A nice cycle is to Duneen Beach, about 13km south of town.

CLONAKILTY TO SKIBBEREEN

Picturesque villages, a fine stone circle and calming coastal scenery mark the lesser-taken route from Clonakilty to Skibbereen. Rather than follow the main N71 all the way, when you get to Rosscarbery turn left onto the R597 at the far end of the causeway (signposted Glandore).

Drombeg Stone Circle

On an exposed hillside, with fields sweeping away towards the coast, the Drombeg stone circle is superbly atmospheric. Its 17 uprights once guarded the cremated bones of an adolescent, discovered during a 1960s excavation. The 9m-diameter circle probably dates from the 5th century AD, representing a sophisticated Iron Age update of an earlier Bronze Age monument.

Just beyond the stones are the remains of a hut and an Iron Age cooking pit, known as a *fulachta fiadh*. Experiments have shown that its heated rocks would boil water and keep it hot for nearly three hours – enough time to cook hunks of meat.

To get there take the signposted left turn off the R597, approximately 4km west of Roscarberry.

Glandore & Union Hall

☎ 028 / pop 250

The pretty waterside villages of Glandore (Cuan Dor) and Union Hall burst into life in summer when fleets of yachts tack into the shelter of the Glandore Harbour inlet.

Union Hall, accessible from Glandore via a narrow road bridge over the estuary, was named after the 1800 Act of Union, which abolished the separate Irish parliament. The lovely 1994 family film *War of the Buttons*, about two battling gangs of youngsters, was filmed here.

There's an ATM, post office and general store in Union Hall and there's food available in both villages. Union Hall has the most choice, with a deli, coffee shop and several pubs, two of which have fantastic waterside terraces.

SIGHTS & ACTIVITIES

Delightful Theresa O'Mahoney runs the **Ceim Hill Museum** (☎ 36280; adult/child €4/2; ◷ 10am-7pm) from her farmhouse off Castletownshend Rd. The small collection of Iron Age bits and bobs is well worth a glance if you're passing.

You can splash round the coast with **Atlantic Sea Kayaking** (☎ 21058; www.atlanticseakayaking .com; Union Hall; 3hr trip €50; ◷ year-round). The night paddles beneath the stars (€45, 2½ hours) are particularly popular.

Colin Barnes runs four-hour **dolphin- and whale-watching cruises** (☎ 086-327 3226; www .whales-dolphins-ireland.com; adult/child €40/30) and shorter coastal trips from Reen Pier, about 3km beyond Union Hall.

SLEEPING

Meadow Camping Park (☎ 33280; meadowcamping@ eircom.net; Rosscarbery road, Glandore; camp sites €17; ◷ Easter & May–mid-Sep) This small idyllic site, in a garden filled with trees and flowers, is 2km east of Glandore on the R597 to Rosscarbery.

Ardagh House (☎ 33571; www.ardaghhouse.com; Union Hall; s/d €40/70; P 🖳) You're soon made to feel part of the family at this restored farmhouse by the harbour. The rooms, many with sea views, are bright and sunny, and there's a garden to lounge in too. The house itself is a bit of a star, having made an appearance in the 1994 flick *War of the Buttons*.

Bay View House (☎ 33115; Glandore; s/d €45/70) This is a place with a rather modest name: Bay View House has *spectacular* views across the bay. Try and snag room 1 for the most jaw-dropping view of all. Bright citrus colours, wood-block flooring, tidy pine furniture and gleaming bathrooms add to the appeal.

GETTING THERE & AWAY

Buses stop in nearby Leap (3km north) where most B&B owners will pick you up if you arrange it in advance.

Castletownshend

☎ 028 / pop 160

With its grand houses and higgledy-piggledy cottages dating back to the 17th and 18th centuries tumbling down the precipitously steep main street, Castletownshend is one of Ireland's most curious villages. At the bottom of the hill is a small quayside and the castle after which the village is named. Once you've seen these, there's zip to do, and that's part of the charm – it's determinedly untouristy.

There are few better places to recharge the batteries so why not stay for a day or two? The **Castle** (☎ 36100; www.castle-townshend .com; €50-80 per person), sitting imposingly on the waterfront, is the stuff of childhood dreams. There are seven guest rooms exuding battered charm, though the real highlight is the wood-panelled living room.

You'll deserve a good meal after panting up the main street to **Mary Ann's** (☎ 36146; www.maryannbarrestaurant.com; lunch €5-12, dinner €15-27). Seafood is the speciality (try the scallops in saffron if available) though there are more predictable staples such as fish and chips, and lamb curry on offer too.

The only way here is by car down the R596. A **taxi** (☎ 21258) from Skibbereen costs €10 to €12.

SKIBBEREEN

☎ 028 / pop 2300

Skibbereen (Sciobairín) is a typical market town: unvarnished, down-to-earth and warmhearted, with a steady influx of tourists stopping on their way to western Cork. There's no real reason to linger other than to pick up info from the tourist office, visit the heritage centre and stay at Bridge House – an event in itself.

COUNTY CORK

History

Skibbereen was one of the most badly affected towns in Ireland during the Famine. Huge numbers of the local population emigrated or died of starvation or disease. 'The accounts are not exaggerated – they cannot be exaggerated – nothing more frightful can be conceived.' So wrote Lord Dufferin and GF Boyle, who journeyed from Oxford to Skibbereen in February 1847 to see if reports of the Famine were true. Their eyewitness account makes horrific reading; Dufferin was so appalled by what he saw that he contributed £1000 (about €100,000 in today's money) to the relief effort.

Orientation

The main landmark in town is a statue in the central square, dedicated to heroes of Irish rebellions against the British. From here, three roads branch off: Market St heads south to Lough Hyne and Baltimore; Main St, the principal shopping street, becomes Bridge St before heading west over the river to Ballydehob and Bantry; and North St heads towards the main Cork road.

Information

The **tourist office** (☎ 21766; skibbereen@skibbereen .corkkerrytourism.ie; North St; ☼ 9am-7pm Jul-Aug, 9am-6pm Mon-Sat Jun & Sep, 9.15am-1pm & 2-5pm Mon-Fri Oct-May) has an excellent pamphlet, the *Skibbereen Trail* (€2), which takes you on a historical walking tour of the town; it's also available from newsagencies and the Heritage Centre. Staff here can book accommodation in Baltimore, and on Sherkin and Clear Islands, advise on local walks, and provide ferry timetables to the islands. You can also find information at www.skibbereen.ie.

There's an Allied Irish Bank with an ATM on Bridge St. For internet access head to the **Flexible Learning IT Centre** (☎ 40297; North St; per min €0.09; ☼ 10am-1.30pm & 2.30-5pm Mon-Fri), on the top floor of the West Cork Arts Centre.

Sights

Constructed on the site of the town's old gasworks, the **Heritage Centre** (☎ 40900; www.skibbheritage.com; Old Gasworks Bldg, Upper Bridge St; adult/child €6/3; ☼ 10am-6pm daily Jun-Sep, 10am-6pm Tue-Sat mid-Mar–May & mid-Sep–Oct, last admission 5.15pm) houses a haunting exhibition about the Famine, with actors reading heart-breaking contemporary accounts. A visit here puts Irish history into harrowing perspective. There's also a smaller exhibition about nearby Lough Hyne, the first marine nature reserve in Ireland, and a genealogical centre.

The **Abbeystrewery Cemetery** is a 1km walk east of the centre, on the N71 to Schull, and holds the mass graves of 8000 to 10,000 local people who died during the Famine.

Tours

Guided **historical walks** (☎ 40900, 087-930 5735; adult/child €4.50/2), lasting 1½ hours, leave from the Heritage Centre at 6.30pm on Tuesday and Saturday April to September. Booking is advised.

Sleeping

Russagh Mill Hostel & Adventure Centre (☎ 22451; www.russaghmillhostel.com; Castletownshend Rd; camp sites €5, dm/d/f €15/40/60) This friendly, frenetic place, 1.5km southeast of town on the R596, occupies an atmospheric old corn mill that has preserved machinery. It caters mainly for school groups, but everyone is welcome. For €20 to €30 you can sample some activities, including a day's kayaking on Loch Hyne or climbing instruction on the centre's climbing wall, taught by experienced practitioners (activities only available to guests staying at the hostel).

ourpick **Bridge House** (☎ 21273; Bridge St; s/d €40/70) You've never stayed anywhere like this before. Mona Best has turned her entire house into a work of art, filling the rooms with fabulous Victorian tableaux and period memorabilia. The whole place bursts at the seams with cherished clutter, crazed carvings, dressed-up dummies and stuff too weird to mention. There's a hearty nod to modernity in the bathroom, which contains a spa bath.

Eldon Hotel (Bridge St), scene of Michael Collins' last meal before being ambushed and killed at Beal-na-Bláth (p224), was under new management and had yet to reopen at the time of writing. Check the tourist office for details.

Eating

There's a **county market** (☼ 12.30-2.30pm) every Friday and a **farmers market** (☼ 10am-1.30pm) every Saturday for all your picnicking needs. If you're in town in September, don't miss the **Taste of West Cork Food Festival** (www.skibbereen.ie), with a lively market and events at local restaurants.

Kalbo's Bistro (☎ 21515; 48 North St; snacks €3-11, dinner €17-28; ☿ noon-3pm & 6.30-9.30pm Mon-Sat year-round, plus 5.30-9.30pm Sun Jul-Aug) This bustling place, with fresh flowers on the tables, serves delicious soup, warm salads, wraps and burgers at lunchtime. When the candles come out, so does the varied evening menu, which offers some particularly delish veggie options, such as sun-dried tomato and mozzarella risotto, alongside meat and fish dishes.

Yassou's (☎ 21157; www.yassouskibbereen.com; Bridge St; lunch €4-10, dinner €10-23; ☿ food served noon-9.30pm) The beamed dining room, slate floor and deep-red trimmings of this Mediterranean restaurant and wine bar make it a top place to settle into. The cuisine is Greek, with lighter dishes such as *spanakopita* and salads for lunch, and big portions of moussaka, meze and meatballs for dinner.

Getting There & Away

Bus Éireann (☎ 021-450 8188; www.buseireann.ie) runs buses to Cork nine times daily Monday to Saturday, and five on Sunday (€13, 1¾ hours); and to Schull eight times daily Monday to Saturday and six times Sunday (€5, 30 minutes) from outside the Eldon Hotel on Main St.

BALTIMORE

☎ 028 / pop 400

Picturesque Baltimore has its sailing hat wedged at a jaunty angle, and a merry whistle on its lips. Its pretty harbour, dominated by the remains of the Dun na Sead (Fort of the Jewels), is the only sight, but its divine coastal setting means there's nowhere better on a sunny day. Watching the boats with a pint of stout in your hand is a fantastically lazy way to spend your time.

Besides idlers, Baltimore attracts sailing folk, anglers, divers and visitors to Sherkin and Clear Islands, meaning that the population swells enormously during the summer months.

Information

There's an information board at the harbour, or check out www.baltimore.ie. The nearest ATM is in Skibbereen. There's internet access (€3.50 per hour) at Casey's hotel.

Activities

There's some excellent diving to be had on the reefs around Fastnet Rock, where the waters are warmed by the Gulf Stream and a number of shipwrecks lie nearby. **Aquaventures Dive Centre** (☎ 20511; www.aquaventures.ie; Stonehouse B&B, Lifeboat Rd) charges €60 for a full day's diving, and also offers diving and accommodation packages in the attached B&B; contact the centre for prices.

Baltimore Sailing School (☎ 20141; www.baltimore sailingschool.com) provides courses (five days for €330) from May to September for beginners and advanced sailors.

For a shorter taste of the sea, contact **Gannets' Way** (☎ 20598; www.gannetsway.com), which offers a day's sailing on a wooden schooner from €85.

Information about other diving, sailing and angling operators is posted by the harbour.

A white-painted landmark beacon (aka Lot's Wife) stands on the western headland of the peninsula and makes for a pleasant **walk**, especially at sunset.

Ten kilometres from Baltimore, on the R585 towards Skibbereen, there's good **walking** around Lough Hyne and the Knockamagh Wood Nature Reserve. Well-marked trails lead round the lake and up a steep hill through the forest. You're rewarded with stunning views at the top.

Festivals & Events

Fiddle Fair (www.fiddlefair.com) In May, with sessions from international and local musicians.

Seafood Festival (www.baltimore.ie) Over the last full weekend of May, jazz bands perform and pubs bring out the mussels and prawns.

Sleeping

Top of the Hill Hostel (☎ 20094; www.topofthehillhostel .ie; dm/d €15/44) Everything, from the exterior to the duvets, is white at this pristine new hostel at the, erm, top of the hill. A good night's rest is assured in sturdy steel bunks, with your possessions safely stowed in individual lockers. The (white) communal areas consist of a lounge, dining room and kitchen and there's a lovely garden to the side.

Rolf's Holidays (☎ 20289; www.rolfsholidays.eu; Baltimore Hill; s €50-60, d €80-100; Ⓟ) Upmarket Rolf's, in an old farmhouse on the outskirts of town, does the lot: there are excellent-value, smartly decorated private rooms, self-catering cottages (from €500 per week), helpful staff and a charming restaurant, Café Art. The whole place is set in peaceful gardens, and is gay-friendly.

COUNTY CORK

our pick Fastnet House (☎ 20515; fastnethouse@
eircom.net; Main St; s/d €50/90) This early-19th-
century house, up from the main harbour, is
another super option. Stone steps lead up to
uncluttered rooms with big windows. There's
an easy-going ambience, and owners Sandra
and Ronnie look after their guests.

Casey's of Baltimore (☎ 20197; www.caseysof
baltimore.com; Skibbereen Rd; s/d €110/182; P 🖳) Ten
of the bedrooms here have estuary views so
gorgeous you'll be caught looking for angels.
If you can prise yourself away from the win-
dowsill, you'll find chipper rooms with huge
beds. Service is ever so friendly, and there are
reasonable discounts offered in the off-season.
Eating here is a delight as well (see below).

Also recommended:

Baltimore Bay Guesthouse (☎ 20600; www.youen
jacob.com; the Quay; s/d €80/120) Large sunny rooms, some
with sea view and balcony, in a cheerful B&B on the harbour.

Baltimore Townhouse (☎ 20197; www.baltimore
townhouse.com; s/d €110/180; P) Immaculate B&B with
luxury trimmings such as king-size beds and LCD TVs.

Eating

Casey's of Baltimore (☎ 20197; sandwiches €4-10, mains
€14-30; 12.30-3pm & 6.30-9pm, bar meals all day) At
Casey's your food comes with fantastic views,
whether you call in for breakfast, sandwiches
or full-on dinner. Seafood includes mussels
fresh from the hotel's own shellfish farm in
Roaringwater Bay and the hotel specialty: crab
claws in garlic butter.

Café Art (☎ 20289; Baltimore Hill; mains €17-26;
lunch & dinner) The kind of place where you
want to kick off your shoes and pad about in
your socks, this place is at once well run and
informal. The staff are merry and the dining
rooms, brightened by candlelight and artwork,
inviting. There's a light European touch to all
the food, be it pork fillet flambéed in brandy or
hake in Pernod. If you like the wine from the
list, you can buy a bottle to take away.

Chez Youen (☎ 20136; www.youenjacob.com; the
Quay; dinner from €30; 6-10pm, closed Nov & Feb)
Terrific seafood is the rule in this Breton-
inspired restaurant where the luscious shellfish platter (€50), containing lobster, prawns,
brown crab, velvet crab, shrimps and oysters, offers the chance to sample shellfish at
its best.

Customs House Restaurant (☎ 20200; www.the
customshouse.com; Main St; set menu €35-45; 7-10pm
Thu-Sun May-Jun & Sep, daily Jul-Aug) Adding to the
area's reputation for gourmet food, Customs

House's modest frontage belies the contemporary interior. The catch of the day and locally sourced, seasonal produce determine
the make-up of the good-value set menus.
Subtle Mediterranean influences pervade
the dishes, such as top-tasting scallops with
chorizo and mushroom risotto with truffle
sauce. Reservations are essential; opening
hours vary year-round so phone ahead to
check.

Drinking

Bushe's Bar (☎ 20125; www.bushesbar.com; the Quay)
The perfect place for sea dogs to chew the
fat after a day on the waves, Bushe's Bar
drips with seafaring paraphernalia. The
benches outside are the best spots in town
for a sundowner.

Getting There & Away

There are four daily buses weekdays and
three times over the weekend between
Skibbereen and Baltimore (€3, 20 minutes).
See opposite for the Schull–Clear Island–
Baltimore ferry service.

CLEAR ISLAND

☎ 028 / pop 150

With its lonely inlets, pebbly beaches, gorse
and heather-covered cliffs, Clear Island
(Oileán Chléire; Cape Clear Island) is an
escapist's heaven. You'll need plenty of time
to suck the full enjoyment from this rugged
Gaeltacht (Irish-speaking) area, the most
southerly inhabited island in the country.
It's a place for quiet walks, hunting down
standing stones and bird-watching.

Facilities are few, but there are a couple of
B&Bs, one shop and three pubs.

Orientation & Information

The island is 5km long and just over 1.5km
wide at its broadest point. It narrows in the
middle where an isthmus divides the northern and southern harbours. There's a **tourist
information post** (☎ 39100; 11am-1pm & 3-6pm
May-Aug) beyond the pier, next to the coffee
shop. There are various leaflets available.
You'll find toilets at the harbour.

The island has its own website: visit www
.oilean-chleire.ie.

Sights

The small **heritage centre** (☎ 39119; admission
€2.50; 2.30-5pm Jun-Aug) has exhibits on the

island's history and culture, and fine views north across the water to Mizen Head.

The ruins of 14th-century **Dunamore Castle**, the stronghold of the O'Driscoll clan, can be seen perched on a rock on the northwestern side of the island (follow the track from the harbour).

Festivals

The **Cape Clear Island International Storytelling Festival** (☎ 39157; http://indigo.ie/~stories; weekend ticket €65) brings hundreds of people to Clear Island for storytelling, workshops and walks, as the nights begin to shorten from late-August to early-September. Check exact dates on the Web and book well ahead for tickets and accommodation.

Activities

BIRD-WATCHING

Cape Clear is one of the top bird-watching spots in Ireland, particularly known for sea birds, including Manx shearwater, gannet, fulmar and kittiwake. Guillemot breed on the island, but other birds head to and fro on hunting trips from the rocky outposts of the western peninsulas. Tens of thousands of birds can pass hourly, especially in the early morning and at dusk. The best time of year for twitching here is October.

The white-fronted **bird observatory** is by the harbour (turn right at the end of the pier and it's 100m along). It's worth calling in to ask about any planned bird-watching trips.

For bird-watching boat trips, phone **MVS Gaisceanán** (☎ 39182).

BirdWatch Ireland (www.birdwatchireland.ie) runs bird-watching field courses to Cape Clear. Details are on the website.

WALKING

There are marked trails all over the island, and B&Bs and the tourist information post can advise on other walks. For **guided walks** covering historical, archaeological or ecological aspects of the island, phone ☎ 39157 (during summer); for walks focused on literature and culture, phone ☎ 39190.

Courses

Comharchumann Chléire Teo (☎ 39119; ccteo@iol .ie) runs Irish-language courses for 12- to 18-year-olds (€730 for three weeks). **Ionad Foghlama Chléire** (☎ 39190; www.cleire.com) runs programmes for adults.

For everything you need to know about goat husbandry, contact Ed Harper at **Chléire Goats** (☎ 39126; goat@iol.ie), based on a farm west of the church. He makes ice cream and cottage cheese, available for tastings, and runs day- and week-long courses on goat-keeping.

Sleeping & Eating

Accommodation on the island is satisfyingly unfancy. Book ahead, especially between May and September.

There's a **camp site** (☎ 39119; per person €7; ☺ Jun-Sep) and An Óige's **Cape Clear Island Hostel** (☎ 41968; www.mamut.com/anoigecapeclear; Old Coastguard Station, South Harbour; dm first night €18, then €16; ▣), which is in a large white building at the south harbour.

Ask for directions to these two friendly B&Bs in typical island houses: **Ard Na Gaoithe** (☎ 39160; ardnagaoithe@hotmail.com; the Glen; s/d €35/70) and **Cluain Mara** (☎ 39153, 39172; www.cape clearisland.com; North Harbour; per person €28-35), which also has self-catering cottages.

Ciarán Danny Mike's (☎ 39172; www.capeclear island.ie; meals €7-12) does bar meals and in summer there's a chip van at the north harbour.

Getting There & Away

From Baltimore, the ferry **Naomh Ciarán II** (☎ 39153; www.capeclearferry.com) takes 45 minutes to cover the 11km journey to Clear Island and it's a stunning trip on a clear day. There are four boats daily between mid-July and mid-August, with the earliest leaving at 11am and the latest returning at 7pm, and at least two per day the rest of the year (departures morning and late-afternoon only). Return fares are €12/6 per adult/child, and bicycles travel free.

GOUGANE BARRA FOREST PARK

Gougane Barra (www.gouganebarra.com) is a truly magical part of inland County Cork. It's almost Alpine in feel, with spectacular vistas of craggy mountain, silver stream and pine forest sweeping down to a mountain lake, the source of the River Lee. St Finbarre, the founder of Cork, established a monastery here in the 6th century. He had a hermitage on the island in **Gougane Barra Lake** (Lough an Ghugain), which is now approached by a short causeway. The small **chapel** on the island has fine stained-glass representations of obscur Celtic saints. A road runs through the park in a loop but you're better off slowing down and walking the well-marked network of paths and nature trails through the forest.

The area cries out for a hostel but the only place to air your hiking boots is the pricy **Gougane Barra Hotel** (☎ 026 47069; www .gouganebarrahotel.com; s/d €75/140). There's an onsite restaurant (serving a two-course dinner for €29), a café and a pub next door, and the hotel runs a summer theatre festival.

Getting There & Away

It ain't easy on public transport. There's a Monday to Saturday bus service (3.15pm, two hours) from Cork to Ballingeary 5km away; if you're staying at the Gougane Barra hotel the staff can pick you up from there.

There's also a Saturday-only 8am Macroom to Ballingeary bus, arriving in time to connect with the 9am Gougane Barra bus. The bus departs from Gougane Barra at 4.40pm Saturday, connecting with the 5pm bus to Macroom.

The Macroom **tourist office** (☎ 026 43280; ☉ summer only) can help with accommodation in town if needed. Alternatively, take a **taxi** (☎ 026 41152) from Macroom for around €30, or organise a tour from Bantry (see p237).

The park is signposted on the R584 after Ballingeary. Returning to the main road afterwards and continuing west, you'll travel over the Pass of Keimaneigh and emerge on the N71 at Ballylickey, midway between the Beara Peninsula and the Sheep's Head Peninsula.

MIZEN HEAD PENINSULA

From Skibbereen the road rolls west through Ballydehob, the gateway to the Mizen, and then on to the pretty village of Schull. Travelling on into the undulating countryside takes you through ever-smaller settlements, to the village of Goleen.

Even here the Mizen isn't done. Increasingly narrow roads head further west to spectacular Mizen Head itself and to the hidden delights of Barleycove Beach and Crookhaven. Without a decent map you may well reach the same crossroads several times.

Heading back from Goleen, you can bear north to join the scenic coast road that follows the edge of Dunmanus Bay for most of the way to Durrus. At Durrus, one road heads for

Bantry while the other turns west to Sheep's Head Peninsula.

SCHULL
☎ 028 / pop 700

Schull (pronounced skul) is a small fishing village where a few vessels still keep the trade alive. The harbour has the satisfying clutter of a working port, and water sports play their part in making Schull a busy tourist attraction. It's particularly crowded during Calves Week, a sailing regatta usually held after the August bank holiday. Out of season the village is even more attractive in some ways, with a strong local community.

Orientation & Information

Most shops and B&Bs line the long Main St.

There's no tourist office, but a very useful booklet, *Schull: A Visitor's Guide*, can be obtained from hotels and some shops, and there's a website (www.schull.ie).

The Allied Irish Bank on Main St has an ATM and bureau de change.

@ Your Service (☎ 28600; Main St; per 30/60min €3/6) Internet access and tourist info.

Chapter One (☎ 27606; www.chapterone.ie; Main St; ☉ closed Wed) A cooperatively run bookshop with a good general collection.

Sights

The Republic's only planetarium, the **Schull Planetarium** (☎ 28552; www.schullcommunitycollege .com; Colla Rd; ☉ 3.30-5pm Sun May, 3-5pm Tue & 7.30-9pm Sat Jun, 7-9pm Mon & Sat Jul-Aug, 3.30-5pm Tue, Thu & Sat & 7.30-9pm Mon & Thu), in the grounds of Schull Community College, has an 8m dome and a video and slide show. It was founded by a German visitor who was charmed by the town. A 45-minute **star show** (adult/child €5/3.50) starts at 4pm or 8pm during opening hours.

The planetarium is at the Goleen end of the village on the Colla road. You can also reach it by walking along the Foreshore Path from the pier.

Activities

There are a number of **walks** in the area including a 13km return trip up Mt Gabriel. The mountain was once mined for copper, and there are Bronze Age remains and 19th-century mine shafts and chimneys. For a gentler stroll try the short 2km Foreshore Path from the pier out to Roaringwater Bay and a view of the nearby islands. These and other walking routes are outlined in the publication *Schull: A Visitor's Guide.*

Schull Watersport Centre (☎/fax 28554; the Pier; ◷ 9.30am-12.30pm Mon-Sat, 2-5pm Sat) hires out sailing dinghies (€50 per half-day) and snorkelling gear (€10 per day), and can arrange sea-kayaking sessions (three-hour session €25) and sailing lessons (€95 for 2½ hours).

Divecology (☎ 28943; www.divecology.com; Cooradarrigan) runs courses and dives (€25) to wreck and reef sites.

For fishing, contact **Schull Angling Centre** (☎ 087-251 7452; mizen@eircom.net) or **Blue Thunder Charters** (☎ 086-386 2876; www.schull-seaangling.com).

Horse- and pony-trekking and trap rides are available at the **Ballycumisk Riding School** (☎ 37246, 087-961 6969; Ballycumisk) outside Schull on the way to Ballydehob, for €25 per hour.

Sleeping

Glencairn (☎ 28007; susanglencairn@yahoo.com; Ardmanagh Dr; s/d €40/70; (P)) Excellent value is the norm at this friendly place, in a peaceful cul-de-sac 100m from Main St. There are some great little touches: Room 4, the only room without a bathroom, has dressing gowns to preserve your dignity while nipping to the detached yet private bathroom. Better still, there are biscuit barrels in all the rooms.

Rookery Cottage B&B (☎ 28660; Air Hill; r €70; (P)) In a quiet spot behind the village, there are bags of comfort at this spruce family B&B. The floorboards that run throughout are so highly polished you can see your face in them, and each of the three rooms (two with bathroom) are lovingly decorated with antiques and quilts.

Grove House (☎ 28067; www.grovehouseschull.com; Colla Rd; s €75-85, d €100-120; (P)) This beautifully restored ivy-covered mansion is the fanciest place to stay in Schull. The house is exquisitely decorated in an easy-going antiques-and-homemade-rugs style. It also has a restaurant (see right).

At the time of writing, the **Harbour View Hotel** (☎ 28101; Main St), formerly the East End Hotel, was under construction. Phone for further information and prices.

Eating

Newman's West (☎ 27776; www.tjnewmans.com; Main St; dishes €6-9; ◷ 9am-11pm) This natty wine bar and art gallery serves nibbles such as soup and salads and enormous chunky sandwiches filled with local cheese and salami. The daily

Western Seaboard specials might include Bantry Bay mussels, fish pie and chowder.

Hackett's (Main St; ◷ lunch noon-3pm daily, dinner Wed-Thu Jul-Aug, Fri-Sat year-round; bar meals €3-7, dinner €15-20) Simplicity is the charm at Hackett's. Black and white photos and tin signs adorn the pub's crooked walls and there's a mishmash of old kitchen tables and benches on the worn stone floor. Weekends brings *un peu de France* to town with cassoulet and stews.

Jagoe's Café & Restaurant (☎ 28028; Main St; lunch €3-11.50, dinner €16-22; ◷ 9.30am-5.30pm Tue-Sat year-round & dinner Jul-Aug) A deli selling artisan produce fronts this delightfully unfussy restaurant strewn with battered wooden furniture. Lunch sees the usual rounds of soup, sandwiches and salads. Things get more interesting at dinner with ingredients such as chicken with saffron, and scallops in cider, artfully combined.

Waterside Inn (☎ 28203; Main St; mains €17-28) The dark interior is a bit of a throwback to the '70s, but the locals stand by the food here all the way. The menu is seafood-oriented, with creative dishes such as monkfish with Gubbeen bacon and chives, but there are good choices for fans of locally reared meat too.

Even if you're not staying at Grove House (see left), you're welcome to eat at its **restaurant** (mains €15-23; ◷ Wed-Mon Jul-Aug & Thu-Sat Sep-Jun). You get to sample local food, such as Gubbeen bacon and Schull eggs for breakfast, and there are French and Swedish dishes for dinner.

SELF CATERING

Picnickers are spoilt for choice: besides the supermarkets on Main St, try the **West Cork Gourmet Store** (☎ 27613; Main St) for its fantastic deli and selection of wines, and **Gwen's Chocolates** (☎ 27853; Main St) for cocoa and cakes. There's also a Sunday **farmers market** (☎ 27824; Pier Rd car park; ◷ 10am-2pm Easter-Christmas).

Getting There & Away

There are two buses daily from Cork to Schull (€15, 2½ hours), via Clonakilty and Skibbereen.

The **Clear Island ferry** (☎ 28278; www.capeclearferries.com; ◷ 11.30am Jun, 10.30am, 2.30pm & 4.30pm Jul-Aug, 2.30pm Sep; adult/child return €13/5) leaves from the pier.

Getting Around

Parking in Schull is difficult in summer. There are three car parks, opposite the Harbour

View Hotel, behind the Allied Irish Bank, and at Pier Rd.

For bus and taxi services, try **Betty Johnson's Bus Hire** (☎ 28410, 086-265 6078).

WEST OF SCHULL TO MIZEN HEAD
☎ 028

If you're driving or cycling, take the undulating coastal route from Schull to Goleen. On a clear day there are great views out to Clear Island and the Fastnet lighthouse. The landscape becomes wilder around the hamlet of Toormore. From Goleen, roads run out to thrilling Mizen Head and to the picturesque harbour village of Crookhaven.

Goleen

Tourism in the Goleen area is handled well by the local community, with the **Mizen Head Signal Station** (opposite) being a token of their commitment and imagination.

SLEEPING & EATING

our pick **Fortview House** (☎ 35324; www.fortview house.ie; Gurtyowen, Toormore; s €45-62, d €90-100; ☺ Mar-Nov; **P**) Out on its own, in terms of location, warmth *and* quality, this lovely house has five antique-filled, flower-themed bedrooms. Hospitable hostess Violet has the most infectious laugh ever, and her breakfast choice is gourmet standard, with eggs from happy hens in the garden. To get there, head along the road that turns off the R592 for Durrus about 1km northeast of Goleen.

Heron's Cove (☎ 35225; www.heronscove.com; Goleen; s/d €50/80; **P**) A delightful location, on the shores of the tidal inlet of Goleen Harbour, makes this fine restaurant and B&B a top choice. Rooms have individual charm and several have balconies overlooking the inlet and the soothing turn of the tide. The homely restaurant has an excellent menu of organic and local food. It's open from 7pm to 9.30pm May to September (and year-round for guests staying at the Heron's Cove). Mains are between €18 and €25.

Rock Cottage (☎ 35538; www.rockcottage.ie; Barna-tonicane, Schull; s/d €95/130; **P**) Rock Cottage is the kind of place where you end up staying longer than you'd intended. The Georgian hunting lodge has three wood-floored guest rooms, which happily mix antique furniture and modern textiles. Rock Cottage is also a working farm and many of the ingredients on the evening set menu (€48) come from the surrounding fields. To find it, continue 1km up the road from Fortview House and go through the gate on your left.

GETTING THERE & AWAY

There are two buses to Goleen from Skibbereen (€8, 70 minutes) via Schull, leaving Skibbereen at 4.05pm and 7.45pm Monday to Saturday, and 11.30am and 1.05pm Sunday. In the other direction, buses leave Goleen at 7.45am and 5.30pm Monday to Saturday (Sunday at 1.35pm and 5.30pm). Buses travel no further down the peninsula than Goleen.

Crookhaven

Onwards from Goleen, the westerly outpost of Crookhaven feels so remote you imagine it's more easily reached by boat than by road. And so it is for some people – in summer there's a big yachting presence and Crookhaven bustles with life. Off season you can stop the world and get off.

In its heyday Crookhaven's natural harbour was an important anchorage. Mail from America was collected here, and sailing ships and fishing vessels found ready shelter. On the opposite shore the gaunt remains of quarry buildings, closed in 1939, lie embedded in the hillside, and are the source of many tall tales by locals in response to curious questions from visitors.

SLEEPING & EATING

Galley Cove House (☎ 35137; www.galleycovehouse. com; s €45-55, d €75-85; **P**) A cheerful welcome complements the secluded location of this modern home, 2km from Crookhaven and with terrific views across the ocean. It's handy for Barley Cove beach, and the pine-floored rooms are clean, airy and filled with light.

O'Sullivan's Bar (☎ 35319; osullivans@crookhaven .ie; snacks €3-11; ☺ noon-8pm) and **Crookhaven Inn** (☎ 35309; mains €4-14; ☺ 12.30-8pm Apr-Oct) are high-spirited pubs on the waterfront. There's live music in summer, when the bars fill with yachtspeople from the nearby sailing club. There's soup, chowder, crab sarnies and quiches on the menu year-round.

Brow Head

This is the most southerly point on the Irish mainland and well worth the walk. As you leave Crookhaven, you'll notice a turn-off to the left marked 'Brow Head'. If travelling by car, park at the bottom of the hill – the track is very narrow and there's nowhere to pull over should you meet a tractor coming the other way. After 1km the road ends. Continue on a path to Brow Head where you'll see an **observation tower**, from which Guglielmo Marconi transmitted his first message (to Cornwall) and received a reply.

Barleycove

Even though this is western Cork's finest beach, it never seems to get overcrowded. It's a great place for youngsters, with gorgeous stretches of golden sand, a safe bathing area where a stream flows down to the sea, lifeguards in July and August, and a Blue Flag award marking the cleanliness of the water. Access is via a boardwalk and pontoon, which protect the surrounding wetlands from the impact of visitors' feet. There's a car park at the edge of the beach, on the south side of the causeway on the road to Crookhaven.

If you can forgive the insensitivity of such a modern and growing development in this heavenly spot, **Barleycove Beach Hotel** (☎ 35234; www.barleycovebeachhotel.com; Barleycove; s/d €80/160, 2-bed self-catering per week €780; **P**) is a mere 200m away from the sand. The rooms are simply done out, with beach views, and there's a bar/restaurant with outdoor seating. Bring ear plugs – the bedroom walls are thin.

Near the beach on the other side of the bay, **Barleycove Holiday Park** (☎ 35302; Barley Cove; camp site €20; ☉ mid-Apr–mid-Sep) is a well-run camping ground with bike rental, shop and children's club.

Mizen Head Signal Station

For the full Mizen experience, don't miss the **Mizen Head Signal Station** (☎ 35225, 35115; www .mizenhead.net; Mizen Head; adult/child 6-12 years €6/3.50; ☉ 10.30am-5pm mid-Mar–May & Oct, 10am-6pm Jun-Sep, 11am-4pm Sat & Sun Nov–mid-Mar). Apart from the thrill of standing on Ireland's most southwesterly point, the walk down to the head and the displays inside the signal station make for a unique attraction.

At the top of the cliffs is **Fastnet Hall** with plenty of information about local ecology, geology and history. From here, take the spectacular **arched bridge** that spans a vast gulf in the cliffs. Far below, seals roll in the dark water when the sea is calm. Beyond the bridge, and

at the far point of the outer rock island, is the **signal station**, containing the keeper's quarters, engine room and radio room of the Mizen Head Fog Signal Station, completed in 1909 and de-staffed and automated in 1993. You can see how the keepers lived and how the station worked, but the real rush (even among crowds on a busy day) is the sense of so much Atlantic beneath vast skies.

Back at the top, the **Mizen Café** is a good place for a bite after all the drama.

NORTHSIDE OF THE PENINSULA

Although the landscape is less dramatic on this side of the peninsula, it's well worth driving along the coast road here for the great views out to Sheep's Head Peninsula and beyond to the magnificent Beara Peninsula.

Durrus

☎ 027 / pop 900

Durrus is a lively little village at the head of Dunmanus Bay and a popular access point for both the Mizen Head and Sheep's Head peninsulas.

Gardeners will be impressed by **Kilravock Garden** (☎ 61111; Ahakista Rd; adult/child €5/3; ☉ 10am-6.30pm Mon-Sat May-Sep), which has been transformed over 17 years from a field to a feast of exotic plants by one green-fingered couple.

Dunbeacon Campsite (☎ 61246; camp sites €14; ☉ Easter–mid-Oct), about 5.5km southwest of Durrus on the R591, has tree-sheltered sites in a cracking location overlooking the bay.

Blairs Cove House (☎ 61127; www.blairscove.ie; s/d €140/220, apt per week from €720; ☉ Mar-Jan) is a Georgian country house set in five acres of land and centred around an exquisite courtyard. Rooms and self-catering apartments display immense elegance and style. The restaurant (open for dinner Tuesday and Saturday and for lunch on Sunday, March to October) in a chandeliered hall, offers a superb set dinner (€55) with local produce given an international treatment. Booking is advised.

Good Things Café (☎ 61426; www.thegoodthingscafe. com; Ahakista Rd; mains €13-28; ☉ 12.30-3pm & 7-9pm Thu-Mon mid-Jun–Dec) is a joyous scoffing place on Dunmanus Bay. It produces some great contemporary dishes from organic, locally sourced ingredients and runs popular cookery courses year-round, covering everything from 'the practical pig' to two-day 'miracle' programmes for beginners.

COUNTY CORK

DURRUS CHEESE

If we were cows, we would be happy grazing in the rugged green fields of West Cork. Irish bovines must agree, because the area is a centre of excellence for artisan dairy production. If you want to see cheese-making in action, call in at **Durrus Cheese** (☎ 027-61100; www.durruscheese .com). Founder Jeffa Gill is happy to talk visitors through the process and there are cheeses on sale. Be sure to call ahead if you want to drop in. Follow the Ahakista road out of Durrus for 500m; turn right at the church and keep going for 3km until you see the dairy's sign.

BANTRY

☎ 027 / pop 3300

Vast Bantry Bay, framed by the craggy Caha Mountains, has an epic quality that you can't help but marvel at. The town's past is one of mixed fortunes: poverty and mass emigration were followed by unexpected prosperity when Gulf Oil built an oil terminal on Whiddy Island. A second source of riches also comes from the bay: you'll see Bantry oysters and mussels on menus throughout County Cork.

The town narrowly missed a place in history during the late 18th century, when storms prevented a French fleet landing to join the United Irishmen's rebellion. A local Englishman, Richard White, was rewarded with a peerage for alerting the British military in

Cork. His grand home is now the town's main attraction.

Orientation & Information

The two main roads into Bantry converge on Wolfe Tone Sq, where the pedestrianised central concourse boasts a statue of Wolfe Tone (see p36).

The helpful **tourist office** (☎ 50229; Wolfe Tone Sq; 🕙 9.15am-5pm Mon-Sat Apr-Oct) is based in the old courthouse. There's a post office on Blackrock Rd, an Allied Irish Bank with ATM on Wolfe Tone Sq, and the **Bantry Laundrette** (☎ 55858; 🕙 9.30am-6pm Mon-Fri, to 5.30pm Sat) in a small courtyard off Barrack St.

Internet access is available at **Fast.Net** (☎ 51624; Bridge St; 10/60 min €1/5; 🕙 9am-6pm Mon-Fri, 10am-5pm Sat).

Sights

With its melancholic air of faded gentility, 18th-century **Bantry House** (☎ 50047; www .bantryhouse.com; Bantry Bay; admission €10, gardens & French Armada Centre only €5, children free; 🕙 10am-6pm mid-Mar–Oct) makes for an intriguing visit. The house has belonged to the White family since 1729 and every room brims with treasures brought back from every generation's travels since then. The entrance is paved with mosaics from Pompeii, French and Flemish tapestries adorn the walls, and Japanese chests sit next to Russian shrines. Upstairs, worn bedrooms look out wanly over an astounding view of the bay – the

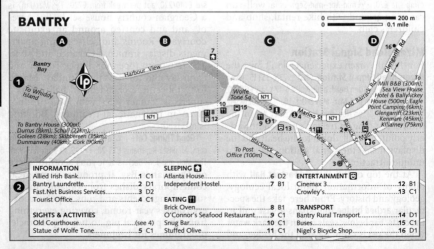

INFORMATION	SLEEPING 🏠	ENTERTAINMENT 🎭
Allied Irish Bank..............................1 C1	Atlanta House...................................6 D2	Cinemax 3......................................12 B1
Bantry Laundrette............................2 D1	Independent Hostel...........................7 B1	Crowley's.......................................13 C1
Fast.Net Business Services................3 D2		
Tourist Office.................................4 C1	EATING 🍴	TRANSPORT
	Brick Oven.....................................8 B1	Bantry Rural Transport......................14 D1
SIGHTS & ACTIVITIES	O'Connor's Seafood Restaurant.........9 C1	Buses..15 C1
Old Courthouse.........................(see 4)	Snug Bar.......................................10 C1	Nigel's Bicycle Shop.........................16 D1
Statue of Wolfe Tone......................5 C1	Stuffed Olive..................................11 C1	

18th-century Whites had ringside seats to the armada (see below). Experienced pianists are invited to tinkle the ivories of the ancient piano in the library. It's possible to stay the night in the wings (see p238).

The **gardens** of Bantry House are its great glory. Lawns sweep down from the front of the house towards the sea, and the formal Italian garden has an enormous 'stairway to the sky', offering spectacular views.

In the former stables you'll find the **1796 French Armada Exhibition Centre**, with its powerful account of the doomed French invasion of Ireland, led by Wolfe Tone. The fleet was torn apart by storms; one frigate, *La Surveillante*, was scuttled by its own crew and today lies 30m down in the bay.

Bantry House is 1km southwest of the town centre on the N71.

Tours

George Plant Minibus Tours (☎ 50654, 087-239 8123; gplant@eircom.net) operates various tours for €20 to €30 from June to September. Trips include Mizen Head, the Beara Peninsula and Gougane Barra Forest Park (p231). They only run if there are sufficient numbers.

Festivals

West Cork Chamber Music Festival (www.westcork music.ie) Held at Bantry House for a week in June/July when the house closes to the public. The garden, craft shop and tearoom remain open.

Sleeping

BUDGET

Independent Hostel (☎ 51140; Harbour View; dm €12.50) The cheapest accommodation in town, this basic hostel on the harbour has two small, cramped dorms. You'll find the owner at Barry's B&B next door.

Eagle Point Camping (☎ 50630; www.eaglepoint camping.com; Glengarriff Rd, Ballylickey; camp sites €23;

☾ end Apr–end Sep) An enviable location at the end of a promontory 6km north of Bantry makes this a popular site. Most spots have sea views, and there's direct access to the pebbly beaches nearby.

MIDRANGE

Atlanta House (☎ 50237; atlantaguesthouse@gmail .net; Main St; s/d €40/60; 🖵) You won't get a more central stay than in this recently refurbished town house, which has good-sized rooms and firm beds piled high with pillows. There's a congenial welcome from the staff and a reassuring sense of comfort and calm.

Mill (☎ 50278; Glengarriff Rd; www.the-mill.net; s/d €45/70; ☾ Easter–Oct; Ⓟ) One of the best B&Bs in the west, this modern house on the immediate outskirts of town oozes individuality. The irrepressible landlady, Tosca, is just part of it. The rooms are full of knick-knacks, and the spacious breakfast and dining room has a wonderful collection of Indonesian puppets and Tosca's art to accompany terrific breakfasts.

TOP END

Ballylickey House (☎ 50071; www.ballylickeymanor house.com; Ballylickey; d €120-130, ste €170; ☾ Mar–Nov; Ⓟ) In a beautiful manor house with manicured lawns overlooking the bay, Ballylickey has two types of accommodation – grand rooms in the house itself or sweet little cottages set round a swimming pool in the gardens. All are spacious and comfortably furnished, with big squishy beds and floral upholstery.

Sea View House Hotel (☎ 50073; www.seaview househotel.com; Ballylickey; s €85-95, d €150-170; Ⓟ) You'll find everything you'd expect from a luxury hotel here: country-house ambience, tastefully decorated public rooms, expansive service and extraordinarily snug bedrooms. The hotel is on the N71, 5km northeast of Bantry.

COUNTY CORK

DETOUR: SHIPLAKE MOUNTAIN HOSTEL

Far up a twisting track lies one of Cork's most unusual hostels. **Shiplake Mountain Hostel** (☎ 023-45750; www.shiplakemountainhostel.com; Dunmanway; camp site €7, dm/s/d €13/18/32; Ⓟ) consists of three brightly coloured gypsy caravans, each with a double bed squeezed in, and two dorm rooms in an old stone cottage. The owners take their environmental responsibility seriously – the showers use local spring water and you can have the hostel's own duck eggs (30c) for breakfast. They can pick you up from nearby Dunmanway, which has an ATM and grocery shops. Once here, chase the ducks, go for walks, borrow a bike (free) or gather round the stove in the common room for a good chinwag.

Bantry House (☎ 50047; www.bantryhouse.com; Bantry Bay; s/d €140/240; ❋ Apr-Oct; Ⓟ) Bantry House's guest rooms, decorated in a warming mixture of antiques and contemporary furnishings, are luxurious places to while away the hours. Rooms 22 and 25 are double aspect, with views of the garden and the bay. Enhance the dream by playing croquet, lawn tennis or billiards and lounging in the house's library once the doors are shut to the public.

Eating

O'Connor's Seafood Restaurant (☎ 50221; www.oconnorseafood.com; Wolfe Tone Sq; lunch €5-13, dinner €18-30; ❋ lunch & dinner daily Mar-Oct, Tue-Sat Nov-Feb; ﴾&﴿) The tank full of lobsters and the wooden sailing ships in the window give the game away – O'Connor's offers Bantry seafood at its best. Mussels are the speciality here and are prepared in a variety of ways – try them cooked in Murphy's stout. It's all ultrafresh, from the food to the soft neutral décor. A two-course set menu is available between 6pm and 7pm for €26.

Brick Oven (☎ 52500; the Quay; mains €9-25; ❋ noon-3pm & 5-9pm Mon-Thu, noon-3pm & 6-10pm Fri-Sat, 1-10pm Sun) Generally rammed to the gills, this is a family favourite thanks to its cunningly divided menu and chirpy atmosphere. Kids can pig out on pizza, while their discerning parents feast on more adult fare such as sun-dried tomato risotto.

Snug Bar (☎ 50027; the Quay; mains €14-23) The aptly named Snug is a cocoon of interesting nooks and crannies, with enamel advertising signs on the walls and one table wrapped around a full-grown tree. Simple bar meals (soups, lasagne and the like) are served at lunch with more ambitious seafood and steaks on the menu at night.

For a wholesome picnic, stock up on artisan produce, salads, sandwiches and wine at the **Stuffed Olive** (☎ 55883; New St).

Entertainment

Crowley's (☎ 50029; Wolfe Tone Sq) is one of the best bars for music, with traditional bands on Wednesday nights.

Cinemax 3 (☎ 55777; www.cinemaxbantry.com; the Quay) shows blockbusters and a Tuesday arthouse programme on its three screens.

Getting There & Away

Bus Éireann (☎ 021-450 8188; www.buseireann.ie) has 12 buses daily Monday to Saturday (four on

Sunday) between Bantry and Cork (€13.50, two hours). In June and August, there's one service daily to Killarney (€13, 12 hours) via Glengarriff and Kenmare.

The private **Berehaven bus** (☎ 70007) links Bantry to Castletownbere via Glengarriff. It leaves from the fire station in Wolfe Tone Sq at noon and 5.50pm on Monday, 3.45pm on Tuesday, Friday and Saturday and 7.45pm Thursday (one way/return €8/15, 75 minutes).

Bantry Rural Transport (☎ 52727; www.ruraltransport.ie; 5 Main St) runs a useful series of circular routes to Dunmanway, Durrus, Goleen, Schull, Skibbereen, and outlying villages. There's a set price of €4/6 one way/return. Services run on set days only. Phone for details.

Getting Around

Bicycles can be hired at **Nigel's Bicycle Shop** (☎ 52657; Glengarriff Rd; per day/week €15/60).

SHEEP'S HEAD PENINSULA

The least visited of Cork's three peninsulas, Sheep's Head Peninsula has a rare charm of its own. There are wonderful seascapes to appreciate from the loop road running along most of its length. A good link road with terrific views, called the Goat's Path Rd, runs between Gortnakilly and Kilcrohane (on the north and south coasts respectively), over the western flank of Mt Seefin.

Ahakista (Atha an Chiste) consists of a couple of pubs and a few houses stretched out along the R591. An ancient **stone circle** is signposted at the southern end of Ahakista; access is via a short pathway. The peninsula's other village is **Kilcrohane**, 6km to the southwest, beside a fine **beach**. You can get pub food in both villages.

For more information about the area, take a look at the website (www.sheepshead.ie).

WALKING & CYCLING

Walkers and cyclists will relish the chance to stretch their legs and enjoy the windswept moors, wild gorse, foxgloves and fuchsias in beautiful solitude. On the Goat's Path Rd, the steep Bantry Kilcohane section requires firm thighs; the Ahakies–Durrus stretch is more gentle. Bantry's tourist office (see p236) can

---

WALK: MT SEEFIN

Make time for an exhilarating 1km stride to the summit of Mt Seefin (345m). It's not challenging but this is open country, where mist can easily descend, so go properly equipped. There's a path, but it fades out in places.

The ascent begins at the top of the Goat's Path Rd, about 2km between Gortnakilly and Kilcrohan. On the roadside is an out-of-place imitation of Michelangelo's Pietà – follow the track that starts opposite the parking area on the south side of the Pietà. Keep to the path along the rocky spine of the hill until you reach a depression. Follow a path up a short gully to the right of a small cliff and then continue, again on the rocky spine of the broad ridge, to a trigonometry point on the summit. Retracing your steps can be challenging. From the trig point it's best to keep high along the broad ridge and not drift too far to the left.

---

book accommodation along the Sheep's Head Way, has lots of info on the peninsula and sells a map and guide (€12.50).

The **Sheep's Head Way** is an 88km walking route around the peninsula, on roads and tracks where possible. Use Ordnance Survey maps 85 and 88 to navigate your way around (see www.osi.ie to purchase maps). There are no camp sites on Sheep's Head Peninsula; camping along the route is allowed with permission from the landowner.

The 120km **Sheep's Head Cycle Route** runs anticlockwise from Ballylickey (north of Bantry), round the coastline of the Sheep's Head Peninsula, back on to the mainland and down to Ballydehob. There are opportunities to take shortcuts or alternative routes (eg over the Goat's Path Rd, or along the coast from Ahakista to Durrus). The widely available brochure, *The Sheep's Head Cycle Route,* has full details.

GETTING THERE & AWAY

Bantry Rural Transport (☎ 027-52727; www.rural transport.ie; 5 Main St) buses run a circular route on Tuesday and Thursday, leaving Bantry at 9.15am and going via the Goat's Path Rd to Kilcrohane and Durrus (one way/return €4/6).

BEARA PENINSULA (RING OF BEARA)

The Beara Peninsula (Mor Choaird Bheara) is the stuff of glossy tourist brochures, a sublime place of rock-studded mountains and green valleys sliding at impossible angles into the Atlantic. Its villages are as friendly and picturesque as you could wish for, and

the thrillingly wobbly cable car at the tip of the peninsula, which takes you and the sheep out to tiny Dursey Island, is a bonus.

Sitting insouciantly astraddle the Cork–Kerry border, Beara is less visited than the Ring of Kerry to the north. You can escape even further into the landscape by strapping on your hiking boots. There's exhilarating hill walking requiring some skill and commitment, as well as proper clothing and navigational experience.

The 196km **Beara Way** is a signposted walk linking Glengarriff with Kenmare (in Kerry) via Castletownbere, Bere Island, Dursey Island and the north side of the peninsula; for more details, see p698. The 138km **Beara Way Cycle Route** takes a similar direction, passing on small lanes through all the villages on Beara. You can find excellent maps and guidebooks in local tourist offices.

ORIENTATION & INFORMATION

A small part of the peninsula lies in Kerry but is dealt with here for the convenience of people travelling the Ring of Beara. Castletownbere in Cork or Kenmare in Kerry make good bases for exploring the area.

In theory you could drive the 137km around the coast in one day, but at the price of omitting a great deal. In particular, you would miss the spectacular **Healy Pass**, which cuts across the peninsula from Cork to Kerry.

The following towns are described in a route that assumes you're starting from Glengarriff and working your way clockwise to Kenmare.

GLENGARRIFF

☎ 027 / pop 1020

Hidden deep in the Bantry Bay area, Glengarriff (Gleann Garbh) is an attractive village with a happy holiday feel. Its weird microclimate stems from its sheltered position and the shallow sea, which in turn encourages exotic plant growth, best seen on Garinish Island and in Bamboo Park (opposite).

The rough, rocky Caha Mountains make for good hill walking. There are plenty of gentler strolls too, in mature oak woodlands and through the coastal Blue Pool Amenity Area where seals, perched on submerged rocks, appear to levitate on the water.

In the second half of the 19th century, Glengarriff became a popular retreat for prosperous Victorians, who sailed across from England, took the train to Bantry, then chugged over to Glengarriff in a paddle steamer. By 1850 the road to Kenmare had been blasted through the mountains and the link with Killarney was established. Today Glengarriff lies on the main Cork to Killarney road; despite drawing crowds, there's still a satisfying back-country feel to the place.

Information

There's a **Fáilte Ireland tourist office** (☎ 63084; Main St; ⊗ 9.15am-1pm & 2-5pm Jun-Aug) and a privately run **tourist office** (⊗ 10am-1pm & 2-6pm Mon-Sat Jun-Aug) beside the Blue Pool Ferries terminal.

There's no bank here but the post office on the main street (which is also the Spar shop) has a bureau de change.

Sights

GARINISH (ILNACULLIN) ISLAND

The magical Italianate **garden** (☎ 63040; adult/senior & child €3.70/2.20; ⊗ 9.30am-6.30pm Mon-Sat & 11am-6.30pm Sun Jul-Aug, 10am-6.30pm Mon-Sat & 11am-6.30pm Sun Apr-Jun & Sep, 10am-4.30pm Mon-Sat & 1-5pm Sun Mar & Oct, last admission 1hr before closing) on Garinish Island is a must. Exotic plants flourish in the rich soil and warm climate. The camellias, magnolias and rhododendrons especially provide a blaze of colour in a landscape usually dominated by greens and browns. There are good views from a **Grecian temple** at the end of a cypress avenue, and a spectacular panorama from the top of the 19th-century **Martello tower**, built to watch out for a possible Napoleonic invasion.

This little miracle of a place was created in the early 20th century, when the island's owner Annan Bryce commissioned the English

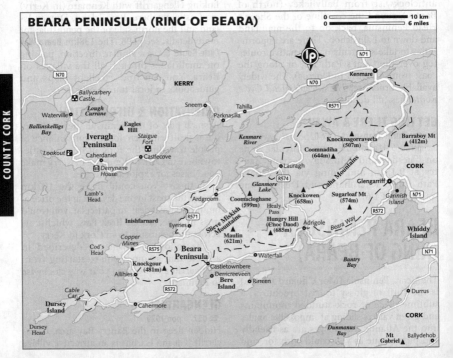

BEARA PENINSULA (RING OF BEARA)

0 ——— 10 km
0 ——— 6 miles

KERRY

Kenmare

N70

N70

Ballycarbery Castle
Waterville
Lough Currane
Eagles Hill
Ballinskelligs Bay
Iveragh Peninsula
Lookout
Caherdaniel
Derrynane House

Sneem
Parknasilla
Tahilla

Staigue Fort
Castlecove

R571

Kenmare River

Laragh

R574

Coomnadiha (644m)

Knocknagorraveela (507m)
Barraboy Mt (412m)

CORK

Caha Mountains

Glengarriff

N71

Lamb's Head

Glanmore Lake

Ardgroom
Coomacloghane (599m)
Knockowen (658m)
Healy Pass

Sugarloaf Mt (574m)
Garinish Island

R572

Inishfarnard

Eyeries

R571

Slieve Miskish Mountains

Maulin (621m)

Hungry Hill (Cnoc Daod) (685m)

Adrigole

Beara Way

Whiddy Island

N71

Copper Mines

Cod's Head

R575

Beara Peninsula

Knockgour (481m)

Allihies

Castletownbere
Derricreeveen
Bere Island

Waterfall

Rirreen

Bantry Bay

Cable Car

Dursey Island

R572

Cahermore

Durrus

CORK

Dursey Head

Dunmanus Bay

Mt Gabriel

Ballydehob

architect Harold Peto to design her a garden on the then-barren outcrop.

Garinish Island is reached by taking a 10-minute boat trip past islands and colonies of basking seals. Three ferry companies leave every 20 to 30 minutes when the garden is open. The return boat fare (adult €8 to €12, child €6) doesn't include entry to the gardens:

Blue Pool Ferries (☎ 63333) From the centre of the village, near the Quills Woollen Market.

Harbour Queen Ferries (☎ 63116, 087-234 5861) From the pier opposite the Eccles Hotel.

Lady Ellen (☎ 087-944 3784) From Ellen's Rock, 1.6km along the Castletownbere road.

BAMBOO PARK

Another garden is **Bamboo Park** (☎ 63570; www .bamboo-park.com; adult/child €5/free; 9am-7pm), which flourishes thanks to Glengarriff's mild, frost-free climate. There are 12 hectares of exotic plants, including palm trees and tree ferns, and coastal woodland walks. Lining the waterfront are 13 ivy-covered stone pillars, the origin of which remains a mystery, even to locals.

GLENGARRIFF WOODS NATURE RESERVE

The 300-hectare ancient **woodland** lining Glengarriff's glacial valley was owned by the White family of Bantry House in the 18th century. The thick tree cover maintains humid conditions which allow ferns and mosses to flourish. Look out especially for rare kidney saxifrage (tiny white flowers on red stems rising from rosettes of leaves).

The woodlands and bogs are also home to Ireland's only arboreal ant and the rare and protected Kerry slug. If you're lucky, you'll see these spotty cream-coloured gastropods chewing on lichen after rainfall.

There are four marked trails through the reserve, separately covering woodland, mountain, river and meadow, and you can combine them to form one big walk (8.5km, three to four hours).

To get to the woods, leave Glengarriff on the N71 Kenmare road. The entrance is about 1km along on the left.

Activities

For deep-sea fishing trips, contact Brendan at **Harbour Queen Ferries** (☎ 63116, 087-234 5861).

Sleeping

Murphy's Village Hostel (☎ 63555; Main St; dm/d €15/40) Right at the heart of Glengarriff, Mur-

phy's is a cheerful, well-run hostel with spacious, bright rooms and comfy pine bunks. The roof terrace, looking over a sea of trees, is a sociable place on warm evenings. The owners also run the cheerful Village Café downstairs; it's open from June to September.

Dowlings Camping & Caravan Park (☎ /fax 63154; Castletownbere Rd; camp sites €18; Easter-Oct) This well set-up park, 4km west of Glengarriff on the road to Castletownbere, is located in a woodland setting. Amenities include a games room and a licensed bar staging traditional music every night from June to August.

River Lodge B&B (☎ 63043; Castletownbere Rd; s/d €50/80; Feb-Nov; **P**) On the edge of Glengarriff, on the Castletownbere road, River Lodge is a modern house surrounded by beautiful gardens. The rooms are plain and old-fashioned but there's a certain muddled charm to the place. The affable hosts serve up home-baked bread for breakfast.

Casey's Hotel (☎ 63010; Main St; s/d €52/92; **P**) Old-fashioned Casey's has been welcoming guests since 1884 and is proud of past visitors such as Eamon de Valera. Rooms are a little dated and some are a touch cramped, but you're treated with immense warmth and there are characterful public spaces and a patio-garden to enjoy.

Eccles Hotel (☎ 63003; www.eccleshotel.com; Glengarriff Harbour; d €126; **P**) The Eccles has a long and distinguished history, counting the British War Office, Thackeray, George Bernard Shaw and WB Yeats as former occupants. The décor is slightly parochial but the rooms are big and sunny and there's a pleasant air of nostalgia about the place. For the best views, ask for a bay-side room on the 4th floor.

Eating

Rainbow Restaurant (☎ 63440; Main St; lunch €9-15, dinner €14-28) Local dishes are the fare here, with the emphasis on seafood. Sitting on the streetside benches and tucking into Bantry Bay mussels or seafood chowder with soda bread is a fine way to spend a sunny evening.

Hawthorne Bar (bar meals €4.50-10, mains €10-16) This less formal establishment, part of the same operation as the Rainbow Restaurant next door, does stonking portions of good-value bar food.

Martello Restaurant (☎ 63860; Garinish Ct, Main St; lunch €11-18, dinner €20-28; 12.30-3.30pm & 6.30-9.30pm Tue-Sat, 12.30-3.30pm Sun Jun-Aug, 6.30-9.30pm Thu-Sat, 12.30-3.30pm Sun Sep-May) This smart but casual bistro serves up Glengarriff's tastiest grub. There are steak sandwiches and pastas for lunch, or you can return later for local dishes such as flambéed Bantry Bay scallops and crab claws. Booking is advised.

Getting There & Away

A bus travels three times daily Monday to Saturday (twice Sunday) from Glengarriff to Bantry (€3, 30 minutes) and Cork (€13.50, 2½ hours). Buses are less frequent in the other direction to Adrigole and Castletownbere. For details of the Berehaven bus service, see p238.

Getting Around

Glengarriff Cabs (☎ 63060, 087-973 0741; www .glengarrifftours.ie) also runs day trips. Contact Gene for details.

GLENGARRIFF TO CASTLETOWNBERE

The landscape becomes more rugged and impressive as you head west from Glengarriff towards Castletownbere. On the highest hills, Sugarloaf Mountain and Hungry Hill, rock walls known as 'benches' snake backwards and forwards across the slopes. They can make walking on these mountains quite challenging, and dangerous in fog. Take a map (Ordnance Survey Discovery series 84 and 85 cover the area) and compass if venturing into the hills, and seek local advice.

Adrigole is a scattered strip of houses, ideal for walkers and sailors who like peace and quiet. The **West Cork Sailing Centre** (☎ 027-60132; www.westcorksailing.com; the Boat House) offers everything from kayak hire to family sailing holidays. A half-day sailing course costs €160, an hour's kayaking €12 and an 'action day' of various watery activities €75.

Hungry Hill Lodge (☎ 027-60228; www.hungryhill lodge.com; Adrigole; camp sites €15, dm €17, d €34-40; **P**) is a well-situated hostel with excellent facilities (and a pub), just beyond Adrigole village. It's in a peaceful location, perfect for walking, cycling and watersports. The owners can organise bike hire for €12.50 per day and refill divers' air bottles for €5.

CASTLETOWNBERE & AROUND

☎ 027 / pop 850

Tourism is not the first concern in Castletownbere (Baile Chais Bhéara), and as a result, there is a refreshing appeal to the everydayness of the place. The town is home to one of Ireland's largest fishing fleets and retains the bustle of a working port.

The helpful **tourist office** (☎ 70054; www.beara tourism.com; Main St; ☒ Tue-Sat) is just outside the Church of Ireland. **Beara Action Group** (☎ 70880; www.bearainfo.com; per 30/60min €3.5/4.5) has internet access. On Main St, you'll find a post office with bureau de change, an Allied Irish Bank with an ATM, and a string of pubs. **O'Shea's Laundrette** (☎ 70966; Main St; ☒ 9am-6pm Mon-Fri, from 9.30am Sat) charges €1 per pound for washing.

Sights

The **Call of the Sea** (☎ 70835; www.callofthesea.com; North Rd; adult/child €4/2; ☒ 10am-5pm Mon-Fri, 1-5pm Sat & Sun Jun-Aug, phone for opening times outside these months) is a small museum with a nautical flavour where the smuggling, mining, fishing and naval history of the Beara Peninsula is explored in a series of interesting, sometimes hands-on exhibitions (try your skills at morse code). It's on the R571 running north from Castletownbere.

On a lonely hill 2km from Castletownbere, the impressive **Derreenataggart Stone Circle**, consisting of 10 stones, can be found close to the roadside. It's signposted at a turn-off to the right at the western end of town. There are a number of other standing stones in the surrounding area.

The remote **Dzogchen Beara Buddhist meditation centre** (☎ 73032; www.dzogchenbeara.org; Garranes, Allihies) is 8km southwest of Castletownbere on top of Black Ball Head. The solitude and some of the best sea views in western Cork set the mood. Accommodation is available in self-catering **cottages** (per week €305-425) or the **hostel** (dm €15). Visitors are welcome to attend sessions, and the retreat offers regular seminars and study groups. Enquire by phone or email.

Activities

Beara Diving & Watersports (☎ 71682, 087-699 3793; www.bearadiving.com; the Square; ☒ 10am-6pm Jun–mid-Sep, noon-5pm Mon-Sat May, 10am-5.30pm Sat rest of year) Runs PADI courses and has boat dives (€49 with equipment) from Easter to mid-September, when you might meet Dirk, the friendly conger eel.

Bike N Beara Bike Hire (☎ 74898, 086-1280 307; per day/week from €12.50/70) Can drop off bikes at your accommodation. Enquiries at SuperValu on Main St.

Sea Kayaking West Cork (☎ 70692, 086-309 8654; www.seakayakingwestcork.com) Takes you out for a paddle for €45 per half day.

COUNTY CORK

DETOUR: BERE ISLAND

Someone stopped the clocks on deliciously remote Bere Island sometime in the 1950s. Or so it feels, with life trundling along at a slower pace than on the mainland. Lying 2km out to sea, separated from Castletownbere by the second deepest natural harbour in the world (after Sydney), the island is home to only 230 residents. In the summer the population swells with holiday-makers who come mainly for the island's relaxed pace of life and unspoilt beauty. If you *must* do something, there are two Martello towers, an abandoned British fort, walking and cycling routes, and plenty of sheltered coves for swimming.

To the east, Rirreen village has the most amenities, with a general store, pub, café and bright, tidy rooms at **Lawrence Cove Lodge** (☎ 027-75988; www.lawrencecovelodge.com; dm/s/d €27/45/70; ☒). The village of Derricreeveen, to the west, has a café and pub.

There are two regular ferry services to the island: **Bere Island Car Ferries** (☎ 027-75009; www.bereislandferries.com) runs from Castletownbere to Derricreeveen, while **Murphy's Ferry Service** (☎ 027-75014; www.murphysferry.com) runs to Rirreen from a pontoon 3km east of Castletownbere. The crossing takes 20 minutes; return tickets are €6 to €8 on foot or €25 in a car.

There's more info about the island at www.bereisland.net.

Silver Dawn (☎ 70979, 086-816 2899; www.ireland seafishing.com) Nifty new boat for deep-sea fishing (€350 per half-day) plus coastal sightseeing (adult/child €25/15).

Sleeping

Harbour Lodge Hostel (☎ 71043; www.harbourlodge .net; Old Convent; dm/d €18/36; ☑ ☒) This large building, situated off Main St, used to be a convent. It's a strange old place: just have a look at the refectory-like dining room. The rooms are worn but spacious, particularly the doubles, which have proper beds rather than the usual bunks.

Rodeen B&B (☎ 70158; www.rodeencountryhouse .com; s/d €45/70; ☑ Mar-Oct; ☑) A delightful haven, tucked away above the eastern approach to town. The bright house has stunning sea views and is surrounded by gardens full of crumbling Delphic columns and other surprises. Flowers from the garden grace the breakfast table, and there are homebaked scones with honey from landlady Ellen's bees.

Cametringane Hotel (☎ 70379; www.camehotel .com; the Harbour; s/d €70/140; ☑) The best thing about this hotel are the rooms with balconies, where you can sit in the sunshine and watch the boats on the harbour. You'll need to book long in advance for these. Everything here feels very fresh. The hotel is on the far side of the harbour.

See also Dzoghen Beara Buddhist Meditation Centre (opposite).

Eating

Copper Kettle (☎ 71792; the Square; mains €10-12; ☑ 10am-5pm) While there are hefty portions of lasagne, stir fries and sandwiches on offer at this convivial little café near the water, the home baking is the clincher. Start with apple pie, continue with scones and finish it all off with chocolate cake.

Olde Bakery (☎ 70869; oldebakerybeara@eircom.net; Castletown House; mains €13-21; ☑ 5.30-9.30pm Tue-Sun, plus noon-4.30pm Sun) One of the best restaurants in town, the Olde Bakery serves good-value portions of standard international grub within its rustic, wood-panelled walls. The seafood dishes are best: try the tiger prawns in satay.

For all the makings of a decent picnic, head to **Taste** (☎ 71842; Main St; ☑ 9.30am-6pm).

Drinking

our pick **McCarthy's Bar** (☎ 70014; Main St) If you're carrying a copy of Pete McCarthy's bestseller, *McCarthy's Bar*, you'll be excited to see the front-cover photo sitting in three dimensions on Main St. McCarthy's is a grocery as well as a pub, so if you fancy a tin of peaches and a bottle of bleach to go with your Beamish, you've come to the right place. There's frequent live music and a wicked wee snug inside the door.

Getting There & Away

Bus Éireann (☎ 021-450 8188) runs three buses from Cork to Castletownbere (€17, 3¼ hours) Monday to Saturday and two on Sunday, via Bantry, Glengarriff and Adrigole. **Harringtons** (☎ 74003) runs a private bus between Cork and Castletownbere at 8am daily except Thursday and Sunday. **O'Donoghue's** (☎ 70007) runs one on Thursday (7.30am) and Sunday (4.50pm) instead. Buses leave from the square.

DURSEY ISLAND

☎ 027 / pop 60

Tiny Dursey Island, at the end of the peninsula, is reached by Ireland's only **cable car** (adult/child return €4/1; ☼ 9-11am, 2.30-5pm & 7-8pm Mon-Sat, 9-10am, 1-2pm, 4-4.30pm & 7-7.30pm Sun), which sways precariously 30m above Dursey Sound. Livestock take precedence over humans in the queue, and bikes are not allowed. The later times shown above are for returning only.

The island, just 6.5km long by 1.5km wide, is a wild bird and whale sanctuary, and dolphins can sometimes be seen swimming in the waters around it. There's no accommodation on the island, but it's easy to find somewhere to camp.

The **Beara Way** loops round the island for 11km, and the signal tower is an obvious destination for a short walk.

NORTHSIDE OF THE BEARA

A single-track road snakes round the northern coast, past boulder-strewn fields tumbling dramatically towards the ocean. It can feel satisfyingly remote – your only company along some stretches are flocks of sheep and the odd sheepdog.

Allihies & the Copper Mines

Copper-ore deposits were first identified on the far Beara in 1810. While mining quickly brought wealth to the Puxley family who owned the land, it brought low wages and dangerous, unhealthy working conditions for the workforce, which at one time numbered 1300. Experienced Cornish miners were brought into the area, and the dramatic ruins of engine-houses replicate those of Cornwall's coastal tin mines. As late as the 1930s, more than 30,000 tonnes of pure copper were exported annually, but by 1962 the last mine was closed. Watch out for hidden mineshafts if you go for a wander.

There are pubs and B&Bs in Allihies (Na hAilichí), and a small tourist information kiosk, beside the church, opens in summer.

Eyeries to Lauragh

Heading north and east from Allihies, a 23km coastal road, with hedges of fuchsias and rhododendrons, twists and turns all the way to **Eyeries**. This cluster of brightly coloured houses overlooking Coulagh Bay is often used as a film set. The town is also home to **Milleens cheese** (☼ 027 74079; www

.milleenscheese.com), from pioneering producer Veronica Steele. She welcomes visitors to her farm – phone ahead.

The coast road rejoins the main road at the small village of **Ardgroom** (Ard Dhór). As you head east towards Lauragh, look for signs pointing to the Ardgroom **stone circle**, an unusual Bronze Age monument with nine tall, thin uprights. There's rough parking at the end of a narrow approach lane. The circle is visible about 200m away and a path leads to it across bogland.

Lauragh (Laith Reach), situated northeast of Ardgroom, is in County Kerry. It's home to the **Derreen Gardens** (☎ 064-83103; adult/child €6/3; ☼ 10am-6pm Apr-Oct), planted by the fifth Lord Lansdowne around the turn of the 20th century. Mossy paths weave through an abundance of interesting plants, including spectacular New Zealand tree ferns and red cedars, and you may see seals on the shore.

From Lauragh, a serpentine road travels 11km south across **Healy Pass** and down to Adrigole, offering spectacular views of the rocky inland scenery. About 1km west of Lauragh, along the R572, is a road to **Glanmore Lake**, with the remains of an old hermitage on a tiny island in the middle. There are walking opportunities in the area, but gaining access can be problematic: ask locally for advice.

Sleeping & Eating

There are pubs and B&Bs in Eyeries, Ardgroom and Allihies. In high season, check with the Castletownbere tourist office (p242).

Glanmore Lake Hostel (☎ 064-83181; www .anoige.ie; Glanmore Lake; dm adult/child €15/12; ☼ end-May–end-Sep; P) A timeless atmosphere and an engaging location at the heart of Glanmore make this remote An Óige hostel an appealing place. It's in Glanmore's old National Schoolhouse, 5.6km from Lauragh. Take the road for Glanmore Lake and keep going.

Allihies Village Hostel (☎ 027-73107; www.allihies hostel.net; Allihies; dm/d/f €18/50/65; ☀) Run by father-and-daughter team Michael and Sarah, this is a model hostel. Gleaming from top to bottom, there are smart wood-floored dorms and public areas, a courtyard and barbecue area. Michael is a mine of information on the area and can advise on local walks and pony-trekking.

our pick Josie's Lakeview House (☎ 064-83155; Glanmore Lake; lunch €3-13, mains €14-24) If there are better views to accompany your food in

Ireland, we've yet to find them. Josie's sits on a hill overlooking Glanmore Lake – come for lunch as the sun sparkles on the water or for dinner as it sets behind the mountains. The philosophy in the kitchen is simple: homely food, well made. Choose from salads and sandwiches during the day or heartier rack of lamb and local seafood specials at night. Josie's is 4km from Lauragh; take the road for Glanmore Lake and follow the signs.

Getting There & Away

The bus service is limited. Bus 282 runs between Kenmare and Castletownbere via Lauragh, twice daily Monday to Saturday in July and August only. Contact **Bus Éireann** (☎ 021-450 8188; www.buseireann.ie) for times and prices. Allihies is served by privately run **O'Donoghue's** (☎ 027-70007).

NORTHERN CORK

Northern Cork lacks the glamour and romance of the county's coastal regions, but there is a pleasant sense of escape from the mainstream, and the area's towns and villages have a refreshing rural integrity.

MALLOW

☎ 022 / pop 7900

Mallow (Mala) is a prosperous town located in the Blackwater Valley, which caters for fans of fishing, golfing and horse racing. Visitors to its spa in the 19th century christened it the 'Bath of Ireland'. The comparison is far-fetched these days though the architecture in the town centre hints at its former grandeur.

The **tourist office** (☎ 42222; www.eastcorktourism .com; ⏰ 9.30am-1pm & 2-5.30pm Mon-Fri) can help with accommodation and activities.

In the town itself, you can spot white fallow deer around the imposing ruins of **Mallow Castle** (Bridge St), which dates back to 1585. Also look out for the distinctive **Clock House** (Bridge St), designed by an amateur architect after an Alpine holiday – you'd never guess.

You can hire fishing rods for €10 to €15 per day from **Country Lifestyle** (☎ 20121; Spa Walk) near the tourist office, and bikes for €15 per day from **Cremin Cycles** (☎ 42465; Bridge St).

A haven of peace, **Ard Na Laoi** (☎ /fax 22317; Bathview, Mallow; s/d €39/60; **P**) is a lovely house in garden surroundings and has big alluring rooms. The hallway and reception rooms have remarkable embossed and painted tin ceilings, an American custom that was introduced by the original owner.

Longueville House (☎ 47156; www.longuevillehouse .ie; s/d €110/260; **P**), 7km from Mallow off the N72, has the timeless atmosphere of all good country-house hotels. The rooms, from the exquisite bedrooms to the renowned President's Restaurant, are opulently decorated. Go fishing, traipse around the gardens, read the papers in front of the fire or just scoff the local produce.

Buses run hourly every day between Mallow and Cork (€7.90, 35 minutes) and trains run every two hours (€8, 25 minutes).

AROUND MALLOW

At Buttevant, about 20km north of Mallow on the N20, are the ruins of a 13th-century **Franciscan abbey**. Between Mallow and Killarney, you might want to divert to see the well-preserved remains of 17th-century **Kanturk Castle**. Inhabited only by crows these days, the castle acted as both fortification and country house from the early 17th century to 1906.

Red deer scamper around the 400 acres of landscaped gardens at **Doneraile Park** (⏰ closes 8pm), 13km northeast of Mallow. There are woodland walkways, cascades and playgrounds to keep the kids happy.

County Kerry

Kerry is as close as you'll get to the mythical Ireland: that Celtic kingdom of misty mountains promised by glossy brochures, Hollywood and our daydreams. Between the county's snow-capped summits are medieval ruins, glacial lakes, coastal peninsulas, blustery beaches, deserted archipelagos, secluded hamlets, and larger towns where live music sparks up every night.

Most visitors touch down in Killarney. The townsfolk know how to run a mean hotel and serve an Atlantic catch or a rack of Kerry lamb. Instead of municipal gardens there's a 10,000-hectare national park, which can be explored by 'jaunting car' (pony and trap) and a boat across the lakes. In the nearby Gap of Dunloe, the road winds crazily beneath the Macgillycuddy's Reeks range, which includes nine of Ireland's 10 highest peaks.

Tourists often arrive at the coast with the idea that the iconic Ring of Kerry is a 'place' they can visit. In fact, it's a 179km circuit of the Iveragh Peninsula, where the mountains-meet-ocean beauty makes for one of the world's great road trips. To paraphrase one pub sign, you'll enjoy Ireland's best known views… fog permitting. Across a dolphin-inhabited bay, the Dingle Peninsula is home to one of the country's highest concentrations of ancient sites and Mt Brandon, Ireland's eighth highest peak.

Such magnificent scenery is, of course, a magnet for buses, but the hordes can be escaped by using back roads and mountain passes. As for the local folk, Kerrymen are famous throughout Ireland for their proud provincialism and country cunning. Just listen to the outrageous yarns told by the 'jarveys' who drive Killarney's jaunting cars.

HIGHLIGHTS

- **Distracted Motorists** The Ring of Kerry drive past mountains and beaches (p258)
- **Salmon or Steak** Celtic hospitality in Killarney (opposite) and Kenmare (p267)
- **Island Hopping** The rocky Skelligs (p262) and evacuated Blaskets (p294)
- **Pint & a Screwdriver** Vibrant Dingle town's pubs that double as hardware shops (p285)
- **Ripping Yarns** Literary Listowel (p281) and the county's many storytellers
- **Hearty Pursuits** Activities on land and sea at Derrynane (p265) and Rough Point (p290)

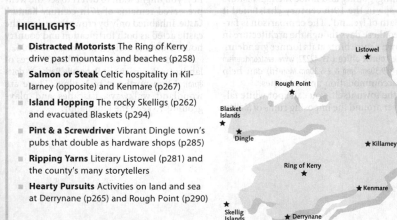

- POPULATION: 139,900
- AREA: 4746 SQ KM

KILLARNEY

☎ 064 / pop 16,800

Killarney is a well-oiled tourism machine in the middle of sublime scenery that looks swell on a postcard. Its manufactured tweeness is renowned – the stream of buses arriving to consume soft-toy shamrocks, the placards on street corners pointing to 'trad' sessions. However, it has many charms beyond its obvious proximity to lakes, waterfalls, woodland and moors dwarfed by 1000m-plus peaks. In a town that's been practising the tourism game for over 250 years, competition keeps standards high, and visitors on all budgets can expect to find superb restaurants, great pubs and good accommodation.

HISTORY

Killarney and its surrounds have been inhabited probably since the Neolithic period and were certainly important Bronze Age settlements, based on the copper ore mined on Ross Island. Killarney changed hands between warring tribes, notably the Fir Bolg ('bag men'), expert stonemasons who built forts (including Staigue), and developed Ogham script.

In the 7th century, St Finian founded a monastery on Inisfallen Island, and Killarney became a focus for Christianity in the region. The O'Donoghue clan

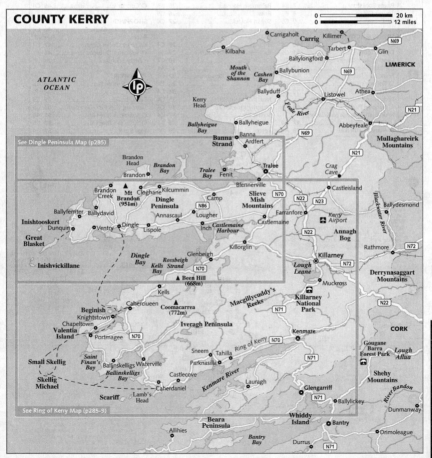

COUNTY KERRY

later ousted the Gaels, before building Ross Castle (in the 15th century).

It wasn't until much later, in the 17th century, that Viscount Kenmare developed the town as a tourist centre, an Irish version of England's Lake District. Among its many notable 19th-century visitors were the Romantic poet Percy Bysshe Shelley, who began *Queen Mab* here, and Queen Victoria.

ORIENTATION

The centre of Killarney is the T-junction where New St meets High and Main Sts. As it heads south, High St becomes Main St, then turns east into Kenmare Place and

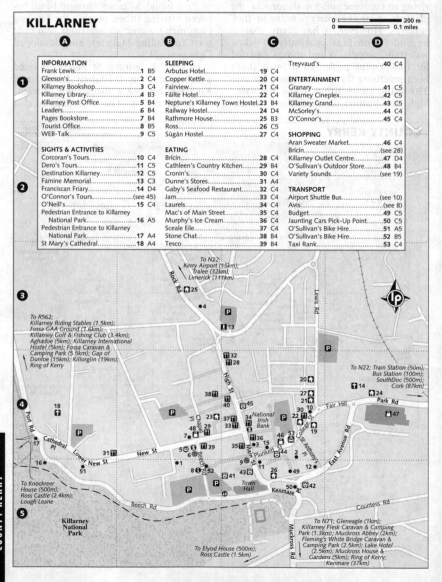

KILLARNEY

INFORMATION		SLEEPING		Treyvaud's.................................40 C4
Frank Lewis.................................1 B5		Arbutus Hotel.............................19 C4		
Gleeson's....................................2 C4		Copper Kettle.............................20 C4		ENTERTAINMENT
Killarney Bookshop.....................3 C4		Fairview.....................................21 C4		Granary......................................41 C5
Killarney Library.........................4 B3		Fáilte Hotel.................................22 C4		Killarney Cineplex......................42 C5
Killarney Post Office....................5 B4		Neptune's Killarney Town Hostel.23 B4		Killarney Grand...........................43 C5
Leaders.......................................6 B4		Railway Hostel............................24 D4		McSorley's..................................44 C4
Pages Bookstore.........................7 B4		Rathmore House.........................25 B3		O'Connor's.................................45 C4
Tourist Office..............................8 B5		Ross...26 C5		
WEB-Talk....................................9 C5		Súgán Hostel..............................27 C4		SHOPPING
				Aran Sweater Market..................46 C4
SIGHTS & ACTIVITIES		EATING		Brícín.......................................(see 28)
Corcoran's Tours.......................10 C4		Brícín...28 C4		Killarney Outlet Centre...............47 C4
Dero's Tours.............................11 C5		Cathleen's Country Kitchen.........29 C4		O'Sullivan's Outdoor Store.........48 B4
Destination Killarney.................12 C5		Cronin's.....................................30 C4		Variety Sounds.........................(see 19)
Famine Memorial.......................13 C3		Dunne's Stores...........................31 A4		
Franciscan Friary.......................14 D4		Gaby's Seafood Restaurant..........32 C4		TRANSPORT
O'Connor's Tours....................(see 45)		Jam..33 C4		Airport Shuttle Bus..................(see 10)
O'Neill's...................................15 C4		Laurels.......................................34 C4		Avis..(see 8)
Pedestrian Entrance to Killarney		Mac's of Main Street...................35 C4		Budget.......................................49 C5
National Park........................16 A5		Murphy's Ice Cream.....................36 C4		Jaunting Cars Pick-Up Point.......50 C5
Pedestrian Entrance to Killarney		Sceale Eile..................................37 C4		O'Sullivan's Bike Hire.................51 A5
National Park........................17 A4		Stone Chat.................................38 B4		O'Sullivan's Bike Hire.................52 B5
St Mary's Cathedral...................18 A4		Tesco...39 B4		Taxi Rank...................................53 C4

East Ave Rd, where the large hotels are. The national park is to the south, while the bus and train stations are east of the centre.

INFORMATION
Bookshops
Killarney Bookshop (☎ 34108; 32 Main St)
Pages Bookstore (☎ 26757; 20 New St)

Emergency
For emergencies (ambulance, fire or police) dial ☎ 999.

Internet Access
Killarney Library (☎ 32655; Rock Rd) Free access.
Leaders (☎ 39635; Beech Rd; per 30 min/1 hr €1.80/3; ⏱ 9.30am-6pm Mon-Fri, 10.30am-5.30pm Sat)
WEB-Talk (☎ 22523; 12 Main St; per 30 min/1 hr €2/4; ⏱ 9.30am-10pm Mon-Sat, 11am-10pm Sun) Also offers cheap phone calls abroad.

Internet Resources
www.corkkerry.ie A useful resource for accommodation and information throughout the southwest.

Laundry
Gleeson's (☎ 33877; Brewery Lane; per 6kg €12; ⏱ 9am-6pm Mon-Sat)

Left Luggage
Left-luggage office (☎ 37509; per bag €2; ⏱ 7am- 6pm Mon-Sat) At the bus station; ask at the coffee shop.

Libraries
Killarney Library (☎ 32655; Rock Rd; ⏱ 10am-5pm Mon, Wed, Fri & Sat, 10am-8pm Tue & Thu)

Medical Services
The closest accident and emergency unit is at Tralee General Hospital (p278).
SouthDoc (☎ 1850-335999; Upper Park Rd) Doctors outside surgery hours.

Money
Many banks have either a bureau de change or an ATM, or both. There is also a bureau de change in the tourist office.

Post
Killarney Post Office (☎ 31461; New St; ⏱ 9am-5.30pm Mon & Wed-Sat, from 9.30am Tue)

Toilets
There are public toilets on Kenmare Place.

Tourist Information
Publisher **Frank Lewis** (☎ 31108; www.guide killarney.com; 6 Bridewell Lane) produces the *Guide Killarney* (€5), a good 'what's on' magazine found in many hotels, B&Bs, hostels and bookshops. It can also be obtained directly from the publisher.
Tourist office (☎ 31633; www.corkkerry.ie; Beech Rd; ⏱ 9am-8pm Jun-Aug, 9.15am-5pm Sep-May) Busy, but efficient; gives out a good, free map of the national park.

SIGHTS
Built between 1842 and 1855, **St Mary's Cathedral** (☎ 31014; Cathedral Pl), at the western end of New St, is a superb example of neo-Gothic revival architecture. The cruciform Augustus Pugin building was inspired by Ardfert Cathedral (p281), near Tralee.

At the northern end of High St is a **Famine Memorial** to victims, which was erected by the Republican Graves Association in 1972. With a determination reflecting the implacable hope for a united Ireland, the inscription reads: 'This memorial will not be unveiled until Ireland is free.'

On Fair Hill is an 1860s **Franciscan friary**, displaying an ornate Flemish-style altarpiece, some impressive tile work and stained glass windows by Harry Clarke. The Dublin artist's organic style was influenced by Art Nouveau, Art Deco and Symbolism.

ACTIVITIES
You can fish for trout and salmon in the Rivers Flesk (per day €10) and Laune (per day €25); a state salmon licence (per 21 days €48) is needed. Or you can fish for brown trout for free in Killarney National Park's lakes. Information, permits, licences and hire equipment can be obtained at **O'Neill's** (☎ 31970; 6 Plunkett St), which looks like a gift shop, but is a long-established fishing centre.

Killarney Riding Stables (☎ 31686; Ballydowney; 1-/2-/3-hr rides €30/50/70) is 1.5km west of the centre on the N72. The well-run complex offers two- and five-day rides through the Iveragh Peninsula for more experienced riders.

Killarney Golf & Fishing Club (☎ 31034; www.kil larney-golf.com; Mahony's Point; green fees per person €40-120, club hire €30-40), 3.4km west of town on the N72, has three courses: two alongside Lough Leane, one with artificial lakes, and all with mountain views.

COUNTY KERRY

SLEEPING
Budget

Some hostels arrange pick-ups from the bus and train stations. Most offer discounted bike hire, horse riding and tours of the Ring of Kerry, the Dingle Peninsula and local attractions. Book ahead during the summer.

Neptune's Killarney Town Hostel (☎ 35255; www .neptuneshostel.com; Bishop's Lane, New St; dm €14-17.50; 🖳) Neptune's mixed dorms can sleep over 150, but the central hostel feels much smaller thanks to the roaring fire in reception, free internet access, and the staff's unfailing helpfulness. Continental breakfast (€2.50) is offered in the large kitchen.

Súgán Hostel (☎ 33104; www.killarneysugan hostel.com; Lewis Rd; dm/tw €15/40) Behind its pub-like front, 250-year-old Súgán is an amiably eccentric hostel with a turf fire in the cosy common room and low ceilings with crazy corners. Manager Pa Sugrue confidently offers to reimburse punters if they're not tickled by his storytelling nights at O'Connor's (p252).

Fossa Caravan & Camping Park (☎ 31497; www .camping-holidaysireland.com; Fossa; camp sites €15, hostel €13-17; 🕑 Easter-Sep). The better of two parks on the N72 to Killorglin, 5.5km west of Killarney, it has a restaurant, and the location is a relaxing spot with views of the Macgillycuddy's Reeks.

Killarney International Hostel (☎ 31240; anoige@killarney.iol.ie; Aghadoe House, Fossa; dm €16-22, tw €46; 🅿 🖳) The Headley barons' former residence, built in the 18th century and set in 75 acres of woodland, is surprisingly homely for a 170-bed hostel. Signposted off the N72, 5km west of central Killarney, the An Óige member offers breakfast (€5 to €7), packed

lunch, a laundry room and a free bus to and from town (June to September).

Railway Hostel (☎ 35299; www.killarneyhostel .com; Fair Hill; dm €16-22, s/d €35/50; 🅿) This modern hostel near the train station is about as inviting as hostels get, with en-suite bathrooms, bunks nestling in nooks, and maps and cycling itineraries adorning the walls. Prices include a basic breakfast.

Killarney Flesk Caravan & Camping Park (☎ 31704; www.campingkillarney.com; Muckross Rd; camp sites €19; 🕑 Easter-Sep) About 1.3km south of town on the N71, the park is surrounded by woods and has great mountain views. Facilities include bike hire, a supermarket, restaurant, bar and café.

Midrange

B&Bs and guesthouses are as thick on the ground in Killarney as jaunting cars. It can be difficult, however, to find a room from June to August, when it's often easiest to let the tourist office find one for you (€4). New Rd, Rock Rd and Muckross Rd (and the roads leading off Muckross Rd) are good places to look.

Rathmore House (☎ 32829; rathmorehousekly@iol.ie; Rock Rd; s/d €50/80; 🕑 Mar-Oct; 🅿) There's a warm welcome at this long-established B&B, one of a group of family-run establishments at the northern entrance to town. The ensuite rooms and their cherrywood furniture are as cheerful as the owners.

Elyod House (☎ 36544; www.elyodhouse.ie; Ross Rd; s/ d €55/72; 🅿) This quietly located modern house is on the road to Ross Castle, and a few minutes walk from town. Rooms are fresh and clean, and the welcome is friendly.

Northwood House (☎ 37181; www.northwoodhouse .com; 5 Muckross View; r €64-80) This B&B in a quiet location to the southeast of town, reached along

---

FOOTBALL CRAZY

Gaelic football clubs are as common in Ireland as green fields and pub signs bearing the 'G' word. However, among Kerrymen, the obsession with the sport reaches fever pitch. Forget about soccer or even hurling; this obsession is akin to rugby in New Zealand and soccer in Brazil.

Run by the GAA (Gaelic Athletic Association), the 15-a-side game is played with a heavy leather ball on a rectangular grass pitch with H-shaped, net-backed goals. Teams score through a confusing combination of kicking, carrying, hand-passing and *soloing* (dropping and toe-kicking the ball into the hands). The game, which closely resembles Australian Rules football, dates back to the 16th century, but took its current form in the 19th century.

If you would like to watch some Gaelic football and you're in town during the season (February to September), head to the Fossa GAA Ground on the N72, 1.6km west of the centre. To learn about the game from some lifelong pub commentators, have a drink at the bar-cum-Gaelic football shrine Jimmy O'Brien's (Fair Hill).

COUNTY KERRY

Countess Rd, has modern rooms with TVs, en suite bathrooms and wonderful views.

Copper Kettle (☎ 34164; Lewis Rd; s/d €70/100; Ⓟ) A grandfather clock in a purpose-built alcove by the entrance sets the tone for this modern B&B, where the comfy rooms have bright wood surrounds. Big breakfasts are served a few metres away at sister guesthouse Fairview.

Fáilte Hotel (☎ 33404; failtehotel@eircom.net; College St; s/d €75/120) Recently refurbished, the Fáilte is not the best value in town, but has a good location, restaurant, and bar, where there's music nightly during the summer. The 15 rooms, particularly number five, are attractively decorated with patchwork quilts, flowers and contemporary canvases.

Top End

ourpick **Fairview** (☎ 34164; www.fairviewkillarney.com; Lewis Rd; s/d €80/130; Ⓟ ♿ 🖳) Alluring touches such as curvy fittings, antique furniture, underfloor heating, Jacuzzi baths and plasma-screen TVs give this guesthouse both comfort and character. The courteous service and the location (walking distance from the centre, but out of the hubbub) are both perfect.

Arbutus Hotel (☎ 31037; www.arbutuskillarney .com; College St; s/d from €80/150; 🕐 Feb-Nov) Bedrooms range from those with 1920s Celtic Deco furniture to more modern rooms with black-and-white bathrooms and the bath in a sweeping alcove. Trad sessions fire up in Buckley's Bar on Saturday and Monday nights and Sunday lunchtimes.

The Ross (☎ 31855; www.theross.ie; Kenmare Pl; tw & d €170-225; Ⓟ 🖳) This unrepentantly modern, 29-room boutique hotel cheekily uses the pool and spa of its older sibling, the Killarney Park hotel. A chic haven, it features a cocktail bar, a restaurant reached by a glass staircase and purple-lit corridors with thick carpets patterned with huge, pink flowers.

EATING
Budget

Jam (☎ 31441; 77 High St; snacks & meals €2-8; 🕐 8am-6pm Mon-Sat) This funky little café is a healthy pit stop for hot meals, soups, salads, sandwiches, and coffee and cake.

Cathleen's Country Kitchen (☎ 33778; New St; breakfast & lunch €3.50-11; 🕐 9am-5.30pm) The place for a breakfast roll, boiled bacon for lunch and no-nonsense service.

Sceale Eile (☎ 35066; 73 High St; mains €6-11; 🕐 9.30am-5pm Mon-Sat) This canteen café, with

Irish literary memorabilia decorating the walls upstairs, energises Killarney's workforce with baguettes, bagels, burgers, lasagna and roasts.

Cronin's (☎ 31521; 9 College St; mains €9-19; 🕐 9am-9.30pm) One of a cluster of eateries in this area, this long-established, family-run restaurant is popular for breakfasts with all the trimmings, roasts lathered in gravy, and sweet pies with dollops of cream. As the curvy lamps and mirrors suggest, it goes upmarket at night.

For homemade ice cream and snacks, head to **Mac's of Main Street** (☎ 35213; Main St) and/or **Murphy's Ice Cream** (☎ 066-9152644; Main St).

Dunne's Stores (☎ 35888; New St) has a well-stocked supermarket with a fill-your-own salad and pasta counter, and there's a **Tesco** on the corner of Beech Rd and New St.

Midrange

Most restaurants offer early-bird specials between 6pm and 7pm.

Laurels (☎ 31149; www.thelaurelspub.com; Main St; mains €14-20; 🕐 12-3pm & 6-9.30pm) Tasty but pricey pub grub such as burgers and pizzas with inventive toppings. Sit in the bar rather than the restaurant to enjoy a setting that mixes a traditional feel with slick, friendly service. The Guinness is smooth, and champ (potatoes mashed with spring onions) is a house speciality.

Stone Chat (☎ 34295; 8 Flemings Lane; mains €14-23; 🕐 12.30-3pm & 6-9pm) This secluded restaurant serves traditional and more cosmopolitan dishes, from Kerry lamb to Moroccan-style monkfish, and chicken wrapped in Parma ham. The great vegetarian selection includes spicy fajitas and a tagliatelle with coconut cream and chilli essence. Try the grilled salmon with crunchy sautéed vegetables.

Treyvaud's (☎ 33062; 62 High St; mains €15-24; 🕐 noon-10.30pm Apr-Sep, check times rest of year) Michael Treyvaud's modish restaurant has a strong reputation for subtle dishes that merge trad Irish with seductive European influences, from prime beef meatballs to deep-fried cannelloni filled with butternut squash.

ourpick **Brícín** (☎ 34902; 26 High St; mains €18-20; 🕐 12.30-3pm & 6-9pm Tue-Sat) Decorated with fittings from a convent, an orphanage and a school, this Celtic Deco restaurant doubles as the town museum, with Jonathan

Fisher's 18th-century views of the national park taking pride of place. Dishes such as Kerry lamb, salmon stuffed with crab meat and house speciality *boxty* (potato pancake) draw a loyal local crowd.

Top End

Gaby's Seafood Restaurant (☎ 32519; 27 High St; mains €18-50; ☸ 6-10pm Mon-Sat) Dissenters mutter that Gaby's is overpriced and overrated, preferring alternatives such as nearby Foley's, but we found the restaurant to be well deserving of its awards, which seem to number one for each of its 31 years of slick but warm service. Peruse the menu by the fire before drifting past the wine cellar to the low-lit dining room, where you'll savour exquisite Gallic dishes such as lobster in a secret sauce that includes cognac and cream. There are even a few choices for non-seafood lovers.

DRINKING & ENTERTAINMENT

Most pubs put on live music, and most nights are lively here – even Mondays, when many of the town's hospitality staff are released to the fun side of the bar. Plunkett and College Sts are lined with pubs.

O'Connor's (☎ 30977; High St) Typically, this tiny pub is one of Killarney's most popular haunts. There's entertainment every night, from trad sessions to stand-up comedy, storytelling and pub theatre.

Killarney Grand (☎ 31159; Main St; music 9pm-2.45am) There's free entry before 11pm to this busy Killarney institution, where trad music gives way to live bands, set dancing on Wednesdays and a nightclub at weekends.

Granary (☎ 20075; Touhills Lane) Hidden down the alley next to the Killarney Grand, this bar/restaurant is one of the coolest hangouts in town, with low lighting, exposed stone walls, and leather sofas. Bands and DJs play at weekends.

McSorley's (☎ 37280; College St) A popular, clubby bar with multicoloured lighting and kilt-clad cover bands.

Gleneagle (☎ 36000; Muckross Rd) You can catch cabaret nightly during the summer, or bop late at O'D's Nightclub on Friday and Saturday nights.

Cinemas

Killarney Cineplex (☎ 37007; Kenmare Pl; adult/child €9/5.50) This four-screener has a good run of contemporary releases.

SHOPPING

Variety Sounds (☎ 35755; 7 College St) An eclectic music shop with a good range of traditional music, instruments, sheet music and learn-to-play books.

Aran Sweater Market (☎ 39756; College St) Aran sweaters galore wrap round you at this well-stocked place.

Killarney Outlet Centre (☎ 36744; Fair Hill) This mall has a number of shops including Lowe Alpine, Nike Factory Store and Blarney Woollen Mills, all selling brand-name clothing and other products at healthy discounts.

O'Sullivan's Outdoor Store (☎ 26927; New St) There's a general selection of activity gear at O'Sullivan's branches.

Brícín (☎ 34902; 26 High St) One of the craft shops offering interesting items such as local craftwork alongside reproduced vintage Guinness advertisements and touristy fare.

GETTING THERE & AWAY

Air

Kerry Airport (☎ 066-9764644; www.kerryairport.com) is at Farranfore, about 15km north of Killarney along the N22 and then about 1.5km along the N23. **Aer Arann** (☎ 0818 210210; www.aerarann .com) has daily flights to Dublin, a Manchester service on Monday, Wednesday and Friday, and a flight to Lorient, France, on Saturday between June and September. **Ryanair** (☎ 0818 303030; www.ryanair.com) operates a daily flight to London Stansted (twice daily Easter to October), and serves Frankfurt–Hahn on Monday, Wednesday, Friday and Sunday.

The small airport has a café, bureau de change, an ATM and wi-fi. Car hire agencies with desks at the airport:

Avis (086-2604454; www.avis.ie)

Budget (064-34341; www.budget.ie)

Dooley Car Rentals (062-53103; www.dooleycarrentals .com)

Europcar (087-2383938; www.europcar.com)

Hertz (064-34126; www.hertz.ie)

Irish Car Rentals (086-1700650; www.irishcarrentals .com)

National and Alamo (086-3846193; www.carhire.ie)

Bus

Bus Éireann (☎ 34777, 30011) operates from next to the train station, with regular links to Tralee (€7.50, 35 minutes, hourly); Cork (€14.50, two hours, 15 daily); Dublin (€22, six hours, six daily); Galway (€20.50, seven hours, seven daily) via Limerick (€15, 2¼ hours); Waterford (€20.50, 4½ hours, hourly); and Rosslare Harbour (€24, six to seven hours, three daily).

From June to mid-September, there are daily Ring of Kerry services (see p259).

Train

Killarney's train station (☎ 31067) is on Park Rd, east of the centre. There are up to three direct trains a day to Cork (€22.50, 1½ hours) and nine to Tralee (€8.50, 45 minutes). There are direct trains to Dublin, but you may have to change at Mallow, while Waterford and Limerick require a few changes.

GETTING AROUND
To/From the Airport

Bus Éireann services between Killarney and the airport run roughly two hourly, every day between June and September. Outside this period, however, there are only one or two daily services, Monday to Saturday. Another option is to catch a bus to Farranfore, 1.5km from the airport.

A private shuttle bus (☎ 36666), geared towards flights from Frankfurt, departs from outside Concoran's (Map p248) at 10.30am and from the airport at noon. Phone ahead to reserve a seat.

A taxi to Killarney costs about €30. The town taxi rank is on College St.

Car

The centre of Killarney can be thick with traffic at times. **Budget** (☎ 34341; Kenmare Pl) is the only car-hire outfit with an office in town; **Avis** (☎ 36655; Beech Rd) has a booth at the tourist office from June to August. Otherwise contact the companies at the airport.

There is a sizeable, free car park next to St Mary's Cathedral. The central car parks cost €1 per hour, 8.30am to 6.30pm Monday to Saturday.

Bicycle

Bicycles are ideal for exploring the scattered sights of the Killarney area, many of which are accessible only by bike or on foot. Several places hire bikes for about €15 per day including pannier bags, tool kit and maps.

O'Sullivan's Bike Hire (☎ 31282) has branches on New Street, opposite the cathedral, and on Beech Rd, opposite the tourist office.

> **DETOUR: AGHADOE**
>
> On a hilltop 5km west of town, Aghadoe's views of Killarney, the lakes and Inisfallen Island have for centuries moved tourists to trek up here. At the eastern end of the meadow, in front of the Aghadoe Heights Hotel, are the ruins of a **Romanesque church** and the 13th-century **Parkavonear Castle**. Parkavonear's keep, still standing, is one of the few cylindrical rather than rectangular keeps built by the Normans in Ireland. Unsurprisingly, its name translates as 'field of the meadow'.
>
> To get there by car from Killarney, turn right off the N72 after the turning for Killarney Riding Stables. Between Monday and Saturday, June to September, four daily buses link Killarney and Aghadoe. Some tours stop there.

Jaunting Car

If you're not on two wheels, Killarney's traditional transport is the horse-drawn **jaunting car** (☎ 33358; www.killarneyjauntingcars.com), which comes with a driver known as a jarvey. The pick-up point, nicknamed 'the Ha Ha' or 'the Block', is on Kenmare Pl. Trips cost €40 to €70, depending on distance; traps officially carry four people. Jaunting cars also congregate in the N71 car park for Muckross House and Abbey, and at the Gap of Dunloe.

AROUND KILLARNEY

KILLARNEY NATIONAL PARK

Any cynicism built up among Killarney's 'My friend kissed the Blarney Stone and all I got was this lousy T-shirt' stores evaporates when you enter the park. Buses rumble up to Ross Castle and Muckross House, but it's possible to flee the rest of tourist-kind in 10,236 hectares, among Ireland's only wild herd of native Red Deer, the country's largest area of ancient Oakwoods and views of most of its major mountains.

The glacial Lough Leane (the Lower Lake or 'Lake of Learning'), Muckross Lake and the Upper Lake make up about a quarter of the park. Their peaty waters are as rich in wildlife as the surrounding soil: cormorants

COUNTY KERRY

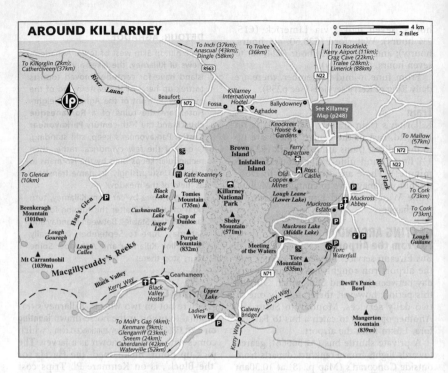

AROUND KILLARNEY

skim across the surface, deer swim out to graze on the islands, and salmon, trout and perch prosper in a pike-free environment.

Designated a Unesco Biosphere Reserve in 1982, the park extends to the southwest of town. There are pedestrian entrances opposite St Mary's Cathedral (Map p248), with other entrances (for drivers) off the N71.

Knockreer House & Gardens

Near the St Mary's Cathedral entrance to the park stands Knockreer House, with gardens featuring a terraced lawn and a summerhouse. Built in the 1870s on the advice of Queen Victoria, the original building burned down and the present incarnation dates from 1958. The house isn't open to the public, but the gardens have views across the lakes to the mountains. From the St Mary's Cathedral entrance, follow the path immediately to your right uphill for about 500m.

Ross Castle

Restored by Dúchas, **Ross Castle** (☎ 35851; Ross Rd; adult/child €5.30/2.10; ◷ 9am-6.30pm Jun-Aug, 9.30am-5.30pm Sep–mid-Oct & mid-Mar–May, 9.30am-4.30pm Tue–

Sun & bank holidays mid-Oct–mid-Nov; P) dates back to the 15th century, when it was a residence of the O'Donoghues. It was the last place in Munster to succumb to Cromwell's forces, thanks partly to its cunning spiral staircase, in which every step is a different height, in order to break an attacker's stride.

According to a prophecy, the castle would be captured only from the water, so in 1652 the Cromwellian commander, Ludlow, had floating batteries brought to Lough Leane from Castlemaine Harbour along the River Laune. Seeing the prophecy about to be fulfilled, the defenders, having resisted the English siege from the land for months, promptly surrendered.

The castle is a 2.4km walk from the St Mary's Cathedral pedestrian park entrance. If you're driving from Killarney, turn right opposite the Esso garage at the start of Muckross Rd. Access is by guided tour only.

Inisfallen Island

The first monastery on Inisfallen Island (at 22 acres, the largest of the national park's 26 islands) is said to have been founded by St

Finian the Leper in the 7th century. The island's fame dates from the early 13th century when the Annals of Inisfallen were written here. The annals, now in the Bodleian Library in Oxford, England, remain a vital source of information on early Munster history. On Inisfallen (the name means 'island') are the ruins of a 12th-century **oratory** with a carved Romanesque doorway and a **monastery** on the site of St Finian's original.

You can hire boats from Ross Castle to row to the island. Alternatively, boaters charge passengers around €7 each for the crossing. Some Gap of Dunloe boats and bus tours also stop here.

Muckross Estate

The core of Killarney National Park is the Muckross Estate, donated to the state by Arthur Bourn Vincent in 1932. **Muckross House** (☎ 31440; www.muckross-house.ie; adult/child/family €5.50/2.25/13.75, combined ticket with farms €8.25/3.75/21; ☯ 9am-6pm Sep-Jun, to 7pm Jul & Aug; P ☝) is a 19th-century mansion, restored to its former glory and packed with contemporaneous fittings. Entrance is by guided tour.

The beautiful gardens sloping down to the lake include a walled garden with ornamental flower beds. A block behind the house contains a restaurant, craft shop and studios where you can see potters, weavers and bookbinders at work. Jaunting cars wait to run you though deer parks and woodland to Torc Waterfall and Muckross Abbey (about €10 each return).

Immediately east of Muckross House are the **Muckross Traditional Farms** (☎ 31440; adult/child/family €5.75/2.35/14.50, combined ticket with Muckross House €8.25/3.75/21; ☯ 10am-6pm Jun-Sep, 1-6pm

May, 1-6pm Sat, Sun & public holidays mid-Mar–Apr & Oct). These reproductions of 1930s Kerry farms, complete with chickens, pigs, cattle and horses, show farming and living conditions before electricity was available.

Muckross House is 5km south of town, signposted from the N71. During the summer, O'Connor's Tours (below) operates a tourist bus, leaving for the house at 1.45pm and returning at 5.15pm (return €10). The house is included in some half-day tours of Killarney, and it would be possible to work it into a circuit of the park and the Gap of Dunloe.

If you're walking or cycling to Muckross, there's a cycle track alongside the Kenmare road for most of the first 2km. A path then turns right into Killarney National Park. Following this path, after 1km you'll come to **Muckross Abbey**, which was founded in 1448 and burned by Cromwell's troops in 1652. William Thackeray called it 'the prettiest little bijou of a ruined abbey ever seen'. Muckross House is another 1.5km from the abbey ruins.

If you're cycling around Muckross lake, it's easier and more scenic to go in an anticlockwise direction. Given that most people choose this direction, this also lessens the chance of collisions between cyclists speeding in opposite directions.

Gap of Dunloe

Geographically, the Gap of Dunloe is outside the Killarney National Park, but most people include it in their visit to the park. In the winter, it's an awe-inspiring mountain pass, overshadowed by Purple Mountain and Macgillycuddy's Reeks. In high summer, it's a bottleneck for the tourist trade, with buses

MUNROS AND HEWITTS

Macgillycuddy's Reeks is the name of the magnificent group of mountains to the southwest of Killarney, concentrated to the west of the Gap of Dunloe. The name Macgillycuddy derives from the ancient Mac Gilla Muchudas clan; *reek* means pointed hill. In Gaeltacht they're known as Na Crucha Dubha (the black tops).

The red sandstone mountains were carved by minor glaciers into elegant forms, such as Carrantuohil's curved outline – referred to in its name, which translates as 'reversed reaping hook'. The mountains are studded with awesome cliffs, the summits are buttressed by ridges of purplish rock and the cupped valleys between are filled with glittering lakes.

The Reeks are Ireland's highest mountain range, featuring nine of its 12 *munros* (a Scottish term meaning a mountain over 900m). These include the country's seven highest peaks, towering alongside roughly half of Ireland's 211 *hewitts* (hills in England, Wales and Ireland that are over 2000 feet, or 610m).

depositing countless visitors at Kate Kearney's Cottage for the one-hour horse-and-trap ride through the Gap.

The best way to see the Gap is to hire a bike from Killarney (p253) and cycle to Ross Castle. Get there before 11am to catch a boat up the lakes to Lord Brandon's Cottage, then cycle through the Gap and back to town via the N72 and a path through the golf course (for bike hire and boat trip, about €30).

The 1½-hour boat ride alone justifies the trip. It crosses all the lakes, passing islands and bridges and winding between the second two lakes via Meeting of the Waters and the Long Range. The proprietor of Brícín restaurant, which is named after the bridge on the Muckross Peninsula, enthuses, 'Get out on an open boat and you'll feel like Robinson Crusoe'.

On land, walking, pony or four-person trap can be substituted for cycling. The Gap pony men charge €50 per hour or €80 for the two-hour trip between Lord Brandon's Cottage and Kate Kearney's Cottage.

Among the tour companies offering the circuit, **O'Connor's Tours** (☎ 30200; www.gapof dunloetours.com; High St) and **O'Donoghue Brothers Boating Tours** (☎ 31068; www.killarneydaytour.com; Muckross Rd) specialise in tours to the Gap and the national park.

Lunch, afternoon tea and dinner are available at the 19th-century pub **Kate Kearney's Cottage** (☎ 44146; lunch €10.50-13), a preferable pit stop to **Lord Brandon's Cottage** (snacks €6.50), an ugly snack bar redeemed only by its views down Upper Lake.

In winter it's possible to drive through the gap, but access is restricted during the summer.

WALKING

There are numerous low-level walking opportunities around Killarney, such as the four-hour circuit of Muckross Lake. The Killarney tourist office and local bookshops stock trekking guides, and the map (Ordnance Survey Map Discovery Series No 78) needed to tackle Carrantuohil (1039m), Ireland's highest peak, and the other mountains.

Ascending Macgillycuddy's Reeks and their neighbours (Purple, Tomies and Shehy mountains, between the Gap of Dunloe and Lough Leane, and Torc and Mangerton mountains, southeast of Muckross Lake) should never be attempted without having the skills to use a map and compass. Weatherproof and water-

proof footwear and clothing are essential at all times of the year. Seek advice locally before attempting mountain walks.

There are several ways up Carrantuohil. Some require reasonable hill-walking ability; others are serious scrambling or rock-climbing routes. You can get a taste of the Reeks at close quarters by walking up Hag's Glen, the beautiful approach valley that leads to the lakes of Callee and Gouragh below the north face of Carrantuohil.

The best approach is from **Cronin's Yard** (☎ 34963; www.croninsyard.com; Mealis), where there's a tearoom, showers and toilets, a public telephone, and packed lunches available on request. It's at the road's end (OS ref 836873), reached from the N72 via Beaufort, west of Killarney. You may be asked to pay a small fee for using the car park. From there, the way lies alongside the Gaddagh River, which you need to ford in places; great care is required if it's in flood. It's just over 3km to the lakes.

The popular, but hair-raising, way to the summit of Carrantuohil from the lakes is via **Devil's Ladder**, a gruelling trudge up a badly eroded gully path, southwest of the lakes. The ground is loose in places, and in wet conditions the way becomes muddy. This takes six hours return from Cronin's Yard.

ORGANISED TOURS

Guided two-hour **national park walks** (☎ 33471, 087-639 4362; www.killarneyguidedwalks.com; adult/child €9/4.50) leave at 11am daily from outside O'Sullivan's at the western end of New Street. Guide Richard Clancy, fresh from his post round, and his Irish red setter Rua, meander through Knockreer gardens, then to spots where Charles de Gaulle holidayed, David Lean filmed *Ryan's Daughter* and Brother Cudda slept for 200 years. Trips are available at other times on request.

A number of Killarney companies run daily day trips by bus around the Ring of Kerry (€25), the Gap of Dunloe (p255) and Dingle Peninsula (€25). Tours run from 10.30am until around 5.30pm. Half-day tours (€17), taking in Aghadoe, Ross Castle, Muckross House and Torc Waterfall also operate daily, as do bike tours and lake cruises. Tour operators include **Dero's Tours** (☎ 31251; www.derostours.com; Main St), **Corcoran's** (☎ 36666; 8 College St) and **O'Connor Autotours** (☎ 34833; Ross Rd). However, unless you're really pushed for time, the tours can be too rushed to do the scenery justice.

Destination Killarney (☎ 32638; East Avenue Rd) and **Killarney Watercoach Cruises** (☎ 31068) operate hour-long lake cruises with commentary (adult/child €8/4). During the summer, they leave from Ross Castle on a roughly hourly basis – check at the tourist office (p249) for departure times.

The **open boats** (☎ 087-6899241) nearby offer more appealing trips for higher prices. While up to 10 boats (seating 12 people) work the lakes in the summer, you'll be lucky to meet a boatman during the winter.

KILLARNEY TO KENMARE

The N71 to Kenmare winds between rock and lake, with plenty of laybys to stop and admire the views. Watch out for the buses squeezing along the road. About 2km south of the entrance to Muckross House, a path leads 200m to the pretty **Torc Waterfall**. After another 8km on the N71 you come to **Ladies' View**, where the fine views along Upper Lake were much enjoyed by Queen Victoria's ladies-in-waiting, who gave the viewpoint its name. There are cafés here and 5km further on at **Moll's Gap**, another good viewpoint.

WALK: REEKS RIDGE

Experienced walkers with confidence over steep ground could consider the longest and most sustained ridge walk in Ireland, a seven-hour, 13km trek with wide-ranging views. The demanding trek scales six 900m-plus peaks – including Knocknapeasta and Maolán Buí, Ireland's fourth- and fifth-highest summits – with a total ascent of 1050m.

The exposed walk should be avoided in windy conditions. In poor weather, or when there is a chance of encountering snow and ice, it is a serious undertaking. An ice axe, and perhaps other mountaineering equipment, should be carried; only those with winter mountaineering experience should attempt it.

From Cronin's Yard, pass through a gate on the right of the yard. Skirt a field on a grass track, cross a stile and follow the stony track that climbs gently above the Gaddagh River. Leave the track where it crosses a tributary of the Gaddagh and head southeast across open ground, climbing the increasingly steep slopes towards the conspicuous summit of **Cruach Mór** (932m). Aim slightly east of the summit to find easier ground. The top, marked by a stone grotto, has impressive views south across the Iveragh Peninsula (1½ to two hours from the start).

However, your attention is likely to be drawn by the rock ridge running south towards the **Big Gun** (939m). Huge blocks of rock (gendarmes) adorn the crest of the ridge, making it initially difficult to keep to the top. Follow informal paths below and to the west of the ridge, being careful not to lose too much height. Scramble back up to the ridge at a notch, then climb – with care – directly along the exciting rocky arête to reach the Big Gun. The ridge now swings southwest towards Knocknapeasta. Stick to the crest as you descend to a col, but where the ridge becomes difficult again you can drop south (left) of the arête before rejoining it just beneath the summit of **Knocknapeasta** (988m; one hour from Cruach Mór).

The views from the highest point on the walk are tremendous, taking in Ireland's three highest summits to the west and, to the east, the serrated ridge you have traversed. To the north, wild cliffs fall away into the dark waters of Lough Cummeenapeasta, with the patchwork fields of north Kerry beyond. To the south, the mountain falls away to Black Valley, and ridge after ridge of mountains extend towards the Atlantic.

Head south from Knocknapeasta along a broad, stony ridge, then bear southwest as you drop to a col and climb a short distance to the summit of **Maolán Buí** (973m). Cross an unnamed top at 926m to reach **Cnoc an Chuillin** (958m), the last major peak on the ridge. Now descend to a col and climb onto another unnamed summit. It is best to descend directly into Hags Glen from here, keeping to the west of steep ground, though some walkers brave Devil's Ladder (opposite) further to the west. Once in Hags Glen, follow the stony track for 4km to the finish (one to 1½ hours).

An alternative route (eight to 10 hours, 15km, 1450m ascent) for very fit walkers extends the route west across Ireland's two highest peaks – Carrauntoohil (1039m) and Beenkeragh (1010m) – before descending to Hags Glen.

RING OF KERRY

This 179km circuit of the Iveragh Peninsula pops up on every self-respecting tourist itinerary for a good reason. The secondary road winds past pristine beaches, the island-dotted Atlantic, medieval ruins, mountains, and loughs (lakes). Even locals stop their cars to gawk at the rugged coastline – particularly between Waterville and Caherdaniel in the southwest of the peninsula, where the beauty dial is turned up to 11.

Although it can be 'done' in a day by car or bus, or three days by bicycle, the more time you take, the more you'll enjoy it. Tour buses travel the Ring in an anticlockwise direction. Getting stuck behind one is tedious, but driving in the opposite direction and meeting one on a blind corner is hair-raising. A good place to escape both scenarios is the tip of the peninsula, where the sleepy Skellig Ring is too narrow for coaches.

There's also little traffic on the Ballaghbeama Gap, which cuts across the peninsula's central highlands with some spectacular views: it's perfect for a long cycle, as is the longer Ballaghisheen Pass to Waterville. The 214km Kerry Way (p699) starts and ends in Killarney.

RING OF KERRY

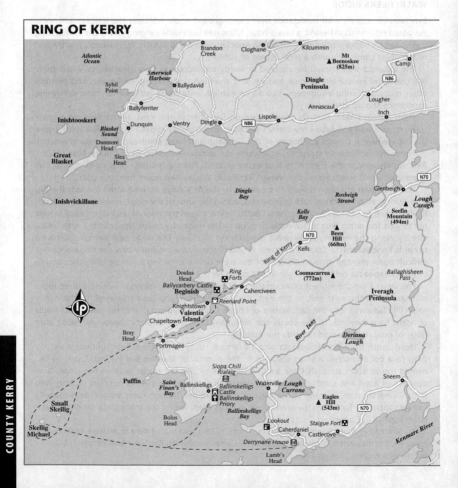

GETTING AROUND

From June to mid-September, Bus Éireann operates a daily Ring of Kerry service (bus 280), leaving Killarney at 1.15pm and returning at 5.40pm. Stops include Killorglin, Glenbeigh, Caherciveen, Waterville, Caherdaniel and Molls Gap. From Monday to Saturday during the same period, bus 279 links Killarney with Waterville and Caherciveen via stops including Killorglin. Services leave Killarney at 9.50am and 3pm, Waterville at 7.30am, and Caherciveen at 12.15pm. For details, ring **Killarney bus station** (☎ 064-30011).

A number of Killarney tour companies also run daily day trips by bus around the Ring of Kerry (€25).

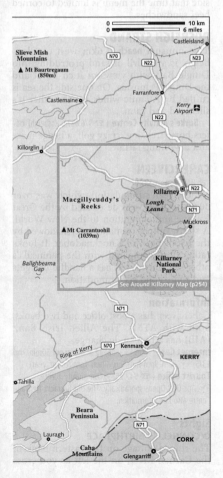

KILLORGLIN

☎ 066 / pop 3870

Travelling anticlockwise from Killarney, the first town on the Ring is Killorglin (Cill Orglan). The town is quieter than the waters of the River Laune that lap against the eight-arched bridge, built in 1885. In August, there's an explosion of time-honoured ceremonies and libations at the famous pagan festival, the Puck Fair. A handsome statue of King Puck (yes, he's a goat) can be seen on the Killarney side of the river. Author Blake Morrison documents his mother's childhood here in *Things My Mother Never Told Me*.

There is a helpful **tourist office** (☎ 976 1451; Library Pl; ☑ 9am-5pm Mon-Sat) with maps, walking guides, pottery and souvenirs for sale, and free internet access at the **library** (☎ 976 1272; Library Pl; ☑ 10am-5pm Tue-Sat). For taxis call **Laune Cabs** (☎ 1800-223 223).

Festivals

The lively **Puck Fair Festival** (Aonach an Phuic; ☎ 976 2366; www.puckfair.ie) takes place 10-12 August. First recorded in 1603, its origins are hazy. It is based around the custom of installing a billy goat (a poc, or puck), the symbol of mountainous Kerry, on a pedestal in the town, its horns festooned with ribbons. Other entertainment ranges from the horse fair and bonny baby competition to street theatre and the pubs staying open until 3am. Accommodation is hard to find if you have not booked in advance.

TOP FIVE KERRY ADVENTURES

- Climb **Mt Carrantuohil** (p256) or **Mt Brandon** (p292), but dress correctly and know how to use a map and compass.

- Try both your hands at rock climbing and canoeing at **Caherdaniel** (p265).

- Pack the seasickness pills and head for the **Skellig Islands** (p262). Who needs Himalayan trekking trips?

- Go horse riding along the western shores and beaches of the **Iveragh Peninsula** (opposite).

- Visit the **Blaskets** (p294). Not as testing as the trip to the Skelligs, but a ticket to a timeless island landscape in its own right.

Sleeping

West's Holiday Park (☎ 976 1240; enquiries@west caravans.com; Killarney Rd; camp sites €18; ✹ Apr-Oct) This small site has views of Carrantuohil across tree-lined fields. On the N72, just under 2km east of the bridge, it has a tennis court and the owners can advise walkers and fishers.

Coffey's River's Edge (☎ 976 1750; www.coffeysrivers edge.com; the Bridge; s/d €50/100; Ⓟ) An unbeatable location right by the bridge over the River Laune on the village side makes this an attractive stop. Rooms are smart and bright.

Eating & Drinking

At the supermarket on the Square, Upper Bridge St, you'll find a help-yourself deli counter.

ourpick **Sol Y Sombra** (☎ 976 2347; Lower Bridge St; dishes €5-13; ✹ Wed-Mon Jun-Aug, Wed-Sun Sep-Jan & Mar-May, closed Feb) This tapas bar, in a beautifully renovated church, transports you to Mediterranean soil with its tapas and larger raciones dishes (for sharing), such as grilled squid, marinated anchovy fillets and pan-fried oyster mushrooms. There are 40 Spanish wines to choose from. Bands play at weekends, with occasional flamenco dancing.

Bunkers Bar & Coffee Shop (☎ 976 1381; Iveragh Rd; mains €7-19; ✹ 9am-10pm) This pub/restaurant pays no dues to smart décor, but offers a good choice of grub from steak to chicken Kiev. Breakfast is about €6.50.

Dev's 'N The Square (the Square; €17-25; ✹ 9am-3pm & 6-10pm) Unpretentious Dev's offers hefty duckling, steak and lamb dishes, accompanied by jacket potatoes with garlic butter. Try the grilled Atlantic salmon with lemon-and-herb couscous.

Nick's Seafood Restaurant (☎ 976 1219; info@nicks .ie; Lower Bridge St; mains €20-38; ✹ 6.30-9.30pm Tue-Sun May-Sep, Wed-Sun Oct-Mar) French–Irish flair makes this fine restaurant an enduring favourite. Dishes such as moules and shellfish mornay get the first-class preparation they deserve; or choose the best Kerry beef and lamb or great vegetarian dishes. The extensive wine list features a seductive house wine.

Pubs include the old and spacious **Clifford's Tavern** (Upper Bridge St), which fills up on Friday and Saturday nights when there are trad sessions. There are Thursday sessions at the **Laune Bar** (Lower Bridge St) on the corner above the bridge.

KERRY BOG VILLAGE MUSEUM

On the N70 between Killorglin and Glenbeigh, the **Kerry Bog Village Museum** (☎ 976 9184; adult/child/family €4.50/4/15; ✹ 9am-7pm Easter-Oct, 9am-6pm rest of year) re-creates a 19th-century bog village, typical of the small communities that carved out a precarious living in the harsh environment of Ireland's ubiquitous peat bogs. There are re-creations of the homes of the turfcutter, blacksmith, thatcher and labourer, and a dairy. Some Kerry Bog ponies are in a field behind the museum.

Next to the museum, the **Red Fox** (☎ 976 9288; Glenbeigh; meals €7-12) serves reasonable nosh between Easter and October, but outside that time the menu is limited to corned beef sandwiches.

ROSBEIGH STRAND

This unusual **beach**, 1.6km west of Glenbeigh, is a tendril of sand protruding into Dingle Bay, with views of Inch Point and the Dingle Peninsula. On one side the sea is ruffled by Atlantic winds; on the other it's sheltered and calm.

Burke's Activity Centre (☎ 976 8872; Rosbeigh) offers horse trekking, crazy golf, a hedge maze and a working farm.

CAHERCIVEEN

☎ 066 / pop 1300

Caherciveen's population, which was over 30,000 in 1841, was desecrated by the Great Famine and emigration to the New World. A sleepy outpost remains, overshadowed by the 688m peak of Knocknadobar. It looks rather dour compared with the peninsula's other settlements, but has a handful of sights and some good accommodation.

Information

Caherciveen has a post office and two banks, both with ATMs. The Allied Irish Bank (AIB) has a bureau de change.

Internet Café (☎ 948 1885; 12 Main St; per 30min/1hr €3/5; ✹ 9am-9pm Jun-Aug, 11am-7pm rest of year)
Tourist office (☎ 947 2589; Community Centre; ✹ Apr-Oct) Opens sporadically. The Old Barracks Heritage Centre also has information.

Sights

O'CONNELL'S BIRTHPLACE

The ruined cottage on the eastern bank of the Carhan River, on the left as you cross the bridge en route from Kells, is the humble birthplace of Daniel O'Connell, 'The Great Liberator' (see p37). On the opposite bank is an amenity area with a handsome bust of the great Catholic leader. There are paths along the river, with boards explaining the area's wildlife.

BARRACKS
The Old Barracks Heritage Centre (☎ 947 2777; off Main St; adult/child €4/2; ⏰ 10am-4pm Mon-Sat Mar-May & Oct-Dec, 10am-6pm Mon-Sat, 1-5pm Sun Jun-Sep) is housed in a tower of the former Royal Irish Constabulary (RIC) barracks. Legend has it that, when the building was reconstructed after anti-Treaty forces burnt it down in 1922, the plans got mixed up with those intended for a barracks in India. There's a definite Northwest Frontier look.

Topped by a spiral staircase ascending to a lookout with underwhelming windows, the museum covers subjects of local and national interest, such as the Fenian Rising, Daniel O'Connell and Caherciveen's other great son, Gaelic football star Jack O'Shea. There are re-creations of a local dwelling at the time of the famine and of the barracks during the 1916 Easter Rising.

BALLYCARBERY CASTLE & RING FORTS
The ruins of Ballycarbery Castle are 2.4km along the road to White Strand Beach from the barracks. The 16th-century castle was inhabited by the McCarthy More chieftains and, later, Sir Valentine Brown, surveyor general of Ireland under Elizabeth I.

Along the same road are two stone ring forts. Cahergall, the larger one, dates from the 10th century and has stairways on the inside walls, a *clochan* (beehive hut), and the remains of a house. The smaller, 9th-century Leacanabuile has the entrance to an underground passage. Their inner walls and chambers give a strong sense of what life was like in a ring fort. If driving, leave your car in the parking area next to a stone wall and walk up the footpaths.

Activities
Local **walks** include the 5½ hour Killelan Mountain circuit, and the less strenuous foreshore walk to the castle and ring forts.

From June to September, a two-hour **guided walk** (☎ 947 3186; adult/child €7/4) to archaeological and historic sites leaves from the UN Bar, opposite the post office, at 11am every morning.

Boat trips (☎ 947 3186; €15; ⏰ Jun-Sep) on the Valentia River are run by the walk organiser each afternoon.

Festivals
Celtic music is a major component of the **Caherciveen Festival of Music & the Arts** (☎ 947 3772; www.celticmusicfestival.com), which takes place over the bank holiday weekend at the beginning of August and features cover bands, busking competitions and set dancing.

Sleeping
Sive Hostel (☎ 947 2717; sivehostel.ie; 15 East End; dm/d €16/44) There is a faint hospital whiff about the pink sheets in this IHH property's small dorms, but the comfortable TV lounge is a winner.

Mannix Point Camping & Caravan Park (☎ 947 2806; www.campinginkerry.com; Mannix Point; camp sites €19; ⏰ Mar-Oct) Mortimer Moriarty's award-winning coastal site has radio piped into the bathrooms, a lounge and music room, an inviting kitchen with gas stoves, a barbecue area, and even a bird-watching platform.

O'Shea's B&B (☎ 947 2402; www.osheasbnb.com; Church St; s/d €37/64; **P**) Four en-suite rooms in a comfortable family house with views of the castle and barracks. A good source of local information, the O'Sheas organise walking and boat trips.

Sea Breeze (☎ 947 2609; seabreezebandb@eircom .net; Reenard Rd; s/d €45/70) This gleaming B&B has a conservatory gazing across the harbour at the castle and Doulus Head. It is 500m southwest of town en route to Reenard Point.

Eating
Helen's Coffee Shop (☎ 947 2056; Main St; snacks €4-6) Helen's is a cheerful gem of a place serving a range of coffees as well as various tasty soups and sandwiches, homemade cakes and confectionary.

Amarantine (☎ 947 3499; 14 Church St; meals & snacks €4-11) This nondescript café-wine bar has a good name locally for its ciabattas, salads, pastries and mains.

Fertha (☎ 947 2023; 20 Main St; bar food €7-12) This is a spacious pub offering a range of steady dishes including roasts and poached salmon.

Entertainment

Trad sessions can be found in An Bonnán Buí, the Anchor, and among the fishing tackle in Mike Murts.

VALENTIA ISLAND

☎ 066 / pop 715

Crowned by Geokaun Mountain, 11km-long Valentia Island (Oileán Dairbhre) is an altogether homier isle than the brooding Skelligs to the southwest. Its hills and fields roll in harmony with those of the mainland, to which it's connected by ferry and bridge. Like the Skellig Ring that it leads to, it's a worthwhile, coach-free detour from the Ring of Kerry. A bracing walk takes in Geokaun Mountain and Fogher Cliff.

Valentia was chosen as the site for the first transatlantic telegraph cable. When the connection was made in 1858, it put Caherciveen in direct contact with New York, although it had no connection with Dublin. The link worked for 27 days before failing, but went back into action years later. The telegraph station operated until 1966.

Portmagee (population 376), overlooking the south side of the island from the mainland, consists of a line of attractive, colourful houses on a single street. On summer mornings, its small pier comes to life with boats embarking on the choppy crossing to the Skellig Islands (right).

Sights & Activities

Immediately across the bridge from Portmagee is an interesting building with turf-covered barrel roofs, a not-entirely-successful re-creation of bygone vernacular buildings. The **Skellig Experience** (☎ 947 6306; adult/child/family €5/3/14; ◷ 10am-7pm Jun-Aug, to 6pm Apr, May & Sep-Nov, last admission 45 min before closing) contains exhibitions on the life and times of the Skellig Michael monks, the history of the island's lighthouses, and the wildlife. If you're planning a trip to the Skelligs, it's worth coming here for background information; if the weather's bad, it may be the closest you get to the islands. Island and harbour cruises are also on offer.

Portmagee holds **set-dancing workshops** (☎ 947 7108) over the May bank holiday weekend, featuring plenty of stomping practice sessions in the town's Bridge Bar.

Sleeping

Spring Acre (☎ 947 6141; rforan@indigo.ie; Knightstown; s/d €35/70) The most remarkable thing about this bungalow overlooking the Valentia Island ferry terminal – and owned by the ferry operator – is its view across the harbour to Killelan Mountain. But if you want to stay on the island, it's in a handy location: near pubs, restaurants, walks and the pier where boats leave from for the Skellig Islands.

The Moorings (☎ 947 7108; www.moorings.ie; Portmagee; s €55-90, d €80-130, tr €120-190, f €100-245) A friendly local gathering point, with 16 rooms split between muted modern choices and more traditional, earthier options. The nautical-themed restaurant (meals €20 to €37) specialises in seafood. There is live music and Irish dancing in the cosy Bridge Bar on Tuesdays in July and August and a Skelligs package available including B&B and trips.

Getting There & Away

Most visitors reach Valentia Island via the bridge from Portmagee. From April to October, there is a **ferry service** (☎ 947 6141) to Knightstown on Valentia Island from Reenard Point, 5km southwest of Caherciveen. The five-minute crossing costs one way/return €5/8 for a car, €2/3 for a cyclist and €1.50/2 for a pedestrian. It operates between 8.15am (9am Sunday) and 10pm.

SKELLIG ISLANDS

gannet pop 45,000

The Skellig Islands (Oileáin na Scealaga) explode out of the Atlantic Ocean with a defiance to match the empty-eyed gannets perching on their barren rocks. They measure up to any of the attractions offered by yellow-bellied landlubbers on the mainland, but you'll need to do your best grisly sea-dog impression on the 12km crossing, which can be rough. There are no toilets or shelter on Skellig Michael, the only island visitors are permitted to land on. Bring something to eat and drink and wear stout shoes and weatherproof clothing, including a waterproof jacket for the wave-spattered boat trip. (The boat operators can also often lend passengers old waterproof jackets and trousers for the crossing.)

Activities

The Skelligs are a **bird-watching** paradise. Keep a sharp lookout during the boat trip and you may spot diminutive storm petrels (also known as Mother Carey's chickens) darting above the water like swallows. Gannets are unmistakable with their savage beaks, imperious eyes, yellow caps and 100cm-plus wing spans. They dive like tridents into the sea, from up to 30m at well over 100km per hour, to snatch fish below the surface. Kittiwakes – small, dainty seabirds with black-tipped wings – are easy to see and hear around Skellig Michael's covered walkway as you step off the boat. They winter at sea then land in their thousands to breed between March and August. Further up the rock you'll see stubby-winged fulmars, with distinctive bony 'nostrils' from which they eject an evil-smelling green liquid if you get too close. Look also for razorbills, black-and-white guillemots, and the delightful puffins with their multicoloured beaks and waddling gait. In May, puffins come ashore to lay a solitary egg at the far end of a burrow, and parent birds can be seen guarding their nests. Puffins stay only until the first weeks of August.

Skellig Michael

The jagged, 217m-high rock of **Skellig Michael** (Archangel Michael's Rock; like St Michael's Mount in Cornwall, England and Mont Saint Michel in Normandy, France) is the larger of the two islands and a Unesco World Heritage site. It looks like the last place on earth that anyone would try to land, let alone establish a community, yet early Christian monks survived here from the 6th until the 12th or 13th century. Influenced by the Coptic Church founded by St Anthony in the deserts of Egypt and Libya, their determined quest for ultimate solitude led them to this remote, windblown edge of Europe.

SCARY SKELLIG

A notice on the island warns of 'an element of danger' in visiting Skellig Michael. It can certainly be an adventurous and sometimes tough trip: not a joyful experience for seasickness sufferers on rock-and-roll days. You also need to be sure-footed on the rocks and stone steps. One boat operator comments, 'On a lot of occasions, I say, "If anyone is of a nervous disposition, do not come". Having said that, it's normally okay.'

The monastic buildings are perched on a saddle in the rock, some 150m above sea level, reached by 600 steep steps cut into the rock face. The astounding 6th-century oratories and beehive cells vary in size; the largest cell has a floor space of 4.5m by 3.6m. You can see the monks' south-facing vegetable garden and their cistern for collecting rain water. The most impressive structural achievements are the settlement's foundations – platforms built on the steep slope using nothing more than earth and dry stone walls.

Little is known about the life of the monastery, but there are records of Viking raids in AD 812 and 823. Monks were kidnapped or killed, but the community recovered and carried on. Legend even has it that the monks converted one of the raiders, Olaf Tryggvesson, and he became Norway's first Christian ruler. In the 11th century a rectangular oratory was added to the site, but although it was expanded in the 12th century, the monks abandoned the rock around this time, perhaps because of particularly ferocious Atlantic storms.

After the introduction of the Gregorian calendar in 1582, Skellig Michael became a popular spot for weddings. Marriages were forbidden during Lent, but since Skellig used the old Julian calendar, a trip to the islands allowed those unable to wait for Easter to tie the knot.

In the 1820s two lighthouses were built on Skellig Michael, together with the road that runs around the base.

The guides on the island ask you to do your picnicking on the way up to the monastery, or at Christ's Saddle just before the last flight of steps, rather than among the ruins. This is to keep sandwich-loving birds and their droppings away from the monument.

Small Skellig

While Skellig Michael looks like two triangles linked by a spur, Small Skellig is longer, lower and much craggier. From a distance it looks as if someone battered it with a feather pillow that burst. Close up you realise you're looking at a colony of over 20,000 pairs of breeding gannets, the second-largest breeding colony in the world. Most boats circle the island so you can see the gannets, and there may be a chance of seeing basking seals. As Small Skellig is a bird sanctuary, no landing is permitted.

Getting There & Away

Because of concerns for the fragility of Skellig Michael there are limits on how many people can visit on the same day. There are 15 boats licensed to carry no more than 12 passengers each, so there should never be more than 180 people there at any one time. Because of these limits, it's wise to book ahead in July and August, bearing in mind that if the weather's bad the boats may not sail. Trips usually start running around Easter, but high seas and bad weather can put them off until May.

Boats leave around 10am and return at 3pm. You can depart from Portmagee (and even Caherciveen), Ballinskelligs or Derrynane. The boat owners try to restrict you to two hours on the island, which is the bare minimum, on a good day, to see the monastery, look at the birds and have a picnic. Check that your boat does actually land on Skellig Michael. The crossing takes about 1½ hours from Portmagee, one hour from Ballinskelligs and 1¾ hours from Derrynane (around €40 return from all places).

Local pubs and B&Bs will point you in the direction of operators, including:

Casey's (☎ 947 2437; Caherciveen)
Des Lavelle (☎ 947 6124; Portmagee)
Eoin Walsh (☎ 947 6327; Valentia Island)
John O'Shea (☎ 087-670 5121; Caherdaniel)
Sea Quest (☎ 947 6214; Reenard Point)
Skellig Cruise (☎ 947 9182; Ballinskelligs)

SKELLIG RING

This 18km detour from the Ring of Kerry links Portmagee and Waterville via a Gaeltacht (Gaeilge-speaking) area centred on Ballinskelligs (Baile an Sceilg). Ballinskelligs' name translates as 'town of the crag', which may elicit sniggers from fans of Father Ted and his Craggy Island pals. The area is as wild and beautiful as anything on Ted's fictional isle, with the ragged outline of Skellig Michael never far from view.

Tourist information is available at Café Coistrá (see right).

Sights

SIOPA CHILL RIALAIG

This contemporary **art gallery** (☎ 947 9297; cillrialaig@easatclear.ie; Dun Geagan; ☉ 10am-7pm Jul-Aug, 11am-5pm rest of year) is packed with work by local artists and talent from around Ireland and the world. It is the shop window of the Cill Rialaig Project, which provides a retreat for creative people on the site of a village abandoned during the famine. Free accommodation and studio space are available to artists, who are invited to donate work to the gallery at the end of their stay. Standards are high and the attractive space houses as fine a collection of pieces as you'd find in a top Dublin gallery.

The gallery is by the R566 at the northeastern end of Ballinskelligs. You'll spot its circular, thatched roofs and the sculpture that resembles a hallucinogenic mushroom. There is a café inside.

BALLINSKELLIGS PRIORY & BAY

The sea and salty air are eating away at the atmospheric ruins of this medieval building, a monastic settlement that was probably associated with the Skellig Michaels monks after they left their rocky outpost in the 12th century. To reach it, follow the sign to the pier at the western end of town and you will see it on the left.

Another sign points to the fine little Blue Flag **beach**. At the western end of the beach are the last remnants of the 16th-century **castle** stronghold of the McCarthys, built on the isthmus as a defence against pirates.

Activities

St Finian's Bay is good for surfing. **Ballinskelligs Water Sports** (☎ 086-389 4849) hires out surfboards, kayaks and windsurfers, and gives lessons. **Sean Feehan** (☎ 947 9182) offers fishing, diving and boat trips to the Skelligs.

Sleeping & Eating

Skellig Hostel (☎ 947 9942; www.skellighostel.com; Ballinskelligs; dm €14.50, s & tw €36, d €44-48, f €60; P &) This modern building is a little characterless, but the rooms, lounge and dining room are comfortable, and it's in an elevated position with sea views.

Ballinskelligs Inn (Cable O'Leary's; ☎ 947 9106; www .ballinskelligsinn.com; s/d €40/80; lunch €9, dinner €12-20; P) A classic rural establishment: the conversation is in Gaeilge and the hot water is shy, though the rooms are comfortable. Food is not its strong point, but there is some interesting history; ask about Cable O'Leary.

Café Coistrá (☎ 947 9323; ☉ 9am-6pm) At the car park for Ballinskelligs strand, this beach-hut café and craft shop is a great place for a coffee and a nose through the old local photos.

WATERVILLE

☎ 066 / pop 550

A line of colourful houses strung between Lough Currane and Ballinskelligs Bay, Waterville lacks its neighbour Caherdaniel's charm. However, the breezy beach resort has attracted famous admirers such as Charlie Chaplin, who stayed at the Butler Arms Hotel and is commemorated in an uncannily lifelike statue. Locals also hope the new Skellig Bay Golf Club will give the town a boost.

There is tourist information and a bureau de change at **Waterville Craft Market** (☎ 947 4212; 🕙 9am-9pm Jun-Aug, 10am-6pm Sep-May).

Sights

At the north end of Lough Currane, **Church Island** has the ruins of a medieval church and beehive cell. Reputedly founded as a monastic settlement by St Finian in the 6th century, it is a good alternative to the Skelligs in choppy weather.

Chartering a three-man boat costs €40 to €50; contact Lakelands B&B (see below).

Activities

Waterville Golf Links (☎ 947 4102) charges a hefty €165 per round, or €115 before 8am and after 4pm Mondays to Thursdays; but it is one of the most stunning links courses in the world and attracts serious golfers from all over. A cheaper alternative is the **Skellig Bay Golf Club** (☎ 947 4133; Mon-Fri €60, Sat & Sun €70).

There is free **fishing** for sea trout on Lough Currane and the other lakes; a state licence is required. Sea angling offers the chance of catching mackerel, pollack and shark. **Tadhg O'Sullivan tackle shop** (☎ 947 4433; Main St) has information.

Sleeping & Eating

O'Dwyer's (☎ 947 4248; Main St; s €30, d & tw €60) A central budget option, above a bar/restaurant, with small en-suite bathrooms, and small beds in the doubles.

Clifford's B&B (☎ 947 4283; cliffordbandb@eircom .net; Main St; s/d €35/60; 🕙 Mar-Oct; ℗) Excellent-value, comfortable house with clear views of the sea from the front upstairs rooms.

Lakelands (☎ 947 4303; www.lakelandshouse.com; Lake Rd; s/d €75/96) A farmhouse B&B offering fishing. The attractive modern building has sweeping views of Lough Currane, and some rooms have Jacuzzis and balconies.

Smuggler's Inn (☎ 947 4330; www.the-smugglers -inn.com; Cliff Rd; s €90-130, d €120-160; 🕙 Apr-Oct; ℗) Standing in splendid isolation between the links and a long, sandy beach, this pleasant guesthouse is among the smart establishments north of town that cater to golfers. Seafood, particularly shellfish, is a speciality in the beach-facing restaurant (mains €20 to €30, bar food €5 to €15).

The Huntsman (☎ 947 4124; huntsmanclub@eircom .net; s/d €125/150; 🕙 Mar-Oct) The five self-catering units opposite St Michael's Church are surprisingly luxurious inside, with saunas, double Jacuzzis and sea-facing balconies. The French-orientated restaurant (mains €15 to €30) is decorated with an amusing hodge-podge of ornaments including fibreglass models of monsters of the deep.

Sheilin (☎ 947 4231; Top Cross; lunch €10, dinner €14-28; 🕙 noon-3pm & 6-10pm) Friendly, if hopelessly eccentric, seafood restaurant split between two houses, serving dishes such as Valentia scallops and fresh crab in wine sauce.

Paddy Frog's (☎ 947 8766; the New Line; mains €25-28; 🕙 6.30-9.30pm March-Oct) This French–Irish gourmet restaurant in an inventively decorated new building is overpriced, but offers a good mix of local seafood and meat.

CAHERDANIEL

☎ 066 / pop 350

Hiding between Derrynane Bay and the foothills of Eagles Hill, Caherdaniel is a tiny hamlet with a surprising vibrancy pulsing along its few streets. It boasts a Blue Flag beach, activities galore and the ancestral seat of Daniel O'Connell, 'The Liberator' (p37). At night, you can toast the village from beneath the driftwood and fishing tackle decorating the Blind Piper pub (p266).

Wave Crest (see p266) offers tourist information.

Sights

DERRYNANE NATIONAL HISTORIC PARK

Derrynane House (☎ 947 5113; Derrynane; adult/child €2.90/1.30; 🕙 9am-6pm Mon-Sat, 11am-7pm Sun May-Sep, 1-5pm Tue-Sun Apr & Oct, 1-5pm Sat & Sun Nov-Mar, last admission 45 min before closing) is the ancestral home of Daniel O'Connell, the campaigner for Catholic emancipation. His family bought the house and surrounding parkland having grown rich on smuggling with France and Spain. It's largely furnished with O'Connell memorabilia, including the restored triumphal chariot in which he lapped Dublin after his release from prison in 1844.

There is a walking track through the gardens – where palms, four-metre tree ferns, gunnera ('giant rhubarb') and South American species grow thanks to the Gulf Stream – to wetlands, beaches and clifftops. You can spot wild pheasants and other birds. The **chapel**, which O'Connell added to Derrynane House in 1844, is a copy of the ruined one on **Abbey Island**, which can usually be reached on foot across the sand.

Look out for the **Ogham stone** on the left of the road to the house. With its carved notches representing the simple Ogham alphabet of the ancient Irish, the stone has several missing letters, but may represent the name of a local chieftain.

Activities

Caherdaniel competes with Valentia Island as the diving base for the Iveragh Peninsula. Try **Activity Ireland** (☎ 947 5277; www.activity-ireland .com), which also organises a range of other outdoor activities including rock-climbing. Popular **Derrynane Sea Sports** (☎ 087-908 1208) organises sailing, canoeing, windsurfing and water-skiing for all levels, operating from the beach between June and August.

Eagle Rock Equestrian Centre (☎ 947 5145) offers beach, mountain and woodland treks for all levels (€25 per hour).

John O'Shea (☎ 087-670 5121; Bunavalla Pier) runs fishing trips and excursions to the Skelligs.

Walkers should head to **Bunavalla Pier**, 3.2km downhill from the N70, west of Caherdaniel. Walk there and you'll descend towards 'Ireland's best known view' (according to the Scarriff Inn's sign at the top) along what could be Ireland's windiest, steepest lane. Keep left and conserve your energy for the slog back uphill.

Sleeping & Eating

Wave Crest (☎ 947 5188; www.wavecrestcamping.com; camp sites €16; ❍ mid-Mar–mid-Oct; 🖵) This friendly site, 1.6km southeast of Caherdaniel, has a superb coastal setting and well-kept facilities. Booking during peak season is advised.

Glenbeg Caravan & Camping Park (☎ 947 5182; glenbeg@eircom.net; camp sites €17; ❍ mid-Apr–early Oct) Some 2.5km east of Caherdaniel on the N70, Glenbeg has an unbeatable seaside location, overlooking a sandy beach with views of the Beara Peninsula.

Travellers' Rest Hostel (☎ 947 5175; dm/d €16.50/39; 🅿) All low ceilings, board games and dried flowers in the grate, Travellers' Rest has the quaint feel of a country cottage. Call at the garage opposite if there's nobody about.

Olde Forge (☎ 947 5140; theoldeforge@eircom.net; s/d €40/70; 🅿) This B&B has six attractive rooms and fantastic views of Kenmare Bay and the Beara Peninsula. It's 1.2km southeast of town on the N70.

Kerry Way B&B (☎ 947 5277; www.activity-ireland .com/bab; s/d €45/60; 🅿) Run by the same people as Activity Ireland, this pleasant old house has good-sized en-suite rooms.

Glaise Rinn (☎ 947 5013; lunch €4-7; ❍ May-Aug) Breakfast, baguettes, homemade quiches and pizzas are served at this deli at the entrance to Wave Crest.

Blind Piper (☎ 947 5126; bar food €10-18; ❍ noon-9.30pm Jun-Aug, to 8.30pm rest of year) This local institution is a great family pub during the day, serving expensive but quality grub. The deep-fried monkfish, Cajun chicken panini and *croque monsieur* with brie are recommended. After dark, locals and visitors crowd in here; music sessions have been known to happen.

A decent place open during the summer, and a cheaper alternative to the pub, is **Courthouse Cafe** (☎ 947 5834; dinner €10; ❍ 11am-4pm & 6pm-10pm Jun-Sep), near the Blind Piper. Fish cakes and chips, and other filling feeds are available to take away or eat upstairs.

STAIGUE FORT

This ring fort is an imposing sight at the head of a valley, and a powerful evocation of late-Iron Age Ireland. Its circular stone wall, up to 6m high and 4m thick, is surrounded by a protective bank and ditch. Steps criss-cross the interior of the wall, which contains two small rooms and a narrow entrance tunnel.

Staigue probably dates from the 3rd or 4th century, and the building's sophistication suggests it belonged to a powerful chieftain. Despite having sweeping views down to the coast, it can't be seen from the sea. It may have been a communal place of refuge, or a cultural and commercial centre where people came to celebrate, exchange goods and stage ceremonies.

The fort is near the village of Castlecove, about 4km off the N70, reached by a pot-holed country lane that narrows as it climbs to a road-end car park beside the site. Traffic jams can occur.

The battered building that would look at home in Havana is the **exhibition centre** (☉ 10am-9pm Easter-Sep), which has a café and an interpretive display.

A scrawled sign, before it descends into a stream of consciousness about trespassing, asks for €1 for access to the Dúchas site across private land.

SNEEM

Halfway between Caherdaniel and Kenmare, Sneem (An tSnaidhm) is a good place to stop for an ice cream and a clamber on the rocks under the bridge (not at the same time). The village's Gaeilge name translates as 'the knot', which is thought to refer to the River Sneem that swirls, knot-like, into Kenmare Bay nearby. It's nicknamed 'the knot in the Ring of Kerry'.

President Charles de Gaulle is among the luminaries who have been attracted to the peaceful spot, and he is commemorated by a statue. In the sculpture park are pieces donated from around the world, including the *Goddess Isis* from Egypt and the *Peaceful Panda* from China.

KENMARE

☎ 064 / pop 2460

The copper-covered limestone spire of Holy Cross Church, drawing the eye to the wooded hills above town, gives Kenmare an alpine appearance. Of course, you couldn't be anywhere other than southwest Ireland with rivers named Finnihy, Roughty and Sheen emptying into Kenmare Bay. Nonetheless, Kenmare is a town of some distinction. Elegant streets with superb restaurants fan out from Fair Green. It does get busy in the summer, but is less hectic than Killarney, and is ideally situated for visiting both the Ring of Kerry and Beara Peninsula.

Orientation

In the 18th century, Kenmare was laid out on an X-plan, with a triangular market square in the centre and Fair Green nestling in its upper V. To the south, Henry and Main Sts are the main shopping and eating/drinking thoroughfares, with Shelbourne St linking them at the southern end. Kenmare Bay stretches out to the southwest, and there are glorious views of the mountains.

Information

The post office on the corner of Henry and Shelbourne Sts has local walking maps and guides, as well as internet access (€1 for 15 minutes). There are two Kenmare websites: www.kenmare.eu and www.kenmare.com.

There's free parking throughout town, with a two-hour limit between 9am and 6pm.

AIB (cnr Main & Henry Sts) ATM and bureau de change.

Bank of Ireland (the Square) Also has ATM and bureau de change.

Finnegan's Taxis & Tours (☎ 41491) Located above the tourist office.

Kenmare Bookshop (☎ 41578; Shelbourne St) Has a wide range of books, including a strong Irish section with maps and guides.

O'Shea's Laundry (☎ 41394; Kenmare Business Park; ☉ 8.30am-6pm Mon-Fri, to 5.30pm Sat; self-service €1) Located 2km north of town on the N71.

Pubic toilets (Old Killareny Rd) Opposite the Holy Cross Church, next to a car park.

Tourist office (☎ 31633; the Square; ☉ Apr-Oct) Gives out free maps detailing a heritage trail around town and longer walks of up to 13km.

Sights

The **Kenmare Heritage Centre** (☎ 41233; the Square; adult/child €2.70/1.30; ☉ 9.15am-7pm Mon-Sat Jul & Aug, to 5.30pm Mon-Sat Easter-Jun & Sep), reached through the tourist office, tells the history of the town from its founding as Neidín by the swashbuckling Sir William Petty in 1670. The centre also relates the story of the Poor Clare Convent, founded in 1861 and still standing behind Holy Cross Church. Local women were taught needlepoint lace-making skills at the convent, and Kenmare was catapulted to international fame through the work produced by the women.

Upstairs, the **Kenmare Lace and Design Centre** (☎ 42978; ☉ 10.15am-5.30pm Mon-Sat Easter-Oct, 10.30am-1.30pm Nov-Mar) has displays including designs for 'the most important piece of lace ever made in Ireland' (in a 19th-century critic's opinion). It's run by lace-maker Nora Finnegan, who was taught by the Poor Clare nuns. Also interesting is the story of Margaret Anna Cusack (1829–99), the Nun of Kenmare and an early advocate of women's rights. She was hounded out of Kenmare, converted to Protestantism and died, embittered, in Leamington, England.

Signposted southwest of the Square is an early Bronze Age **stone circle**, one of the biggest in southwest Ireland. Fifteen stones ring a boulder dolmen, a burial monument rarely found outside this part of the country.

Built in 1862, the **Holy Cross Church** on Old Killarney Rd boasts a splendid wooden roof with 14 angel carvings. There are fine mosaics in the aisle arches and around the stained-glass window over the altar. The architect was Charles Hansom, collaborator and brother-in-law of Augustus Pugin (the architect behind London's Houses of Parliament).

Activities

Kenmare Golf Club (☎ 41291; 18 holes Mon-Fri €50, Sat & Sun €55) has its entrance on the R569, about 100m from the top of Main St.

Star Sailing (☎ 41222; Dauros), on the R571, offers activities including sailing, sea kayaking, diving, windsurfing, pony trekking, cycling and hillwalking for novices and experts.

Warm yourself on tea, coffee, rum and the captain's sea shanties on a two-hour quest to spot sea cubs and other sea life with **Seafari** (☎ 42059; Kenmare Pier; adult/child €20/12.50). Reservations are advised.

For fishing, try **Kenmare Bay Angling & Sightseeing Cruises** (☎ 087-2592209; Kenmare Pier).

For horse riding, there's **Dromquinna Stables** (☎ 41043; Templenoe), 10km west of town on the Ring of Kerry (N70).

The tourist office has details of walks around Kenmare Bay and into the hills, on sections of the Kerry Way (see p699) and Beara Way (see p698).

Sleeping
BUDGET

Kenmare Lodge (☎ 40662; 27 Main St; dm €15-20, tw €34, d €50) This pleasant, modern hostel has a patio, and cream walls enlivened by Modernist reproductions. There are laundry facilities and a roomy kitchen and dining area.

Ring of Kerry Caravan & Camping Park (☎ 41648; Reen; camp sites €18-20; ☻ Apr-Sep) Mountains and sea surround this beautiful site in wooded country. It's 3.5km west of town and 1km down a side road, off the north side of the Sneem road.

MIDRANGE

Hazelwood (☎ 41420; www.kenmare-bnb.com; s/d €45/70; P) Some 3.5km southwest of town at the beginning of the Ring of Beara (R571), this family-run B&B was built to resemble an African bungalow by owner Miffy's grandfather.

Grab a tome from the bookshelf and lounge by the fire or in the conservatory overlooking Kenmare Bay.

Whispering Pines (☎ 41194; wpines@eircom.net; s/d €45/80; ☻ Easter-Nov; P) In a quiet location near the pier, with four immaculate rooms and a cheerful welcome. Breakfasts range from stewed prunes and apricots to Kenmare smoked salmon and scrambled eggs.

Hawthorn House (☎ 41035; www.hawthornhouse kenmare.com; Shelbourne St; s/d €55/80; P) This stylish house has seven spacious rooms, including a majestic family room, all named after local towns and decked out in light pine. Chatty owner Mary is a fount of local information.

Rose Cottage (☎ 41330; the Square; d €70-80; P) This picturesque building set back from Fair Green has old-fashioned but comfortable and homely rooms. The Poor Clare nuns stayed here when they arrived in Kenmare, then had to leave just as the apples were ripening in the orchard. Note that rooms are double only: no singles are allowed.

TOP END

Sheen Falls Lodge (☎ 41600; www.sheenfallslodge .ie; r from €445; breakfast €24; ☻ Feb-Dec; P) The Marquis of Landsdowne's former summer residence still feels like an aristocrats' playground. Oscar's bar/bistro is named after the local heron, and there's a 1920s Buick that is used to go on picnics. Beyond such flourishes, the lodge is a luxurious retreat with a spa and 66 rooms with DVD players and Italian marble bathrooms. With views of the falls and across Kenmare Bay to Carrantuohil, it's a beautiful place to escape the less amusing aspects of the 21st century.

Eating

Kenmare has a deserved reputation for its fine eateries.

BUDGET

For self-caterers, there's a **SuperValu** (☎ 41307; Main St) supermarket

Jam (☎ 41591; Henry St; meals & snacks €2-9; ☻ 8am-5pm) Funky, comfy Jam offers filo pastry and quiches brimming with goodness, and a long list of increasingly elaborate coffees.

(Continued on page 277)

The Irish Kitchen

Gourmet heaven at Bushmills Inn (p662), County Antrim

LOCAL IRISH PRODUCE

'Local is by far the sexiest word in food, even sexier than organic,' enthuses Darina Allen, chef at Ballymaloe House (p216), teacher and all-round champion of everything that's good about Irish food. 'Before now, we had this dreadful attitude that homemade butter or home-cured bacon was of less value than something wrapped up in plastic on supermarket shelves.'

This new-found sexiness of local produce and traditional production makes it a great time to visit Ireland. Farmers markets are springing up all over the country, local produce is readily available in every town, and the artisan producers actively encourage visitors to come and see them at work.

Frank Hederman, Belvelly smokehouse (p215), County Cork

JOHN ANGERSON / ALAMY

TRADITION REBORN

It hasn't always been the case. Until the end of the 20th century, the Irish were cooking less and buying more convenience food, and Ireland's traditional food culture had all but died. Then came the revolution, prompted in part by the Irish economic renaissance. 'There was more money around, people travelled more, ate out more, and so become more adventurous and discerning with their food,' says Darina. At the same time, following BSE (mad cow disease), people in Europe began to care about how their food was produced.

Darina's own interest in food is rooted in her childhood. 'When I was a child, we had a kitchen garden, a house cow, a fruit garden and hens. We'd hatch the chicks, fatten them up and then you'd have them on the table. There was always cooking going on around me. I remember coming home from school and there'd be a tray of scones coming out of the oven, or in the afternoons we'd go on picnics.'

Meet the locals at McDonagh's (p411), County Galway

OLIVER STE

ade locally – a selection of Irish cheeses

OLIVER STREWE

There's a growing desire among the Irish to hark back to happier, gentler times by recapturing such traditional food values. At Ballymaloe House, 'forgotten skills' courses, covering such delights as pig-curing, bee-keeping and butter-making, are one sign of this. 'Fifteen years ago, no one would have come,' says Darina. But now the courses are attracting a steadily rising number of people, and in particular the young.

A similar passion is often cited as the driving force behind the artisan producers themselves, but the reality is a little more prosaic. Says Frank Hederman of the Belvelly smokehouse (p215), 'Passion had nothing to do with it. It's a question of economics. When I started in the early '80s, my credit card was about to be cut up and I had a family to support. I knew that if you took a fish and added value to it, you could sell it for more. Back then, I was making a living rather than making food.'

The return to local production was a necessarily creative response to new farming regulations brought in when the Irish joined the EU. 'The Irish are very attached to their land,' explains Darina. 'The economics of farming had changed so much that people really had to rack their brains to see how they could remain on their land, and the way to do it was to add value to their food. Twenty-five years ago, the matriarch of cheese production, Veronica Steel, started to make cheese and it snowballed.'

Fresh from the oven at Ballymaloe House (p216), County Cork

OLIVER STREWE

The kitchen garden, Ballymaloe House (p216) County Cork

DESIGN PICS INC. / ALAMY

Artistic dishes at Kirwan's Lane Creative Cuisine (p411), County Galway

OLIVER STREWE

Veronica, of Milleens cheese (p244) in Cork, remembers the time well. 'It was simple. I had a cow that produced too much milk for me to drink. There's only one thing you can do with surplus milk and that is to make cheese. Hikers would stop by the farmhouse and take the cheese away with them and a local chef started using it in her restaurant. And then I got another cow, and other farmers became interested in what I was doing and started making their own cheese too.'

Over the following decades, the small producers battled regulations that favoured the monolithic producers over small family operations. A lot of the artisan production started in Munster and the Cork area, and still thrives there today. 'A lot of this had to do with Myrtle Allen [Darina's mother-in-law] of Ballymaloe,' explains Frank. 'She was hugely supportive, using a lot of local produce in her restaurant and encouraging local production.'

After years of lobbying, changes were finally made to the agricultural policy, with the EU paying for quality rather than quantity. At the same time, the Irish government recognised that local food production could play a big role in triggering rural redevelopment. 'There's

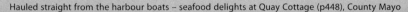

Hauled straight from the harbour boats – seafood delights at Quay Cottage (p448), County Mayo

HOLGER L.

ARTISANS IN HEAVEN

Darina Allen: 'The greatest satisfaction is teaching someone how to cook. You show them how to make a soup or a jam and you're giving them a gift, a skill for life that touches every day of their lives. My joy when someone takes their first loaf of bread out of the oven, the look of delight on their face, that keeps me going.'

Frank Hederman: 'My idea of heaven would be to stay at the smokehouse and salt and smoke fish rather than do all the other business stuff around it. I love going out and meeting the guy who gets the eels and the guy who supplies the mackerels. And I love the farmers markets – the interaction you have with people who are buying your produce is hugely satisfying and rewarding.'

Veronica Steele: 'In the actual cheese-making process, watching this lump of "stuff" become a beautiful orange cheese under your hand is extraordinary. And then people are eating it and enjoying it. That's magic.'

Seamus O'Hara: 'The most satisfying thing in the world is going into a bar, whether it's in Dublin or Manhattan, and seeing people drinking and enjoying your beer on draught.'

much more support and appreciation of this type of food at an official level than there used to be. Artisan food is now valued by the Irish food board,' says Darina.

'it's vitally important to preserve our food culture'

THE FUTURE'S BRIGHT

There are many reasons to be confident about the future of Irish cuisine. Frank believes that the acceptance of it, both at home and abroad, is a huge reflection of how far Ireland has come. 'We're making an impact and people are coming to Ireland for the food, not for soccer or rugby or Guinness or that horrible phrase craic. You can come to Ireland for good restaurants, you can visit smokehouses and you can visit cheese producers.'

Darina finds reasons for optimism in the growth of the farmers markets, as it means local people can get local and seasonal produce (unheard of in the supermarkets), and a renewed interest in centuries-old production methods. 'Artisan food production is valued on so many levels, from a health point of view as well as for the craft and flavour. It's now accepted that it's vitally important to preserve and value our traditional food culture.'

It's this fundamental change of approach that Veronica believes is responsible for restoring some confidence and pride to her country. 'There are some extraordinary good new cheeses coming up all the time. All we had before was absolute crap, dreadful stuff. It's exciting that the food-making knowledge and skills are there and growing. As an island that's a very important security to have.'

Darina Allen, Ballymaloe House (p216), County Cork

BALLYMALOE COOKERY SCHOOL

VISITING ARTISAN PRODUCERS

We've included details of local producers in the regional chapters but these are just the tip of the iceberg. Use the following resources and ask in local shops to track down others. Be sure to phone before turning up so the producers can set aside time to show you around.

- **www.bestofbridgestone.com** – extensive coverage of artisan producers plus the best restaurants serving their produce
- **www.bordbia.ie** – Irish food board website, with a few local producers listed
- **Good Food in Cork** – excellent annual booklet detailing artisan producers in Cork, established by Myrtle Allen; pick it up from the Farmgate Café (p207) in Cork city; also available online at www.corkfreechoice.com
- **www.irelandmarkets.com** – definitive list of local farmers markets
- **www.irishcheese.ie** – the farmhouse cheese-makers association, with every small dairy covered
- **www.slowfoodireland.com** – organisation supporting small producers, with social events across Ireland

MODERN IRISH CUISINE

The confidence in the natural produce hewn from land and sea has led to an unflowery, down-to-earth modern cuisine. You'll find local produce name-checked on menus across the country, from Dublin Bay prawns and Connemara salmon to Skeaghanore duck and Kilbritain lamb. Ireland's finest chefs take the best-quality produce and cook it well and simply. According to Darina, 'I can't do twiddles and bows and I'm not interested in intricate things with 90 things on one plate. The bows and twiddles just compensate for poor produce. My message is: For God's sake, keep it simple.'

Best of all, the visitor doesn't need to spend big in elaborate restaurants to partake of the feast – small restaurants, delis and cafés the country over have fallen in love with good, fresh Irish produce and it's easy to find well-cooked, homely food far from the tourist trail.

Fresh, local produce at Fenn's Quay (p208), County Cork

OLIVER STR

mpting appetisers, Longueville House (p245), County Cork

OLIVER STREWE

MICROBREWERIES FIGHT BACK

Up until the 1980s, the outlook for Ireland's brewing industry looked even bleaker than it did for its food. Sure, everyone knows about Guinness, but over the previous 100 years it had developed at the expense of hundreds of smaller breweries. Ironically, Ireland has clung on to its reputation as a country with a strong beer heritage, but until recently the modern reality was severely lacking – all Irish beer came from only three breweries, none of which is currently Irish-owned.

The experience of the Carlow Brewing Company (p349) is typical of the revival of interest in microbrewing. Says founder Seamus O'Hara, 'I had the opportunity to travel in Europe, and it opened my eyes to the fact that there was a lot more to beer than the two or three brands available in Ireland. I went to the US and the microbrewery scene there that had started up in the 1980s led us to believe that we could set up a small brewery and be commercially successful too.' In the mid-'90s, other small breweries started up and a pioneering industry developed.

The commercial environment was loaded against new companies though, with high customs and excise levied against the smaller breweries. 'Many breweries were driven by passion and an interest in brewing, and we were all a bit wide-eyed about the commercial side of the business,' says Seamus. Some breweries have fallen by the wayside since those pioneering first days, and now there are nine left from an original 12.

It's a hard job...sampling stout at the Carlow Brewing Company (p349), Central South

CARLOW BREWING COMPANY

Carlow Brewing survived those early years by exporting up to 75% of its produce. 'Overseas, people are more used to trying different beers, so there was always going to be a market for a genuine Irish beer at the speciality end in terms of quality and flavour.' As with food, extensive lobbying of the industry regulators reaped rewards, and the excise has now been reduced by 50% for small producers. The market is still dominated by the big breweries, but people's attitudes are changing: the number of speciality beers coming into the country and being produced are educating beer-drinkers and broadening the market. 'The Irish beer drinker is more discerning and demanding now that they're aware there are other choices. It's similar to what happened with Irish food – there's just a bit of a lag with beer.'

FINDING THE BEST IRISH FOOD & DRINK

The best advice for unearthing the best of Ireland's food and drink will also add to your enjoyment of the country as a whole. Try and visit one of the artisan producers, like a cheese-makers', smokehouse or brew-pub; most producers are happy to talk you through the process and offer tastings.

The next best thing is to go to a farmers' market and get a real insight into what's being grown in the area and what's in season. Ask the stall-holders, usually the producers themselves, what the best local food is and which restaurants are doing it justice.

If you keep your eyes open, you'll realise there's more to Irish beer than just the popular mainstream brands. Look out for those pubs serving speciality beers on draught – it shows they're serious about their brews.

Finally, go off the beaten track – wander away from the main tourist centres and you'll find some delightful hidden pubs, farm shops and restaurants waiting to be discovered.

A food lover's paradise – the English Market (p207), County Cork

CHRIS ROUT / AL

(Continued from page 268)

Café Mocha (☎ 42133; the Square; meals & snacks €4-13; ☯ 9am-5.30pm) Soup, salads, sandwiches, breakfast and homemade ice cream are on the menu in this popular café with painterly canvases decorating the yellow walls.

Purple Heather Bistro (☎ 41016; Henry St; meals & snacks €5-15; ☯ 10.45am-6pm Mon-Sat) With a great atmosphere and comfy traditional décor, this Kenmare favourite serves a great range of tasty sandwiches and Irish dishes with a dash of European cuisine. There are good veggie options and the homemade desserts are a real flourish.

MIDRANGE
Horseshoe (☎ 41553; 3 Main St; mains €12-26; ☯ 5-10pm) The decent vegetarian options at this gastro-pub include spinach and wild-onion risotto, while steaks, scallops, burgers and mussels are prepared using simple, traditional recipes.

our pick Bácús (☎ 49300; Main St; mains €13-25; ☯ 8.30am-9.30pm) Everything's homemade; the produce is local and seasonal; the ales are from microbreweries; the décor is Art Deco lamps and black-and-white French photos. This could be Ireland's best midrange restaurant –it's certainly great value. The bouillabaisse is recommended, as is Sunday brunch (9am to 4pm).

PF McCarthy's (☎ 41516; 14 Main St; dinner €13-27; ☯ noon-3pm Mon-Sat, 5-9pm Tue-Sat) A convivial pub with German and Czech beers on tap, and dishes such as Thai crab lasagna and Moroccan bean stew alongside the usual hostelry fare.

TOP END
Packies (☎ 41508; Henry St; mains €13-30; ☯ 6-10pm Mon-Sat Mar-Oct, Thu-Sat Nov-Feb) This stylish, award-winning restaurant underpins Mediterranean flair with tried-and-tested Irish methods. Seafood matters here, and there's a strong bias towards organic produce. There are also chicken, lamb and tagliatelle choices.

Mulcahy's Restaurant (☎ 42383; 36 Henry St; mains €17-29; ☯ 6.30-10pm Wed-Mon Apr-Sep, Thu-Mon Oct-Mar) Acclaimed Mulcahy's brings world style to Kenmare. The food is satisfyingly modernist, with sushi starters and Pacific Rim flair, but with inventive Irish touches. Vegetarians and wine buffs are well catered for.

D'Arcy's Oyster Bar and Grill (☎ 41589; mains €19-31; ☯ 6.30-9.30pm) Newspapers have raved about D'Arcy's, but a sign hanging in the window summarises its charms: 'Eat fish – your heart will love you for it'. Lobster and red snapper are among the fresh catches served in modern, low-key surrounds. Landlubber dishes such as Irish T-bone and Kerry lamb are available from the grill.

Entertainment
For good trad sessions try Crowley's on Henry St, while Florry Batt's in the same street sees a cheerful crowd and occasional sing-alongs. A wide range of acts plays PF McCarthy's on Main Street (Thursday to Saturday).

Shopping
Kenmare has a disproportionate number of quality craft shops. There's a **market** (☎ 84236; the Square) on Wednesday mornings (closed from December to January). On August 15 every year, marketers from throughout Ireland, with crafts, local produce, ponies, cattle, sheep, bric-a-brac, etc come to town.

PFK Gold & Silversmith (☎ 42590; pfkelly@indigo.ie; 18 Henry St) Minimilastic jewellery by Paul Kelly and contemporary Irish designers. Check out the salt servers with enamel linings by West Cork designer Marika O'Sullivan. Prices start at €80; Kelly also takes commissions.

Soundz of Muzic (☎ 42268; 9 Henry St) Has a selection of Irish and contemporary music.

Noel & Holland (☎ 42464; 3 Bridge St) Find that elusive favourite at this excellent secondhand bookshop that sells some rare editions and also has a terrific range of paperbacks, all neatly collated.

Kerry Wool Market (☎ 89168; Henry St) A mountain of Aran jumpers.

Getting There & Away
There are twice-daily buses to Killarney (€7.60, 50 minutes), where you can change for Tralee. On Friday afternoon buses go to Sneem, and to Lauragh and Ardgroom on the Beara Peninsula. Twice-daily buses carry on to Castletownbere during the summer. Buses stop outside Roughty Bar (Main St).

Getting Around
Finnegan's Cycle Centre (☎ 41083; Shelbourne St) is the Raleigh Rent-a-Bike dealer, with bikes costing €15/85 per day/week.

NORTHERN KERRY

The landscape of Northern Kerry is often dull compared with the glories of the Iveragh and Dingle Peninsulas, Killarney and Kenmare. There are some fascinating places all the same with enough compelling history to reward a few days exploration. Ballybunion and the blustery beaches south of the Shannon estuary are certainly worth a look.

TRALEE

☎ 066 / pop 22,070

Despite being the county town, Tralee is dismissed in the rest of Kerry as an overflow valve for Limerick and its social problems. Tralee is certainly a down-to-earth place, more engaged with the business of everyday life than the tourist trade. A request for a cigarette is never far away and you should take care after dark. However, if you've just emerged from Kerry's rural areas, this is a refreshingly lively, heterogeneous spot with some friendly pubs and worthwhile attractions.

Founded by the Normans in 1216, Tralee has a long history of rebellion. In the 16th century the last ruling earl of the Desmonds was captured and executed here. His head was sent to Elizabeth I, who spiked it on London Bridge. The Desmond castle once stood at the junction of Denny St and the Mall, but any trace of medieval Tralee that survived the Desmond Wars was razed during the Cromwellian period.

Orientation

You'll find most things you need along the Mall and its continuation, Castle St. Elegant Denny St and Day Place are the oldest parts of town, with 18th-century buildings. Ashe St is home to the circular Courthouse, a solemn, fortresslike building. The tourist office is at the southern end of Denny St. The bus and train stations are a five-minute walk northeast of the town centre. The Square, just south of the Mall, is a pleasant open space with a contemporary style.

Information

On Castle St you'll find banks with ATMs and bureaux de change. The big car park opposite the Brandon Hotel costs €3 per day, Monday to Saturday. The metered parking in the rest of town is €1.20 per hour.

Antech (☎ 719 1441; 40 Bridge St; per hr €4) For internet access, cheap international calls, Western Union transfers, photocopying and mobile top-up.

Luggage storage (per item €2.50; ☼ 7am-5pm) At the train station.

Polymaths (☎ 712 5035; 1-2 Courthouse Lane) New bookshop with a good selection of books on Kerry.

Post office (Edward St) Off Castle St.

Public toilets (Denny St)

Tourist office (☎ 712 1288; Denny St) Helpful office at the side of Ashe Memorial Hall.

Tralee General Hospital (☎ 7126222; Boherbee) Has an accident and emergency unit.

Sights & Activities

Housed in the Ashe Memorial Hall is the **Kerry County Museum** (☎ 712 7777; Denny St; adult/child/family €8/5/22; ☼ 10am-4.30pm Tue-Fri Jan-Mar, 9.30am-5pm Tue-Sat Apr, May & Sep-Dec, 9.30am-5.30pm Jun-Aug). It has excellent interpretive displays on Irish historical events and trends, with an emphasis on Kerry. The **Tom Crean Room** celebrates the local hero (see boxed text, p286) who accompanied both Scott and Shackleton on epic Antarctic expeditions. Also here is the **Medieval Experience**, an enjoyable multimedia presentation re-creating life (smells and all) in Tralee in 1450. Children love strolling the medieval streets and there's a commentary in various languages.

Blennerville used to be the chief port of Tralee, though it has long since silted up. A 19th-century flour **windmill** has been restored and is the largest working mill in Ireland and Britain. The modern **visitor centre** (☎ 712 1064; adult/child/family €5/3/15; ☼ 9.30am-5.30pm May-Oct) houses an exhibition on grain-milling, and on the thousands of emigrants who boarded 'coffin ships' from what was then Kerry's largest embarkation point. There's also a database of the Irish émigrés who flocked to America. The admission price includes a 30-minute guided tour of the windmill, which is 1km southwest of Tralee on the N86.

Between 1891 and 1953 a narrow-gauge **steam railway** connected Tralee with Dingle. The last surviving steam engine on this line runs along the restored Tralee–Blennerville section of the track, but at the time of research it was indefinitely closed for repair.

Tralee's water-fun centre, **Aquadome** (☎ 712 8899; www.aquadome.ie; off South Circular Rd; adult/child

€12/10; ⏰ 10am-10pm Jul & Aug, 10am-10pm Mon, Wed & Fri, noon-10pm Tue & Thu, 11am-8pm Sat & Sun rest of the year), has gushers, geysers, sauna and steam room as well as plenty of water just to swim in.

Festivals

The declining **Rose of Tralee** (www.roseoftralee.ie; Ashe Memorial Hall, Denny St) festival is at the end of August. Community arts group **Samhlaíocht** (www.samhlaiocht.com) organises cultural festivals throughout the year.

Sleeping

Bayview Caravan & Camping Park (☎ 712 6140; bayviewtralee@eircom.net; Killeen; camp sites €14; ⏰ Apr-Oct) This small park in a pleasant tree-lined

location has good facilities. It's 1.5km north of the centre on the R556.

Finnegan's Holiday Hostel (☎ 712 7610; www .finneganshostel.com; 17 Denny St; dm/s €17/30) Don't be deterred by the elegant Georgian façade – this is a hostel. Inside, the grandeur has faded, but there are a sizeable kitchen and lounge. The dorms, named after Irish scribblers, have en-suite bathrooms.

Conn Oriel (☎ 712 5359; www.connoriel.com; 6 Pembroke Sq, Pembroke St; s/d €40/70; Ⓟ) One of a line of B&Bs, this friendly mother/daughter operation has cheery decorative art on the yellow walls.

Imperial Hotel (☎ 712 7755; www.imperialtralee .com; Denny St; s/d €65/120) The friendly, family-run Imperial is not as stylish as the Grand but

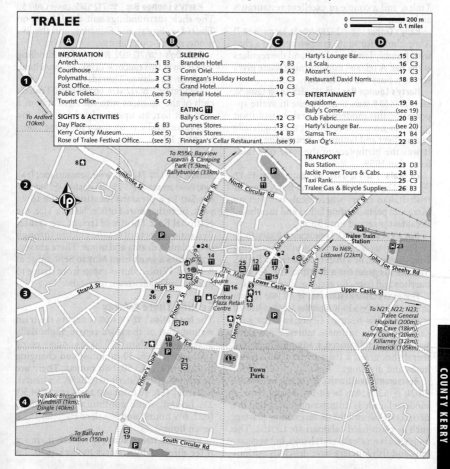

TRALEE	0 ___ 200 m / 0 ___ 0.1 miles

INFORMATION
Antech...................................1 B3
Courthouse...........................2 C3
Polymaths.............................3 C3
Post Office............................4 C3
Public Toilets.....................(see 5)
Tourist Office........................5 C4

SIGHTS & ACTIVITIES
Day Place..............................6 B3
Kerry County Museum........(see 5)
Rose of Tralee Festival Office...(see 5)

SLEEPING
Brandon Hotel.......................7 B3
Conn Oriel............................8 A2
Finnegan's Holiday Hostel......9 C3
Grand Hotel.........................10 C3
Imperial Hotel......................11 C3

EATING 🍴
Baily's Corner.......................12 B3
Dunnes Stores......................13 C2
Dunnes Stores......................14 B3
Finnegan's Cellar Restaurant...(see 9)

Harty's Lounge Bar...............15 C3
La Scala...............................16 C3
Mozart's..............................17 C3
Restaurant David Norris.........18 B3

ENTERTAINMENT
Aquadome............................19 B4
Baily's Corner....................(see 19)
Club Fabric...........................20 B3
Harty's Lounge Bar.............(see 20)
Siamsa Tíre..........................21 B4
Séan Óg's............................22 B3

TRANSPORT
Bus Station...........................23 D3
Jackie Power Tours & Cabs.....24 B3
Taxi Rank.............................25 C3
Tralee Gas & Bicycle Supplies...26 B3

has modern bedrooms and good facilities, including a wood-panelled bar offering trad sessions on Friday and Saturday.

Grand Hotel (☎ 712 1499; www.grandhoteltralee.com; Denny St; s/d €85/130; **P**) Built in 1928, the Grand's prices are a trifle grand, but it maintains the feel of a proper county-town hotel in its public rooms and pleasantly aged bedrooms.

Brandon Hotel (☎ 712 3333; www.brandonhotel.ie; Prince's St; s €105-145, d €160-240; **P**)) If you want corporate big-hotel anonymity, the Brandon is the place. Pricey but with good facilities, including a spa and leisure centre, the smart rooms have cream colour-schemes.

Eating

There are plenty of lunchtime eateries in Tralee, and a couple of excellent restaurants and pubs.

Baily's Corner (☎ 712 6230; Ashe St; bar meals €4-7) A top choice for soup, sandwiches and a chat with friendly landlord Garry and the regulars at the bar. A relaxed mid-morning scene gives way to a busy rest-of-the-day.

Harty's Lounge Bar (☎ 712 5385; Lower Castle St; bar meals €4.50-9, mains €9-22) Despite its svelte appearance, this modernised Tralee institution serves no-nonsense nosh, but with tagliatelle joining beef and Guinness stew on the menu. It was the birthplace of the Rose of Tralee festival in 1959.

La Scala (☎ 712 2477; the Square; mains €6-19; ☯ 10am-12am Fri & Sat, 10am-11pm Sun-Thu) A popular Irish-Italian eatery where locals banquet on pizza and pasta, sizzling fajitas and meatballs. Breakfast is served until 5pm.

Mozart's (☎ 712 7977; 4 Ashe St; snacks & mains €8-20; ☯ 9am-6pm Mon-Sat) Not content with composing Don Giovanni, he's inspired a bistro in Tralee. Mozart's is great for a daytime bite, serving burritos and baps, focaccias and croissants.

Finnegan's Cellar Restaurant (☎ 718 1400; 17 Denny St; mains €15-24; ☯ 5.30-10.30pm May-Sep, Wed-Mon rest of year) In a low-beamed Georgian cellar with candles on the intimate tables, Finnegan's serves reasonably priced, traditional meat and fish dishes given a twist by unusual sauces, herbs and dressings.

Restaurant David Norris (☎ 718 5654; Ivy Tce; mains €18-24; ☯ 5.30-9.30pm Tue-Fri, Sat 7-9.30pm) Norris' modern façade is uninspiring, but inside the décor is stylish and the menu exciting. Starters such as crisp-fried calamari are terrific. The emphasis is on steaks and shanks, but vegetarians and fish fanciers have delicious options

too. A €25, four-course early bird special is available until 7pm Monday to Friday.

Dunnes Stores (the Mall) is the perfect place for self-caterers. There's also a branch on North Circular Rd.

Entertainment

PUBS & CLUBS

Castle St is thick with pubs, many of them offering live entertainment. There are some reasonable café/bars on the Square where you could easily pass an afternoon watching Tralee coming and going.

Baily's Corner (☎ 712 6230; Ashe St) Baily's is deservedly popular for its traditional sessions, with local musicians performing original material most weeknights.

Harty's Lounge Bar (☎ 712 5385; Lower Castle St) The slick surroundings suit the DJ sets on Thursday, Friday and Saturday, and the live modern music on Sunday.

Seán Óg's (☎ 712 8822; Bridge St) Fair diddling trad is on at this raucous 'drinking consultant' bar from Sunday to Thursday.

Club Fabric (☎ 712 4174; Godfrey Place) Tralee's club of the moment with the right mix of a chill-out bar, an upstairs level for '70s and '80s faves, and a main disco for some floor-burning DJs.

THEATRE

Siamsa Tíre (☎ 712 3055; www.siamsatire.com; Town Park; shows per person €15-25; booking office ☯ 9am-6pm Mon-Sat) In a pleasant location in the town park, near the tourist office, Siamsa Tíre, the National Folk Theatre of Ireland, re-creates dynamic aspects of Gaelic culture through song, dance, drama and mime. There are several shows a week from May to September at 8.30pm. Winter shows range from dance to drama and mainstream musicals.

Getting There & Away

The **bus station** (☎ 716 4700) is next to the train station, east of the town centre. Eight daily buses run to Dublin (€20.50, six hours), going via Listowel (€5, 30 minutes) and changing in Limerick (€13.50, two hours). There are hourly buses to Waterford (€20.50, 5½ hours), Killarney (€6, 40 minutes) and Cork (€14.50, 2½ hours), some continuing to Wexford (€22, 6½ hours) and Rosslare Harbour (€23, seven hours).

From the **train station** (☎ 712 3522) there are three direct daily services to Cork (€30, 2¼ hours), nine to Killarney (€8.50, 45 minutes) and one to Dublin (€44, four hours). More trains pass through Mallow (€20, 1½ hours).

Getting Around
There's a taxi rank on the Mall, or try **Jackie Power Tours & Cabs** (☎ 712 9444; 2 Lower Rock St). **Tralee Gas & Bicycle Supplies** (☎ 712 2018; Strand St) hires out bikes.

AROUND TRALEE
Crag Cave
This **cave** (☎ 714 1244; Castleisland; adult/child €12/5; ☼ 10am-6pm Wed-Sun Jan & Feb, 10am-6pm mid-Mar–Jun & Sep-Dec, 10am-6.30pm Jul & Aug) was discovered in 1983, when problems with water pollution led to a search for the source of the local river. In 1989, 300m of the 4km-long cave were opened to the public; admission is by 30-minute guided tour. The remarkable rock formations include a large, wine bottle-shaped stalagmite in the 'Kitchen Cave'; the 'Crystal Gallery', with its thousands of straw-thin stalactites; and a stalagmite shaped like a statue of the Madonna.

The cave is signposted from both Castleisland and the Abbeyfeale–Castleisland stretch of the N21. Castleisland is well connected with both Tralee and Killarney by bus.

Ardfert
☎ 066 / pop 940
Ardfert (Ard Fhearta), about 10km northwest of Tralee on the Ballyheigue road, is most notable for the Dúchas-owned **Ardfert Cathedral** (☎ 713 4711; adult/child €2/1; ☼ 10am-6.30pm May-Sep; last admission 45 min before closing). Most of the building dates back to the 13th century, but it incorporates elements of an 11th-century church. Set into one of the interior walls is an effigy, said to be of St Brendan the Navigator, who was educated in Ardfert and founded a monastery here. The grounds contain the ruins of two other churches, 12th-century Templenahoe and 15th-century Templenagriffin, and a small visitor centre with an exhibition on the cathedral's history.

Turning right in front of the cathedral and going 500m down the road brings you to the extensive remains of a **Franciscan friary**, dating from the 13th century, but with 15th-century cloisters.

Ardfert Indoor Market (☎ 087-920 9673; Community Centre; ☼ 11am-2pm Sun) sells organic produce as well as bric-a-brac.

During the week, Bus Éireann 274, between Tralee and Ballyheigue, stops in Ardfert once daily in either direction; more frequently on Sundays, and in June and September.

LISTOWEL
☎ 068 / pop 3900
The late writer Bryan MacMahon said of Listowel: 'I harbour the absurd notion of motivating a small town in Ireland, a speck on the map, to become a centre of the imagination.' Listowel certainly has more literary credentials than your average provincial town, with connections to such accomplished scribes as John B Keane, Maurice Walsh, George Fitzmaurice and Brendan Kennelly. Keane wrote with wry humour about subjects ranging from Limerick's beggars to the perils of giving up porter as a New Year's resolution. Outside these connections and a few venues, however, the town is little more than some tidy Georgian streets and a riverside park.

Orientation & Information
The Square is the main focus of the town. At its centre is the St John's Theatre and Arts Centre, formerly St John's Church. Most pubs and restaurants are on Church and William Sts, north from the Square, while a short walk southeast along Bridge Rd takes you to the River Feale and Childers Park. The river can also be reached down the road alongside the castle.

There's metered parking in the main square and free parking, downhill to the right of the castle.

Ó Hannán's Book Shop is opposite where William St joins Main St. The Kerry Literary & Cultural Centre bookshop also stocks titles by local writers
Bank of Ireland (the Square) Has an ATM and bureau de change.
North Kerry Together (☎ 23429; 58 Church St; 15min/1hr €1/3; ☼ 9.30am-6pm Mon-Thu, 9.30am-1pm Fri)
Post office (William St) At the northern end of the street.
Tourist office (☎ 22590; ☼ 9.30am-1pm & 2-5.15pm Mon-Sat May-Sep) Housed in the St John's Theatre & Arts Centre.

Sights
Kerry Literary & Cultural Centre, with its audiovisual **Writers' Exhibition** (Seanchaí; ☎ 22212; www.kerrywritersmuseum.com; 24 the Square; adult/child

€5/3; ◷ 10am–5pm Mon-Sat Jun-Sep, to 4.30pm Mon-Fri Oct-May; ⊛), is an absolute gem that gives due prominence to Listowel's heritage of literary observers of Irish life. Rooms are devoted to local greats such as John B Keane and Bryan MacMahon, with simple, haunting tableaus narrating their lives and recordings of them reading their work. There is a café and a performance space where events are sometimes staged.

St Mary's Church, in the Square, was built in 1829 in the neo-Gothic style. It has some lovely mosaic work over the altar and a vaulted roof with timber beams.

The 12th-century **Listowel Castle**, behind the Kerry Literary & Cultural Centre, was once the stronghold of the Fitzmaurices, the Anglo–Norman lords of Kerry. The castle was the last in Ireland to succumb to the Elizabethan attacks during the Desmond revolt. What remains of the castle has been thoroughly restored. Free guided tours are available between June and September.

In Childers Park is the **Garden of Europe**, opened in 1995. Its 12 sections represent the 12 members of the EU of the day. There is a fine bust of the poet Schiller and, strikingly, Ireland's only public monument to those who died in the Holocaust, and to all victims of injustice.

On Church St there is a **literary mural** depicting famous local writers and their pronouncements.

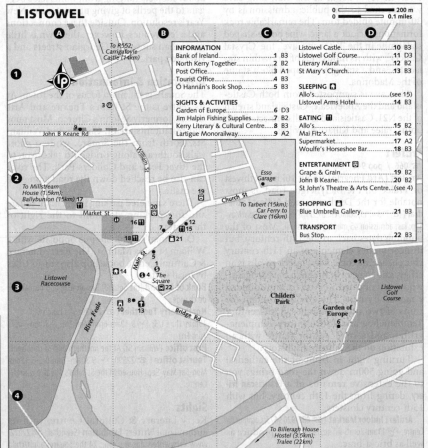

LISTOWEL

0 — 200 m
0 — 0.1 miles

INFORMATION	
Bank of Ireland	1 B3
North Kerry Together	2 B2
Post Office	3 A1
Tourist Office	4 B3
Ó Hannán's Book Shop	5 B3

SIGHTS & ACTIVITIES	
Garden of Europe	6 D3
Jim Halpin Fishing Supplies	7 B2
Kerry Literary & Cultural Centre	8 B3
Lartigue Monorailway	9 A2

Listowel Castle	10 B3
Listowel Golf Course	11 D3
Literary Mural	12 B2
St Mary's Church	13 B3

SLEEPING ⌂	
Allo's	(see 15)
Listowel Arms Hotel	14 B3

EATING ⊞	
Allo's	15 B2
Mai Fitz's	16 B2
Supermarket	17 A2
Woulfe's Horseshoe Bar	18 B3

ENTERTAINMENT ⊟	
Grape & Grain	19 B2
John B Keane	20 B2
St John's Theatre & Arts Centre	(see 4)

SHOPPING ⌂	
Blue Umbrella Gallery	21 B3

TRANSPORT	
Bus Stop	22 B3

To R552;
Carrigafoyle
Castle (14km)

John B Keane Rd

To Millstream
House (1.5km);
Ballybunion (15km) 17

Market St

Esso
Garage

Church St

To Tarbert (15km);
Car Ferry to
Clare (16km)

William St

Listowel
Racecourse

River Feale

The
Square

Main St

Bridge Rd

Childers
Park

Garden of
Europe

Listowel
Golf
Course

To Billeragh House
Hostel (3.5km);
Tralee (22km)

Activities

Lartigue Monorailway (☎ 24393; John B Keane Rd; adult/child €6/3; ☼ 2-4pm May-Sep) was designed by Frenchman Charles Lartigue. This unique survivor of Victorian railway engineering operated between the town and Ballybunion on the coast. The renovated section of line is short but fascinating, with manual turnstiles at either end for swinging the train round.

Listowel Golf Course (☎ 21592; per 9 holes €30), on the banks of the River Feale, is about 2km west of the centre off the N69 to Tarbert. You can also walk through Childers Park and the 'Garden of Europe' to get there.

The River Feale provides many opportunities for angling year round. For licences and information, contact **Jim Halpin Fishing Supplies** (☎ 22392; 24 Church St), which also sells angling equipment.

The tourist office has leaflets on **walks** such as the 3.5km river walk and the 10km Sive walk, which takes in John B Keane Rd, a disused railway track and a bog.

Festivals & Events

Writers' Week (☎ 21074; www.writersweek.ie; 24 the Square) takes place in May. Readings, poetry, music, drama, seminars, storytelling and many other events are held at various places around town. The festival attracts an impressive list of writers that in recent years has included Roddy Doyle, DBC Pierre, journalist Robert Fisk, and Joe Simpson, author of the mountaineering epic *Touching the Void*, who has family connections in Listowel.

Listowel Food Fair (☎ 23034; www.listowelfoodfair .com) takes place in November. The four-day event includes a farmhouse cheesemaker competition, a market featuring local producers, cookery demonstrations and tastings of all sorts of goodies.

Listowel Races (☎ 21144) take place over Whit weekend in June, and for a week during the harvest festival in September.

Sleeping

Billeragh House Hostel (☎ 40321; billeraghhousehostel@ yahoo.com; dm/s/d/f €15/20/35/50) Housed in an ivy-clad Georgian hall, this hostel is 3.5km south of Listowel on the N69. Facilities include en-suite bathrooms, a kitchen and dining room, and a laundry room.

Millstream House (☎ 21129; Greenville; s/d €30/60) This excellent B&B, 1.5km from the centre, has blanket warmers and power showers.

The welcoming Sheahans make you feel instantly at home.

Listowel Arms Hotel (☎ 21500; the Square; www .listowelarms.com; s €85-100 d €140-170; **P**) Listowel's only hotel is a family-run affair in a Georgian building that balances touches of grandeur with country charm. Antiques, marble sinks and power showers abound in the rooms, some of which overlook the river and the racecourse. There's a palatial restaurant and the bar is a good place to find music in the summer.

There are three rooms above the bar/bistro **Allo's** (☎ 2288; Church St; s/d €50/100)

Eating

Listowel has several good eateries and a supermarket on Market St.

Mai Fitz's (☎ 23144 William St; lunch €4-9, mains €12-23; ☼ noon-9pm Tue-Sun) A pleasant, small pub serving chowder, breaded mushrooms and the like. After 3pm, more solid dishes such as Dingle Bay scampi are available.

Allo's (☎ 22880; Church St; mains €12-29; ☼ noon-9pm Tue-Sat) A popular bar/bistro with an intimate feel created by the wooden booths and saloon-style doors. As well as hake, monkfish and duck breast, the more expensive a la carte menu (from 7pm) features continental dishes such as pork fillet wrapped in Serrano ham.

Woulfe's Horseshoe Bar (☎ 21083; 14 Lower William St; bar food €13-20, dinner €18-28; ☼ noon-9pm) Enjoy the cosiness of the downstairs bar or the upstairs restaurant at this long-established place. The menu offers meat, chicken and fish dishes with international touches.

Entertainment

Listowel has plenty of pubs, several with live music and traditional sessions during the week.

John B Keane (37 William St) Once run by the late writer himself, this small, unassuming bar is swathed in Keane memorabilia. At 9.15pm on Tuesday and Thursday during July and August, his son performs sketches, and excerpts from his plays are acted.

St John's Theatre & Arts Centre (☎ 22566; the Square) The centre hosts drama, music and dance events as well as art exhibitions.

Grape & Grain (☎ 23001; Church St) Music can be found at the weekends at this refurbished Listowel institution, a good place for a pint and a bite.

Shopping

Blue Umbrella Gallery (21 Church St; ☺ 10-6pm Tue-Sat) An arts and crafts cooperative opposite the large Archangel gallery. There are changing exhibitions and lots of work for sale.

Getting There & Away

There are frequent daily buses to both Tralee (40 minutes, €5) and Limerick (1½ hours, €13). In July and August there is one daily service to the Cliffs of Moher and Galway. The bus stop is on the northern side of the Square.

AROUND LISTOWEL
Ballybunion

There are a surprising number of reasons to visit this one-seahorse beach town, 15km northeast of Listowel on the R553. Beyond the statue of a club-swinging Bill Clinton, commemorating his visit to the local golf club in 1998, there are two Blue Flag **beaches**.

Overlooking the southern beach are the remains of **Ballybunion Castle**, the 16th-century seat of the Fitzmaurices. There's an underground passage leading from the castle to the cliff.

The **Ballybunion Bachelor Festival** takes place in June. The 30-year-old event sees 15 tuxedo-clad bachelors from across Ireland vying to impress the judges, while the town enjoys a long weekend of street entertainment and celebrations.

In July and August there are two buses from Listowel to Ballybunion daily, Monday to Saturday.

Carrigafoyle Castle

A fine location on the Shannon Estuary adds to the romantic drama of this late-medieval **castle** (☎ 43304; 9am-6pm May-Sep). Its name comes from Carragain Phoill (Rock of the Hole); it's built in a channel between the mainland and Carrig Island. Built by the O'Connors, who ruled most of northern Kerry, the castle was besieged by the English in 1580, retaken by O'Connor, and finally destroyed by Cromwell's forces in 1649. You can climb the spiral staircase to the top for a good view of the estuary.

The castle is 2km west of the village of Ballylongford (Bea Atha Longphuirb). On Tuesday and Thursday, between September and June, two buses link Ballylongford with Tralee via Listowel.

Tarbert

☎ 068 / pop 810

Tarbert is 16km north of Listowel on the N69. **Shannon Ferry Limited** (☎ 905 3124; one way/return bicycle & foot passengers €4/6, motorcycles €8/12, cars €15/25; ☺ 7am-9.30pm Mon-Sat, 9am-9.30pm Sun Apr & Sep, 10.30am-6pm May-Sep, 7am-7.30pm Mon-Sat, 9am-7.30pm Sun Oct-Mar) runs a half-hourly ferry between Tarbert and Killimer in County Clare, useful if you want to avoid congested Limerick city. The ferry dock is 2.2km west of Tarbert and is clearly signposted.

If you have some time before you catch your ferry, you should visit the renovated **Tarbert Bridewell Jail & Courthouse** (☎ 36500; adult/child €5/2.50; ☺ 10am-6pm Apr-Oct), which has exhibits on the social and political conditions of the 19th century. From the jail, the 3.8km **John F Leslie Woodland Walk** runs along Tarbert Bay towards the mouth of the Shannon.

There are buses on Tuesday and Thursday mornings and Friday night to Tralee (one hour), and Sunday afternoon to Limerick (1¼ hours).

DINGLE PENINSULA

The northern-most promontory in Kerry and Cork's proud collection, the Dingle Peninsula also has the subtlest charms. Its mellow landscape is one of green hills and golden sands, and culminates in Europe's most westerly point, gazing across the sound at the ghost town on Great Blasket Island. Of course, the friendly hills have their mountainous areas, such as Mt Brandon and the Connor Pass, but, on the whole, this is calming country.

Centred on pretty Dingle town, the peninsula has a high concentration of ring forts and other ancient ruins. Activities on offer range from diving to playing the bodhrán. There's an alternative way of life here in the craft shops and cultural centres, trad sessions and folkloric festivals found in the Dingle's tiny settlements.

Tours

A number of Killarney companies run daily day trips by bus around the Dingle Peninsula (€25). Alternatively, Dingle-based outfits operate guided two-hour minibus tours of the peninsula from €15 per person.

DINGLE PENINSULA

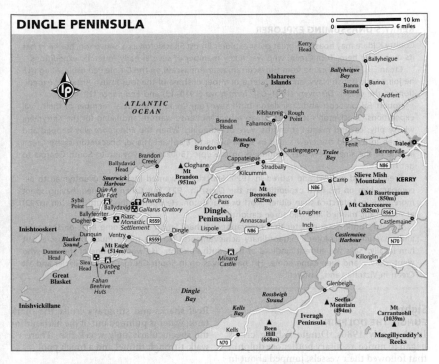

0 — 10 km
0 — 6 miles

Moran's Slea Head Tours (☎ 086-275 3333; Moran's Garage) Leaves the pier at 10am and 2pm daily.
O'Connor's Slea Head Tours (☎ 087-248 0008) Departs from Dingle pier at 11am and 2pm daily.
Sciúird (Map p287; ☎ 915 1606) Has 3½-hour archaeological tours leaving Dingle at 10.30am daily, with a minimum of six people. The tours explore the prehistoric sites, Ogham stones and monastic ruins in the western part of the peninsula. Check for departure point when booking.

DINGLE

☎ 066 / pop 1775

The peninsula's capital is a very special place indeed. It's one of Ireland's largest Gaeltacht towns and a friendly dolphin called Fungie has lived in the bay for 25 years. Many pubs double as shops, so you can enjoy Guinness and a sing-along among screws and nails, wellies and horseshoes. These charms have long drawn runaways from across the world, making the port town a surprisingly cosmopolitan, creative place. It's a popular stomping ground for stag and hen parties, as well as the Fungie-hunting hordes.

Information

The banks on Main St have ATMs and bureaux de change. The post office is off Lower Main St. Parking is free throughout town and €1 per hour in the car park at the harbour.

An Café Liteártha (☎ 915 2204; Dykegate Lane) Bookshop specialising in Irish history.
Dingle Bookshop (☎ 915 2433; Green St) Has a good collection of new and used books, including books on travel and local interest.
Dingle Cleaners (☎ 915 0680; Mail Rd; ⏰ 9.30am-6pm Mon-Sat)
Dingle Internet Café (☎ 915 2478; Lower Main St; per hr €4; ⏰ 10am-10pm Mon-Fri May-Sep, to 6pm rest of year)
The Old Forge (☎ 915 0523; Holyground; per hr €4; ⏰ 10.30am-7.30pm Mon-Sat, 9.30am-10pm Jun-Aug, 12.30pm-7.30pm Sun) Internet café; also cheap international calls.
Tourist office (☎ 915 1188; the Pier; ⏰ 9am-7pm Jun-Sep, 9am-1pm & 2.15-5pm Mon-Sat Oct-May) Busy but helpful, this place has maps, guides and plenty of information on the entire peninsula. It books accommodation for a €4 fee.

KERRY'S UNASSUMING EXPLORER

County Kildare may boast the great polar explorer Ernest Shackleton as a native son, but Kerry has its own polar hero, Tom Crean, who was a key member of several early Antarctic expeditions.

Crean (1877–1938) came from Gurtacurran, near Annascaul on the Dingle Peninsula. At age 15 he joined the British Navy, and was later a member of three of the four British Antarctic expeditions in the vessels *Discovery* (1901–04), *Terra Nova* (1910–13) and *Endurance* (1914–16).

Robert Falcon Scott and Shackleton both saw Tom Crean as a crucial member of their rival expeditions. Shackleton's letters to Crean reflect immense warmth and liking for the Kerryman, whose physical and mental strengths were outstanding. When the *Endurance* was trapped and crushed in ice and the crew sailed in small boats to Elephant Island, Shackleton chose Crean as one of the small crew that continued on the epic 1300km sea voyage to South Georgia to get help.

Crean served in WWI and retired in 1920. Shackleton wanted his fellow countryman to accompany him on his final expedition on the *Quest* in 1921, but Crean declined, having spent more time in Antarctica than either Scott or Shackleton. He opened the South Pole Inn (p292) at Annascaul, married and had three daughters.

It wasn't until decades later that biographer Michael Smith shone some light on the quiet and unassuming explorer's extraordinary achievements. 'No one made much of a fuss about him locally,' says the current landlord of the South Pole Inn. 'He was just one of the lads who went away… and then came home.' His name lives on in South Georgia's Crean Glacier and Mt Crean in Victoria Land, Antarctica.

Sights

FUNGIE THE DOLPHIN

In the early 1980s, Dingle fishing crews began to notice a solitary bottlenose dolphin that followed their vessels, jumped about in the water and sometimes leapt over smaller boats. When an American tourist offered to pay a boatman to take him to visit the large, friendly dolphin, an industry was born. Eleven boats now go out every day in the summer, and the Dingle dolphin is an international celebrity.

Boats leave the pier daily for one-hour dolphin-spotting trips; call **Dingle Boatmen's Association** (☎ 915 2626; adult/child €16/8). It's free if Fungie doesn't show, but he usually does. The association also runs a daily two-hour boat trip for enthusiasts who want to **swim with Fungie** (per person €25, plus wetsuit hire adult €25, child €15-20; ☾ 8am Jun-Aug, 9am rest of the year). Organise it in advance through **Brosnan's** (☎ 915 1967; Coleen), where you can hire wetsuits and snorkelling gear.

DINGLE OCEANWORLD

This **aquarium** (☎ 915 2111; www.dingle-oceanworld .ie; Dingle Harbour; adult/child/family €11/6.50/30; ☾ 10am-8.30pm Jul & Aug, to 6pm rest of year) is a lot of fun. Psychedelic fish glide through tanks re-creating environments such as Lake Malwai, the River Congo and the piranha-filled Amazon.

Reef sharks and stingrays cruise the shark tank; water is pumped out of the harbour for the spectacularly ugly wreck fish. There's a walk-through tunnel and a touch pool.

OTHER SIGHTS

Next to **St Mary's Church** on Green St is the **Trinity Tree**, a sculpture representing the Holy Trinity, made from an unusual three-trunk sycamore. With its carved faces, it looks something out of a fairy tale.

In the former convent, on the other side of the church, is the Celtic culture centre **Díseart** (☎ 915 2476; adult/child/family €3.50/2/10; ☾ 9am-1pm & 2-5pm), which has stained-glass windows by Harry Clarke (p249).

Every second weekend in August the **Dingle Races** bring crowds from far and wide. The racetrack is 1.6km east of town on the N86.

The **Dingle Regatta**, a race in the harbour in traditional Irish *currach* (or *naomhóg*) canoes, is Kerry's largest such event, held at the end of August.

Activities

Mountain Man Outdoor Shop (☎ 915 2400; Strand St) is a shopfront for **Adventure Dingle** (www .adventuredingle.com), which offers all sorts of adventure packages including rock climbing, sailing, horse riding, multi-adventure and boat trips to the Blaskets. It also takes

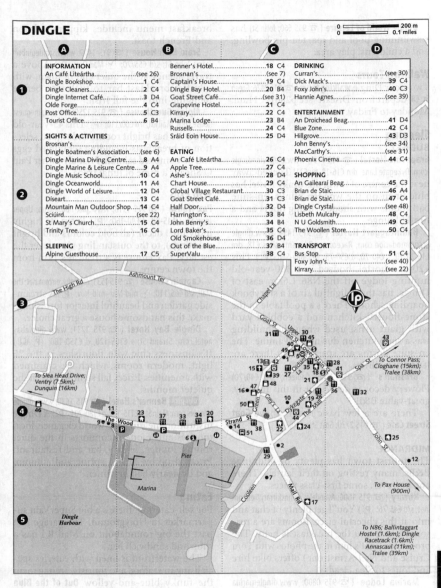

DINGLE

| 0 | 200 m |
| 0 | 0.1 miles |

INFORMATION
An Café Liteártha.........................(see 26)
Dingle Bookshop.....................**1** C4
Dingle Cleaners......................**2** C4
Dingle Internet Café................**3** D4
Olde Forge...........................**4** C4
Post Office..........................**5** C3
Tourist Office.......................**6** B4

SIGHTS & ACTIVITIES
Brosnan's............................**7** C5
Dingle Boatmen's Association......(see 6)
Dingle Marina Diving Centre.......**8** A4
Dingle Marine & Leisure Centre....**9** A4
Dingle Music School................**10** C4
Dingle Oceanworld...................**11** A4
Dingle World of Leisure............**12** D4
Díseart.............................**13** C4
Mountain Man Outdoor Shop.......**14** C4
Sciúird............................(see 22)
St Mary's Church...................**15** C4
Trinity Tree........................**16** C4

SLEEPING
Alpine Guesthouse..................**17** C5

Benner's Hotel.....................**18** C4
Brosnan's..........................(see 7)
Captain's House...................**19** C4
Dingle Bay Hotel...................**20** B4
Goat Street Café..................(see 31)
Grapevine Hostel...................**21** C4
Kirrary............................**22** C4
Marina Lodge.......................**23** B4
Russells...........................**24** C4
Sráid Eoin House...................**25** D4

EATING
An Café Liteártha..................**26** C4
Apple Tree.........................**27** C4
Ashe's.............................**28** D4
Chart House........................**29** C4
Global Village Restaurant..........**30** C3
Goat Street Café..................**31** C4
Half Door..........................**32** D4
Harrington's.......................**33** B4
John Benny's.......................**34** B4
Lord Baker's.......................**35** C4
Old Smokehouse.....................**36** D4
Out of the Blue....................**37** B4
SuperValu..........................**38** C4

DRINKING
Curran's...........................(see 30)
Dick Mack's........................**39** C4
Foxy John's........................**40** C3
Hannie Agnes.......................(see 39)

ENTERTAINMENT
An Droichead Beag..................**41** D4
Blue Zone..........................**42** C4
Hillgrove..........................**43** D3
John Benny's.......................(see 34)
MacCarthy's........................(see 31)
Phoenix Cinema.....................**44** C4

SHOPPING
An Gailearaí Beag..................**45** C3
Brian de Staic.....................**46** A4
Brian de Staic.....................**47** C4
Dingle Crystal.....................(see 48)
Lisbeth Mulcahy....................**48** C4
N U Goldsmith......................**49** C3
The Woollen Store..................**50** C4

TRANSPORT
Bus Stop...........................**51** C4
Foxy John's........................(see 40)
Kirrary............................(see 22)

To Slea Head Drive;
Ventry (7.5km);
Dunquin (16km)

Ashmount Ter

The High Rd

Chapel La

Goat St

Upper Main St

Lower Main St

Orchard La

Dykegate La

Green St

Grey's La

Strand St

The Wood

Pier

Marina

Dingle
Harbour

The Mall

Spa St

John St

Mall Rd

Cooleen

To Connor Pass;
Cloghane (15km);
Tralee (38km)

To Pax House
(900m)

To N86; Ballintaggart
Hostel (1.6km); Dingle
Racetrack (1.6km);
Annascaul (11km);
Tralee (39km)

bookings for **Dingle Horse Riding** (☎ 915 2199; Ballinaboola; 1hr €30), which organises mountain treks, beach rides and peninsula tours.

Snorkelling and scuba diving in Dingle Bay and around the Blasket Islands, courses and wreck dives can be arranged at **Dingle Marina Diving Centre** (☎ 915 2789; the Wood).

Dingle Marine & Leisure (☎ 915 1344; the Wood) runs full- and half-day deep-sea angling trips from €45.

In July and August, **Dingle Music School** (☎ 086-319 0438; Dykegate Lane) offers beginners' workshops in bodhrán (from €12; noon Tue, Wed & Thu, 11am Sat) and tin whistle (€25; 11am Mon). Bodhráns are supplied.

Dingle World of Leisure (☎ 915 660; John St) has a swimming pool and spa, ten-pin bowling, and a childrens' play area.

Walking Tours

Two-hour Dingle **walking tours** (☎ 915 2476; Green St; €8) depart from Díseart (see p286) at 11am, Monday to Friday.

Sleeping

BUDGET

Grapevine Hostel (☎ 915 1434; www.grapevinedingle .com; Dykegate Lane; dm €16-18, tw €21) Tucked away near the centre of town, this dinky hostel has blue linen on the wooden bunks, en-suite bathrooms with shoddy sliding doors and a fire-lit lounge.

Ballintaggart Hostel (☎ 915 1454; www.dingle accommodation.com; Racecourse Rd; camp sites €18, dm €13.20-20, s €40-70, d €50-75; ✆ May-Sep; Ⓟ) This 120-bed hostel, housed in a 300-year-old hunting lodge off the N86 1.6km east of Dingle, has the delightful air of a storybook boarding school. There's a pool table in the stone-floored kitchen and a cobbled yard with giant urns, used when the building was a soup kitchen during the Famine. The en-suite dorms are spacious and there are laundry facilities.

Brosnan's (☎ 915 1146; Cooleen; s/d €40/70) Flowery décor is *de rigueur* in this friendly, great-value B&B.

There are a few basic rooms above **Goat Street Café** (☎ 915 2770; Goat St; r €20).

MIDRANGE

The tourist town has plenty of midrange B&Bs, many resting on their laurels. There are, however, some first-class places.

Kirrary (☎ 915 1606; Avondale; collinskirrary@eircom .net; s/d €45/76; Ⓟ) You'll get plenty of chat and info at this cheerful place. Rooms are a reasonable size and the breakfast is hefty. The proprietor (that's him in the photos with Tom Cruise and Neil Armstrong) offers bike hire and tours to Slea Head.

Marina Lodge (☎ 915 0800; www.dinglemarina lodge.com; the Wood; s/d €50-60/100-120; Ⓟ ⌨) A clean-cut building on the waterfront with a neat, modern interior. This is the sprightliest B&B in town.

Russells (☎ 915 1747; maryr@iol.ie; the Mall; s/d €50/80) The welcome is lukewarm in this lime-green B&B, but the modern rooms are tastefully decorated and the extensive breakfast menu includes kippers, salmon and French toast.

Sráid Eoin House (☎ 915 1409; www.sraideoinbnb .com; John St; s/d €55/70; ✆ Mar-Oct; Ⓟ) Above a travel agency at the quiet end of town, with a buffet breakfast bar to tuck into before plunging into the full Irish.

Alpine Guesthouse (☎ 915 1250; www.alpineguest house.com; Mail Rd; s/d €60/110; Ⓟ) This 45-year-old favourite has bright rooms and a good selection of breakfasts including scrambled eggs and oak-smoked salmon. Friendly owner Paul O'Shea is a mine of fungi trivia.

TOP END

Pax House (☎ 915 1518; www.pax-house.com; Upper John St; s €45-80, d €90-160; Ⓟ) From its highly individual décor (all bold colours and bright paintings), to the outstanding views over the estuary, Pax House is a treat. It's 1km from the town centre.

Captain's House (☎ 915 1531; captigh@eircom.net; the Mall; s/d €65/110; ✆ mid-Mar–mid-Nov; Ⓟ) A streamside garden and beautiful interior furnishings make this handsome house a great choice.

Dingle Bay Hotel (☎ 915 1231; www.dinglebay hotel.com; Strand St; s €105-120, d €150-180; Ⓟ ⌨) It's business chic with flourishes in the 25 light, modern rooms, which are crammed with amenities. Prices fall significantly in the quieter months.

ⓞⓤⓡⓟⓘⓒⓚ Benner's Hotel (☎ 915 1638; www.dingle benners.com; Main St; s €115-127, d €180-204; Ⓟ) A Dingle institution melding old-world elegance, local touches and modern comforts in the quiet rooms, lounge, library, bar and restaurant. Prices drop by 20% in spring and autumn, and by nearly half in winter.

Eating

For self-catering, there's a big SuperValu supermarket in Holyground. The garage just past the big roundabout on Mail Rd has a shop and sandwich bar.

The waterfront is lined with eateries specialising in seafood and tourists, among them the funky blue-and-yellow **Out of the Blue** (☎ 915 0811) and Apple Tree's sister establishment **Harrington's** (☎ 915 1985).

BUDGET

John Benny's (☎ 915 1215; Strand St; snacks €3-5, mains €10-17.50; ✆ 12.30pm-9.15pm) Friendly Benny's manages to not be too touristy despite its seafront location. The popular pub rolls out stodgy classics including fillets, ribs, strip loins, curries, stews, bacon and cabbage, fish and chips, and sandwiches.

An Café Liteártha (☎ 915 2204; Dykegate Lane; snacks €3-6; ⏱ 9am-6pm) Prices don't change much at this delightful spot where you can relax at the back of a bookshop, engulfed in the spirit of literary Dingle.

Goat Street Café (☎ 915 2770; Goat St; snacks & mains €4-11; ⏱ 10.30am-5pm Mon-Sat) This cheerful little café struggles when busy, but is a popular pit stop for soups and salads, tarts and tagine.

Apple Tree (☎ 915 0804; Orchard Lane; mains €7-10; ⏱ 9am-6pm) Homemade chips and desserts, including deep-fried Mars Bars, make this a top-notch no-frills café.

MIDRANGE

Old Smokehouse (☎ 915 1061; Lower Main St; lunch €6-10, dinner €15-23; ⏱ 6.30pm-10pm Apr-May & Sep-Oct, 12.30pm-10pm Jun-Aug) The food, like the décor and service, is unfussily pleasant. Meat dishes, such as local lamb with sage and mustard dumplings, outnumber the seafood choices. Get there early to grab a table in the conservatory overlooking the stream.

Ashe's (☎ 915 0989; Main St; mains €16-29; ⏱ noon-3pm & 6-9pm Mon-Sat) Owned by a distant relation of Gregory Peck, this gastro-pub serves modern cuisine in old-fashioned surrounds. The universally recommended food ranges from beef and Guinness stew to Spanish fish stew. Vegetarians and seafood-lovers will be happy.

Lord Baker's (☎ 915 1277; Lower Main St; bar menu €7-24, mains €17-30; ⏱ 6-10pm Fri-Wed) Established as a pub in 1890 by its namesake, this Dingle institution has a cheerful turf fire and a splendid menu that wastes no energy on purple prose. The excellent choice includes brill, salmon and lobster, Kerry lamb, steak and poultry.

our pick Global Village Restaurant (☎ 915 2325; Main St; mains €18-24, early bird €21-23; ⏱ 6-9.30pm Mar-May, 5-10pm Jun-Sep) With the sophisticated feel of a continental bistro, this restaurant offers a fusion of global recipes gathered by the well-travelled owner-chef, whose CD and art collections are also eclectic. Vegetarians are well catered for. Try the Glenbeigh oysters starter.

The Chart House (☎ 915 2255; Mail Rd; mains €19-29; ⏱ 6.30-10pm Wed-Sun, closed Jan) This low-lying stone building near the roundabout is regarded locally as the place to spoil yourself. Book ahead to ensure you don't miss out on

dishes such as Blasket Islands lamb, tartlet of wild mushroom and tarragon, turbot, sea bass and skate.

Half Door (☎ 915 1600; John St; mains €22-50, set menu €25; ⏱ 12.30-2.30pm Mon-Sat, 5.30-10pm Mon-Sun) Fish and shellfish are superbly presented at this outstanding seafood restaurant, which is among a cluster of quality eateries. Spoil yourself and go for lobster thermidor, or mussels in a garlic and wine sauce. There are meat and duck dishes too, and the surroundings are suitably cosy.

Drinking

Dingle has over 50 pubs, many of them mongrel affairs that double as shops. Two wonderful examples of this on Main Street are **Foxy John's** (☎ 915 1316) and **Curran's** (☎ 915 1110), which respectively sell hardware and outdoor clothing. At night, you can sit behind the shop counters.

Dick Mack's (☎ 915 1960; Green St) Announced by stars in the pavement bearing the names of its celebrity customers from Robert Mitchum to Julia Roberts, this lively pub and leather shop sees impromptu sessions.

Hannie Agnes (☎ 087-949 0832; Green St) Local haunt that's known for its smooth Guinness and, during the summer, trad sessions and Irish coffee. It used to be the coffin-maker's shop; the coffins are reinstalled for the Halloween party.

Entertainment

MacCarthy's (☎ 915 1205; www.maccacrthyspub.com; Goat St) Popular bar containing one of Ireland's smallest venues. There is music at the weekends – check the website .

John Benny's (☎ 915 1215; Strand St) Lively trad, set dancing and signing are on offer from 9.30pm Monday, Wednesday, Friday and Saturday.

An Droichead Beag (Small Bridge Bar; ☎ 915 1723; Lower Main St) Traditional music kicks off at 9.30pm nightly at this raucous pub by the bridge.

Blue Zone (☎ 915 0303; Green St; ⏱ 6pm-1am Tue-Thu, 6pm-2am Fri & Sat, 6pm-12.30am Sun) Late-night hangout with Coronoa, San Miguel and pizzas on the menu, and live music on Tuesday and Thursday.

Hillgrove (☎ 915 1131; Spa St) There's a break from traditional Dingle at nightclub Hillgrove, where chart sounds rule nightly in summer, and at weekends the rest of the year.

CINEMAS

Phoenix Cinema (☎ 915 1222; Dykegate Lane; ticket €6.50) Screens Hollywood films.

Shopping

The Woollen Store (☎ 915 0692; Green St) Has a great selection of hats, jumpers, hooded tops and shawls, some with fleece linings to prevent that wool itch.

Lisbeth Mulcahy (☎ 915 1688; Green St) Beautiful scarves, rugs and wall hangings are created on a 150-year-old loom by this long-established designer. Also sold here are ceramics by her husband, who has a workshop at Louis Mulcahy Pottery (p295), west of Dingle.

An Gailearaí Beag (☎ 915 2976; Main St) A showcase for the work of the West Kerry Craft Guild, selling ceramics, paintings, wood carvings, photography, batik, jewellery, stained glass and much more.

N U Goldsmith (☎ 915 2217; Green St) Original jewellery by Niamh Utsch is on display at this stylish little gallery. Individual pieces start at €40 and keep rising.

Brian de Staic (☎ 915 1298; www.briandestaic.com; Green St) This local jewellery designer's exquisite modern Celtic work includes symbols, crosses and standing stones. The company also has a shop on the Wood.

Dingle Crystal (☎ 915 1550; Green St) Biker-cum-master craftsman Seán Daly worked at Waterford Crystal for 15 years before setting up here 10 years ago. There are demonstrations on the premises and tours of the nearby workshop.

Getting There & Away

Bus Éireann (☎ 712 3566) buses stop outside the car park behind the supermarket. There are four buses daily Monday to Saturday from Dingle to Tralee, and three on Sunday (€9). Between Monday and Saturday, June to September, four daily services link Dingle and Killarney (€11) via Inch. Otherwise, change in Tralee.

There are eight buses a week to Dunquin and Ballydavid, on Monday, Tuesday, Thursday and Friday.

Getting Around

Dingle is easily navigated on foot. For a taxi call **Dingle Co-op Cabs** (☎ 087-2225777), which can also give private tours of the peninsula.

Bike-hire places include **Kirrary** (☎ 915 1606; Avondale; per day €8) and **Foxy John's** (☎ 915 1316; Main St; per day €10).

NORTHSIDE OF THE PENINSULA

There are two routes from Tralee to Dingle, both following the same road out of Tralee past the Blennerville Windmill. Near the village of Camp, a right fork heads to the Connor Pass, while the N86 via Annascaul takes you to Dingle more quickly. The Connor Pass route is much more beautiful. At Kilcummin, a road heads west to the quiet villages of Cloghane and Brandon, and finally to Brandon Point and its fine views of Brandon Bay.

Castlegregory

☎ 066 / pop 940

Castlegregory (Caislean an Ghriare), which once rivalled Tralee as a busy local centre, is a quiet village enlivened only by the occasional souped-up car, driven by young men desperately searching for kicks among the hedgerows. However, things change when you drive up the sandstrewn road along the Rough Point peninsula, the broad spit of land between Tralee Bay and Brandon Bay. Up here, it's a playground. Not content with being a prime windsurfing location, the peninsula sees strange new sports like wavesailing and kitesurfing. Divers can glimpse pilot whales, orcas, sunfish and dolphins. In the pub, the many-accented babble tells of a community of people who came for a day and couldn't face leaving the playground.

Jamie Knox Watersports (☎ 713 9411; www .jamieknox.com; Brandon Bay) offers surf, windsurf, kitesurf, canoe and pedaloe hire and lessons. Halfway along the peninsula, the centre runs a B&B (s/d €48/76) between Easter and November.

Beyond Rough Point are the seven **Maharees Islands**. The largest of the 'hogs', as the islands are known locally, is Illauntannig. The remains of a 6th-century monastic settlement there include a stone cross, a church and beehive huts. Two small adjoining islands can be reached on foot from Illauntannig at low tide, but make sure you know exactly what the tide is doing. The islands are privately owned, but trips (taking about 10 minutes) can be arranged through Castle House (opposite), or through Harbour House (below) in conjunction with a **scuba diving** trip. There is great underwater visibility, making this one of Ireland's best diving areas.

SLEEPING & EATING

Anchor Caravan Park (☎ 713 9157; www.caravanparks ireland.net; camp sites €16-18; ☯ Easter-Sep) A park with well-kept facilities. Set in a sheltered wooded area near the beach, it's signposted from the R560 southeast of Castlegregory.

Castle House (☎ 713 9183; www.castlehouse-bnb .com; s/d €50/75; **P**) Located at the start of the road along the Rough Point peninsula, this handsome house has six rooms with antique dressers, comfortable chairs and sparkling bathrooms. The beach is minutes away on a path through the fields.

Harbour House (☎ 713 9292; www.maharees.ie; Scraggane Pier; s/d €57/94; **P**) This busy B&B and its attached restaurant are in a great position overlooking the Maharees Islands, 5km north of Castlegregory near the end of the peninsula. It's also a diving centre, running PADI courses, and has excellent facilities, including an indoor pool and fitness room.

Spillane's (☎ 713 9125; Fahamore; bar meals €6-23, mains €11-22; ☯ 4pm-9pm Apr & May, Sep & Oct, 1pm-9pm Jun-Aug, 6pm-9pm Nov-Mar) Outside tables overlook the beach, bay and mountains; inside, the usual bar-propping Guinness-swillers look on as feral children tear past waitresses serving scampi, burgers and all the pub stalwarts. You have to shout to get served in this place.

GETTING THERE & AWAY

On Fridays, the Tralee–Cloghane bus stops in Castlegregory, leaving at 8.55am and 2pm. In the other direction, it stops in Castlegregory at 10.35am. More services pass through Camp, 10km southeast on the N86.

Cloghane

☎ 066 / pop 275

Cloghane (An Clochán) is another little piece of utopia hiding on the Dingle Peninsula. The village's friendly pubs and accommodation nestle between Mount Brandon and Brandon Bay, with views across the water to the Stradbally mountains. If you don't fancy scaling Mount Brandon, there are plenty of coastal strolls.

On the last weekend in July, Cloghane celebrates the ancient Celtic harvest festival **Lughnasa** (☎ 713 8277; www.irishcelticfest.com), with events both in the village and atop Mount Brandon. In late August, the Brandon Regatta is a race in traditional *currach* canoes.

Cloghane has a **tourist office** (☎ 713 8137; ☯ May-Sep) opposite the church. Its roof had blown off at the time of research, but the villagers were fixing it. You can buy the *Cloghane and Brandon Walking Guide* (€4), with details of the trails you'll see signposted, and *Loch a'Dúin Archaeological and Nature Trail* (€4) at the tourist office, or at accommodation in the village.

There is a post office in the village shop, attached to Mount Brandon Hostel.

The vacuum-silent **St Brendan's Church** has a stained-glass window showing the Gallarus Oratory and Ardfert Cathedral.

SLEEPING & EATING

Mount Brandon Hostel (☎ 713 8299; www.mount brandonhostel.com; dm/s/tw €18/25/40; ☯ Mar-Jan **P** ⬚) A small, simple hostel with scrubbed wooden floors and furniture, and a patio overlooking the bay. Treatments such as Shiatsu massage are available.

Benagh (☎ 713 8142; mcmorran@eircom.net; s/d €35/70; **P**) At the foot of Mt Brandon, 500m northeast of the village, this purpose-built B&B has four breezy rooms with skylights in the low pine ceilings and sweeping bay views. The friendly owners have great knowledge of local archaeology and ecology, and can organise guided walks.

O'Connors (☎ 713 8113; www.cloghane.com; s €40-50, d €70-90; meals €14-17; **P**) Book ahead to bag a room or a table in this welcoming village pub, which serves evening meals made with local produce from salmon to steak between 7pm and 9.30pm. Landlord Michael is an opencast mine of local information. There is also a camp site with pressurised showers (€7 per person).

Crutch's Hillville House Hotel (☎ 713 8118; www.irishcountryhotels.com; Connor Pass Rd, Kilcummin; s/d €50/100; mains €17-23; **P**) Built in 1833 by alcoholic aristocracy and later tinkered with by a retired army captain who used railway tracks for beams, this blue-and-white, creeper-covered hotel is a bastion of upper-crust eccentricity. Many of the modern rooms have four-poster beds. Breakfast is included in the room rate; dinner is available in the restaurant overlooking the sycamore-ringed lawn.

WALK: MT BRANDON

At 951m, **Mt Brandon** (Cnoc Bhréannain) is Ireland's 8th highest peak. It's made up of a beautiful series of high summits that lie along the edge of a spectacular series of east-facing cliffs and steep ridges above a rocky lake-filled valley. An ascent of the mountain is a serious all-day trip. You should be well-equipped with weatherproof clothing and mountain boots, even in summer. Above all you should be experienced in the use of a map (Ordnance Survey Map No 70) and compass because thick mist can develop quickly, as can wind and rain. Allow at least six to seven hours return.

A popular route from the west is the Saint's Rd, which starts at Kilmalkedar Church (p296). To avoid 274m-high Reenconnell, start the trail at the large Mt Brandon car park, signposted from the Dingle–Feohanagh road. It's a straightforward 6km slog there and back, well marked with 14 crosses interspersed with white markers, and takes five hours return.

The classic way up Mt Brandon starts from Faha (OS reference 493120) above Cloghane. (You can drive there. If you walk, the steep 2km adds a couple of hours onto the six-hour there-and-back climb from Faha.) To reach Faha, take the turn left (signposted 'Cnoc Bhréanainn'), about 200m northeast of Cloghane school, and follow the narrow lane to a T-junction. Turn left again and carry on until you reach the Faha road-end parking area. From here, it's a fairly tough 7km to the summit and back.

Walk left up the track above the car park and follow the obvious path past a grotto onto the open mountain. The rocky path is very clear. Occasional guide poles mark the way along a rising grassy ridge, with a magnificent line of cliffs and ridges ahead. The path contours around rocky slopes before descending into the glaciated wilderness at the valley head, from where it winds between great boulders and slabs. Yellow arrows on the rocks point the way.

When the back wall is reached, the path zigzags very steeply to the rim of the great cliffs. Turn left at the top and head for the summit of Mt Brandon, marked by a trigonometry point or pillar, a wooden cross, and the remains of Teampaillín Breanainn (St Brendan's Oratory). The views in clear weather from the summit are reverie-inducing, but be alert to the sudden edge of the cliffs. You can continue along the cliffs' edge to the subsidiary summits and Brandon Peak, 2km south, but this will add a couple of hours. Retracing your steps requires care and concentration on the initial steep zigzags. The rest of the way back to Faha is freewheeling.

GETTING THERE & AWAY

On Friday, bus 273 leaves Tralee at 8.55am and 2pm for Cloghane (1¼ hours). Returning, it leaves Cloghane at 10.05am and 3.10pm.

CONNOR PASS

At 456m, the Connor (or Conor) Pass is the highest in Ireland and offers spectacular views of Dingle Harbour to the south and Mt Brandon to the north. On a foggy day you'll see nothing but the road just in front of you. When visibility is good, the 10-minute climb from the car park near the summit is well worthwhile to see the tip of the peninsula spread out below you. The road has been improved on the south side but drivers should still take great care, particularly when descending.

TRALEE TO DINGLE VIA ANNASCAUL

For drivers, the N86 has little to recommend it other than being faster than the Connor Pass

route. By bike it's less demanding. On foot, the Dingle Way (p699) runs near the road for the first three days.

The main reason to pause in Annascaul (Abhainn an Scáil), also spelled Anascaul, is to visit the **South Pole Inn** (☎ 066-915 7388; Main St; bar meals €8-20; ☻ noon-8pm). Antarctic explorer Tom Crean (p286) ran the pub in his retirement. Now it's a regular Crean museum and giftshop, as well as a cracking pub serving hearty mains, puddings and a respectable Irish coffee. Ask to have the 'polar experience'.

Monday to Saturday, eight daily buses stop in Annascoul en route to Tralee or Dingle (six on Sunday).

KILLARNEY TO DINGLE VIA CASTLEMAINE

☎ 066

The quickest route from Killarney to Dingle passes through Killorglin and Castlemaine. At

Castlemaine, head west on the R561. You'll soon meet the coast, then go through Inch before joining the N86 to Dingle.

Castlemaine is well connected with Tralee, Killorglin, and Limerick via Killarney, but there are no buses from Castlemaine to Annascaul via Inch.

Mt Caherconree

About 11km west of Castlemaine is the turn-off for Mt Caherconree (825m), signposted as the scenic drive to Camp. About 4km along this road coming from the south is an Iron Age promontory fort that may have been built by Cúror MacDáine, king of Munster. Whichever direction you come from, there are stunning views of Caherconree's sweeping slopes and the surrounding countryside. The narrow, exposed road demands concentration from drivers, so pull over if you want to take in the views.

Phoenix Vegetarian Restaurant & Accommodation (☎ 976 6284; www.thephoenixorganic.com; Shanahill East, Castlemaine; camp sites incl shower €14, r with/without bathroom €28/35, gypsy caravan €30; lunch €4-10, dinner €10-20; ☿ Easter-Oct; ℗) is a centre for all things creative and quirky, announced by a colourful mural overlooking the R561. The dance-teaching owner Lorna runs a dance centre here and there's a film club. The restaurant, open all year, specialises in vegetarian dishes using produce from the organic gardens. The rooms are delightful; sadly, the gypsy caravans and outside toilets were in an appalling state when we visited, though there were plans to do them up.

Inch

Inch's 5km-long **sand spit** was a location for both the leprechaunish *Ryan's Daughter* and more muscular *Playboy of the Western World*. Sarah Miles, love interest in the former film, described her stay here as 'brief but bonny'.

The dunes are certainly bonny, scattered with the remains of shipwrecks and Stone Age and Iron Age settlements. The west-facing beach is also a hot surfing spot; waves average 1m to 3m. **Westcoast Surf School** (☎ 086-306 7053) offers lessons and five-day kids' camps.

Cars are allowed on the beach, but be careful because vehicles regularly get stuck in the wet sand.

Sammy's (☎ 915 8118), at the entrance to the beach, is the nerve centre of the vil-

lage. The beach-facing bar/restaurant serves tucker from sandwiches and pasta to fresh oysters and mussels. There's a shop, tourist information, internet access (per hour €5), and trad sessions during the summer. The Pakistani–Irish proprietor's real name is Mahmood Hussein.

Camping (camp sites from €10) is possible in a field above the beach – ask at Sammy's. You can also camp in the dunes, which provide excellent shelter.

Moan Laur (☎ 915 8957; www.moanlaur-bnb.com; Slieve East; s/d €35/60), on the N86 to Camp, is a whitewashed, modernised cottage with views of the Slieve Mish Mountains, run by a friendly English couple.

Inch Beach Guest House (☎ 915 8333; www.inchbeachguesthouse.com; s €47-67, d €70-110) is all skylights, sea views and *Ryan's Daughter* memorabilia. The general breeziness is completed by attractive modern fittings.

Foley's (☎ 915 8117) is a popular watering hole overlooking grassy dunes.

WEST OF DINGLE

☎ 066

At the tip of the peninsula is the Slea Head drive along the R559. It has the greatest concentration of ancient sites in Kerry, if not the whole of Ireland. Specialist guides on sale in An Café Liteártha (p285) and the tourist office (p285) in Dingle list the most interesting and accessible sites.

This part of the peninsula is a Gaeltacht (Irish-speaking) area. The landscape is dramatic, escpecialy in shifting mist, although full-on sea fog obliterates everything. For the best views, it's best to follow the Slea Head drive in a clockwise direction. Cross the bridge west of Dingle and keep straight on to Ventry (p294). Beyond Ventry the road hugs the coast past Dunbeg Fort (p294), then rou nd the rocky outposts of Slea Head (p294) and Dunmore Head (p294). Continuing along the coast to Dunquin (p294), then turning east to Ballyferriter (p295), the views of the Blasket Islands (p294) give way to views of 951m-high Mt Brandon (opposite) and its neighbours. Beyond Ballyferriter is the Gallarus Oratory (p296) and numerous other historic sites, not to mention a confusing clutter of lanes. From Gallarus, the R599 circles back to Dingle.

Ventry

pop 410

The village of Ventry (Ceann Trá) is next to a wide sandy bay.

A great base for exploring the area is **Ceann Trá Heights** (☎ 915 9866; www.iol.ie/~ventry; s/d €50/72; ☼ Mar-Nov), a comfortable, modern guesthouse overlooking Ventry Harbour.

Near Ceann Trá Heights is **Long's Riding Stables** (☎ 915 9723; 1hr/day €30/125), which offers mountain and beach treks.

Slea Head & Dunmore Head

Overlooking the mouth of Dingle Bay, Slea Head has fine beaches, good walks, and views of Mount Eagle and the Blasket Islands. It's understandably popular with coach parties.

Dunmore Head is the western-most point on the Irish mainland and the site of the wreckage in 1588 of two Spanish Armada ships.

About 7km southwest of Ventry on the road to Slea Head is the Iron Age **Dunbeg Fort**, a dramatic example of a promontory fortification, perched atop a sheer sea cliff. The fort has four outer walls of stone. Inside are the remains of a house and a beehive hut, as well as an underground passage.

On the inland side of the road is a car park and the **Stonehouse Restaurant** (☎ 915 9970; lunch €5-10, dinner €16-23), built in the Gallarus Oratory style. It has a good choice of coffee and cake, cream tea, and more substantial dishes.

The Slea Head area is dotted with **beehive huts**, **forts**, **inscribed stones** and **church sites**. The **Fahan huts**, including two fully intact huts, are 500m west of Dunbeg Fort on the inland side of the road.

When the kiosks are open, you'll be charged about €2 to €3 for entrance to the sights.

Dunquin

The main reason to come to Dunquin, a scattered village beneath Mount Eagle and Croaghmarhin, is to visit the Blasket Centre or catch a boat to the islands. A scenic road climbs through the mountains from Dunquin to Ventry.

The **Blasket Centre** (Ionad an Bhlascaoid Mhóir; ☎ 915 6444; adult/child €3.70/1.30; ☼ 10am-6pm Easter-Jun, Sep & Oct, 10am-7pm Jul & Aug, last admission 45 min before closing) is a wonderful interpretive centre in a long, white hall ending in a wall-to-ceiling window overlooking the islands. Great Blasket's rich community of storytellers and musicians is profiled along with its literary visitors like John Millington Synge, writer of *Playboy of the Western World*. The more prosaic practicalities of island life are covered by exhibits on shipbuilding and fishing. There's a café with Blasket views, and a small bookshop.

Dunquin Hostel (☎ 915 6121; oigedun@eircom.net; dm €16; ☼ Feb-Nov; P) has a terrific location, near the Blasket Centre and not too far from Dunquin Pier. There are stunning views. The An Óige member closes between 10am and 5pm.

Mustard-coloured **De Mórdha** (☎ 915 6276; ardaingeal@hotmail.com; s/d €40/60; ☼ Easter-Oct; P) is a pleasant little B&B with all mod cons and great views.

An Portán (☎ 915 6212; www.anportan.com; lunch from €12, dinner €15-25; ☼ Easter-Sep; P) serves traditional Irish meals with an international flavour. It has rooms in a complex separate from the restaurant.

Blasket Islands

The Blasket Islands (Na Blascaodaí), 5km out into the Atlantic, are the most westerly islands in Europe. At 6km by 1.2km, Great Blasket (An Blascaod Mór) is the largest and most visited, and is mountainous enough for strenuous walks, including a good one detailed in Kevin Corcoran's *Kerry Walks*. All of the Blaskets were inhabited at one time or another; there is evidence of Great Blasket being inhabited during the Iron Age and early Christian times. The last islanders left for the mainland in 1953 after the government and the remaining inhabitants agreed that it was no longer feasible to live in such remote and harsh conditions.

You could camp on the islands, but there are no facilities. There's accommodation in Dunquin.

GETTING THERE & AWAY

Weather permitting, ferries to Great Blasket operate Easter to September (return adult/child €30/15, 20 minutes). Boats leave Dunquin every 30 minutes, 9.55am to 6pm. **Dingle Marine & Leisure** (☎ 915 1344) operates ferries from Dingle (return adult/child €35/25, 35 minutes). Check on arrival when the last boat back is expected to leave.

Dingle Marine & Leisure, **Blasket Islands Eco Ventures** (☎ 915 6422) and **Blasket Islands Tours** (☎ 915 4864) offer 2½ hour cruises around the

---

THE BLASKET WEAVER

The deserted village on Great Blasket might not look like the most inviting place to live, but for some 20 years Welsh immigrant Sue Redican has occupied one of the cottages between April and October.

Europe's most western resident has no electricity or phone line, but has candles for light, gas for cooking, and a mobile phone and VHF radio for communication. She stays there for as much of the year as she can, and once stayed for 10 months, although bad weather can cut her off from the mainland. 'I'd rather get stuck in than stuck out,' she says. Blasket inhabitants traditionally speak of going 'out' to the mainland and coming 'in' to the island.

'I feel alone rather than lonely here,' she says. 'You can have 400 seals on the beach sitting up and watching you, and in the past few weeks we've seen basking sharks and killer whales.' Sue also gets plenty of human company during the summer, when she sells her weaving to day-trippers and delivers her scones to the Blasket Islands Eco Ventures boat.

---

archipelago (adult/child €40/25), departing from Dunquin.

Ballyferriter

Continuing north from Dunquin, you pass the tiny settlement of Clogher, where the road turns inland to reach the Ballyferriter (Baile an Fheirtearaigh). It's named after Piaras Ferriter, a poet and soldier who emerged as a local leader in the 1641 rebellion and was the last Kerry commander to submit to Cromwell's army.

One of the most interesting potteries on the peninsula, **Louis Mulcahy Pottery** (☎ 915 6229; Clogher; ✆ 9am-5.30pm Mon-Fri, 10am-5.30pm Sat, 11am-5.30pm Sun Nov-Easter) has all sorts of pots, jugs, plates and some handsome clocks. Pieces have been sold or given to the likes of Bill Clinton and the Pope. Opening hours are longer in summer and autumn.

Just before Ballyferriter proper, a sign points to **Ceann Sibéal Golf Links** (☎ 915 6255; Jun-Sep €65, Oct-May €45, plus club hire year round €25), a wild and windy course adjoining **Ferriter's Cove**.

About 2.5km northeast of Ferriter's Cove is **Dún an Óir Fort** (Fort of Gold), the scene of a hideous massacre during the 1580 Irish rebellion against English rule. The fort was held by Sir James Fitzmaurice, who commanded an international brigade of Italians, Spaniards and Basques. On 7 November, English troops under Lord Grey attacked the fort; within three days the defenders surrendered. 'Then putt I in certeyn bandes who streight fell to execution. There were 600 slayne', said the poet Edmund Spenser, who was secretary to Lord Grey and patently not in a lyrical mood at the time.

All that remains of the fort is a network of grassy mounds, but it's a pretty spot overlooking Smerwick Harbour. About 2.5km north of Ballyferriter, near the golden Beal Bán beach, it's reasonably signposted from the main road. In the car park, opened in the 1980s by then-President Charles Haughey, there's a handsome memorial sculpture by Cliodna Cussen.

Dingle Peninsula Museum (Músaem Chorca Dhuibhne; ☎ 915 6100; adult/child €2.50/1.50; ✆ 10am-6pm Apr-Oct, by appointment rest of year) is housed in the 19th-century schoolhouse. It has displays on archaeology and ecology of the peninsula.

Friendly **Ferriter's Cove** (☎ 915 6295; ferriterscove@eircom.net; Ballyyoughtra; s/d €40/70; P) has sunny rooms with cheerful bedspreads and bay views. To get there, follow the signs to the golf club.

Free camping is possible near Ferriter's Cove but there are no facilities; ask locally before pitching.

In **Murphy's Bar** (Tigh Uí Mhurchú; ☎ 915 6224; snacks & mains €4-11; ✆), a stuffed fox with a pheasant in its jaws looks down on Gaeilge-speaking locals of all ages tucking into basic pub grub.

Riasc Monastic Settlement

The remains of this 5th- or 6th-century monastic settlement are one of the peninsula's more impressive and haunting sites, particularly the pillar with beautiful Celtic designs. Excavations have also revealed the foundations of an oratory first built with wood and later stone, a kiln for drying corn and a cemetery. The ruins are signposted as 'Mainistir Riaisc' along a narrow lane off the R559, about 2km east of Ballyferriter.

COUNTY KERRY

Gallarus Oratory

This dry-stone oratory is quite a sight, standing in its lonely spot beneath the brown hills as it has done for some 1200 years. It has withstood the elements perfectly, apart from a slight sagging in the roof. Traces of mortar suggest that the interior and exterior walls may have been plastered. Shaped like an upturned boat, it has a doorway on the western side and a round-headed window on the eastern side. Inside the doorway are two projecting stones with holes that once supported the door.

The oratory is signposted off the R559, about 2km further on from the Riasc Monastic Settlement turn-off. The community-run **visitor centre** (☎ 915 5333; adult/child €3/2.50; ☺ 9am-8pm) charges for access to the oratory, car park and a 15-minute audio-visual display. It has a shop and seasonal café.

You can access the oratory for free by continuing uphill to a small parking area on the left. However, in the summer it's worth noting that this parking space is limited and congestion caused by cars in the lane is a problem.

Europe's most westerly camp site, **Oratory House Camping** (Campaíl Teach An Aragail; ☎ 915 5143; www.dingleactivities.com; Gallarus; camp sites from €17; ☺ Apr-Sep), is 300m from the Gallarus Oratory. It's a source of much local information on a mass of activities, especially walking.

Bus 277 leaves Dingle at 9am and drops off at Gallarus 10 minutes later on Tuesday and Friday only. From Gallarus it leaves at 1.25pm.

Kilmalkedar Church

This 12th-century church was once part of a complex of religious buildings. The characteristic Romanesque doorway has a tympanum with a head in the centre. There is an Ogham stone, pierced by a hole, in the grounds, as well as a very early sundial. Nearby is a restored two-storey building known as **St Brendan's House**, which is believed to have been the residence of the medieval clergy. The track to the right of this is the **Saint's Rd**, the traditional approach to Mt Brandon (p292). Parking is limited.

From Gallarus Oratory, the R559 goes north to the little village of Murreagh. The church is about 2km east of the village.

Following the R559 southeast for 8km from Kilmalkedar takes you back to Dingle.

Getting There & Away

Two Buses leave Dingle on Monday and Thursday for Dunquin via Ballyferriter. One of them also stops in Ventry. There are two buses on Tuesday and Friday to Ballydavid, one via Gallarus. The services return the same day. For more details contact **Bus Éireann** (☎ 716 4700) in Tralee.

Counties Limerick & Tipperary

From marching ditties to bad puns on bathroom walls, the names Tipperary and Limerick are part of the lexicon. But, as is so often the truth, the reality bears little relationship to the lore.

Limerick is a city with a history as dramatic as Ireland's. In a nation of hard knocks, it seems to have had more than its share. This is where generations of people fled from as soon as they could. But today it's a place where you can enjoy the delights of modern, urban Ireland, all near the shores of the Shannon Estuary.

Tipperary is surprisingly beautiful – not that Ireland has its dogs of counties – but the rolling hills, rich farmland and river valleys bordered by soaring mountains make every exploration a delight. This is a place to get near the ground; to follow a river to its source; to climb a stile to see that lonely ruin.

Both counties are places to revel in the Irish past. Ancient Celtic sights, medieval abbeys and other relics endure in solitude, waiting for discovery. Sights like the monumental Rock of Cashel and Cahir Castle are on many an itinerary, but despite their popularity are still able to move and inspire. In fact, you might find yourself whistling a merry tune as you explore Limerick and Tipperary – just leave those bathroom walls alone.

HIGHLIGHTS

- **Surprising City** The pubs and restaurants in Limerick (p302), plus the delightful Hunt Museum (p300)

- **At Waters Edge** The narrow roads and Shannon vistas of the drive west of Limerick to Foynes, and its new flying boat museum (p306)

- **Over Hill and Dale** Exploring the wilds of Tipperary, from the Glen of Aherlow (p309) to the River Suir valley (p314)

- **Boiling Oil** Walking the walls and keep of Cahir's authentic and preserved castle (p314)

- **On Top of the World** Views of County Tipperary from the ancient monuments on the Rock of Cashel (p310)

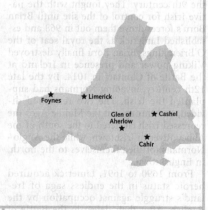

- **POPULATION: 262,000**

- **AREA: 6989 SQ KM**

COUNTY LIMERICK

Limerick's low-lying farmland is framed on its southern and eastern boundaries by swelling uplands and mountains. Limerick city is boisterously urban in contrast and has enough historic and cultural attractions for a day's diversion. About 10km south of the city lie the haunting archaeological sites around Lough Gur and just a few kilometres southwest is the tourist-pleasing village of Adare, with its twee 19th-century rusticity.

LIMERICK CITY

☎ 061 / pop 56,200

With flashy developments along its waterfront, new top-end hotels and a splash of style from an embryonic café culture, Limerick is striving to bury its unfortunate 'stab city' moniker and join the march of Ireland to the future. Still, it's easy to see traces of the squalor, as portrayed graphically by Frank McCourt in his novel *Angela's Ashes*. Until beautification schemes take hold, the main drag, O'Connell St, remains rooted in the city's past. But that doesn't mean you should pass up the Republic's fourth largest city. It has an intriguing castle, interesting museum and several good restaurants and pubs. Perhaps nowhere else can you so easily sense the Irish transition from old to new.

History

Viking adventurers established a settlement on an island in the River Shannon in the 9th century. They fought with the native Irish for control of the site until Brian Ború's forces drove them out in 968 and established Limerick as the royal seat of the O'Brien kings. Brian Ború finally destroyed Viking power and presence in Ireland at the Battle of Clontarf in 1014. By the late 12th century, invading Normans had supplanted the Irish. The two remained divided, and throughout the Middle Ages the repressed Irish clustered to the south of the Abbey River in Irishtown, while the Anglo–Normans fortified themselves to the north, in Englishtown.

From 1690 to 1691, Limerick acquired heroic status in the endless saga of Ireland's struggle against occupation by the English. After their defeat in the Battle of the Boyne in 1690, Jacobite forces withdrew west behind the famously strong walls of Limerick town. Months of bombardment followed and eventually the Irish Jacobite leader Patrick Sarsfield sued for peace. The terms of the Treaty of Limerick, 1691, were then agreed, and Sarsfield and 14,000 soldiers were allowed to leave the city for France. The Treaty of Limerick guaranteed religious freedom for Catholics, but the English later reneged on it and enforced fierce anti-Catholic legislation, an act of betrayal that came to symbolise the injustice of British rule.

During the 18th century, the old walls of Limerick were demolished and a well-planned and prosperous Georgian town developed. Such prosperity had waned by the early 20th century, as traditional industries fell on hard times. Several high-profile nationalists hailed from here, including Eamon de Valera. These days, technological and service industries are major employers. Call a helpline somewhere in the world and you may be speaking to someone in Limerick – if not India.

Orientation

Limerick straddles the Shannon's broadening tidal stream, where the river swings west to join the Shannon Estuary. The city has a clearly defined grid of main streets. The central thoroughfare runs roughly north to south and its name changes from Rutland St in the north to Patrick St, O'Connell St, the Crescent and Quinlan St. It then exits south along O'Connell Ave onto the Cork and Killarney roads. The main places of interest are clustered to the north on King's Island (the oldest part of Limerick and once part of Englishtown); to the south around the Crescent and Pery Sq (the city's noteworthy Georgian area); and along the riverbanks. The joint train and bus station lies southeast, off Parnell St.

Traffic is often coagulated. A welcome new bypass south of town will join the N7 (itself being improved), N18, N20 and N24.

Information

BOOKSHOPS

Eason (☎ 419 588; 9 O'Connell St) A good place to source newspapers and magazines.

O'Mahony's (☎ 418 155; 120 O'Connell St) Ireland's largest independent bookshop has occupied these premises for over 100 years, with an excellent selection of books of local and regional interest.

COUNTY LIMERICK

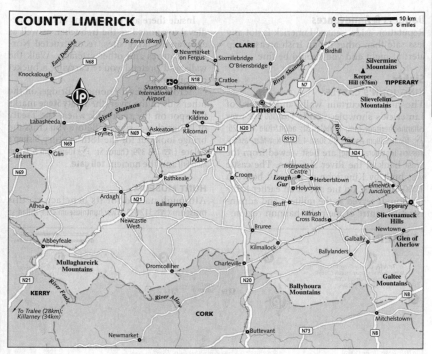

0 — 10 km
0 — 6 miles

INTERNET ACCESS

Check at the tourist office for new access points. There's also internet access at Limerick City Library, below.

Netlink (☎ 467 869; 11 Sarsfield St; per 15min €2; ⏰ 9am-9pm) Small and busy.

LAUNDRY

Superwash Launderette (☎ 414 027; 19 Ellen St; per load €8-18; ⏰ 9am-6pm Mon-Sat)

LEFT LUGGAGE

Limerick Train Station (☎ 217 331; Colbert Station, Parnell St; per item 24hr €2.50; ⏰ 8am-6pm & 6.30pm-8.30pm Mon-Fri, 9.30am-6pm Sat & Sun)

LIBRARIES

Limerick City Library (☎ 407 501; The Granary, Michael St; ⏰ 10am-5.30pm Mon & Tue, to 8pm Wed-Fri, to 1pm Sat)

MEDICAL SERVICES

Both of the following hospitals have accident and emergency departments.

Midwestern Regional Hospital (☎ 482 219, 482 338; Dooradoyle)
St John's Hospital (☎ 415 822; John's Sq)

MONEY

ATMs can be found at shopping complexes, and bus and train stations.

AIB (☎ 414 388; 106/108 O'Connell St) ATMs and bureau de change.
Ulster Bank (☎ 410 200; 95 O'Connell St) Also has ATMs and bureau de change.

POST

Main Post Office (☎ 316 777; Lower Cecil St)

TOILETS

Toilets (Arthur's Quay; admission €0.20)

TOURIST INFORMATION

Limerick Tourist Office (☎ 317 522; www.shannon regiontourism.ie; Arthur's Quay; ⏰ 9.30am-1pm & 2-5.30pm Mon-Fri, 9.30am-1pm Sat) A large, impressive facility with regional information; open longer hours in summer. Ask here about *Angela's Ashes* tours. Also look around town for red-clad 'street ambassadors' offering advice and info.

Dangers & Annoyances

Reputation aside, central Limerick is not any less safe than other urban Irish areas. Keep alert at night and you should be fine.

Sights

KING JOHN'S CASTLE

The massive curtain walls and towers of Limerick's showpiece **castle** (☎ 360 788; www .shannonheritage.com; Nicholas St; adult/child €9/5.25; ☽ 10am-5.30pm Apr-Oct, 10.30am-4.30pm Nov-Mar, last admission 1hr before closing) are best viewed from the west bank of the River Shannon. The castle was built by King John of England between 1200 and 1212 on the site of an earlier fortification. It served as the military and administrative centre of the rich Shannon region.

Inside there are re-creations of brutal medieval weapons like the trebuchet, as well as excavated Viking sites, reconstructed Norman features and other artefacts. Walk the walls and pretend you're carrying a bucket of boiling oil.

Across medieval Thomond Bridge, on the other side of the river, the **Treaty Stone** marks the spot on the riverbank where the Treaty of Limerick was signed. Before you cross the bridge look out for the 18th-century **Bishop's Palace** (☎ 313 399; Church St; ☽ 10am-1pm & 2-4pm Mon-Fri) and the ancient **toll gate**.

HUNT MUSEUM

Although named for its benefactors, this **museum** (☎ 312 833; www.huntmuseum.com; Palladian

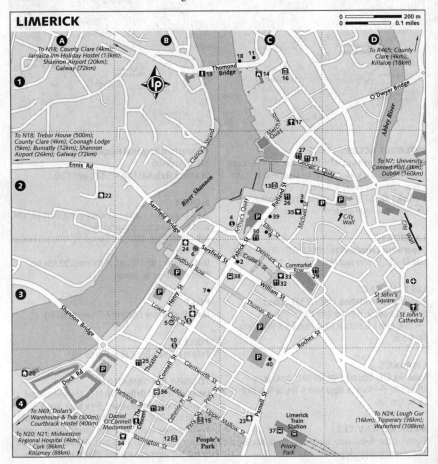

Custom House, Rutland St; adult/child €7.50/3.75; ⏰ 10am-5pm Mon-Sat, 2-5pm Sun) might well be named for the kind of hunt you do for treasure. Visitors are encouraged to open drawers and otherwise poke around the finest collection of Bronze Age, Iron Age and medieval treasures outside Dublin. The 2000-plus items are from the private collection of the late John and Gertrude Hunt, antique dealers and consultants, who championed historic preservation throughout the region. Look out for a tiny, but exquisite, bronze horse by da Vinci, and a Syracusan coin thought to have been one of the 30 pieces of silver paid to Judas for his betrayal of Christ. Cycladic sculptures, a Giacometti drawing and paintings by Renoir, Picasso and Jack B Yeats add to the feast. Guided tours from the dedicated and colourful volunteers are available.

The museum has an excellent in-house restaurant, DuCartes (see p303).

GEORGIAN HOUSE & GARDEN

There is an engaging eeriness about the lofty, echoing rooms of the restored **Georgian House** (☎ 314 130; 2 Pery Sq; adult/child €6/4; ⏰ 9.30am-4.30pm Mon-Fri), a re-creation showing how Limerick's swells once lived. Lavish marble, stucco and wall decorations adorn the main rooms, while things are decidedly downscale when you reach the bare boards and dusty furnishings of the servants' quarters. You'll say 'Brace yourself, Bridget!' reading the hackneyed but entertaining limericks on various wall plaques. The restored back garden leads to a coach house that contains a photographic memoir of Limerick. Things get truly downscale in the small but evocative **Ashes Exhibition**, which features a recon-

struction of the childhood home of novelist Frank McCourt.

LIMERICK CITY GALLERY OF ART

A mix of traditional paintings from the last 300 years covers every inch of wall space in the **Limerick City Gallery of Art** (☎ 310 633; Carnegie Bldg, Pery Sq; admission free; ⏰ 10am-6pm Mon-Wed & Fri, to 7pm Thu, to 1pm Sat). The gallery is beside the peaceful People's Park, at the heart of Georgian Limerick. The permanent collection features work by Sean Keating and Jack B Yeats. Check out Keating's atmospheric *Kelp Burners* and Harry Kernoff's *The Turf Girl*; both infuse their traditional subjects with great energy and joy. The gallery also stages changing exhibitions of often pseudo-scandalous works and is the home of **ev+a** (www.eva.ie), a long-running city-wide contemporary art exhibition held each spring.

ST MARY'S CATHEDRAL

Limerick's ancient **cathedral** (☎ 310 293; Bridge St; admission by €2 donation; ⏰ 9.30am-4.30pm Mon-Sat May-Nov, to 1pm Sat Dec-Apr) was founded in 1168 by Domhnall Mór O'Brien, king of Munster. Parts of the 12th-century Romanesque western doorway, nave and aisles survive, and there are splendid 15th-century black-oak misericords (support ledges for choristers), unique examples of their kind in Ireland. It's worth checking if there are any musical events scheduled.

LIMERICK CITY MUSEUM

This small **museum** (☎ 417 826; Castle Lane; admission free; ⏰ 10am-1pm & 2.15-5pm Tue-Sat) is beside King John's Castle. Exhibits include Stone

Age and Bronze Age artefacts, the civic sword, samples of Limerick silver, and examples of Limerick's lace- and kid-glove manufacturing. There are also exhibits from the late 19th century.

Walking Tours

A local development group runs two-hour walking tours (☎ 318 106; per person €10). One, a popular tour of Limerick locations mentioned in *Angela's Ashes*, starts and ends at the tourist office on Arthur's Quay (tour starts at 2.30pm). The second historical walking tour, beginning at 11am and 2.30pm Monday to Friday, has a start point by arrangement. Confirm both with the tourist office.

Sleeping

If you can find a place to stay near the city centre, you can walk around to enjoy the nightlife. Otherwise you'll be on or near approach roads, so you may wish to opt for something more bucolic.

BUDGET

Jamaica Inn Holiday Hostel (☎ 369 220; www.jamaica inn.ie; Mount Levers, Sixmilebridge, Co Clare; dm €18-19, d €27-29; P ☐) A good option 13km northwest of the city. Rooms range from en suite singles to 10-bed dorms. There are bus connections daily (except Sunday) to Limerick and Shannon Airport.

Courtbrack Hostel (☎ 302 500; www.courtbrack accom.com; Courtbrack Ave; dm/s/d €24/30/52; ⊙ Jun-Aug; ☐) A few minutes walk along Dock Rd from the Shannon Bridge. Rates include a light breakfast, and there's a kitchen, internet room and laundry.

MIDRANGE

Alexandra Terrace on O'Connell Ave has several midrange B&Bs. Ennis Rd, leading northwest towards Shannon, also has a selection, although most are a kilometre or so from the centre.

Trebor House (☎ 454 632; www.treborhouse.com; Ennis Rd; s/d €45/64; ⊙ May-Sep; P) The McSweeney family offer a warm welcome in this classic suburban townhouse (note the pebbledash exterior), a 10-minute walk from the city centre. The five rooms are basic but have TVs.

Glen Eagles (☎ 455 521; gleneaglesbandb@eircom.net; 12 Vereker Gardens, Ennis Rd; r €45-70; ⊙ Feb-Nov; P) Across the river from the city centre, Glen Eagles is on a peaceful cul-de-sac and has

four decent-sized, comfortable rooms and a cheerful welcome.

Coonagh Lodge (☎ 327 050; www.coonaghlodge.com; r €45-75; P ☐) A cute little B&B with a traditional high-pitched roof, the six rooms here vary from singles to rather sizeable family rooms. All have wi-fi. It's in Coonagh, a small town off the N18 west of Limerick.

Railway Hotel (☎ 413 653; www.railwayhotel .ie; Parnell St; r €46-92; P) Right across from the bus and train station, this long-established hotel is busy and shows the wear, but the location is uberconvenient. The 30 rooms are good-sized.

Sarsfield Bridge Hotel (☎ 317 179; www.tsbh.ie; Sarsfield Bridge; r €67-125; P ☐) A new and stylish place right on the river, this hotel eschews frills in order to keep prices moderate. Many of the 55 somewhat compact rooms have good views.

TOP END

George (☎ 460 400; www.thegeorgeboutiquehotel.com; O'Connell St; r €100-200; P ☐) Opened in 2006, this sleek place has a popular atrium lobby and small terrace above the busy streets of the city centre. The design looks like something out of a Sunday supplement – all warm colours with luxurious touches. The 127 rooms have wi-fi, iPod docks and more.

Clarion Hotel (☎ 469 555; www.clarionhotellimerick .com; r from €100; P ☐) A bold exclamation mark on the waterfront development, this striking hotel has modernist accents and is a vision of polished metal and glass. Rooms at the end of corridors seem to hover over the river. There's wi-fi throughout and many business facilities.

Eating

Seafood is *the* thing in Limerick and there's a few quite notable options. On weekends be sure to book for the better places. George's Quay has some continental flair and tables along the water. Locals call it 'first-date row'.

BUDGET

O'Connors Bakery (☎ 417 422; Cruises St; lunch €4-7) The local branch of the tasty regional chain of bakeries, family-run O'Connors has classic fresh-from-the-oven smells as you walk in. Find more than you expected in Limerick? They are renowned for wedding cakes.

Mojo Café Bar (☎ 410 898; 15 Patrick St; mains €4-10) This busy bar and café has sandwiches, paninis, toasted sandwiches and a long list of daily hot lunch specials. The coffee is a cut above the norm.

Chimes (☎ 319 866; Belltable Arts Centre, 69 O'Connell St; breakfast €4, mains €6-9; ☒ 8.30am-5pm Mon-Fri) The art centre's basement café has the sort of creative, healthy fare you'd expect. Good specials.

MIDRANGE

DuCarts (☎ 312 662; Hunt Museum, Rutland St; meals €5-12; ☒ 10am-5pm Mon-Sat, 2-5pm Sun) Window seats overlooking a grassy verge and the Shannon are bathed with light even on the gloomiest of days. The food does the cultural surroundings proud, with a changing selection of salads, soups, sandwiches and hot dishes. But try to forgo something at the start in order to enjoy a delicious dessert finish.

Locke Bar (☎ 413 733; George's Quay; mains €9-15) When the Atlantic gusts abate, enjoy the tables waterside at this sprawling café-cum-bar. You can get lost in the maze of rooms and bars. Enjoy the pub menu of pasta, fish and chips, burgers and more amidst the scrum, or in more refined quarters upstairs.

Green Onion (☎ 400 710; Old Town Hall, Rutland St; mains €10-20; ☒ noon-10pm Tue-Sat) Located in what was once Limerick's 19th-century town hall, the menu at Green Onion is as eclectic as the interior design and often just as striking. Food is served all day and includes a creative range of sandwiches and salads. Think modern Irish with global influences. At night, there's a changing line-up of finely crafted choices and you can enjoy three courses for under €30.

Moll Darby's (☎ 411 511; George's Quay; mains €12-30; ☒ noon-2pm Mon-Fri, 5.30-10pm daily) Exposed brick, dark wood and bundles of nautical schtick make Moll's an attractive and atmospheric choice on George's Quay. The red-checked tablecloths add a jaunty air which will only deepen as you slurp down the superb oysters and other seasonal seafood delights.

TOP END

Brûlée's (☎ 319 931; cnr Henry & Mallow Sts; mains from €20; ☒ 5.30-9pm Tue-Sat) From outside, you get a glimpse of white tablecloths and candles inside this elegant old house. The food lives up to the setting and is best described as modern Irish with plenty of European accents. Mediterranean flavours abound and there's a good and varying selection of local seafood.

Market Square Brasserie (☎ 316 311; 74 O'Connell St; mains from €20; ☒ 5:30-10pm Tue-Sat) Tucked away in the basement of an attractive Georgian house, the food here is carefully prepared and artfully presented. Expect Irish meats and seafood in interesting sauces and surprising flavours. Service is smooth and the setting intimate. Be sure to book in advance.

SELF-CATERING

Pick from local produce and foods like cheese at the **Milk Market** (☎ 415 180; Cornmarket Row; ☒ 8am-noon), a traditional farmer's market held in Limerick's old market buildings.

Drinking & Entertainment

Limerick nightlife features local acts and visiting headliners; you'll find everything from trad Irish to trash rock, indie, chart, soul, reggae, drum 'n bass, jazz and classical, as well as theatre and stand-up comedy. Most clubs have strict door checks. The free *Limerick Event Guide* (LEG; www.eightball.ie/leg.php) can be found in pubs, eateries and hotels all over town.

Dolan's Warehouse (☎ 314 483; www.dolanspub .com; 3/4 Dock Rd) Limerick's best venue for live music promises an unbeatable gig list that has featured everyone from Roper, Kate McGarry and folk legends The Fureys, to The Twang, as well as cutting-edge stand-ups. The Warehouse nightclub is grafted on to the atmospheric Dolan's Pub, where you're guaranteed authentic trad music sessions most nights. There's usually live jazz upstairs.

Trinity Rooms (☎ 411 177; www.trinityrooms.ie; The Granary, Michael St) Three venues in one reflect the name of this vast club in a 300-year-old waterside building. The Green Room front-of-house bar is open for food and drink all day, and has DJs and live bands after dark. The Quarter Club is a late-night chill-out lounge with R&B emphasis, while the Main Room blasts into the early hours with a hot list of DJs. Courtyards rock on mild nights and there's often barbecues.

Nancy Blake's (☎ 416 443; Upper Denmark St) There's a dusting of sawdust on the floor and peat on the fire in the cosy front pub of this old stand-by. Out back is a vast covered drinking zone where there's often live music or televised matches.

South's (☎ 318 850; 4 Quinlan St) The *Angela's Ashes* connection is played up here (the loos are named Frank and Angela). But the current upscale mirrors and glass motif bears little resemblance to the pub where Frank's father knocked 'em back. Enjoy a traditional pint in a posh setting.

Belltable Arts Centre (☎ 319 866; www.belltable.ie; 69 O'Connell St) The Belltable covers everything in theatre, visual arts, music, film and comedy – you're as likely to catch a classic work as something cutting edge. There's an art gallery too, and the Belltable's annual festival of fringe theatre, Unfringed (January and February), gets better every year.

University Concert Hall (UCH; ☎ 322 322; www.uch.ie; University of Limerick) Permanent home of the Irish Chamber Orchestra, the UCH adds lustre to Limerick's cultural scene with visits from world-class performers and regular concerts, opera, drama and dance events. Look for comedy too from the likes of Jon Kenny.

Getting There & Away

AIR
Shannon Airport (see p375) in County Clare handles domestic and international flights. A taxi from Limerick city to the airport costs €32.

BUS
Bus Éireann (☎ 313 333; Parnell St) services operate from the bus and train station near the city centre. There are regular services to Dublin (one way, €11.30 1¼ hours), Tralee (€13.50, two hours), Cork (€10.80, 1¾ hours, Galway, Killarney, Rosslare, Ennis, Shannon, Derry and most other centres. You can also get off in Limerick at the bus stop on O'Connell St.

TRAIN
There are regular trains to all the main towns from **Limerick Railway Station** (☎ 315 555; Parnell St): six trains daily to Dublin Heuston (€43, 2½ hours) and eight trains daily to Ennis (€8.20, 40 minutes). Other routes including Cork, Tralee, Tipperary, Cahir and Waterford involve changing at Limerick Junction, 20km southeast of Limerick.

Getting Around
Regular buses connect Limerick's bus and train station with Shannon Airport (€5 one way), while a taxi from the city centre to the airport costs €32. The airport is 26km northwest of Limerick, about 30 minutes by car.

Limerick is small enough to get around easily on foot or by bike. To walk across

town from St Mary's Cathedral to the train station takes about 15 minutes.

Taxis can be found outside the tourist office, the bus and train station, and in Thomas St.

Scratch card parking discs (€2 per hour) are available from most newsagents and corner shops. There are numerous parking garages around the city at varying rates.

Bikes can be hired at **Emerald Alpine** (☎ 416 983; www.irelandrentabike.com; 1 Patrick St; per day/week €20/80). The company will also retrieve or deliver a bike from anywhere in Ireland for €25. **McMahons Cycle World** (☎ 415 202; www.mcmahonscycleworld.com; 30 Roches St; per day/week €20/80) offers free delivery and collection in the Limerick area, Shannon Airport and Galway.

AROUND LIMERICK CITY
To the south of the city there's a clutch of outstanding historic sites that reward a day visit by car or a couple of days by bike. Only the larger villages are served by bus. For many, the main trip out of town involves Bunratty Castle (see p376) in nearby County Clare.

Lough Gur
The area around this horseshoe-shaped lake has dozens of intriguing archaeological sites. **Grange Stone Circle**, known as the Lios, is a superb 4000-year-old circular enclosure made up of 113 embanked uprights. It is the largest prehistoric circle of its kind in Ireland. There's roadside parking and access to the site is free. To get there, leave Limerick on the N24 road south to Waterford. Look for a sign to Lough Gur indicating a right turn at the roundabout outside town. This takes you onto the R512. In about 18km you reach the stone circle.

Around 1km further south along the R512, at Holycross garage and post office, a left turn takes you towards Lough Gur, past a ruined 15th-century **church**, and a **wedge tomb** on the other side of the road.

Another 2km leads to a car park by Lough Gur and the thatched replica of a Neolithic hut containing the **Lough Gur Stone Age Centre** (☎ 360 788; www.shannonheritage.com; adult/child €5/3; ◷ 10am-5.30pm early May–mid-Sep; **P**). The centre has a good exhibit on prehistoric Irish farms (meaning pre-potato-era) and a small **museum** displaying Neolithic artefacts and a replica of the Lough Gur shield that's now in the National Museum in Dublin. Other displays explain recent emigration from the area, which included a number of future American mobsters.

There are short walks along the lake's edges that take you to burial mounds, standing stones, ancient enclosures and other points of interest. Admission to these sites is free. The whole area is ideal for picnics.

Kilmallock

☎ 063 / pop 1400

The scattering of medieval buildings here is reason for a visit and confirms the town's status during the Middle Ages as Ireland's third-largest town (after Dublin and Kilkenny). Kilmallock developed around a 7th-century abbey, and from the 14th to the 17th centuries it was the seat of the Earls of Desmond. The village lies beside the River Lubach, 26km south of Limerick, a world away from the city's urban racket.

Coming into Kilmallock from Limerick, the first thing you'll see (to your left) is a **medieval stone mansion** – one of 30 or so that housed the town's prosperous merchants and landowners. Further along, the street dodges around the four-storey **King's Castle**, a 15th-century tower house with a ground-floor archway through which the pavement now runs. Across the road, a lane leads down to the tiny **Kilmallock Museum** (☎ 91300; Sheares St; admission free; ⏱ 11am-3pm). It houses a random collection of historical artefacts, a model of the town in 1597 and information for a walking tour around town.

Beyond the museum and across the River Lubach are the moody and extensive ruins of the 13th-century **Dominican priory**, which boasts a splendid five-light window in the choir.

Returning to the main street, head back towards Limerick city, then turn left into Orr St, which runs down to the 13th-century **Collegiate Church**. This has a round tower dating probably to an earlier, pre-Norman monastery on the site.

Further south along the main street, turn left (on foot, the road is one-way against you) into Wolfe Tone St. On the right, just before the bridge, you'll see a plaque marking the house where the Irish poet Aindrias Mac Craith died in 1795. Across the road, one of the pretty, single-storey cottages (the fifth one from the bridge) preserves a 19th-century interior. Obtain the key from next door.

Off the other side of the main street, in Emmet St, is **Blossom Gate**, the one surviving gate of the original medieval town wall.

Kilmallock has an excellent facility in its **Friars' Gate Theatre and Arts Centre** (☎ 98727; www .friarsgate.ie; Main St), where you can also find tourism information about the village. The centre hosts art exhibitions and has a fine little theatre in which it stages plays and music events.

Deebert House (☎ 98106; www.deeberthouse.com; r €30-70; ⏱ Feb-Nov; P ⌨) is a grand Georgian mansion with five rooms (most have an en suite), gorgeous gardens and a playground. It's best heard from the southern exit of the village by turning off down the road signed 'Tipperary'. Deebert House is on the corner at the next junction. Inquire about rates for the two self-catering apartments.

Two Bus Éireann buses run Monday to Saturday from Limerick to Kilmallock (€8.70, one hour).

ADARE & AROUND

☎ 061 / pop 1150

Tourists are drawn to Adare by the busload, which is sort of a shame as the roads are already pretty clogged. But suffer the traffic in high season and you'll be rewarded by scores of medieval buildings and rows of thatched cottages that look, ahem, like they are right out of an English village (blame the 19th-century English landlord, the Earl of Dunraven). Underneath the crowds is a charming Irish village and during slack times its inherent charm is undeniable. Note: this is Ground Zero for many a wedding portrait; expect a passel of glowing brides, frantic grooms and pained fathers.

Located on the River Maigue, Adare lies 16km southwest of Limerick on the busy N21. There's street-side parking in the village, but the best bet is a free car park behind the heritage centre.

Information

AIB Near the tourist office; has an ATM and bureau de change.

Farrier's Internet Café (☎ 396 163; Main St; per 15min €2; ⏱ 10am-6pm) Has good coffee drinks.

Tourist office (☎ 396 255; www.shannonregion tourism.ie; Adare Heritage Centre, Main St; ⏱ 9am-1pm & 2-5pm Mon-Sat, closed Jan) Open longer in summer.

Sights

ADARE HERITAGE CENTRE

In the middle of the village is the **heritage centre** (☎ 396 666; Main St; adult/child €5/3.50; ⏱ 9am-6pm). The centre's audiovisual presentation and exhibits explain the history and the medieval context of Adare's buildings in an entertaining way (note the happy horse). Admission includes entry fee and tour of Adare Castle (right). In winter the centre may close at 4pm.

RELIGIOUS HOUSES

Before the Tudor dissolution of the monasteries (1536–39), Adare had three flourishing religious houses, the remains of which can still be seen. In the village itself, next to the heritage centre, the dramatic tower and southern wall of the **Church of the Holy Trinity** date from the 13th-century Trinitarian priory that was restored by the first earl of Dunraven. Holy Trinity is now a Catholic church. There's a restored 14th-century **dovecote** down the side-turning next to the church.

The ruins of a **Franciscan friary**, founded by the earl of Kildare in 1464, stand in the middle of Adare Manor golf course beside the River Maigue. Public access is assured, but let them know of the clubhouse that you intend to visit. A track leads away from the clubhouse car park for about 400m – watch out for flying golf balls. There's a handsome tower and a fine sedilia (row of seats for priests) in the southern wall of the chancel.

South of the village, on the N21 and close to the bridge over the River Maigue, is the Church of Ireland parish church, once the **Augustinian friary**, founded in 1316. It was also known as the Black Abbey. The interior of the church is pleasantly cavernous, but the real joy is the atmospheric little cloister.

A pleasant **riverside path**, with wayside seats, starts from just outside the friary gates. Look for a narrow access gap and head off alongside the river. After about 250m, turn left along the road to reach the centre of Adare, where the main road intrudes noisily.

ADARE CASTLE

Dating back to around 1200, this picturesque **feudal ruin** (admission & tour incl with Heritage Centre admission; ◯ 10am-6pm Jul-Oct) saw rough usage until it was finally wrecked for good by Cromwell's troops in 1657. By then it had already lost its strategic importance. Restoration work is ongoing; look for the ruined great hall with it's early 13th-century windows. When tours are not on, you can view the castle from the busy main road, or more peacefully from the riverside footpath or the grounds of the Augustinian friary.

CELTIC THEME PARK & GARDENS

About 8km northwest of Adare there's an interesting collection of re-created 'Celtic' structures (plus a few originals) at **Celtic Park** (☎ 394 243; Kilcornan; adult/child €6/free; ◯ 9.30am-6pm mid-Mar–mid-Oct). The park is located on the site of an original Celtic settlement. There's an extensive rose garden and planting of rare local plants including orchids.

Sleeping

There's no shortage of B&Bs about. There are also a few large hotels with plenty of room for bus parking.

Adare Camping & Caravan Park (☎ 395 376; www .adarecamping.com; Adare; camp sites €20) This sheltered, uncrowded site is about 4km south of Adare off the N21 and R519. You can fondle the friendly donkey.

Smithfield House (☎ 64114; gklowe@eircom.net; Croagh, Rathkeale; r €40-70; P) Some 4km west of Adare on the N21, this 1780 Georgian farmhouse has four comfy rooms and a bucolic farm setting. Visit with the many dairy cows or make friendly with some of the numerous horses.

DETOUR: SCENIC N69

Narrow and generally peaceful, the N69 road follows the Shannon Estuary due west from Limerick for 65km to Listowel (see p281). You'll enjoy some great views of the water and seemingly endless rolling green hills laced with stone walls. You'll also discover a number of tiny heritage museums and gardens (most usually only open in the peak season). However, at Foynes there's a major attraction in the **Foyne's Flying Boat Museum** (☎ 069-65416; www.flyingboatmuseum.com; adult/child €8/5; ◯ 10am-6pm Apr-Oct). From 1939 to 1945 this was the landing place for the flying boats that linked North America with the British Isles. Big Pan Am clippers – there's a replica here – would set down in the estuary and refuel. The flights were often filled with wartime intrigue.

Elm House (☎ 396 306; Mondellihy; s/d €47/68; Ⓟ) A peaceful location behind a grove of trees adds to the friendly, relaxed atmosphere. There are four rooms, one with en suite. The B&B is located 1km north of the village

Berkeley Lodge (☎ 396 857; www.adare.org; Station Rd; r €55-80; Ⓟ) One of several nice B&Bs on Station Rd close to the village, this six-room house has TVs in the rooms, great breakfasts and welcomes early arrivals from Shannon Airport.

Dunraven Arms (☎ 396 633; www.dunravenhotel .com; Main St; s/d €170/190; Ⓟ 🖳 🖵) The high-class choice of Adare, this 1792 inn sits discreetly behind extensive plantings. All 86 rooms have wi-fi and a high standard of traditional luxury. The leisure centre boasts a pool and other watery delights.

Eating & Drinking

Food choices lean towards the kind of twee places that one would expect in such a haven for cuteness.

Dovecot (☎ 396 449; Adare Heritage Centre, Main St; lunch €4-12; ⊗ 9am-5pm) This bright and airy cafeteria packs 'em in for typical, if good, breakfast and lunch fare.

Seán Collins (☎ 396 400; Main St; meals €5-10) Adare's most traditional pub – despite a recent refurbishment – has a good menu of pub favourites that you can enjoy at the tables out front. On Sunday there's trad music (more often in summer).

Inn Between (☎ 396 633; Main St; mains €12-22; ⊗ noon-3pm & 6.30-9.30pm) In an oh-so-quaint thatched cottage across from its parent, the Dunraven Arms Hotel, the Inn Between has a creative modern Irish menu created by chef Sandra Earl. Best bets are game, roasts and local seafood.

Wild Geese (☎ 396 451; Main St; mains €20-30; ⊗ 6.30-10pm Tue-Sat) In a town of tough competition in the charming cottage sweepstakes, this one may be the winner – certainly it is for food. The ever-changing menu celebrates the best of Southwest Ireland's foods, from scallops to sumptuous rack of lamb. The preparations are imaginative, the service smooth and polished.

Bill Chawke Lounge Bar (☎ 396 160; Main St) There's trad music every Thursday night and a sing-along on Friday nights (or any other night that the pints loosen up the baritones). There's a beer garden too.

Getting There & Away

Hourly buses link Adare to Limerick (€4, 25 minutes). Many continue on to Tralee (€13.50, 1¾ hours). Others serve Killarney (€13.50, 1¾ hours). Pick up a timetable from the tourist office or check at the bus stop.

COUNTY TIPPERARY

Landlocked Tipperary boasts the sort of fertile soil that farmers dream of. There's still an upper-crust gloss to traditions here. Local fox hunts are in full legal cry during the winter season and the villages can look like something out of the English shires. The central area of the county is low-lying, but rolling hills spill over from adjoining counties. There's good walking, especially in the Glen Of Aherlow near Tipperary town. Of course, the real crowd-pleasers are iconic Cashel, and the Cahir and its castle. In between, you'll find delights along pretty much any country road you choose.

TIPPERARY TOWN

☎ 062 / pop 4600

Tipperary (Tiobrad Árann) has a storied name, largely due to the WWI song. And indeed, you may find it a long road to Tipperary as the N24 and a web of regional roads converge on the centre and traffic often moves at the same speed as the armies at Verdun. The town itself has few pretensions but it's a useful stop for exploring the Slievenamuck Hills, Galtee Mountains and the Glen of Aherlow.

The **tourist office** (☎ 80520; Excel Heritage Centre, Mitchell St; ⊗ 9.30am-5.30pm Mon-Sat) is reached via St Michael's St, a side street leading 200m off the northern side of Main St. There's a car park alongside the heritage centre, which also has a small gallery, movie theatre, good **genealogy centre** (☎ 80552; ⊗ 9.30-4.40pm Mon-Fri) and **internet access** (per 10min €1).

Banks, ATMs, bureau de change and all manner of shops can be found along Main St. The post office is on Davis St, off the north side of Main St.

Midway along Main St, there's a **statue of Charles T Kickham** (1828–82), a local novelist (author of *Knocknagow*, a novel about rural life) and Young Irelander. He spent four years in London's Pentonville Prison in the 1860s for treason.

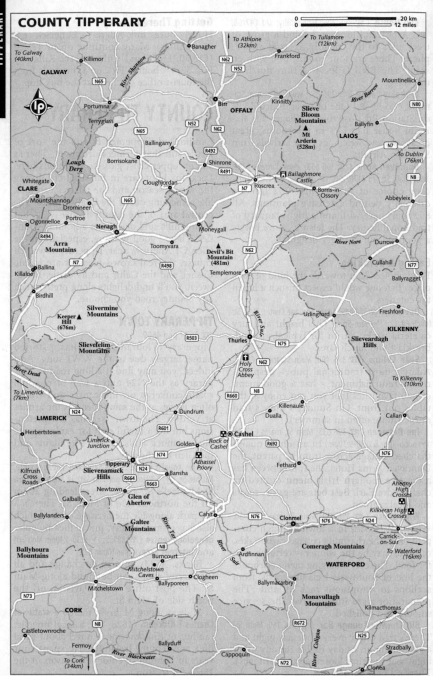

COUNTY TIPPERARY

Sleeping

There's not a lot to choose from in Tipperary town, but standard B&Bs can be found along the N24 on either side of town.

Ach na Sheen (☎ 51298; www.achnasheen.net; Bansha Rd; r €50-90; **P**) An excellent choice, this place is on the immediate outskirts of town, on the N24 towards Bansha. It's got a lovely garden setting and the eight rooms are equipped with TVs and other niceties.

Aisling (☎ 33307; www.aislingbedandbreakfast.com; R664; r €45-65; **P**) There's statuary in the expansive gardens, and flowers in bloom much of the year. The four rooms are country-cosy and all the fresh air will ready you for a hearty breakfast. It's on the road to the Glen of Aherlow.

Eating

There's a regular food market in and around the Excel Heritage Centre's parking lot.

Tipp's Sporting Pub (☎ 51716; 50 Main St; mains €7-15) Also known as the Kirkham House in honour of the local patriot, this old pub has carvery lunches that include smoked haddock and cod pie. On Tuesday nights there are trad music sessions.

Entertainment

Tipperary Racecourse (☎ 51357; www.tipperaryraces .com; Limerick Rd) One of Ireland's leading tracks, it's 3km out of town and has regular meetings during the year. See the local press for details. The course is within walking distance of Limerick Junction station. On race days there are minibus pick-ups from Tipperary town; phone for details.

Getting There & Away

BUS

Most buses stop on Abbey St beside the river. Bus Éireann runs up to eight buses daily on the Limerick–Waterford route (€8.10, two hours) via Cahir and Clonmel. Service is also frequent to Limerick (€4.50, 40 minutes). **Bernard Kavanagh** (☎ 51563; www.bkavcoaches.com) runs one morning service, Monday to Saturday, to Dublin via Cahir and Cashel (€6, 50 minutes). Buses leave at 7.40am from outside the Marian Hall at the northern end of St Michael's St.

Rafferty Travel (☎ 51555; Main St) does bookings for Bus Éireann and for Iarnród Éireann.

TRAIN

To get to the train station, head south along Bridge St. Tipperary is on the Waterford–Limerick Junction line. There are two daily services to Cahir (25 minutes), Clonmel, Carrick-on-Suir, Waterford and Rosslare Harbour, and multiple connections to Cork, Kerry and Dublin from **Limerick Junction** (☎ 51406), barely 3km from Tipperary station along the Limerick road.

Getting Around

BICYCLE

Springhouse Bicycle Hire (☎ 31329; gmrbailey@eircom .net; Kilshane; rental day/week €20/80) has bikes and can offer cycling advice for the region. They also have a small B&B and are located on the N24, just southeast of Tipperary.

GLEN OF AHERLOW & GALTEE MOUNTAINS

South of Tipperary are the shapely Slievenamuck Hills and Galtee Mountains, separated by the broad, chequered valley of the Glen of Aherlow. A 25km scenic drive through the Glen is signposted from Tipperary town. At the eastern end of the Glen, between Tipperary and Cahir, is Bansha (An Bháinseach). The village marks the start of a 20km trip west to Galbally, an easy bike ride or scenic drive along the R663 that takes in the best of the county's landscapes.

The R663 and the R664 south from Tipperary converge at Newtown at the **Coach Road Inn** (☎ 56240), a fine old pub that's popular with walkers and a good source of information on the area. Another good resource is the local visitor information website (www.aherlow. com). The terrain through the area ranges from the lush riverbanks of the Aherlow River to pine forests in the hills and windswept, rocky grasslands that seem to stretch on forever.

There's also excellent walking throughout the area and the views from the hills across the Glen are always spectacular (when it's not raining that is). There's a popular **lookout** and historic **statue of Christ** just north of Newtown on the R664.

Sleeping

The B&Bs near Tipperary (left) are all convenient to the Glen. In addition there's a good range of rural accommodation – much of it catering to walkers. Most places also have self-catering accommodation for longer stays.

Ballinacourty House Camping Park & B&B (☎ 56559; www.camping.ie; Glen of Aherlow; camp sites €18, r €45-80; ♥ mid-Apr–Sep; **P**) Set against a great backdrop of the Galtees, this attractive site is

10km west from Bansha, and past Newtown. It has excellent facilities, as well as a fine garden, restaurant, wine bar and tennis court. An old, stone house has been renovated and now offers B&B accommodation.

Bansha House (☎ 54194; www.tipp.ie/banshahs .htm; Bansha; s/d €50/90; ℗) Period elegance and high ceilings characterise this Georgian country house in spacious grounds. Set amidst farmland and close to walking paths, it's a great getaway. The house is signposted and is 250m along a lane at the western entrance to Bansha.

Rathellen House (☎ 54376; www.rathellenhouse .com; Raheen, Bansha; r €90-190; ℗ 🖵) This purpose-built Georgian-style guesthouse is just south of Bansha and east of the N24. It's open grounds are surrounded by beautiful stone walls, and it's set in the midst of verdant farm country. The seven rooms have heated bathroom floors and numerous other luxuries. Breakfast is a bounteous thing of beauty.

Aherlow House Hotel (☎ 56153; www.aherlow house.ie; Newtown; s/d €105/180; ℗) This 1928 mansion was originally a mountain retreat and guesthouse. In the 1970s it was developed into a hotel and later self-catering cabins were added. It's often the host to local walking festivals.

Getting There & Away
The frequent Bus Éireann link from Tipperary to Waterford stops in Bansha. From here it's a walk or bike ride into the hills. See p309 for bike rental information, otherwise a rental car will let you explore far and wide between walks.

CASHEL
☎ 062 / pop 2500

Cashel (Caiseal Mumhan) owes its great popularity to the dramatic Rock of Cashel and the clutch of historical religious buildings that crowns its breezy summit like a magical extension of the rocky landscape itself. This Irish icon draws visitors by the droves but Cashel manages to maintain a certain charm as a smallish market town. Still, benefits from the hordes include a great range of eating and sleeping places.

Orientation
A bypass on the Dublin–Cork route has eased some of the town's congestion by diverting heavy lorries (and has given hope to places like Tipperary that are waiting for their bypasses). The Rock and its inspiring buildings stand loftily above it all. Reasonable photo opportunities for framing the Rock can be had on the road into town from the Dublin Rd roundabout or the little roads just west of the centre. Much better is to shoot from inside the ruins of Hore Abbey (see opposite).

Parking in Cashel can be tight. Avoid the parking lot closest to the Rock as it's a bit of a scam–you have but one option for parking: €3 for all day and no option for less time. Better are the street spots nearby and throughout town that allow you to only pay for as much time as you need.

Information
AD Weblink (☎ 63304; 102a Main St; per 20min €1; 🕑 10am-7pm) On the backside of Main St.

Book Nook (☎ 64947; 79 Main St) Has a good selection of local interest, general and travel books.

Cashel Heritage Town Centre (☎ 62511; www .cashel.ie; Town Hall, Main St; 🕑 9.30am-5.30pm mid-Mar–Sep, closed weekends Oct–mid-Mar) Helpful and outgoing staff make this a great place to get information. It also has a museum.

Police station (☎ 62866) Behind the post office at the bottom of Main St.

Sights
ROCK OF CASHEL
The **Rock of Cashel** (☎ 61437; www.heritageireland .com; adult/child €5.30/2.10; 🕑 9am-7pm mid-Jun–mid-Sep, to 4.30pm mid-Sep–mid-Mar, to 5.30pm mid-Mar–mid-Jun, final admission 45min before closing) is one of Ireland's most spectacular archaeological sites. The 'Rock' is a prominent green hill, banded with limestone outcrops. It rises from a grassy plain on the outskirts of the town and bristles with ancient fortifications – the word 'cashel' is an anglicised version of the Irish word *caiseal*, meaning 'fortress'. Sturdy walls circle an enclosure that contains a complete round tower, a roofless abbey and the finest 12th-century Romanesque chapel in Ireland. For more than 1000 years the Rock of Cashel was a symbol of power, the seat of kings and churchmen who ruled over the region.

It's a five-minute stroll from the town centre to the rock and you can take some pretty paths including the Bishop's Walk, which ends in the gardens of the Cashel Palace Hotel. There are a couple of parking spaces for visitors with disabilities at the top of the approach road to the ticket office; otherwise see Orientation, opposite, for details on Cashel parking. The Rock is a major draw for coach parties for most of the year and is extremely busy during July and August. The sweeping views allow you to see a tour bus approaching from any direction. The scaffolding moves from place to place each year as part of the never ending struggle to keep the Rock caulked.

History

In the 4th century the Rock of Cashel was chosen as a base by the Eóghanachta clan from Wales, who went on to conquer much of Munster and become kings of the region. For some 400 years it rivalled Tara (see p549) as a centre of power in Ireland. The clan was associated with St Patrick, hence the Rock's alternative name of St Patrick's Rock.

In the 10th century the Eóghanachta lost possession of the rock to the O'Brien (or Dál gCais) tribe under Brian Ború's leadership. In 1101 King Muircheartach O'Brien presented the Rock to the Church, a move designed to curry favour with the powerful bishops and to end secular rivalry over possession of the Rock with the Eóghanachta, by now known as the MacCarthys. Numerous buildings must have occupied the Rock over the years, but it is the ecclesiastical relics that have survived even the depredations of the Cromwellian army in 1647.

Hall of the Vicars Choral

The entrance to the Rock of Cashel is through this 15th-century building, once home to the male choristers who sang in the cathedral. It houses the ticket office. The exhibits in the adjoining undercroft include some very rare silverware, Bronze Age axes and St Patrick's Cross – an impressive, although eroded, 12th-century crutched cross with a crucifixion scene on one face and animals on the other. A replica stands outside, in the castle courtyard. The kitchen and dining hall upstairs contain some period furniture, tapestries and paintings beneath a fine carved-oak roof and gallery. A 20-minute audiovisual presentation on the Rock's history runs every half hour. Showings are in English, French, German and Italian.

The Cathedral

This 13th-century Gothic structure overshadows the other ruins. Entry is through a small porch facing the Hall of the Vicars Choral. The cathedral's western location is formed by the **Archbishop's Residence**, a 15th-century, four-storey castle that had its great hall built over the nave. Soaring above the centre of the cathedral is a huge, square tower with a turret on the southwestern corner.

Scattered throughout are monuments, panels from 16th-century altar tombs and coats of arms. If you have binoculars, look for the numerous stone heads on capitals and corbels high above the ground.

Round Tower

On the northeastern corner of the cathedral is an 11th- or 12th-century round tower, the earliest building on the Rock of Cashel. It's 28m tall and the doorway is 3.5m above the ground – perhaps for structural rather than defensive reasons.

Cormac's Chapel

If the Rock of Cashel boasted only Cormac's Chapel, it would still be an outstanding place. This compelling building dates from 1127, and the medieval integrity of its trans-European architecture survives. It was probably the first Romanesque church in Ireland. The style of the square towers that flank it to either side may reflect Germanic influences, but there are haunting similarities in its steep stone roof to the 'boat-hull' shape of older Irish buildings, such as the Gallarus Oratory in County Clare and the beehive huts of the Dingle Peninsula.

The true Romanesque splendour is in the detail of the exquisite doorway arches, the grand chancel arch and ribbed barrel vault, and the outstanding carved vignettes that include a trefoil-tailed grotesque and a Norman-helmeted centaur firing an arrow at a rampaging lion. The chapel's interior is tantalisingly dark, but linger for a while and your eyes adjust. Inside the main door, on the left, is the sarcophagus said to house King Cormac, dating from between 1125 and 1150. Frescoes once covered the walls, but only vestigial elements of these survive. The southern tower leads to a stone-roofed vault and a croft above the nave (no access).

HORE ABBEY

Cashel throws in another bonus for the heritage lover. This is the formidable ruin of 13th-century Hore Abbey, located in flat farmland just under 1km north of the Rock. Originally Benedictine and settled by monks from Glastonbury in England at the end of the 12th century, it later became a Cistercian house, gifted to the order by a 13th-century archbishop who expelled the Benedictine monks after dreaming that they planned to murder him. The complex is enjoyably gloomy, and from its interior there are superb photo ops of the Rock of Cashel with creative foregrounds, if you get it right.

BRÚ BORÚ

Cashel's heritage and cultural centre, **Brú Ború** (☎ 61122; www.comhaltas.ie; ⊗ 9am-5pm Jun-Sep, closed weekends Oct-May) is in a modern building next to the car park below the Rock of Cashel. The centre offers an absorbing insight into Irish traditional music, dance and song. It has a shop and café, but its main daytime attraction is **Sounds of History**, an exhibition in a subterranean chamber where the story of Ireland and its music is told through imaginative audio displays. In the summer there is a traditional show at night in the centre's theatre. There are also daytime theatrical performances. Admission to events varies from €10 for daytime events to over €40 for the dinner shows.

OTHER SIGHTS

The **Cashel Heritage Town Centre** (☎ 62511; www .casheltc.ie; Town Hall, Main St; admission free; ⊗ 9.30am-5.30pm mid-Mar–Sep, closed weekends Oct–mid-Mar) is located in the town hall. It has a model and displays showing how Cashel looked in the 1640s.

The **Cashel Folk Village** (☎ 62525; Dominic St; adult/child €4/2; ⊗ 9.30am-7.30pm May-Oct, 10am-6pm Mar & Apr) is an engaging exhibition of old buildings and shopfronts from around

the town, plus local memorabilia and an IRA museum.

The **Bolton Library** (☎ 61944; John St; adult/child €3/2; ⊗ 10am-4pm Mon-Fri) is in a forbidding 1836 stone building, and houses a splendid collection of books, maps and manuscripts from the dawn of printing onwards. There are works by writers from Chaucer to Swift.

Sleeping
BUDGET

O'Brien's Holiday Lodge & Camping Park (☎ 61003; www.cashel-lodge.com; Dundrum Rd; camp sites per person €8, dm €18, s €40, d €55-60; P) This first-class IHH hostel, in a converted coach house northwest of town, is friendly, relaxing and well equipped. It has high-standard dorms and rooms, and a camp site. Terrific views of the Rock and Hore Abbey are bonuses, as is the attractive bare stone and wood interior.

Cashel Holiday Hostel (☎ 62330; www.cashelhostel .com; 6 John St; dm €16-18, s €25, d €40) This is a friendly, central, budget option in a quiet, three-storey Georgian terrace off Main St. It has 52 beds in four- to eight-bed rooms as well as a recreation room, kitchen and laundry.

MIDRANGE

The sweet spot for Cashel accommodation is right in the middle of town, and you'll find a huge range of choices, all an easy walk to town and the Rock.

Kearney's Castle Hotel (☎ 61044; Main St; s/d €40/70) Right across from the Cashel Heritage Town Centre, the owners modestly dismiss their building as 'just an old house' even though parts comprise a medieval fortified tower. The 12 simple rooms are sprightly decorated in blue and beige, and have TVs.

Bruden Fidelma Bed & Breakfast (☎ 62330; www .sisterfidelmabandb.com; 5 John St; s/d €50/80; P) 'The chief poet of the tribe earns 21 cows...' is but

---

CASHEL'S CRIME-FIGHTING NUN

'There seems to be some sort of scuffle taking place beneath the abbey wall,' says Sister Fidelma, master of the banal and Cashel's claim to fictional fame. The creation of Canadian author Peter Tremayne (real name Peter Berresford Ellis), the virtuous Fidelma travels 7th-century Ireland from her base in Cashel. Along the way this Miss Marple of the Dark Ages solves mysteries, murders and crimes. In 17 novels (starting with *Absolution by Murder*, quoted here) she preaches law, figures out who offed errant monks and enjoys the company of vaguely oafish Brother Eadulf. Cashelites are used to breathless tourists asking where Sister Fidelma lived and you can buy the books all over town. Soon you too can be thrilling to lines like: 'And I can see why the brethren chose this place to perform their defecations. It is continually washed by the sea.'

one of the multitude of old Irish bromides that adorns the walls of this seven-room B&B which has a snazzy new décor that in some rooms includes huge soaking tubs. As you may have surmised, the B&B is officially sanctioned to exploit Cashel's fictional crime-fighting nun Sister Fidelma (see boxed text, opposite). It is run by the same cheerful management as the Cashel Holiday Hostel next door.

Ladyswell House (☎ 62985; www.ladyswellhouse.com; Ladyswell St; r €50-80) Barely a five-minute walk to the Abbey, this five-room B&B is spotless. Some bathrooms have skylights. The owners are total charmers and will organise custom tours as well as Shannon Airport pick-ups.

Ashmore House (☎ 61286; www.ashmorehouse.com; John St; s/d €60/70; P) Look for the vivid yellow door on this Georgian town house. There are five big, high-ceilinged rooms and gardens out back. It's located on a quiet street just off Main St.

Hill House (☎ 61277; www.hillhousecashel.com; Palmershill; r €60-100; P) It actually could be called Amazing View House, as this Georgian charmer has magnificent views across to the Rock. Set back in gardens, the house is about 400m uphill from Main St. The extraordinary breakfasts made with locally sourced foods may make you forget the Rock entirely.

TOP END

Baileys of Cashel (☎ 61937; www.baileys-ireland.com; Main St; s/d €95/150; P 🖳 🗟) This elegant 1709 building has 19 rooms, all with wi-fi and featuring soaking tubs and an elegant modern design blending dark woods with light walls. There's a good candle-lit wine bar in the basement, a fine restaurant and a leisure centre.

Cashel Palace Hotel (☎ 62707; www.cashel-palace .ie; Main St; r €140-280; P 🖳) The Cashel Palace, a handsome red-brick, late-Queen Anne house, is a local landmark. Fully restored, it has 23 rooms (some with wi-fi) oozing with luxuries like trouser presses (as if you wouldn't have someone else attend to that). Built in 1732 for a Protestant archbishop, the rooms are in the gracious main building or quaint mews.

Eating

Cashel is an excellent place for a meal, even if you're just passing through. Locals favour the €10 bar lunch specials at the Cashel Palace Hotel (see above). Look for the excellent local blue cheese on many menus.

Henry's Fine Foods (☎ 086 894 3707; 5 Main St; meals from €5; ⊙ 9am-6pm) And fine it is. Local ham and cheese features in many a lunch item; definitely partake. The eggs are free-range and there's housemade jellies, jams and chutneys for sale.

Bake House (☎ 61680; 7 Main St; meals €5-8; ⊙ 9am-5.30pm) Head for this busy café for tea and coffee, breakfast or a light lunch. Try the tasty Cashel blue-cheese quiche. Across from the Cashel Heritage Town Centre, ponder the passing parade at tables out front.

our pick **Café Hans** (☎ 63660; Dominic St; mains €8-14; ⊙ noon-5.30pm Tue-Sat) Competition for the 32 seats is fierce at this casual café run by the same family who run Chez Hans (below). There's a terrific selection of salads, open sandwiches and fish, shellfish, lamb and vegetarian dishes, with a discerning wine selection and eye-watering desserts. Get there early or after the rush, or expect to queue.

Chez Hans (☎ 61177; Dominic St; 3 courses €33; ⊙ 6-10pm Tue-Sat) Since 1968 this former church has been a place of worship for foodies from all over Ireland and, for that matter, the world. Still as fresh and inventive as ever, this superb restaurant gives its blessing to all manner of local foods with dishes like its renowned seafood cassoulet and various preparations of local meats. Vegetarian menus are heavenly. Little touches abound, including the homemade chocolates with your coffee. Book ahead.

Drinking

Cashel has a number of quality pubs.

Davern's (☎ 61121; 20 Main St) This bar is popular for a good chat. There's live music some nights, which you may or may not hear tucked away in one of the many crags and corners of this old, old pub.

Ryan's (☎ 62688; Ladywell St) Locals chew the fat, share the gossip and gulp the pint at this congenial place with a beer garden.

Getting There & Away

Bus Éireann runs eight buses daily between Cashel and Cork (€9.50, 1½ hours, eight daily) via Cahir (€3.90, 15 minutes) and Fermoy. There are three buses daily to Roscrea (€8.80, 1¼ hours) and Birr. The bus stop for Cork is outside the Bake House on Main St. The Dublin stop (€9.50, three hours, six daily) is opposite. Tickets are available from the nearby Spar shop or you can buy them on the bus.

Bernard Kavanagh (☎ 51563; www.bkavcoaches
.com) runs one evening service Monday to
Saturday to Tipperary (€6, 50 minutes).

The nearest train stations are at Cahir,
where there are bus connections to Cashel.

AROUND CASHEL

The atmospheric – and delightfully creepy
at dusk – ruins of **Athassel Priory** sit in the
shallow and verdant River Suir Valley, 7km
southwest of Cashel. The original buildings
date from 1205, and Athassel became one of
the richest and most important monasteries
in Ireland. What survives is substantial: the
gatehouse and portcullis gateway, the cloister
and stretches of walled enclosure, as well as
some medieval tomb effigies.

To get there take the N74 to the village of **Golden**, then head south, along the
narrow road signed Athassel Abbey, for
2km. Roadside parking is limited and
very tight. The Priory is reached across
often-muddy fields.

CAHIR

☎ 052 / pop 2850

Every bit as worth a stop as Cashel, Cahir
(An Cathair; pronounced care) is a compact
and attractive town that encircles its namesake castle. Replete with towers, a moat and
various battlements, it's everything a castle
fanatic could ask for. There's a town square
lined with pubs and cafés, and good walking
paths along the banks of the River Suir.

WALK: TIPPERARY HERITAGE WAY

Extending a distance of 55km from a place
called The Vee in the south to Cashel in the
north, the **Tipperary Heritage Trail** takes in
some beautiful river valleys and ruins. The
30km segment running north from Cahir to
Cashel is the best segment as it takes in
the verdant lands around the River Suir and
passes close to highlights such as Athassel
Priory. The best stretches around Golden
are off roads. Expect to see a fair amount of
wildlife as the paths and very minor roads
follow the waters and pass through woodlands. There's an excellent website (www
.tipperaryway.com) that has downloadable
maps for the entire route. You can also use
public transport to return to either Cashel
or Cahir when you're done.

Cahir is 15km south of Cashel, at the eastern tip of the Galtee Mountains.

Orientation

Buses stop in Castle St near a large car park
alongside the river and castle (car parking
here costs €1 for two hours). East of Castle St is the centre of town, eponymously
named the Square. There's street parking
throughout the town.

Information

AIB (Castle St) Has an ATM and bureau de change.

Cahir Communications (☎ 42555; the Square; per
15min €1; ☺ 10am-9pm) Internet access and services.

Post office (Church St) North of the Square.

Public toilets Located next to the tourist office.

Tourist office (☎ 41453; Main St; ☺ 9.30am-6pm
Mon-Sat Apr-Sep) Has leaflets and information about the
town and region.

Sights

CAHIR CASTLE

Cahir's awesome **castle** (☎ 41011; www.heritage
ireland.ie; Castle St; adult/child €2.90/1.30; ☺ 9am-7pm mid-
Jun–mid-Sep, 9.30am-5.30pm Apr–mid-Jun & mid-Sep–mid-
Oct, to 4.30pm mid-Oct–Mar) is feudal fantasy in a big
way. A river-island site, rocky foundations,
massive walls, turrets and towers, defences
and dungeons are all there. This castle is one of
Ireland's largest. Founded by Conor O'Brien in
1142, it was passed to the Butler family in 1375.
In 1599 it lost the arms race of its day when the
Earl of Essex used cannons to shatter the walls,
an event explained with a huge model.

The castle was surrendered to Cromwell
in 1650 without a struggle; its future usefulness may have discouraged the usual
Cromwellian 'deconstruction'. It is largely
intact and formidable still, and was restored
in the 1840s and again in the 1960s when it
came under state ownership.

There's a 15-minute audiovisual show
that puts Cahir in context with other Irish
castles. The buildings within the castle are
sparsely furnished, although there are good
displays. The real rewards come from simply
wandering through this remarkable survivor
of Ireland's medieval past. There are frequent
guided tours, and several good guides are for
sale at the entrance.

SWISS COTTAGE

A pleasant riverside path from behind the town
car park meanders 2km south to Cahir Park

and the **Swiss Cottage** (☎ 41144; www.heritageireland.ie; Cahir Park; adult/child €2.90/1.30; ☒ 10am-6pm mid-Apr–mid-Oct, 10am-1pm & 2-6pm Tue-Sun mid-Mar–mid-Apr, to 4.30pm Tue-Sun mid-Oct–mid-Nov). This place is an exquisite, thatched-cottage fantasy, surrounded by roses, lavender and honeysuckle. It is the best in Ireland, and was built in 1810 as a retreat for Richard Butler, 12th Baron Caher, and his wife. The design was by London architect John Nash, creator of the Royal Pavilion at Brighton and London's Regent's Park. The cottage-orné style emerged during the late 18th and early 19th centuries in England in response to the prevailing taste for the picturesque. Thatched roofs, natural wood and carved weatherboarding were characteristics, and most were built as ornamental features on estates.

There could not be a more lavish example of Regency Picturesque than the Swiss Cottage. It is more of a sizable house than a cottage and has extensive facilities. The 30-minute (compulsory) guided tours are thoroughly enjoyable, although you may have to wait for one in the busier summer months. Note that at the time of research, the cottage was closed while locals quarrelled over bridge access, so check locally before visiting.

Sleeping

Apple Caravan & Camping Park (☎ 41459; www .theapplefarm.com; Moorstown; camp site per adult/child €6/4; ☒ May-Sep) This quiet and spacious camp site on a farm of apple orchards is on the N24 between Cahir (6km) and Clonmel (9km). The place has a delightful fruity ambience and there's free use of a tennis court and racquets.

Lisakyle (☎ 41963; Ardfinnan Rd; dm/s/d €14/18/36; ℗) Some 2km south of town, past the Swiss Cottage on the R670, this charmer of a hostel also offers tent space (€8) amidst pretty gardens. Maurice offers a warm welcome and 21 beds.

Tinsley House (☎ 41947; www.tinsleyhouse.com; The Square; r €35-65; ☒ May-Sep) This mannered house has a great location and four well-furnished rooms. There's a roof garden and the owner, Liam Roche, is an expert on local history and can recommend walks and other activities.

Cahir House Hotel (☎ 43000; www.cahirhousehotel.ie; the Square; €90-130; ℗ ⌨) On a prominent corner of the centre, this landmark hotel has a relaxed vibe. The 42 rooms have wi-fi and a rather bold yellow-and-red décor – think of it as a visual wake-up call.

Eating

Lazy Bean Café (☎ 42038; the Square; snacks €3-7; ☒ 9am-6pm Mon-Sat, 10.30am-6pm Sun) Busy, breezy little café that dishes out loads of tasty sandwiches, snacks and ice cream. A sign says: 'Chocolates, coffee, men. Some things are just better rich.'

River House (☎ 41951; 1 Castle St; meals €7-12; ☒ 9am-5pm) Fortify yourself for an assault on the castle across the street at this modern and very appealing lunch spot. There's a wide selection of cold and hot dishes as well as a large selection of cookbooks (obviously the better ones are in use in the kitchen).

Cahir's **farmers market** (Craft Yard; ☒ 9am-1pm Sat) boasts several stalls of organic food.

Getting There & Away

BUS

Cahir is a hub for several Bus Éireann routes, including Dublin–Cork, Limerick–Waterford, Galway–Waterford, Kilkenny–Cork and Cork–Athlone. There are eight buses per day Monday to Saturday, and six buses on Sunday to Cashel (€3.90, 15 minutes). Buses stop in the car park beside the tourist office.

TRAIN

From Monday to Saturday, the Limerick Junction–Waterford train stops three times daily in each direction.

MITCHELSTOWN CAVES

While the Galtee Mountains are mainly sandstone, a narrow band of limestone along the southern side has given rise to the **Mitchelstown Caves** (☎ 052-67246; Burncourt; adult/child €5/2.50; ☒ 10am-6pm). Superior to Kilkenny's Dunmore Cave (p337) and yet less developed for tourists, these caves are among the most extensive in the country with nearly 3km of passages, and spectacular chambers full of textbook formations with names such as the Pipe Organ, Tower of Babel, House of Commons and Eagle's Wing. Tours take about 30 minutes.

The caves are near Burncourt, 16km southwest of Cahir and signposted on the N8 to Mitchelstown (Baile Mhistéala).

Sleeping

Mountain Lodge Hostel (☎ 052-67277; www.anoige .ie; Burncourt; dm €11-15; ☒ Apr-Sep; ℗) This 24-bed An Óige hostel (housed in an attractive, one-time shooting lodge), is 6km north of the caves, and is a handy base for exploring the Galtee Mountains. It lies to the north of the N8 Mitchelstown–Cahir road.

Getting There & Away

Daily **Bus Éireann** (☎ 062-51555) buses from Dublin to Cork or Athlone drop off at the Mountain Lodge Hostel gate.

CLONMEL

☎ 052 / pop 15,900

Clonmel (Cluain Meala; 'Meadows of Honey') is Tipperary's largest and most commercial town. It's worth a stop for a quick stroll or for supplies. Laurence Sterne (1713–68), author of *A Sentimental Journey* and *Tristram Shandy*, was a native of the town. However, the commercial cheerleader for Clonmel was Italian-born Charles Bianconi (1786–1875), who, at the precocious age of 16, was sent to Ireland by his father in an attempt to break his liaison with a woman. Bianconi later channelled all his frustrated passion into setting up a coach service between Clonmel and Cahir; his company quickly grew to become a nationwide passenger and mail carrier. For putting Clonmel on the map, Bianconi was twice elected mayor.

Orientation

Clonmel's centre lies on the northern bank of the River Suir. Set back from the quays and running parallel to the river, the main street runs east–west, starting off as Parnell St and becoming Mitchell St and O'Connell St before passing under West Gate, where it changes to Irishtown and Abbey Rd. Running north from this long thoroughfare is Gladstone St, which has hotels and pubs.

There's a confounding system of one-way streets; you'll find refuge in the vast parking lot off Gladstone and Mary Sts.

Information

Allied Irish Bank (AIB; O'Connell St) Has an ATM and bureau de change.

Circles Internet (☎ 23315; 16 Market St; per 10min €1; ⏱ 11am-11pm) Speedy connections will divert you from the acerbic staff.

Post office (Emmet St)

Sophie's Bookshop (☎ 80752; 15 Mitchell St) Cute; has a good selection of general and travel books, as well as books of local interest.

Tourist office (☎ 22960; www.clonmel.ie; St Mary's Church, Mary St; ⏱ 9.30am-1pm & 2-4.30pm Mon-Fri) Set in quiet church grounds; ask for the *Clonmel Heritage Trail* map.

Sights

At the junction of Mitchell and Sarsfield Sts is the beautifully restored **Main Guard** (☎ 27484; www.heritageireland.ie; Sarsfield St; adult/child €2.10/1.10; ⏱ 9.30am-6pm mid-Mar–Oct), a Butler courthouse dating from 1675 and based on a design by Christopher Wren. The columned porticos are once again open (after renovations) and exhibits include the ubiquitous model of Clonmel as a walled 17th-century town.

In Nelson St, south of Parnell St, is the refurbished **County Courthouse**, designed by Richard Morrison in 1802. It was here that the Young Irelanders of 1848, including Thomas Francis Meagher, were tried and sentenced to transportation to Australia.

West along Mitchell St (past the town hall with its statue commemorating the 1798 Rising) and south down Abbey St is the **Franciscan friary**. Inside, near the door, is a 1533 Butler tomb depicting a knight and his lady. There's some fine modern stained glass, especially in St Anthony's Chapel to the north.

Turn south down Bridge St and cross the river, following the road round until it opens out at **Lady Blessington's Bath**, a picturesque stretch of the river that is just right for picnicking.

The **County Museum South Tipperary** (☎ 25399; The Borstal, Market Place; admission free; ⏱ 10am-5pm Tue-Sat) has displays on the history of County Tipperary from Neolithic times to the present, and hosts changing exhibitions.

Sleeping

There are several B&Bs on Marlfield Rd, due west of the centre.

Fennessy's Hotel (☎ 23680; fennessyshotel.com; Gladstone St; r €50-120; Ⓟ) Saints Peter & Paul Church, across from this hotel, will provide courage should you have immoral thoughts in any of the 10 rooms at this attractive four-story central hotel. Extras include room safes and whirlpool tubs in some rooms.

Mulcahy's Hotel (☎ 25054; www.mulcahys.ie; 47 Gladstone St; r €55-95; 🖳) Centrally located. The 10 rooms have wi-fi and are part of a complex of bars and bistros. It's good value but beware of weekend noise.

ourpick Hotel Minella (☎ 22388; www.hotel minella.ie; Coleville Rd; r €120-250; P 🖵 🕿) What can you say about a luxury hotel that has a sheep dog named Sparky to greet you at the door, but 'cool!' Unpretentious yet refined, this family-run hotel sits amidst extensive grounds on the south bank of the River Suir, 2km east of the centre. The 90 rooms are divided between those in an 1863 mansion and those in a new wing. The latter boast almost every kind of convenience, including sybaritic private hot tubs on terraces overlooking the river.

Eating

O'Gorman's Bakery (☎ 21380; 61-62 O'Connell St; lunch €5-7; 🕑 8am-6pm Mon-Sat) The scones sell out early at this locally beloved bakery. Get sandwiches to go or tuck into some warming shepherd's pie in the tearoom.

Mulcahy's (☎ 25054; 47 Gladstone St; meals €7-20; 🕑 carvery 8.30am-9.30pm) This vast, rambling pub has a carvery at lunch and a more trad restaurant at dinner.

Angela's (☎ 26899; 14 Abbey St; meals €7-10; 🕑 9am-5.30pm Mon-Sat) The full coffee bar draws people all day at this always buzzing café in the centre. Hot and cold meals feature organic and locally grown ingredients. Salads, soups, sandwiches and hot dishes such as casseroles and pasta are delightfully creative.

Befani's (☎ 77893; 6 Sarsfield St; meals €10-30; 🕑 9am-9.30pm) Just down the street from the Main Guard, Befani's brings the Mediterranean to Clonmel. Brightly flavoured dishes delight at lunch and dinner. Through the day there's a long tapas menu, perfect for accompanying a sherry hailed from the small bar. Breakfasts are a cure for the black-pudding blues.

Drinking

The main bar at Mulcahy's (see above) is dark enough for a boozy assignation even at midday. You may not need a room upstairs.

Two traditional pubs almost next to each other on Parnell St (near Nelson St) are the diminutive **Phil Carroll** (☎ 25215), Clonmel's most atmospheric old boozer and **The Coachman** (☎ 21299), which has also escaped the crimes of modernisation.

Entertainment

Clonmel has a fast-changing line-up of clubs. Ask around for which one's hot.

There's an excellent programme of art exhibitions, plays and films at the **South Tipperary Arts Centre** (☎ 27877; Nelson St), the focus of the arts in Tipperary.

North of town is the **Powerstown Park Racecourse** (☎ 21422; www.powerstownpark.com; Powerstown Park). It holds 13 meetings a year on its 1¼-mile track.

Getting There & Away

BUS

Bus Éireann has buses to Cahir (€4.20, 30 minutes, eight daily); Cork (€13.50, two hours, three daily); Kilkenny (€6.80, one hour, 12 daily); Waterford (€5.40, one hour, eight daily); and a number of other places. Tickets can be bought at the train station on Prior Park Rd, where the buses stop.

TRAIN

The **train station** (☎ 21982) is on Prior Park Rd. Head 1km north along Gladstone St, past the Oakville Shopping Centre and it's just after the petrol station. Monday to Saturday, the Limerick Junction–Waterford train stops three times daily in each direction.

AROUND CLONMEL

Directly south of Clonmel, over the border in County Waterford, are the Comeragh Mountains. There's a scenic route south to Ballymacarbry and the Nire Valley. For more details, see p198.

The East Munster Way (see p699) passes through Clonmel. Heading east towards Carrick-on-Suir, the way follows the old towpath along the River Suir. At Sir Thomas Bridge it cuts south away from the river and into the Comeraghs and through Gurteen Wood to Harney's Crossroads. It rejoins the River Suir again at Kilsheelan Bridge, from where it follows the towpath all the way to Carrick-on-Suir. Going west from Clonmel, the way first leads south into the hills and then descends to Newcastle and the river once more. The route east is pleasant for a short there-and-back outing from Clonmel.

FETHARD

☎ 052 / pop 1400

Fethard (Fiodh Ard) is a quiet, cute little village with a surprising number of medieval ruins scattered about its compact centre. Located 14km north of Clonmel on the River Clashawley, it has a good slice of its old walls still intact. Driving north on the R689 you cross a small ridge and see Fethard in the emerald valley below, looking much as it would have to travellers centuries ago. Its wide main street testifies to its historic role as an important market town.

You can get information and local info from the cheery office of the **Tirry Community Centre** (☎ 31000; Barrack St; 🕓 9am-5pm Mon-Fri). Ask for the walking-tour leaflet. You can also find good information at www.fethard.ie.

The post office is on Main St, and there's an ATM in Kenny's Foodmarket, about 50m northeast along the road from the Tirry Community Centre.

Sights

Fethard's **Holy Trinity Church** and **churchyard** (☎ 26643; Main St; admission free) lie within a captivating little time warp. The church is right off Main St and is reached through a cast-iron gateway. Getting inside is part of the adventure: get the keys from the XL Stop & Shop (aka Whyte's) on Main St, 50m west of the gate.

The main part of the building dates from the 13th century, but its ancient walls have been rather blighted by being covered with mortar for weatherproofing. The handsome west tower was added later and has had its sturdy stonework uncovered. It looks more like a fortified tower house and has savage-looking finials on its corner turrets. The interior of the church has an aisled nave and a chancel of typical medieval style, but it is sparsely furnished. A ruined chapel and sacristy adjoin the south end of the church. It is the context of the entire churchyard that is the real winner. Old gravestones descend in ranks to a refurbished stretch of medieval wall complete with a guard tower and a parapet, from where you can look down on the gentle River Clashawley between its horse-trod banks.

Close to the church in Main St is the 17th-century **town hall**, with some fine coats of arms mounted on the façade.

Fethard's main concentration of medieval remains (some of which have been incorporated into later buildings) are just south of the church at the end of Watergate St. Beside Castle Inn are the ruins of several fortified 17th-century **tower houses**. Just under the archway

to the river bank and Watergate Bridge is a fine **sheila-na-gig** (a sexually explicit medieval depiction of a woman) embedded in the wall to your left. You can stroll the river bank, provided the resident geese are feeling copasetic. From here, the backs of the Abbey St houses, although much added to and knocked about in places, once again display the pleasing irregularities of typical medieval building style.

East along Abbey St is the 14th-century **Augustinian friary**, which is now a Catholic church, with some fine, medieval stained glass and another in-your-face **sheila-na-gig** in its east wall.

Sleeping & Eating

Gateway (☎ 31701, 087-780 6842; www.gatewaybandb .com; Rocklow Rd; r €30-60; **P**) Tucked away just north of Main St, alongside the ruined 15th-century North Gate, this little house is a pleasant stopover with a sunny breakfast room. Rooms are eclectic.

McCarthy's (☎ 31149; Main St; lunch €3-8) A classic that deserves national acclaim and preservation, McCarthy's proclaims itself as Pub, Restaurant and Undertaker – and not necessarily in that order. This timeless joint has closely spaced wooden booths and tables amidst a thicket of treasures dating back to 1840 that will prod your imagination. And yes, it is an efficient set-up for wakes; arrangements are made downstairs.

Sadels (☎ 31176; Main St; mains €12-22; 🕓 5-9pm Wed-Sun) An offshoot of McCarthy's, this classy dinner spot has an ambitious French-influenced menu and a prim setting of white tablecloths and candles.

Getting There & Away

There's no public transport to Fethard but it would make a pleasant cycle from Cashel (p310), 15km to the west.

CARRICK-ON-SUIR

☎ 051 / pop 5700

The unassuming market town of Carrick-on-Suir (Carraig na Siúire), 20km east of Clonmel, boasted twice its present population during the late-medieval period when it was a centre of the brewing and wool industries. The modern town makes a good pit stop – if for no other reason than to escape the local traffic and Byzantine traffic patterns.

Carrick-on-Suir was quick to honour local boy Sean Kelly, one of the world's greatest cyclists, in the late 1980s. The town square bears his name, as does the sports centre. Carrick is also the birthplace of the singing Clancy Brothers, who, with Tommy Makem and assorted Aran Island sweaters, did much to popularise folk music in the 1960s.

From Carrick-on-Suir, the East Munster Way (p699) winds west to Clonmel before heading south into Waterford.

Information

Main St has banks, ATMs and other services.

The **Splash & Chat** (☎ 649 911; 86 Main St; per hr €5; ⊙ 10am-8pm Mon-Sat, noon-5pm Sun) has internet access and a laundry. Email old flames while your undies come clean.

The **Tourist office** (☎ 640 200; www.carrickonsuir.ie; ⊙ 10am-5pm Mon-Fri May-Sep, to 4pm Tue-Fri Oct-Apr) is off Main St, through a narrow entranceway. An old church houses this helpful office as well as a Heritage Centre.

Sights

Carrick-on-Suir was once the property of the Butlers, the Earls of Ormond, who built the **Ormond Castle** (☎ 640 787; www.heritageireland .ie; Castle St; admission free; ⊙ 10am-6pm mid-Jun–early Sep) on the banks of the river in the 14th century. Anne Boleyn, the second of Henry VIII's wives, may have been born here, though other castles also claim this worthy distinction, possibly hoping to boost their own sales of knick-knacks celebrating the beheaded. The Elizabethan mansion next to the castle was built by the 10th Earl of Ormond, Black Tom Butler, in long-term anticipation of a visit by his cousin, Queen Elizabeth I, who rather thoughtlessly never turned up.

Some rooms in this Dúchas-owned edifice have fine 16th-century stuccowork, especially the Long Gallery with its depictions of Elizabeth and the Butler coat of arms.

Sleeping & Eating

Main St has numerous lunch joints, and pubs with food.

Fatima House (☎ 640 298; www.fatimahouse.com; John St; s/d €36/68; P) Located about 500m west of the Greenside bus stop, this B&B is housed in a 100-year-old farmhouse. Furnishings have been accumulating in the rooms for that entire time.

Bell & Salmon Arms (☎ 641 293; www.bellsalmon hotel.com; Main St; s/d €50/90, meals €8-15; P) The

13 rooms here have a simple, pink-accented décor and are modern. The pub boasts trad music some Mondays and Wednesdays; later in the week there's live rock and DJs. Meat, seafood and bowls of boiled potatoes may just cause you to lose your head at – we're not making this up – Anne Boleyn's Restaurant.

Getting There & Away

BUS
Buses stop at Greenside, the park beside the N24 road. Follow New St north from Main St, then turn right.

Bus Éireann (☎ 879 000) has numerous buses serving Carrick-on-Suir. The Limerick–Waterford line serves Cahir and Clonmel (€4.50, 25 minutes) up to nine times daily. There's also a frequent service to Kilkenny (€6.80, 45 minutes).

TRAIN
The station is north of Greenside, off Cregg Rd. From Monday to Saturday, the Limerick Junction–Waterford train stops three times daily in each direction.

THURLES & AROUND
☎ 0504 / pop 6900
Thurles (Durlas) is a busy market town, 22km north of Cashel. It was founded by the Butler family during the 13th century. It is a down-to-earth place and holds little reason for an inordinate pause. In 1884 the *Cumann Lúthchleas Gael* (Gaelic Athletic Association; GAA) was founded, and today the town's famous Semple Stadium rivals Croke Park Stadium in Dublin as a holy ground of Gaelic sports like hurling and Gaelic football.

The centre of town is the long, spacious and traffic-choked Liberty Square. Tourist information can be found at **Lár na Páirc** (☎ 22702; http://tipperary.gaa.ie; Slievenamon Rd), the shop of the GAA, which is redolent in the blue, black and gold of the local team. The **visitor centre** (exhibits adult/child €4/2; ⊙ 10am-5.30pm) is fully dedicated to sport but offers free regional info as well.

The highlight of the area is the Cistercian **Holy Cross Abbey** (⊙ 9am-8pm), 6km southwest of Thurles beside the River Suir. The large buildings that survive today date from the 15th century, although the abbey was founded in 1168. Look for the ornately carved 'Sedelia' near the altar and pause to appreciate the early form of 'stadium seating'. The abbey contains two relics of the True Cross of varying pedigree. A bookshop is open irregular hours.

ROSCREA

☎ 0505 / pop 5600

The pleasant little town of Roscrea (Ros Cré) is a useful pit stop on the journey between Dublin and the west. It has some interesting ruins and couple of good places for a bite to eat.

Roscrea owes its beginnings to a 5th-century monk, St Crónán, who set up a way station for the travelling poor. Most of the historical structures are on or near the main street, Castle St.

The Bank of Ireland on Castle St has an ATM. The town is protected from the busy traffic of the N7 by a bypass.

Sights

Roscrea Castle, a 13th-century stone edifice right in the town centre, was started in 1213 and is remarkably intact. There's two fortified stone towers, surrounded by walls. Look closely and you can see where the original drawbridge was installed. Inside the courtyard stands **Damer House**, the Queen Anne-style residence of the Damer family. Built in the early-18th century, it no doubt had few problems with burglars owing to its location.

Inside you'll find the **Roscrea Heritage Centre** (☎ 21850; Castle St; adult/concession €3.70/1.30; 10am-6pm Apr-Oct, 9.30am-4.30pm Sat & Sun Nov-Mar). The centre contains some interesting exhibitions, including one on the medieval monasteries of the midlands and another on early-20th-century farming life. There's a peaceful walled garden by the house.

Sleeping & Eating

Quigley's Bakery (☎ 23313; Roscrea Shopping Centre; Castle St; meals from €3) Does great sandwiches and other snacks for picnicking.

Tower (☎ 21774; www.thetower.ie; Church St; s/d €42/75; P) The Tower is an excellent choice for a pause lasting through lunch or overnight. The 10 rooms have full facilities and are attractive yet unpretentious. The restaurant wins plaudits for its careful cooking of Irish standards such as roasts and seafood. The pub looks out onto the castle and has good casual lunches.

Getting There & Away

Up to 12 Bus Éireann buses stop at Roscrea between Dublin (€9.30, 2½ hours) and

Limerick (€6.80, 1½ hours). There are three buses daily to Cashel (€8.80, 1¼ hours).

Dublin trains require a connection in Ballybrophy. Limerick trains (€8.30, 1½ hours) stop at Roscrea twice a day from Monday to Saturday, and once on Sunday.

AROUND ROSCREA

In the hinterlands southwest of Roscrea, **Fiacri Country House Restaurant** (☎ 43017; www.fiacrihouse.com; set menu €50; 7-9pm Wed-Sat) is a pink-hued oasis among the peat bogs and dairy farms. There's a high order of cooking here, using local ingredients in creative and ever-changing ways. Meats, seafood and vegetables (vegetarians will do well here) are prepared simply yet with bold and interesting flavours. The setting, like the hosts, is relaxed yet correct. View the garden from the impeccably set dining area.

There's also a **cookery school** (€60; 10am-2pm Tue). Phone ahead to confirm course times. To get here, look for signs and expect to ask for directions.

NENAGH & AROUND

Nenagh is a pretty place with a violent past. It was a garrison town in the 19th century and before that it was the site of a dominant castle. You can see evidence of all this just north of the centre on O'Rahilly St; look for the tall steeple of St Mary's of the Rosary church. **Nenagh Castle** looks like the prototype for the rook in chess and is surrounded by cawing crows and coughing teens. The tower dates from the 13th century and has walls 30m thick.

DETOUR: FAMINE WARHOUSE

From Roscrea, take the R491 10km to Shinrone, then continue on over smaller roads for another 10km to tiny Ballygarry. Here is a relic of one of Ireland's darkest chapters, the **Famine Warhouse** (☎ 087-908 9972; www.heritageireland.ie; 2.30-5.30pm Wed-Sun Apr-Sep, 2-4pm Sat & Sun Oct-Mar), the site of the 1848 rebellion when rebels besieged police who had barricaded themselves inside, taking children hostage. Exhibits put the events in context. Afterwards, you can take the N52 to Nenagh or Birr.

Nearby, the civic centre is an imposing complex of dark-stone buildings from the 19th century. The one that looks like an old **gaol** is just that. Next door, there's a prison of a different kind: an old convent is home to the 1840 **Round House**, a pretty stone building that now houses the **Nenagh Heritage Centre** (☎ 31610; ☿ 9.30am-5pm Mon-Fri), which has tourist info and genealogy services.

There are a couple of good lunch spots in town. **Cinnamon Alley** (☎ 33923; Hanly's Place; meals €5-9; ☿ 9am-5pm Mon-Sat) is on a little alley just west of the castle and gaol. It has creative sandwiches, soups and hot dishes, plus a full coffee bar.

Country House (☎ 32596; 25 Kenyon St; meals €6-12; ☿ 9am-5pm Mon-Sat) is a place of pilgrimage for lovers of really great Irish artisan foods. You can sample a delightful lunch menu in the café or browse the extensive deli area with

housemade preserves, cheeses and other treats. Can you spell p-i-c-n-i-c?

Nenagh is the gateway to the eastern shore of **Lough Derg**, a popular boating and fishing area. About 9km northwest on the R495, is the waterfront hamlet of **Dromineer**, a good place to sample lakeside life. There are plenty of visiting boats in summer and you can swim, fish or charter a yacht. Inquire at **Shannon Sailing** (☎ 067-24499; www.shannonsailing.com).

The **Dromineer Bay Hotel** (☎ 067-24114; www.dromineerbay.com; r €60-130; Ⓟ ▣) is a busy and attractive lakeside place with 20 bright rooms that feature wi-fi. The hotel's bar does good sandwiches for €4 and the upstairs **Gillies Restaurant** (mains €15-35) offers more complex fish and meat dishes.

An interesting, scenic lakeside drive from Nenagh is the 24km R494 that winds around to Killaloe and Ballina (see p378).

County Kilkenny

For many, County Kilkenny is all that they hope for in Ireland. It's a place of rolling green hills where you'll soon run out of adjectives for green. Tiny roads wander the valleys beside swirling rivers and moss-covered stone walls. Relics of centuries of Irish religious history dot the landscape as if part of one great beautiful design.

Wanderers and ramblers are rewarded by characterful pubs and exquisite restaurants scattered across the countryside, seemingly placed to reward those willing to take the road less travelled. Shamrock-cute Inistioge may be star of many a movie, but it's the real deal, and you'll soon find your own rhythm among the tidy shop fronts, mannered square and surging River Nore.

Perhaps Kilkenny's beauty and its inherent reward of discovery is why so many artists and craftspeople make their home in the county. In towns like Bennettsbridge and Thomastown, you'll find wonderfully skilled people busy creating in their studios. Or maybe they're just inspired by Kilkenny's pride itself, its namesake city.

An enduring gift of the Normans, Kilkenny city lures visitors by the score who find it hard to escape its pleasures. Medieval alleys wind among its castle, cathedral and ruined abbeys. But it's no static postcard – an alluring mix of superb restaurants, beguiling pubs and artisan vendors keeps things dynamic.

From bucolic delights to citified fun, Kilkenny is a dream.

HIGHLIGHTS

- **Consumption** Enjoying bounteous food and drink in medieval Kilkenny city (p330)
- **Creation** Admiring the creative arts found at the Kilkenny Design Centre (p332)
- **Erection** Discovering the moody Cistercian ruins of Jerpoint Abbey (p334)
- **Perambulation** Enjoying walks in and around cute little Inistioge (p335) and tongue-twisting Graiguenamanagh (p336)
- **Predilection** Shopping for the crafts and produce of creative locals in Thomastown (p334) and Bennettsbridge (p333)

★ Kilkenny
★ Bennettsbridge
Graiguenamanagh ★
Thomastown ★
Jerpoint Abbey ★ ★ Inistioge

- POPULATION: 75,500
- AREA: 1274 SQ KM

COUNTY KILKENNY

KILKENNY CITY

☎ 056 / pop 9100

Kilkenny figures high on many an itinerary to Ireland and for good reason: it's a fairly compact showplace with easily enjoyed heritage, a castle, interesting shops, a wide range of restaurants, lots of pubs and many inviting places to stay.

You can cover pretty much everything on foot in a couple of hours, but sampling the many delights will take much longer. There's an elegance and vibrancy that give the town (oops, locals insist on 'city') a timeless appeal.

Much of Kilkenny's architectural charm owes a huge debt to the Middle Ages, when the city was a seat of political power. But time has not passed the city by. Kilkenny remains a cultural centre, renowned for its devotion to the arts. Its cobbled pedestrian passageways and old-fashioned shop fronts may look like the way to a mysterious time-warp realm, but in reality they lead to cool bars, stylish boutiques and interesting restaurants. Kilkenny has plenty of modern allure, but it didn't sell out its traditional charms to get here.

Kilkenny's 60-odd licensed pubs and bars are a cheery mix of its gregarious citizens and the hordes of out-of-town merrymakers there for a fun-filled weekend. Along High St, every odd address appears to be a pub, and visitors staying near the centre can carouse from watering hole to watering hole.

Presiding over the town is a splendid medieval cathedral, named after St Canice (Cainneach or Kenneth), who founded a monastery here in the 6th century; hence the city's Irish name, Cill Chainnigh. The town's other 'must-see' attraction is its mighty castle (although it's more mansion than fortress), which sits majestically on a sweep in the River Nore.

As if being medieval isn't enough, Kilkenny is also sometimes called the 'marble city' because of the local black limestone, which resembles a slate-coloured marble. This attractive stone is seen to most striking effect in the cathedral, and is used on floors and in decorative trim all over town.

Kilkenny can get crowded. If possible, try for a weekday or sometime out of season, when you'll have more opportunity to appreciate the timeless charms.

HISTORY

In the 5th century, St Kieran is said to have visited Kilkenny and, on the site of the present Kilkenny Castle, challenged the chieftains of Ossory to accept the Christian faith. Subsequently, St Canice established his monastery here. Kilkenny consolidated its importance in the 13th century under William Marshall, the earl of Pembroke and son-in-law of the Anglo–Norman conqueror Strongbow. Kilkenny Castle was built to secure a crossing point on the Nore.

During the Middle Ages, Kilkenny was intermittently the unofficial capital of Ireland, with its own Anglo–Norman parliament. In 1366 the parliament passed the so-called Statutes of Kilkenny, a set of Draconian laws aimed at preventing the assimilation of the increasingly assertive Anglo–Normans into Irish society. Anglo–Normans were prohibited from marrying the native Irish, taking part in Irish sports, speaking or dressing like the Irish or playing any Irish music. Any breach of the law was to result in the confiscation of Anglo–Norman property and death to the native Irish. Although the laws remained theoretically in force for more than 200 years, they were never enforced with any great effect and did little to halt the absorption of the Anglo–Normans into Irish culture.

During the 1640s, Kilkenny sided with the Catholic royalists in the English Civil War. The 1641 Confederation of Kilkenny, an uneasy alliance of native Irish and Anglo–Normans, aimed to bring about the return of land and power to Catholics. After Charles I's execution, Cromwell besieged Kilkenny for five days, destroying much of the southern wall of the castle before Ormond surrendered. The defeat signalled a permanent end to Kilkenny's political influence over Irish affairs.

Today Kilkenny enjoys a vibrant economy thanks to all those visitors crowding the streets. There's also a fair number of service industries about and it's the regional centre for more traditional pursuits like agriculture (you'll see farmers on tractors stoically dodging tour buses).

ORIENTATION

At the junction of several major highways, Kilkenny straddles the River Nore, which

COUNTY KILKENNY

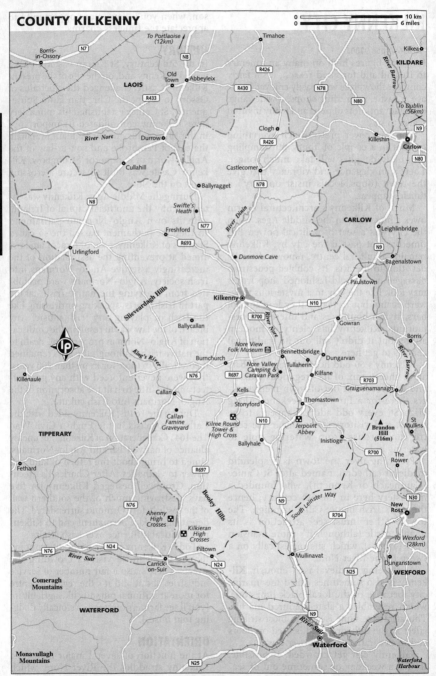

flows through much of the county. St Canice's Cathedral sits on the northern bank of the River Bregagh (a tributary of the Nore) to the north of the town centre outside the town walls. Kilkenny's main thoroughfare, Parliament and High Sts, runs southeast from the cathedral. Kilkenny Castle, on the banks of the River Nore, dominates the town's southern side. John St is the main road on the east side of the River Nore and links up with Dublin Rd at MacDonagh train station with its vast new shopping mall.

INFORMATION
Bookshops
Kilkenny Book Centre (☎ 776 2117; 10 High St) This, the largest bookshop in town, stocks a range of titles, as well as periodicals and a big range of maps. There's a good café upstairs.

Emergency
Police station (☎ 999, 22222; Dominic St)

Internet Access
Café Net (☎ 777 0051; 4 Patrick St; per hr €4; ⏰ 8am-9pm Mon-Sat, noon-9pm Sun)
E-centre (☎ 776 0093; 26 Rose Inn St; per hr €6; ⏰ 9am-9pm)

Laundry
Bretts Launderette (☎ 63200; Michael St; per load €15; ⏰ 8.30am-8pm Mon-Sat) Self-service and drop-off.

Medical Services
St Luke's Hospital (☎ 775 1133; Freshford Rd)
Sam McCauley Pharmacy (☎ 775 0122; 33 High St) A large shop; one of many pharmacies on High St.

Money
All of Ireland's big banks have branches, with ATMs, on High St.

Tourist Information
Tourist office (☎ 775 1500; Rose Inn St; www .kilkenny.ie; ⏰ 9.15am-1pm & 2-5pm Mon-Sat Sep-Jun, 9am-7pm Mon-Sat, 11am-5pm Sun Jul & Aug) In the listed 1582 Shee Alms House, the office sells excellent guides to the town and inexpensive walking maps of the county.

SIGHTS
Kilkenny Castle
On a lovely bend of the Nore stands **Kilkenny Castle** (☎ 772 1450; www.heritageireland.ie; adult/child €5.30/2.10; ⏰ 9.30am-7pm Jun-Sep, 10.30am-12.45pm & 2-5pm Oct-Mar, 10.30am-5pm Apr & May), one of Ireland's

most popular heritage sites and Kilkenny's premier tourist attraction. The first structure on this strategic site was a wooden tower built in 1172 by Richard de Clare, the Anglo–Norman conqueror of Ireland better known as Strongbow. In 1192 Strongbow's son-in-law, William Marshall, erected a stone castle with four towers, three of which survive. The castle was bought by the powerful Butler family in 1391, and their descendants continued to live there until 1935. Maintaining such a structure became a big financial strain and most of the furnishings were sold at auction. The castle was handed over to the city in 1967 for the princely sum of £50.

One glance should tell you that the castle has been modified through the centuries. First of all it's missing a wall – a key defensive deficiency. Second, there's all those windows – perfect targets, say, for a catapult. Most of the changes visible today date from the 19th century when efforts were made to banish the gloom and bring in the cheer. By then the only real defensive worry was a peasant flinging a rotten potato.

There are regular 40-minute guided tours that focus on the **Long Gallery**, in the wing of the castle nearest the river. The gallery, which showcases stuffy portraits of the Butler family members over the centuries, is an impressive hall with high ceilings vividly painted with Celtic and Pre-Raphaelite motifs. Work to restore the castle to its Victorian splendour is ongoing, and more rooms are continuously being opened for the tours. Most of the furnishings are not original to the castle, although a few items have been purchased back. What you do see are Victorian antiques that would evoke gasps from viewers of the *Antiques Roadshow*.

The castle basement is also home to the **Butler Gallery** (☎ 776 1106; www.butlergallery.com; admission free), one of the country's most important art galleries outside Dublin. Small exhibitions featuring the work of contemporary artists are held throughout the year; the space was refurbished in 2007. Also in the basement, the castle kitchen houses a popular summertime café. You can head directly to either the Butler Gallery or the café without paying the tour admission price.

About 20 hectares of **parkland** (admission free; ⏰ 10am-8.30pm summer) extend to the southeast, with a Celtic cross–shaped rose garden, a fountain to the northern end and a children's

KILKENNY

0 _____ 300 m
0 _____ 0.2 miles

COUNTY KILKENNY

INFORMATION
Bretts Launderette.........................1 C4
Café Net...2 B5
E-centre...3 B5
Kilkenny Book Centre....................4 B5
Police Station.................................5 A5
Sam McCauley Pharmacy..............6 B5
Tourist Office.................................7 B5

SIGHTS & ACTIVITIES
Black Abbey...................................8 A4
Black Freren Gate..........................9 A4
Confederation Hall Monument....10 B4
Gardens.......................................11 B5
Grace's Castle..............................12 A4
Kilkenny Castle............................13 C5
Kilkenny College..........................14 C5
National Craft Gallery...................15 B5
Rothe House................................16 B4
Shee Alms House....................(see 7)
Smithwick Brewery......................17 B4
St Canice's Cathedral...................18 A4
St Francis' Abbey..........................19 B4
St John's Priory............................20 C4
St Mary's Cathedral.....................21 A5
Tholsel (City Hall)........................22 B5

SLEEPING
Butler Court.................................23 B5
Butler House................................24 B5
Celtic House.................................25 B4
Cleere's B&B................................26 B3
Daley's B&B.................................27 C5
Darcy's Guest House....................28 A5
Kilford Arms Hotel..................(see 56)
Kilkenny Inn Hotel.......................29 A3
Kilkenny River Court....................30 B5
Kilkenny Tourist Hostel................31 B4
Lacken House...........................(see 41)
Langton House Hotel...................32 C4
Macgabhainn's Hostel.................33 A3
Rafter Dempsey's.........................34 B5

EATING
Café Sol.......................................35 B5
Chez Pierre............................(see 16)
Dunnes Stores.............................36 B5
Edward Langton's...................(see 32)
Fléva...37 B5
Gourmet Store.............................38 B4
Kilkenny Design Centre Café.......39 B5
Kyteler's Inn...............................40 B4
Lacken House...............................41 D5

Lautrec's Brasserie.......................42 B5
Marble City Bar............................43 B4
Pordylos.......................................44 B5
Rinuccini.....................................45 B5
The Pantry...................................46 B4
Zuni...47 B5

DRINKING
Ana Conda............................(see 48)
Hibernian Bar.......................(see 55)
John Cleere.................................48 A4
O'Riada.......................................49 B4
Pumphouse..................................50 B4
Tynan's Bridge House...................51 B5

ENTERTAINMENT
James Park...................................52 A3
Kilkenny Cineplex........................53 A5
Morrisey's Club............................54 B4
Morrison's Bar.............................55 B5
O'Faolain's...................................56 C4
Watergate Theatre.......................57 B4

SHOPPING
Kilkenny Design Centre................58 B5
Mac Donagh Junction..................59 C4
Market Cross................................60 B5

TRANSPORT
Buggys Coaches Stop....................61 B5
JJ Wall & Son...............................62 C4
McDonagh Bus Station.................63 C4

To St Luke's
Hospital (5km)

New Rd

To N77; N78;
Dunmore Cave (4km);
Castlecomer (16km);
Dublin (100km)

Greens
Bridge

Greensbridge St

Castlecomer Rd

Vicar St

Dean St

Irishtown

Michael St

Wolfe Tone St

Butts Green

River Breagh

Abbey St

Parliament St

Blackmill St

High St

Bateman's Quay

John's Quay

John St

McDonagh
Train Station

Maudlin St

Dublin St

River Nore

Dominic St

Kickham St

James St

St Kieran's St

Williams St

Rose Inn St

The Parade

Parnell St

Friary St

Ormonde St

New St

College Rd

Gaol Rd

Walkin St

Stephen St

Patrick St

Castle Rd

To N76;
Ballycallan (8km);
Callan (16km);
Cork (120km)

To N10; R697;
Waterford (44km)

To R700; Tree Grove
Caravan & Camping Park
(1.5km); Nore Valley (11km);

playground to the south. The castle's former stables are now home to the intriguing Kilkenny Design Centre (see p332).

St Canice's Cathedral

Soaring over the north end of the centre is Ireland's second-largest medieval cathedral (after St Patrick's in Dublin), **St Canice's Cathedral** (☎ 776 4971; www.stcanicescathedral.ie; St Canice's Pl; adult/child €4/3; ☺ 9am-1pm & 2-6pm Mon-Sat, 2-6pm Sun Apr-Sep, 10am-1pm & 2-4pm Mon-Sat, 2-4pm Sun Oct-Mar). This Gothic edifice with its iconic round tower has had a long and fascinating history. Legend has it that the first monastery was built here in the 6th century by St Canice, Kilkenny's patron saint. Records show that a wooden church on the site was burned down in 1087.

The existing structure was raised between 1202 and 1285, but then endured a series of catastrophes and resurrections. The first disaster, the collapse of the church tower in 1332, was the consequence of one of the city's more intriguing events. Dame Alice Kyteler, along with her maid, was convicted of witchcraft. Dame Alice's nephew, William Outlawe, also was implicated. The unfortunate maid was burned at the stake, but Dame Alice escaped to London and William spared himself by offering to re-roof part of St Canice's Cathedral with lead tiles. Town officials unwisely took him up on the offer and the new roof proved too heavy, bringing the church tower down with it.

In 1650 Cromwell's forces defaced and damaged the church, using it to stable their horses. Repairs began in 1661 and are still ongoing. The beautiful roof in the nave was completed in 1863. Also worth a look is a model of Kilkenny as it was in 1642 – things haven't changed that much.

Outside the cathedral, a 30m-high **round tower** (admission €3; ☺ Apr-Oct) rises amid an odd array of ancient tombstones and is the oldest structure within the grounds. It was built sometime between AD 700 and 1000 on the site of an earlier Christian cemetery. Apart from missing its crown, the round tower is in excellent condition and those older than 12 can admire a fine view from the top. It's a tight squeeze and you'll need both hands to climb the 100 steps up steep ladders. The approach to the cathedral on foot from Parliament St leads you over Irishtown Bridge and up St Canice's Steps, which date from 1614; the wall at the top contains fragmentary medieval carvings. On gloomy days the leaning tombstones scattered about the grounds prompt you to look at the very least for a black cat.

Inside, highly polished ancient **grave slabs** are set on the walls and the floor. On the northern wall, opposite the entrance, a slab inscribed in Norman French commemorates Jose de Keteller, who died in 1280; despite the difference in spelling he was probably the father of Alice Kyteler. The stone chair of St Kieran embedded in the wall dates from the 13th century. The fine 1596 monument to Honorina Grace at the western end of the southern aisle is made of beautiful local black limestone. In the southern transept, a handsome **black tomb** has effigies of Piers Butler, who died in 1539, and his wife, Margaret Fitzgerald. Tombs and monuments (listed on a board in the southern aisle) to other notable Butlers crowd this corner of the church.

Rothe House

The best surviving example of a 16th-century merchant's house in Ireland is **Rothe House** (☎ 772 2893; www.rothehouse.com; Parliament St; adult/child €4/3, combo tickets with the cathedral are available; ☺ 10.30am-5pm Mon-Sat, 3-5pm Sun Apr-Oct, 10.30-4.30pm Mon-Sat Nov-Mar). The fine Tudor house was built around a series of courtyards and now houses a museum with a sparse collection of local artefacts, including a well-used Viking sword found nearby and a grinning head sculpted from a stone by a Celtic artist. The fine king-post roof of the 2nd floor is a meticulous and impressive reconstruction. A costume exhibit on the 1st floor is primarily good for mild laughs, with its cordon of oddly shaped mannequins looking very uncomfortable in period attire. A re-created medieval garden is due to open in 2008.

In the 1640s, the wealthy Rothe family played a part in the Confederation of Kilkenny, and Peter Rothe, son of the original builder, had all his property confiscated. His sister was able to reclaim it, but just before the Battle of the Boyne (1690) the family supported James II and so lost the house permanently. In 1850 a Confederation banner was discovered in the house. It's now in the National Museum, Dublin.

There's an excellent range of books on the region for sale at the entrance.

Black Abbey

This Dominican abbey on Abbey St was founded in 1225 by William Marshall and takes its name from the monks' black habits. In 1543, six years after Henry VIII's dissolution of the monasteries, it was turned into a courthouse. Following Cromwell's visit in 1650, it remained a roofless ruin until restoration in 1866. Much of what survives dates from the 18th and 19th centuries, but pieces of more ancient archways are still evident within the newer stonework. Open for daily mass, look for the 13th-century coffins near the entrance.

National Craft Gallery

This **gallery** (☎ 776 1804; www.ccoi.ie; Castle Yard; admission free; ⏰ 10am-6pm Mon-Sat, 11am-6pm Sun), opposite Kilkenny Castle, showcases contemporary Irish crafts. It's part of the former stables that also house the Kilkenny Design Centre (see p332). The high-quality exhibitions highlight the diversity and imagination of crafts in contemporary Ireland. Ceramics dominate, but exhibits regularly feature furniture, jewellery and weaving from the members of the Crafts Council of Ireland. There are regular classes in pottery and jewellery-making.

Behind the complex, look for the walkway that extends into the beautiful **gardens** of Butler House, a hotel you can exit through to Patrick St. Look for the fountain made from remnants of the British-built Nelson Column, blown up by nationalists in Dublin almost 100 years ago.

Other Sights

Shee Alms House, on Rose Inn St, was built in sturdy local stone in 1582 by local benefactor Sir Richard Shee and his wife to provide help for the poor. It continued as a hospital until 1740 but now houses the tourist office. The **Tholsel**, or City Hall, on High St was built in 1761 on the spot where Dame Alice Kyteler's maid, Petronella, was burned at the stake in 1324.

Next to the Tholsel is **Butter Slip**, a narrow and dark walkway that connects High St with Low Lane (now St Kieran's St). It was built in 1616 and once was lined with the stalls of butter vendors. With its arched entry and stone steps, Butter Slip is by far the most picturesque of Kilkenny's many narrow medieval corridors.

Black Freren Gate on Abbey St is the only gate from the old Norman city walls still standing, albeit with the help of metal bracing to ensure the safety of those who pass through. Crumbling sections of the old walls remain throughout the central city.

On the corner of Parliament St and the road leading down to Bateman's Quay, the **Confederation Hall monument** (really just a fragment) beside the Bank of Ireland marks the site where the national Parliament met from 1642 to 1649. Nearby is the ramshackle **Grace's Castle**, originally built in 1210, but lost to the family and converted into a prison in 1568, and then in 1794 into a courthouse, which it remains today. Rebels from the 1798 Rising were executed here.

The 19th-century **St Mary's Cathedral** is visible from most parts of town. A plaque at the entrance notes: 'The construction of the cathedral began in 1843 and continued during the famine years, the years of emigration, coffin ships, starvation, and even despair because of the many thousands of our people who died of hunger and disease…', before going on to list yet more tribulations.

Across the river stand the ruins of **St John's Priory**, which was founded in 1200 and was noted for its many beautiful windows until Cromwell's visit. Nearby **Kilkenny College**, on John St, dates from 1666. Its students included Jonathan Swift and the philosopher George Berkeley, but it now houses Kilkenny's county hall.

TOURS

Central Kilkenny city is small and well suited to comprehensive walking tours.

Tynan Tours (☎ 087 265 1745; adult/student €6/5.50; ⏰ numerous times daily mid-Mar–Oct) conducts hour-long walking tours that meander through Kilkenny's narrow lanes, steps and pedestrian passageways. Smart, witty guides recount the intriguing stories these buildings might tell if they could talk. Tours may also be offered in the off season; ask about a group rate if you're travelling with friends.

FESTIVALS & EVENTS

Kilkenny is rightly known as the festival capital of Ireland, with several world-class events throughout the year that attract thousands of people.

Kilkenny Rhythm & Roots (☎ 779 0057; www .kilkennyroots.com) In early May, more than 30 different venues participate in hosting Ireland's biggest music festival, with country and 'old-timey' American roots music strongly emphasised.

Cat Laughs Comedy Festival (☎ 776 3416; (www .thecatlaughs.com) Cat Laughs is a much-acclaimed gathering of world-class comics; late May to early June.

Kilkenny Arts Festival (☎ 775 2175; www.kilkenny arts.ie) The city comes alive with theatre, cinema, music, literature, visual arts, children's events and street spectacles for 10 action-packed days in mid-August. Accommodation at this time is like gold, and you're seriously advised to book well in advance.

Kilkenny Celtic Festival (www.celticfestival.ie) A celebration of all things trad Irish, especially the language. Performances, exhibits, seminars and more. Held in late September to early October.

SLEEPING

If you're arriving in town with no room booked (an unwise move at weekends when rates soar and in summer), the tourist office runs an efficient accommodation booking service costing €4.

Budget

Tree Grove Caravan & Camping Park (☎ 777 0302; www.treegrovecamping.com; New Ross Rd; camp sites per person from €7) This camping ground in a small park is 1.5km south of Kilkenny off the R700. Follow a river path there.

Macgabhainn's Hostel (www.hostelworld.com; 24 Vicar St; dm €15-18) This tidy little 16-bed hostel is truly a no-frills charmer. Breakfasts are cold and the back 'garden' is a work in progress, but it's friendly, there's a laundry and is usually quiet.

Kilkenny Tourist Hostel (☎ 776 3541; www.hostels -ireland.com; 35 Parliament St; dm €16-20; 🖳) Inside the ivy-covered walls, you'll find things relaxed and friendly at this IHH hostel. It's on the main street of Kilkenny, within a few steps of half a dozen clubs and several good restaurants. There's a large kitchen and an atmospheric dining room, while the sitting room is outfitted with couches and a fireplace. The 60 beds are mostly in four- to eight-bed rooms. There's free wi-fi.

Daley's B&B (☎ 776 2866; 82 John St; r €32-60; 🅿) Hidden away behind a dense row of pubs and shops, Daley's is very basic and feels a bit motel-like. It's an adequate cheapie, with eight decent rooms and a convenient location.

Midrange

Cleere's B&B (☎ 772 1210; cleere102@hotmail.com; New Rd; r €45-70; 🅿) A short walk to town, this B&B is very straight-forward: the rooms are clean and comfy and have TVs.

Rafter Dempsey's (☎ 772 2970; www.accommodation kilkenny.com; 4 Friary St; r €45-130) There's basic B&B accommodation in 16 rooms above a simple pub of the same name just off High St. The colour scheme can best be described as 'dog's breakfast' but you may not notice as you squint to see the tiny ceiling-mounted TVs.

our pick Celtic House (☎ 776 2249; john376@gofree .indigo.ie; 18 Michael St; r €50-80; 🅿) Angela Byrne is literally Ireland's goodwill ambassador to the world and she extends a wonderful welcome to guests at this clean-as-a-whistle B&B. Rooms are bright, some have sky-lit bathrooms, others have views of the castle. When not charming the masses, Angela is a landscape painter, her works adorn many a wall here.

Darcy's Guest House (☎ 777 0219, 777 0087; James St; r €50-90; 🅿) This cheery, yellow stucco

---

BAD BREW

If you smell something funny in the air, it may be the Budweiser being brewed under licence in the **Smithwick Brewery** (☎ 772 1014; Parliament St). Now owned by drinks giant Diageo (Guinness, Harp and lots of spirits), the brewery is no longer the civic icon it once was. The tours once – enjoyed by generations are now a thing of the past, in their place are sporadic summertime showings of a promotional video. Enjoy! What's worse is that right in the middle of the complex is **St Francis' Abbey**, which was founded by William Marshall in 1232, but desecrated first by Cromwell in 1650 and then by Diageo. It's an intriguing structure but it's now off limits. When we asked at the gate to see this amazing relic, the guard told us in no uncertain terms to 'go look at one of the other old places in town'.

Note that Smithwick's Irish Ale is also known as Kilkenny Ale, the name it's sold under at scores of fake Irish bars in Europe. Locally, most people still drink its corporate cousin, Guinness.

house is right off High St. Flower boxes enliven the views from the 11 rooms, which have cable TV and a muted décor that complements the exterior.

Kilford Arms Hotel (☎ 776 1018; www.kilfordarms .ie; John St; r €60-160; **P** 🖵) A stuffed and rather mangy 150-year-old Bengal tiger mounted in the lobby sets the tone at this slightly offbeat hotel. While the attitude and authority of the feline is faded, you'll find vibrant colour and flair in the 53 rooms.

Butler Court (☎ 776 1178; www.butlercourt.com; Patrick St; r €70-130; 🖵) Where the locals stash their guests, this friendly guesthouse has 10 nicely appointed rooms opening onto a restful courtyard. Breakfasts are continental and there's a fridge in every room.

Kilkenny Inn Hotel (☎ 777 2828; www.kilkennyinn .com; 15-16 Vicar St; r €70-150; **P** 🖵) A modern 30-room hotel right below the cathedral, this friendly place has broadband internet in the slightly small rooms. The décor is a stylish mix of light woods and pastels.

Lacken House (☎ 776 1085; www.lackenhouse.ie; Dublin Rd; r €95-170; **P** 🖵) Just out of town, this beautiful 10-room, Victorian-era guesthouse exudes grace and charm. There's a superb breakfast and the restaurant is highly regarded. The ornate rooms have free wi-fi and its only a 10-minute walk to the centre.

Top End

Langton House Hotel (☎ 776 5133; www.langtons.ie; 69 John St; r €80-200; **P** 🖵) Perched atop the cavernous public spaces of this Kilkenny landmark are 30 rooms of varying standard. Although the building is dated, the décor has been updated with rather dark browns and beiges. The bathrooms are spotless and large, although the tubs have a podlike shower contraption that will recall the 'Rock 'n Roll Creation' routine from *This is Spinal Tap*.

Kilkenny River Court (☎ 772 3388; www.kilrivercourt .com; John St; r per person from €110; **P** 🖵) Along the Nore, by the bridge, this hotel has 90 modern rooms in a purpose-built wing fronted by a courtyard. There's free wi-fi and decent views from some rooms. The riverside terrace is a choice spot for a drink when the weather's fine.

Butler House (☎ 772 2828; www.butler.ie; 16 Patrick St; r €125-250; **P** 🖵) Once home of the earls of Ormonde (who built the nearby castle), this gracious townhouse is now a luxurious hotel with aristocratic trappings including

sweeping staircases, marble fireplaces, an art collection and impeccably trimmed gardens (see p328). The 13 generously sized rooms have new bathrooms and wi-fi.

EATING

There's a good range of choices in Kilkenny but note that at quiet times, places often close by 8.30pm. Picnickers can pick up groceries from **Dunnes Stores** (☎ 776 1756; St Keiran's St; 🕙 24hr).

Cafés

St Keiran's St has a number of continental-style cafés with outdoor tables.

Gourmet Store (☎ 777 1727; 56 High St; sandwiches €4; 🕙 9am-6pm Mon-Sat) In this crowded little deli, takeaway sandwiches are assembled from choice, imported meats and cheeses (plus a few top-notch locals).

Chez Pierre (☎ 776 4655; 17 Parliament St; mains €3-8; 🕙 10am-5pm) It's all brightness and yellow skies at this sunny-sweet French café, next to Rothe House. The menu offers an assortment of sandwiches, soups and sweets you can enjoy at timeless, simple wooden tables.

The Pantry (☎ 776 2250; St Keiran's St; mains €6-12; 🕙 8am-6pm) Break soda bread (well at least butter it up) and sip a range of coffees at this old-fashioned bakery and tearoom. Those filling, hot meals of your youth are here, ready and waiting.

Restaurants

our pick Kilkenny Design Centre Café (☎ 772 2118; Castle Yard; meals €6-12; 🕙 10am-7pm) Upstairs from the stylish shops is this equally stylish café. The food is artful, often organic and always healthful (OK, maybe not the sumptuous desserts but who wants healthy?). Breads are baked in-house and go well in sandwiches, with soups and alongside salads. The hot specials are superb.

Marble City Bar (☎ 776 1143; 66 High St; meals €6-15; 🕙 food served 10am-9pm) This stylishly mod bar manages to stand out. Usual bar standards such as sausage with mash and fish and chips are elevated above the norm through the use of excellent ingredients. A lower-level café facing St Kieran's St has breakfasts, coffees and outdoor tables.

Edward Langton's (☎ 776 5133; 69 John St; mains €8-22; 🕙 noon-10pm Mon-Sat, noon-9pm Sun) Langton's is an enormous, snazzy pub with a good restaurant that seems able to seat much of the town.

Certainly most everybody's here for Sunday lunch when tipsy blondes totter past gossiping grannies. The food is trad Irish; expect bowls of boiled potatoes and veg to come in never-ending supply.

Fléva (☎ 777 0021; 84 High St; meals €8-28; ♥ 12.30-2.30pm & 6-9.30pm Tue-Sat) Regional ingredients combine for a fusion of global flavours. There's a merry vibe about this somewhat formal (white tablecloths) yet quirky (eclectic local art on the walls) restaurant. Vegetarians will blossom after reading the many choices and anyone who likes wine will find much to sip.

Kyteler's Inn (☎ 772 1064; 27 St Kieran's St; mains €9-20; ♥ noon-10pm) Dame Alice Kyteler's old house, built in 1224, is one of the tourist magnets in town. The Dame had four husbands, all of whom died in suspicious circumstances. Having acquired some powerful enemies, she was charged with witchcraft in 1323. The food is pub-standard (the menu boasts a 'healthy' option: baked potato filled with baked beans), but tourists of all ages whoop it up in the dungeon-like basement.

Lautrec's Brasserie (☎ 776 2720; 9 St Kieran's St; mains €10-26; ♥ 5-10pm) The name should clue you right in – this is a lovely little romantic French bistro. Hold hands at the tiny tables in the tiny dining room and partake of the wine selections. Mains range from delicate pizzas to seafood to continental classics.

Pordylos (☎ 777 0660; Butter Slip; meals €10-30; ♥ 12.30-3pm & 5.30-10pm) You'll feel you've slipped into a French country home as you enter from shadowy Butter Slip. The seafood comes from Dunmore East and the excellent meats are sourced locally. Good French vintages soon loosen the spirits and you'll feel in the midst of a highly successful dinner party.

our pick **Café Sol** (☎ 776 4987; William St; dinner mains €16-28; ♥ noon-3pm & 6-9pm Mon-Sat) Noel McCarron, the proprietor, lists the local sources for many of the foods used on the seasonally changing menu. The bold and edgy artwork on the walls, like the food, shows surprising combinations. There are more flavours and elements than you might expect but it all works together in symphonic harmony. Three-course set menus (€23) are great value.

Rinuccini (☎ 776 1575; 1 The Parade; mains €16-28; ♥ noon-2pm & 6-9pm) Enjoy gracious dining in the shadow of the castle at this lower-level restaurant in an elegant townhouse. The menu is classic Italian and everything from minestrone to pastas to fine veal and seafood, is just so.

Zuni (☎ 772 3999; www.zuni.ie; 26 Patrick St; dinner €19-30; ♥ 12.30-2.30pm Tue-Sat, 6.30-10pm Mon-Sat, 1-3pm & 6-9pm Sun) Among Kilkenny's most stylish and busy restaurants, Zuni manages to stay at the cutting edge it pioneered when it opened just before the Millennium. Dark leathers and fabrics on the seating contrasts with lighter natural materials on the tables and walls.

Lacken House (☎ 776 1085; www.lackenhouse.ie; Dublin Rd; set 4 courses €43, set 5 courses €59; ♥ 6-9.30pm Tue-Sat) In the gracious guesthouse of the same name, this candlelit, intimate dining room is one of the most romantic spots in town. Foods are sourced locally and are organic when possible. Preparations are traditional with modern, creative touches. The wine list is extensive.

DRINKING

There are a few places that do after-hours lock-ins on weekends.

Tynan's Bridge House (☎ 772 1291; St John's Bridge) Conversation is generally audible in this grand old Georgian pub, the best trad bar in town. The 300-year-old building has settled a bit over the years, but then so have many of the customers. Survey the craic from the tables in front or settle out back in the – of all things – olive-tree festooned patio.

O'Riada (27 Parliament St) The lowest-key bar in Kilkenny. The only dashes of flash are an electric light and a TV set. The joint fills up and gets pretty lively when there's a game on the tube, but most of the time you can ponder your pint and strike up a conversation with anyone – including yourself.

Pumphouse (☎ 776 3924; 26 Parliament St) With live rock groups like Kopek many nights a week, the Pumphouse is one of Kilkenny's livelier bars. When there's no band, music comes from a free jukebox that doesn't have a bad song on it. It's a large place with pool tables and big TVs. Smokers hang out on the roof.

Ana Conda (☎ 777 1657; Parliament St) A frequent winner in local polls, locals enjoy the tiled floors, comfy banquettes, Friday night céilidh sessions and Saturday night rock shows. The covered beer garden is popular among smokers.

John Cleere (☎ 776 2573; 22 Parliament St) One of Kilkenny's best venues for live music, this long bar has blues, jazz and rock, including local

---

CRAFTY KILKENNY

Across The Parade from Kilkenny Castle are the elegant former castle stables (1760), which have been extensively renovated. Besides the National Craft Gallery (p328), the buildings are home to a number of local craftspeople, such as the voluble A Byrne, a silversmith.

The front building holds gallerylike shops of the **Kilkenny Design Centre** (☎ 772 2118; www .kilkennydesign.com; Castle Yard), where you can find all manner of top-end Irish crafts and artwork for sale. From County Kilkenny, look for the spongeware pottery of Nicholas Moss, the handblown crystal of Jerpoint Glass, the luscious leather bags of Chesneau Leathers and the handmade beads of All That Glistens. Overall there are at least 130 fulltime craftspeople and artists working commercially in the county, one of the highest concentrations in Ireland. Reasons for this vary, but the nexus of culture afforded by high-brow Kilkenny is a major factor. Bennettsbridge and Thomastown are two other good places for top quality crafts.

---

favourites Bone. Especially in the summer, this is the place to look for trad music sessions.

Hibernian Bar (☎ 777 1888; Hibernian Hotel, Patrick St) There may come a time when having yet another pint in an atmospheric pub might be just one too many. Take refuge here at this swanky hotel bar with deep, comfy leather banquettes and a long list of proper cocktails.

ENTERTAINMENT

For information on local events, check out the weekly *Kilkenny People* newspaper. A good website is www.whazon.com.

Cinema & Theatre

Kilkenny Cineplex (☎ 772 3111; Fair Green, Gaol Rd) Four screens here blare with the latest Hollywood releases.

Watergate Theatre (☎ 776 1674; www.watergatekil kenny.com; Parliament St) Recently spiffed up, this theatre hosts drama, comedy and musical performances. Why is it that intermissions seem to last 18 minutes?

Nightclubs

Kilkenny is the regional hub of clubbing; check to see what's hot now.

O'Faolain's (☎ 776 1018; Kilford Arms Hotel, John St; admission €8-12) The club itself is an attraction: it's built on three levels around an old stone church that was brought over from Wales. There are live DJs most nights, starting around 10.30pm and weekend club nights.

Morrison's Bar (☎ 777 1888; 1 Ormonde St; ☿ 5pm-1am) In the cellar of the Hibernian Hotel there's this stylish hideaway, with its atmospheric lighting and snazzy *belle époque* décor. DJs spin an eclectic mix for an up-market crowd that actually cares about getting spilled on.

Morrisey's Club (☎ 777 0555; 40 Parliament St; admission €8; ☿ 8pm-late Thu-Sun) In a basement a few doors from the Kilkenny Tourist Hostel, this club usually doesn't really get cranking until around 10pm (those who show up earlier get in free). DJs rule but there are also live acts many nights. Sunday nights get a barely-18 crowd.

Sport

Locals drool over the results of the regular dog races at **James Park** (☎ 772 1214; Freshford Rd; ☿ 8pm Wed & Fri).

SHOPPING

Kilkenny is the regional centre for shopping. You'll find an interesting mix of chain and local stores along High St, and in **Market Cross**, a multilevel mall behind a row of High St shops. Opening by 2008, a flashy new shopping mall, **MacDonagh Junction**, will be the largest in the region.

GETTING THERE & AWAY

Driving from Dublin is easy: take the M7 motorway to the M9 and head south. Work is ongoing to extend the M9 all the way south past Carlow, which will greatly relieve the busy parallel N9. At Paulstown, the N10 branches off for the 17km run west to Kilkenny. When road work is done, the city will be well under two hours from Dublin.

Bus

Bus Éireann (☎ 776 4933; www.buseireann.ie) operates from a shelter about 200m east of John St adjacent to the train station – which also sells tickets. Bus Éireann also picks up and drops off passengers at the very central Café Net on St Patrick's St. There are services to

Carlow (€6.30, one hour, 12 daily), Clonmel (€6.80, one hour, 12 daily), Cork (€14.90, three hours, two daily), Dublin (€9.80, 2¼ hours, five daily) and Waterford (€8.40, one hour, two daily).

JJ Kavanagh & Sons (☎ 883 1106; www.jjkavanagh .ie) has two buses per day Monday to Saturday to Carlow city (€5, 50 minutes) in County Carlow and Portlaoise (€7, 1½ hours).

Train

The train station (☎ 772 2024) has been shoved 200m back from John St to make way for the vast new mall. Kilkenny sees five trains daily for Dublin (€22, 1¾ hours) and Waterford (€9.80, 50 minutes).

GETTING AROUND

There are large parking lots and garages off both sides of High St. Other lots are scattered in all areas.

JJ Wall & Son (☎ 772 1236; 86 Maudlin St) rents out bikes at €20 per day. The circuit around Kells, Inistioge, Jerpoint Abbey and Kilfane makes a fine day's ride. It also sells lawn mowers if you've finally had enough of all that green.

For a cab, call **Danny's Taxis** (☎ 223 8887).

CENTRAL KILKENNY

The area south – and most notably southeast – of Kilkenny city is laced with country roads and dotted with cute villages overlooking the rich, green Barrow and Nore valleys. Riverside towns like Graiguenamanagh and Inistioge have superb scenery. This is prime walking country, with beautiful trails running alongside the rivers and between the towns. And in places like Bennettsbridge, you can visit the workshops of some of the county's most notable craftspeople.

KELLS & AROUND

Kells (not to be confused with Kells in County Meath) is a mere widening of the road, a hamlet with a fine stone bridge on a tributary of the Nore. However, in Kells Priory, the village has one of Ireland's most impressive and romantic monastic sites. The village is 13km south of Kilkenny city on the R697.

Kells Priory

This is the best sort of ruin, where visitors can amble about as they like, whenever they like, with no tour guides, tours, ropes or restrictions. With no hours or fees, it's almost a religious experience. At dusk on a vaguely sunny day the old priory is simply beautiful. Most days you stand a chance of exploring the site alone, with only the company of bleating sheep.

The earliest remains of this gorgeous monastic site date from the late 12th century, while the bulk of the present ruins are from the 15th century. In a sea of rich farmland, a carefully restored protective wall connects seven dwelling towers. Inside the walls are the remains of an **Augustinian abbey** and the foundations of some chapels and houses. It's unusually well fortified for a monastery and the heavy curtain walls hint at a troubled history. Indeed, within a single century from 1250, the abbey was twice fought over and burned down by squabbling warlords. It went into permanent decline beginning when it was suppressed in 1540.

The ruins are 800m east of Kells on the Stonyford road.

Kilree Round Tower & High Cross

About 2km south of Kells (signposted from the priory car park) there's a 29m-high round tower and a simple early high cross, which is said to mark the grave of a 9th-century Irish high king, Niall Caille. He's supposed to have drowned in the King's River at Callan some time in the 840s while attempting to save a servant, and his body washed up near Kells. His final resting place lies beyond the church grounds because he wasn't a Christian.

Callan Famine Graveyard

West of Kilree, and signposted off the main road 2km south of Callan, is a **cemetery** where the local victims of the Great Famine (p46) are buried. It isn't much to look at, but the unmarked graves are a poignant reminder of the anonymity of starvation.

BENNETTSBRIDGE & AROUND

☎ 056 / pop 950

In a scenic setting on the River Nore 7km south of Kilkenny city on the R700, Bennettsbridge is an arts and crafts treasure chest. The multi-arched stone bridge is a work of art itself.

In a big mill by the river west of town is **Nicholas Mosse Irish Country Shop** (☎ 772-7105; www.nicholasmosse.com; ☺ 10am-6pm Mon-Sat, 1.30-5pm Sun), a pottery shop that specialises in handmade spongeware – creamy-brown pottery that's covered with sponged patterns. It also sells linens and other handmade craft items (although some hail from lands of cheap labour far from Ireland). A seconds shop yields huge savings. Upstairs, the **café** is the best choice locally for lunch, with a creative line-up of soups, sandwiches, hot dishes etc. It's renowned for its scones.

Just up the road, **Keith Mosse Wood Working** (☎ 772 7948; www.keithmosse.com) is home to the eponymous craftsman, who takes fine woods from five continents and turns them into simply elegant furniture and decorator items.

Yet another few hundred metres away, by the bridge, **Moth to a Flame** (☎ 772 7826) is in an old garage after its old factory went up in smoke. The air is redolent with the wax used in creating elaborate candles; hundreds line tables throughout the workshop.

For fine leather, check out the factory boutique of **Chesneau** (☎ 772 7456; www.chesneau design.com), near the village centre. Stylish bags and accessories are on offer in a rainbow of colours – emerald-green numbers are big sellers. Most of the designs are created locally and sold internationally.

On a small road above Nicholas Mosse, the **Nore View Folk Museum** (☎ 27749; Danesfort Rd; admission free;) is a privately owned folk museum displaying local items of interest, including old farming tools and other bric-a-brac.

Nore Valley Camping & Caravan Park (☎ 972 7229; http://norevalleypark.tripod.com; Annamult; day admission €4; camp sites from €8; ☺ 9am-7pm Mon-Sat Apr-Sep) is a 2-hectare farm that suits kids and campers. Kids can caress goats, cuddle rabbits, navigate a maze and jump on a straw bounce. There is a tearoom and picnic area. If you're coming into Bennettsbridge from Kilkenny along the R700, turn right just before the bridge; the park is signposted.

Besides the café at Nicholas Mosse, the central **Italian Affair** (☎ 770 0988; 4 Chapel St; mains €8-25; ☺ noon-3pm & 5-9pm Tue-Sun) has a good menu of pizza, pasta and more. The coffee bar is always popular.

THOMASTOWN & AROUND
☎ 056 / pop 1750

Thomastown is a small market town known for its crafts. Nicely situated by the Nore, the Dublin–Waterford road (N9) runs right through the centre and the traffic can be awful. Named after Welsh mercenary Thomas de Cantwell, Thomastown has some fragments of a medieval wall and the partly ruined 13th-century **Church of St Mary**. Down by the bridge, **Mullin's Castle** is the sole survivor of the 14 castles that were originally here.

Ignore the traffic and explore the compact centre, which has a surprising assortment of intriguing shops and cafés. **Clay Creations** (☎ 772 4977; Low St) displays the works of local artist Brid Lyons. Her whimsical ceramics and sculptures include an iconic dog captured mid-snarl.

Food For Thought (☎ 779 3297; Market St) is a shrine to Irish artisan foods. Some of the local products carried include G's Preserves (made from their own organic raspberries), Knockdrinna Farmhouse Cheese (fresh goat-milk cheese), Carlow Cheese (an amazing hard cheese made with nettles) and chocolates from the Truffle Fairy.

Jerpoint Abbey

One of Ireland's finest Cistercian ruins, **Jerpoint Abbey** (☎ 24623; www.heritageireland.ie; Hwy N9; adult/child €2.90/1.30; ☺ 9.30am-6pm Jun-Sep, 10am-4pm Oct-May) is about 2.5km southwest of Thomastown on the N9. It was established in the 12th century and has been partially restored. The fine tower and cloister are late 14th or early 15th century. The roofless outline of the cloisters are perfectly atmospheric; look for the series of often amusing figures carved on the pillars, including a knight. There are also stone carvings on the church walls and in the tombs of members of the Butler and Walshe families. Faint traces of a 15th- or 16th-century painting remain on the northern wall of the church. This chancel area also contains a tomb thought to be that of the hardheaded Felix O'Dullany, Jerpoint's first abbot and bishop of Ossory, who died back in 1202. Ask for a free guided tour; there is a small exhibit on other historic ruins in the region.

According to local legend, St Nicholas (or Santa Claus) is buried near the abbey. While retreating in the Crusades, the knights of Jerpoint removed his body from Myra in modern-day Turkey and reburied him in the **Church of St Nicholas** to the west of the abbey.

The grave is marked by a broken slab decorated with a carving of a monk.

Stonyford

On the N10, a few kilometres northwest of the abbey and Thomastown, is the small village of Stonyford. The local highlight, the nationally renowned **Jerpoint Glass Studio** (☎ 24350; www.jerpointglass.com), is housed here in an old stone-walled farm building. Most days, you can watch workers craft molten glass into exquisite artistic and practical items.

Kilfane

The village of Kilfane, 3km north of Thomastown on the N9 (Dublin road), has a small, ruined **13th-century church** and **Norman tower**, 50m off the road and signposted. The church has a remarkable stone carving of Thomas de Cantwell called the Cantwell Fada or Long Cantwell. It depicts a tall, thin knight in detailed chain-mail armour brandishing a shield decorated with the Cantwell coat of arms.

Kilfane Glen & Waterfall (☎ 24558) is a pretty spot with wooded paths winding through its wild 6-hectare gardens, which date from the 1790s. An elaborately decorated thatched cottage is worth hiking to. Note it was closed in 2007; check for its reopening. Kilfane Glen is 2km north of town along the N9.

Gowran

Some 14km northeast of Thomastown on the N9 (and 14km east of Kilkenny), the small village of Gowran is notable for the Heritage Service–run **St Mary's Church** (☎ 772 6894; www.heritageireland.ie; adult/child €1.60/1; ☺ 9.30am-6pm Jun–mid-Sep), a 13th-century house of worship for clerics living in a loose community. Much modified through the years, a 19th-century church grafted onto one side.

Sleeping & Eating

In an idyllic location 7km southeast of Thomastown off the R700, **Ballyduff House** (☎ 775 8488; www.ballyduffhouse.com; s/d €55/90; P) overlooks the River Nore. There are three large rooms in the 18th-century mansion; common rooms are welcoming with a range of timeless overstuffed furniture to welcome weary souls.

Ethos Bistro (☎ 775 4945; Low St, Thomastown; meals €6-22; ☺ noon-8pm Wed-Sat, noon-3pm Sun) is a new place winning plaudits for its creative, natural fare. As you'd expect, local ingredients star and the eclectic menu changes often. It's always busy, so you should book for dinner. There are tables on a back patio.

Hudsons (☎ 779 3900; Station Rd, Thomastown; set dinner €28; ☺ 6-9pm Wed-Sun) Overlooking an intricate garden, Hudsons mixes frill with a stylish, modern dining room. Popular classics, such as grilled meats, seared salmon and Caesar salad, make regular appearances on a daily menu that emphasises fresh local ingredients.

Getting There & Away

Bus Éireann (☎ 64933) runs two buses daily linking Thomastown to Bennettsbridge (€4, 10 minutes) and Kilkenny (€6, 20 minutes). There are also numerous services to Dublin and Waterford. Buses stop outside O'Keeffe's supermarket on Main St in Thomastown.

The train station is 1km west of town past Kavanagh's supermarket. Five trains daily stop on the Dublin–Waterford route via Kilkenny.

INISTIOGE

☎ 056 / pop 714

The little village of Inistioge (in-ish-teeg) is picture-perfect. It has an 18th-century, 10-arch stone bridge spanning the River Nore and vintage shops facing a tranquil square. Somewhere so inviting could hardly hope to escape the attention of movie-location scouts: Inistioge's film credits include *Widow's Peak* (1993), *Circle of Friends* (1994) and *Where the Sun Is King* (1996). There are picnic tables on the river.

With a scenic stretch of the South Leinster Way coursing through town, this is a good base for exploring the region. The R700 from Thomastown makes for a lovely **scenic drive** through the river valley. For variety, try some of the small roads that lead off this into the verdant countryside – you can't get lost for long. Better yet, try the **hiking trails** that follow the river. Side trails lead up into the hills.

Approximately 1km south, on Mt Alto, is **Woodstock Gardens** (☎ 779 4000; parking €4; ☺ 9am-8pm Apr-Sep, 9am-4pm Oct-Mar). The hike up is well worth the effort for the panorama of the valley below, and the heavily forested park itself is a beauty, with expanses of gardens, picnic areas and trails.

Like many neighbouring places, the **Woodstock Arms** (☎ 775 8440; www.woodstockarms .com; Inistioge; s/d c40/70) has tables outside overlooking the square. The interior of this pub has been rather plainly remodelled, but the

COUNTY KILKENNY

seven simple rooms upstairs are unfussy and sparkly clean.

Just north of town, **Motte Restaurant** (☎ 775 8655; Plas Newydd Lodge; set menu €35; ☽ 7-9.30pm Wed-Sat) has a delightful contemporary Irish menu that features a nightly menu that takes global inspiration. It's welcoming and relaxed, and diners can linger over cordials and conversation long after supper is over.

Just outside Woodstock Gardens, John Bassett has turned his family home into an exciting dining experience. Where once was his teenage bedroom there now sits a keg. The restaurant, **our pick** **Bassetts at Woodstock** (☎ 775 8820; www.bassetts.ie; mains €25-28; ☽ noon-2pm Wed-Sun, 6-10pm Wed-Sat), is a constantly evolving creative experience. Lunches may feature tapas (€10 each) and Saturday nights various tasting menus paired with wines. The food is fresh, local and inventive. Future meals graze right outside the door.

Getting There & Away

This is car, bike or hike country. Weekly (!) buses operate to New Ross and Kilkenny.

GRAIGUENAMANAGH
☎ 059 / pop 1700

Graiguenamanagh (pronounced 'greg-na-mana') is a pretty little riverside town on the Barrow, 23km southeast of Kilkenny. The town's best feature is its six-arch stone bridge that is illuminated at night. Along the river there's a serene wooded walk, of about 1½ hours, to St Mullins, just a few kilometres downstream from town, and another up Brandon Hill (516m), about 6km away.

Dating back to 1204, **Duiske Abbey** (☎ 24238; ☽ 8am-6pm) was once Ireland's largest Cistercian abbey. What you see today is the result of 800 years of additions and changes and it is very much a working parish (come at the right time and you'll interrupt the kids' choir practice, much to their delight). The simple exterior and whitewashed interior only hint at its long history. To the right of the entrance look for the Knight of Duiske, a 14th-century, high-relief carving of a knight in chain mail who's reaching for his sword. On the floor nearby, a glass panel reveals some of the original 13th-century floor tiles, now 2m below the present floor level. In the grounds stand two early high crosses, brought here for protection in the last century. The smaller Ballyogan Cross has panels on the eastern side depicting the crucifixion, Adam and Eve, Abraham's sacrifice of Isaac, and David playing the harp. The western side shows the massacre of the innocents.

Around the corner, the **Abbey Centre** (☽ 9am-1pm Mon-Fri, some days longer) houses a small exhibition of Christian art, plus pictures of the abbey in its unrestored state.

Down by the boats tied up along the river, the **Waterside** (☎ 792 4246; www.watersideguesthouse .com; Quay Graiguenamanagh; set dinner €36; ☽ restaurant 6.30-9.30pm Mon-Sat, 12.30-2.30pm Sun, weekends only Oct-Apr) is a popular guesthouse housed in an impressive 19th-century corn warehouse. Built solidly of stone, it has 10 modest rooms (€57 to €110) and received a refurbishment in 2007. The restaurant is well-regarded for its interesting modern Irish menu. Look for the local speciality smoked eel paired with horseradish. There are tables outside in summer.

WALK: COUNTY KILKENNY

South Leinster Way slices through the hilly southern part of County Kilkenny, from Graiguenamanagh through Inistioge, down to Mullinavat and westward to Piltown. It looks attractive on the map, but in reality much of it is paved highway, and not particularly good for walking. Stick with the prettiest part, a stretch of some 13km, beginning on the River Barrow. It links Graigue and Inistioge, two charming villages with amenities for travellers. In either village you can reward yourself with a top-notch meal.

Alternatively, along this path branch off onto **Brandon Way** (4km south of Graigue), which scales **Brandon Hill** (516m). The broad moorland summit is easily reached and affords a lovely view of the Blackstairs Mountains and Mt Leinster to the east. A return trip from Graigue is a fairly relaxed 12km walk.

The trail down **River Barrow** from Graigue to St Mullins is equally beautiful, with a firm path wending past canals and through some wooded country and pleasant grassy picnic areas. **St Mullins** itself is an interesting destination).

For fishing tackle, baked beans and a pint of stout, head to **Mick Doyle's** or **Mick Ryan's**, two old pubs on Abbey St that admirably attempt to address their customers' basic needs. There's a good used bookstore in between.

ST MULLINS

A tranquil spot about 6km downstream from Graiguenamanagh, St Mullins (on the County Carlow line) is good for a relaxing getaway, a picnic, or as rewarding destination on a long walk from Graigue. The river snakes through here in the shadow of Brandon Hill, and from it a trail winds uphill to the ruined hulk of an old monastery surrounded by the graves of 1798 rebels. A 9th-century Celtic cross, badly worn down over the centuries, still stands beside the monastery. Nearby, St Moling's Well is a holy well that seems to attract spare change.

Mulvarra House (☎ 051-424 936; www.mulvarra .com; s/d €50/80; ℗) is a B&B just up the hill from the river. It's modern and comfortable, a good base for exploring the area and you can partake of the body treatment centre.

NORTHERN KILKENNY

The rolling green hills of northern County Kilkenny are perfect for leisurely drives with the makings of a picnic stowed away in the boot. There's not a whole lot going on in this part of the county, but the picturesque towns of Ballyragget and Castlecomer are sure to tempt the traveller to pull over for a brief stroll. Dunmore Cave is the most frequently visited sight in these parts, but you'll enjoy the region best by taking the smallest roads you can find and making your own discoveries.

CASTLECOMER & AROUND

☎ 056 / pop 2400

Castlecomer is on the gentle River Dinin, some 18km north of Kilkenny. The town became a centre for anthracite mining after the fuel was discovered nearby in 1636; the mines closed for good in the mid-1960s. The anthracite, very hard form of coal, was widely regarded as being Europe's best, containing very little sulphur and producing almost no smoke.

Local fossil fuels are celebrated in the new **Castlecomer Discovery Park** (☎ 444 0707), set to open by the end of 2007. It will have an exhibition on coal mining set among lush woodlands.

You can best enjoy the area by just wandering about. Drive the back roads, enjoying the scenery and discovering little villages like **Clogh**, which has a lovely country pub, **Joyce's**, run by the charming John Coffey.

About 8km west of Castlecomer is Ballyragget, with an almost-intact square tower in the 16th-century **Butler Castle** (closed to the public).

Almost 2km south of Ballyragget is **Swifte's Heath**, home to Jonathan Swift during his school years in Kilkenny. The 'e' was evidently dropped from the name before the satirist gained notoriety as the author of *Gulliver's Travels* and *A Modest Proposal*.

Foulksrath Castle Hostel (☎ 67674; www.anoige .ie; Ballyragget; dm €12-15; ℗) is a busy An Óige hostel near Ballyragget with a superb setting, and surely rates among Ireland's best budget accommodation. The 44 beds are in a 16th-century Norman tower that's reputed to be haunted by more than tales of blown travel budgets.

Getting There & Away

Bus Éireann (☎ 64933) has five buses daily to Kilkenny (€4.30, 20 minutes). **Buggys Coaches** (☎ 444 1264) has three to four buses daily (€3.50) to a stop in Kilkenny outside the castle and to a stop 300m from Foulksrath Castle Hostel.

DUNMORE CAVE

Striking calcite formations enliven **Dunmore Cave** (☎ 056-67726; www.heritageireland.ie; Ballyfoyle; adult/child €2.90/1.30; ☼ 10am-6.30pm Jun-Sep, 10am-5pm Oct-May), some 6km north of Kilkenny on the Castlecomer road (N78). According to sources, marauding Vikings killed 1000 people at two ring forts near here in 928. When survivors hid in the caverns, the Vikings tried to smoke them out by lighting fires at the entrance. It's thought that they then dragged off the men as slaves and left the women and children to suffocate. Excavations in 1973 uncovered the skeletons of at least 44 people, mostly women and children. They also found coins dating from the 920s, but none from a later date. One theory suggests that the coins were dropped by the Vikings (who often carried them in their armpits, secured with wax) while enthusiastically engaged in the slaughter. However, there are few marks of violence on the skeletons, lending weight to the theory that suffocation was the cause of death.

The cave is well lit and spacious although, like so many caves, damp and cold. After a steep descent you enter caverns full of stalactites, stalagmites and columns, including the 7m Market Cross, Europe's largest freestanding stalagmite. The compulsory guided tours are worthwhile.

Buggys Coaches (☎ 056-444 1264) runs three to four buses daily (€3.50) from a stop in Kilkenny outside the castle.

Central South

Derided by some as the 'hole in the donut', the four counties here in the heart of Ireland are a delight to anyone who understands that the donut hole can be the best part.

The four midland counties of Kildare, Carlow, Laois and Offaly combine lush rolling fields, tree-covered hills, expanses of wildlife-filled bog and a history rich in artefacts. From the grand estates of the landlord days, with their Georgian homes, to the ancient and beguiling Clonmacnoise, Ireland's most magnificent monastic site, there's much that will surprise and delight as you explore the little lanes of the region.

And those explorations may yield the region's great pleasure: getting lost. Though you can't ever get really lost, just temporarily uncertain of your location. And who cares? It's hard to find a bad location and best of all, you can use it as an excuse to ask directions. Where else in the world will the way be so jovially explained like this: 'Well you just go up the wee road there until you come to the big tree, not the one big tree mind you but the other big tree, the one where Brigit O'Neill a few years back had quite the time…'

You'll want to record it. And the struggle of finding your way will get you ready for the many magnificent meals found in this centre of Ireland's growing food movement. Those lush lands produce some wonderful delights that will make this hole in the donut the best tasting around.

HIGHLIGHTS

- **Bogged Down** County Kildare's huge tracks of fecund land at the Bog of Allen (p344)
- **Horsin' Around** Learning the real meaning of the Irish National Stud in Kildare (p346)
- **Gardens Aplenty** Delighting in fine old estates and lush plantings in and around Ballon (**p352**)
- **Monastic Life** Letting your soul guide you around Ireland's finest monastic site, Clonmacnoise (p362)
- **Pearl Necklace** Exploring the ring of sights old and natural around Portlaoise (p354)

- POPULATION: 333,000
- AREA: 6301 SQ KM

GRAND & ROYAL CANALS

Starting in the late 1700s, a web of canals were dug extending west from Dublin (the starting point was the Guinness brewery). The goal was to link burgeoning industrial centres with ocean ports. Two of the most ambitious were the Grand and Royal Canals, which revolutionised transport in Ireland in the early 19th century, but their heyday was short-lived and the railways soon superseded them. Today they're favoured for cruising and fishing, and for their walking and cycling. Many waterfront villages can be found along their waters. Recent restorations have made them appealing recreational destinations.

For history, canal maps, coarse fishing, and ecology information, try the *Guide to the Grand Canal of Ireland* and the *Guide to the Royal Canal of Ireland,* both sold in tourist offices and bookshops in the region. **Waterways Ireland** (www.waterwaysireland.org) is charged with developing the waterways and has a wealth of info and publishes *Ireland's Waterways, Map and Directory.*

GRAND CANAL

The Grand Canal threads its way from Dublin to Robertstown in County Kildare, where one branch continues west through Tullamore before joining the River Shannon at Shannonbridge (p362), part of a region in County Offaly with many waterway diversions. The

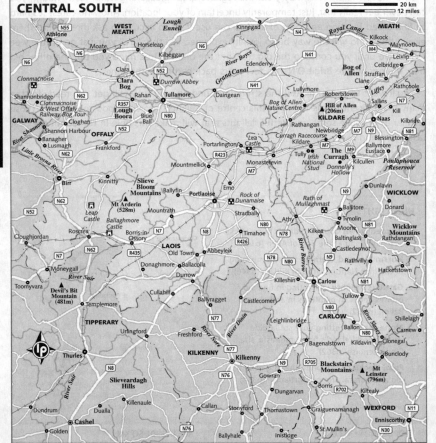

CENTRAL SOUTH

other turns south to join the River Barrow at the cute town of Athy (p347); a total of 130km in all.

The canal passes through relatively unpopulated countryside. Flowers, fens, picturesque villages and 36 finely crafted locks line the journey; if you're lucky you'll see otters. Near the village of Sallins, the graceful seven-arched **Leinster Aqueduct** carries the canal across the River Liffey, while further south sections of the River Barrow are particularly delightful.

Huge engineering difficulties, including the riddle of how to cross the Bog of Allen, meant that the canal took 23 years to build, finally opening in 1779. Passenger services continued until the 1850s. A trickle of commercial traffic carried turf, porter, coal and grain until 1960; the last shipment was a bargeful of Guinness!

For detailed information on the section of the canal between Robertstown and Lullymore, see p344.

ROYAL CANAL

Fourteen years behind the Grand Canal and duplicating its purpose, the 145km Royal Canal was always a loss-maker. It follows Kildare's northern border, passing an impressive backdrop of historical landmarks and stately homes, including St Patrick's College in Maynooth and Castletown House. There's a massive **aqueduct** near Leixlip, before it joins the River Shannon at Cloondara (or Clondra) in County Longford.

The canal has become a popular amenity for thousands of residents along the north Kildare commuter belt. Consequently, bus and rail services are good, and a leisurely walk between Leixlip and Maynooth is an easy day trip from Dublin. Although the towpaths are open all the way to the Shannon, the canal itself is navigable only as far as Ballymahon in County Longford. But restoration continues (in 2007 an important stretch at Abbeyshrule in County Longford reopened) and the entire waterway should be navigable when the final 18km to Clondra reopens in 2008.

BARGES & BOATS

The canals offer a relaxing way to drift across the country in warmer months; you can hire narrow boats at several locations. Two-/eight-berth boats cost from €800/1600 in September and about €1200/1800 in July and August but rates vary widely.

Barrowline Cruisers (☎ 0502-25189; www.barrow line.ie; Vicarstown Inn, Vicarstown, Co Laois) Grand Canal and River Barrow.

Canalways (☎ 045-524 646; www.canalways.ie; Spencer Bridge, Rathangan, Co Kildare) Grand Canal and River Barrow.

Tranquil Holidays (☎ +44-1788 824 664; www .tranquilholidays.org; Twelfth Lock, Dublin 15) One of the few companies servicing the Royal Canal.

Banagher (p361) is also a good place for Grand Canal rentals.

WALKING THE TOWPATHS

Canal towpaths are ideal for leisurely walkers and there are numerous access points along both canals. Robertstown is a good starting point for long-distance rambles. The village is the hub of the Kildare Way and River Barrow towpath trails, the latter stretching all the way to St Mullin's, 95km south in County Carlow. From there it's possible to connect with the South Leinster Way (p700) at Graiguenamanagh, or the southern end of the Wicklow Way (p701) at Clonegal, north of Mt Leinster.

A variety of leaflets detailing the paths can be picked up at most regional tourist offices. Waterways Ireland is also a good source.

COUNTY KILDARE

Once a backwater from Dublin, County Kildare (Cill Dara) is now prime suburbia. Charming towns like Maynooth and Kildare city are becoming bedrooms for commuters and it seems the continuous road construction is always one step behind the latest surge in traffic.

Kildare is one of the most prosperous counties in Ireland and it has some of the most lucrative thoroughbred stud farms in the world. The multimillion-pound industry thrives in the county – partly because Irish law levies no taxes on stud fees (thanks to former prime minister and horse owner Charles J Haughey). There are many ties to the horse-breeding centre of Kentucky in the US.

Geographically, the county has some of the best farmland in Ireland, as well as a vast swathe of bog to the northwest and the sweeping grasslands of the Curragh to the south.

Although not over-stuffed with must-see attractions, Kildare does have a number of

CENTRAL SOUTH

diversions for a day-trip out of Dublin or a stop on your way west.

MAYNOOTH

☎ 01 / pop 10,300

The university gives the town of Maynooth (Maigh Nuad) a lively feel. The pretty tree-lined main street has stone-fronted houses and shops, there's easy access to the Royal Canal and good transport thanks to the legions of barristers and other swells hurrying to the city.

Orientation & Information

Main St and Leinster St join and run east–west, while Parson St runs south to the canal and the train station (accessed via a couple of footbridges), and Straffen Rd runs south to the M4.

Tech Store (☎ 629 1747; www.techstore.ie; Unit 5, Glenroyal Shopping Centre; ☽ 10am-10pm Mon-Fri, noon-8pm Sat & Sun) Full line of services, including internet access (per hr €6); just off Straffen Rd.

Sights

ST PATRICK'S COLLEGE

Turning out Catholic priests since 1795, **St Patrick's College & Seminary** (☎ 628 5222; Main St) was ironically founded by the English in an attempt to steer Irish priests away from the dangerous ideals of revolution and republicanism being taught in France. The college joined the National University in 1910 and currently has about 5500 students. However, the number of young men studying for the priesthood continues to dwindle and there's just a few dozen now.

The college buildings are impressive – Pugin had a hand in designing them – and well worth an hour's ramble. You enter the college via Georgian Stoyte House, where the **accommodation office** (☎ 708 3576; ☽ 8.30am-5.30pm & 8-11pm Mon-Fri, 8.30am-12.30pm & 1.30-11pm Sat & Sun) sells booklets (€4) for guiding yourself around. In summer there's also a **visitor centre** (☽ 11am-5pm Mon-Fri, 2-6pm Sat & Sun May-Sep) and a small **science museum** (admission by donation; ☽ 2-4pm Tue & Thu, 2-6pm Sun May-Sep). The college grounds contain a number of lofty Georgian and neo-Gothic buildings, gardens and squares, but the highlight of the tour has to be the **College Chapel**. Pull open the squeaky door and you enter the world's largest choir chapel, with stalls for more than 450 choristers and some magnificent ornamentation.

MAYNOOTH CASTLE

Near the entrance to St Patrick's College you can see the ruined gatehouse, keep and great hall of 13th-century **Maynooth Castle** (☎ 628 6744; admission free; ☽ 10am-6pm Mon-Fri, 1-6pm Sat & Sun Jun-Sep, 1-5pm Sun Oct), home of the Fitzgerald family. The castle was dismantled in Cromwellian times, when the Fitzgeralds moved to Kilkea Castle (p348). Entry is by a 45-minute guided tour only; there's a small exhibition on the castle's history in the keep.

Activities

Leixlip, on the River Liffey between Maynooth and Dublin, is an important canoeing centre and the starting point of the annual 28km **International Liffey Descent Race** (www.liffey descent.com). Usually held in early September, the race attracts more than 1000 competitors. For more information on canoeing in Ireland, try **Canoeing Ireland** (www.canoe.ie).

Sleeping

Maynooth has limited choices for lodging.

NUI Maynooth (☎ 708 6200; www.maynooth campus.com; dm/s/d from €23/57/70; **P**) The university campus can accommodate 1000 guests in a wide variety of rooms. Most are in the mid-1970s North Campus, but rooms are better in the South Campus, where the accommodation office is. These are strewn around the courts and gardens of atmospheric St Patrick's College. Availability is best in the summer months.

Glenroyal Hotel & Leisure Club (☎ 629 0909; www.glenroyal.ie; Straffan Rd; r from €85-130; **P** 🖳 🏊) This modern 113-room hotel is tailored to business travellers and weddings. The design is bog standard but the rooms are spacious and spotless, have high-speed internet, and there are *two* swimming pools.

Carton House (☎ 505 2000; www.cartonhouse.com; r from €140; **P** 🖳 🏊) It really doesn't get any grander than this vast, early-19th-century estate set on lavish grounds. Although its history was a chequered mix of owners, Carton House was recently fully rebuilt into a spacious 147-room hotel. The interiors belie the exterior and are stylishly minimalist. Rooms have wi-fi, lavish baths and modern accoutrements like flat-screen TVs. To reach the hotel, follow the R148 east towards Leixlip along the Royal Canal.

Eating

Kehoe's (☎ 628 6533; Main St; meals €5-8; ☺ 8am-4pm Mon-Sat) The place for a classic Irish breakfast, Kehoe's offers a warm, trad welcome to its small and cosy quarters. There are numerous daily lunch specials.

Meghna (☎ 505 4868; Main St; meals €10-20; ☺ noon-2.30pm & 5-11pm) Several cuts above the usual curry joint, Meghna has a wide range of excellent South Asian dishes. The dining room has a gracious air and it's a floor above the street. For a kick in the old massalla, try the chicken chilli version.

Getting There & Away

Dublin Bus (☎ 873 4222; www.dublinbus.ie) runs a service to Maynooth (€3.10, one hour) leaving several times an hour from Pearse St in Dublin.

Maynooth is on the main Dublin–Sligo line, with regular trains in each direction: to Dublin (€2.70, 35 minutes, one to four per hour); to Sligo (€35, two hours 40 minutes, four per day).

AROUND MAYNOOTH

Celbridge

After the flowery excess of the Baroque era, the architectural pendulum swung far with Palladianism, a neoclassical style that favoured balance, austerity and porticos – lots of porticos. In the early 18th century, Italian architects brought an especially pure form to Ireland and **Castletown House** (☎ 628 8252; adult/child €3.70/1.30; ☺ 10am-6pm Mon-Fri, 1-6pm Sat & Sun Easter-Sep, 10am-5pm Mon-Fri, 1-5pm Sun Oct), a massive country house, is one of Ireland's finest examples. A lengthy tree-lined avenue leads up to the imposing façade, and the exquisite interior has been completely restored. Entry is by one-hour guided tour only.

The house was built between 1722 and 1732 for William Conolly, a humble publican's son who became speaker of the Irish House of Commons and the richest man in Ireland. It was designed by Alessandro Galilei, and his avant-garde building (a central block flanked by curved curtain walls) soon became the model for many of Ireland's country houses. In the US, Thomas Jefferson became a Palladian acolyte and much of official Washington DC is in this style.

There are two follies in the grounds commissioned by Conolly's widow, Katherine, to give employment to the poor after the 1739 famine. The **obelisk** can be seen from the Long Gallery at the back of the house, while the Heath-Robinsonesque **Wonderful Barn**, six teetering storeys wrapped by an exterior spiral staircase, is on private property just outside Leixlip. Those fins you see circling are developer sharks hoping to surround the barn with houses.

Buses 120 and 123 run from Dublin to Celbridge (€3, 30 minutes, every half-hour Monday to Friday, hourly Saturday, six buses Sunday).

Larchill Arcadian Gardens

These **gardens** (☎ 628 7354; www.larchill.ie; Kilcock; adult/child €7.50/5.50; ☺ noon-6pm Tue-Sun Jun-Aug, noon-6pm Sat & Sun Sep) are Europe's only example of a mid-18th-century *ferme ornée* (ornamental farm). A 40-minute walk takes you through beautiful landscaped parklands, passing eccentric follies, classic 18th-century formal plantings, gazebos and a lake. Children will be chuffed with the adventure playground, maze and winsome farm animals.

The gardens are 5km north of Kilcock on Dunsaughlin Rd (R125).

STRAFFAN

☎ 01 / pop 400

Teeny Straffan has a few attractions for the young and one huge one for the old.

Located in an old church, mechanical fanatics worship at the **Steam Museum & Lodge Park Walled Garden** (☎ 627 3155; www.steam-museum.ie; adult/concession €7.50/5; ☺ 2-6pm Wed-Sun Jun-Aug), which traces the history of steam power and the Industrial Revolution. The collection includes working steam engines from breweries, distilleries, factories and ships. Next door, the 18th-century walled garden has traditional fruits, flowers and formal plantings.

Just down the road at the **Straffan Butterfly Farm** (☎ 627 1109; www.straffanbutterflyfarm.com; Ovidstown; adult/child €7/4.50; ☺ noon-5.30pm Jun-Aug), you can wander through a tropical greenhouse full of enormous exotic butterflies, or commune with critters like Larry, the leopard gecko.

Two of Ireland's best-known golf courses can be found at the **K Club** (Kildare Hotel & Country Club; ☎ 601 7200; www.kclub.ie; Straffan; r from €250; Ⓟ ☐ Ⓡ), a Georgian estate and golfers' paradise. Inside there are 92 well-appointed rooms and lots of public spaces for having a drink and lying about your exploits outside.

There are two golf courses: one, with Arnold Palmer's design imprimatur, is one of the best in Ireland and has been the home of the European Open since 1995; the second course opened in 2003. Green fees are stiff (from €250) but reserve in advance. In 2006, this is where the European team won its third Ryder Cup in a row.

Bus Éireann (☎ 836 6111; www.buseireann.ie) runs buses from Dublin (€3.30, 30 minutes, every half hour, six buses Sunday).

ALONG THE GRAND CANAL

Heading west from Straffan, there are some interesting sites as you follow the banks of the Grand Canal. Just past Clane it's worth making the short detour to tiny, tranquil **Robertstown**. This picturesque village has remained largely untouched and is dominated by the now-dilapidated Grand Canal Hotel, built in 1801. It's a good place to start a canal walk (see p341).

Just southwest of Robertstown and at the centre of the Kildare flatlands, the **Hill of Allen** (206m) was a strategic spot through the centuries due to its 360-degree view. Today the top is marked by a 19th-century folly and the ruins of some Iron Age fortifications said to mark the home of Fionn McCumhaill.

Further west you'll find the wonderfully interpretive **Bog of Allen Nature Centre** (☎ 045-860 133; www.ipcc.ie; R414, Lullymore; adult/child €5/free; ☒ 9.30am-5pm Mon-Fri), a fascinating institution run by the nonprofit Irish Peatland Conservation Council. The centre traces the history of bogs and peat production, and has the largest carnivorous plant collection in Ireland, including sundews, butterwort and other bog-native protein-eaters. Much funding comes from the Netherlands, where the historic bogs are all gone. It's common to find dew-eyed Dutch volunteers assisting in the ongoing renovations. A nearby boardwalk extends into the Bog of Allen.

A rather mangy rabbit mascot greets visitors to the cheerful **Lullymore Heritage & Discovery Park** (☎ 045-870 238; Lullymore; adult/child €9/8; ☒ 10am-6pm Mon-Sat, 11am-6pm Sun Easter-Oct, 11am-6pm Sat & Sun Nov-Easter), about 1km south of the Bog of Allen Nature Centre. Aimed right at kids, a woodland trail leads you past various dwellings (including Neolithic huts, a not-so-festive Famine-era house and an enchanting fairy village), and there's crazy golf and a road train. Should the unthinkable

happen and it rains, the Funky Forest is a vast indoor playground.

For information on hiring narrow boats on the canal, see p341.

NEWBRIDGE & THE CURRAGH
☎ 045 / pop 15,900

The fairly unremarkable town of Newbridge (Droichead Nua) is near the junction of the M7 and M9. Many tourists flock to the **Newbridge Silverware Showroom** (☎ 431 301; www.new bridgecutlery.com), a purely commercial venture that trades on the area's metalwork heritage as it peddles vast quantities of silver-plated spoons, forks and whatnots. Remarkably rude staff took the shine off our visit the day we were there.

Silverware aside, the town is more famous as the gateway to the Curragh, one of the country's largest pieces of unfenced fertile land and the centre of the Irish horse industry. It's renowned for its **racecourse** (☎ 441 205; www.curragh.ie; admission €15-50; ☒ mid-Apr–Oct), the oldest and most prestigious in the country. Even if you're not a horsey type, it's well worth experiencing the passion, atmosphere and general craic of a day at the races, which can verge on mass hysteria. If you miss the chance to hear the hooves, you can still see some action: if you get up early or pass by in the late evening, you'll see the thoroughbreds exercising on the wide-open spaces surrounding the racecourse.

BOG OF ALLEN

Stretching like a brown, moist desert through nine counties, including Kildare, Laois and Offaly, the Bog of Allen is Ireland's best-known raised bog, and once covered much of the midlands. Unfortunately, in a pattern repeated across Ireland, the peat is rapidly being turned into potting compost and fuel. Once Ireland had almost 17% of its land covered in bogs; today it's less than 2%. Bogs are home to a wide range of plants and animals, including cranberries, insect-eating sundews, all manner of frogs and butterflies.

There are various ways to discover this rich land. For details of the Clonmacnoise & West Offaly Railway Bog Tour see p362. The Bog of Allen Nature Centre is right along the Grand Canal.

CHRISTY MOORE: A NEW TRADITION FOR TRADITIONAL MUSIC

A native of Newbridge, County Kildare, Christy Moore is one of Ireland's best-known, and certainly best-loved, traditional singers. Combining a ready wit and puckish charm, he has produced more than 23 solo albums of songs that are easy on the ear if not the mind.

The causes he has championed – travellers, antinuclear protests, South Africa, Northern Ireland – might give one the wrong impression: Christy is equally at home singing tender love songs (Nancy Spain), haunting ballads (Ride On), comic ditties (Lisdoovarna) and bizarre flights of lyrical fancy (Reel in the Flickering Light). He was also influential as a member of Planxty and Moving Hearts, as Ireland experimented during the 1970s and 1980s with its traditional musical forms to combine folk, rock and jazz in a heady and vibrant fusion.

Born in 1945, Moore grew up the son of a grocer and was influenced early in his musical career by a Traveller, John Riley. He was denied the musical opportunities he craved in Ireland and left in 1966 for England, where he quickly became popular on the British folk scene in Manchester and West Yorkshire.

Moore's first big break came with *Prosperous* (named after the Kildare town), on which he teamed up with the legendary Donal Lunny, Andy Irvine and Liam O'Flynn. They went on to form Planxty and recorded three ground-breaking albums.

Moore has done much to breathe life into traditional music. His work is always entertaining but like any good pub ballad, there's far more to his lyrics than you might first suspect. He's passionate, provocative and distinctive; you'll hear the influences of others as diverse as Jackson Browne and Van Morrison.

Certainly, even as he curtails his live performances to write, he is an iconic figure among Irish trad musicians and fans. He has built an international reputation as a writer and interpreter of a living tradition, at the head of the table of Irish traditional music.

Recommended listening: *The Christy Moore Collection, 1981–1991*.

The M7 runs through the Curragh (exit 12) and Newbridge from Dublin. There is frequent Bus Éireann service between Dublin's Busáras bus station and Newbridge (€6.80, 90 minutes). From Newbridge, buses continue on to the Curragh racecourse (€1.30, 10 minutes) and Kildare city. There are extra buses on race days.

The Dublin–Kildare **train** (☎ 01-836 6222) runs from Heuston train station and stops in Newbridge (€11.30, 30 minutes, hourly).

DETOUR: BALLYMORE EUSTACE

The village of Ballymore Eustace is home to one of Ireland's best modern pubs, the **Ballymore Inn** (☎ 045-864 585; www.ballymoreinn .com; meals €10-30). The richly tiled interior is warmed by small fireplaces, which flicker against the wicker and leather seating. The food ranges from pizza to amazing steaks. You can opt for a more formal experience in the dining room at lunch or dinner or settle back in the large pub, where pub food is served all day. Food is sourced from a stellar cast of local suppliers.

Check the timetable for trains that stop at the racecourse.

South Kildare Community Transport (☎ 871 916; www.skct.ie) runs a local bus service on two routes that serve Athy, Ballitore, Castledermot, Kildare city and Moone and Newbridge among others (one way €3.50; up to five times daily).

KILDARE CITY
☎ 045 / pop 5800

Unassuming Kildare is a small cathedral and market town, strongly associated with one of Ireland's high-profile saints, St Brigid. Its busy, compact triangular square is a pleasant place outside rush hour.

Information

The **Tourist Office & Heritage Centre** (☎ 521 240; www.kildare.ie; Market House, Market Sq; ☼ 9.30am-1pm & 2-5.30pm Mon-Sat May-Sep, 10am-1pm & 2-5pm Mon-Fri) has an exhibition (admission €1) outlining Kildare's history. There's local art for sale.

Sights
ST BRIGID'S CATHEDRAL

The solid presence of 13th-century **St Brigid's Cathedral** (☎ 521 229; Market Sq; admission by donation;

(✓) 10am-1pm & 2-5pm Mon-Sat, 2-5pm Sun May-Sep) looms over Kildare Sq. Look out for a fine stained-glass window inside that depicts the three main saints of Ireland: Patrick, Brigid and Colmcille. The church also contains the restored tomb of Walter Wellesley, Bishop of Kildare, which disappeared soon after his death in 1539 and was only found again in 1971. One of its carved figures has been variously interpreted as an acrobat or a sheila-na-gig.

The 10th-century **round tower** (admission €4) in the grounds is Ireland's second highest at 32.9m, and one of the few that you can climb, provided the guardian is around. Its original conical roof has been replaced with an unusual Norman battlement. Near the tower is a **wishing stone** – put your arm through the hole and touch your shoulder and your wish will be granted. On the north side of the cathedral are the heavily restored foundations of an ancient **fire temple** (see the boxed text, below).

IRISH NATIONAL STUD & GARDENS

With highlights like the 'Teasing Shed', you shouldn't miss the **Irish National Stud** (☎ 521 617; www.irish-national-stud.ie; Tully; adult/child €10/5; (✓) 9.30am-6pm mid-Feb–Dec, last admission 5pm), about 3km south of Kildare, which was founded by Colonel Hall Walker (of Johnnie Walker whiskey fame) in 1900. He was remarkably successful with his horses, but his eccentric

breeding technique relied heavily on astrology: the fate of a foal was decided by its horoscope and the roofs of the stallion boxes opened on auspicious occasions to reveal the heavens and duly influence the horses' fortunes. Today the immaculately kept centre is owned and managed by the Irish government. It breeds high-quality stallions to mate with mares from all over the world.

There are **guided tours** (many of the guides have a real palaver) of the stud every hour on the hour, with access to the intensive-care unit for newborn foals. If you visit between February and June, you might even see a foal being born. Alternatively, the foaling unit shows a 10-minute video with all the action. You can wander the stalls and go eye-to-eye with famous stallions. Less vigorous are the retirees like Vintage Crop, who won the Melbourne Cup in 1993. Given that most are now geldings, they probably have dim memories of their time in the aforementioned Teasing Shed, the place where stallions are stimulated for mating, while dozens look on. The cost: tens of thousands of euros for a top horse.

The revamped **Irish Horse Museum** celebrates championship horses and more mundane examples such as farmhouse nags.

The delightful **Japanese Gardens** (part of the complex) are considered to be the best of their kind in Europe. Created between 1906 and 1910, they trace the journey from birth to

---

ST BRIGID

St Brigid is one of Ireland's best-known saints, hailed as an early feminist but also known for her compassion, generosity and special ways with barnyard animals. Stories about her are both many and mythical. All agree that she was a strong-willed character: according to one legend, when her father chose her an unwanted suitor, she pulled out her own eye to prove her resolve never to wed. After she had taken her vows, and was mistakenly ordained a bishop rather than nun, her beauty was restored. Another has her being shipped off to a convent after she compulsively gave away the family's wealth to the poor. (One tale even has Brigid being spirited to Ireland from Portugal by pirates.)

Brigid founded a monastery in Kildare in the 5th century for both nuns and monks, which was unusual at the time. One lurid account says it had a perpetual fire tended by 20 virgins that burned continuously until 1220 when the Bishop of Dublin stopped the tradition, citing it as 'un-Christian'. The supposed fire pit can be seen in the grounds of St Brigid's Cathedral where a fire is lit on 1 February, St Brigid's feast day. Nonvirgins are welcome.

Brigid was a tireless traveller, and as word of her many miracles spread, her influence stretched across Europe. Yet another legend claims that the medieval Knights of Chivalry chose St Brigid as their patron, and that it was they who first chose to call their wives 'brides'.

Brigid is remembered by a simple reed cross first woven by her to explain the redemption to a dying chief. The cross, said to protect and bless a household, is still found in many rural homes. She is also the patron of travellers, chicken farms and seamen, among others.

death through 20 landmarks, including the Tunnel of Ignorance, the Hill of Ambition and the Chair of Old Age.

St Fiachra's Garden is another bucolic feature, with a mixture of bog oak, gushing water, replica monastic cells and an underground crystal garden of dubious distinction. Both gardens are great for a relaxing stroll.

The large **visitor centre** houses an excellent café, shop and children's play area. A tour of the stud and gardens takes about two hours.

Lying outside the site, behind the museum, are the ruins of a 12th-century **Black Abbey**. Just off the road back to Kildare is **St Brigid's Well**, where five stones represent different aspects of Brigid's life.

Sleeping

Silken Thomas (☎ 522 232; www.silkenthomas.com; Market Sq; s/d from €45/70; **P**) This local institution includes clubs, bars and an 18-room hotel. There's a modern wing and an 18th-century town house. Rooms are unfrilly but comfortable; try for one away from the action.

Derby House Hotel (☎ 522 144; www.derbyhouse hotel.ie; s/d from €60/100; **P** 🖵) This old hotel has 20 decent rooms right in the centre of town. It's an easy walk from here to bars, restaurants and all the St Brigid lore you could hope for. There's wi-fi throughout.

Martinstown House (☎ 441 269; www.martinstown house.com; the Curragh; s/d €145/220; 🏵 mid-Jan–mid-Dec; **P**) This beautiful 18th-century country manor is built in the frilly 'strawberry hill' Gothic style and set in a 170-acre estate and farm surrounded by trees. The house has four rooms filled with antiques; children are banned – darn. You can arrange for memorable dinners in advance (€55); ingredients are drawn from the kitchen garden.

Eating

Fittingly enough there's a market on Market Sq every Thursday, although the selection can vary; when we asked what was grown locally we got this response: 'potatoes'.

Agape (☎ 533 711; Station Rd; meals €5-10; 🏵 9am-6pm Mon-Sat) Just off Market Sq, this trendy little café has a fine range of homemade food. There's a full coffee bar and a menu of salads, soups, sandwiches and tasty hot specials.

Chapter 16 (☎ 522 232; Market Sq; mains €12-25; 🏵 6-10pm) Part of the Silken Thomas empire, this ambitious restaurant serves steaks, seafood and modern Irish fare in an attrac-

tive setting. The vast pub has a popular carvery lunch.

Getting There & Away

There is frequent Bus Éireann service between Dublin Busáras and Kildare city (€8.80, 1¾ hours). Buses continue on to Limerick (€11.30, 2½ hours, four daily). Some Dublin buses also service the Stud.

The Dublin–Kildare **train** (☎ 01-836 6222) runs from Heuston train station and stops in Kildare (€12.80, 35 minutes, one to four per hour). This is a major junction and trains continue on to numerous places including Ballina, Galway, Limerick and Waterford.

South Kildare Community Transport (☎ 045-871 916; www.skct.ie) runs a local bus service on two routes that serve Athy, Ballitore, Castledermot, Kildare city, Moone and Newbridge among others (one way €3.50, up to five times daily).

ATHY

☎ 059 / pop 6200

Strategically placed at the junction of the River Barrow and the Grand Canal, the Anglo-Norman settlement of Athy (Áth Í; a-*thigh*) shows little of its long history.

Athy was founded in the 12th century and later became an important defence post. Many of the town's older buildings remain, including the impressive **White's Castle**, a tower built in 1417 to house the garrison. The castle is next to Crom-a-boo Bridge, named after what must be the world's worst battle cry, hollered by the local Geraldine family.

The **Tourist Office & Heritage Centre** (☎ 863 3075; Emily Sq; admission Heritage Centre adult/child €3/2; 🏵 10am-5pm Mon-Fri, 2-4pm Sat & Sun May-Oct, 10am-5pm Mon-Fri Nov-Apr) gives good walking recommendations. The heritage centre traces the history of Athy and has a fascinating exhibit on Antarctic explorer Sir Ernest Shackleton (1874–1922), who was born in nearby Kilkea. On display is one of Shackleton's sledges, acquired from New Zealand where he sold it to pay off his debts.

Activities

Athy is a popular place for pike, salmon and trout fishing. For equipment and information try **Griffin Hawe Hardware** (☎ 863 1221; www.griffinhawe.ie; 22 Duke St). There's a wide range of fly rods and gear.

Sleeping & Eating

Coursetown House (☎ 863 1101; fax 863 2740; Stradbally Rd; s/d €75/120; ℗) This 200-year-old farmhouse is just east of Athy off the R428. It's set among gorgeous gardens, which provide a lot of the produce that makes the breakfasts here so bountiful in season. The five rooms exude country charm and have powerful showers for washing the grime off after a long walk in the countryside.

Carlton Abbey Hotel (☎ 863 0100; www.carltonabbey hotel.com; town centre; r from €80; ℗ 🖳 🐾) Once as stolid as the morals of its residents, this old convent has been converted into a most inviting boutique hotel. There are 40 rooms with dark woods and light linens and mod cons such as high-speed internet. There's a popular pub, a good restaurant and a 21m pool.

Getting There & Away

Bus Éireann (☎ 01-836 6111; www.buseireann.ie) has six buses to/from Dublin (€9.30, 1½ hours) and Clonmel (€11.70, two hours).

South Kildare Community Transport (☎ 045-871 916; www.skct.ie) runs a local bus service on two routes that serve Athy, Ballitore, Castledermot, Kildare city, Moone and Newbridge among others (one way €3.50, up to five times daily).

DONNELLY'S HOLLOW TO CASTLEDERMOT

This 25km stretch south towards Carlow contains some interesting detours to tiny towns bypassed by the speedy but unlovely N9.

South Kildare Community Transport (☎ 045-871 916; www.skct.ie) runs a local bus service on two routes that serve Athy, Ballitore, Castledermot, Kildare city, Moone and Newbridge among others (one way €3.50; up to five times daily).

Donnelly's Hollow

Dan Donnelly (1788–1820) is revered as Ireland's greatest bare-knuckle fighter of the 19th century. He's also the stuff of legend – his arms were so long, he could supposedly tie his shoelaces without having to bend down. This spot, 4km west of Kilcullen on the R413, was his favourite battleground, and the obelisk at the centre of the hollow details his glorious career.

Ballitore

☎ 059 / pop 750

Low-key Ballitore is the only planned and permanent Quaker settlement in Ireland. It was founded by incomers from Yorkshire in the early 18th century. A small **Quaker Museum** (☎ 862 3344; ballitorelib@kildarecoco.ie; Mary Leadbeater House, Main St; admission by donation; ☿ noon-5pm Tue-Sat year-round, 2-6pm Sun Jun-Sep), in a tiny restored house, documents the lives of the community (including the namesake former owner who was known for her aversion to war). There's a Quaker cemetery and Meeting House, and a modern **Shaker Store** (☎ 862 3372; www.shaker store.ie; Main St; ☿ 10am-6pm Mon-Fri, 2-6pm Sat & Sun), which sells delightfully humble wooden toys and furniture. It has a tearoom.

About 2km west is **Rath of Mullaghmast**, an Iron Age hill fort and standing stone where Daniel O'Connell, champion of Catholic emancipation, held one of his 'monster rallies' in 1843.

Moone

☎ 059 / pop 380

Just south of Ballitore, the unassuming village of Moone is home to one of Ireland's most magnificent high crosses. The unusually tall and slender **Moone High Cross** is an 8th- or 9th-century masterpiece, which displays its carved biblical scenes with the confidence and exuberance of a comic strip. The cross can be found 1km west of Moone village and the N9 in an atmospheric early Christian churchyard. Old stone ruins add to the mood of the drive.

The solid and stone 18th-century **Moone High Cross Inn** (☎ 862 4112; Bolton Hill; s/d from €50/80; ℗), 2km south of Moone, has five rooms decorated in quaint country-house style. The delightful bar downstairs serves good pub lunches and there's a proper restaurant (open 6pm to 8.30pm, mains €12 to €35), which uses local and organic ingredients. The inn revolves around a Celtic theme, celebrating pagan festivals and hoarding healing stones, lucky charms and even a 'love stone' in the outside courtyards.

Kilkea Castle

Built in the 12th century, **Kilkea Castle Hotel** (☎ 059-914 5156; www.kilkeacastle.ie; Castledermot; r from €160; ℗ 🖳) is Ireland's oldest continuously inhabited castle. It's the kind of place where you'll find a suit of armour in a nook in the hall and looks like a castle right out of central casting. It was once the second home of the Maynooth Fitzgeralds, and the grounds are supposedly haunted by Gerald the Wizard Earl, who rises every seven years from the Rath of Mullaghmast to free Ireland from its enemies – a pretty good trick considering he was buried in London.

The castle was completely restored in the 19th century and is now an exclusive hotel and golf club. Among its exterior oddities is an **Evil Eye Stone**, high up at the back of the castle. Thought to date from the 14th or 15th century, it depicts some very weird goings-on between nightmarish creatures that may be a woman, wolf and cock. Another carving depicts a monkey in bondage; definitely fertile grounds for voyeurs.

De Lacy's (set dinner from €50), the restaurant, serves complex and formal meals in elegant surroundings.

The castle is 5km northwest of Castledermot on the Athy road (R418).

Castledermot
☎ 059 / pop 1160

Castledermot was once home to a vast ecclesiastical settlement, but all that remains of St Diarmuid's 9th-century **monastery** is a 20m round tower topped with a medieval battlement. Nearby are two well-preserved, carved 10th-century granite high crosses, a 12th-century Romanesque doorway and a medieval Scandinavian 'hogback' gravestone, the only one in Ireland. Reach the ruins by entering the rusty gate on all-too-busy Main St (N9), then walking up the tree-lined avenue to St James' church. At the southern end of town, the ruins of an early 14th-century **Franciscan friary** can be seen by the road.

Schoolhouse Restaurant (☎ 914 4098; Main St; ☽ 6-9pm Tue-Sat, noon-2pm & 6-9pm Sun) is, as you might guess, based in a 1920s school. The dining room is elegant, with cream-coloured walls and dark wood. The food is modern Irish and makes full use of regional ingredients. At times, simple B&B rooms may be available.

COUNTY CARLOW

Carlow (Ceatharlach), Ireland's second-smallest county, has a beauty all of its own. Dotted around are strings of quietly picturesque villages such as Rathvilly, Leigh-

linbridge and Borris, which have scarcely changed in the past hundred years. The most dramatic chunk of history in these parts is Europe's biggest dolmen, just outside Carlow town. From history to gardens, you'll find much to delay your exit from this county.

The scenic Blackstairs Mountains dominate the southeast: the highest, Mt Leinster (796m), is one of Ireland's premier hang-gliding sites, with stunning views from the summit. The website (www.carlowtourism .com) has scads of local info.

CARLOW TOWN
☎ 059 / pop 13,400

The winding streets and lanes of Carlow give it just a bit of a 'Kilkenny Lite' feel. Or maybe it's just Kilkenny cheap. There's enough heritage to keep you wandering for an afternoon, and a ripple of trendy cafés and solid nightlife may keep you in town past dusk. But you're unlikely to feel besieged by the tour bus hordes.

Orientation & Information

Dublin St is the city's principal north–south axis, with Tullow St, the main shopping street, running off it at a right angle.

Post office (cnr Kennedy Ave & Dublin St)

Tourist office (☎ 913 1554; cnr Tullow & College Sts; ☽ 9.30am-1pm & 2-5.30pm Mon-Fri year-round, 10am-5.30pm Sat Jun-Aug) A useful source of information. A county museum (www.carlowcountymuseum.com) is in the works for an adjoining space.

Webtalk (☎ 913 9721; 44 Tullow St; per hr €6; ☽ 9.30am-6pm Mon-Sat) Full internet services.

Sights

Follow the walking tour (p350) to hit Carlow's highlights.

If you're feeling more thirsty than energetic, visit the **Carlow Brewing Company** (☎ 913 4356; www.carlowbrewing.com; the Goods Store, Station Rd; admission €7). This small microbrewery has been hugely successful since it opened in 1998; its award-winning O'Hara's Celtic Stout bursts with flavour and blows away that *other* Irish stout. Arrange tours in advance.

Activities

The River Barrow is popular with canoeists, kayakers and rowers. **Adventure Canoeing Days** (☎ 087-252 9700; www.gowiththeflow.ie) does

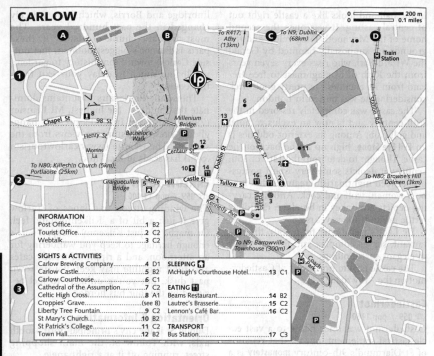

CARLOW

INFORMATION
Post Office.................................**1** B2
Tourist Office.............................**2** C2
Webtalk....................................**3** C2

SIGHTS & ACTIVITIES
Carlow Brewing Company...............**4** D1
Carlow Castle............................**5** B2
Carlow Courthouse......................**6** C1
Cathedral of the Assumption.........**7** C2
Celtic High Cross........................**8** A1
Croppies' Grave......................(see 8)
Liberty Tree Fountain...................**9** C2
St Mary's Church.......................**10** B2
St Patrick's College.....................**11** C2
Town Hall................................**12** B2

SLEEPING 🏠
McHugh's Courthouse Hotel..........**13** C1

EATING 🍴
Beams Restaurant......................**14** B2
Lautrec's Brasserie.....................**15** C2
Lennon's Café Bar.....................**16** C2

TRANSPORT
Bus Station..............................**17** C3

weekend trips that tackle the rather tame white-water (from €50) and rents out canoes (from €50 per day). Book in advance.

Walking Tour

Start your walk at the tourist office on College St. Just to the right is the elegant Regency Gothic **Cathedral of the Assumption (1)**, which dates from 1833. The cathedral was the brainchild of Bishop Doyle, a staunch supporter of Catholic emancipation. His statue inside includes a woman said to represent Ireland rising up against her oppressors. The church also has an elaborate pulpit and some fine stained-glass windows.

Next door is **St Patrick's College (2)**, Ireland's first post-penal seminary. Opened in 1793 (but now closed to the public), it is thought to have been in use for longer than any other seminary in the world.

Walking north along College St then turning left on Dublin St, you'll come to the impressive **Carlow Courthouse (3)**, at the northern end of Dublin St. Designed by William Morrisson in 1830, this elegant building is modelled on the Parthenon and is considered to

be one of the most impressive courthouses in the country. Carlow got it through an administrative mix-up – the building was originally intended for Cork.

Walk down Dublin St and turn right into Centaur St and past the **Town Hall (4)**, dating from 1884. When you reach the river, cross the **Millennium Bridge (5)** and walk across the park to 98 St where you'll find the **Celtic high cross (6)** that marks the mass Croppies' Grave. Here 640 United Irish rebels were buried following the bloodiest fighting of the 1798 Rising. The name 'croppie' came from the rebels' habit of cropping their hair to indicate their allegiance.

From here turn back into Maryborough St and walk south to the five-arched **Graiguecullen Bridge (7)**, thought to be the oldest and lowest bridge over the River Barrow. Cross the bridge and continue east to the ruins of 13th-century **Carlow Castle (8)**, built by William de Marshall on the site of an earlier Norman motte-and-bailey fort. The castle survived Cromwell's attentions but succumbed to the grand plans of a certain Dr Middleton, who decided to convert it into

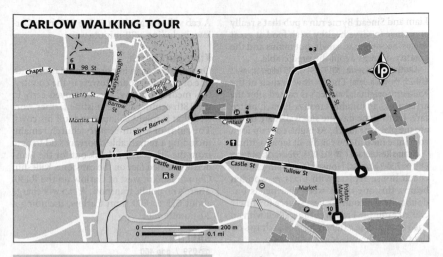

CARLOW WALKING TOUR

WALK FACTS

Start Tourist office
Finish Liberty Tree fountain
Distance 2.5km
Duration One hour

a lunatic asylum. Proving the cliché about the lunatics running the asylum, he blew up much of the castle in 1814 in order to 'remodel' it. All that is left is a single wall flanked by two towers.

Continue up Castle Hill and take the fork to your left onto Castle St. On your left you will see **St Mary's Church (9)**, built in 1727 (the tower and spire were added later, in 1834), with a number of statues by Richard Morrison.

Walk on up Tullow St, the town's principal shopping thoroughfare, and take the second right into Potato Market. At the end of the lane is a small square. The bronze statue in the middle of the fountain is the **Liberty Tree (10)**, designed by John Behan to commemorate the 1798 Rising.

Festivals & Events

Every summer (usually in mid-June) Carlow town celebrates the 10-day **Éigse Carlow Arts Festival** (☎ 914 0491; www.eigsecarlow.ie), when musicians, writers, actors and street performers take over the town. Artists and groups come not just from Ireland but also countries as far away as South Korea and India.

Sleeping

Diminutive County Carlow has many charming inns, making it easy to stay out in the lovely countryside, popping into town for food and culture.

McHugh's Courthouse Hotel (☎ 913 3243; www .mchughscourthousehotel.com; 38-39 Dublin St; s/d from €50/90; **P**) The look is sort of pseudo-old but the interior of the rooms is very much modern-nondescript. The pub is large and woodsy, the bathrooms large and tile-y while the singles are tiny.

Barrowville Townhouse (☎ 914 3324; www.barrow villehouse.com; Kilkenny Rd; s/d from €60/110; **P**) This attractive 18th-century town house has been meticulously restored and converted into a classy B&B, under five minutes' walk south of town. The seven rooms vary in size but are all perfectly atmospheric for curling up with a book or… Enjoy breakfast in the open and airy conservatory.

Eating & Drinking

Watch for new cafés opening in the centre. This is the nightlife hub for those stuck out in the sticks; ask around to find out what the clubs of the moment are. There's usually something on along Tullow St and Thursday night is popular for live music. Carlow's **farmers market** (⊗ Sat) is fittingly on the Potato Market.

Lennon's Café Bar (☎ 913 1575; 121 Tullow St; meals €5-15; ⊗ food served 9am-4pm Mon-Sat, 6-10pm Thu & Fri) Trendy and stylish, Lennon's is a sure sign that the times may be a-changin' in Carlow.

Liam and Sinéad Byrne run a pub that's really an excuse to serve healthy fresh food at great prices. Sandwiches, salads, hot mains and the creative dinners avoid the predictable.

Lautrec's Brasserie (☎ 914 3455; 115 Tullow St; meals €10-25; ⏰ noon-9pm) The Carlow branch of the Kilkenny original, Lautrec's is named after the artist and has suitably creative French bistro fare. During the day the sidewalk café tables are the place for lunch. At night, cosy up for a romantic meal at the candle-lit tables within.

Beams Restaurant (☎ 913 1824; 59 Dublin St; set dinner €40; ⏰ 7.30-9.30pm Sat) Housed in an 18th-century coach house replete with massive wooden beams, this one-day-a-week charmer is undoubtedly the county's best source for finely crafted exquisite French cuisine, albeit with an Irish accent. The extensive wine list draws on the stock of the subsidiary wine shop.

Getting There & Away
BUS
Bus Éireann runs buses to Dublin (€9.30, two hours, 10 daily), to Cork (€14.90, 3½ hours, one daily) via Kilkenny (€6.30, 35 minutes) and to Waterford (€9.30, 1½ hours, seven daily).

JJ Kavanagh & Sons (☎ 914 3081; www.jjkavanagh .ie) has several buses per day to Dublin (€11, two hours) and Dublin Airport (€16, three hours). There are two buses per day Monday to Saturday to Kilkenny (€5, 50 minutes) and Portlaoise (€6, one hour).

Buses for both companies leave from the bus station located at the eastern end of Kennedy Ave.

TRAIN
The **train station** (☎ 913 1633; Station Rd) is to the northeast of town. Carlow is located on the Dublin–Waterford line with five trains daily in each direction Monday to Saturday (four Sunday). One way to Dublin or Waterford (both 1¼ hours) costs €12.80.

AROUND CARLOW TOWN
Browne's Hill Dolmen
This 5000-year-old granite monster is Europe's largest **portal dolmen** and one of Ireland's most famous. The capstone alone weighs well over 100 tonnes and would originally have been covered with a mound of earth. The dolmen is 3km east of town on the R726 Hackettstown road; a path leads round the field to the dolmen. There's no public transport.

A cab will charge about €15 to €20 from Carlow, including a 20-minute wait.

Killeshin Church
Once the site of an important monastery with one of the finest round towers in the country, this medieval marvel was destroyed early in the 18th century by a Philistine farmer worried that it might collapse and kill his cows. The ruins of a 12th-century church remain, including a remarkable doorway said to date from the 5th century. Look out for the wonderful bearded face on the capstone. Killeshin Church is 5km west of Carlow on the R430. There's no public transport. A cab will charge about €15 to €20 from Carlow, including a 20-minute wait.

BALLON
☎ 059 / pop 400
Out among the best of Carlow's rolling countryside, there are numerous estates and gardens near the small village of Ballon, located on the N80.

Altamont Gardens (☎ 915 9444; www.heritageireland .ie; admission free; ⏰ 9am-5pm Mon-Fri, 2-5.30pm Sat & Sun; P) is one of Ireland's most magnificent old walled formal gardens. Run by the Heritage Service, the 40-acre garden has a design dating to Victorian times. From the car park, just follow your nose to what's in bloom. There's a small nursery selling plants found inside. The gardens are 5km east of Ballon.

Only 600m south of Altamont Gardens, **Sherwood Park House** (☎ 915 9117; www.sherwoodpark house.ie; s/d from €60/100; P) is a Greystone Georgian manor dating from 1730. The five rooms are huge and boast such period niceties as four-poster beds. You can make arrangements for dinner. This is prime walking country.

The **Ballykealey Manor Hotel** (☎ 915 9288; www .ballykealeymanorhotel.com; Ballon; s/d from €90/140; P) is an early 19th-century pastiche of Tudor and Gothic details. Inside this elegant stone manor are 12 luxurious rooms (with more coming). It's all on a fine country estate and there's a popular restaurant, the **Oak Room** (meals €15-30; ⏰ noon-2.30pm Sun, 6-9pm Wed-Sun) with high-end cuisine.

BORRIS
☎ 059 / pop 590
This seemingly untouched Georgian village on a hill has a dramatic mountain backdrop and

traditional main street. A huge stone railway viaduct on the edge of town has been disused since the idiotic line closures of the 1950s.

Borris is full of character, with plenty of atmospheric bars known for summertime trad music.

Sights & Activities

At the opposite end of the village from the graceful 16-arch railway viaduct is the dramatic **Borris House** (☎ 977 3105), a beautiful Tudor-style residence and one of Ireland's most majestic stately homes. Tours by appointment only.

At the bottom of the hill, **Mill Gardens** (☎ 977 3132; admission €5; ☒ call for arrangements) mixes Victorian formality with orchards and modern ornamental plants.

Borris is a starting point for the 13km **Mt Leinster Scenic Drive** (it can also be walked) and is also on the South Leinster Way (see p700). Alternatively, there's a lovely 10km walk along the **River Barrow towpath** to picturesque Graiguenamanagh, just inside County Kilkenny.

Sleeping & Eating

There are several magnificent and memorable places to stay in and around Borris.

Step House (☎ 977 3209; www.thestephouse.com; 66 Main St; s/d from €55/90; **P**) This Georgian home right in the centre of town is a vision in cheery yellow, even on a grey day. Inside, antiques abound in the common spaces and in all 20 bedrooms. It's a dream both for dysfunctional collectors and adults looking to lose the kids (they're not allowed). Many rooms have views of the large gardens out back framed by Mt Leinster.

Lorum Old Rectory (☎ 977 5282; www.lorum.com; s/d from €95/150; ☒ Mar-Nov; **P**) Halfway between Borris and Bagenalstown off the R705, this historic manor house sits on a prominent knoll east of the road. The gardens stretch in all directions, offering good views from each of the five rooms. The cooking here is renowned (much of it organic); ask about arrangements when you book.

our pick **Kilgraney Country House** (☎ 0503-75283; http://indigo.ie/~kilgrany; s/d from €100/130; ☒ Mar-Nov; **P**) The River Barrow burbles away down the shallow valley from this six-room Georgian manor. The owners, veteran travellers, have created a fabulous interior that's a refuge for those who have OD'd on chintz.

DETOUR: CLONEGAL

Located off winding local roads some 5km east of Kildavin and the N80, the minute village of Clonegal is all moody atmosphere. Expect a headless horseman to gallop by as you explore the paths around **Huntington Castle** (☎ 054-77552) in the heart of the moors. It's open sporadically but you're really here for an atmospheric – if hair-raising – wander, before retreating to one of the cute village pubs.

They've decorated using goods collected from places as far as the Philippines. There's a spa, a herb garden and six-course meals (from €48). This is the classic Dublin escape; it's off the R705 halfway between Borris and Bagenalstown, north of the Lorum Old Rectory.

M O'Shea (☎ 977 3106; Main St) This place is a mix of general store, modern grocery and pub. Spare parts hang from the ceiling, while you can pick up bananas next door. Surprises abound in the warren of rooms; should you get peckish you can strap on a feedbag of horse chow that's for sale not far from the stout tap (or be dull and order the tasty pub grub). There are tables out the back on sunny days.

Getting There & Away

Borris is on the east–west R702, which links the N9 with the N11 in County Wexford. Heading north, the R705 follows the scenic River Barrow Valley 12km to Bagenalstown.

MT LEINSTER

At 796m, Mt Leinster offers some of Ireland's finest **hang-gliding**. It's also worth the hike up for the panoramic views over Counties Carlow, Wexford and Wicklow. To get there from Borris, follow the Mt Leinster Scenic Drive signposts 13km towards Bunclody in County Wexford. It takes a good two hours on foot or 20 minutes by car.

SOUTH LEINSTER WAY

Southwest of Clonegal, on the northern slopes of Mt Leinster, is the tiny village of Kildavin, the starting point of the South Leinster Way. For details see p700.

CENTRAL SOUTH

COUNTY LAOIS

Most people see Laois (pronounced 'leash') as a green blur outside the car window as they zoom along the N7 or N8 to sexier sites west. But get off the main roads, and you'll discover the hidden corners of Ireland's heartland: surprising heritage towns, the unspoiled Slieve Bloom Mountains and a lace-work of rivers and walkways.

For all you need to know about the county, check out www.laoistourism.ie. Look for the excellent booklet *Laois Heritage Trail* at tourist offices, which does a good job of tying the county's heritage together.

PORTLAOISE

☎ 057 / pop 3600

Portlaoise's two main edifices could be called 'nuts and bolts' – the large mental asylum and maximum-security prison. Unless you're planning to lose the plot or commit murder, there's very little to keep you here as a visitor. However, the Slieve Bloom Mountains (p356) to the west and the impressive Rock of Dunamaise (opposite) to the east are well worth a visit.

Information

Dunamaise Arts Centre (☎ 866 3355; Church St; per hr €5; ☯ 8.30am-5.30pm Mon-Sat) Has Internet access.

Tourist office (☎ 862 1178; James Fintan Lawlor Ave; ☯ 9.30am-1pm & 2-5.30pm Mon-Fri Oct-May, Mon-Sat Jun-Sep) In the shopping-centre car park beside the bypass; delightful staff.

Sleeping & Eating

Portlaoise can fill your plate; there's a good selection of lunch spots. Many are on the characterful Main St. To get there, cut through Lyster's Lane from the charmless strip mall and parking lot with the tourist office off the bypass.

O'Loughlin's Hotel (☎ 862 1305; www.oloughlins hotel.ie; 30 Main St; s/d from €60/100; Ⓟ ▣) This heritage building is home to a simple but comfortable hotel. The 20 rooms have wi-fi and past the little fireplace in the lobby is a large pub popular at lunch.

Egan's Hostelry (☎ 862 1106; Main St; meals €7-12; ☯ 9am-9.30pm) This pub is always busy thanks to its good-value buffet line. There are numerous tasty and traditional hot choices daily and all come with an array of sides that overwhelm the plate.

Kitchen & Foodhall (☎ 866 2061; Hyand's Sq; mains €7-12; ☯ 9am-5.30pm Mon-Sat) Choose from a bountiful array of fresh salads at the buffet at this renowned purveyor of creative and healthy foods. There are daily hot specials and items like chutney and jam are all house-made. Bright, cheery and child-friendly, it's just off Main St and is a good spot for picnic stock-ups.

Entertainment

Dunamaise Arts Centre (☎ 866 3355; www.dunamaise .ie; Church St) The county's purpose-built theatre and arts centre presents a varied programme of national and international performances and visual arts, comedy and films.

Getting There & Away

BUS

Portlaoise is at the busy junctions of the M7, N7 and N8.

Bus Éireann runs frequent buses on three main routes: to Cork (€9.50, three hours) via Abbeyleix, Cashel and Cahir; to Dublin (€9.30, 1¾ hours) via Kildare city; and along the N7 to Limerick (€11.30, three hours) via Mountrath, Borris-in-Ossory and Roscrea.

JJ Kavanagh & Sons (☎ 056-883 1106; www.jj kavanagh.ie) runs two buses per day Monday to Saturday to Carlow (€6, one hour) and Kilkenny (€7, 1½ hours).

TRAIN

Portlaoise, just 70 minutes from Dublin (€18.50, 14 daily), is on the lines to Cork, Limerick and Tralee. The small **train station** (☎ 862 1303; Railway St) is a five-minute walk north of the town centre.

AROUND PORTLAOISE

Within a 20km radius of Portlaoise are a range of towns, attractions and features that date as far back as the 2nd century, often include gorgeous gardens and attest to the local influence of the Vikings, French and others. Running roughly in a circle from the north clockwise to the south, you can easily enjoy the variety of sights by car in a day. It would also be a not-horribly-difficult bike ride; by public transport you can only reach a few towns easily.

Mountmellick

☎ 057 / pop 2600

Incorrectly called the 'Manchester of Ireland' (it's smaller and nicer), Mountmellick is a quiet Georgian town on the River Owenass. It was renowned for its linen production in the 19th century and owes much of its history to its Quaker settlers.

A 4km looped and signed **heritage trail**, beginning in the square, leads you on a walking tour of the most important landmarks. There's a display of superbly subtle Mountmellick embroidery at the **Mountmellick Museum** (☎ 862 4525; www.mountmellickdevelopment.com; Mountmellick Development Association, Irishtown; admission €3; ⊗ 9am-1pm Mon-Fri year-round, 2-4.30pm Jun-Sep). Be sure to pick up the excellent *Mountmellick Heritage Trail* booklet. Various linens and quilts still being made by locals are for sale here.

Mountmellick is on the N80, 10km north of Portlaoise.

Portarlington

pop 3300

Portarlington (Cúil an tSúdaire) grew up under the influence of French Huguenot and German settlers and has some fine 18th-century buildings along French and Patrick Sts, although many have been neglected. The 1851 **St Paul's Church** (admission free; ⊗ 7am-7pm), on the site of the original 17th-century French church, was built for the Huguenots, some of whose tombstones stand in a corner of the churchyard. It's about 18km northwest of Portlaoise.

About 4km east of town are the impressive ivy-covered ruins of 13th-century **Lea Castle** on the banks of the River Barrow, once the stronghold of Maurice Fitzgerald, second baron of Offaly. The castle consists of a fairly intact towered keep with two outer walls and a twin-towered gatehouse. Access is through a farmyard 500m to the north off the main Monasterevin road (R420).

Emo Court

The unusual, green-domed **Emo Court** (☎ 086-810 7916; www.heritageireland.ie; Emo; adult/child €2.90/1.30, grounds free; ⊗ 10.30am-6.30pm Tue-Sun mid-Jun–mid-Sep, last admission 5.45pm, grounds open daylight hr year-round) is an impressive house, designed by James Gandon (architect of Dublin's Custom House) in 1790. It was originally the country seat of the first earl of Portarlington. After many years as a Jesuit novitiate,

the house, with its elaborate central rotunda, was impressively restored.

The extensive grounds contain over 1000 different trees (including huge sequoias) and shrubs from all over the world, and are littered with Greek statues. You'll say 'mother!' when you see 'The Clucker', an impressive ornamental garden. Enjoy a picnic or a long walk through the woodlands to Emo Lake.

Emo is about 13km northeast of Portlaoise, just off the R422, 2km west of the M7.

Rock of Dunamaise

The **Rock of Dunamaise** (admission free; ⊗ daylight hr; Ⓟ) is an arresting sight, dramatically perched on a craggy limestone outcrop. It was first recorded on Ptolemy's map of AD 140 and suffered successive waves of Viking, Norman, Irish and English invasion and occupation. Cromwell's henchmen finally destroyed the site in 1650.

Stabilisation of the ruins is ongoing and, for now, require a dose of imagination. However, the views from the summit are sweeping on a clear day; bring a picnic. If you're lucky you'll be able to see Timahoe round tower to the south, the Slieve Blooms to the west and the Wicklow Mountains to the east.

The rock is situated 6km east of Portlaoise along the Stradbally road (N80). **Portlaoise Taxi Service** (☎ 057-866 2270) will take you out there for about €20 return.

Stradbally

☎ 057 / pop 1200

Strung out along the N80, the pretty village of Stradbally, 10km southeast of Portlaoise, is home to the annual **Electric Picnic** (www.electric picnic.ie), an open-air music concert over three days that bills itself as 'boutique' because admission is limited to 32,000 (three-day pass: €220). Rocking the grounds of Stradbally Estate are the likes of Björk, Jarvis Cocker, Primal Scream and Josh Wink.

Appealing to a rather different crowd, the **Stradbally Steam Museum** (☎ 864 1878; www .stradballysteammuseum.com; admission €5; ⊗ 10am-4pm Sat & Sun) is a haven for steam enthusiasts, with a collection of lovingly restored fire engines, steam tractors and steamrollers. During the August bank-holiday weekend the museum hosts a two-day rally where the 40-hectare estate of Stradbally Hall is taken over by steam-operated machinery and vintage cars.

CENTRAL SOUTH

The 1895 Guinness Brewery steam locomotive in the village is closely associated with the museum and is used for trips on a short stretch of volunteer-built **narrow-gauge railway** (www.irishsteam.ie; admission varies; 🕑 2.30-5pm Sun & Mon bank holiday weekends Easter-Oct).

JJ Kavanagh & Sons (☎ 056-883 1106; www.jjkavanagh.ie) runs Portlaoise–Kilkenny buses that pass through Stradbally (from Portlaoise €3.50, 15 minutes, two daily Monday to Saturday).

Stradbally is also on the Bus Éireann Waterford–Longford service (two buses daily Monday to Saturday, one Sunday), which also passes through Kilkenny, Carlow, Portlaoise (€3.20, 15 minutes) and Athlone.

Timahoe
pop 500

Tiny Timahoe casts a real charm, even if the village is nothing more than a handful of houses fronting a grassy triangle. Screened by a babbling stream, and straight out of a fairytale, is a tilting 30m-tall, 12th-century **round tower** – all it needs is Rapunzel to complete the picture. The tower, with its unusual carved Romanesque doorway high up on the side is part of an ancient site that includes the ruins of a 15th-century church. The entire place has a certain magical quality, enhanced by a dearth of visitors most times.

Timahoe is 13km southeast of Portlaoise on the R426.

MOUNTRATH
☎ 057 / pop 1400

Another once-prosperous 18th-century linen centre, Mountrath is a low-key village where the highlight is a regular cattle market. Both St Patrick and St Brigid are supposed to have established religious houses here, although no trace of either remains.

Today, the local place of pilgrimage is the 6th-century monastery of St Fintan at Clonenagh, 3km east on the Portlaoise road. Its claim to fame is **St Fintan's Tree**, a large sycamore with a groove filled with water in one of its lower branches and said to have healing properties.

Ballyfin House (8km north of Mountrath) is an architectural treasure, designed by Richard Morrison in 1850. It's closed to visitors as it undergoes the fate of many a historic Irish mansion: conversion to upscale hotel.

ourpick **Roundwood House** (☎ 873 2120; www.roundwoodhouse.com; Slieve Blooms Rd; s/d from €100/150,

weekly rates available; 🕑 Feb-Dec) is the country estate you wish your rich friends owned. It's a superb 17th-century Palladian villa set on verdant grounds at the end of a tree-lined drive. Ten rooms are scattered between the period-piece of a main house and a slightly more modern adjoining structure. Books abound and you can relax and read by a fire in the lounge. Kids love the grounds and cheery dogs. Dinner (per person €30 to €50) is a country treat of local foods; the cheese board is a delight. After dinner, your host Frank Kennan (wife Rosemary handles the cuisine) is ready to share tales while enjoying a few from the well-stocked bar; just be careful how you say 'Bush'.

Mountrath is on the main Bus Éireann Dublin–Limerick route, with up to 14 buses daily in each direction.

SLIEVE BLOOM MOUNTAINS

One of the best reasons for visiting Laois is to explore the Slieve (shlee-ve) Bloom Mountains. Although not as spectacular as some Irish ranges, their sudden rise from a great plain, and the absence of visitors, make them highly attractive. You'll get a real sense of being away from it all as you tread the deserted mountaintop blanket bogs, moorland, pine forests and isolated valleys.

The highest point is Mt Arderin (528m), south of the Glendine Gap on the Offaly border, from where, on a clear day, it's possible to see the highest points of all four of the ancient provinces of Ireland. East is Lugnaquilla in Leinster, west is Nephin in Connaught, north is Slieve Donard in Ulster and southwest is Carrantuohil in Munster.

If you're planning a walking tour, Mountrath to the south and Kinnitty to the north, are good bases. For leisurely walking, **Glenbarrow**, southwest of Rosenallis, has an interesting trail by the cascading River Barrow. Other spots to check out are **Glendine Park**, near the Glendine Gap, and the **Cut mountain pass**.

You can pick up a *Laois Walks Pack* (€2), which has information on more than 30 waymarked walks around the county, from the tourist office in Portlaoise.

The **Slieve Bloom Way** (p700) is a 77km signposted trail that does a complete circuit of the mountains, taking in most major points of interest. You can walk alone, or from May to October you could join a guided group walk organised by the **Slieve Bloom Walking Club** (☎ 0509-37299; www.slievebloom.ie; per person €5-20; ⏲ Sun Jun-Nov). Lengths range from 10km to 20km.

WESTERN LAOIS

About 3km west of Borris-in-Ossory, and once a major coaching stop, is **Ballaghmore Castle** (☎ 0505-21453; www.castleballaghmore.com; Ballaghmore; adult/child €5/3; ⏲ 10am-5pm). This square tower fortress from 1480 is soaked in atmosphere, with heavy, creaking wooden doors, cold stone walls and a mysterious sheila-na-gig. It's all colourfully restored and available to rent for €2000 per weekend. If that's out of your budget, you could stay in the grounds at **Manor Guest House** (per person €60) and self-catering **Rose Cottage** (per week €500).

ABBEYLEIX

☎ 057 / pop 2400

Abbeyleix (abbey-*leeks*), 15km south of Portlaoise, is a pretty tree-lined heritage town with neat houses and a lot of traffic. The original settlement, which grew up around a 12th-century Cistercian monastery, wasn't here at all: local 18th-century landowner Viscount de Vesci levelled the village and moved it to its present location owing to frequent floods in the old location. During the Famine, de Vesci proved a kinder landlord than many, and the fountain obelisk in the square was erected as a thank you from his tenants.

Sights

In an old school building at the northern end of Main St is **Heritage House** (☎ 873 1653; adult/child €4/2; ⏲ 10am-5pm Mon-Sat, 1-5pm Sun Mar-Oct, 9am-5pm Mon-Fri Nov-Feb; Ⓟ), a museum and tourist office that details the town's colourful history. It contains some examples of the Turkish-influenced carpets woven in Abbeyleix from 1904 to 1913 – they even created some for the *Titanic*.

De Vesci's mansion, **Abbeyleix House**, was designed by James Wyatt in 1773. It's 2km southwest of town on the Rathdowney road, but is not open to the public.

Much more ore accommodating are the lavish **Heywood Gardens** (☎ 087-667 5291; www.heritageireland.ie; admission free; ⏲ 8am-9pm May-Aug, to 7pm Apr & Sep, to 5.30pm Oct-Mar; Ⓟ), a Heritage Service–managed property 4.5km southeast of town.

Sleeping & Eating

Farren House Farm Hostel (☎ 873 4032; www.farmhostel.com; dm €20; Ⓟ) In a restored limestone grain loft on a working family farm (tours available), this quirky independent hostel has 45 beds in 14 en-suite rooms. When you call, a) ask about meals, and b) ask about directions. It's about 6km west of Abbeyleix in rural farm country.

Fountain House B&B (☎ 873 1231; Main St; s/d €30/60; Ⓟ) For more than 40 years this friendly little B&B has offered clean lodging right in the centre.

Abbeyleix Manor Hotel (☎ 873 0111; www.abbeyleixmanorhotel.com; s/d €75/130; Ⓟ 💻) The charmless generic exterior here hides 46 spacious, modern rooms with wi-fi inside. Get one in the back, away from the road.

Morrissey's (☎ 873 1281; Main St) This half-pub, half-shop and former travel agency and undertaker is a past winner of the Pub of the Year award. In the half-light you can cradle a pint at the sloping counter while you soak up the atmosphere in the ancient pew seats in front of the potbelly stove. Soak up the pints with a sandwich or other pub snack.

Getting There & Away

Abbeyleix is on the Bus Éireann route to Dublin (€9.30, 1¾ hours) via Portlaoise and Cork (€9.50, 2¾ hours) via Cashel and Cahir. There are six buses each way daily.

DURROW

☎ 057 / pop 1200

Neat rows of houses, pubs and cafés surround Durrow's manicured green. On the western side stands the unmissably imposing gateway to 18th-century **Castle Durrow**, a large Palladian villa. It's now an upmarket 98-room **hotel** (☎ 873 6555; www.castledurrow.com; s/d from €140/200; Ⓟ) and even if you can't stay here, it's well worth nipping into this elegantly restored greystone edifice for a snack on the terrace or a walk through the 30 acres of gardens and woodland. The excellent restaurant (set menu €50, open 7pm to 8.45pm) is supplied by the castle's organic kitchen garden. Rooms vary greatly in style; ask to see a few.

Durrow is 10km south of Abbeyleix, and is accessible by bus (Dublin–Cork route) from the town (€3.10, 10 minutes, six buses daily in each direction).

COUNTY OFFALY

Even if the green and watery county of Offaly seems to slip your itinerary, it won't be for long once you realise it's the home of the ecclesiastical city of Clonmacnoise, one of Ireland's most famous sights. But beyond this must-see attraction, Offaly has much to offer: its lowlands are dotted with monastic ruins, its towns are steeped in history and it has a burgeoning foodie culture.

Geographically, Offaly is dominated by the low-lying bogs. Enormous expanses like the Bog of Allen and the Boora Bog, where peat is extracted on an industrial scale, are horribly scarred. However, in the northeast corner of the county, 665-hectare Clara Bog is remarkably untouched and recognised internationally for its plant and animal life. It's under consideration for Unesco recognition.

To the east the rugged Slieve Bloom Mountains (p356) provide excellent walking, while fishing and water sports are popular on the River Shannon and the Grand Canal. Access www.offaly.ie and www.ireland.ie/offaly for more information.

BIRR

☎ 057 / pop 3650

The warm welcome in Birr belies its name and will make you go 'ahhh'. Two- and three-storey pastel Georgian buildings line its streets. You'll find good accommodation, eating and drinking options and some interesting shops. You'll also find Birr Castle, with its surrounding craggy walls and many attractions, right in the centre.

History

Birr started life as a 6th-century monastic site founded by St Brendan. By 1208 the town had acquired an Anglo-Norman castle, home of the O'Carroll clan who reigned over the surrounding territory.

During the Plantation of 1620, the castle and estate were given to Sir Laurence Parsons, who changed the town's fate by carefully laying out streets, establishing a glass factory and issuing a decree that anyone who 'cast dunge rubbidge filth or sweepings in the forestreet' would be fined four pennies. He also banned barmaids, sentencing any woman caught serving beer to the stocks (obviously he was a Philistine). The castle has remained in the family for 14 generations, and the present earl and his wife still live on the estate.

Orientation

All the main roads converge on Emmet Sq, with its erect column honouring martyred Irish patriot Robert Emmet. In one corner, Dooly's Hotel, dating from 1747, was once a coaching inn on the busy route to the west.

Information

The post office is in the northeastern corner of Emmet Sq.

Tourist office (☎ 932 0110; Castle St; ☉ 9.30am-1pm & 2-5.30pm Mon-Sat May-Sep) Has good regional info as well as that for Birr.

Sights

BIRR CASTLE DEMESNE

It's easy to spend half a day exploring the attractions and gardens of **Birr Castle Demesne** (☎ 932 0336; www.birrcastle.com; adult/child €9/5.50; ☉ 9am-6pm). The 'castle' (all those windows mean 'mansion') itself, however, is a private home and cannot be visited. Most of the present building dates from around 1620, with additional alterations made in the early 19th century.

The 50-hectare castle surroundings are famous for their magnificent **gardens** set around a large artificial lake. They hold over 1000 species of plants in all sizes from all over the world; something always seems to be in bloom. Look for the world's tallest box hedges, planted in the 1780s and now standing 12m high, and the romantic Hornbeam cloister.

The Parsons were a remarkable family of pioneering Irish scientists, and their work is documented in the **historic science centre**. Exhibits include the massive **telescope** built by William Parsons in 1845. The 'leviathan of Parsonstown', as it was known, was the largest telescope in the world for 75 years and attracted a wide variety of scientists and astronomers. It was used to map the moon's surface, and made innumerable discoveries, including the spiral galaxies. After the death of William's son, the telescope, unloved and untended, slowly fell to bits. A huge restoration scheme in the 1990s rebuilt the telescope: it's now fully operational, and demonstrations are held three times daily in high season.

OTHER BUILDINGS & MONUMENTS
Birr has no shortage of first-class Georgian houses; just stroll down tree-lined **Oxmantown Mall**, which connects Rosse Row and Emmet St, or **John's Mall**, to see some of the best examples.

The tourist office hands out a walking map that details the most important landmarks, including a **statue** of the third earl of Rosse, the megalithic **Seffin Stone** (said to have marked the centre of Ireland) and **St Brendan's Old Churchyard**, reputedly the site of the saint's 6th-century settlement.

Activities
A beautiful tree-lined **riverside walk** runs east along the River Camcor from Oxmantown Bridge to Elmgrove Bridge.

If you're feeling more energetic, **Birr Outdoor Education Centre** (☎ 912 0029; www.oec.ie; Roscrea Rd) offers hill walking, rock climbing and abseiling in the nearby Slieve Blooms, as well as canoeing and kayaking on local rivers.

Birr Equestrian Centre (☎ 912 1961; www.birr equestrian.ie; Kingsborough House; treks per hr €25), 3km outside Birr on the Clareen road, runs treks in the surrounding farmland and forests.

Sleeping
Birr has a good range of central accommodation at moderate prices.

Maltings Guesthouse (☎ 912 1345; themaltings birr@eircom.net; Castle St; s/d from €50/80; P) Based in an 1810 malt storehouse once used by Guinness, this place has a serene location right by the castle and the River Camcor. The 13 tastefully decorated rooms are fine value and there's a popular restaurant downstairs.

Stables Guesthouse (☎ 912 0263; www.thestables restaurant.com; 6 Oxmantown Mall; s/d from €50/80) Located on one of Birr's finest streets, this graceful, greystone Georgian town house is full of character. The six rooms are nicely decorated and if your luggage is light, there's a well-regarded boutique.

Walcot B&B (☎ 912 1247; walcot@hotmail.com; cnr Oxmantown Mall & Ross Row; s/d from €50/90; P) Right across from the castle, this solid B&B has a simple elegance, exemplified by the formal dining room for breakfast. The six plush rooms overlook a tranquil private garden.

Dooly's Hotel (☎ 912 0032; www.doolyshotel.com; Emmet Sq; r from €65-150; P ▯) This local landmark couldn't be more central. Few vestiges of its coach-house past remain and its 18 modern rooms have broadband internet access.

Eating & Drinking
You can eat and drink well in Birr at interesting restaurants and in often-music-filled pubs.

Emma's Café & Deli (☎ 912 5678; 31 Main St; meals €4-8; ⏱ 9.30am-6pm Mon-Sat year-round, 12.30-5.30pm Sun Jun-Aug) Good smells waft out onto Birr's main shopping street from this simple yet stylish café. Huddle around wooden tables inside or out front to enjoy organic soup, paninis and warm, homemade scones.

Riverbank (☎ 912 1528; Riverstown; meals €8-28; ⏱ 12.30-2.30pm & 5.30-10pm Tue-Sun) As the name implies, this casually elegant place is right on a stretch of the pretty River Brosna, 1.5km south of the centre off the N52. Tables outside let you hear the flowing water over a drink. The food changes seasonally and is a creative take on modern Irish.

Spinners (☎ 912 1673; Castle St; meals €12-30; ⏱ 4-9pm Wed-Mon, 12.30-2.30pm Sun) Hidden behind the thick walls of this beautifully restored woollen mill is a fine restaurant with a varied and seasonal menu with many dishes sourced locally. Solid meaty fare mingles with seafood and veggie options. The courtyard terrace is a summertime delight.

Thatch (☎ 912 0682; Crinkill; set dinner €40; ⏱ Tue-Sat) Some 2km southeast of Birr off the N62, this gorgeous 200-year-old eponymously

---

DETOUR: GHOSTS AT LEAP CASTLE

Ireland's most haunted castle, **Leap Castle** (☎ 057-913 1115; seanfryan@oceanfree.net; R421; admission €6; ✆ call for opening times) originally kept guard over a crucial route between Munster and Leinster. The castle was the scene of many dreadful deeds, and has quaint features like dank dungeons and a 'Bloody Chapel'. It's famous for its eerie apparitions – the most renowned inhabitant is the 'smelly ghost', a spirit that leaves a horrible stench behind after sightings.

Renovations are ongoing but you can visit. It lies about 12km southeast of Birr between Kinnitty and Roscrea (in Tipperary) off the R421. If it looks familiar, it's because an especially creepy image of Leap Castle was used on the cover of several editions of Tim Winton's The Riders.

---

roofed pub is a country delight. Enjoy a perfectly poured pint at picnic tables or inside at the bar, which defines the phrase 'Irish pub'. The food lives up to the surroundings: lots of simply prepared meats and seafood with the seasons. Pub grub is also available; book.

Craughwell's (☎ 21839; Castle St) Stop for a snootful at Craughwell's, renowned for its rollicking traditional session on Friday night and impromptu sing-along sessions on Saturday.

Chestnut (☎ 912 2011; Green St) Easily the most appealing pub in the centre, the Chestnut dates to 1823. The current incarnation mixes style with hops, both on full display in the hidden garden. Summer sees regular barbecue nights.

Entertainment

Besides the places listed above, you'll find many more humble boozers about Birr.

Melba's Nite Club (☎ 912 0032; Emmet Sq; ✆ Fri-Sun) In the basement of Dooly's Hotel, this dance place gives fine insight into the potato- and stout-fuelled mating habits of rural Ireland.

Birr Theatre & Arts Centre (☎ 912 2911; www.birr theatre.com; Oxmantown Hall) A vibrant place with a regular line-up of films, local drama, well-known musicians and more.

Getting There & Away

Bus Éireann runs buses on three main routes: to Dublin (€13.20, 3½ hours, one daily) via Tullamore, to Limerick (€14.20, 1¼ hours, five daily) and to Athlone (€8.20, one hour, five daily).

Kearns Transport (☎ 0509-22244; www.kearns transport.com) has three to four buses daily to Tullamore and Portumna plus a weekend service to Galway.

All buses depart from Emmet Sq; look for signs with the latest schedules.

KINNITTY

☎ 057 / pop 500

Kinnitty is a quaint little village that makes a good base for the Slieve Bloom Mountains (p356). Driving out of Kinnitty, the roads across the mountains to Mountrath and Mountmellick, both in County Laois, are particularly scenic.

Look out for the bizarre 10m-high **stone pyramid** in the village graveyard behind the Church of Ireland. In the 1830s, Richard Bernard commissioned this scale replica of the Cheops pyramid in Egypt for the family crypt.

The shaft of the 9th-century **Kinnitty High Cross** was nabbed by Kinnitty Castle in the 19th century and is now displayed on the hotel's terrace. Adam and Eve and the Crucifixion are clearly visible on either face.

Sleeping & Eating

Ardmore House (☎ 913 7009; www.kinnitty.net; the Walk; s/d from €45/70; P ☐) Fresh air, turf fires and home-made brown bread are the order of the day at this lovely Victorian stone farmhouse with five simple guest rooms. Numbers two and five have views of the weird pyramid and the heathery mountains. If you're a rambler, ask about their walking packages. The B&B is set off the R440, about 200m east of Kinnitty.

Kinnitty Castle Demesne (☎ 913 7318; www .kinnittycastle.com; r from €215; P ☐) This former O'Carroll residence, rebuilt in neo-Gothic style in the 19th century, is one of Ireland's most renowned mansions. Set on a vast estate, it is now a luxury hotel much in demand for weddings of those who have accountants to ponder the bill. You can act the lord and try your hand at falconry or archery, walk the mannered grounds or just relax in one of the 37 luxurious rooms (all with wi-fi). The Georgian-style restaurant (mains €20 to €30) is a formal feast; there's traditional music in the Dungeon Bar Friday nights. The castle is 3km southeast of town off the R440.

BANAGHER & AROUND
☎ 057 / pop 1800

Pastel-fronted vintage buildings march down Banagher's long main street to the banks of the River Shannon. It's popular with boaters, thanks to the modern marina. The town is pretty laid-back but has some impressive fortifications on the west bank of the river and some bits of literary history.

Charlotte Brontë had her honeymoon in Banagher in 1854 – no one links her untimely death nine months later to the place. Thirteen years earlier, Anthony Trollope, fresh from inventing the pillarbox, took up a job as a post-office clerk in the village; in his spare time he managed to complete his first novel, *The Macdermots of Ballycloran*.

Information
Tourist office (☎ 915 2155; offalywest@hotmail.com; Crank House, Main St; ☼ 9am-1pm & 2-5pm Mon-Fri) Inside an unusual bow-fronted Georgian town house, this office provides information about Banagher and the surrounding region. Internet access is available for €1 per 15 minutes.

Sights
Sited at a crossing point over the River Shannon, Banagher was a place of enormous strategic importance during turbulent times. **Cromwell's Castle** was built in the 1650s, but modified during the Napoleonic Wars, when **Fort Eliza** (a five-sided gun battery whose guardhouse, moat and retaining walls can still be seen), a **military barracks** and **Martello Tower** were also built.

St Paul's Church at the top of Main St contains a resplendent stained-glass window originally intended for Westminster Abbey.

Many while away an afternoon on the trails and roads along the marshy banks of the Rivers Shannon and Little Brosna.

About 3km south of Banagher off the R439 in Lusmagh is **Cloghan Castle** (☎ 915 1650; Lusmagh; per person €10; ☼ by prior arrangement), in use for nearly 800 years. The castle has seen more than its fair share of bloodshed, beginning life as a McCoghlan stronghold and later becoming home to the mighty O'Carroll clan. Today the castle consists of a well-preserved Norman keep and an adjoining 19th-century house full of interest-ing antiques and armaments. The tour takes about an hour.

About 8km south of Banagher, along tiny tracks on the County Galway side of the border, is the 15th-century **Meelick Church**, one of the oldest churches still in use in Ireland.

Activities
In mild months, look for canoes for rent down by the marina. On calm summer days the waters here are perfect for a paddle.

A number of companies rent out beefier cruisers that you can use to navigate Ireland's waterways, including the Royal and Grand Canals (see p340); prices shown are for high season:

Carrick Craft (☎ 01-278 1666; www.cruise-ireland .com; the Marina) Four- to eight-person berths ranging from €1000 to €2500 per week.

Silverline Cruisers (☎ 915 1112; www.silverline cruisers.com; the Marina) Two- to eight-person berths from €900 to €2700 per week.

Sleeping & Eating
Unless you're making like Seaman Staines and bedding down in your own berth, choices locally are limited.

Crank House Hostel (☎ 915 1458; abguinan@eircom .net; Crank House, Main St; dm €14; P) This Independent Holiday Hostels of Ireland (IHH) facility is Offaly's only hostel. It has 40 beds in a variety of decent two- and four-bed rooms, a laundry, a kitchen and a pottery studio ('dude, nice pot').

Charlotte's Way (☎ 915 3864; charlottesway@hotmail .com; the Hill; s/d €40/70; P) This nicely restored former rectory offers four comfy good-value rooms. Breakfasts star eggs fresh from the hens outside. A honeymooning Charlotte Brontë was a frequent visitor and, after her death, her husband Arthur lived here as the rector.

Brosna Lodge Hotel (☎ 915 1350; www.brosnalodge .com; Main St; s/d from €50/90; P) This family-run hotel in the centre of town has 14 decent-sized rooms decorated in nautical colours, and offers good value for money. The restaurant (mains €9 to €16) and pub enjoy limited competition; there's a beer garden.

Heidi's Irish Coffee Shop (☎ 956 2680; mains €4-10; ☼ 9am-6pm) Around the corner from the tourist office, Heidi's name may refer to the time when a daring sandwich ingredient was margarine. Popular with locals; conversation stops when a visitor enters.

CENTRAL SOUTH

DETOUR: SHANNON HARBOUR

Just 1km east of where the Grand Canal joins the River Shannon, **Shannonbridge** is a tiny town that is fun for a stop or a stay. Locks regulate the waters and you can see far across the marshy plains. Walking paths stretch in all directions.

High above it all, the 1806 **Harbour Master's House** (☎ 057-915 1480; gkirwan@iol.ie; s/d from €50/80; ☼ Mar-Dec; Ⓟ) overlooks the canal. It is run by the daughter of an actual harbour master and has five nice rooms of varying sizes. Nearby are two pubs whose appeal varies by season: Gleeson's has a beer garden while the Harbour has a fireplace and food.

The village is about 10km east of Banagher off the R356. Nearby, 16th-century **Clonony Castle** is enclosed by an overgrown castellated wall. Tales that Henry VIII's second wife, Anne Boleyn, was born here are unlikely to be true, but her cousins Elizabeth and Mary Boleyn are buried beside the ruins.

Entertainment

JJ Hough (☎ 915 1893; Main St) Rivalling the river as Banagher's most appealing feature, Hough's is a 250-year-old pub with vines on that vintage covering the front. Renowned for music, there are trad sessions most nights in summer and on weekends in winter. Or entertain yourself absorbing the artefact-covered walls or counting stars in the beer garden.

Getting There & Away

Kearns Transport (☎ 0509-22244; www.kearnstransport .com) links Banagher to Birr one time daily.

SHANNONBRIDGE

☎ 090 / pop 380

Perfectly picturesque, Shannonbridge gets its name from a narrow 16-span, 18th-century bridge that crosses the river into County Roscommon. It's a small, sleepy village with just one main street and two pubs (the Village Tavern is great for trad music). A sometime tourist office operates at the east end of the bridge.

You can't miss the massive 19th-century **fortifications** on the western bank, where heavy artillery was installed to bombard Napoleon in case he was cheeky enough to try to invade by the river. The fort has been reincarnated as the **Old Fort Restaurant** (☎ 967 4973; mains €15-28; ☼ 5-9.30pm Wed-Sat, 12.30-2.30pm Sun year-round), which serves pricey versions of Irish standards. Tables outside have bridge views.

Clonmacnoise & West Offaly Railway Bog Tour

Ride a train into the heart of the Blackwater Bog on this **tour** (Bord Na Móna; ☎ 967 4450; www

.bnm.ie; adult/child €7/5; ☼ 10am-5pm Mon-Fri Apr, May & Sep, daily Jun-Aug; Ⓟ), which runs on a narrow-gauge railway line once used to transport peat. The diesel locomotive moves at around 10km/h – slow enough to take in the landscape and its special flora, which has remained unchanged for thousands of years. Stops let you try peat cutting.

To get there from Shannonbridge, follow the R357 east towards Cloghan for about 5km, then take the signposted turn north and follow the road for another 3km.

CLONMACNOISE

☎ 090 / pop 320

Gloriously placed overlooking the River Shannon, **Clonmacnoise** (☎ 967 4195; www.heritageireland .ie; adult/child €5.30/2.10; ☼ 9am-7pm Jun–mid-Sep, 10am-6pm mid-Sep–Oct & mid-Mar–May, 10am-5pm Nov–mid-Mar, last admission 45min before closing; Ⓟ) is one of Ireland's most important ancient monastic cities. The site is enclosed in a walled field and contains numerous early churches, high crosses, round towers and graves in astonishingly good condition. The surrounding marshy area is known as the Shannon Callows, home to many wild plants and one of the last refuges of the seriously endangered corncrake (a pastel-coloured relative of the coot).

History

Roughly translated, Clonmacnoise (Cluain Mhic Nóis) means 'Meadow of the Sons of Nós'. The marshy land would have been impassable for early traders, who instead chose to travel by water or on *eskers* (raised ridges formed by glaciers). When St Ciarán founded a monastery here in AD 548 it was the most important crossroads in the country, the intersection of the north–south River

Shannon, and the east–west Esker Riada (Highway of the Kings).

The giant ecclesiastical city had a humble beginning and Ciarán died just seven months after building his first church. Over the years Clonmacnoise grew to become an unrivalled bastion of Irish religion, literature and art and attracted a large lay population. Between the 7th and 12th centuries, monks from all over Europe came to study and pray here, helping to earn Ireland the title of the 'land of saints and scholars'. Even the high kings of Connaught and Tara were brought here for burial.

Most of what you can see today dates from the 10th to 12th centuries. The monks would have lived in small huts scattered in and around the monastery, which would probably have been surrounded by a ditch or rampart of earth.

The site was burned and pillaged on numerous occasions by both the Vikings and the Irish. After the 12th century it fell into decline, and by the 15th century it was home only to an impoverished bishop. In 1552 the English garrison from Athlone reduced the site to a ruin: 'Not a bell, large or small, or an image, or an altar, or a book, or a gem, or even glass in a window, was left which was not carried away,' was reported at the time.

Among the treasures that survived the continued onslaughts are the crosier of the abbots of Clonmacnoise in the National Museum, Dublin, and the 12th-century *Leabhar na hUidhre* (The Book of the Dun Cow), now in the Royal Irish Academy in Dublin.

Information

There's an excellent on-site museum and café; a regional **tourist office** (☎ 967 4134; ☻ 10am-5.45pm Easter-Oct) is near the entrance. If you want to avoid summer crowds it's a good idea to visit early or late; the tiny country lanes nearby can clog with coaches. Plan on a visit of at least a couple of hours.

Sights

MUSEUM

Three connected conical huts near the entrance house the museum and echo the design of early monastic dwellings. The centre's 20-minute audiovisual show is an excellent introduction to the site.

The exhibition area contains the original high crosses (replicas have been put in their former locations outside), and various artefacts uncovered during excavation, including silver pins, beaded glass and an ogham stone. It also contains the largest collection of early Christian grave slabs in Europe. Many are in remarkable condition, with inscriptions clearly visible, often starting with *oroit do* or *ar* (a prayer for).

HIGH CROSSES

Well done to the museum for their moody display: there's a real sense of drama as you descend to the foot of the imposing sandstone **Cross of the Scriptures**, one of Ireland's finest. It's

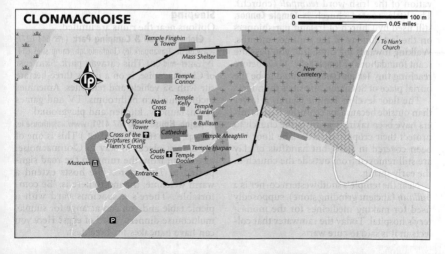

CLONMACNOISE

0 — 100 m
0 — 0.05 miles

Temple Finghin & Tower
Mass Shelter
Temple Connor
North Cross
Temple Kelly
Temple Ciarán
O'Rourke's Tower
Bullaun
Cross of the Scriptures (King Flann's Cross)
Cathedral
South Cross
Temple Meaghlin
Temple Hurpan
Temple Doolin
Temple Dowling
Entrance
Museum
New Cemetery
To Nun's Church
P

very distinctive, with unique upward-tilting arms and richly decorated panels depicting the Crucifixion, the last judgement, the arrest of Jesus and Christ in the tomb. A couple of figures with natty beards have been interpreted as Abbot Cólman and King Flann, who erected the 4m-high cross.

Only the shaft of the **North Cross**, which dates from around AD 800, remains. It is adorned by lions, convoluted spirals and a single figure, thought to be the Celtic god Cerrunnos, or Carnunas, who sits in a Buddha like position. The richly decorated **South Cross** has mostly abstract carvings – swirls, spirals and fretwork – and, on the western face, the Crucifixion plus a few odd critters cavorting.

CATHEDRAL

The biggest building at Clonmacnoise, the cathedral was originally built in AD 909, but was significantly altered and remodelled over the centuries. Its most interesting feature is the intricate 15th-century Gothic doorway with carvings of Sts Francis, Patrick and Dominic. A whisper carries from one side of the door to the other, and this feature was supposedly used by lepers to confess their sins without infecting the priests.

The last high kings of Tara – Turlough Mór O'Connor (died 1156) and his son Ruairí, or Rory (died 1198) – are said to be buried near the altar.

TEMPLES

The small churches are called temples, a derivation of the Irish word *teampall* (church). The little, roofed church is **Temple Connor**, still used by Church of Ireland parishioners on the last Sunday of the summer months. Walking towards the cathedral, you pass the scant foundations of **Temple Kelly** (1167) before reaching tiny **Temple Ciarán**, reputed to be the burial place of St Ciarán, the site's founder.

The floor level in Temple Ciarán is lower than outside because for centuries local farmers have been taking clay from the church to protect their crops and cattle. The floor has been covered in slabs, but handfuls of clay are still removed from outside the church in the early spring.

Near the temple's southwestern corner is a *bullaun* (ancient grinding stone), supposedly used for making medicines for the monastery's hospital. Today the rainwater that collects in it is said to cure warts.

Continuing round the compound you come to 12th-century **Temple Melaghlin**, with its attractive windows, and the twin structures of **Temple Hurpan** and **Temple Doolin**.

ROUND TOWERS

Overlooking the River Shannon is the 20m-high **O'Rourke's Tower**. Lightning blasted the top off the tower in 1135, but the remaining structure was used for another 400 years.

Temple Finghin and its round tower are on the northern boundary of the site, also overlooking the Shannon. The building dates from around 1160 and has some fine Romanesque carvings. The herringbone-patterned tower roof is the only one in Ireland that has never been altered. Most round towers became shelters when the monasteries were attacked, but this one was probably just used as a bell tower since the doorway is at ground level.

OTHER REMAINS

Beyond the site's boundary wall, about 500m east through the modern graveyard, is the secluded **Nun's Church**. From here the main site, including the towers, is invisible. The church has wonderful Romanesque arches with minute carvings; one has been interpreted as Ireland's earliest sheila-na-gig, but is more probably an acrobat.

To the west of the site, on the ridge near the car park, is a motte with the oddly shaped ruins of a 13th-century **castle**, where the walls need team-effort to stay erect.

Sleeping

Options near the ruins are limited.

Glebe Caravan & Camping Park (☎ 643 0277; www.glebecaravanpark.ie; Clonfanlough; camp sites €14; ☒ Easter–mid-Oct) This caravan park, 5km east of Clonmacnoise, is on a pretty three-hectare site with 35 vehicle and tent sites. Amenities include modern bathrooms, TV and games room, laundry, kitchen and playground.

Kajon House (☎ 967 4191; www.kajonhouse.ie; Creevagh; d from €67; ☒ Feb–Oct; ℗) This is one of the closest places to stay to Clonmacnoise: just 1.5km from the ruins on the road signposted to Tullamore. The hosts extend a warm welcome; the motto here is: 'Be comfortable'. There's a spacious yard with a picnic table and you can arrange for simple, multicourse dinners. Tired of eggs? Here you can have pancakes for breakfast.

Getting There & Away

Clonmacnoise is 7km northeast of Shannon-bridge on the R444 and about 24km south of Athlone in County Westmeath. By car you can explore this interesting and evocative area at leisure.

Paddy Kavanagh (☎ 087-240 7706; pkmail@eircom .net) in Athlone runs private tours to Clonmacnoise and the Clonmacnoise & West Offaly Railway bog tour. Prices are subject to variation depending on the number of people and how long you want to be at the site.

There are river cruises to Clonmacnoise from Athlone in County Westmeath (see p500).

A **taxi** (☎ 090-647 4400) from Athlone will cost roughly €50, including an hour's wait.

TULLAMORE

☎ 057 / pop 10,400

Tullamore (Tulach Mór), Offaly's county town, is a busy place with a burgeoning population of fortune-seekers from Eastern Europe. This is the place to get a *perogi* with your pint.

The town suffered two strange setbacks in its history. In 1764, the earl drowned in a freak accident. As his son was only six months old at the time, and unable to grant new building leases until he was of legal age, the town did a Rip Van Winkle for the next 21 years. It was rudely awakened by a second freak accident, when a hot-air balloon crashed in 1785 and burnt down most of the town.

In the long run, the effect was negligible: Tullamore is prosperous and famous for smooth Tullamore Dew whiskey. Despite one minor detail (production has moved to County Tipperary), you can still visit the old distillery on the banks of the Grand Canal and have a snifter of the amber liquid.

Information

Post office (O'Connor Sq)
Tourist office (☎ 932 5015; tullamoredhc@eircom .net; Bury Quay; ⏰ 9am-6pm Mon-Sat & noon-5pm Sun May-Sep, 10am-5pm Mon-Sat & noon-5pm Sun Oct-Apr) Somewhat inconveniently located away from parking inside the Tullamore Dew Heritage Centre.
Tullamore Internet Cafe (☎ 936 0387; 5 Kilbridge St; per 15min €1; ⏰ 10am-11pm) Near the tourist office.

Sights

TULLAMORE DEW HERITAGE CENTRE

Located in an 1897 canalside whiskey warehouse, the **heritage centre** (☎ 932 5015; www .tullamore-dew.org; Bury Quay; adult/child €6/3.20; ⏰ 9am-6pm Mon-Sat & noon-5pm Sun May-Sep, 10am-5pm Mon-Sat & noon-5pm Sun Oct-Apr) mixes intriguing local history with booze propaganda. Fortunately the emphasis is on the former, and engaging exhibits show the local role of the Grand Canal, which passes out the front. This is the place to first get the lowdown on the 1785 balloon conflagration, then down a shot of whiskey.

CHARLEVILLE FOREST CASTLE

Spires, turrets, clinging ivy and creaking trees combine to give this hulking structure a haunted feel. **Charleville Forest Castle** (☎ 932 3040; www.charlevillecastle.com; 1- to 2-person admission €16, per additional person €8; ⏰ regular tours Jul & Aug, by appointment Sep-Jun) was the family seat of the Burys, who commissioned the design in 1798 from Francis Johnston, one of Ireland's most famous architects. The interior is spectacular, with stunning ceilings and one of the most striking Gothic-revival galleries in Ireland. The kitchen block was built to resemble a country church.

Admission is by 35-minute tour only. If you'd like to help restore this pile, you can join groups of international volunteers; contact the castle for details (and also to confirm opening hours). The entrance is off the N52, south of Tullamore. Frustration ensues if you go too far and reach Blue Ball, a village with hairy traffic.

Activities

For information on hiring narrow boats on the canal, see p341.

DETOUR: LOUGH BOORA

Much of County Offaly's once extensive bogs were stripped of peat for electricity generation during the 20th century. One area, **Lough Boora** (www.loughbooraparklands.com), is now the focus of a scheme to restore its environment. Located 5km east of Blue Ball off the N357, the lough comprises 2000 hectares. Over 50km of trails have been built and there are bird-watching spots and other places where you can pause and see nature reclaiming this land. Numerous large environmental sculptures by noted artists are scattered about.

Sleeping

Ask at the tourist office for a list of simple B&Bs.

Moorhill Hotel (☎ 932 1395; www.moorhill.ie; Clara Rd; s/d from €80/100; **P** 🖵) This Victorian retreat has 42 rooms in a complex of two-storey wings. Furnishings are a mix of modern and antique; there's wi-fi throughout. The hotel is set amid chestnut trees about 3km north of town on the N80. Guests enjoy the Irish-French restaurant (mains from €18).

Tullamore Court Hotel (☎ 934 6666; www.tullamore courthotel.ie; O'Moore St; r €80-200; **P** 🖵) This modern hotel on the edge of the centre brings a dash of style to workman-like Tullamore. The 104 rooms are spacious and well-equipped for business with features such as wi-fi. Best are luxurious suites in a new wing that overlook the town.

Eating & Drinking

There's a good farmers market every Saturday on Millennium Sq and Main St.

Mezzo (☎ 932 9333; Patrick St; mains €10-16; ☼ 5-9pm) Not vastly authentic (note the fajitas and the Thai chicken this and that), but the mostly Italian menu at this attractive little bistro is good and portions are huge. Pasta is garlicky, pizzas crispy and the seafood better than average. Bring your own booze.

Brewery Tap (☎ 932 1131; O'Connor Sq) One of several atmospheric boozers in the centre, this one gets gregarious, has live music many nights and pours an honest pint.

Getting There & Away

BUS

Bus Éireann stops at the train station, located south of town. From Tullamore there are buses to Dublin (€12.60, two hours, three daily), to Portumna (€4.20, 40 minutes, one daily) via Birr and to Waterford (€16.70, 3¼ hours, two daily) via Portlaoise, Carlow and Kilkenny.

Kearns Transport (☎ 912 0124; www.kearnstransport .com) also serves Birr and Dublin with several buses daily.

TRAIN

There are fast trains east to Dublin (€16.50, 1¼ hours, 10 daily) and west to Galway (€17.50, 1½ hours, six daily) as well as Westport and Sligo. The station is on the southwest edge of the centre on Cormac St.

DURROW ABBEY

Founded by St Colmcille (also known as St Columba) in the 6th century, Durrow Abbey is most famous for producing the illustrated *Book of Durrow*. The 7th-century text is the earliest of the great manuscripts to have survived – a remarkable feat considering it was recovered from a farm where it was dipped in the cattle's drinking water to cure illnesses. It can be seen today at Trinity College, Dublin.

The site contains five early-Christian gravestones and Durrow's splendid 10th-century **high cross**, whose complex, high relief carvings depict the sacrifice of Isaac, the Last Judgement and the Crucifixion; it was possibly created by the same stonemason who carved the Cross of the Scripture at Clonmacnoise. In 2003 the government bought the site and has begun a laborious process of restoration. Various areas may be closed to visitors.

The path north past the church leads to **St Colmcille's Well**, a place of pilgrimage marked by a small cairn of stones.

Durrow Abbey is 7km north of Tullamore down a long lane west off the N52.

County Clare

Clare (An Clár) is a trip in itself. It combines an Atlantic-pounded coast, and dramatic and unique wind-swept landscapes with artefacts from prehistory through medieval times. Of course all this physical attraction is fine, but what will really get into your soul is that Clare carries a song in its heart. This is the centre for traditional Irish music. From tiny village pubs to large venues, you'll hear the county's musicians not just keeping the legacy of song alive but refining and developing it.

Ennis is the main city. From this hub of narrow streets and nightlife, the entire county is a short trip away. But you'll want to take your time becoming part of Clare's fabric. Wander the coast. The desolate barrens south of Kilkee to Loop Head have dramatic cliffs and sweeping vistas and a surprising paucity of visitors. North, you'll find absolutely wonderful villages such as Miltown Malbay, Ennistymon and Kilfenora, where you'll find character and characters ready to make you feel right at home.

The iconic headlands of the Cliffs of Moher and the music-filled pubs of Doolin are a draw for many. Use them as an excuse to plunge further, for you'll be right on the edge of the Burren, a stark, alien landscape of wild beauty and delightful villages such as Corofin.

Learn the fabric of this water-dashed, windswept land and soon you'll be singing your own songs of joy.

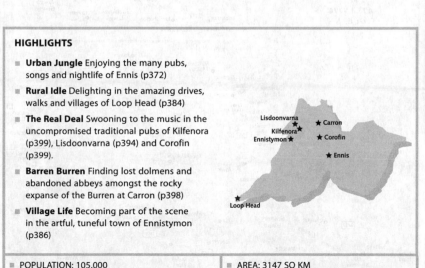

HIGHLIGHTS

- **Urban Jungle** Enjoying the many pubs, songs and nightlife of Ennis (p372)

- **Rural Idle** Delighting in the amazing drives, walks and villages of Loop Head (p384)

- **The Real Deal** Swooning to the music in the uncompromised traditional pubs of Kilfenora (p399), Lisdoonvarna (p394) and Corofin (p399).

- **Barren Burren** Finding lost dolmens and abandoned abbeys amongst the rocky expanse of the Burren at Carron (p398)

- **Village Life** Becoming part of the scene in the artful, tuneful town of Ennistymon (p386)

Lisdoonvarna ★
★ Carron
Kilfenora ★
Ennistymon ★
★ Corofin
★ Ennis
★
Loop Head

- POPULATION: 105,000   - AREA: 3147 SQ KM

COUNTY CLARE

ENNIS & AROUND

ENNIS

☎ 065 / pop 18,900

Ennis (Inis) is a busy commercial centre and lies on the banks of the River Fergus, which runs east, then south into the Shannon Estuary.

It's the place to stay if you want a bit of urban flair; from Ennis, you can reach any part of Clare in under two hours. Short on sights, the town's strengths are its food, lodging and traditional entertainment. The town centre, with its narrow, pedestrian-friendly streets, is home to large, modern stores.

History

The town's medieval origins are indicated by its irregular, narrow streets. Its most important historical site is Ennis Friary, founded in the 13th century by the O'Briens, kings of Thomond, who also built a castle here in the 13th century. Much of the wooden town was destroyed by fire in 1249 and again in 1306, when it was razed by one of the O'Briens.

Orientation

The old town centre is on the Square, and the principal streets, O'Connell St, High St (becoming Parnell St), Bank Pl and Abbey St, radiate from there. There has been an effort to create some pedestrian quarters around Parnell St with mixed results. The large but fairly

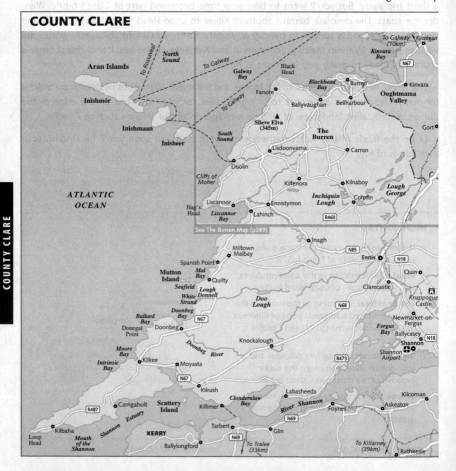

COUNTY CLARE

mundane cathedral (1843) is at the southern end of O'Connell St; its spire is a useful landmark from afar.

The completion of the N18 bypass east of the city has done much to improve traffic, although trips to the coast still take you through the centre.

Information
BOOKSHOPS
Abbey News Agency (36 Abbey St) Good selection of local and international newspapers. It also sells Ordnance Survey maps.

Ennis Bookshop (☎ 682 9000; 13 Abbey St) Good independent shop for maps and books of local interest.

O'Mahony's (☎ 682 8355; Merchant Sq) Large local branch of 100-year-old Limerick store.

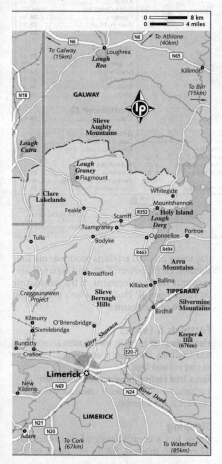

INTERNET ACCESS
Linkserve (☎ 689 3767; 4A Lower Market St; per hr €1; 🕑 10.30am-9pm) Upstairs, bargain prices on surfing and internet calling.

LIBRARIES
De Valera Library (☎ 682 1616; Harmony Row; 🕑 10am-5.30pm Mon, Wed & Thu, to 8pm Tue & Fri, to 2pm Sat) Offers one hour of free internet access. Also has dedicated email screens for short-term use.

MEDICAL SERVICES
Cassidy's Pharmacy (☎ 682 8765; 10 O'Connell St; 🕑 8am-6pm)

MONEY
You can change money and use ATMs at various banks on the Square.

POST
The post office is on Bank Pl, northwest of the Square.

TOURIST INFORMATION
Ennis tourist office (☎ 682 8366; www.shannon regiontourism.ie; Arthur's Row; 🕑 9.30am-5.30pm Jul & Aug, 9.30am-1pm & 2-5.30pm Mon-Sat Mar-Jun & Sep-Dec, 9.30am-1pm & 2-5.30pm Mon-Fri Jan & Feb) Very helpful and efficient. Can book accommodation for a €4 fee; lots of green blarney gifts.

Sights
MONUMENTS & SCULPTURES
In the town centre, the Square, is a **Daniel O'Connell monument**. His election to the British parliament by a huge majority in 1828 forced Britain to lift its bar on Catholic MPs and led to the Act of Catholic Emancipation a year later. The 'Great Liberator' stands on an extremely high column, so far above the rest of us you would hardly know he was there. Eamon de Valera was *teachta Dála* (TD; member of the Irish Parliament) for Clare from 1917 to 1959. There's a **bronze statue** of him near Ennis courthouse.

Numerous **modern sculptures** can be found scattered around the centre. Works such as the *Weathered Woman* on Old Barrack St are both interesting and provide a handy place to sit. Get the *Ennis Sculpture Trail* map from the tourist office.

ENNIS FRIARY
Just north of the Square is **Ennis Friary** (☎ 682 9100; Abbey St; adult/child €1.50/0.75; 🕑 10am-6pm

COUNTY CLARE

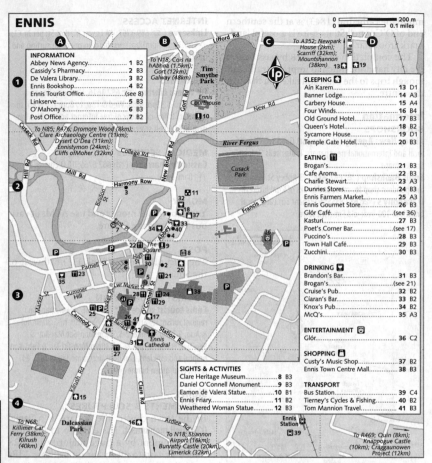

ENNIS

0 ——— 200 m
0 ——— 0.1 miles

INFORMATION
Abbey News Agency.................. 1 B2
Cassidy's Pharmacy.................. 2 B3
De Valera Library...................... 3 B3
Ennis Bookshop....................... 4 B2
Ennis Tourist Office.............(see 8)
Linkserve................................ 5 B3
O'Mahony's............................. 6 B3
Post Office.............................. 7 B3

SLEEPING ◘
Aín Karem............................. 13 D1
Banner Lodge........................ 14 A3
Carbery House....................... 15 A4
Four Winds............................ 16 B4
Old Ground Hotel................... 17 B3
Queen's Hotel........................ 18 B3
Sycamore House..................... 19 D1
Temple Gate Hotel................. 20 B3

EATING ◘
Brogan's................................. 21 B3
Cafe Aroma............................ 22 B3
Charlie Stewart...................... 23 A3
Dunnes Stores........................ 24 B3
Ennis Farmers Market............ 25 A3
Ennis Gourmet Store.............. 26 B3
Glór Café..........................(see 36)
Kasturi.................................. 27 B3
Poet's Corner Bar..............(see 17)
Puccino's............................... 28 B3
Town Hall Café...................... 29 B3
Zucchini................................ 30 B3

DRINKING ◘
Brandon's Bar........................ 31 B3
Brogan's............................(see 21)
Cruise's Pub.......................... 32 B2
Cíaran's Bar........................... 33 B2
Knox's Pub............................ 34 B2
McQ's.................................... 35 A3

ENTERTAINMENT ◘
Glór...................................... 36 C2

SHOPPING ◘
Custy's Music Shop................. 37 B2
Ennis Town Centre Mall.......... 38 B3

TRANSPORT
Bus Station........................... 39 C4
Tierney's Cycles & Fishing....... 40 B2
Tom Mannion Travel............... 41 B3

SIGHTS & ACTIVITIES
Clare Heritage Museum................ 8 B3
Daniel O'Connell Monument......... 9 B3
Eamon de Valera Statue.............. 10 B1
Ennis Friary............................. 11 B2
Weathered Woman Statue........... 12 B3

Jun–mid-Sep, to 5pm Apr, May & mid-Sep–Oct). It was founded by Donnchadh Cairbreach O'Brien, king of Thomond, sometime between 1240 and 1249, but a lot of what you see now was completed in the 14th century. Although it pales compared to ruins elsewhere in Clare, it does has a graceful five-section window dating from the late 13th century, and a McMahon tomb (1460) with alabaster panels depicting scenes from the Passion.

CLARE HERITAGE MUSEUM

Sharing the same building as the tourist office is this diverting little **museum** (☎ 682 3382; Arthur's Row; admission free; ☼ 9.30am-1pm, 2-5.30pm Tue-Sat). The 'Riches of Clare' exhibition tells the story of Clare from 8000 years ago to the present day using original artefacts grouped into four themes: earth, power, faith and water. It also recounts the development of the submarine by Clare-born JP Holland, who's good for at least two of the themes.

Festivals & Events

Fleadh Nua (☎ 682 4276; www.fleadhnua.com) A lively traditional music festival held in late May, with singing, dancing and workshops.
Ennis Trad Festival (www.ennistradfestival.com) Traditional music is performed in venues across town for one week in mid-November.

Sleeping

Ennis has a great variety of places to stay. There are modest B&Bs on most of the main roads into town, some are an easy walk to the centre. Many people come here straight from Shannon Airport, less than 30 minutes south.

BUDGET

The long-running Abbey Tourist Hostel on Harmony Row closed in 2006 and there's no sign of a replacement.

Aín Karem (☎ 682 0024; 7 Tulla Rd; s/d €45/62; P) Northeast of the centre, this modern two-storey house is pleasantly furnished and rooms are standard size. This neighbourhood has several other B&Bs; it's a 10-minute walk to the centre.

Sycamore House (☎ 682 1343; smsfitz@gofree.indigo .ie; Tulla Rd; s/d from €45/62; P) Right across from Aín Karem, there are four modest rooms in this B&B that's in a unassuming modern, one-storey typical Irish house. It's clean and friendly – what more do you want?

MIDRANGE

Banner Lodge (☎ 682 4224; www.bannerlodge.com; Market St; s/d from €45/80) You can't really get more central than this – and what a price! Some of the eight rooms are pretty tight, but given the location it is a fair trade-off. The décor in the 2nd-storey inn is dominated by the bold blue carpet. Service is minimal.

Carbery House (☎ 682 4046; Kilrush Rd; s/d €50/90; P) About a 10-minute walk south from the centre, this orderly B&B has two fireplaces to provide atmosphere – for real warmth, however, crank up the electric blankets on the bed. Early arrivals from the airport are OK, space permitting and credit cards are accepted.

Four Winds (☎ 682 9831; Clare Rd; s/d €50/80; mid-Mar–mid-Oct; P) This is a pleasant two-story house with decent rooms. There's a nice back garden. The friendly owners accept credit cards.

Queens Hotel (☎ 682 8963; www.irishcourthotels.com; Abbey St; s/d from €65/90; P 🖳) Discreetly aged outside, this corner hotel is perfect for those seeking an anonymous stay. The 48 rooms are standard motel in design, with a timeless red and yellow motif. The lobby has wi-fi and, like your internet connection, you can slip through unobserved.

Newpark House (☎ 682 1233; www.newparkhouse .com; s/d €65/100; Easter–Oct; P) A vine-covered country house dating from 1650, Newpark is 2km north of Ennis. The six rooms are a mix of furnishings old and new with many engravings on the walls. To get here go along Tulla Rd to Scarriff road (R352) and turn right at the Roselevan Arms.

TOP END

ourpick **Old Ground Hotel** (☎ 682 8127; www.flynn hotels.com; O'Connell St; s/d from €90/150; P 🖳) The lobby at this local institution is always a scene: old friends sprawl on the sofas, deals are cut at the tables and ladies from the neighbouring church's altar society exchange gossip over tea. Parts of this rambling landmark date back to the 1800s. The 83 rooms vary greatly; some are very nice and have wi-fi.

Temple Gate Hotel (☎ 682 3300; www.templegate hotel.com; the Square; s/d €120/170; P 🖳) Hidden off O'Connell St, you won't get a more central location than at this modest-looking up-market hotel. Inside, the 70 modern rooms have wi-fi. Service is good and should suit business travellers.

Eating

Ennis has a good mix of restaurants, cafés and bars that serve food. The enormous **Dunnes Stores** (☎ 684 0700; Ennis Town Centre Mall; 24hr) has everything from prepared foods to groceries. The **Ennis Farmers Market** (Upper Market St car park; 8am-2pm Fri) lures some of Clare's best producers.

BUDGET

Puccino's (☎ 689 1665; 41 O'Connell St; snacks €2-6; 8am-6pm Mon-Sat) This tiny nook on the main drag has a full coffee bar and blends up fresh fruit smoothies and juices. Jaws need a workout? There are sandwiches.

Glór Café (☎ 684 3103; Friar's Walk; mains €3.75-8.50; 10am-5pm Mon-Sat) The café at Glór, the local arts centre, is suitably artistic. Soups, salads, sandwiches, hot dishes and desserts are creative and enticing. Lots of veggie options.

Ennis Gourmet Store (☎ 684 3314; 1 Old Barrack St; snacks €4-10; 9am-7pm Mon-Sat, noon-6pm Sun) Enjoy a warm drink from the full coffee and tea bar at an outside table at this little gem. There's a range of soups, sandwiches and hot specials plus a deli-cade of Irish cheeses, preserves, good wines and more.

Cafe Aroma (☎ 684 2703; Bank Pl; meals €4-10; 8am-7pm) Spread over three levels, this popular spot always bustles with locals grabbing a freshly made sandwich (try the bacon, avocado and garlic spread wonder) or settling back for something more substantial.

MIDRANGE

Poet's Corner Bar (☎ 682 8127; Old Ground Hotel, O'Connell St; meals €6-12; ⏰ 12.30-9pm) This famous old bar has a deserved reputation for its traditional dishes, from boiled bacon and cabbage with parsley sauce to a thick seafood chowder that transcends its local cliché. The dark surroundings are vintage Clare.

Charlie Stewart (☎ 684 8477; 76 Parnell St; meals €7-18; ⏰ noon-9pm) Burgers, nachos, pastas and other bar foods flesh out the long menu of popular choices at this big, open pub. The kitchen closes ahead of live rock some nights.

Brogan's (☎ 682 9859; 24 O'Connell St; meals €8-20; ⏰ 10am-10pm) The peas at this popular old pub are always well cooked, the supply of spuds never-ending. Classics like bacon and cabbage get top billing although you can ferret out more modern fare.

Kasturi (☎ 684 8060; Carmody St; meals €10-20; ⏰ noon-2.30pm & 6-11pm Mon-Sat, 1-4pm Sun) Indian cuisine is excellent at this most accommodating of restaurants. The staff are gracious, constantly serving the large, mannered dining room. Classics such as tandoori chicken are served with flair.

TOP END

Town Hall Café (☎ 682 8127; O'Connell St; lunches €6-14, dinners €20-35; ⏰ 10am-4.45pm & 6-9.30pm) Adjacent to, and affiliated with, the Old Ground Hotel, this excellent bistro is in the stylishly resurrected old town hall. High ceilings allow large artwork while the spare settings don't compete with the food: casual and creative during the day, more formal and surprising at night. Seafood is excellent.

Zucchini (☎ 686 6566; 7 High St; mains €25-30; ⏰ 5-9.30pm) The vivid-red front tells you that this place is a standout. The ever-changing menu is ambitious: look for interesting options such as local oysters baked with rocket and roasted halibut with saffron. Everything is sourced locally and you'll enjoy handmade breads and desserts plus seafood caught offshore.

Drinking & Entertainment

As the capital of a renowned music county, Ennis is not short of pubs with trad music as well as some contemporary clubs. Where's best changes often but one interesting source is the weekly *Claire People*, which has a colourful column on pubs by local raconteur Cormac MacConnell.

PUBS

Brogan's (☎ 682 9859; 24 O'Connell St) Brogan's sees a fine bunch of musicians ripping the roof off from about 9pm on Tuesday and Thursday plus more nights in summer. On the corner of Cooke's Lane, it's a big pub that stretches a long way back from the street.

Brandon's Bar (☎ 682 8133; O'Connell St) Still holds its own for trad sessions, on Monday nights especially (from about 9.30pm). Brandon's also stages live music, including blues, rock and disco (!).

Cruise's Pub (☎ 684 1800; Abbey St) Cruise's friendly bar has a long side courtyard that's perfect for enjoying a fresh-air pint in the shadow of the old friary. There are trad music sessions most nights from 9.30pm.

Ciaran's Bar (☎ 684 0180; Francis St) Slip into this small place by day and you can be just another geezer pondering a pint. At night there's trad music Wednesday to Sunday.

Knox's Pub (☎ 682 2871; Abbey St) Knox's gives it all its got if you're looking for chart sounds, DJs riffing, full-on football megascreen action and a raucous crowd. Mr Knox, the original coffee, wine and spirits merchant, is no doubt spinning in his grave to the beat of the music. It's open late past midnight.

McQ's (☎ 682 4608; 78 Parnell St) Aromatic peat fires warm this cosy pub that's a haven on a rainy day. There's good food and a few simple B&B rooms upstairs.

VENUES

Cois na hAbhna (☎ 682 0996; ceoltrad@eircom.net; Gort Rd) This pilgrimage point for traditional music and culture is housed in a custom-built pentagonal hall 1.5km north of town along the N18. It has performances and a full range of classes in dance and music. You can hear music on Wednesday nights and there's music and dancing some Saturdays. The archive is a resource centre and a library of Irish traditional music, song, dance and folklore relating mainly to County Clare; books and recordings are on sale.

Glór (☎ 684 3103; www.glor.ie; Friar's Walk) Clare's cultural centre is in a striking modern building. Art, traditional music, theatre, dance, photography and film are some of the programmes offered. There's a strong Irish bias but international influences are celebrated.

COUNTY CLARE

Shopping

Ennis has the best shopping in the county; stock up on essentials in the vast **Ennis Town Centre Mall** with its Dunnes Stores just behind O'Connell St. Look for a discreet passage in. On Saturday morning, there is a market at Market Pl. O'Connell St has the best selection of shops.

Custy's Music Shop (☎ 682 1727; www.custysmusic .com; Francis St) The top place for a terrific stock of Irish music, instruments, other musical items and general info about the scene. Has a shop on the web as well.

Getting There & Away

BUS

The **bus station** (☎ 682 4177) is beside the train station. Buses run from Ennis to: Cork (€11.70, three hours, nine daily); Doolin (€8.80, 1½ hours, three daily) via Corofin, Ennistymon, Lahinch and Liscannor; Galway (€9, 1½ hours, hourly) via Gort; Limerick (€6.30, 40 minutes, hourly) via Bunratty; and to Shannon Airport (€5.40, 50 minutes, hourly). To reach Dublin, connect through Limerick.

TRAIN

From **Ennis station** (☎ 684 0444) there are nine trains daily to Limerick (€8.20, 40 minutes), where you can connect to trains to places further afield like Dublin. There are welcome plans afoot to restore service on the line from Ennis to Galway.

Getting Around

For a taxi call **Burren Taxis** (☎ 682 3456) or pick one up at the taxi stands at the train station and beside the Daniel O'Connell Monument.

Tierney's Cycles & Fishing (☎ 682 9433; 17 Abbey St; ☺ 9am-6pm Mon-Sat) has well-maintained mountain bikes costing €20/80 per day/week to hire, which includes a helmet, lock and repair kit. Staff will recommend routes where you're less likely to end up as road kill.

Tom Mannion Travel (☎ 682 4211; www.tmt-ireland. com; 71 O'Connell St) rents cars.

Parking is fairly good in Ennis. There's a big car park behind the tourist office in Friar's Walk and one alongside the river just off Abbey St. It's pay and display for about €1 per hour.

AROUND ENNIS

North of Ennis is the early Christian site of Dysert O'Dea; to the southeast are several fine castles. Note that much of the county can be enjoyed as a day trip from Ennis.

Local and express buses cover most areas around Ennis, but their frequency varies; many buses run only May to September (some only July and August) and on certain days. Before making plans confirm times and destinations with **Ennis bus station** (☎ 065-682 4177; www.buseireann.ie).

Dysert O'Dea

You can feel the past as you navigate the narrow tracks with grass in the middle to **Dysert O'Dea** (Map p389), where St Tola founded a monastery in the 8th century. The church and high cross, the White Cross of St Tola, date from the 12th or 13th century. The cross depicts Daniel in the lion's den on one side and a crucified Christ above a bishop carved in relief on the other. Look for carvings of animal and human heads in a semicircle on the southern doorway of the Romanesque church. There are also the remains of a 12m-high round tower.

In 1318 the O'Briens, who were kings of Thomond, and the Norman de Clares of Bunratty fought a pitched battle nearby, which the O'Briens won, thus postponing the Anglo-Norman conquest of Clare for some two centuries. The 15th-century O'Dea Castle nearby houses the **Clare Archaeology Centre** (☎ 065-683 7401; adult/child €4/3.50; ☺ 10am-6pm May-Sep). A 3km history trail around the castle passes some two dozen ancient monuments – from ring forts and high crosses to an ancient cooking site. A further 5km walk along a medieval road takes you to another stone fort.

East of Dysert O'Dea is **Dromore Wood** (Map p389; ☎ 065-683 7166; www.heritageireland.ie; Ruan; admission free; ☺ visitor centre 10am-6pm mid-Jun–mid-Sep). This Dúchas nature reserve encompasses some 400 hectares as well as the ruins of the 17th-century O'Brien Castle, two ring forts and the site of Kilakee church.

GETTING THERE & AWAY

Dysert O'Dea is 1.7km off the Corofin road (R476), 11km north of Ennis. Dromore Wood is 8km east, off the N18.

Bus Éireann (☎ 065-682 4177) generally runs one bus daily from Ennis to Doolin, which will stop along the R476.

COUNTY CLARE

Quin

☎ 065 / pop 460

Quin (Chuinche), a tiny village 10km southeast of Ennis, was the site of the Great Clare Find of 1854 – the most important discovery of prehistoric gold in Ireland. Greed and need beat out any good deed and only a few of the several hundred torques, gorgets and other pieces, discovered by labourers working on the Limerick to Ennis railway, made it to the National Museum in Dublin; most were sold and melted down. The source of this and much of ancient Ireland's gold may have been the Wicklow Mountains on the east coast.

The Franciscan friary **Quin Abbey** (☎ 684 4084) was founded in 1433 using part of the walls of an older de Clare castle built in 1280. Despite many periods of persecution, Franciscan monks lived here until the 19th century. The last friar, Father Hogan, who died in 1820, is buried in one corner. The splendidly named Fireballs McNamara, a notorious duellist and member of the region's ruling family, is also buried here. An elegant belfry rises above the main body of the abbey, and you can climb the narrow spiral staircase to look down on the fine cloister and surrounding countryside. The site is always open and you can ponder the encroaching modern graves.

Beside the friary is the 13th-century Gothic **Church of St Finghin**.

Numerous cafés and pubs line the quiet streets near the ruins. On the Ennis side of the village, look for **Zion** (☎ 682 5417; Ennis Rd; meals €6-20; ⏰ 8am-5pm Mon-Wed, to 10pm Thu-Sat). There are good alternative abbey views nearby and you can fortify with excellent coffees, teas and juices. During the day breakfast and fresh and creative lunches are available. Weekend dinners are also creative.

Knappogue Castle

About 3km southeast of Quin is **Knappogue Castle** (☎ 061-368 103; www.shannonheritage.com; adult/child €7/3.35; ⏰ 9.30am-4pm Apr-Oct). It was built in 1467 by the McNamaras, who held sway over a large part of Clare from the 5th to the mid-15th century and built 42 castles in the region. Knappogue's walls are intact, and it has a fine collection of period furniture and fireplaces.

When Oliver Cromwell came to Ireland in 1649, he used Knappogue as a base, which is one of the reasons it was spared from destruction. The McNamara family regained the castle after the Restoration in 1660, since then windows and other features have been added to make it more 'liveable'.

There's the expected souvenir shop in the courtyard. Knappogue also hosts touristy **medieval banquets** (☎ 061-360 788; adult/child €52/26; ⏰ 5.30pm & 8.45pm Apr-Oct). Unlike Bunratty Castle (p377), Knappogue lays out knives and forks!

Craggaunowen

For more ancient Irish heritage spiffed up for the masses, visit **Craggaunowen** (☎ 061-367 178; www.shannonheritage.com; adult/child €8.50/5; ⏰ 10am-6pm May-Aug). Around 6km southeast of Quin, the project includes re-created ancient farms, dwellings such as a *crannóg* (artificial island) and a 5th-century ring fort, plus real artefacts including a 2000-year-old oak road. Craggaunowen Castle is a small, well-preserved McNamara fortified house. With lots of animals like snot-nosed boars, this is a good place for kids who like dirty critters.

Craggaunowen has a pleasant little café. Nearby Cullaun Lake is a popular boating and picnic spot, and there are forest trails nearby.

DETOUR: REAL BEER

A splendid antidote to Ireland's dismal beer scene (yeah, we know about Guinness but what about some variety, huh?) can be found right at the intersection of the Ennistymon (N85) and the Kilfenora (R481) roads in Inagh, 16km northeast of Ennis. **Biddy Early Brewery** (☎ 065-683 6742; www.beb.ie) is a rarity for the Emerald Isle: a great microbrewery serving its own range of beers. The Black Biddy Irish Stout recalls every bit of bold flavour that's been mass-marketed out of the corporate stouts. All beers are made with natural ingredients and there's often season specials. Enjoy a pint in the airy pub or outside at tables; there's food most months. Ask about the Biddy Early legend and you'll understand why this detour could be a one-way trip.

EASTERN & SOUTH-EASTERN CLARE

Away from the Atlantic coast and the rugged Burren uplands, Clare rolls gently eastward through low-lying green countryside that is given emphasis by the occasional range of smooth hills. The county's eastern boundary is the River Shannon and the long, wriggling inland waterway of Lough Derg, which stretches 48km from Portumna in County Galway, to just south of Killaloe. Lakeside villages such as Mountshannon seem in a different country from the rugged, evocative west of Clare, but this is a delightful, intimate countryside of water, woods and panoramic views. Southeastern Clare, where the Shannon swells into its broad estuary, is a plain landscape dotted with farms and small villages. Overhyped Bunratty Castle is a major attraction and nearby Shannon Airport is an important entry point.

SHANNON AIRPORT

☎ 061

Shannon, Ireland's second-largest airport, used to be a vital fuelling stop on the transatlantic air route for piston-engine planes without enough range to make it across the Atlantic to the European mainland. Today Shannon (Sionainn) is a low-stress gateway to the region.

About 3km from the airport, **Shannon town**, built to serve airport workers, has the feel of one of those old planned Soviet industrial cities – albeit with more reliable hot water. Don't linger.

Information

Shannon Town Centre (an enclosed shopping mall), off the N19, has banks, basic stores and fast food.

The **airport terminal** (☎ 742 6666; www.shannonairport.com) has many facilities, including a nice, free observation area for those stuck waiting. Almost everything is on one level. You can park close to the terminal (€1 per 15 minutes); more remote areas are much cheaper.

Aer Rianta (☎ 712 000) This desk provides airport and flight information.

Bank of Ireland (☎ 471 100) Open from the first flight (about 6.30am) to 5.30pm; there also currency exchanges and ATMs.

Internet access The terminal has free wi-fi throughout. Terminals are available outside the Hughes & Hughes Bookshop (per 15min €1.50).

Tourist office (☎ 471 664; www.shannonregiontourism.ie; ☽ 6.30am-6pm May-Sep, 7am-5.30pm Oct-Apr) Near the arrivals area, it has vast regional info and books rooms (€4 fee).

Sleeping & Eating

There's B&B accommodation 3km from the airport in Shannon town but Ennis, Limerick and much prettier towns – even Bunratty – can be reached in 30 minutes. Chains and modern pubs can be found in Shannon town. The airport terminal has one big and often crowded buffet-style restaurant.

Moloney's B&B (☎ 364 185; 21 Coill Mhara St; s/d €38/65; P) The four rooms at this cheery B&B in Shannon town are spotless. Coming from the airport turn right off the N19 at the big

---

SHANNON'S SIREN SONG

Long after Shannon Airport was no longer a vital refuelling stop, it prospered thanks to Irish laws that required international flights to Dublin to also stop here. Crafty locals were ready to relieve travellers forced into a visit of any spare change and it's here that Duty Free shopping was invented. The airport also takes credit for Irish coffee – that whiskey-laced creamy brew popular with Americans (although in 2007 you couldn't actually get one at the airport due to labour disputes).

The lovely attributes of Western Ireland aside, forcing travellers to land in Shannon was always a scam. In recent years some North American flights have been allowed to serve Dublin non-stop, but the last vestige of the mandatory Shannon stopover was swept away in 2007 by the EU open-skies deal with the USA. A predictable chorus of local officials decried the deal and worried that tourists might no longer come to the region if their plane wasn't forced to land. This argument, of course, ignores the fact that Shannon Airport is a delightful and civilised facility and that western Ireland will still attract hordes of visitors.

COUNTY CLARE

roundabout by the town centre. Keep on past the centre and at a crossroads go left down a slip road. Continue left past a school and the Shannon Leisure Centre. At the next junction go right, and then take the first left.

Park Inn Shannon Airport (☎ 471 122; www.parkinns .com; r €155; P ⌨) In a parking lot in front of the terminal, this bog-standard motel has views of the bogs. The 115 rooms are business-friendly and have wi-fi. This is an option if you have an early flight and want to lose the rental car. Look for specials.

Getting There & Around

AIR
Time will tell how many flights to the US continue to serve Shannon Airport (SNN) once the Open Skies agreement comes into full effect in 2008. The airport is proving popular with low-cost carriers like Ryanair, which serves its usual mixed bag of European destinations like Hahn in Germany – which despite its 75km distance away the airline calls 'Frankfurt'. Services to London's Heathrow Airport are in flux.

Airlines with direct flights to Shannon:

Aer Lingus (☎ 0818 365 000; www.aerlingus.ie) Dublin, Boston, New York, Chicago, Los Angeles.

American Airlines (☎ 01-602 0550; www.aa.com) Chicago.

Central Wings (www.centralwings.com) Warsaw.

Continental (☎ 1890 925 252; www.continental.com) Newark.

Delta Air Lines (☎ 1800 768 080; www.delta.com) Atlanta, New York.

Ryanair (☎ 0818 303 030; www.ryanair.com) London, Glasgow and numerous secondary European airports.

BUS
Bus Éireann (☎ 474 311; www.buseireann.ie ⌚ 8am-5pm May-Sep, Mon-Fri Oct-Apr) has a ticket office near the arrivals area in the terminal. If it's closed you can buy tickets from the driver. Destinations served by direct buses include Cork (€11.70, 2½ hours, hourly), Ennis (€5.40, 50 minutes, hourly), Galway (€10.80, 1¾ hours, hourly) and Limerick (€5, 30 to 55 minutes, two per hour). Some frequencies are reduced on Sundays.

TAXI
A taxi to the centre of Limerick or Ennis costs about €32 if booked at the taxi desk inside the airport. You may pay more at the outside rank. The taxi desk opens with first flights.

BUNRATTY
☎ 061
Conveniently located beside the N18 motorway and with plenty of bus-sized parking, Bunratty – home to government schemes to promote (milk?) tourism – draws more tourists than any other place in the region. The namesake castle has stood over the area for centuries. In recent decades it's been tarted up and surrounded by attractions. A theme park re-creates a clichéd Irish village of old (where's the horseshit we ask?) and each year more and more shops crowd the access roads – many selling authentic Irish goods just off the boat from China. There are some rather pricey group-dining options that are big with the bus crowd.

Buses and groups lay siege to Bunratty April to October. With all the hoopla, it's easy to overlook the actual village, which is at the back of the theme park. It is a pretty place and has numerous leafy places to stay and eat. It's a good place if you want something close to Shannon Airport, only 5km west.

There's a small **visitor information office** (☎ 364 321; ⌚ 9am-5.30pm Mon-Fri all year, Sat & Sun mid-May–Sep) in Bunratty Village Mills, a strip mall near the castle. There are ATMs and exchange services.

Bunratty Castle & Folk Park
There's a joint-entry-fee ticket to **Bunratty Folk Park** and **Bunratty Castle** (☎ 360 788; www .shannonheritage.com; adult/child €14/9). You can get separate entrance tickets to the park when the castle is closed; all the prices are slightly less off-season.

A gift shop guarding the entrance has an especially garish selection of green schlock including a 'Top of the Morning' alarm clock. (A sign inside the park reads 'Exit to Car Park through shop'.)

BUNRATTY CASTLE
Big, square and hulking, **Bunratty Castle** (⌚ 9am-4pm) certainly is well suited for its role. The Vikings built a fortified settlement on this spot, a former island surrounded by a moat. Then came the Normans, and Thomas de Clare built the first stone structure on the site in the 1270s. The present castle is the fourth incarnation to occupy the location beside the River Ratty. It was built in the early 1400s by the energetic McNamara family, but fell shortly thereafter to the O'Briens, kings of

Thomond, in whose possession it remained until the 17th century. Admiral Penn, father of William Penn who was the Quaker founder of the US state of Pennsylvania and the city of Philadelphia lived here for a short time.

A complete restoration was carried out more recently, and today the castle is full of fine 14th- to 17th-century furniture, paintings and wall hangings. Most aren't original to the castle but are similar to objects you would have found in the day, with the exception of the odd pot of boiling oil.

BUNRATTY FOLK PARK

The **folk park** (adult/child €8.85/5.25; ⊙ 9am-6pm Jun-Aug, 9am-5.30pm Sep-May, last admission 45min before closing) adjoins the castle. It is a reconstructed traditional Irish village with cottages, a forge and working blacksmith, weavers and pie-makers. There's a complete village street with post office, pub and small café.

A few of the buildings were brought here from elsewhere, but most are re-creations of the real thing. In peak season, four or five employees in period garb can be found explaining the warm family-friendly aspects of the late 19th century (there are no poor people, trigger-happy English etc). The entire place is attractive in the way that Disneyland has its own charm. But you'll find far more surviving authenticity of rural village Ireland in a place like Ennistymon than you will here.

The **Traditional Irish Night** (☎ 360 788; adult/child €46/23; ⊙ 7-9.30pm Apr-Oct) is held in a corn barn in the folk park. Lots of red-haired (real or fake, it's clearly a big help in securing employment) servers dish up trad music, dancing, Irish stew, apple pie and soda bread. There's nontraditional wine as well, which may put you in the mood for the sing-along.

MEDIEVAL BANQUETS

If you skip the high-jinks in the corn barn, you may opt for a **medieval banquet** (☎ 360 788; adult/child €55/27.50; ⊙ 5.30pm & 8.45pm), replete with harp-playing maidens, court jesters and food with a medieval motif (lots of meaty items, but somehow we think the real stuff would empty the place right out). It's all washed down with mead, a kind of honey wine and you eat with your fingers. The banquets are very popular with coach parties so it's advisable for independent travellers to book well ahead. Various actors interact with choral singers.

The banquets at Knappogue Castle (p374) and Dunguaire Castle (in Galway; p437) are similar but more sedate.

Sleeping

Bunratty has a few hotels and dozens of B&Bs. A big map by the park entrance shows locations; most are away from the castle, park and shop scrum.

Briar Lodge (☎ 363 388; www.briarlodge.com; Hill Rd; s/d from €50/65; P) On a quiet cul-de-sac 1.6km from the castle, this traditionally styled house makes for a good refuge. All three rooms have little extras like curling irons (for that grand banquet entrance!).

Tudor Lodge (☎ 362 248; Hill Rd; s/d €50/75; P) Just a few minutes' stroll from the centre, this handsome house has a faux-Tudor motif. The five rooms are comfortable and good value.

Bunratty Castle Hotel (☎ 478 700; www.bunratty castlehotel.com; s/d from €80/150; P ▯ ☎) Right at ground zero, every touristy place in Bunratty is but a short walk from this modern, boutique hotel. All 144 rooms have wi-fi and are luxuriously appointed. It's an attractive place and there's a spa.

Eating & Drinking

Most of the food choices – especially in the malls – are geared to the masses.

Durty Nelly's (☎ 364 861; Bunratty House Mews; bar meals €5-12, restaurant mains from €20) Thronged with tourists all summer long, Nelly's manages to provide some charm amidst the hubbub, right across from the castle. Meals are better than you'd expect, although the pub is more enjoyable than the restaurant upstairs. A few locals (unpaid volunteers?) can be found with pints in corners near the bar and there are trad sessions many nights.

Red Door (☎ 466 993; Bunratty House, Hill Rd; mains €10-25; ⊙ noon-3pm & 6.45-9pm Tue-Sun) Near the real Bunratty village behind the folk park, this top-notch restaurant serves creative local fare on the grounds of an old estate. The menu has international influences but you'll always go right with local meats or seafood.

Mac's Bar (☎ 361 511; Bunratty Folk Park) This engaging place is actually part of the Folk Park village. It has traditional music many evenings June to September, and on weekends the rest of the year. Ignore it during the day, but after the park closes (you can still get in) it starts to feel real.

COUNTY CLARE

Getting There & Away

Bunratty is on the busy Bus Éireann Limerick–Shannon Airport route. Service to both is at least hourly and trips take less than 30 minutes and cost under €5. There's at least five direct buses daily to Ennis (€6.20, 30 minutes). Buses stop outside the Fitzpatrick Bunratty Shamrock Hotel near the castle.

KILLALOE & BALLINA

☎ 061 / pop 1750

Facing each other across a narrow channel, Killaloe and Ballina are really one destination, even if they have very different personalities (and counties). A fine old 13-arch bridge spans the river, linking the pair. You can walk it in five minutes.

Killaloe (Cill Da Lúa) is picturesque Clare at its finest. It lies on the western banks of lower Loch Deirgeirt, the southern extension of Lough Derg, where the loch narrows at one of the principal crossings of the River Shannon. The village lies snugly against the Slieve Bernagh Hills that rise abruptly to the west. The Arra Mountains create a fine balance to the east and all of Lough Derg is at hand. The village is also on the 180km East Clare Way.

Not as quaint as Killaloe, Ballina is in County Tipperary and actually manages to have some of the better pubs and restaurants. It lies at the end of a scenic drive from Nenagh along Lough Derg on the R494, see p321.

From Killaloe and Ballina, the Shannon is navigable all the way north to Lough Key in County Sligo; in summer the towns are jammed with weekend sailors.

Orientation & Information

In Ballina, Main St is the focus; it's up the hill from the water. The busy narrow street running from the river on the Killaloe side is Bridge St, which turns right and becomes Main St.

The **tourist office** (☎ 376 866; Brian Boru Heritage Centre; ☼ 10am-6pm May–mid-Sep) is on a tiny island off the bridge on the Killaloe side and shares space with the heritage centre and the **library** (☎ 376 062; ☼ 10am-1.30pm & 2.30-5.30pm Mon, Tue & Thu, 10am-5.30pm & 6.30-8pm Wed & Fri, 10am-2pm Sat), which has free internet access.

The AIB bank at the bottom of Church St in Killaloe has an ATM.

Whelan's Foodstore (☎ 376 159; Church St, Killaloe) has a substantial selection of newspapers and magazines.

There's parking on both sides of the river and that's just what you'll want to do as soon as you arrive. Pretty as it is, the bridge is really a traffic nightmare; its one lane and the complex local traffic patterns mean that you can wait 10 minutes or more to drive across. Use your feet. There are toilets on the Killaloe side in the car park.

Sights & Activities

Killaloe Cathedral (St Flannan's Cathedral; ☎ 376 687; Limerick Rd) dates from the early 13th century and was built by the O'Brien family on top of a 6th-century church. Inside, magnificent carvings decorate the Romanesque southern doorway. Next to the doorway is the shaft of a stone cross, known as Thorgrim's Stone. It dates from the early Christian period and is unusual in that it bears both the old Scandinavian runic and Irish ogham scripts. In the cathedral grounds is St Flannan's Oratory, of 12th-century Romanesque design.

The **Brian Boru Heritage Centre** (☎ 376 866; www.shannonheritage.com; Lock House, Killaloe; adult/child €3.20/1.65; ☼ 10am-6pm May-Sep) is named for the local boy who made good as the king who is purported to not only have unified Ireland but freed it from the Viking scourge. (Recently such claims have been ascribed to political spinmeisters, the Karl Roves of their day.) The centre does much to celebrate the legends.

For all your fishing needs go to **TJ's Angling Centre** (☎ 376 009; Main St, Ballina). You can rent fishing tackle for €10 per day and catch your limit in free advice. It also organises fishing trips, although you can catch trout and pike right here.

Whelan's Boat Hire (☎ 086 391 9472; Whelan's Food Store, Church St, Killaloe) rents out 19ft lake boats for €15/50 per hour/day, including all equipment and fishing rods.

To cruise the waters, the **Spirit of Killaloe** (☎ 086 814 0559; Bridge St, Killaloe; tickets €10) does hour-long trips.

Sleeping

There are lots of B&Bs in the area, especially on the roads along the lough. Book ahead in summer.

Arkansas B&B (☎ 376 485; arkans@eircom.net; Main St, Ballina; s/d €40/65; P) There are four basic rooms at this well-located simple B&B. And the name? The lovely owner says she once saw a fishing trawler named Arkansas and she liked the sound.

Kincora House (☎ 376 149; www.kincorahouse.com; Church St, Killaloe; s/d €40/70) This simple place in a centuries-old townhouse is right in the heart of Killaloe. The traditional-style rooms have a simple, older style and could belong to a favoured aunt.

Lakeside Hotel (☎ 376 122; www.lakeside-killaloe .com; Ballina; s/d from €70/130; P ⊡ ⊠) In a great location on the Ballina side of the bridge, this gentrified waterfront hotel has several attractive public areas and the grounds good for strolling. The 46 rooms vary greatly, prices work in direct ratio to view.

Kincora Hall Hotel (☎ 061-376 000; www.kincorahall .com; Killaloe; r €80-200; P) This handsome hotel sits right on the water and has its own marina. There's a comfy away-from-it-all feel to everything; rooms are big and are stylishly done out and there's a plush library for relaxing. It's 1.3km north of the bridge.

Eating & Drinking

Molly's Bar & Restaurant (☎ 376 632; Ballina; meals €8-24; ⊙ food served noon-10pm) Right at the base of the bridge, this riverside pub has a very nice rooftop deck which puts you high above the coagulated traffic. Molly's gets very busy and offers Irish standards such as bacon and cabbage plus pub classics such as pizzas and sandwiches. On weekend nights there's a disco, live music and DJs.

River Run (☎ 376 805; www.riverruncafe.com; Main St, Ballina; mains €10-16; ⊙ noon-10pm) Small, smart and stylish, this bistro has food as creative as the art on the walls. The selections are kept short but always include good seafood, fish, various meats and veggie options. Desserts are tops, the wine list long.

Gooser's Bar & Eating House (☎ 376 791; Main St, Ballina; dinner mains €18-28; ⊙ noon-10pm Mon-Sat, 12.30-9.30pm Sun) Only the masses of funseekers on busy weekends diminishes the Gooser's experience. This is a hugely popular place, noted for its big selection of fish. Sailors make mirth and plough into the hefty seafood platter. Want to avoid a wait? Dine at the bar (meals €9.50 to €24), and save a few euros.

Anchor Inn (☎ 376 108; Bridge St, Killaloe) The raucous Anchor Inn stages traditional music sessions on Wednesday night, and there's live music at weekends. It's right at the bridge and an easy hop from Molly's.

Liam O'Riains (☎ 376 722; Main St, Ballina) At the area's most atmospheric pub you're greeted by a cow-eyed, 12kg pike mounted on a wall near the entrance. He's an ugly mother. Everything else here, however, is lovely. Candles glow softly and windows overlook the river below.

Getting There & Away

There are four **Bus Éireann** (☎ 313 333) services a day Monday to Saturday from Limerick to Killaloe (€5.40, 45 minutes). The bus stop is outside the cathedral.

KILLALOE TO MOUNTSHANNON

The journey north to Mountshannon along Lough Derg is scenic; there are good viewpoints and picnic spots. To get to Mountshannon from Killaloe take the R463 to Tuamgraney, then turn east on the R352.

About 2km north of Killaloe, **Beal Ború** is an earthen mound or fort said to have been Kincora, the fabled palace of the famous Irish king Brian Ború, who, besides lending his name to bad Irish bars the world over, took on the Vikings at the Battle of Clontarf in 1014. Traces of Bronze Age settlement have been found. With its commanding view over Lough Derg, this was obviously a site of strategic importance.

About 3.5km north of Killaloe is the **University of Limerick Activity Centre** (☎ 061-376 622; www .ulac.ie; Two Mile Gate). Here individuals and groups can learn water-based skills, such as canoeing, sailing and windsurfing. Land-based activities include archery, orienteering and forest games. There's a very impressive, high-rig frame on which to get to grips with rope work. A weekend water-based skills course costs from €200 per person.

About 4.5km north of Killaloe is Cragliath Hill, which has another fort, **Gr9ananlaghna**, named after Brian Ború's great-grandfather, King Lachtna.

Tuamgraney, at the junction of the road to Mountshannon, has an interesting old church, St Cronan's, with a small museum, the **East Clare Heritage Centre** (☎ 921 351; www.eastclareheritage.com).

Sleeping & Eating

Lough Derg Holiday Centre (☎ 061-376 777; www .loughderg.net; Scarriff Rd, Killaloe; cottages per week from €400; ⊙ mid-May–mid-Sep) Six kilometres north of Killaloe, near the lake shore, the cottages at the Holiday Cenre have three bedrooms. It's a fun place and you can do most things aquatic such as rent a boat. The campground, however, is now closed.

Lantern House (☎ 061-923 034; www.lantern house.com; Scarriff Rd, Ogonnelloe; s/d from €45/90; P) About 10km north of Killaloe, and in a lofty location overlooking much of Lough Derg, this modern six-room house is beautifully surrounded by gardens of heather. There's a restaurant (mains €12 to €24; open 6pm to 9pm March to October) attached that offers distinctive modern Irish cuisine. Booking ahead is advised.

MOUNTSHANNON & AROUND
☎ 061 / pop 330
Winner of many a 'Tidy Town' award, the village of Mountshannon (Baile Uí Bheoláin), on the southwestern shores of Lough Derg, was founded in 1742 by an enlightened landlord to house a largely Protestant community of flax workers.

The harbour is host to a fair number of fishing boats, and visiting yachts and cruisers in summer. It is the main centre for trips to Holy Island, one of Clare's finest early Christian settlements.

There's great fishing around Mountshannon, mainly for brown trout, pike, perch and bream. Ask at your lodging about boat hire and equipment.

There are toilets by the harbour.

Holy Island
Lying 2km offshore from Mountshannon, Holy Island (Inis Cealtra) is the site of a **monastic settlement** thought to have been founded by St Cáimín in the 7th century. On the island you will see a round tower that is more than 27m tall (though missing its top storey). You'll also find four old chapels, a hermit's cell and some early Christian gravestones dating from the 7th to 13th centuries. One of the chapels has an elegant Romanesque arch. Inside the chapel is an inscription in Old Irish, which translates as 'Pray for Tornog, who made this cross'.

The Vikings treated this monastery roughly in the 9th century, but under the crowd-pleasing protection of Brian Ború and others, it flourished.

From Mountshannon harbour you can take a cruise around the island with **Ireland Line Cruises** (☎ 375 011; adult/child €8/4; ☼ late Apr-Oct). Trips can also be arranged from Mount-

shannon through the East Clare Heritage Centre (see p379) in Tuamgraney.

Sleeping & Eating
Lakeside Holiday Park (☎ 927 225; www.lakeside ireland.com; camp sites €15; ☼ May-Oct) This spacious park has a fine lakeside location with 35 camp sites and a few holiday trailers (€250 per week). It hires out boats and equipment for windsurfing, rowing and sailing. From Mountshannon, head north along the Portumna road (R352) for 2km and take the first turn-off on the right.

Derg Lodge (☎ 927 319, 927 180; bridgebarbb@mail .com; Whitegate Rd, Mountshannon; s/d €40/60; P) This pleasant four-room B&B is about 500m from the village. It hires boats for €35 per day, €65 with a *gillie* (boatperson).

Hawthorn Lodge (☎ 927 120; www.mountshannon-clare.com; s/d from €45/60; P) Just 1km from the village, this tidy cottage is everybody's idea of a low-key country retreat. Set your electric blanket on high and you may never emerge into the chilly albeit fresh morning air.

Mountshannon Hotel (☎ 927 162; www.mount shannon-hotel.ie; Main St; s/d €50/80; ☼ Mar-Oct; P) This little heritage hotel is as tidy as the town. The 14 rooms are good value for the money and there's a good bar with tables out front.

An Cupán Caifé (☎ 927 275; Main St; meals €8-18; ☼ noon-9pm May-Aug, 12.30-9pm Sep-Apr, closed Wed) This café-restaurant has a charmingly casual atmosphere. There's a varied menu of surf and turf, with a smattering of Irish-ised Italian choices. Daily specials usually involve local fish.

Harbour Restaurant (☎ 927 162; Mountshannon Hotel, Main St; mains €10-20) This hotel restaurant is justifiably popular. People book well in advance to enjoy the creative seafood dishes available.

Getting There & Away
Swimming or driving are your best ways to reach Mountshannon. Bus Éireann runs one bus to here each Saturday from Limerick.

NORTH TO GALWAY
North of Mountshannon, the R352 follows Lough Derg to Portumna in Galway. Inland is an area known as the Clare Lakelands, based around Feakle, where numerous lakes offer good coarse fishing.

SOUTHWESTERN & WESTERN CLARE

One look at the map and you can see that Loop Head on Clare's southwestern tip is giving the finger to the Atlantic. OK, it's a stubby finger but still it's emblematic of the never-ceasing titanic struggle between land and sea along this stretch of Irish coast.

The soaring cliffs south of the beach resort of Kilkee to Loop Head are both striking and underappreciated by many visitors. Most save their energies for the iconic Cliffs of Moher. Marching in geologic lockstep, the formations are undeniably stunning, although in summer you may be marching in lockstep with hordes of other visitors.

South of the cliffs to Kilkee are the low-key beach towns of Lahinch, Miltown Malbay and Doonbeg. No part of this coast is remotely tropical, but there's a stark wind-blown beauty that stretches to the horizon. Many a hapless survivor of the Spanish Armada washed ashore here 400 years ago. Tales of their offspring still titillate locals.

Your best days here may be spent on the smallest roads you can find. Make your own discoveries, whether it's your own stretch of lonely beach or something more settled, like the charming heritage town of Ennistymon.

Getting There & Away

BOAT

Shannon Ferry Limited (☎ 905 3124; www.shannonferries.com) runs a 20-minute car ferry from Killimer, across the Shannon Estuary, to Tarbert in County Kerry. You pay on board. See p284 for fares and times. It's a real time-saver over detouring through Limerick.

BUS

You can usually count on a Bus Éireann service or two linking all the main towns in the region each day. From Limerick routes run along the Shannon to Kilrush and Kilkee, as well as through Corofin, Ennistymon, Lahinch, Liscannor and on to the Cliffs of Moher and Doolin. Buses from Ennis follow the same pattern. On the coast between Kilkee and Lahinch services average twice daily in summer. There are a few other routes but they are not daily and are geared to school kids.

KILRUSH

☎ 065 / pop 2700

Kilrush (Cill Rois) is an interesting small town that overlooks the Shannon Estuary and the hills of Kerry to the south. The main street, Frances St, runs directly to the harbour. It is more than 30m wide, reflecting Kilrush's origins as a port and market town in the 19th century, when there was much coming and going between land and sea. It has the western coast's biggest **marina** (www.kilrushcreekmarina.ie) at Kilrush Creek.

Kilrush's tourist office (☎ 905 1577) moves from year to year but is usually on or near Frances St and is open roughly May to September.

In Market Sq there's an ACC bank with an ATM and on Frances St you'll find the post office and an AIB bank with an ATM. **KK Computing** (☎ 905 1806; Frances St; per hr €5; ⊙ 10am-10pm, shorter hours in winter) has internet access.

Sights & Activities

St Senan's Catholic church (Toler St) contains eight detailed examples of stained glass by well-known early-20th-century artist Harry Clarke. East of town is **Kilrush Wood**, which has some fine old trees and a picnic area.

Vandeleur Walled Garden (☎ 905 1760; adult/child €5/2; ⊙ 10am-6pm Apr-Oct, to 4pm Nov-Mar) is a remarkable 'lost' garden. It was the private domain of the wealthy Vandeleur family, merchants and landowners who engaged in harsh evictions and forced emigration of local people in the 19th century. The gardens lie within a large walled area and have been redesigned and planted with colourful tropical and rare plants. There are woodland trails around the area and there's also a café.

Near the marina is **Kilrush Creek Adventure Centre** (☎ 905 2855; www.kilrushcreekadventure.com; Kilrush Creek). It offers a range of watery activities including windsurfing, kayaking, sailing and power boating. Call for rates and hours.

More than 100 dolphins live in Shannon Estuary. Weather permitting, you can do a two- to 2½-hour trip to see them with **Dolphin Discovery** (☎ 905 1327; www.discoverdolphins.ie; Kilrush; adult/child €19/10). Boats leave from Kilrush Creek Marina.

Sleeping & Eating

B&Bs are about as common as driftwood on a beach.

COUNTY CLARE

Katie O'Connor's Holiday Hostel (☎ 905 1133; katieoconnors@eircom.net; Frances St; dm/d €17/36; ☺ mid-Mar–Oct) This fine old main-street house dates from the 18th century, and was one of the town houses of the Vandeleur family. These days Masie extends an amazing welcome. These are 16 beds in two rooms at this IHH-affiliated hostel.

our pick **Crotty's** (☎ 905 2470; www.crottyspubkilrush .com; Market Sq; s/d from €45/70) Brimming with character, Crotty's has an old-fashioned high bar, tiled floors and a series of snugs decked out with traditional furnishings. You can enjoy music many nights in summer. Food is served daily (meals €6 to €16) and is a high-end version of pub fare. Daily specials are excellent value and reflect what's fresh. Upstairs are seven traditional rooms that are small and clean. Service is excellent and the owners are real pros.

Hillcrest View (☎ 905 1986; www.hillcrestview.com; Doonbeg Rd; s/d from €50/64; **P**) This large house, at the top of the hill where the Doonbeg road climbs out of Kilrush, is about 1km from the centre. The six rooms have lovely furnishings, and breakfast is served in a bright conservatory.

Harbour Restaurant (☎ 905 2836; Creek Marina; meals €8-25; ☺ noon-9pm) Right on the, er, harbour, this modern bistro has a long and appealing menu. There's everything from massive sandwiches to all manner of local seafood. Tables outside are popular in summer and you can also just relax with a suitable sunset beverage.

Getting There & Around

Bus Éireann has one or two buses daily to Limerick (1¾ hours), Ennis (one hour) and Kilkee (15 minutes). Fares average €6.

You can hire bikes at **Gleeson's Cycles** (☎ 905 1127; Henry St; per day/week €20/80, day deposit €40).

SCATTERY ISLAND

This uninhabited, windswept, treeless island, 3km southwest of Kilrush in the estuary is the site of a Christian settlement founded by St Senan in the 6th century. Its 36m-high **round tower** is one of the tallest and best preserved in Ireland, and the entrance is at ground level instead of the usual position high above the foundation. There are remains of five **medieval churches**, including a 9th-century cathedral. This is a great and evocative place to wander about.

An exhibition on the history and wildlife of the Heritage Service–administered island is housed in the **Scattery Island Visitor Centre** (www .heritageireland.ie; admission free).

Scattery Island Ferries (☎ 065-905 1327; Kilrush Creek Marina; adult/child €12/6; ☺ Jun-Sep) runs boats from Kilrush to the island. There's no strict timetable as the trips are subject to tidal and weather conditions. There's a stay of about 1hr on the island. You can buy tickets at the small kiosk at the marina.

KILKEE

☎ 065 / pop 1300

During the summer, Kilkee's wide beach is thronged with day-trippers and holidaymakers. Kilkee (Cill Chaoi) first became popular in Victorian times when rich Limerick families built seaside retreats here. Today, it is well supplied with guesthouses, amusement arcades and takeaways, although good taste – mostly – prevails and there are few real visual horrors.

LAST CALL FOR THE WEST CLARE RAILWAY?

Running on a roundabout route from Ennis to Kilrush and Kilkee, the narrow-gauge West Clare Railway was sort of the line that barely could. It ran from 1892 until 1961 and during that time reached its greatest notoriety when popular early-20th-century musician Percy French mocked it in the song *Are Ye Right There Michael*. It seems the perennially late WCR caused French to miss a paying gig in Kilkee. After taking his revenge via song the railway management – so the oft-told tale goes – sued for libel. Percy triumphed because after he was late for a court appearance, the judge asked for an explanation. His reply: 'I took the West Clare Railway your honour.' The case was thrown out and he was awarded costs.

Today a 2km vestige of the **line** (☎ 905 1284; www.westclarerailway.ie; adult/child €6/3; ☺ 10am-6pm May-Sep) survives near Moyasta on the Kilkee Rd (N67) 6km northwest of Kilrush. Run by volunteers, the steam-powered trains shuttle back and forth over the open land. And if some local boosters get their way the line will be restored between Kilrush and Kilkee. However there's one obstacle: like seemingly everywhere else in Ireland, the route is under threat from new home construction.

The semicircular bay has high cliffs on the north end and tidal rocks to the south. The sea puts on a show anytime as waves pound the shore.

Information

Bank of Ireland (O'Curry St) Has an ATM.

Post office (O'Connell St) Across from the library.

Tourist office (☎ 905 6112; O'Connell St; 9.30am-5.30pm Jun-Aug) Near the seafront.

Sights & Activities

Many visitors come for the fine sheltered **beach** and the **Pollock Holes**, natural swimming pools in the Duggerna Rocks to the south of the beach. **St George's Head**, to the north, has good cliff walks and scenery, while south of the bay, the **Duggerna Rocks** form an unusual natural amphitheatre. Further south is a huge **sea cave**. These sights can be reached by driving to Kilkee's West End area and following the coastal path.

Kilkee is a well-known **diving** centre. There are shore dives from the Duggerna Rocks fringing the western side of the bay, and boat dives on the Black Rocks further out. Experience and local knowledge or guidance is strongly advised. Right at the tip of the Duggerna Rocks is the small inlet of Myles Creek, out from which there's excellent underwater scenery. **Oceanlife Ireland** (☎ 905 6707; www.diveireland.com; George's Head, Kilkee), by the harbour, has tanks and other equipment for hire and runs basic courses.

All that surf means that folks with boards (and extra thick wetsuits) will be very happy. **Kilkee Surf School** (☎ 087-995 6231; lessons per day from €30) is run by veteran local surfers and takes students to where the waves are best each day.

Sleeping

There are plenty of guesthouses and B&Bs in Kilkee, though during the high season rates can soar and you may have a problem finding a vacancy.

Green Acres Caravan & Camping Park (☎ 905 7011; Doonaha, Kilkee; camp sites €18; early Apr-Sep) Beside the Shannon, 6km south of Kilkee on the R487, this is a small peaceful park with 40 sites.

Bayview (☎ 905 6058; www.bayviewkilkee.com; O'Connell St; s/d from €45/64; P) A central guesthouse right on the main drag, Bayview has

good views over the bay from its front rooms. The eight guest rooms vary considerably in décor, although you won't be tempted to cart anything home. The breakfast room has a heritage feel.

Strand Guest House (☎ 905 6177; www.thestrandkilkee.com; The Strand; s/d from €45/74; P) Right across from the water, this six-room guesthouse is a veteran of many a summer. The rooms are simply decorated, but do have telephones. Some have great views as does the lounge, which has picnic tables outside for a little salt-spray in your stout.

Stella Maris Hotel (☎ 905 6455; www.stellamarishotel.com; O'Connell St; s/d from €55/120; P) There are 20 modern rooms in the year-round choice for lodging in Kilkee. Some rooms on the top floor have views of the surf and some have high-speed internet. The hotel is right in the centre and has good food.

Halpin's Townhouse Hotel (☎ 905 6032; www.halpinsprivatehotels.com; Erin St; s/d from €80/100; mid-Mar–mid-Nov; P) A smart Georgian townhouse has been turned into a plush 12-room hotel. Close to the centre, it eschews the salt-stained furnishings of many a beach-town place for a stylish look. Residents enjoy the basement bar with its gracious airs and good wine list.

Eating

Kilkee has several markets; in summer the ranks of eateries swell.

Pantry (☎ 905 6576; O'Curry St; meals €6-12; 10am-10pm) This simple caff goes one better than the competition with its flawless preparations of classics like lasagne, burgers, and fish and chips.

Stella Maris (☎ 905 6455; O'Connell St; meals €10-25; noon-9pm) The popular hotel has a good menu of local foods on offer through the day. Enjoy great seafood or one of many daily specials in the bright and simple dining room or in the usually crowded pub.

Murphy Blacks (☎ 905 6854; The Square; mains €16-28; 5-9.30pm Wed-Sun Apr-Oct) How do you ensure that you're getting the best fish? Go to a place owned by an ex-fisherman. This deservedly popular dinner spot is booked up solid night after night for its amazing seafood dishes that are executed with colour and flair. Tables outside are a summer-night treat.

Entertainment

Myle's Creek (☎ 905 6771; O'Curry St) Music plays most nights from June to August in this

---

DETOUR: CLIFFS OF AMAZEMENT

On the south side of Kilkee's bay, look for a sign that reads 'Scenic Loop'; it's an understatement. A narrow track curves around the coast for 10km south until it joins the R487, the Loop Head Rd. Along the way you will be struck by one stunning vista of soaring coastal cliffs after another. Some have holes blasted through by the surf, others have been separated from land and now stand out in the ocean as lonely sentinels. One even has an old house perched on top–how did that get there? Plan on puttering along, blasting through your camera's memory chip and pausing for passing cows.

---

simple place. very quiet in the off-season, it attracts a playful and gregarious crowd in summer. On some nights there's not a fiddle in sight and amped guitars rule.

Mary O'Mara's (☎ 905 6286; O'Curry St) A basic pub with popular trad music nights through the summer.

Getting There & Away
Bus Éireann has one to two buses daily to Kilkee from Limerick (€13.50, two hours) and Ennis (€10.50, 1¼ hours). Both routes pass through Kilrush.

KILKEE TO LOOP HEAD
The land from Kilkee south to Loop Head has subtle undulations that suddenly end in dramatic cliffs falling off into the Atlantic. It's a windswept place with timeless striations of old stone walls. You can literally see for miles and there is a rewarding sense of escape from the mainstream. It's good cycling country and there are coastal walks; which is just as well as there's no public transport.

Carrigaholt
☎ 065 / pop 100
On 15 September 1588, seven tattered ships of the Spanish Armada took shelter off Carrigaholt (Carraig an Chabaltaigh), a tiny village inside the mouth of the Shannon Estuary. One, probably the *Annunciada*, was torched and abandoned, sinking somewhere out in the estuary. Today Carrigaholt has one of the simplest and cutest main streets you'll find. The substantial remains of a 15th-century

McMahon castle with a square keep overlook the water.

To view resident bottlenose dolphins (there are more than 100 in the Shannon Estuary), head for **Dolphinwatch** (☎ 905 8156; www.dolphin watch.ie; Carrigaholt; adult/child €22/11). Opposite the post office, Dolphinwatch runs two-hour trips in the estuary from April to October, weather permitting. Ask about Loop Head sunset cruises.

Long Dock (☎ 905 8106; West St; meals €6-24; ☼ food served 11am-9pm) is an atmospheric pub-restaurant combo. Stone walls and floors and a welcoming fire are only the start. Fresh fish is the thing here; you'll see the purveyors out working in the estuary or even drinking at the bar.

Like Carrigaholt, **Morrissey's Village Pub** (☎ 905 8041; West St) hasn't changed much in a long time and is all the better for it. Get your feet ready for music and dancing many nights through the year. Picnic tables take full advantage of the corner location.

Kilbaha
☎ 065 / pop 50
The land at this minute waterfront village is as barren as the soul of a 19th-century landlord who burned down the local church so his workers wouldn't waste productive hours praying. Even today the scars are felt. Gazing up at the ruins of his house far up the hillside, a local says: 'Yeah, we got rid of him', as if the events of 150 years ago were yesterday.

You can learn more about this story and other aspects of local life from a unique modern-day **scroll**, an open-air sculpture that relates local history.

The **Lighthouse Inn** (☎ 905 8358; www.thelight houseinn.ie; s/d €30/60; P) is a stolid place right on the water. It has 11 basic and clean rooms. The pub serves sandwiches and the like through the year and more complex seafood dinners (from €12) in summer. There are live sessions many nights.

Loop Head
On a clear day, Loop Head (Ceann Léime), Clare's southernmost point, has magnificent views south to the Dingle Peninsula crowned by Mt Brandon (951m), and north to the Aran Islands and Galway Bay. There are bracing walks in the area and a long hiking trail runs along the cliffs to Kilkee. A working **lighthouse** (complete with Fresnel lens) is the punctuation on the point.

COUNTY CLARE

The often deserted wilds of Loop Head are perfect for a little DIY fun. **Loop Head Adventures** (☎ 905 8875; loopheadsports@eircom.net; ✆ May-Oct) rents gear and gives advice for cycling (bikes €15 per day), fishing (rods and gear €15 per day) and snorkelling (drysuits and gear €30 per day). It's located a short distance from the lighthouse.

KILKEE TO ENNISTYMON

North of Kilkee, the land flattens and you enjoy vistas that sweep across pastures and dunes. The N67 runs inland for some 32km until it reaches Quilty. Take the occasional lane to the west and search out unfrequented places such as White Strand, north of Doonbeg. **Ballard Bay** is 8km west of Doonbeg, where an old telegraph tower looks over some fine cliffs. **Donegal Point** has the remains of a promontory fort. There's good fishing all along the coast, and safe beaches at Seafield, Lough Donnell and Quilty. Off the coast of the latter, look for **Mutton Island**, a barren expanse sporting an ancient tower.

Doonbeg

☎ 065 / pop 610

Doonbeg (An Dún Beag) is a tiny seaside village about halfway between Kilkee and Quilty. Another Armada ship, the *San Esteban,* was wrecked on 20 September 1588 near the mouth of the Doonbeg River. The survivors were later executed at Spanish Point. Note the surviving wee little 16th-century **castle tower** next to the graceful seven-arch stone bridge over the Doonbeg River.

White Strand (Trá Bán) is a quiet beach, 2km long and backed by dunes. It's north of town and hard to miss as it's now been surrounded by the snooty – and hulking – Doonbeg Golf Resort and Lodge. From the public car park (protected from the adjacent resort hotel by a stout fence, no doubt so the swells won't steal your iPod), you follow a break in the dunes to a perfect crescent of sand.

SLEEPING & EATING

For campers there are often spots on the side roads around Doonbeg that make a good pitch, with glorious sunsets as a bonus. The town has two popular rural pubs where locals celebrate anything they can think of.

Whitestrand B&B (☎ 905 5347; whitestrand bandb@eircom.net; Killard; s/d €30/60; P) Is this the deal of the coast? A large, modern house looks over a perfect little cove of beach across to the sweep of the White Strand. The two rooms are comfortable and have views. Remote – at times you can hear cows mooing over the surf – the B&B is just south of town, then 2km to the water.

Morrissey's (☎ 905 5304; www.morrisseysdoonbeg .com; Main St; s/d €70/100; ✆ Mar-Oct; P 💻) Under its fourth-generation owner, this old pub has been reborn as one of the hippest places on the coast. The seven rooms feature queen beds, flat-screen TVs and wi-fi. The pub-restaurant is renowned for its casual but enticing seafood, from fish and chips to barbecued salmon. Outside there's a terrace overlooking the river, inside colours reminiscent of a box of good bon-bons mingle with stark white walls. Meals range from €8 to €20.

Miltown Malbay

☎ 065 / pop 1600

Like Kilkee, Miltown Malbay was a resort favoured by well-to-do Victorians, though the town isn't actually on the sea: the beach is 2km south at Spanish Point. A classically friendly place in the chatty Irish way, Miltown Malbay has a thriving music scene. Every year it hosts a **Willie Clancy Irish Music Festival** (☎ 708 4148) as a tribute to a native son and one of Ireland's greatest pipers. The festival is usually the first or second week in July, when the town is overrun with wandering minstrels, the pubs are packed, and Guinness is consumed by the barrel. Workshops and classes underpin the event; don't be surprised to attend a recital with 40 noted fiddlers.

For local information, drop by **An Ghiolla Finn Gift Shop** (☎ 688 9239; Main St). The wonderful Maureen Kilduff knows everything and everybody.

Possibly the friendliest welcome in town is at **An Gleann B&B** (☎ 708 4281; angleann@oceanfree.net; Ennis Rd; s/d €40/70; P). Off the R474 a kilometre from the centre, the rooms here are basic and comfy and owner Mary Hughes is a delight. Cyclists are catered for.

You'll no longer be mystified about how the pros do it after a stay at the **Berry Lodge** (☎ 708 7022; www.berrylodge.com; Annagh; s/d €52/80; P), which runs a serious cooking school. Students get in-depth instruction – often over more than one day. Packages include lodging and meals, roughly €100 per person per day. Those with a scholarly bent can simply avail themselves of the five cheery rooms and excellent meals. It's just south of Miltown Malbay.

Across the road from the gift shop, **Baker's Cafe** (☎ 708 4411; Main St; meals €4; ☯ 7am-7pm Mon-Sat) has excellent baked goods and creates enormous sandwiches – perfect for seaside picnics.

Not far away, the **Old Bake House** (☎ 708 4350; Main St; meals €6-14; ☯ noon-9pm) wins awards for its simple yet exceptional cooking. There's a new menu every day. Highlights might include a hummus salad with garlic bread, seafood of many stripes or a surprising combination of sandwiches. It has a kids' menu.

O'Friel's Bar (☎ 708 4275; The Square) is one of a couple of genuine old-style places with occasional trad sessions.

Bus Éireann service is paltry. Expect one or two buses daily north and south along the coast and inland to Ennis.

Lahinch
☎ 065 / pop 625

Lahinch (Leacht Uí Chonchubhair) owes its living to beach-seeking tourists pure and simple. You might find a beady-eyed greed in the eyes of the locals you won't find at village just a mile or two inland. The town sits on protected Liscannor Bay and does have a fine beach. Free-spending mobs descend in summer, many wielding golf clubs for play at the famous Lahinch Golf Club.

The tourist office, **Lahinch Fáilte** (☎ 708 2082; www.lahinchfailte.com; The Dell; ☯ 9am-8pm Jun-Aug, 10am-5pm Sep-May), is off the northern end of Main St and is part of a well-stocked gift shop. There's an ATM outside the tourist office and the office has a bureau de change. You can park at both ends of town near the water.

Like swells after a storm, the surfing scene keeps getting bigger, you can get lessons from about €30 an hour. **Lahinch Surf Shop** (☎ 708 1108; www.oceanscene.ie; Church St) runs regular classes for all levels and sells gear.

Lahinch Surf School (☎ 087-960 9667; www.lahinchsurfschool.com; Beach Hut, Lahinch Prom) offers lessons and various multiday packages.

SLEEPING & EATING
Lahinch Hostel (☎ 708 1040; www.visitlahinch.com; Church St; dm €17, r €20-45) This well-run hostel has clean, bright rooms with a total of 55 beds. It's close to the beachfront and has surfboard and bicycle storage.

Auburn House (☎ 708 2890; www.auburnhouse.ie; School Rd; s/d from €45/62; ☯ Feb-Oct) An absolute find – but you might miss it because you'll be enjoying the view and not looking for the house, this brilliantly run six-room gem is right at the south entrance to town, across from the cliffs. There are great views and the centre is a three-minute walk.

Atlantic Hotel (☎ 708 1049; www.atlantichotel.ie; s/d from €99/130; ℗ ▣) There's still a pleasant air of bygone times in the reception rooms and bars at this town-centre veteran. The 14 rooms are well-appointed. There's food in the bar and the restaurant offers of the expected fine seafood choices (mains from €29).

Barrtra Seafood Restaurant (☎ 708 1280; Miltown Malbay Rd; mains €16-28) The menu item 'Seafood Symphony' says it all at this rural repose 3.5km south of Lahinch. Enjoy views over pastures to the sea from the homey dining rooms. The cooking eschews flash and lets the inherent tastiness of the food shine.

GETTING THERE & AWAY
Bus Éireann runs one or two buses daily through Lahinch on the Doolin–Ennis/Limerick routes and one or two daily south along the coast to Doonbeg in summer.

ENNISTYMON
☎ 065 / pop 880

Ennistymon (Inis Díomáin) is a timeless country village just 4km inland from Lahinch, but worlds away in terms of atmosphere. People go about their business (which involves a lot of cheerful chatting) barely noticing the characterful buildings lining Main St. And behind this façade there's a surprise: the roaring **Cascades**, the stepped falls of the River Inagh. After heavy rain the falls surge, beer-brown and foaming, and you risk getting drenched on windy days in the flying drizzle. You'll find them through an arch by Byrne's Hotel.

The **library** (☎ 707 1245; ☯ 10am-1.30pm & 2.30-5.30pm Mon, Tue & Thu, 10am-5.30pm & 6.30-8pm Wed & Fri, 10am-2pm Sat), just down from the Square, offers free internet access. The Bank of Ireland, in Parliament St, has a bureau de change and an ATM.

Besides excellent pubs and good sleeping options, Ennistymon has a burgeoning arts scene. **Courthouse Studios & Gallery** (☎ 707 1630; Parliament St) is an impressive new facility with ever-changing exhibitions by local and international artists. It provides studio space for several artists in residence such as film-maker Fergus Tighe. Just south of town on the N85, artists Eamon Doyle and Phillip Morrison have studios and a **gallery** (☎ 707 2787; ☽ 10am-6pm).

Sleeping & Eating

Byrne's (☎ 707 1080; Main St; r €80-120) The Cascades are just out back at this historic guesthouse and restaurant. When the air is not heavy with mist, you can have a drink at a back deck table. The menu is substantial and there's plenty of seafood specials (mains €15-25). There are six comfortable rooms up the creaky heritage stairs. The restaurant is open noon to 9pm Monday to Saturday May to October, and 6pm to 9pm, Wednesday to Saturday during the rest of the year.

Falls Hotel (☎ 707 1004; www.fallshotel.ie; s/d from €85/120; P ☐ ☙) This handsome Georgian house, built on the ruins of an O'Brien castle, has 140 rooms that exude gracious charm. Fittings throughout are heavy and traditional. The view of the Cascades from the entrance steps is breath-taking, and there are walks around the 20 hectares of wooded gardens.

Café Eclipse (☎ 087-977 5226; Parliament St; lunch mains €8-10; ☽ 8.30am-5pm Mon-Sat) This busy little place is the local choice for a full trad breakfast. The rest of the day there's a standard line-up of tasty sandwiches and hot specials.

Holywell Italian Restaurant (☎ 707 2464; Church St; mains €10-12; ☽ noon-11pm) At the north end of the centre, this dark and casual restaurant is the place to spool pasta or knock back a pizza over romantic whispers.

Entertainment

Eugene's (☎ 707 1777; Main St) Not to be missed, Eugene's is a classic pub that defines craic. It's intimate, cosy and has a trademark collection of visiting cards covering its walls, alongside photographs of famous writers and musicians. There is an inspiring collection of whiskey (Irish) and whisky (Scottish) over which you can smoothly debate their competing qualities.

Cooley's House (☎ 707 1712; Main St) Another great old pub, but with music most nights in summer and on Wednesday (trad night) in winter.

Getting There & Away

Bus Éireann runs one or two buses daily through Ennistymon on the Doolin–Ennis/

> **THE POET & THE PRIESTS**
>
> Ennistymon has more than its fair share of cultural associations. The Welsh poet Dylan Thomas lived at what is now the Falls Hotel when the house was the family home of his wife Cáitlín McNamara. There's plenty of Thomas memorabilia, and a Dylan Thomas Bar, at the hotel. At the other end of the scale is *Father Ted*, the enduring British TV comedy set around the highjinks of three Irish priests living on the fictional Craggy Island. Most of the locations used in the show are around Ennistymon (Eugene's pub was used as a location and the cast drank here) and Kilfenora. The lonely Father Ted house is near Kilnaboy.

Limerick routes and one or two daily south along the coast to via Lahinch to Doonbeg in summer. Buses stop in front of Aherne's on Church St.

LISCANNOR & AROUND

☎ 065 / pop 380

This small, seaside village overlooks Liscannor Bay where the road (R478) heads north to the Cliffs of Moher and Doolin. Liscannor (Lios Ceannúir) has given its name to a type of local stone, slatelike and with a rippled surface, that is used for floors, walls and even roofs.

John Philip Holland (1840–1914), the inventor of the submarine, was born in Liscannor. He emigrated to the USA in 1873, and dreamed that his invention would be used to sink British warships. There's a rather silly statue of the man (or is it a walrus?) in front of the Cliffs of Moher Hotel.

Sleeping & Eating

Moher Lodge Farmhouse (☎ 708 1269; www.cliffsofmoher-ireland.com; s/d €45/70; ☽ Apr-Oct; P) This big bungalow is in a great position overlooking the owner's open farmlands and the sea. The four rooms are welcoming after a day rambling. It's 3km northwest of Liscannor, 1km from the Cliffs of Moher.

Cliffs of Moher Hotel (☎ 708 6770; www.cliffsofmoherhotel.ie; Main St; s/d from €50/80; P ☐) A modest yet modern inn right in the centre, this hotel has 23 nicely furnished and comfortable rooms. Local icons above and below the sea are recalled in the Puffin Bar and Submarine Restaurant.

COUNTY CLARE

Vaughan's Anchor Inn (☎ 708 1548; Main St; mains €12-25; ☻ noon-9.30pm) Noted for its excellent seafood, Vaughan's is a popular place. When it rains, you can settle in by a peat fire, when it shines (sometimes 15 minutes later) you can take in the air at a picnic table. The pub stays open past the kitchen.

Joseph McHugh's Bar (☎ 708 1163; Main St) Lots of courtyard tables and regular trad sessions make this old pub a winner.

Getting There & Away

Bus Éireann runs one to three buses daily through Liscannor on the Doolin–Ennis/ Limerick routes.

HAG'S HEAD

Forming the southern end of the Cliffs of Moher, Hag's Head is a dramatic place from which to view the cliffs.

There's a huge sea arch at the tip of Hag's Head and another arch visible to the north. The signal tower on the Head was erected in case Napoleon tried to attack on the western coast of Ireland. The tower is built on the site of an ancient promontory fort called Mothair, which has given its name to the famous cliffs to the north. A walking trail links the head with the cliffs and Liscannor.

CLIFFS OF MOHER

Star of a million tourist brochures, the Cliffs of Moher (Aillte an Mothair, or Ailltreacha Mothair) are one of the most popular sights in Ireland. But like many an ageing star, you have to look beyond the glitz to appreciate the inherent attributes behind the cliché.

The cliffs rise to a height of 203m. They are entirely vertical and the cliff edge abruptly falls away into the constantly churning sea. A series of heads, the dark limestone seems to march in a rigid formation that amazes, no matter how many times you look.

Such appeal comes at a price, however: mobs. This is check-off tourism big time and busloads come and go constantly in summer. To handle the crowds, a vast new visitor centre opened in 2007. Set back into the side of a hill, it's impressively unimpressive – it blends right in. However, as part of the development, the main walkways and viewing areas along the cliffs have been surrounded by a 1.5m-high wall. It's lovely stone but it's also way too high and set too far back from the edge. The entire reason for coming

here (the view – unless you're a bus-spotter) is obscured.

However, like so many oversubscribed natural wonders, there's relief and joy if you're willing to walk 10 minutes away. Past the end of the 'Moher Wall' south, there's still a trail along the cliffs to Hag's Head – few venture this far. There's also a path heading north but you're discouraged from it, so use your common sense. With binoculars you can spot the more than 30 species of birds, including puffins, that make their homes among the craggy cliff-faces. On a clear day you'll channel Barbra Streisand as you can see forever; the Aran Islands stand etched on the waters of Galway Bay, and beyond lie the hills of Connemara in western Galway.

For uncommon views of the cliffs and wildlife you might consider a cruise. Most of the boat operators in Doolin (p394) offer tours of the cliffs. **Cliffs of Moher Cruises** (☎ 065-707 5949; www.mohercruises.com; Doolin Pier; adult/child €20/10; ☻ Apr-Oct) is a popular choice.

Information

The new **visitor centre** (☎ 065-708 6141; www.cliffsof moher.ie; ☻ 8.30am-9pm Jun-Aug, 8.30am-7pm May & Sep, 9am-6pm Mar, Apr & Oct, 9.30am-5pm Nov-Feb) – actually, in a sign of the times, it's called the 'Cliffs of Moher Visitor Experience' – has exhibitions about the cliffs and the environment called the 'Atlantic Edge' (adult/child €4/2.50). Staff lead tours outside and they answer questions but tend to freeze up when you get beyond the top five things someone on a bus tour might ask (such as where you can hike).

The car park costs €8 – be sure to pay for your ticket before you leave. Vendors of 'authentic' sweaters and other tat have stalls near the cars and buses. The café is not impressive.

Getting There & Away

Bus Éireann runs one to three buses daily past the cliffs on the Doolin–Ennis/Limerick routes. Waits between buses may exceed your ability to enjoy the spectacle so you might combine a bus with a walk.

THE BURREN

The Burren region is rocky and windswept, an apt metaphor for the hardscrabble lives of those who've eked out an existence here. It stretches across northern Clare, from

COUNTY CLARE

the Atlantic coast to Kinvara in County Galway, a unique limestone landscape that was shaped beneath ancient seas, and then forced high and dry during some great geological cataclysm. The sea is not muted here by offshore islands or muffled promontories, as it sometimes is on the coasts of Kerry and Galway. In the Burren, land and sea seem to merge into one vast, exhilarating space beneath huge skies.

Boireann is the Irish term for 'rocky country', a plain but graphic description of the Burren's acres of silvery limestone karst pavements. The pavements, known as 'clints', lie like huge, scattered bones across the swooping hills. Between the seams of rock lie narrow fissures, known as 'grykes'. Their humid, sheltered conditions support exquisite wild flowers in spring, lending the Burren its other great charm: brilliant, if ephemeral, colour amid so much arid beauty. There are also intriguing villages to enjoy, especially along the coast and in the south Burren. These include Doolin on the west coast, Kilfenora inland and Ballyvaughan in the north, on the shores of Galway Bay. The Burren's coastline is made up of rocky foreshores, occasional beaches and bare limestone cliffs, while inland lies a haunting landscape of rocky hills peppered with ancient burial chambers and medieval ruins. If driving, take any road – the smaller the better – and see what you discover: you'll never be lost for long.

Large areas of the Burren, about 40,000 hectares in all, have been designated as Special Areas of Conservation. Apart from being against the law, it makes ecological sense not to remove plants or to damage walls, ancient monuments or the landscape itself. Visitors are also asked to resist the temptation to erect 'sham' replicas of dolmens and other monuments, however small, including *Spinal Tap* size.

Information

Generally there is a wealth of literature about the Burren and it's best to trawl the bookshops of Ennis and any local heritage centres for long-standing, but still relevant, publications such as Charles Nelson's *Wild Plants of The Burren and the Aran Islands*. The Tír Eolas

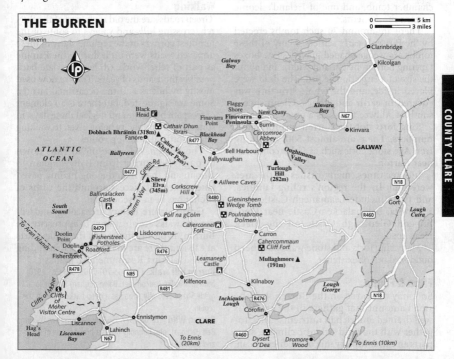

THE BURREN

series of foldout maps, *A Rambler's Guide & Map,* shows antiquities and other points of interest. The *Burren Journey* books by George Cunningham are excellent for local lore, but you may have to search for them. The visitor centre in Ennis is another good source; the booklet *The Burren Way* has good walking routes. Look for wonderfully detailed maps by Tim Robinson.

Archaeology

The Burren's bare limestone hills were once lightly wooded and covered in soil. Towards the end of the Stone Age, about 6000 years ago, nomadic hunter-gatherers began to develop a settled lifestyle of farming and hunting. They cleared the woodlands and used the hills for grazing. Over the centuries, much soil was eroded and the limestone bones of the country became increasingly exposed.

Despite its apparent harshness, the Burren supported quite large numbers of people in ancient times, and has more than 2500 historic sites. Chief among them is the 5000-year-old Poulnabrone Dolmen, the framework of a Neolithic/Bronze Age chamber tomb, and one of Ireland's iconic ancient monuments.

There are around 70 such tombs erected by the Burren's early settlers. Many of these tombs are wedge-shaped graves, stone boxes tapering both in height and width, and about the size of a large double bed. The dead were placed inside, and the whole structure was covered in earth and stones. Gleninsheen, south of Aillwee Caves, is a good example.

Ring forts dot the Burren in prodigious numbers. There are almost 500, including Iron Age stone forts such as Cahercommaun near Carron.

In later times, many castles in the area were built by the region's ruling families, and these include Leamanegh Castle near Kilfenora, Ballinalacken Castle near Doolin and Gleninagh Castle on the Black Head road.

Many ring forts and stone walls have been bulldozed out of existence.

Flora & Fauna

Soil may be scarce on the Burren, but the small amount that gathers in the cracks is well drained and rich in nutrients. This, together with the mild Atlantic climate, supports an extraordinary mix of Mediterranean,

Arctic and Alpine plants. Of Ireland's native wild flowers, 75% are found here, including a number of beautiful orchids, the creamy-white burnet rose, the little starry flowers of mossy saxifrage and the magenta-coloured bloody cranesbill.

The Burren is a stronghold of Ireland's most elusive mammal, the weasel-like pine marten. It's rarely seen, although there are certainly some living in the Caher Valley. Badgers, foxes and even stoats are common throughout the region. Otters and seals haunt the shores around Bell Harbour, New Quay and Finavarra Point.

The estuaries along this northern coast are rich in birdlife and frequently attract Brent geese during the winter. More than 28 of Ireland's 33 species of butterfly are found here, including one endemic species, the Burren green.

As always, modern farming and 'land-improvement' grants have had their effect on the Burren. Weedkillers, insecticides and fertilisers favour grass and little else, often fatally undermining fragile ecological systems.

Walking

'Green roads' are the old highways of the Burren, crossing hills and valleys to some of the remotest corners of the region. Many of these unpaved roads were built during the Famine as part of relief work, while some date back possibly thousands of years. They're now used mostly by hikers and the occasional farmer. Some are signposted, but there is an element of footpath blockage and neglect these days, in spite of much publicity being given to walking and to 'official' walking routes.

The Burren Way (see p698) runs down through the Burren from Ballyvaughan to Doolin and then inland along mainly paved lanes, since cliff access around the Cliffs of Moher has been discouraged.

Guided nature, history, archaeology and wilderness walks are great ways to appreciate the Burren. Typically the cost of the walks starts at €15 and there are many options, including individual trips. Recommended guides:

Burren Hill Walks (☎ 065-707 7168, 088-265 4810; burrenhillwalks@eircom.net; Ballyvaughan) Run by local guide Shane Connolly, who has a deep background in the region.

Burren Wild (☎ 087 877 9565; www.burrenwalks.com; Bell Harbour) John Connolly offers a broad range of walks and packages.

Getting There & Away

Various buses pass through the Burren. The main routes include one from Limerick and Ennis to Corofin, Ennistymon, Lahinch, Liscannor, the Cliffs of Moher, Doolin and Lisdoonvarna; another connects Galway with Ballyvaughan, Lisdoonvarna and Doolin. Usually there are one to three buses daily, with the most in summer.

Getting Around

By car you can cover a fair amount of the Burren in a day and have a chance to explore some of the many unnamed back roads. Mountain bikes are an excellent means of getting off the main roads; ask about rentals at your accommodation. Finally, walking is a superb way to appreciate the subtle beauty and dramatic landscapes.

DOOLIN

☎ 065 / pop 250

Doolin gets plenty of press and chatter as a centre of Irish traditional music, owing to a couple of pubs that have sessions through the year. It's also known for its setting – 6km north of the Cliffs of Moher, the land is windblown, with huge rocks exposed by the long-vanished top soil. It's a place to get boats to the Aran Islands offshore.

Given all its attributes, you might be surprised when you realise that Doolin as it's known barely exists. Rather, when you arrive you might be forgiven for exclaiming 'there's no there here!' For what's called Doolin is really three infinitesimally small neighbouring villages. **Fisherstreet** is right on the water, Doolin itself is about 1km east on the little Aille River and **Roadford** is another 1km east. None has more than a couple of buildings, which gives the place known as Doolin a scattered appearance, without a centre.

Still, the area is hugely popular with backpackers and more affluent travellers (ex-backpackers with jobs). There are scores of hostels and B&Bs widely spread about the rough landscape and a pretty good scene – usually with music – develops in the local pubs, at night.

Orientation & Information

Doolin's three parts are easily reached. From the north and Black Head the R479 first hits Roadford, with its hostels and two pubs. From the east, the R479 heads down into Doolin village

from a junction with the R478, where there's a market. Doolin village has a couple of new hotels and developments. From the south, take a small road off the R478 north of the cliffs of Moher and follow it down to Fisherstreet, with its postcard-perfect row of shops and pub. From here the harbour and ferries are 1.5km.

There is no post office or bank in Doolin. Many places will change money and offer internet access. Try **Doolin Internet Cafe** (per 30min $3; ☒ 8am-10pm) in the Doolin Activity Lodge (p393). For tourist info, there's a self-service area in the Hotel Doolin (p393).

Activities

One of the most enjoyable ways to pass your time in Doolin is by walking the windswept country. Tracks and paths radiate in all directions; the Cliffs of Moher are 6km south.

The Doolin area is popular with cavers. The **Fisherstreet Potholes** are nearby, and **Poll na gColm**, 5km northeast of Lisdoonvarna, is Ireland's longest cave, with more than 12km of mapped passageways; see www .cavingireland.org for more details. A little over 1km north of Roadford you'll find **Doolin Cave** (☎ 707 5761; www.doolincave.ie; adult/child €15/8), which boasts an enormous stalactite that looks like a giant squid. The main entrance is at the Fisherstreet Potholes; tour times vary by season.

The rocks to the north of Doolin Harbour are honeycombed with an unusual system of undersea caves called the **Green Holes of Doolin**. They're the longest known undersea caves in temperate waters. Nondivers can look, with care, into Hell, a large gash in the rocks, north of the harbour and about 50m from the sea. The gash is about 6m wide, and the heaving water at the bottom leads to a maze of submarine passages.

The unguided caves mentioned here require experience and full equipment.

Sleeping

A new place to stay seems to open in Doolin about as often as some drunken tourist requests 'Danny Boy' at a trad music session. Despite this you should book ahead in summer.

BUDGET

Doolin has an excellent range of hostels.

Nagles Doolin Caravan & Camping Park (☎ 707 4458; www.doolincamping.com; camp sites from €15;

COUNTY CLARE

VOICES: JAMES CULLINAN, DOOLIN MUSICIAN

James Cullinan has been playing the fiddle for 35 years. He's a noted musician in County Clare and can often be heard playing in Doolin's pubs. 'It's bit impromptu', he says, 'I'll be out with friends, have two or three pints, hear some music and the next thing you know I've run home, got the fiddle and I'm back playing music.' Unplanned, pint-fuelled sessions aside, his playing is kept in check by his work as chef and owner of the well-regarded guesthouse and restaurant that bears his name. Outside of summer, however, he's a regular at area music festivals. He took a few moments to answer our questions about music.

How did Doolin become known for music? In the 1970s Michael Russell and his brothers really began reviving the old songs. They had a farm here but weren't very good farmers – if they heard of a session, they'd go play and leave the hay in the field. Pretty soon they had a reputation and people started coming here to hear them. Over time people began to expect music here, so publicans would pay a few guys each night just to get something going. It was a good way to get free pints.

How did you start playing? I had a great music teacher. It was the early 1970s and Irish music was becoming cool again. He gave everybody a tin whistle and if you showed any talent you got a fiddle.

Why did you stick with the fiddle? It has endless possibilities for how you play it. I can play the same song at every session here but each time will be different. It can depend on where you sit, who else is playing, what the crowd's like and more.

What kind of crowd is best? Loud. You just want to feel like you're playing amongst people.

Does Doolin or Clare have a unique style? Yes, we do a lot of jigs and reels here. In other counties you'll hear more polkas or other influences but Clare musicians are pretty conservative. Older people come here and know everything we play. We play around with the old stuff and have fun with that.

What's the worst thing that can happen in a pub session? Somebody starts to sing. We keep the jigs and reels going because otherwise after a few pints everybody thinks they can sing and they take over. We're there playing for ourselves, not to back-up drunks.

The second worst thing? Some guy always comes up and asks for 'Devil Came Down to Georgia'. They must play it a lot in bad Irish bars in America.

Apr-Sep) With full-on views of the Cliffs of Moher, and Doolin only a short distance away, this is an appealing site. The 60 sites are open to the elements, so pin those pegs down.

Aille River Hostel (☎ 707 4260; ailleriver@esatclear .ie; Roadford; dm/d €14/33; mid-Mar–Dec;) In a picturesque spot by the river in the upper village, this converted 17th-century farmhouse is a great choice. There are turf fires, hot showers and free laundry. This IHH hostel has 30 beds and camp sites (from €14).

Rainbow Hostel (☎ 707 4415; Roadford; dm/d from €14/34;) Many a friendship has started in the cosy lounge here. IHH-affiliated, this hostel has 30 beds and is in an old farmhouse by the road.

Paddy's Doolin Hostel (☎ 707 4421; www .doolinhostel.com; Fisherstreet, Doolin; dm/r €15/40;) This place, also known as Paddy Moloney's, is a modern, IHH-affiliated hostel. There are 90 beds in four- and eight-bed rooms. Private rooms with bathrooms are also available.

Doolin Cottage (☎ 707 4762; caroldoolin@hotmail .com; Roadford; s/d from €34/56; Mar-Nov;) This charming little old house has a peaceful and friendly atmosphere and is good value. The three rooms vary greatly in size.

COUNTY CLARE

MIDRANGE

Most places to stay in this price range are in houses on large plots of land. There are many choices.

Doolin Activity Lodge (☎ 707 4888; www.doolin lodge.com; Fisherstreet; s/d from €40/60; (P) (□)) This impressive purpose-built guesthouse occupies a large compound; the solid stone buildings are quite attractive. There are 14 newly furnished rooms, some with skylights for watching the rain blow past, as well as self-catering apartments.

Dubhlinn House (☎ 707 4770; www.dubhlinnhouse .com; Doolin; s/d from €45/64; (P)) This bright and airy B&B is as cheery as it looks, and has good views down towards the water. The three rooms are simply decorated while the breakfasts are lavish; choose from a variety of meals including a puffed savoury omelette.

O'Connors Guesthouse (☎ 707 4498; www.oconnors doolin.com; Doolin; s/d from €45/68; (P)) On a bend in the Aille, this working farm has 10 rooms of varying sizes in a rather plush farmhouse. Fresh baked breads in the morning may put you in the mood for chores, but you're on holiday, so don't. Stretch your legs in the large gardens and say 'hi' to a cow.

Doonmacfelim House (☎ 707 4503; www.doonmac felim.com; Roadford; s/d from €55/70; (P)) Decorated as you'd expect from a favourite aunt, the rooms are comfortable. There's a bit of history as well: prehistoric artefacts including a stone axe on display were found during construction of this red stucco house.

Cullinan's Guest House (☎ 707 4183; www.cullinans doolin.com; Doolin; s/d from €60/80; (P)) The eight B&B rooms here are all to a high standard, with power showers and various extras. Right on the Aille (two rooms have balconies), it has a lovely back terrace for enjoying the views. The restaurant is one of the best. The owner is a well-known local musician (see the boxed text, opposite).

Sea View House (☎ 707 4826; www.ireland-doolin.com; Fisherstreet; s/d from €60/80; (P)) On high ground right above Fisherstreet village, this big house has sweeping ocean views. The common lounge has a telescope for enjoying the vantage point. The four rooms make the same bold use of colours that gives the public areas a sense of style.

TOP END

Hotel Doolin (☎ 707 4111; www.hoteldoolin.ie; Doolin; Coast Rd, Doolin; s/d €80/130; (P)) Part of a new development that may put a little 'there' in Doolin village, this upmarket boutique hotel has 17 well-appointed rooms. Creams and coffee tones are accented by rich colours. Service is good and there's a modern bar for those who want sport instead of music.

Eating

For self-catering, the well-stocked Doolin Deli is just down from O'Connor's pub in Fisherstreet on the road to the pier.

McGann's (☎ 707 4133; Roadford; meals €6-15) McGann's does a good job with cheap and cheerful pub grub. You can order through a window and dine at a picnic table.

O'Connor's (☎ 707 4168; Fisherstreet; meals €8-18) The town's most popular pub makes a fine job of Irish standards. The seafood chowder, bacon and cabbage and fish and chips are all excellent. Beware, however, of bus crowds.

Cullinan's (☎ 707 4183; 1-/2-/3-courses €25/32/40; Doolin; ⏱ 6-9pm Thu-Tue) Attached to the guesthouse of the same name, this excellent restaurant offers delicious seafood as well as meat and poultry dishes. The short menu changes depending on what's fresh, but is always creative. Bold combinations are favoured and there's a long wine list.

Drinking & Entertainment

Doolin's rep is largely based on music. There are a lot of musicians who live in the area and they have a symbiotic relationship with the tourists: each desires the other and each year things grow a little larger. But given the heavy concentration of visitors it's inevitable that standards don't always hold up to those in some of the less trampled villages in Clare (see the boxed text, p394). Still, in the off-season, this is where you'll always be able to hear a trad session.

Doolin's three pubs are listed below in order of their importance to the music scene.

O'Connor's (☎ 707 4168; Fisherstreet) This sprawling favourite packs them in and has rollicking atmosphere when the traditional music, singing and drinking are all in full swing. The food is good; it's right on the water.

McGann's (☎ 707 4133; Roadford) McGann's has all the classic touches of a full-on Irish music pub with the action often spilling out onto the street. Food is also served here and it has a small outside covered area.

MacDiarmada's (☎ 707 4700; Roadford) Also known as MacDermott's, this simple red

---

WHEN SESSIONS GO BAD

It was an off-season night in Doolin's popular O'Connor's pub. There was a good crowd listening to three old-timers work their way through old classics. Mid-song they were joined by an American tourist who pulled a guitar out of an expensive custom case still wearing fresh bag tags from the flight over. Like any good session, the three incumbents made room for the newcomer. They soon regretted this. During the next pause, the guitar-wielding bloke said, 'Follow me!' and proceeded into an earnest and somewhat off-key version of 'Eight Days a Week', a song seldom heard at trad sessions. The three locals exchanged glances that said they'd smelled something out of the wrong end of a cow. Eventually they regained some control and as the American tried gamely to follow their songs, he said repeatedly to his camera-flashing partner: 'Look, I'm playing with real Irish musicians!'

At this point an Italian tourist wandered over and said loudly 'I shall join you in song.' Grabbing a mike while the old guys exchanged more dubious glances, he leaned back to belt out a croon but slipped, hitting the table and spilling all the beer. Amid the chaos, the American looked at his spilled pint and said over and over: 'That was going to be my first Guinness ever!'

---

and white old pub can be the rowdy favourite of locals. The music sessions are up to Doolin standards.

Getting There & Away

BOAT
Doolin is the ferry departure point to the Aran Islands from April to October. There are three ferry companies offering numerous departures in season. It takes around 20 minutes to cover the 8km to Inisheer (€30 return), the smallest and closest of the three Aran Islands. A boat to Inishmór takes 90 minutes with an Inisheer stop (€40 return). Ferries to Inishmaan are infrequent. Note that sailings are often cancelled due to high seas. Call and confirm times and book in advance.

Doolin Ferries (☎ 707 4455, 707 4466; www.doolin ferries.com; Doolin Pier)

Doolin Ferry (☎ 707 5555, 707 1710; www.doolinferry .com; Doolin Pier)

Jack B (☎ 707 5949; www.mohercruises.com; Doolin Pier; ☾ Apr-Oct) Offers combined Aran Islands trips with Cliffs of Moher cruises.

BUS
Bus Éireann runs one to three buses daily to Doolin from Ennis (€8.80, 1½ hours) and Limerick (€13, 2½ hours) via Corofin, Lahinch and the Cliffs of Moher. Buses also go to Galway (€12, 1½ hours, one or two daily) via Ballyvaughan.

In the summer, various backpackers shuttles often serve Doolin from Galway and other points in Clare. These are amply marketed in hostels.

Getting Around
Several hostels and B&Bs rent bikes; ask around.

LISDOONVARNA
☎ 065 / pop 950
Lisdoonvarna (Lios Dún Bhearna), often just called 'Lisdoon', is well known for its mineral springs. For centuries people have been visiting the local spa to swallow its waters. Posh in the Victorian era, the town is now a much more plebeian and friendly place. It's a very good base for exploring the Burren.

The town was once a centre for *basadóiri* (matchmakers) who, for a fee, would fix up a person with a mate. Most of the mainly male hopefuls would hit town in September, feet shuffling, cap in hand, after the hay was in. Today, true matchmaking is unlikely, but the **Lisdoonvarna Matchmaking Festival** (www .matchmakerireland.com), held throughout September and early October, is a great excuse for daftness, drinking, merrymaking, music and, of course, moneymaking.

Orientation & Information
Lisdoonvarna is essentially a one-street town with a square in the centre from where you turn west for Doolin and the coast. The town has plenty of shops, pubs, B&Bs and hotels with some fine restaurants. You can

change money at the post office on Main St to the north.

There's internet access at the **Internet Shop** (☎ 707 5005; Main St; per 20min €2; ☑ 9am-6pm Mon-Sat May-Sep).

Sights & Activities

At the southern end of town is a spa, with a sulphur spring, a Victorian pumphouse and an agreeable, wooded setting. The iron, sulphur, magnesium and iodine in the water are supposed to be good for rheumatic and glandular complaints. There's just one hitch: in 2007 the spa centre was closed as various renovation schemes (most involving the word 'upscale') were debated. But you can still drink the water, even if it's not exactly a vintage wine–tasting experience. Look for a trail beside the Roadside Tavern that runs 400m down to **two wells** by the river. One is high in sulphur, the other iron. Mix and match for a cocktail of minerals.

You can learn about the ancient Irish art of oak-smoking salmon from a video (six languages) at the **Burren Smokehouse visitor centre** (☎ 707 4432; www.burrensmokehouse.ie; Kincora Rd; admission free; ☑ 10am-5pm Apr-May, 9am-6pm Jun-Oct, 10am-4pm Nov-Mar). Tasty smoked salmon and other fishies in a myriad of forms are offered for free tasting – perhaps you'll even buy some? Good coffee and tea are for sale along with other deli-type foods and local arts and crafts. Tourist information is available. The centre is on the edge of Lisdoonvarna on the Kincora road (N67).

Sleeping & Eating

Book during September's Matchmaking Festival; B&Bs are like mushrooms after the rain.

Sleepzone (☎ 707 7168; www.sleepzone.ie; Doolin Rd; dm/s/d €15/35/50; P ☐) What a hostel! This former posh hotel is now a 124-bed hostel. The grounds reflect its past and there are all the usual facilities – except these are very nice indeed – as well as wi-fi and free continental breakfasts. There's a shuttle bus between here and a sister hostel in Galway (March to October).

Kincora House and Art Gallery (☎ 707 4300; www .kincorahotel.ie; s/d from €45/70; ☑ Mar-Oct; P) On the west side of town, this country charmer is covered in flowering vines. The 1860 building underneath attests to the spa-driven affluence of the era. The 14 rooms are cute

as you'd expect, local art abounds and the pub and restaurant are appealing.

Sheedy's Country House Hotel & Restaurant (☎ 707 4026; www.sheedys.com; Sulphur Hill, Lisdoonvarna; s/d from €90/140; ☑ Mar-Oct; P) Sheedy's stands in a splendid location amid flower, vegetable and herb plots. The 11 rooms are individually and stylishly designed and the public areas are full of character. The restaurant (dinner mains €20 to €28) offers modern Irish cuisine at its best.

our pick **Roadside Tavern** (☎ 707 4084; meals €6-12) Down by the river, this place is pure craic. Third-generation owner Peter Curtin knows every story worth telling. There are trad sessions daily in summer and during the weekends in winter. Imbibing musicians can be found here anytime. A sample of pub conversation we overhead – man to publican: 'I'll have half a sandwich.' Man's wife to publican: 'Oh give him a whole one so I won't have to cook tonight.'

Getting There & Around

Bus Éireann runs one to three buses daily to Doolin via Lisdoonvarna from Ennis, and to Limerick via Corofin, Lahinch and the Cliffs of Moher. Buses also go to Galway via Ballyvaughan and Black Head.

FANORE

☎ 065 / pop 150

Fanore (Fan Óir), 5km south of Black Head, is less a village and more a stretch of coast with a shop, a pub and a few houses scattered along the main road (R477). It has a fine sandy beach with an extensive backdrop of dunes. Surfers flock here through the year; there's extensive parking and there are toilets open in summer. An incursion of holiday homes could mean that even this sleepy corner of Clare is in for changes.

There's a well-stocked shop, **Siopa Fan Óir** (☎ 707 6131; ☑ 9am-9pm summer, to 7pm winter), just across from O'Donohue's pub, where you can buy fishing tackle, walking maps, boogie boards, cheap sand buckets etc.

There are few accommodation options and eateries in the Fanore area. One, **Rocky View Farmhouse** (☎ 707 6103; www.rockyviewfarmhouse.com; s/d €38/64; P), is a charming house at the heart of the coastal Burren. Its six open and airy rooms are suited to this especially barren end of the burren. Organic food is grown and used in the breakfasts.

COUNTY CLARE

In many ways, the community centre, **O'Donohue's** (☎ 707 6119; meals €6-12; ☺ Apr-Oct), 4km south of the beach, offers no-nonsense soup, hot dishes and sandwiches along with its genuine local character. Done up in blue and white, it looks out over the grey sea.

Bus Éireann runs one to three buses daily from Galway via Black Head and through Fanore to Lisdoonvarna.

BLACK HEAD

Atlantic storms have stripped the land around the unfortunately named Black Head down to bare rock. Grass and the occasional shrub cling to crevices. Standing like sentinels, boulders and the odd cow dot the landscape here, Clare's northwesternmost point.

The main road (R477) curves around the head just above the sea. There's good shore **angling** for pollock, wrasse, mackerel – and sea bass if you're lucky – from the rocky platforms near sea level. These can be fatally dangerous waters, even for those with long-standing local knowledge. Even in apparently calm conditions, watch for sudden surges.

BALLYVAUGHAN & AROUND

☎ 065 / pop 200

All the charm of the Burren is distilled into its favoured location, Ballyvaughan (Baile Uí Bheacháin), where the hard land of the hills gives way to a quiet leafy corner of Galway Bay. It makes an excellent base for visiting the northern part of the Burren. You'll be reluctant to leave.

The centre of the village is located at the junction of the N67 and the coastal R477. Going south and inland on the N67 brings you to the centre of the Burren. Turning west leads you to the magnificent coast road (R477) around Black Head and south towards Doolin.

Just west of the junction, on the R477, is the quay, built in 1829 at a time when boats traded with the Aran Islands and Galway, exporting grain and bacon and bringing in turf – a scarce commodity in the Burren.

A few metres past the harbour, a signposted track leads to a seashore bird shelter from where there is a good view of tidal shallows.

Information

The new **visitor centre** (☎ 707 7464; www.bally vaughantourism.com; ☺ 9am-9pm Mar-Oct, 9am-5pm Thu-Mon Nov-Feb) is in a vast gift shop. **Brendan's Boat** (☎ 707 7337; www.brendansboat.ie; ☺ 9.30am-6.30pm Apr-Dec) is a renowned local leather-maker. On the south side of the centre, it offers internet access and shares the building with a laundry and bike rental place.

Sights & Activities

About 6km south of Ballyvaughan on the Lisdoonvarna road (N67) is a series of severe bends up **Corkscrew Hill** (180m). The road was built as part of a Great Famine relief scheme in the 1840s. From the top there are spectacular views of the northern Burren and Galway Bay, with Aillwee Mountain and the caves on the right, and Cappanawalla Hill on

---

CLIMBING THE AGES

An exhilarating outing is the climb up Black Head to the Iron Age **ring fort of Cathair Dhún Iorais**. There's no path, so it's essential to take a map (Ordnance Survey Discovery Series No 51) and compass. The ground is very rocky in places, so strong footwear is essential. Be prepared for wet, windy and potentially cold conditions, even in summer. It's a steep 1.5km to the fort.

Start from just above the lighthouse on the northern tip of Black Head. There's limited parking on the inland side of the road. Head due south up the rocky hillside from the road, negotiating between rock shelves, to reach an old green track. Cross the track and continue directly to where things level off and Cathair Dhún Iorais stands amid a sea of limestone pavements. It's not the most dramatic of ring forts, but the setting is magnificent. The views to Galway and Connemara are breathtaking in clear weather.

From the fort you can bear southeast to skirt the limestone cliffs that run in an unbroken wall to the west. This takes you onto the broad shoulder that leads south, in 1.3km, to the summit of **Dobhach Bhráinín**, one of the highest points in the Burren at 318m. Again, skilled use of map and compass is essential in case of sudden mist, when careless descent from Dobhach Bhráinín may land you above the cliffs. It's best to return to the fort and descend the way you came.

the left, and with the partially restored 16th-century Newtown Castle, erstwhile residence of the O'Lochlains, at its base.

There's a lot to see in the frigid waters off the Clare coast, including some very large crabs – the kind that have been gracing your plate. **Burren Adventure Dive Centre** (☎ 707 7921; www.burrenadventures.com; Main St) offers lessons and a full range of gear. Discovery dives for novices cost €95.

Sleeping & Eating
There are several simple B&Bs close to the centre. Ballyvaughan's **farmers market** (◷ 10am-2pm Sat) celebrates the huge range of quality produce and products from local producers.

Ballyvaughan Lodge (☎ 707 7292; www.ballyvaughanlodge.com; s/d from €45/70; **P**) Set in nice gardens, this B&B has a fine patio for sniffing the floral fragrances. The 11 rooms are comfortable.

Hyland's Burren Hotel (☎ 707 7037; www.hylandsburren.com; Main St; s/d €65/80; **P**) An appealing place, this central hotel has 30 large rooms and manages to retain a local feel alongside its corporate motif. There's a bar and a restaurant. Ask for the hotel's *Walks* leaflet.

Rusheen Lodge (☎ 707 7092; www.rusheenlodge.com; Lisdoonvarna Rd; s/d €70/100; ◷ Feb-Nov; **P** 🖳) Stylish, imaginative furnishings make this nine-room guesthouse a winner. There's wi-fi inside and colourful gardens outside. It's about 750m south of the village on the N67.

Monk's Bar & Restaurant (☎ 707 7059; Old Pier; mains €10-20; ◷ kitchen noon-8pm) Famed for its excellent seafood, Monk's is a cheerful, spacious and comfortable place. Peat fires warm in winter while sea breezes cool you at the outdoor tables in summer. The pub is open late and there are trad sessions some nights in high season.

Ólólainn (Main St) A tiny place on the left as you head out to the pier, Ólólainn (o-*loch*-lain) is the place for a timeless moment or two in old-fashioned snugs. Look for the old Bushmill's sign out front.

Getting There & Away
Bus Éireann runs one to three buses daily from Galway through Ballyvaughan and around Black Head to Lisdoonvarna and Doolin.

CENTRAL BURREN
The road through the heart of the Burren, the R480, travels through harsh but inspiring scenery. This is the barren Burren at its best. Amazing prehistoric stone structures can be found throughout the region.

South from Ballyvaughan the R480 branches off the N67 at the sign for Aillwee Caves. The R480 goes past Gleninsheen Wedge Tomb and Poulnabrone Dolmen before reaching Leamanegh Castle, where it joins the R476, which runs southeast to Corofin. At any point along here, try a small road – especially those to the east – for an escape into otherworldly solitude.

Aillwee Caves
Popular with kids, **Aillwee Caves** (☎ 065-707 7036; www.aillweecave.ie; Ballyvaughan; adult/child €12/5.50; ◷ from 10am) is a large tourist attraction. The main cave penetrates for 600m into the mountain, widening into larger caverns, one with its own waterfall. The caves were carved out by water some two million years ago. Near the entrance are the remains of a brown bear, extinct in Ireland for more than 10,000 years. You can only go into the cave as part of a guided tour (phone for exact times). Often crowded in summer, there's a café and other time-killers on site.

Gleninsheen Wedge Tomb
One of Ireland's most famous prehistoric grave sites, Gleninsheen lies beside the R480 just south of Aillwee Caves. It's thought to date from 4000 to 5000 years ago. A magnificent gold torque (a crescent of beaten gold that hung round the neck) was found nearby in 1930 by a young boy called Paddy Dolan, who was hunting rabbits. Dating from around 700 BC, the torque is reckoned to be one of the finest pieces of prehistoric Irish craftwork and is now on display at the National Museum in Dublin (p96). Note: the gate giving access to the Gleninsheen tomb may be locked.

Poulnabrone Dolmen
Also known as the Portal Tomb, Poulnabrone Dolmen is one of Ireland's most photographed ancient monuments – a classic tourist icon. The dolmen (a large slab perched on stone uprights) stands amid a swathe of rocky pavements, for all the world like some surreal bird of prey about to take off. The capstone weighs five tonnes. The

site is 8km south of Aillwee and is visible from the R480. A path leads to it from the roadside.

Poulnabrone was built more than 5000 years ago. It was excavated in 1986, and the remains of 16 people were found, as well as pieces of pottery and jewellery. Radiocarbon dating suggests that they were buried between 3800 and 3200 BC. When the dead were originally entombed here, the whole structure was partially covered in a mound of earth, which has since worn away. It's your guess as to how they built it.

Caherconnell Fort

For a look at a well-preserved *caher* (walled homestead) of the late Iron Age–Early Christian period, stop at **Caherconnell Fort** (☎ 708 9999; adult/child/family €5/3/12; ☼ 9.30am-6.30pm Jul & Aug, 10am-5pm Mar-Jun, Sep & Oct; Ⓟ), a privately run heritage attraction. Exhibits show how the evolution of these defensive settlements may have reflected territorialism and competition for land among a growing, settling population. The drystone walling of the fort is in excellent condition. There is a visitor centre with information on the many other monuments in the area. It's about 1km south of Poulnabrone on the R480.

Carron & Around

The tiny village of Carron ('Carran' on some maps; 'An Carn' in Gaelic), a few kilometres east of the R480, is a wonderfully remote

spot. Vistas of the rocky Burren stretch in all directions from its elevated position.

A must-see stop, the **Burren Perfumery & Floral Centre** (☎ 065-708 9102; Carron; ☼ 9am-7pm Jun-Sep, to 5pm Oct-May) is the real deal. It uses wild flowers of the Burren to produce its scents, and it's the only handicraft perfumery in Ireland. There's a free audiovisual presentation on the flora of the Burren, which have a diversity that may surprise. One example: the fragrant orchid that grows amongst the rocks. The centre has an organic-tea café and native gardens. Look for perfumery signs at the T-junction near Carron church, which note that tour buses *aren't* welcome.

Below Carron lies one of the finest turloughs in Ireland. It's known as the **Carron Polje**. Polje is a Yugoslav term used universally for these shallow depressions that flood in winter and dry out in summer, when the lush grass that flourishes on the surface is used for grazing.

Stretching south from Carron almost to Kilnaboy is land best suited for growing rocks. Take any narrow track you find, and every so often you'll see an ancient **dolmen**.

About 3km south of Carron and perched on the edge of an inland cliff is the great stone fort of **Cahercommaun**. It was inhabited in the 8th and 9th centuries by people who hunted deer and grew a small amount of grain. The remains of a souterrain (underground passage) lead from the fort to the outer cliff face. To get there, go south from Carron and take a left turn for Kilnaboy. After 1.5km a path on

---

ROCK LEGENDS

The geology of the Burren may seem like a load of old rocks, but there is immense drama and excitement in the primeval adventures that produced the exquisite landscape that we see today. The Burren is the most extensive limestone region, or karst (after the original Karst in Slovenia), in Ireland or Britain. It consists almost entirely of limestone, except for a cap of mud and shale that sits on the higher regions.

During the Carboniferous period 350 million years ago, this whole area was the bottom of a warm and shallow sea. The remains of coral and shells fell to the sea bed, and coastal rivers dumped sand and silt on top of these lime deposits. Time and pressure turned the layers to stone, with limestone below and shale and sandstone above.

Massive shifts in the earth's crust some 270 million years ago buckled the edges of Europe and forced the sea bed above sea level. At the same time the stone sheets were bent and fractured to form the long, deep cracks so characteristic of the Burren today, each one a stone trench crammed full of wild flowers, and nurtured on tenuous soil and a microclimate of sweet, damp air.

During numerous Ice Ages, glaciers scoured the hills, rounding the edges and sometimes polishing the rock to a shiny finish. The glaciers also dumped a thin layer of rock and soil over the region. Huge boulders were carried by the ice, incongruous aliens on a sea of flat rock. Seen all over the Burren, these 'glacial erratics' are often a visibly different type of rock.

the left leads up to the fort. Look for a good info board at the start of the path.

Clare's Rock Hostel (☎ 065-708 9129; www.claresrock .com; Carron; dm/d €14/38; ☺ May-Sep; ℗ ☐) is an imposing building in grey exposed stone. It has 30 beds, big spacious rooms and excellent facilities. Guests can hire bikes or cavort with the trolls on the outdoor garden gnome chessboard.

Cassidy's (☎ 065-708 9109; Carron; bar mains €4.50-9.50; ☺ daily May-Sep, weekends Oct-Apr) serves up a good range of pub dishes, several with witty names reflecting the pub's previous incarnation as a British RIC station, and then as a Garda barracks. Enjoy trad music and dancing some weekends.

KILFENORA
☎ 065 / pop 360

Kilfenora (Cill Fhionnúrach) lies on the southern fringes of the Burren, 8km southeast of Lisdoonvarna. It's a small place, like its diminutive 12th-century cathedral. There are several high crosses in its churchyard. Low polychromatic buildings surround its compact centre.

The town has a strong music tradition that rivals that of Doolin, but without the crowds. The **Kilfenora Céili Band** (☎ 684 2228; www.kilfenora ceiliband.com) is a celebrated community that's been playing for 100 years. Its traditional music features fiddles, banjos, squeezeboxes and more. It often plays Wednesday nights at Linnane's (see right).

Sights
The **Burren Centre** (☎ 708 8030; www.theburrencentre .ie; Main St; adult/child €7/4; ☺ 9.30am-6pm Jun-Aug, 10am-5pm mid-Mar–May, Sep & Oct) has a series of entertaining and informative displays on every aspect of the Burren past and present. There's a tea room and a shop that sells local products.

In the past the ruined 12th-century **cathedral** at Kilfenora was an important place of pilgrimage. St Fachan (or Fachtna) founded the monastery here in the 6th century, and it later became the seat of Kilfenora diocese, the smallest in the country. The cathedral is the smallest you're ever likely to see. Only the ruined structure and nave of the more recent Protestant church are actually part of the cathedral. The chancel has two primitive carved figures on top of two tombs.

Kilfenora is best known for its **high crosses**, three in the churchyard and a large 12th-century example in the field about 100m to the west. The most interesting one is the 800-year-old **Doorty Cross**, standing prominently to the west of the church's front door. It was lying broken in two until the 1950s, when it was re-erected. A panel in the churchyard does an excellent job of explaining the carvings that adorn the crosses.

Sleeping & Eating
Kilfenora has two fabulous pubs.

Kilfenora Hostel (☎ 708 8908; www.kilfenorahostel .com; Main St; dm/s/d €20/25/50; ℗ ☐) Affiliated with Vaughan's Pub next door, rates here include a pint of Guinness. This new hostel has 46 beds in nine rooms. Extras include wi-fi, laundry and a big kitchen. Weary travellers in the lounge may feel they've fallen into the hand of god.

Murphy's B&B (☎ 708 8040; lika@eircom.net; Main St; s/d from €40/60; ☺ mid-Feb–Nov) Right on the main street, Mrs Mary Murphy runs a fine little B&B with the kind of simple rooms you could call your own. She has two more houses nearby.

Linnane's (☎ 708 8157; Main St; meals €5-12; ☺ kitchen: noon-8pm) Irish standards like bacon and cabbage, stew, smoked salmon and more are fully honoured here. Peat fires warm the almost bare interior, with not a frill in sight. There's trad music many nights in summer.

our pick Vaughan's Pub (☎ 708 8004; Main St; meals €9-12; ☺ kitchen: 10am-9pm) What a place! Seafood, traditional foods and local produce feature on the appealing menu. The pub has a big reputation in Irish music circles. There's music in the bar every night during the summer and on many nights the rest of the year. The adjacent barn is the scene of terrific set-dancing sessions on Thursday and Sunday nights. Enjoy the beer garden under the big tree out front.

Getting There & Away
Kilfenora does not have a useful bus service.

COROFIN & AROUND
☎ 065 / pop 420

Corofin (Cora Finne), also spelled Corrofin, is a quiet village on the southern fringes of the Burren. It's low-key but it's also a classic place to sample the rhythms of Clare life. The surrounding area features a number of turloughs. There are several O'Brien castles in the area, two on the shores of nearby Inchiquin Lough.

Corofin is home to the interesting **Clare Heritage Centre** (☎ 683 7955; www.clareroots.com; Church St; adult/concession €4/2; ☺ 9.30am-5.30pm Apr-Oct). Housed in an old church, it has a display covering the horrors of the Potato Famine. More than 250,000 people lived in Clare before the Famine; today the county's population stands at about 95,000 – a drop of some 62%. In a separate building nearby, the **Clare Genealogical Centre** (☎ 683 7955; ☺ 9am-5.30pm Mon-Fri) has facilities for people researching their Clare ancestry.

About 4km northwest of Corofin, on the road to Leamanegh Castle and Kilfenora (R476), look for the small town of **Kilnaboy**. The ruined church here is well worth seeking out for the sheila-na-gig (explicit carved female figure) over the doorway.

Sleeping & Eating

Corofin Village Hostel (☎ 683 7683; www.corofin camping.com; Main St; camp sites, dm/d €14/€16/22; P) Camp sites out back have nice open spaces, and inside there are 30 beds. The large common room at this IHH-affiliated hostel has a pool table. Hot showers are free for all.

Lakefield Lodge (☎ 683 7675; www.lakefieldlodge bandb.com; Ennis Rd; s/d from €46/64; ☺ Mar-Oct) A well-run place near the southern edge of the village. There are four comfy rooms and a cheery welcome at this pleasant bungalow that's surrounded by gardens.

Fergus View (☎ 683 7606; www.fergusview.com; s/d €52/74; P 🖥) Got the black pudding blues? Here there's a huge choice for breakfast. This lovely home has views over the surrounding farms to the rocky hills beyond. All six rooms have wi-fi. Test your knowledge against the vintage lesson plans left by a previous schoolteacher owner. It's 3km north of Corofin on the R476.

Inchiquin Inn (☎ 683 7713; Main St; lunch €6-10; ☺ kitchen 9am-6pm) Locals follow the horses at this oh-so-local pub with a great kitchen. The seafood chowder and bacon and cabbage are some of the best you'll find. The former is thick, tangy and redolent with smoked fish. There's trad music some summer nights.

Corofin Arms Restaurant (☎ 683 7373; Main St; meals €8-20; ☺ 5.30-9pm Wed-Mon, noon-9pm Sun) Locally sourced foods are the speciality at this sprightly little bistro that's very popular. Look for dishes made with tangy Kilnaboy cheese that's made just up the road. Seafood

is the star, anything with the housemade garlic sauce a celebrity.

Getting There & Away

Bus Éireann has an infrequent service some weekdays between Corofin and Ennis.

NORTHERN BURREN

Low farmland stretches south from County Galway until it meets the bluff limestone hills of the Burren, which begin west of Kinvara and Doorus in County Galway.

From Oranmore in County Galway to Ballyvaughan, the coastline wriggles along small inlets and peninsulas; some, such as Finavarra Point and New Quay, are worth a detour. Here, narrow roads traverse the low rocky windswept hills that are dotted with old stone ruins that have yielded to nature.

Inland near Bell Harbour is the largely intact Corcomroe Abbey, while the three ancient churches of Oughtmama lie up a quiet side valley. Galway Bay forms the backdrop to some outstanding scenery: bare stone hills shining in the sun, with small hamlets and rich patches of green wherever there's soil.

Buses don't reach these Clare recesses. It's car, bike or foot country.

New Quay & the Flaggy Shore

New Quay (Ceibh Nua), on the **Finavarra Peninsula**, is about 1km off the main Kinvara–Ballyvaughan road (N67) and is reached by turning off at Ballyvelaghan Lough 3km north of Bell Harbour.

Smack on the water, **Linnane's Bar** (☎ 065-707 8120; New Quay; meals €9-20; ☺ noon-8pm), not surprisingly, is known for seafood. For centuries this area was famous for its oysters; shellfish are still processed here and you can sometimes buy them from the little processing works behind the pub.

The **Flaggy Shore**, west of New Quay, is a particularly fine stretch of coastline where limestone terraces step down to the sea. About 500m west of Linnane's, at a crossroads, the **Russell Gallery** (☎ 065-707 8185; New Quay) specialises in *raku* (Japanese lead-glazed earthenware) work. The airy gallery has a range of other works by Irish artists for sale along with books on the region.

Nearby, just off the N67, **Wilde & Wooley** (☎ 707 8042; Burren) is the name for Antoinette Hensey's shop where she makes custom knitwear from beautifully dyed wool. The designs are complex and beautiful; a sweater costs between €150 to €200.

Turn north off the N67 for the Flaggy Shore. The road hugs the shoreline going west, then curves south past **Lough Muirí**, where you're likely to see a number of wading birds, as well as swans. There are said to be otters in the area. At a T-junction just past the lough, a right turn leads to a rather dingy-looking **Martello tower** on Finavarra Point, a relic of the paranoia over the Napoleonic threat.

Bell Harbour

No more than a crossroads with a growing crop of holiday cottages and a pub, Bell Harbour (Beulaclugga) is about 8km east of Ballyvaughan. There's a pleasant walk along an old green road that begins behind the modern Church of St Patrick, 1km north up the hill from the Y-junction at Bell Harbour, and threads north along Abbey Hill.

Inland from here are the ruins of Corcomroe Abbey, the valley and churches of Oughtmama, and the interior road that takes you through the heart of the Burren.

Corcomroe Abbey

The beautiful and atmospheric Corcomroe, a former Cistercian abbey 1.5km inland from Bell Harbour, lies in a small, tranquil valley surrounded by low hills. It is a marvellous place, one of the finest buildings of its kind. It was founded in 1194 by Donal Mór O'Brien. His grandson, Conor na Siudaine O'Brien (died 1267), king of Thomond, is said to occupy the tomb in the northern wall, and there's a crude carving of him below an effigy of a bishop armed with a crosier, the pastoral staff that was carried by a bishop or abbot. The surviving vaulting in the presbytery and transepts is very fine and there are some striking Romanesque carvings scattered throughout the abbey. The abbey began a long decline in the 15th century. Often-touching modern graves crowd the ruins.

Oughtmama Valley

Small ancient churches lie hidden in this lonely, deserted valley. To get there turn inland at Bell Harbour, then go left at the Y-junction. In just under 1km you reach a house amid trees, on the right at Shanvally. A rough track leads inland from just beyond the house for about 1.5km to the churches. Roadside parking is very limited, but there is a large roadside area about 400m before Shanvally, back towards the Y-junction, with views of Corcomroe. The churches at **Oughtmama** were built in the 12th century by monks in search of solitude. Look for the Romanesque arch in the westernmost – and largest – church. It's a hardy walk up **Turlough Hill** behind the chapels, but the views are tremendous. Near the summit are the remains of a **hill fort**.

County Galway

Western Ireland's heartland, County Galway has a spellbinding beauty.

The beating heart of the county itself is Galway city. Lined by colourful narrow shop fronts and pubs, this vibrant tangle of cobbled lanes has an intimate, villagelike atmosphere and an absolutely phenomenal live-music scene that attracts traditional and contemporary musicians – along with artists, writers, poets and assorted wayfarers – from all over the country and beyond.

Radiating from Galway city are the main arterial links to some of Ireland's most heart-stopping scenery. Northwest of Galway city, the fabled Connemara region harbours one of the country's largest and most important Gaeltacht (Irish-speaking) areas. Woven with hiking and biking trails, the region's weathered mountains, sheep-grazing pastures, bogs, and remote villages are raggedly stitched together by stone walls, while along Connemara's coastline white-sand beaches offer invigorating swimming in summer and windswept walks in winter. South of Galway city there are medieval churches and castles, Norman towers and oyster beds in abundance, and eastwards of the city farming fields roll seamlessly to the country's bucolic midlands.

Offshore, lashed by the unforgiving Atlantic, the rocky Aran Islands and Inishbofin are anchored by enduring traditions: pony traps, hand-knitted fishermen's sweaters, and age-old legends and lore. Scrubbed clean by the elements, relics on the islands include ancient cliff-top ringforts and rusted shipwrecks that serve as a reminder of the perilous seas.

The county's wild landscapes and thriving traditions invariably claim visitors' hearts, and chances are your first visit won't be your last.

HIGHLIGHTS

- **Getting Hooked...** Sip Galway city's local ale, Galway Hooker (p413)
- **...And Hooked Again** Sail around the picturesque coastline near Roundstone on a traditional Galway Hooker fishing boat (p429)
- **Jammin'** Catch live-music sessions at the legendary Tigh Hughes (p426) in Spiddal
- **Island Dreaming** Escape contemporary life on Inishmaan (p421), the island time forgot
- **Sky Walking** Stroll (or cycle) above the thundering Atlantic along Sky Rd (p431), near Clifden

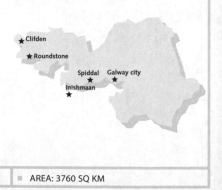

- ★ Clifden
- ★ Roundstone
- Spiddal ★   Galway city ★
- Inishmaan ★

■ POPULATION: 208,800	■ AREA: 3760 SQ KM

GALWAY CITY

☎ 091 / pop 65,800

Arty and bohemian, Galway (Gaillimh) is legendary around the world for its entertainment scene. Brightly painted pubs heave with live music on any given night. Cafés spill out onto winding cobblestone streets filled with a frenzy of fiddles, banjos, bagpipes, harps, tin whistles, guitars and *bodhráns* (hand-held goatskin drums), and jugglers, painters, poets, puppeteers and magicians in outlandish masks enchant passers-by. Actors in traditional Irish theatre tread also the boards around town.

Galway's streets are steeped in history, yet have a contemporary vibe. Students make up a quarter of the city's population, while the remains of the medieval town walls lie between shops selling Aran sweaters, handcrafted Claddagh rings, and stacks of secondhand and new books. Bridges arc over the salmon-filled River Corrib, and a long promenade leads to the seaside suburb of Salthill, where at night the moon's glow illuminates Galway Bay, where the area's famous oysters are produced.

The city's smorgasbord of eating and drinking options ranges from the market – where farmers in Wellington boots unload soil-covered vegetables – to adventurous new restaurants redefining Irish cuisine. Sprawling superpubs with wooden staircases serve frothy Guinness, Galway Hooker ale and Irish coffees.

Even by Irish standards, Galway is renowned for its rainfall. This is a city where locals don't say 'It's forecast to rain tomorrow,' but rather more dubiously, 'It's not forecast to rain *until* tomorrow.' To be fair, you can be lucky with the weather, and on a sunny day the city is positively hopping. But the rain scarcely dampens Galway's atmosphere, which is exuberant at any time of year – and especially during its myriad festivals.

Galway is often referred to as the most 'Irish' of Ireland's cities (and it's the only one where you're likely to hear Irish spoken in the streets, shops and pubs), but some locals lament that these may be the last days of 'old' Galway before it absorbs the effects of the country's globalised economy. But for now at least, Galway remains true to its spirited roots.

HISTORY

Galway's Irish name, Gaillimh, originates from the Irish word *gaill*, meaning 'outsiders' or 'foreigners', and the term resonates throughout the city's history.

From humble beginnings as a tiny fishing village at the mouth of the River Corrib, it grew into an important town when the Anglo-Normans, under Richard de Burgo (also spelled de Burgh or Burke), captured territory from the local O'Flahertys in 1232. Its fortified walls were built from around 1270.

In 1396, Richard II granted a charter transferring power from the de Burgos to 14 merchant families or 'tribes' – hence its enduring nickname of the City of the Tribes. (Each of the city's roundabouts is named for the one of the tribes.) These powerful, mostly English or Norman families clashed frequently with the leading Irish families of Connemara.

A massive fire in 1473 destroyed much of the town but created space for a new street layout, and many solid stone buildings were erected in the 15th and 16th centuries.

Galway maintained its independent status under the ruling merchant families, who were mostly loyal to the English Crown. Its coastal location encouraged a huge trade in wine, spices, fish and salt with Portugal and Spain, rivalling London in the volume of goods passing through its docks. Its support of the Crown, however, led to its downfall; the city was besieged by Cromwell in 1651 and fell the following year. In 1691 William of Orange's militia added to the destruction. Trade with Spain declined and, with Dublin and Waterford taking most sea traffic, Galway stagnated for centuries.

The early 1900s saw Galway's revival as tourists returned to the city and student numbers grew. In 1934, the cobbled streets and thatched cabins of Claddagh were tarred and flattened to make way for modern, hygienic buildings, and construction has boomed since.

Just three hours from Dublin, Galway's population today continues to swell with an influx of new residents, making it the fastest-growing city in Europe.

ORIENTATION

Galway's compact town centre straddles Europe's shortest river, the Corrib, which connects Lough Corrib with the sea. Most shops and services congregate on the river's eastern bank, while some of the city's best music pubs and restaurants are huddled to its west. From this area, known locally as the West Side, a 10-minute walk leads you out to the beginning of the seaside suburb of Salthill.

Running west from the grassy Eyre Sq, the city's pedestrianised primary shopping street starts as Williamsgate St, becomes William St and then Shop St, before forking into Mainguard St and High St. Just east of Eyre Sq is the combined bus and train station, half a block northeast of which is the main tourist office.

INFORMATION

A plethora of internet cafés around town charge around €5 per hour. Places open up and close down quickly, but you'll have no problems finding somewhere to log on.

Irish banks have branches with ATMs in the city centre.

Allied Irish Bank (Lynch's Castle, cnr Shop & Upper Abbeygate Sts)

Bank of Ireland (Eyre Sq) Two branches on the square.

Charlie Byrne's (☎ 561 766; Cornstore, Middle St) Huge collection of secondhand and discounted books in a succession of rambling rooms.

Eason's (☎ 562 284; Shop St) Superstore with a large selection of travel guides, and Galway's biggest periodicals rack.

Ireland West Tourism (☎ 537 700; www.irelandwest .ie; Forster St; ☼ 9am-5.45pm Easter-Sep, 9am-5.45pm Mon-Fri, 9am-noon Sat Oct-Easter) Large, efficient information centre that can help arrange local accommodation, and regional bus tours and ferry trips. It also changes

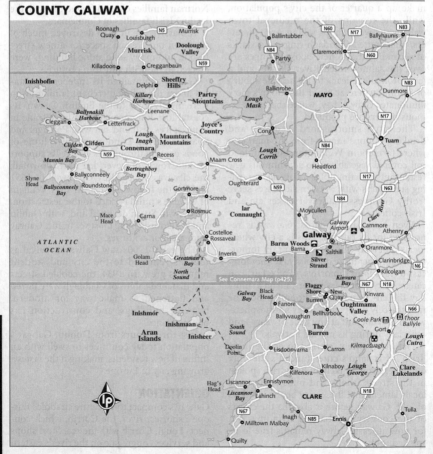

COUNTY GALWAY

money. A row of telephones is available for free calls to local car rental agencies.

Laundrette (☎ 584 524; 4 Sea Rd; per load €8)

Post office (☼ 9am-5.30pm Mon-Sat) Also changes money.

Prospect Hill Laundrette (☎ 568 343; Prospect Hill; per load €8).

Tourist Information Booth (Eyre Sq; ☼ 1.30-5.30pm Oct-Easter, 9am-5.30pm Easter-Sep) Operated by the main tourist office; dispenses free city maps and local info.

USIT (☎ 565 177; www.usit.ie; 16 Mary St) Organises travel throughout Ireland and abroad.

SIGHTS & ACTIVITIES
Collegiate Church of St Nicholas of Myra

Crowned by a pyramidal spire, the **Collegiate Church of St Nicholas of Myra** (☎ 564 648; Market St;

admission by donation; ☼ 9am-5.45pm Mon-Sat, 1-5pm Sun Apr-Sep, 10am-4pm Mon-Sat, 1-5pm Sun Oct-Mar) is Ireland's largest medieval parish church still in use. Dating from 1320, the church has been rebuilt and enlarged over the centuries, though much of the original form has been retained.

Christopher Columbus reputedly worshipped in the church in 1477. One theory suggests that the story of Columbus' visit to Galway arose from tales of St Brendan's 6th-century voyage to America (see p439). Seafaring has long been associated with the church – St Nicholas, for whom it's named, is the patron saint of sailors.

After Cromwell's victory, the church was used as a stable, and damaged stonework is still visible today. But St Nicholas was relatively fortunate: 14 other Galway churches were razed to the ground.

Parts of the church's floor are paved with gravestones from the 16th to 18th centuries, and the Lynch Aisle holds the tombs of the powerful Lynch family. A large block tomb in one corner is said to be the grave of James Lynch, a mayor of Galway in the late 15th century who condemned his son Walter to death for killing a young Spanish visitor. So the tale goes, none of the townsfolk would act as executioner and the mayor personally acted as hangman, after which he went into seclusion. Outside on Market St is a stone plaque on the **Lynch Memorial Window**, which relates this legend and claims to be the spot where the gallows stood.

The two church bells date from 1590 and 1630.

Lynch's Castle

Considered the finest town castle in Ireland, the old stone town house **Lynch's Castle** (cnr Shop & Upper Abbeygate Sts; admission free) was built in the 14th century, though much of what you see today dates from around 1600. The Lynch family was the most powerful of the 14 ruling Galway 'tribes', and members of the family held the position of mayor no fewer than 80 times between 1480 and 1650.

Stonework on the castle's façade include ghoulish gargoyles, and the coats of arms of Henry VII, the Lynches and the Fitzgeralds of Kildare. The castle is now a branch of the Allied Irish Bank, and you can peer into its old fireplace while withdrawing money from the foyer's ATMs.

COUNTY GALWAY

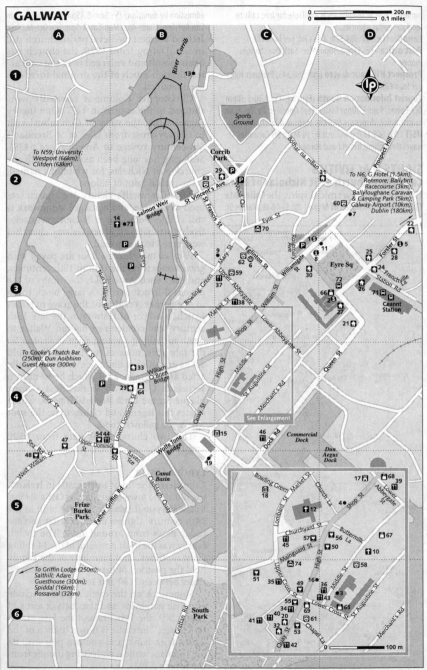

GALWAY

0 ————— 200 m
0 ————— 0.1 miles

Spanish Arch & Medieval Walls

Framing the river east of Wolfe Tone Bridge, the Spanish Arch (1584) is thought to be an extension of Galway's medieval walls. The arch appears to have been designed as a passageway through which ships entered the city to unload goods such as wine and brandy from Spain.

During the drawn-out renovations of Eyre Sq, the arch and its lawns became the main open-air communal space. Its ongoing popularity sees locals gather on summer evenings for impromptu events such as screenings of films, which are projected onto the arch's façade.

Although a 1651 drawing of Galway clearly shows its extensive fortifications, the visits of Cromwell and William of Orange and subsequent centuries of neglect saw the walls almost completely disappear. Another surviving portion has been artfully incorporated into the modern shopping mall, Eyre Square Centre, complete with a **tarot-card reader** (☎ 556 826, 087 902 4776; ☻ by appointment Mon & Thu-Sat) installed in the basement in a former turret.

Galway City Museum

Adjacent to the Spanish Arch, the **Galway City Museum** (☎ 567 641; Spanish Pde; adult/child €5/2.50; ☻ 11am-1pm & 2-5pm Tue-Sun; ☒) permanently opened in its new location in mid-2007. It houses an array of artefacts interpreting the city's history, including some military items from the War of Independence, as well as research facilities, a coffee shop and superb vantage points looking out over the city and bay.

Galway Cathedral

Lording over the River Corrib, the imposing **Galway Cathedral** (☎ 563 577; www.galwaycathedral.org; Gaol Rd; admission by donation; ☻ 8am-6pm) was dedicated by the late Cardinal Richard Cushing of Boston in 1965. The cathedral's full name is the unwieldy Catholic Cathedral of Our Lady Assumed into Heaven and St Nicholas, but its high, curved arches and central dome have a simple, solid elegance, as well as superb acoustics that are best appreciated during an **organ recital**. Programme dates are posted on the website.

From the Spanish Arch, a riverside path runs upriver and across the Salmon Weir Bridge to the cathedral.

Eyre Square

For years the restoration of Galway's central public square turned the city's showpiece

COUNTY GALWAY

into a construction site and created traffic chaos. But the end result – an open green space with sculptures and pathways – is worth it. Its lawns are formally named Kennedy Park in commemoration of President John F Kennedy's 1963 visit to Galway, though you'll rarely, if ever, hear locals refer to it as anything but Eyre Sq.

The street running along the southwestern side of the square has now been pedestrianised, while the eastern side is taken up almost entirely by the Hotel Meyrick (formerly the Great Southern Hotel), an elegant grey limestone pile restored to its Victorian glory. Guarding the upper side of the square, **Browne's Doorway** (1627), a fragment from the home of one of the city's merchant rulers, looks like the remains from a carpet-bombing raid but is a classy touch nevertheless.

Salmon Weir

Upstream from the Salmon Weir Bridge, which crosses the River Corrib just east of the cathedral, the waters of the Corrib cascade down the great weir, one of their final descents before reaching Galway Bay. The weir controls the water levels above it, and when the salmon are running you can often see shoals of them waiting in the clear waters before rushing upriver to spawn.

The salmon and sea-trout seasons usually span February to September, but most fish pass through the weir during May and June. To obtain fishing permits and book a time, contact the manager at **Galway Fisheries** (☎ 562 388; Nun's Island) by post or phone several months ahead of your visit.

Kenny Gallery

Established in 1968, West Ireland's first **gallery** (Kenny's; ☎ 562 739; www.kennys.ie; High St; ☯ 9.30am-6pm Mon-Sat) displays an exceptional collection of Irish art in a higgledy-piggledy terrace house. Look out for work by up-and-coming Galway artists, including Charlotte Kelly's abstract landscapes, Kieran Tuohy's bog-oak sculptures (crafted from bog-oak roots preserved in the oxygen-resistant turf for thousands of years), Jennifer Cunningham's prints and Liam Butler's welded copper.

All works are for sale, but even if you're not here to buy, Kenny's offers a glimpse into the future of Galweigan art. Proprietor Tom Kenny is a fount of information on the local scene.

Kenny's also trades antiquarian books online, including many Irish-language titles.

Nora Barnacle House

James Joyce courted his future wife Nora Barnacle (1884–1951) at this little **house** (☎ 564 743; 8 Bowling Green), beginning in 1909. It's now a privately owned museum displaying the couple's letters and photographs among evocatively arranged furniture. Hours are erratic; call ahead or check with the tourist office. Expect to pay around €3 admission.

Salthill

A favourite pastime for Galweigans and visitors alike is walking along the **Prom**, the seaside promenade running from the edge of the city along Salthill. Local tradition dictates 'kicking the wall' across from the diving boards (a 30- to 45-minute stroll from town) before turning around. At the time of writing, plans were underway to extend the Prom all the way from Salthill to Silver Strand – about 7.5km all up.

In and around Salthill are plenty of cosy pubs from where you can watch storms roll over the bay. Between May and September, you can also catch the traditional Irish dance and music spectacular, **Trad on the Prom** (☎ 087 238 8489; www.tradontheprom.com). The website posts show times and ticket information including various dinner-and-show packages.

TOURS

If you're short on time, bus tours departing from Galway are a good way to see Connemara, the Burren or the Cliffs of Moher, while boat tours take you to the heart of Lough Corrib. Tours can be booked direct or at the tourist office, and bus tours leave from outside Kinlay House Hostel on Merchants Rd.

Burren Wild Tours (☎ 087 877 9565 or 086 060 7858; www.burrenwalks.com; adult/student €22/18) Seasonal bus tours to the Burren and Cliffs of Moher incorporating an easy 90-minute guided mountain walk.

Corrib Princess (☎ 592 447; www.corribprincess.ie; Woodquay; adult/family €14/35; ☯ May-Sep) Two to three 1½-hour cruises on the River Corrib and Lough Corrib per day, departing from Woodquay, just beyond Salmon Weir Bridge.

Lally Coaches (☎ 562 905; www.lallytours.com; adult/child/student €22/13.50/16) Entertaining, informative bus tours of Connemara, or the Burren and Cliffs of Moher with local guides.

O'Neachtain Tours (☎ 553 188; www.galway.net /pages/oneachtain-tours; adult/student €22/16) Runs coach tours of Connemara, or the Burren and Cliffs of Moher. Family rates available on request.

SLEEPING

You'll find B&Bs lining the major approach roads, including many in Salthill, but to take full advantage of Galway's tightly packed attractions try for a room in the city centre. If you're planning to stay in Galway for an extended period, Wednesday's edition of the free *Galway Advertiser* (www.galwayadvertiser.ie) lists rental properties.

Galway's festivals (below) and easy striking distance from Dublin make it *hugely* popular year-round, especially on weekends. Accommodation often fills months in advance – book ahead!

Most of our accommodation recommendations have private parking or offer discounted parking at nearby car parks. Enquire when you book.

Budget

Ballyloughane Caravan & Camping Park (☎ 755 338; galwcamp@iol.ie; Ballyloughane Beach, Renmore; camp sites €7-10; ☺ Apr-Sep) This family-run camping ground is clean, peaceful and secure, and its beachside lo-

cation gives it sweeping views across the bay. It's off the Dublin road (N6), 5km from Galway.

Salmon Weir Hostel (☎ 561 133; www.salmonweirhostel.com; 3 St Vincent's Ave; dm €10-18, d €36-40) Galway's hippie vibe finds its spiritual home in the Salmon Weir's guitar-strewn lounge room, where informal jam sessions take place most nights. The hostel has a share-house feel, including shared bathrooms for all rooms. There's no breakfast, although coffee and tea are free; watch out the 3am curfew doesn't leave you sleeping in the rain.

Barnacle's Quay Street House (☎ 568 644; www.barnacles.ie; 10 Quay St; dm €12.50-23, d €52-56; ☐ ☺) Surrounded by the pubs, restaurants and cafés you came to Galway for, this well-run hostel is housed in a medieval building with a 1990s extension. Barnacle's horseshoe-shaped kitchen has toasted-sandwich makers and a dishwasher, and there's a warm common room with a big gas fireplace. Breakfast includes scones and soda bread.

Kinlay House (☎ 565 244; www.kinlayhouse.ie; Merchant's Rd; dm €14-23, d €50-62; ☐ ☺) Easy-going staff, a full range of facilities and an ultra-central location just off Eyre Sq make this Galway's all-round best hostel. Spanning two huge brightly lit floors, Kinlay House

---

PARTY ON...AND ON

Galway's packed calendar of festivals turns the city and surrounding communities into what feels like one nonstop party – streets overflow with revellers, and pubs and restaurants often extend their opening hours.

Highlights include the following:

- **Cúirt Poetry & Literature Festival** (☎ 565 886; www.galwayartscentre.ie/cuirt) Top-name authors converge on Galway in April for Ireland's premier literary festival, featuring poetry slams, theatrical performances and readings.

- **Galway Arts Festival** (☎ 566 577; www.galwayartsfestival.ie) A two-week extravaganza of theatre, music, art and comedy in mid-July.

- **Galway Film Fleadh** (☎ 751 655; www.galwayfilmfleadh.com) One of Ireland's biggest film festivals, held in July around the same time as the arts festival.

- **Galway Race Week** (☎ 753 870) Horse races in Ballybrit, 3km east of the city, are the centre-piece of Galway's biggest, most boisterous festival of all. The week occurs in late July or early August.

- **Galway International Oyster Festival** (☎ 527 282; oysters@iol.ie) Oysters are washed down with plenty of pints in the last week in September.

Also see p437 for information on Galway Hooker boat races, p437) for more oyster-related events, p422 for *bodhrán* (hand-held goatskin drum) workshops and p419 for the Aran Islands' rollicking *Father Ted* festival.

still manages to feels personal thanks to social common areas (with free wi-fi), two self-catering kitchens and two cosy TV lounges. You can book regional day trips here, which depart right outside the building.

Other recommendations:

Sleepzone (☎ 566 999; www.sleepzone.ie; Bóthar na mBan; dm €13-28, d €52-76; 🖳) Big, busy backpacker base with free internet and wi-fi, a bureau de change, pool table and BBQ terrace. Party-goers beware: no alcohol is allowed on the premises.

Galway City Hostel (☎ 566 959; www.galwaycity hostel.com; Eyre Sq; dm €13.50-23, d €44-60; 🖳) Friendly spot next door to the bus-train station, with all-new bunks, renovated bathrooms and a breezy balcony.

Claddagh Hostel (☎ 533 555; www.claddagh hostelgalway.com; Queen St; dm from €15, tw from €50; 🖳) Small, central multilevel terrace house with glassed-in lounge-cum-TV-room and spotless kitchen/dining room. Free internet terminals and wi-fi.

Midrange

St Martin's B&B (☎ 568 286; www.stmartins.ie; 2 Nun's Island Rd; s €35-45, d €40-70; 🚳) A welcoming cup of tea is the start of a memorable stay at this central, beautifully kept house, which has a flower-filled garden overlooking floodlit waterfalls cascading into the Corrib. Kindly hosts Mary and Donie Sexton serve freshly squeezed orange juice and home-baked brown bread, and in winter Mary wraps up hot-water bottles to tuck into your bed.

Griffin Lodge (☎ 589 440; griffinlodge@eircom.net; 3 Father Griffin Pl; s €35-50, d €55-70; 🅿🚳) You'll be welcomed like a long-lost friend at this completely renovated B&B, which has eight immaculate rooms in soothing shades of spearmint and moss green. Frills are kept to a minimum, with just a few elegant framed prints and crocheted cotton bedspreads.

Dun Aoibhinn Guest House (☎ 583 129; www .dunaoibhinnhouse.com; 12 St Mary's Rd; s/d from €39/58; 🅿🖳) Pronounced doon-ay-ven, this restored town house with original lead-light windows and floorboards is less than five minutes' stroll from the West Side's music pubs. Antique-filled rooms come with flat-screen satellite TVs, free wi-fi, laptop safes and fridges. Tea, coffee and biscuits are included; otherwise breakfast means nipping over the road to buy fresh croissants.

Galway Arms Inn (☎ 565 444; http://galwayarmsinn .ie; 65 Lower Dominick St; s/d from €40/80) Rooms on the upper floors of this down-to-earth pub on the corner of Mill St have balconies, and some

have river views. A hearty Irish breakfast is served between 9am and 10.30am, giving you a chance for a lie-in after a night downstairs in the bar. Wi-fi's free.

Adare Guesthouse (☎ 582 638; adare@iol.ie; 9 Father Griffin Pl; s €50-90, d €80-120; 🅿) Overlooking a football pitch and children's playground, this barn-style place has 10 generously sized rooms and service that runs like clockwork. Sift through a dozen menu choices at breakfast including French toast, pancakes, smoked salmon and steaming bowls of porridge.

Spanish Arch Hotel (☎ 569 600; www.spanisharch hotel.ie; Quay St; s €75-85, d €99-145) In a sensational spot on the main drag, this 20-room boutique hotel is housed in a 16th-century former Carmelite convent. The hotel's solid-timber bar has a great line-up of live music, so rooms at the back, while smaller, are best for a quiet night's sleep. There's also an excellent on-site restaurant, which provides room service.

Skeffington Arms Hotel (☎ 563 173; www.skeffington .ie; Eyre Sq; d from €99; 🚳) Rooms at the Skeff, overlooking Eyre Sq, recently underwent extensive renovations, lifting them to an even higher standard. But the main reason to stay here is still the time-honoured pub below, which also has a lunchtime carvery, an evening restaurant (serving stand-out seafood chowder with a shot of Guinness) and a classy nightclub, Karma.

Garvey's Inn (☎ 562 224; www.garveysinn.com; Eyre Sq; d €110-120; 🚳) Set over an authentic timber pub dating from 1861, this comfortable family-owned hotel has a bird's-eye view over Galway's oasislike square, and snug rooms stocked with everything you're likely to need, including irons, ironing boards and trouser presses.

Top End

Hotel Meyrick (☎ 564 041; www.greatsouthernhotel galway.com; Eyre Sq; s/d/ste from €120/135/150; 🅿🖳) Known as the Railway Hotel when it opened in 1852, and later as the Great Southern Hotel, this stately showpiece drips with chandeliers, tasselled velvet curtains, bevelled mirrors, and luxuries such as a rooftop hot tub; all 99 guest rooms include bathtubs. Its corridors were built to accommodate women's hooped ball gowns.

Forster Court Hotel (☎ 564 111; www.forstercourt hotel.com; Eyre Sq; d €145; 🖳🚳) What sets this sleek, modern hotel apart is a host of thoughtful little details such as bottle openers attached to the walls of its spiffy navy-and-gold rooms, free broadband and wi-fi, and a decadently late checkout of 2pm on Sundays. All but two rooms have bathtubs, and 20 have balconies. Room rates drop by up to 50% on weekdays during winter.

Park House Hotel (☎ 564 924; www.parkhousehotel .ie; Park Lane, Fair Green Rd; d from €198; P ⌷) Housed in an old farm-feed wholesale warehouse, this privately owned hotel boasts regal guest rooms and a sumptuous lobby stuffed with embroidered armchairs. Luxurious touches include a turndown service, Molton Brown bath products, free broadband, morning and evening newspapers, and air conditioning (not that Galway needs it, but hey, just in case).

ourpick **G Hotel** (☎ 865 200; www.theghotel.ie; Wellpark; d/ste from €200/340; P ⌷ ⌷) Galway didn't know what hit it when this ubercontemporary hotel opened inside a nondescript business complex. Avant-garde interiors designed by Galweigan milliner-to-the-stars Philip Treacy include a grand salon with 350 suspended silver balls, a Schiaparelli-pink cocktail lounge, and a restaurant with purple banquettes styled like oversize seashells. The G's on-site spa looks out on a bamboo-planted forest, and you can watch flat-screen TVs from the bathtub of most suites. Valet parking and wi-fi are free.

EATING

Seafood is Galway's specialty, whether fish and chips, ocean-fresh chowder or sea bass cooked to perfection. Galway Bay oysters can also be found locally and at nearby Clarinbridge. The city's bohemian bent means vegetarians are spoilt for choice from cafés through to high-end restaurants.

Restaurants

ourpick **Ard Bia** (☎ 539 897; www.ardbia.com; 2 Quay St; café dishes €6-12, lunch mains €10-14, dinner mains €16-26; ⓨ café 10am-5pm, lunch served noon-3pm, restaurant 6.30-10.30pm Tue-Sat) In Irish, Ard Bia means 'High Food', which sums up both the 1st-floor location and the cuisine of this café-restaurant. Ard Bia's owner also runs a gallery in town, and this funky dining space showcases contemporary art and local pottery. Blackboard lunch specials are complemented by staples as such beef-and-rosemary burgers; dinner choices run from smoked-paprika lamb to tabouli-and-tofu cake.

McDonagh's (☎ 565 001; 22 Quay St; fish & chips from €7.50, restaurant mains €15-23; ⓨ café & takeaway counter noon-midnight Mon-Sat, 5-11pm Sun, restaurant 5-10pm Mon-Sat) A trip to Galway isn't complete without stopping at McDonagh's. Divided into two parts, with a takeaway counter and a café with long communal wooden tables (great for meeting locals) on one side, and a more upmarket restaurant on the other, Galway's best chipper churns out battered cod, plaice, haddock, whiting and salmon nonstop, all accompanied by homemade tartare sauce.

Mustard (☎ 566 400; Middle St; mains €8-13; ⓨ noon-10pm) This exciting new spot serves select wines and inventive dishes such as crispy aromatic duck pizzas with plum sauce, and lentil kofta burgers.

Druid Lane Restaurant (☎ 563 015; 9 Quay St; lunch mains €8-13, dinner mains €15-27; ⓨ 5pm-late Mon-Fri, 1-4pm & 5pm-late Sat & Sun) Signature main courses at this intimate restaurant include saddle of rabbit, and roasted duck breast. And while starters such as Thai fish cakes with lemongrass dip have an international flavour, homemade desserts such as Baileys bread-and-butter pudding are as Irish as it gets.

Finnegan's (☎ 564 764; 2 Market St; mains €10; ⓨ 9am-10pm Mon-Sat, 11am-10pm Sun) Authentic, utterly unpretentious Irish cooking and an equally authentic clientele make this a wonderful spot for comfort food. Finnegan's homemade shepherd's pie comes piping hot from the oven, its traditional Irish stew will stick to your ribs, and desserts include Baileys cheesecake. Full Irish breakfasts are served all day.

Kirwan's Lane Creative Cuisine (☎ 568 266; Kirwan's Lane; lunch mains €10-16, dinner mains €18-28; ⓨ noon-2pm & 6-10pm Mon-Sat) Kirwan's Lane isn't complacent about its reputation as one of the city's best and most inventive restaurants. The menu combines Irish produce with Asian spices, service is attentive without being intrusive, and the two-storey space is minimalist and elegant. Definitely book ahead.

Da Tang Noodle House (☎ 561 443; Middle St; mains €11.50-18.50; ⓨ noon-3pm & 5.30-10pm Mon-Sat, 5.30-10.30pm Sun) This place on Middle St does light, healthy Chinese stir-fries and satays in a stylish paper-lantern-lit interior.

Oscar's Restaurant (☎ 582 180; Upper Dominick St; dish of the day €17, mains €25-29.50; ⓨ from 7pm Mon-Fri, from 6pm Sat) Opening hours can be erratic, but no matter – the flamboyant and fun atmosphere at Oscar's is consistently matched by adventurous cooking, such as seared king scallops with pistachios, and roast rabbit with apricot. Meals are presented with an eye for aesthetics and served with theatrical flair.

Cafés

Food 4 Thought (☎ 565 854; Lower Abbeygate St; mains €4-7; ☽ 7.30am-6pm Mon-Fri, 8am-6pm Sat, 11.30am-4pm Sun) In addition to providing organic and vegetarian sandwiches, savoury scones, and wholesome dishes such as cashew-nut roast and moussaka made with textured vegetable protein, this New Age-y place is great for finding out about energy workshops and yoga classes around town.

Le Journal (☎ 568 426; Quay St; lunch mains €4-9, dinner mains €10-22; ☽ 9am-6pm Oct-Apr, 9am-10pm May-Sep) Lined with leather-bound books and decorated with painted quotations of the opening phrases of classic novels, this chef-run place is an inexpensive café by day and a *très* elegant bistro on summer nights.

Goya's (☎ 567 010; 2 Kirwan's Lane; dishes €4.50-9.50; ☽ 9.30am-6pm Mon-Sat) As evidenced by the confections on display, the cakes are supreme at Goya's, a Galway treasure hidden on a narrow walkway. Its cool pale blue décor, Segafredo coffee and sweet treats including a towering lemon meringue pie make it a perfect spot to take some time out. Goya's also serves one lunchtime special (€8).

Delight (☎ 567 823; 29 Upper Abbeygate St; dishes €5-10; ☽ 9am-6pm Mon-Fri, closed Christmas period & Race Week) The name's an understatement: this hole-in-the-wall gourmet food bar is sheer heaven for sandwiches and wraps bursting with sprouts, as well as wheat-grass shots, juices and baked goods including a gooey chocolate pudding to die for. Everything, including the breakfast muesli, is made on the premises. The shop has a roaring takeaway trade, but there's also a clutch of tables.

Sheridans on the Docks (☎ 564 905; 3 New Docks; dishes from €6; ☽ 4.30-11.30pm Mon-Thu, 12.30pm-12.30am Fri, 10am-12.30am Sat) This waterfront bar is a chic yet relaxed spot for cheese platters from the family's cheese shop, Sheridans Cheesemongers, as well as wines by the glass and boutique beers.

Busker Brownes (☎ 563 377; Upper Cross St; dishes around €10; ☽ 10.30am-11.30pm Mon-Thu, 10.30-12.30am Fri & Sat, 12.30-11.30pm Sun) Smartly done out in brown-on-brown tones, this suave café-bar does fine pub fare and hangover breakfasts. It's also a prime spot to catch live ragtime jazz.

Self-Catering

Richard McCabe's Bakery (☎ 865 641; www.mccabescakes.net; Cornstore, Cross St; ☽ 6am-6pm Mon-Sat) To pack a beach picnic, head to the bakery of five-time world-champion pastry chef Richard McCabe for crusty fresh bread and sausage rolls.

Sheridan's Cheesemongers (☎ 564 829; 14 Churchyard St; ☽ 9.30am-6pm Mon-Fri, 9am-6pm Sat) Sheridan's Cheesemongers has local and international cheeses, and top drops in its upstairs wine-bar-cum-shop (open 2pm to 9pm Tuesday to Friday, noon to 8pm Saturday).

DRINKING

Galway's nickname of the City of Tribes sums up its drinking and entertainment scene. For its size the city has surprisingly distinct areas where you'll encounter different crowds: Eyre Sq and its surrounds tends to be the domain of retail and office workers and tourists; the main shopping strip draws hip young professionals; the Woodquay area, near Salmon Weir bridge, is where rural salt-of-the-earth folk congregate when in town; and the West Side attracts boho artists and musicians. Wherever you go, you won't be bored (or thirsty).

Most of Galway's pubs see musicians performing at least a couple of nights a week, whether in an informal session or as a headline act, and many swing to live music every night.

Séhán Ua Neáchtain (☎ 568 820; 17 Upper Cross St) Painted a bright cornflower blue, this 19th-century pub, known simply as Neáchtain's (*nock*-tans), has Galway Hooker on tap and a truly fabulous atmosphere.

Crane Bar (☎ 587 419; 2 Sea Rd) An atmospheric old pub west of the Corrib, the Crane is the best spot in Galway to catch an informal céilidh (session of traditional music and dancing) most nights. It also hosts a structured line-up of talented bands in its rowdy, good-natured upstairs bar.

Róisín Dubh (☎ 586 540; Upper Dominick St) Despite being schmicked up in recent years and becoming somewhat more like a superpub (complete with a vast rooftop terrace), Róisín Dubh is still *the* place to see emerging alternative and rock acts before they hit the big time.

Blue Note (☎ 589 116; 3 West William St) This jazzy pub-cum-dance-bar has a great summer beer garden and usually no cover charge.

HOOKED

Launched in 2006, Galway's local beer might have been called Cuckoo if founders Ronan Brennan and Aidan Murphy had their way – given that this is what their friends and family called them when they announced they were starting up their own brewery. (Creating a new beer in Guinness-drinking Ireland is like selling ice to Eskimos, surely.)

Instead, the two cousins (their mums are identical twins), who come from hospitality and brewing backgrounds respectively, threw the name open via a website competition. Galway Hooker (after the bay's iconic fishing boats) was the hands-down consensus.

Choosing a name was one thing, but starting a brewing company wasn't straightforward. As Ronan says, 'Eventually we found an existing brewery which had been dormant for five years and needed to be completely recommissioned including new machinery, which meant a lot of begging, borrowing and stealing.'

The pale ale is chemical free, since, according to Ronan, 'We couldn't afford chemicals.' On a serious note, Aidan adds, 'We're putting the flavour in the way it's meant to be. There's a love of good beer in this country, but a lack of variety. People are slow to change their drinking habits. We were careful which pubs we put it into – places where people are open-minded and it didn't outlast its keg life (about a month). The integrity of the beer is everything – we wanted to create the best beer possible for the people of Galway.'

And they have.

Galway Hooker is on tap around town including most West Side pubs. Should you get hooked, international exports are in the works.

Tig Cóilí (Mainguard St) Two live céilidhs a day draw the crowds to this authentic fire-engine-red pub, just off High St. Inside, black-and-white photos take you back into Galway's past.

Cooke's Thatch Bar (☎ 521749; 2 Newcastle Rd) Warm, welcoming and not even remotely touristy, this 18th-centuy thatched-roofed local has fantastic Guinness, a heated internal courtyard and live music at least once a week.

Living Room (www.thelivingroom.ie; 5 Bridge St; admission free; ☙ 10.30am-11.30pm Mon-Wed, 10.30am-2am Thu-Sun) With glam red-and-orange décor, original '50s and '60s retro furniture, DJs, and modish bar food until 6pm, the Living Room is home away from home for Galway's hipsters.

Monroe's Tavern (☎ 583 397; Upper Dominick St) A reliable spot for traditional music and ballads, Monroe's remains the only pub in the city for regular Irish dancing (on Tuesday). You can take pizzas through to the bar from Galway's best pizza joint, the attached Monroe's Pizza Cabin (☎ 582 887; small/medium/large pizzas from €6/12.50/15; open from 4pm to midnight Monday to Wednesday, 4pm to 1am Thursday to Sunday).

Other recommendations:

Quays (☎ 568 347; Quay St) Enormous tavern with endless timber-panelled rooms and passageways, and great vantage points from which to watch live music (ranging from traditional to pop) most nights.

Front Door (☎ 563 757; High St) Heated balconies and cosy timber booths make this a popular spot for a pint.

King's Head (☎ 566 630; 15 High St) Mainstream, commercial superpub within a 17th-century stone house, hosting rock bands most nights and a popular jazz session on Sunday 'morning' (usually noon to 4pm).

Taaffe's Bar (☎ 564 066; 19 Shop St) Stripped of some of its original period detail but still well loved for its nightly Irish music sessions beginning at 5pm.

ENTERTAINMENT

Most pubs in Galway have live music at least a couple of nights a week. Thursday's edition of the free *Galway Advertiser* (www.galway advertiser.ie) lists what's on in the city.

Nightclubs

Clubs generally get cranking around 11pm and wind down around 2am. Admission prices vary according to the nightly programme.

Central Park (☎ 565 976; www.centralparkclub.com; 36 Upper Abbeygate St; ☙ 11pm-2am) With seven bars and a capacity of 1000 people, CPs is a Galway institution, especially among the professional crowd.

cuba (☎ 565 991; www.cuba.ie; Eyre Sq; admission €5-15; ☙ 8pm-late) Chances are you'll spot this place by the crowds milling out front. House-spinning DJs and live acts fill the dance floor.

GPO (☎ 563 073; www.gpo.ie; 21 Eglinton St; admission €6-10) GPO cranks out '80s and '90s tunes

---

CLADDAGH RINGS

The fishing village of Claddagh once had its own king as well as its own customs and traditions. Now subsumed into the Galway city centre, virtually all remnants of the original village are gone, but Claddagh rings survive as a timeless reminder.

Popular as an engagement or wedding ring (or just as a memento of your visit), these rings depict a heart (symbolising love) between two outstretched hands (friendship), topped by a crown (loyalty). Rings are handcrafted at jewellers around town, and start from about €15 for a silver band to well over €1000 for a diamond-set platinum version.

Jewellers include Ireland's oldest jewellery shop, **Thomas Dillon's Claddagh Gold** (☎ 566 365; www.claddaghring.ie; 1 Quay St), which was established in 1750. It has some vintage examples in its small back-room 'museum'.

---

on Wednesday, and house, R&B, indie and hip-hop the rest of the week. It's a favourite with students, who get free admission most nights.

Karma (☎ 563 173; www.karma.ie; Eyre Sq; admission €6-10; ⏰ 11pm-late Thu-Sun) Part of the Skeffington Arms Hotel, Karama draws a sophisticated crowd who dress to impress.

Theatre

Druid Theatre (☎ 568 617; www.druidtheatre.com; Chapel Lane) This long-established theatre is famed for showing experimental works by young Irish playwrights.

Town Hall Theatre (☎ 569 777; Courthouse Sq) The Town Hall Theatre features Broadway and West End shows, and visiting singers.

An Taibhdhearc na Gaillimhe (☎ 562 024; Middle St) Stages plays in Irish.

SHOPPING

Galway has an enticing array of specialty shops dotting its narrow streets, stocking cutting-edge fashion, Irish woollens (including Aran sweaters), outdoor clothing and equipment, local jewellery, art and, of course, music.

Galway market (Churchyard St; ⏰ 7.30am-3pm Sat & Sun) Galway's festive market is filled with buskers and stalls selling farm-fresh produce, crafts, jewellery and hot food. At the time of writing, plans were underway for the markets to operate from Thursday to Sunday – check with the tourist office for updates. Saturday usually offers the widest choice of stalls and liveliest crowds.

P Powell & Sons (☎ 562 295; powellsmusicshop@eircom .net; William St) You can pick up tin whistles, *bodhráns* and other instruments here, as well as sheet music.

Mulligan Records (☎ 564 961; 5 Middle St) Drop into Mulligan Records for recorded Irish

music and folk music from around the world.

General purpose shopping centres include the Eyre Square Centre, with a large Dunne's supermarket; Bridge Mills, in an old mill building by the river at the western end of William O'Brien Bridge; and the Cornstore on Middle St.

GETTING THERE & AWAY

Air

British Airways (www.britishairways.com) has limited services to **Galway airport** (GWY; ☎ 800 491 492; www.galwayairport.com; Carnmore) from London, Manchester and Glasgow. **Aer Arran** (www .aerarran.com) offers cheap flights between Galway and London Luton, Edinburgh, Manchester and Birmingham, as well as Lorient in France.

The closest major airport is **Shannon airport** (SNN; ☎ 061-712 000; www.shannonairport.com), served by domestic and international carriers including Ryanair. **Knock airport** (NOC; ☎ 094-67222; www.knockairport.com) is also within easy reach of Galway.

Bus

From the **bus station** (☎ 562 000), just off Eyre Sq, there are frequent **Bus Éireann** (www.buseireann .ie) services to all major cities in the Republic and the North. The one-way fare to Dublin (3¾ hours) is €13.

A lot of private companies are also represented. **Bus Nestor** (☎ 797 484; busnestor@eircom.net) runs five to eight daily services to Dublin (€10) via Dublin airport (€10). Buses leave from outside the tourist office every couple of hours or so between 6.30am and 5.25pm. Hourly buses to Dublin (€12) and Dublin airport (€17), run by **City Link** (☎ 564 163; www.citylink.ie), depart from the tourist office daily. **Michael Nee**

Coaches (☎ 095-51082) runs two or three daily services to towns throughout Connemara. Buses depart from the tourist office.

Train
From the **train station** (☎ 564 222), just off Eyre Sq, there are up to five trains daily to/from Dublin's Heuston Station (one way from €29, three hours). Connections with other train routes can be made at Athlone (one hour).

GETTING AROUND
To/From the Airports
Just one bus per day runs between Galway airport and Galway from Monday to Saturday (none on Sunday). It leaves the airport at 1.25pm, and leaves Galway bus station at 12.50pm. A taxi to/from the airport costs about €18, which can be ordered from a bank of free phones at the airport. Some B&Bs and hotels can arrange pick-up.

Bus Éireann (www.buseireann.ie) operates 11 daily services from Shannon airport to Galway (€14.50) bus stop (via Ennis, €5.70) from 7.55am to 8.55pm (from 7.05am to 8.05pm from Galway to Shannon airport). **Citylink** (www.citylink.ie) also runs five services a day between Galway tourist office and Shannon airport (€15). The journey takes just under two hours.

Knock airport is linked by a shuttle bus with Charlestown, from where there are direct Bus Éireann services to/from Charlestown and Galway (1¾ hours).

There are also frequent daily Citylink services between Dublin airport and Galway (€17). Direct journeys take 3¼ hours; some make a stop in central Dublin and take 3¾ hours.

Bicycle
Europa Bicycles (☎ 563 355; Hunter's Bldg; ☒ Mon-Sat), on Earl's Island, opposite Galway Cathedral, hires bikes for €10 for 24 hours.

Bus
You can walk to almost everything in Galway, including out to Salthill, but you'll also find regular buses departing from Eyre Sq. For Salthill, take bus 1 (€1.20).

Car
Parking throughout Galway's streets is metered and costs €1 for the first 30 minutes and €0.80 for every hour thereafter. There

are several multistorey and pay-and-display car parks around town.

Galway's unprecedented growth and the resulting lack of infrastructure serving its urban sprawl means that traffic in and out of the city centre can bank up alarmingly. For a stress-free holiday, try to leave the roads to commuters at peak hours if possible.

Taxi
Taxi ranks are located on Eyre Sq, on Bridge St, and next to the bus-train station. You can also catch a cab by dropping by a taxi office. Try **Abbey Cabs** (☎ 569 469; Eyre St) or **Galway Taxis** (☎ 561 111; Dominick St).

ARAN ISLANDS
☎ 091
Just a 40 minute boat ride from the mainland, the desolate beauty of the Aran Islands feels far removed from contemporary life.

An extension of the limestone escarpment that forms the Burren, the island has shallow topsoil scattered with yellow buttercups, white-petalled daisies and spring gentian, and jagged cliffs that are pounded by surf. On the cliff tops, ancient forts such as Dún Aengus on Inishmór and Dún Chonchúir on Inishmaan are some of the oldest archaeological remains in Ireland.

A web of ancient stone walls (1600km in all) ensnares all three islands like a stone fishing net. These walls serve the dual purpose of keeping sheep and ponies in, and providing a repository for stone dug from the ground to make way for grazing and harvests. The islands also have a smattering of early *clocháns* (dry-stone beehive huts from the early-Christian period), resembling igloos made from stone.

Inishmór (Arainn in Irish, meaning 'Big Island') is the largest and most easily accessible from Galway. The island is home to one of Ireland's most important and impressive archaeological sites, as well as some lively pubs and restaurants, particularly in its little township Kilronan. The smallest island, Inisheer (Inis Oírr; 'Eastern Island'), with an impressive arts centre, is also easily reached from Galway year-round and from Doolin in the summer months. Hence Inishmaan (Inis Meáin; 'Middle Island'), in the centre, tends to be bypassed by the majority of tourist traffic, preserving its age-old traditions and evoking a sense of timelessness.

Although high summer brings a maddening number of tourists, services on the islands are few. Only Inishmór has an ATM (with limited hours and a propensity to run out of cash), and the majority of places don't accept credit cards (always check ahead). Restaurants, including pubs that serve food, often reduce their opening hours or shut completely during winter. However, winter lets you experience the islands at their wild, windswept best.

History

Almost nothing is known about the people who built the massive Iron Age stone structures on Inishmór and Inishmaan. These sites are commonly referred to as 'forts', but are actually believed to have served as pagan religious centres. In folklore, the forts are said to have been built by the Firbolgs, a Celtic tribe who invaded Ireland from Europe in prehistoric times.

It is believed that people came to the islands to farm, which was a major challenge given the rocky terrain. Early islanders augmented their soil by hauling seaweed and sand up from the shore. People also fished the surrounding waters on long *currachs* (rowing boats made of a framework of laths covered with tarred canvas), which remain a symbol of the Aran Islands.

Christianity reached the islands remarkably quickly, and some of the earliest monastic settlements were founded by St Enda (Éanna) in the 5th century. Enda appears to have been an Irish chief who converted to Christianity and spent some time studying in Rome before seeking out a suitably remote spot for his monastery. Any remains you see today are from the 8th century onwards.

From the 14th century, control of the islands was disputed by two Gaelic families, the O'Briens and the O'Flahertys. The English took over during the reign of Elizabeth I, and in Cromwell's times a garrison was stationed here.

As Galway's importance waned, so did that of the islands, and their isolation meant islanders maintained a traditional lifestyle well into the 20th century. Up to the 1930s, people wore traditional Aran dress: bright red skirts and black shawls for women, baggy woollen trousers and waistcoats with *crios* (colour-

ful belts) for men. The classic heavy cream-coloured Aran sweater knitted in complex patterns originated here, and it is still hand-knitted on the islands.

Until the last few decades the islands were, if not centuries from civilisation, then at least a perilous all-day journey in unpredictable seas. Fast ferries have now made for a quick (albeit sometimes still rough) crossing. But island life changed forever with the commencement of air services on 15 August 1970. It's a day that sticks in the minds of locals, who recall that a hurricane blew up and they were called down from their houses to sit in the plane to prevent it from being blown away. For many years afterwards, when the power went out, locals were again called down to the airstrips to line up their car headlights either side of the runway so pilots could land.

There are now secondary schools on all three islands, but as recently as a decade ago, students on the two smaller islands had to move to boarding school in Galway to complete their education, which involved an abrupt switch from speaking Irish to English. Farming has all but died out on the islands and tourism is now the primary source of income; while Irish remains the local tongue, most locals speak English with visitors and converse with each other in Irish.

Getting There & Away

AIR

All three islands have landing strips. The mainland departure point is Connemara regional airport at Minna, near Inverin (Indreabhán), about 35km west of Galway. **Aer Arann** (☎ 593 034; www.aerarannislands.ie) offers return flights to any of the islands five times daily (hourly in summer) for €45/25/37 per adult/child/student; the flights take just seven minutes, and groups of four or more can ask about group rates. You may find yourself sitting in the cockpit next to the pilot of the tiny planes (scary at first, but the views are stunning). A bus from outside Galway's Kinlay House Hostel to the airport costs €6 return.

BOAT

Weather permitting, there's at least one boat a day heading out to the Aran Islands. Around Galway's Eyre Sq are several ferry offices that can set you up with a boat ride as well as accommodation. Galway's tourist office will do the same.

Island Ferries (☎ 568 903, 572 273; www.aranisland ferries.com; adult/child/concession €25/13/20) and **Aran Direct** (☎ 566 535; www.arandirect.com; return adult/child/concession €25/15/20) have quick 40-minute crossings from Rossaveal, about 40km west of Galway. The Galway–Rossaveal bus trip costs €6/2.50 per adult/child return and leaves Galway's Kinlay House Hostel 1½ hours before the ferry's scheduled departure. If you're driving to Rossaveal, you can park in the car park near the ferry offices. Transporting a car costs upwards of €160 and is only available on some crossings, but in any case you won't need one on the islands.

Ferries to Inisheer also operate from Doolin (p394).

Getting Around

The ferry companies run interisland services in high season only; from October to April connections require a trip back to Rossaveal.

INISHMÓR

☎ 099 / pop 1300

Most visitors who venture out to the islands don't make it beyond Inishmór (Árainn) and its main attraction, Dún Aengus, the stone fort perilously perched on the island's towering cliffs. Tourism turns the wheels of the island's economy: an armada of tour vans greet each ferry at the wharf, offering a ride round the sights (not a bad idea if you're doing a quick day trip). The arid landscape west of Kilronan (Cill Rónáin), the island's main settlement, is dominated by stone walls, boulders, scattered buildings and the odd patch of deep-green grass and potato plants.

Orientation

Inishmór is 14.5km long and 4km at its widest stretch. All boats arrive and depart from Kilronan, on the southeastern side of the island. The airstrip is 2km further southeast of town; a shuttle to Kilronan costs €5 return. One principal road runs the length of the island, intersected by small lanes and paths of packed dirt and stone.

Information

Staffed by lifelong islanders, the **tourist office** (Map p418; ☎ 61263; Kilronan; ⏰ 11am-7pm Jun-Sep, 11am-1pm & 2-5pm Mon-Fri, 10am-1pm & 2-5pm Sat & Sun Oct-May), on the waterfront west of the ferry pier in Kilronan, also changes money. The **Bank of Ireland** (Map p418; Kilronan; ⏰ 10am-12.30pm & 1.30-3pm Wed), north of the village centre, doesn't have an ATM, but you'll find one in Kilronan's small **Spar supermarket** (Map p418; Kilronan; ⏰ 9am-6pm Mon-Wed, 9am-7pm Thu-Sat, 10am-5pm Sun Jun-Aug).

LITERARY ARAN

The Aran Islands have sustained a strong creative streak, partly as a means for entertainment during long periods of isolation and partly, in the words of one local composer, to 'Make sure the rest of the country doesn't forget we're here'. Artists and writers from the mainland have similarly long been drawn to the elemental nature of island life.

Dramatist JM Synge (1871–1909) spent a lot of time on the islands (listening to the local dialect through the floorboards of his room), and his play *Riders to the Sea* (1905) is set on Inishmaan. His book *The Aran Islands* (1907) is the classic account of life here and remains in print.

American Robert Flaherty came to the islands in 1934 to film *Man of Aran*, a dramatic account of daily life. It became a classic and is regularly screened in Kilronan on Inishmór.

The mapmaker Tim Robinson has written a wonderful two-volume account of his explorations on Aran called *Stones of Aran: Pilgrimage* and *Stones of Aran: Labyrinthe*. His book *The Aran Islands: A Map and Guide* is superb.

Two other excellent publications are *The Book of Aran*, edited by Anne Korf, consisting of articles by 17 specialists covering diverse aspects of the islands' culture, and *Aran Reader*, edited by Breandán and Ruairí O hEither, with essays by various scholars on the islands' history, geography and culture.

Local literary talent includes the writer Liam O'Flaherty (1896–1984) from Inishmór. O'Flaherty, who wandered around North and South America before returning to Ireland in 1921 and fighting in the Civil War, is the author of several harrowing novels, including *Famine*.

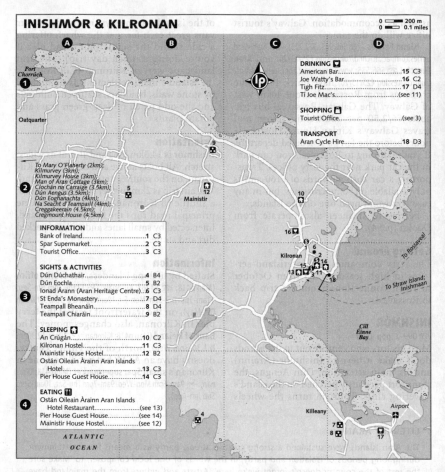

INISHMÓR & KILRONAN

0 —— 200 m
0 —— 0.1 miles

DRINKING 🍺
American Bar...15 C3
Joe Watty's Bar.....................................16 C2
Tigh Fitz...17 D4
Tí Joe Mac's.....................................(see 11)

SHOPPING 🛍
Tourist Office....................................(see 3)

TRANSPORT
Aran Cycle Hire....................................18 D3

Port Chorrúch ①

Oatquarter

To Mary O'Flaherty (2km);
Kilmurvey (3km);
Kilmurvey House (3km);
Man of Aran Cottage (3km);
Clochán na Carraige (3.5km);
Dún Aengus (3.5km);
Dún Eoghanachta (4km);
Na Seacht d'Teampaill (4km);
Creggakeerain (4.5km);
Cregmount House (4.5km)

Mainistir

INFORMATION
Bank of Ireland......................................1 C3
Spar Supermarket...................................2 C3
Tourist Office...3 C3

SIGHTS & ACTIVITIES
Dún Dúchathair......................................4 B4
Dún Eochla..5 B2
Ionad Árann (Aran Heritage Centre)...6 C3
St Enda's Monastery...............................7 D4
Teampall Bheanáin.................................8 D4
Teampall Chiaráin...................................9 B2

SLEEPING 🛏
An Crúgán..10 C2
Kilronan Hostel......................................11 C3
Mainistir House Hostel..........................12 B2
Ostán Oileain Àrainn Aran Islands
    Hotel...13 C3
Pier House Guest House.........................14 C3

EATING 🍴
Ostán Oileain Àrainn Aran Islands
    Hotel Restaurant.........................(see 13)
Pier House Guest House....................(see 14)
Mainistir House Hostel......................(see 12)

Kilronan

To Rossaveal
To Straw Island; Inishmaan

Cill Éinne Bay

Killeany

Airport

ATLANTIC OCEAN

Sights

Three spectacular forts stand guard over Inishmór, each believed to be around 2000 years old. Chief among them is **Dún Aengus** (Dún Aonghasa; ☎ 61008; adult/child/family €2.10/1.10/6; ⏱ 10am-6pm), with a remarkable *chevaux de frise*, a dense series of defensive stone spikes that surely helped deter ancient armies considering invading the site. The powerful swells pounding the sheer cliff face are awe-inspiring, particularly if you're here at a quiet time, such as the evening. Any time of day, take care: there are no guard rails and the winds can be strong; visitors have been blown off and killed on the rock shelf below.

Along the road between Kilronan and Dún Aengus is the smaller, perfectly circular fort,

Dún Eochla. Dramatically perched on a cliff-top promontory directly south of Kilronan is **Dún Dúchathair**.

The ruins of numerous stone churches trace the island's monastic history. The small **Teampall Chiaráin** (Church of St Kieran), with a high cross in the churchyard, is near Kilronan. To the southeast, near Cill Éinne Bay, is the early-Christian **Teampall Bheanáin** (Church of St Benen). Near the airstrip are the sunken remains of a church; the spot where it's located is said to have been the site of **St Enda's Monastery** in the 5th century. Past Kilmurvey is the perfect **Clochán na Carraige**, an early-Christian stone hut that stands 2.5m tall, and various small early-Christian ruins known rather inaccurately as the **Na Seacht**

O FATHER WHERE ART THOU?

Devotees of the late 1990s cult TV series *Father Ted* might recognise 'Craggy Island' – the show's fictional island setting off Ireland's west coast – from its opening sequence showing the *Plassy* shipwreck (p422) on Inisheer. However, apart from this single shot, the sitcom was mostly filmed in London studios, with additional location shots in Counties Clare, Wicklow and Dublin. Alas, the Parochial House and Vaughan's pub are nowhere to be found here (instead you'll find them around Lisdoonvarna in County Clare).

This hasn't stopped the Aran Islands from embracing the show as their own – although which of the islands has the rightful claim to the 'Craggy Island' title is hotly disputed. Things heated up even more when Inishmór recently hosted its first *Father Ted* festival, **Ted Fest** (www.friendsofted .org), with madcap festivities including breakfast-time charades, sketches performed in Irish by local schoolchildren, a Father Jack cocktail night (in honour of the show's cantankerous alcoholic elderly priest), fancy-dress guided walks around the island, and a Ted trivia night.

Besides being an excuse to party island style, the festival was organised to commemorate actor Dermot Morgan (Ted), who died in 1998 from a heart attack aged 45. Proceeds are donated to Croi, the West of Ireland Cardiology Foundation.

The inaugural event was a sell-out and Ted Fest is set to become an annual pilgrimage for fans. Future festivals may be held on more than one island to cope with demand – and to appease the long-running 'Craggy Island' debate. Check the website for dates and bookings.

dTeampaill (Seven Churches), comprising a couple of ruined churches, monastic houses and some fragments of a high cross from the 8th or 9th century. To the south of the ruins is **Dún Eoghanachta**, another circular fort.

There's a Blue Flag beach (a clean, safe beach given the EU Blue Flag award) at **Kilmurvey**, peacefully situated west of bustling Kilronan. In the sheltered little bay of **Port Chorrúch**, up to 50 grey seals sun themselves and feed in the shallows.

For an informed appreciation of all three islands' history, geology and wildlife, stop in at the **Aran Heritage Centre** (Ionad Árann; Map p418; ☎ 61355, 61354; www.visitaranislands.com; Kilronan; adult/child €5.50/4; ☼ 11am-1pm & 2-5pm Mon-Fri, 10am-1pm & 2-5pm Sat & Sun), just off the main road leading out of Kilronan. The admission fee covers regular screenings of Robert Flaherty's 1934 film *Man of Aran*. The centre also has a coffee shop.

Sleeping

The tourist office can book rooms for a €4 fee. Advance bookings are advised, particularly in high summer.

Kilronan Hostel (Map p418; ☎ 61255; www.kilronan hostel.com; Kilronan; dm/tw from €15/40) You'll see the pistachio green Kilronan Hostel perched above Tí Joe Mac's pub even before your ferry docks at the pier, a two-minute walk away. Fortunately the floors have been insulated, so there's very little pub noise. The

hostel lends out fishing rods for free and can teach you to play hurling on the beach out front.

Mainistir House Hostel (☎ 61169; www.mainistir housearan.com; Mainistir; dm/s/d €16/40/50) Quirky and colourful, this 60-bed hostel on the main road north of Kilronan is a fun place both for young travellers and for families. Fresh morning pastries and free pick-up are included in the rates, and you only have to head as far as the dining room for renowned home cooking.

Kilmurvey House (☎ 61218; www.kilmurveyhouse .com; Kilmurvey; s €55-60, d €90-100; ☼ Apr-Sep) On the path leading to Dún Aengus is this grand 18th-century stone mansion. It's a beautiful setting, and the rooms are well maintained. Hearty meals (dinner €25) incorporate home-grown vegetables, and fresh fish and meats. You can swim at a pretty beach that's a short walk from the house.

Man of Aran Cottage (☎ 61301; www.manofaran cottage.com; Kilmurvey; s/d €55/80; ☼ Mar-Oct) Built for the 1930s film of the same name, this thatched B&B doesn't trade on past glories – its authentic stone-and-wood interiors are well maintained, and are decorated with soft, printed cotton fabrics. It has a genuinely homey feel.

Cregmount House (☎ 61139; Creggakeerain; d €64-70; ☼ May-Oct) Situated refreshingly far from the tourist crowds at the northwestern end of the island, Cregmount House is a pleasant

COUNTY GALWAY

three-room B&B with quality cooking (dinner €26) and views across Galway Bay.

An Crúgán (☎ 61150; www.ancrugan.com; Kilronan; d €70, cottages per week €450-550; ☯ Apr-Oct) Located off the main road north of Kilronan, An Crúgán has six well-appointed rooms. If you're after more privacy, a two-bedroom self-catering cottage is available to rent year-round.

Pier House Guest House (Map p418; ☎ 61416; www .pierhousearan.com; Kilronan; s €90-100, d €110-120; ☯ Mar-Oct; ⚅) Captivating views and light-filled interiors splashed with colour make this double-decker guesthouse a pierside haven.

Ostán Oileain Árainn Aran Islands Hotel (Map p418; ☎ 61104; www.aranislandshotel.com; Kilronan; d from €118; ☯ closed early Jan–mid-Feb; ⚅) Inishmór's only hotel has generously appointed guest rooms in warm russet and navy tones; with plush carpets, gleaming timber furniture, and all the mod cons of a mainland hotel. The owner, PJ O'Flaherty, is also the creative force behind the traditional Irish dancing spectacular *Ragús*, and the show is regularly performed on the island when not touring abroad. Contact the hotel for performance dates.

Eating

Mainistir House Hostel (☎ 61169; www.mainistirhouse aran.com; Mainistir; buffet €16; ☯ from 8pm summer, from 7pm winter) Mainistir House Hostel cooks up fab organic, largely vegetarian fare such as pea-and-leek tart, and pear cheesecake made with crushed Amaretti biscuits. Nonguests are welcome, but be sure to book ahead.

Man of Aran Cottage (☎ 61301; www.manofarancot tage.com; Kilmurvey; sandwiches from €3, set dinner €35; ☯ lunch & dinner Jun-Sep, dinner only Mar-May & Oct) This historic whitewashed cottage is an idyllic setting in which to savour freshly caught fish, and flavourful organic vegetables and herbs grown in the cottage's garden. Reservations are essential.

Ostán Oileain Árainn Aran Islands Hotel Restaurant (Map p418; ☎ 61104; www.aranislandshotel.com; Kilronan; mains €15.50-34.50; ☯ 12.30-4pm & 5-9pm) The superb seafood at this smart restaurant includes cracked-crab-claw salad, whole rainbow trout and lobster. Afterwards, unwind over an Irish coffee in the timber bar, which has traditional live music most nights. Check ahead for low-season opening hours.

Pier House Guest House (Map p418; ☎ 61416; www .pierhousearan.com; Kilronan; mains €22-28; ☯ lunch & dinner May-Oct) Has a well-regarded restaurant.

Drinking

Tigh Fitz (☎ 61213; Killeaney) Near the airport, this jovial pub has traditional sessions every weekend and does excellent bar food (noon to 5pm) from June to August. It's 1.6km from Kilronan (about a 25-minute walk).

Joe Watty's Bar (Map p418; ☎ 61155; Kilronan) The best pub in Kilronan is Joe Watty's, with traditional sessions most nights and pub food (noon to 8pm) from June to August.

Tí Joe Mac's (Map p418; ☎ 61248; Kilronan) Informal music sessions and pub food served all year make Tí Joe Mac's a dependable favourite.

American Bar (Map p418; ☎ 61130; Kilronan) No one knows how it got its New World name, but this locally run island stalwart hosts great live music at least a couple of nights a week, and serves lunch and dinner daily in summer.

Shopping

Shops around Kilronan mostly sell machine-knitted Aran sweaters. For a much heavier, hand-knitted version, visit **Mary O'Flahrety** (☎ 61117; Oat Quarter). Chances are you'll see Mary knitting when you call in. Expect to pay around €100 for a genuine hand-knitted sweater.

The **tourist office** (Map p418; ☎ 61263; Kilronan; ☯ 11am-7pm Jun-Sep, 11am-1pm & 2-5pm Mon-Fri, 10am-1pm & 2-5pm Sat & Sun Oct-May) sells greeting cards featuring evocative impressionist paintings by local artist Michaél Ó Ceallaigh, and can give you details about buying original works.

Getting Around

Aran Cycle Hire (Map p418; ☎ 61132; per day €10), near the pier, hires out sturdy bikes, which it'll deliver to your accommodation anywhere on the island. You can also bring your own bicycle on the ferry for free.

Year-round, numerous **minibuses** (tours €10) greet each ferry arrival and offer a 2½-hour island tour that provides a good overview of the main sights.

To see the island at a gentler pace, **pony traps** (☯ Mar-Nov) with a driver are available for trips between Kilronan and Dún Aengus; the return journey costs between €60 and €100 for up to four people. If the pony traps are not waiting by the pier, walk to the tourist office to ask where they're stationed.

INISHMAAN

☎ 099 / pop 200

The least-visited of the islands, with the smallest population, Inishmaan (Inis Meáin) is, perhaps not surprisingly, the most tranquil. Early Christian monks seeking solitude were drawn to Inishmaan, as was the author JM Synge, who spent five summers here over a century ago. The island they knew largely survives today: docile farm animals, impressive old forts, and warm-hearted locals who may tell you with a glint in their eye that they had a hard night on the whiskey the previous evening (there are no *garda* on the island to enforce closing times). Inishmaan's scenery is breathtaking, with a jagged coastline of startling cliffs and empty beaches.

To their credit, Inishmaan's down-to-earth islanders are largely unconcerned with the prospect of attracting tourist euros, so facilities are few and far between.

Orientation & Information

Inishmaan is roughly 5km long by 3km wide. Most of its buildings are spread out along the road that runs east–west across the centre of the island. The principal boat landing is on the eastern side of the island, while the airstrip is in the northeastern corner. In An Córa, the helpful **Inishmaan Island Co-operative** (☎ 73010; ☯ 9am-1pm & 2-5pm Mon-Fri), northwest of the pier and post office, dispenses tourist information. There's no ATM; the bank visits on the second Tuesday of each month.

Sights

Glorious views of the island's limestone valleys extend from the elliptical stone fort **Dún Chonchúir**, thought to have been built sometime between the 1st and 7th centuries. **Teach Synge** (☎ 73036; admission €3; ☯ by appointment), a thatched cottage on the road just before you head up to the fort, is where the writer JM Synge spent his summers between 1898 and 1902.

Cill Cheannannach is a rough 8th- or 9th-century church, south of the pier. The well-preserved stone fort **Dún Fearbhaigh**, a short distance west, dates from the same era.

At the desolate western edge of the island, **Synge's Chair** is a lookout at the edge of a sheer limestone cliff with the surf from Gregory's Sound booming below. The cliff ledge is often sheltered from the wind, so do as Synge did and find a comfortable seat to take it all in.

On the walk out to Synge's Chair, a sign points the way to a **clochán**, hidden behind a house and shed.

In the east of the island, about 500m north of the boat landing stage, is **Trá Leitreach**, a safe, sheltered beach.

Sleeping & Eating

Most B&Bs serve evening meals, usually using organically grown food. Meals generally cost around €22 to €25.

Máire Mulkerrin (☎ 73016; s/d €25/40) Now in her 80s, Mrs Mulkerrin is a local icon in her skirts and shawls. She keeps a cosy, spick-and-span home, filled with faded family photos, and her stove warms the kitchen all day.

Ard Alainn (☎ 73027; s/d with shared bathroom €25/50; ☯ May-Sep) Signposted just over 2km from the pier, Ard Alainn has five simple rooms, all with shared bathroom. The breakfasts by hostess Maura Faherty will keep you going all day.

Tig Congaile (☎ 73085; tigcongaile@eircom.net; Moore Village, Inishmaan; s €40, d €54-70) Not far from the pier, Guatemalan-born Vilma Conneely adds unexpected diversity to the local dining scene (lunch dishes from €5, dinner from €20; open 10.30am to 9pm), making the most of limited local ingredients. She does a fine sea vegetable soup and her vegetable-and-herb quiche is wonderful. Guest rooms are modern and comfortable.

An Dún (☎ 73047; anduninismeain@eircom.net; s €45-60, d €70-100) Opposite the entrance to Dún Chonchúir, modern An Dún has comfortable en-suite rooms and a sauna. It serves very hearty set dinners and nonguests are welcome, though you must make a reservation. An Dún also has a handy little grocery shop, good for buying essentials for your day hike.

Óstán Inismeáin (☎ 73020; bfaherty@iol.ie; s €38-58, d €64-90) At the northern end of the island, out on the bare limestone flats, this pink-painted motel-style building has 10 rooms, a pub (dishes €5 to €9) and a large formal dining room (lunch and dinner, mains €13 to €32). Bar food and á la carte plates showcase the freshest of ingredients.

Teach Anna (☎ 73054; d €70) Run by islander Anna Byrne (whom you'll also meet at the post office, where she works by day), this homey B&B is five minutes' walk from the beach and has four rooms. The multiskilled

Anna cooks bargain-priced evening meals (€12) on request.

Teach Ósta (☎ 73003; mains from €10; ⊗ noon-late) This terrific little pub hums on summer evenings and supplies snacks, sandwiches, soups and seafood platters. Though the pub often keeps going until the wee hours, food service generally stops around 7pm and may not be available in the winter months.

Shopping

The knitwear factory **Cniotáil Inis Meáin** (☎ 73 009) exports fine woollen garments to some of the world's most exclusive shops. You can buy the same sweaters here; call before visiting.

Getting Around

Walking is a fine way to explore the island's sights, but you may also be able to get an informal tour with locals from around €5.

INISHEER

☎ 099 / pop 300

Although Inisheer (Inis Oírr) is only 8km off the coast from Doolin in County Clare, the absence of tourist amenities nevertheless keeps visitor numbers down. The smallest of the Aran Islands has a palpable sense of enchantment, enhanced by the island's deep-rooted mythology and ethereal landscapes.

The wheels of change turn very slowly here. Electricity didn't come to the island until the 1970s and even then only by generator. It was connected to the mainland's electricity via an underwater cable in 1997.

Inisheer boasts a surprisingly large state-of-the-art community arts centre, which sits out on an exposed stretch of the northern side of the island as a beacon of the island's artistic traditions.

Information

In July and August a small **kiosk** (⊗ 10am-6pm) at the harbour provides tourist information. Like Inishmaan, there's no ATM; the bank visits on the fourth Tuesday of each month.

Online, www.inisoirr-island.com is a handy resource for planning your trip.

Sights & Activities

The majority of Inisheer's sights are in the north of the island. The 15th-century **O'Brien's Castle** (Caisleá'n Uí Bhriain), a 100m climb uphill to the island's highest point, has dra-

matic views over clover-covered fields to the beach and harbour. It was built within the remains of a ringfort called Dún Formna, dating from as early as the 1st century AD. The gate is sometimes locked, but if it's open you can explore the remains freely. Nearby is an 18th-century signal tower.

On the Strand (An Trá) is the 10th-century **Teampall Chaoimháin** (Church of St Kevin), named for Inisheer's patron saint, who is buried close by. On the eve of his 14 June feast day a mass is held here in the open air at 9pm. Those with ailments sleep here for the night to be healed.

West of the small, sandy beach next to the pier, **Inisheer Heritage House** (☎ 75021; Inisheer; admission €2; ⊗ 2-4pm Jul & Aug or by appointment) is a traditional stone-built thatched cottage with some interesting old photographs. It also has a craft shop and café.

Cill Ghobnait (Church of St Gobnait), southwest of Inisheer Heritage House, is a small 8th- or 9th-century church named for Gobnait, who fled here from Clare while trying to escape an enemy who was pursuing her.

About 2km southwest of the church is the **Tobar Éinne** (Well of St Enda). Locals still carry out a pilgrimage known as the *turas,* which involves, over the course of three consecutive Sundays, picking up seven stones from the ground nearby and walking around the small well seven times, putting one stone down each time, while saying the rosary until an elusive eel appears from the well's watery depths. If, during this ritual, you're lucky enough to see the eel, it's said your tongue will be bestowed with healing powers, literally enabling you to lick wounds.

The signposted 10.5km **Inis Oírr Way** (Inisheer Way) walking path brings you past the rusting hulk of the **Plassy**, a freighter wrecked in 1960 and thrown high up onto the rocks. Miraculously, all on board were saved; Tigh Ned's pub has a collection of photographs and documents detailing the rescue. An aerial shot of the wreck was used in the opening sequence of the iconic TV series *Father Ted* (see O Father where art Thou?, p419). The uninhabited **lighthouse** (1857) on the island's southern tip is off limits.

Festivals & Events

One of the arts centre's highlights is its week-long **Craiceann Inis Oírr International Bodhrán Summer School** (☎ 75067; www.craiceann.com) in June, which includes *bodhrán* masterclasses, lectures and workshops, as well as related events such as Irish dancing. Craiceann takes its name from the Irish word for 'skin', referring to the goat skin used to make these circular drums, which are held under one arm and played with a wooden beater. The festival is headed up by Inisheer local Micheal O hAlmhain, who has performed with Irish bands including the Chieftains. During Craiceann, nightly drumming sessions take place in the island's pubs.

Sleeping & Eating

Brú Radharc Na Mara Hostel (☎ 75024; maire .searraigh@oceanfree.net; dm €15; ☾ Mar-Oct) Hand-

ily located next to a pub and by the pier, this spotless Independent Holiday Hostels of Ireland (IHH) hostel has ocean views, a self-catering kitchen and bikes for hire. The owners also run the adjacent B&B (rooms €40), with basic en-suite rooms.

Ard Mhuire (☎ 75005; unamcdonagh@hotmail.com; s/d €35/70; ☾ closed 10 Dec-10 Jan) As central as it gets, this 1934 double-decker house is to the left of the pier. It's home to the Conneely family, who have refurbished the guest rooms and put on a fine breakfast; dinner can also be arranged.

Óstán Inis Oírr (☎ 75020; s/d from €33/63; ☾ Apr-Sep) The Flaherty family's modern hotel, just

---

WALK: INISHEER

This moderate 12km (five hour) walk takes in many of Inisheer's sights. It virtually circumnavigates the island, taking you through the settled northern fringe, past the stone-walled fields in the centre and south, and around the wild and rocky south coast. For all but 2km along the southern shore, the walk follows quiet lanes. You'll come across yellow blazes on some sections of the walk, marking the Inis Oírr Way, which confines itself to the northern two-thirds of the island.

From the Inisheer ferry pier, walk west along the narrow road parallel to the shore and continue past Fisherman's Cottage Bistro. Ignore the waymarker pointing left at the next junction and go on straight ahead to the small fishing pier at the northwest corner of the island. Continue along the road, now with a gravel surface, past another acute-angled junction on the left (where the waymarkers reappear). Here the shingle shore is on one side of the road, and a dense mosaic of fields, enclosed by remarkably intact stone walls, is on the other.

About 1km from the acute junction, turn left with the painted sign; about 100m along the paved lane is the Tobhar Eínne.

Return to the coast road and continue southwest as it becomes a rough track. After about 600m, head roughly south across the limestone pavement and strips of grass to the shore. Follow the gently sloping rock platform around the southwestern headland (Ceann na Faochnaí) and walk east to the lighthouse near Fardurris Point (two hours from the ferry pier).

Walk around the wall enclosing the lighthouse and use a stile to cross another wall by the entrance gate. Now back on a level surface, follow the road generally northeast as it climbs gradually. Access to Cill na Seacht Ninion (the Church of the Seven Daughters) is from a point 1.5km from the lighthouse, almost opposite two metal-roofed sheds on the right; a pillar next to a gate bears the chapel's name and an arrow points vaguely in its direction. Use stiles to cross three fields to a rusty gate in the ivy-clad walls around the chapel site. In the largest stone enclosure are five grave slabs, one of which still has a faint incised cross.

Back on the road, continue northeast to the village of An Formna. Take the right fork, then turn right again at a T-junction and head south along the road above Lough More. Keep left at a track junction and continue to the Atlantic shore with the wreck of the *Plassy* just ahead (one hour from the lighthouse).

Head north, following the track, which then becomes a sealed road at the northern end of Lough More. Continue following the road along the northern shore of the island, past the airstrip.

At the airstrip you can diverge, if you wish, to the sandy hummock that shelters the ancient Teampall Chaomháin. A little further along the road, turn left to reach O'Brien's Castle. From here, follow the narrow road northwest, turn right at a T-junction and then make your way to Cnoc Rathnaí, a Bronze Age burial mound (1500 BC), which is remarkably intact considering it was buried under the sand until the 19th century, when it was rediscovered. Continue towards the beach; the pier is to your left through a maze of lanes.

COUNTY GALWAY

up from the Strand, has homey rooms and serves hearty meals in its pub and restaurant (mains €8 to €14, open lunch and dinner, April to September).

Radharc an Chláir (☎ 75019; bridpoil@eircom.net; s/d €38/70) This pleasant B&B near O'Brien's Castle has views of the Cliffs of Moher and Galway Bay. You'll need to book several weeks ahead, as hostess Brid Poil's home cooking draws many repeat visitors. Guests can hire bikes (€10 per day) and arrange evening meals (€20).

Fisherman's Cottage (☎ 75073; mains €12-20; ☽ Apr-Oct) Cosy Fisherman's Cottage, near the pier, specialises in tasty, fresh seafood and organically grown vegetables.

Drinking

Tigh Ned (☎ 75004) Here since 1897, Tigh Ned is a welcoming, unpretentious place with lively, traditional music and inexpensive lunchtime fare.

Tigh Ruairí (☎ 75020) Rory Conneely's atmospheric digs hosts live music sessions.

Óstán Inis Oírr (☎ 75020) The hotel's pub is also a friendly spot for a pint.

Getting Around

Bikes can be rented from **Rothair Inis Oírr** (☎ 75033; per day €10; ☽ May-Sep). **Brú Radharc Na Mara Hostel** (☎ 75024; maire. searraigh@oceanfree .net; per day €10; ☽ Mar-Oct) also hires bikes to nonguests.

You can take a tour of the island on a **pony trap** (per hr €5-10) in summer, or on an atmospheric tractor-drawn thatched-cottage-style **wagon** (☎ 086 607 3230; per hr €5-10).

CONNEMARA

In Irish, Connemara (Conamara) means 'Inlets of the Sea', which is borne out by the region's filigreed coastline.

The coastal road west of Spiddal (R336) winds around small bays and coves reminiscent of eastern Canada's remote reaches of Nova Scotia and Newfoundland (minus the moose). It strings together a succession of seaside hamlets, including the jewel-like fishing harbour at Roundstone, and sleepy Lennane on Killary Harbour, the country's only fjord. Clifden, Connemara's largest town, is spectacularly sited on a hill, while offshore lies the idyllic island of Inishbofin.

Connemara's interior is a kaleidoscope of rusty bogs, lonely valleys and shimmering black lakes. At its heart are the Maumturk Mountains and the pewter-tinged quartzite peaks of the Twelve Bens mountain range, with a network of scenic hiking and biking trails. It's dazzling at any time of day but especially as the sun starts its descent, when the landscape glows as if filtered through a topaz-coloured lens.

One of the most important Gaeltacht (Irish-speaking) areas in the country begins around Spiddal and stretches along the coast as far as Cashel. Ireland's national Irish-language radio station, Radio na Gaeltachta (www.rte.ie/rnag) and Irish-language TV station, TG4 (www.tg4.ie), are both based in the region, as is the Irish-language weekly newspaper Foinse (www .foinse.ie in Irish).

If you intend any detailed exploration of the area, the excellent *Connemara: Introduction and Gazeteer*, by Tim Robinson, is a must. *Connemara: A Hill Walker's Guide*, by Robinson and Joss Lynam, is also invaluable.

Galway's tourist office (p404) has a wealth of information on the area. Online, **Connemara Tourism** (www.connemara-tourism.org) and **Go Connemara** (www.goconnemara.com) have region-wide info and links.

Getting There & Around

BUS

Organised bus tours from Galway (p408) are plentiful and offer a good overview of the region, though ideally you'll want more than one day to absorb the area's charms.

Bus Éireann (☎ 091-562 000; www.buseireann .ie) serves most of Connemara. Services can be sporadic, and many buses operate May to September only, or July and August only. Some drivers will stop in between towns if arrangements are made at the beginning of the trip.

Michael Nee Coaches (☎ 095-51082) is an independent line that specifically serves Connemara, with daily buses beginning in Galway, and connections within the area. Connemara towns served include Maam Cross, Recess, Cashel, Clifden, Letterfrack, Tully Cross and Cleggan. If you're going somewhere in-between towns (a hostel in the countryside, for example) you might be able to arrange a drop-off with the driver.

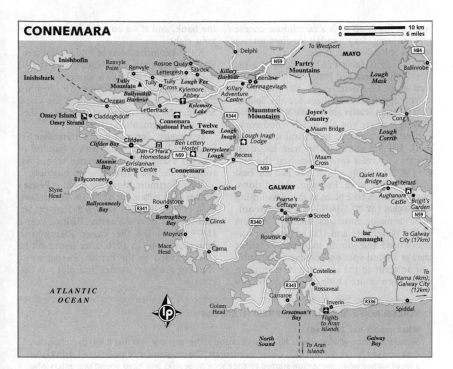

CONNEMARA

0 ——— 10 km
0 ——— 6 miles

ATLANTIC
OCEAN

CAR

Your own wheels are the best way to get off this scenic region's beaten track – though watch out for the narrow roads' stone walls, just waiting to scrape the sides of your car.

Keep an eye out too for meandering Connemara sheep – characterised by thick creamy fleece and black faces and legs – which frequently wander onto the road. Even Connemara's flattest stretches of road tend to be bumpy due to the uneven bog beneath the tarmac.

Heading west from Galway, you can either take the coast road (R336) through Salthill, Barna and Spiddal, or the direct inland route (N59) through Oughterard. The journey from Maam Cross northwest to Leenane (R336) or northeast to Cong (R345) takes you through the stunning mountainous region of Joyce country.

Many road signs in this area are in Irish only, so take note of the Irish place names (in parentheses) that are also listed in this section.

COASTAL DRIVE – GALWAY CITY TO MACE HEAD

The slow coastal route between Galway and Connemara takes you past picturesque seascapes and villages.

Opposite the popular Blue Flag beach **Silver Strand**, 4.8km west of Galway, are the **Barna Woods**, a dense, deep green forest perfect for rambling and picnicking. Conserved by the Galway County Council, the woods contain the last natural growing oaks in Ireland's west.

The once unspoilt village of Barna, a further 3km west, has been inundated by recent development (to the chagrin of locals, who campaigned passionately and ultimately futilely against it). Barna is, however, home to some of the greater Galway area's best seafood at **O'Grady's on the Pier** (☎ 091-592223; www .ogradysonthepier.com; mains €15-30; ☯ from 6pm Mon-Sat, 12.30-2.45pm & from 6pm Sun). Daily specials include ocean-fresh catches such as grilled monkfish with sautéed potatoes and mushroom cream, and there are plenty of choices for carnivores. Michael O'Grady's vanilla-nut ice-cream cluster with caramel sauce is sublime; otherwise

COUNTY GALWAY

you can finish off with a farmhouse cheese platter. Long, lazy Sunday lunches attract legions of locals; book ahead.

West again, **Spiddal** (An Spidéal) is a refreshingly untouched little village, and the start of the Gaeltacht region. On your right as you approach the village are the **Spiddal Craft & Design Studios** (☎ 091-553376; www.spiddal craftvillage), where you can watch woodworkers, leatherworkers, sculptors and weavers at work, buy a T-shirt with an Irish-language slogan, or have a spot of lunch at the bistro (☎ 091-55030), which is in fact the best place to eat in town. Exceptional traditional music sessions take place at the unassuming **Tigh Hughes** (☎ 091-553447) – it's not uncommon for major musicians, such as members of the Waterboys and U2, to turn up unannounced and join in the craic. Sessions start at around 9pm on Tuesdays. The pub's just adjacent to the main street; turn right at the town centre's little crossroads next to the bank, and it's a couple of doors up on your right.

A few kilometres west of Spiddal, the scenery becomes more dramatic, with parched fields crisscrossed by low stone walls rolling to a ragged shore. **Carraroe** (An Cheathrú Rua) has fine beaches, including the Coral Strand, which is composed entirely of shell and coral fragments.

Lettermore, **Gorumna** and **Lettermullen** islands are low and bleak, with a handful of farmers eking out an existence from tiny, rocky fields. Fish farming is big business.

Near Gortmore, along the R340, is **Pearse's Cottage** (Teach an Phiarsaigh; ☎ 091-574 292; adult/family €1.50/4.25; ⊙ 10am-6pm Easter & mid-Jun–mid-Sep, 10am-5pm Sat & Sun spring & autumn). Pádraig Pearse (1879–1916) led the Easter Rising with James Connolly in 1916; after the revolt he was executed by the British. Pearse wrote some of his short stories and plays in this cottage.

VOICES: AOIFE NÍ THUAIRISG, PRESENTER, TG4

What impact has TG4 had?

Before the station was launched, the national image of the language was that it was parochial, that it was spoken by people who didn't want to integrate. The programme commissioners didn't have a lot of money when the station started so they took huge risks and hired young presenters who weren't afraid to stand up and voice strong opinions. Now you see shops and restaurants using Irish in their business names, and posh yummy mummies enrolling their children at expensive Irish-language schools. It's completely changed – it's become fashionable.

Is Irish your first language?

Yes. I'm from Connemara and we always spoke Irish at home, and I was educated completely in Irish. I loved Big Bird on *Sesame Street* as a kid, but my mum had to translate what he was saying because it was in English. Now the station addresses programming for kids, so they can watch shows like *SpongeBob SquarePants* in their own language.

Where is the dubbing done?

In studios all over Ireland – a nationwide industry has come out of the TV station. Irish has totally different dialects around the country – totally different phrasing – so we cover them all.

Are the voice-over talent and presenters all native Irish speakers?

No, a lot have learnt Irish. Sometimes people are intimidated talking to me because I'm a native speaker and they think their Irish isn't good enough, but it's great to talk to people in Irish and for them to realise their Irish doesn't have to be 'perfect' for them to feel comfortable using it. I'm very proud of the language. A lot of people my age learnt Irish at school, where learning derived from focusing on grammar; it was drummed into them. I'm glad that people can now experience the language in a way that's different and relevant.

In addition to television broadcasts, TG4's website (www.tg4.ie) streams programmes and has online archives of shows including episodes of Aoife's *Paisean Faisean* (with subtitles in English).

If you're keen to learn the language, you can enrol in short courses at the International Summer School of the **National University of Ireland, Galway** (☎ 091-495 442; www.nuigalway.ie/iss) and **Cnoc Suain Cultural Centre** (☎ 091-555 703; www.cnocsuain.com) in Spiddal.

Continuing along the R340 brings you to **Carna**, a small fishing village from where there are pleasant walks out to **Mweenish Island** or north to Moyrus and out to **Mace Head**. This wild headland is best known for its research station (closed to the public), which measures changes in the global atmosphere and their effect on weather and climate.

The following places are worth hitting the brakes for if you aren't planning to make Roundstone or beyond by nightfall.

Inland from Spiddal village on a trout-filled river, **Spiddal Caravan & Camping Park** (Pairc Saoire an Spidéil; ☎ 091-553 372; pairics aoire@eircom .net; River Rd, Spiddal; camp/caravan sites €12/22; ☒ mid-Mar–Oct) has modern facilities, including clean, free showers.

The best thing about the whitewashed **Buninvhir B&B** (☎ 091-574 238; www.buninvhir.com; Derryrush, Rosmuc; s/d €35/58; ☒ Easter-Sep) is its uninterrupted view over Kilkieran Bay from the front terrace – which is to take nothing away from the cosy home's patchwork-quilted beds, flowering garden, and delicious evening meals (€20), which are served on the terrace in fine weather. Credit cards aren't accepted.

Set in a storybook garden roamed by ducks and chickens, **Cloch na Scíth** (☎ 091 553 364; www .thatchcottage.com; Kellough, Spiddal; d €64-68, cottages from €250; ℗) is a century-old thatched cottage with a warm, friendly host, Nancy, who cooks bread in an iron pot over the peat fire (as her grandmother taught her) and serves Baileys by the fire. A separate self-catering thatched cottage on the property makes a great base for families.

At the head of Cashel Bay, **Cashel House Hotel** (☎ 095-31001; www.cashel-house-hotel.com; Cashel; s €95-135, d €190-310; ℗) is a *Great Gatsby*–style mansion with 32 period rooms surrounded by 17 hectares of woodland and gardens. It also has a stable of Connemara ponies (riding lessons available), a superb dining room and even a small private beach.

Guests can go fly fishing in the grounds of the majestic **Ballynahinch Castle Hotel** (☎ 095-31006; www.ballynahinch-castle.com; Recess; d €210-360; ☒ Mar-Nov; ℗), southwest of Recess, and anyone can stop by for a drink in the bar. Rooms are dressed in olive and gold fabrics (many with four-poster beds), from where you can gaze out at the river, mountains or stately courtyard. Seasonal closing dates vary – phone for details.

OUGHTERARD & AROUND
☎ 091 / pop 2400

The writer William Makepeace Thackeray sang the praises of the small town of Oughterard (Uachtar Árd), saying, 'A more beautiful village can scarcely be seen'. Fortunately, little has changed in the intervening years. Just 27km along the main road from Galway to Clifden, near Lough Corrib, this pretty gateway to Connemara is one of Ireland's principal angling centres.

Immediately west of Oughterard, the countryside opens up to sweeping panoramas of lakes, mountains and bogs that get more spectacular the further west you travel.

Nearby attractions include Aughanure Castle, a spiritual Celtic garden, the Quiet Man Bridge, and the scenic drive along the Glann road to a vantage point overlooking the Hill of Doon.

Information
Bank of Ireland (Main St) Has an ATM and bureau de change.
Post office (Main St)
Tourist office (☎ 552 808; www.connemarabegins. com; Main St; ☒ 9.30am-5.30pm Mon-Fri) Also offers internet access at €1 per 15 minutes.

Sights
AUGHANURE CASTLE
Built in the 16th century, this bleak **fortress** (☎ 552 214; adult/child €2.75/1.25; ☒ 9.30am-6pm Apr-Oct) was home to the 'Fighting' O'Flahertys, who controlled the region for hundreds of years after they fought off the Normans. The six-storey tower house stands on a rocky outcrop overlooking Lough Corrib and has been extensively restored. Surrounding the castle are the remains of an unusual double bawn (area surrounded by walls outside the main castle, and acting as a defence and a place to keep cattle in times of trouble), and underneath the castle the lake washes through a number of natural caverns and caves.

Aughanure Castle is 3km east of Oughterard, off the main Galway road (N59).

BRIGIT'S GARDEN
Halfway between the villages of Moycullen and Oughterard is the magical **Brigit's Garden** (☎ 091-550 905; www.galwaygarden.com; Polagh, Roscahill; adult/child €7/4; ☒ 10am-5.50pm mid-Apr–Sep; ℗ ☒). Named for the Celtic goddess governing the life-cycle, it has four seasonal gardens based

around Celtic festivals, mythology and lore, along with Ireland's largest sundial. A nature trail meanders through woodlands and wildflower meadows, and a teashop serves homemade food sourced from the gardens. At various times, you might also catch New Age cookery classes, yoga workshops and pagan festivals. Best of all, Brigit's Garden is a not-for-profit initiative that's run to allow visitors to appreciate the area's cultural and environmental heritage. If you're coming on the Galway–Clifden bus, get off at the Roscahill post office, from where it's a signed 2km walk southeast, or call ahead and someone can usually pick you up from the bus stop.

QUIET MAN BRIDGE
Just 3km outside Oughterard (on your left as you head northwest) is the Quiet Man Bridge, which featured in the 1952 film of the same name starring Maureen O'Hara and John Wayne. Visible from the main road, you can turn down the short lane to walk over the quaint stone bridge and meditate on the surrounding 'Quiet Man Country'. (Though it's decidedly less quiet when bus tours pull up.)

Much of the film was shot in and around Ashford Castle in the town of Cong in neighbouring county Mayo.

Sleeping & Eating
Canrawer House (☎ 552 388; oughterardhostel.com; Station Rd; dm €15-17; ☯ Feb-Oct; Ⓟ) Dorms and family rooms are bright and clean, and there's an outdoor patio where you can chat with other guests. If you want to catch the area's wild brown trout for dinner, the owner of this chaletlike timber-panelled hostel can take you. Lessons cost €25 per hour, and full-day guided lake tours including all gear cost €140.

Waterfall Lodge (☎ 552 168; www.waterfalllodge .net; Glann Rd; s/d €50/80; Ⓟ) Decorated in rose-coloured hues and lit by glowing lamps, this double-fronted Victorian B&B stands amid wooded gardens beside a brook a few moments' stroll from the village centre. Breakfast choices include kippers, homemade pancakes or melt-in-your-mouth French toast.

Boat Inn (☎ 552 196; www.theboatinn.com; Market Sq; d €90-120) In addition to providing comfy rooms, this inn (mains around €20; open lunch and dinner) serves traditional Irish stew to warm you up after a day's fishing and other family-friendly fare including sizzling fajitas, enormous beef burgers with home-

made sauce, and a crumble of the day with custard made on the premises. The bar hosts regular live music.

Currarevagh House (☎ 552 312; www.currarevagh .com; d €184-198; ☯ Mar–mid-Oct; Ⓟ) You'd be hard pressed to find a more romantic place than this rambling 19th-century mansion on the shore of Lough Corrib. You can take afternoon tea (€9.90) by the open fire and dine on exquisite five-course dinners (€45; nonguests welcome). Currarevagh House can also pack picnic lunches (€13.50) to take fishing or on a day hike.

White Gables (☎ 555 744; Moycullen; set dinner menu €44.50, set Sun lunch menu €24.50, mains €24.50-29.50; ☯ from 7pm Tue-Sat, from 12.30pm & from 7pm Sun mid-Feb–mid-Dec) This candlelit restaurant inside a 1920s stone cottage is where Connemara families come together to celebrate special occasions. Twists on nostalgic favourites include pork schnitzel, chicken Kiev, seafood cocktail and a signature half roast duck with orange sauce, all accompanied by well-chosen wines. Dinner is served daily in July and August. The restaurant is in Moycullen village, 13km northwest of Galway on the N59.

Drinking
Power's Bar (☎ 557 047; Market Sq) Head to this thatched pub for a good pint and live music on weekends.

Getting There & Away
Bus Éireann has buses from Galway to Oughterard every three or four hours. If driving from Galway, take Newcastle road (N59) in the direction of Clifden.

LOUGH CORRIB
The Republic's biggest lake, Lough Corrib virtually cuts off western Galway from the rest of the country. Over 48km long and covering some 200 sq km, it encompasses over 360 islands; Inchagoill, the largest island, has a monastic settlement that visitors can visit from Oughterard or Cong.

Lough Corrib is world famous for its salmon, sea trout and brown trout. The highlight of the **fishing** calendar is the mayfly season, when zillions of the small bugs hatch over a few days (usually in May) and drive the fish and anglers into a frenzy. The hooks are baited with live flies, which join their cousins dancing on the surface of the lake. Salmon begin running around June. The owner of Oughterard's **Can-**

rawer House (☎ 552 388; oughterardhostel.com; Station Rd; ⏰ Feb-Oct, is a good contact for information and boat hire; fishing lessons cost €25 per hour, and full-day guided lake tours including all fishing gear cost €140. You can buy fishing supplies from **Thomas Tuck** (☎ 552 335; Main St, Oughterard; ⏰ 9am-6.30pm Mon-Sat).

The largest island on Lough Corrib, Inchagoill is a lonely place hiding many ancient remains. Most fascinating is an obelisk called **Lia Luguaedon Mac Menueh** (Stone of Luguaedon, Son of Menueh) marking a burial site. It stands about 75cm tall, near the Saints' Church, and some people claim that the Latin writing on the stone is the second-oldest Christian inscription in Europe, after those in the catacombs in Rome. **Teampall Phádraig** (St Patrick's Church) is a small oratory of a very early design with some later additions. The prettiest church is the Romanesque **Teampall na Naoimh** (Saints' Church), probably built in the 9th or 10th century. There are carvings around the arched doorway.

Inchagoill can be reached by boat from Oughterard (or Cong in County Mayo). **Corrib Cruises** (☎ 092-46029; www.corribcruises.com) sail from Oughterard to Inchagoill (adult/child €13/6) and on to Cong (€20/9). Departures are at 11am, 2.45pm and 5pm from May to October.

LOUGH INAGH VALLEY
☎ 091

The journey north along the Lough Inagh Valley, just north of the N59, is one of the most scenic in Ireland (a big call, we know). There are two fine approaches up valleys from the south, starting on either side of Recess, and the sweep of Derryclare and Inagh Loughs accompanies you most of the way. On the western side is the brooding **Twelve Bens** mountain range, while just beyond the valley on the northern side is a picturesque drive beside Kylemore Lake.

Towards the northern end of the valley, a track leads west off the road up a blind valley, which is also well worth exploring.

You'll wake up to the sound of sheep bleating at the spotless **Ben Lettery Hostel** (☎ 51136; www.anoige.ie/hostels/ben-lettery; Ballinafad; dm €12-17; ⏰ Mar-Nov; Ⓟ). On the main Clifden road, in the heart of the Connemara wilderness, it has a tidy, homey kitchen and living room, and is an excellent base to explore the Twelve Bens and Lough Inagh Valley. The hostel is 8km west of

Recess and 13km east of Clifden. Michael Nee Coaches will stop here if you arrange it with the driver, but note that it's only possible to check in between 5pm and 10pm.

Steeped in Victorian grandeur, the atmospheric **Lough Inagh Lodge** (☎ 34706; www.loughinaghlodgehotel.ie; s €104-138, d €168-240, dinner €43; Ⓟ) is about 7km north of Recess on the R344. It serves dinner (€43), and in the quieter months it organises watercolour classes from €450 per person, including three nights' B&B accommodation plus two evening meals and three days' tuition; contact the lodge for course dates.

ROUNDSTONE
☎ 095 / pop 400

Clustered around a boat-filled harbour, Roundstone (Cloch na Rón) is one of Connemara's gems. Colourful terrace houses and inviting pubs overlook the dark recess of Bertraghboy Bay, which is home to lobster trawlers and traditional *currachs* with tarred canvas bottoms stretched over wicker frames. The idyllic surroundings continue to lure film makers, artists and musicians.

Sights & Activities

Just south of the village in an old Franciscan monastery is Malachy Kearns' **Roundstone Musical Instruments** (☎ 35808; www.bodhran.com; Michael Killeen Park; ⏰ 9am-7pm Jul-Sep, 9.30am-6pm May-Jun & Sep-Oct, 9.30am-6pm Mon-Sat Nov-Apr). Kearns is Ireland's only full-time maker of traditional *bodhráns*. He made the drums for *Riverdance* here, and he sells tin whistles, harps and inexpensive booklets filled with Irish ballads; there's also small free folk museum and a coffee shop. Adjacent **craft shops** sell everything from teapots to sweaters.

Looming above the stone pier is **Mt Errisbeg** (298m), the only significant hill along this section of coastline. The pleasant walk from Roundstone to the top takes about two hours. Follow the small road past O'Dowd's pub in the centre of the village. From the summit there are wonderful views across the bay to the distant humps of the Twelve Bens.

Galway Hooker sailing trips (☎ 21034; www.truelight.ie; half-/full-day trip €45/65; ⏰ Apr-Oct) on a beautifully-restored traditional boat built in 1922 take you around Connemara's seal- and porpoise-inhabited inlets and bays.

WHERE THERE'S SMOKE, THERE'S SALMON

If you're curious to discover how the area's famous salmon is smoked, you can tour the family-run **Connemara Smokehouse** (☎ 095-23739; www.smokehouse.ie; Bunowen Pier, Ballyconneely; ☷ tours 3pm Wed Jun-Aug). Free tours show you the hand filleting, traditional preparation, slicing and packing of the wild and organic salmon, and shed light on various smoking methods before finishing up with a tasting. Advance reservations are essential. Outside high season it's usually possible to stop by the smokehouse and stock up if you call ahead.

Festivals & Events

The **Roundstone Arts Week** (www.roundstonearts week.com), usually held late June or early July, gathers together local artists, musicians and writers.

Sleeping & Eating

Gurteen Beach Caravan & Camping Park (☎ 35882; www.gurteenbay.com; Roundstone; camp sites €10) This peaceful, well-equipped camping ground is in a great spot 2.5km west of town, near the beach.

Angler's Return (☎ 31091; www.anglersreturn.itgo .com; Toombeola; d from €90; ☷ Mar-Nov; P) Less than 10 minutes' drive out of Roundstone along the R341, this garden-set B&B is perfect for those who fish – or for anyone seeking time out in the tranquil beauty of Bertraghboy Bay. Most of the cosy rooms have shared bathrooms, and evening meals can be arranged on request. The home is not suitable for children under four.

St Joseph's (☎ 35865; www.connemara.net/st josephs; Main St; d €64-72; ☷ closed late Dec; P) Christina Lowry's central B&B offers a warm welcome and beautiful views over the harbour.

O'Dowd's (☎ 35809; Main St; mains €12-20; ☷ restaurant noon-10pm Apr-Sep, noon-3pm & 6-9.30pm Oct-Mar) This well-worn, comfortable old pub hasn't lost any of its authenticity since it starred in Hollywood flick *The Matchmaker*. It's a great spot to nurse a pint. Specialities at its adjoining restaurant include hot-buttered lobster and 'ocean rolls' (fillets of plaice stuffed with seafood in dill sauce). Cheaper bar food (€8 to €17) is available until 9pm.

ROUNDSTONE TO CLIFDEN

The R341 shadows the coast from the harbourside hamlet of Roundstone to Clifden. Along this scenic stretch, beaches for summertime frolicking or spectacular wintry walks include the white sands of **Trá Mhóir** (Great Beach), **Gurteen Bay** (sometimes spelt Gorteen Bay) and **Dog's Bay**. Trá Mhóir is off the highway, but well worth the slight detour; to get there, turn off at Ballyconneely, heading south towards the Connemara Golf Club. You will pass the ruins of **Bunowen Castle** before reaching the shore.

Kite-surfing and buggy-boarding lessons are available along Connemara's coast; contact **Connemara Kite Sports** (☎ 095-43793, 087-9673077; www.connemarakitesports.com) for seasonal info.

Away from the coast, there is an alternate route between Roundstone and Clifden, which connects with the N59 east of Clifden. The old road is a bumpy ride, passing through the eerie, rust-collared wilderness of **Roundstone Bog**. Locals who believe the bog is haunted won't drive this road at night; indeed, the roughness of the road is reason enough to avoid it after dark. In summer, you might see turf being manually harvested, as blanket bogs cannot be cut mechanically.

CLIFDEN & AROUND

☎ 095 / pop 1900

Connemara's 'capital', Clifden (An Clochán), presides over the head of the narrow bay where the River Owenglin tumbles into the sea. Its Victorian houses and church spires rise on the horizon as you approach the town from the coast road, and the surrounding countryside offers walks through woods and above the shoreline.

Though the summer months clog Clifden's streets with tourists, winter gives the town a faded, forgotten charm. Year-round, its easy access by public or private transport (about 80km from Galway city) and good facilities make it a useful stop while exploring the region.

Information

There are banks with ATMs around Market Sq, as well as a large supermarket.

Post office (Main St)

Shamrock Washeteria (Market Sq) Wash those dirty clothes here.

Tourist office (☎ 21163; clifden@irelandwest.ie; Galway road; ☷ 10am-5pm Mon-Sat Easter-Jun & Sep, 10am-5pm Jul & Aug)

Two Dog Internet Café (☎ 22186; Church Hill; per hr €5)

Sights & Activities

Connemara's past comes to life at **Dan O'Hara's Homestead** (☎ 21808; www.connemaraheritage.com; Lettershea; adult/under 12yr €7.50/4; ☉ 10am-6pm Apr-Oct, by appointment Nov-Mar). Farmer Dan O'Hara lived here until his eviction from the farm and subsequent immigration to New York, where he ended up selling matches on the street. Its present owners have restored the property, turning it into an illuminating heritage centre with varied activities such as demonstrations of bog cutting, thatching, sheep shearing and so on. You can pop in just to have a coffee or browse the craft shop. It's also possible to stay at the farmhouse; call for more information. The homestead's 7km east of town on the N59.

Heading directly west from Clifden's Market Sq, **Sky Road** traces a spectacular loop out to the township of Kingston and back to Clifden, taking in some rugged, stunningly beautiful coastal scenery en route. The round trip of about 12km can easily be walked or cycled, but if you're short on time you can also drive.

Books and maps outlining the area's myriad of walking routes are available at the **Connemara Walking Centre** (☎ 21379; walkwest@indigo.ie; Market St; ☉ Mar-Sep). Tourist offices throughout County Galway also have information and sell detailed maps of routes, including the new 250km **Slí Chonamara** walking route, which has a variety of spur trails in the region.

If you'd rather not go it alone, field archaeologist and Connemara local **Michael Gibbons** (☎ 21492; www.walkingireland.com) leads day walks as well as longer 'walking festivals' coinciding with the Celtic calendar; contact him directly for prices and dates. **Connemara Safari** (☎ 21071; www.walkingconnemara.com) also conducts walking tours, including island-hopping tours. Prices start from €599 for five-day tours, including meals and accommodation.

And if you prefer to let someone else do the walking, you can ride gentle Connemara ponies from **Errislannan Riding Centre** (☎ 21134; info@connemara-tourism.org; Ballyconneely road). Guides provide lessons, and lead treks along the beach and up into the hills. Rates depend on type and length of ride you want to take. The centre is about 3.5km south of Clifden on the R341.

Sleeping

Some of the most appealing accommodation nestles around in the town's scenic outskirts.

Brookside Hostel (☎ 21812; www.brooksidehostel .com; Fairgreen; dm €13.50-15, d €36-40; ☉ Mar-Oct; Ⓟ) Run by Richard Bartley, who built it from scratch, this IHH hostel is located in a peaceful spot off the bottom of Market St, with the River Owenglin trickling past. Guided walks are available, and there's a bright, clean self-catering kitchen.

Clifden Town Hostel (☎ 21076; www.clifdentown hostel.com; Market St; dm €15-17, d €36-40; Ⓟ) Right in the centre of town, and a stone's throw from Clifden's cafés, restaurants and pubs, this cheery IHH hostel is set in a cream-coloured house framed by big picture windows. It has 34 beds in its sunlit rooms.

Ben View House (☎ 21256; www.benviewhouse .com; Bridge St; s €30-55, d €60-80) This central 1848 town house has an antiquated charm provided by timber beams, polished floorboards and old-fashioned hospitality.

Seamist House (☎ 21441; Market St; www.connemara .net/seamist; s €50-70, d €70-100) Right in town but opening onto a private fairy tale garden (which also provides fruit for homemade jam spread on your freshly baked scones), this stone house has immaculate rooms and a homey atmosphere. Highly recommended.

Mallmore House (☎ 21460; www.mallmorecountry house.com; Ballyconneely road; d €70-80; ☉ Mar-Sep; Ⓟ) Unbeatable for the price, this colonnaded snow white Georgian manor house is set in 14 hectares of woodland about 2km from town. Its spacious rooms are elegantly furnished, and bountiful breakfasts include pancakes and smoked salmon.

Foyle's (☎ 21801; www.foyleshotel.com; Main St; s €72, d €114-170; ☉ Jun-Aug) A white-trimmed, Wedgwood blue landmark in the centre of town, Clifden's oldest hotel has 30 flowing rooms in romantic shades such as rose and olive, and a well-regarded on-site restaurant (mains €15 to €20) specialising in seafood. Unwind on the flower-filled patio garden or in the lively pub.

Quay House (☎ 21369; www.thequayhouse.com; Beach Rd; s €95-115, d €140-180; ☉ mid-Mar–mid-Nov) Location and history make this a charmed spot. More than 200 years old, this place right on the water used to house the harbour master, but it was converted into a choice 14-room hotel long ago. Rooms are large and furnished with antiques, and some have working fireplaces and views of the harbour. Breakfast is served in a vine-draped glass conservatory.

Abbeyglen Castle (☎ 21201; www.abbeyglen.ie; Sky Rd; s/d from €144/239; ☺ Feb-Dec; ℙ) Should you be arriving by private helicopter, you can land on the lawns of this magnificent chateau. If not, don't worry, you'll still feel entirely welcome in the historic home of Clifden founder John d'Arcy. Tear yourself from its immense, sumptuously furnished rooms to play billiards, dine at the restaurant or drink in the chummy pub.

Eating & Drinking

Pubs and restaurants cluster around Clifden's town centre. As elsewhere in these parts, seafood reigns supreme.

Two Dog Café (☎ 22186; 2 Church Hill; dishes €4-7) Painted bright orange and blue, this hip spot has good, strong coffee, fresh-baked goods, and light fare such as tortilla wraps. The upstairs internet terminals make this Europe's westernmost internet café.

Lowry's Bar (☎ 21347; Market St; meals €4-9; ☺ 10.30am-midnight Mon-Thu, 10.30am-1am Fri & Sat, 10.30am-11.30pm Sun) A time-worn local, Lowry's traditional pleasures extend from the age-old, unadorned look of the place to its céilidh sessions, which take place at least a couple of nights a week. The food is 'unpretentious Irish' (eg bangers and mash).

EJ Kings (☎ 21330; Market Sq; mains €13.50-22; ☺ 10.30am-11pm Sat-Thu, 10am-12.30am Fri & Sat) A busy old pub established in 1852, EJ Kings serves soups (including somewhat watery chowder), oak-smoked-salmon and crab-meat platters, and a fine Irish stew. Vegetarian options include tortillas stuffed with spinach and ricotta.

D'Arcy Inn (☎ 21146; Main St; mains around €15; ☺ 10.30am-late) Live music and poetry readings make Darcy's a sociable spot for seafood or just for a pint. During the winter months it's best to call ahead to check it's open.

Fogerty's (☎ 21427; Market St; mains €17.50-25; ☺ 5.30-10pm Thu-Tue) In a thatched stone house brightened by blue-painted window frames, Fogerty's cooks up traditional Irish and seafood dishes including a guaranteed-to-be-good catch of the day.

Abbeyglen Castle (☎ 21201; www.abbeyglen.ie; Sky Rd; set menu €49; ☺ 7-9pm Feb-Dec) If staying in Clifden's grand castle isn't an option, you can reserve ahead to dine here on Connemara

lamb, salmon, or crustaceans plucked from the live tank.

Getting There & Away

Buses including Bus Éireann services from Galway stop on Market St near the library.

Michael Nee Coaches (☎ 51082) runs between Clifden's main square and Galway three times daily, June to September. During the same period there are two buses daily to Cleggan (twice weekly from October to May), from where the ferry sails to Inishbofin.

Getting Around

The compact town centre is easy to cover on foot. **John Mannion & Son** (☎ 21160; Bridge St) hires out bicycles for €10 per day. The **Connemara Walking Centre** (☎ 21379; walkwest@indigo.ie; Market St; ☺ Mar-Sep) can also arrange bike hire.

CLAGGAGHDUFF & OMEY ISLAND

Following the fretted coastline north of Clifden brings you to the tiny village of **Claddaghduff** (An Cladach Dubh), which is signposted off the road to Cleggan. If you turn west here down by the Catholic church you will come out on **Omey Strand**, and at low tide you can drive or walk across the sand to **Omey Island** (population 20), a low islet of rock, grass, sand and a handful of houses. During summer, horse races are held on Omey Strand.

CLEGGAN

☎ 095 / pop 300

Most visitors whiz through Cleggan (An Cloiggean), a small fishing village 16km northwest of Clifden, to hop on the Inishbofin ferry. While here, however, you can experience Ireland's 'wild west' at **Cleggan Riding Centre** (☎ 44746; prices vary), which offers horseback adventures including three-hour treks to Omey Island via the sandy causeway.

INISHBOFIN

☎ 095 / pop 200

By day sleepy Inishbofin is a haven of tranquillity. You can walk or bike its narrow, deserted lanes, green pastures and sandy beaches, with farm animals and seals for company. But with no garda on the island to enforce closing times at the pub, by night – you guessed it – Inishbofin has mighty fine craic.

Information

Inishbofin's small post office has a grocery shop and a currency-exchange facility. Pubs and hotels will usually change travellers cheques.

Sight & Activities

Situated 9km offshore, Inishbofin is compact – 6km long by 3km wide – and its highest point is a mere 86m above sea level. Just off the northern beach is **Lough Bó Finne**, from which the island gets its name; *bó finne* means 'white cow'.

St Colman exiled himself to Inishbofin in AD 664, after he fell out with the Church over its adoption of a new calendar. He set up a monastery, supposedly northeast of the harbour, where the more recent ruins of a small 13th-century **church** still stand. Grace O'Malley, the famous pirate queen, used Inishbofin as a base in the 16th century, and Cromwell's forces captured Inishbofin in 1652, building a star-shaped prison for priests and clerics. Just behind the pier, the small but comprehensive **heritage museum** (www.inishbofin .com; admission free; ☉ hr vary) gives an overview of the island's history. Displays include the contents of an old house, photographs, and traditional farming and fishing equipment.

The island's pristine waters offer superb **scuba diving** (see p434).

Festivals & Events

Inishbofin well and truly wakes up during the May **Inishbofin Arts Festival** (☎ 45861; www .inishbofin.com), which features events such as accordion workshops, archaeological walks, art exhibitions and concerts by high-profile Irish bands such as the Frames.

Sleeping & Eating

You can pitch a tent on most unfenced ground, but not on or near the beaches.

Inishbofin Island Hostel (☎ 45855; www.inishbofin-hostel.ie; camp sites €7, dm €15, d €36-40; ☉ early Apr-Sep) In an old farmhouse, this snug IHH hostel has glassed-in common areas with panoramic views and equally scenic camp sites. It's 500m up from the ferry dock.

Doonmore Hotel (☎ 45804; s €60-70, d €90-120; ☉ Apr-Sep) Close to the harbour, Doonmore has comfortable, unpretentious rooms. Lunch (€15) and dinner (€30) in the dining room take advantage of the abundance of locally caught seafood, and the hotel can

pack lunches for you to take while exploring the island.

Day's Inishbofin House (☎ 45809; www.inishbofin house.com; d €110-240) You can nurture both body and soul at this revamped hotel – whether it's in the Egyptian linen-draped rooms (most with sea views from balconies or terraces), the on-site marine spa or the restaurant (meals €25 to €45), which serves Mediterranean fare such as roast-butternut-squash-and-mascarpone risotto, or pheasant-and-foie gras terrine.

Getting There & Around

Ferries from Cleggan to Inishbofin take 30 to 45 minutes and cost €15 return. Dolphins often swim alongside the boats. Confirm ahead, as ferries may be cancelled when seas are rough.

Island Discovery (☎ 45894, 45819; www.inishbofin islanddiscovery.com) runs daily from Cleggan to Inishbofin.

Inishbofin Ferries (☎ 45903, 45806, 45831; inishbofin ferry@eircom.net) operates the *Galway Bay* twice daily April to October, and three times daily June to August. This line also runs the older *Dún Aengus* mail boat (11.30am Monday to Saturday year-round).

Inishbofin Cycle Hire (☎ 45833), at the pier, hires out bicycles for €15 per day.

LETTERFRACK & AROUND

☎ 095 / pop 200

Founded by Quakers in the mid-19th century, Letterfrack (Leitir Fraic) is ideally situated for exploring Connemara National Park, Renvyle Point and Kylemore Abbey. The village is barely more than a crossroads with a few pubs and B&Bs, but the forested setting and nearby coast are a magnet for outdoors adventure seekers. Letterfrack is 15km northeast of Clifden on the N59.

Sights

KYLEMORE ABBEY

A few kilometres east of Letterfrack stands **Kylemore Abbey** (☎ 41146; www.kylemoreabbey.com; adult/under 12yr/student €12/free/7; ☉ abbey 9am-5.30pm mid-Mar–mid-Nov, 10am-4.30pm mid-Nov–mid-Mar, gardens 10am-5pm mid-Mar–Nov). Magnificently sited on the shores of a lake, this 19th-century neo-Gothic mansion was built for a wealthy English businessman, Mitchell Henry, who spent his honeymoon in Connemara; his wife died tragically young. Both now rest in a small **mausoleum** in the grounds, not far from a small, restored **neo-Gothic chapel**, which can also be visited.

During WWI, a group of Benedictine nuns left Ypres in Belgium and set up in Kylemore Abbey. The nuns established an exclusive convent boarding school here, but the school will be closing in 2010 and, at the time of writing, Kylemore's long-term future was uncertain.

Until the school's closure, some sections of the abbey remain open to the public, displaying a couple of roped-off period-furnished rooms. Admission also covers the abbey's **Victorian walled gardens**.

Without paying admission, you can stroll around the lake and surrounding woods. There's also an on-site craft shop and a cafeteria-style **restaurant** (dishes €4-7; 9.30am-5.30pm) where you can get sandwiches and a couple of hot dishes such as spaghetti bolognaise.

Kylemore's tranquillity is shattered in high summer with the arrival of up to 55 tour coaches per day, each one followed through the gates by an average of 50 cars (yes, about 2750 cars every day). At this time of year especially, one of the most peaceful ways to experience the area's surrounds is with **Kylemore Abbey Fishery** (41178; www.kylemore abbeyfishery.net; per day fishing from €35, gear rental from €15), which arranges local lake and river fishing trips for salmon and trout.

CONNEMARA NATIONAL PARK
Immediately southeast of Letterfrack, **Connemara National Park** (41054; www.heritageireland .ie; Letterfrack; adult/child €2.90/1.30; visitors centre & facilities 10am-5.30pm Mar-May, 9.30am-6.30pm Jun-Aug, 10am-5.30pm Sep-early Oct, grounds open year-round) spans 2000 hectares of bog, mountain and heath. The headquarters and visitor centre are housed in old buildings just south of the crossroads in Letterfrack.

The park encloses a number of the **Twelve Bens**, including Bencullagh, Benbrack and Benbaun. The heart of the park is **Gleann Mór** (Big Glen), through which flows the River Polladirk. There's fine walking up the glen and over the surrounding mountains. There are also short, self-guided walks and, if the Bens look too daunting, you can hike up **Diamond Hill** nearby.

The visitor centre offers an introduction to the park's flora, fauna and geology, and visitors can scrutinise maps and various trails here before heading out into the park. Seeing

the exhibits on bog biology, and the video *Man and the Landscape* will make walking the park a more rewarding experience. The centre has an indoor eating area and rudimentary kitchen facilities for walkers.

Guided nature walks (incl in admission; walks 11am Mon, Wed & Fri Jun, 11am Mon, Wed & Fri-Sun Jul & Aug) depart from the visitor centre. They cover rough, boggy terrain – bring sturdy boots and rain gear.

Activities
Along the coast north of Letterfrack, especially from Tully Cross east to Lettergesh and Salrock, there are expanses of pure white sand, including **Glassillaun Beach**. Scuba-diving company **Scuba Dive West** (43922; www.scuba divewest.com; Letterfrack) is based at Glassillaun Beach, and runs courses and dives around the surrounding coastlines and islands. A full day with guide and equipment costs €99/119 for shore/boat diving. There are also stunning beaches at **Gurteen** and at **Lettergesh**, where the beach horse-racing sequences for *The Quiet Man* were shot.

Invigorating **walks** can be enjoyed all along the coast, including around Renvyle Point to Derryinver Bay. An excellent hill walk, which takes four to five hours each way, starts from the post office at Lettergesh and heads up Binn Chuanna and Maolchnoc, and then down to Lough Fee. A 4km walk from Letterfrack to the peak of Tully Mountain takes 30 minutes and affords wonderful ocean views.

Courses
The thatched-cottage restaurant **Pangur Ban** (41243; www.pangurban.com; Letterfrack) makes a cosy setting for cookery courses. Two-day weekend courses start at €160 (you'll need to arrange your own accommodation), and cover a specific theme. 'Breads and cakes', for example, teaches you how to make yeast bread, traditional brown soda bread, zucchini-and-walnut bread, cranberry-and-nut bread, flourless almond tarts and coffee cake. Courses are limited to four to six people; Pangur Ban's website lists programme dates.

Sleeping & Eating
Renvyle Beach Caravan & Camping (43462; Renvyle; hiker & cyclist sites €8, camp sites €16; Easter-Sep) This camping ground, 1.5km west of Tully Cross, is in an enviable location, with direct access to the sandy beach.

Old Monastery Hostel (☎ 41132; www.oldmonastery hostel.com; Letterfrack; camp sites from €9, dm €13-15, d €40-50; P 🖳 ♿) Down a wooded track (400m from the Letterfrack crossroads), this 19th-century stone house has been restored (including adding free wi-fi) without sacrificing its rustic charm. The hostel's book-filled parlour is lit by candles and a fireplace; there's a vegetarian buffet (€10) and the staff organise regular boat trips to remote islands.

Renvyle House Hotel (☎ 43511; www.renvyle.com; Renvyle; d €110-240; P 🐾) Allegedly haunted, this 56-room converted country house was once owned by the poet Oliver St John Gogarty. Even if you're not staying here, it makes an atmospheric stop for a drink or snack after a walk along the peninsula. If you are, you can also play tennis or enjoy a round of golf on the hotel's nine-hole course.

Pangur Ban (☎ 41243; www.pangurban.com; Letterfrack; mains €15-24; 🕑 5.30-9.30pm Jul-Aug, 5.30-9.30pm Tue-Sat Mar-Jun & Sep-Dec) In a 300-year-old thatched cottage 100m west of the Letterfrack crossroads, Pangur Ban has captured the imagination of Ireland's foodies with inventive Irish cuisine such as lamb shanks braised in Guinness, and

---

WALK: KILLARY HARBOUR

This easy 18km walk (approximately seven hours) takes in the natural splendour and poignant human history of the area around Killary Harbour. The total ascent is 130m; Salrock Pass marks the modest high point of the circuit at 130m, making this route an ideal option if clouds are lying low over higher peaks in the area. The terrain covered is a mixture of quiet tarmac lanes, grassy *boreens* (small lanes or roadways) and rugged paths; boots are a good idea as sections of the trail can become boggy or muddy.

The route starts and finishes 3km southwest of Leenane, at the quarry situated 20m southwest of the River Bunowen on the main Leenane–Clifden road (N59). There's ample parking at the quarry, but getting here first requires your own wheels.

When you come out of the quarry, you turn left, walk onwards for 400m and then take the first right. Heading down that road, you'll soon come to two gates and a sign that indicates that private vehicles may not proceed further. Pass through the right-hand gate and continue along the lane for a little over 1km. Lines of floats securing mussel beds bob in the harbour to the north and will be a constant presence for the first half of the route. The lane soon becomes a gravel track, and then, after passing through a couple of gates and crossing a bridge, which spans a waterfall, it narrows again to become a grassy *boreen*.

This area was badly affected by the Great Famine, and around 3km from the start of the walk you'll come to the first of several ruinous stone buildings that once made up the village of Foher, which was depopulated during the Famine. Follow the *boreen* along the front of the ruins, and pass over a stone stile in the wall to the west. The *boreen* now dwindles to a single-file path, and climbs up and around a rock outcrop. The retaining walls of the Famine road, which was constructed by locals in return for rations, are obvious at the side of the path.

The rugged landscape is now dotted with boulders and bands of rock, although the buildings and boats of Rosroe soon come into view ahead (1½ to two hours from the start). Pass along the south side of a large stone wall enclosing a field, and exit the *boreen* beside a cottage. Join the minor road leading to Rosroe harbour; the pier is about 200m along the road to the right, and well worth the short detour.

From the pier, retrace your steps along the road, continuing past the point where you came down off the *boreen*. Killary Harbour Little (or Little Killary) is the picturesque inlet to the south, its shape mimicking the larger-scale fjord further north. Follow the road for around 1km, climbing to a sharp right turn. Leave the lane here, continuing ahead (east) through a wooden gate. A short but steep ascent now leads to Salrock Pass, from where Killary Harbour and Little Killary are both visible.

The descent on the eastern side of the pass is even steeper, but you'll soon come to a junction of a fence and stone wall on your right. Head through a wooden gate on the left, and walk along a rough track that runs over Salrock, from where you follow a line of electricity poles all the way to the deserted village of Foher, which you passed on your outward journey. Trace the wall as it descends gradually through the ruins, rejoining the *boreen* at the eastern end of the hamlet. Retrace your initial steps back to the road and your starting point.

pot roast pheasant with apples, cider, and parsnip mash. If you want to recreate them yourself, Pangur Ban runs cookery courses.

Getting There & Away

Bus 420, run by **Bus Éireann** (☎ 091-562 000), travels year-round between Galway and Clifden (one way adult/child €9.80/6.10), calling at Salruck, Lettergesh, Tully Church, Kylemore, Letterfrack, Cleggan and Claddaghduff en route.

LEENANE & KILLARY HARBOUR

☎ 095

The small village of Leenane (also spelled Leenaun) drowses on the shore of Killary Harbour. Dotted with mussel rafts, the harbour is widely believed to be Ireland's only fjord. Slicing 16km inland and more than 45m deep in the centre, it certainly looks like a fjord, although some scientific studies suggest it may not actually have been glaciated. Mt Mweelrea (819m) towers to its north.

Leenane boasts both stage and screen connections. It was the location for *The Field* (1989), based on John B Keane's poignant play about a tenant farmer's ill-fated plans to pass on a rented piece of land to his son. The village's name made it onto the theatrical map with the success in London and New York of Martin McDonagh's play *The Beauty Queen of Leenane*.

Information

There's no bank or ATM, but the post office changes foreign currency.

Sights

After surveying the countryside studded with sheep, you can roam among them at the **Sheep & Wool Centre** (☎ 42323, 42231; www.sheepandwool centre.com; admission €4; ☷ 9am-6pm Apr-Oct). You can also see spinning and weaving demonstrations, learn about the history of dyeing at the little museum, and feed the farm animals – then dine yourself on homemade cakes, pies and Irish stew at the café. The centre's shop sells locally made handcrafts, as well as topographical walking maps. If you're here in the low season, it's still worth phoning as you may be able to pop by if the family is around.

Activities

Canoeing, sea kayaking, sailing, rock climbing, clay-pigeon shooting, windsurfing, water-skiing, archery, day hikes and outdoor combat laser games are just some of the activities on offer at **Killary Adventure Centre** (☎ 43411; www .killary.com; half/full day from €40/80; ☷ 10am-5pm), approximately 3km west of Leenane on the N59. Between April and September, be sure to pack insect repellent to keep midges at bay.

From Nancy's Point, about 2km west of Leenane, **Killary Cruises** (☎ 091-566 736; www.killary cruises.com; adult/child/family €19/9/42) offers 1½-hour cruises of Killary Harbour aboard a catamaran. Dolphins leap around the boat, which passes by a mussel farm and stops at a salmon farm, where you'll see the fish being fed. There are four cruises per day from April to October.

There are several excellent **walks** from Leenane, including one to **Aasleagh Waterfall** (Eas Liath), about 3km away on the north-eastern side of Killary Harbour. Also from Leenane, the road runs west for about 2km along the southern shore. Where the highway veers inland, walkers can continue on an old road along the shore to the tiny fishing community of **Rosroe Quay** (population 11); see p435 for a detailed route description. For guided day and overnight walks in the region, Gerry Greensmyth from **Croagh Patrick Walking Tours** (☎ 098-26090; www.walkingguideire land.com) has a wealth of local expertise.

Sleeping & Eating

Sleepzone Connemara (☎ 42929; www.sleepzone.ie; camp sites €10, dm €13-22, s €30-40, d €44-60; ☷ Mar-Oct; ⓟ ▣) This 19th-century property has been converted to clean dorms and modernised private rooms. If you want to commune with the great outdoors, you can also pitch a tent here. Free wi-fi is available, along with a bar, barbecue terrace, tennis court and bike hire. The hostel runs a handy shuttle service to/from Galway (one way/return €8/12; Sleepzone guests only).

Killary Adventure Centre (☎ 43411; www.killary adventure.ie; dm €18-24, d €64-70; ⓟ) For those wanting to sleep and breathe the action lifestyle, the adventure centre has clean, spartan dorms and double rooms, as well as a restaurant (dinner €25) and bar with panoramas of Killary Harbour. Package rates are available for families.

Killary House (☎ 42254; www.connemara.com /killaryhouse; Leenane; d €50-60; ⓟ) On a working farm just a short walk from Leenane, this cosy B&B looks out to the bay from its front rooms, and up to the hills in its rear rooms. Cheaper rooms share a bathroom. Ask about on-site meals, including children's menus.

Blackberry Cafe (☎ 42240; Leenane; café dishes €4.50-11, dinner mains €14-25; ☻ noon-4.30pm & 6-9pm Jul & Aug, noon-4.30pm & 6-9pm Wed-Mon Easter-Jun & Sep) The unexpectedly contemporary Blackberry Café serves fabulous fresh seafood, such as Connemara smoked salmon or steamed mussels in garlic and white wine sauce.

Drinking

Farmers and other locals come for quiet pints and warming Irish coffees at a couple of authentic dark wood-panelled pubs with enormous open fireplaces on Leenane's main street.

SOUTH OF GALWAY CITY

Visitors often pass through this region en route to or from County Clare without stopping, but it's a charming spot to explore if you have time. If you're basing yourself in Galway city and you have wheels, its oyster restaurants merit a visit in their own right.

CLARINBRIDGE & KILCOLGAN
☎ 091 / pop 2100

An easy 16km south of Galway, Clarinbridge (Droichead an Chláirin) and Kilcolgan (Cill Choglán) are at their busiest during the **Clarinbridge Oyster Festival** (www.clarinbridge.com), held during the second weekend of September. However, the oysters are actually at their best from May and through the summer. Clarinbridge is also good for rummaging the antique stores along the main road.

For a homey cup of tea served in china cups at frilly tables, stop in at **Claire's Tea Rooms** (☎ 776606; Clarinbridge; snacks €3-8; ☻ 10.30am-5pm Tue-Sat, 1-5pm Sun), set inside an old stone cottage.

The oyster festival is run by the folk at **Paddy Burke's Oyster Inn** (☎ 796 107; Clarinbridge; 6 oysters €10, mains €10-24; ☻ 12.30-10pm), an old-fashioned thatched inn by the bridge dishing up heaping servings of seafood.

Signposted near the post office just north of neighbouring Kilcolgan, **Moran's Oyster Cottage** (☎ 976 113; The Weir, Kilcolgan; 6 oysters €12, mains €13-20; ☻ noon-10pm Mon-Sat, 10am-10pm Sun)

is an atmospheric thatched pub and restaurant overlooking Dunbulcaun Bay, where the oysters are reared before they arrive on your plate.

Clarinbridge is on the main Galway–Gort–Ennis–Limerick road (N18) and is served by numerous Bus Éireann buses from Galway. Kilcolgan is also on the N18.

KINVARA
☎ 091 / pop 400

The small stone harbour of Kinvara (sometimes spelt Kinvarra) lolls at the southeastern corner of Galway Bay, which accounts for its Irish name, Cinn Mhara (Head of the sea). Traditional Galway Hooker sailing boats race here each year on the second weekend in August in the **Cruinniú na mBáid** (Gathering of the Boats).

Kinvara's other big date on its annual calendar is **Fleadh na gCuach** (Cuckoo Festival), a traditional music festival in late May that features over 100 musicians performing at upwards of 50 organised sessions. Spin-off events include a parade.

Details of both festivals are available on Kinvara's **website** (www.kinvara.com).

Sights & Activities

The chess piece-style **Dunguaire Castle** (☎ 637 108; adult/child €4/2; ☻ 9.30am-5.30pm May-Oct) was erected around 1520 by the O'Hynes clan and is in excellent condition following extensive restoration. It is widely believed that the castle occupies the former site of the 6th-century royal palace of Guaire Aidhne, the king of Connaught. Dunguaire's owners have included Oliver St John Gogarty (1878–1957) – poet, writer, surgeon and Irish Free State senator.

The most atmospheric way to visit the castle is to attend a **medieval banquet** (☎ 061-360 788; www.shannonheritage.com; banquet €48.95; ☻ 5.30pm & 8.45pm May-Oct). These intimate banquets include music, storytelling, a hearty chicken dinner, wine and a jug of mead.

Sleeping & Eating

Doorus House (☎ 637 512; doorushouse@kinvara.com; Doorus; dm €15-16; P ▣) History fills the air of this lovely An Óige hostel, 6km northwest of Kinvara. It's in an old mansion once owned by Count Floribund de Basterot, who entertained here such notables as WB Yeats, Lady

---

DETOUR: GORT & AROUND

If you're a fan of WB Yeats (and you have wheels), two sights connected to the great poet near the highway town of Gort are a worthwhile detour on your way to or from Galway.

A 16th-century Norman tower known as **Thoor Ballylee** (☎ 631 436; Peterswell; admission €6; 🕙 10am-6pm Mon-Sat May-Sep) was the summer home of WB Yeats from 1922 to 1929, and was the inspiration for one of Yeats' best-known works, *The Tower*. The restored 16th-century tower contains the poet's furnishings and you can see an audiovisual presentation on his life. From Gort take the Loughrea road (N66) for about 3km and look for the sign.

About 3km north of Gort is **Coole Park** (☎ 631 804; www.coolepark.ie; admission €2.90; 🕙 10am-5pm Apr-May & Sep, 10am-6pm Jun-Aug). It was the home of Lady Augusta Gregory, co-founder of the Abbey Theatre and a patron of Yeats. An exhibition focuses on the literary importance of the house, and the flora and fauna of the surrounding nature reserve. The main attraction on the grounds is the autograph tree, on which many of Lady Gregory's esteemed literary guests carved their initials. Coole Park's restaurant (mains €8 to €12), in the property's former stables, serves wholesome wraps and homemade burgers.

In the same area, about 5km southwest of Gort, is the extensive monastic site of **Kilmacduagh**. Beside a small lake is a well-preserved 34m-high round tower, the remains of a small 14th-century cathedral (Teampall Mór MacDuagh), an oratory dedicated to St John the Baptist, and other little chapels. The original monastery is thought to have been founded by St Colman MacDuagh at the beginning of the 7th century. There are fine views over the Burren from here and you can visit any time.

If you happen to be passing through Gort in mid-June, you may think you've arrived in Rio. Gort has the highest Brazilian population per capita in Ireland, and its **Brasilian Festival** (http://brasilianfestivalgort.blogspot.com) fills the town with samba beats, *capoeira* (a combination of martial arts and dance) and Brazilian food.

Augusta Gregory, Douglas Hyde and Guy de Maupassant. Dorms are basic but spotless. The hostel's signposted off the main road to Ballyvaughan (N67).

Burren View (☎ 637 142; www.kinvara.com/burren-view; Doorus; d with shared/private bathroom €60/65; 🕙 Apr-Sep; 🅿) About 6km northwest of Kinvara, the O'Connor family's farmhouse rests on a secluded peninsula with glorious views across Galway Bay to the Burren. A short stroll from the house is a Blue Flag beach.

Keough's (☎ 637 145; Main St, Kinvara; mains €8-15) This friendly local, where you'll often hear Irish spoken, serves up a fresh battered cod and pints of the good stuff. Traditional music sessions take place on Mondays and Thursdays, while Saturday nights swing with old-time dancing.

Getting There & Away

Bus 423, which links Galway with towns in county Clare, stops in Kinvara. From late May to late November, Bus Éireann's Galway–Killarney bus 50 stops in Kinvara three to four times daily Monday to Saturday, and twice on Sunday. For more details contact **Galway bus station** (☎ 091-562 000).

EASTERN GALWAY

Lough Corrib separates eastern Galway from the dramatic landscape of Connemara and the county's western coast, and this region is markedly different. Eastern Galway is relatively flat, and its underlying limestone has provided it with well-drained, fertile soil that is ideal for farming, giving it more in common with the country's midlands.

Getting There & Away

Bus Éireann (☎ 091-562 000) services connect Galway with Athenry, Ballinasloe, and Loughrea. Services from Galway to/from Portumna require a change at Kilbeggan.

ATHENRY

☎ 091 / pop 2200

The name Athenry is synonymous with the stirring song 'The Fields of Athenry', composed by Pete St John in the 1970s, which recounts incarceration resulting from the Famine. Often thought to be adapted from an 1880s ballad (disputed by St John), it's been covered by countless artists, and is sung by passionate crowds at sporting matches, including in adapted forms such as Liverpool Football Club's anthem, 'The Fields of Anfield Road'.

The walled town, 16km east of Galway, takes its own name from a nearby ford (*áth* in Irish), which crossed the River Clare east of the settlement and was the meeting point for three kingdoms, hence Áth an Rí (Ford of the Kings).

The informative **Athenry Arts & Heritage Activity Centre** (☎ 844 661; www.athenryheritagecentre .com; The Square; ☽ 10am-2pm Mon-Fri) has in-depth background on the town's sights and can outline walking itineraries. The **town website** (www.athenry.net) lists sleeping and eating options, and **Galway East Tourism** (☎ 850 687; www .galwayeast.com) also has information.

Touted as Ireland's most intact collection of medieval architecture, the city holds a number of preserved buildings, including a restored **Norman Castle**, the **Medieval Parish Church of St Mary's**, a **Dominican Priory** with superb masonry on its occupational gravestones, and an original **market cross**.

LOUGHREA & AROUND
☎ 091 / pop 4000

Named for the little lake at its southern edge, Loughrea (Baile Locha Riach) is a bustling market town 26km southeast of Galway. Loughrea has Ireland's last functioning medieval **moat**, which runs from the lake at Fair Green near the cathedral to the River Loughrea north of town.

Not to be confused with St Brendan's Church on Church St, which is now a library, **St Brendan's Catholic Cathedral** (☎ 841 212; Barrack St; admission free; ☽ 11.30am-1pm & 2-5.30pm Mon-Fri), dating from 1903, is renowned for its Celtic revival stained-glass windows, furnishings and marble columns.

Near Bullaun, 7km north of Loughrea, is the pillar-like **Turoe Stone**, covered in delicate La Téne–style relief carvings. It dates from between 300 BC and AD 100. The Turoe Stone wasn't set here originally, but was found at an Iron Age fort a few kilometres away.

On the road east to Ballinasloe, 6.5km from Loughrea, the **Dartfield Horse Museum & Park** (☎ 843 968; www.dartfieldhorsemuseum.com; adult/child €8/5; ☽ 9.30am-6pm) allows horse-lovers to learn about horse breeding, carriages, the colourful racing industry and the horse's role in Irish history. Pony and carriage rides can be arranged.

our pick **Meadow Court Hotel** (☎ 841 051; www .meadowcourthotel.com; Clostoken; d from €116; **P**), a cherry red country manor 3.2km west of Loughrea, is an exceptional place to dine (mains €16 to €29; open lunch and dinner) and/or rest your head. It gets our pick for the most flawless sea bass in the west, fragranced with garlic and lime, while starters such as deep-fried mushrooms are also expertly prepared and presented, and the wine list is outstanding. Dreamy guest rooms come with canopied four-poster beds, broadband and room service.

BALLINASLOE
☎ 0509 / pop 6000

On the main Dublin–Galway road (N6), Ballinasloe (Béal Átha na Sluaighe) is famed for its historic October **horse fair** (www.ballinasloe .com), which dates right back to the High Kings of Tara. Attending the horse fair invariably involves sloshing through muddy fields – bring Wellington boots and don't wear white! But don't let the mud deter you: the fair has an old-time carnival atmosphere, created by the 80,000-plus horse traders and merrymakers who roll into town. They include Ireland's Travelling community, who camp nearby in traditional barrel-topped wagons. To learn more about Traveller culture, the websites of the **Irish Traveller Movement** (www.itmtrav.ie), **University College Dublin** (www.ucd.ie/folklore) and **Pavee Point Travellers Centre** (www.paveepoint.ie) are all excellent sources of information.

Around 6km southwest of town on the N6, Aughrim was the site of the bloodiest battle ever fought on Irish soil, which ended in a crucial victory by William of Orange over the Catholic forces of James II. The **Battle of Aughrim Visitor Centre** (☎ 73939; Aughrim; adult/child €4/3; ☽ 10am-6pm Tue-Sat, 2-4pm Sun Jun-Aug; ♿) helps place it within the framework of the War of the Two Kings. Signposts from the interpretive centre indicate the actual battle site.

Hyne's Hostel (☎ 73734; info@auldshillelagh.com; Aughrim, Ballinasloe; dm €12-15; **P** ♿) has just 12 beds, so you'll need to book well ahead for summer or the horse fair. It hires out bikes and can arrange pick-up around the area.

CLONFERT CATHEDRAL
Heading 21km southeast of Ballinasloe brings you to the tiny 12th-century **Clonfert Cathedral**.

COUNTY GALWAY

It's on the site of a monastery said to have been founded in AD 563 by St Brendan 'the Navigator', who is believed to be buried here. Although the historical jury is out on whether St Brendan 'the Navigator' reached America's shores in a tiny *currach* (rowing boat made of a framework of laths covered with tarred canvas), there are Old Irish Ogham (the earliest form of writing in Ireland) carvings in West Virginia that date from as early as the 6th century, suggesting an Irish presence well before Columbus set foot there.

The main attraction is the six-arch Romanesque doorway, adorned with surreal human heads. The cathedral is off the R256; you'll need your own car to get here.

PORTUMNA

☎ 0509 / pop 1900

In the southeast corner of the county, the lakeside town of Portumna is popular for boating and fishing. **Lough Derg Holiday Park** (☎ 061-376 329; www.loughderg.net) rents boats for €45/65/190 per half-day/day/week.

Impressive **Portumna Castle** (☎ 41658; Castle Ave; adult/child €2/1; 10am-6pm Apr-Oct) was built in 1618 by Richard de Burgo (or Burke) and boasts an elaborate, geometrically laid-out garden.

Counties Mayo & Sligo

They're just a few hours by road from Dublin, yet Mayo and Sligo have a genuine off-the-beaten-track feel to them. Both are rural, sparsely populated and blessed with beguiling natural beauty. A traveller looking to get away from the modern pace of life need only make a beeline for Mayo and Sligo's remote islands, deserted beaches, desolate bogs and humble Gaeltacht enclaves populated by maybe a few hundred souls.

Mayo is the more rugged of the two counties. It juts further into the Atlantic, and most of the county is covered by an impressively harsh, boggy terrain. The words 'To hell or to Connacht' – not necessarily meant as a compliment – may well have been referring to Mayo's nether regions. But while the land isn't heavenly for farmers, it dazzles the eye with its stark rock formations and subtle hues. And a preponderance of the evidence suggests that living here builds character, for you won't meet a hardier, friendlier bunch anywhere.

Sligo also has its share of natural wonderment. Its magnificent flat-top mountains and verdant pastoral scenes directly inspired the poet William Butler Yeats to compose some of Ireland's most ardent verse. But Sligo presents a more worldly face. Its coast has become a haven for international surfers, and Sligo Town, with its complementary blend of international restaurants, art galleries and mod hotels, is as sophisticated as many cities. The county boasts an improbable bounty of prehistoric sites, and is home to some of Ireland's finest traditional musicians.

If you're looking to raise your blood pressure, there are better places to go, but for remote country lodgings; relaxed drives behind slow-moving tractors; placid, fish-filled lakes; and a warm-hearted welcome, Mayo and Sligo are your ticket.

HIGHLIGHTS

- **Tragic Beauty** Jaw-dropping Doolough Valley (p450), site of the desperate Famine Walk
- **Island Escape** Ruggedly remote Achill Island (p452), off western Mayo
- **Sing Along** Raise a glass, and your voice, at Matt Molloy's pub (p449) in Westport
- **Maeve's Grave** Hike up the rock pile said to cover a legendary queen's remains at Knocknarea (p469)
- **Surfin' Sligo** Year-round waves at Strand-hill (p469) and Easky (p471)

POPULATION: 178,900 (COMBINED)   AREA: 7195 SQ KM

COUNTY MAYO

In terms of topography and history, much of Mayo (Maigh Eo), particularly along its coast, is a continuation of the wilds of Connemara. It's Connacht to the core, and with only a fraction of the tourists who flood into County Galway's rugged hinterland each summer. Though it's not one of Ireland's famously green counties, Mayo does have a flair for the dramatic, particularly in the stunningly beautiful Doolough Valley. In the farthest reaches of the county you can really shake free of the world's cares.

Of course, Mayo's history does not paint a picture of the easy country life. The ravages of the Potato Famine – which provoked the refrain 'County Mayo, Mayo, God help us!' – were harshest here. Due to emigration, many overseas Irish can trace their roots to this once-plagued land. The population has never rebounded to its pre-Famine numbers.

While the county lags behind the rest of Ireland in terms of economy, it is by no means a down-trodden place. The pace of life is slower here, which is precisely what attracts many travellers out this way. The further west you go, the more rugged it gets.

CONG
☎ 094 / pop 185

Cong does its best to comply with romantic notions of what a traditional country Irish

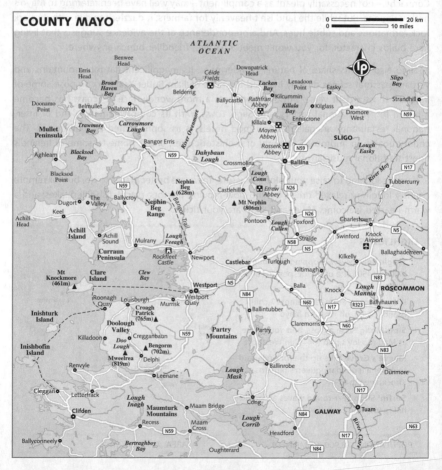

village ought to look like. Time appears to have stood still here ever since *The Quiet Man* was filmed in and around the village in 1951. But while it still more or less fits the bill for an ordinary little village surrounded by some particularly enticing rural scenery, the town lacks an authentic pulse. Very few people actually live in the town proper, and photos of John Wayne gaze out from shop windows. In summer, the arrival of the morning's first tour bus instantly doubles the number of people walking the town's streets.

Obviously, Cong is out of step in every way with modern Ireland. Come here either as a fan of the film and appreciate it the way you might enjoy a visit to a Hollywood backlot, or shield yourself with a postmodern fascination for the way in which reality and fiction tend to blur. If you're here for the quietude of spring or fall, simply amble the wooded trails between the lovely old abbey and fantastic Ashford Castle. Cong is blessed with tranquil streams, attractive stone bridges and forested parklands.

Cong is just east of the border with County Galway and lies on the narrow isthmus between Lough Corrib and Lough Mask.

Information
The **tourist office** (Map443; ☎ 954 6542; Abbey St; ☻ 10am-6pm Mar-Nov) is in the old courthouse building opposite Cong Abbey. Film fanatics may want to equip themselves with a copy of *Complete Tour Guide to the Quiet Man Locations* (€5).

There are no banks, but you can change money at the post office on Main St, or in the tourist office.

Sights
CONG ABBEY
An evocative reminder of ecclesiastical times past, the weathered shell of Cong's 12th-century **Augustinian abbey** (Map p443; admission free; ☻ dawn-dusk) is scored by wizened lines from centuries of exposure to the elements. Nevertheless, several finely sculpted features have survived, including a carved doorway, windows and lovely medieval arches (touched up in the 19th century).

Founded by Turlough Mór O'Connor, high king of Ireland and king of Connaught in 1120, the abbey occupies the site of an earlier 6th-century church. The community once gathered in the **Chapter House** to confess their sins publicly. Nowadays, many of those same people are trying to rest in peace here, for over the years a graveyard has spread around the abbey's hull and within it as well.

From the abbey, moss-encrusted trees guard a path to the river. Here lies the site's most memorable feature – a diminutive 16th-century **monk's fishing house** (Map p443) built midway over the river so that the monks could haul their catch straight up through a hole in the floor. There would have once been a cord to a bell in the kitchen, letting the cooks know to get the pot on.

CONG

0 _____ 200 m
0 _____ 0.1 miles

INFORMATION
Post Office...1 B1
Tourist Office..2 B2

SIGHTS & ACTIVITIES
Cong Abbey...3 B2
Monk's Fishing House...........................4 A2
Quiet Man Heritage Cottage...............5 A2

SLEEPING 🏠
Danagher's Hotel...................................6 B2
Lydon's Lodge.......................................7 A1
Ryan's Hotel......................................(see 8)

EATING 🍴
Fennel Seed...8 B1
Hungry Monk..9 B2

TRANSPORT
Bus Stop...10 B1

To Pigeon Hole Cave (1.5km)
To Clonbur (6km); Leenaun (28km)
Risings
To Captain Webb's Hole (300m); Cong Caravan & Camping Park (2km); Cong Hostel (2km); Neale (5km); Ballinrobe (10km); Galway (34km)
Circular Rd
Salmon Hatchery
Main St
The Lane
Dry Canal
Abbey St
River Cong
To Ashford Castle (900m); Corrib Cruises (900m)
To Ashford Castle (900m); Corrib Cruises (900m)

QUIET MAN HERITAGE COTTAGE

Cong's most over-the-top nod to its own cel-
luloid glory is the **Quiet Man Heritage Cottage**
(Map p443; ☎ 954 6089; Circular Rd; adult/child/student
€3.75/2/3; ☑ 10am-5pm Mar-Oct), modelled on Sean
Thornton's White O' Mornin' Cottage from
the film. The cottage also contains a regional
archaeological and historical exhibition, which
crams items from 7000 BC to the 19th century into a very small space.

ASHFORD CASTLE

Just beyond Cong Abbey, the village abruptly
ends and the woodlands surrounding **Ashford Castle** (Map p445; ☎ 954 6003; www.ashford.ie)
begin. First built in 1228 as the seat of the
de Burgo family, the castle changed hands
several times and was added onto and rebuilt on a few occasions. Among its owners
were the Guinness family, whose stout ruled
Ireland for well over a century. Arthur Guinness turned the castle into a regal hunting
and fishing lodge, which it remains today.
The castle is an impressive sight, with battlements towering over the Cong River, and
visitors can peek into its immaculately restored interior parlours. The real attraction,
however, is the surrounding estate – 350
acres of parkland, covered with forests,
streams, bridle paths and a golf course. A
walk through the Kinlough Woods gets you
away from the golfers and out to the shores
of Lough Corrib. You can also walk along
the banks of the river back to the monk's
fishing house (p443).

Activities
CRUISES

In the centre of Lough Corrib is the island
of Inchagoill. **Corrib Cruises** (Map p445; ☎ 954
6029; www.corribcruises.com; Cong) offers 1½ hour
boat tours from the Ashford Castle pier to
Inchagoill (€15, 11.15am and 2.45pm, April
to October), with a 30 minute guided tour of
the Island's Monastic sites. Some boats also
continue on to Oughterard (€20, 11.15am,
June to September) in County Galway (see
p427). Tickets can be purchased on board.
The company also runs 45-minute mini
tours and live-music cruises at night. Ask
at the tourist office for details.

FALCONRY

As if Ashford Castle wasn't already medieval
and aristocratic enough, it is also home to

Ireland's first **falconry school** (Map p445; ☎ 954
6820; www.falconry.ie). It's hard to imagine a more
magnificent setting to learn this ancient art.
Set deep in the castle's magnificent estate, the
school will teach anyone over the age of seven
how to handle and fly Harris hawks. An in-
troductory lesson lasting 45 minutes costs €60
per person, although there are reduced rates
for two or more people. A lengthier 'hawk
walk' lesson lasts for 90 minutes (€90). Call
ahead to make an appointment.

Sleeping
BUDGET

Cong Caravan & Camping Park (Map p445; ☎ 954 6089;
www.quietman-cong.com; Quay Rd, Lisloughrey; camp/cara-
van sites €15/20) This agreeable camping ground
has thick lawns on which to pitch your tent
(read: soft ground for sleeping). It is operated by the same family that run the hostel, and all the same amenities are available
to campers.

Cong Hostel (Map p445; ☎ 954 6089; www.quiet
man-cong.ie; Quay Rd, Lisloughrey; dm/s/d €15/25/50; ℗)
Well-run and friendly, Cong Hostel is 2km
outside Cong village, past the main gate to
Ashford Castle. It has an array of tidy dorms
and private rooms and offers laundry facilities, a screening room for *The Quiet Man*, and
hires bikes. It's affiliated with both An Óige
and Independent Holiday Hostels of Ireland
(IHH). To find it, head east from town along
the Galway road (R346) and when you see the
signs turn right onto the side road.

MIDRANGE

Lydon's Lodge (Map p443; ☎ 46053; lydonslodge@eircom
.net; Circular Rd; s/d from €40/80; ☑ Mar-Oct; ℗) This
rambling family-run lodge by the river has
comfy but plain rooms and a laidback bar with
an open fire and occasional music. DJ King
Cong makes regular weekend appearances.
Breakfast is included in the room rates.

Michaeleen's Manor (Map p445; ☎ 954 6089; www
.quietman-cong.com; Quay Rd, Lisloughrey; s/d €50/70; ℗)
Owners Margaret and Gerry Collins give the
warmest welcome in town, and if you're crazy
about *The Quiet Man*, here's one Irish couple
who can actually outmatch your enthusiasm.
Their home is large and modern, but they've
turned it into a museum of film memorabilia.
Gerry proudly boasts blood ties to most of the
film's supporting cast. The home is exceedingly comfortable and Margaret's breakfast
will sustain you through walking the grounds

of the nearby castle. There's also a hot tub and tennis court.

Danagher's Hotel (Map p443; ☎ 954 6028; fax 954 6495; Abbey St; s/d €50/80) Upstairs from a nice old pub, and overlooking the town's main junction, Danagher's has 11 en-suite rooms, some with views of the countryside. It is named for the Victor McLaglen character from the movie (we'll assume you know *which* movie). The pub serves traditional Irish fare.

Ryan's Hotel (Map p443; ☎ 954 6243; www.ryanshotel cong.ie; Main St; s/d €55/100; P) The social hub of Cong may well be this hotel, on the main drag and sporting a pub and a fine restaurant. Rooms, while clean and presentable, are nothing to shout about. All are en suite.

TOP END

Ashford Castle (Map p445; ☎ 954 6003; www.ashford .ie; d from €310/750 weeknight/weekend; P) Break the bank and you'll feel like a king or a queen for a night or two. Or at least a celebrity. (Flip through the guest book to see if you recognise any of the names signed therein.) Rooms and service are exquisite and rates include breakfast and dinner in the castle's George V restaurant.

Eating

Cullen's at the Cottage (Map p445; ☎ 954 5332; Ashford Castle; mains €7-25; ⏲ 12.30-9.30pm Thu-Mon) A viable excuse to visit Ashford Castle for anyone staying in a far cheaper B&B, Cullen's is a comfortable little house that serves delicious seafood, steaks and vegetarian dishes. You

can also drop by for a light lunch after hiking the surrounding forest.

Fennel Seed (Map p443; ☎ 954 6004; Ryan's Hotel, Main St; bar food €8-12, mains €17-25; ⏲ 7-10pm Mon-Sat, 1-7pm Sun) Two chefs used to cooking for the upper-crust at Ashford Castle have brought their culinary skills to the village, with great success. The dining room combines elegance and hominess. Steaks and lamb shanks are excellent, but vegetarians are also catered for. Above-average bar food is served in the adjacent Crow's Nest Pub until 7pm.

Hungry Monk (Map p443; ☎ 954 5842; Abbey St; sandwiches €6-8, salads €8-14; ⏲ 10am-6pm Mon-Sat Mar-Oct; 🖳) This cheery little coffee shop offers a smart selection of delicious sandwiches, soups and salads. Your sandwich might contain slick slices of home-baked ham served with mango chutney. The joint also brews the best coffee in town.

Getting There & Away

Bus Éireann (☎ 096-71800; www.buseireann.ie) has regular service from Galway (one way/return €9/14) and Westport (€8/13). The bus stops in front of the Quiet Man Coffee Shop on Main St.

If you're travelling by car or bike further into County Mayo, eschew the main N84 to Castlebar and take the longer, but much more attractive, route west to Leenaun (starting with the R345) and north to Westport via Delphi. This will take you through the Doolough Valley.

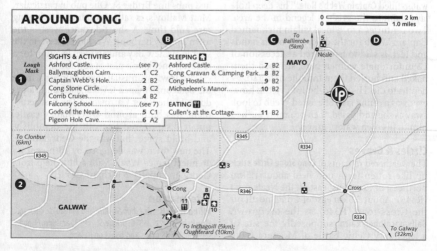

AROUND CONG

| | | | | | 0 ——— 2 km |
| | | | | | 0 ——— 1.0 miles |

SIGHTS & ACTIVITIES		SLEEPING 🛏	
Ashford Castle..................(see 7)		Ashford Castle..................7 B2
Ballymacgibbon Cairn..........1 C2		Cong Caravan & Camping Park....8 B2
Captain Webb's Hole..........2 B2		Cong Hostel..................9 B2
Cong Stone Circle..........3 C2		Michaeleen's Manor..........10 B2
Corrib Cruises..........4 B2		
Falconry School..................(see 7)		EATING 🍴
Gods of the Neale..........5 C1		Cullen's at the Cottage..........11 B2
Pigeon Hole Cave..........6 A2		

COUNTIES MAYO & SLIGO

LOCAL PROTEST YIELDS NEW WORD

It was near the unassuming little village of Neale that the term boycott came into use. In 1880, the Irish Land League, in an effort to press for fair rents and improve the lot of workers, withdrew field hands from the estate of Lord Erne, who owned much of the land in the area. When Lord Erne's land agent, Captain Charles Cunningham Boycott, evicted the striking labourers, the surrounding community began a campaign to ostracise the agent. Not only did farmers refuse to work his land, Boycott was refused local services, and people in the town refused to talk to him or sit next to him in church. The incident attracted attention from the London papers, and soon Boycott's name was synonymous with such organised, nonviolent protests. Within a few months, Boycott gave up and left Ireland.

Getting Around

Bikes can be hired from the Cong Hostel or from Lisloughery House, on the grounds of Ashford Castle (p444).

AROUND CONG
Caves

The Cong area is honeycombed with limestone caves, each of which – in true Irish style – has a colourful legend or story to its credit.

One of the best is **Pigeon Hole**, a deep limestone gash in pine forest about 1.5km west of Cong. It can be reached by road or by the walking track from across the river. Steep and slippery stone steps lead down into the cave, where subterranean water flows in winter. Keep an eye out here for the white trout of Cong – a mythical woman who turned into a fish to be with her drowned lover.

A short distance to the west of the village, though somewhat tricky to find, is the water-filled **Captain Webb's Hole**. This deep hole lays claim to the grisliest legend in the area. Two centuries ago, a local villain nicknamed Captain Webb for the deformity of his hands and feet, is said to have lured a succession of 12 unfortunate women here, stripped them naked and hurled them into the hole's soggy depths to die. His would-be 13th victim however was a canny lass. She asked Webb to look away as she undressed, then promptly pushed him to his own watery grave.

Circles & Graves

The weathered remains of **Cong Stone Circle** stick up like rotten teeth in a field about 1.5km northeast of Cong, just east off the Neale road (R345). About 3.5km east of Cong, north off the Cross road (R346), is the overgrown **Ballymacgibbon Cairn**, supposedly the site of a legendary Celtic battle of Moytura (take the track signposted and watch for a stile to your right).

Neale

If you take the turn-off at the northern end of the village of Neale, 6km northeast of Cong, you will find the curious, carved stone known as the **Gods of the Neale**. It's about 200m east of the main road, through an unsigned gateway on the left. This mysterious slab, which is dated 1757, is carved with figures of a human, an animal and a reptile.

WESTPORT
☎ 098 / pop 5315

It's perhaps the ultimate twee 'tidy town,' and its gentility is sometimes disturbed by hens and stags flying in for a weekend of partying – yet Westport (Cathair na Mairt) has an undeniable appeal. Its broad Georgian streets and shaded lime-flanked riverside mall are about as photogenic as Ireland gets, and spirited pubs line Bridge St. One pub in particular, Matt Malloy's, is rather conducive to having rare auld time. A short distance west is the town's pretty harbour, Westport Quay, on the shores of Clew Bay and an ideal location for a leisurely meal, or a pint at sundown.

The town's unusual layout unfurls from the octagonal-shaped town square, and slopes down to the River Carrowbeg. The first settlement was built around an O'Malley castle, but it disappeared beneath the demolish-and-build spree that was the Georgian era. The new town was designed by 18th-century architect James Wyatt, with a little help from Georgian superstar Richard Castle.

Information

Allied Irish Bank (Shop St) ATM and bureau de change.
Bookshop (☎ 26816; Bridge St; ☻ 11am-6pm) Good selection of OS maps and books on Ireland.

Gavin's Video & Internet Cafe (☎ 26461; Bridge St; per hr €4; ☽ 10am-10pm) Internet access.

Gill's Launderette (☎ 25819; James St; per load from €5.35; ☽ 9am-6pm Mon-Sat) Will recycle your dirty laundry.

Tourist office (☎ 25711; www.irelandwest.ie, www .visitmayo.com, www.westporttourism.com; James St; ☽ 9am-6pm Mon-Sat, 10am-6pm Sun Jul & Aug, 9am-5.45pm Mon-Sat Apr-Jun & Sep, 9am-12.45pm & 2-5pm Mon-Fri rest of year)

Sights

WESTPORT HOUSE & COUNTRY PARK

The charms of this glorious country **mansion** (☎ 25430; www.westporthouse.ie; Quay Rd; admission to house & gardens adult/child/student €11.50/6.50/9, attractions extra; ☽ 11.30am-5pm Apr-Sep, Sat & Sun only Mar & Oct; ℗) outshine its commercial overhaul of recent years. Built in 1730, it was once one of the country's most dignified country homes, but it has since sold its soul to become a kind of stately-home theme-park hybrid. A fake 'dungeon' sits below the house; unnerving waxworks dot the upper galleries; plastic swans drift on the elegantly landscaped lake; and a minirailway and water slides are tucked into the once tranquil gardens. Clearly this

place wasn't always fun for the entire family, but it learned its lesson.

Head out of Westport on Quay Rd towards Croagh Patrick and Louisburgh. After 1km, just before Westport Quay, take a small road to the right and through the grand gateway.

The octagon monument, standing at the nexus of the town, was erected in 1845 in honour of eminently forgettable George Clendening, a local banker. His statue stood upon the podium until 1922, when its head was lopped off during the Civil War. In 1990 a Roman-looking statue of St Patrick, complete with serpent-entwined staff, replaced the unfortunate capitalist.

Activities

For tackle, camping gear and information about fishing, enquire at **Hewetson** (☎ 26018; Bridge St; ☽ 10am-5pm Mon-Sat).

Carrowholly Stables (☎ 27057; www.carrowholly -stables.com; Carrowholly) has horses and ponies at the ready for guided treks along trails overlooking Clew Bay. All levels are accommodated for. The stables are 3km north of the

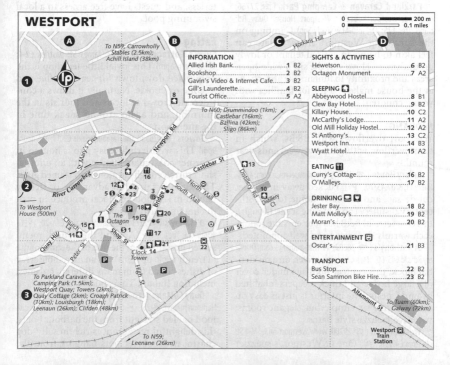

WESTPORT

0 —————— 200 m
0 —————— 0.1 miles

INFORMATION		SIGHTS & ACTIVITIES	
Allied Irish Bank...................1 B2		Hewetson...................6 B2
Bookshop...........................2 B2		Octagon Monument.........7 A2
Gavin's Video & Internet Cafe...3 B2		
Gill's Launderette...............4 B2		**SLEEPING** 🏠
Tourist Office....................5 A2		Abbeywood Hostel.........8 B1
		Clew Bay Hotel.............9 B2
		Killary House..............10 C2
		McCarthy's Lodge..........11 A2
		Old Mill Holiday Hostel...12 A2
		St Anthony's...............13 C2
		Westport Inn...............14 B3
		Wyatt Hotel................15 A2
		EATING 🍴
		Curry's Cottage............16 B2
		O'Malleys.................17 B2
		DRINKING 🍷 🍸
		Jester Bay.................18 B2
		Matt Molloy's.............19 B2
		Moran's...................20 B2
		ENTERTAINMENT 🎬
		Oscar's...................21 B3
		TRANSPORT
		Bus Stop..................22 B2
		Sean Sammon Bike Hire....23 B2

To N59; Carrowholly Stables (2.5km); Achill Island (38km)

Horkans Hill

To N60; Drummindoo (1km); Castlebar (16km); Ballina (42km); Sligo (86km)

Newport Rd

St Mary's Cres

River Carrowbeg

Castlebar St

North Mall

South Mall

Distillery Rd

Distillery Ct

Mill St

To Westport House (500m)

James St

Bridge St

The Octagon

Shop St

Peter St

Church Hill

Quay Hill

Clock Tower

High St

To Parkland Caravan & Camping Park (1.5km); Westport Quay; Towers (2km); Quay Cottage (2km); Croagh Patrick (10km); Louisburgh (18km); Leenaun (26km); Clifden (48km)

To N59; Leenane (26km)

Altamount St

To Tuam (60km); Galway (72km)

Westport 🚆 Train Station

town centre, next to Westport Golf Club, off the N59 to Newport. Call ahead.

Sleeping

The tourist office books rooms (€4 service fee).

BUDGET

Old Mill Holiday Hostel (☎ 27045; oldmillhostel@eircom .net; Barrack Yard, James St; dm/d/tr €17.50/48/66; ☒ closed Christmas day; ℗) This hostel is housed in an impressively repurposed mill, with stone walls and rooms that are well attended to, and the location couldn't be more convenient. The IHH property has inviting communal areas that make for a laidback social vibe. It's also family-friendly.

Abbeywood Hostel (☎ 25496; www.abbeywood house.com; Newport Rd; dm €18-22, d €50; ☒ daily May-Sep, weekends only Oct-Dec & Mar-Apr, closed Jan & Feb; ℗ ▣) Set back from the road on the northern end of town is this characterful old house and gardens, originally part of a monastery. It still boasts some stained glass, wood floors and high ceilings. A light breakfast is available daily.

Parkland Caravan & Camping Park (☎ 27766; camping@westporthouse.ie; Westport House, Quay Rd; camp sites €25; ☒ mid-May–early Sep) Camping on the sprawling Westport House estate can feel akin to being an evicted tenant or lowly groundsman. However, the site's wide-open areas and proximity to funfair-like attractions at the house make it a hit for families with young children.

MIDRANGE

Westport overflows with B&Bs, which in turn overflow with guests at weekends year round.

Killary House (☎ 27457; killaryhouse@msn.com; 4 Distillery Ct; s/d €45/70; ℗) Tucked away in a quiet cul-de-sac, and formerly home to an 18th-century distillery (no lingering scent, though), this characterful B&B has four en-suite rooms, each warmly decorated and well appointed.

St Anthony's (☎ 28887; www.st-anthonys.com; Distillery Rd; s/d €45/80; ℗) Over the river, on a residential block, this genteel B&B sits under cover of a large hedge and thick creepers inhabited by birds' nests. The interior is just as easy on the eye, with six simple but elegant rooms; two have Jacuzzi-style baths.

Westport Inn (☎ 29200; www.westportinn.ie; Mill St; s/d from €49/98; ℗) One of Westport's snazzier

choices, this hotel has comfortably appointed rooms and is just around the corner from the main drag. Some rooms have four-poster beds and Jacuzzi tubs. Rooms in the front may get noisy when the nightclub next door closes.

McCarthy's Lodge (☎ 27050; www.mccarthyslodge .com; Quay St; s/d €50/90) It's upstairs from a pub, but McCarthy's is no flop for drunks. Rooms are as tidy as the town, and as bright and orderly as an Ikea showroom. It's just a few paces up from the Octagon. Breakfast is included.

TOP END

Clew Bay Hotel (☎ 28088; www.clewbayhotel.com; James St; s/d from €70/140; ℗) A smart choice for anyone looking for stylish digs in the heart of town, this hotel has a good restaurant (breakfast included with the price), an art gallery and a fully equipped gym next door (to which guests have free access).

Wyatt Hotel (☎ 25027; www.wyatthotel.com; the Octagon; s/d €110/180; ℗) Other than its position smack in the middle of town, it's the quality of service that really distinguishes this pleasant hotel. Rooms are comfortable though characterless, and guests have free access to a local swimming pool.

Eating

Curry's Cottage (☎ 25297; James St; pastries €2-4; ☒ 9.30am-6pm) This jovial little tea shop is the only place downtown for tea or coffee and a scone or cookie. Naturally it draws a considerable crowd of locals and tourists in the morning, and again around snack time in the afternoon.

Towers (☎ 26534; the Harbour; mains €9-17; ☒ noon-9pm) This wonderfully cosy pub is housed in a former coastguard station with an unusual short turret, rough cut stone and stained glass. The kitchen takes full advantage of freshly hauled in seafood and local produce in producing fine Irish cuisine.

O'Malley's (☎ 27307; Bridge St; mains €11-20; ☒ 6-10pm Thu-Tue) The 'Around the World' menu served upstairs from the pub of the same name (a trendy pick-up joint) has an incredible array of dishes culled from many different cuisines, including Italian, Thai and Mexican.

Quay Cottage (☎ 26412; www.quaycottage.com; the Harbour; mains €18-25; ☒ 6-11pm Tue-Sat) Serving seafood hauled straight from the harbour boats, this delightful restaurant is rich in salty-dog charm, with lobster pots hanging from the roof beams. There are a few meat and vegetarian dishes offered 'for landlubbers' too. It's on the road that leads to Westport House.

Drinking

our pick **Matt Molloy's** (☎ 26655; Bridge St) Matt Molloy, the fife player from the Chieftains, opened this pub years ago and the good times haven't let up. It's a good old fashioned pub, nothing glamorous or trendy about it. Head straight to the back room around 9pm and you'll catch live traditional ceili music. Or perhaps an old man will simply slide into a chair and croon a few dozen classics.

Moran's (☎ 26320; Bridge St) Westport being a well-preserved specimen, it stands to reason a traditional pub such as this one would still be in operation. It's a holdover from the days when a pub was also a shop, and buying groceries was occasion to have a few pints before heading home without the groceries. Don't shy away from the private façade.

Jester Bar (☎ 29255; Bridge St) Westport flashes its contemporary side in this hipster hangout. If you're looking sharp, you'll fit right in. No céilidhs, no talk of fishing – urban grooves set the pace here.

Getting There & Away

Bus Éireann (☎ 096-71800) travels to Achill Island (€11, 30 minutes, two daily), Dublin (€16, five hours, three daily), Galway (€13, two hours, eight daily) and Sligo (€15, two hours, two daily). Buses depart from and arrive at the Mill St stop. There are limited services on Sunday.

The **train station** (☎ 25253) is 800m from the town centre. There are three daily connections to Dublin (adult/child €30/15, 3½ hours).

Getting Around

For a cab call **Moran's Executive Taxis** (☎ 25539) or **O'Toole Taxis** (☎ 087-243 2600). **Sean Sammon** (☎ 25471; James St) hires out bikes for €10 per day.

AROUND WESTPORT

If you're heading by car or bicycle from Westport to Connemara, in County Galway, or to Cong, in the Eastern part of Mayo, take the Quay Hill route past the harbour and fol-

low the coast highway to Louisburgh. Then turn onto the R335 through the Doolough Valley. It's stunningly beautiful.

Croagh Patrick

St Patrick couldn't have picked a better spot for a pilgrimage than this conical mountain (also known as 'the Reek') just 8km southwest of Westport. On a clear day the tough two-hour climb rewards with a stunning view of Clew Bay and its innumerable sandy islets.

It was on Croagh Patrick that Ireland's patron saint fasted for 40 days and nights, and where he reputedly banished venomous snakes. Climbing the 765m holy mountain is an act of penance for thousands of pilgrims on the last Sunday of July (Reek Sunday). The truly contrite make the trek along Tóchar Phádraig (Patrick's Causeway), the original 40km route from Ballintubber Abbey, and ascend the mountain barefoot.

The trail taken by less contrite folk begins beside Campbell's pub in the village of Murrisk (Muraisc). There's no mistaking the route. At the start of the path you'll find a **visitor centre** (☎ 098-64114; www.croagh-patrick.com; ⏰ 11am-5pm mid-Mar–Oct).

Opposite the car park is the **National Famine Memorial**, a spine-chilling sculpture of a three-masted ghost ship wreathed in swirling skeletons, commemorating the lives lost on so called 'coffin ships' employed to help people escape the Famine (1845–49). The path down past the memorial leads to the scant remains of **Murrisk Abbey**, founded by the O'Malleys in 1547.

Louisburgh

☎ 098 / pop 210

Gateway village to the Doolough Valley, the small village of Louisburgh (Cluain Cearbán) was founded under curious circumstances in 1795. Based on a simple four-street system known as the Cross, the whole town was designed and built as a living memorial to a relative of the first marquess of Sligo, Lord Altamont (John Browne): his kinsman was killed at the Battle of Louisburgh in Nova Scotia, 1758.

The **Famine Museum & Granuaile Visitors Centre** (☎ 66134; Church St, Louisburgh; adult/child/concession €3.50/1.50/2.50; ⏰ 11am-4pm Tue, 3-7pm Thu, noon-4pm Fri & Sat), in the library, offers a quick glimpse into the life and times of Grace O'Malley (Gráinne Ní Mháille or Granuaile, 1530–1603) the infamous pirate queen of

Connaught. It also recounts local memories of the famine, which hit hard in this part of Mayo.

There are some excellent Blue Flag **beaches** in the vicinity. Old Head Beach, 4km from Louisburgh, just off the main road to Westport, is particularly sandy and safe.

Old Head Forest Caravan & Camping Park (☎ 087-648 6885; Old Head, Louisburgh; camp sites €12; ☼ Jun-Sep) is a medium-sized camping park in woodland, a short walk from its namesake beach, where there is a pier and a slipway with a lifeguard on duty.

Bus Éireann (☎ 096-71800) service 450 links Westport and Louisburgh (€6.50, 35 minutes, up to five times daily Monday to Saturday) via Murrisk.

Killadoon

Panoramic ocean views and vast sandy beaches, almost always empty, can be found at the tiny village of Killadoon. Look for Tallabawn and Dooarghtry beaches, which are reached by a narrow coastal road heading south from Louisburgh, or by turning west off the R335 at Cregganbaun.

Bus Éireann (☎ 096-71800) service 450 from Westport and Louisburgh continues to Killadoon twice daily Monday to Saturday. The trip takes about 15 minutes.

Doolough Valley

One of Ireland's most dramatic drives is through the Doolough Valley, along the R335 scenic route from Westport and Leenane (County Galway). It was the site of a legendary famine walk, which took place in 1849. In icy weather, 400 hundred people died along the road as they walked from Louisburgh to Delphi and back. They had hoped to receive food and aid from a landlord, but were refused. Read up on this history or visit the Famine Museum in Louisburgh before taking this route, as it greatly enhances the impact. Failing that, however, Doolough is still special.

Drive at as leisurely a pace as you can get away with (early morning traffic is usually light). It's mostly a pristine and desolate terrain that continually unfolds as hills part along the road and new hills fill the horizon. Most of the valley is free of housing, cut turf or even stone walls. Black **Doo Lough** (Dark Lake) gives way to **Bundorragha River**, where you can count on seeing people fishing for salmon. It goes on and on like this, and is very satisfying.

It is possible to park your car near the lake and take a stroll along the road to Delphi. To really immerse yourself in the valley's splendour, stay a night or two in Delphi, and organise a fishing excursion from there.

DELPHI (COUNTY GALWAY)

☎ 095

It's no accident that one of the country's top spas chose to locate itself in Delphi. This starkly beautiful swathe of mountainous moorland is ideal get-away-from-it-all territory. Miles from any significant settlements, you can toss aside that mobile phone, forget your troubles and set about the serious business of relaxing.

The area was named by its most famous resident, the second Marquess of Sligo, who was convinced that the land strongly resembled the area around Delphi, Greece.

our pick **Delphi Lodge** (☎ 42222; www.delphilodge .ie, www.delphi-salmon.com; Leenane; s/d €130/200, cottages per week for 4 or more from €800; P ▣) feels more like a congenial house party than a hotel, with communal dining often utilising the lodgers' catch. This lakeside Georgian lodge is a popular retreat for well-heeled fishermen, walkers and seekers of tranquillity. It was once the sporting lodge of the Marquis of Sligo. Self-catering cottages offer the best deal for families. Fishing holidays can be arranged through the lodge (enquire when making reservations).

The **Delphi Mountain Resort & Spa** (☎ 42987, 42208; www.delphiescape.com; Leenane; s/d with breakfast & activities from €200/300; P ▣) is built from rough-cut stone and honey-coloured wood. This world-class spa-hotel hits the perfect note between modern chic and rustic glow – even if the exterior somewhat resembles a hobbit hole. Day programmes for nonguests cost from €80 to €230.

Delphi Adventure Centre (☎ 42208; www.delphiad ventureholidays.ie), alongside the lodge, offers over 25 outdoor activities from hill walking to raft building to cross-country assault courses.

CLARE ISLAND

☎ 098 / pop 130

Clew Bay is dotted with some 365 islands, presided over by mountainous Clare Island, 5km offshore at the mouth of the bay. Dominated by rocky **Mt Knockmore** (461m), the island's trails and roads offer varied terrain, and are terrific for walking and climbing. Getting lost is never a worry. It also has several safe, sandy beaches to its credit.

The island has the ruins of the Cistercian **Clare Island Abbey** (c 1460) and **Granuaile's Castle**, both associated with the piratical Grace O'Malley. The tower castle was her stronghold, although it was altered considerably when the coastguard took it over in 1831. Grace is said to be buried in the small abbey, which contains a stone inscribed with her family motto: 'Invincible on land and sea'.

The island is also one of the dwindling number of places where you can find choughs, which look like blackbirds but have red beaks.

Fishing and scuba diving can be arranged through the Bay View Hotel & Hostel (below).

Sleeping & Eating

Bay View Hotel & Hostel (☎ 26307; clareislhotel@hotmail.com; dm/s/d €20/40/70; s/d with bathroom €50/90; ☻ May-Oct) The island's only hotel overlooks the harbour, with a sunset view of the mainland that is simply sublime. It has a restaurant and bar, and is a bit of a social centre for the island.

Cois Abhainn (☎ 26216; fax 26250; Toremore; s/d €35/70; ☻ May-Oct) Alternatively, for that 'ends-of-the-earth' feeling, you could head to the windswept southwestern corner of the island, 5km from the harbour. This B&B has sensational views of Inishturk Island. Not all rooms are en suite. Evening meals can be arranged, often involving freshly caught fish.

If you're just going for the day, consider taking your own food, though pub grub is available at the Bay View Hotel & Hostel, and B&Bs do evening meals (from €15).

Getting There & Away

The nearest mainland point is Roonagh Quay, 8km west of Louisburgh. **Clare Island Ferries** (☎ 28288, 087-241 4653; www.clareislandferry.com) and **O'Malley's Ferries** (☎ 25045, 086-600 0204; www.omalleyferries.com) make the 15-minute trip from Roonagh (adult/child return €15/8). There are 15 sailings daily in July and August, and from three to six daily the rest of the year.

Getting Around

You can hire **bikes** (☎ 25640) from opposite the pier for €10 per day. Enquire at the pier if you need taxi service.

INISHTURK ISLAND
☎ 098 / pop 100

Still further off the beaten track is ruggedly beautiful Inishturk, which lies about 12km off Mayo's western coast. It is a sparsely populated and little visited island, despite the two **sandy beaches** on its eastern side, impressive **cliffs**, wonderful **flora and fauna**, and a rugged, hilly landscape that's ideal for **walking.** In fact, ambling the island's maze of country roads is a perfect way to familiarise yourself with the pace of life here.

Accommodation and meals are available at the colourful **Harbour Lodge** (☎ 45610; s/d incl breakfast & dinner €35/70), a short walk from the ferry, and the more remote but scenically positioned **Teach Abhainn** (☎ 45510; s/d €30/50; dinner €25; ☻ Apr-Oct), a working farm 1.5km west of the harbour.

John Heanue operates a **ferry** (☎ 45541, 086-202 9670; Roonagh; adult/child return €25/12.50; ☻ 11am & 6.30pm) from Roonagh Quay, near Louisburgh. There is also a twice weekly service to Cleggan in County Galway; call for details of departure times.

NEWPORT
☎ 098 / pop 530

Newport (Baile Uí Fhiacháin), 12km north of Westport, is a picturesque 18th-century village in which there really isn't much to do other than catch fish in streams, lakes or Clew Bay. The town's most striking feature is a seven-arch viaduct built in 1892 for the Westport–Achill Railway; the trains stopped in 1936 and the bridge has since become a pedestrian walkway. The main attraction in town is stately Newport House, a fine Georgian estate, where most visitors stay. The Bangor Trail (see p456) and Foxford Trail, both end near the town, draw many walkers. Achill Island (p452) is a short drive away.

The **tourist office** (Main St; ☻ 10am-3pm Mon-Fri) has information on fishing. The post office and bureau de change are across the river. There are no banks.

Sleeping & Eating

Newport House (☎ 41222; www.newporthouse.ie; Main St; s €136-188, d €220-324; dinner €63; ☻ Mar-Sep; (P) (💻)) This magnificent Georgian mansion, strangled by ivy that turns crimson in fall, is one of the top country hotels in Ireland. Every room in the hotel is beautifully appointed and includes breakfast, but

Newport House is especially known for its contemporary Irish cuisine and a vintage wine list that will make you drool. The bar and the surrounding gardens are also worth checking out, even if you're not a guest. The hotel staff can help arrange fishing excursions.

Hotel Newport (☎ 41155; www.hotelnewportmayo .com; Main St; s/d from €80/120; P) In the heart of the town, this hotel has updated rooms and a fine restaurant that specialises in local seafood (meals are included in the room rate), and a pub.

Getting There & Away

The frequent **Bus Éireann** (☎ 096-71800) services between Westport and Achill Island pass through Newport, though you'll need to request a stop here.

NEWPORT TO ACHILL ISLAND
Burrishoole Abbey

From a distance, the eerie shell of this windbattered **abbey** (admission free; ☾ dawn-dusk) resembles a 2D film set. It was founded in 1486 by the Dominicans. In a strange twist of fate, the abbey actually plunged the surrounding devout community into holy hot water, when Rome threatened them with excommunication for not consulting them on the abbey's creation.

About 2.5km northwest towards Achill a sign points the way to the abbey, from where it's a further 1km.

Rockfleet Castle

Also known as **Carrigahowley**, this bluff 15thcentury tower is one of the most tangible spots to be associated with 'pirate queen' Granuaile (see p449). She married her second husband, Richard an-Iarrain (impressively nicknamed 'Iron Dick' Burke) to gain control of this castle, and famously fought off an English attack here.

The tower is in a quiet outlet of Clew Bay. Turn south at the sign, about 5km west of Newport on the Achill road.

Mulrany

This elongated hillside village (An Mhala Raithní) is a great spot to try counting the approximately 365 saucer-sized islands that grace Clew Bay. Mulrany stands on the isthmus with Bellacagher Bay and boasts a stun-

ning, wide Blue Flag beach. Take the steps opposite the Park Inn, or the path beside the service station.

Sleeping

Midrange accommodation is best on Achill, but a few forlorn B&Bs with spectacular views can be found in Mulrany.

Traenlaur Lodge (☎ 098-41358; www.anoige.ie; Lough Feeagh, Newport; dm €15; ☾ Jun-Sep) A gorgeous An Óige hostel in a former fishing lodge with its own harbour on Lough Feeagh. It's often full of walkers resting their weary feet from the Western Way or Bangor Trail. It is 8km from Newport, signposted from the Achill road.

Park Inn Mulrany (☎ 098-36000; www.parkinnmul ranny.ie; N59, Mulrany; s/d from €100/180; P ☐ ☒) Established in 1897, the Park Inn sits amid 42 wooded acres and boasts one of the most magical coastal views in Ireland. Room décor is up to date, the restaurant is highly regarded, and guests can keep in shape in the swimming pool and gym. Low-season midweek packages can bring the price way down.

ACHILL ISLAND
☎ 098 / pop 960

Ireland's largest off-shore island, Achill (An Caol), is connected to the mainland by a short bridge, making it accessible by car or bus. Despite this convenience, Achill has plenty of that far-flung island feeling. It is blessed with breathtaking cliff scenery, rocky headlands, sheltered sandy beaches, broad expanses of blanket bog and rolling mountains. It also has an interesting history, having been a frequent refuge during Ireland's numerous rebellions. It's at its most dramatic during winter, when high winds and a lashing sea can make the island seem downright inhospitable. The year-round population, though, remains as welcoming as ever. Few visitors choose to appreciate this temperamental side of Achill, however, preferring its milder summers, when the island spruces up with purple heather, rhododendrons and wildflowers. If it's beach weather, count on Achill's sprinkling of holiday chalets (some nicknamed the Toblerones), hotels and camping grounds reaching full occupancy.

A quiet hamlet known as the Valley is the island's most traditional quarter, and has a historic hostel. The village of Keel is the island's main centre of activity.

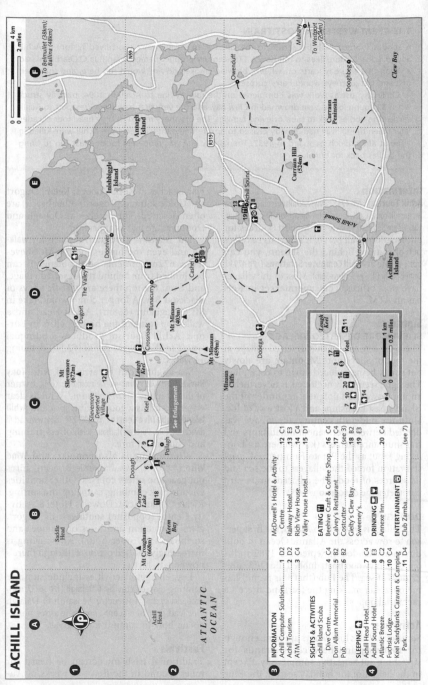

ACHILL ISLAND

INFORMATION
Achill Computer Solutions......1 D2
Achill Tourism..........................2 D2
ATM..3 C4

SIGHTS & ACTIVITIES
Achill Island Scuba
  Dive Centre.............................4 C4
Don Allum Memorial................5 B2
Pub...6 B2

SLEEPING
Achill Head Hotel.....................7 C4
Achill Sound Hotel...................8 E3
Atlantic Breeze.........................9 C2
Fuchsia Lodge.........................10 C4
Keel Sandybanks Caravan & Camping
  Park......................................11 D4

McDowell's Hotel & Activity
  Centre.................................12 C1
Railway Hostel.......................13 E3
Rich View House....................14 C4
Valley House Hostel...............15 D1

EATING
Beehive Craft & Coffee Shop...16 C4
Calvey's Restaurant...............17 C4
Costcutter..........................(see 3)
Gielty's Clew Bay..................18 B2
Sweeney's..............................19 E3

DRINKING
Annexe Inn............................20 C4

ENTERTAINMENT
Club Zamba......................(see 7)

THE GREAT WESTERN GHOST TRAIN

A spooky footnote can be added to the Great Western Railway's short-lived history in Achill Sound. Local folklore likes to tell how a 17th-century prophet named Brian Rua O'Cearbhain had a vision that one day 'carts on wheels, blowing smoke and fire' would run here, and that their first and last journeys would carry corpses.

Chillingly, just as work was completed on the railway line to Achill in 1894, tragedy struck when 32 young locals were drowned in Clew Bay, and the very first train from Westport to Achill carried the bodies back to their grieving families. The prophecy reared its ugly head four decades later when the railway had already ceased to run. Ten migrant workers from Achill were killed in a fire at Kirkintilloch, Scotland in 1937. The railway line was reopened for one last run to bring the bodies back for burial.

Information

Achill Tourism (☎ 47353; www.achilltourism.com, www.visitachill.com; Cashel; ☽ 9am-6pm Mon-Fri Jul & Aug, 10am-4pm Sep-Jun) is one of the best sources for information in all Mayo. It's next to Lavelle's petrol station. Behind the station, you can get on line at **Achill Computer Solutions** (☎ 47940; Cashel; per hr €4; ☽ 9.30am-5pm). Most of the villages have post offices. The supermarket in Keel has an ATM.

Sights

SLIEVEMORE DESERTED VILLAGE

The eerie remains of this deserted village at the foot of Slievemore Mountain are slowly but surely being reduced down to rock piles. The sight, seemingly neglected, is nevertheless an impressive and poignant reminder of the island's past hardships and a lost way of life. Until the mid-19th century, the village was divided between permanent inhabitants and transhumance farmers (known here as 'booleying'), but as the Potato Famine took grip, starvation forced the villagers to the sea and its sources of food. The adjacent graveyard completes the desolation.

DOOAGH

This village is where Don Allum, the first person to row across the Atlantic Ocean in both directions, landed in September 1982 in his 6m-long plywood boat, dubbed the *QE3*, after 77 days at sea. The Pub (that's its name) has memorabilia marking the feat, and there's a memorial opposite.

Activities

Some of Achill's lovely bays are tame enough for **swimming** and have clean strands for stretching out beneath a summer sky. Except in the height of the holiday season, the Blue Flag beaches at Keel, Dooega, Keem, Dugort and Golden Strand (Dugort's other beach) are often deserted. The beaches at Dooagh and Dooniver are just as appealing.

The island is a wonderful place for **walking** and even the highest point (Mt Slievemore, 672m) presents no problems. It can be climbed from behind the deserted village, and from the top there are terrific views of Blacksod Bay. A longer climb would take in Mt Croaghaun (668m), Achill Head and a walk atop some of the highest cliffs in Europe. Achill Tourism produces a bilingual *Guide to Walking in Achill* (€3.50) detailing 14 walks.

Sea-angling can be arranged with **Tony Burke** (☎ 47257; tmburke@eircom.net; Keel), owner of the 10-metre *Cuan na Cuime*. With its clear waters Achill is a good diving spot and **Achill Island Scuba Dive Centre** (☎ 087-234 9884; www.achilldivecentre.com; Purteen Harbour, Keel) offers training and equipment hire.

Windsurfing is also popular, and **Wind Wise** (☎ 43958; www.windwise.ie; Bunacurry) hires out gear and offers courses. Other activities include rock climbing, canoeing and surfing. Richie O'Hara at McDowell's Hotel & Activity Centre (opposite) southwest of Dugort, gives instruction and hires out canoes and surfboards (€15 per hour). Kite-surfing is increasingly spotted offshore, though there's nowhere to hire gear.

Less energetic activities include summer painting classes run by **Ó'Dálaigh** (☎ 36137; www.achillpainting.com). Instructor Seosamh Ó Dálaigh will lead you to a scenic spot and offer pointers on how to commit it to canvas.

Festivals

Traditional Irish music can be heard for miles around in the first two weeks of Au-

gust, during the **Scoil Acla Festival** (www.visitachill
.com; ☎ 43063). The event also promotes Irish
dancing, culture and music through numerous workshops (swiftly relocating to pubs
come the evening).

Sleeping
BUDGET
Keel Sandybanks Caravan & Camping Park (☎ 094-
903 2054; www.achillcamping.com; Keel; camp sites €10;
☺ June–mid-Sep) This camping ground is on
a trim patch of greenery overlooking Keel
Strand, a Blue Flag beach. It's a short stroll
from the town. It has a lounge and a laundry
room.

ourpick **Valley House Hostel** (☎ 47204; www.valley
-house.com; the Valley; camp sites/dm/d €10/15/36, f from
€39.50; P) A hostel in a great old mansion
that's gone just a tad to seed, Valley House
adds to its charm with unruly gardens and
a licensed pub with patio tables. Old stone
houses dot the rugged terrain of the surrounding Valley. The hostel has still more in its
favour – its infamous history. In 1894, the
landlady was brutally attacked by a local man
and JM Synge based his play *The Playboy of
the Western World* on his misadventures. The
subsequent film *Love and Rage* (1999) was
also partially shot here. Take the road to Keel
and turn right (northeast) at the Bunacurry
junction signposted for Dugort.

Railway Hostel (☎ 45187; Achill Sound; camp sites/dm
€10/15 P) Once a railroad station, this place
now serves as a no-frills hostel. You're barely
poking Achill with your big toe if you stay
here, but in peak season it'll get you near
enough to the island's top sights. It's just
before the bridge you cross to reach the
island.

Rich View House (☎ 43462; richviewhostel@hotmail
.com; Keel; s/d €15/30) Facilities at this relaxed hostel-
cum-home-stay are simple, even scarce, but
the jolly live-in owner is extremely knowledgeable about Achill and quick to invite guests
to the pub.

MIDRANGE
Atlantic Breeze (☎ 43189; www.atlantic-breeze.com;
Pollagh, Keel; s/d €35/60; ☺ Apr–Oct; P) Welcoming
Mary Sweeny's award-winning B&B has three
rooms and lovely views from its conservatory.
It's just a little ways beyond Keel.

Fuchsia Lodge (☎ 43350; fuchsialodge@eircom.ie; Keel;
s/d €40/60; P ♿) This popular and convenient
B&B is a short walk outside the village of Keel.

It has four cosy bedrooms, including two connecting rooms ideal for a family. It is one of
few B&Bs open all year round.

McDowell's Hotel & Activity Centre (☎ 43148;
Slievemore Rd, Dugort; s/d €50/100; P) Set inland,
McDowell's makes up for its lack of sea
views by offering a host of activities, including surfing, sailing and currach rowing. The
hotel has 10 reasonable rooms, a decent bar-
restaurant and can be a lively spot during July
and August. It's within spitting distance of
hill-walking trails.

Achill Sound Hotel (☎ 45245; www.achillsoundhotel
.com; Achill Sound; s/d €55/100; P) Near the bridge,
on the island side, this family-run hotel offers very basic but orderly rooms, some with
fine views of the sound. There is a bar and
restaurant off the lobby.

Achill Head Hotel (☎ 43108; www.achillhead
.com; Pollagh, Keel; s/d €65/100; P) This medium-
sized hotel has 19 modern rooms, some
with rather grandiose four-poster beds and
patchwork-style quilts. The hotel is in the
heart of Keel and close to the seafront, though
not so well located as its website would have
you believe.

Eating
Most hotels will serve lunch or dinner to nonguests.

Beehive Craft & Coffee Shop (☎ 43018; Keel; snacks
around €7; ☺ 10.30am-6pm Apr-Oct; P) As much a
craft shop as a café, the Beehive dishes up
wonderful homemade soups served with
brown scones, and a more sinful selection of
homebaked cakes.

Calvey's Restaurant (☎ 43158; Keel; mains €6-18;
☺ 6-10pm Mon-Sat) This award-winning restaurant serves up a mix of fresh local seafood and
meat from its attached butchery. Its signature
dish is local lamb, but there are also a few
nonmeat dishes for vegetarians.

Gielty's Clew Bay (☎ 43119; www.gieltys.com; Dooagh;
sandwiches €4-7, mains €10-14; ☺ 10am-9pm) It's modern and basically characterless, but Gielty's is
an exceedingly friendly pub that churns out
good Irish food. You can do a light lunch or
a full-on meal here. On summer evenings, the
place serves as one of the island's bigger live
music venues, with trad céilidh jams several
nights a week.

If you're camping or hostelling, stock up
at **Sweeney's supermarket** (☎ 45211), just across
the bridge as you enter Achill, or at **Costcutter**
(☎ 43125), a deli and supermarket in Keel.

Drinking & Entertainment

From May to September, most pubs and hotels have live music.

Annexe Inn (☎ 43268; Keel) This cosy little pub delivers the best traditional music sessions all year round. It has music almost nightly in July and August, and on weekends the rest of the year.

Club Zamba (☎ 43108; Achill Head Hotel, Pollagh, Keel) Achill's most happening nightclub is strung with video screens and swirling lights. It has a text-message request-service to the DJ, so it's no good using the old 'not my kind of music' excuse to avoid dancing.

Getting There & Around

Bus Éireann (☎ 096-71800) services run from Ballina and Westport Monday to Saturday year-round, with nine stops on the island, including at Dooagh, Keel, Dugort, Cashel and Achill Sound. Check the current schedule with the tourist office.

Bikes can be hired from **O'Malley's Island Sports** (☎ 43125; jomalley@eircom.net; Keel; ☽ Jun-Aug). Call ahead, as bikes go quickly during peak season. It's next to the post office in Keel.

BANGOR ERRIS

☎ 097 / pop 270

This unexceptional little village is the start or end point for the 48km **Bangor Trail**, which connects Bangor (Bain Gear) and Newport. It's an extraordinary hike that takes walkers through some of the bleakest, most remote countryside in Ireland. Unfortunately, you'll need several 1:50,000 OS maps to cover the trail (see p710).

Bus Éireann (☎ 096-71800) runs an evening bus Monday to Saturday (and an additional midday bus in July and August) from Ballina (€11, one hour).

BALLYCROY NATIONAL PARK

Ballycroy National Park, comprising one of Europe's largest expanses of blanket bog, was founded in 1998, but at the time of writing the park was not yet fully operational. It is a gorgeously scenic region in which the Owenduff River wends its way through intact bogs. Many migratory birds roost here. A visitor centre is due to be completed sometime in 2008, in the nearby town of Ballycroy. You'll be able to stop here for information on the natural environment as well as some of the area's history and culture. Presumably, there will be guided walks as well as trails on which visitors can explore the park on their own, but very little information was available at the time of research.

MULLET PENINSULA

☎ 097

The Mullet Peninsula dangles some 30km out into the Atlantic, connected to the mainland by a flake of boggy earth. It feels more cut off than some islands, and has much of the same bleakness. Needless to say, it's thinly populated and infrequently visited, which is part of its appeal. The real draw, however, are the pristine beaches along its sheltered eastern shore. The peninsula is Irish speaking and the functional little town of **Belmullet** (Béal an Mhuirthead) is the main settlement.

Information

Atlantek Computers (☎ 82255; Carter Sq; per hr €6; ☽ 10am-6pm Mon-Sat) For internet access.

Bank of Ireland (Carter Sq) Has an ATM and bureau de change.

Erris tourist office (☎ 81500; Barrack St; ☽ 9.30am-4.30pm Mon-Fri Easter-Sep)

Post office (Main St)

Blacksod Point & Around

The road south from Belmullet loops round the tip of the peninsula to rejoin itself at Aghleam. Near the point are the remains of an old **church**, and the view across the bay takes in the spot where *La Rata Santa Maria Encoronada*, part of the 1588 Spanish Armada, came in and was later burned by its captain.

The road to Blacksod Point passes **Elly Bay**, a pleasant beach and a favourite haunt of birdwatchers. Further south it passes stunning **Mullaghroe Beach**. In the early years of the 20th century, a whaling station operated at Ardelly Point, just north of here.

The weather centre here determined the eventual date for the D-Day Normandy landing.

Sleeping & Eating

Western Strands Hotel (☎ 81096; www.westernstrandshotel.com; Main St, Belmullet; s/d €48/70) A cheerful atmosphere predominates in this fairly large hotel, upstairs from an old-timey pub. It's smack-dab in the centre of tiny Belmullet, and offers an array of services – while checking-in, enquire about fishing, cycling, beaches etc. En-suite rooms are straightforward without being flashy, and good food is available in the bar.

Chez Nous (☎ 82167; chez_nous_belmullet@esatclear .ie; Church Rd, Belmullet; s/d €40/70; ☿ Mar–Dec; ℗) Wonderfully snug rooms with cheerful colour schemes can be found at this modern B&B; take the road signposted Garda. It's a five-minute walk to the town's central roundabout.

Getting There & Around

Monday to Saturday **Bus Éireann** (☎ 096-71800) runs an evening bus (and an additional midday bus in July and August) from Ballina to Belmullet (€11, 1¼ hours), continuing on to Blacksod Point.

McNulty's Coaches (☎ 81086; www.mcnultycoaches .com; Chapel St), with an office near the Belmullet post office, runs daily buses to and from Castlebar. The 1½-hour trip costs €9/13 one way/return.

POLLATOMISH

☎ 097 / pop 150

Irresistibly remote and pretty, Pollatomish (Poll an Tómais), also spelled Pullathomas, sits in a serene bay some 16km east of Belmullet, signposted on the road to Ballycastle (R314). There's a pleasant sandy **beach** and walks up to **Benwee Head** from where there are terrific views.

our pick **Kilcommon Lodge Hostel** (☎ 84621; www .kilcommonlodge.net; Pollatomish; dm/d €12/30; ℗), in a lovely setting, evokes quiet, somewhat quirky country living. The surrounding gardens are cluttered with unusual bric-a-brac, including whale bones, and the beach is just a short stroll away. It's family-run, and friendly. Evening meals are available.

BALLYCASTLE & AROUND

☎ 096 / pop 250

Fifty years ago, just one megalithic tomb was recorded in the region around Ballycastle (Baile an Chaisil). Now, the area claims one of the greatest concentrations of such tombs in Europe. It is also blessed with breathtaking coastal scenery. The pretty village consists of one sloping street. It's very quiet, with an unfussed, old-fashioned feel to it.

Sights

CÉIDE FIELDS

A famous wit once described archaeology as being all about 'a series of small walls'.

Well it's not often that such walls have had experts hopping up and down with such excitement than at **Céide Fields** (Achaidh Chéide; www.museumsofmayo.com; ☎ 43325), 8km northwest of Ballycastle.

During the 1930s, a local man, Patrick Caulfield, was digging in the bog when he noticed a lot of piled-up stones buried beneath it. About 40 years later, his son Seamus, who had become an archaeologist on the basis of his father's discovery, began extensive exploration of the area. What he, and later others, uncovered was the world's most extensive Stone Age monument, consisting of stone-walled fields, houses and megalithic tombs – reckoned to total about half a million tonnes of stone. Astonishingly, five millennia ago a thriving farming community lived here, growing wheat and barley, grazing sheep and cattle, and fencing off land with an impressive level of planning.

Even for nonarchaeologists, the award-winning **Interpretive Centre** (☎ 43325; ceidefields@opw .ie; R314; adult/child under 6/student/concession incl tour €3.50/ free/1.25/2.50; ☿ 10am-6pm Jun-Sep, 10am-5pm mid-Mar– May, Oct & Nov, groups only rest of year), in a glass pyramid overlooking the site, gives a fascinating glimpse into the past of 5500 years ago. However, it's recommended that you take a guided tour of the site itself, or it may seem nothing more than, well, a series of small walls.

Activities

The **Heathfield Lodge Stables** (☎ 43350; liz@heath fieldstables.com; Ballycastle) offers riding lessons, childrens' pony rides and trail rides through beautiful coastal hill country near Ballycastle. It's not quite 1km down the road towards Killala.

Sleeping & Eating

Stella Maris (☎ 43322; www.stellamarisireland.com; Ballycastle; s/d from €155/200; dinner around €50) Originally a British Coast Guard station, and later a nunnery, this grand old building has been successfully converted into one of Mayo's finest lodgings. Rooms were designed with a nice complement of antiques and stylish modern furnishings, and the restaurant is top notch. The setting is what really sells it, though. It's 2.5km outside the town, overlooking the ocean amid rolling green hills and fields of sheep.

Mary's Cottage Kitchen (☎ 43361; Lower Main St; dishes €2.50-11.50; ☿ 10am-3pm Mon-Sat Oct-Mar, 10am-6pm Apr-Sep) Cosy grey-stone cottages like this are always appealing, and never more so than when they house a bakery that advertises its wares with the ambrosial scent of apple pie. In addition to cakes and tea, the kitchen serves up light meals. During the summer tables are set up out back in a leafy garden. Evening meals are sometimes served during peak season.

Getting There & Away
Bus Éireann (☎ 71800) runs between Ballycastle and Ballina (€9, 30 minutes) twice a day, Monday to Friday.

KILLALA & AROUND
☎ 096 / pop 650

The town itself is pretty enough, but Killala (Cill Alaidh or Cill Ála) is more famous for its namesake bay nearby, and its role in the French invasion and rebellion of Wolfe Tone in 1798.

It's claimed that St Patrick founded Killala, and the Church of Ireland cathedral sits on the site of the first Christian church. The 25m round tower still looms over the town's heart; it was struck by lightning in 1800 and the cap was later rebuilt. A seasonal **tourist office** (☎ 32166; ☻ 10am-5pm Jun-Sep) is located 500m outside town on the Ballina road.

Rathfran Abbey
The remains of this remote Dominican friary, dating from 1274, can be both tranquil and downright eerie. The silence is broken only by the cawing of crows and the whistling wind. In 1590 the friary was burned by the English, but the resilient monks stayed nearby until the 18th century.

Take the R314 road north out of Killala and, after 5km and crossing the River Cloonaghmore, turn right. After another 2km turn right at the crossroads.

Moyne Abbey
This 15th-century Franciscan structure is impressive, though it too was torched, by Richard Bingham in the 16th century. Reaching this lonely ruin requires trekking a little ways through private farmland. You'll reach Moyne Abbey by heading north from Ballina. It's 3km north of Rosserk Abbey (p460); you'll see it on the right across a field.

Breastagh Ogham Stone
This lonely lichen-covered stone, the height of a basketball player, is etched with an obscure ogham script but the weathered markings are all but invisible. It's in a field left of the R314, just past the turning for Rathfran Abbey. Cross the ditch where the sign points to the stone.

Lackan Bay
Flush with revolutionary fervour and eager to hurt the English in their own backyard, on 22 August 1798 more than 1000 French troops commanded by General Humbert landed at Kilcummin in Killala Bay. It was hoped (or rather promised by Irish patriot Wolfe Tone) that their arrival would inspire the Irish peasantry to revolt against the English.

A right turn off the main R314 is signposted for Kilcummin. On the R314 just after the turning to Lackan Bay a **sculpture** of a French soldier helping a prostrate Irish peasant marks the place where the first French soldier died on Irish soil. Lackan Bay **beach** is a stunning expanse of golden sand, ideal for young children.

Getting There & Away
The Ballina–Ballycastle bus runs twice a day Monday to Friday, stopping outside McGregor's newsagency in Killala. Ring **Bus Éireann** (☎ 71800) for details.

BALLINA
☎ 096 / pop 9478

The bustling, workaday town of Ballina (Béal an Átha; balli-*nagh*) is the largest in the county. It's a convenient base for exploring northern Mayo, and is particularly attractive if you're interested in catching salmon. You'll be able to stock up on fishing supplies here. The town itself is not particularly pretty, though its streets retain traces of Victorian and Edwardian elegance, and the River Moy pumps right through the town's heart.

Information
Atlantek Computers (☎ 70658; Circular Rd; per hr €6; ☻ 10am-6pm Mon-Sat) An internet café.

AIB (Pearse St) With ATM and bureau de change.

Moy Valley Resources (☎ 70848; Cathedral Rd; per hr €9; ☻ 9am-1pm & 2-5.30pm) Internet access in same building as the tourist office.

Post office (O'Rahilly St) On the southern extension of Pearse St.

Tourist office (☎ 70848; Cathedral Rd; ☻ 10am-5.30pm Mon-Sat Apr-Oct, closed Nov-Mar) Across the River Moy from the centre.

Activities

In season, you'll see green-garbed waders heading for the River Moy in droves. This is one of the most prolific **salmon-fishing** rivers in Europe, and you can often see the scaly critters jumping in the Ridge (salmon pool), with otters and grey seals in pursuit.

A list of fisheries and permit contacts is available at the tourist office. The season is February to September, but the best fishing is June to August. Information, supplies and licensing are available at **Ridge Pool Tackle Shop** (☎ 72656; Cathedral Rd; ☽ 8am-5pm). Fly-casting lessons can also be arranged.

Lough Conn, southwest of Ballina, is an important brown-trout fishery, and there's no shortage of places with boats and *ghillies* (guides) round the lake. Pontoon, near Foxford, is a better base for **trout fishing** in both Lough Conn and Lough Cullen.

Festivals

One of the best outdoor parties in the country, the town's annual knees-up is the **Ballina Street Festival** (☎ 79814; www.ballinastreetfestival.ie), which lasts for a full two weeks in early July. It's a bit of everything, with parades, dances, cart racing, traditional dress-up days and a 'teenage gladiator' tournament.

Sleeping

Belleek Caravan & Camping Park (☎ 71533; www.belleekpark.com; Ballina; camp sites €18; ☽ Mar-Nov) This well-manicured, grassy site is a 1st-class choice for campers. It has a laundry, kitchen and plenty of space for the children to play. It's 2km from Ballina, 300m off the Killala road.

The Loft B&B (☎ 21881; www.theloftbar.ie; Pearse St; d €80) In the heart of town, this sleek and stylish hotel affords modern accommodation above one of Ballina's livelier pubs. Rooms in front may get noisy around closing time, but in the back it's quiet. The building has wireless internet access.

Belleek Castle (☎ 22400; www.belleekcastle.com; s/d from €100/150; ☽ Apr-Dec; P) A fabulously over-the-top neo-Jacobean manor, set deep in a 1000-acre woodland outside Ballina. It's a luxuriant romantic getaway, with four-poster beds and loads of historic artefacts. Organic foodies will love the restaurant, Granuailes, which along with the Armada bar is designed to look like the inside of a Spanish galleon.

Eating

Gaughan's (☎ 70096; O' Rahilly St; lunch €3-10; ☽ food served 11am-3pm) It's a dark old pub favoured by locals, but don't shy away. You'll get a good home-cooked lunch here.

Dillon's Bar & Restaurant (☎ 72230; Dillon's Tce; mains €14-25; ☽ food served 3-9pm Mon-Thu, 12.30-9pm Fri-Sun) This restaurant's vine-covered cobbled courtyard makes it everybody's favourite find, especially on a warm evening when the atmosphere is romantic. The menu exploits local produce, and the al fresco seating is a bonus in summer. Turn right at the south end of Pearse St and enter an arch to your left.

Drinking

Pub-crawlers will be kept busy in Ballina, which has some 60 watering holes to tick off. Many have traditional music sessions on Wednesday and Friday evenings.

GETTING IN TOUCH WITH YOUR NAME

Many people left Mayo during the Famine years, establishing family roots elsewhere in the world. If your family name is Barrett, Brennan, Dogherty, Doyle, Foy, Gallagher, Harkin, Henry, Kelly, Lavelle, McNulty or McNicholas, there's a more than strong chance that your people originally hailed from north Mayo. (The Lavelles, interestingly, are believed to be of French origin – some say they arrived on Achill Island around the time of the 1798 Rebellion.) You can get in touch with your roots at the **Mayo North Family Heritage Centre** (☎ 096-31809; Enniscoe, Castlehill, Ballina; ☽ 9.30am-6pm Mon-Fri Apr-Sep; P), beginning with an initial assessment (€75). Attached is a piece-meal **museum** (adult/student museum only €4/2, museum & garden €8/3; ☽ 10am-6pm Mon-Fri, 2-6pm Sat & Sun Apr-Sep) of old farm machinery and domestic implements. The tea room spills into walled gardens from Enniscoe House.

If your family name is Burke, Duffy, Gallagher, Joyce, Kelly, Moran, Murphy, O'Connor, O'Malley or Walsh, your people may have come from south Mayo. You can dig up information at the **South Mayo Family Research Centre** (☎ 094-954 1214; Main St, Ballinrobe).

An Bolg Buí (Yellow Belly; ☎ 22561; Tolan St) This well-worn, all-wood pub by the bridge is a great spot to savour a pint and swap fish tales. On Wednesday traditional musicians have a session here.

Getting There & Away

Bus Éireann runs daily express services from the **bus station** (☎ 71800; Kevin Barry St) to Westport (€10, one hour). Buses also go to Achill Island (€13, two to three hours, two daily), Sligo (€11, 1½ hours, five daily) and Dublin (€16, 3½ hours, six daily).

Trains to Dublin (€30, 3½ hours, three daily) leave from the **train station** (☎ 71818; Station Rd), at the southern extension of Kevin Barry St. Ballina is on a branch of the main Westport–Dublin line, so you'll have to change at Manulla Junction.

AROUND BALLINA
Rosserk Abbey

Dipping its toes into the River Rosserk, a tributary of the Moy, this handsome Franciscan abbey dates from the mid-15th century. There's an eye-catching double piscina (perforated stone basin) in the chancel: look for the exquisite carvings of a round tower and several angels. Rosserk was destroyed by Richard Bingham, the English governor of Connaught, in the 16th century.

Leave Ballina on the R314 for Killala and after 6.5km turn right at the sign and then left at the next crossroads. Continue for 1km, then turn right.

North Mayo Sculpture Trail

This trail of 15 outdoor sculptures essentially follows the R314 from Ballina to Blacksod Point. It was inspired by the discoveries at Céide Fields and was inaugurated in 1993 to mark 5000 years of Mayo history. Leading artists from eight different countries were commissioned to create sculptures reflecting the beauty and wilderness of the northern Mayo countryside.

The North Mayo Sculpture Trail (Tír Sáile) is a 60-page book detailing each sculpture. It's available from tourist offices and bookshops. The trail is about 90km and can be walked.

CROSSMOLINA & AROUND
☎ 096 / pop 940

It's a quiet country town and near the Lough Conn, but Crossmolina (Crois Mhaoiliona)

offers little in the way of services, which is perhaps why most visitors bypass it. If you're in a thoughtful frame of mind (as you may well be if you're whiling away your time at the end of a fishing pole) then perhaps this is your spot.

There's a Bank of Ireland with an ATM opposite Hiney's pub. For fishing gear you'll need to go to Ballina (p459). Crossmolina is 13km west of Ballina.

Sights & Activities

It's a rough 800m scramble over farmland to reach the ruined **Errew Abbey**, but you'll be rewarded by the picturesque location cupped on three sides by mirror-like Lough Conn. The disintegrating remains include a 13th-century house for Augustinian monks built on the site of a 7th-century church.

Take the Castlebar road south, and 1km past the heritage centre turn left at the sign and keep going for 5km. The entrance is by a farm.

To stretch your legs and get your heart pounding a little you can always take the scenic two-hour trek up to the top of **Mt Nephin** (806m).

Sleeping & Eating

Enniscoe House (☎ 31112; www.enniscoe.com; Castlehill; d €180-224, 2br apt per week €450-600; dinner €48; ☺ Apr-Oct; ℗) Life in a stately country manor, surrounded by hills and forests – it doesn't get much better. Built in 1750, Enniscoe House is truly impressive, and the interior has been kept up nobly. You can stay in the big house, or settle into a courtyard apartment (also historic) on a weekly basis. Its Victorian walled garden is only a tiny portion of the sprawling estate, which includes wild woodland walks and large grassy expanses.

Mount Falcon Country House Hotel (☎ 74472; www.mountfalcon.com; Foxford Rd; d €180-280; ℗ ⚟) If Enniscoe House can be topped, Mount Falcon just may pull it off. Hidden within 100 acres of woods between Lough Conn and the River Moy, the mansion has exquisite guest rooms, a spa and a fine restaurant. It has its own exclusive fishery along the river.

Healy's Restaurant and Country House Hotel (☎ 56443; www.healyspontoon.com; Pontoon, Foxford; s/d from €65/90; mains €10-27; ℗) Staring at the lake and backed by forest and hills, Healy's has the look of a relaxed country holiday spot. It's in an 1840s lodge, very sporting in look, and features modestly updated rooms and two elegant dining rooms that squarely emphasise surf and turf classics. If not staying here or nearby, the wood tables out front are a tempting pit stop for a cool drink.

Dolphin Hotel (☎ 31270; www.thedolphin.ie; Crossmolina; s/d €60/90; dishes €8-17; ⏰ food 8am-10pm) Looking like a very proud and trim country inn, the Dolphin offers comfortable B&B, a good restaurant, and one of the liveliest live music venues all in one building. The menu ranges from a carvery lunch to carefully prepared Irish dishes with local produce. National bands perform in the club several nights weekly.

Getting There & Away

There are regular **Bus Éireann** (☎ 71800) buses to Ballina and Castlebar. The bus stop is outside Hiney's on Main St.

CASTLEBAR & AROUND

☎ 094 / pop 10,290

Castlebar (Caisleán an Bharraigh's) has an up-and-coming feel to it, with construction sites at every turn and more energy on its streets than you'll find in just about any other Mayo town. Apart from a handful of hotels and eateries, most of what will interest a tourist here is actually outside the town, which means that, despite the town's hustle and bustle, the best reason to stop is if you're on your way somewhere else nearby.

Castlebar's place in Irish history was cemented in 1798, when General Humbert's outnumbered army of French revolutionary soldiers and Irish peasants pulled off an astonishing victory here. The ignominious cavalry retreat of the British became known as the Castlebar Races.

Orientation & Information

The main thoroughfare changes its name from Ellison St to Main St to Thomas St as you head north. The Mall is to the east.

Allied Irish Bank (Main St) ATM and bureau de change.

Chat'rnet (☎ 903 8474; New Antrim St; per hr €3.60; ⏰ 10.30am-10.30pm) Internet café opposite the tourist office.

Tourist office (☎ 902 1207; Linenhall St; ⏰ 9.30am-1pm & 2-5.30pm May-Sep) West off the northern end of Main St.

Sights

NATIONAL MUSEUM OF COUNTRY LIFE

This fine **museum** (☎ 903 1755; www.museum.ie; Turlough Park, Turlough; admission free; ⏰ 10am-5pm Tue-Sat, 2-5pm Sun; Ⓟ Ⓖ) is not a nostalgic remembrance of a worry-free past, of course, but nor is it a gloomy Paddy-in-the-dung-heap equivalent of *Angela's Ashes*. What we have are four floors of very smartly presented, level-headed displays. A branch of the National Museum of Ireland (the other three are all in Dublin), this museum sets out to engender an enduring respect for the cultural richness of a way of life that hasn't yet faded from memory. Good timing! Many of the traditions and skills celebrated here (from wickerwork to boatbuilding), while not entirely obsolete, are certainly on their way out. If there is a message, or a point of view, it's one of admiration for the resourcefulness, ingenuity and self-sufficiency of the Irish people. The exhibits concentrate on the period from 1850 to 1950.

The extensive lakeside grounds invite picnics, and part of Turlough's 19th century manor is open for snooping. Interesting demonstrations and workshops are organised for Wednesdays and Sundays – see the website for schedules.

The museum is signposted off the N5, 5km northeast of Castlebar.

TURLOUGH ROUND TOWER

This impenetrable 9th-century tower calls to mind the fairy tale *Rapunzel* with its single lofty window. It stands on a hilltop by a ruined 18th-century church, a short distance northeast of the National Museum of Country Life.

MICHAEL DAVITT MEMORIAL MUSEUM

Housed in a pre-penal church where the man himself was christened (and next to the Straid Abbey, in which he was buried) is this small but passionate **museum** (☎ 903 1022; www.museumsofmayo.com; Straide; adult/child €4/2; ⏰ 10am-6pm; Ⓟ). The man we're talking about, of course, is Michael Davitt (1846–1906), a Fenian and zealous founding member of the Irish National Land League. Davitt's family was brutally evicted from his childhood home near here.

Take the N5 east and turn left onto the N58 to Straide (Strade on some maps). It's 16km from Castlebar.

BALLINTUBBER ABBEY

The history of this delightful little **abbey** (☎ 903 0934; www.ballintubberabbey.ie; Ballintubber; admission free; ⏰ 9am-midnight; Ⓟ) reads like a collection of far-fetched folk tales. Commonly referred to as 'the abbey that refused to die', this is the only church in Ireland founded by an Irish king that is still in use. It was set up in 1216 next to the site of an earlier church founded by St Patrick after he came down from Croagh Patrick.

The abbey was burned by Normans, seized by James I and suppressed by Henry VIII. The nave roof was only restored in 1965 after the original was burned down by Cromwell's soldiers in 1653. Mass was outlawed and priests hunted down. Yet worship in the roofless remains continued against all the odds.

Take the N84 south towards Galway and after about 13km turn left at the Campus service station; the abbey is 2km along.

Sleeping & Eating

Imperial Hotel (☎ 902 1961; www.imperialhotelcastlebar .com; the Mall; s/d Sun-Thu €55/90, Fri & Sat €65/110) Established in 1795, and presiding over the Mall, Castlebar's oldest hotel still has a good dose of old-world character, reflected in its chequered floors and cosy old bar. Its spacious rooms, however, have been revamped to a wholly modern standard.

Welcome Inn Hotel (☎ 22288; cb.welcome@mayo -ireland.ie; s/d €60/120; **P**) Castlebar's second-largest hostelry, this kitschy mock-Tudor establishment is almost as expensive as the Imperial but not nearly as nice. But it's right in the heart of town, and rooms are clean and upbeat.

Café Rua (☎ 902 3376; New Antrim St; dishes €3-12; 9.30am-6pm Mon-Sat) This bright little coffee shop wins loyal support for its menu of filling and healthy Irish dishes and pastries. On your way in you might catch a whiff of a house specialty: champ, comprising of mashed potatoes and onions. It does a mean breakfast, and good coffee, too.

Getting There & Around

Bus Éireann (☎ 096-71800) travels to Westport (€4, 20 minutes, 10 daily), Dublin (€16, 4½ hours, one daily) and Sligo (€13, 1½ hours, three daily). Services on Sunday are less frequent. Buses stop on Market St.

McNulty's Coaches (☎ 902 9948; www.mcnulty coaches.com) runs daily buses to and from Belmullet. The 1½-hour trip costs €9/13 one way/return. The company also runs several buses to Galway on Friday and Sunday. Call for details.

The Westport–Dublin train stops at Castlebar (€30, 3½ hours) three times daily. The station is just out of town on the N84 towards Ballinrobe.

KNOCK
☎ 094 / pop 595
Perhaps you've heard of the shrine at Knock (Cnoc Mhuire), Ireland's answer to Lourdes and Fatima. It's a serious mecca for the faithful, particularly those in need of a miracle, and for that reason the elderly and infirm flock to Knock in droves.

Knock was nothing but a rather downtrodden rural village until 1879, when a divine apparition propelled this little settlement to become one of the world's most sacred Catholic shrines. The influx of earnest pilgrims naturally means big business for some (well, *most*) of the vendors here, adding a discordant note of cynicism to the place.

The Knock Marian Shrine consists of several churches and shrines in the town centre. Nearby are clustered shops, restaurants and the **tourist office** (☎ 938 8193; 10am-6pm May-Sep). The Bank of Ireland has an ATM.

Sights
CHURCH OF THE APPARITION
The story goes thus: in drenching rain during the evening of 21 August 1879, two young Knock women were startled by a vision of Mary, Joseph and St John the Evangelist freeze-framed in dazzling white light against the southern gable of the parish church. They were soon joined by 13 more villagers, and together they all gazed at the heavenly apparition for hours as the daylight faded.

A Church investigation quickly confirmed it as a bona fide miracle, and a sudden rush of other Vatican-approved miracles followed as the sick and disabled claimed amazing recoveries upon visiting the spot. Today, dutiful worshippers are always found praying at the modern chapel enclosing the scene of the apparition. Seemingly floating above the altar are ethereal sculptures of the apparition, carved from snow-white marble. Near the church is the enormous spiky-topped **Basilica of Our Lady, Queen of Ireland**.

KNOCK FOLK MUSEUM
A short stroll from the basilica, this petite **museum** (☎ 938 8100; adult/child/concession €4/3.50; 10am-6pm May-Oct, noon-4pm Nov-Apr) does its

best to encapsulate the Knock phenomenon. It follows the story from the first witnesses, through the miraculous cures, the repeated Church investigations and finally to the visit of Pope John Paul II on the event's centenary. One striking photograph shows rows of crutches left behind by miraculously cured pilgrims.

Sleeping

Pilgrims periodically swamp Knock, so there is no shortage of digs.

Belmont Hotel (☎ 938 8122; www.belmonthotel.ie; s/d €55/90; P 💻) This old hotel is slightly dated but well run, which merely complements its conservative atmosphere. It's about 800m southeast of the shrine.

Knock House Hotel (☎ 938 8088; www.knockhousehotel.ie; Ballyhaunis Rd; s/d from €66/110; P) It's a modern pile of stone and glass, with a few odd angles thrown in, making Knock House the most stylish place to stay in town. It's about 500m east of town.

Getting There & Away

Knock Airport (☎ 936 7222; www.knockairport.com), 15km north by the N17, has daily flights to Dublin (Aer Arann) and London Stansted (Ryan air). In May 2007, flyglobespan began direct flights to New York's JFK airport (three times weekly) and Boston (twice weekly). A €10 development fee is payable on departure.

Bus Éireann service 21 connects Knock's town centre with Westport (€9, one hour), Castlebar (€7, 45 minutes) and Dublin (€16, four hours) three times daily (and once Sunday).

Getting Around

A shuttle bus service is run by **Bus Éireann** (☎ 096-71800) to and from Knock airport and Charlestown (€4, 20 minutes), where connections can be made.

COUNTY SLIGO

Tiny County Sligo (Sligeach) packs as much poetry, myth and folklore into its lush landscape as any shamrock lover could ever hope for. This was the place that most inspired the Nobel laureate, poet and dramatist William Butler Yeats (1865–1939), who helped cement Sligo's pastoral reputation with such verses as 'The Lake Isle of Inisfree', in which he mused about the simple country life. That lake isle really exists, and the county's countryside retains much of its verdant splendour. Sligo also has a wealth of impressive prehistoric sites, and a pair of lovely flat-topped mountains, Knocknarea and Benbulben, that seem to loom over the entire county. But Sligo is not a complacent backwater. Sligo town hops with a worldly-wise confidence, and the beautiful coast is home to an imported passion for surfing.

SLIGO TOWN

☎ 071 / pop 18,480

Sligo town is no 'tidy town' slumbering in dreams of past glories. To be sure, it's nicely arranged around the River Garavogue, with stone bridges, historic buildings, pedestrian streets and inviting shop fronts. But, displaying a modern vitality, Sligo dares to mix it up, thrusting glass towers upon prominent corners. Its citizens love to dine out in an impressive array of international eateries. The town seems quite comfortable with itself, in no hurry to shed its vaunted cultural traditions and seeing no need to be overly protective of them, either. The arts and nightlife here simmer with a healthy mix of excellent céilidh sessions and genre bending contemporary paintings. On warm days, it can seem like all the town is seated at restaurant tables along the quay. For so compact a burgh, there's an awful lot going on in Sligo.

Information

Bank of Ireland (Stephen St) ATM and bureau de change.

Cafe Online (☎ 914 4892; 1 Calry Crt, Stephen St; per hr €3.50; 🕑 10am-11pm Mon-Sat, noon-11pm Sun) It's possible to plug your laptop into the broadband connection here.

Keohane's Bookshop (☎ 914 2597; Castle St) Great Irish interest section, and finely chosen fiction recommendations.

North-West Regional Tourism office (☎ 916 1201; www.irelandnorthwest.ie; Temple St; 🕑 9am-6pm Mon-Fri, 10am-6pm Sat & Sun Jun-Sep, 9am-5pm Mon-Fri Oct-May) South of the centre, especially useful if you need help finding accommodation.

Post office (Wine St)

Wash & Dry Laundrette (☎ 914 1777; Connolly St; from €8; 🕑 9am-6pm Mon-Sat)

Sights

SLIGO COUNTY MUSEUM

The main appeal of this **museum** (☎ 914 1623; Stephen St; admission free; 🕑 10.30am-12.30pm &

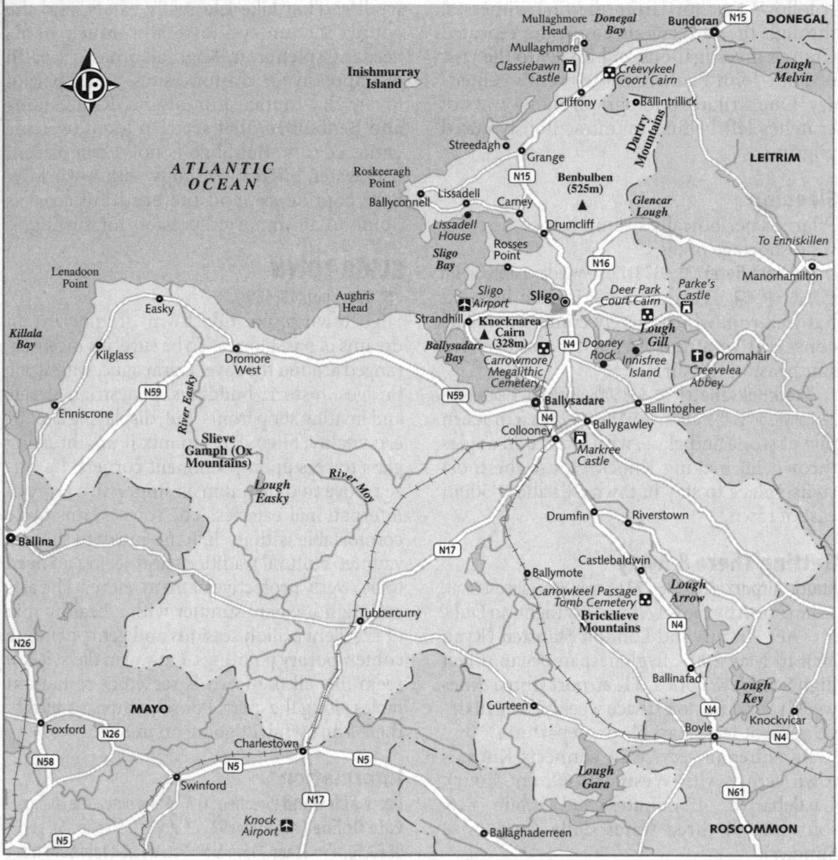

COUNTY SLIGO

2.30-4.30pm Mon-Sat Jun-Sep, 2-5pm Tue-Sat Apr, May & Oct) is the Yeats room. There are photographs, letters and newspaper cuttings connected with the poet WB Yeats, and drawings by Jack B Yeats, his brother. The room across the hall contains a prison apron dress worn by Countess Constance Markievicz after the 1916 Rising. The upstairs galleries exhibit contemporary art, mostly regional.

MODEL ARTS & NILAND GALLERY

In contrast to its imposing 19th-century façade, the interior of Sligo's excellent **gallery** (☎ 914 1405; www.modelart.ie; the Mall; admission free; ⏰ 10am-5.30pm Tue-Sat, 11am-4pm Sun; ♿) is pleasantly airy and contemporary. The wide-ranging collection includes works by Charles Lamb and Sean Keating as well as Jack B Yeats, one of Ireland's most important modern artists (who said he never painted anything without putting a thought of Sligo into it). The gallery also hosts a rich schedule of travelling exhibitions, readings, film and music events. There's also a gourmet café, the Atrium (p467).

SLIGO ABBEY

The handsome husk that is Sligo's **abbey** (☎ 914 6406; Abbey St; adult/child €2/1.25; ⏰ 10am-6pm mid-Mar–Oct, 9.30am-4.30pm Fri-Sun Nov–mid-Mar) has enjoyed the best and worst of luck. It was first built by the town's founder, Maurice FitzGerald, around 1252 for the Dominicans, but it burned down in the 15th century and was rebuilt. Friends in high places then saved the abbey from the worst ravages of the Elizabethan era, and rescued the only sculpted altar to survive the Reformation. However, the abbey's fortunes reversed when it was put to the torch in 1641, and subsequently raided for stone. The doorways reach only a few feet high at the abbey's rear, and the ground around it was swollen by the mass graves from years of famine and war.

YEATS BUILDING
On the corner of Lower Knox and O'Connell Sts, near Hyde Bridge, the Yeats Building houses the hit-and-miss **Sligo Art Gallery** (☎ 914 5847; www.sligogallery.com; Lower Knox St; admission free; ☙ 10am-5pm Mon-Sat), with travelling exhibitions. There's a pleasant café with windows overlooking the busy street corner.

Festivals
Sligo kicks up its heels every now and then, with a couple of standout festivals.

Sligo Live (www.sligolive.ie) Live music festival features roots music and popular offshoots at the Sligo Race Course; in the first week of June.

Yeats Festival (www.yeats-sligo.com) Irish poetry, music and culture is celebrated with three weeks of performances and events around town. Held late July–mid-August.

Sleeping
BUDGET
Eden Hill Holiday Hostel (☎ 914 3204; edenhill@eircom .net; Pearse Rd; camp sites per person €9, dm €11-15, d €36-40; **P**) Sharing honours as best hostel in Sligo, this converted Victorian home, originally owned by members of the Yeats family, has a cheery atmosphere, spotless dorms and an enormous communal kitchen. It's 1.5km from the station, but pick up may be arranged by phoning ahead to the hostel.

White House Hostel (☎ 914 5160; fax 914 4456; Markievicz Rd; dm €14; ☙ Mar-Oct; **P**) To stay closer to the action and mingle with more fellow hostellers, you could try this laid-back central spot. It looks a little rundown from the outside, but its dorm rooms are perfectly acceptable.

Harbour House (☎ 917 1547; www.harbourhouse hostel.com; Finisklin Rd; dm €18-25, s/d €28/44; **P**) If you prefer mod-cons to quirkiness, then you'll be more than happy with this excellent, well-equipped IHH hostel, less than 1km northwest of the centre. It offers a

little budget luxury, in the form of colourful en-suite rooms with TV and firm beds.

MIDRANGE
B&Bs line Pearse Rd.

our pick **Pearse Lodge** (☎ 916 1090; pearselodge@ eircom.net; Pearse Rd; s €42-45, d €72; **P**) A smart choice. Its owners not only attend to details in upkeep and service, but are also up on what's happening in town. Rooms are impeccably clean and tastefully furnished, and the breakfast is superb, with a menu including smoked salmon, pancakes and vegetarian options. Good family choice.

McGettigan's (☎ 916 2857; www.bandbsligo.ie; Connolly St; standard/en suite s €45/58, d €75/85; **P**) This unfussy lodging's big selling point is its central location, near the centre of the action. It's not a private home, but does include a nice breakfast menu that offers grilled plaice (flatfish).

St Ann's (☎ 914 3188; Pearse Rd; d €70; **P** 🕳) With an al-fresco swimming pool (unheated), neatly snipped topiary and frilly feminine rooms, this well maintained B&B comes highly recommended.

Inisfree House (☎ 256 2532; High St; d €110; **P**) Projecting a nonchalant air, this hotel doesn't try to charm its guests, but it does win them over with its central location and neat rooms. The downstairs pub is cool, and handy for a last round.

TOP END
Sligo Southern Hotel (☎ 916 2101; www.sligosouthern hotel.com; Strandhill Rd; s/d €95/150; **P** 🕳 🖥 ♿) The courtly gardens of this elegant hotel border the bus and train stations. Its boldly coloured interior manages to combine superb facilities (including swimming pool, plasma TV and broadband internet access) with comfortable charm.

The Glass House (☎ 919 4300; www.theglasshosue.ie; Swan Point; s/d €130/218; **P**) Central Sligo's boldest architectural statement is this svelte study in glass and geometry. It overlooks the river, so you can't miss it. Guest rooms are genuinely stylish and afford excellent views, and the hotel has a great bar and restaurant. You're at the cutting edge and smack in the middle of things here.

Eating
Coach Lane (☎ 916 2417; www.coachlane.com; 1-2 Lord Edward St; mains €14-28; ☙ 5.30-11pm) Consistently rated among Sligo's best dining options,

SLIGO TOWN

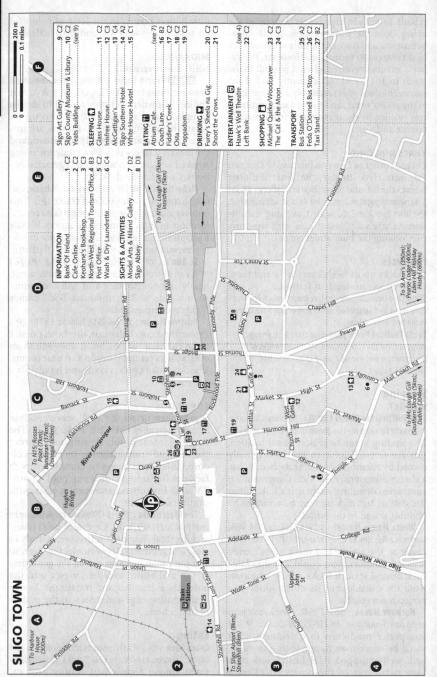

INFORMATION
Bank Of Ireland............................	1 C2
Cafe Online.................................	2 C2
Keohane's Bookshop....................	3 C3
North-West Regional Tourism Office.	4 B3
Post Office..................................	5 C4
Wash & Dry Laundrette................	6 C4

SIGHTS & ACTIVITIES
Model Arts & Niland Gallery.........	7 D2
Sligo Abbey................................	8 D3

Sligo Art Gallery..........................	9 C2
Sligo County Museum & Library.....	10 C2
Yeats Building.............................	(see 9)

SLEEPING
Glass House................................	11 C2
Innisfree House...........................	12 C2
McCettigan's..............................	13 C4
Sligo Southern Hotel...................	14 A2
White House Hostel.....................	15 C1

EATING
Atrium Cafe................................	(see 7)
Coach Lane................................	16 B2
Fiddler's Creek............................	17 C2
Osta..	18 C2
Poppadom..................................	19 C3

DRINKING
Furey's Sheela na Gig..................	20 C2
Shoot the Crows.........................	21 C3

ENTERTAINMENT
Hawk's Well Theatre....................	(see 4)
Left Bank....................................	22 C2

SHOPPING
Michael Quirke/Woodcarver..........	23 C2
The Cat & the Moon....................	24 C3

TRANSPORT
Bus Station.................................	25 A2
Feda O'Donnell Bus Stop.............	26 C2
Taxi Stand.................................	27 B2

Coach Lane does top-notch Irish and international cuisine. The restaurant shares its kitchen with Donaghy's Pub, but make sure you're seated in the dining room, where the atmosphere is superior. The seafood-slanted menu features juicy Lissadell clams and mussels, and there are some intriguing wild-card specials, such as roast Tipperary ostrich.

Atrium Cafe (☎ 914 1405; Model Arts & Niland Gallery; sandwiches & snacks €6-10; ☒ 10am-4pm Tue-Sat, 11am-3pm Sun) To enjoy a healthy bite while hobnobbing with the Sligo art set, head to this gourmet gallery café. It's understandably popular for Sunday brunch. Also good for coffee and dessert.

Fiddler's Creek (☎ 914 1866; www.fiddlerscreek.ie; Rockwood Pde; mains €9-23; ☒ food served noon-3pm & 5.30-10pm) This riverside pub has an excellent menu that isn't limited to the usual meat and potato standards. The bar atmosphere is lively, despite the dark medieval stonework. The adjacent dining room, for contrast, is lit by windows overlooking the quay.

Poppadom (☎ 914 7171; www.poppadom.ie; 34 O'Connell St; mains €10-20; ☒ 5-11.30pm) Excellent Indian cuisine makes it worth the trek upstairs to Poppadom. The atmosphere is a real surprise: minimalist elegance rather than the usual exotica. Service is smooth and professional. If you're staying in a hostel, the take-away menu's prices are greatly reduced (€6 to €13).

Osta (Hyde Bridge, Left Bank; light meals €5-10; ☒ 8am-9pm) Osta is a café and a wine bar, and it's well suited to both callings. It's intimate and well lit, and has a prime location for gazing at the river as it charges beneath Hyde Bridge. Quay tables make this a choice spot on warm days.

Drinking

Sligo enjoys some of the best night-time fun in Ireland's northwest, with impromptu sessions striking up at every opportunity, although the town also has a reputation for late-night wildness.

Shoot the Crows (☎ 916 2554; www.shootthecrows .ie; Castle St) This dark and somewhat dishevelled old pub oozes bohemian atmosphere. Early evening draws a good-natured crowd of regulars, and even when the place is packed to the gills it generally has an easy going vibe. Sing-alongs and sessions happen frequently here. You'll know you've found it when you spot the nude women painted on the façade.

Furey's Sheela na Gig (☎ 914 3825; Bridge St) Named after a Gaelic fertility symbol of a naked woman, this old-style bar is Irish traditional band Dervish's local watering hole, and has superb traditional music most nights.

Entertainment

Left Bank (☎ 914 0100; 15 Stephen St) With its long bar and casual wide-open space, Left Bank is among Sligo's best venues for live music performances. The place often books bands on the cool, modern end of the jazz spectrum, and even when there's no band the place generates a happening, upbeat vibe.

Hawk's Well Theatre (☎ 61526; www.hawkswell.com; Temple St) This well-regarded theatre presents a varied programme of concerts, dance and drama.

Shopping

The Cat & the Moon (☎ 914 3686; www.thecatandthe moon.com; 4 Castle St; ☒ 9am-6pm) Quality Irish crafts and arts are sold here – no cheesy shamrock stuff. Designer jewellery is a specialty, but you'll also find fine woollen goods, and objects to pretty up the home.

Getting There & Away

AIR

From **Sligo Airport** (☎ 916 8280; www.sligoairport .com; Strandhill Rd) there are direct Aer Arann flights to Dublin twice daily (from €25; 40 minutes).

BUS

Bus Éireann (☎ 916 0066) leaves from the terminal below the train station, on Lord Edward St. Destinations include Ballina (€11, 1½ hours, five daily), Westport (€15, two hours, twice daily) and Dublin (€16, four hours, four daily). Services are less frequent on Sunday.

Feda O'Donnell (☎ 074-954 8114; www.fedaodonnell .com) operates a service between Crolly (County Donegal) and Galway via Donegal town and Sligo twice daily (four times Friday). The buses leave by Matt Lyon's shop on the corner of Wine and Quay Sts.

TRAIN

Trains leave the **station** (☎ 916 9888) for Dublin (€26, 3½ hours, four or five daily) via Boyle, Carrick-on-Shannon and Mullingar.

Getting Around

Local buses run to Strandhill (€2.70, five to seven Monday to Saturday) and sometimes continue to the airport. A taxi to the airport costs about €15. There's a taxi stand on Quay St. **Feehily's Taxis** (☎ 914 3000) offer a 24-hour service.

AROUND SLIGO TOWN
Rosses Point
☎ 071 / pop 780

Rosses Point (An Ros) is a picturesque seaside resort with a lovely Blue Flag beach, grassy dunes rolling down to the strand, birdlife and Benbulben, Sligo's most recognisable landmark, arching skywards in the distance. It holds special appeal for the golf-minded traveller, as some of the prime real estate here is dominated by lovingly trimmed greens. It's expensive to stay here, unless you're camping. Rosses Point is Sligo town's backyard, so you can pop in for the day or for dinner.

ACTIVITIES

Established in 1894, **County Sligo Golf Course** (☎ 917 7134; www.countysligogolfclub.ie) is one of Ireland's most challenging and renowned links courses, attracting golfers from all over Europe. Its position on the peninsula is simply stunning. Green fees cost from €70 Monday to Thursday, and €85 Friday to Sunday; fees are less in the winter.

SLEEPING & EATING

Greenlands Caravan & Camping Park (☎ 917 7113; noelineha@eircom.net; camp sites per person €11; ⊗ Easter–mid-Sep) Peering over the Atlantic from the point's extreme, with easy access to the beaches, this site manages to feel isolated despite its proximity to local amenities. You'll just need to keep your head down if errant golfers are swinging nearby.

Yeats Country Hotel (☎ 917 7211; www.yeats countryhotel.com; s/d from €90/140; P ⚲) There isn't much of a town centre, so this huge three-star hotel more or less stands in for the heart of Rosses Point. It has a commanding presence, overlooking the beach and the golf course, and attracts golfers and families. Rooms are large and many afford sea views.

Waterfront (☎ 917 7122; mains €13-28; ⊗ 5-9.30pm) One of the drawing cards of Rosses Point is this pub/restaurant, overlooking the estuary and Oyster Island. It has a spirited atmosphere, and naturally the kitchen conjures up excellent seafood. The menu also offers a few worthy vegetarian dishes and children's portions.

Deer Park Court Cairn

A 10-minute walk from the car park through pine-scented forest leads to this enigmatic court tomb (also called Magheraghanrush). Dating from around 3000 BC, the crumbling

---

VOICES: MICHAEL QUIRKE, THE WOODCARVER OF WINE ST

While strolling Sligo's streets, be sure to duck into the shop of Michael Quirke, a woodcarver, raconteur and local character. Mr Quirke's studio, you'll notice, is a converted butcher shop, and among the stumps of beechwood are some of the implements of the butcher's trade, including an electric bone saw. Quirke, himself formerly a butcher, began to use his tools for cutting and carving wood in 1968. He divided his time between his twin callings for 20 years, after which he gave up meat, so to speak.

Much of his art is inspired by Irish mythology, a subject about which he is passionate and knowledgeable. He seems pleased to hold court with the customers and the curious who enter his shop.

'Irish mythology, unlike Greek mythology, is alive and constantly changing,' he says. 'It's not set in stone, and that's why it's interesting.' To demonstrate what he means, as he talks Quirke makes unforced connections between Irish myths, music, history, flora, fauna and contemporary events. He goes on frequent tangents, and often makes a point of debunking misconceptions. For instance: 'You'll hear talk about bunnies in Ireland, but in fact we have hares, which are very different. Bunnies are nervous, skittish animals. That's why they live in holes. On the other hand, the Irish hare has nerves of steel. It does not hide in burrows, and when it runs it does not hesitate. When I walk my dog, if a hare runs by, no more than 20 feet away, my dog will never notice it. It's a grey streak.'

Quirke talks while he carves. When he's done talking to you, he will put down his carving, shake your hand and tell you it's been lovely to chat.

structure is comparable to a crude human form, with a large belly-like central court and several protruding burial chambers positioned as though the head and legs.

Take the N16 east from Sligo and turn onto the R286 for Parke's Castle. Almost immediately, turn left at the Y-junction onto a minor road for Manorhamilton. Continue for 3km to the car park, then follow the trail for 50m before veering right up a small hill.

Knocknarea Cairn

Sligo's ultimate rock pile, 2km northwest of Carrowmore, Knocknarea is deeply mired in myth. The cairn is popularly believed to be the grave of legendary Queen Maeve (Queen Mab in Welsh and English folk tales). The 40,000 tonnes of stone have never been excavated, despite speculation that a tomb on the scale of the one at Newgrange lies buried below.

The enormous stone heap, perched high atop its limestone plateau (328m), seems to be looking over your shoulder everywhere you dare tread in its ancestral backyard. It's a 45-minute trek to the top, from which a spectacular panoramic view pulls in Ben Bulben, Rosses Point and the Atlantic Ocean beyond.

Leave Sligo as though for Carrowmore, then follow signs to Knocknarea. Or from Carrowmore, continue down the road, turn right by a church then follow signs.

Carrowmore Megalithic Cemetery

The largest Stone Age cemetery in Ireland and the second-biggest in Europe, **Carrowmore** (☎ 916 1534; adult/child/concession €2.10/1.10/1.30; ✆ 10am-6pm Easter-Sep; Ⓟ) impresses for its variety as well as its scale. Everywhere you look the gently rolling hills are beaded with stone circles, passage tombs and dolmens – there are about 60, all told.

Attempts to date the site have had both diverse and divisive results. The conventional wisdom is that the site pre-dates Newgrange in County Meath by some 700 years. Over the centuries, many of the stones have been destroyed, and several remaining stones are on private land.

The delicately balanced dolmens were originally covered with stones and earth, so it requires some effort to picture what this 2.5km-wide area might once have looked like. To help (or some would say hinder) the imagination, the Dúchas-operated site has launched a decapitated reconstruction of

one cairn, caged by wire and sliced open by a gaping entrance. An exhibit in the roadside visitor centre gives the full low-down on this fascinating site.

To get there, leave town by Church Hill and continue south for 5km; the route is clearly signposted.

Strandhill

☎ 071 / pop 1000

The great Atlantic rollers that sweep into the long, red-gold beach by Strandhill (An Leathras), 8km west of Sligo off the R292 airport road, have made it a surfing mecca of international renown. Its handy 24-hour **surfcam** (www.strandhillsurfcam.com) brings enthusiasts scurrying whenever the surf's good.

Enquire at **Perfect Day Surf Shop** (☎ 087-202 9399; www.perfectdaysurfing.com; Shore Rd) for gear and lessons. The **Strandhill Surf School** (☎ 916 8483; www.strandhillsurfschool.com; Beach Front) is another helpful resource, especially for beginners or intermediate surfers.

Another of Strandhill's big attractions is the **Celtic Seaweed Baths** (☎ 916 8686; www.celticseaweedbaths.com; Shore Rd; s/tw bath €18/22; ✆ 11am-8pm), which caters to the growing number of people who crave the sensation of skinny dipping in a tub filled with cool seaweed. It's sort of a mermaid fantasy. This is a modern facility that inspires with its high standards of sanitation.

A few kilometres towards Sligo, there is a point from which, at low tide, you can walk to **Coney Island**: its New York namesake was supposedly named by a man from Rosses Point. The island's wishing well is reputed to have been dug by St Patrick (who, if all these tales are to be trusted, led a *very* busy life).

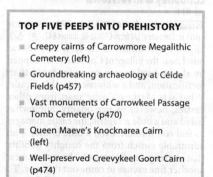

TOP FIVE PEEPS INTO PREHISTORY

- Creepy cairns of Carrowmore Megalithic Cemetery (left)
- Groundbreaking archaeology at Céide Fields (p457)
- Vast monuments of Carrowkeel Passage Tomb Cemetery (p470)
- Queen Maeve's Knocknarea Cairn (left)
- Well-preserved Creevykeel Goort Cairn (p474)

SLEEPING

Strandhill Caravan & Camping Park (☎ 916 8111; sxl@iol.ie; camp sites per person €11; Jun-Sep) Ideally positioned by the long beach, separated only by grassy dunes. This large flat camp site has 100 sites and good facilities.

Strandhill Lodge & Hostel (☎ 9168313; www.strandhill accommodation.com; Shore Rd; dm/d €15/30; **P**) This cheerful and orderly budget haunt, just a few paces from the strand, is the place to mingle with surfer dudes and dudettes. It has 33 beds distributed between dorms of different sizes, a few twin rooms, and a self-catering kitchen.

Dunes Tavern (☎ 916 8131; www.accommodation strandhill.com; Top Rd; dm/d €20/35) Along the main highway, this tavern offers the traditional sleeps-over-a-pub combo. All rooms are ensuite, very clean and have views of the beach or Knocknarea. The pub, with billiards and the odd céilidh session, is a social spot.

DRINKING

Strand Bar (☎ 916 8140; Shore Rd) A terrific pub with snugs, décor worth studying and music on the weekends. It's also a great place to glean the surfing low-down, as it is run by three Irish champions. There's a seafood restaurant above.

Getting There & Away

Bus Éireann (☎ 916 0066) buses run from Sligo to Strandhill and Rosses Point (€2.70, five to seven Monday to Saturday), but there's no public transport to other places of interest in the area. While it's possible to walk to Carrowmore and Knocknarea from town, it's a long day's return trek.

SOUTH OF SLIGO TOWN
Colloney & Riverstown
☎ 071

our pick **Markree Castle** (☎ 071-916 7800; www.markree castle.ie; Colloney; s/d from €100/140; dinner €47; **P** **⑤**), Sligo's oldest inhabited castle, is a three-star hotel near the village of Colloney. It's topped by showy battlements, more for fancy than fortification, and a whimsical Gothic façade. What sets Markree Castle apart from other castles, however, is personality. Somewhat faded and a little eccentric, the castle manages to feel comfortable, even a little homey – an admirable switch from the haughty nobility that castles generally project. The restaurant is another fine excuse to come out this way. To get here, follow the N4 to the roundabout in Colloney. It's not signposted at the roundabout, but if you follow the sign to the Castle Dargon, you'll reach the gate to Markree Castle, about 1km up the road.

The exceedingly charming **Sligo Folk Park** (☎ 916 5001; www.sligofolkpark.com; Millview House, Rivers town; adult/child €5/3; 10am-4.30pm Mon-Sat, 12.30-5pm Sun May-Oct, Dec) revolves around an immaculately restored 19th-century cottage. A number of humble, thatched structures complement this centrepiece, along with scattered farm tools and an exhibit that honours the old country life. In December, the park sets up Santa Town, which just may be pushing things a bit too far.

Every summer the town kicks up its heels for the **James Morrison Traditional Music Festival** (www.morrison.ie; first week of Aug). It's a three-day weekend filled with live music in a dancehall setting. Just as fun are informal seminars on how to sing *sean nós* ballads or perform traditional Irish reels on instruments such as the button accordion and the fiddle.

Coopershill House (☎ 916 5108; www.coopershill .com; Riverstown; s/d €145/230; 5-course dinner from €45; Apr-Oct; **P**), a grey-stone mansion, seems to exist in a world of its own. It's an idyllic Georgian retreat in an estate speckled by wildflowers, alive with birdsong and home to a deer farm. Most of the eight bedrooms have lovely canopy beds.

Carrowkeel Passage Tomb Cemetery

With a God's-eye view of the county from high in the Bricklieve Mountains, there's little wonder why this hill-top site was sacred in prehistoric times. The windswept location is simultaneously uplifting and downright eerie, dotted with around 14 cairns, dolmens and the scattered remnants of other graves. It's possible to squeeze into at least one limestone chamber, although bigger folk are liable to get stuck. The place has been dated to the late Stone Age (3000 to 2000 BC).

West off the N4 road, Carrowkeel is closer to Boyle than Sligo town. If coming from the latter, turn right in Castlebaldwin, then left at the fork. The site is 2km uphill from the gateway. You can take an Athlone bus from Sligo and ask to be dropped off at Castlebaldwin.

Ballymote
☎ 071 / pop 980

This pretty little town merits a visit if only to see the immense ivy-covered shell of **Ballymote Castle**. It was from this early-14th-century castle, fronted by formidable drum towers, that O'Donnell marched to disaster at the Battle of Kinsale in 1601. It's on the Tubbercurry road.

Temple House (☎ 918 3329; www.templehouse.ie; Ballymote; s/d €85/170; dinner €35; ☺ Apr-Nov; P) is a glorious Georgian mansion surrounded by 1000 acres of woods, sheep-studded fields and a crystalline lake. Also on the grounds is a 13th-century Knights Templar castle. The house itself is packed with period décor, dusty natural-history collections and decapitated hunting trophies. It's 4km northwest of Ballymote, close to the N17.

Tubbercurry
☎ 071 / pop 1170

Sleepy Tubbercurry (Tobar an Choire), also spelled Tobercurry, is shaken awake in mid-July, when the week-long **South Sligo Summer School** (☎ 912 0912; www.ssssschool.org) celebrates Irish music and dance with infectious gusto. Try your hand at anything from the tin whistle to an Irish jig, or simply enjoy the eruption of local concerts and recitals.

Easky & Enniscrone
☎ 096

Easky (Eascaigh) is little more than a widening along the coast road, but it gets singled out as one of Europe's best year-round surfing destinations. In summer the little town can be overrun with wetsuited Aussies and Californians. The helpful **Easky Surfing & Information Centre** (Irish Surfing Association; ☎ 49428; www.isasurf.ie) ought to be your first stop if you're planning on hitting the waves anywhere near here.

South at Enniscrone (Innis Crabhann), a stunning Blue Flag beach known as the Hollow stretches its sandy arm for 5km. The town is also famous for its seaweed baths (see boxed text, below).

Atlantic Caravan & Camping Park (☎ 36132; atlanticcaravanpk@eircom.net; Enniscrone; camp sites €10-15, caravans per week €205-420; ☺ Mar-Sep), a sandy two-star camping ground, is a spit from Hollow beach. For the tentless, it has furnished caravans that can sleep four or more.

Getting There & Away
Bus Éireann (☎ 071-916 0066) express service 23 to Sligo from Dublin (€16, 3½ hours) and service 64 between Galway (€13, 2½ hours) and Derry (€18, three hours) stop outside Quigley's in Collooney. On Saturday only, the Sligo–Castlerea bus 460 stops at Collooney (€3, 15 minutes), Ballymote (€5, 30 minutes) and Tubbercurry (€7, 40 minutes). Buses run from Sligo to Collooney, Monday to Saturday. From Easky, buses run four times daily (once on Sunday) to Sligo (€8, 50 minutes) and Ballina (€5, 30 minutes). From Enniscrone, buses also run four times daily (once on Sunday) to Sligo (€9, 65 minutes) and Ballina (€2.50, 15 minutes).

The Sligo train stops at Collooney and Ballymote en route to Dublin (both €24, four to six five times daily). Call **Sligo station** (☎ 071-916 9888) for times.

LOUGH GILL

The mirror-like 'Lake of Brightness', Lough Gill is home to as many legends as fish; one that can be tested easily is the story that

---

MERMAID DREAMS

Sinking into a sea-water bath and slathering yourself with seaweed may sound like madness, but in Ireland it's considered to be good for the health. Seaweed baths have been part of Irish homeopathy for centuries and are considered a cure for rheumatism and arthritis, even hangovers. Although some claims are unproven, one thing's for sure – a single session wallowing in the soupy waters will leave your skin feeling baby-soft. Seaweed's silky oils contain a massive concentration of iodine, a key presence in most moisturising creams.

Several places offer seaweed baths in Sligo, but two spots stand out. **Kilcullen's Seaweed Baths** (☎ 36238; www.kilcullenseaweedbaths.com; Enniscrone; s/tw bath €17/27.50, 30min massage €25; ☺ 10am-9pm May-Oct, noon-8pm Mon-Fri, 10am-8pm Sat & Sun Nov-Apr) is the most traditional. Set within a grand Edwardian structure, Kilcullen's has loads of character, with original gigantean porcelain baths and stout brass taps still operating.

For a more modern setting, **Celtic Seaweed Baths** (☎ 916 8686; www.celticseaweedbaths.com; Shore Rd, Strandhill; s/tw bath €18/22; ☺ 11am-8pm) inspires confidence with its high standards of sanitation.

a silver bell from the abbey in Sligo was thrown into the lough and only those free from sin can hear it pealing. We didn't hear it, but perhaps you will? Yeah, right.

The lake, southeast of Sligo, and other attractions are all within a day trip of anywhere in the county. A return trip of 48km takes in most of the lough and Parke's Castle, which, though in County Leitrim, is included here.

Dooney Rock

This huge limestone knoll bulges awkwardly upward by the lough's southern shore. Yeats immortalises it in *The Fiddler of Dooney*. There's a good lake view from the top, and tranquil woodland walks below its fissured flanks.

Leave Sligo south on the N4, but turn left at the sign to Lough Gill. Another left at the T-junction brings you onto the R287 towards Dooney car park.

Innisfree Island

This pint-sized island (Inis Fraoigh) lies tantalisingly close to the lough's southeastern shore. Its air of tranquillity so moved Yeats that he famously wrote *The Lake Isle of Innisfree:*

I will arise and go now, and go to Innisfree,
And a small cabin build there, of clay and wattles made;
Nine bean rows will I have there, a hive for the honey bee,
And live alone in the bee-loud glade.

Continue east from Dooney Rock and turn left at the crossroads. After 3km turn left again for another 3km. A small road leads down to the lake.

Creevelea Abbey (County Leitrim)

A short riverside walk from Dromahair village leads to the ruinous remains of this unfortunate Franciscan friary. A monument to bad timing, the abbey was founded just a few decades before the orders were suppressed in 1539. Yet despite being gutted by fire on several occasions, and desecrated by Richard Bingham and later Cromwell, the hardy monks kept coming back. The cloister has some curious carvings of St Francis, one displaying stigmata and another depicting the saint preaching to birds.

From Innisfree, return to the R287 and follow signs to Dromahair and the abbey.

Parke's Castle (County Leitrim)

The tranquil surrounds of **Parke's Castle** (☎ 071-916 4149; Fivemile Bourne; adult/child €2.75/1.25; ☼ 10am-6pm mid-Mar–Oct; ℗), with swans drifting by on Lough Gill and neat grass cloaking the old moat, belies the fact that its early Plantation architecture was created out of an unwelcome English landlord's insecurity and fear.

The thoroughly restored, three-storey castle forms part of one of the five sides of the bawn, which also has three rounded turrets at its corners. Join one of the entertaining guided tours after viewing the 20-minute video.

From Creevelea Abbey, continue east along the R287, turn left towards Dromahair and continue northwards. To return to Sligo from Parke's Castle turn west onto the R286.

Rose of Innisfree

The **Rose of Innisfree** (☎ 071-916 4266; www.roseofinnisfree.com; adult/child €12/6) offers live recitals of Yeats' poetry accompanying music during 1½-hour cruises on Lough Gill that run from Parke's Castle at 11am, 12.30pm, 1.30pm, 3.30pm and 4.30pm Easter to October. The company runs a bus from Sligo to the castle. Call for departure times and location.

Getting There & Away

CAR & BICYCLE

Leave Sligo east via the Mall past the hospital, and turn right off the N16 onto the R286, which leads to the northern shore of Lough Gill. The southern route is less interesting until you reach Dooney Rock.

NORTH OF SLIGO TOWN

Drumcliff & Benbulben

Visible all along Sligo's northern coast, and one of the most recognisable hills in Ireland, is the limestone plateau of Benbulben (525m). Its high plateau is uncommonly flat for Ireland, and its near-vertical sides are scored by earthen ribs that make the mountain appear to be straining against unseen forces pulling it down.

Benbulben's extraordinary beauty was not lost on WB Yeats. Before the poet died in Menton, France, in 1939, he had requested: 'If I die here, bury me up there on the mountain, and then after a year or so, dig me up and bring me privately to Sligo'. His wishes weren't honoured until 1948, when his body was interred in the churchyard at Drumcliff, where his great-grandfather had been rector.

EXTREME COPYRIGHT

We might take plagiarism seriously these days, but we ain't got nothing on the early Irish church. What might incur a hefty fine and slap on the wrist in the modern day cost the lives of 3000 men in battle in the year AD 561. The aptly named 'Battle of the Book' took place in Cooldrumman, near Drumcliff, after St Colmcille (or Columba) provoked rage by copying rare religious manuscripts. The matter initially went to the local king to settle, who famously declared 'to every cow its calf, to every book its copy', siding against St Colmcille. But the matter persisted, and the battle commenced. It's said that the ensuing loss of life drove St Colmcille to devote himself to saving as many souls as had been lost in the bloody battle. Thus he founded the Drumcliff monastery and set about spreading Christianity far and wide.

Yeats' grave is next to the Protestant church's doorway, and his youthful bride Georgie Hyde-Lee is buried alongside. Almost three decades her senior, Yeats was 52 when they married. The poet's epitaph is from his poem *Under Ben Bulben:*

Cast a cold eye
On life, on death.
Horseman, pass by!

Visiting the grave is somewhat disturbed by traffic noise along the N15 that no doubt has Yeats rolling over.

In the 6th century, St Colmcille chose the same location for a monastery. You can still see the stumpy remains of the **round tower**, which was struck by lightning in 1936, on the main road nearby. Also in the churchyard is an extraordinary 11th-century **high cross**, etched with intricate biblical scenes.

In summer, the church shows a 15-minute audiovisual on Yeats, St Colmcille and Drumcliff. There's also a little tea shop in which to browse at books, pick up local ceramics and peruse novelty shamrock badges.

SLEEPING & EATING

Benbulben Farm (☎ 071-916 3211; hennigan@eircom.net; Barnaribbon, Drumcliff; s/d €45/66; ✆ Mar-Oct; **P**) If you want to slumber in the heart of Yeats Country, you can't do much better than this isolated farmhouse B&B, at the base of Benbulben. It's 2km north of Drumcliff.

Yeats Tavern (☎ 071-916 3117; N15, Drumcliff; mains €11-24; ✆ noon-9.30pm; **P**) This vast and popular pub/restaurant is the top road stop in northern Sligo. You'll get a quality pint of Guinness or Irish coffee, but most come for the food. The menu covers all the local surf and turf bases, and a few pasta and vegetarian selections. It's about 300m north from Yeats' grave.

Glencar Lough

As well as **fishing**, a feature of this lake is the beautiful **waterfall**, signposted from all directions. Yeats refers to this picturesque spot in *The Stolen Child*. The surrounding countryside is best enjoyed by walking east and taking the steep trail north to the valley.

From Drumcliff it's less than 5km to the lake, and there's a **Bus Éireann** (☎ 071-60066) service from Sligo. Call for details.

Lissadell House

The building is nearly as foreboding as a prison, but don't be put off by the grim, exterior of **Lissadell House** (☎ 087-629 6928; www.lissadell house.com; Lissadell; adult/child €6/3; ✆ 11am-6pm Mar-Oct; **P**) or you'll miss out on a fascinating peek into the life of one of Ireland's most colourful families.

The house was built by Sir Robert Gore-Booth back in 1830, and it reflects a taste for Georgian architecture that must have appeared stodgy even then. The interior has all the pomp missing from the bunker-like exterior. However, the family itself is remembered more for its activism than for its affluence.

Sir Robert took to calling himself 'Count Markiewicz', an affectation that passed onto his famous granddaughter Constance Gore-Booth (1868–1927). She was a committed activist for Irish independence, and earned a death sentence (later commuted) for her part in the Easter Rising. In 1918 she became the first woman elected to the British House of Commons but – like most Irish rebels – refused to take her seat.

Her sister Eva was just as fiery a character, an ardent suffragette and poet. WB Yeats immortalised his close friendship with the Markievicz women in the verse *In Memory of Eva Gore-Booth and Con Markievicz.*

The 45-minute guided tour is filled with stories of the family's adventures, quirks and peccadillos. The murals of domestic servants standing alongside family members in the dining hall are just one illustration of how they liked to thumb their noses at convention.

To get there, follow the N15 north from Sligo and turn west at Drumcliff, just past Yeats Tavern.

Streedagh

From the village of Grange, signs point towards Streedagh Beach, a grand crescent of sand that saw some 1100 sailors perish when three ships from the Spanish Armada were wrecked nearby. Swimming is dangerous, but the beach is ideal for horse riding. **Island View Riding Stables** (☎ 916 6156; www.islandviewriding stables.com; Grange; adult/child per hr €20/15) offers a variety of riding opportunities, including equestrian holiday packages.

Mullaghmore

The delightful **beach** at Mullaghmore (An Mullach Mór) is a sweeping arc of dark-golden sand and shallow waters, wide and safe. Mind you, it wasn't so safe for poor old Lord Mountbatten. It was in this bay that the IRA rigged his boat with explosives and assassinated him in 1979.

The road loops around Mullaghmore Head, where wide shafts of rock slice into the Atlantic surf. It also passes the rather smug-looking **Classiebawn Castle** (closed to the public) a neo-Gothic turreted pile built for Lord Palmerston in 1856 and later home to the ill-fated Lord Mountbatten.

Creevykeel Goort Cairn

Shaped like a lobster's claw, this intriguing prehistoric **court tomb** (admission free; ☼ dawn-dusk) encloses several burial chambers. The structure was originally constructed around 2500 BC, with several more chambers added later. Once in the unroofed oval court, smaller visitors can duck under the stone-shielded entrance to reach the site's core.

The tomb is north of Cliffony on the N15.

Sleeping

Benwiskin Centre (☎ 071-917 6721; www.benwiskin centre.com; Ballintrillick; dm/f €15/60; P &) In the nether reaches of the county, 4km east of Cliffony, this superb hostel-cum-community-centre is worth seeking out. The setting couldn't be more picturesque, and the hostel has impeccable en-suite dorms, and leafy garden. Book ahead in summer. Take the lane by Creevykeel and follow signs.

Getting There & Away

Bus Éireann (☎ 071-916 0066) buses run from Sligo to Drumcliff (€3, 15 minutes), Grange (€4, 20 minutes) and Cliffony (€5, 25 minutes), as most buses to Donegal and Derry follow the N15. In Drumcliff the bus stop is near the church; in Grange it's outside Rooney's newsagency; and in Cliffony it's O'Donnell's Bar. The North-West Regional Tourism office (p463) has schedules.

DETOUR: INISHMURRAY ISLAND

It takes some trouble to arrange a visit to **Inishmurray**, an island that was abandoned in 1948. Early-Christian remains sit cheek-by-jowl with fascinating pagan relics on this uninhabited isle. There are three well-preserved **churches**, **beehive cells** and **open-air altars**. The old monastery is surrounded by a thickset oval wall. It was founded in the early-6th century by St Molaise, and his wooden statue once stood in the main church, but is now in the National Museum in Dublin.

The pagan relics were also assembled by Inishmurray monks. There's a collection of cursing stones: those who wanted to lay a curse did the Stations of the Cross in reverse, turning the stones as they went. There were also separate burial grounds for men and women, and a strong belief that if a body was placed in the wrong ground it would move itself during the night.

Only 6km separates Inishmurray from the mainland, but there's no regular boat service, and the lack of a harbour makes landing subject to the weather. Excursions can be arranged for €30 return with **Lomax Boats** (☎ 071-916 6124; tlomax@eircom.net; Mullaghmore) or **Joe McGowan** (☎ 071-916 6267; www.sligoheritage.com; Streedagh Point) in July and August. McGowan, in fact, is an enthusiastic historian and a fine source of information. Trips can also be arranged throughout spring and autumn, but get a group together as you'll be asked to cough up a collective €300 for the boat hire.

Central North

The six central northern counties – Cavan, Monaghan, Roscommon, Leitrim, Longford and Westmeath – might be a long way from the country's coveted coastline (in Irish terms, at least), but with the mighty River Shannon surging through wooded countryside interspersed with trout-teeming lakes, there's no shortage of water in these parts.

There is, however, a refreshing lack of tourists. That's not to say there's nothing here for visitors to see. Cavan and Monaghan border Northern Ireland, forming part of the province of Ulster along with the North's six counties, and the central north has some major museums interpreting Ireland's colonial past. It also has some significant Celtic sites. Chief among them is the awe-inspiring Cruachan Aí in County Roscommon, spattered with barrows, cairns and standing stones. There's plenty for visitors to do, too, especially outdoors, including mountain hikes along pristine trails and – thanks to all that water – fishing, boating and water sports.

Although it's well off the well-trampled tourist track, the central north is not cocooned from the country's transformed landscape. Ireland's skyrocketing real estate prices have put the coast beyond the reach of many would-be home- and business- owners. As a result, sea-changers are now seeking out previously unimagined possibilities in the country's centre. In turn, these inland areas are starting to see some of the cosmopolitan changes and economic effects that the rest of the country experienced over a decade ago.

But the central north's abundance of water, vast tracts of bog, unfolding fields and mist-shrouded forests means it remains, perhaps, Ireland's final frontier; and a perfect place to retreat.

HIGHLIGHTS

- **Take to the Water** Cruise the Shannon-Erne Waterway (p493) at Carrick-on-Shannon
- **Scale New Heights** Get a bird's eye view of Lough Key's lakes and woodlands on a treetop canopy walk (p490)
- **Backtrack** Contemplate the 148 BC–built oak trackway unearthed in County Longford's bogland (p495)
- **Say Cheese** Buy prized Corleggy Cheese direct from the farm or learn how to make it yourself during a cheese-making course (p481) at Belturbet
- **Hit the Literary Trail** Follow Patrick Kavanagh's footsteps around Inniskeen (p487)

- POPULATION: 291,650
- AREA: 9302 SQ KM

CENTRAL NORTH

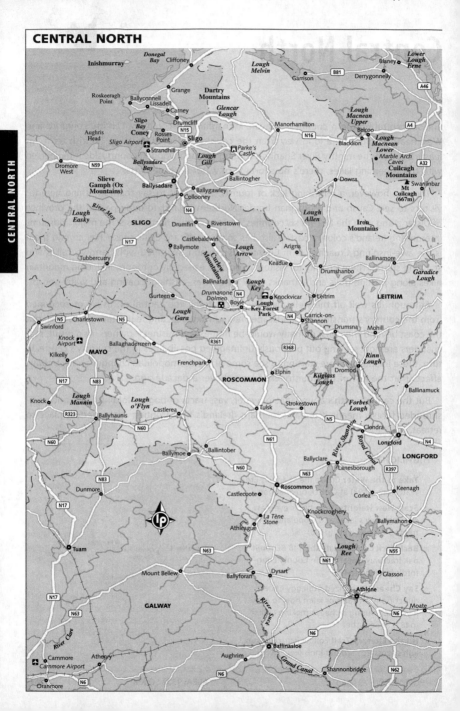

COUNTY CAVAN

Cavan's Irish name, An Chabháin, means 'the hollow', and there's not a lot of solid ground here, to be sure. Cavan is known as 'the Lake Country' as it's said there are no fewer than 365 lakes – one for every day of the year. (Some residents claim it has 366, allowing for leap years, too.) Unsurprisingly, Cavan is paradise for anglers, whose luck would have to be running very dry not to land a catch here.

Cavan has some spectacular paths leading through the wild Cuilcagh Mountains, which are the source of the 300km River Shannon. If too much water's barely enough, you can rent a boat at Belturbet to cruise the Shannon-Erne Waterway.

History

Magh Sleacht, a plain in the northwest near the border village of Ballyconnell, was a hugely important 5th-century druidic centre. The principal Celtic deity, Crom Cruaich, diminished rather swiftly in significance as St Patrick set about spreading the Christian word.

In the 12th century, the Anglo-Normans tried to get a foothold in Cavan, but the landscape foiled them and the region remained under the control of the Gaelic O'Reilly clan. The O'Reillys ruled until the 16th century, when they joined the other Ulster lords to fight the Nine Years' War (1594–1603) against the English and were defeated.

As part of the Ulster Plantation, Cavan was divided up among English and Scottish settlers. In the 1640s, taking advantage of England's troubles, Owen Roe O'Neill led a rebellion against the settlers. O'Neill died in 1649 of suspected poisoning in Clough Oughter Castle near Cavan.

After the War of Independence in 1922, the Ulster counties of Cavan, Monaghan and Donegal were incorporated into the South. With the border so close, republicanism is strong here but with border points now removed you may not even notice crossing between the two.

Activities

FISHING

Exceptional lake fishing reels in anglers from all over Europe to the county's southern and western borders. It's primarily coarse fishing, but there's also some game angling for brown trout in Lough Sheelin. Most lakes are well signposted, and the types of fish available are marked.

For more information, contact **North West Tourism** (☎ 049-433 1942) or the **Northern Regional Fisheries Board** (☎ 049-37174), both in Cavan town.

WALKING

The highlight for many walkers in the region is the Cavan Way (p699), traversing 26km between the hamlets of Blacklion and Dowra through the Cuilcagh Mountains. Heading south from Blacklion, it takes you through an area known locally as the Burren, which is dotted with prehistoric monuments; past the Shannon Pot, the source of Ireland's longest river; then by road to Dowra, passing over the Black Pigs Dyke, an ancient fortification that once divided Ireland in two.

Maps of the Cavan Way are on display in Blacklion and Dowra. Detailed route information (including downloadable pdf maps) is available online at www.cavantourism.com.

At Blacklion you can also pick up the Ulster Way (p700).

CAVAN TOWN

☎ 049 / pop 3550

According to its residents, the county town of Cavan has boomed over the last few years. Thankfully, one person's boom is another's tranquil escape: Cavan is still the sort of place where strangers say 'hello' to you in the street.

Sparkling crystalware is a speciality here, as are Cavan's gleaming horses.

Orientation & Information

Cavan centres on two parallel streets, country town–like Main St and the more elegant Farnham St, with its Georgian houses, large courthouse and garda station, and imposing cathedral.

Cavan tourist office (☎ 433 1942; www.cavan tourism.com; Farnham St; ☺ 9am-5pm Mon-Fri) Located above the library on the first floor.

Ego Internet Café & Coffee House (☎ 437 3488; Convent Bldgs, Main St; ☺ 9am-7pm Mon-Sat) Check your email here.

Genealogical Research Centre (☎ 436 1094; cavangenealogy@eircom.net; Farnham St; assessment fee €95, single search €25; ☺ 9am-5pm Mon-Fri) In the same offices as the tourist office, this centre can access over one million records for you and is a handy resource if you don't want to spend days tracking down files yourself.

Sights

The **grave** of 17th-century rebel leader Owen Roe O'Neill is in Abbey St's cemetery. Nearby, an ancient **bell tower** is all that remains of the 13th-century Franciscan friary the town grew up around.

The town's famous crystal is displayed (with price tags) at the **Cavan Crystal Showroom** (☎ 433 1800; www.cavancrystaldesign.com; Dublin Rd; admission free; ☽ 9.30am-6pm Mon-Fri, 10am-5pm Sat, noon-5pm Sun). It also sells a wide variety of local crafts, from pottery to candles. The showroom is about 2km southeast of the town centre on the N3.

Cavan Equestrian Centre (☎ 433 2017; www.cavan equestrian.com; Ballyhaise Rd; 1.5km north of town off the N3, is the largest in the country, with showjumping events most weekends and auctions six times a year. Events are posted on the website.

Sleeping

Glendown House (☎ 433 2257; www.glendownhouse .com; 33 Cathedral Rd; s €40-45, d €70; ℗) Tom and Eileen Flynn make their warm, cosy home feel like your home too. If you've overdosed on fried breakfasts, there's a wonderful fruit-and-yoghurt alternative. It's gay-friendly.

Farnham Arms Hotel (☎ 433 2577; www.farnhamarms hotel.com; Main St; s €65-130, d €99-150, tr €150-180, bar menu €7.50-12, dinner €35; ℗) A typical, welcoming provincial main-street hotel, the Farnham Arms' clean, spacious rooms are endearingly a little battered at the edges. The lounge serves carvery lunches; dinner at the restaurant includes old favourites like a Farnham grill or chicken Maryland, while the bar has good all-day hot snacks and sandwiches.

Cavan Crystal Hotel (☎ 436 0600; www.cavancrystal hotel.com; Dublin Rd; s/d from €110/170, dinner €45; ℗ ☙) Adorned with glittering Cavan Crystal chandeliers, this luxurious 85-room hotel contains a fine restaurant and offers onsite beauty treatments.

Farnham Estate (☎ 437 7700; www.farnhamestate .com; Cavan; s €125-165, d €150-190; ℗ ⌨ ☙ ☖) Within misty woodlands, this sprawling 16th-century estate was recently given the royal treatment by the Radisson SAS group. Rooms synthesise contemporary style with the ancient forested surrounds, there's a garden-view restaurant and an indoor/outdoor swim-

ming pool as well as mind-blowing spa facilities (also open to nonguests). The estate's 3km east of town on the R198.

Eating & Drinking

McMahons Café Bar (☎ 436 5484; www.mcmahonscafe bar.com; Main St; café dishes €4-5.50, pizzas €6-12; ☽ café 11am-6pm Mon-Sat, bar 10am-11.30pm daily) This hip establishment could easily hold its own in Dublin. Upstairs there's a funky little café whipping up squeezed-on-the-spot juices and fresh-filled bagels. Downstairs the cavernous tiered bar has live bands on Friday and Sunday and cutting-edge DJs on Thursday and Saturday. There's also a late-night pizza menu (served until 10pm) and over 200 cocktails.

Melbourne Bakery (☎ 436 1266; Main St; mains €6-10; ☽ 9.30am-5.30pm Mon-Fri) A friendly local clientele and a delicious array of pastries make this old-world bakery-canteen a treat for breakfast and lunch or just a cuppa.

Side Door (☎ /fax 433 1819; Drumalee Cross; mains €15-29; ☽ 5.30-10.30pm Tue-Sat, 12.30-4pm & 5.30-9.30pm Sun) It's worth heading 1km out of town to this sophisticated spot with a seductive sax-and-strings soundtrack, local contemporary art on the walls, and an upbeat world menu ranging from fajitas to curries and char-grilled steaks.

Abbey Bar (☎ 433 1650; Coleman Rd) An unreconstructed old-men's pub, Abbey has lots of dark wood, tatty seats and a row of proper characters having slightly surreal conversations.

Getting There & Around

Buses arrive at and depart from the small **bus station** (☎ 433 1353; Farnham St; ☽ 7.30am-8.30pm Mon-Sat).

Cavan is on the Dublin–Donegal, Galway–Belfast and the Athlone–Belfast bus routes. Buses to Dublin (two hours, 6am to 10pm Monday to Saturday, 8am to 8pm Sunday) leave on the hour. There are buses to Belfast (three hours, two per day Monday to Saturday, one Sunday), to Galway (3¼ hours, two per day Monday to Saturday, one Sunday) and to Donegal (2¼ hours, four daily).

Bus Éireann (☎ 433 1353; www.buseireann.ie; Farnham St) also has services running to various small towns throughout the county including four services daily to Bawnboy, Ballyconnell and Belturbet, and buses leaving on the hour to Virginia, Kells, Dunshaughlin, Navan and Cootehill.

LAKE ESCAPES

Favoured by renegades, rebels and reclusive royal residents, crannógs (meaning 'small islands built with young trees') were the escapists' homes of choice. These artificial islands, particularly popular in times of political instability, had a surprisingly long life, and were made throughout the 6th to the 17th centuries.

Overgrown now with trees and brambles, it's sometimes hard to see crannóg remains as the amazingly dogged pieces of engineering that they are. Using the simplest tools, the islands were built from scratch from layers of wood, peat, stone, heather and soil. Crannóg dwellers made access even trickier by palisading the islands, and by using zigzagging causeways or submerged stepping stones as a front path. Sometimes canoe-like boats were the only way to get across.

Crannógs were used as defended farmsteads, craft centres and storage places for valuables (for example, during 9th-century Viking raids). They were important rebel hide-outs during the Nine Years' War: the English realised this, and made crannógs a serious target in their northerly Irish assaults.

There are over 1200 crannógs in Ireland (mainly in Cavan, Monaghan, Leitrim and over the border in Fermanagh), but few have been properly excavated. Those that have give tantalising glimpses of crannóg life: manacled, mutilated skeletons of slaves and hostages, for example, highlight their turbulent histories.

Taxis can be ordered on ☎ 433 1172 or ☎ 433 2876.

AROUND CAVAN TOWN
Lough Oughter & Killykeen Forest Park

Rod-wielding anglers congregate at Lough Oughter, which splatters across the map like spilt liquid. Coarse fishing aside, the wildlife-rich lough is also idyllic for naturalists, walkers and anyone wanting to vanish into a landscape of shimmering waters and cathedral-like aisles of trees. It's best accessed via **Killykeen Forest Park** (☎ 049-433 2541; car €5, pedestrians & cyclists free), 12km northwest of Cavan, where various nature trails (from 1.5km to 5.8km) lead you through the woods and along the shore. Keep an eye out for stoats, badgers, foxes, grey squirrels and hedgehogs, as well as some amazing birdlife.

Many of the low overgrown islands in the lake were crannógs (fortified, artificial islands). The most spectacular is **Clough Oughter Castle**, a 13th-century circular tower perched on a tiny speck of land. It was used as a lonely prison, then as a stronghold by rebel leader Owen Roe O'Neill, who was (probably) poisoned there in 1649, before it was destroyed by Cromwell's army in 1653. Although the castle lies out of reach over the water, it's worth getting near for the view: go on foot via the forest trails, or get a closer look by car by turning left out of the Killykeen park exit and following the narrow road running north from the village of Garthrattan.

Butlersbridge & Cloverhill

These two blink-and-you'll-miss-them townships are well placed for breaking your journey through the central north.

The pretty hamlet of Butlersbridge (8km north of Cavan), on the River Annalee, makes a pleasant spot for a riverside picnic. If it's not picnic weather, pop into the **Derragarra Inn** (☎ /fax 049-433 1003), an ivy-covered pub with a wood-beamed interior, beer garden, live music at weekends and good bar food.

At Cloverhill (9km north of Cavan), the multi-award-winning **Olde Post Inn** (☎ 047-55555; www.theoldepostinn.com; s/d €50/100, 5-course dinner €53; ⏱ 6.30-9pm Tue-Sat, 12.30-2.30pm & 6.30-8.30pm Sun; Ⓟ) has outstanding fare. Gearóid Lynch's menu revolves around old Irish favourites such as suckling pig, venison, pheasant and steak. For dessert, his warm fig tart with caramelised banana and banana ice cream involves an extra wait, but it's worth it. Afterwards, retire to one of the inn's six comfortable rooms in the post master's former residence.

To experience life on a working farm, head to **Fortview House** (☎ 049-433 8185; fortviewhouse@hotmail.com; Drumbran; d from €60; Ⓟ), which arranges guided fishing trips, and free use of boats on the main lakes. From Butlersbridge take the N54 to Cloverhill, turning right just after the Olde Post Inn. The farm is a further 2km along this lane.

CHEESE-MAKING

Hard pasteurised goat's milk cheese is something of a rarity in the cheese world, and prize-winning **Corleggy Cheese** (☎ 952 2930; www.corleggy.com; Belturbet) is particularly rare due to its small production runs. Corleggy uses vegetarian rennet and is washed in sea brine, with subtle flavours thanks to the grassy grazing pastures surrounding the farmhouse where the cheese is handmade. Its flavours are brought out when accompanied by fruit like fresh figs or plums. A number of other cheeses including cow's and sheep's milk cheeses are also produced here, with flavours including garlic and red pepper, smoked cheese, cumin, and green peppercorn.

You can stop by the farmhouse between 3pm and 6pm each Thursday to buy Corleggy cheese direct from the source. Otherwise, visit cheese-maker Silke Cropp at her weekly stall at Dublin's Meetin House Sq Market in Temple Bar (p139).

If you want to learn how to make this cheese yourself, Silke runs half-a-dozen **cheese-making courses** each summer. Courses take place on Sundays from 10am to 5pm and cost €150, which includes coffee and treats on arrival and an organic lunch with wine while the cheese-making process takes place. Afterwards you'll have your own kilo of cheese to take with you. BYO bucket.

Corleggy's farmhouse is located 2.5km north of Belturbet village. Coming from the direction of Cavan on the N3 into Belturbet village, turn right at the point the main road takes a sharp left, then take your first left and follow it for just on 2.5km; you'll see Corleggy's sign on your left.

CENTRAL NORTH

Belturbet

☎ 049 / pop 1300

In a prime position on the Shannon-Erne Waterway, this charming, old-fashioned settlement, 16km northwest of Cavan, is a fisherman's favourite. It's also a busy base for cruise boats, and the start of many a cycle trip along the canal and river system. **Emerald Star** (☎ 952 2933; www.emeraldstar.ie; ☉ Apr–Oct) has several hire boats that you can sail between Belturbet and Belleek. A two- to three-berth boat costs from €1050 per week in the high season; two- to five-berth boats start from €1505.

You can hire bicycles and get route advice from Padraig Fitzpatrick at **Fitz Hire** (☎ 952 2866, 086-804 7521; fitzpatrickhire@eircom.net; Belturbet Business Park, Creeney; per day/week €15/45). For an additional €10 per bike, you can cycle one way along the waterway and have Padraig collect your bikes from your final destination.

Belturbet is home to celebrated Corleggy cheese (above), which is served in some of the country's top restaurants.

Trains used the **Belturbet Railway Station** (☎ 952 2074; www.belturbet-station.com; Railway Rd; adult/child/student €2.50/1.30/2; ☉ 9.30am–5pm Jun–Sep) from 1885 until 1959, after which it languished for 40 years, at times sheltering cattle. Volunteers have painstakingly restored the old station building, which is built of cut stone from the nearby River Erne.

The cosiest accommodation option in town is the cherry-coloured **Church View Guest House** (☎ 952 2358; www.churchviewguesthouse.com; 8 Church St;

s €32, d €50; ℗), but book ahead as it's perennially busy with anglers thanks to its cold storeroom and proximity to the lakes.

Bus Éireann (☎ 433 1353) bus 30 runs through Belturbet, stopping outside the post office (on the Diamond) six times per day Monday to Saturday (four Sunday). The main towns on this route are Dublin (two hours), Cavan (15 minutes) and Donegal (2¼ hours).

SOUTHERN CAVAN
Ballyjamesduff

☎ 049 / pop 870

As its name suggests, Ballyjamesduff was the one-time home of the earl of Fife, James Duff, an early Plantation landlord. His descendant, Sir James Duff, commanded English troops during the suppression of the 1798 Rebellion.

These days the town is best known as the home of the **Cavan County Museum** (☎ 854 4070; ccmuseum@tinet.ie; Virginia Rd; adult/child €3/1.50; ☉ 10am–5pm Tue–Sat year-round, 2–6pm Sun Jun–Sep), located inside a forbidding former convent. Highlights include the Pighouse Collection (18th-, 19th- and 20th-century costumes and folk items), and an array of relics from the Stone, Bronze, Iron and Middle Ages, including a 1000-year-old boat excavated from Lough Erril. There's also a large feature on Irish sports.

Pigs might not fly but they get a fair bit of speed up during the three-day **Ballyjamesduff International Pork Festival** (☎ 087 419 1859; cciarans goreilly@eircom.net; ☉ mid-Jun), where thousands

CENTRAL NORTH

BALLY WHO?

All over Ireland you'll see the town prefix 'Bally' (and variations thereof, such as Ballyna and Ballina). The ubiquitous term originates from the Irish phrase 'Baile na'. It's often mistranslated as 'town', but there were few-to-no towns in Ireland when the names came about. A closer approximation is 'place of' (similar to the French expression *chez*). Hence Ballyjamesduff, for example, means Place of James Duff (or James Duff's place). Dublin's Irish name was Baile Átha Cliath (Place of the Hurdle Ford). If it was anglicised, it too would be a Bally; spelt something like 'Ballycleeagh'.

Other common place names, especially in the central northern counties, include Carrick (or Carrig), meaning 'rock' in Irish; such as Carrickmacross (Rock of MacRoss/MacRoss' rock) in County Monaghan.

And a prefix you'll encounter particularly often in the province of Connaught (Connacht in Irish) is Clon (or Cloon), which is Irish for 'dry place' – something in short supply and hence highly coveted in damp Connaught counties like Leitrim.

---

gather to watch pig races, as well as to dine on giant spit roasts and to take part in pork-cooking competitions.

There are no buses to Ballyjamesduff; the closest bus stops in Virginia and from there it costs around €10 euros by taxi.

Lough Sheelin
☎ 049

Trout fishing is at its best in May and June along the tree-lined banks of Lough Sheelin. Any time of year the leafy setting is ideal for horse riding, walking or splashing about in boats far from, well, anything.

Peaceful accommodation options exist at opposite ends of the 6km-long lough in the villages of Finnea (in County Westmeath) and Mountnugent (about 24km south of Cavan).

Ross House (☎/fax 854 0218; www.ross-house.com; Mountnugent; d €76, apt €180; P) is a refined period farmhouse in mature grounds on the lake's edge with a free tennis court, horse riding (from €17 per hour) and boat hire (from €20 per day). Some of Ross House's half-a-dozen spacious rooms have fireplaces and/or their own conservatories. In addition to high tea (€15), or a four-course dinner (€22), you can get a packed lunch (€5) to take out boating.

Crover House Hotel (☎ 854 0206; www.croverhouse hotel.ie; Mountnugent; d from €140; P) is a grand 40-room complex with a golf course, graceful gardens and panoramic lake views from the bedrooms. Boat hire's available from the hotel's private jetty, and if you're really travelling in style, you can land a helicopter here.

EASTERN CAVAN
Many settlements in the county's east, such as **Virginia** (pronounced *ver*-ginee), were laid

out as 17th-century Plantation estates. While in the area, it's worth stopping at **Kingscourt** (population 1307) to visit **St Mary's Catholic Church**, with superb 1940s stained-glass windows made by artist Evie Hone.

Just northwest of Kingscourt is the 225-hectare **Dún an Rí Forest Park** (☎ 042-966 7320; car/pedestrian €5/free). There are colour-coded forest walks (all under 4km long), with picnic places and a wishing well. Along the river, look out for mink and otters. Bordering the forest, **Cabra Castle** (☎ 966 7030; www.manorhouse hotels.com; s from €112, d from €173, dinner €42; P), about 3km out of Kingscourt on the Carrickmacross road, was put together in the 19th century, since Cromwell battered the original castle to pieces. It's now a deluxe 80-room hotel decked out in plush period furnishings with a fine restaurant and a nine-hole golf course.

WESTERN CAVAN
Set against the dramatic backdrop of the Cuilcagh Mountains, the remote western stretch of the county straddles the border with the North.

Few buses serve this isolated fragment of the county. The express Donegal–Dublin buses pass through Ballyconnell, Bawnboy and Swanlinbar four times daily. The Galway–Belfast bus goes via Sligo and stops in Blacklion four times Monday to Saturday (twice Sunday). Contact **Bus Éireann** (☎ 433 1353) in Cavan for schedules.

Ballyconnell
☎ 049 / pop 1100

The Shannon-Erne Waterway wends its way through the village of Ballyconnell, which has a couple of restorative spots to spend the night.

Within a converted farmhouse, Cavan's only hostel, the independently-run **Sandville House** (☎ 952 6297; http://homepage.eircom.net/~sandville; dm from €15, d from €30; ☯ Easter-Oct; P), has its own meditation room as well as a self-catering kitchen (though no breakfast). The hostel's set in silent fields 5km southeast of the village (signposted off the R200). The Dublin to Donegal bus stops on request at the Slieve Russell Hotel, from where you can pre-arrange for the hostel to pick you up. Check ahead as it's often closed for private spiritual retreats.

For relaxation of an altogether more luxurious kind, the **Slieve Russell Hotel** (☎ 952 6444; www.quinnhotels.com; Cranaghan; d from €198; P ⊒ ⊡), 2km southeast of town, is famed for its marble columns, fountains, restaurants, bars, and an 18-hole golf course. Spa treatments include flotation tanks, a herbal sauna and a salt grotto.

Blacklion & Around
☎ 071 / pop 170
Traversed by the Cavan Way (p699), the area between Blacklion and Dowra is spotted with prehistoric monuments, including the remains of a *cashel* (ringfort) and the ruins of several sweathouses, used mostly in the 19th century.

Dedicated foodies make the pilgrimage to Blacklion's **MacNean House & Bistro** (☎ 985 3022; fax 985 3404; Main St; s/d €60/120, dinner menu €35-55, mains €20-24.50; ☯ restaurant sittings from 7pm Thu & Fri, from 6.30pm & 9.30pm Sat, 12.30pm, 3.30pm & 7pm Sun; P), run by award-winning TV chef Neven Maguire, who grew up in this gorgeous country house and has turned it into one of the country's finest restaurants. The food is

truly outstanding: feast on crab ravioli, succulent lamb with truffle juice, or vegetarian fare including avocado spring rolls. Overnighting here gives you the chance to taste Maguire's steaming porridge with cream and honey at breakfast.

Sligo–Belfast buses stop in Blacklion four times every day from Monday to Saturday (twice on Sunday). Buses stop in front of Maguire's pub.

Cuilcagh Mountain Park
The border between the Republic and Northern Ireland runs along the ridge of Mt Cuilcagh, the distinctive summit of this park. Its lower slopes are important protected peatland habitats. The visitor centre and the park's biggest attraction, the Marble Arch Caves (p688), lie a short hop over the border from Blacklion, in County Fermanagh.

GETTING THERE & AWAY
Bus Éireann (☎ 01-836 6111) express buses on the Dublin–Donegal route pass through Virginia, but only pick up going north and drop off going south. Bus 109 from Dublin to Cavan stops in Virginia (1¾ hours, hourly). A Cavan–Dundalk bus passes through Kingscourt (one hour) on Tuesday and Thursday. There's also a Dublin–Navan–Kingscourt (1¾ hours) service, with two buses per day Monday to Saturday (one Sunday).

COUNTY MONAGHAN

If you're one of the few visitors who passes through Monaghan (Muineachán), you'll immediately notice the rippling landscape's tiny rounded hills, resembling bubbles in badly pasted wallpaper. Known as drumlins, the

---

DETOUR: JAMPA LING BUDDHIST CENTRE

If you're on a quest for enlightenment, or just seeking some time out, the **Jampa Ling Buddhist Centre** (☎ 952 3448; www.jampaling.org; Owendoon House, Bawnboy; dm/s/d incl meals €32/39/68), in a beautiful country setting, is peace on earth. Jampa Ling, meaning 'Place of Loving Kindness', offers courses (from about €45 per day) in Galupa Buddhism, philosophy and meditation, though you don't have to take part in a course to stay here. All meals, which are included in the day courses and for overnight guests, are vegetarian. Occasional weekend workshops range from yoga to medicinal and culinary herbs, and visitors can stay as long as they like. From Ballyconnell, follow the signs to Bawnboy. In the village, turn left at the petrol station and follow the small road for 3km. Continue past the lake and a series of bends; you'll see the centre's stone gates a further 250m ahead on your right.

bumps are the result of debris left by retreating glaciers during the last Ice Age.

Unlike much of the province, Monaghan was largely left alone during the Ulster Plantation. After the Cromwellian wars, though, local chieftains were forced to sell their land for a fraction of its true value, or have it seized and redistributed to Cromwell's soldiers.

Poet Patrick Kavanagh (1905–67) was born in Inniskeen, and the village's literary resource centre offers an evocative insight into his life and work.

County Monaghan is famed for its lace, and this eye-straining craft continues in Clones and Carrickmacross, centres of the industry since the early 19th century.

MONAGHAN TOWN
☎ 047 / pop 5720
It may be the county town, but Monaghan's residents live their lives utterly unaffected by tourism. The main visitor attraction is the county museum, containing an extensive regional collection, but it's also pleasant to wander the streets admiring the elegant 18th- and 19th-century limestone buildings.

The MacMahon family ruled this area for centuries: in Convent Lake, just behind St Louis Convent, there is a small overgrown *crannóg* that served as the family headquarters in the 14th century. After the turbulent wars of the 16th and 17th centuries, the town was settled by Scottish Calvinists.

Monaghan lies 141km northwest of Dublin, but just 8km from the border with Northern Ireland.

Orientation & Information
Monaghan is squashed between two small lakes, Peter's Lake to the north, and Convent Lake in the southwest. Its principal streets form a rough arc, broken up by the town's three main squares. From east to west these are Church Sq, the diamond (the Ulster name for a town square) and Old Cross Sq.

To the west of this arc, at the top of Park St, are Market Sq and the **tourist office** (☎ 81122; www.monaghantourism.com; 6 Castle Meadow Ct; ☒ 9am-5pm Mon-Fri May–mid-Oct). For help with genealogies, contact the **Monaghan Ancestral Research Group** (☎ 82304; 6 Tully St).

Sights & Activities
Monaghan County Museum & Gallery (☎ 82928; comuseum@monaghancoco.ie; 1-2 Hill St; admission free;

☒ 11am-5pm Mon-Fri, noon-5pm Sat) is an excellent regional museum, containing over 70,000 artefacts in its permanent collection from the Stone Age to modern times. Its crowning glory is the 14th-century **Cross of Clogher**, an oaken altar cross encased in decorative bronze panels. Other impressive finds include the Lisdrumturk and Altartate Cauldrons, medieval *crannóg* artefacts, a still-functioning original lock and key from Monaghan Gaol, and some frightening knuckle-dusters and cudgels relating to the border with the North.

Eye-catching edifices around town include the **Dawson Monument** (1857), in Church Sq – a hefty obelisk commemorating Colonel Dawson's unfortunate demise in the Crimean War. Overlooking it is the Gothic **St Patrick's Church** and a stately Doric **courthouse** (1829). The most striking is the **Rossmore Memorial** (c 1875), an over-the-top Victorian drinking fountain that dominates the diamond. The town also has a number of buildings with gently rounded corners, which is an unusual architectural feature in Ireland.

Just out of the centre of town on the Dublin road is another piece of Victorian whimsy, the mock-14th-century **St Macartan's Catholic Cathedral** (1861), topped by a teetering 77m-high, needle-sharp spire.

Fine fishing abounds in the area; contact Dick Kernan at **Venture Sports** (☎ 81495; 71 Glaslough St) for permits, tackle and local knowledge.

Sleeping & Eating
Glendrum House (☎ 82347; Cootehill Rd, Drumbear; s/d €40/65; ℗) There are five comfortable rooms in this modern home, a 10-minute walk from the town centre (on the R188). And for 'a good walk spoilt', there's a golf course practically within putting distance.

Four Seasons Hotel (☎ 81888; www.4seasonshotel.ie; Coolshannagh; d from €140; ℗ ⓦ) Unconnected to the similarly named international chain, this is a large, modern establishment with a full complement of fitness facilities including a Jacuzzi, sauna and gym. Service is both affable and professional. The hotel is less than 1km from town on the N2.

Andy's Bar & Restaurant (☎ 82277; 12 Market St; mains €13-22, set dinner menus €20-30; ☒ restaurant 4-10.15pm Tue-Fri, noon-10.15pm Sat, 3.30-10pm Sun) You can barely see Andy's Bar for the plaudits that plaster its exterior. Most of these relate to its dark, old-fashioned interior and top-quality beer, but the deep-fried Irish brie served with warm wine, and Andy's signature monkfish and crab claws sautéed in lime deserve a wholehearted mention too. Inexpensive but delicious bar food is available in the Victorian pub, which also offers a good children's menu.

Mediterraneo (☎ 82335; 58 Dublin St; mains €15-30; ⏰ 6-11pm Tue, 6-10pm Wed-Sun) The two-sittings system on busy nights shows you just how popular this colourful bistro is. There's a good fish selection, as well as decent Italian staples including pizza and pasta. You'll need to reserve at the weekend, and turn up on time or risk having your table given away.

Paramount (☎ 77333; 30 Market St; mains €16-30; ⏰ 6.30-10pm Wed-Mon) This classy, minimalist restaurant over Cooper's pub serves excellent seafood and steak, and vegetarians will find at least a couple of options on the menu.

Drinking & Entertainment

Sherry's (☎ 81805; 24 Dublin St) Walking into Sherry's, one of Monaghan's oldest bars, is like stepping back into a spinster's parlour of the 1950s. The old tiled floor, beauty board and dusty memorabilia probably haven't been touched in decades.

Squealing Pig Bar & Restaurant (☎ 49550; the Diamond) Monaghan's nightlife revolves around this triple-decker place, which has a young, fun vibe and decently priced diner-style food.

An Póc Fada (☎ 77952; North Rd) Named after an Irish hurling term (essentially translating as 'the long shot'), this good-time pub has live music mostly of the rock variety.

Market House (☎ 38158; www.themarkethouse.ie; Market St; admission free-€10) This restored 18th-century market hall–turned–arts venue hosts traditional, classical and jazz music concerts, poetry readings and drama events, and the occasional film and art exhibition.

Getting There & Around

From the **bus station** (☎ 82377; North Rd), there are numerous daily intercity services within the Republic and into the North. These include 12 buses Monday to Saturday (seven Sunday) to Dublin (two hours); six to Derry (two hours) via Omagh; five (four Sunday) to Belfast (two hours); and nine (eight Sunday) to Armagh (40 minutes). There are also frequent daily local services to the nearby towns of Castleblayney, Ballybay, Carrickmacross and Ardee.

McConnon's (☎ 82020) private bus company runs buses to Dublin (two Monday to Friday, one Saturday and Sunday), which serve Castleblayney, Carrickmacross and Slane en route. They leave from outside Ronaghan's chemist on Church Sq.

ROSSMORE FOREST PARK

Crumbling remains of the Rossmore family's 19th-century castle, including its entrance stairway, buttresses and the family's pet cemetery can be seen at **Rossmore Forest Park** (☎ 047-433 1046; car/pedestrian €5/free; ⏰ Jul & Aug). Rhododendrons and azaleas blaze with colour in early summer.

Along with forest walks and pleasant picnic areas, the park contains several giant redwoods, a fine yew avenue and Iron Age tombs. A gold collar (known as a lunula) from 1800 BC was found here in the 1930s and is now on display in the National Museum in Dublin. The park is located 3km southwest of Monaghan on the Newbliss road (R189).

CLONES & AROUND

☎ 047 / pop 1720

There must be something in the water at Clones (Cluain Eois). It's the hometown of both the 'Clones Colossus', heavyweight Kevin McBride, whose defeat of Mike Tyson in 2005 was so crushing that it prompted Tyson's immediate retirement; and the 'Clones Cyclone', former featherweight boxer Barry McGuigan, who won the world championship in 1985. McGuigan went on to train Daniel Day-Lewis for six months for the 1997 film *The Boxer*.

The year 1997 also saw Clones make cinematic headlines with the release of Neil Jordan's *The Butcher Boy*, which was shot on location here and featured many of the townspeople as extras. *The Butcher Boy* was based on Patrick McCabe's dark novel of the same name, which is set in the town. McCabe also hails from Clones.

Clones was once the site of an important 6th-century monastery that later became an Augustinian abbey, and its main sights are ecclesiastical. There's a well-preserved 10th-century **high cross** on the Diamond, decorated with drama-charged biblical stories such as Daniel in the lion's den.

Along with the remains of the **abbey** founded by St Tiernach on Abbey St, there's a truncated 22m-high **round tower** in the cemetery south of town, from the early 9th century. Nearby is the supposed burial place of Tiernach himself, a chunky 9th-century **sarcophagus** with worn animal-head carvings.

The bus stop, post office and banks are in the central diamond. There's no tourist office but you can pick up information at the **Ulster Canal Stores** (☎ 52125; Cara St; ☼ 9am-5pm Mon-Fri Sep-Jun, 9am-5pm daily Jul & Aug), which also displays locally made traditional crocheted lace. Over 120 different pieces are available to buy; prices range from €8 to €125.

Aside from boxing, Clones is fanatical about Gaelic football and consistently punches above its weight in the national sport.

Sleeping & Eating

Lennard Arms Hotel (☎ 51075; www.lennardarms.com; the Diamond; d €70; **P**) A welcoming, home-spun country hotel, the Lennard Arms has 11 comfortably refurbished rooms. Snacks and more substantial meals are available all day from the bar. Specials including a fishing package from €100 per person including two nights' B&B, dinner, and a fishing trip on the owners' boat.

Hilton Park (☎ 56007; www.hiltonpark.ie; d €220-300, dinner €55; ☼ Apr-Sep; **P**) This glamorous country home's interior was transformed into an Italianate palazzo in the 1870s, and light streams through stained glass into antique-filled rooms. Top-class cuisine, much of it produced in the estate's organic gar-dens, is served in regal surroundings (book 24 hours ahead for dinner), and there's an 18-hole golf course. Hilton Park is 5km south of Clones along the L46 towards Scotshouse.

Getting There & Around

Bus Éireann (☎ 82377) runs a service from Clones to Monaghan (30 minutes, five buses Monday to Saturday, one Sunday), with connections on to Castleblayney, Carrickmacross, Slane and Dublin.

Ulsterbus (☎ 048-9066 6630) has one direct service per day between Clones and Belfast (2¾ hours), and another service that requires a change in Monaghan, running Monday to Friday.

McConnon's (☎ 82020) runs a bus to Dublin (two hours), leaving Clones at 8.20am Monday to Saturday, which stops in Monaghan, Castleblayney, Carrickmacross and Slane.

Collins Coaches (☎ 042-966 1631) operates a bus to Dublin (2½ hours) at 7.45am from Monday to Saturday, and at 5.45pm on Sunday that stops at various towns including Carrickmacross.

CARRICKMACROSS & AROUND
☎ 042 / pop 1965

Until recently, the centre of Carrickmacross (Carraig Mhachaire Rois) was clogged with highway traffic. But a new bypass has

---

DETOUR: CASTLE LESLIE

Sir Paul McCartney and Heather Mills' doomed nuptials took place at **Castle Leslie** (☎ 88109; www.castleleslie.com; Glaslough; d from €290) but don't let that dissuade you – the castle has a weird and wonderful history, and activities for both guests and nonguests.

The Leslie family (who trace their ancestors to Attila the Hun) acquired the castle in 1665 and still run it today. The castle's kooky history comes into its own in its 14 guest rooms. Each has a unique character and story to tell. The Red Room, used by WB Yeats, contains the first bath plumbed in Ireland. In Uncle Norman's Room, guests claim to have been levitated in the Gothic four-poster bed. And Desmond's Room recalls this particularly eccentric member of the Leslie family. A *bon vivant* who palled around with Mick Jagger and Marianne Faithful, Desmond made sci-fi films, composed experimental early electronic music and wrote several novels including the early 1950s bestseller *Flying Saucers Have Landed*.

Candlelit banquets (from €52 for guests and nonguests) at the castle are a sumptuous, communal affair. Castle Leslie also offers an extensive programme of year-round **cookery courses** with master chef Noel McMeel. Themed courses cover everything from 'Irish cooking by seasons' to 'death by chocolate' and 'food and erotica'. Prices start from €65 for evening courses, to €185 for one-day courses and €350 for two-day courses (excluding accommodation).

Guests and nonguests can also **fish** on the estate's private lake, or saddle up at the newly restored **equestrian centre** (☎ 88100; per hr from €30) to ride through 40km of trails in the demesne.

There's a minimum two-night stay on weekends; children under 18 aren't allowed.

breathed new life into the town, making it a peaceful spot to wander.

Father Ted fans may know Carrickmacross as the birthplace of Ardal O'Hanlon aka Father Dougal McGuire in the TV series. O'Hanlon's first novel *The Talk of the Town* was set in 'Castlecock', a thinly-veiled version of the town.

Carrickmacross was first settled by early English and Scottish Planters, and its broad main street is dotted with some elegant Georgian houses. Delicate Carrickmacross lace, an industry revived in 1871 by the St Louis nuns, is a world-famous export.

There's no tourist office, but the tourism section of the town's website, www.carrick macross.ie, has visitor information.

Sights & Activities

In the town's former cattle yards, a local cooperative runs the **Carrickmacross Lace Gallery** (☎ 62506; Market Sq; ☒ 9.30am-5.30pm Mon-Thu, 9.30am-5pm Fri Apr-Sep), which sells the distinctive gossamer-like designs. Unlike Clones' crocheted lace, here designs are appliquéd on organza using thick thread and close stitches. Excess organza is cut away and the work is embellished with a variety of point stitches, guipure, pops and the lace's distinctive loop edge. Most famously, Carrickmacross lace graced the sleeves of Princess Diana's wedding dress.

Craftsmanship also shines at **St Joseph's Catholic Church** (O'Neill St), with 10 windows designed by Harry Clarke, Ireland's most renowned stained-glass artist.

There's fantastic **fishing** in many of the lakes around Carrickmacross, including Loughs Capragh, Spring, Monalty and Fea; contact **Peader O'Brien** (☎ 966 3207) for angling information.

Sleeping & Eating

Red Door B&B (☎ 969 0691; www.thereddoor.ie; 51-53 Main St; s €70, d €100, f ste from €120) Situated on the wide main street in a stately town house, you'll instantly recognise this glossy new B&B by its scarlet door. Contemporary interiors blend with original period detail, and family suites have baths with spa jets.

Grenmount Restaurant (☎ 966 1357; Main St; mains €5.50-12.50; ☒ 9am-8.30pm Mon-Fri, 9am-8pm Sat, 10am-8pm Sun) This old-time split-level café is where locals congregate over lunch for a chat or bring the kids for an early dinner. Rib-sticking food

includes battered fresh cod (though other seafood such as scampi is frozen). Vinyl booths are big and comfy, and friendly staff can fill you in on the goings-on around town.

Molly's Restaurant (☎ 969 2540; 1 Monaghan St; lunch mains €7-14, dinner mains €16-22; ☒ 9am-4pm Mon, 9am-4pm & 6-10pm Tue-Sat, 1-8pm Sun) Carrickmacross' newest restaurant is this chic little spot run by Moira and Declan Dunne. The modern Irish menu has some interesting world influences, ranging from a Portuguese prawn hot pot to roast pork fillet with truffled mash or honey roast chicken breast with spicy parsnip puree. For dessert, don't pass up the divine blackberry and almond frangipane tart with vanilla-bean ice cream.

Getting There & Away

Four **Bus Éireann** (☎ 01-836 6111) routes connecting Dublin with Letterkenny, Derry, Armagh and Portrush pass through Carrickmacross (two hours, 11 daily Monday to Saturday, six Sunday).

Collins Coaches (☎ 966 1631) runs a service to Dublin (five daily Monday to Friday, four Saturday, two Sunday).

McConnon's (☎ 047-82020) has a bus service that passes through Carrickmacross on its Dublin–Monaghan–Clones route, with two buses per day on weekdays leaving Carrickmacross at 7.15am and 9.35am, and on Saturday at 9.35am.

Matthews Coach Hire (☎ 042 937 8188; www.matthews coach.com) runs limited services to Dublin, and also serves Inniskeen.

The bus stop is outside O'Hanlon's shop on Main St.

INNISKEEN
☎ 042 / pop 310

Acclaimed poet Patrick Kavanagh (1904–67) was born in the village of Inniskeen (Inis Caoin), which lies 10km northeast of Carrickmacross. The **Patrick Kavanagh Rural & Literary Resource Centre** (☎/fax 937 8560; www .patrickkavanaghcountry.com; adult/child under 12/student €5/free/3; ☒ 11am-4.30pm Tue-Fri year-round, call for summertime weekend opening hr) is housed in the old parish church where the poet was baptised, and the staff have a passion for his life and work that is contagious.

Kavanagh's long work *The Great Hunger* (1942) blasted away the earlier clichés of Anglo-Irish verse and revealed Ireland's poor farming communities as half-starved, 'broken-backed' and sexually repressed. His best-known poem, *On Raglan Road* (1946), was an ode to his unrequited love. It doubled as the lyrics for the traditional Irish air 'The Dawning of the Day'; performed by Van Morrison, Mark Knopfler, Billy Bragg, Sinéad O'Connor and countless others.

Actor Russell Crowe's passion for Kavanagh's writing ran so high at the BAFTA awards a few years back that when his recital of Kavanagh's poem *Sanctity* (1937) was cut from the telecast of his Best Actor acceptance speech, he infamously threw the awards' director against a wall, kicking over chairs in the process; vowing he'd see to it that the director would never work in Hollywood.

Information on **guided literary tours** around town is posted on the resource centre's website. Otherwise you can buy a copy of the *Patrick Kavanagh Trail Guide* (€0.70) and walk or drive around the sites in and around the village and picturesque surrounding countryside (5.6km all up).

The centre hosts an annual **Patrick Kavanagh Weekend** in November and an annual **Writers' Weekend** in August. Contact the centre for booking information.

There are three or four Bus Éireann buses daily, Monday to Saturday, between Dundalk and Inniskeen (20 minutes). **Matthews Coach Hire** (☎ 042 937 8188; www.matthewscoach.com) has limited services from Carrickmacross (15 minutes).

COUNTY ROSCOMMON

In a county composed of one-third bog, studded by island-scattered lakes and cleaved by the Rivers Shannon and Suck, fishing is, naturally enough, the main lure for visitors here. But Roscommon is also home to a couple of excellent museums as well as over 5000 megalithic tombs, ring forts and mounds.

STROKESTOWN & AROUND
☎ 078 / pop 630

Strokestown (Béal na mBuillí), about 18km northeast of Roscommon town, is worth at least a half-day visit for its grand estate and Famine Museum. The broad main street in town was designed by one of the early Mahons to be Europe's widest.

Over the May Bank Holiday weekend, Gaelic and English poetry and music are performed at the **International Poetry Festival** (☎ 947 4123; www.strokestownpoetry.org). If you're poetically inclined, the website has details on entering the International Poetry Competition.

Strokestown Park House & Famine Museum

At the end of Strokestown's main avenue, three Gothic arches lead to **Strokestown Park House** (☎ 33013; www.strokestownpark.ie; house, museum & gardens €11, house or museum only €4.50, gardens only €4; ☒ 10am-5.30pm mid-Mar–Oct, tours 11.30am, 2pm & 4pm Mon-Fri, 5pm Sat & Sun).

The original 12,000-hectare estate was granted by King Charles II to Nicholas Mahon for his support in the English Civil War. Nicholas' grandson Thomas commissioned Richard Cassels to build him a Palladian mansion in the early 18th century. Over the centuries, the estate decreased along with the family's fortunes. When it was eventually sold to a local garage in 1979, it had been whittled down to 120 hectares. The estate was bought as a complete lot, so virtually all of its contents are intact.

Admission to the house is by a 50-minute **guided tour**, taking in a galleried kitchen with state-of-the-art clockwork machinery, and a child's bedroom complete with 19th-century toys and fun-house mirrors.

The **walled garden** contains the longest herbaceous border in Ireland and Britain, which blooms in a rainbow of colours in summer.

In direct and deliberate contrast to the splendour of the house and its grounds is the harrowing **Strokestown Famine Museum**, a must for anyone seeking to understand the devastating 1840s potato blight. The museum takes an unblinking look at the starvation of the poor, and the ignorance, callousness and cruelty of those who were in a position to help. Strokestown landlord Major Denis Mahon ruthlessly evicted starving peasants who couldn't pay their rents, chartering boats to transport them away from Ireland. Almost 600 of these 1000 emigrants died on the overcrowded 'coffin ships'. Perhaps unsurprisingly, Mahon was assassinated by some of his tenants in 1847. The museum also opens visitors' eyes to present-day famine around the world.

Cruachan Aí Visitor Centre

Anyone with an interest in Celtic mythology will be enthralled by the area around the village of Tulsk, which contains 60 ancient national monuments including standing stones, barrows, cairns and fortresses, making it the most important Celtic royal site in Europe. The landscape and its sacred structures have lain largely undisturbed for the past 3000 years. The **Cruachan Aí Visitor Centre** (☎ 071-963 9268; www.cruachanai.com; Tulsk; adult/child €5/2.75; ⏲ 9am-6pm Mon-Fri, 10am-6pm Sat, 1-4pm Sun Jun-Oct, 9am-5pm Mon-Sat Nov-May) has audiovisual displays and informative panels and maps, and can let you know the current status of access to the (privately owned) sites.

According to the legend of *Táin Bó Cúailnge* (Cattle Raid of Cooley), Queen Maeve (Medbh) had her palace at Cruachan. The Oweynagat Cave (Cave of the Cats), believed to be the entrance to the Celtic otherworld, is also situated here.

Tulsk is 10km west of Strokestown on the N5. Bus Eirran's frequent Dublin to Westport route stops right outside the visitor centre.

BOYLE & AROUND
☎ 071 / pop 2200

At the foot of the Curlew Mountains, Boyle (Mainistir na Búille) has been somewhat usurped in recent years by Carrick-on-Shannon in terms of development. There's plenty to interest visitors here, though, including the hands-on King House Interpretive Centre, a 4000-year-old dolmen, an island-scattered forest park and beautiful Boyle Abbey.

If you're here at the end of July, you can catch the lively **Boyle Arts Festival** (☎ 966 3085; www.boylearts.com), which features music, theatre, storytelling and contemporary Irish art exhibitions.

History
The history of Boyle is the history of the King family. In 1603, Staffordshire-born John King was granted land in Roscommon with the aim of 'reducing the Irish to obedience'. Over the next 150 years, through canny marriages and cold-blooded conquests, his descendants made their name and fortune, becoming one of the largest landowning families in Ireland. The town of Boyle grew around their estate.

King House was built in 1730, and in 1780 the family moved to the grander Rockingham House, built in what is now Lough Key Forest Park, and which was destroyed by fire in 1957.

Actress Maureen O'Sullivan (Mia Farrow's mum), was born in a house on Main St opposite the Bank of Ireland in 1911.

Information
Tourist office (☎ 966 2145; cnr Military Rd & Main St; ⏲ 10am-5.30pm Mon-Sat Jun-early Sep) In King House; when it's closed, calls are diverted to Galway tourist office (p404).

Úna Bhán Tourism Centre (☎ 966 3033; www.unabhan.net; ⏲ 9am-6pm daily May-Aug, 9am-6pm Mon-Fri Sep-Apr) Also in King House, you can seek assistance here if the tourist office is closed.

Sights & Activities
KING HOUSE INTERPRETIVE CENTRE
After the King family moved to Lough Key, the imposing Georgian mansion King House became a military barracks for the fearsome Connaught Rangers from 1788 until Irish independence in 1922. The county council bought the property in 1987, and spent several years and €3.8 million turning it into the inspired **King House Interpretive Centre** (☎ 966 3242; www.kinghouse.ie; Main St; adult/child/family €7/4/18; ⏲ 10am-6pm Apr-Sep; ♿). Sinister-looking dummies from various eras tell the turbulent history of the Connaught kings, the town of Boyle and the King family, including a grim tale of tenant eviction during the Famine. Kids can try on ancient Irish cloaks, brooches and leather shoes, write with a quill, play a regimental drum, and build a vaulted ceiling from specially designed blocks.

The mansion's sheltered walled courtyard hosts an **organic market** (⏲ 10am-2pm Sat). Green-and-white-striped tented stalls sell a fantastic array of organic produce including meat, over

CENTRAL NORTH

CLOSE ENCOUNTERS

Perhaps the most intriguing thing about Boyle and its surrounds is a rash of reported UFO sightings in recent years, particularly along the quiet little back road north to Ballinafad. The **UFO Society of Ireland** (☎ 966 2844) launched in Boyle in 1997 following a particularly mysterious crash in the nearby mountains. A few kilometres away, the Roscommon side of Carrick-on-Shannon is home to **Golden UFO Investigations** (☎ 086 684 7866). Of course, there are plenty of sceptics, but you might want to keep your eyes peeled, just in case.

26 varieties of fresh fish, vegetables, cheeses, chutneys and breads, as well as hot soups to warm you up.

BOYLE ABBEY

Gracing the River Boyle is the finely preserved (and reputedly haunted) **Boyle Abbey** (☎ 966 2604; adult/child/family €2/1/5.50; 🕒 10am-6pm Easter-end Oct, last admission 45 min before closing). Founded in 1161 by monks from Mellifont in County Louth, the abbey captures the transition from Romanesque to Gothic, best seen in the nave, where a set of arches in each style face each other. Unusually for a Cistercian building, figures and carved animals decorate the capitals to the west. After the Dissolution of the Monasteries, the abbey was occupied by the military and became Boyle Castle; the stone chimney on the southern side of the abbey (once the refectory) dates from that period.

Guided tours of the abbey are available on the hour until 5pm.

LOUGH KEY FOREST & LEISURE PARK

Sprinkled with small islands, **Lough Key Forest & Leisure Park** (☎ 966 2363; www.loughkey.ie; forest admission free; 🕒 forest 10am-6pm Mon-Thu, to 9pm Fri & Sun Jul & Aug, 10am-6pm daily Sep-Jun) has long been popular for its picturesque ruins, including a 12th-century abbey on tiny Trinity Island, and a 19th-century castle on Castle Island. It's also a time-honoured favourite with kids for its wishing chair, bog gardens, fairy bridge, and viewing tower over the lake. Deer roam freely, and there are several marked walking trails.

The park recently received a boost with the addition of a brand-new **visitor centre**, and the **Lough Key Experience** (adult/student/child €7.50/6.50/5), incorporating a panoramic, 250m-long treetop canopy walk, which rises 7m above the woodland floor and offers superb lake views. Other new attractions include the **Boda Borg Challenge** (adult/child €16/12, min 3 people) – a series of rooms filled with activities and puzzles (great for sudden bursts of rain); and an outdoor **adventure playground** (adult/child free/€5). Attractions are open 10am to 6pm Monday to Thursday, and to 9pm from Friday to Sunday in July and August. From April to June, and in September, hours are from 10am to 6pm daily. It's advisable to check opening hours before visiting.

In summer, **Lough Key Boats** (☎ 086-816 7037; www.loughkeyboats.com) provides water-skiing lessons, on-the-hour commentated boat trips aboard the *Trinity*, rowing-boat hire and fishing advice (record-breaking pike have been caught here). Contact Lough Key Boats for prices and seasonal operating hours or ask at the visitor centre.

The 350-hectare park was once part of the Rockingham estate, owned by the King family from the 17th century until 1957. Rockingham House, designed by John Nash, was destroyed by a fire in the same year; all that remains are some stables, outbuildings and tunnels leading to the lake – built to hide the servants from view.

If you want to pitch up, there's an onsite caravan and camping park (opposite).

Lough Key is 3km east of Boyle on the N4. The Bus Éireann Sligo to Dublin service has frequent services from Boyle to Lough Key.

DRUMANONE DOLMEN

This astonishing portal **dolmen**, one of the largest in Ireland, measures 4.5m by 3.3m and was constructed before 2000 BC. It can be tricky to find: follow Patrick St west out of town for 2km, then bear left at the junction signposted to Lough Gara. Follow this road for another kilometre, passing under a railway arch. A sign indicates the path across the railway line. Take extra care crossing the busy line, as trains are frequent.

DOUGLAS HYDE INTERPRETIVE CENTRE

The life of Roscommon native Dr Douglas Hyde (1860–1949), poet, writer and first president of Ireland, is celebrated at the **Douglas Hyde Interpretive Centre** (Gairdín an Craoibhín; ☎ 094-987 0016; Frenchpark; admission free; 🕒 2-5pm Tue-Fri, 2-6pm Sat & Sun May-Sep). Outside the political arena, Hyde cofounded the Gaelic League in 1893 and spent a lifetime gathering Gaelic poems and folklore that might otherwise have been lost forever.

The centre is housed in the former Protestant church at Frenchpark, 12km southwest of Boyle on the R361. Call ahead to make sure it's open.

ARIGNA MINING EXPERIENCE

Ireland's first and last coal mine (1600s to 1990) is remembered at the **Arigna Mining Experience** (☎ 964 6466; www.arignaminingexperience.ie; adult/child €8/5; 🕒 10am-5pm), set in the hills above Lough Allen. The highlight is the 40-minute underground tour, which takes you 400m

---

HARP & SOUL

The blind harpist Turlough O'Carolan (1670–1738) is celebrated as the last of the Irish bards, but his biggest entry in the history books is for composing the tune of 'The Star-Spangled Banner'.

Most of O'Carolan's life was spent in Mohill (County Leitrim) where his patron Mrs MacDermott-Roe lived. He later moved to the pretty village of Keadue (County Roscommon), where the **O'Carolan International Harp Festival & Summer School** (☎ 071-964 7204; www.keadue.harp.net; late Jul-early Aug) is held in his honour. Over the course of a week, the festival's programme includes harp workshops, recitals and lectures. The festival is preceded by a week-long summer school of music and dancing classes.

O'Carolan is buried in the 12th-century Kilronan church just west of the village on the R284 to Sligo.

---

down to the coal face. Tours are led by ex-miners, who really bring home the gruelling working conditions and dangers of their job. Wear sturdy shoes for the tour, as it can be wet and muddy underfoot.

ARIGNA MINERS WAY & HISTORICAL TRAIL
Covering 118km of north Roscommon, east Sligo and mid-Leitrim, these well-signposted tracks and hill passes cover the routes taken by miners on their way to work. A guide-book with detailed maps is available from local tourist offices or the **Arigna Miners Way & Historical Trail office** (☎ 078-47212; www.arignaminers wayandhistoricaltrail.com; Keadue Presbytery, Keadue).

Sleeping & Eating
Lough Key Caravan & Camping Park (☎ 966 2212; camp sites from €12; May-Aug) Right inside the picturesque Lough Key Forest Park, excellent facilities at this camp ground include a recreation room, a laundry and a children's play area. The tourist office at King House can also provide details.

Royal Hotel (☎ 966 2016; fax 966 4949; Bridge St; d €80-130, mains €8-15; P) In the town centre, this old-fashioned 18th-century country hotel has 22 plain but comfy rooms (some overlooking the river), great craic in the bar, and a restaurant, open daily, serving honest-to-goodness home cooking.

Stone House Café (Bridge St; lunch €5-8; 9.30am-6pm Mon-Fri, 10am-6pm Sat Jun-Aug, 9.30am-5pm Mon, Tue & Thu-Sat, 9.30am-3pm Wed Sep-May) This charming little building on the river was once the gate lodge to the private mansion Frybrook House. It's an atmospheric spot to enjoy a range of soups, *panini* and puddings while watching the water rushing past.

Chambers (☎ 966 3614; Bridge St; mains €14-24; 6-10pm Tue-Sun) High-quality modern Irish cuisine

at Chamber's smart new premises includes wild boar, and ostrich served with *rösti* (a side dish of fried, grated potatoes) along with plenty of fish.

Drinking & Entertainment
Moving Stairs (☎ 966 3586; the Crescent) The most lively evening joint in Boyle has a great line-up of live music – everything from jazz to traditional to rock, depending on the night.

Wynne's Bar (☎ 086-821 4736; Main St) Don't be surprised if you bump into Irish actor Brendan Gleeson, who often pops by this quaint old bar in the centre of town. Its trad music session, from 10pm on Friday, is the most respected in Boyle – come early if you want to sit down.

Alongside Moving Stairs are a couple of other small pubs which are popular with locals seeking a quiet pint.

Getting There & Around
Bus Éireann (☎ 916 0066) buses leave for Sligo (50 minutes, six Monday to Saturday, four Sunday) and Dublin (three hours, five Monday to Saturday, four Sunday). Buses pull up just near the Royal Hotel on Bridge St.

Boyle **train station** (☎ 966 2027) is on Elphin St. Trains leave three times daily to Sligo (40 minutes) and Dublin (three hours) via Mullingar.

You can order a taxi on ☎ 966 3344 or ☎ 966 2119.

ROSCOMMON TOWN
☎ 090 / pop 1625
The county town of Roscommon (Ros Comáin) is very much a place of local business and commerce, rather than a tourist stop, but it has a small, stately centre, and a couple of really lovely accommodation options.

Roscommon's seasonally opening **tourist office** (☎ 662 6342; www.irelandwest.ie; John Harrison Hall, the Square; ☺ 10am-1pm & 2-5pm Mon-Sat Jun-Aug) is next to the post office.

Sights & Activities

In the former Presbyterian church, **Roscommon County Museum** (☎ 662 5613; the Square; adult/child €2/1; ☺ 10am-3pm Mon-Fri Jun–mid-Sep) contains some interesting pieces, including an inscribed 9th-century slab from St Coman's monastery and a medieval sheila-na-gig from Rahara. The unusual Star of David window supposedly represents the Trinity.

The Norman **Roscommon Castle**, built in 1269, was almost immediately destroyed by Irish forces. Its turbulent 'knocked-down, put-up-again' history continued until the final surrender to Cromwell in 1652. The massive walls and round bastions, standing alone in a field to the north of town, look mighty impressive as you approach…although the castle's as hollow as an Easter egg inside.

At the southern end of town, the 13th-century **Dominican priory**, off Circular Rd, merits a quick visit for its unusual 15th-century carving of eight *gallóglí* ('gallowglasses' or mercenary soldiers). Wielding seven swords and an axe, they protect an earlier effigy of the priory's founder, Felim O'Conor, set in the north wall.

Roscommon's central square is dominated by its former courthouse (now the Bank of Ireland). Opposite, all but the façade of its **old jail** was demolished around a decade ago to make way for a dismal shopping arcade.

Ask at the tourist office for a map of the **Suck Valley Way**, a 75km walking trail along the River Suck. The river has an abundance of rudd, tench, pike and perch. En route you may pass **La Tène Stone** in Castlestrange, 7km southwest of town on the R366, a rare Iron Age spiral-inscribed stone.

Sleeping & Eating

Gleeson's Guesthouse (☎ 662 6954; www.gleesons townhouse.com; the Square; s/d from €55/110, café mains €8-15, restaurant mains €14-35, restaurant set menus from €30; ☺ café 8am-6pm, restaurant 12.30-2.30pm & 6.30-9.30pm; ℗ 🖳) There's a wonderfully warm welcome at this listed 19th-century town house, set back from the square in its own fairy-lit courtyard. Rooms are decorated in bright Mediterranean colours and babysitting can be organised on request. At the same premises, Eamonn and Mary Gleeson also run a bustling café and

the excellent Manse restaurant, serving delicious fare like crispy duck salad, and mustard-encrusted spring lamb.

Castlecoote House (☎ 666 3794; www.castle cootehouse.com; Castlecoote; s €95-115, d from €150/190; ℗) About 8km southwest of Roscommon, this wedding-cake-white Georgian Palladian mansion (c 1570) has five impossibly romantic rooms with antique furnishings and views over the orchard, croquet lawn, ruined castle or river. A couple also come with four-poster beds and chandeliers. You can play tennis on two courts on the grounds. From Roscommon town, take the R366 signposted to Fuerty and follow it to Castlecoote. As you go over the bridge into the village, the double gates of Castlecoote House are on your right.

Drinking & Entertainment

JJ Harlow's (☎ 663 0869; the Square) Converted from a family drapery, this old-style bar has shelves full of provisions and hardware items, and hosts live music including bluegrass and jazz.

Roscommon Arts Centre (☎ 662 5824; www.roscom monartscentre.ie; Circular Rd) There's an impressive range of independent cinema and touring comedy, theatre and music at this auditorium. Check the website for programmes.

Getting There & Around

Bus Éireann (☎ 071-916 0066) express buses between Westport (2¼ hours) and Dublin (three hours) via Athlone stop in Roscommon three times daily (once on Sunday). Buses stop on the square.

Roscommon train station is in Abbeytown, just west of the town centre near the Galway road; there are three trains daily (four Friday) on the line from Dublin (two hours) to Westport (1½ hours).

Order taxis on ☎ 087-979 1406.

COUNTY LEITRIM

Split almost in two by Lough Allen, locals say that land in Leitrim (Liatroim) is sold by the gallon, and they're only half joking. Leitrim suffered hugely from emigration because of its terrible soil fertility. Even today it has the smallest population (around 25,800) of all the counties. On the flip side, it has the most pubs per capita in Ireland.

A far-sighted renovation project, completed in 1994, saw the creation of a symbolic link between southern and northern Ireland, when the 19th-century Ballyconnell–Ballinamore Canal was reopened as the Shannon-Erne Waterway. It joins Ireland's two main river systems (the Shannon and the Erne) to create an amazing 750km network of rivers, lakes and artificial navigations. The waterway runs from the River Shannon beside the village of Leitrim, 4km north of Carrick-on-Shannon, through northwestern County Cavan to the southern shore of Upper Lough Erne, just over the Northern Ireland border in County Fermanagh.

Lively Carrick-on-Shannon is the ideal gateway for exploring both the waterway and the county.

CARRICK-ON-SHANNON

☎ 071 / pop 1850

Since the completion of the Shannon-Erne Waterway, Carrick-on-Shannon (Cora Droma Rúisc) has become a major marina, and a recent influx of international business centres has seen the town's population surge. Tourism remains Carrick's main industry, however, and its charming village centre and riverside location make a popular weekend destination, so you'll need to plan your visit well ahead.

During the 17th century and most of the 18th it was a Protestant town, but Catholics were permitted to live in the area known as 'the Liberty' on the Roscommon side of the river.

Orientation & Information

Carrick's main L-shaped layout (Main St, then the right-angled turn onto Bridge St) is in Leitrim; the town's continuation over

---

RIVER'S WISDOM

According to Irish mythology, the River Shannon's name comes from Princess Sinann, granddaughter of Lír (the 'father god of the sea'). So the story goes, in pursuit of mystic knowledge, Sinann plunged into a well where the salmon of wisdom swam. The well boiled up into a raging flood, surging into the great river.

A plaque on Carrick-on-Shannon's main street opposite Market Yard commemorates the legend.

---

the bridge is in County Roscommon. Market Yard is situated at the corner of the 'L'.

Allied Irish Bank (AIB; Main St)

Post office (Bridge St) Opposite Flynn's Corner House bar.

Internet café (☎ 962 1103; gartlans@eircom.net; Bridge St; per 15min €2; ♑ 9.30am-7pm Mon-Sat) Above Gartlan's Newsagents.

Tourist office (☎ 962 0170; www.leitrimtourism.com; Old Barrel Store, Carrick-on-Shannon Marina; ♑ 9.30am-5pm Easter-Oct) Has a walking-tour booklet, which takes in Carrick's places of interest. If you're here out of season, the Sligo tourist office (p463) has information.

Trinity Rare Books (☎ 96 22144; Bridge St) Stocks over 20,000 antiquarian and second-hand books including some hard-to-come-by first editions and a huge collection of Irish-interest titles.

Sights

Europe's smallest chapel is the teensy **Costello Chapel** (Bridge St), measuring just 5m by 3.6m. It was built by Edward Costello in 1877, distraught at the early death of his wife Mary. Both husband and wife now rest within the grey limestone interior, lit by a single stained-glass window. Their embalmed bodies were placed in lead coffins, which sit on either side of the door under slabs of glass. If the door is locked, ask the tourist office to open it.

Carrick has some above-par examples of early-19th-century architecture on St George's Terrace. Have a glance at **Hatley Manor**, home of the St George family; the **Old Courthouse** (now the seat of the county council), whose underground tunnel led convicts from the dock to the (demolished) jail; and stop by the craft shops and cafés in the recently refurbished **Market Yard**.

Activities

The 110-seater boat **Moon River** (☎ 962 1777; www.moon-river.net; the Quay) runs one-hour cruises on the Shannon. There are one or two sailings per day (€12) between Easter and October, rising to four sailings during June, July and August: check the information board on the quay for details. The boat also has late-night cruises – see the listing under Drinking & Entertainment, p495.

If you prefer to sail under your own steam, Carrick is the Shannon-Erne Waterway's **boat-hire** capital, with several companies based at the Marina. The canal's 16 locks are fully automated, you don't need a licence, and you're given full instructions on handling your boat before you set out. Make sure you pick up a chart of the waterway (available from bookshops and boat-hire companies), showing the depths and locations of locks. High-season prices start at around €1000 per week for a four-berth cruiser.

Hire companies:

Carrick Craft (☎ central reservations 01-278 1666, Carrick office 962 0236; www.carrickcraft.com; the Marina)

Crown Blue Line (☎ 962 7634; www.crownblueline .com; the Marina)

Emerald Star (☎ 962 0234; www.emeraldstar.ie; the Marina)

The annual regatta run by **Carrick Rowing Club** (☎ 962 0532) takes place on the first Sunday in August and draws a big crowd.

For information on fishing, contact the **Carrick-on-Shannon Angling Association** (☎ 962 0489; Gortmor House, Lismakeegan).

Sleeping

Camping is free on the Roscommon side of the riverbank, though there are no facilities. Tokens for the showers at the nearby Marina can be purchased from the Marina office.

An Oiche Hostel (☎ 962 1848; Bridge St; dm €20; P) Tucked above a vet's surgery a couple of doors towards town from the river, this tiny hostel has four plain, single-sex dorms that are comfortable, if on the pricey side. There's a small kitchen and sitting room, but no breakfast.

Four Seasons (☎ 962 1333; Main St; s €35-40, d €70-80) Within a period town house, this beautifully kept B&B is exactly the kind of place you'd hope to find in such a pretty country town, run with pride by its courteous host, Mr Lannon.

Hollywell (☎ 962 1124; hollywell@esatbiz.com; Liberty Hill; s €70-90, d €100-140; ☑ early Feb-early Nov; P) This beautiful ivy-covered Georgian country house, on the Roscommon side of the river, has spacious, restful bedrooms with huge beds. Two rooms have splendid views of the Shannon and its ever-changing light. Hollywell's hosts are full of local knowledge and put on superb breakfasts including freshly baked bread. The antique furnishings and proximity to the water mean the house isn't suitable for children.

Bush Hotel (☎ 962 0014; www.bushhotel.com; Main St; s €75-89, d €89-159; P) This centrally located old stagecoach inn has warm furnishings but a frosty welcome. If traffic noise annoys you, ask for a room at the back overlooking the garden. There's an all-day coffee shop and a good restaurant (with friendlier service).

Eating

Coffey's Pastry Case (☎ 962 0929; Bridge St; dishes €3.50-8.25; ☑ 8.30am-7pm Mon-Sat, 9.30am-7pm Sun) Cakes, quiches and other inexpensive fare are made on the premises of this coffee shop. Upstairs, its large dining room has polished linoleum floors, some great black-and-white photographs of the town, and big timber-framed windows overlooking the river.

Oarsman Bar & Boathouse Restaurant (☎ 962 1139; Bridge St; lunch mains €8-10, dinner €16-24; ☑ noon-3.30pm Mon-Wed, noon-2.30pm Thu-Sat, dinner 7-9.30pm Thu-Sat) The Oarsman pours a fine pint, but the pub grub here is also surprisingly good, including classy dishes like turkey with date-and-chestnut stuffing accompanied by cranberry compote and sage-and-onion *jus*.

Cryan's (☎ 962 0409; Bridge St; mains €10-15; ☑ 8am-9.30pm) Cryan's serves up Irish breakfasts and schoolboys' favourites like bacon and cabbage and sherry trifle in truly enormous portions at wooden booths lit by tasselled lamps. Vegan alert: check when ordering as even the vegetable soups are generally made with meat stock. The attached pub has traditional music sessions on Saturday and Sunday nights.

Vittos (☎ 962 7000; Market Centre; mains €10.50-20.50; ☑ 12.30-2.30pm & 5-10pm Mon-Fri, 12.30-10.30pm Sat, 12.30-9.30pm Sun Jun-Aug, 12.30-2.30pm & 6-9.30pm Mon, Thu & Fri, 12.30-10pm Sat, 12.30-9pm Sun Sep-May) In a wood-beamed barn, this family-friendly restaurant has over 50 dishes on its Ireland-meets-Italy menu, including chicken, vegetarian and Atlantic seafood risottos. Service is fast and friendly, and there is such a thing as a free lunch (for kids on weekends in the winter months).

Victoria Hall Restaurant (☎ 962 0320; Victoria Hall, Quay Rd; mains €18-29; ☑ 12.30-10pm) Plasma TVs screening footage of flickering open fireplaces make for a bizarrely cosy atmosphere in this graceful old parochial hall. You can watch Victoria Hall's chefs turn out Asian-inspired dishes like sea bass and king prawns in panang curry butter sauce in the open kitchen. Bento boxes (€9 to €15) are available at lunch.

Drinking & Entertainment

Flynn's Corner House (☎ 962 1139; cnr Main & Bridge Sts) This authentic corner house has a good drop of Guinness and live music on Friday night. Savour it before it's modernised.

Moon River (☎ 962 1777; www.moon-river.net; the Quay; admission €12) Local bands make Saturday nights aboard this 110-seater cruiser a great alternative to hitting the pubs. Boarding is at 11.30pm; the boat then sets sail along the Shannon until 3am, returning to dry land between 1.30am and 2am for those who want to get off.

Carrick's **cinema** (Carrick Cineplex; ☎ 967 200; www .carrickcineplex.ie; Boyle Rd) screens new releases. In your travels around the area, you may also spot the **mobile cinema** (www.leitrimcinema.ie): a capsule that contains a full set of seats as well as a giant screen. The tourist office can tell you where you can catch it and what's playing.

Getting There & Away

The bus stop is outside Coffey's Pastry Case. **Bus Éireann** (☎ Dublin 01-836 6111, 916 0066) express service 23 between Dublin (2¾ hours) and Sligo (one hour) stops here six times in each direction Monday to Saturday (five Sunday). The service stops at several large towns en route, including Boyle, Longford and Mullingar.

The **train station** (☎ 962 0036) is a 15-minute walk over on the Roscommon side of the river. Turn right across the bridge, then left at the service station onto Station Rd. Carrick has three trains daily to Dublin (2¼ hours) and Sligo (55 minutes), with an additional one to Sligo on Friday.

Leitrim Way

The **Leitrim Way** walking trail begins in Drumshanbo and ends in Manorhamilton, a distance of 48km. For more detailed information get a copy of *Way-Marked Trails of Ireland*, by Michael Fewer, from the tourist office.

COUNTY LONGFORD

County Longford (An Longfort) is a quiet farming county largely off the tourist map – to the delight of those who come for the superb fishing around Lough Ree and Lanesborough.

If you fancy a walking holiday with a difference, consider exploring the region on the towpath of the 145km-long **Royal Canal** (see p341), which runs from Dublin to meet the River Shannon near Clondra, west of Longford town.

One of the three biggest portal **dolmens** in Ireland, with an improbably balanced top stone, lies at Aughnacliffe in the north; it's thought to be around 5000 years old.

Longford suffered massive emigration during the Famine of the 1840s and 1850s, and it's never really recovered. Many Longford migrants went to Argentina, where one of their descendants, Edel Miro O'Farrell, became president in 1914.

LONGFORD TOWN & AROUND
☎ 043 / pop 6830

Longford's county town is a solidly work-a-day place that offers easy access to its star visitor attraction, the Iron Age Corlea Trackway bog road.

Literati converge on the town each February for the **Longford National Writers Group Festival**, which attracts novelists, short-story and screen writers and poets from around the country.

County-wide information is available at Longford's friendly **tourist office** (☎ 42577; www .longfordtourism.com; Market Sq; ☼ 9am-5.30pm Mon-Sat summer, winter hr vary).

Sights

In the mid-1980s, excavations of Longford's vast bogland revealed an extraordinary oak *togher* (trackway) dating back to 148 BC. An 18m stretch of the historic track has now been preserved in a humidified hall at the **Corlea Trackway Visitor Centre** (☎ 22386; Keenagh; adult/child/family €3.70/1.30/8.70; ☼ 10am-6pm Apr-Sep; ☀). The fascinating 45-minute tour details the bog's unique flora and fauna, and fills you in on how the track was discovered, and methods used to preserve it. Wear a wind-proof jacket as the bogland can get blowy. The centre is 15km south of Longford on the Ballymahon road (R397).

The discovery of the ancient road has inspired bog oak sculptures such as the works of local artist **Michael Casey** (☎ 25297; www.michael caseysculptor.com).

Goldsmith Country (p502) straddles the Longford/Westmeath border.

Sleeping & Eating

Viewmount House (☎ 41919; www.viewmounthouse .com; Dublin Rd; s €50-60, d €90-100, ste €110-120, dinner €50; ☼ restaurant 6-9pm; **P**) This sensitively restored Georgian residence, about 1km out

CENTRAL NORTH

of town, is the pick of the Longford crop. Five peaceful bedrooms, filled with period furniture including solid wooden beds, look out over manicured gardens. Breakfast is served in the eggshell-blue, cross-vaulted dining room; alternatives to the Irish fry include homemade muesli and pecan pancakes. Viewmont's intimate restaurant in the former coach house is open to nonguests.

Aubergine Gallery Café (☎ 48633; 17 Ballymahon St; mains €12-18; ☽ noon-5pm Tue, noon-5pm & 6-8pm Wed & Thu, noon-4pm & 6-9.30pm Fri & Sat, 2-8pm Sun) Above a fashion boutique on the main street is this young and cheerful restaurant. Dishes are mainly contemporary Mediterranean affairs, and there are several good vegetarian options.

Getting There & Away

Bus Éireann (☎ 090-648 4406) operates services from Longford to Athlone (one hour, six daily Monday to Saturday), Carrick-on-Shannon (40 minutes, six daily Monday to Saturday, five Sunday), Dublin (two hours, 13 daily Monday to Saturday, 11 Sunday), Galway (2½ hours, three daily Monday to Saturday, one Sunday) and Sligo (1½ hours, six daily Monday to Saturday, five Sunday). Buses stop outside Longford train station.

Longford **train station** (☎ 45208), off New St, has trains to Dublin (one hour and 40 minutes, four daily) and Sligo (1¼ hours, three daily Monday to Saturday, four Sunday), with an extra one to Sligo on Friday.

COUNTY WESTMEATH

Characterised by lakes and pastures grazed by beef cattle, Westmeath (An Iarmhí) has a wealth of attractions ranging from a wonderful whiskey distillery to the miraculous Fore Valley; an ecological estate where you can learn ancient Irish crafts; and the country's oldest pub in the county town, Athlone. Regular river trips explore Lough Ree and its Viking heritage.

MULLINGAR & AROUND

☎ 044 / pop 8820

Humming with the activity of locals going about their daily lives, Mullingar (An Muileann gCearr) is a prosperous regional town. In the greater area, you can visit fish-filled lakes, a pewter factory, and the area's

main draw – a fantastical mansion with an odious history.

The town itself is one of the few places outside Dublin that James Joyce visited, and it appears in both *Ulysses* and *Finnegans Wake*. Restored sections of the Royal Canal (p341) extend in either direction from Mullingar.

Information

There are several banks on the main street (which changes name five times).

East Coast & Midlands Tourism (☎ 934 8761; www .eastcoastmidlands.ie; Dublin Rd; ☽ 9.30am-1pm & 2-5.15pm Mon-Fri) About 1.5km east of town and opened year-round.

Laundrette (☎ 934 3045; Dublin Bridge; ☽ 8.45am-6.15pm Mon-Sat) Wash your travel-weary clothes at this place in town.

Market House tourist office (☎ 934 8650; cnr Mount & Pearse Sts; ☽ 9.30am-5.15pm Mon-Fri Jun-Sep) Central but seasonal.

Post office (Dominick St)

Sights

Most of Mullingar's interesting sights lie a few kilometres outside the town centre.

In town, at the northern end of Mary St, the immense **Cathedral of Christ the King** was built just before WWII and has large mosaics of St Anne and St Patrick by Russian artist Boris Anrep. There's a small **ecclesiastical museum** (☎ 934 8338; adult/child €1.25/0.65; ☽ 3-4pm Sat & Sun Jul-Aug) over the sacristy, entered from the side of the church, which contains vestments worn by St Oliver Plunkett.

MULLINGAR PEWTER

Pewterware is Mullingar's best-known export. At the **Mullingar Pewter visitor centre** (☎ 934 8791; www.mullingarpewter.com; Great Down, the Downs), you can tour the **factory floor** (☽ 9.30am-4pm Mon-Thu, 9.30am-12.30pm Fri) and see artisans turning the matt-grey metal into goblets, tankards, candlesticks and *objets d'art*. The centre is about 6km southeast of Mullingar on the Dublin road (N4).

BELVEDERE HOUSE & GARDENS

Don't miss the magnificent **Belvedere House Gardens & Park** (☎ 934 9060; www.belvedere-house.ie; adult/child €8.75/4.75; ☽ house, shop & café 10.30am-5pm Mar-Apr & Sep-Oct, 10am-5pm May-Aug, 10.30am-4.30pm Nov-Feb, gardens 10.30am-7pm Mar-Apr & Sep-Oct, 9.30am-9pm May-Aug, 10.30am-4.30pm Nov-Feb), an immense

1740-built hunting lodge set in 65 hectares of gardens overlooking Lough Ennell. More than a few skeletons have come out of Belvedere's closets: the first earl, Lord Belfield, accused his wife and younger brother Arthur of adultery. She was placed under house arrest here for 30 years, and Arthur was jailed in London for the rest of his life. Meanwhile, the earl lived a life of decadence and debauchery. On his death, his wife emerged dressed in the fashion of three decades earlier, still protesting her innocence.

Lord Belfield also found time to fall out with his other brother George, who built a home nearby. Ireland's largest folly, a ready-made 'ruin' called the **Jealous Wall**, was commissioned by the earl so he wouldn't have to look at George's mansion.

Designed by Richard Cassels, Belvedere House contains some delicate rococo plaster-work in the upper rooms. The gardens, with their Victorian glasshouses and lakeshore setting, make for wonderful walking on a sunny day. Kids will enjoy tram rides around the grounds, which hold an **animal sanctuary** full of donkeys, ponies and goats.

Note that the last admission to both the house and gardens is one hour prior to closing.

Belvedere House is 5.5km south of Mullingar on the N52 to Tullamore.

LOUGH ENNELL

This lough is renowned for its brown trout and coarse fishing. It's also the area where Jonathan Swift first dreamed up *Gulliver's Travels* (1726), hence its park's name, **Jonathan Swift Park**.

The park is 10km south of Mullingar on the N52.

Activities
FISHING

Trout fishing is popular in the loughs around Mullingar, including White, Mt Dalton and Pallas Lakes, and Loughs Owel, Derravaragh, Glore, Lene, Sheelin and Ennell. The largest trout (11.9kg) ever caught in Ireland was landed in Ennell in 1894.

The fishing season runs from 1 March or 1 May (depending on the lake) to 12 October. The **Shannon Regional Fisheries Board** (☎ 934 8769) control all lakes except Lough Lene.

For further information contact East Coast & Midlands Tourism, or the helpful

David O'Malley's Fishing Tackle Shop (☎ 934 8300; 33 Dominick St) in Mullingar.

HORSE RIDING

Mullingar Equestrian Centre (☎ 934 8331; www .mullingarequestrian.com; Athlone Rd; **P**), southwest of Mullingar on the Athlone road (R390), offers riding packages starting at €90 including a lesson, lunch and a two-hour cross-country ride; or €275 for two nights' accommodation including all meals and five hours' riding tuition.

WATERSPORTS

Swimming is possible in Loughs Ennell, Owel and Lene (which has a Blue Flag award – an EU award given to clean, safe swimming spots – and lifeguards on duty in July and August), but Derravaragh is very deep with no shallows.

At Lough Ennell you can rent boats from **Lilliput Boat Hire** (☎ 26167; lilliputboathire@ireland .com; boat hire per day from €20) in Jonathan Swift Park. At the same location, **Lilliput Adventure Centre** (☎ /fax 26789; www.lilliputadventure.com) organises kayaking, as well as land-based activities such as gorge walking and abseiling courses; a day's mixed-activity package costs €40. It's also possible to get a dorm bed here (including activities €65), or to camp (including activities €37).

Festivals & Events

The inaugural **Hi:Fi festival** (www.hififestival .ie) rocked Mullingar's Belvedere House in August 2007, with indie artists including The Prodigy and The Streets and DJs such as Sasha. Tune into the website for upcoming dates and ticket info.

Sleeping & Eating

There are few B&Bs in the centre, but you'll find them on the approach roads from Dublin and Sligo.

Lough Ennell Caravan & Camping Park (☎ /fax 934 8101; eamon@caravanparksireland.com; Tudenham; camp sites from €15; ☺ Apr-Sep; **P**) Eight hectares of woodland surround this peaceful camp site. It's right on the shore of Lough Ennell, and is within walking distance of Belvedere House. The site is 5km south of town on the N52 to Tullamore.

Greville Arms Hotel (☎ 48563; www.grevillearms hotel.com; Pearse St; s €65-80, d €120-140; **P**) If James Joyce dropped by today, he would find this atmospheric maze of wooden staircases and landings much the same as it was when he described it in *Ulysses*.

Gallery 29 (☎ 49449; 16 Oliver Plunkett St; lunch mains €4-9, dinner mains €14-22; ☑ 9.30am-5.30pm Mon-Wed & Sat, 9.30am-late Thu & Fri) Classy and creative, Gallery 29 is a buzzing café of increasing fame, picking up awards for its health-conscious fare. Its homemade baked goods look as artistic as the artworks on display, and you can get full hot meals like oven-baked salmon at lunch as well as soups and salads.

Ilia (☎ 40300; 28 Oliver Plunkett St; light meals €4.25-12; ☑ 9am-6pm Mon-Sat) Croissants, full Irish, pancakes with maple syrup, and bacon and eggs make this sweet two-storey café Mullingar's most popular spot for breakfast. It's also a good bet for lunches like prawn and avocado salad or toasted bagels.

Con's (☎ 934 0925; 22 Dominick St; mains €7-12; ☑ carvery noon-3pm) Con's is best known for its huge carvery lunches and hearty sandwiches, and it's a fun spot for a pint too.

Oscar's (☎ 44909; 21 Oliver Plunkett St; mains €15-25; ☑ 6-9.30pm Mon-Thu, 6-10pm Fri & Sat, 12.30-2.15pm & 6-8.15pm Sun) If you ask anyone in Mullingar where you should go for dinner, chances are they'll send you here. The menu mostly skirts the Mediterranean (pastas, quality pizzas and French-inspired meat and poultry), and the wine list is the best in town.

Drinking & Entertainment

Yukon Bar (☎ 934 0251; 11 Dominick St) The fortune-teller at this pub is a real draw – hours can vary and it's hard to get an appointment, but between 2.30pm and 4.30pm on Tuesday is your best bet. There's also a Monday- and Thursday-night soul, blues and rock session in the front bar, while the small venue at the back, Stables, has occasional gigs.

Danny Byrne's (☎ 934 3792; 27 Pearse St) This renovated pub draws passionate crowds when it screens football and rugby matches. There's traditional music on Wednesday nights.

Mullingar Arts Centre (☎ 934 7777; www.mullingar artscentre.ie; County Hall, Lower Mount St) The centre runs a regular programme of music, comedy, drama and art exhibitions.

Getting There & Away

Bus Éireann (☎ 01-836 6111) runs services to Athlone (one hour, two Monday to Saturday, one Sunday), Ballina (three hours, three Monday to Saturday, four Sunday)

and Dundalk (2½ hours, two Monday to Saturday, one Sunday). There's also a frequent commuter service to and from Dublin (1½ hours), reduced at weekends to around eight buses on Saturday and five on Sunday. All stop at Austin Friar St and the train station.

The **train station** (☎ 934 8274) sees three or four trains daily in each direction on the line from Dublin (one hour) to Sligo (two hours).

KILBEGGAN & AROUND

Little **Kilbeggan** (population 652) has two big claims to fame: a restored whiskey facility–turned-museum, and Ireland's only National Hunt racecourse.

Industrial technology enthusiasts (and/or whiskey enthusiasts) will get a kick out of **Locke's Distillery** (☎ 057-933 2134; Kilbeggan; adult/child €6.25/free; ☑ 9am-6pm Apr-Oct, 10am-4pm Nov-Mar). This 1757-established whiskey producer is believed to be the oldest licensed pot still in the world before it ceased operation two centuries later. Today you can marvel at hulking machinery, visit a cooper's room and warehouse, and listen to the creaks and groans of the working mill wheel. Guided tours last 50 minutes; finishing off with a whiskey tasting.

Punters from all over the country attend the old-time evening meetings at the **Kilbeggan Races** (☎ 057-933 32176; www.kilbegganraces.com; tickets €15; ☑ approx fortnightly May-Sep).

About 6.5km west of Kilbeggan (1.5km west of Horseleap), just off the N6, is the blissful spa retreat **Temple House & Health Spa** (☎ 057-933 35118; www.templespa.ie; s from €145, d from €250, restaurant mains €23.50-30; ☑ Tue-Sun, day spa Wed-Sun, restaurant 7-9pm Tue-Thu, 7-9.30pm Fri & Sat, 12.30-2pm Sun; ⓟ ⌨) The 250-year-old house is set in 40 hectares of grounds, on the site of an ancient monastery. Food is locally sourced (with herbs fresh from the garden), and wine's served with dinner. Both the restaurant and the day spa are open to nonguests – 'relaxing days' start at €140, while all-out 'pampering days' start from €220.

NORTH OF MULLINGAR
Crookedwood & Around

The small village of Crookedwood hugs the shore of Lough Derravaragh. The 8km-long lake is associated with the legend of the children of Lír, who were turned into swans here. Stepmums get a bad rap in lore (Cinderella et al), and Irish mythology is no exception – the transformation of Lír's children is said to have been inflicted by their jealous stepmother. Each winter, the legend is recalled by thousands of snow-white migratory swans who flock from as far away as Russia and Siberia.

About 3km west of Crookedwood is the **Multyfarnham Franciscan friary**. In the present church, the remains of a 15th-century church still stand, and there are outdoor Stations of the Cross set beside a stream.

East of Crookedwood, a small road leads 2km to the ruins of the fortified 15th-century **St Munna's Church**, built in a lovely location on the site of a 7th-century church founded by St Munna. Keys to the church are available from the nearby bungalow.

Tullynally Castle Gardens

The seat of the Pakenham family is the imposing Gothic revival **Tullynally Castle** (☎ 044-61159; www.tullynallycastle.com; Castlepollard; gardens adult/child/family €6/3/16; ☺ 2-6pm Jun-Aug). The castle itself is closed to visitors, but you can roam its 12 hectares of gardens and parkland containing ornamental lakes, a Chinese and a Tibetan garden and a wonderful stretch of 200-year-old yews.

To get here, take the N4 from Mullingar, then the R394 at Edgeworthstown to Castlepollard, from where the castle and gardens are signposted 2km to the northwest.

Fore Valley

Near the shores of Lough Lene, the emerald-green Fore Valley is a superb place to explore by bicycle or on foot. In AD 630, St Fechin founded a monastery just outside the village of Fore. There's nothing left of this early settlement, but three later buildings in the valley are closely associated with 'seven wonders' said to have occurred here.

The **Fore Abbey Coffee Shop** (☎ 044-61780; foreabbeycoffeeshop@oceanfree.net; ☺ 11am-6pm daily Jun-Sep, 11am-5pm Sun Oct-May), on the edge of Fore village, acts as a tourist information office and screens a 20-minute video about the wonders. Guided tours of Fore can be arranged by contacting the coffee shop in advance.

From Mullingar, take the N4 then the R394 northeast to Castlepollard. The road to Fore is signposted from there.

THE SEVEN WONDERS OF FORE

The oldest of the three buildings is St Fechin's Church, containing an early-13th-century chancel and baptismal font. Over the cyclopean entrance is a huge lintel stone carved with a Greek cross and thought to weigh about 2.5 tonnes. It's said to have been put into place by St Fechin's devotions – the wonder of the **stone raised by prayer**.

A path runs from the church to the attractive little anchorite cell – the **anchorite in a stone** – which dates back to the 15th century and was lived in by a succession of hermits. The Seven Wonders pub in the village holds the key.

On the other side of the road near the car park is **St Fechin's Well**, filled with **water that will not boil**. Cynics should beware of testing this claim, as it's said that if you try it, doom will come to your family. Nearby is a branch from the **tree that will not burn**; the coins pressed into it are a more contemporary superstition.

Further over the plain are the extensive remains of a 13th-century Benedictine priory, the **Monastery of the Quaking Scraw**, miraculous because it was built on what once was a bog. In the following century it was turned into a fortification, hence the loophole windows and castlelike square towers. The western tower is in a dangerous state – keep clear.

The last two wonders are the **mill without a race** and the **water that flows uphill**. The mill site is marked, and legend has it that St Fechin caused water to flow uphill, towards the mill, by throwing his crosier against a rock near Lough Lene, about 1.5km away.

Rockfield Ecological Estate

This **ecological estate** (☎ 043-76025; imeldadaly@eircom.net; Rathowen; tour €10, mains €20-25; ☺ by appointment) gives you an inspiring insight into sustainable living as well as traditional Irish culture and crafts. In addition to two-hour tours of the working farm, you can dine on nutritious homemade food utilising organic produce from the rambling gardens (while sitting on a chair fashioned from fallen tree branches); or take part in full-day **courses** (per person incl lunch €100) such as spinning, weaving, basket making, wood carving and stone sculpting. Irish bands sometimes play here, and onsite accommodation is in the works.

From Mullingar, take the Longford road (N4) northwest for 28km through the village of Rathowen. At the end of the village turn left for 1km until you reach a bend, then follow the road around to the left for a further 1km; the farm's signposted on your left.

ATHLONE

☎ 090 / pop 7350

The location of Athlone (Baile Átha Luain), smack-bang in the centre of the country, is both a blessing and a curse for Westmeath's county town. A curse because it's easily bypassed on intercoastal journeys, and infrastructure is often allocated elsewhere (Athlone, for example, has long been pushing for an international airport, but it's unlikely since it would take business away from those on the coast). But on balance it's a blessing because it's within easy reach of Ireland's major cities by rail and road, with none of the traffic congestion and all of the benefits of small-town life.

The Shannon splits this former garrison town in two. Most businesses and services sit on the river's eastern bank. In the shadow of Athlone Castle, the western (left) bank is an enchanting jumble of twisting streets, colourfully painted houses, historic pubs, antique shops, and old book binders, as well as some outstanding restaurants.

In true 'if you can't join them, beat them' spirit, Athlone is in the midst of building what's slated to be the country's biggest shopping centre in the town's heart, as well as maintaining its campaign for city status.

Orientation & Information

Athlone is on the main Dublin–Galway road (N6). The Shannon flows through the centre from Lough Ree; major landmarks Athlone Castle and Sts Peter and Paul Cathedral are prominently situated on the river's western bank.

The websites www.athlone.ie and www.westmeathtourism.com are good sources of information; while the website www.acis.ie has a downloadable pdf version of the *Athlone & District Tourist Guide* including walking tours of the town.

Bank of Ireland (Northgate St) At the start of Northgate St, just up from Custume Pl.

Information office (☎ 647 3173; Lloyds Lane; ⏰ 9am-5pm) Run by the local chamber of commerce.

Post office (Barrack St) Beside the cathedral.

Tourist office (☎ 649 4630; Athlone Castle; ⏰ 9.30am-1pm & 2-5.15pm Mon-Fri May-Sep) Inside the castle guardhouse.

Sights & Activities

ATHLONE CASTLE VISITOR CENTRE

The Normans built their castle here in 1210, at this important crossroads formed by the river and the ford across it. Over the centuries it was much squabbled over, particularly during the turbulent 17th century. In 1690 the Jacobite town survived a siege by Protestant forces, but a year later it fell, under a devastating bombardment of 12,000 cannonballs, to William of Orange's troops. Major alterations to the castle took place between the 17th and 19th centuries.

The **Athlone Castle Visitor Centre** (☎ 649 2912; adult/child/family €5.50/1.60/12; ⏰ 10am-4.30pm May-Sep) contains some informative displays on the 1691 Siege of Athlone, the flora and fauna of the Shannon, and the Shannon's hydroelectricity role. Other highlights are an old gramophone that belonged to the great Athlone tenor John McCormack (1884–1945); and a military and folk museum with two sheila-na-gigs. An hour is probably enough time to take it all in.

RIVER CRUISES

Viking Tours (☎ 086-262 1136; vikingtours@ireland.com; 7 St Mary's Pl; ⏰ May-Sep) offers cruises on the River Shannon aboard a replica Viking longship complete with costumed staff and helmets, and swords and shields for kids. Tours sail north to Lough Ree (adult/child/family €12/10/40, 1½ hours), and south to Clonmacnoise (adult/child/family €20/15/60, 4½ hours) in County Offaly. There are usually daily sailings in June, July and August, plus sailings most days in May and September; call or ask the tourist office about schedules.

New outfit **Shannon Safari** (☎ 647 9558; www.shannonsafari.ie; 36 Silverquay) offers private hourlong powerboat cruises year-round for €80 per couple or €100 per family, with longer cruises available. Boats depart beside the Radisson hotel.

FISHING

Information and permits are available from the friendly **Strand Tackle Shop** (☎ 647 9277; powell@iol.ie; the Strand), on the eastern bank of the river opposite the castle.

Sleeping

Bastion B&B (☎ 649 4954; www.thebastion.net; 2 Bastion St; s €40-50, d €60-70) In a converted draper's shop, this funky B&B's white-on-white interiors are a canvas for eclectic artwork, cacti collections and Indian wall hangings. The five rooms (three with private bathroom) are crisp and clean, with neatly folded fluffy towels, and there's an arty lounge-breakfast room where you can kick-start your day with cereal, fruit, ground coffee, fresh bread and a cheeseboard.

our pick Coosan Cottage Eco Guesthouse (☎ 647 3468; www.ecoguesthouse.com; Coosan Point Rd; s/d €50/80, snacks €2-3.50; P ♿) Built from scratch by its owners, this beautiful cottage is completely ecofriendly, utilising wind-generated electricity, rain water and sawdust pellet–fuelled heating. Home comforts include cooked breakfasts such as salmon fishcakes, an onsite sauna, and a bar (with great Guinness on tap). If you're not staying here, you can pop by from 1pm for a cuppa or a wholesome bowl of chowder and a chat. The cottage is set in peaceful horse paddocks 2.5km from the town centre, with free pick-up if you're coming by train or bus. Credit cards aren't accepted.

Prince of Wales Hotel (☎ 647 6666; www.theprinceofwales.ie; Church St; d from €120; P 💻) Former guests – including US President Martin Van Buren, who stayed here in 1853 – wouldn't recognise the Prince of Wales since it's ultra-contemporary strip-and-refit. Chocolate-and-cream bedrooms are equipped with state-of-the-art entertainment systems and black marble bathrooms; the latest addition is a gleaming restaurant, the Corvus. Lunch and dinner are served Saturday and Sunday only (main course, dessert and tea or coffee €32.50); cheaper bar food is available for lunch and dinner during the rest of the week. The hotel is on the eastern riverbank in the centre of town.

Eating

Athlone's culinary excellence continues apace; scout around the western bank's backstreets and you'll unearth some gems.

our pick Left Bank Bistro (☎ 649 4446; Fry Pl; snacks €3-6, mains €20-29; 🕑 snacks 10.30am-noon, lunch noon-5pm & dinner 5.30-10.30pm Tue-Sat) With airy, whitewashed interiors, shelves of gourmet goods, and a menu combining superior Irish ingredients with Mediterranean and Asian influences, this sophisticated deli-bistro attracts coffee-sipping web designers as well as power-lunching business types. There's a lengthy wine list, some extraordinary desserts, such as dark chocolate truffle torte with raspberry and Bushmills sauce, and staff who really know their stuff.

Olive Grove (☎ 647 6946; Custume Pl; mains €14-22.50; 🕑 noon-4pm & 5.30-10pm Tue-Sun) Another mover and shaker on Athlone's dining scene, this stylised restaurant by the river gets creative with starters like deep-fried mozzarella sticks with spicy peach salsa, and mains such as chicken breast stuffed with smoked cheese, or pistachio-encrusted oven-baked cod.

Le Chateau (☎ 649 4517; Peter's Port; mains €22-30; 🕑 lunch from 12.30pm, dinner from 5.50pm) Many Athlone locals regard this converted church as their favourite restaurant, and it's easy to understand why: the split-level timber dining room glows with flickering candles at night, and classy comfort food includes tender roast beef and rack of lamb.

Hip left-bank cafés include **Slice of Life** (☎ 649 3970; Bastion St; mains €3-7; 🕑 9am-6pm Mon-Sat) and **Foodies** (☎ 649 8576; Bastion St; sandwiches €4-7; 🕑 9.30am-5.30pm Mon-Sat), which has a soothing wood stove, good coffee (Illy – yay!), and muffins bursting with fruit. In the same creaking wooden building as Foodies, there's a New Age-ish gift shop filled with Celtic charms, candles, crystals and local art.

A market sets up between the cathedral and Athlone Castle on the first weekend of the month.

Drinking & Entertainment

Sean's Bar (☎ 649 2358; Main St) Age certainly hasn't wearied Sean's Bar. Dating *way* back to AD 900, Sean's stakes its claim as Ireland's oldest pub. Its log fires, uneven floors, sawdust, rickety piano and curios collected over the years attest to the theory, which is backed up by the *Guinness Book of Records*. The riverside beer garden has live music most nights in summer; to really see things in full swing, turn up at about 5.30pm on a Saturday.

Dean Crowe Theatre (☎ 649 2129; www.deancrowetheatre.com; Chapel St) This refurbished theatre has wonderful acoustics, and runs a broad programme of theatrical and musical events year-round.

Getting There & Around

Athlone's **bus depot** (☎ 648 4406) is beside the train station. Express buses stop there on many east–west routes. There are 15 buses daily to

Dublin (two hours) and Galway (1¼ hours); three from Monday to Saturday (one Sunday) to Westport (2¾ hours) in County Mayo; and three Monday to Saturday (one Sunday, plus an extra bus Friday) to Mullingar (one hour).

From **Athlone train station** (☎ 647 3300), there are nine trains daily Monday to Saturday (seven Sunday) to Dublin (1¾ hours); three or four daily to Westport (two hours); and four to six daily to Galway (1¼ hours). The train station is on the eastern bank on Southern Station Rd. To get here, follow Northgate St up from Custume Pl. Its extension, Coosan Point Rd, joins Southern Station Rd near St Vincent's Hospital.

You can order a taxi on ☎ 647 4400.

LOUGH REE & AROUND

Many of the 50-plus islands within **Lough Ree** were once inhabited by monks and their ecclesiastical treasures, drawing Vikings like moths to a flame. These days, its visitors are less bloodthirsty, with sailing, trout fishing and bird-watching the most popular pastimes. Migratory birds that nest here include swans, plovers and curlews.

Poet, playwright and novelist Oliver Goldsmith (1728–74), author of *The Vicar of Wakefield,* is closely associated with the area running alongside the eastern shore of Lough Ree. Known as **Goldsmith Country**, the region is beautifully captured in his writings. The *Lough Ree Trail: a Signposted Tour,* by Gearoid O'Brien, is available from the tourist offices in Athlone and Mullingar. Ideal for cycling, this 32km tour runs through Glasson (which Goldsmith called the 'loveliest village of the plain') and around the shores of Lough Ree, and into County Longford.

Situated 8km northeast of Athlone on the N55, **Glasson** (population 816) is well worth a stop for its good restaurants and lively pubs. Nearby, **Wineport Restaurant** (☎ 648 5466; www.wineport.ie; d €150-350, mains €24-29, dinner menu €55; ⏱ 5-10pm Wed-Sat, 12.30-9pm Sun), in a lakeside cedar lodge, showcases chef Feargal O'Donnell's fêted modern Irish cuisine. Despite its fame, the atmosphere remains relaxed and little gourmets are made welcome. The lodge's 10 rooms are named after wines and champagnes (with a tipple on arrival), and boat hire can be arranged.

Getting There & Away

Bus Éireann (☎ 647 3322) service 466 from Athlone to Longford has two trips daily from Monday to Saturday, stopping outside Grogan's pub in Glasson.

County Donegal

You could spend weeks losing yourself in wild and woolly Donegal. The county's stark beauty captivates you and, over time, seeps down to your core. Tortuous country roads skirt stark mountains, rugged sea cliffs, craggy peninsulas, remote Gaeltacht communities, sheep-studded pastures, pristine strands, icy streams and horizons carpeted with bog and heather. Reaching up to the island's northernmost point, the county seems eternally braced to hold its own on its own. For although political and economic turmoil have eased off, the county endures its fair share of Atlantic squalls to stave off complacency.

Due to its isolation, Ireland's second-largest county (only Cork is larger) feels like its own country. It was severed from its traditional province when most of Ulster became Northern Ireland, and it is cut off from the rest of the Republic by the extended finger of County Fermanagh. Donegal was always a stubbornly independent land, largely ignored by those in Dublin's distant driving seat.

The Donegal experience is largely about weather, for here there's no need to set sail to brave the sea – the sea charges ashore and its mists ride stiff winds over fields and into the towns. Storms arrive unannounced, and just as abruptly break into brilliant sunshine, transforming the blue and grey into sparkling greenery. When the weather is kind, Donegal's better beach resorts can rival any in Europe, and make perfect destinations for a summer getaway. Once you've attained the proper come-what-may attitude, you'll know you've been tamed by this uncompromising land.

COUNTY DONEGAL

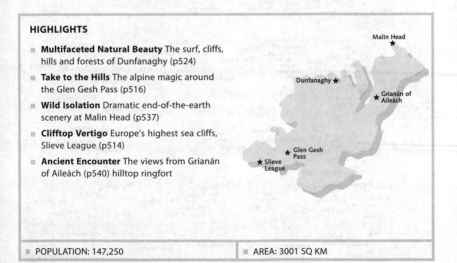

HIGHLIGHTS

- **Multifaceted Natural Beauty** The surf, cliffs, hills and forests of Dunfanaghy (p524)
- **Take to the Hills** The alpine magic around the Glen Gesh Pass (p516)
- **Wild Isolation** Dramatic end-of-the-earth scenery at Malin Head (p537)
- **Clifftop Vertigo** Europe's highest sea cliffs, Slieve League (p514)
- **Ancient Encounter** The views from Grianán of Aileách (p540) hilltop ringfort

Malin Head ★

Dunfanaghy ★

Grianán of Aileách ★

Glen Gesh Pass ★

★ Slieve League

- POPULATION: 147,250
- AREA: 3001 SQ KM

History

Donegal is covered with pre-Christian tombs and other prehistoric titbits dating back as much as 9000 years. The arrival of the Celts and their fort-building endeavours provided the origins of the county's Irish name, Dun na nGall (Fort of the Foreigner). Christianity is also a strong suit in the county's history, thanks to St Colmcille, a local man who not only spread the good word here, but exported it across the sea to Scotland too.

Until the early 17th century, the county was roughly divided between two clans, the O'Donnells and the O'Neills, but the Plantation of Ulster that followed their defeat and flight from Ireland reduced the county to a subservient misery. The partition of Ireland in 1921 compounded Donegal's isolation, as it was cut off from Derry, which it served as a natural hinterland. Many locals along the coast have benefited from rising real-estate values, and pockets feel like an affluent vacationland. While inland communities remain largely rural, the growth of Letterkenny, near the border of Northern Ireland, indicates the Republic's economic upturn has reached this far-flung region.

Climate

In many ways, Donegal seems to defy its northerly location; its thermometers rarely drop below zero, and in summer the temperature can top 25°C. This is largely due to the warm caress of the Atlantic Gulf Stream

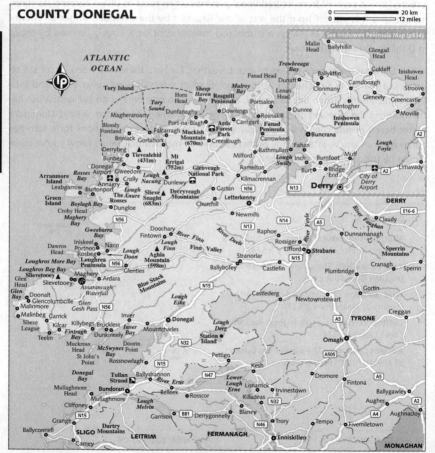

along the county's vast coastline. But when the winter winds and heavy rain are ripping through your semiprotective parka, it doesn't really matter that the 'official' temperature is a tolerable 4°C – it can feel arctic. Conversely, when the summer gauge shows that it's less than 20°C, you'll soon find yourself stripping down to your swimsuit.

Language

Roughly one-third of the county lies in the Gaeltacht, where Irish is the lingua franca and road signs challenge the reader to perform linguistic gymnastics to get the right pronunciation. Donegal Irish has a markedly different pronunciation from that spoken elsewhere, and even native speakers from southern Ireland can have difficulty understanding the local vernacular. Rest assured, however, that virtually everyone speaks English and will do so without hesitation. It would behove you, though, to familiarise yourself with the Irish place names; although we use English transliterations, their Irish names are included in brackets.

Getting There & Away

Donegal Airport (☎ 074-954 8284; www.donegalairport .ie; Carrick Finn) has flights to/from Dublin (from €30, 50 minutes, daily) and flights to Glasgow Prestwick (from €65, Friday and Sunday). It's in the townland of Carrick Finn (Charraig Fhion) about 3km northeast of Annagry along the northwestern coast. There is no public transport to the airport, so you'll have to get there by your own steam; there are car-rental desks in the terminal.

The **City of Derry Airport** (☎ 028-7181 0784; www .cityofderryairport.com) is just beyond the county's eastern border, in Northern Ireland.

Getting Around

The bus is your main transport option if you don't have your own car.

Private bus company **Lough Swilly** (in Letterkenny ☎ 074-912 2863, in Derry 028-7126 2017; http:// home.clara.net/sjp/nibus/lswilly.htm) traverses the county thoroughly.

Private coaches operated by **Feda O'Donnell** (☎ 954 8114; www.fedaodonnell.com) serve the western half of the county from Crolly to Bundoran.

This is very much walking and cycling country. Plenty of Donegal walking guides can be found in tourist offices and larger bookshops. Recommended companions include *New Irish Walks: West and North* by Tony Whilde and Patrick Simms and *Hill Walkers' Donegal* by David Herman, which have details of many walks mentioned in this chapter.

When driving, be prepared for switchback roads, directions only in Irish, signs hidden behind vegetation, signs pointing the wrong way, signs with misleading mileage or no signs at all. Most of all, prepare yourself for reckless young drivers, who casually put the lives of their fellow motorists at risk.

DONEGAL TOWN

☎ 074 / pop 2450

It's picturesque enough, but Donegal town is more of a gateway to the county than a destination in itself. The town has plenty of hotels and pubs, and an old castle guards a bend in the River Eske, just a block from the central diamond. County Donegal's true treasures are just a few hours drive to the northwest of here.

This spot was once a stamping ground of the O'Donnells, the great chieftains who ruled the northwest from the 15th to 17th centuries. These days it's a far more sedate spot. If you're coming from the south, Donegal town makes a pleasant pit stop.

INFORMATION

Bank of Ireland (the Diamond) One of several banks with ATM and bureau de change.

Blueberry Cybercafe (☎ 972 2933; Castle St; per hr €4; ⏲ 9am-7.30pm Mon-Sat) Internet café above the

---

TOP FIVE SCENIC RIDES

- ■ The coast highway from Dunfanaghy (p524) to Gweedore (p520)
- ■ The 100-mile loop of isolated Inishowen Peninsula (p534)
- ■ The vertiginous heights of Horn Head (p524)
- ■ The lingering arc through stunning Glenveagh National Park (p530)
- ■ The snaking switchbacks of Glen Gesh Pass (p516)

COUNTY DONEGAL

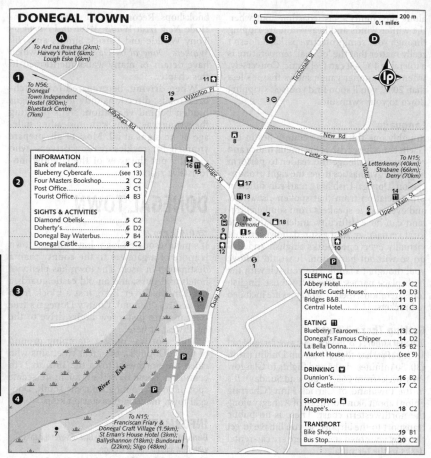

DONEGAL TOWN

To Ard na Breatha (2km);
Harvey's Point (6km);
Lough Eske (6km)

To N56;
Donegal
Town Independent
Hostel (800m);
Bluestack Centre
(7km)

To N15;
Letterkenny (40km);
Strabane (66km);
Derry (70km)

INFORMATION
Bank of Ireland	1 C3
Blueberry Cybercafe	(see 13)
Four Masters Bookshop	2 C2
Post Office	3 C1
Tourist Office	4 B3

SIGHTS & ACTIVITIES
Diamond Obelisk	5 C2
Doherty's	6 D2
Donegal Bay Waterbus	7 B4
Donegal Castle	8 C2

SLEEPING
Abbey Hotel	9 C2
Atlantic Guest House	10 D3
Bridges B&B	11 B1
Central Hotel	12 C3

EATING
Blueberry Tearoom	13 C2
Donegal's Famous Chipper	14 D2
La Bella Donna	15 B2
Market House	(see 9)

DRINKING
Dunnion's	16 B2
Old Castle	17 C2

SHOPPING
Magee's	18 C2

TRANSPORT
Bike Shop	19 B1
Bus Stop	20 C2

To N15;
Franciscan Friary &
Donegal Craft Village (1.5km);
St Ernan's House Hotel (3km);
Ballyshannon (18km); Bundoran
(22km); Sligo (48km)

Blueberry Tearoom. Check in at the counter downstairs before going up.

Four Masters Bookshop (☎ 972 1526; the Diamond) A good spot for books, maps and travel guides.

Post office (Tirchonaill St) North of the diamond.

Tourist office (☎ 972 1148; donegal@failteireland .ie; Quay St; ☒ 9am-6pm Mon-Sat, noon-4pm Sun Jul-Aug, 9.30am-5.30pm Mon-Sat Sep-Jun) South of the diamond.

SIGHTS
Donegal Castle
Overlooking a wicked bend of the Eske, **Donegal Castle** (☎ 972 2405; Castle St; adult/child €3.70/1.30; ☒ 10am-6pm mid-Mar–Oct, 9.30am-4.30pm Nov-Dec) remains an imperious monument to both Irish and English might. Built by the O'Donnells in

1474, it served as the seat of their formidable power until 1607, when the English decided to be rid of pesky Irish chieftains once and for all. Even in defeat, Rory O'Donnell was no pushover, though. To stop the English getting their grubby hands on it, he torched his own castle before fleeing to France in the infamous Flight of the Earls. Their defeat paved the way for the Plantation of Ulster by thousands of newly arrived Scots and English Protestants, thereby creating the divisions that still afflict the island to this day.

The castle was rebuilt in 1623 by Sir Basil Brooke, along with the adjacent three-storey Jacobean house. Much of the castle is gutted today, but enough has been preserved that it's worth a look-see.

Diamond Obelisk

In 1474 Red Hugh O'Donnell and his wife, Nuala O'Brien, founded a **Franciscan friary** by the shore south of town. It was accidentally blown up in 1601 by Rory O'Donnell while laying siege to an English garrison, and little remains. What makes it famous is that four of its friars, fearing that the arrival of the English meant the end of Celtic culture, chronicled the whole of known Celtic history and mythology from 40 years before the Flood to AD 1618 in *The Annals of the Four Masters*, still one of the most important sources of early Irish history. The **obelisk** (1937), in the diamond, commemorates the work, copies of which are displayed in the National Library in Dublin.

ACTIVITIES
Boat Trips

A fantastic way to explore the highlights of Donegal Bay is to take one of the boat tours run by **Donegal Bay Waterbus** (☎ 972 3666; www .donegalbaywaterbus.com; Donegal Pier; adult/child €10/5). Aboard a 20m tour boat, the 1¼-hour tour covers everything from historic sites to seal-inhabited coves, stopping to admire an island manor and a ruined castle along the way. The tour runs up to five times daily during the summer and at least once a day the rest of the year, depending on the weather. Call to check departure times.

Fishing

Permits are required for fishing in the local rivers. Kits and information are available from **Doherty's** (☎ 972 1119; Main St; ☾ 9am-6pm Thu-Tue).

SLEEPING

B&Bs are plentiful around Donegal town, and the tourist office can assist with making bookings.

Budget

Donegal Town Independent Hostel (☎ 972 2805; lincunn8@eircom.net; Killybegs Rd, Doonan; dm/d €16/40; P) Privately operated by a friendly couple and their dog, this Independent Holiday Hostels of Ireland (IHH) hostel, 1.2km northwest of town off the Killybegs Rd (N56), has gaudily painted, but exceptionally clean dorms and private rooms. It's within walking distance of town. Pick up can be arranged.

Bluestack Centre (☎ 973 5564; www.donegal bluestacks.com; Drimarone; dm/f €16/50; P ⅏) This is a remote country hostel-cum-community centre with squeaky-clean rooms and a basketball court. It's also a handy point for hikers tackling the Bluestack Mountains. It's often left unmanned, however, so call ahead. It's 7km north of town, signposted from the roundabout northwest of town.

Midrange & Top End

Atlantic Guest House (☎ 972 1187; Main St; s/d from €35/45; P) It's not homey or particularly friendly, but this busy old guesthouse, just a block from the diamond, is a convenient and reasonable choice. It has 16 cheery and clean rooms, some with private bathroom. Mattresses are a little thin.

Bridges B&B (☎ 972 1082; Waterloo Pl; s/d €40/70) Facing the castle and the river, this small, family-run B&B is simply tidy, quiet and comfy.

Ard na Breatha (☎ 972 2288; www.ardnabreatha.com; Drumrooske Middle; s/d €65/130; P) This is a terrific little guesthouse, with a more countrified setting 2.4km out of town. It has modern rooms furnished to the highest standard and charming service. The restaurant is open for dinner at weekends (reservations required). It's signposted off the road to Lough Eske.

Abbey Hotel (☎ 972 1014; www.whites-hotelsireland .com; the Diamond; s/d from €70/130; P ⅏) In a great stone building (118 rooms) at the heart of town, the Abbey offers a bit of snazzy, contemporary flair on the inside. Rooms out the back overlook the river. The hotel offers access to a gym and has a stylish restaurant and bar.

Central Hotel (☎ 972 1027; www.centralhoteldonegal .com; the Diamond; s/d €80/140; P ⅏) The Abbey's twin is another impressive stone building that presides over the town centre. It offers all the comfort and mod cons of a contemporary establishment. Back rooms have river views and the bar features live music. Enticing specials are offered in winter.

St Ernan's House Hotel (☎ 972 1065; www.saint ernans.com; R267; s/d from €150/230, dinner €52; ☾ May-Oct; P) If you've ever dreamt of having your own private island, you'll love this place. This magnificent country hotel (built by a nephew of Wellington in 1836) is set on its own wooded islet about 3km south of Donegal town, signposted off the road to Laghey and accessible via a causeway. It's hard not to feel serene with lapping water on all sides. Children under six are not catered for.

COUNTY DONEGAL

EATING

Donegal's Famous Chipper (☎ 972 1428; Upper Main St; fish & chips €5-6; ⏰ 12.30-11.30pm Thu-Tue) You've probably never heard of this joint, whose fame spreads as far as the town limit, but it's an excellent place to grab an order of fried cod. You can eat at the Formica counter or take yours to a nearby pub (of which there are plenty).

Blueberry Tearoom (☎ 972 2933; Castle St; mains €7-9; ⏰ 9am-7pm Mon-Sat) Piping hot baked goodies, *panini* (type of Italian sandwich) and excellent pies make this snug tearoom a local favourite at any time of the day. Its lunchtime specials are also worth fighting your way in for, and it dabbles in everything from French to Cajun dishes.

Market House (☎ 972 1014; the Diamond; mains €15-25; ⏰ noon-2pm, 5-9pm) With tartan carpeting and stone walls, the Market House somehow manages to not feel touristy or old-fashioned. The kitchen tackles surf and turf mainstays with a contemporary ethos: fresh, light and, above all, fine tasting.

La Bella Donna (☎ 972 5790; Bridge St; mains €10-25; ⏰ noon-5pm & 7-9.30pm) The Irish enthusiasm for Italian is not lost on far-flung Donegal, as the lively and well-dressed weeknight crowds at this snazzy place attest. Drop by for pizzas, pastas and steaks. Lunchtime *panini* and espressos are a forte.

DRINKING

Donegal's nightlife is a bit hit and miss. Any place with a live-music session on is likely to be your best bet.

Dunnion's (Bridge St) The owner of this old-school pub, next to the river, plays the button-box accordion, and his pals join him in a céilidh most nights. It often has the best craic in town.

Old Castle (☎ 972 1062; Castle St) A grey-stone pub built to match the neighbouring castle with attractive stonework, corbel windows and a low wooden ceiling. It's a relaxing spot to enjoy a sip of stout and swap banter with locals.

SHOPPING

Donegal Craft Village (☎ 972 2225; Ballyshannon Rd; ⏰ 9am-6pm Mon-Sat, 11am-6pm Sun) There's not a single canned leprechaun or Guinness T-shirt in sight at this complex of craft studios, 1.5km south of town. Instead, it showcases quality pottery, crystal, hand-woven fab-

rics, jewellery and more – look for the Raw Studio, selling sculpted bogwood by Michael Griffin.

Magee (☎ 972 2660; www.mageedonegal.com; the Diamond; ⏰ 9.30am-6pm Mon-Sat) Magee is a small department store with a room devoted to Donegal tweed.

GETTING THERE & AWAY

Frequent **Bus Éireann** (☎ 913 1008; www.bus eireann.ie) services connect Donegal with Sligo (€11, 1¼ hours, six daily), Galway (€17 3½ hours, two to three daily) and Killybegs (€6, 35 minutes, three daily) to the west; Derry (€11.50, 1½ hours) and Belfast (€16, 3½ hours) in the North; and Dublin (€16, four hours, six daily) in the southeast. The bus stop is on the western side of the diamond.

Feda O'Donnell (☎ 954 8114; www.fedaodonnell .com) runs to Galway (single/return €15/22, 3½ hours, twice daily, three on Friday and Sunday) via Ballyshannon, Bundoran and Sligo. Departures are from the tourist office. Fares within Donegal range from €6 to €10.

McGeehan Coaches (☎ 954 6150; www.mgbus .com) runs buses to Dublin's Busáras bus station (single/return €16/23, four hours, two daily Monday, Friday, Saturday and Sunday, one daily Tuesday to Thursday) from in front of the garda barracks across from the tourist office.

GETTING AROUND

Head to the **Bike Shop** (☎ 972 2515; Waterloo Pl; per day/week €10/60) for bike hire and information on cycling in the area.

AROUND DONEGAL TOWN

LOUGH ESKE

Despite its optimistic name, meaning 'Lake of the Fish', this picturesque spot northeast of Donegal town isn't the fishpond it once was, but it's still terrific territory for cycling or walking over the majestic Blue Stack Mountains.

Sleeping & Eating

Ardeevin Guest House (☎ 074-972 1790; http://ardeevin .tripod.com; Lough Eske; s/d €50/75; ℗) Great views of the lake are just one of this B&B's selling points. Running for 40 years, it has evolved into a large rambling house with charming rooms and an old-fashioned garden. It's 4km north of Donegal town off the Letterkenny road (N15). Take the second left and follow the signs.

Harvey's Point Country Hotel (☎ 074-972 2208; www.harveyspoint.com; Harvey's Point; d €199-299, 4-course dinner €50; P ⌨) This is an elite retreat. With expansive grounds lapping the edge of the lake, it has large guestrooms, Jacuzzi baths, a top-notch French restaurant and a helicopter pad that's not just for show. Harvey's is 6km north of Donegal town.

Getting There & Away

From the diamond in Donegal, take the N56 to Killybegs. About 300m past the bridge, turn right following the signs to Harvey's Point.

ROSSNOWLAGH

☎ 071 / pop 50

The old-world resort of Rossnowlagh (Ross Neamblach), southwest of Donegal town, has a dazzlingly white Blue Flag beach, which extends for nearly 5km and is a popular **surfing** spot (gentle rollers here). The huge Sandhouse Hotel stands beside a humble caravan park along the beach, and that's about it, really. But if you're after some relaxing rays, this may be your spot.

Deep in the adjacent forest is a **Franciscan friary** (☎ 985 1342; admission free; ⏰ 10am-8pm Mon-Sat) with tranquil gardens; the way of the cross takes you through a hillside smothered with rhododendron to spectacular hill-top views.

Smugglers Creek (☎ 985 2367; smugcreek@eircom .net; s/d €45/80; ⏰ Easter-Oct; P) is perched dramatically on the hillside above the bay. This pub, restaurant and guesthouse is justifiably popular for its excellent food and sweeping views. Room 4 has the best vantage point and a balcony into the bargain. The pub features live music on summer weekends.

Once an extravagant 19th-century fishing lodge, the **Sandhouse Hotel** (☎ 985 1777; www.sand house-hotel.ie; d €189-319; ⏰ Apr-Dec; P ♿) continues to project a festive atmosphere and is a fine beach getaway.

BALLYSHANNON

☎ 071 / pop 2230

Pretty Ballyshannon (Béal Átha Seanaidh), crawling up a steep incline above the River Erne, is a world away from the tacky excess of nearby Bundoran, and makes a more tranquil base to explore the coastline.

Information

Bank of Ireland (Market St) Has an ATM.

Post office (Market St) Near the junction.

Tourist information centre (⏰ 9.30am-1pm, 2-5pm, closed Oct-Apr) A skeletal operation at the bus station.

WALK: BLUE STACK MOUNTAINS

If you're not satisfied with admiring the Blue Stack Mountains from a distance, you can take a rewarding, though difficult, trek along a circuitous 18km path through wild and rugged terrain. A complete circuit should take about seven hours, and entails summiting several peaks topping 600m. The highest of these, at 674m high, is **Blue Stack**, from which the views of southern Donegal are spectacular. Alternatively, you can walk the short (though steep) distance to **Eas Doonan waterfall**, which drops some 30m and is truly spectacular after a good rain. This walk can be done in about one hour. Note that in wet weather the trail can be a bit boggy, surely slowing you down.

The trail head is easy to find, though it sounds complicated. Off the N15 from Donegal Town, look for the signs for Lough Eske. There are three turnoffs, all leading to Lough Eske Dr. Follow the road counterclockwise towards the northern end of the lake, where the road hairpins twice. Off the second hairpin take the small road leading to Edergole, where you'll find a walker sign and space to park your car.

It would be wise to collect more detailed information and perhaps a map before attempting the full circuit. The OSI 1:50,000 map No 11 covers this territory. The information centre in Donegal Town (see p506) is excellent. The Mountain Views website (http://mountainviews .ie) is a useful resource with input from hikers who have explored the Blue Stacks and other mountains in Ireland.

COUNTY DONEGAL

Sights & Activities
ALLINGHAM'S GRAVE
As a kid, the poet William Allingham (1824–89) scribbled his first attempts at verse on a window in the AIB bank on Castle St where his dad was the manager. The wordsmith, who is best remembered for his poem *The Fairies*, is now buried in the graveyard beside **St Anne's Church**, the grave marked simply 'poet'. The church is signposted left off Main St after Dorrian's Imperial Hotel.

ABBEY MILLS
Waterwheels have been harnessing the river's power for centuries at **Abbey Assaroe** (☎ 985 8966; Abbeylands; admission free; ☼ 11am-7pm Jun-Sep, 2.30-7pm Sun Oct-May; P). The site was founded in the late 12th century by Cistercian monks from County Roscommon. Now restored to working order, the mills are open as a heritage centre. Take the road to Rossnowlagh (R231) and after 2km, signs indicate Abbey Mills on the left.

Festivals & Events
The exuberant **Ballyshannon Folk & Traditional Music Festival** (www.ballyshannonfolkfestival.com) arrives for the last weekend in July or the first in August. The schedule is available online.

Sleeping & Eating
Lakeside Caravan & Camping (☎ 985 2822; lakesidecentre@eircom.net; Belleek Rd; camp sites from €17 ☼ Mar-Sep) Nestling on the shore of Assaroe Lake, this four-star camping ground is worth the trip. It's especially well equipped for kids. From Ballyshannon, take the N3 for 1km towards Belleek.

Breesy Centre (☎ 982 2925; www.breesycentre.com; Cashelard; dm/d €20/40, breakfast €5; P &.) This remote country hostel has sparkly and cheerful dorms with private bathrooms, and a tranquil village setting 6km northeast of Ballyshannon. Head north on the N15, turn east after 5km (there's a sign for Cashelard) and continue 1km. You'll see the hostel, opposite a modern-looking pub.

Cavangarden House (☎ 985 1365; www.littleireland .ie/cavangardenhouse; Donegal Rd; s/d €44/70; P) This Georgian country house is a beauty amid expansive lawns trees alive with birdsong. Guestrooms have sturdy antique beds, and evening meals can be arranged. To find it, take the N15 3km north of town and look for the signs.

Shannon's Corner (☎ 985 1180; Main St; mains €6-10; ☼ 8.30am-4.30pm) In-the-know locals pile into this unassuming bistro for its home-cooked lunches and smashing sarnies.

Drinking
Fin McCool's (☎ 985 2677; Main St) A traditional pub with occasional music sessions.

Thatch Pub (Bishop St) This picturesque place, just off the top of Main St, is a great place to grab a pint and a few snapshots.

Getting There & Away
There are regular daily **Bus Éireann** (☎ 074-912 1309) services to Bundoran (€2.10, 10 minutes), Sligo (€9, 50 minutes), Galway (€17, 3½ hours), Donegal (€5, 25 minutes), and Dublin (€16, 4½ hours; via Enniskillen, Cavan and Navan). The bus station is between the bridge and the Gallogley Jewellers clock tower.

Feda O'Donnell (☎ 074-974 8114) buses depart from opposite the bus station for Donegal (€5, 15 minutes) and Letterkenny (€6, one hour) twice daily, four times on Friday. For Sligo (€6, 45 minutes) and Galway (€15, three hours) they leave from outside Maggie's Bar, south of the river near the roundabout, twice daily, three times Friday and Sunday.

BUNDORAN
☎ 071 / pop 1680
It's one of Ireland's tackiest holiday resorts, with an assortment of unappealing arcades and fast-food diners, but not all is lost in Bundoran (Bun Dobhráin). The big draw here is the surf, for which Bundoran is renowned. The strand and nearby dunes are beautiful, offering scenic spots for walking, sunbathing and horse riding. If you stay here, mosey over to the less commercial west end of town.

Information
AIB Bank (Main St) Has an ATM and bureau de change.
Post office (Main St)
Tourist office (☎ 984 1350; bundoran@irelandnorth west.ie; the Bridge, Main St; ☼ 10am-5pm Mon-Fri mid-Mar–Sep, 10am-4pm Fri & Sat Oct–mid-Mar) Seasonal office opposite the Holyrood Hotel.

Activities
SURFING & KITE-SURFING
The breaks of Tullan Strand, just north of the town centre, offer some of the best surfing in Europe, and Bundoran hosts the annual Irish National Surfing Championships,

which are usually held in April. For more information, check out the website of the **Irish Surfing Association** (www.isasurf.ie).

The youth-oriented **Donegal Adventure Centre** (☎ 984 2418; www.donegal-holidays.com; Bay View Ave; surf lessons per 3hr €35) rents gear and runs all-year surf tuition. It also offers kayaking and gorge walking, and for those taking courses, dorm beds are available (€25).

Bundoran Surf Co (☎ 984 1968; www.bundoransurfco.com; ⏰ 9.30am-7pm) offers lessons in kite-surfing and power-kiting. A day-long lesson costs €120. The company also rents standard surf gear (board and wetsuit per half day €30) and gives surf lessons (per three hours €35). Surf and accommodation packages can be arranged (see the website for details).

HORSE RIDING
Family-run, friendly and efficient **Donegal Equestrian Holidays** (☎ 984 1977; www.donegalequestrianholidays.com), just outside the town, is Bundoran's big draw for nonsurfers. The centre offers rides over the dunes and along the beach, lessons for all levels and pony camps for families. Call ahead for reservations. A one-hour trail ride (€45) is your simplest option, but longer rides are available.

WATER ACTIVITIES
Bundoran's beach isn't safe for swimming, so the place to get wet is **Waterworld** (☎ 984 1172; www.waterworldbundoran.com; adult/child under 8 €8.50/3.50), a fun facility with a swimming pool and water slides. It's on the beach. Also on the premises, **Aquamara** (☎ 984 1173; baths from €18; ⏰ 11am-7pm) provides a decidedly more sedate form of bathing in its seaweed baths. See the boxed text, p471, for more on Irish seaweed therapy.

Sleeping
All of the following are in the more pleasant west end of town.

Homefield Hostel (☎ 984 1288; homefield@indigo.ie; Bayview Ave; dm/d €18/40; ℗) This 260-year-old building was once Viscount Enniskillen's holiday play pad, and later served as an altogether more restrained convent. It now has the look and feel of a fun and well-lived-in, budget-oriented lodge. The six-bed dorms and private rooms are in good nick and there are lots of cosy lounges.

Bay View B&B (☎ 984 1237; Main St; s/d €40/64; ℗) Facing the beach, this stately Edwardian town house has a historic feel but is no less inviting for it. Guestrooms are a bit utilitarian, but all are en suite and those in front have unobstructed views of waves crashing ashore.

Fitzgerald's Hotel (☎ 984 1336; www.fitzgeraldshotel.com; s/d €65/110; ℗) Bundoran's most polished operation is this small hotel, across the street from the strand. It's an older building that has been thoroughly updated with ample personality. Rooms are spacious and many have excellent views. The hotel has an excellent restaurant-bistro.

Eating
La Sabbia (☎ 984 2253; Bay View Ave; lunch €6-9, dinner €9-24; ⏰ 9am-late) This colourful Mediterranean bistro has tables spilling out onto the front porch and attracts a lively, upbeat crowd. The menu features seafood specialties (the oyster bar is a good starting point) along with tasty pastas and pizzas. It's also a good spot for strong coffee or a *panini*.

COUNTY DONEGAL

SURF'S UP

It isn't exactly a secret (among surfers, anyway) that the west coast of Ireland offers some of the best surf breaks in Europe. Travellers from as far off as Australia and South Africa regularly arrive in towns like Bundoran and Easky (County Sligo) with their minds singularly focused on the beach breaks, reef breaks and point breaks for which the coast is known.

Towns noted for their surfing activity in Donegal include Rossnowlagh (p509), Bundoran (opposite) and Dungloe (p519). In Sligo, the surf is often up in Strandhill (p469) and Easky (p471). Achill Island (p454) in County Mayo also has good surfing. All of these places have outfitters that can take care of the needs of the travelling surfer. If you're not a surfer, many companies will teach you how to do it. All levels can be accommodated for.

The Irish Surfing Association has a useful website at www.isasurf.ie. Surfers can also get recent information from fellow travellers at www.globalsurfers.com. See p702 for more on surfing and swimming.

Fitzgerald's Bistro (☎ 984 1336; Main St; mains €16-24; ☽ 6.30-9pm Wed-Sun Easter-Oct, Fri & Sat only Oct-Easter) Hidden within Fitzgerald's Hotel, this popular bistro looks a little like a hunting lodge, but with cosy plush booths and a friendly staff. Although seafood is the specialty, the kitchen is equally adept with meat and veg. A fun spot.

Drinking

Brennan's (☎ 984 1810; Main St; ☽ midnight-4am Fri-Sun) is a quiet and neighbourly old pub in the heart of town. It's a refreshing departure from the brash and spangly places up the street.

Getting There & Away

Bus Éireann (☎ 074-912 1309) buses stop on Main St. There are direct daily services to Sligo (€8, 45 minutes), Galway (€17, 2¼ hours), Donegal (€6, 40 minutes) and more. **Ulsterbus/Translink** (☎ 028-9066 6630; www.ulsterbus.co.uk) has three services daily Monday to Friday (one Saturday) to Belfast (€17.50, 3½ hours) via Enniskillen (€12.50, 1¼ hours). **Feda O'Donnell** (☎ 074-974 8114) buses from Crolly (€6, 2½ hours) travelling to Galway (€14, three hours) stop in Bundoran outside the Holyrood Hotel twice daily, three times on Friday and Sunday.

SOUTHWESTERN DONEGAL

MOUNTCHARLES TO BRUCKLESS

Donegal's scenery-o-meter starts to crank up when you reach the coast, just to the west of Donegal town, and it steadily intensifies as you head north. The first coastal communities you'll reach are tiny but no less beautiful. Apart from a scattering of pubs and cafés in Mountcharles and Dunkineely, there are few places to eat (especially in winter), so stock up before leaving Donegal town or Killybegs.

Mountcharles

☎ 074 / pop 430
This hillside village of Mountcharles (Moin Séarlas) is the first settlement along the coastal road (N56) southwest of Donegal town. About 2km south of the village is a safe, sandy beach. The shiny-green **pump** at the top of this hillside village was once the backdrop for stories of fairies, ghosts, historic battles and mythological encounters. For it was at this point that local boy Séamus MacManus, a poet and *seanachaí* (storyteller) of international repute, practised the ancient art in the 1940s and 1950s.

Dunkineely

☎ 074 / pop 350
The dozy little village of Dunkineely (Dún Cionnfhaolaidh or Dún Cionnaola) is situated a little further west. From here, a minor road runs down the improbably thin finger of land poking into the sea at **St John's Point**. There's a beach with a little bit of sand and sweeping coastal views, and the waters around the point are a prime diving site.

Blue Moon Hostel (☎ 973 7264; http://homepage .eircom.net/~bluemoonhostel; Main St; camp sites per person €5, dm/d €12/30; **P**) is an Independent Hostel Owners of Ireland (IHO) hostel that looks unexceptional, even a little dowdy. Its three-tier bunk beds are comfy enough and it offers two kitchens, a washer/dryer and plenty of information on local goings-on such as deep-sea diving and sea angling.

Castle Murray (☎ 973 7022; www.castlemurray.com; St John's Point; s/d €90/140; mains €17-24; ☽ 6.30-9.30pm; **P**) Overlooking the sea cliffs, this is no castle, but a rather small and welcoming hotel in an old beach house. It has 10 playfully updated guestrooms, each conveying a cultural theme – the décor is sure to date badly, but the rooms are unquestionably comfortable and the sunset views can't be beat. Breakfast is superb, and it's little wonder, for the place is equally known for its restaurant, which specializes in seafood with some admirable French influences. Prawns and monkfish in garlic butter is a specialty.

Bruckless

☎ 074 / pop 180
The scattered settlement of Bruckless (An Bhroclais) is the next stop, about 2km west of Dunkineely. Horse riding and pony trekking are available at **Deane's Equestrian Centre** (☎ 973 7160; deanesequestrian@eircom.net; Darney, Bruckless; ☽ 10am-4pm), including lessons, five-minute pony rides for children (€5) and longer excursions (adult/child from €17/20). Advance booking is required.

The luxury, ivy-clad, Georgian B&B **Bruckless House** (☎ 973 7071; www.iol.ie/~bruc/bruckless

.html; d €120; Apr-Sep; (P)) is simply gorgeous. Fronted by a traditional cobbled farmyard, it is home to a stud farm for Connemara ponies. Guests will enjoy wandering its 18 acres of gardens, which lope down to the shore. The interior is furnished with antique oriental influences. It's signposted off the main road approximately 3km after Dunkineely.

Getting There & Away

Bus Éireann (972 1008) bus 490 from Donegal to Killybegs stops near the Village Tavern in Mountcharles, the Inver post office in Bruckless and the Dunkineely Furniture Centre in Dunkineely.

KILLYBEGS

074 / pop 1400

A fishy fragrance welcomes you to Killybegs (Ceala Beaga), Ireland's most important fishing port and home to a large fishmeal processing plant. Apart from that, it's a fairly charming town, with a number of oddly angled streets colliding at its diamond, a block from the pier. Deep-sea angling is the top tourist activity here, but Killybegs is also a convenient base for the spectacular cliff scenery beyond Kilcar.

The community-run **tourist office** (973 2346; Quay St; 9.30am-5.30pm Mon-Fri) is in a cabin near the harbour. The **Bank of Ireland** (Main St) has an ATM and bureau de change.

Sights & Activities

A right turn in town up a steep hill brings you to **St Mary's Church**, outside which stands the extraordinary **tombstone of Niall Mór Mac-Sweeney**, head of the MacSweeney clan, one of Donegal's ruling families before 1607. It clearly depicts a chain-mailed warrior with a plumed helmet, his battle-axe raised and sword at the ready. This warlike figure is a *gallowglass*, a Scottish mercenary who first came to the north and west of Ireland in the late 13th century.

Several operators offer **fishing** expeditions with the opportunity to catch pollock, cod and whiting. **Killybegs Angling Charters** (973 1144; www.killybegsangling.com; Blackrock Pier) runs fishing charters (€400 for the boat). The **Harbour Store** (973 1569; the Harbour), by the wharf, sells fishing gear.

The wild, secluded **Fintragh Bay**, about 3km west and down a big-dipper of a road, is fun to explore and the water is clean and safe for swimming.

Sleeping

Ritz (973 1309; www.theritz-killybegs.com; Chapel Brae; dm/d/f €20/60/70; (P)) For the price, this place ain't at all bad. It is an IHO hostel, but rooms provide the privacy and comfort of a hotel. It has an enormous modern kitchen, colourful rooms with private bathroom and TV, and cosy common areas. A light breakfast is included. It's a good family choice.

Seawinds B&B (973 2003; www.seawindsireland.com; the Diamond; s/d €40/60; (P)) In the heart of town, this friendly B&B has basic and cheery rooms, all with no-fuss holiday-home décor. Another good choice for families.

Tara Hotel (974 1700; www.tarahotel.ie; Main St; s/d €80/120;) Just a few skips from the harbour, this thoroughly modern hotel gives Killybegs an unexpected tinge of minimalist swank. Guestrooms come with the usual frills (including TV and internet). Ask for one of six sea-view rooms with balcony (costing €10 extra in summer).

Eating

Shines (973 1996; Killybegs; fish & chips €6; 11am-2pm, 4-11.30pm Wed-Sat, 3-11.30pm Sun) If the official town aroma has you craving something with gills and fins, this spic-and-span chip shop can take care of your needs without further ado. It does a brisk takeaway business. Salt yours down and take it to the beach.

22 Main Street (973 2876; www.22mainstreet.com; Main St; mains €11-22; 5-10pm) If you crave something other than seafood but your partner has to have something fished from the local waters, then this Mediterranean-style bistro's your ticket. In the heart of the town, it cranks out pizzas and pastas, along with piping hot seafood pies, fish and chips and prime Irish beef.

Kitty Kelly's (973 1925; www.kittykellys.com; Kilcar Rd; 6.30-9.30pm daily Easter-Sep, Thu-Sun Oct-Mar) Run by a gregarious local celebrity, this 200-year-old farmhouse restaurant puts on what feels like an intimate dinner party. As you would expect in such a setting, the menu is traditional Irish, with some praiseworthy seafood selections. It's on the coast road, 5km west of Killybegs. Reservations recommended.

COUNTY DONEGAL

Getting There & Away

Bus Éireann (☎ 912 1008) service 492 to Donegal (€6, 30 minutes) from Killybegs runs four times daily Monday to Saturday. Bus 490 heads west to Kilcar (€4, 20 minutes) and Glencolumbcille (€8, 45 minutes) once daily Monday, Wednesday and Friday, and twice on Tuesday, Thursday and Saturday. In July and August an extra bus runs daily, and buses continue to Malinmore twice daily, Monday to Saturday.

KILCAR & CARRICK

☎ 074 / pop 260

Kilcar (Cill Chártha) and its more attractive neighbour Carrick (An Charraig) are small country towns that make good bases for exploring the breathtaking coastline of southwestern Donegal, especially the stunning sea cliffs at Slieve League. Kilcar is also famous for the manufacture of Donegal tweed. Just outside Kilcar is a small, sandy beach.

This is lovely walking country, particularly if you don't mind hoofing up and down a few hills. Kilcar Tourism has some pointers for walking the Kilcar Way; ask at the **Aísleann Cill Cartha** (☎ 973 8376; Main St; ⏲ 9am-5.30pm Mon-Fri), a community centre that provides information for tourists.

More tourist information is available from the cultural centre, **Ionad Cultúrach Sliabh Liag** (Slieve League Cultural Centre; ☎ 973 9077; www.sliabhleague.com; Teelin, Carrick), which also has a pleasant coffee shop. There are no banks. The post office is off Main St past O'Gara's pub.

Sights

STUDIO DONEGAL

Beside the community centre is the **Studio Donegal** (☎ 973 8194; www.studiodonegal.ie; the Glebe Mill, Kilcar; admission free; ⏲ 10am-5.30pm Mon, 9am-5.30pm Tue-Thu, 9.30am-5pm Fri), a shop where tweeds are spun and loomed by hand. Sometimes visitors are invited upstairs to see spinners and weavers in action.

SLIEVE LEAGUE

The Cliffs of Moher get more attention from photographers, but the Slieve League is higher. Driving up to these spectacular polychrome sea cliffs, the highest in Europe dropping some 600m into the sea, is a hair-raising – but exhilarating – experience. From the car park, there's a path skirting up around the near-vertical rock face to the aptly named **One Man's Pass**.

Take the turn-off signposted Bunglass from the R263 at Carrick, 5km northwest of Kilcar, and continue beyond the narrow track signposted Slieve League to the one that's signposted Bunglass.

Activities

Three walks that start in Kilcar are collectively known as the **Kilcar Way**. From Teelin, experienced walkers can spend a day walking north via Bunglass and the cliff-top One Man's Path – not for the faint hearted – to Malinbeg, near Glencolumbcille. It shouldn't be attempted in windy conditions or if bad weather is likely to impede visibility.

Sleeping & Eating

Dún Ulún House (☎ 973 8137; dunulunhouse@eircom .net; Coast Rd; camp sites €10, dm €15, d €45; P) The sweeping view down to a ruined ringfort is what strikes you first about this inn, run by an older couple. If you're a single traveller open to sharing a room, they'll arrange a bed for the night, hostel-style. Accommodation is simple but homey, and the owners can be helpful with travel plans, Gaelic lessons and genealogy. Breakfast (€7.50) is optional. A little camping ground is ensconced in the tiered hillside. The house is 1km west of the village.

Derrylahan Hostel (☎ 973 8079; derrylahan@eircom .net; Derrylahan, Kilcar; camp sites €12, dm/d €14/36; P) The best option for hostellers and campers is this friendly IHH hostel. It's a working farm, and the hostel is very well run and friendly. The dorms are comfortable, there are plentiful cooking facilities and a 20-person group house. It also rents bikes. It's 3km west of the village on the coast road. Pick-ups can be arranged.

Ostan Sliabh Liagh (☎ 973 9973; www.ostansliabh liag.com; Carrick; s/d €35/70; bar food €4-9; P) In the heart of the sweet little hamlet of Carrick, this B&B is above the town's largest pub and offers rooms that are barebones but pass military inspection for tidiness. Most rooms are en suite. The pub grub isn't bad, either.

Blue Haven (☎ 973 8090; Kilcar-Killybegs Rd; mains €12-25; ⏲ 6-10pm, noon-3pm Sun) It's modern and stylish, but this restaurant aspires merely to serve 'home cooking' prepared with fresh local produce. The place can be quite festive, and its sunset views are stunning.

Getting There & Away

Bus Éireann (☎ 912 1309) service 490 connects Kilcar and Carrick with Killybegs and Glencolumbcille once daily Monday to Friday (twice daily Saturday, once Sunday). In July and August an extra bus runs Monday to Saturday. **McGeehan Coaches** (☎ 954 6150) has a daily service from Glencolumbcille to Dublin that stops at Carrick and Kilcar. There are extra buses in summer.

GLENCOLUMBCILLE & AROUND

☎ 074 / pop 255

It's not much more than a gash in the rocks, making Glencolumbcille (Gleann Cholm Cille, 'Glen of Columba's Church') a remote and starkly beautiful coastal haven. Approaching the town via the Glen Gesh Pass perfectly illustrates how cut off Glencolumbcille is from the rest of the world, as you drive through miles and miles of hills and bogs before the ocean appears – and there you'll see a narrow, green valley and the small Gaeltacht village within it.

This spot has been inhabited since 3000 BC and you'll find plenty of Stone Age remains throughout the collection of tiny settlements. It is believed that the 6th-century St Colmcille (Columba) founded a monastery here (hence the valley's name) and incorporated Stone Age standing stones called *turas* into Christian usage by inscribing them with a cross.

At midnight on **Colmcille's Feast Day** (9 June) penitents begin a walkabout of the *turas* and the remains of Colmcille's church before attending Mass at 3am in the local church.

Information

Teach Alasa (☎ 973 0116; Cashel; ☙ 10am-6pm Mon-Sat, 1-5pm Sun Apr, Jun & Sep–mid-Nov, 9.30am-9pm Mon-Sat, noon-6pm Sun Jul & Aug) dispenses limited tourist information. There are no banks or ATMs but the post office has a bureau de change.

Sights & Activities

FATHER MCDYER'S FOLK VILLAGE

A museum with a mission, this **folk centre** (☎ 973 0017; www.glenfolkvillage.com; Doonalt; adult/child €3/2; ☙ 10am-6pm Mon-Sat, noon-6pm Sun Easter-Sep; P) was established by the forward-thinking Father James McDyer in 1967 to freeze-frame traditional folk life for posterity. It's housed in a huddle of replicated thatched cottages of the 18th and 19th centuries, with genuine period fittings. The *shebeen* (illicit drinking

place) sells unusual local wines (made from ingredients such as seaweed and fuchsias) alongside marmalade and whisky truffles. Admission includes a tour. It's 3km west of the village, by the beach.

BEACHES

There are two sandy beaches with brisk waves in **Doonalt**, immediately west of the village. Another gorgeous little beach can be found at **Malinbeg**, a perfect sheltered bay bitten out of low cliffs and filled with firm red-tinged sand. Its just down the coast road, in the direction of Slieve League.

WALKING

A couple of loop walks will get you off into the blustery wilds beyond the town. The **Tower Loop** (10km, two to three hours) takes you up over some stunning coastal cliffs, while the more arduous **Drum Loop** (13km, three to four hours) heads into the hills, northeast of the town. Both walks start and finish at Colmcille's church. At the time of research, finishing touches were being put on a new **walking centre** (☎ 973 0302), near the beach, which will offer information, guided walks and showers.

Courses

Oideas Gael (☎ 973 0248; www.oideas-gael.com; ☙ mid-Mar–Oct), at the Foras Cultúir Uladh (Ulster Cultural Foundation) 1km west of the village centre, offers a range of 'cultural activity holidays' – adult courses in Irish language and traditional culture, including dancing, pottery and music. The centre also leads hillwalking programmes in the Donegal highlands. Three-day courses cost from €100. Accommodation can be arranged – you'll have a choice of homestay or self-catering, with prices of around €20 to €40 per person per night.

Sleeping

Dooey Hostel (☎ 973 0130; www.dooeyhostel.com; camp sites/dm/d 7.50/13/28; P) This ageing IHO hostel has character in spades, in part because it's owned by an elderly, wildhaired chainsmoker who calls herself 'Mad' Mary O'Donnell. The hostel is actually built *into* the hillside, with rock and dripping greenery bulging into its inner corridor. It has a superb hilltop view to boot. Facilities are rustic, but each dorm has its own bath and kitchen. A group house for 20 is available. Drivers should take the turn beside the Glenhead Tavern for 1.5km; walkers can take a short cut beside the Folk Village. Cash only.

Malinbeg Hostel (☎ 973 0006; www.malinbeghoste .com; Malinbeg, Glencolumbcille; dm/s/d €16/25/40; ✆ closed Dec & early Jan; P) The Dooey's opposite is the thoroughly modern and comfortable Malinbeg. It sports spotless rooms with private bathroom and scores big for its proximity to a beautiful beach, a food store and restaurant. Call ahead for a pick-up.

Glencolumbcille Hotel (Óstán Ghleann Cholm Cille; ☎ 973 0003; www.glenhotel.com; s/d €60/110; P) This canary-coloured hotel stands amid the rolling countryside, with its own golf course slowly taking shape at its rear. Its 40 classy rooms are extremely spacious. For something special, request the suite facing the coast. To get there, continue past the folk museum towards Malinbeg.

Eating

During the winter there are few eating options within the town itself. The food store, next to the Malinbeg Hostel, can provide ready-made sandwiches.

An Cistin (the Kitchen; ☎ 973 0213; Glencolumbcille; mains €10-22; ✆ 9am-9pm Easter-Oct) You won't find a better spot to chow down than this café-restaurant attached to Oideas Gael. It serves up a surprisingly gourmet selection, including superb seafood, to a soundtrack of mellow jazz.

Silver Strand House (☎ 973 0220; Malinbeg; mains €15-20; ✆ 9am-9.30pm daily May-Sep, Sat & Sun Oct-Apr; P) For those staying towards the tip of Malinbeg, this catch-all restaurant by the beach proffers a great fisherman's platter so you can sample most of the local haul.

Shopping

Glencolumbcille Woollen Mill (☎ 973 0070; www.rossan knitwear-glenwoolmill.com; Malinmore; ✆ 10am-8pm Mar-Oct, to 5.50pm Nov-Feb) is the place to stock up on woollies. Rossan knitwear is manufactured locally, but you can also pick up Donegal tweed jackets, caps and ties alongside lamb's-wool scarves and shawls. It's 3km southwest of Cashel.

Getting There & Away

Bus Éireann (☎ 912 1309) service 490 leaves for Killybegs daily (€8, 45 minutes) with an extra service on Saturday and in July and August.

McGeehan Coaches (☎ 954 6150) leaves from 's Pub for Killybegs (€5, one hour) and Dublin

(€20, five hours, twice daily). McGeehan also runs to Ardara, Dungloe and Glenties.

MAGHERY & THE GLEN GESH PASS
☎ 074 / pop 640

A tiny village on the northern edge of the peninsula, Maghery has a picturesque waterfront, and if you follow the strand westward, you'll get to a rocky promontory full of caves. During Cromwell's 17th-century 'Irish destruction tour', 100 villagers sought refuge here but all except one were discovered and massacred.

About 1.5km east of Maghery is enchanting **Assarancagh Waterfall**, beyond which is the beginning of a 10km marked trail to the **Glen Gesh Pass** (Glean Géis, meaning 'Glen of the Swans'), one of the most beautiful spots in Europe. It's almost alpine in appearance; cascading mountains and lush valleys dotted with isolated farmhouses and small lakes. If you're driving or cycling, you can get to the pass directly from Glencolumbcille by following the road signs for Ardara.

ARDARA
☎ 074 / pop 580

Exquisite and scenically positioned Ardara (Árd an Rátha) represents the heart of Donegal's knitwear and hand-woven tweed tradition. There isn't a whole lot going on here, although the town has a couple of sterling pubs. Once you've restocked on winter woollies, head for the switchbacks of the beautiful Glen Gesh Pass, which begins just west of the town.

Tourist information is available from the Triona Design visitor centre (see Shopping, opposite). On the diamond there's an Ulster Bank with an ATM; the post office is a short walk away on Main St.

Festivals & Events

The trad-music **Cup of Tae Festival** (www.cupof taefestival.com) takes place at the end of April or early May. It includes a school of music, as well as dancing and storytelling.

Sleeping & Eating

Drumbarron Hostel (☎ 954 1200; jfeeneyardara@eircom .net; the Diamond; dm/d €16/36) This Georgian-style two-storey house has utilitarian dorms furnished with comfortable bunk beds. It's equipped with a large kitchen and has a welcoming parlour. Knock at the B&B opposite if there's nobody in the hostel. Cash only.

Drumbarron House (☎ 954 1200; jfeeneyardara@eircom.net; the Diamond; s/d €40/70) In the family for three generations, this large B&B is efficiently run and cosy. Its owner is an artist, who has hung modern art all over the house. Cash only.

Green Gate (☎ 954 1546; http://thegreengate.eu; Ardvally, Ardara; s/d from €40/70; P) This idyllic hill-top B&B is owned by a gregarious Frenchman named Paul Chatenoud, and if you stay here chances are you'll get to know him rather well (he's a character who likes to spend time with his guests). Accommodation is spread out over several patchily restored cottages and the compound has hares who casually trim the grass and sweeping views down to the bay. Follow the tiny pictorial signs of a gate beyond Woodhill House.

Woodhill House (☎ 954 1112; www.woodhillhouse.com; d €98-150; P) This 17th-century manor house is rich in history and old-world style. The courtly gardens are a huge bonus, and its cosy restaurant has a wine list to leave any connoisseur drooling. It's 400m southeast of the centre.

Nancy's Bar (☎ 954 1187; Front St; mains €8-12) This pub-restaurant successfully makes its guests feel as though they're sitting in Nancy's living room. It serves superb seafood and chowder, and is also the best place in town to savour a social pint or two.

Entertainment

Corner House (☎ 954 1736; the Diamond) is a good spot to listen to an Irish music session (nightly from June to September) while savouring a drop or two of the black stuff. Occasionally, someone will spontaneously break out in song, and if the mood is right the rest of the pub will join in.

Shopping

Ardara is a great place to stock up on winter woollens and warm tweed. There are half a dozen outlets specialising in local knitwear.

Triona Design (☎ 914 1422; www.trionadesign.com; Main St; ☼ 9am-7pm) There is a staff of weavers here who keep traditional skills alive while demonstrating their techniques for visitors. It's a good place to learn about the profession's rich history and purchase quality items.

Kennedy's (☎ 954 1106; Front St) In business for over a century, Kennedy's helped establish Ardara's reputation as a sweater mecca.

Getting There & Away

In July and August, **Bus Éireann** (☎ 912 1309) service 492 from Killybegs (€4, 25 minutes) stops three times daily Monday to Friday, in each direction, outside O'Donnell's in Ardara. June to mid-September **McGeehan Coaches** (☎ 954 6150) runs a service to Dublin (€17.50, 4½ hours) twice daily via Donegal (€4, 50 minutes).

Getting Around

Don Byrne's of Ardara (☎ 954 1638; Main St), east of the centre, rents bikes for €15/60 per day/week.

DAWROS HEAD

The outer reaches of beautiful Loughrea Peninsula, north of Ardara, glistens with a multitude of tiny lakes cupped by gentle, undulating hills. The twin resort towns of **Narin** and **Portnoo** also tend to be swamped with summer weekenders, attracted by the beautiful wishbone-shaped Blue Flag beach at Narin.

The beach's sandy tip points towards the protective bulk of **Iniskeel Island**, and at low tide you can walk out to this island. St Connell, a cousin of St Colmcille, founded a monastery here in the 6th century. Hardly any trace of the monastery remains but the island is nevertheless studded with interesting early medieval Christian remains.

Another adventurous diversion is to track down **Lough Doon**, 3km south of Narin, in the centre of which sits the 2000-year-old **Doon Fort**, a fortified oval settlement. To reach the fort, you need to hire a rowing boat (around €10) from an adjacent farm. Pick a day that's not too windy.

If the fort whets your appetite for archaeology, pay a visit to the **Dolmen Ecocentre** (☎ 074-954 45010; www.dolmencentre.com; Kilclooney; ☼ 9am-5pm Mon-Fri), which can point you towards several other prehistoric sites, including a delightful tortoiselike passage tomb a short walk up a track left of the church.

Also on the peninsula, hemmed in by grassy dunes, is **Tramore Beach**. In 1588 part of the Spanish Armada ran aground here. The survivors temporarily occupied O'Boyle's Island in Kiltoorish Lake, but then marched to Killybegs, where they set sail again in the

COUNTY DONEGAL

Girona. The *Girona* met a similar fate that year in Northern Ireland, with the loss of over a thousand crew (see the boxed text, p661).

Sleeping

Narin and Portnoo have B&Bs aplenty, which are generally open from April to September.

Tramore Beach Caravan & Camping Park (☎ 074-955 1491; campbella@eircom.net; Rosbeg; camp sites €14) This remote place has 24 sandy camp sites sheltered amid dunes, just a short hop from the beach. Take the road from Ardara to Narin then turn left, following the signposts to Tramore Beach.

Lackagh Mor Cottages (☎ 074-954 5935; mgyo@eircom.net; Lackagh; s/d €35/60; **P**) This assemblage of stone cottages makes a great romantic getaway or family vacation spot. The ocean is a short walk from here, or you can just admire it from your cottage. It's just outside the village of Portnoo.

Getting There & Away

From Monday to Saturday in July and August, **Bus Éireann** (☎ 074-912 1309) service 492 runs between Killybegs and Portnoo (€9, 55 minutes, twice daily).

GLENTIES
☎ 074 / pop 790

This sure is a tidy town, just as the sign informs you as you roll in on the highway. Glenties (Na Gleannta) may be a little too fussily kept up – you have the feeling an old lady will follow you around with a broom and a dustpan – but there's no denying its beautiful location at the foot of two valleys with a southern backdrop laid on by the Blue Stack Mountains. It's a good spot for **fishing** and there are some cracking **walks** in the surrounding countryside.

A **summer school** (www.patrickmacgill.com) is held in August in honour of plucky Patrick MacGill (1891–1963), the 'navvy poet' who was sold by his parents at a hiring-fair, later escaped and eventually ended up writing for the English *Daily Express*. Glenties is also linked with playwright Brian Friel, whose play (and later star-studded film), *Dancing at Lughnasa,* is set in the town.

On the main street there's a Bank of Ireland, with an ATM and bureau de change, and a post office.

St Connell's Museum & Heritage Centre (☎ 955 1227; Main St; adult/child €2.50/1; ⏱ 10am-1pm & 2-4.30pm Mon-Sat Apr-Sep), beside the old courthouse at the western end of town, has a fusty ragbag of local artefacts.

Sleeping & Eating

Campbell's Holiday Hostel (☎ 955 1491; www.campbell ireland.com; dm/d €12/28; ⏱ Apr-Oct; **P**) A spic-and-span hostel with colour-coded six-bed dorms and comfortable doubles, plus a couple of kitchens and a laundry. It's hidden behind the museum as you enter from Ardara town on the N56.

Brennan's B&B (☎ 955 1235; Main St; s/d €45/70; **P**) This family run B&B is right on the main drag, among a crop of inviting pubs and shops. Guest rooms are comfortable and lovingly tended to by the elderly matron of the house.

Highlands Hotel (☎ 955 1111; http://homepage.eir com.net/~highlandshotel; Main St; s/d €52/96; mains €12-24) This laid-back country hotel dominates the western end of town. It serves excellent all-day food in substantial proportions using the freshest of produce. Rooms are nothing fancy, but are properly kept up and spacious.

Entertainment

Spot the thatched roof and you might assume **Paddy's Bar** (☎ 955 1158; Main St) is a relic favoured by old men. Inside, though, it's completely remodelled and seems to attracts all ages. It has a pool table and features traditional céilidh sessions several nights a week.

Getting There & Away

Bus Éireann (☎ 912 1309) service 492 from Donegal to Dungloe stops off in Glenties (€7, 45 minutes) one to two times daily Monday to Friday.

FINN VALLEY & AROUND

Off the beaten track, even by Donegal standards, the Finn valley makes a serene escape for fishing, hill walking or cycling. The River Finn is a good **salmon-fishing** river. There's also good **hill walking** on the Blue Stack Mountains and along the Ulster Way (p700), but you do need to be equipped with maps and provisions. Finn Farm Hostel can dispense maps and advice for the area. A long, one-day trek could start from the hostel and end in Glenties.

The main town is **Ballybofey** (Bealach Féich), linked to adjoining **Stranorlar** by an arched bridge over the Finn. There's a locally run **tourist office** (☎ 074-913 2377; Main St; ⏱ 9am-5pm Mon-Fri) in the Ballybofey Balor

Theatre. In Ballybofey's Protestant church is the **grave** of Isaac Butt (1813–79), founder of the Irish Home Rule movement.

Sleeping & Eating

Finn Farm Hostel (☎ 074-913 2261; Cappry, Ballybofey; camp sites/dm/d €10/15/30; **P**) This hostel occupies a working farm, replete with horse stables. The place exudes old Irish character, and is quite friendly, though finicky guests sometimes complain it's run down. It also offers horse-riding lessons and organised walks. Finn Farm is about 2km southwest of Ballybofey; the turning is signposted simply 'Hostel' off the N15 Donegal road.

Getting There & Away

Bus Éireann (☎ 074-912 1309) express service 64 between Galway (€17, 4¾ hours) and Derry (€7, 35 minutes) via Sligo (€12, two hours), Donegal (€6, 30 minutes) and Letterkenny (€5, 25 minutes) stops up to six times daily in Ballybofey. Local buses connect Ballybofey with Killybegs and also Letterkenny.

McGeehan Coaches (☎ 074-954 6150) runs services from Glencolumbcille (€8, 1¾ hours) to Letterkenny (€5, 35 minutes), with a stop in front of the Fintown post office at 8.40am and 1.20pm Monday to Saturday and 5.55pm Sunday. Going the other direction, it stops in Fintown at 11.35am and 5.45pm Monday to Saturday, 3pm Sunday.

NORTHWESTERN DONEGAL

There are few places in Ireland that are more savagely beautiful than northwestern Donegal. Humans have been unable to tame the wild and breathtakingly spectacular landscape. The rocky Gaeltacht area between Dungloe and Crolly is known as the Rosses (Na Rossa), and contains numerous tiny lakes and a coastline of clean, sandy beaches. Further northwest, between Bunbeg and Dunfanaghy, the scenery is softer but more stunning – to many visitors, this is the epitome of what unspoilt Ireland should look like. Offshore, the islands of Arranmore and Tory are both beautiful and fascinating to those eager for a glimpse of a more traditional way of life.

DUNGLOE & AROUND

☎ 074 / pop 950

A Number One pop song from the late 1960s, 'Mary from Dungloe', by Emmet Spiceland, helped put this little pit stop on the map. Each year the town hosts an international film festival, during which a 'new Mary' is crowned, keeping the flame alive after all these years. Apart from that, though, don't expect too much greatness from Dungloe (An Clochán Liath). It's standout feature is that it's the hub of the Rosses, with ample lodging and services for anyone visiting this spectacular locale. The nearby village of **Kincasslagh** is far more picturesque.

The **tourist office** (☎ 952 1297; ⏱ 10am-2pm & 3-6pm Mon-Sat, 11am-5pm Sun Jun-Sep) is off Main St behind the Bridge Inn. The **Bank of Ireland** (Main St) has an ATM and bureau of change. The **post office** (Quay Rd) is off Main St.

Activities

Fishing for salmon and trout on Dungloe River and Dungloe Lough is popular and you can get tackle and permits from **Bonner's** (☎ 21163; Main St). The nearest good beach is 6km southwest of town at **Maghery Bay**.

Kevin Tobin, a former national surf champ, runs the local **Dooey Surf School** (Scoil na dTonn; ☎ 952 2468; www.dooeysurfschool.com; 2hr lesson €25).

Festivals & Events

Crooner Daniel O'Donnell, pin-up to pensioners across England and Ireland, returns to his home town to host the 10-day **Mary from Dungloe Festival** (☎ 952 1254; www.maryfrom dungloe.com) in late July/early August. Thousands pack the town for all kinds of revels culminating in a pageant where the year's 'Mary' is selected.

Sleeping & Eating

Iggy's B&B (☎ 954 3112; Main St, Kincasslagh; s/d €25/50; ⏱ Jun-Sep; **P**) This country inn is a treasure. Rooms are kept tidy with grandmotherly care and the downstairs pub is a right social spot, with old Iggy himself pulling pints. Seafood dishes are also served here. Nothing fancy, just heart-warming.

Carey's Viking House Hotel (☎ 954 3295; careysvikinghouse@eircom.net; Kincasslagh; s/d €60/80; **P**) This family-run hotel is a polished operation with a restaurant, views of the beach and proximity to a challenging golf course.

COUNTY DONEGAL

It's a modern hotel, but small and with a traditional approach. Rooms are impeccable and cheerful.

Riverside Bistro (☎ 952 1062; Main St; mains €14-24; ☺ 12.30-3pm & 6-10pm) A lively French theme pervades this colourful little bistro, which is a good spot for candle-lit dinners and a choice of surprisingly daring Irish and international dishes, including a few for vegetarians.

Getting There & Away

McGeehan Coaches (☎ 954 6150) runs a service from Dungloe to Dublin (€17.50, 4½ hours, two daily, three Sunday) via Glenties (€4, 30 minutes) and Donegal (€6, one hour). No transit serves Kincasslagh.

BURTONPORT

☎ 074 / pop 345

This pocket-sized port village is the embarkation point for Arranmore Island, which looks near enough to wade to. Burtonport (Ailt an Chorráin) has attracted some famously off-the-wall characters over the years. In the 1970s, the Atlantis commune was established here, and practised a primal therapy that earned it the nickname 'the Screamers'. Eventually it relocated to the Colombian jungle. Later, the three Silver Sisters chose Burtonport to live out their Victorian lifestyle, complete with Victorian dress. The town seems perfectly ordinary today, though it is pretty.

For **fishing** trips contact **Inishfree Charters** (☎ 954 2245; www.burtonport.com; boat per day €270). It'll do half-day excursions. Alternatively, you can check in at the cabins by the pier.

The giant fibreglass lobster clinging precariously to the outer wall at **Lobster Pot** (☎ 954 2012; Main St; mains €10-20; ☺ noon-2pm & 6-9.30pm) is an unsubtle clue to the menu here: freshly netted seafood. It's a fine, neighbourly sort of place with an obsession for football.

Lough Swilly (☎ 912 2863) buses stop in Burtonport en route from Dungloe to Derry.

ARRANMORE ISLAND

☎ 074 / pop 600

Blessed by dramatic cliff faces, sea caves and clear sandy beaches, the small island of Arranmore (Árainn Mhór) lies a short ferry trip from the mainland. Measuring just 9km by 5km, the island has been inhabited since the early Iron Age (800 BC), and a prehistoric triangular fort can be seen on the southern side. The western and northern parts are wild and rugged, with few houses to disturb the sense of isolation. A walking path, the **Arranmore Way**, circles the island (allow three to four hours) and off the southwestern tip is **Green Island**, a bird sanctuary for corncrakes, snipes and a variety of seabirds that you can see from Arranmore (but not visit). You'll hear mostly Irish spoken on Arranmore Island, although most of the people are bilingual.

Sleeping & Eating

Arranmore Hostel (☎ 952 0015; www.arainnmhor.com; Leabgarrow; dm/d €14/32) A short walk left of the ferry terminal, and beautifully positioned next to a beach, is this civilised 30-bed hostel. Originally a post office, its owners live off-site so call ahead.

Arranmore House Hotel (☎ 952 0918; www.arranmorehousehotel.ie; Plohogue; d €40-60; mains €11-19) A modern and perky hotel, with a fine little restaurant and comfortable rooms. It's near the beautiful beach at Aphort Strand.

Entertainment

The island's all-night festivities are renowned. Half a dozen pubs put on turf fires and traditional music sessions, and some stay open 24 hours a day to sate thirsty fishermen.

Getting There & Around

The **Arranmore Ferry** (☎ 952 0532; www.arainnmhor.com/ferry) plies the 1.5km from Burtonport to Leabgarrow (€9 return; 25 minutes; seven Sunday, eight Monday to Saturday July and August and three Sunday, five Monday to Saturday September to June). It also takes cars (€26 return).

Once there, you can save your legs by taking an island tour with **O'Donnell Taxis** (☎ 087-260 6833). **Bikes** (per day €15) can be hired at the port.

GWEEDORE & AROUND

☎ 074 / pop 1390

The Irish-speaking district of Gweedore (Gaoth Dobhair) is a loose assembly of small towns between the coast and the impressive peak of Mt Errigal. The area is commonly used as a base for trips to Tory Island and Glenveagh National Park. Its rugged coast, dotted with white, sandy beaches, has been overrun by holiday-home mania. Consequently, Derrybeg (Doirí Beaga) and Bunbeg (Bun Beag) virtually run into each other along the R257. A few kilometres east on the R258, a few hotels are scattered along the roadside – that's Gweedore for you.

Thankfully, the developers haven't yet ventured inland. Away from the coast, habitations are few and far between, and the only feature breaking up the bleak landscape is the presence of dozens of small fishing lakes.

On the main road in Bunbeg there's an National Irish Bank with an ATM and bureau de change, while Derrybeg has a post office. Ferries depart Bunbeg for Tory Island (see right).

Activities

The most beautiful walking trail in the area is the **Tullagobegley Walk** (Siúlóid Tullagobegley), a historical trample over **Tievealehid** (Taobh an Leithid; 431m), which was used for centuries by locals carrying corpses to the 13th-century graveyard in Falcarragh. The 5½-hour walk begins at Lough Nacung (Loch na Cuinge), just east of Gweedore off the N56. The path brings you past some 19th-century silver mines to Keeldrum, a small townland on the outskirts of Gortahork, before finishing up at the Tullagobegley graveyard in Falcarragh.

Unfortunately, the walk is not waymarked so we strongly advise that you carry an OS Sheet 1 of the area.

Sleeping & Eating

Screag an Iolair Hil Hostel (☎ 954 8593; isai@eircom .net; Tor, Crolly; dm/d €12.50/36; ☷ Mar–Oct) This is an enchanting little farmyard hostel enveloped in the remote, rocky landscape 5km above Crolly, southwest of Gweedore on the N56. It combines unforced rustic charm with knowledgeable owners who welcome guests as old friends – highly recommended.

Sleepy Hollows Campsite (☎ 954 8272; www .sleepyhollows.ie; Meenaleck, Crolly; camp sites €18; ☷) The grassy camp sites here are in secluded woods, thoughtfully removed from the ungainly caravan parking lot. It's 200m past Leo's Pub in the village of Crolly.

Bunbeg House (Teach na Céidhe; ☎ 953 1305; www .bunbeghouse.com; s/d €50/80) This is a sweet, sweet spot. In a converted corn mill, this B&B sits directly by Bunbeg harbour, within earshot of wooden boats knocking against each other. It's a cosy place filled with wood panelling and rattan furniture, and was immortalised in Tony Hawke's much-loved *Round Ireland with a Fridge* travelogue.

Seaview Hotel (Óstán Radharc na Mara; ☎ 953 1159; www.visitgweedore.com/seaview.htm; Bunbeg; s/d from €80/140; ☷) This historic hotel, on the main road, was revamped and brought up to date just a few years ago. It retains much of its historic appeal, and its beachfront location is unbeatable. It has 40 spacious rooms.

Tábhairne Hughie Tim (mains €12-26; ☷ 1-9.30pm) Attached to the Seeview Hotel, this place whips up good bar food.

Gola Bistro (dinner €45; ☷ 6-10pm) An elegant place to enjoy a relaxed four-course meal. Leo's Tavern also does good food.

Entertainment

You never know who'll drop by for a sing-along at **Leo's Tavern** (☎ 954 8143; Meenaleck, Crolly), Donegal's most famous pub. It is owned by Leo and Baba Brennan, parents of Máire, Ciaran and Pól, who were the core of the group Clannad. Another sibling, Enya, needs no introduction to fans of contemporary Irish music. The pub glitters with gold, silver and platinum disks and various other mementos of the successful kids. It is in the townland of Meenaleck, about 3km south of Gweedore. At Crolly, take the R259 1km towards the airport, and look for the signs for Leo's.

Getting There & Away

Feda O'Donnell (☎ 954 8114) runs a service twice daily (three Friday and Sunday) from Gweedore to Letterkenny (€5, 1½ hours), Donegal (€6, 1¾ hours), Sligo (€10, 3¼ hours) and Galway (€20, 5½ hours).

BLOODY FORELAND

Named for the crimson colour of the rocks at sunset, Bloody Foreland (Cnoc Fola) is a dramatic stretch of coast that regularly bears the full brunt of the Atlantic's fury. Unfortunately, vacation homes have entered into the scenery here. In any case, the foreland is little more than something to admire on your way elsewhere. The coast road to the north and south of here nevertheless remains wonderfully remote, scenic and ideal for cycling.

TORY ISLAND

☎ 074 / pop 190

Swept by sea winds and stung by salt spray, the remote crag of Tory Island (Oileán Thoraí) has taken its fair share of batterings. With nothing to shield it from savage Atlantic squalls, it's a tribute to the hardiness of Tory Islanders that

---

THE BUNGALOW BLITZ

Although Donegal is Ireland's most remote corner, it hasn't been spared the real estate boom, and in spots its coastline has fallen prey to an insidious invasion – a bungalow blight. As rows of kit housing have gone up, the natural beauty of some parts of the county have clearly diminished over the past 15 years. Areas such as the Bloody Foreland, long celebrated for its stunning sunset views, are now known as 'Legoland'.

Around two-thirds of construction undertaken in Donegal today is aimed at the second-home market. Already, almost a quarter of the county's homes lie empty for much of the year. In an effort to limit the damage to Donegal's natural environment, county officials have pressed for tighter zoning laws that stipulate future development be restricted to full-time residents. Construction of holiday homes can be expected to continue for some time, though, as a backlog of permits has already been issued.

---

the island has been inhabited for over 4500 years. Although it's only 11km north of the mainland, the rough sea has long consolidated the island's staunch independence.

So it's no surprise that Tory is one of the last places in Ireland that holds onto, rather than simply paying lip service to, traditional Irish culture. The island has its own dialect of Irish and even has an elected 'king', and over the decades its inhabitants had a reputation for distilling and smuggling contraband *poitín* (a peaty whisky). However, the island is perhaps best known for its 'naïve' (or outsider) artists, many of whom have attracted the attention of international collectors (see boxed text, right).

In 1974, after an eight-week storm that lashed the island mercilessly, the government made plans to evacuate Tory permanently. Thankfully this did not happen, due in part to the efforts of Father Diarmuid Ó Peícín, who spearheaded an international campaign to raise funds, create a proper ferry service, establish an electrical supply and more. The demise of the fishing industry has brought its own share of problems, but the community still doggedly perseveres.

The island has just one pebbly beach and two recognisable villages: West Town (An Baile Thiar), containing most of the island's facilities, and East Town (An Baile Thoir). Its eastern end is dominated by jagged quartzite crags like colossal keys, while the southwest slopes down to wave-washed bedrock.

Information is available from the **Tory Island Co-op** (Comharchumann Thoraí Teo; ☎ 913 5502; www.oileanthorai.com).

Sights & Activities

Cottages mingle with ancient ecclesiastical treasures in West Town. St Colmcille is said to have founded a monastery here in the 6th century, and reminders of the early church are scattered throughout the town. One example is the 12th-century **Tau Cross**, an odd, T-shaped cruciform that suggests the possibility of seafaring exchanges with early Coptic Christians from Egypt. The cross greets passengers disembarking from the ferry. Also nearby is a 6th- or 7th-century **round tower**, with a circumference of nearly 16m and a round-headed doorway high above the ground.

The island is a wondrous place for **bird-watching**: over 100 species of sea bird inhabit the island, and among the cliffs in the northeast you can see colonies of puffin (around 1400 are thought to inhabit the island).

Sleeping & Eating

Teach Bhillie (☎ 916 5145; www.toraigh.net; West Town; s/d €25/40) From the ferry, walk 300m left to this unmarked, yellow B&B. It contains spartan but spotless rooms enlivened with bright splashes of colour, and welcomes guests with genuine warmth.

Graceanne Duffy's (☎ 913 5136; East Town; s/d €30/56, dinner €13; ✆ May-Oct) A B&B in the smaller of Tory's two villages, Graceanne's has three simple but comfortable bedrooms (two with showers) and meals include organic produce.

Tory Hotel (Óstán Thoraí; ☎ 913 5920; www.toryhotel .com; West Town; s/d €75/120, mains €8-11; P) Located by the pier, this is a modern, 14-room hotel where you can stay in pastel-coloured rooms, get the low-down on Tory from helpful staff, and enjoy good pub food or full meals. Two- and three-night packages are far more economical. It also has a club (at the People's Bar) for island music and dance.

TORY ISLAND 'NAIVE' ART

You expect to encounter unique cultures on remote islands, but rarely does that include a distinctive school of painters that have come to be internationally recognised. The Tory Island painters lack formal training, but they have cultivated a style that's both folksy and expressive.

In the 1950s the English painter Derrick Hill began to spend much of his time on the island, where he produced many paintings. The islanders took an natural interest in Hill, often watching him as he worked. As the story goes, one of the islanders approached Hill and said, 'I can do that.' He was James Dixon, a self-taught painter who used boat paint and made his own brushes with donkey hairs. Hill was impressed with the 'painterly' quality of Dixon's work and the two formed a lasting friendship. Other islanders were soon inspired to follow suit, each forging unique styles while portraying rugged island scenes. These included Ruari Rodgers, Anton Meenan and Patsy Dan Rodgers, who along with Dixon began to exhibit overseas in the late 1960s. Their work has shown in Chicago, New York, Belfast, London and Paris and fetches impressive prices at auctions. Patsy Dan has ridden his fame to the furthest possible extent, having been elected 'King' of Tory Island.

Many of these artists are still painting (Dixon passed away in 1970, age 93) and their work is frequently shown at the **Dixon Gallery** (☎ 916 5420) by the Tory Hotel. On the mainland, you can always see Tory Island work at the Glebe Gallery (p529), which also shows the work of Derrick Hill.

Entertainment

Club Sóisialta Thórai (Tory Social Club; ☎ 916 5121; West Town) The island's social life revolves around this merry club, which presents regular céilidhs.

People's Bar (☎ 913 5920; West Town) The pub at the Tory Hotel is a relaxed place to enjoy a drop of the black stuff, swap stories and listen to traditional music sessions.

Getting There & Away

Bring waterproofs for the trip – it can be a wild ride. **Donegal Coastal Cruises** (Turasmara Teo; ☎ 953 1340) runs boats to Tory (adult/child/student return €22/11/16.50) from Bunbeg (daily June to September, Monday to Friday October to May) and Magheraroarty (two daily June to September, with an extra trip daily July and August). Magheraroarty is reached by turning off the N56 at the western end of Gortahork near Falcarragh; the road is signposted Coastal Route/Bloody Foreland.

There's also a seasonal service from Portna-Blagh, 2km east of Dunfanaghy (same price, Wednesday July and August).

Call ahead, as weather and tides affect sailings. It's not uncommon for travellers to be stranded on the island in bad weather.

Getting Around

Bike hire is available from **Rothair ar Cíos** (☎ 916 5614; West Town; per day €10).

FALCARRAGH & GORTAHORK

☎ 074 / pop 850

The Irish-speaking Falcarragh (An Fál Carrach) and neighbouring Gortahork (Gort an Choirce) are small workaday settlements. You'll find more tourist amenities up the road in Dunfanaghy, but these towns afford an opportunity to experience life in the Gaeltacht region and there's a good beach nearby.

The 19th-century police barracks now houses **Falcarragh Visitor's Centre** (An tSean Bheairic; ☎ 918 0888; 🕑 9am-5pm Mon-Fri, noon-5pm Sat & Sun), which has tourist information and a café. The Bank of Ireland at the eastern end of Main St has an ATM and bureau de change, and the post office is at Main St's western end in Falcarragh.

Sights & Activities

It's 4km to the windswept **beach**; follow the signs marked Trá from either end of Main St. The beach is superb for walking, but currents make swimming unsafe.

The grey bulk of **Muckish Mountain** (670m) dominates the coast between Dunfanaghy and the Bloody Foreland. The top has sweeping views to Malin Head and Tory Island. It can be climbed from southeast of Falcarragh by way of the inland road through Muckish Gap.

Sleeping & Eating

Loistin Na Seamroige (Shamrock Lodge; ☎ 913 5057; Main St, Falcarragh; dm/d €15/40; 🕑 mid-Jan–mid-Dec)

This independent hostel is upstairs from Falcarragh's best pub. Dorms are very basic but decent. The owner, Margaret, grew up on the premises, and on a good night her pub will seem like the town's living room.

Óstán Loch Altan (☎ 913 5267; www.ostanlochaltan .com; Gortahork; s/d €55/110, mains €14-21; P) Resembling an American chain hotel, the rooms here lack personality, but make up for it with comfort. The restaurant (open from April to October) dishes up decent local fare.

Maggie Dan's (☎ 916 5022; www.maggiedans.ie; An Phanc, Gortahork; pizzas €5-10; ☾ 6pm-midnight; P) A piano player tinkles the ivory most nights in this excellent pizzeria. It's a little bit of bohemia in the countryside, with occasional theatre performances put on by the Maggie Dans Café Theatre Group. Facing the Market Sq, it's one of the few places open year-round along this stretch of the coast.

Entertainment
Teach Ruairi (☎ 913 5428; Beltany, Gortahork) is a traditional bar about 1km west of Gortahork, signposted off the Gweedore road. There is live acoustic music most nights, and the atmosphere is as authentic as can be.

Getting There & Away
The **Feda O'Donnell** (☎ 954 8114) bus from Crolly stops on Main St, Falcarragh (twice daily, Monday to Saturday, three Friday and Sunday). From Falcarragh it travels on to Letterkenny (€5, one hour) and Galway (€20, 5¼ hours).

The **John McGinley** (☎ 913 5201) bus from Anagry to Dublin stops at Gortahork (4.50am, 7.15am & 3.35pm) and Falcarragh (ten minutes after Gortahork; €16, five hours). There are additional trips Friday and Sunday.

DUNFANAGHY & AROUND
☎ 074 / pop 300
This is a beautiful spot. The village is attractive, but more importantly the coast and the surrounding terrain offer a varied range of natural settings. Beautiful beaches, stunning coastal cliffs, mountain trails and even a forest are all within a few kilometres of the town centre. Add to that some fine dining options and one of Ireland's more intriguing hostels, and you've got an unbeatable package.

Information
The Allied Irish Bank, opposite the Carrig Rua Hotel, has no ATM, but you'll find one in Ramsey's Shop on the waterfront. The **post office** (Main St; ☾ 9am-1pm & 2-5.30pm Mon-Sat) has a bureau de change.

Sights
HORN HEAD
The towering headland of **Horn Head** (Corrán Binne) has some of Donegal's most spectacular coastal scenery and plenty of birdlife. Its dramatic quartzite cliffs, covered with bog and heather, rear over 180m high, and the view from their tops is heart-pounding.

Go by bike or car from the Falcarragh end of Dunfanaghy. The road circles the headland (best to approach it in a clockwise direction) and offers tremendous views on a fine day: Tory, Inishbofin, Inishdooey and tiny Inishbeg islands to the west; Sheep Haven Bay and the Rosguill Peninsula to the east; Malin Head to the northeast; and even the coast of Scotland beyond. Take care in bad weather as the route can be perilous.

ARDS FOREST PARK
This forested **park** (☎ 912 1139; admission free), about 5km southeast of Dunfanaghy off the N56, is crisscrossed by marked nature trails varying in length from 2km to 13km. It covers the northern shore of the Ards Peninsula and there are walks to its clean beaches. The woodlands are home to several native species, including ash, birch and sessile oak. Introduced species, both broadleaf and conifer, also proliferate, and you may even encounter foxes, hedgehogs and otters. In 1930 the southern part of the peninsula was taken over by Capuchin monks; the grounds of their friary are open to the public.

DUNFANAGHY WORKHOUSE
This grim building was the local workhouse, built to keep and employ the destitute. Conditions were excessively harsh. Men, women, children and the sick were separated from one other, and their lives were dominated by gruelling work. Dunfanaghy's workhouse was soon inundated with starving people as the Famine took grip. Just two years after it opened in 1845, it accommodated some 600 people – double the number originally planned.

The workhouse, west of the centre up past the post office, is now a **heritage centre** (☎ 913 6540; simmonsjanis@hotmail.com; Main St; adult/child €4.50/2; ☾ 10am-5pm Mon-Fri, noon-5pm Sat & Sun mid-Mar–Sep), which tells the history of 'Wee

Hannah's' and her passage through the institution. On some mornings the place is overrun with busloads of school children.

DUNFANAGHY GALLERY

Just up the road from the heritage centre, **Dunfanaghy Gallery** (☎ 913 6224; Main St; admission free; ⏰ 10am-6pm Mon-Sat) started life as a fever hospital. The gallery has several rooms, which showcase paintings old and new, historic photos printed from original glass plates, hand-woven tweeds, pottery, jewellery and books.

DOE CASTLE

The early 16th-century **Doe Castle** (Caisléan na dTuath; Creeslough) was the stronghold of the Scottish MacSweeney family until it fell into English hands in the 17th century. The castle is picturesquely sited on a low promontory with water on three sides and a moat hewn out of the rock on the landward side. The best view is from the Carrigart–Creeslough road. The interior isn't open to the public.

The castle is around 16km from Dunfanaghy on the Carrigart road and is clearly signposted.

CREESLOUGH & MUCKISH MOUNTAIN

The distinctive shape of Muckish Mountain (670m) – when it's not shrouded in the cloud and mist that locals call *smir* – is an eye-catching landmark and a good climb. You can get to it via the village of Creeslough, 11km south of Dunfanaghy on the N56, and home to an extraordinary **modern church**, resembling a half-melted sugar cube, whose snowy bulk is intended to mirror the mountain's shape. To get to Muckish, take a right about 2km northwest of the village and continue for about 6km, where a rough track begins the ascent.

BEACHES

Dunfanaghy is blessed with the fabulous **Killyhoey Beach**, a wide, sandy, virtually empty beach that leads right into the heart of the village. **Marble Hill Beach**, about 3km east of town in Port-na-Blagh, is more secluded but very popular, and is usually crammed in summer. Reaching Dunfanaghy's loveliest spot, **Tramore Beach**, requires hiking 20 minutes through the grassy dunes immediately south of the village (see Walking, right).

Activities
WALKING

For an exhilarating hike, take the road from Dunfanaghy towards Horn Head until the bridge. After crossing, go through the gate on your left and stroll along the track until you reach the dunes. A well-beaten path will lead you to the magnificent **Tramore Beach**. Turn left and follow it to the end, where you can find a way up onto a path leading north to **Pollaguill Bay**. Continue to the cairn at the end of the bay and follow the coastline for a stupendous view of the 20m **Marble Arch**, carved out by the sea.

A shorter walk begins at Marble Hill Beach in Port-na-Blagh. Take the path on the left side of the beach past the cottage and work your way about 500m through the brush and along the top of the cliff until you reach **Harry's Hole**, a small crevice in the cliff that is popular with daredevil kids, who dive 10m into the water below.

GOLF

Dunfanaghy Golf Club (☎ 913 6335; www.dunfanaghy golfclub.com) is a stunning waterside 18-hole links course just outside the village on the Port-na-Blagh road.

HORSE RIDING

This is a terrific way of exploring the expansive beaches and surrounding countryside. It can be arranged through **Dunfanaghy Stables** (☎ 910 0980; www.dunfanaghystables.com; Main St; per hr €25).

SEA ANGLING & DIVING

Richard Bowyer (☎ 913 6640; Port-na-Blagh) organises sea-angling trips from the small pier in Port-na-Blagh between Easter and September. Local diving trips are also run by **Diveology** (☎ 086-809 5737; www.diveology.com).

WINDSURFING & KITE-SURFING

Windsurfing lessons and gear hire are available through **Marble Hill Windsurfing** (☎ 913 6231; richardharshaw@eircom.net; the Cottage, Marble Hill, Port-na-Blagh; ⏰ daily Jul & Aug, by appointment May, Jun & Sep). Lessons start from €40.

Sleeping

The Mill House (☎ 913 6409; www.corcreggan.com; Corcreggan Mill, Dunfanaghy; camp sites per person €8, dm €20, d €40-55, tr €70; P) Part of the busy Corcreggan Mill compound (but owned and operated separately) is the lovingly rebuilt Mill House, just a few paces from the railway car hostel. It has spotless dormitory-style accommodation (with firm mattresses), along with private rooms for couples and families (one room even has a crib for babies). Campers can pitch tents on a cushy lawn beside an organic vegetable garden. There's lots going on amid several comfortable sitting rooms and halls, with music sessions, massage services and meditation seminars. Throw in a continental/full breakfast for an additional €5/7. It's 4km southwest of Dunfanaghy on the Falcarragh road (N56). Buses stop outside.

ourpick The Carriage Hostel (☎ 910 0814; www .the-carriage-hostel-corcreggan.com; Corcreggan Mill, Dunfanaghy; dm €14-17; s €25-35, d €35-42; **P**) If you're after ordinary dormitory accommodation, look elsewhere. The Carriage Hostel, on the site of an historic mill, comprises of a 19th-century mahogany railway carriage parked alongside an old kiln. You have a choice of shacking up in the railway's private cabins – not luxurious, but a cool experience and open year round – or in the rustic old stone Kiln House (open May to September). Be sure to specify your preference. Dorms have just three or four beds. Cosy sitting rooms exude historic Irish comfort.

Rosman House (☎ 913 6273; www.rosmanhouse.ie; Figart, Dunfanaghy; s/d €45/60; **P**) With six flowery, spotless rooms, this B&B is very homey – in fact, a family of six live here. It's surrounded by fields and gardens. You'll find it just down the road from the workhouse.

Arnold's Hotel (☎ 913 6208; www.arnoldshotel.com; Main St; s €92-109, d €124-158; ☽ Apr-Oct; **P**) Open since 1922, Arnold's is a self-assured, 30-room hotel overlooking the waterfront in Sheep Haven Bay. Strewn with deep armchairs and backed by neatly trimmed terrace gardens, it is a relaxing place to stay. However, it also offers all manner of activity holidays (see the website).

Shandon Hotel (☎ 913 6137; www.shandonhotel.com; Sheep Haven Bay, Dunfanaghy; d €250, 2-night min; **P** ☽) Donegal's swankiest modern accommodation is to be had at this hilltop hotel-spa, with a spectacular vantage of Marble Hill Beach. Rooms, all facing the ocean, are spacious and elegantly attired. However, it's the spa that's the class of the outfit. It has a stylishly designed pool, a children's pool, steamrooms and a fully equipped gym, and guests can pamper themselves with a range of health treatments. A good choice for families.

Eating

Muck 'n' Muffins (☎ 913 6780; Main Sq; sandwiches & snacks €3-8; ☽ 10am-5pm Mon-Sat, 11am-5pm Sun, wine bar from 8pm daily Aug, Fri & Sat Sep-Jul) A 19th-century rough-stone grain store now hosts this three-storey café and craft shop by the waterfront. The perfect place for healthful sandwiches, tempting cakes and muffins. During summer it opens some evenings as a wine bar, serving tapas and cheeseboards.

Mill (☎ 913 6985; www.themillrestaurant.com; Figart, Dunfanaghy; 3-course dinner €39; ☽ 7-9pm Tue-Sun Mar-Dec) An exquisite country setting and perfectly composed meals make this friendly spot a treat. It occupies an old flax mill that was for many years the home of Frank Eggington, a locally renowned painter. It's just south of the town on the Falcarragh road. Book ahead. It also offers a high-class B&B (single/double €65/95).

ourpick Cove (☎ 913 6300; Rockhill, Port-na-Blagh; 4-course dinner €40; ☽ 6-10pm Wed-Mon, 1-4pm Sun) For a fun and stylish evening out, you can do no better. Owners Siobhan Sweeney and Peter Byrne are perfectionists who tend to every detail in the kitchen, the dining room and, most importantly, on your plate. Food is inventive and deceptively simple – you may discover subtle Asian influences. After dinner, retire to the elegant lounge upstairs. It's on the coast road in Port-na-Blagh.

Getting There & Away

Feda O'Donnell (☎ 954 8114) buses from Crolly (€5, 40 minutes) to Galway (€20, five hours) stop in Dunfanaghy square twice daily Monday to Saturday, three Friday and Sunday.

John McGinley (☎ 913 5201) buses to Dublin stop in Dunfanaghy (€16, 4¾ hours). The **Lough Swilly** (☎ 912 2863) Dungloe–Derry bus stops in Dunfanaghy (€7, 1½ hours) twice daily Monday to Friday, three times on Saturday.

EASTERN DONEGAL

LETTERKENNY

☎ 074 / pop 12,000

Donegal's largest town is growing rapidly, and it has the traffic congestion to prove it. Letterkenny (Leitir Ceanainn) is undergoing great change as the local economy picks up, which is obviously great for most of its inhabitants. Expect even more growth in the years ahead if plans materialize for a new tech-oriented industrial development on Letterkenny's outskirts.

The town is also enjoying a cultural up-swing, particularly in the form of its esteemed theatre, and pubs and clubs buzz with students and young professionals. But the town's energy, while novel to its inhabitants, won't necessarily entice visitors. Most passers-through will be on their way to Donegal's more alluring northern corners. Letterkenny is particularly relevant as a gateway to the remote Inishowen Peninsula. Travellers using public transport are likely to stop here for at least a short period.

Orientation

Main St, said to be the longest high street in Ireland, runs from Dunnes Stores at one end to the courthouse at the other, and divides into Upper and Lower Main Sts. At the top of Upper Main St there is a Y-junction: High Rd veers left, while Port Rd goes right to the bus station and the road out to Derry.

Information

Check out www.destinationletterkenny.com for some useful information.

AIB (Main St) Bank branch with ATM.

Bank of Ireland (Main St)

Cyberworld (☎ 912 0440; Lower Main St; per hr €2) Internet café.

Duds 'n' Suds Laundrette (☎ 912 8303; Pearse Rd; load from €8)

Northwest Tourist Office (☎ 912 1160; www .donegaldirect.ie; Neil Blaney Rd; ☽ 9am-5pm Mon-Fri, noon-3pm Sat & Sun Jun & Aug, 9am-5pm Mon-Fri Sep-May) Run by Fáilte Ireland (Irish Tourist Board), this office is far inferior to the tourist office in Donegal town. It's 1km southeast of town at the end of Port Rd.

Post office (Upper Main St)

Sights & Activities

Dominating the town's hillside profile, the enormous Gothic-style **St Eunan's Cathedral** (1901) thrusts skyward on Sentry Hill Rd (take Church Lane up from Main St) and contains much intricate Celtic carving.

Outside the town, salmon and trout populate the rivers and lakes. Equipment and information is available from **Top Tackle** (☎ 916 7545; 55 Port Rd; ☽ 9.30am-5.30pm Mon-Sat).

Festivals & Events

The **Letterkenny Festival** (☎ 912 7856) is a four-day international festival of music and dance held at the end of August.

Sleeping

Port Hostel (☎ 912 5315; www.porthostel.ie; Port Rd; camp sites €20, dm €15, d €36-40; ℗) This purpose-built hostel, though modern, has a well-used college dormitory atmosphere, especially in the huge downstairs dorm. It attracts a steady stream of visitors from Northern Ireland, especially on holiday weekends, when all Letterkenny takes on a holiday atmosphere. Then, this hostel can feel like the centre of the action. Its setting is appealing, though: it's up a crooked lane that swerves uphill behind the An Grianán Theatre. Karen, the gregarious owner, is a good source of Donegal info.

Letterkenny Court Hotel (☎ 912 2977; www.let terkennycourthotel.com; Main St; s/d from €49/98; ℗) In a historic building that sports a bright, colourful paint job, this hotel is a polished operation on the main drag. Service, style and location are its selling points. Rooms have a pastel, fresh-as-spring feel, and about a dozen pubs are within a few staggers of the front door.

Cove Hill House (☎ 912 1038; Port Rd; with/without bathroom s €45/35, d €60/50; ℗) This B&B has a comfortable and cheerful feel. It's on the tolerable side of dainty, crammed with homey knickknacks and nuzzled by a beautiful garden. Credit cards are accepted. It's behind the theatre and next to Port Hostel.

Castle Grove (☎ 915 1118; www.castlegrove.com; Ramelton Rd; s/d €105/170; ℗) Ignore Letterkenny's slew of swanky business hotels. The place for a luxurious stay is this grandiose Georgian manor 5km out towards Ramelton. Its enormous estate rolls down unimpeded to the estuary and the impossibly neat lawn seems cut with nail clippers. Award-winning Irish/French food in its restaurant clinches the deal.

Eating

Simple Simon's (☎ 912 2382; St Oliver Plunkett Rd; soups & salads €3-6.50; ☽ 9am-6pm Mon-Sat) 'Genetically modified' is a dirty term at this passionate natural-products shop and attached café. The on-site bakery produces delightful treats for every special diet imaginable and it stocks a good selection of organic veggies.

Sienna (☎ 912 8535; Upper Main St; mains €5-9; ☽ 9am-6.30pm Mon-Sat, 10.30am-5.30pm Sun) Tops

COUNTY DONEGAL

among Letterkenny's stylish contemporary eateries, Sienna is a great spot for ciabatta and *panini* sandwiches and strong coffee during the daytime. At night, the place becomes dimly lit and romantic, and the menu converts to more sophisticated Mediterranean fare. A nice wine selection and live jazz complement the cosmopolitan vibe.

Brewery (☎ 912 7330; Upper Main St; bar food around €8, mains €13-26; ⏰ 3-9pm) There's a choice between top-notch bar food downstairs or enormous platters upstairs at this happening pub-restaurant overlooking the small square.

Yellow Pepper (☎ 912 4133; www.yellowpepper restaurant.com; 36 Lower Main St; dinner mains €16-20; ⏰ noon-10pm) A popular place among locals not looking to impress each other. It's family-run, and feels like it – it's cheery and comfortable. Don't be misled, however: this place is often touted as Letterkenny's best restaurant. It stakes its reputation on excellent fish dishes.

Drinking

Cottage Bar (☎ 912 1338; 49 Upper Main St) Watch your head on entering Letterkenny's most appealing pub. From the low ceilings hang all manner of interesting bric-a-brac. Once you're safely seated with a pint, you'll enjoy studying the stuff. If it's nippy out, try to snag a seat by the open fire. Thursday night music sessions sweeten the deal.

Entertainment

Casbah (Main St) Letterkenny's most happening club draws a diverse (though generally young) crowd. The place rocks when live shows are on in its basement.

An Grianán Theatre (☎ 912 0777; www.angrianan .com; Port Rd) An Grianán Theatre is both a community theatre and major arts venue for the northwest, presenting national and international drama, comedy and music. It also has a good café and bar.

Getting There & Away

Letterkenny is a major bus hub for northwestern Ireland. The bus station is by the roundabout at the junction of Ramelton Rd and the Derry road. It will look after luggage for €2.

Bus Éireann (☎ 912 1309) express bus 32 runs to Dublin (€16, four hours) six times daily (four on Sunday) via Omagh (€11, one hour) and Monaghan (€13, 1¾ hours). The Derry (€7, 35 minutes) to Galway (€15, 4¾ hours) bus 64 stops at Letterkenny three times daily

(twice on Sunday) before continuing to Donegal (€8, 50 minutes), Bundoran (€12, 1½ hours), Sligo (€12, 2¼ hours) and Galway (€17, 3½ hours) The Derry–Cork express bus 53 connects Letterkenny and Donegal (45 minutes), and Sligo (€12, two hours). It runs three times daily (once on Sunday).

John McGinley (☎ 913 5201) buses run twice daily Sunday to Thursday (three times Friday, once on Saturday) from Annagry to Dublin (€15, 3¾ hours) through Letterkenny and Monaghan.

Lough Swilly (☎ 912 2863) has regular services from Derry (€6.60, one hour) to Dungloe (€8, two hours), via Letterkenny and Dunfanaghy, as well as direct to Letterkenny.

Feda O'Donnell (☎ 954 8114) runs a bus from Crolly (€5, 1½ hours) to Galway (€16, four hours) twice daily via Letterkenny, Donegal, Bundoran and Sligo. Buses stop on the road outside the bus station.

McGeehan Coaches (☎ 954 6150) runs a service from Letterkenny to Glencolumbcille (€10, 2¼ hours) daily except Sunday.

Getting Around

Taxis can be ordered from **A Cabs** (☎ 912 2272). There are taxi stands on Main St opposite the square, and opposite the bus station.

LOUGH GARTAN
☎ 074

The patriarch of Irish monasticism, St Colmcille (or Columba), was born in a lovely setting near the glassy Lough Gartan, and some isolated stone structures and crosses remain from his lifetime. The lake is 17km northwest of Letterkenny. It's beautiful driving country.

Colmcille Heritage Centre

This **heritage centre** (☎ 913 7306; Gartan; adult/concession €2/1.50; ⏰ 10.30am-6.30pm Mon-Sat, 1-6.30pm Sun, May-Sep), on the shore of Lough Gartan, is Colmcille's Hall of Fame, with a lavish display on the production of illuminated manuscripts.

Colmcille's mother, on the run from pagans, supposedly haemorrhaged during childbirth and her blood is believed to have changed the colour of the surrounding Gartan Clay from brown to pure white. Ever since, the clay has been regarded as a charm. Ask nicely and the staff may produce some from under the counter.

On the way to the heritage centre you'll also see signs to the stone pile that once was

Colmcille's Abbey. Further down the road, on hillside overrun by bleating sheep, is the **saint's birthplace**, marked by a hefty cross. Beside it is an intriguing prehistoric tomb strewn with greening coppers that's popularly known as the Flagstone of Loneliness, on which Columba supposedly slept. The chunky slab was once believed to cure homesickness.

To reach the heritage centre, leave Letterkenny on the R250 road to Glenties and Ardara. After a few kilometres, turn right on the R251 to Churchill village and follow the signs. Alternatively, from Kilmacrennan on the N56, turn west and look for signs.

Gartan Outdoor Education Centre
Courses including rock climbing, sea kayaking, sailing, surfing, windsurfing, hill climbing and more are offered for both adults and children at this **adventure centre** (☎ 913 7032; www.gartan.com; Gartan, Churchill). It's located 18km northwest of Letterkenny, and set in its own 35-hectare estate on the shores of Lough Gartan.

Glebe Gallery & House
The English painter Derrick Hill bought historic **Glebe House** (☎ 913 7071; Churchill; adult/ child/concession €2.75/1.25/2; ☀ 11am-6.30pm daily Easter, Sat-Thu only mid-May–Sep; Ⓟ Ⓖ) in 1953, providing him with a gorgeous base on the Irish mainland, not far from his beloved Tory Island. Before Hill arrived, the house served as a rectory and then a hotel. The mansion is sumptuously decorated, alive with colour, flair and an evident love of all things exotic.

The house's real appeal, however, is Hill's astonishing art collection. In addition to works by Hill and the 'naive' artists of Tory Island (see the boxed text, p523) are works by Picasso, Landseer, Hokusai, Jack B Yeats and Kokoschka. The woodland gardens are also wonderful. A guided tour of the house takes about 45 minutes.

DUNLEWY & AROUND
☎ 074 / pop 700
Blink and you could miss the tiny village of Dunlewy (Dún Lúiche), sitting at the foot of Mt Errigal beside Lough Dunlewy. You won't miss Mt Errigal, however, which towers over the town. It's a modest little gateway to Glenveigh National Park.

Sights & Activities
DUNLEWY LAKESIDE CENTRE
The catch-all **lakeside centre** (Ionad Cois Locha; ☎ 953 1699; www.dunleweycentre.com; Dunlewy; admission house & grounds or boat trip adult/child €5.75/3.75, combined ticket €9.50/6.50; ☀ 10.30am-6pm Mon-Sat, 11am-6pm Sun Easter-Oct) offers something for everybody, especially kids. It includes the thatched cottage of Manus Ferry, a local weaver who earned world renown for his tweeds (he died in 1975). It's also an activity centre with a petting zoo, lakeside walks, pony trekking and, best of all, excellent boat trips on the lake with a storyteller who vividly brings to life local history, geology and ghoulish folklore. In summer there are traditional music concerts. There's also a good café with a turf fire and craft shop. The centre is currently expanding, and will soon include a theatre and concert venue.

MT ERRIGAL & THE POISONED GLEN
Scree-scarred Mt Errigal (752m) is one of Ireland's highest peaks. It looms over Dunlewy, seemingly daring walkers to attempt the tough but beautiful climb to its conical peak. Anyone keen to take on the challenge should pay close attention to the weather. It's a dangerous climb on misty or wet days, when the mountain is shrouded in cloud and visibility is minimal.

There are two paths to the summit: the easier route, which covers 5km and takes around two hours; and the more difficult 3.3km walk along the northwestern ridge, which involves scrambling over scree for about 2½ hours. Details of both routes are available at the Dunlewy Lakeside Centre.

Legend has it that the stunning ice-carved rock-face of the Poisoned Glen got its sinister name when the ancient one-eyed giant king of Tory, Balor, was killed here by his exiled grandson, Lughaidh, whereupon the poison from his eye split the rock and poisoned the glen. The less interesting truth, however, lies in a cartographic gaffe. Locals were inspired to name it An Gleann Neamhe (the Heavenly Glen), but when an English cartographer mapped the area, he carelessly marked it An Gleann Neimhe – the Poisoned Glen.

The R251 has several viewpoints overlooking the glen. It's possible to walk through it, although the ground is rough and boggy. From the lakeside centre a return walk along the glen is 12km and takes two to three hours. Just watch out for the green lady – the resident ghost!

Sleeping

Errigal Hostel (☎ 953 1180; www.errigalhostel.com; Dunlewy; dm/d €18/50; P) Just 2km north of Dunlewy at the base of Mt Errigal, this purpose-built, modern An Óige hostel was under construction at the time of research. It is due to open by the time you read this. Ring ahead to reserve a bed.

Radharc an Ghleanna (☎ 953 1835; radharcang@ hotmail.com; Moneymore, Dunlewy; s/d €35/60; P) The four comfy rooms at this country bungalow are as clean as laboratories, while the views over the lough and to the Poisoned Glen are eye-popping. It's down a small lane a short drive east of the hostel.

GLENVEAGH NATIONAL PARK

Lakes cluster like dew in the mountainous valley of **Glenveagh National Park** (Pairc Naísúnta Ghleann Bheatha; glenveaghnationalpark@duchas.ie; admission free; 10am-6pm Feb-Nov, last admission 5pm), one of the most beautiful spots in Ireland. Alternating between great knuckles of rock, green-gold swathes of bog and scatterings of oak and birch forest, the 16,500-sq-km protected area makes wonderful walking country. It is also home to a variety of wildlife, including the golden eagle, which was hunted to extinction here in the 19th century but was reintroduced in 2000.

Yet such serenity came at a heavy price. The land was once farmed by 244 tenants, who were forcibly evicted by landowner John George Adair in the winter of 1861 following what he called a 'conspiracy', but really because their presence obstructed his vision for the valley.

Adair put the final touches on his paradise (1870–73) by building the spectacular lakeside Glenveagh Castle, while his wife, Adelia, introduced two things that define the national park's appearance: the herd of red deer and the rhododendrons. Green fingers and a love of animals notwithstanding, the Adair name still meets with dripping scorn. However, a rather poetic revenge was enacted when Adair's body was to be buried in 1885. As the funeral cart rolled up to his grave, it's said they found a donkey already occupying his would-be home for eternity.

If anything, things got even more surreal after Adair's death. The castle was briefly oc-cupied by the IRA in 1922. Then in 1929 the property was acquired by Kingsley Porter, professor of art at Harvard University, who mysteriously disappeared in 1933 (presumed drowned, but rumoured to have been spotted in Paris afterwards). Six years later the estate was bought by his former student, Henry McIlhenny, once described by Andy Warhol as 'the only person in Philadelphia with glamour'. In 1975 McIlhenny sold the whole kit and caboodle to the Irish government and it is now administered by Dúchas, the Heritage Service.

The park features nature trails along lakes, through woods and blanket bog, as well as a viewing point that's a short walk behind the castle.

The **Glenveagh Visitor Centre** (☎ 074-913 7090; Churchill) has a 20-minute audiovisual display on the ecology of the park and the infamous Adair. The restaurant serves hot food and snacks, and the reception sells the necessary midge repellent, as vital in summer as walking boots and waterproofs are in winter. Camping is not allowed.

Glenveagh Castle

This delightfully showy **castle** (adult/child €3/1.50; 10am-6pm Easter-Oct) was modelled in miniature on Scotland's Balmoral Castle. Henry McIlhenny made it a characterful home with liberal reminders of his passion for hunting deer. In fact you'll be hard pressed to find a single room without a representation – or taxidermied remains – of a stag.

An entertaining guided tour takes in a series of flamboyantly decorated rooms that look as if McIlhenny just left them. The most eye-catching, including the tartan- and-antler-covered music room and the pink candy-striped room demanded by Greta Garbo whenever she stayed here, are in the round tower. The drawing room has a splendid 300-year-old fireplace bought by McIlhenny from the Ards estate near Dunfanaghy.

The exotic gardens are similarly spectacular. They've been nurtured for decades and boast a host of terraces, an Italian garden, a walled kitchen garden, and the Belgian Walk, built by Belgian soldiers who stayed here during WWI. Their cultured charm is in marked contrast to the wildly beautiful landscape that enfolds the area.

The last guided tours of the castle leave about 45 minutes before closing time. **Mini-**

buses (adult/child return €2/1) run from the visitor centre to the castle roughly every 15 minutes. The last one returns from the castle at 6pm.

DOON WELL & ROCK OF DOON

In centuries past wells were commonly believed to cure afflictions and judging by the shimmering rosaries, multicoloured rags and trinkets bejewelling nearby bushes, many still believe this to be true of **Doon Well** (Tobar an Duin). Despite its decoration, the well itself looks more like a kitchen cupboard than a wishing well.

A sign points to the overgrown **Rock of Doon** (Carraig an Duin), which has some far-reaching views. This is where the O'Donnell kings were crowned – presumably so they could get a squiz at what they were inheriting.

Take the signposted turn-off from the N56 just north of Kilmacrennan. The well and rock are about 1.5km north of the village.

LIFFORD

☎ 074 / pop 1400

Nudging the border by Strabane in County Tyrone, the dwindling town of Lifford (Leifear) was formerly the judicial capital of Donegal. While its powerful past is long gone, its spirit lives on in the daunting 18th-century **Old Courthouse** (☎ 914 1733; www.liffordold courthouse.com; adult/concession €5/3; ☑ 10am-4.30pm Mon-Fri, 12.30-4.30pm Sun; P). The courthouse is home to an excellent **heritage centre** with creepily lifelike re-creations that use actors' faces projected onto waxworks. In this manner, Manus O'Donnell tells the story of Donegal's Gaelic chieftains and several bona-fide trials are re-enacted in the austere courtroom (including that of Napper Tandy, John 'half-hanged' McNaughten and the Lord Leitrim murder). A guard will take you down to the prison cells, accompanied by sounds of banging doors and ominous footsteps, to be locked up for sheep-stealing or the like.

Getting There & Away

Bus Éireann's (☎ 912 1309) express service 32 from Dublin (€16, 3¼ hours) to Letterkenny (€6.50, 20 minutes) stops in Lifford up to five times daily. Local buses connect Lifford with Letterkenny, Ballybofey and Strabane.

NORTHEASTERN DONEGAL

ROSGUILL PENINSULA

☎ 074

The best way to explore Rosguill's rugged splendour is by driving, cycling or even walking the 15km Atlantic Dr, signposted to your left as you come into the sprawling village of **Carrigart** (Carraig Airt) from the south. There are plenty of pubs in the village to cure your thirst and a nice, secluded beach at **Trá na Rossan**. On no account should you swim in Boveeghter or Mulroy Bay – both are unsafe. Perhaps this is why the summer crowds don't linger here, preferring instead to travel 4km northward to **Downings**, where the beach is spectacular but the village has a slightly abused feel to it.

Activities

The superb links of **Rosapenna Golf Club** (☎ 915 5301; www.rosapennagolflinks.ie; Downings; green fees €50-75), designed by St Andrew's Old Tom Morris in 1891 and remodelled by Harry Vardon in 1906, is one of the outstanding seaside courses in Ireland. The scenery is spectacular as is the layout, which can challenge even the lowest handicapper.

Sleeping

Casey's Caravan Park (☎ 915 5301; rosapenna@eircom .net; Downings; camp sites €10-20; ☑ Apr-Sep) You won't get closer to Downing's Blue Flag beach than at this extremely popular camp site right beside the dunes. The village is just around the corner. Book ahead.

Trá na Rosann Hostel (☎ 915 5374; www.anoige .ie; Downings; dm €15; ☑ Apr-Oct) Knockout views and a terrific atmosphere are the biggest draws at this chalet-like former hunting lodge, now an An Óige hostel. The one drawback is that it's 6km east of Downings and you'll have to hitch if you don't have your own wheels.

Beach Hotel (Óstán na Trá; ☎ 915 5303; beachhoteldonegal@eircom.net; Downings; s/d €45/80; ☑ Apr-Oct; P) For more of a personal touch, come to this family-run hotel, which has 20 pristine rooms close to the beach. Ask for one of the new rooms, most of which have sea views.

Downings Bay Hotel (☎ 915 5586; www.downings bayhotel.com; Downings; s/d from €65/100; P   &) This classic beach resort hotel has been thoroughly updated, offering contemporary luxury just a few steps from the strand. Rooms are spacious, comfortable and immaculate. It's very reasonably priced for what it offers, and even better deals can be had in winter.

Eating

Old Glen Bar & Restaurant (☎ 915 5130; Glen, Carrigart; mains €14-23; ☯ 6-11pm) This wonderful pub is entirely authentic and serves a sensational pint. At the back of the pub, though, modernity rules with a contemporary restaurant serving up a fabulous menu of fish, seafood and meat. The tiny hamlet of Glen is signposted off the R245 between Creeslough and Carrigart, about 6km south of the latter.

Haven Restaurant (☎ 915 5586; bar food €10-20, restaurant mains €16-25; ☯ 6.30-9.30pm) In the Downings Bay Hotel, this restaurant deals up above-average meals. Bar food can be ordered in JC's Bar.

Getting There & Around

A local bus connects Carrigart and Downings, but it's of limited use for visitors. You really need your own transport for this area.

FANAD PENINSULA

The second-most northern point in Donegal, Fanad Head thrusts out into the Atlantic to the west of Rosguill. The peninsula curls around the watery expanses of Mulroy Bay to the west, and Lough Swilly to the east, the latter trimmed by high cliffs and sandy beaches. Most travellers stick to the peninsula's eastern flank, visiting the beautiful beach and excellent golf course at Portsalon, and the quiet heritage towns of Ramelton and Rathmullan. Accommodation is relatively limited, so book ahead in summer.

Portsalon & Fanad Head

Once named the second most beautiful beach in the world by British newspaper the *Observer,* the tawny-coloured Blue Flag beach in Ballymastocker Bay, which is safe for swimming, is the principle draw of tiny Portsalon (Port an tSalainn). For golfers, however, the main attraction is the marvellously scenic **Portsalon Golf Club** (☎ 915 9459; Portsalon).

Knockalla Caravan & Camping Park (☎ 074-915 9108; Portsalon; camp sites €14-20; ☯ mid-Mar–mid-Sep) is a short walk from the beach on the lower slopes of Knockalla Mountain and fills up quickly in summer. It has a kitchen, a laundry, a shop, a games room and an outdoor play area.

It's another 8km to the lighthouse on the rocky tip of Fanad Head, the best part of which is the scenic drive there. Driving the rollercoaster road that hugs the cliffs back to Rathmullan, you'll pass the early 19th-century **Knockalla Fort**, built to warn off any approaching French ships.

GETTING THERE & AWAY

The **Lough Swilly** (☎ 074-912 2863) bus leaves Letterkenny twice daily for Milford (€3.50, one hour) and continues from Milford to Portsalon (€9, 35 minutes, morning bus only).

Rathmullan

☎ 074 / pop 520

The refined little port of Rathmullan (Ráth Maoláin) has a tranquillity about it that belies the momentous events that took place here from the 16th to 18th centuries. In 1587, Hugh O'Donnell, the 15-year-old heir to the powerful O'Donnell clan, was tricked into boarding a ship here and taken to Dublin as a prisoner. He escaped four years later on Christmas Eve and, after unsuccessful attempts at revenge, died in Spain, aged only 30. In 1607, despairing of fighting the English, Hugh O'Neill, the earl of Tyrone, and Rory O'Donnell, the earl of Tyrconnel, boarded a ship in Rathmullan harbour and left Ireland for good. This decisive act, known as the Flight of the Earls, marked the effective end of Gaelic Ireland and the rule of Irish chieftains. Large-scale confiscation of their estates took place, preparing for the Plantation of Ulster with settlers from Britain. Also in Rathmullan, Wolfe Tone, leader of the 1798 Rising, was captured.

SIGHTS

The picturesque Carmelite **Rathmullan Friary** is so covered in vines that it would probably crumble should they be cleared away. It was founded around 1508 by the MacSweeneys, and was still used in 1595 when English commander, George Bingham, raided the place and took off with the communion plate and priestly vestments. Bishop Knox then renovated the friary in 1618 in order to use it as his own residence.

SLEEPING & EATING
Dinner at the hotels costs from €40 to €45; there are several pubs in town serving bar food.

Knoll (☎ 915 8241; Main St; s/d €35/70; P) This genteel black-and-white house was built to house the commander of the North Atlantic Fleet in 1780, and has since been reincarnated as everything from a police station to a post office. Happily for travellers, it now houses a cosy three-room B&B, fronted by beautifully maintained gardens. It's just half a block from the sea.

Rathmullan House (☎ 915 8188; www.rathmullan house.com; s/d €115/230; P ⌨ &) Just north of town, on the shores of Lough Swilly, this luxurious country house boasts an indoor heated swimming pool, a sauna and tennis courts, and is set in a beautifully wooded garden by the water. Its restaurant, the Weeping Elm, is highly regarded for its innovative use of organic ingredients.

Fort Royal (☎ 915 8100; www.fortroyalhotel.com; s/d €130/190; ☾ Apr-Oct; P) This more down-to-earth but equally exclusive waterside hotel has 15 old-fashioned rooms, a wonderful restaurant and rambling gardens that feel as old as the house, built in 1805. Private cottages, oozing traditional rural simplicity, rent for €500-700 per week. The grounds extend to a private beach, and also include a tennis court and pitch-and-putt course.

GETTING THERE & AWAY
The **Lough Swilly** (☎ 912 2863) bus from Letterkenny arrives in Rathmullan (€5, 45 minutes, twice daily) en route to Milford and Portsalon (morning bus only).

Ramelton
☎ 074 / pop 1050
The sweet little town of Ramelton (Ráth Mealtain, also sometimes called Rathmelton) is the first community you come to if you're approaching the peninsula from the east. It's a picture-perfect spot, with rows of handsome Georgian houses and rough-walled stone warehouses following the curve of the River Lennon. If the doctor ordered you to steer clear of any form of excitement, you had probably better drop your bags here for a few days.

The **National Irish Bank** (the Mall), by the River Lennon, has a bureau de change but no ATM. The **post office** (Castle St) is off the Mall.

SIGHTS
Housed in a restored warehouse on the riverfront, the **Donegal Ancestry Family Research Centre & Heritage Centre** (☎ 915 1266; www.donegalancestry .com; the Quay; adult/child €4/2; ☾ 9am-4.30pm Mon-Thu, 9am-4pm Fri) has an exhibition on the history of Ramelton, and also does genealogical research. It costs €15 for an initial consultation.

The ruined **Tullyaughnish Church**, on the hill, is also worth a visit because of the Romanesque carvings in the eastern wall, which were taken from a far older church on nearby Aughnish Island, on the River Lennon. Coming from Letterkenny turn right at the river and follow it round for about 400m.

SLEEPING & EATING
Lennon Lodge (☎ 915 1227; Market Sq; s/d €30/60; P) This is a family-run B&B upstairs from a pub. It has basic but clean rooms, a laundry, a large common room and TVs in every room. The pub has live music Friday to Sunday nights, and regular darts competitions.

Crammond House (☎ 915 1055; crammondhouse@ ramelton.net; Market Sq; s/d €35/64; ☾ Apr-Oct; P) An old-fashioned welcome is found at this sedate Georgian town house at the northern end of Ramelton. Rooms are large and elegantly furnished.

Tanyard (☎ 915 1029; www.thetanyard.com; Bridgend, Ramelton; apt per week €255-470; P) If your doctor really did advise you spend a few days in a quiet place like Ramelton, you couldn't do much better than the apartments in this converted Georgian warehouse. It's right on the river, with the water lapping the building's stone back side, and a wee walk from the heart of the town. Apartments sleep up to four people, have kitchens and are rather stylish.

Mirabeau Steak House (☎ 915 1138; the Mall; mains €9-18; ☾ 6-10pm) This dimly lit restaurant claims the old living room of a Georgian house on the riverfront. The cuisine is French with an emphasis on steak and seafood, and portions are colossal.

Bridge Bar (☎ 915 1119; Bridgend; mains €13-25; ☾ 6-11pm) Just over the bridge, about 100m from downtown, the Bridge Bar is one of those lovely old country pubs you came to Ireland for. It has a cosy 1st-floor

COUNTY DONEGAL

restaurant with good seafood dishes, such as roasted swordfish.

GETTING THERE & AWAY

Lough Swilly (☎ 912 2863) buses connect Rathmelton with Letterkenny (€2.85, 30 minutes, three times daily from Monday to Saturday).

INISHOWEN PENINSULA

The sprawling Inishowen (Inis Eoghain) Peninsula, with Lough Foyle to the east and Lough Swilly to the west, reaches just far enough out into the Atlantic to qualify as Ireland's northernmost point: Malin Head. It is remote, rugged, desolate and sparsely populated, making it a special and quiet sort of place. Ancient sites and ruined castles abound,

as do traditional thatched cottages that aren't yet being used as storage sheds.

The towns in the next section are part of a route that follows the road west of Derry up the coast of Lough Foyle to Moville and then northwest to Malin Head, before heading down the western side to Buncrana. If you're coming from Donegal, the peninsula can be approached from the southwest by turning off for Buncrana on the N13 road from Letterkenny to Derry.

Moville & Around

☎ 074 / pop 1470

Inishowen's best-looking town is Moville (Bun an Phobail), which essentially amounts to a couple of roads meeting beside a harbour.

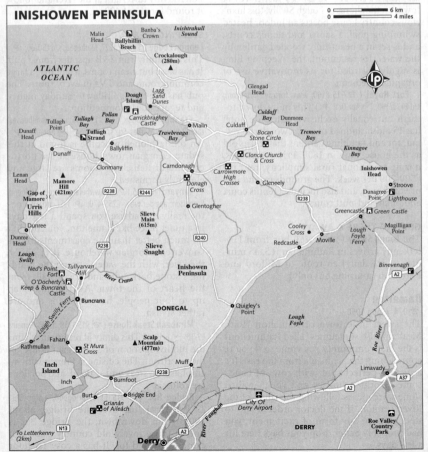

Nearly every building is old and well kept up in a way that's more proud than prissy. It can be rather sleepy, but on holiday weekends tourists from Northern Ireland flood the town. Moville was a busy port during the 19th and early 20th centuries, when thousands of emigrants set sail for America from here. The **coastal walkway** from Moville to Greencastle takes in the stretch of coast where the steamers used to moor, and also affords some rewarding **bird-watching** opportunities. There's **fishing** off the pier for mackerel, mullet and coalfish.

Main St has several banks with ATMs and the post office.

SIGHTS

By the gate of the Cooley gravehouse is an unusual 3m-high **cross**. Note the ringhole in its head – through it, the hands of negotiating parties are said to have clasped to seal an agreement. Whether they were uncommonly tall or stood on boxes remains a mystery. In the graveyard is the **Skull House**, which is associated with St Finian, the monk who accused Colmcille of plagiarising one of his manuscripts in the 6th century. He lived in a monastery here that was founded by St Patrick and survived into the 12th century.

Approaching Moville from the south, look out for a turning on the left that has a sign on the corner for the Cooley Pitch & Putt. If you pass a church, you've gone too far. The graveyard is just over 1km up this road on the right.

FESTIVALS

The cross-border **Foyle Oyster Festival** (☎ 938 2753; Main St) sees much scoffing of seafood in late September.

SLEEPING & EATING

Moville Holiday Hostel (☎ 938 2378; Malin Rd; dm €15; Ⓟ) A private, unpaved road curves off the main highway heading west of town, leading into a grove of trees and this secluded hostel. It's in an old stone house beside a bubbling brook. Very peaceful and near enough the main drag to walk.

Barron's Café (☎ 938 2472; Lower Main St; s/d €28/56) The café isn't much to write home about (though it may be convenient), but the guestrooms upstairs are happy little dens and very tidy. It's run by a friendly older couple.

Naomh Mhuíre (☎ 938 2091; catherinemcgroarty@eir com.net; Main St; with/without bathroom s €40/35, d €70/60; Ⓨ Mar-Sep) This pleasant town house sits on a street corner in the heart of the town. It has six plain but well-kept rooms, most of which use a shared bathroom.

Carlton Redcastle Hotel (☎ 938 5555; www.carlton redcastlehotel.com; d €200, mains €14-27; Ⓟ) The peninsula's flashiest luxury resort is along the lough, just north of Moville. It's rooms are indeed

COUNTY DONEGAL

TWITCHING ON INISHOWEN

Because it is surrounded by vast estuarine areas and pokes into the sea at Ireland's northernmost point, the Inishowen Peninsula naturally attracts a lot of birdlife. The variety of species is tremendous, with well over 200 species passing through or residing permanently on the peninsula. Inishowen regularly receives well-travelled visitors from Iceland, Greenland and North America. Thanks to irregularities in the Atlantic winds, rare and exotic species blow in from time to time.

Along the peninsula's Lough Foyle side, particularly north of Moville, a twitcher may hope to spot swans and geese in great numbers, along with cormorants diving into the lough for fish. The gannet, with its 1.8m wingspan, is among Ireland's most impressive birds. Coal tits, herons and puffins all appear along the shore here. Turning to the land, you are likely to see magpies, starlings, wrens, plovers and turtledoves. Sparrow-hawks and peregrine falcons sometimes hover above, in search of prey.

Many of these same species, including the gannet, also appear on Malin Head, the island's northern tip. Here, many birds nest on the cliffs, including guillemots, fulmars and shags. In autumn, manx shearwaters stop on Malin Head, before continuing their long migration to South America.

Inch Island, sitting off the peninsula's Lough Swilly shore, is a protected bird sanctuary that attracts whooper swans by the dozen.

A helpful resource for birders is *Ireland's Birds*, by Eric Demsey and Michael O'Clery. Online, visit www.birdsireland.com.

comfortable and classy, and the resort's Thalasso Spa is a major draw. If you don't require so much pampering, but consider yourself a gastronome, drop in for a meal at the lauded Waters Edge Restaurant, overlooking the estuary. It's in an exquisite setting and the menu fully exploits the local bounty.

DRINKING

There are a couple of friendly pubs along the Malin Rd, less than a block from the Market Sq. **Rawdon's** (☎ 938 2225; Malin Rd) features live music on Friday night. Even better is **Rosato's** (☎ 938 2247; Malin Rd), a smart old joint that also does good Italian food along with bar standards. It has live music on summer weekends.

GETTING THERE & AWAY

Lough Swilly (☎ 912 2863) runs four buses daily Monday to Saturday to Moville (€7, 45 minutes) from Derry.

Greencastle

☎ 074 / pop 570

Seals can be spotted bobbing their smooth heads hopefully in the busy little fishing port of Greencastle (An Cáisleán Nua), north of Moville. The town gets its name from the castle built in 1305 by Richard de Burgo, known as the Red Earl of Ulster because of his florid complexion. The Green Castle was a supply base for English armies in Scotland, and for this reason was attacked by Robert Bruce in the 1320s. The castle's vine-netted hulk survives.

A disarmingly eccentric collection of artefacts can be found at the **Inishowen Maritime Museum and Planetarium** (☎ 938 1363; www.inishowen maritime.com; museum adult/child €5/3, planetarium €10/6; ☑ 10am-6pm Mon-Sat, noon-6pm Sun Apr-Sep, to 5pm Oct-Mar), in a former coastguard station next to the harbour. The most fascinating exhibits are from the sunken wrecks of Lough Foyle, including, in pride of place, a pair of perfectly preserved military-issue boxer shorts salvaged by marine archaeologists from a ditched WWII bomber. The demise of the Spanish Armada and the departure from these waters of Irish immigrants are two of the museums more compelling themes. Take caution if visiting on a day when local children are testing their home-made rockets out front.

The simple, harbour-side **Kealy's Seafood Bar** (☎ 938 1010; mains €11-27; ☑ 12.30-3pm & 7-10pm Jun & Aug, Thu-Sun only Sep-May) is decorated with awards for its seafood. If the catch came any fresher you'd have to fight the seals for it.

Five **Lough Swilly** (☎ 912 2863) buses travel daily, Monday to Saturday, between Derry and Shrove, passing through Greencastle (€7.50, one hour).

Lough Foyle Ferry (☎ 938 1901; www.loughfoyleferry .com) also has a car-ferry service to Magilligan roughly every 25 minutes from outside the museum. Single fares per car/motorbike/ adult/child cost €9/4.50/2/1, and the crossing takes just 15 minutes. It runs every 15 minutes from 7.20am Monday to Saturday and 9am Sunday year-round. The last ferry is at 9.50pm, April to September, and 7.50pm, October to March.

Inishowen Head

A right turn outside Greencastle leads to Stroove; a sign indicating Inishowen Head is 1km along this road. It's possible to drive or cycle part of the way, but it's also an easy walk to the headland, from where you can see (on a clear day) the Antrim coast as far as the Giant's Causeway. A more demanding walk continues to the sandy beach of **Kinnagoe Bay**.

Culdaff & Around

☎ 074 / pop 180

This is a lovely spot, where sheep vastly outnumber the people. The sleepy, secluded, resort village of Culdaff (Cúil Dabhcha) is surrounded by several ancient sites, but the main draw is a country inn with an impressive live-music venue. The village is on the main Moville–Carndonagh road (R238).

SIGHTS & ACTIVITIES

Sheep now wander the remains of the **Clonca church and cross**. Inside, an intricately carved tombstone sporting a sword and hurling-stick motif was erected by one Magnus MacOrristin. The carved lintel over the door is thought to come from an earlier church. Outside, the remains of the cross show the miracle of the loaves and fishes on the eastern face and geometric designs on the sides.

Look for the turn-off to Culdaff, on the right if coming from Moville, on the left after about 6km if coming from Carndonagh. The Clonca church and cross are 1.5km on the right behind some farm buildings. A necklace of around 30 prehistoric stones, called the **Bocan Stone Circle**, embroiders a farmer's field east of Clonca Church. From Clonca, continue along the road until you reach a T-junction with a modern church facing you. Turn right here and after about 500m turn left (no sign). The Bocan Stone Circle is inside the first heather-covered field on the left.

The plain stumpy-armed **Carrowmore High Crosses** are all that remain of an ancient monastic site straddling a small lane. One is basically a decorated slab showing Christ and an angel, while the other is a taller, unadorned cross.

From Bocan Stone Circle and Clonca Church, retrace the route back to the main Carndonagh–Moville road and turn left, then almost immediately right.

Culdaff has a beach that's good for **swimming** and **windsurfing** and, from Bunagee Pier, **sea angling** and **diving** are popular.

SLEEPING & EATING

McGrory's of Culdaff (☎ 937 9104; www.mcgrorys.ie; Culdaff; s/d €70/120, mains €9-23; ✆ bar food 12.30-8pm, restaurant 6.30-9 Tue-Sat, 1-3pm & 6-8.30pm Sun; P) This is a good place to count sheep. It has 17 spiffy rooms, all smartly decorated with a modern eye. Before sleeping, however, head downstairs to catch live music in Mac's Backroom, which books international singer-songwriters. An old stone pub and restaurant serves traditional Irish food.

Malin Head
☎ 074
If you've already seen Ireland's southernmost point and its westernmost point, you'll still be impressed when you lay eyes on Malin Head (Cionn Mhálanna), the island's northern extent. The head's rocky, weather-battered slopes feel like they're being dragged unwillingly into the sea. It's great for wandering on foot, absorbing the stark natural setting and pondering deep subjects as the wind tries to blow the clothes off your back. There are a smattering of farm houses and few services, so pack what you'll be needing.

On the northernmost tip, called **Banba's Crown** (Fíorcheann Éireann), stands a cumbersome cliff-top **tower** that was built in 1805 by the British admiralty and later used as a Lloyds signal station. Around it are unattractive concrete huts that were used by the Irish army in WWII as lookout posts. To the west from the fort-side car park, a path leads to **Hell's Hole**, a chasm where the incoming waters crash against the rocky formations.

To the east a longer headland walk leads to the **Wee House of Malin**, a hermit's cave in the cliff face.

Several endangered bird species thrive here. This is one of the few places in Ireland where you can still hear the call of the endangered corncrake in summer. Other birds to look out for are choughs, snow bunting and puffins.

The Plantation village of **Malin** (Málainn), on Trawbreaga Bay, 14km south of Malin Head, has a pretty movie-set quality. Walkers can head out from the tidy village green on a circular route that takes in **Knockamany Bens**, a local hill with terrific views, as well as **Lagg Presbyterian Church** (3km northwest from Malin), the oldest church still in use on the peninsula. The massive sand dunes at Five Fingers Strand, another 1km beyond the church, are a dog's dream.

SLEEPING & EATING

Sandrock Holiday Hostel (☎ 937 0289; sandrockhostel@eircom.net; Port Ronan Pier, Malin Head; dm €10-12; P ♿) Visitors are welcomed like family at this perennially popular IHH hostel on the western side of the headland. It's situated in a rocky bay, where seafood can sometimes be bought straight off the boats. Sandrock has 20 remarkably cosy beds, laundry facilities, pick-up and bike hire (€9 per day).

Malin Head Hostel (☎ 937 0309; www.malinhead hostel.com; Malin Head; dm/d €13/36; ✆ Jul-Sep; P) The picture of orderliness, this friendly 20-bed IHH hostel has free hot showers and an organic garden where you can buy fruit and vegetables. There's also aromatherapy and reflexology treatments (per reflexology/full-body massage €35/45). There's a shop nearby and local buses stop at the hostel.

Malin Hotel (☎ 937 0606; info@malinhotel.ie; Malin; s/d from €65/110, mains €10-23; ✆ bar food 12.30-3pm, restaurant 6-10pm) From the street you'll first spot the old pub, but look beyond it and you'll also see a modern, boxlike hotel piled up to the rear. It has lavishly decorated rooms, and the pub-restaurant serves up good Irish food. There's entertainment at the weekend.

GETTING THERE & AWAY

The best way to approach Malin Head is by the R238/242 from Carndonagh, rather than up the eastern side from Culdaff. **Lough Swilly** (☎ 912 2863) operates a bus that runs on Monday, Wednesday and Friday at 11am between Derry and Malin Head via Carndonagh (€4, 30 minutes); on the same days a bus leaves Carndonagh at 3pm for Malin Head. There are three buses from Derry to Malin Head on Saturday.

Carndonagh

☎ 074 / pop 1680

Carndonagh (Cardomhnach), surrounded by hills on three sides, is a busy commercial centre serving the local farming community. It's not a choice locale in these parts, but convenient for gathering information and provisions.

The helpful, locally run **Inishowen tourism office** (☎ 937 4933; www.visitinishowen.com; Chapel St; 9.30am-5.30pm Mon-Fri Sep-May, 9.30am-7pm Mon-Fri, 11am-4pm Sat Jun & Aug), southwest of the diamond, also sells fishing licences for all of Donegal. There are three banks on the diamond and AIB has an ATM; the post office is in the shopping centre halfway down Bridge St towards the Donagh Cross.

SIGHTS

Once an important ecclesiastical centre, Carndonagh has several early Christian stone monuments. Not least, the delightful 7th-century **Donagh Cross** stands under a shelter by an Anglican church at the Ballyliffin end of town. It's carved with a darling short-bodied, big-eyed figure of Jesus, smiling impishly. Flanking the cross are two small pillars, one showing a man, possibly Goliath, with a sword and shield, the other, David and his harp. In the graveyard there's a pillar with a carved marigold on a stem and nearby a crucifixion scene.

SLEEPING & EATING

If you're off to Malin Head for the day or going on to the camping ground at Clonmany, stock up with provisions at the Costcutter supermarket in the large shopping centre on Bridge St.

Ashdale House (☎ 937 4017; www.ashdalehouse .net; s/d €47/64; Mar-Nov; P) This large family home, 1km out of town on the road towards Malin, is Carndonagh's best B&B. It's a cheerful modern house that modestly evokes an Irish traditional manor.

Arch Inn (☎ 937 3209; the Diamond; snacks around €5) In the main square, the Arch does good soup and sandwiches by day and hosts a traditional music session on Sunday evening.

GETTING THERE & AWAY

A **Lough Swilly** (☎ 912 2863) bus leaves Buncrana for Carndonagh (€5.30, 45 minutes) three times daily (except Tuesday and Wednesday, when it departs once each day) and Sunday (no service). On weekdays they return from Carndonagh three times daily. Lough Swilly also runs a bus between Derry (€8, 55 minutes) and Malin Head via Carndonagh daily Monday, Wednesday and Friday and three times Saturday.

Ballyliffin & Clonmany

☎ 074 / pop 700

For such a diminutive and remote seaside resort, easygoing Ballyliffin (Baile Lifin) does a roaring summer trade. It has a handful of good hotels, which somehow soak up an army of Northern Irish holidaymakers, who come to play golf on the two championship 18-hole courses, and enjoy the local beaches.

Both villages have post offices but no banks.

SIGHTS

About 1km north of Ballyliffin is the lovely, sandy expanse of **Pollan Strand**, but the crashing breakers make it unsafe for swimming. A walk along the dunes to the north of this beach brings you to **Doagh Island** (now part of the mainland), where the matchbox ruin of 16th-century **Carrickbraghey Castle** (Carraic Brachaide) is continually battered by the ocean.

Also on the island is the enthusiastically thrown-together **Doagh Famine Village** (☎ 937 8078; www.doaghfaminevillage.com; Doagh Island; adult/child €6/4; 10am-5.30pm Apr-Sep) in a reconstructed village of thatched cottages. It runs a terrific tour packed with entertaining titbits about a disappearing way of life, and takes a refreshing approach to the Famine by making insightful comparisons with famine-stricken countries today. Tea and scones are included in the admission fee. Call ahead to book the tour.

The other beach is at **Tullagh Strand**. It's great for an exhilarating walk and, although swimming is possible, the current can be strong and it isn't recommended when the tide is going out. There are walks to **Butler's Glen** and **Dunaff Head** from Clonmany.

ACTIVITIES

With two championship courses, **Ballyliffin Golf Club** (☎ 937 6119; www.ballyliffingolfclub.com; Ballyliffin; green fees weekday/weekend Old Links €50/55,

Glashedy €65/75) is among the best places to golf in Donegal. The scenery is so beautiful that it can distract even the most focused golfer.

SLEEPING & EATING

Tullagh Bay Camping & Caravan Park (☎ 937 8997; Tullagh Bay; camp sites €14; ☯ Easter-Sep) About 5km from Clonmany, this windy but flat park is ideal for the bucket-and-spade brigade as it's just behind the vast, dune-backed Tullagh Strand.

Rossaor House (☎ 937 6498; rossaor@gofree.indigo.ie; Ballyliffin; s €45-50, d €70-80; P) It's worth the extra few euros to stay at this above-average B&B just outside town. Quite apart from its wonderful views, pristine rooms and leafy little garden, where else can you request home-produced honey on your freshly baked scones?

Ballyliffin Lodge (☎ 937 8200; www.ballyliffinlodge.com; d from €200, bar food €6-14, restaurant mains €16-30) This spa hotel was the class of Ballyliffin. Guests are treated to panoramic views, lavishly decorated rooms and mod amenities. The resort's leisure facilities include a state-of-the-art spa and a golf course. The hotel's Holly Tree Restaurant oozes cosmopolitan sophistication, while its bar, Mamie Pat's, is a more laidback spot for a straightforward pub meal.

GETTING THERE & AWAY

Lough Swilly (☎ 912 2863) buses run between Clonmany and Carndonagh (€3.50, 20 minutes); see opposite.

Clonmany to Buncrana

There are two routes from Clonmany to Buncrana: the scenic coastal road via the Gap of Mamore and Dunree Head, and the speedier inland road (R238). The **Gap of Mamore** (elevation 262m) descends dramatically between Mamore Hill and Croaghcarragh on its way to Dunree (An Dún Riabhach), where the **Guns of Dunree military museum** (☎ 074-936 1817; www.dunree.pro.ie; ☯ 10.30am-6pm Mon-Sat, 1-6pm Sun Jun-Sep, 10.30am-4.30pm Mon-Fri, 1-6pm Sat & Sun Oct-May) sits on a rocky outcrop in a 19th-century fort. It's a beautiful spot. If the guns don't impress you, the scenery and birdlife will.

Buncrana

☎ 074 / pop 3490
Buncrana (Bun Cranncha) is not the wild side of the peninsula, and feels much more connected with the outside world. It's a comely town with its fair share of pubs. A 5km sandy

beach on the shores of Lough Swilly is the town's main attraction, and in summer hordes flock in from Derry.

INFORMATION

Bank of Ireland (Lower Main St) ATM and bureau de change.
Post office (Upper Main St)
Tourist office (☎ 936 2600; Derry Rd; ☯ 11am-3.30pm Fri, 11.30am-2pm Sat summer) One kilometre south of the town centre.
Ulster Bank (Upper Main St) ATM and bureau de change.
Valu Clean (☎ 936 2570; Lower Main St; laundry from €6) Laundry service.

SIGHTS

At the northern end of the seafront the early-18th-century, six-arched Castle Bridge leads to **O'Docherty's Keep**, a tower house built by the O'Dochertys, the local chiefs, in 1430. It was burned by the English and then rebuilt for their own use. At its side is the manor-like **Buncrana Castle**, built in 1718 by John Vaughan, who also constructed the bridge; Wolfe Tone was imprisoned here following the unsuccessful French invasion in 1798. Walking 500m further from the keep (turn left and stick to the shoreline) brings you to **Ned's Point Fort** (1812), built by the British and now under siege from graffiti artists.

SLEEPING & EATING

B&Bs abound, but they can fill up quickly during August.

Tullyarvan Mill (☎ 936 1613; www.tullyarvanmill.com; Carndonagh Rd; dm/d/q €15/40/60; ☯ year-round; P ☐ ☻) Amid beautiful riverside gardens, this historic mill has a modern, purpose-built hostel attached to it. Dorms are clean as army barracks and each bed has a locker beside it for personal storage. The compound has a lively vibe, due to the cultural events and conferences that seem to be happening all the time. Head north out of town on the R238 and follow the signs.

Caldra B&B (☎ 936 3703; caldrabandb@eircom.net; Lisnakelly; s/d €25/50, mains €5-15; ☯ food served 8.15am-8pm Mon-Thu, to 9pm Fri & Sat, 10.30am-9pm Sun) This large, modern B&B faces Lough Swilly. Guestrooms are decorated with flair. It's just north of town.

Lake of Shadows Hotel (☎ 936 1005; www.lakeofshadows.com; Grianán Park; s €54-62, d 88-104; P) A fine Victorian façade brings to mind past generations coming to 'take the sea air' here. Its

23 modern, but fading, flowery rooms help maintain the image. To get here from Main St, head down Church St towards the bay.

Beach House (☎ 936 1050; www.thebeachhouse.ie; the Pier, Swilly Rd; mains €11-23; ☑ 5pm-late Tue-Fri, noon-late Sat & Sun) With plate glass windows facing the lough, the location here couldn't be better. The dining room projects an elegant simplicity that complements the contemporary Irish cuisine. Service is friendly and attentive.

ENTERTAINMENT
Dating from 1792, the **Atlantic Bar** (☎ 932 0880; Upper Main St) is Buncrana's oldest pub. Chummy older gents keep the bar, and young and old swill pints.

GETTING THERE & AROUND
From Buncrana, **Lough Swilly** (☎ 912 2863) buses run several times daily to Derry and less often to Carndonagh.

Lough Swilly Ferry (☎ 938 1901; www.loughfoyleferry .com) runs from Buncrana to Rathmullan (30 minutes, nine daily, single car/motorbike/ adult/concession €12/6/3/2) from mid-June to September. Pick up a current timetable at the tourist office.

South of Buncrana
FAHAN
A monastery was founded in Fahan by St Colmcille in the 6th century. Among its ruins is the beautifully carved, 7th-century **St Mura Cross** in the graveyard beside the church. Each face is decorated with a cross, in intricate Celtic weave, and the barely discernible Greek inscription is the only one known from this early Christian period.

GRIANÁN OF AILEÁCH
This amphitheatre-like stone **fort** (admission free; ☑ 10am-6pm; P) encircles the top of Grianán Hill like a halo, 18km south of Buncrana near Burt, signposted off the N13. In many ways it's a very theatrical place, offering eye-popping views of the surrounding loughs and all the way to distant Derry. And its miniarena can resemble a circus whenever a tour bus rolls up and spills its load inside the 4m-thick walls.

The fort may have existed at least 2000 years ago, but it's thought that the site itself goes back to pre-Celtic times as a temple to the god Dagda. Between the 5th and 12th centuries it was the seat of the O'Neills, before being demolished by Murtogh O'Brien, king of Munster. Most of what you see now is a reconstruction built between 1874 and 1878.

The merry-go-round-shaped **Burt Church** at the foot of the hill was modelled on the fort by Derry architect Liam McCormack and built in 1967.

INCH ISLAND
Few tourists make it to tranquil Inch Island, accessible from the mainland by a causeway, but it does have plenty of birdlife, including a sanctuary for swans, two small beaches and the remains of an old fort. **Inch Island Stables** (☎ 074-936 0335) organises horse-riding lessons and trips around the island.

Counties Meath & Louth

History's march has left a trail across the adjoining counties of Meath and Louth. At Brú na Bóinne and Loughcrew you'll find the amazing relics of the earliest Irish who, some 4000 years ago, built tombs that are the Pyramids of Ireland. At Monasterboice, Mellifont and Kells, the first Christians created abbeys, towers and other religious structures that survive today and recall a time lit only by fire. In recent centuries, the counties have been the location of often violent conflicts between the locals and the invaders from across the Irish Sea; much of the fighting was along the River Boyne, and places such as Drogheda still bear the scars.

Today the invasions are much more local. The counties are becoming Dublin suburbs as cityfolk search for affordable housing – something that is both a blessing and a curse, as the greater range of activities and nightlife is offset by urban sprawl and congestion. History and preservation have run headlong into the demands of sprawl and convenience in the Tara Valley with controversy around the new M3 motorway.

Although the top sites in the region can easily be explored as day trips from Dublin, you'll find greater rewards by spending some time in the counties. Drogheda makes an excellent base for must-see sights such as Newgrange, while Carlington has a scenic location near the border and hosts many activities on both land and sea. Or, better yet, wander the back roads of the counties – you'll find some surprising bit of history around every corner.

COUNTIES MEATH & LOUTH

HIGHLIGHTS

- **Egyptian Ireland** Extraordinary prehistoric remains underground at Newgrange (p543) and Knowth (p544) in the richly interesting Brú na Bóinne

- **Lost Ireland** The surprising and rarely visited ancient sites known as the Loughcrew Cairns (p557)

- **Fortified Ireland** The authentic walled castle at Trim (p553)

- **Modern Ireland** The many pleasures to be found in cosmopolitan Drogheda (p558)

- **Summer Ireland** A backdrop of multihued hills and sun-dappled waters in Carlingford (p574)

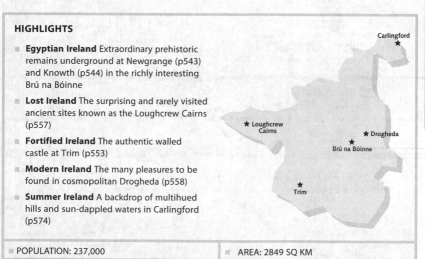

★ Carlingford

★ Loughcrew Cairns

★ Drogheda

★ Brú na Bóinne

★ Trim

■ POPULATION: 237,000　　　　　■ AREA: 2849 SQ KM

COUNTY MEATH

In the original Gaelic divisions of Ireland, Meath (An Mhí) was Mide, 'the Middle Kingdom', and one of five provinces. The seat of the high kings until the 6th century, Meath was a fairly heavy hitter in Irish affairs.

These days, Meath's influence doesn't extend far beyond agricultural matters, but in that domain it still packs a solid punch: a farm in Meath is worth two in any other county, so goes the old saying. The fecund earth has attracted settlers since earliest times, and Meath's principal attractions are its don't-miss ancient sites in the Boyne Valley and among the hills of Tara, and the surprising town of Trim.

The county's towns have experienced rapid growth in the last decade, as Dubliners searching for affordable housing have invaded Navan, Slane and Kells. The changes brought by the cityfolk are mixed. You'll see new houses and businesses, and have plenty of time to ponder them as you sit in traffic.

Meath's tourism authority is one of the best in Ireland. Its publications are of a high standard; you'll get loads of info at www.meathtourism.ie.

History

Meath's rich soil, laid down during the last Ice Age, attracted settlers as early as 8000 BC. They worked their way up the banks of

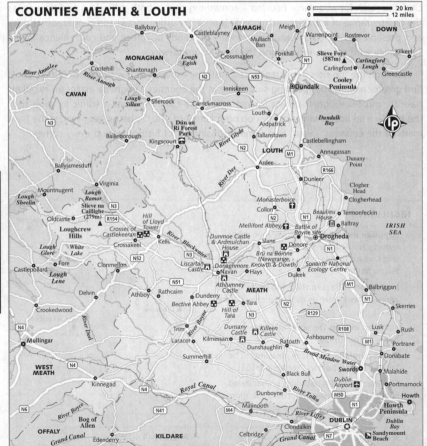

COUNTIES MEATH & LOUTH

the River Boyne, transforming the landscape from forest to farmland. The extensive necropolis at Brú na Bóinne, dating from when the Egyptian pyramids were still but a dream, lies on a meandering section of the Boyne between Drogheda and Slane. There's a group of smaller passage graves in the Loughcrew Hills near Oldcastle.

For a thousand years the Hill of Tara was the seat of power for Irish high kings (*ard ríthe*), until the arrival of St Patrick in the 5th century. Later, Kells became one of the most important and creative monastic settlements in Ireland, and lent its name to the famed *Book of Kells*, a 9th-century illuminated manuscript now displayed at Trinity College, Dublin.

BRÚ NA BÓINNE

Not to be missed, the vast Neolithic necropolis known as Brú na Bóinne (the Boyne Palace) is one of the most extraordinary sites in Europe. A thousand years older than Stonehenge, this is a powerful and evocative testament to the mind-boggling achievements of prehistoric humans.

The complex was built to house the remains of the people who were at the top of the social heap. Its tombs were the largest artificial structures in Ireland until the construction of the Anglo-Norman castles 4000 years later. Over the centuries the tombs decayed, were covered by grass and trees and were plundered by everybody from Vikings to Victorian treasure hunters, whose carved initials can be seen on the great stones of Newgrange. The countryside around the tombs is littered with countless other ancient mounds (tumuli) and standing stones.

The area consists of many different sites, with the three principal ones being Newgrange, Knowth and Dowth.

Orientation & Information

To keep visitors from mucking up the ruins, all visits to Brú na Bóinne have to start at the **Brú na Bóinne visitor centre** (☎ 041-988 0300; www.heritageireland.ie; Donore; adult/child visitor centre €2.90/1.60, visitor centre, Newgrange & Knowth €10.30/4.50; 🕑 9am-7pm Jun-Sep, 9.30am-5pm Oct-Apr). Happily, this is a superb interpretive centre with an extraordinary series of interactive exhibits on the passage tombs and prehistoric Ireland in general. The building is a stunner, picking up the spiral design of Newgrange.

It has regional tourism info, a good café and a bookshop.

You should allow plenty of time to visit Brú na Bóinne. If you're only planning on taking the guided tour of the interpretive centre, give yourself about an hour. If you plan a visit to Newgrange or Knowth, allow at least two hours. If, however, you want to visit all three in one go, you should plan at least half a day. In summer, particularly at the weekend, and during school holidays, the place gets very crowded, and you will not be guaranteed a visit to either of the passage tombs; call ahead to book a tour as there are 750 slots and on peak days 2000 people show up. In summer, the best time to visit is midweek or early in the morning.

The important thing to note is that if you turn up at either Newgrange or Knowth (Dowth is not open for tourists) first, you'll be sent to the visitor centre. Tours depart from a bus stop that you reach by walking across a spiral bridge over the River Boyne, and the buses take just a few minutes to reach the sites. Technically you can walk the 4km to either site from the visitor centre but you're discouraged from doing this as you might get mowed down on the very narrow lanes by the tour bus you've chosen not to take.

The visitor centre is on the south side of the river. It's 2km west of Donore and 6km east of Slane, where bridges cross the river from the N51. Newgrange itself lies just north of the River Boyne, about 13km southwest of Drogheda and around 5km southeast of Slane; Dowth is between Newgrange and Drogheda; while Knowth is about 1km northwest of Newgrange, or almost 4km by road.

Sights

NEWGRANGE

Even from afar, you know that **Newgrange** (adult/child visitor centre & Newgrange €5.80/2.90) is something special. Its white, round stone walls topped by a grass dome look otherworldly, and just the size is impressive: 80m in diameter and 13m high. But underneath it gets even better. Here lies the finest Stone Age passage tomb in Ireland, and one of the most remarkable prehistoric sites in Europe. It dates from around 3200 BC, predating the Pyramids by some six centuries. The purpose for which it was constructed remains uncertain. It could have been a burial place for kings or a centre for ritual – although the alignment with the sun at the time of the winter solstice also suggests it was designed to act as a calendar.

The name derives from 'New Granary' (the tomb did in fact serve as a repository for wheat and grain at one stage), although a more popular belief is that it comes from the Irish for 'Cave of Gráinne', a reference to a Celtic myth taught to every Irish child. *The Pursuit of Diarmuid and Gráinne* tells of the illicit love between the woman betrothed to Fionn McCumhaill (or Finn McCool), leader of the Fianna, and Diarmuid, one of his most trusted lieutenants. When Diarmuid was fatally wounded, his body was brought to Newgrange by the god Aengus in a vain attempt to save him, and the despairing Gráinne followed him into the cave, where she remained long after he died. This suspiciously Arthurian tale (for Diarmuid and Gráinne read Lancelot and Guinevere) is undoubtedly a myth, but it's still a pretty good story. Newgrange also plays another role in Celtic mythology, as the site where the hero Cúchulainn was conceived.

Over time, Newgrange, like Dowth and Knowth, deteriorated and was even used as a quarry at one stage. The site was extensively restored in 1962 and again in 1975.

A superbly carved kerbstone with double and triple spirals guards the tomb's main entrance. The front façade has been reconstructed so that tourists don't have to clamber in over it. Above the entrance is a slit, or roof box, which lets light in. Another beautifully decorated kerbstone stands at the exact opposite side of the mound. Some experts say that a ring of standing stones encircled the mound, forming a Great Circle about 100m in diameter, but only 12 of these stones remain, with traces of some others below ground level.

Holding the whole structure together are the 97 boulders of the kerb ring, designed to stop the mound from collapsing outwards. Eleven of these are decorated with motifs similar to those on the main entrance stone, although only three have extensive carvings.

The white quartzite was originally obtained from Wicklow, 70km to the south – in an age before horse and wheel, it was transported by sea and then up the River Boyne – and there is also some granite from the Mourne Mountains in Northern Ireland. Over 200,000 tonnes of earth and stone also went into the mound.

You can walk down the narrow 19m passage, lined with 43 stone uprights (some of them engraved), which leads into the tomb chamber about one-third of the way into the colossal mound. The chamber has three recesses, and in these are large basin stones that held cremated human bones. As well as the remains, the basins would have held funeral offerings of beads and pendants, but these were stolen long before the archaeologists arrived.

Above, the massive stones support a 6m-high corbel-vaulted roof. A complex drainage system means that not a drop of water has penetrated the interior in 40 centuries.

At 8.20am during the winter solstice (19 to 23 December), the rising sun's rays shine through the slit above the entrance, creep slowly down the long passage and illuminate the tomb chamber for 17 minutes. There is little doubt that this is one of the country's most memorable, even mystical, experiences; be sure to add your name to the list that is drawn by lottery every 1 October. Even if you miss out, there is a simulated winter sunrise for every group taken into the mound.

KNOWTH

Northwest of Newgrange, the burial mound of **Knowth** (Cnóbha; visitor centre & Knowth adult/child €4.50/1.60; ☯ Easter–Oct) was built around the same time and seems set to surpass its better-known neighbour in both its size and the importance of the discoveries made here. It has the greatest collection of passage-grave art ever uncovered in Western Europe, and has been under excavation since 1962.

The excavations soon cleared a passage leading to the central chamber, which at 34m is much longer than the one at Newgrange.

NEWGRANGE FARM

Here's one for the kids. Situated a few hundred metres down the hill to the west of Newgrange tomb is a 135-hectare **working farm** (☎ 041-982 4119; www .newgrangefarm.com; Newgrange; adult €8, family €12-30; ☯ 10am-5pm Easter-Aug). The truly hands-on family-run farm allows visitors to feed the ducks and lambs, and stroke the bunnies. Amiable Farmer Bill keeps things interesting, and demonstrations of threshing, sheepdog work and shoeing a horse are absorbing. You reach the farm by following signs off the N51.

In 1968 a 40m passage was unearthed on the opposite side of the mound. Although the chambers are separate, they're close enough for archaeologists to hear each other at work. Also in the mound are the remains of six early-Christian souterrains (underground chambers) built into the side. Some 300 carved slabs and 17 satellite graves surround the main mound.

Human activity at Knowth continued for thousands of years after its construction, which accounts for the site's complexity. The Beaker folk, so called because they buried the dead with drinking vessels, occupied the site in the Bronze Age (c 1800 BC), as did the Celts in the Iron Age (c 500 BC). Remnants of bronze and iron workings from these periods have been discovered. Around AD 800 to 900, it was turned into a *ráth* (earthen ringfort), a stronghold of the very powerful Uí Néill (O'Neill) clan. In 965, it was the seat of Cormac MacMaelmithic, later Ireland's high king for nine years. The Normans built a motte (raised, flattened mound with a keep on top) and bailey (outer wall of a castle) here in the 12th century. In about 1400 the site was finally abandoned.

Further excavations are likely to continue at least for the next decade, and one of the thrills of visiting Knowth is being allowed to watch archaeologists at work (although given the cramped conditions inside, you won't be jealous!).

DOWTH

The circular mound at **Dowth** (Dubhadh, meaning 'Dark') is similar in size to Newgrange – about 63m in diameter – but is slightly taller at 14m high. It has suffered badly at the hands of everyone from road builders and treasure hunters to amateur archaeologists, who scooped out the centre of the tumulus in the 19th century. For a time, Dowth even had a tearoom ignobly perched on its summit. Relatively untouched by modern archaeologists, Dowth shows what Newgrange and Knowth looked like for most of their history. Because it's unsafe, Dowth is closed to visitors, though the mound can be viewed from the road. Excavations began in 1998 and will continue for years to come.

There are two entrance passages leading to separate chambers (both sealed), and a 24m early-Christian underground passage at either end, which connect up with the western passage. This 8m-long passage leads into a small cruciform chamber, in which a recess acts as an entrance to an additional series of small compartments, a feature unique to Dowth. To the southwest is the entrance to a shorter passage and smaller chamber.

North of the tumulus are the ruins of **Dowth Castle** and **Dowth House**.

Tours

Brú na Bóinne is one of the most popular tourist attractions in Ireland, and there are oodles of organised tours transporting busloads of eager tourists to the visitor centre (everybody must access the sites through there), especially from Dublin.

The **Mary Gibbons Tours** (☎ 01-283 9973; www.new grangetours.com; tour €35) are highly recommended. Tours depart from numerous Dublin hotels, beginning at 9.30am Monday to Saturday, and take in the whole of the Boyne Valley, including Newgrange, and the Hill of Tara. The expert guides offer a fascinating insight into Celtic and pre-Celtic life in Ireland, and you'll get access to Newgrange even on days when all visiting slots are filled.

Bus Éireann (☎ 01-836 6111; www.buseireann.ie; adult/child €29/18; ☼ Mon-Thu, Sat & Sun mid-Mar–Sep) runs Newgrange and the Boyne Valley tours departing from **Busáras** (Map pp82-3; Store St) in Dublin at 10am, returning at approximately 5.45pm.

Sleeping & Eating

Drogheda is close to Brú na Bóinne and has many hotels, while the nearby village of Slane is especially good for lunch. There are some excellent sleeping options close to the sites, and Brú na Bóinne itself has a good café.

Newgrange Lodge (☎ 041-988 2478; www.new grangelodge.com; dm/d €15/50; ℗ 🖳) A beautiful new place just east of the Brú na Bóinne visitor centre, this place has dorm beds and hotel-standard rooms with TVs. Reception is open 24 hours, and there is a café, outdoor patios, bicycle hire and much more.

Rossnaree (☎ 041-982 0975; rossnaree@eircom.net; Newgrange; s/d €100/160; ☼ mid-Mar–Oct; ℗) At a sharp corner on the narrow road between Donore and Slane is this magnificent Italianate country house overlooking the Boyne and surrounded by a working farm. The three bedrooms are quite luxurious, and you can book dinner (€45) a day in advance. The

FIONN & THE SALMON OF KNOWLEDGE

One of the best-known stories in the Fenian Cycle tells of the old druid Finnegan, who struggled for seven years to catch a very slippery salmon that, once eaten, would bestow enormous wisdom on the eater, including the gift of foresight. The young Fionn McCumhaill arrived at his riverside camp one day looking for instruction, and no sooner did the young hero arrive than Finnegan managed to land the salmon. As befits the inevitable tragedy of all these stories, Finnegan set the fish to cook and went off for a bit, ordering Fionn to keep an eye on it without eating so much as the smallest part. You'd think that after all these years of labour Finnegan could have put off his errand until after dinner, but it wasn't to be: as Fionn turned the fish on the spit a drop of hot oil landed on his thumb, which he quickly put in his mouth to soothe. Finnegan returned, saw what had happened and knew that it was too late; he bade Fionn eat the rest of the fish, and so it was that Fionn acquired wisdom and foresight.

events related in *Fionn and the Salmon of Knowledge* are said to have taken place in this very spot (above).

Glebe House (☎ 041-983 6101; www.glebenouse.ie; Dowth; r €120; **P**) This charming 17th-century, wisteria-clad country house has four gorgeous rooms with open, log fires and vibrant purple carpet. It is 7km west of Drogheda, and has views of Newgrange and Dowth. Children under 10 are not allowed.

Getting There & Away

From Drogheda, **Bus Éireann** (☎ 041-983 5023) runs a service that drops you off at the entrance to the visitor centre (€2, 20 minutes, four to six daily).

Newgrange Shuttlebus (☎ 1800 424 252; return ticket €18) runs one or two trips daily to the Brú na Bóinne visitor centre from central Dublin. Book in advance.

BATTLE OF BOYNE SITE

More than 60,000 soldiers of the armies of King James II and King William III fought on this patch of farmland on the border of counties Meath and Louth in 1690; in the end, William prevailed and James sailed off to France. Today the **battle site** (☎ 041-980 9950; www.battleoftheboyne.ie; 🕙 10am-6pm May-Sep) is part of the Oldbridge Estate farm. The Heritage Service is slowly developing the area and there are plans for a visitor centre and exhibits. In the meantime, the site is eerily low-key. You can wander the fields and think about the events that saw Protestant interests remain in Ireland – although the roar you hear isn't the ghosts of the soldiers, it's the M1. The site, 3km north of Donore, is signposted off the N51.

SLANE

☎ 041 / pop 900

Pretty little Slane (Baile Shláine) grew up around the enormous castle whose grounds dominate the town; the massive grey gate to the privately owned castle lies southwest of the town centre, which is made up of pleasant 18th-century stone houses and cottages. At the junction of the main roads are four identical houses facing each other: local lore has it that they were built for four sisters who had taken an intense dislike to one another and kept a beady-eyed watch from their individual residences.

Slane is a convenient base for Newgrange, located 6km east.

Orientation

Slane is perched on a hillside at the junction of the N2 and N51, some 15km west of Drogheda. To the south, at the bottom of the hill, the Boyne glides by under a narrow bridge. The hairpin turn on the northern side of the bridge is considered to be one of the most dangerous in the country, as there is a steep hill preceding it. Throughout the day, there's a fair amount of traffic here.

Sights

HILL OF SLANE

About 1km north of the village is the Hill of Slane, a fairly plain-looking mound that only stands out for its association with a thick slice of Celto-Christian mythology. According to legend, St Patrick lit a paschal (Easter) fire here in AD 433 to proclaim Christianity throughout the land. Patrick's fire infuriated Laoghaire, the pagan high king of Ireland, who had expressly ordered that no fire be lit within sight of the Hill of Tara. Thankfully –

at least for the future of Irish Christians – he was restrained by his far-sighted druids, who warned that 'the man who had kindled the flame would surpass kings and princes'. Laoghaire went to meet Patrick, and all but one of his attendants – a man called Erc – greeted Patrick with scorn.

Here the story *really* gets far-fetched. During the meeting, Patrick killed one of the king's guards and summoned an earthquake to subdue the rest. After his Herculean efforts, Patrick calmed down a little and plucked a shamrock from the ground, using its three leaves to explain the paradox of the Holy Trinity – the union of the Father, the Son and the Holy Spirit in one Godhead. Laoghaire wasn't convinced, but he agreed to let Patrick continue his missionary work. Patrick's success that day – apart from keeping his own life, starting an earthquake and giving Ireland one of its enduring national symbols – was good old Erc, who was baptised and later became the first bishop of Slane. To this day, the local parish priest lights a fire here on Holy Saturday.

The Hill of Slane originally had a church associated with St Erc and, later, a round tower and monastery, but only an outline of the foundations remains. Later a motte and bailey were constructed, and are still visible on the western side of the hill. The ruined church, tower and other buildings here once formed part of an early-16th-century Franciscan friary. On a clear day, you can see the Hill of Tara and the Boyne Valley from the top of the tower, which is always open, as well as (it's said) seven Irish counties.

St Erc is believed to have become a hermit, and the ruins of a small Gothic **church** (15 Aug) mark the spot where he is thought to have spent his last days, around AD 512 to 514. It's on the northern riverbank, behind the Protestant church on the Navan road, and lies within the private Conyngham estate.

SLANE CASTLE

The private residence of Lord Henry Conyngham, earl of Mountcharles, **Slane Castle** (988 4400; www.slanecastle.ie; adult/child €7/5; noon-5pm Sun-Thu May-early Aug) is west of the town centre along the Navan road and is best known in Ireland as the setting for major outdoor rock concerts.

Built in 1785 in the Gothic revival style by James Wyatt, the building was later altered by Francis Johnson for George IV's visits to Lady

Conyngham. She was allegedly his mistress, and it's said the road between Dublin and Slane was built especially straight and smooth to speed up the randy king's journeys.

U2 fans may recognise the castle from the cover of their 1984 album *The Unforgettable Fire*, which was recorded here. Seven years later, a *really* unforgettable fire gutted most of castle, whereupon it was discovered that the earl was underinsured. A major fundraising drive – of which the summer concerts were a part – led to a painstaking restoration and the castle finally reopened for tours in 2001.

LEDWIDGE MUSEUM

Simple yet moving, the **Ledwidge Museum** (982 4544; www.francisledwidge.com; Janesville; adult/child €2.50/1; 10am-1pm & 2-5pm) is located in the birthplace of poet Francis Ledwidge (1891–1917). He died on the battlefield at Ypres, having survived Gallipoli and Serbia. A keen political activist, Ledwidge was thwarted in his efforts to set up a branch of the Gaelic League in the area, but he found an outlet in verse:

> A blackbird singing,
> I hear in my troubled mind,
> Bluebells swinging
> I see in a distant wind,
> But sorrow and silence
> are the wood's threnody,
> the silence for you,
> and the sorrow for me.

Lethbridge aside, the cottage is a good example of how farm labourers lived in the 19th century. It is about 1.5km northeast of Slane on the Drogheda road (N51).

Sleeping & Eating

Slane Farm Hostel (988 4985; www.slanefarmhostel .ie; Harlinstown House, Navan Rd; dm/s/d €18/35/50) These former stables, built by the marquis of Conyngham in the 18th century, have been converted into a fabulous hostel that is part of a working farm surrounding Harlinstown House, where the owners reside. Our readers consistently rave about this place and we concur. It's 2.5km west from Slane and also has self-catering cottages – contact the hostel for rates.

Conyngham Arms Hotel (982 4155; www.conyng hamarms.com; s/d from €75/140) This fairly elegant 19th-century hotel maintains that village-inn feel and look. The four-poster bed in each room is a real treat. The hotel's restaurant serves up a menu of Irish favourites (mains €9 to €13; open noon to 8pm), and the lovely back garden is a fine place for a pint.

our pick **Millhouse Boutique Hotel** (☎ 982 0878; www.themillhouse.ie; r €160-220; P 💻) Set in the 18th-century Georgian manor house of the bossman for the nearby mill, this newly opened hotel is a stunner. The 10 rooms are luxurious, and are decorated in stylish combinations of taupes, creams and mauves. Many have huge tubs and some have sweeping views of the River Boyne. Guests can enjoy artful meals here after time in the sauna. The hotel is 500m downhill from town, right before the N2 bridge.

Boyle's Licensed Tea Rooms (☎ 982 4195; Main St; snacks from €3; 🕑 10am-5pm) Guaranteed to make any granny swoon, this tearoom and café lies behind a beautiful shop front decorated with gold lettering. The menu – written in 12 languages – is strictly of the tea-and-scones type, but people come here for the ambience, which is straight out of the 1940s.

George's (☎ 982 4493; Chapel St; meals €4-8; 🕑 9am-6pm Tue-Sat) This deli-patisserie is just east of the crossroads. Creative organic soups, salads and sandwiches are on offer, as are luscious scones, tortes and cakes. Get your picnic here.

Getting There & Away

Bus Éireann has four to six buses daily to Drogheda (€2.50, 35 minutes), Dublin (€8.20, one hour) and Navan (€2, 20 minutes).

SLANE TO NAVAN

The 14km journey southwest on the N51 from Slane to Navan is dotted with a few manor houses, ruined castles, round towers and churches don't get too excited, however, as they're not nearly as impressive as sites elsewhere in Meath.

Dunmoe Castle lies down a poorly signposted cul-de-sac to the south, 4km before reaching Navan. This D'Arcy family castle is a 16th-century ruin with good views of the countryside and the impressive red-brick **Ardmulchan House** (closed to the public), on the opposite side of the River Boyne. Cromwell is supposed to have fired at the castle from the riverbank in 1649, and local legend holds that a tunnel used to run from the castle vaults under the river.

You can't miss the fine 30m-high round tower and 13th-century church of **Donaghmore**, on the right, 2km nearer to Navan. The site has a profusion of modern gravestones, but the 10th-century tower with a Crucifixion scene above the door is interesting, and there are carved faces near the windows and the remains of the church wall.

NAVAN

☎ 046 / pop 3400

You won't want to waste too much time in Navan (An Uaimh), Meath's main town and the crossroads of the busy Dublin road (N3) and the Drogheda–Westmeath road (N51). You might find yourself here changing buses.

If you need local information, the **tourist office** (🕑 10am-6pm Mon-Sat) is in the impressive new **Solstice Arts Centre** (☎ 909 2300; cnr Railway St & Circular Rd), which has a gallery and live acts.

Under 2km from town, **Athlumney Manor** (☎ 907 1388; www.athlumneymanor.com; Athlumney, Duleek Rd; s/d from €50/70; P 💻) is a large, modern house with six well-appointed, comfortable rooms. In the centre, **Newgrange Hotel** (☎ 353 4690; www.newgrangehotel.ie; Bridge St; r from €90; P 💻) is a posh place with 62 rooms and a good old-style pub.

Ryan's Pub (☎ 902 1154; 22 Trimgate St; bar food from €4; 🕑 noon-8pm) is Navan's best trad pub. The food is good, especially the smoked salmon. Ask if they have a Felix special.

Bus Éireann has hourly service here on route the from Dublin (€9, 50 minutes) to Cavan via Kells (€3.30, 15 minutes).

AROUND NAVAN

The impressive and relatively intact **Athlumney Castle** lies about 2km southeast of town. It was built by the Dowdall family in the 16th century, with additions made a hundred years later. After King James' defeat at the Battle of the Boyne, Sir Lancelot Dowdall set fire to the castle to ensure that James' conqueror, William of Orange, would never shelter or confiscate his home. He watched the blaze from the opposite bank of the river before leaving for France and then Italy. As you enter the estate, take a right toward the Loreto Convent, where you can pick up the keys to the castle. In the convent yard is another **motte**, which at one time it had a wooden tower on it.

There are some pleasant **walks** around Navan, particularly the one following the towpath that runs along the old River Boyne canal towards Slane and Drogheda. On the southern bank, you can go as far as Stackallen and the Boyne bridge (about 7km), passing Ardmulchan House and, on the opposite bank, the ruins of Dunmoe Castle (opposite).

Close to the Kells road (N3), 5km north-west of Navan, is the large ruin of a castle that once belonged to the Talbot family. **Liscartan Castle** is made up of two 15th-century square towers joined by a hall-like room.

TARA

It's Ireland's most sacred stretch of turf, a place at the heart of Irish history, legend and folklore. It was the home of the mystical druids, the priest-rulers of ancient Ireland, who practised their particular form of Celtic voodoo under the watchful gaze of the all-powerful goddess Maeve (Medbh). Later it was the ceremonial capital of the high kings – 142 of them in all – who ruled until the arrival of Christianity in the 6th century. It is also one of the most important ancient sites in Europe, with a Stone Age passage tomb and prehistoric burial mounds that date back up to 5000 years.

The **Hill of Tara** (Teamhair) may look like a bumpy pitch 'n' putt course, but its historic and folkloristic significance is immense: it is Ireland's own Camelot. And like Camelot it's had a lot of drama, most recently when a proposed route for the new M3 motorway would have gone right through the site. Years of arguing resulted in the government mostly ignoring the concerns of preservationists and deciding to ram the road right through the valley. Many laughed derisively when on the very first day of digging in 2007, an ancient site that could rival Stonehenge was uncovered. Work on the M3 was halted, although the government still seems set to put the needs of sprawl over the needs of heritage.

From the site, there are expansive views of the rolling green countryside and its web of hedgerows.

History

The Celts believed that Tara was the sacred dwelling of the gods and the gateway to the otherworld. The passage grave was thought to be the final resting place of the Tuatha de Danann, the mythical fairyfolk – who were real enough, but instead of pixies and brownies, they were earlier Stone Age arrivals on the island.

As the Celtic political landscape began to evolve, the druids' power was usurped by war-like chieftains who took kingly titles; there was

no sense of a united Ireland, so at any given time there were countless *rí tuaithe* (petty kings) controlling many small areas. The king who ruled Tara, though, was generally considered the big kahuna, the high king, even though his direct rule didn't extend too far beyond the provincial border. The most lauded of all the high kings was Cormac MacArt, who ruled during the 3rd century.

The most important event in Tara's calendar was the three-day harvest *feis* (festival) that took place at Samhain, a precursor to modern Halloween. During the festival, the high king pulled out all the stops: grievances would be heard, laws passed, and disputes settled amid an orgy of eating, drinking and all-round partying.

When the early Christians hit town in the 5th century, they targeted Tara straight away. Although the legend has it that Patrick lit the paschal fire on the Hill of Slane (p546), some people believe that Patrick's incendiary act took place on Tara's sacred hump. The arrival of Christianity marked the beginning of the end for Celtic pagan civilisation, and the high kings began to desert Tara, even though the kings of Leinster continued to be based here until the 11th century.

In August 1843, Tara saw one of the greatest crowds ever to gather in Ireland. Daniel O'Connell, the 'Liberator' and the leader of the opposition to union with Great Britain, held one of his monster rallies at Tara, and up to 750,000 people came to hear him speak.

Information

A former Protestant church (with a window by the well-known artist Evie Hone) is home to the useful **Tara Visitor Centre** (☎ 046-902 5903; www.heritageireland.ie; adult/child €2.10/1.10; ☉ 10am-6pm mid-May–mid-Sep, last admission 5.15pm), where a 20-minute audiovisual presentation about the site, *Tara: Meeting Place of Heroes*, is shown. Tara itself is always open and there's no charge; people walk their dogs here. There are good explanatory panels by the entrance, and a shop and café are nearby.

Sights
RÁTH OF THE SYNODS
The names applied to Tara's various humps and mounds were adopted from ancient texts, and mythology and religion intertwine with the historical facts. The Protestant church grounds and graveyard spill onto the remains

COUNTIES MEATH & LOUTH

of the **Ráth of the Synods**, a triple-ringed fort where some of St Patrick's early synods (meetings) supposedly took place. Excavations of the enclosure suggest that it was used between AD 200 and 400 for burials, rituals and living quarters. Originally the ring fort would have contained wooden houses surrounded by timber palisades.

During a digging session in the graveyard in 1810, a boy found a pair of gold torques (crescents of beaten gold hung around the neck), which are now in the National Museum in Dublin. Later excavations discovered Roman glass, shards of pottery and seals, showing links with the Roman Empire even though the Romans never extended their power into Ireland.

The poor state of the enclosure is due in part to a group of British 'Israelites' who in the 1890s dug the place up looking for the Ark of the Covenant, much to the consternation of the local people. The Israelites' leader claimed to see a mysterious pillar on the enclosure, but unfortunately it was invisible to everyone else. After they failed to uncover anything, the invisible pillar moved to the other side of the road but, before the adventurers had time to start work there, the locals chased them away.

ROYAL ENCLOSURE

To the south of the church, the **Royal Enclosure** (Ráth na Ríogh) is a large, oval Iron Age hill fort, 315m in diameter and surrounded by a bank and ditch cut through solid rock under the soil. Inside the Royal Enclosure are smaller sites.

Mound of the Hostages

This bump (Dumha na nGiall) in the northern corner of the enclosure is the most ancient known part of Tara and the most visible of its remains. Supposedly a prison cell for hostages of the 3rd-century king Cormac MacArt, it is in fact a small Stone Age passage grave dating from around 1800 BC that was later used by Bronze Age people. The passage contains some carved stonework, but it's closed to the public.

The mound produced a treasure trove of artefacts, including some ancient Mediterranean beads of amber and faïence (glazed pottery). More than 35 Bronze Age burials were found here, as well as a mass of cremated remains from the Stone Age.

Cormac's House & the Royal Seat

Two other earthworks found inside the enclosure are Cormac's House (Teach Cormaic) and the Royal Seat (Forradh). Although they look similar, the Royal Seat is a ringfort with a house site in the centre, while Cormac's House is a barrow (burial mound) in the side of the circular bank. Cormac's House commands the best views of the surrounding lowlands of the Boyne and Blackwater Valleys.

Atop Cormac's House is the phallic **Stone of Destiny** (Lia Fáil), originally located near the Mound of the Hostages, which represents the joining of the gods of the earth and the heavens. It's said to be the inauguration stone of the high kings, although alternative sources suggest that the actual coronation stone was the Stone of Scone, which was removed to Edinburgh, Scotland, and used to crown British kings. The would-be king stood on top of the Stone of Destiny and, if the stone let out three roars, he was crowned. The mass grave of 37 men who died in a skirmish on Tara during the 1798 Rising is next to the stone.

ENCLOSURE OF KING LAOGHAIRE

South of the Royal Enclosure is the **Enclosure of King Laoghaire** (Ráth Laoghaire), a large but worn ringfort where the king, a contemporary of St Patrick, is supposedly buried dressed in his armour and standing upright.

BANQUET HALL

North of the churchyard is Tara's most unusual feature, the **Banquet Hall** (Teach Miodhchuarta, meaning 'House of Meadcircling'). This rectangular earthwork measures 230m by 27m along a north–south axis. Tradition holds that it was built to cater for thousands of guests during feasts. Much of this information comes from the 12th-century *Book of Leinster* and the *Yellow Book of Lecan,* which even includes drawings of the hall.

Opinions vary as to the site's real purpose. Its orientation suggests that it was a sunken entrance to Tara, leading directly to the Royal Enclosure. More recent research has uncovered graves within the compound, and it's possible that the banks are in fact the burial sites of some of the kings of Tara.

GRÁINNE'S FORT

Gráinne was the daughter of King Cormac who was betrothed to Fionn McCumhaill (Finn McCool) but eloped with Diarmuid

ÓDuibhne, one of the king's warriors, on her wedding night, becoming the subject of the epic *The Pursuit of Diarmuid and Gráinne*. **Gráinne's Fort** (Ráth Gráinne) and the northern and southern **Sloping Trenches** (Claoin Fhearta) off to the northwest are burial mounds.

Tours
The **Mary Gibbons Tours** (☎ 01-283 9973; www.new grangetours.com; tour €35) to Brú na Bóinne take in the whole of the Boyne Valley, including the Hill of Tara.

Bus Éireann tours to Newgrange and the Boyne Valley (see p545) include a visit to Tara on certain days.

Drinking
O'Connell's (☎ 046-902 5122; Skryne) An unspoilt and atmospheric country pub with all the essentials – a nice open fire, friendly service and plenty of local lore on the walls. It is in Skryne, not far from Tara.

Getting There & Away
Tara is 10km southeast of Navan, just off the Dublin–Cavan road (N3). **Bus Éireann** (☎ 01-836 6111) services linking Dublin and Navan pass within 1km of the site (€8.40, 40 minutes, hourly Monday to Saturday and four times on Sunday). Ask the driver to drop you off at the Tara Cross and then follow the signs.

AROUND TARA
See how the other 1% lives at **Dunsany Castle** (☎ 046-902 5198; www.dunsany.net; Dunsany; adult/child €15/free; ❧ summer). It's the residence of the lords of Dunsany, the former owners of the lands around Trim Castle. The Dunsanys are related to the Plunkett family, the most famous of whom is St Oliver, whose head is kept in a church in Drogheda (p559). As it's very much a lived-in property, opening hours vary in accordance with the family's schedule; major refurbishment has limited hours even further. Call for details.

There's an impressive private art collection and many other treasures related to important figures in Irish history, such as Oliver Plunkett and Patrick Sarsfield, leader of the Irish Jacobite forces at the siege of Limerick in 1691. A number of upstairs bedrooms have been restored and are now included in an expanded tour (though there's an extra charge to visit these). Maintenance and restoration are ongoing (as it would be in a castle built in

1180!) and different rooms are open to visitors at different times.

Housed in the old kitchen and in part of the old domestic quarters is a **boutique** (☎ 902 6202; ❧ 10am-5pm) that proudly sells the Dunsany Home Collection – it's your chance to buy an item that will make you feel like the other 1%. Locally made table linen and accessories are featured, as well as various articles for the home designed by Lord Dunsany himself, known to plebeians as Edward C Plunkett.

About 1.5km northeast of Dunsany is the ruined **Killeen Castle**, the seat of another line of the Plunkett family. The 1801 mansion was constructed around a castle built by Hugh de Lacy, lord of Meath, originally dating from 1180. It comprises a neo-Gothic structure between two 12th-century towers. It is closed to the public.

The castles are about 5km south of Tara on the Dunshaughlin–Kilmessan road.

TRIM
☎ 046 / pop 1600
The snoozy but most worthy town of Trim (Baile Átha Troim, meaning 'Town at the Ford of the Elder Trees') was at one time a major player in local affairs, and a cursory exploration of the town will reveal some inviting relics of its medieval past, none more so than the very obvious and very big castle that was Ireland's largest Anglo Norman fortification. The medieval town was a busy jumble of streets, and once had five gates and as many as seven monasteries in the immediate area.

It's hard to imagine nowadays, but a measure of Trim's importance was that Elizabeth I genuinely considered building Trinity College here. One student who did go to school here – at least for a short time – was Arthur Wellesley, the duke of Wellington, who studied in Talbot Castle and St Mary's Abbey. Local legend has it that the duke was born in a stable round these parts, which would explain the duke's famous exclamation that simply being born in a stable doesn't make one a horse. Sadly for the legend, if he did say it – which is hardly definite – he didn't mean it literally: for stable and horse read Ireland and Irish, for he was in fact born in Dublin. The local burghers dedicated a **Wellington column** at the junction of Patrick and Emmet Sts, which was less a tribute to his views on his own birth and more to the fact that his impressive career did actually benefit Ireland. After defeating

COUNTIES MEATH & LOUTH

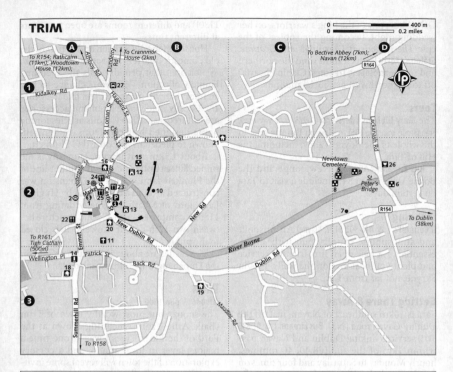

TRIM

Napoleon at the Battle of Waterloo, the Iron Duke went on to become prime minister of Great Britain and in 1829 passed the Catholic Emancipation Act, which repealed the last of the repressive penal laws.

Trim was home to the county jail, giving rise to the ditty: 'Kells for brogues, Navan for rogues and Trim for hanging people'.

Today Trim's history is everywhere. The streets, still lined with tiny old workers cottages, are seeing a few new developments aimed at realising the area's huge tourism potential.

Orientation & Information

Almost everything commercial in Trim is on or near Market St. That huge steeple you see just south belongs to **St Patrick's Church**, parts of which date to the 15th century.

Bank of Ireland (Market St) Exchanges money and has an ATM.

Post office (cnr Emmet & Market Sts; ☼ 9.30am-6pm Mon-Fri, 9.30am-1pm Sat)

Silkweb Design (☎ 948 1599; Market St; per 15 min €1; ☼ 9.30-6pm Mon-Fri, 10am-4pm Sat) Offers internet access from its upper-floor location.

Tourist office (☎ 943 7227; Town Hall, Castle St; ◷ 9.30am-5.30pm Mon-Sat, noon-5.30pm Sun) Has useful info and is part of the Trim Heritage Centre (right). You can buy a handy little walking-tour booklet, *Trim Tourist Trail* (€4), upstairs in the genealogy section.

Sights

TRIM CASTLE

This remarkably preserved edifice is proof of Trim's medieval importance. Hugh de Lacy founded **Trim Castle** (King John's Castle; ☎ 943 8619; www.heritageireland.ie; adult/child €3.70/1.30, grounds only €1.60/1; ◷ 10am-6pm Apr-Oct, Sat & Sun Nov-Mar) in 1173, but Rory O'Connor, said to have been the last high king of Ireland, destroyed this motte and bailey within a year. De Lacy did not live to see the castle's replacement, and the building you see today was begun around 1200. It has hardly been modified since then – certainly there's none of those windows and other niceties that have spoiled the real defensive nature of other places calling themselves 'castles'. The small booklet sold at the castle is quite good.

A keen eye might recognise the castle from Mel Gibson's 1996 movie *Braveheart,* in which it served as a 'castle double' for the castle at York. The interesting historical coincidence is that Queen Isabella's real lover, Roger de Mortimer, earl of March, actually lived in the castle between 1316 and 1320.

Although King John visited Trim in 1210 to bring the de Lacy family into line – hence the building's alternative name of King John's Castle – he never actually slept in the castle. On the eve of his arrival, Walter de Lacy locked it up tight and left town, forcing the king to camp in the nearby meadow.

Throughout Anglo-Norman times the castle occupied a strategic position on the western edge of the Pale, the area where the Anglo-Normans ruled supreme; beyond Trim was the volatile country where Irish chieftains and lords fought with their Norman rivals and vied for position, power and terrain.

Trim was conquered by Silken Thomas in 1536 and again in 1647 by Catholic Confederate forces, opponents of the English Parliamentarians. In 1649 it was taken by Cromwellian forces, and the castle, town walls and Yellow Steeple were damaged.

The grassy two-hectare enclosure is dominated by a massive stone keep, 25m tall and mounted on a Norman motte. Inside are three lofty levels, the lowest one divided in two by a central wall. Just outside the central keep are the remains of an earlier wall.

The principal outer-curtain wall, some 500m long and for the most part still standing, dates from around 1250 and includes eight towers and a gatehouse. It also has a number of sally gates from which defenders could exit to confront the enemy. The finest stretch of the outer wall runs from the River Boyne through Dublin Gate to Castle St.

Within the northern corner was a church and, facing the river, the Royal Mint, which produced Irish coinage (called 'Patricks' and 'Irelands') into the 15th century. The Russian cannon in the car park is a trophy from the Crimean War and bears the tsarist double-headed eagle.

In 1465, Edward IV ordered that anyone who had robbed or 'who was going to rob' should be beheaded, and their heads mounted on spikes and publicly displayed as a warning to other thieves. In 1971 excavations in the castle grounds near the depression south of the keep revealed the remains of 10 headless men, presumably the hapless (or wannabe) criminals.

At night the castle walls are moodily lit by coloured spotlights.

TRIM HERITAGE CENTRE

Sharing space in the town hall with the tourist office is the informative **Trim Heritage Centre** (☎ 943 7227; Town Hall, Castle St; admission by donation; ◷ 9.30am-5.30pm Mon-Sat, noon-5.30pm Sun). *The Power and the Glory,* a 20-minute video outlining the medieval history of Trim, is shown on demand. Highlights include the medieval plague of rats.

The **genealogy and heritage section** (☎ 943 6633; www.meathroots.com; Town Hall, Castle St; initial consultation €30; ◷ 9am-5pm Mon-Thu, 9am-2pm Fri) of the heritage centre is in the town hall. It has an extensive genealogical database for people trying to trace Meath ancestors.

TALBOT CASTLE & ST MARY'S ABBEY

Across the River Boyne from the castle are the ruins of the 12th-century Augustinian **St Mary's Abbey**, rebuilt after a fire in 1368 and once home to a wooden statue of Our Lady of Trim, which was revered by the faithful for its miraculous powers. In 1649 Cromwell's soldiers set fire to the statue in front of their injured commander, General Croot, a rather poignant slap in the face of Catholic belief.

COUNTIES MEATH & LOUTH

Just in case the locals didn't get the symbolism of the gesture, the soldiers destroyed the abbey as well. An artists' rendition of the statue is by the roadside in front of the ruins.

Part of the abbey was converted in 1415 into a fine manor house by Sir John Talbot, then viceroy of Ireland; it came to be known as **Talbot Castle**. The Talbot coat of arms can be seen on the northern wall. Talbot went to war in France, where in 1429 he was defeated at Orleans by none other than Joan of Arc. He was taken prisoner, released and went on fighting the French until 1453. He was known as 'the scourge of France' or 'the whip of the French', and Shakespeare wrote of this notorious man in Henry VI: 'Is this the Talbot so much feared abroad/That with his name the mothers still their babes?'

Talbot Castle was owned in the early 18th century by Esther 'Stella' Johnson, the mistress of Jonathan Swift. She bought the manor house for £65 sterling and lived there for 18 months before selling it to Swift for a tidy £200 sterling; he lived there for a year. Swift was rector of Laracor, 3km southeast of Trim, from around 1700 until 1745, when he died. From 1713 he was also – and more significantly – dean of St Patrick's Cathedral in Dublin.

Just northwest of the abbey building is the 40m **Yellow Steeple**, once the bell tower of the abbey, dating from 1368 but damaged by Cromwell's soldiers in 1649. It takes its name from the colour of the stonework at dusk.

Part of the 14th-century town wall stands in the field to the east of the abbey, including the **Sheep Gate**, the lone survivor of the town's original five gates. It used to be closed daily between 9pm and 4am, and a toll was charged for sheep entering to be sold at market.

NEWTOWN

About 1.5km east of town on Lackanash Rd, Newtown Cemetery contains an interesting group of ruins. What had been the **parish church of Newtown Clonbun** contains the late-16th-century tomb of Sir Luke Dillon, chief baron of the Exchequer during the reign of Elizabeth I, and his wife Lady Jane Bathe. The effigies are known locally as the Jealous Man and Woman, perhaps because of the sword lying between them.

Rainwater that collects between the two figures is claimed to cure warts. Place a pin in the puddle and then jab your wart. When the pin becomes covered in rust your warts will vanish. Some say you should leave a pin on the statue as payment for the cure.

The other ruins here are Newtown's **Cathedral of Sts Peter and Paul**, and the 18th-century **Newtown Abbey** (Abbey of the Canons Regular of St Victor of Paris). The cathedral was founded in 1206 and burned down two centuries later. Parts of the cathedral wall were flattened by a storm in 1839, which also damaged sections of the Trim Castle wall. The abbey wall throws a superb echo back to **Echo Gate** across the river.

Southeast of these ruins, and just over the river, is the **Crutched Friary**. There are ruins of a keep, and traces of a watchtower and other buildings from a hospital set up after the Crusades by the Knights of St John of Jerusalem, who wore a red crutch (cross), on their cassocks. **St Peter's Bridge**, beside the friary, is said to be the second-oldest bridge in Ireland.

Sleeping

Bridge House Tourist Hostel (☎ 943 1848; silvertrans@ eircom.net; Bridge St; dm/d from €20/50; Ⓟ) Each night global travellers gather here to say something along the lines of 'I hadn't known Trim would be so cool'. Dorm beds are tight, the private rooms not bad at all.

White Lodge (☎ 943 6549; www.whitelodgetrim.com; New Rd; s/d €44/64; Ⓟ ☒) This American-style house has lines that may cause some to whistle the *Brady Bunch* theme, albeit with a brogue. The six light-filled rooms are quite spacious. It's 500m east of the centre at the northern end of New Rd.

Woodtown House (☎ 943 5022; woodtown@iol.ie; Athboy; r €45-76; Ⓟ) It's well worth the 12km trip on the R154 north out of Trim to stay at this relaxing country house. The restored 18th-century interiors compete with the beautiful, tree-filled grounds for your attention. Of the four rooms, two are en suite.

Crannmór House (☎ 943 1635; www.crannmor.com; Dunderry Rd; s/d from €50/68; Ⓟ) Five acres of rolling farmland and paddocks surround this vine-covered period residence about 2km along the road to Dunderry. The owner will arrange guided fishing trips.

Tigh Cathain (☎ 943 1996; www.tighcathaintrim .com; Longwood Rd; s/d €50/76; Ⓟ) A Tudor-style country house about 1km southwest of the town centre, Tigh Cathain has three pastel bedrooms decorated in pink, yellow and blue. The house is surrounded by a handsome 1-acre garden.

Brogan's Guesthouse (☎ 943 1237; www.brogans.ie; High St; s/d from €55/75; P 💻) Brogan's has been taking care of its guests since 1915, both in the handsome pub and in the attractive, comfortable rooms. Of the 14 rooms, eight are in the converted stables out the back and the rest are in the main building. Note: those easily made bilious should avoid the hotel's brochure.

Highfield House (☎ 943 6386; www.highfieldguest house.com; Maudlins Rd; s/d from €55/80; P) This elevated, elegant 18th-century country house has lavish common spaces that have been restored to their former grandeur. There are seven comfortable rooms – get one away from road noise.

Castle Arch Hotel (☎ 943 1516; www.castlearch hotel.com; Summerhill Rd; s/d from €60/100; P 💻) The 22 rooms at this modern business-class hotel have a posh, heavy-drapery design accented with vintage touches. The namesake arch nicely frames the entrance. Breakfasts are good.

Trim Castle Hotel (☎ 948 3000; www.trimcastlehotel .com; Castle St; s/d from €85/120; P 💻) This stylish new boutique hotel is part of a development that is spiffing up an area close to the castle. The 68 rooms here have wi-fi, and a compact but comfortable modern design. There are interesting features such as terraces and balconies with views of the castle.

Eating & Drinking

Most pubs do decent food, and the stirrings of tourism are broadening the choice of restaurants.

Egos Lunch Club (☎ 948 6731; Emmet St; meals €5-10; 🕙 9am-5pm Mon-Sat) Boast about your accomplishments at this bright and open modern café. It has a full coffee bar and a long menu of hot specials, sandwiches and salads.

Sally Rodgers (☎ 943 8926; Bridge St; meals €6-15; 🕙 kitchen 5-9pm) The generic bar here is saved by the random statuary and tables overlooking the River Boyne. Upstairs there's a restaurant where the Malaysian chefs prepare Asian food that's more interesting than usual, as well as some excellent fish and chips.

Watson's Elementary Café (Market St; meals €7-10; 🕙 9am-9pm Mon-Sat) You don't have to be a Sherlock to find this quality café with solid renditions of standards ranging from omelettes to shepherd's pie.

Franzini O'Brien's (☎ 943 1002; French Lane; mains €12-20; 🕙 6.30-10pm Tue-Sat, 1-9pm Sun) The Irish menu at this bistro-cum-bar has global in-

fluences. It's always gourmet night here, and you can enjoy some fine seafood and other interesting fare made from locally sourced produce; on the other hand you may just want to enjoy a pint and some nachos at the bar.

Marcy Regan's (☎ 943 6103; Lackanash Rd, Newtown, Trim; 🕙 Thu-Tue) This small pub beside St Peter's Bridge claims to be Ireland's second-oldest pub. Many Fridays see trad music sessions.

Getting There & Away

The influx of commuters means that Bus Éireann runs a bus at least once an hour between Dublin and Trim (one way €8, 70 minutes). Buses stop in front of the newsagent at the northern end of Haggard St.

AROUND TRIM

There are a couple of evocative Anglo-Norman remains in the area around Trim. Some 7.5km northeast of Trim on the way to Navan is **Bective Abbey**, founded in 1147 and the first Cistercian offspring of magnificent Mellifont Abbey in Louth. The remains seen today are 13th- and 15th-century additions, and consist of the chapter house, church, ambulatory and cloister. In 1543, after the Dissolution of the Monasteries, it was used as a fortified house and the tower was built.

In 1186, Hugh de Lacy, lord of Meath, began demolishing the abbey at Durrow in County Offaly in order to build a castle. A workman, known both as O'Miadaigh and O'Kearney, was so offended by this desecration that he lopped off de Lacy's head and fled. Although de Lacy's body was interred in Bective Abbey, his head went to St Thomas' Abbey in Dublin. A dispute broke out over who should possess all the bodily remains, and it required the intervention of the pope to, well, pontificate on the matter, with a ruling in favour of St Thomas' Abbey.

Some 12km northwest of Trim, on the road to Athboy, is **Rathcairn**, the smallest Gaeltacht (Irish-speaking) district in Ireland. Rathcairn's population is descended from a group of Connemara Irish speakers, who were settled on an estate here as part of a social experiment in the 1930s.

KELLS

☎ 046 / pop 2400

Kells is best known for the magnificent illuminated manuscript that bears its name, and which so many visitors queue to see on their

COUNTIES MEATH & LOUTH

visits to Trinity College in Dublin. Generally, they don't make the trip to where it was
stashed from the end of the 9th century until
1541, when it was removed by the Church.
Apart from the remnants of the monastic site
that housed the *Book of Kells* – some interesting high crosses and a 1000-year-old round
tower – there's not a lot to see or do here.

Information

The **tourist office** (☎ 924 9336; Kells Heritage Centre,
Headfort Pl; ☑ 10am-5.30pm Mon-Sat, 1.30-5.30pm Sun
May-Sep, 10am-5pm Mon-Fri Oct-Apr) is in the heritage
centre, located behind the town hall. It can
help with info on some Meath's remote sights,
such as Loughcrew Cairns.

Sights

KELLS HERITAGE CENTRE

Spread across two detail-packed floors, the
town's **heritage centre** (☎ 924 9336; Headfort Pl; adult/
child €4/3; ☑ 10am-5.30pm Mon-Sat, 1.30-5.30pm Sun May-
Sep, 10am-5pm Mon-Fri Oct-Apr) has a rather beautiful
copy of the area's most famous object, the
Book of Kells, which was brought here from
the monastery on Iona in Scotland in 807 after
a Viking raid. Surrounding the book are various 6th- to 12th-century relics and artefacts,
as well as a highly detailed scale model of the
town in the 6th century.

MARKET CROSS

Until 1996, the **Market Cross** had stood for
centuries in Cross St, at the heart of the
town centre. Besides inviting the pious admiration of the faithful, the cross was used
as a gallows in the aftermath of the 1798
revolt; the British garrison hanged rebels
from the crosspiece, one on each arm so
the cross wouldn't fall over. But what 1000
years of foul weather and the sacrilegious
British couldn't do, a careless bus driver
did with one bad turn-and-reverse – in
1996, the cross was toppled. It was eventually repaired and re-erected outside the Kells
Heritage Centre.

On the eastern side of the Market Cross
are depictions of Abraham's sacrifice of
Isaac, the brothers Cain and Abel, the Fall of
Adam and Eve, guards at the tomb of Jesus
and a wonderfully executed procession of
horsemen. On the western face, the Crucifixion is the only discernible image. On the
northern side is a panel of Jacob wrestling
with the angel.

ROUND TOWER & HIGH CROSSES

The Protestant church of **St Columba** (admission
free; ☑ 10am-1pm & 2-5pm Mon-Sat, services only Sun),
west of the town centre, has a 30m-high 10th-
century **round tower** on the southern side. It's
without its conical roof, but it's known to date
back at least as far as 1076, when Muircheartach Maelsechnaill, the high king of Tara, was
murdered in its confined apartments.

Inside the churchyard are four 9th century
high crosses in various states of repair. The
West Cross, at the far end of the compound
from the entrance, is the stump of a decorated
shaft, which has scenes of the baptism of Jesus,
the Fall of Adam and Eve, and the Judgement
of Solomon on the eastern face, and Noah's
ark on the western face. All that is left of the
North Cross is the bowl-shaped base stone.

Near the tower is the best preserved of the
crosses, the **Cross of Patrick and Columba**, with its
semi-legible inscription *Patrici et Columbae
Crux* on the eastern face of the base. Above
it are scenes of Daniel in the lions' den, the
fiery furnace, the Fall of Adam and Eve, and
a hunting scene. On the opposite side of the
cross are depictions of the Last Judgement,
the Crucifixion, and riders with a chariot, as
well as a dog on the base.

The other surviving cross is the unfinished
East Cross, with a carving of the Crucifixion and
a group of four figures on the right arm.

ST COLMCILLE'S HOUSE

From the churchyard exit on Church St, **St
Colmcille's House** (admission free; ☑ 10am-5pm Sat &
Sun Jun-Sep) is left up the hill, among the row of
houses on the right side of Church Lane. It is
usually open in summer; otherwise, pick up
the keys from **Mrs Carpenter** (☎ 924 1778; 1 Lower
Church View), at the brown-coloured house as
you ascend the hill.

This squat, solid structure is a survivor
from the old monastic settlement. Its name
is a misnomer, as it was built in the 10th century and St Colmcille was alive in the 6th
century. Experts have suggested that it was
used as a scriptorium, a place where monks
illuminated books.

Sleeping & Eating

Teltown House B&B (☎ 902 3239, 087-665 9022; Teltown;
s/d €45/90; Ⓟ) History abounds at this three-
room B&B set in a restored ivy-covered stone
farmhouse: Ireland's own Olympic games
were held here 2000 years ago, and some 2000

years before *that*, somebody carved classic circular art into a rock next to the B&B. Read about it at www.mythicalireland.com/ancient sites/news/teltown-rock-art.htm. The B&B is 6km south of Kells, east of the N3 at the Silver Tankard pub.

Headfort Arms Hotel (☎ 924 0063; www.headfort arms.ie; John St; s/d from €70/120; P 💻) Family run and right in the town centre, the Headfort Arms has 45 modern rooms with wi-fi; 32 are in a new wing, while the rest are in a charming old building. It hosts the Vanilla Pod restaurant (below).

In the Dock (☎ 924 7840; Kells Heritage Centre, Headfort Pl; meals €5-8; 💬 10am-5.30pm Mon-Sat, 1.30-5.30pm Sun May-Sep, 10am-5pm Mon-Fri Oct-Apr) Fresh banana smoothies are just one of the treats at this popular café in the heritage centre.

Vanilla Pod (☎ 924 0084; Headfort Arms Hotel, John St; mains €11-17; 💬 5.30-9.30pm, noon-3pm Sun) Located in the Headfort Arms Hotel but independently run, this bistro wins plaudits for its interesting international variations on regional foods.

Getting There & Away

Bus Éireann (☎ 01-836 6111) has services from Kells to Dublin (€9.80, one hour, hourly) via Navan. There are also buses to Cavan (€9, 45 minutes, hourly).

AROUND KELLS
Hill of Lloyd Tower

It's easy to see why this 30m-high **tower** (☎ 924 0064; adult/child €3/2; 💬 by appointment) on the Hill of Lloyd became known as the 'inland lighthouse'. Built in 1791 by the earl of Bective, in memory of his father, it has been renovated, and if it's open you can climb to the top or picnic in the surrounding park. The tower is 3km northwest of Kells, off the Crossakeel road.

Crosses of Castlekeeran

Lost in the ruins of an ancient hermitage are the **Crosses of Castlekeeran**. They're not overly impressive in themselves – three plainly carved, early-9th-century crosses (one in the river) – but there's something invitingly peaceful about the quiet, overgrown cemetery that surrounds them. The **ruined church** in the centre has some early grave slabs and an Ogham stone (stone inscribed with Ireland's earliest form of writing).

To get to the crosses, head through a farmyard about 2km further down the Crossakeel road from the Hill of Lloyd tower.

LOUGHCREW CAIRNS

With all the hoopla over Brú na Bóinne, this amazing place is often overlooked. That's just as well because it means you can enjoy Loughcrew Cairns in peace. There are 30-odd Stone Age passage graves strewn about three summits of the Loughcrew Hills, but they're hard to get to and relatively few people ever bother. But this is about as moody and evocative place as you'll want to find, and it's well worth the effort.

The hills, also known as Slieve (Sliabh) na Caillighe and the Mountains of the Witch, are northwest of Kells, along the R154, near Oldcastle. From here there are some splendid views of the surrounding countryside. The main passage graves are grouped on three summits – Carnbane East (194m), Carnbane West (206m) and Patrickstown (279m) – although the last has been so ruined by 19th-century builders that there's little to see.

Like Brú na Bóinne, the graves were all built around 3000 BC, but, unlike their better-known and better-excavated peers, were used at least until 750 BC. As at Newgrange, larger stones in some of the graves are decorated with spiral patterns. Some of the graves look like large piles of stones, while others are less obvious, their cairn having been removed. Archaeologists have unearthed bone fragments and ashes, stone balls and beads.

Carnbane East

Carnbane East has a cluster of sites; **Cairn T** (☎ 049-854 2009; www.heritageireland.ie; admission free; 💬 10am-6pm mid-Jun–Aug; P) is the biggest at about 35m in diameter and has numerous carved stones. One of its outlying kerbstones is called the Hag's Chair, and is covered in gouged holes, circles and other markings. You need the gate key to enter the passageway and a torch to see anything in detail. It takes about half an hour to climb Carnbane East from the car park. From the summit on a reasonably clear day, you should be able to see the Hill of Tara to the southeast, while the view north is into Cavan, with Lough Ramor to the northeast, and Lough Sheelin and Oldcastle to the northwest.

In summer, access to Cairn T is controlled by the Heritage Service, which provides guides. But locals are passionate about the place and at any time of the year you can arrange for guides who will not only show you Cairn T but take you to some of the other cairns as well. Enquire at the **Loughcrew Historic Garden** (☎ 049-854 1060; ☷ noon-5pm mid-Mar–Sep, 1-4pm Sun Oct–mid-Mar) or at the Kells tourist office.

Carnbane West

From the car park, it takes about an hour to reach the summit of Carnbane West, where Cairn D and L, both some 60m in diameter, are located. Cairn D has been disturbed in an unsuccessful search for a central chamber. Cairn L, northeast of Cairn D, is also in poor condition, though you can enter the passage and chamber, where there are numerous carved stones and a curved basin stone in which human ashes were placed.

Cairn L is administered by the Heritage Service, which only gives out the key to those with an authentic research interest.

COUNTY LOUTH

The Wee County is a sobriquet borne with pride round these hardscrabble parts. And if you don't like it, well, take this! The coast has an industrial legacy but Drogheda is emerging from its sweaty past to become an appealing regional town and a good base for visiting nearby Brú na Bóinne, just over the border in County Meath. Other attractions include the prehistoric and monastic sites north and east of the Boyne Valley, such as Mellifont Abbey and Monasterboice. In the north, there's the lonely and evocative Cooley Peninsula, north of Dundalk.

History

As part of the ancient kingdom of Oriel, Louth is the setting for perhaps the most epic of all Irish mythological tales, the *Táin Bó Cúailnge* (Cattle Raid of Cooley), which includes a starring role for Ireland's greatest mythological hero, *Cúchulainn*. *The Táin*, by Thomas Kinsella, is a modern version of this compelling and bloody tale.

Louth is home to a number of monastic ruins dating from the 5th and 6th centuries; the monastery at Monasterboice and the later Cistercian abbey at Mellifont, both near Drogheda, are Louth's most interesting archaeological sites.

The arrival of the Normans in the 12th century ushered in a period of great change

and upheaval; attracted by the fertile plains of the Boyne, the Anglo-Norman gentry set about subduing the local population and building mighty houses and castles. The Norman invaders were responsible for the development of Dundalk and the two towns on opposite banks of the Boyne that united in 1412 to become what is now Drogheda.

DROGHEDA

☎ 041 / pop 30,200

Surprising Drogheda. There, we wrote them a new slogan. Long dismissed by some, Drogheda is easily the most interesting town north of Dublin. This once fortified town straddling the River Boyne has a clutch of fine old buildings, a handsome cathedral and a riveting museum that offers at least a partial insight into the city's eventful past, while an ongoing spate of development and a rising population of Dublin commuters have slowly begun to breathe new life into the place.

With its wonderful old pubs, fine restaurants, narrow streets, good transport and numerous sleeping options, Drogheda is an excellent base for exploring the world-class attractions that surround it in the Boyne Valley. Brú na Bóinne is only 7km west.

History

This bend in the Boyne has been desirable right back to 910, when the Danes built a fortified settlement here. In the 12th century, the Normans added a bridge and expanded the two settlements on either side of the river. They also built a large defensive motte-and-bailey castle on the southern side at Millmount. By the 15th century, Drogheda was one of Ireland's four major walled towns and a major player in Irish affairs.

In 1649, Drogheda was the scene of Cromwell's most notorious Irish slaughter (see p560) and things went from bad to worse in 1690 when the town backed the wrong horse at the Battle of the Boyne and surrendered the day after the defeat of James II.

Despite a boom in the 19th century, when Drogheda became a textile and brewing centre, the town has never really hit its stride and today it struggles to break the shackles of a century-long torpor, although the current economy is starting to make some big differences.

DROGHEDA

INFORMATION	
Post Office	1 B3
Surf City	2 A3
Tourist Office	3 B3
Wise Owl Bookshop	4 B3

SIGHTS & ACTIVITIES	
Butter Gate	5 B3
Church of Our Lady of Lourdes	6 B1
Courthouse	7 B2
Highlanes Gallery	8 B3
Governor's House	(see 10)
Magdalene Tower	9 B2
Millmount Museum & Tower	10 B3
St Laurence's Gate	11 C2
St Peter's Church of Ireland	12 B2
St Peter's Roman Catholic Church	13 B3
Tholsel	14 B3

SLEEPING	
D Hotel	15 C3
Green Door Hostel	16 B3
Westcourt Hotel	17 B3

EATING	
Art Café	(see 8)
Bella Atina	18 C3
Kierans Deli	19 B3
La Pizzeria	20 B3
Monks	21 B3

DRINKING	
C Ní Cairbre	22 C2
Patrick Clarke & Sons	23 B2
Peter Matthews	24 B2

ENTERTAINMENT	
Drogheda Arts Centre	25 B3
Fusion	26 A2
Redz	27 B3

SHOPPING	
Laurence Town Centre	28 B2
Scotch Hall Shopping Centre	29 C3

TRANSPORT	
Bus Station	30 B3
Quay Cycles	31 C3

Orientation

Drogheda sits astride the River Boyne, with the principal shopping area on the northern bank along West and Laurence Sts. South of the river is the site of some trendy new developments, and is where you'll find the mysterious Millmount mound. The M1 motorway to Belfast skirts round the town to the west, and there's traffic congestion in the city centre. There's parking in small lots scattered everywhere.

Information

Post office (West St) Next to the Westcourt Hotel.
Surf City (☎ 983 6826; 45 West St; per 30min €3; ☻ 10am-6pm) Internet access.
Tourist office (☎ 983 7070; www.drogheda.ie; Mayoralty St; ☻ 9am-5pm Mon-Fri, 9am-4.30pm Sat) On

the northern side of the river, just off the docklands. There is also a good regional office at Brú na Bóinne (p543).
Wise Owl Bookshop (☎ 984 2847; The Mall; ☻ 9am-5pm Mon-Sat) A large store with good local books and maps.

Sights

ST PETER'S ROMAN CATHOLIC CHURCH

The shrivelled little head of the martyr St Oliver Plunkett (1629–81) is the main draw of the 19th-century **Catholic church** (West St), which is actually two churches in one: the first, designed by Francis Johnston in classical style and built in 1791; and the newer addition, built in the Gothic style visible today. Plunkett's head – from which the rest of him was separated following his hanging in 1681 – is in a glittering brass-and-glass case in the north transept. The stained-glass windows glow at night.

ST LAURENCE'S GATE

Astride the eastwards extension of the town's main street is St Laurence's Gate, the finest surviving portion of the city walls.

The 13th-century gate was named after St Laurence's Priory, which once stood outside the gate; no traces of it now remain. The gate consists of two lofty towers, a connecting curtain wall and the entrance to the portcullis. This imposing pile of stone is not in fact a gate but instead a barbican, a fortified structure used to defend the gate, which was further behind it. When the walls were completed in the 13th century, they ran for 3km around the town, enclosing 52 hectares.

HIGHLANES GALLERY

A new and impressive **gallery** (☎ 980 3311; www .highlanes.ie; St Laurence St; admission free; ☽ 10am-6pm, 10am-8pm Thu, noon-6pm Sun), the Highlanes is in a massively rebuilt 19th-century monastery, which is on the site of a 15th-century monastery. All the visual arts can be found here, as well as a good permanent collection of paintings. There are regular special exhibits and the entire complex is worth a look – as is the view down to the Boyne.

MILLMOUNT MUSEUM & TOWER

Across the river from town in a villagelike enclave amid a sea of dull suburbia, is Millmount, an artificial hill overlooking the town. Although it may have been a prehistoric burial mound along the lines of nearby Newgrange, it has never been excavated. There is a tale that it was the burial place of Amergin, a warrior-poet who arrived in Ireland from Spain around 1500 BC. Throughout Irish history, poets have held a special place in society, and have been both venerated and feared.

The Normans constructed a motte-and-bailey fort on top of this convenient command post overlooking the bridge. It was followed by a castle, which in turn was replaced by a **Martello tower** in 1808. The tower played a dramatic role in the 1922 Civil War – there are fine views over the town from the top. Admission is included as part of entry to the Millmount Museum (below).

It was at Millmount that the defenders of Drogheda, led by the governor Sir Arthur Ashton, made their last stand before surrendering to Cromwell. Later, an 18th-century English barracks was built round the base, and today this houses craft shops, museums and a restaurant.

A section of the army barracks is now used as the **Millmount Museum** (☎ 983 3097; www.mill mount.net; adult/child €4.50/2.50; ☽ 10am-6pm Mon-Sat, 2.30-5.30pm Sun), with interesting displays about the town and its history. Displays include three wonderful late-18th-century guild banners, perhaps the last in the country. There is also a room devoted to Cromwell's siege of Drogheda and the Battle of the Boyne. The

---

BE GOOD OR CROMWELL WILL GET YOU

England's first democrat and protector of the people is an Irish nightmare, and the name Oliver Cromwell (1599–1658) is still used to scare children at bedtime.

Cromwell hated the Irish. To him, they were treacherous infidels, a dirty race of papists who had sided with Charles I during the Civil War. When 'God's own Englishman' landed with his 12,000 troops at Dublin in August 1649, he immediately set out for Drogheda, a strategic fort town and bastion of royalist support.

When Cromwell arrived at the walls of Drogheda, he was met by 2300 men led by Sir Arthur Aston, who boasted that 'he who could take Drogheda could take hell'. After Aston refused to surrender, Cromwell let fly with heavy artillery and after two days the walls were breached. Hell, it seems, was next.

In order to set a terrifying example to any other town that might resist his armies, Cromwell taught the defenders a brutal lesson. Over a period of hours, an estimated 3000 were massacred, mostly royalist soldiers but also priests, women and children. Aston was bludgeoned to death with his own leg. Of the survivors, many were captured and sold into slavery in the Caribbean.

Cromwell defended his action as God's righteous punishment of treacherous Catholics, and he was quick to point out that he had never ordered the killing of noncombatants: it was the 17th century's version of 'collateral damage'.

pretty cobbled basement is full of gadgets and kitchen utensils from bygone times, including a cast-iron pressure cooker and an early model of a sofa bed. There's also an excellent example of a coracle. Across the courtyard, the **Governor's House** opens for temporary exhibitions.

You can drive up to the hilltop or climb Pitcher Hill via the steps from St Mary's Bridge.

The 13th-century **Butter Gate**, just northwest of Millmount, is the only surviving genuine town gate in Drogheda. This tower, with its arched passageway, predates the remains of St Laurence's Gate by about a century.

OTHER STRUCTURES

Tholsel (cnr West & Shop Sts), an 18th-century limestone town hall, is now occupied by the Bank of Ireland.

North of the centre is **St Peter's Church of Ireland** (William St), containing the tombstone of Oliver Goldsmith's uncle Isaac, as well as another image on the wall depicting two skeletal figures in shrouds, dubiously linked to the Black Death. This is the church whose spire was burned by Cromwell's men, resulting in the death of 100 people seeking sanctuary inside. Today's church (1748) is the second replacement of the original destroyed by Cromwell. It stands in an attractive close approached through lovely wrought-iron gates. Note the old 'Blue School' of 1844 on one side. Off Hardmans Gardens is the rather charming and more recent **Church of Our Lady of Lourdes**.

At the time of writing, the modest 19th-century **courthouse** (Fair St) was being renovated. It is home to the sword and mace presented to the town council by William of Orange after the Battle of the Boyne.

Topping the hill behind the main part of town is the 14th-century **Magdalene Tower**, the bell tower of a Dominican friary founded in 1224. Here, England's King Richard II, accompanied by a great army, accepted the submission of the Gaelic chiefs with suitable ceremony in 1395, but peace lasted only a few months and Richard's return to Ireland led to his overthrow in 1399. The earl of Desmond was beheaded here in 1468 because of his treasonous connections with the Gaelic Irish; the tower is also reputed to be haunted by a nun.

Finally, you can't help but admire the 1855 **Boyne Viaduct** carrying trains over the river east of the centre. Each of the 18 beautiful stone arches has a 20m span; erecting the piers bankrupted one company.

Sleeping

Most of the B&Bs are slightly out of town; the only centrally located options are the hostel and a business hotel.

Green Door Hostel (☎ 983 4422; www.greendoor ireland.com; 13 Dublin Rd; dm/d from €18/52) This long-running hostel has moved to improved digs in a heritage building some 250m from the train station towards the town centre. Dorm rooms have from four to 10 beds, and some doubles come with TVs and bathrooms. There are summer shuttles to Newgrange and other sites.

Killowen House B&B (☎ 983 3547; www.killowen -house.net; Woodgrange, Dublin Rd; s/d from €45/66; P) The formal exterior of the suburban home tells you that you're at a well-run place, and this will be confirmed once you step inside. The four rooms here are spick-and-span, and there's lots of Boyne Valley tour info available.

Orley House (☎ 983 6019; www.orleyhouse.com; Bryanstown, Dublin Rd; s/d from €45/70; P) This very professional B&B is about 2km out of town on the Dublin road. Rooms are well furnished, and breakfast is in a sun-filled conservatory.

Westcourt Hotel (☎ 983 0965; www.westcourt.ie; West St; s/d from €65/130; P ☐) A rambling veteran, the Westcourt is located in the dead centre of town. The 27 rooms have wi-fi and a timeless décor that could be from any time in the last 40 years. It's a popular place and has several venues from café to pub.

D Hotel (☎ 987 7700; www.thed.ie; Scotch Hall; s/d from €90/150; P ☐) Flash comes to Drogheda – or, in this hotel's parlance, the 'big D'. Part of a swish new development on the south bank of the Boyne, this place has 104 rooms, all with wi-fi and most with cool views of the city. Everything's stylish, sometimes excessively so: some lamps look like an exploding H-bomb in a marshmallow factory.

Eating

You'll find a good variety of foods throughout the centre.

Monks (☎ 984 5630; 1 North Quay; mains €6-9; ☻ 8.30am-6pm Mon-Sat, 10.30am-5pm Sun) At the southern end of Shop St, on the corner of North Quay, this lovely espresso bar and café is a local institution. The sandwiches are inventive and the coffee's good.

COUNTIES MEATH & LOUTH

Art Café (☎ 980 3295; Highlanes Gallery, St Laurence St; meals €6-10; ☱ 9am-5pm Mon-Sat) Located in the impressive new Highlanes Gallery, this lunch spot is breath of fresh air. Everything is homemade and you're sure to get a tasty bowl of soup, sandwich or hot special. There's wi-fi.

Kierans Deli (☎ 983 8728; 15 West St; meals €6-12; ☱ 8.30am-5.30pm Mon-Sat) When you think pork, think Kierans. This renowned deli is well known for its bacon, ham, pasties and perfect picnic food. Its café out the back has a full coffee bar, excellent salads and a good line-up of daily specials.

Bella Atina (☎ 984 4878; The Mall; mains €9-15; ☱ 6-10.30pm Mon-Sat) Old Country charm combines with new ideas at this excellent Italian place down by the river. It's red, red, red inside – and that's before you spill marinara sauce on your shirt. Pastas are fresh and the cannelloni is a treat.

La Pizzeria (☎ 983 4208; St Peter St; pizzas €10; ☱ 5-10pm Thu-Tue) Watch the dough fly as beautiful pizzas are handcrafted in the traditional open kitchen up front. With wine bottles hanging from the ceiling, this is an Italian joint straight out of central casting. It's busy when everywhere else is empty.

Drinking & Entertainment
PUBS
Drogheda has dozens of bars and pubs. Check the tourism **website** (www.drogheda .ie) for a full schedule of live music around town. There's usually at least one trad session every night.

our pick C Ní Cairbre (Carberry's; ☎ 984 7569; North Strand) This pub is a national treasure. Owned by the same family since 1880, C Ní Cairbre has brown walls that look every decade of their age, and old newspaper clips and long-faded artwork covering most surfaces. But the real joy here is the music. This is the centre for traditional music in the region. There's not a mike in sight – rather, musicians find a table and start playing, just as it should happen in a proper session. You're likely to hear music most nights; however, Wednesday is always devoted to singing and Sunday night is often bluesy.

Peter Matthews (McPhail's; ☎ 984 3168; Laurence St) Popular with those on the make, McPhail's (as it's always called, no matter what the sign says) favours a poppy, chart-oriented soundtrack. Some nights feature live music, mostly cover bands.

Patrick Clarke & Sons (☎ 983 6724; St Peter St) This wonderful old boozer is right out of a time capsule. The unrestored wooden interior features snugs and leaded-glass doors that read Open Bar. The pints just taste better at this corner classic.

VENUES
Fusion (☎ 983 5166; www.fusiononline.ie; 12 George's St) The beer garden is a big pull here, as is the heaving disco, which runs from Thursday to Sunday night with a mix of '60s, rock, house and dance music. Can you say alcopop?

Redz (☎ 983 5331; 79 West St) A small, chilled-out bar at the front hides a big club out back. DJs, live acts and lots of people getting down keep things going until late.

Drogheda Arts Centre (☎ 983 3946; www.droichead .com; Stockwell Lane) Theatrical and musical events are staged in this lively public cultural centre. There are often late-night sessions of trad, rock, jazz, samba and more.

Shopping
Large glitzy malls are coming to Drogheda. Located on the south bank with the D Hotel is **Scotch Hall Shopping Centre** (Marsh Rd); looking down from the centre is the equally large **Laurence Town Centre** (Laurence St), which was once a grammar school.

Getting There & Away
BUS
Drogheda is only 48km north of Dublin, on the main M1 route to Belfast. The bus station is just south of the river on the corner of John St and Donore Rd. This is one of the busiest bus routes in the country, and **Bus Éireann** (☎ 983 5023) regularly serves Drogheda from Dublin (€6.30, one hour, one to four hourly). Drogheda to Dundalk is another busy route (€4.50, 30 minutes, hourly).

From Drogheda you can get a bus that drops you off at the entrance of the Brú na Bóinne visitor centre (€2, 20 minutes, four to six daily).

TRAIN
The **train station** (☎ 983 8749) is just south of the river and east of the town centre, off the Dublin road. Drogheda is on the main Belfast–Dublin line (Dublin €12, 30 minutes; Belfast €24, 1½ hours), and there are five or six express trains (and many slower ones) each way, with five on Sunday. This

is the best line in Ireland, with excellent on-board service.

Getting Around

Drogheda itself is excellent for walking, and many of the surrounding region's interesting sites are within easy cycling distance. **Quay Cycles** (☎ 983 4526; 11A North Quay; per day from €20), near the bridge, rents bikes.

AROUND DROGHEDA

There are a number of stellar attractions around Drogheda. A few kilometres north of town, Mellifont and Monasterboice are two famous monastic sites that are definitely worth the visit. Drogheda is also a good base for exploring the Boyne Valley; Brú na Bóinne and the Battle of Boyne site are just a few minutes west over the border in County Meath. If you're travelling on to Dundalk and into Northern Ireland, you can go for one of three routes: the quicker but duller M1; the circuitous inland route via Collon and Ardee, along which you can also visit Monasterboice and Mellifont; or the scenic coastal route that leads you up to Carlingford.

Beaulieu House

Before Andrea Palladio and the ubiquitous Georgian style that changed Irish architecture in the early decades of the 18th century, there was the Anglo-Dutch style, a simpler, less ornate look that is equally handsome. **Beaulieu House** (☎ 041-984 5051; www.beaulieu .ie; house & garden €12, garden only €6; ☼ 11am-5pm Mon-Fri May–mid-Sep, 1-5pm Jul & Aug), about 5km east of Drogheda on the Baltray road, is a particularly good example of the style and – apparently – the first unfortified mansion to be built in Ireland, which doesn't say a lot for neighbourliness up to that time. It was built between 1660 and 1666 on lands confiscated from the Plunkett family (the family of the headless Oliver) by Cromwell and given to the marshal of the army in Ireland, Sir Henry Tichbourne. The red-brick mansion, with its distinctive steep roof and tall chimneys, has been owned by the same family ever since.

Besides the house and elegant gardens, the real draw is the superb art collection spread about the stunning interior, a motley collection ranging from lesser Dutch masters to 20th-century Irish painters.

Mellifont Abbey

In its Anglo-Norman prime, **Mellifont Abbey** (☎ 041-982 6459; www.heritageireland.ie; Tullyallen; adult/child €2.10/1.10; ☼ visitor centre 10am-6pm May-Sep; **P**) was the Cistercians' first and most magnificent centre in the country. Although the ruins are highly evocative and worth exploring, they don't do real justice to the site's former significance.

In the mid-12th century, Irish monastic orders had grown a little too fond of the good life and were not averse to a bit of corruption. In 1142 Malachy, bishop of Down (later canonised for his troubles), was at the end of his tether and he invited a group of hard-core monks from Clairvaux in France to set up shop in a remote location, where they would act as a sobering influence on the local monks. The Irish monks didn't quite get on with their French guests, and the latter soon left for home. Still, the construction of Mellifont – from the Latin *mellifons* (honey fountain) – continued, and within 10 years nine more Cistercian monasteries were established. Mellifont was eventually the mother house for 21 lesser monasteries, and at one point as many as 400 monks lived here.

Mellifont not only brought fresh ideas to the Irish religious scene, it also heralded a new style of architecture. For the first time in Ireland, monasteries were built with the formal layout and structure that was being used on the Continent. Only fragments of the original settlement remain, but the plan of the extensive monastery can easily be traced.

Like many other Cistercian monasteries, the buildings clustered round an open cloister. To the northern side of the cloister are the remains of a principally 13th-century cross-shaped church. To the south, the chapter house has been partially floored with medieval glazed tiles, originally found in the church. Here also would have been the refectory, kitchen and warming room – the only place where the austere monks could enjoy the warmth of a fire. The eastern range would once have held the monks' sleeping quarters.

Mellifont's most recognisable building, and one of the finest pieces of Cistercian architecture in Ireland, is the lavabo, an octagonal washing house for the monks. It was built in the early 13th century and used lead pipes to bring water from the river. A number of other buildings would have surrounded this main part of the abbey.

After the Dissolution of the Monasteries, a fortified Tudor manor house was built on the site in 1556 by Edward Moore, using materials scavenged from the demolition of many of the buildings.

In 1603 this house was the scene of a poignant and crucial turning point in Irish history. After the disastrous Battle of Kinsale, the vanquished Hugh O'Neill, last of the great Irish chieftains, was given shelter here by Sir Garret Moore until he surrendered to the English lord deputy Mountjoy. After his surrender, O'Neill was pardoned but, despairing of his position, fled to the Continent in 1607 with other old-Irish leaders in the Flight of the Earls. In 1727 the site was abandoned altogether.

The visitor centre next to the site describes monastic life in detail. The ruins themselves are always open and there's good picnicking next to the rushing stream. It's about 1.5km off the main Drogheda–Collon road (R168). A back road connects Mellifont with Monasterboice. There is no public transport to the abbey.

Monasterboice

Crowing ravens lend just the right atmosphere to **Monasterboice** (Mainistir Bhuithe; admission free; sunrise-sunset; P), an intriguing monastic site containing a cemetery, two ancient church ruins, one of the finest and tallest round towers in Ireland, and two of the best high crosses. The site can be reached directly from Mellifont via a winding route along narrow country lanes.

Down a leafy lane and set in sweeping farmland, Monasterboice has a special atmosphere, particularly at quiet times. The original monastic settlement at Monasterboice is said to have been founded in the 5th or 6th century by St Buithe, a follower of St Patrick, although the site probably had pre-Christian significance. St Buithe's name somehow got converted to Boyne, and the river is named after him. It's said that he made a direct ascent to heaven via a ladder lowered from above. An invading Viking force took over the settlement in 968, only to be comprehensively expelled by Donal, the Irish high king of Tara, who killed at least 300 of the Vikings in the process.

The high crosses of Monasterboice are superb examples of Celtic art. The crosses had an important didactic use, bringing the gospels alive for the uneducated – a type of cartoon of the Scriptures, if you like. Like Greek statues, they were probably brightly painted, but all traces of colour have long disappeared.

The cross near the entrance is known as **Muirdach's Cross**, named after a 10th-century abbot. The subjects of the carvings have not been positively identified. On the eastern face, from the bottom up, are thought to be the Fall of Adam and Eve, the murder of Abel, the battle of David and Goliath, Moses bringing water from the rock to the waiting Israelites, and the three wise men bearing gifts to Mary and Jesus. The Last Judgement, with the risen dead waiting for their verdict, is at the centre of the cross and further up is St Paul in the desert.

The western face relates more to the New Testament, and from the bottom depicts the arrest of Christ, Doubting Thomas, Christ giving a key to St Peter, the Crucifixion, and Moses praying with Aaron and Hur. The cross is capped by a representation of a gabled-roof church.

The **West Cross** is near the round tower and stands 6.5m high, making it one of the tallest high crosses in Ireland. It's much more weathered, especially at the base, and only a dozen or so of its 50 panels are still legible. The more distinguishable ones on the eastern face include David killing a lion and a bear, the sacrifice of Isaac, David with Goliath's head, and David kneeling before Samuel. The western face shows the Resurrection, the crowning with thorns, the Crucifixion, the baptism of Christ, Peter cutting off the servant's ear in the garden of Gethsemane, and the kiss of Judas.

A third, simpler cross in the northeastern corner of the compound is believed to have been smashed by Cromwell's forces and has only a few straightforward carvings. Photographers should note that this cross makes a great evening silhouette picture, with the round tower in the background.

The **round tower**, minus its cap, stands in a corner of the complex. It's closed to the public but is still over 30m tall – imagine being at the top and seeing some Vikings headed your way. Records suggest the tower interior went up in flames in 1097, destroying many valuable manuscripts and other treasures.

(Continued on page 573)

Ireland Outdoors

Walk for a day or a week along one of Ireland's spectacular waymarked ways (p568)

GARETH MCCORMACK

WALKING & CYCLING

Driving Ireland's twisting two-lane highways often gives visitors the feeling that they are missing half the point of travelling in this wildly beautiful country. You'll soak in more scenery and become more attuned to Ireland's traditional pace if you hit the pavements and trails on foot or two wheels. The country's varied terrain amply rewards the patient and observant. Though the island is not large, it encompasses rolling hills of green; lush riparian woods; rugged limestone escarpments; broad sandy beaches; coastal islands; canal towpaths; stunning sea cliffs; and blanket bogs stretching as far as the eye can see.

Stroll solo along the Beara Way (p698), County Cor

Cyclists for the most part must share the highway with those pesky autos, but the country possesses no shortage of scenic routes, some of them through sparsely populated countryside or along rugged coasts.

Day Walks

In just about any part of Ireland you can take a leisurely day hike. The wooded trails around Glendalough (p154) in County Wicklow lure many a traveller from nearby Dublin for a few hours. Along the River Barrow in Counties Kilkenny and Carlow, perfectly pleasant walks can be had along the towpath from Borris (p353) to Graiguenamanagh (p336). Also in County Kilkenny, the prettiest section of the South Leinster Way (p336) is a 13km hike between the charming villages of Graiguenamanagh and Inistioge. In either direction, a pleasant meal awaits at the end of the trail. In County Galway, Clifden's Sky Road (p431) yields views of the Connemara coast; it's suitable for walking or cycling. Anyone roaming

What goes up the Gap of Dunloe (p255) must come down

Where the mountain meets the sea – Mt Mweelrea (p436), County Galway
GARETH MCCORMACK

the woods around Lough Key (p490), in County Roscomon, should take advantage of the park's unique canopy walk.

The Coast

Ireland's coastlines are naturally conducive to long and reflective walks with or without shoes on. If that sounds like your particular nirvana, the coast of County Galway's Connemara and the pristine beaches of Counties Mayo and Sligo beckon. Some coastal walks, however, present unexpected challenges. County Antrim, in Northern Ireland, is rife with rocky trails above the surf. Particularly spectacular is the final 16.5km, starting from Carrick-a-Rede, on the Causeway Coast Way (p663). The Wexford Coastal Walk (p167) isn't quite so treacherous, but it is long, following 221km of trails overlooking the bones of old shipwrecks.

Mountains

Ireland's mountain ranges aren't as magnificent as the Alps, but they do offer gratifying hillwalking opportunities, many of which can be done in a day. County Donegal's Blue Stack Mountains (p509) encompass varied terrain and dramatic peaks. The Brandon Way (p336), in County Kilkenny, wends up through woodlands and moorlands from the River Barrow to picturesque Brandon Hill (516m). Mt Leinster (p183) in County Wexford affords views of five coun-

The long route to Brandon Peak (p292), County Kerry
GARETH MCCORMACK

ties from its 796m summit. You'll find Northern Ireland's best hill-walking in the Mourne Mountains (p627) of County Down. In this range, Northern Ireland's highest peak, Slieve Donard (853m; p628), is within reach on a day's walk from the town of Newcastle.

Killarney National Park in County Kerry offers superb and challenging routes for the walker and cyclist. The top walk, of course, is up Mt Carrantuohil (1039m; p256), the highest peak in all Ireland. The park also has an adventurous 55km bike route. On the nearby Dingle Peninsula, Mt Brandon (951m; p292) offers spectacularly rugged trails that yield jaw-dropping views.

Take in the views along the Wicklow Way (p701)

EOIN CLARKE

'The Burren Way takes in County Clare's unique landscape'

Waymarked Ways

The country's network of long-distance 'waymarked ways' can keep a traveller walking for a week or longer. Though many of these run on for several hundred kilometres, you can jump in or jump out as you see fit. The Beara Way (p698), in West Cork, is an unstrenuous loop of 196km that follows historic routes and tracks. The Burren Way (p698), at 35km, is far shorter and takes in County Clare's unique, rocky landscape, the Cliffs of Moher and the musical town of Doolin.

Cavan Way (p699) is not long, either – just 26km – but it packs impressive topographic variety, taking in bogs, Stone-Age monuments and the source of the River Shannon. In County Kerry, the 168km Dingle Way (p699) loops round one of Ireland's most beautiful peninsulas. Starting in County Tipperary and ending up in County Waterford, the East Munster Way (p699) is a 70km walk through forest and open moorland, and along the towpath of the River Suir. The 214km Kerry Way (p699) takes in the spectacular Macgillycuddy's Reeks (p256) and the Ring of Kerry coast.

To the north, the Ulster Way (p700) makes a circuit around the six counties of Northern Ireland and Donegal. In total, the footpath covers more than 900km, but it can easily be

Cruise the Irish Sea under paddle power (p701)

RICHARD WAREHAM FOTOGRAFIE / ALAMY

TOP ADVENTURE CENTRES

Adventure centres can be found around Ireland, especially near the coast. These centres make it easy for a traveller to indulge in activities such as canoeing, surfing, kayaking, orienteering, hiking, climbing and other sports. Some also provide accommodation. Here's a select list:

- Killary Adventure Centre, County Galway (p436)
- Delphi Adventure Centre, County Galway (p450)
- Dunmore East Adventure Centre, County Waterford (p190)
- Kilrush Creek Adventure Centre, County Clare (p381)
- University of Limerick Activity Centre, County Clare (p379)

A surfers' paradise – Bundoran (p510), County Donegal

GARETH MCCORMACK

broken down into smaller sections. The popular 132km Wicklow Way (p701) starts in southern Dublin and ends in Clonegal in County Carlow.

The Kingfisher Trail (p677) is a waymarked, long-distance cycling trail stretching some 370km along the back roads of Counties Fermanagh, Leitrim, Cavan and Monaghan.

WATERSPORTS

Travelling in a small island nation has its natural advantages if you're into watersports. Ireland has 3100km of coastline, and numerous rivers and lakes, so no matter where in the country you may be, you're never far from a place to surf, windsurf, scuba dive, paddle a canoe, swim or simply cast a line into a cool stream ribboned with salmon. Most of these activities are already exceedingly popular in Ireland, and those that aren't appear headed that way. Outfitters and information sources abound.

Surfing & Windsurfing

Surfing is all the rage on the coast, especially in the west. The town of Bundoran (p510) in County Donegal is home to the Irish national championships each April. For the rest of the year, surfers of all levels paddle out to catch the waves. Down in County Sligo, Easky (p471) and Strandhill (p469) are famous for their year-round surf, and have facilities for travellers who seek room and board (with the room being optional). County Clare has nice breaks at Kilkee (p382), Lahinch (p386) and Fanore (p395).

Over on the east coast, some fine surfing is to be had at County Waterford's Tramore Beach (p191), a coastal resort that's home to Ireland's largest surf school. In County Wexford, surfing is popular at Rosslare Strand (p173).

> ### HANG-GLIDING & PARAGLIDING
>
> If walking and biking are too terrestrial for your taste, you can always take to the skies and ride the wind. Some of Ireland's finest hang-gliding and paragliding is found at Mt Leinster (p183) in County Wexford; Great Sugarloaf Mountain (p160) in County Wicklow; Benone and Magilligan beaches (p655) in County Derry; and Achill Island (p452) in County Mayo. Check the **Irish Hang Gliding & Paragliding Association** (www.ihpa.ie) and **Ulster Hang Gliding & Paragliding Club** (www.uhpc.co.uk) websites for local pilots.

Get up close and personal with a four-legged friend (p697)

HOLGER LEUE

The beaches around Portrush (p659), County Antrim, afford good surfing and body-surfing. The swells are highest and the water warmest in September and October.

Windsurfing is also gathering momentum along Ireland's coasts, especially in the shallow bay off County Wexford's Rosslare Strand (p173) and off Achill Island (p452) in County Mayo. Windsurfing and kitesurfing are equally popular around Portna-Blagh (p525), County Donegal.

Canoeing & Kayaking

Ireland's indented coastline makes it ideal for canoeing and kayaking expeditions. The type of canoeing in Ireland and degree of difficulty varies from gentle paddling to white-water canoeing and canoe surfing. The best time for white water is winter (December to February), when the heavier rainfall swells the rivers. In County Carlow, the River Barrow (p349) is a dream setting for canoeists and kayakers. A canoe and paddle also provide the only means for exploring the backwaters of Lough Erne (p687).

Scuba Diving

With little sewage from cities to obscure the waters, Ireland's west coast has some of the best scuba diving in Europe. The offshore islands and rocks host especially rich underwater life. The

HORSE RIDING

Unsurprisingly, considering the Irish passion for horses, riding is a popular pastime. There are dozens of centres throughout Ireland, offering possibilities ranging from hiring a horse for an hour (from €25/£15) to fully packaged, residential equestrian holidays.

Many a traveller seeks the opportunity to ride Connemara ponies (see also p73), and this can be arranged at the Errislannan Riding Centre (p431) near Clifden in County Galway. Reputable outfits can be found all around the country, including friendly Donegal Equestrian Holidays (p511) in Bundoran, County Donegal, and Killarney Riding Stables (p249), which offers multiday rides through County Kerry's stunning Iveragh Peninsula.

'The watery sport for which Ireland is best known is fishing'

best period for diving is roughly March to October. Visibility averages more than 12m, but can increase to 30m on good days. Scuba Dive West (p434), in Letterfrack, County Galway, is one of the country's best outfitters and can organise diving expeditions along the west coast.

Fishing

The watery sport for which Ireland is best known is the traditional pastime of fishing, be it from a boat on the deep seas or on a quiet spot along a river. The country is justly famous for its coarse fishing (which is generally free), covering bream, pike, perch, roach, rudd, tench, carp and eel. Freshwater game fish include salmon, sea trout and brown trout. Some managed fisheries also stock rainbow trout.

The enormous Shannon and Erne river systems, stretching southwards from Counties Leitrim and Fermanagh, are prime angling spots, and Cavan (p478), the 'Lake County', is a favourite with hardcore fishers. In the west, the great lakes of Corrib (p428), Mask (p442) and Conn (p459) have plenty of lakeshore B&Bs, good sturdy boats and knowledgeable boaters.

WATCHING WILDLIFE

Spotting animals in the wild is often a highlight on a walk through Ireland's diverse natural settings. The country's forests, lakes, bogs, wetlands and coastal islands are rife with birds, furtive furry creatures and sea mammals. In many parts of the country your chances of spotting wildlife is quite high.

Land Mammals

Killarney National Park (p253), in County Kerry, has been designated a Unesco Biosphere Reserve for its bounty of intriguing plant and animal species. It is home to the only wild herd of red deer, Ireland's most magnificent native mammal. Steely-nerved hares are commonly observed along many of Ireland's rural walkways.

Water Mammals

Aquatic mammals are commonly spotted around Ireland's periphery, as well in some of its streams. Whales, including fin whales, humpbacks and minke whales, are

Hare (p72) RICHARD MILLS

Red deer (p72), people-watching RICHARD MILLS

Seal (p72), flat out! RICHARD MILLS

often spotted off the coast of West Cork during summer, when they come to feed offshore. Dolphins and porpoises are year-round residents of Irish waters, particularly favouring the natural harbours of Counties Kerry and Cork.

Seals live all around Ireland's perimeter. You're likely to encounter them on the island of Inishbofin (p432) off the coast of Galway; near Portaferry (p616) in County Down; on Rathlin Island (p668) off the Antrim coast; and around Greencastle (p536) in Donegal's Inishowen Peninsula. One of Ireland's prized animals is the river otter, which has survived here long after disappearing from much of the rest of Europe. They are extremely shy, but a sharp-eyed walker may get lucky along the streams of Connemara (p424) in County Galway. Some otters have been known to leave the water to search for food in boglands in the west of Ireland. You're more likely to spot scratched markings left on turf piles, or tiny otter footprints.

Birds

Birds, of course, proliferate in huge numbers and are not generally shy, making Ireland a hot destination for birders. Ireland is also home to some rare and endangered species. For a description of some birds found in Ireland, see p72.

Ireland is a stopover for migrating birds, many of them from the Arctic, Africa and North America. Additionally, irregular winds frequently deliver exotic blowovers rarely seen in western Europe. Birders on Ireland's coasts and islands are always on the lookout for breeding seabirds such as the gannet, kittiwake, cormorant and heron. The rare corncrake often appears along the west coast. Large colonies of puffins inhabit coastal cliffs, particularly on islands off Donegal and Northern Ireland. Peregrine falcons, long ago hunted out, were reintroduced to Donegal's Glenveagh National Park in 2001, and since then the species has shown signs that it will re-establish itself in Ireland.

The birding is good just about everywhere in Ireland. There are more than 70 reserves and sanctuaries in Ireland, many of them open to the public. Good places to go are the Inishowen Peninsula (p535) in County Donegal; the Skellig Islands (p262) off the coast of County Kerry; the Cooley Birdwatching Trail (p575) in County Louth; and Castle Espie (p620) in County Down.

A perennial favourite – the puffin (p72)
RICHARD MILLS

Peregrine falcon (p72)
RICHARD MILLS

(Continued from page 564)

The church ruins are from a later era and are of less interest, although the modern gravestones are often quite sad.

There's a small gift shop outside the compound in summer. There are no set hours but come early or late in the day to avoid the crowds. It's just off the M1 motorway, about 8km north of Drogheda.

DUNDALK
☎ 042 / pop 28,200

Dundalk is all business and always has been. Not as grim as it once was, the town is a pleasant enough place for those who live here. It has a couple of interesting sites, and you may pause as you hurry along the M1 or drop down as a day trip from Carlingford.

The town grew under the protection of a local estate controlled by the de Verdon family, who were granted lands here by King John in 1185. In the Middle Ages, Dundalk was at the northern limits of the English-controlled Pale, strategically located on one of the main highways heading north.

The **tourist office** (☎ 933 5484; www.eastcoast midlands.ie; Jocelyn St; ❂ 9am-5pm Mon-Fri year-round, plus 9am-1pm & 2-5.30pm Sat Jun–mid-Sep) is next to County Museum Dundalk.

Right in the centre, the richly decorated 19th-century **St Patrick's Cathedral** was modelled on King's College Chapel in Cambridge, England. In front of it is the **Kelly Monument** (Jocelyn St), in memory of a local captain drowned at sea in 1858. Also here is the interesting **County Museum Dundalk** (☎ 932 7056; Jocelyn St; adult/concession €4/2.50; ❂ 10.30am-5.30pm Mon-Sat, 2-6pm Sun, closed Mon Oct-Apr). Different floors in the museum are dedicated to the town's early history and archaeology, and to the Norman period. One floor deals with the growth of industry in the area, from the 1750s up to the 1960s – including the cult classic Heinkel Bubble Car, which was manufactured in the area.

The **courthouse** (cnr Crowe & Clanbrassil Sts) is a fine neo-Gothic building with large Doric pillars designed by Richard Morrison, who also designed the courthouse in Carlow. In the front square is the stone **Maid of Éireann**, commemorating the Fenian Rising of 1798.

Should you need sustenance, **Rosso** (☎ 935 6502; 5 Roden Pl; lunch €10, dinner mains €20-24; ❂ noon-2.30, 5.30-9.30pm Sun-Fri) is one of several restaurants of distinction here. Across from St Patrick's Cathedral, Rosso has popular lunch specials, such as creamy risottos; dinners are elegant and feature local seafood. Its modern stylish interior contrasts nicely with the heritage exterior.

Bus Éireann (☎ 041-982 8251) runs an almost hourly service to Dublin (one way/return €6.30, 1½ hours) and a less frequent one to Belfast. The **bus station** (☎ 933 4075; Long Walk) is near the courthouse. If you're connecting to, say, Carlingford, the bus station's address is all too appropriate, as the **Clarke Train Station** (☎ 933 5521) is 900m west of the bus station and centre on Carrickmacross Rd. It has trains to Dublin (€18.50, one hour, 10 daily) on the Dublin–Belfast line.

DETOUR: THE COAST ROAD

Most people just zip north along the M1 motorway but if you want to double your travel time, see some sea and enjoy a little rural Ireland – at least before Dubliners put up houses everywhere – then opt for the R166 from Drogheda north along the coast.

The sleepy little village of **Termonfeckin** (Tearmann Féichín) was, until 1656, the seat and castle of the primate of Armagh. The 15th-century **castle** (admission free; ❂ 10am-6pm), or tower house, is tiny and worth a five-minute stop.

About 2km further north is the busy seaside and fishing centre of **Clogherhead** (Ceann Chlochair), with a good, shallow Blue Flag beach. Try to ignore the caravan parks.

The 33km route comes to an end in **Castlebellingham**. The village here grew up around an 18th-century crenulated **mansion**, and generations of mud farmers served the landlord within. Buried in the local graveyard is Dr Thomas Guither, a 17th-century physician supposed to have reintroduced frogs to Ireland by releasing imported frog spawn into a pond in Trinity College, Dublin. Frogs, along with snakes and toads, had supposedly received their marching orders from St Patrick a thousand years earlier.

From here you can continue 12km north to Dundalk along the suburban R132 or join the M1 and zip off.

COOLEY PENINSULA

There is an arresting beauty in the forested slopes rising out of the dark waters of Carlingford Lough up to the sun-dappled, multihued hills of the peninsula. There are crisp views across the waters to Northern Ireland's Mourne Mountains and good views across the windswept land here. Tiny country lanes wind their way down to 'beaches' where there are stones of every size. You'll feel solitude and maybe even calm.

But there's something unsettling about the place too. Isolated and remote, the Cooley Peninsula may be a political part of the Republic of Ireland, but its spirit is in the wilds of South Armagh, a fiercely independent territory in Northern Ireland that is deeply suspicious of outsiders, and a bastion of republican support.

Carlingford

☎ 042 / pop 1400

The Cooley Peninsula's mountains and views display themselves to dramatic effect in Carlingford (Cairlinn). This pretty three-street village, with its cluster of whitewashed houses, nestles on Carlingford Lough, beneath Slieve Foye (587m). Hard though it is to believe, not much of this was appreciated until the late 1980s, when the villagers got together to show what can be done to revive a dying community. The story of their efforts is vividly told in the heritage centre. Today this is an excellent stop on your journey to/from the north, particularly on long summer evenings, when you'll pub-hop along the stony streets.

INFORMATION

The **tourist office** (☎ 937 3033; www.carlingford.ie; 🕙 10am-5pm, closed Tue Oct-Mar) is in an old train station right next to the bus stop on the waterfront. It has parking.

SIGHTS

Holy Trinity Heritage Centre

The **heritage centre** (☎ 937 3454; Churchyard Rd; adult/concession €3/1.50; 🕙 10am-12.30pm & 2-4pm Mon-Fri, noon-4.30pm Sat & Sun) is in the former Holy Trinity Church. The information boards are encased within closable doors so that the centre can double as a concert hall outside visiting hours. A mural shows what the village looked like in its heyday, when the Mint and Taafe's Castle were right on the water-

front, and a short video describes the village history and explains what has been done to give it new life in recent years.

King John's Castle

Carlingford was first settled by the Vikings, and in the Middle Ages became an English stronghold under the protection of the castle, which was built on a pinnacle in the 11th to 12th centuries to control the entrance to the lough. On the western side, the entrance gateway was built to allow only one horse and rider through at a time.

King John's name stuck to quite a number of places in Ireland, given that he spent little time in or near any of them! In 1210 he spent a couple of days here en route to a battle with Hugh de Lacy at Carrickfergus Castle in Antrim. It's suggested by boosters that the first few pages of the Magna Carta, the world's first constitutional bill of rights, were drafted while he was here.

Other Sights

Near the tourist office is **Taafe's Castle**, a 16th-century tower house that stood on the water-front until the land in front was reclaimed to build a short-lived train line. The **Mint**, near the square, is of a similar age. Although Edward IV is thought to have granted a charter to a mint in 1467, no coins were produced here. The building has some interesting Celtic carvings round the windows. Near it is **Tholsel**, the only surviving gate to the original town, although it was much altered in the 19th century, when its defensive edge was softened in the interests of letting traffic through.

West of the village centre are the remains of a **Dominican friary**, built around 1305 and used as a storehouse by oyster fishermen after 1539.

Carlingford is the birthplace of Thomas D'Arcy McGee (1825–68), one of Canada's founding fathers. A bust commemorating him stands opposite Taafe's Castle.

ACTIVITIES

For a wide range of activities, including rock climbing, orienteering, hiking and windsurfing, contact the **Carlingford Adventure Centre** (☎ 937 3100; www.carlingfordadventure.com; Tholsel St).

Carlingford is the starting point for the 40km **Táin Trail**, which makes a circuit of the Cooley Peninsula through the Cooley Mountains. The route is a mixture of surfaced roads, forest tracks and green paths. For more information contact the tourist office here (opposite) or the **Dundalk tourist office** (☎ 042-933 5484; www.eastcoastmidlands.ie; Jocelyn St; ☯ 9am-5pm Mon-Fri year-round, plus 9am-1pm & 2-5.30pm Sat Jun–mid-Sep).

Carlingford Pleasure Cruises (☎ 937 3239; adult/child €12/6) runs one-hour cruises between May and September; there's no set time as departure depends on the tides.

Feel like a bit of peeping? The tourist office has full details on the **Cooley Birdwatching Trail**. Much of the area is protected and among the species you can see are godwits, red-breasted mergansers, buzzards, tits and various finches.

FESTIVALS & EVENTS
Almost every weekend from June to September, Carlingford goes event crazy: there are summer schools, medieval festivals, leprechaun hunts, homecoming festivals and anything that'll lure folks in off the M1. The mid-August **Oyster Festival** is a favourite.

SLEEPING & EATING
Carlingford is a far nicer option for a night's sleep than Dundalk, but it gets pretty crowded during summer, especially at weekends; book well in advance. As for food, you won't go far wrong: excellent seafood dominates virtually every menu.

Carlingford Adventure Centre (☎ 937 3100; www.carlingfordadventure.com; Tholsel St; dm/s/d €22/35/56) Popular with groups, the dorms are often filled by mobs of school kids that flood here during summer. Individual travellers not put off by the hullabaloo downstairs can stay in simple singles and doubles on the second floor.

McKevitt's Village Hotel (☎ 937 3116; www.mckevittshotel.com; Market Sq; s/d €60/90; P) With 17 modern rooms all kitted out in light creams and whites, this hotel offers quality accommodation, as well as a lovely bar that draws lots of locals and a well-respected seafood restaurant, Schooners (dinner €20 to €25).

Beaufort House (☎ 937 3879; www.beauforthouse.net; Ghan Rd; r €65-100; P 🖳) This spacious six-room B&B with stunning front-lawn views of the sea is along the road towards the pier. Its main business is taking care of guests – which

it does with considerable skill – but it also runs a yacht charter and sailing school.

Oystercatcher Lodge & Bistro (☎ 937 3989; www.theoystercatcher.com; Market Sq; s/d from €70/125) Renowned for the superb quality of its oysters, this white-tablecloth restaurant does local seafood just right (mains from €15; open 6.30pm to 9.30pm Monday to Saturday, 5pm to 8.30pm Sunday). Upstairs are seven comfortable and large rooms. On weekends there's a two-night minimum; midweek the rates are much less.

Ghan House (☎ 937 3682; www.ghanhouse.com; Main Rd; s/d from €75/190; P 🖳) This magnificent 18th-century Georgian house is about 1km outside the village, just off the Dundalk road. There are 12 rooms, each tastefully decorated with period antiques and original artworks, though many guests prefer the four original rooms in the main house. There's wi-fi throughout. The exceptional restaurant (five-course set menu from €45; open 7pm to 9.30pm Monday to Saturday, 12.30pm to 3.30pm Sunday) features a classical menu of traditional dishes, most made with foods sourced locally; learn its secrets in the cooking school.

Magee's Bistro (☎ 937 3751; Tholsel St; mains €20-24; ☯ 10am-9pm) Full Irish breakfasts start the day before the huge lunch menu takes over. There are loads of specials, depending what's fresh each day. Dinner sees more complex and interesting creations. Tables outside make this a true bistro.

DRINKING
This tiny village supports a few pubs, although most are nothing special.

PJ O'Hares (☎ 937 3106; Newry St) Behind the old-style grocery at the front is a classic, stone-floor pub where a peat fire burns and drinkers sit in animated conversation over a cool pint. The owners have done a good job of melding a modern bar and outdoor seating with the original, untouched pub. This is the place for summertime music.

GETTING THERE & AWAY
Bus Éireann (☎ 933 4075) has services to Dundalk (€5, 50 minutes, four to five daily Monday to Saturday). There are no Sunday services.

COUNTIES MEATH & LOUTH

Belfast

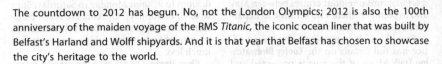

The countdown to 2012 has begun. No, not the London Olympics; 2012 is also the 100th anniversary of the maiden voyage of the RMS *Titanic*, the iconic ocean liner that was built by Belfast's Harland and Wolff shipyards. And it is that year that Belfast has chosen to showcase the city's heritage to the world.

It may seem strange for a city to identify with a ship that is famous for sinking on its maiden voyage, but Belfast built what was the most advanced piece of technology in the world at that time and takes pride in the innovation, skill and engineering genius that went into making the *Titanic*. And as the locals constantly remind you, 'She was fine when she left here'.

Once lumped with Beirut, Baghdad and Bosnia as one the four 'B's for travellers to avoid, Belfast has pulled off a remarkable transformation from bombs-and-bullets pariah to hip-hotels-and-hedonism party town. The city's skyline is in a constant state of flux as redevelopment continues apace. The old shipyards are giving way to the luxury waterfront apartments of the Titanic Quarter, and Victoria Sq, Europe's biggest urban regeneration project, has added a massive city-centre shopping mall to a list of tourist attractions that includes Victorian architecture, a glittering waterfront lined with modern art, foot-stomping music in packed-out pubs and the UK's second-biggest arts festival.

So as 2012 approaches it seems somehow fitting that Belfast should celebrate the *Titanic's* creation, building new pride and optimism out of the wreckage of past disaster. Get here early and enjoy it before the rest of the world arrives.

HIGHLIGHTS

- **Ah Go On, Take A Drink** Supping a Guinness or three in Belfast's beautiful Victorian pubs (p600)
- **The Writing on the Walls** The powerful political murals in West Belfast (p589)
- **Titanic Town** Learning about the shipyards that gave birth to the *Titanic* on a boat trip around Belfast's docklands (p593)
- **Head for the Hills** A panoramic view over the city from the top of Cave Hill (p588)
- **Back to the Future** The iconic DeLorean DMC at the Ulster Transport Museum (p609)

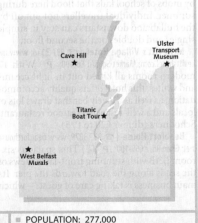

- TELEPHONE AREA CODE: 028 FROM BRITAIN AND REST OF WORLD, 048 FROM REPUBLIC OF IRELAND
- POPULATION: 277,000

HISTORY

Belfast is a relatively young city, with few reminders of its pre-19th-century history. The city takes its name from the River Farset (from the Gaelic *feirste*, meaning sandbank, or sandy ford) which flows into the River Lagan at Donegall Quay (it is now channelled through a culvert). The old Gaelic name, Beál Feirste, means 'Mouth of the Farset'.

In 1177 the Norman lord John de Courcy built a castle here, and a small settlement grew up around it. Both were destroyed 20 years later, and the town did not begin to develop in earnest until 1611 when Baron Arthur Chichester built a castle and promoted the growth of the settlement.

The early-17th-century Plantation of Ulster brought in the first waves of Scottish and English settlers, followed in the late 17th century by an influx of Huguenots (French Protestants) fleeing persecution in France, who laid the foundations of a thriving linen industry. More Scottish and English settlers arrived, and other industries such as rope-making, tobacco, engineering and shipbuilding developed.

With its textile mills and shipyards, Belfast was the one city in Ireland that felt the full force of the Industrial Revolution. Sturdy rows of brick terrace houses were built for the factory and shipyard workers, and a town of around 20,000 people in 1800 grew steadily into a city of 400,000 by the start of WWI, by which time Belfast had nearly overtaken Dublin in size.

The partition of Ireland in 1920 gave Belfast a new role as the capital of Northern Ireland. It also marked the end of the city's industrial growth, although decline didn't really set in until after WWII. With the outbreak of the Troubles in 1969, the city saw more than its fair share of violence and bloodshed, and shocking news images of terrorist bombings, sectarian murders and security forces' brutality made Belfast a household name around the world.

The 1998 Good Friday Agreement, which laid the groundwork for power-sharing among the various political factions in a devolved Northern Ireland Assembly, raised hopes for the future and since then Belfast has seen a huge influx of investment, especially from the EU. Massive swathes of the city centre have been (or are being) redeveloped, unemployment is low, house prices continue to rise faster than in any other UK city, and tourism has taken off.

A historic milestone was passed on 8 May 2007 when the Reverend Ian Paisley (firebrand Protestant preacher, and leader of the Democratic Unionist Party) and Martin McGuinness (Sinn Fein MP and former IRA commander) were sworn in at Stormont as first minister and deputy first minister of a new power-sharing government.

There are still plenty of reminders of the Troubles – notably the 'peace lines' that still divide communities – and the passions that have torn Northern Ireland apart over the decades still run deep. But despite occasional

---

BELFAST IN...

One Day

Start your day with breakfast in one of the many cafés on Botanic Ave – **Maggie May's** (p599) will do nicely – then stroll north into the city centre and take a free guided tour of **City Hall** (p582). Take a black-taxi tour of the **West Belfast murals** (p589), then ask the taxi driver to drop you off at the **John Hewitt Bar & Restaurant** (p599) for lunch. Catch a 2pm **Titanic Tour** (p593) boat trip around the harbour, then walk across the **Lagan Weir** (p585) to visit the **Odyssey Complex** (p586). Round off the day with dinner at **Deane's Restaurant** (p598) or **Roscoff** (p598).

Two Days

On your second day take a look at **Queen's University** (p586), wander around the Early Ireland exhibit in the **Ulster Museum** (p587) and stroll through the **Botanic Gardens** (p587), then walk south along the river for lunch at **Cutters River Grill** (p600). In the afternoon either continue walking south along the **Lagan Towpath** (p587) to Shaw's Bridge and catch a bus back to town, or go for a hike up **Cave Hill** (p588). Spend the evening crawling traditional pubs such as the **Crown Liquor Saloon** (p601), **Kelly's Cellars** (p601) and the **Duke of York** (p601).

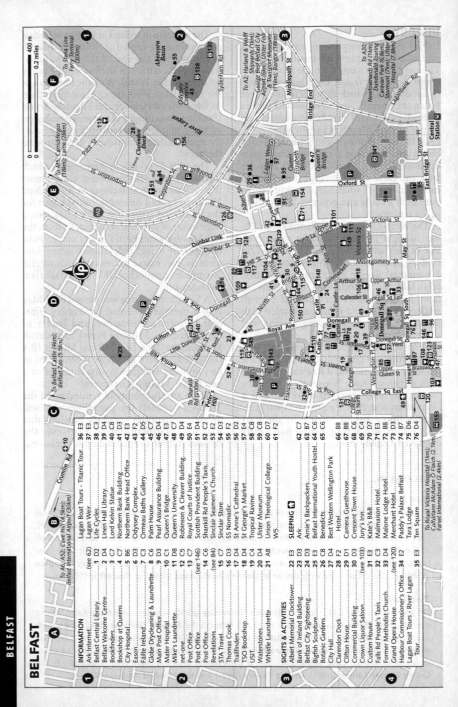

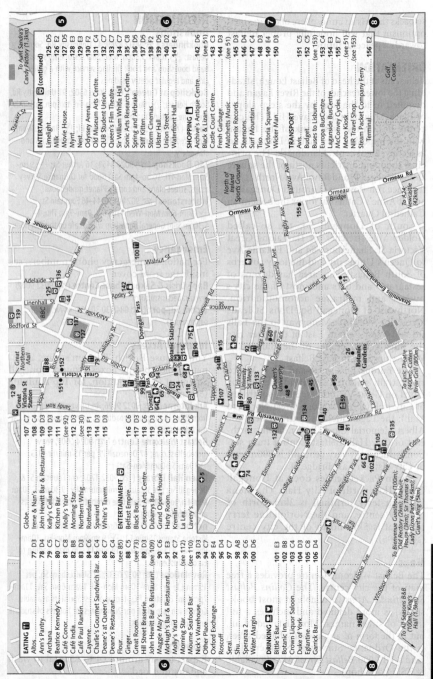

setbacks there is an atmosphere of determined optimism that will hopefully propel Belfast towards a peaceful future.

ORIENTATION

Belfast sits at the head of Belfast Lough, straddling the lower reaches of the River Lagan and hemmed in to the west by the steep slopes of Black Mountain and Cave Hill. The city centre lies on the west bank of the Lagan, with the imposing City Hall in Donegall Sq as a convenient central landmark. The principal shopping district is north of the square along Donegall Pl and Royal Ave. North again, the once run-down area around Donegall St and St Anne's Cathedral forms the bohemian Cathedral Quarter.

South of Donegall Sq, the so-called Golden Mile stretches for 1km along Great Victoria St, Shaftesbury Sq and Botanic Ave to Queen's University and the leafy suburbs of South Belfast. This area has dozens of restaurants and bars and most of the city's budget and midrange accommodation. Northwest of Donegall Sq, Divis St leads across the Westlink Motorway to the Falls Rd and West Belfast. East of the river rise the huge yellow cranes of the Harland & Wolff shipyards in East Belfast.

The Europa BusCentre and Great Victoria St train station are behind the Europa Hotel on Great Victoria St, 300m southwest of City Hall (access through Great Northern Mall); the Laganside BusCentre is near the Albert Memorial Clock Tower, 600m northeast of City Hall. Belfast Central train station (which isn't very central!) is 800m east of City Hall on East Bridge St.

Steam Packet ferries dock at Donegall Quay, 1km north of City Hall. The Stena Line car-ferry terminal is 2km north of the city centre, and the Norfolkline ferry terminal is 5km north of the city centre (see p605).

Maps

The Belfast Welcome Centre provides a free map of the city centre. The *Collins Belfast Streetfinder Atlas* (available at most bookshops) is more detailed and includes a full index of street names. Most detailed of all, but in the form of an unwieldy folded sheet, is the Ordnance Survey of Northern Ireland's 1:12,000 *Belfast Street Map* (available at TSO bookshop).

INFORMATION
Bookshops
Bookfinders (☎ 9032 8269; 47 University Rd, South Belfast; ◷ 10am-5.30pm Mon-Sat) A studenty second-hand bookshop and book-finding service with a gallery, café and regular poetry readings.

Bookshop at Queen's (☎ 9066 6302; 91 University Rd, South Belfast; ◷ 9am-5.30pm Mon-Fri, to 5pm Sat) Irish literature, history and politics.

Eason (☎ 9023 5070; 20 Donegall Pl; ◷ 9am-5.30pm Mon-Wed, Fri & Sat, to 9pm Thu) Books, magazines and stationery.

TSO Bookshop (☎ 9023 8451; 16 Arthur St; ◷ 9am-5pm Mon-Fri, 10am-4pm Sat) Good for Ordnance Survey maps, street plans and Lonely Planet guidebooks.

Waterstones (☎ 9024 0159; 44-46 Fountain St; ◷ 9am-6pm Mon-Wed, Fri & Sat, 9am-9pm Thu, 1-5.30pm Sun) General bookshop with a café on the first floor.

Emergency
For national emergency phone numbers, see inside the front cover.

Rape Crisis & Sexual Abuse Centre (☎ 9032 9002; www.rapecrisisni.com)

Victim Support (☎ 0845 30 30 900; www.victimsupport.org)

Internet Access
You can use British Telecom's blue, internet-enabled phone boxes around Donegall Sq and at Central Station, for 10p a minute (50p minimum).

Ark Internet (☎ 9032 9626; 44 University St; per min from 2.1p) High speed broadband, no minimum charge. At the Ark Hostel.

Belfast Welcome Centre (☎ 9024 6609; www.gotobelfast.com; 47 Donegall Pl; per 15 min/hr £1/3; ◷ 9am-5.30pm Mon-Sat)

Linen Hall Library (☎ 9032 1707; cnr Fountain St & Donegall Sq; per 30min £1 minimum; ◷ 9.30am-5.30pm Mon-Fri, to 4.30pm Sat) One computer on each floor; ask at desk before using.

net-one (☎ 9032 5400; Great Northern Mall, Great Victoria St; per 15min £1; ◷ 9am-9pm Mon-Fri, 10am-9pm Sat, 11am-9pm Sun) Twelve PCs; in mall leading to Europa BusCentre.

Revelations (☎ 9032 0337; 27 Shaftesbury Sq; per 15min £1; ◷ 8am-10pm Mon-Fri, 10am-6pm Sat, 11am-7pm Sun) Eighteen PCs, laptop access, printers available. Concession rate of £1 per 20 minutes for holders of student and hostelling ID cards.

Laundry
Expect to pay around £4 to £5 total to wash and dry one load.

Globe Drycleaning & Laundrette (37 Botanic Ave)
Mike's Laundrette (46 Agincourt Ave, South Belfast)
Whistle Laundrette (160 Lisburn Rd, South Belfast)
Offers service washes only; no self-service.

Left Luggage

Because of security concerns, there are no left-luggage facilities at Belfast's airports, train stations and bus stations. However, most hotels and hostels allow guests to leave their bags for the day, and the Belfast Welcome Centre (below) also offers a daytime left-luggage service.

Libraries

Belfast Central Library (☎ 9050 9150; Royal Ave; ☯ 9am-8pm Mon, Wed & Thu, to 5.30pm Tue & Fri, to 4.30pm Sat)
Linen Hall Library (☎ 9032 1707; cnr Fountain St & Donegall Sq; ☯ 9.30am-5.30pm Mon-Fri, to 4.30pm Sat) See p582.

Medical Services

Accident and emergency services are available at these hospitals:
City Hospital (☎ 9032 9241; 51 Lisburn Rd)
Mater Hospital (☎ 9074 1211; 45-51 Crumlin Rd) Near the junction of Antrim Rd and Clifton St.
Royal Victoria Hospital (☎ 9024 0503; 274 Grosvenor Rd) West of the city centre.
Ulster Hospital (☎ 9048 4511; Upper Newtownards Rd, Dundonald) Near Stormont Castle.

For advice on medical and dental emergencies, call **NHS Direct** (☎ 0845 4647; ☯ 24hr).

Money

There are plenty of ATMs around town. There are currency-exchange facilities at the Belfast Welcome Centre, the post offices on Bridge St and Shaftesbury Sq, and the Thomas Cook branches.

Post

Post office Main post office (12-16 Bridge St; ☯ 9am-5.30pm Mon-Sat); Bedford St (16-22 Bedford St); Botanic Gardens (cnr University Rd & College Gardens, South Belfast); Shaftesbury Sq (1-5 Botanic Ave)

Tourist Information

Belfast Welcome Centre (☎ 9024 6609; www .gotobelfast.com; 47 Donegall Pl; ☯ 9am-7pm Mon-Sat, noon-5pm Sun Jun-Sep, 9am-5.30pm Mon-Sat Oct-May) Provides information about the whole of Northern Ireland, and books accommodation anywhere in Ireland and Brit-

ain. Services include left luggage (not overnight), currency exchange and internet access.
Cultúrlann McAdam Ó Fiaich (☎ 9096 4188; 216 Falls Rd; ☯ 9.30am-5.30pm Mon-Fri) This cultural centre (p588) in West Belfast has a Tourist information desk.
Fáilte Ireland (Irish Tourist Board; ☎ 9032 7888; www .ireland.ie; 53 Castle St; ☯ 9am-5pm Mon-Fri year-round, to 12.30pm Sat Jun-Aug) Can book accommodation in the Republic of Ireland.
Tourist information desks Belfast City Airport (☎ 9045 7745; ☯ 5.30am-10pm); Belfast International Airport (☎ 9448 4677; ☯ 24hr)

Travel Agencies

STA Travel (☎ 9024 1469; 92-94 Botanic Ave; ☯ 9.30am-5.30pm Mon-Fri, 10am-5pm Sat)
Thomas Cook City centre (☎ 9088 3900; 11 Donegall Pl; ☯ 9am-5.30pm Mon-Wed, Fri & Sat, 10am-5.30pm Thu); Belfast International Airport (☎ 9442 2536; ☯ 5.30am-9.30pm Mon-Fri, to midnight Sat & Sun) Times vary slightly in winter and during the summer peak to reflect flight activity.
Trailfinders (☎ 9027 1888; 47-49 Fountain St; ☯ 9am-7pm Mon-Fri, 9am-6pm Sat, 10am-6pm Sun)
USIT (☎ 9032 7111; 13b Fountain Centre, College St; ☯ 9.30am-5pm Mon-Fri, to 12.30pm Sat)

DANGERS & ANNOYANCES

Even at the height of the Troubles, Belfast wasn't a particularly dangerous city for tourists, and today you're less at risk from crime here than you are in London. It's best, however, to avoid the so-called 'interface areas' – near the Peace Lines in West Belfast, Crumlin Rd and the Short Strand (just east of Queen's Bridge) – after dark; if in doubt about any area, ask at your hotel or hostel.

One irritating legacy of the Troubles is the absence of left-luggage facilities at bus and train stations. You will also notice a more obvious security presence than elsewhere in the UK and Ireland, in the form of armoured police Land Rovers, fortified police stations, and security doors on some shops (mostly outside the city centre) where you have to press the buzzer to be allowed in. There are doormen on many city-centre shops.

If you want to take photos of fortified police stations, army posts or other military or quasi-military paraphernalia, get permission first to be on the safe side. In the Protestant and Catholic strongholds of West Belfast it's best not to photograph people without permission; always ask first and be prepared to accept a refusal. Taking pictures of the murals is not a problem.

SIGHTS

City Centre

CITY HALL

The Industrial Revolution transformed Belfast in the 19th century, and its rapid rise to muck-and-brass prosperity is manifested in the extravagance of **City Hall** (☎ 9027 0456; www.belfastcity .gov.uk; Donegall Sq; admission free; ☽ guided tours 11am, 2pm & 3pm Mon-Fri, 2pm & 3pm Sat). Built in classical Renaissance style in fine, white Portland stone, it was completed in 1906 and paid for from the profits of the gas supply company. It is equipped with facilities for the disabled. (Note that City Hall will be closed for major renovation work until summer 2009.)

The hall is fronted by a statue of a rather dour 'we are not amused' **Queen Victoria**. The bronze figures on either side of her symbolise the textile and shipbuilding industries, while the child at the back represents education. At the northeastern corner of the grounds is a statue of **Sir Edward Harland**, the Yorkshire-born marine engineer who founded the Harland & Wolff shipyards and who served as mayor of Belfast in 1885–86. To his south stands a memorial to the victims of the *Titanic*.

The **Marquess of Dufferin** (1826–1902), whose career included postings as ambassador to Turkey, Russia, Paris and Rome, governor-general of Canada and viceroy to India, has an ornate, temple-like memorial flanked by an Indian and a Turkish warrior, on the western side of the City Hall. By the time this book is published, the marquess should be joined by a life-size bronze statue of George Best (1946–2005), Northern Ireland's most famous footballer. Belfast's City Airport has already been renamed in his honour.

The highlights of the free **guided tour** of City Hall include the sumptuous, wedding-cake

Italian marble and colourful stained glass of the entrance hall and rotunda, an opportunity to sit on the mayor's throne in the council chamber, and the idiosyncratic portraits of past lord mayors. Each lord mayor is allowed to choose his or her own artist, and the variations in personal style are intriguing.

LINEN HALL LIBRARY

Opposite City Hall, on North Donegall Sq, is the **Linen Hall Library** (☎ 9032 1707; www.linenhall .com; 17 Donegall Sq N; admission free; ☽ 9.30am-5.30pm Mon-Fri, to 1pm Sat; ☽). Established in 1788 to 'improve the mind and excite a spirit of general inquiry', the library was moved from its original home in the White Linen Hall (the site is now occupied by City Hall) to the present building a century later. Thomas Russell, the first librarian, was a founding member of the United Irishmen and a close friend of Wolfe Tone – a reminder that this movement for independence from Britain had its origins in Belfast. Russell was hanged in 1803 after Robert Emmet's abortive rebellion.

The library houses some 260,000 books, more than half of which are part of its important Irish and local-studies collection. The political collection consists of pretty much everything that has been written about Northern Irish politics since 1966. The library also has a small **coffee shop** (☽ 10am-4pm Mon-Fri, to 12.30pm Sat) and all the daily newspapers. The visitors' entrance is on Fountain St, around the corner from the main door.

OTHER DONEGALL SQ BUILDINGS

On Donegall Sq West is the ornate **Scottish Provident Building** (1897–1902). It's decorated with a veritable riot of fascinating statuary, including several allusions to the industries that

---

RED HAND OF ULSTER

According to legend, the chief of a raiding party – O'Neills or O'Donnells, take your pick – approaching the coast by boat decided to fire up his troops by decreeing that Ulster would belong to the first man to lay his right hand upon it. As they neared land one particularly competitive chap cut off his own right hand and lobbed it to the shore, thus claiming Ulster as his own. The O'Neill clan later adopted the Red Hand as their emblem and it went on to become the symbol of the Irish province of Ulster.

You'll see the Red Hand of Ulster in many places: on the official Northern Irish flag, in the Ulster coat of arms, above the entrance to the Linen Hall Library (above) on Donegall Sq, and laid out in red flowers in the garden of Mount Stewart House & Gardens (p618) in County Down. It also appears in many political murals in the badges of loyalist terrorist groups, and as a clenched red fist in the badge of the Ulster Volunteer Force (UVF).

assured Victorian Belfast's prosperity, as well as sphinxes, dolphins and lions' heads. The building was the work of the architectural partnership of Young and MacKenzie, who counterbalanced it in 1902 with the red sandstone **Pearl Assurance Building** on Donegall Sq East. Also on the east side of the square is the Classical Greek portico of the former **Methodist Church** (1847), now occupied by the Ulster Bank.

On the north side of square is the equally fine **Robinson & Cleaver Building** (1888), once the Royal Irish Linen Warehouse and later home to Belfast's finest department store (now occupied by Marks & Spencer). There are 50 busts adorning the façade, representing patrons of the Royal Irish Linen company – look out for Queen Victoria and the Maharajah of Cooch Behar, both former customers.

CROWN LIQUOR SALOON

There are not too many historical monuments that you can enjoy while savouring a pint of beer, but the National Trust's **Crown Liquor Saloon** (☎ 9027 9901; 46 Great Victoria St; admission free; ⏰ 11.30am-11pm Mon-Sat, 12.30-10pm Sun) is one. Belfast's most famous bar was refurbished by Patrick Flanagan in the late 19th century and displays Victorian decorative flamboyance at its best (your man was looking to pull in a posh clientele from the new-fangled train station and Grand Opera House across the street).

The exterior (1885) is decorated with ornate and colourful Italian tiles, and a mosaic of a crown on the pavement outside the entrance. Legend has it that Flanagan, a Catholic, argued with his Protestant wife over what the pub's name should be. His wife prevailed and it was named the Crown in honour of the British monarchy. Flanagan took his sneaky revenge by placing the crown mosaic where customers would tread it underfoot every day.

The interior (1898) sports a mass of stained and cut glass, marble, ceramics, mirrors and mahogany, all atmospherically lit by genuine gas mantles. A long, highly decorated bar dominates one side of the pub, while on the other is a row of ornate wooden snugs. The snugs come equipped with gun-metal plates (from the Crimean War) for striking matches, and bell-pushes that once allowed drinkers to order top-ups without leaving their seats (alas, no longer).

Above the Crown is **Flannigan's** (☎ 9027 9901), another interesting bar with *Titanic* and other maritime memorabilia.

GRAND OPERA HOUSE

One of Belfast's great Victorian landmarks is the **Grand Opera House** (☎ 9024 1919; www.goh.co.uk; Great Victoria St; guided tours adult/child £5/3; ⏰ tours available 11am-noon Wed-Sat), across the road from the Crown Liquor Saloon. Opened in 1895, and completely refurbished in the 1970s, it suffered grievously at the hands of the IRA, having sustained severe bomb damage in 1991 and 1993. It has been suggested that as the Europa Hotel next door was the home of the media during the Troubles, the IRA brought the bombs to them so they wouldn't have to leave the bar.

The interior has been restored to its original, over-the-top Victorian pomp, with swirling wood and plasterwork, fancy gilt-work in abundance and carved elephant heads framing the private boxes in the auditorium. See also p604.

ORMEAU BATHS GALLERY

Housed in a converted 19th-century public bathhouse, the **Ormeau Baths Gallery** (☎ 9032 1402; www.ormeaubaths.co.uk; 18a Ormeau Ave; admission free; ⏰ 10am-5.30pm Tue-Sat) is Northern Ireland's principal exhibition space for contemporary visual art. The gallery stages changing exhibitions of work by Irish and international artists, and has hosted controversial showings of works by Gilbert and George, and Yoko Ono. The gallery is a few blocks south of Donegall Sq.

THE ENTRIES

The oldest part of Belfast, around High St, suffered considerable damage from WWII bombing. The narrow alleyways running off High and Ann Sts, known as the Entries, were once bustling commercial and residential centres: **Pottinger's Entry**, for example, had 34 houses in 1822.

Joy's Entry is named after Francis Joy, who founded the *Belfast News Letter* in 1737, the first daily newspaper in the British Isles (and still in business). One of his grandsons, Henry Joy McCracken, was executed for supporting the 1798 United Irishmen's revolt.

The United Irishmen were founded in 1791 by Wolfe Tone in Peggy Barclay's tavern in **Crown Entry**, and used to meet in Kelly's Cellars

(1720; p601) on Bank St, off Royal Ave; see p36 for more on the United Irishmen).

White's Tavern (1630; p601), on **Wine Cellar Entry**, is the oldest tavern in the city and is still a popular lunch-time meeting spot.

Cathedral Quarter

The district north of the centre around St Anne's Cathedral, bounded roughly by Donegall, Waring, Dunbar and York Sts, has been promoted as Belfast's Left Bank, a bohemian district of restored red-brick warehouses and cobbled lanes lined with artists' studios, design offices, and stylish bars and restaurants. It's home to the Cathedral Quarter Arts Festival (p594).

Built in imposing Hiberno-Romanesque style, **St Anne's Cathedral** (☎ 9033 2328; www .belfastcathedral.org; Donegall St; admission free, donations accepted; ⏲ 10am-4pm Mon-Fri; ♿) was started in 1899 but did not reach its final form until 1981. As you enter you'll see the black-and-white marble floor is laid out in a maze pattern – the black route leads to a dead end, the white to the sanctuary and salvation. The 10 pillars of the nave are topped by carvings symbolising aspects of Belfast life; look out for the Freemasons' pillar (the central one on the right, or south, side). In the south aisle is the tomb of unionist hero Sir Edward Carson (1854–1935). The stunning mosaic of *The Creation* in the baptistry contains 150,000 pieces of coloured glass; it and the mosaic above the west door are the result of seven years' work by sisters Gertrude and Margaret Martin.

A 10-minute walk northwest from the cathedral along Donegall and Clifton Sts leads to **Clifton House** (2a Hopewell Ave, Carlisle Circus), built in 1774 by Robert Joy (Henry Joy McCracken's uncle) as a poorhouse. The finest surviving Georgian building in Belfast, it now houses a nursing home.

South of the cathedral at the end of Donegall St lies the elegant Georgian **Commercial Building** (1822) ahead, easily identified by the prominent name of the Northern Whig Printing Company, with a modern bar on the ground floor. Opposite is the **Northern Bank Building**, the oldest public building in the city, which started life as the one-storey Exchange in 1769, became the Assembly Rooms with the addition of an upper storey in 1777, and was remodelled in Italianate style in 1845 by Sir Charles Lanyon, Belfast's

pre-eminent Victorian architect, to become a bank.

The most flamboyant legacy of Belfast's Victorian era is the grandiose **Ulster Bank Building** (1860), now home to the Merchant Hotel (p595), this Italianate extravaganza has a portico of soaring columns and sculpted figures depicting Britannia, Justice and Commerce, and iron railings decorated with the Red Hand of Ulster and Irish wolfhounds.

To the west of the cathedral, at the junction of Royal Ave and North St, is the **Bank of Ireland Building** (1929), a fine example of Art Deco architecture. The former **Sinclair Store** (1935), diagonally opposite the bank, is also in Deco style.

Laganside & Lanyon Place

The ambitious **Laganside Project** (www.laganside .com) to redevelop and regenerate the centre of Belfast saw the building of the Waterfront Hall, British Telecom's Riverside Tower and the Belfast Hilton in the 1990s. Projects completed since then include several clusters of riverside apartments, the Lanyon Quay office development next to the Waterfront Hall and the restoration of listed buildings such as McHugh's bar on Queen's Sq, the ornate Victorian warehouses now housing the Malmaison Hotel on Victoria St and the Albert Memorial Clock Tower.

The latest stage is the 29-storey **Obel**, Belfast's tallest building, which soars above the waterfront at Donegall Quay. All 182 apartments in the building were sold in advance, within 48 hours of being released; it's due for completion some time in 2008.

A few blocks to the south is the brand new £320 million retail complex of **Victoria Square** (www.victoriasquare.com), whose centrepiece is a shopping mall topped by a vast glass dome (due to open in 2008).

CLARENDON DOCK

Near the ferry terminal on Donegall Quay is the Italianate **Harbour Commissioner's Office** (1854). The striking marble and stained-glass interior features art and sculpture inspired by Belfast's maritime history. The captain's table built for the *Titanic* survives here – completed behind schedule, it never made it on board. Guided tours of the office are available during the Belfast Maritime Festival in early July. It's also open on European Heritage Open Days, which take place over a weekend in

September or October (see the Events section on www.ehsni.gov.uk).

Sinclair Seamen's Church (☎ 9086 8568; Corporation Sq; admission free; ☒ 2-4pm Wed, 11.30am-7pm Sun), next to the Harbour Commissioner's Office, was built by Charles Lanyon in 1857–58 and was intended to meet the spiritual needs of visiting sailors. Part church, part maritime museum, it has a pulpit in the shape of a ship's prow (complete with red-and-green port and starboard lights), a brass ship's wheel and binnacle (used as a baptismal font) salvaged from a WWI wreck and, hanging on the wall behind the wheel, the ship's bell from HMS *Hood*.

North of the Harbour Commissioner's Office is the restored **Clarendon Dock**. Leading off it are the dry docks where Belfast's shipbuilding industry was born – No 1 Dry Dock (1796–1800) is Ireland's oldest, and remained in use until the 1960s; No 2 (1826) is still used occasionally. Between the two sits the pretty little **Clarendon Building**, now home to the offices of the Laganside Corporation.

CUSTOM HOUSE SQ

South along the river is the elegant **Custom House**, built by Lanyon in Italianate style between 1854 and 1857; the writer Anthony Trollope once worked in the post office here. On the waterfront side the pediment carries sculpted portrayals of Britannia, Neptune and Mercury. The Custom House steps were once Belfast's equivalent of London's Speakers' Corner, a tradition memorialised in a bronze statue preaching to an invisible crowd.

Looking across the River Lagan from the Custom House, East Belfast is dominated by the huge yellow cranes of the Harland & Wolff shipyards. The modern Queen Elizabeth Bridge crosses the Lagan just to the south, but immediately south again is **Queen's Bridge** (1843) with its ornate lamps, Sir Charles Lanyon's first important contribution to Belfast's cityscape.

QUEEN'S SQ

At the east end of High St is Belfast's very own leaning tower, the **Albert Memorial Clock Tower**. Erected in 1867 in honour of Queen Victoria's dear departed husband, it is not so dramatically out of kilter as the more famously tilted tower in Pisa but does, nevertheless, lean noticeably to the south – as the locals say, 'Old Albert not only has the time, he also has the

inclination.' Restoration work has stabilised its foundations and left its Scrabo sandstone masonry sparkling white.

Many of the buildings around the clock tower are the work of Sir Charles Lanyon. The white stone building immediately north of the clock tower was completed in 1852 by Lanyon as head office for the **Northern Bank**.

South of the tower on Victoria St is the Malmaison Hotel (1868; p595), formerly two seed warehouses – look for the friezes of exotic birds, plants and nut-munching squirrels on the left half of the façade.

LAGAN WEIR

Across the street from the Custom House is *Bigfish* (1999), the most prominent of the many modern artworks that grace the riverbank between Clarendon Dock and Ormeau Bridge. The giant ceramic salmon – a symbol of the regeneration of the River Lagan – is covered with tiles depicting the history of Belfast.

It sits beside **Lagan Weir**, the first stage of the Laganside Project, completed in 1994. Years of neglect and industrial decline had turned the River Lagan, the original lifeblood of the city, into an open sewer flanked by smelly, unsightly mudflats. The weir, along with a programme of dredging and aeration, has improved the water quality so much that salmon, eels and sea trout migrate up the river once again.

For details of the boat tours that depart from here, see p593.

LANYON PLACE

A five-minute walk south from the Lagan Weir leads to Lanyon Pl, the Laganside Project's flagship site, dominated by the 2235-seat Waterfront Hall (p603). Across Oxford St lie the neoclassical **Royal Courts of Justice** (1933), bombed by the IRA in 1990 but now emerging from behind the massive security screens that once concealed them.

South of the courts is the elegant Victorian **St George's Market** (☎ 9043 5704; cnr Oxford & May Sts; admission free; ☒ 6am-1pm Fri, 9am-3pm Sat), built in 1896 for the sale of fruit, butter, eggs and poultry, and the oldest continually operating market in Ireland. Restored in 1999, it now hosts a variety market on Friday, selling fresh flowers, fruit, vegetables, meat and fish, plus general household and second-hand goods, and the City Food and Garden Market on

Saturday. There's also a two-day Christmas Fair and Market in early December.

Titanic Quarter

Belfast's former shipbuilding yards – the birthplace of the RMS *Titanic* – stretch along the east side of the River Lagan, dominated by the towering yellow cranes known as Samson and Goliath. The area is currently undergoing a £1 billion regeneration project known as **Titanic Quarter** (www.titanicquarter.com), which plans to develop the long-derelict docklands over the next 15 to 20 years.

There are plans to build an 'iconic attraction' in the Titanic Quarter in time for the centenary of the *Titanic*'s launch in 2012. In the meantime, the informative and entertaining commentary on the Lagan Boat Company's Titanic Tour (p593) is the best way to learn about the history of the shipyards.

ODYSSEY COMPLEX

The Odyssey Complex is a huge sporting and entertainment centre on the eastern side of the river across from Clarendon Dock. The complex features a hands-on science centre, a 10,000-seater sports arena (home to the Belfast Giants ice-hockey team), a multiplex cinema with an IMAX screen, a video-games centre and a dozen restaurants, cafés and bars.

Also known as whowhatwherewhenwhy, **W5** (☎ 9046 7700; www.w5online.co.uk; adult/child £6.50/4.50, 2 adults & 2 children £19; ☽ 10am-6pm Mon-Sat & noon-6pm Sun, last admission 1hr before closing; &.) is an interactive science centre aimed at children of all ages. Kids can compose their own tunes by biffing the 'air harp' with a foam rubber bat, try to beat a lie detector, create cloud rings and tornadoes, and design and build their own robots and racing cars.

The Odyssey Complex is a five-minute walk across the weir from the Lagan Lookout. Metro bus 26 from Donegall Sq West to Holywood stops at the complex (£1, 5 minutes, hourly Monday to Friday only); the rather inconspicuous bus stop is on Sydenham Rd.

SS NOMADIC

In 2006 the **SS Nomadic** (☎ 9024 6609; www.save nomadic.com; adult/child £5/3; ☽ 10am-6pm May-Sep) – the only surviving vessel of the White Star Line (the shipping company that owned the *Titanic*) – was rescued from the breaker's yard and brought to Belfast where she is being restored. The little steamship, which once served

as a tender ferrying first- and second-class passengers between Cherbourg harbour and the giant Olympic Class ocean liners (which were too big to dock at the French port), will eventually be berthed in the Hamilton Dock, just north of the Odyssey Complex. In the meantime, she can be visited at the quay next to the Odyssey Complex.

South Belfast

The Golden Mile – the 1km stretch of Great Victoria St and Shaftesbury Sq that links the city centre to the university district – was once the focus for much of Belfast's nightlife. These days, with the regeneration of the city centre, it's more tarnished brass than gold, but it still has several decent pubs and eateries.

Metro buses 8A, 8B and 8C run from Donegall Sq East along Bradbury Pl and University Rd to Queen's University.

QUEEN'S UNIVERSITY

If you think that Charles Lanyon's Queen's College (1849), a Tudor Revival building in red brick and honey-coloured sandstone, has something of an Oxbridge air about it, that may be because he based the design of the central tower on the 15th-century Founder's Tower at Oxford's Magdalen College. Northern Ireland's most prestigious university was founded by Queen Victoria in 1845, one of three Queen's colleges (the others, still around but no longer called Queen's colleges, are in Cork and Galway) created to provide a nondenominational alternative to the Anglican Church's Trinity College in Dublin. In 1908 the college became the Queen's University of Belfast, and today its campus spreads across some 250 buildings. Queen's has around 25,000 students and enjoys a strong reputation in medicine, engineering and law.

Just inside the main entrance is a small **visitor centre** (☎ 9097 5252; www.qub.ac.uk/vcentre; University Rd; admission free; ☽ 10am-4pm Mon-Sat May-Sep, 10am-4pm Mon-Fri Oct-Apr; &.) with exhibitions and a souvenir shop. You can arrange a guided tour by phoning in advance.

The university quarter is an attractive district of quiet, tree-lined streets. Georgian-style **University Sq** (1848–53), on the northern side of the campus, is one of the most beautiful terraced streets in Ireland. Opposite its eastern end is the grand, neo-Renaissance

Union Theological College (1853), originally the Presbyterian College and yet another Lanyon design. It housed the Northern Ireland Parliament from the partition of Ireland until 1932, when the Parliament Buildings at Stormont were opened.

BOTANIC GARDENS

The green oasis of Belfast's **Botanic Gardens** (☎ 9031 4762; Stranmillis Rd; admission free; ⊗ 7.30am-sunset) is a short stroll away from the university. Just inside the Stranmillis Rd gate is a statue of Belfast-born William Thomson, **Lord Kelvin**, who helped lay the foundation of modern physics and who invented the Kelvin scale that measures temperatures from absolute zero (-273°C or 0°K).

The gardens' centrepiece is Charles Lanyon's beautiful **Palm House** (admission free; ⊗ 10am-noon & 1-5pm Mon-Fri, 2-5pm Sat, Sun & bank holidays, closes 4pm Mon-Fri Oct-Mar), built in 1839 and completed in 1852, with its birdcage dome, a masterpiece in cast-iron and curvilinear glass. Nearby is the unique **Tropical Ravine** (admission free; ⊗ same as Palm House), a huge red-brick greenhouse designed by the garden's curator Charles McKimm and completed in 1889. Inside, a raised walkway overlooks a jungle of tropical ferns, orchids, lilies and banana plants growing in a sunken glen.

ULSTER MUSEUM

If the weather washes out a walk in the gardens, head instead for the nearby **Ulster Museum** (☎ 9038 3000; www.ulstermuseum.org.uk; Stranmillis Rd; admission free; ⊗ 10am-5pm Mon-Fri, 1-5pm Sat, 2-5pm Sun). Note that the museum will be closed for redevelopment until spring 2009.

Don't miss the **Early Ireland gallery**, a series of tableaux explaining Irish prehistory combined with a spectacular collection of prehistoric stone and bronze artefacts that help provide a cultural context for Northern Ireland's many archaeological sites. The exhibits are beautifully displayed – the Malone Hoard, a clutch of 16 polished, Neolithic stone axes discovered only a few kilometres from the museum, looks more like a modern sculpture than a museum exhibit.

Other highlights include the **Industrial History gallery**, based around Belfast's 19th-century linen industry, and the **Treasures of the Armada**, a display of artefacts and jewellery recovered from the 1588 wreck of the *Girona* (see the boxed text, p661) and other Spanish Armada vessels. Among the treasures is a ruby-encrusted golden salamander.

The centrepiece of the **Egyptian collection** is the mummy of Princess Takabuti. She was unwrapped in Belfast in 1835, the first mummy ever to be displayed outside Egypt; more recently, her bleached hair has led the locals to dub her 'Belfast's oldest bleached blonde'.

The top floors are given over to 19th- and 20th-century **Irish and British art**, notably the works of Belfast-born Sir John Lavery (1856–1941), who became one of the most fashionable and expensive portraitists of Victorian London.

West Belfast

Though scarred by three decades of civil unrest, the former battleground of West Belfast is one of the most compelling places to visit in Northern Ireland. Recent history hangs

---

WALK: LAGAN TOWPATH

Part of Belfast's Laganside redevelopment project has been the restoration of the towpath along the west bank of the River Lagan. You can now walk or cycle for 20km along the winding riverbank from central Belfast to Lisburn. The Belfast Welcome Centre provides the *Lagan Valley Regional Park – Towpath Leaflet,* which has a detailed map.

A shorter walk (10km) that you can easily do in half a day starts from **Shaw's Bridge** on the southern edge of the city. Take bus 8A or 8B from Donegall Sq East to the stop just before the Malone roundabout (where Malone Rd becomes Upper Malone Rd). Bear left at the roundabout (signposted Outer Ring A55) and in five minutes or so you will reach the River Lagan at Shaw's Bridge.

Turn left and follow the cycle-/walkway downstream on the left bank of the river (waymarked with red '9' signs). After 30 minutes you will arrive at the most attractive part of the walk: **Lagan Meadows**, a tree-fringed loop in the river to the right of the path and a good place for a picnic on a summer's day. Another half-hour will bring you to **Cutters River Grill** (p600), a great place for a lunch break. From the pub it's another hour of pleasant walking to Lagan Weir in the city centre.

heavy in the air, but there is a noticeable air of optimism and hope for the future.

The main attractions are the powerful murals that chart the history of the conflict as well as the political passions of the moment, and for visitors from mainland Britain there is a grim fascination to be found in wandering through the former 'war zone' in their own backyard.

West Belfast grew up around the linen mills that propelled the city into late 19th-century prosperity. It was an area of low-cost, working-class housing and even in the Victorian era was divided along religious lines. The advent of the Troubles in 1968 solidified the sectarian divide, and since 1970 the ironically named 'Peace Line' has separated the Loyalist and Protestant Shankill district from the republican and Catholic Falls.

Despite its past reputation the area is safe to visit. The best way to see West Belfast is on a black-taxi tour (see p593). The cabs visit the more spectacular murals as well as the Peace Line (where you can write a message on the wall) and other significant sites, while the drivers provide a colourful commentary on the history of the area.

There's nothing to stop you visiting under your own steam, either walking or using the shared black taxis along the Falls or Shankill Rds (see the boxed text, p607). Alternatively, buses 10A to 10F from Queen St will take you along the Falls Rd; buses 11A to 11D from Wellington Pl go along Shankill Rd.

You can also pick up a free *West Belfast and Shankill Arts and Heritage Trail* leaflet at the Belfast Welcome Centre, which has maps detailing two waymarked walks around the Falls and Shankill districts. It doesn't list political murals.

FALLS ROAD

Although the signs of past conflict are inescapable, the Falls today is an unexpectedly lively, colourful and optimistic place. Local people are friendly and welcoming, and community ventures such as Conway Mill, the Cultúrlann centre and black-taxi tours have seen tourist numbers increase dramatically in recent years.

The focus for community activity is the Irish language and cultural centre **Cultúrlann McAdam Ó Fiaich** (☎ 9096 4180; www.culturlann.ie; 216 Falls Rd; ✆ 9am-9pm Mon-Fri, 10am-6pm Sat). Housed

in a red-brick, former Presbyterian church, it's a cosy and welcoming place with a tourist information desk, a shop selling a wide selection of books on Ireland, Irish-language material, crafts, and Irish music tapes and CDs, and an excellent café-restaurant (p600). The centre also has an art gallery and a theatre that stages music, drama and poetry events.

A few blocks away is **Conway Mill** (☎ 9024 7276; www.conwaymill.org; 5-7 Conway St; admission free; ✆ 10am-5pm Mon-Fri, to 3pm Sat), a 19th-century flax mill that now houses more than 20 small shops and studios making and selling arts, crafts and furniture, an art gallery and an exhibition on the mill's history. There's also the **Irish Republican History Museum** (✆ 10am-2pm Tue-Sat), a collection of artefacts, newspaper articles, photos and archives relating to the republican struggle from 1798 to the Troubles.

See also the Walking Tour, p591.

SHANKILL ROAD

Although the Protestant Shankill district (from the Irish *sean chill,* meaning 'old church') has received less media and tourist attention than the Falls, it also contains many interesting murals. The people here are just as friendly, but the Shankill has far fewer tourists than the Falls. Loyalist communities seem to have more difficulty in presenting their side of the story than the republicans, who have a far more polished approach to propaganda and public relations.

To reach Shankill Rd on foot, set off north from City Hall along Donegall Pl and Royal Ave, then turn left on Peter's Hill and keep straight on across the Westlink dual carriageway.

Beyond Shankill Rd, about 500m up Glencairn Rd, is **Fernhill House: The People's Museum** (☎ 9071 5599; www.fernhillhouse.co.uk; Glencairn Rd; adult/child £2/1; ✆ 10am-4pm Mon-Sat, 1-4pm Sun). Set in a wealthy Victorian merchant's villa, the museum contains a re-creation of a 1930s working-class terraced house, exhibitions detailing the history of the Shankill district and the Home Rule crisis, and the largest collection of Orange Order memorabilia in the world. To get there, take bus 11B, 11C or 11D from Wellington Pl, at the northwest corner of Donegall Sq.

Outside the Centre
CAVE HILL

The best way to get a feel for Belfast's natural setting is to view it from above. In the

THE MURALS OF BELFAST

Belfast's tradition of political murals is a century old, dating from 1908 when images of King Billy (William III, Protestant victor over the Catholic James II at the Battle of the Boyne in 1690) were painted by unionists protesting against home rule for Ireland. The tradition was revived in the late 1970s as the Troubles wore on, with murals used to mark out sectarian territory, make political points, commemorate historical events and glorify terrorist groups. As the 'voice of the community' the murals were rarely permanent, but changed to reflect the issues of the day.

Republican Murals

The first republican murals appeared in 1981, when the hunger strike at the Maze prison saw the emergence of dozens of murals supporting the hunger strikers. In later years republican muralists broadened their scope to cover wider political issues, Irish legends and historical events. After the Good Friday Agreement of 1998, the murals came to demand police reform and the protection of nationalists from sectarian attacks.

Common images seen in republican murals include the phoenix rising from the flames (symbolising Ireland reborn from the flames of the 1916 Easter Rising), the face of hunger-striker Bobby Sands, and scenes and figures from Irish mythology. Common slogans include 'Free Ireland', the Irish Gaelic 'Éirí Amach na Cásca 1916' (The Easter Rising of 1916) and 'Tíocfaidh Ár Lá' ('Our Day Will Come').

The main areas for republican murals are Falls Rd, Beechmount Ave, Donegall Rd, Shaw's Rd and the Ballymurphy district in West Belfast; New Lodge Rd in North Belfast; and Ormeau Rd in South Belfast.

Loyalist Murals

Whereas republican murals were often artistic and rich in symbolic imagery, the loyalist ones have traditionally been more militaristic and defiant in tone. The loyalist battle cry of 'No Surrender!' is everywhere, along with red, white and blue painted kerbstones, paramilitary insignia and images of King Billy, usually shown on a prancing white horse.

You will also see the Red Hand of Ulster, sometimes shown as a clenched fist (the symbol of the Ulster Freedom Fighters, UFF), and references to the WWI Battle of the Somme in 1916 in which many Ulster soldiers died; it is seen as a symbol of Ulster's loyalty to the British crown, in contrast to the republican Easter Rising of 1916. Common mottoes include 'Quis Separabit' (Who Shall Divide Us?), the motto of the Ulster Defence Association (UDA); and the defiant 'We will maintain our faith and our nationality'.

Murals Today

In recent years there has been a lot of debate about what to do with Belfast's murals. Some see them as an ugly and unpleasant reminder of a violent past, others claim they are a vital part of Northern Ireland's history. There's no doubt they have become an important tourist attraction, but there is now a move to replace the more aggressive and militaristic images with murals dedicated to local heroes and famous figures such as footballer George Best and *Narnia* novelist CS Lewis.

There are also some off-beat and amusing artworks, including one that has been baffling passers-by for years. A gable-end on Balfour Ave, off the Ormeau Rd, asks the question 'How can quantum gravity help explain the origin of the universe?' It was part of an art installation in 2001, one of 10 questions selected by scientists as the most important unsolved problems in physics. Perhaps it has survived so long as it reflects the still unsolved and – to outsiders, equally baffling – problem of Northern Ireland's sectarian divide.

If you want to find out more about Northern Ireland's murals, look out for the books *Drawing Support* (three volumes) by Bill Rolston, *The Peoples' Gallery* by the Bogside Artists and the Mural Directory website (www.cain.ulst.ac.uk/murals).

absence of a private aircraft, head for Cave Hill (368m) which looms over the northern fringes of the city. The view from its summit takes in the whole sprawl of the city, the docks and the creeping fingers of urbanisation along the shores of Belfast Lough. On a clear day you can even spot Scotland lurking on the horizon. For information on climbing to the summit, see the boxed text, below.

The hill was originally called Ben Madigan, after the 9th-century Ulster king, Matudhain. Its distinctive, craggy profile, seen from the south, has been known to locals for two centuries as 'Napoleon's Nose' – it supposedly bears some resemblance to Bonaparte's hooter, but you might take some convincing. On the summit is an Iron Age earthwork known as McArt's Fort where members of the United Irishmen, including Wolfe Tone, looked down over the city in 1795 and pledged to fight for Irish independence.

Cave Hill Country Park (☎ 9077 6925; Antrim Rd; admission free; ☯ 7.30am-dusk) spreads across the hill's eastern slopes, with several waymarked walks and an adventure playground for kids aged three to 14 years.

To get there, take buses 1A to 1H from Donegall Sq West to Belfast Castle or Belfast Zoo.

BELFAST CASTLE
Built in 1870 for the third Marquess of Donegall, in the Scottish Baronial style made fashionable by Queen Victoria's then recently built Balmoral, the multiturreted pomp of **Belfast Castle** (☎ 9077 6925; www.belfastcastle.co.uk; Antrim Rd; admission free; ☯ 9am-10pm Mon-Sat, to 5.30pm Sun) commands the southeastern slopes of Cave Hill. It was presented to the City of Belfast in 1934.

Extensive renovation between 1978 and 1988 has left the interior comfortably modern rather than intriguingly antique, and the castle is now a popular venue for wedding receptions. Upstairs is the **Cave Hill Visitor Centre** with a few displays on the folklore, history, archaeology and natural history of the park. Downstairs is the Cellar Restaurant and a small **antiques shop** (☯ noon-10pm Mon-Sat, to 5pm Sun).

Legend has it that the castle's residents will experience good fortune only as long as a white cat lives there, a tale commemorated in the beautiful formal gardens by nine portrayals of cats in mosaic, painting, sculpture and garden furniture.

BELFAST ZOO
Belfast Zoo (☎ 9077 6277; www.belfastzoo.co.uk; Antrim Rd; adult/child Apr-Sep £7.80/4.10, Oct-Mar £6.30/3.20, children under 4, senior & visitors with disabilities free; ☯ 10am-7pm Apr-Sep, to 4pm Oct-Mar, last admission 2hr before closing) is one of the most appealing zoos in Britain and Ireland, with spacious enclosures set on an attractive, sloping site; the sea lion and penguin pool with its underwater viewing is particularly good. Some of the more unusual animals include tamarins,

---

WALK: CAVE HILL

Start from the public car park just before the gates of Belfast Castle. Take the path that leads up from the car park. After 150m you reach a horizontal path at a T-junction; go right and follow this trail as it continues uphill through the woods. After about 800m you emerge from the trees beneath Cave Hill's eastern crags. Fork left beneath the obvious caves that give the hill its name; if you keep straight on here, the path continues north for 1km to the Belfast Zoo car park and traverse to the north (right) beneath the cliffs then climb up to a shoulder (muddy). The path then doubles back to the south (left) and follows the cliff tops to the summit.

A little bridge and some steps lead up to the summit proper, an Iron Age fort surrounded by crags. There's a superb view across the city, harbour and lough, with Scrabo Hill and Tower prominent on the eastern horizon, and the rounded forms of the Mourne Mountains far away to the south.

Continue south then west on a broad, well-made trail for almost 1km. At a sharp bend to the right, beside a wooden bench, leave the trail on the left via a stile, and go downhill on a faint path through a field. Pass through another stile at an old quarry and turn left, keeping the quarry on your left. The path then descends more steeply through woods; at a T-junction go left on a better path which leads to the T-junction above the castle car park; turn right here to finish. (Total 5.5km; allow two hours)

spectacled bears and red pandas, but the biggest attractions are 'Jack' the blue-eyed white tiger, the ultracute meerkats and the colony of ring-tailed lemurs.

MALONE HOUSE

Malone House (☎ 9068 1246; www.malonehouse.co.uk; Upper Malone Rd; admission free; ⏰ 9am-5pm Mon-Sat, 11am-5pm Sun) is a late-Georgian mansion in the grounds of Barnett Demesne. Built in the 1820s for local merchant William Legge, the house is now used mainly for social functions and conferences, with art exhibitions staged in the Higgin Gallery. The surrounding gardens are planted with azaleas and rhododendrons, with paths leading down to the Lagan Towpath (see boxed text, p587).

The house is about 5km south of the centre; take bus 8A or 8B to Dub Lane, Upper Malone Rd.

SIR THOMAS & LADY DIXON PARK

This **park** (Upper Malone Rd; admission free; ⏰ 7.30am-dusk year round) consists of rolling meadows, woodland, riverside fields and formal gardens. The main draw is its spectacular **Rose Garden**, which contains more than 20,000 blooms. Among other displays, a spiral-shaped garden traces the development of the rose from early shrub roses up to modern hybrids; the roses are in bloom from late July. The park also contains a walled garden, a Japanese-style garden, a children's playground and a café.

The park is 1.5km south of Malone House.

GIANT'S RING

This huge **prehistoric earthwork** (admission free; ⏰ 24hr), nearly 200m in diameter, is a circular Neolithic ritual complex with a dolmen (known as the Druid's Altar) in the centre. Prehistoric rings were commonly believed to be the home of fairies and consequently treated with respect, but this one was commandeered in the 19th century as a racetrack, the 4m-high embankment serving as a natural grandstand. The site is 6.5km south of Belfast city centre, off Milltown Rd near Shaw's Bridge.

STORMONT

The dazzling white neoclassical façade of **Parliament House** at Stormont is one of Belfast's most iconic buildings; in the North, 'Stormont' carries the same connotation as 'Westminster' does in Britain and 'Washing-

ton' in the USA – the seat of power. For 40 years, from its completion in 1932 until the introduction of direct rule in 1972, it was the seat of the parliament of Northern Ireland. More recently, it returned to the forefront of Irish politics when Ian Paisley and Martin McGuinness – who had been the best of enemies for decades – laughed and smiled as they were sworn in as first minister and deputy first minister respectively.

The building occupies a dramatic position at the end of a gently rising, 1.5km-long avenue and is fronted by a defiant statue of the arch unionist Sir Edward Carson. Parliament House is not open to the public, but you are free to walk around the extensive grounds, and you can take a virtual tour at www.niassembly .gov.uk. Nearby, 19th-century **Stormont Castle** is, like Hillsborough in County Down, an official residence of the Secretary of State for Northern Ireland.

Stormont is 8km east of the city centre, off the A20 Newtonards road. Take bus 4A or 4B from Donegall Sq West.

WALKING TOUR

WALK FACTS

Start City Hall
End Milltown Cemetery
Distance 4km
Duration one hour

This walk leads through the heart of republican West Belfast from the city centre to Milltown Cemetery. Starting from **City Hall** (p582) go north along Donegall Pl and turn left on Castle St. Keep straight ahead along Divis St.

As you cross the busy Westlink dual carriageway you will see the infamous **Divis Tower**, a 20-storey apartment block. The security forces took over the top two floors of the tower block as an observation post in the 1970s, and continued to use it to monitor people's movements until it was decommissioned in 2005.

As you pass the Divis Tower, look to the right along the side street opposite and you'll see steel gates that mark the beginning of the so-called **Peace Line**, the 6m-high wall of corrugated steel, concrete and chain link that has divided the Protestant and Catholic communities of West Belfast for almost 40 years. Begun in 1970 as a 'temporary measure', it has now outlasted the Berlin Wall, and zigzags for some 4km from the Westlink to the lower slopes of Black Mountain. These days the gates in the wall remain open during the day, but most are still closed from 5pm to 8am. There are now more than 20 such barriers in Belfast, and a total of more than 40 throughout Northern Ireland, the most visible sign of the divisions that have scarred the province for so long.

Next, you pass the **Solidarity Wall**, a collection of murals expressing republican sympathies with, among others, the Palestinians, the Kurds and the Basques, along with several anti-George W Bush murals. Just past here Divis St becomes Falls Rd, and Conway St, on the right at the Celtic Bar, leads to **Conway Mill** (p588).

On the corner of Falls Rd and Sevastopol St is the red-brick **Sinn Féin headquarters**, with its famous mural of a smiling Bobby Sands, the hunger striker who was elected as MP for West Belfast just a few weeks before he died in 1981. The text reads, in Sands' own words, 'Our revenge will be the laughter of our children'. A few blocks further on, on the right between Waterford St and Springfield Rd, look out for the **Ruby Emerald Take-Away** at 105 Falls Rd – it was on the pavement outside this shop (known as Clinton's Hot Food from 1996 to 2003) that the historic handshake between Sinn Féin leader Gerry Adams and US president Bill Clinton took place in November 1995.

On the left now are the artwork railings of the **Royal Victoria Hospital**, dating from 1906 and claiming to be the world's first air-conditioned building. Known locally as the RVH, it played an important role in creating the first ever portable defibrillator and, in the 1970s and '80s, developed a well-earned reputation for expertise in the treatment of gunshot wounds. The wavy form of the railings mimics the structure of DNA – look for the little yellow Xs and Ys for X- and Y-chromosomes – and the portraits (laser-cut in sheet steel) chart the progress of a human life from birth to the age of 100. Just beyond the hospital is the **Cultúrlann MacAdam ÓFiaich** (p588).

All along Falls Rd you'll see republican murals, as well as memorials in honour of people who have died during the conflict. At Islandbawn St on the right, the **Plastic Bullet Mural** commemorates the 17 people, including eight children, who were killed by plastic baton rounds (now banned) fired by the se-

curity services. Two streets on, on the right, is **Beechmount Ave**, with a huge 'Éirí Amach na Cásca' (Easter Rising) mural. Look at the street name – a hand-painted sign reads 'RPG Avenue'. 'RPG' stands for 'rocket-propelled grenade', and the street earned its nickname because it offered a line of sight for IRA rocket attacks on the security forces base in nearby Springfield Rd.

Another 15 minutes of walking will take you past the **City Cemetery** and Falls Park to **Milltown Cemetery** where the 1981 hunger strikers are buried. You'll see lots of green Hs attached to lamp posts (in memory of the H-blocks at the Maze prison where the hunger strikers were incarcerated); at Hugo St, opposite the City Cemetery, there's a large mural entitled 'St James's Support the Hunger Strikers'.

Return by the same route or catch any bus or taxi back to the city centre. There's a bus stop across the road from the Milltown Cemetery entrance.

BELFAST FOR CHILDREN

W5 (p586) is the city's biggest draw for kids – it's hard to drag them away once they get started on the hands-on exhibits – and the Odyssey Complex houses other attractions including a video-games arcade, a ten-pin bowling rink and an IMAX cinema. **Belfast Zoo** (p590) is a perennial favourite, and the **Ulster Museum** (p587) also has plenty of exhibits and special events designed for children of all ages.

For outdoor fun, head for the **Botanic Gardens** (p587), or the adventure playground in **Cave Hill Country Park** (p590). Or you can try crazy golf with a difference at **Pirates Adventure Golf** (☎ 9048 0220; www.piratesadventuregolf.com; 111A Dundonald Touring Caravan Park, Dundonald Rd; adult/child £5.50/3.75; ☺ 10am-10pm), a landscaped, 36-hole course decked out with waterfalls, fountains and a giant pirate ship.

Sweeties may not be at the top of parents' shopping lists these days, but you might be prepared to make an exception for **Aunt Sandra's Candy Factory** (☎ 9073 2868; www.irishcandyfactory.com; 60 Castlereagh Rd; ☺ 9.30am-5pm Mon-Fri, 10am-4.30pm Sat). This 1950s-style shop sells fudge, candy, chocolates, toffee apples and other traditional sweets which have been made by hand, and you can get a tour of the workshop before buying the goods.

Located outside of town but near enough for a day trip, you'll find the **Ulster Folk & Trans-**

VOICES: KEN HARPER, BLACK-TAXI DRIVER

What do you do for a living? I do black-taxi tours. I started work in Belfast in 1968 – that was just the start of the so-called Troubles – and qualified as a taxi driver in 1979. I remember, just before the ceasefires of 1994, the odd tourist coming through Belfast and asking me for a tour. Now it's a major industry.

What do people want to see?
The most popular sights, without doubt, are the Shankill Rd and Falls Rd areas. For example, the murals, the so-called peace line and the general area around those roads which the Troubles affected greatly.

Do visitors understand the situation here?
Some tourists do and some don't understand the conflict and divisions in Northern Ireland, but I can explain to the majority of my tourists the background to the problem. The daftest question I have been asked was, 'Who is Sinn Fein?', thinking it was a person. Another tourist asked, on seeing a statue of Queen Victoria, 'Is that the bad Queen?'.

---

port Museums (p609), and the **Ark Open Farm** (p619), both of which are hugely popular with kids.

The free monthly *Whatabout?* booklet (available from the Belfast Welcome Centre) has a 'Family Fun' section, which lists events and attractions of interest to travellers with children. If you're in town in late May, look out for the **Belfast Children's Festival** (www.belfast childrensfestival.com), which is packed with cultural and educational events.

TOURS

You can find full details of organised tours at the Belfast Welcome Centre (p580). If you want to hire a personal guide, call the Welcome Centre or contact the **Northern Ireland Tourist Guide Association** (☎ 9753 3370; www.bluebadgeireland .org; half-/full-day tours £75/130).

Boat Tours

Lagan Boat Company (☎ 9033 0844; www.laganboat company.com; adult/child £8/6) offers two 1¼-hour boat tours: the **River Lagan Tour** (☼ 2pm & 3.30pm Mon, 12.30pm, 2pm & 3.30pm Tue-Thu Apr-Sep, 12.30pm & 2pm Tue-Thu Mar & Oct) heads upstream to Stranmillis, departing from the Lagan Lookout.

The excellent **Titanic Tour** (☼ 12.30pm & 2pm Fri-Mon Mar-Oct, Sat & Sun only Nov & Dec, also 3pm Fri-Mon May-Sep) explores the derelict docklands downstream of the weir, taking in the huge dry-dock where the liners *Titanic* and *Olympic* could fit with just nine inches to spare. The Titanic Tour departs from Donegall Quay near the *Bigfish* sculpture, and picks up passengers at the Odyssey Complex.

These tours are popular – it's safest to book in advance.

Bus Tours

Belfast City Sightseeing (☎ 9045 9035; www .belfastcitysightseeing.com; adult/child £11/5) Runs 1¼-hour open-top bus tours that take in City Hall, the Albert Clock, the Titanic Quarter, the Botanic Gardens, and the Falls Rd and Shankill Rd murals in West Belfast. There are departures from Castle Pl every 30 minutes from 9.30am to 4.30pm from May to September, hourly from 10am to 4pm from October to March.

Belfast International Youth Hostel (☎ 9032 4733; www.minicoachni.co.uk; 22 Donegall Rd; tour adult/child £9/6) Recommended by many readers for its two-hour minibus tour that takes in all the city's main sights. Tours depart from the hostel (p595) daily at noon, and can be booked at the Belfast Welcome Centre.

Cycling Tours

Life Cycles (☎ 9043 9959; www.lifecycles.co.uk; 36-37 Smithfield Market; per person £12-16) Offers three-hour guided tours (minimum five people) of the city centre, South Belfast and the Lagan Towpath. The cost includes bike and helmet rental. Call to arrange a tour at least one day in advance. There are entrances on West St and Winetavern St.

Taxi Tours

Black-taxi tours of West Belfast's murals – known locally as the 'bombs and bullets' or 'doom and gloom' tours – are being offered by an increasing number of taxi companies and local cabbies. These can vary in quality and content, but in general they're an intimate and entertaining way to see the sights and can be customised to suit your own interests. There are also historical taxi tours of the city centre. For a one-hour tour expect to pay £25 total for one or two people, and £8 per person for three to six. Call and they will pick you up anywhere in the city centre.

The following are recommended.

Harpers Taxi Tours (☎ 9074 2711, 07711-757178; www.harperstaxitours.co.nr)

Official Black Taxi Tours (☎ 9064 2262, toll-free ☎ 0800 052 3914; www.belfasttours.com)

Original Belfast Black Taxi Tours (☎ 9058 6996, 07751-565359)

Walking Tours

Belfast Pub Tours (☎ 9268 3665; www.belfastpub tours.com; per person £6; ⊙ departs 7pm Thu & 4pm Sat May–Oct) A two-hour tour (not including drinks) taking in six of the city's historic pubs, departing from the Crown Dining Rooms, above the Crown Liquor Saloon (p601) on Great Victoria St.

Blackstaff Way (☎ 9029 2631; per person £6; ⊙ departs 11am Sat) A fascinating 1½-hour historical tour through the city along the route of the Blackstaff River, which was channelled underground in 1881. Departs from the Belfast Welcome Centre.

Historic Belfast Walk (☎ 9024 6609; per person £6; ⊙ departs 2pm Wed & Fri-Sun) A 1½-hour tour that explores the architecture and history of the Victorian city centre and Laganside. Departs from the Belfast Welcome Centre.

Titanic Trail (☎ 9024 6609; one/two people £8/10) A state-of-the-art, self-guided trail which allows you to explore the city centre and Titanic Quarter at your own pace. A hand-held media player provides an audio-visual commentary, and shows you where to go using GPS technology. On hire from the Belfast Welcome Centre (two people can share one media player).

FESTIVALS & EVENTS

The **Belfast City Council** (☎ 9024 6609; www.belfast city.gov.uk/events) organises a wide range of events throughout the year, covering everything from the St Patrick's Day parade to the Lord Mayor's Show, and has a very useful online events calendar.

March

Between the Lines (Crescent Arts Centre; ☎ 9024 2338; www.crescentarts.org) Ten-day literary festival.

St Patrick's Carnival (☎ 9031 3440; www.feilebelfast .com) A celebration of Ireland's patron saint marked by various community festivals and culminating in a grand city-centre parade on 17 March.

Belfast Film Festival (☎ 9032 5913; www.belfast filmfestival.org) A week-long celebration of Irish and international film-making held in late March.

April

Titanic Made In Belfast Festival (☎ 9024 6609) A week-long celebration of the world's most famous ship, and the city that built her, with special exhibitions, tours, lectures and film screenings. First half of April.

May

Belfast Marathon (☎ 2587 2828; www.belfastcity marathon.com) First Monday in May. Runners from across the globe come to compete but it's also a people's event, with a walk and fun run as well.

Cathedral Quarter Arts Festival (☎ 9023 2403; www.cqaf.com) Twelve days of drama, music, poetry, street theatre and art exhibitions in and around the Cathedral Quarter. Held in early May.

June

City Dance (Crescent Arts Centre; ☎ 9024 2338; www .crescentarts.org) Dance festival held at the Arts Centre.

July

Belfast Maritime Festival (☎ 9024 6609) A two-day festival at the beginning of July, centred on Queen's Quay and Clarendon Dock, with sailing ships, street entertainment, seafood festival and live music. In 2009 the festival will coincide with Belfast being one of the host ports for the Tall Ships Atlantic Challenge (www.sailtraininginter national.org).

August

Féile an Phobail (☎ 9031 3440; www.feilebelfast .com) Said to be the largest community festival in Ireland, the Féile takes place in West Belfast over 10 days in early August. Events include an opening carnival parade, street parties, theatre performances, concerts and historical tours of the City and Milltown cemeteries.

October

Belfast Festival at Queen's (☎ 9097 1197; www .belfastfestival.com) The UK's second-largest arts festival held in and around Queen's University during three weeks in late October and early November.

Halloween Carnival (☎ 9024 6609) Held from 27 to 31 October, with special events across the city, including a carnival parade, ghost tours and fireworks.

December

Christmas Festivities (☎ 9024 6609) A range of events from late November to 31 December, including carol singing, lamplight processions, a street carnival and a huge outdoor ice rink at the Odyssey Complex.

SLEEPING

From backpacker hostels to boutique hotels, the range of places to stay in Belfast gets wider every year. The traditional accommodation scene – red-brick B&Bs in the leafy suburbs of South Belfast and city-centre business hotels – has been lent a splash of colour in the form of stylish hotel-restaurant-nightclub combos such as Benedicts, and elegant but expensive boutique hotels set in refurbished historic buildings such as Ten Square and the Merchant Hotel.

Most of Belfast's budget and midrange accommodation is south of the centre, in the university district around Botanic Ave, University Rd and Malone Rd. This area is also crammed with good-value restaurants and pubs, and is mostly within a 20-minute walk of City Hall. You can expect to pay around £11 for a dorm bed in a hostel, approximately £45 to £65 for a double room in a good B&B or guesthouse, and about £70 to £100 for a double in a luxurious midrange hotel. The top-end and more expensive midrange places attract a business clientele during the week, and usually offer lower rates at weekends (Friday to Sunday nights).

Book ahead in summer or during busy festival periods. The Belfast Welcome Centre will make reservations for a fee of £2. You can also book accommodation through the **Lonely Planet website** (lonelyplanet.com).

City Centre

BUDGET

Belfast International Youth Hostel (☎ 9032 4733; www.hini.org.uk; 22-32 Donegall Rd; dm £8.50-12, s/d from £18/26; 🖳 🕭) Belfast's modern Hostelling International (HI) hostel is conveniently located just off Shaftesbury Sq, which means it can be a bit noisy at night when the pubs and clubs empty. The hostel has a kitchen, a laundry, a café and free linen; rates are slightly higher on Friday and Saturday nights. Take bus 9A or 9B from Donegall Sq East or Great Victoria St (across from the Europa BusCentre) to Bradbury Pl.

MIDRANGE

Benedicts (☎ 9059 1999; www.benedictshotel.co.uk; 7-21 Bradbury Pl; s/d from £65/75; 🖳) Set bang in the middle of the Golden Mile, Benedicts is a modern, style-conscious hotel at the heart of Belfast's nightlife. The rooms are above a huge Gothic bar and restaurant (where you also have breakfast), so don't expect peace and quiet till after 1am. Free wi-fi.

Jury's Inn (☎ 9053 3500; www.jurysdoyle.com; Fisherwick Pl, Great Victoria St; r £69-89; 🖳) Jury's bland modernity is more than made up for by its top location – only three minutes from City Hall and close to loads of good pubs and restaurants – and good value. Fixed room rates apply for anything up to three adults, or two adults and two kids. Breakfast is optional and costs £9 extra.

TOP END

Malmaison Hotel (☎ 9022 0200; www.malmaison-belfast.com; 34-38 Victoria St; r from £135, ste from £255; 🖳) Housed in a pair of beautifully restored Italianate warehouses (originally built for rival firms in the 1850s), the Malmaison is a luxurious haven of king-size beds, deep leather sofas and roll-top baths big enough for two, all done up in a decadent décor of black, red, dark chocolate and cream. The massive, rock-star penthouse suite has a giant bed (almost 3m long), a bathtub big enough for two and, wait for it … a billiard table. With purple baize.

our pick **Ten Square** (☎ 9024 1001; www.tensquare.co.uk; 10 Donegall Sq S; r from £165; 🖳) A former bank building to the south of City Hall that has been given a designer feng-shui makeover, Ten Square is an opulent, Shanghai-inspired boutique hotel with friendly and attentive service. Magazines such as *Cosmopolitan* and *Conde Nast Traveller* drool over the dark lacquered wood, cream carpets, low-slung futon-style beds and sumptuous linen, and the list of former guests includes Bono, Moby and Brad Pitt.

Merchant Hotel (☎ 9023 4888; www.themerchanthotel.com; 35-39 Waring St; r from £220, ste from £290; 🖳 ℗) Belfast's most flamboyant Victorian building, the old Ulster Bank head office, has been converted into the city's most flamboyant boutique hotel, a fabulous fusion of old-fashioned elegance and contemporary styling.

South Belfast

To get to places on or near Botanic Ave, take bus 7A or 7B from Howard St. For places on or near University and Malone Rds take bus 8A or 8B, and for places on or near Lisburn Rd take bus 9A or 9B; both depart from Donegall Sq East, and from the bus stop on Great Victoria St across from the Europa BusCentre.

AIRPORT ACCOMMODATION

Park Plaza Hotel (☎ 9445 7000; www.park plazabelfast.com; Belfast International Airport, Aldergrove; s/d £105/120; 🖳 Ⓟ) Immediately opposite the terminal at Belfast International Airport, the 106-room Park Plaza has a business centre, conference facilities and free courtesy transport to the city centre.

Park Avenue Hotel (☎ 9065 6520; www .parkavenuehotel.co.uk; 158 Holywood Rd; s/d £79/99; Ⓟ) The classy 56-room Park Avenue is the nearest hotel to Belfast City Airport (3km away), and 3km east of the city centre.

BUDGET

Paddy's Palace Belfast (☎ ☎ 9033 3367; www.paddys palace.com; 68 Lisburn Rd; dm £6-13.50, s/d £27/37; 🖳 Ⓟ) A newish kid on the block, Paddy's offers clean and comfortable dorms, a big, well-equipped kitchen and a bright and homely common room, though the dorms are a bit gloomy. It has free internet and friendly staff who are happy to point you to the best local pubs. There's no sign outside, so it's easy to miss – bang on the door at the corner of Lisburn Rd and Fitzwilliam St.

Arnie's Backpackers (☎ 9024 2867; www.arniesback packers.co.uk; 63 Fitzwilliam St; dm £9-11; 🖳) This long-established hostel is set in a quiet terraced house in the university area, with plenty of lively bars and restaurants nearby. It's a bit on the small side, but real coal fires, a friendly crowd, and the ever-helpful Arnie himself (and his two cute Jack Russell terriers) make it more cosy than cramped.

our pick Ark (☎ 9032 9626; www.arkhostel.com; 44 University St; dm £11, s/d £20/32; 🖳) The Ark has moved to a snazzy new home on the corner of University St and Botanic Ave (look for the tiny sign above the door), bang in the heart of Queens student quarter. It's small, convivial and newly kitted out with modern fittings. It has its own internet café, and is more family friendly than other hostels; there's also a 2am curfew.

Kate's B&B (☎ 9028 2091; katesbb127@hotmail .com; 127 University St; s/d £25/50) Kate's is a homely kind of place, from the window boxes bursting with colourful flowers to the cute dining room crammed with bric-a-brac and a couple of resident cats. The bedrooms are basic but comfortable, and the showers are

a bit cramped, but at this price – and only a few minutes' walk from Botanic Ave – we're not complaining.

All Seasons B&B (☎ 9068 2814; www.allseasonsbelfast .com; 356 Lisburn Rd; s/d/f £30/50/60; Ⓟ) Away from the centre, but right in the heart of trendy Lisburn Rd, All Seasons is a red-brick villa with bright, colourful bedrooms, modern bathrooms, a stylish little breakfast room and a comfortable lounge. Take bus 9A or 9B from the city centre; the house is between Cranmore Ave and Cranmore Gardens, 150m past the big police station.

MIDRANGE

Bienvenue Guesthouse (☎ 9066 8003; bienvenueguest house@aol.com; 8 Sans Souci Park; s/d £42/60; 🖳 Ⓟ) Set in a grand Victorian house with a tree-lined garden in a quiet side street off Malone Rd, the Bienvenue's four rooms offer hotel-standard accommodation, with period antiques (including a half-tester bed in one room), direct-dial phones, 24-hour reception and daily newspapers.

our pick Old Rectory (☎ 9066 7882; www.anold rectory.co.uk; 148 Malone Rd; s/d £46/66; Ⓟ) A lovely red-brick Victorian villa with lots of original period features, this former rectory has four spacious bedrooms, a comfortable drawing room with a leather sofa and fancy breakfasts (venison sausages, scrambled eggs with smoked salmon, freshly squeezed OJ). It's a 10-minute bus ride from the centre – the inconspicuous driveway is on the left, just past Deramore Park South.

Camera Guesthouse (☎ 9066 0026; camera _gh@hotmail.com; 44 Wellington Park; s/d £50/68) A cosy, welcoming Victorian B&B with an open fire in the drawing room, the Camera is set in yet another of South Belfast's peaceful, tree-lined terraces. The tasty breakfasts are prepared using organic produce, and the friendly couple who own the place are a fount of knowledge on what to see and do in town.

TOP FIVE BELFAST RESTAURANTS

- Beatrice Kennedy's (p600)
- Cayenne (p598)
- Deane's Restaurant (p598)
- Roscoff (p598)
- Shu (p600)

Tara Lodge (☎ 9059 0900; www.taralodge.com; 36 Cromwell Rd; s/d/tr £65/75/105; 🖳 🅿) This B&B is a cut above your average South Belfast guesthouse, with its stylish, minimalist décor; friendly, efficient staff; delicious breakfasts; and 18 bright and cheerful rooms. Great location too, on a quiet side street just a few paces from the buzz of Botanic Ave.

Crescent Town House (☎ 9032 3349; www.crescent townhouse.com; 13 Lower Cres; s/d/tr from £90/110/130; 🖳 ♿) Another stylish boutique hotel with a perfect location, the Crescent is an elegant Victorian town house transformed into a den of designer chic, with its finger on the pulse of the city's party zone. Rooms have silky, Ralph Lauren–style décor and luxury bathrooms with Molton Brown toiletries and walk-in rain-head showers.

TOP END

our pick **Malone Lodge Hotel** (☎ 9038 8000; www .malonelodge.com; 60 Eglantine Ave; s/d/apt from £85/120/109; 🖳 🅿) The centrepiece of a tree-lined Victorian terrace, the modern Malone Lodge has pulled in many plaudits for its large, luxurious rooms with elegant gold and navy décor, good food and pleasant, helpful staff. It also offers five-star self-catering apartments (one-, two- and three-bedroom).

Best Western Wellington Park Hotel (☎ 9038 1111; www.wellingtonparkhotel.com; 21 Malone Rd; s/d from £105/120; 🖳 🅿 ♿) A modern makeover with sunny yellow décor and designer frills has made the Wellie Park into a family-friendly, business-friendly place that appeals to a wide range of people, and provides the little luxuries that make you want to come back – overstuffed sofas, bathrobes and slippers, newspapers delivered to your room. Beware, though – it can be noisy at weekends, when the hotel pulls in more of a party crowd.

Outside the Centre

Dundonald Touring Caravan Park (☎ 9080 9100; www.theicebowl.com; 111 Old Dundonald Rd, Dundonald; camp/caravan sites £9.50/16.50; ☾ Mar-Sep) This small site (22 pitches) in a park next to the Dundonald Icebowl is the nearest camping ground to Belfast, 7km east of the city centre and south of the A20 road to Newtownards.

Farset International (☎ 9089 9833; www.farset international.co.uk; 446 Springfield Rd; s/d £34/48; 🅿 ♿) This is a community-run venture in West Belfast, best described as a posh hostel. The

bright and cheerful modern complex is set in grounds overlooking a small lake, and has 38 en-suite rooms with TV. Rates include breakfast, and in the evening you can eat in the restaurant or use the self-catering kitchen.

EATING

In the last five years or so Belfast's restaurant scene has been totally transformed by a wave of new restaurants whose standards now compare with the best eating places in Europe.

City Centre

The main shopping area north of Donegall Sq becomes a silent maze of deserted streets and steel shutters after 7pm, but during the day the many pubs, cafés and restaurants do a roaring trade. In the evening, the liveliest part of the city centre stretches south of Donegall Sq to Shaftesbury Sq.

BUDGET

Charlie's Gourmet Sandwich Bar (☎ 9024 6097; 48 Upper Queen St; mains £1-4; ☾ 8am-5pm Mon-Sat) Charlie's is good place for cheap, healthy and filling sandwiches, and also serves a range of breakfasts from toasted soda bread to the full Ulster fry.

Ann's Pantry (☎ 9024 9090; 29-31 Queen's Arcade; mains £1.20-5; ☾ 9am-5.30pm Mon-Sat) A tiny bakery with next-door coffee shop, Ann's serves superb home-made soups, pies (try the steak and Guinness), cakes and choose-your-own sandwiches to take away or sit in.

Café Paul Rankin (☎ 9031 5090; 27-29 Fountain St; mains £2-5; ☾ 7.30am-6pm Mon-Wed, Fri & Sat, 7.30am-9pm Thu) Owned by Northern Ireland's best-known celebrity chef, this café has comfy benches and sofas for lounging on, and serves quality coffee, cakes, focaccias, soups, pastas and salads.

our pick **Flour** (☎ 9033 9966; 46 Upper Queen St; mains £4-5; ☾ 7.30am-5.30pm Mon-Wed, Fri & Sat, to 10.30pm Thu) This funky little creperie tempts in hungry shoppers with a range of baguettes and sweet and savoury pancakes with healthy fillings such as olives, feta cheese and sun-dried tomatoes. Home-made soups and freshly squeezed juices are also on the menu.

Morning Star (☎ 9023 3976; 17 Pottinger's Entry; mains £5-15; ☾ food served noon-9pm Mon-Sat) This former coaching inn is famed for its all-you-can-eat lunch buffet (£5). The upstairs restaurant features traditional Irish beef (big 700g steaks cost £15), mussels, oysters and eels, as well as more unusual things like alligator and ostrich. See also under Drinking, p601.

MIDRANGE

Altos (☎ 9032 3087; Anderson McCauley Bldg, Fountain St; mains £6-10; ☼ 10am-5pm Mon-Wed, to 8pm Thu, to 6pm Fri & Sat) This popular, high-ceilinged bistro is decked out in giant, modern-art canvases and bright ochre and turquoise colours that match the Mediterranean influence on the menu, which includes a good selection of vegetarian dishes.

Archana (☎ 9032 3713; 53 Dublin Rd; mains £6-11; ☼ noon-2pm & 5pm-midnight Mon-Sat, 5-11pm Sun) A cosy and unpretentious Indian restaurant, Archana offers a good range of vegetarian dishes from its separate 'Little India' menu. The *thali* – a platter of three curries with rice, naan bread, pakora and dessert – is good value at £13/9 for the meat/veggie version.

ourpick Mourne Seafood Bar (☎ 9024 8544; 34-36 Bank St; mains £9-14; ☼ noon-6pm Mon, noon-9pm Tue, noon-9.30pm Wed & Thu, noon-10.30pm Fri & Sat, 1-6pm Sun) This informal, publike space, all red brick and dark wood with old oil lamps dangling from the ceiling, is tucked behind a fishmonger's shop, so the seafood is as fresh as it gets. On the menu are oysters served *au naturel* or Rockefeller, meltingly sweet scallops with saffron linguini, salt and chilli squid, and roast gurnard with mustard and dill cream. Hugely popular, so best book ahead, especially on Sunday.

Speranza 2 (☎ 9023 0213; 16-19 Shaftesbury Sq; mains £9-15; ☼ 5-11.30pm Mon-Sat, 12.30-2.30pm & 3-10pm Sun) A local institution – it's been around for more than 20 years – the recently revamped Speranza is a big, buzzing Italian restaurant that complements traditional pizzas and pastas with more sophisticated dishes. It's family friendly, with a kids' menu, high-chairs, colouring books and crayons. They only take reservations for groups of six or more; otherwise, pop in and wait in the bar for a table.

Water Margin (☎ 9032 6888; 159-161 Donegall Pass; mains £11-16; ☼ noon-11pm) You can worship at the altar of Cantonese cuisine in this stylishly converted church, a five-minute walk east of Shaftesbury Sq. Expect authentic Chinese food from the Cantonese chefs and friendly, professional service.

Oxford Exchange (☎ 9024 0014; 1st fl, St George's Market, Oxford St; mains £11-17; ☼ noon-10pm Mon-Thu,

noon-11pm Fri & 5-11pm Sat) Smart and stylish with bare pine floors, chocolate brown chairs, white linen napkins and a yellow tulip on each table, the Oxford has breezy charm and a menu of high-end comfort food – try the beer-battered cod with mushy peas, and chunky chips served in a twist of newspaper.

Cayenne (☎ 9033 1532; 7 Ascot House, Shaftesbury Sq; mains £12-20, 2-/3-course lunch £13/16; ☼ noon-2.15pm Mon-Fri, 6-10.15pm Mon-Thu, 6-11.15pm Fri & Sat, 6-8.45pm Sun) Behind an anonymous frosted-glass façade lurks a funky, award-winning restaurant operated by TV celebrity chef, Paul Rankin, decked out in designer black and amber and clad in conceptual art. The menu concentrates on quality Irish produce prepared with an Asian or Mediterranean twist.

Ginger (☎ 9024 4421; 7-8 Hope St; mains £14-18; ☼ noon-3pm & 5-10pm Mon-Sat) Ginger is one of those places you could walk right past without noticing, but if you do you'll be missing out. It's a cosy and informal little bistro with an unassuming exterior, serving food that is anything but ordinary – the flame-haired owner-chef (hence the name) really knows what he's doing, sourcing top-quality Irish produce and turning out exquisite dishes such as salad of seared sirloin steak with sweet pickled onion, wasabi and mango purée, and oyster mushroom tartlet with creamy green peppercorn puy lentils and parsnip chips.

TOP END

Deane's Restaurant (☎ 9033 1134; 34-40 Howard St; mains £15-20, 2-/3-course lunch £16/20; ☼ noon-3pm & 5.30-10pm Mon-Sat) Chef Michael Deane heads the kitchen in Northern Ireland's only Michelin-starred restaurant, where he takes the best of Irish and British produce – beef, game, lamb, seafood – and gives it the gourmet treatment. Typical dishes include pan-fried scallops with pickled carrots, watercress purée and orange vinaigrette, and rack of venison with baked potato purée, red cabbage marmalade and spiced pear *confit*. Revamped in 2007, the ultracool dining room is open-plan and minimalist.

ourpick Roscoff (☎ 9031 1150; 7-11 Linenhall St; mains £16-22; ☼ noon-2.15pm Mon-Fri, 6-10.15pm Mon-Thu, 6-11.15pm Fri & Sat) A muted décor in shades of slate blue, white and dark grey, with polished wood floors and white linen, puts the food squarely centre stage in this sophisticated and smoothly run restaurant. Part of the Paul Rankin stable, Roscoff takes inspiration from Irish produce and French cuisine, with dishes such as *carpaccio* (very thin slices of raw meat) of venison with celeriac remoulade, and pot roast turbot with mussels and tarragon cream. There's a two-/three-course lunch menu for £16/20, and a three-course dinner menu for £25 (Monday to Thursday only).

Great Room (☎ 9023 4888; Merchant Hotel, 35-39 Waring St; 2-/3-course lunch £16/20, mains £23-25; 🕒 7am-11pm) Set in the former banking hall of the Ulster Bank head office, the Great Room is a jaw-dropping extravaganza of gilded stucco, red plush, white marble cherubs and a vast crystal chandelier glittering beneath a glass dome. The menu matches the décor, decadent but delicious, a French-influenced catalogue of political incorrectness laced with foie gras, veal, truffles and caviar.

Cathedral Quarter & Around

John Hewitt Bar & Restaurant (☎ 9023 3768; 51 Donegall St; mains £5-7; 🕒 food served noon-3pm Mon-Sat) Named for the Belfast poet and socialist, this is a modern pub with a traditional atmosphere and a well-earned reputation for excellent food. The menu changes weekly, but includes inventive dishes such as broccoli and Cashel blue cheese tart with sauté potatoes and dressed salad. It's also a great place for a drink (see p601).

McHugh's Bar & Restaurant (☎ 9050 9999; 29-31 Queen's Sq; mains lunch £5-7, dinner £8-15; 🕒 food served noon-10pm Mon-Sat, noon-9pm Sun) This restored pub has a traditional feel with its old wooden booths and benches, and boasts one of the city's best bar-restaurants, serving traditional pub grub downstairs (till 7pm) and fancier dishes in the mezzanine restaurant upstairs (from 5pm). The house speciality is oriental stir-fries.

Hill Street Brasserie (☎ 9058 6868; 38 Hill St; mains lunch £5-7, dinner £14-22; 🕒 noon-3pm Mon-Sat, 5-11pm Tue-Sat) in keeping with the design studios and art galleries that throng the nearby streets, this little brasserie is desperately trendy, from the slate-and-wood floor to the aubergine-and-olive colour scheme. Dinner is a bit overpriced, but the lunch menu is a bargain offering a choice of home-made burgers, risotto of the day and a flavoursome and filling seafood chowder.

Nick's Warehouse (☎ 9043 9690; 35-39 Hill St; mains £10-19; 🕒 food served noon-2.30pm Mon-Fri, 6-9.30pm Tue-Sat) A Cathedral Quarter pioneer (opened in 1989), Nick's is an enormous red-brick and blonde-wood wine bar and restaurant buzzing with happy drinkers and diners. The menu is strong on inventive seafood and veggie dishes, such as grilled swordfish on coconut rice with a pineapple, chilli, and sweetcorn relish, and spinach, red pepper and parmesan roulade with a tomato sauce and basil pesto.

South Belfast

BUDGET

Maggie May's (☎ 9032 2662; 50 Botanic Ave; mains £3-6; 🕒 8am-10.30pm Mon-Sat, 10am-10.30pm Sun) This is a homely little café with two rows of cosy wooden booths, colourful murals of old Belfast, and a host of hungover students wolfing down huge Ulster fries at lunchtime. The all-day breakfast menu runs from tea and toast to pancakes and maple syrup, while lunch can be soup and a sarnie or steak-and-Guinness pie; puddings include Dime Bar and sticky toffee. BYOB.

Other Place (☎ 9020 7200; 79 Botanic Ave; mains £7-9; 🕒 8am-5pm) This is another student favourite where you can linger over the Sunday papers amid red brick, orange pine and antique *objets*, or damp down a rising hangover with big plates of lasagne, cajun pitta or home-made hamburgers. Breakfast served till 11am.

MIDRANGE

our pick **Molly's Yard** (☎ 9032 2600; 1 College Green Mews; lunch mains £5-8; 2-/3-course dinner £20/25; 🕒 noon-9.30pm Mon-Sat) A restored Victorian stables courtyard is the setting for this superb restaurant, with a cosy bar-bistro on the ground floor, outdoor tables in the yard and a rustic dining room in the airy roof space upstairs. The menu is seasonal and sticks to half a dozen each of starters and mains, ranging from gourmet confections such as penne and shredded confit duck with roast garlic and parmesan cream to hearty comfort food such as cottage pie. It also has its own microbrewery (see p602).

Café India (☎ 9066 6955; 42-46 Malone Rd; mains £7-10; 🕒 noon-2.30pm & 5-11.30pm Mon-Thu, noon-midnight Fri & Sat, 1-11.30pm Sun) A cut above your average curry house, Café India is a big, split-level barn of a place with a high, raftered ceiling and lots of varnished wood. The food is exceptionally good – we can recommend the *palok chaat* (spiced spinach and onion fritters) and chicken tikka *achari zeera* (tandoori chicken in a tangy sauce flavoured with cumin and pickles).

Deane's at Queen's (☎ 9038 2111; 1 College Gardens; mains £8-14; 🕒 11.30am-9pm Mon & Tue, 11.30am-10pm Wed-Sat, 1-5pm Sun) A chilled-out bar and grill from Belfast's top chef, Michael Deane, this place focuses on what could be described as good-value, gourmet pub grub, with a list of dishes that includes mussels in cider, leek and Gruyère tart, Lyonnaise sausage and mash with *choucroute* (shredded, pickled cabbage), and haddock and chips with mushy peas and dill tartare.

Café Conor (☎ 9066 3266; 11A Stranmillis Rd; mains £8-15; ⏲ 9am-11pm) Set in the glass-roofed former studio of William Conor, a Belfast artist, this is a laid-back bistro with a light and airy dining area dominated by a portrait of Conor himself. The menu offers a range of pastas, salads, burgers and stir-fries, along with Irish favourites such as sausage and champ with onion gravy. The breakfast menu, which includes waffles with bacon and maple syrup, is served till noon on weekdays, 3pm at weekends.

Serai (☎ 9032 4000; 1 University St; mains £10-12; ⏲ noon-2.30pm & 5.30-11pm Sat, noon-2.30pm & 5.30-10.30pm Sun) Crammed with well-heeled students gabbing over glasses of Chilean Sauv Blanc, Serai is a stylish bar-restaurant with an intriguing Asian fusion menu ranging from succulent chicken satay with salad dressed in soy sauce and sesame seeds, to stir-fried squid with lemongrass and chilli, and *ikan kukus* (fish steamed in banana leaf with hot-and-sour sauce). The early-bird menu, served 5.30pm to 7pm, offers a two-course dinner including one drink for £12.50.

Shu (☎ 9038 1655; 253 Lisburn Rd; mains £10-18; ⏲ noon-2.30pm & 6-9pm Mon-Fri, 7-9.30pm Sat) If you want to know who to blame for all those copycat designer restaurants with the dark-wood-and-chocolate-brown-leather look, then look no further. Lording it over the hipper-than-than-thou Lisburn Rd since 2000, Shu is the granddaddy of Belfast chic, a stylish restaurant with a basement bar that is still regularly winning awards for its food. The French-influenced menu includes frogs' legs and foie gras and dishes such as roast corn-fed chicken with ragout of white beans and lemon thyme, and wild mushroom, squash and ricotta *pithivier* (pastry parcel) with parsnip purée.

our pick Beatrice Kennedy's (☎ 9020 2290; 44 University Rd; mains £14-17; ⏲ 5-10.15pm Tue-Sat, 12.30-2.30pm & 5-8.15pm Sun) This is where Queen's students take their parents for a smart dinner. It offers a candle-lit Edwardian drawing-room décor of burgundy, bottle green and bare red brick, with polished floorboards, starched white linen and brown leather chairs, and

TOP FIVE TRADITIONAL PUBS

- Bittle's Bar (opposite)
- Crown Liquor Saloon (opposite)
- Duke of York (opposite)
- Kelly's Cellars (opposite)
- Morning Star (opposite)

a simple menu of superb cuisine, including home-made bread and ice cream. Enjoy dishes such as smoked trout and crab tart, and roast monkfish with butternut squash purée and fennel. There's a separate vegetarian menu with dishes such as spinach and apple tart with potato gratin and fennel salad. From 5pm to 7pm you can get a two-course dinner for £13.

Outside the Centre

An Caife (☎ 9096 4184; Cultúrlann MacAdam ÓFiaich, 216 Falls Rd, West Belfast; mains £5-7; ⏲ 9am-9pm Mon-Sat, 10am-6pm Sun) If you're exploring West Belfast, drop in to the café in this Irish language and arts centre (see p588) for some good home-cooked food – the menu includes stews, soups, pizzas, cakes, scones and fresh pastries.

Cutters River Grill (☎ 9080 5100; 4 Lockview Rd, Stranmillis; mains lunch £8-13, dinner £9-19; ⏲ food served noon-10pm) One of the few bar-restaurants in Belfast with a waterside setting, Cutters has a terrace overlooking the River Lagan where you can enjoy lunch – try home-made lasagne or smoked chicken salad – while watching sculls and eights from the nearby rowing club messing about on the river.

DRINKING

Belfast's pub scene is lively and friendly, with the older traditional pubs complemented – and increasingly threatened – by a rising tide of stylish designer bars.

Standard opening hours are 11am or 11.30am to midnight or 1am, and 12.30pm to 11pm or midnight Sunday; some pubs remain closed all day Sunday, or don't open till 4pm or 6pm.

The worst thing about drinking in Belfast is getting past the bouncers on the door – the huge number of security staff employed in the city means that polite, well-trained doormen are a rarity. Some of the flashier bars have a dress code – usually no training shoes, no jeans, no baseball caps (so that the security cameras can get a clear shot of your face) and definitely no football colours. A few even specify 'No political tattoos'.

City Centre

Crown Liquor Saloon (☎ 9024 9476; 46 Great Victoria St) Belfast's most famous bar has a wonderfully ornate Victorian interior. Despite being a tourist attraction (see p583), it still fills up with crowds of locals at lunchtime and in the early evening.

Garrick Bar (☎ 9032 1984; 29 Chichester St) Established in 1870, but recently refurbished, the Garrick hangs on to a traditional atmosphere with acres of dark wood panelling, tiled floors, a pillared bar and old brass oil lamps. There are snug booths with buttoned leather benches, and a real coal fire in each room. There's traditional music sessions in the front bar from 9pm on Wednesdays, and 5pm to 9pm Fridays.

Irene & Nan's (☎ 9023 9123; 12 Brunswick St) Named after two pensioners from a nearby pub who fancied themselves as glamour queens, Irene & Nan's typifies the new breed of Belfast bar, dripping with designer chic and tempting your taste buds with an in-bar bistro. It's a laid-back place with a 1950s retro theme, good food and good cocktails.

Morning Star (☎ 9023 5986; 17 Pottinger's Entry) One of several traditional pubs hidden away in the pedestrian alleys off High St, the Morning Star dates back to at least 1810 when it was mentioned in the *Belfast News Letter* as a terminal for the Dublin to Belfast stage coach. It has a big sweeping horseshoe bar, and cosy snugs for privacy. See also p597.

White's Tavern (☎ 9024 3080; 1-4 Wine Cellar Entry) Established in 1630 but rebuilt in 1790, White's claims to be Belfast's oldest tavern (unlike a pub, a tavern provided food and lodging). Downstairs is a traditional Irish bar with open peat fire and live folk music Wednesday to Saturday, upstairs is all red brick, pine and polished copper, with DJs playing from Thursday to Saturday.

Kelly's Cellars (☎ 9032 4835; 1 Bank St) Kelly's is Belfast's oldest pub (1720) – as opposed to tavern; see White's Tavern – and was a meeting place for Henry Joy McCracken and the United Irishmen when they were planning the 1798 Rising. The story goes that McCracken hid behind the bar when British soldiers came for him. It remains resolutely old-fashioned, with vaulted ceiling and elbow-worn bar, is crammed with bric-a-brac and pulls in broad cross-section of Belfast society.

Bittle's Bar (☎ 9031 1088; 103 Victoria St) A cramped and staunchly traditional bar that occupies Belfast's only 'flat iron' building, Bittle's is a 19th-century triangular red-brick building decorated with gilded shamrocks. The wedge-shaped interior is covered in paintings of Ireland's literary heroes by local artist Joe O'Kane. Pride of place on the back wall is taken by a large canvas depicting Yeats, Joyce, Behan and Beckett at the bar with glasses of Guinness, and Wilde pulling the pints on the other side.

Cathedral Quarter & Around

John Hewitt Bar & Restaurant (☎ 9023 3768; 51 Donegall St) The John Hewitt is one of those treasured bars that have no TV and no gaming machines; the only noise here is the murmur of conversation. As well as Guinness, the bar serves Hilden real ales from nearby Lisburn, plus Hoegaarden and Erdinger wheat beers. There are regular sessions of folk, jazz and bluegrass from 6pm on Saturday, 3pm Sunday, and around 9pm the rest of the week. See also p599.

Northern Whig (☎ 9050 9888; 2 Bridge St) A stylish modern bar set in an elegant Georgian printing works, the Northern Whig's airy interior is dominated by three huge Socialist-Realist statues rescued from Prague in the early 1990s. Its relaxing sofas and armchairs in fashionable chocolate and café-au-lait colours encourage serious afternoon loafing, though the pace hots up considerably after 5pm on Friday and Saturday when the stag- and hen-party crowd starts knocking back the WKDs and Bacardi Breezers.

Duke of York (☎ 9024 1062; 11 Commercial Ct) Hidden away down an alley in the heart of the city's former newspaper district, the snug, traditional Duke was a hang-out for print workers and journalists and still pulls in a few hacks. One claim to fame is that the Sinn Féin leader, Gerry Adams, worked behind the bar here during his student days.

Spaniard (☎ 9023 2448; 3 Skipper St) Forget 'style': this narrow, crowded bar, which looks as if it's been squeezed into someone's flat, has more atmosphere in one battered sofa than most 'style bars' have in their shiny entirety. Friendly staff, good beer, an eclectic crowd and cool tunes played at a volume that still allows you to talk: bliss. On Sunday from 9pm to midnight is You Say We Play, with the DJ playing requests only.

Rotterdam (☎ 9074 6021; 54 Pilot St) The Rotterdam is a purist's pub, unrepentantly old-fashioned and wonderfully atmospheric, with stone floors, an open fire, low ceilings and perfectly poured Guinness. It's famed for the quality of its live-music sessions – jazz, folk, rock or blues plays most nights, and in summer the tables, and the gigs, spill outdoors.

South Belfast

Eglantine (☎ 9038 1994; 32 Malone Rd) The 'Eg' is a local institution, and widely reckoned to be the best of Belfast's student pubs. It serves good beer and good food, and there are DJs spinning most nights. Wicked Wednesday pulls in the crowds with an electric rodeo bull, bouncy boxing, sumo-wrestler suits and other fun, and Tuesday is the big music and entertainment quiz night. Expect to see a few stag and hen parties stagger through at weekends.

Botanic Inn (☎ 9050 9740; 23-27 Malone Rd) The 'Bot' is the second pillar of Malone Rd's unholy trinity of student pubs, along with the 'Eg' and the 'Welly Park' (Wellington Park). The latter has sadly been renovated into airport-departure-lounge anonymity, but the Bot is still a wild place, with dancing in the upstairs Top of the Bot club Thursday to Saturday (people queue down the street to get in), live folk music from 9pm on Wednesday, and big-screen sport when there's a match on.

Globe (☎ 9050 9848; 36 University Rd) This popular student pub seems to be the karaoke capital of Belfast, with sing-it-yourself sessions almost every night; the pseudo-1970s décor goes well with the wild retro sessions on Wednesday nights. On Saturday afternoons sport is the order of the day with football or rugby blaring on half a dozen giant screens.

Molly's Yard (☎ 9032 2600; 1 College Green Mews; ♥ closed Sun) This atmospheric restaurant-bar (see also p599) is home to Northern Ireland's first microbrewery, producing three varieties of real ale – Belfast Blonde (a continental-style lager), Molly's Chocolate Stout and Headless Dog, a dark amber ale with a refreshingly hoppy and slightly flowery flavour.

ENTERTAINMENT

The Belfast Welcome Centre issues *Whatabout?*, a free monthly guide to Belfast events, with pub, club and restaurant listings. The Thursday issue of the *Belfast Telegraph* has an Entertainment section with club, gig and cinema listings, as does the Scene section in Friday's *Irish News*.

The **Big List** (www.thebiglist.co.uk) is a weekly freesheet, published on Wednesday, that covers pubs, clubs and music events all over Northern Ireland, although the emphasis is heavily on Belfast. The **Belfast Beat** (www.adman publishing.com) is a free monthly guide listing what's on where on Friday and Saturday. **ArtsListings** (www.artslistings.com) is another free monthly that covers the arts scene throughout the whole of Northern Ireland.

Clubbing

Club hours are generally 9pm to 3am, with no admittance after 1am.

Milk (☎ 9027 8876; www.clubmilk.com; Tomb St; admission £5-10; ♥ Wed-Sun) Set in a converted red-brick warehouse, Milk has maintained its position as one of Belfast's hottest and most sophisticated clubs. Snatch on Thursday is the city's biggest R&B and hip-hop night, Fridays are for disco, house and electro, and on Saturday resident and guest DJs play house.

La Lea (☎ 9023 0200; www.lalea.com; 43 Franklin St; admission £2-5; ♥ from 9pm Wed-Sat) Billed as Belfast's most prestigious nightclub, La Lea caters to a cocktail-sipping, style-conscious over-23 crowd (which translates as 'no students'), with a strict door policy to keep out the riff-raff. Impressive décor with space-age lighting and huge Cambodian stone heads.

QUB Student Union (☎ 0870 241 0126; www.qub students.com; Mandela Hall, Queen's Students Union, University Rd) The student union has various bars and music venues hosting club nights, live bands and stand-up comedy. The monthly Shine (www.shine.net; first Saturday of the month; admission £19) is one of the city's best club nights with resident and guest DJs pumping out harder and heavier dance music than most of Belfast's other clubs.

Stiff Kitten (☎ 9023 8700; www.thestiffkitten.com; Bankmore Sq, Dublin Rd; admission £5-10; ♥ 11am-1am Mon-Wed, to 2am Thu, to 2.30am Fri, to 3am Sat, to midnight Sun) If the student union is too grungy a venue for your tastes head for the Stiff Kitten, a stylish new bar and club under the same management as Shine. Same serious attitude to the music, but distinctly glitzier, appealing to an over-25 crowd.

Gay & Lesbian Venues

Belfast's rapidly expanding gay scene is concentrated in the Cathedral Quarter. For information on what's happening, check out www.gaybelfast.net and www.queerni.com.

Kremlin (☎ 9080 9700; www.kremlin-belfast.com; 96 Donegall St; ☽ 9pm-2.30am Tue, 9pm-3am Wed-Sun) Gay-owned and operated, the Soviet-kitsch-themed Kremlin is the heart and soul of Northern Ireland's gay scene. A statue of Lenin guides you into Tsar, the pre-club bar, from where the Long Bar leads into the main clubbing zone, Red Square. There's something going on seven nights a week – Event Horizon (admission £5, midnight to 6am) on Saturdays is the city's only all-night club.

Dubarrys Bar (☎ 9032 3590; www.dubarrysbar .co.uk; 10-14 Gresham St) One of Belfast's newest gay venues, Dubarrys is aimed at a slightly older, more sophisticated crowd who are looking for designer décor, cool tunes and conversation rather than flashing lights and banging dance music. Lick! (www.lick-women.com) is a lesbian club night, held at Dubarrys the third Friday of the month.

Mynt (☎ 9023 4520; www.myntbelfast.com; 2-16 Dunbar St) Another new club complex with a vast, luxurious lounge bar and two club spaces, Mynt provides entertainment all through the week, culminating in hilarious Sunday-night game shows hosted by Belfast's favourite drag queen, Baroness Titti von Tramp.

Union Street (☎ 9031 6060; www.unionstreetpub .com; 8-14 Union St) A stylish modern bar with retro styling and lots of bare brick and dark wood – check out the Belfast sinks in the loo – Union Street pulls in a mixed gay and straight crowd, attracted by the laid-back atmosphere and good food.

Other gay-friendly pubs include the **Nest** (☎ 9032 5491; 22-28 Skipper St), the John Hewitt (p601) and the Spaniard (p601).

Live Music & Comedy

Big-name bands and performers play to sell-out crowds at the Ulster Hall, Waterfront Hall, Odyssey Arena or King's Hall.

MAJOR VENUES

Waterfront Hall (☎ 9033 4455; www.waterfront.co.uk; 2 Lanyon Pl) The impressive 2235-seat Waterfront is Belfast's flagship concert venue, hosting local, national and international performers from pop stars to symphony orchestras.

Odyssey Arena (☎ 9073 9074; www.odysseyarena .com; 2 Queen's Quay) The home stadium for the Belfast Giants ice-hockey team is also the venue for big entertainment events such as rock and pop concerts, stage shows and indoor sports.

King's Hall (☎ 9066 5225; www.kingshall.co.uk; Lisburn Rd) Northern Ireland's biggest exhibition and conference centre hosts a range of music shows, trade fairs and sporting events. It's accessible by any bus along Lisburn Rd or by train to Balmoral Station.

ROCK

Belfast Empire (☎ 9024 9276; www.thebelfastempire .com; 42 Botanic Ave; admission £4-10) A converted late-Victorian church with three floors of entertainment, the Empire is a legendary live-music venue. The regular Thursday night Gifted session showcases the best of new talent, both local and UK-wide, while Saturday is either big-name bands or tribute bands. There's stand-up comedy every Tuesday.

Limelight (☎ 9032 5942; www.the-limelight.co.uk; 17-19 Ormeau Ave) This combined pub and club along with next-door venue the Spring and Airbrake (under the same management) is one of the city's top venues for live rock and indie music, having hosted bands from Oasis to Franz Ferdinand, the Manic Street Preachers and the Kaiser Chiefs. It's also home to alternative club night Helter Skelter (admission £5, from 10pm every Saturday) and Belfast's biggest student night Shag (admission £3, from 10pm every Tuesday).

Lavery's (☎ 9087 1106; www.lavs.co.uk; 14 Bradbury Pl) Managed by the same family since 1918, Lavery's is a vast, multilevel, packed-to-the-gills boozing emporium, crammed with drinkers young and old, from students to tourists, businessmen to bikers. The Back Bar has live acoustic music from local singer-songwriters on Wednesday and live indie and alternative bands on Thursday, while the Bunker stages various local and touring bands Sunday to Thursday and DJs Friday and Saturday.

FOLK, JAZZ & BLUES

Pubs with regular live sessions of traditional Irish music include the Botanic Inn, the Garrick Bar, White's Tavern, the John

Hewitt, Kelly's Cellars and the Rotterdam (see Drinking).

For jazz and blues, head for the John Hewitt, McHugh's, the Rotterdam (all under Drinking), the Crescent Arts Centre (right) or the **Kitchen Bar** (☎ 9032 4901; www.thekitchenbar .com; 38 Victoria Sq).

CLASSICAL MUSIC

Ulster Hall (☎ 9032 3900; www.ulsterhall.co.uk; Bedford St) Ulster Hall (built in 1862) is a popular venue for a range of events including rock concerts, lunch-time organ recitals, boxing bouts and performances by the Ulster Orchestra (www .ulster-orchestra.org.uk). It's closed for renovations until the end of 2008.

Queen's University's **School of Music** (☎ 9033 5337; www.music.qub.ac.uk; University Rd) stages free lunchtime recitals on Thursday and regular evening concerts in the beautiful, hammer-beam-roofed Harty Room (School of Music, University Sq), and at the Sonic Arts Research Centre (Cloreen Park), with occasional performances in the larger Sir William Whitla Hall (University Rd). You can download a programme from the website.

COMEDY

There's no dedicated comedy club in the city, but there are regular comedy nights at various venues including the **Spring and Airbrake** (Ormeau Ave), the Belfast Empire (p603), and the QUB Student Union (p602).

Theatre & Opera

Grand Opera House (☎ 9024 1919; www.goh.co.uk; 2-4 Great Victoria St; ☷ box office 8.30am-9pm Mon-Fri, to 6pm Sat) This grand old venue plays host to a mixture of opera, popular musicals and comedy shows. The box office is across the street on the corner of Howard St.

Lyric Theatre (☎ 9038 1081; www.lyrictheatre.co.uk; 55 Ridgeway St; ☷ box office 10am-7pm Mon-Fri, 4-7pm Sat) On the riverside south of the Botanic Gardens, the Lyric stages serious drama and is a major venue for the Belfast Festival at Queen's (see p594). Hollywood star Liam Neeson, who first trod the boards here, is a patron.

Old Museum Arts Centre (☎ 9023 3332; www.old museumartscentre.org; 7 College Sq N; ☷ box office 9.30am-5.30pm Mon-Sat, to 7.30pm before a performance) The Old Museum stages an exciting programme of drama and comedy, with occasional prose and poetry readings and dance performances.

Crescent Arts Centre (☎ 9024 2338; www.crescentarts .org; 2-4 University Rd) The Crescent hosts a range of concerts, plays, workshops, readings and dance classes, and there's a regular club night called New Moon (10pm to late, admission £6, first Saturday of each month), which showcases live bands, with DJs playing afterwards. The Crescent also stages a 10-day literary festival called Between the Lines each March, and a dance festival, City Dance, in June.

Black Box (☎ 9024 4400; www.blackboxbelfast.com; 18-22 Hill St) Describing itself as a 'home for live music, theatre, literature, comedy, film, visual art, live art, circus, cabaret and all points in between', Black Box is a new and intimate venue in the heart of the Cathedral Quarter.

Cinemas

Movie House (☎ 9024 5700; www.moviehouse.co.uk; 14 Dublin Rd) A convenient city-centre 10-screen multiplex.

Queen's Film Theatre (☎ 9097 1097; www.queens filmtheatre.com; 20 University Sq) A two-screen arthouse cinema close to the university, and a major venue for the Belfast Film Festival.

Storm Cinemas (☎ 9073 9134; www.stormcinemas .co.uk; Odyssey Pavilion) Belfast's biggest multiplex, with 12 screens and stadium seats throughout; part of the Odyssey Complex.

Sport

Rugby, soccer, Gaelic football and hockey are played through the winter, cricket and hurling through the summer.

Windsor Park (☎ 9024 4198; off Lisburn Rd) International soccer matches take place here, south of the centre; for details of Northern Ireland international matches, see www.irishfa.com.

Casement Park (☎ 9038 3815; www.antrimgaa.net; Andersonstown Rd) In West Belfast, you can see Gaelic football and hurling here.

Odyssey Arena (☎ 9073 9074; www.odysseyarena .com; 2 Queen's Quay) The Belfast Giants ice-hockey team draws big crowds to the area at the Odyssey Complex; the season is September to March. The arena also hosts indoor sporting events including tennis and athletics.

SHOPPING

For general shopping you'll find all the usual high-street chains and department stores in the compact central shopping area north of City Hall. The main shopping malls are the **Castle Court Centre** (Royal Ave) and the brand new **Victoria Square** (btwn Ann & Chichester St). There's late-night shopping till 9pm on Thursdays.

Newer shopping districts include the ultra-hip Lisburn Rd (from Eglantine Ave out to Balmoral Ave) – a straggling strip of red-brick and mock-Tudor façades lined with fashion boutiques, interior-design shops, art galleries, delicatessens, espresso bars, wine bars and chic restaurants – and the unexpected concentration of designer fashion shops (about a dozen of them) on Bloomfield Ave in East Belfast.

Items particular to Northern Ireland that you may like to look out for include fine Belleek china, linen (antique and new) and Tyrone crystal.

Wicker Man (☎ 9024 3550; 12 Donegall Arcade; ☻ 9am-6pm Mon-Wed & Fri, 9am-9pm Thu, 9am-5.30pm Sat, 1-5pm Sun) This shop sells a wide range of contemporary Irish crafts and gifts, including silver jewellery, glassware and knitwear.

Fresh Garbage (☎ 9024 2350; 24 Rosemary St; ☻ 10.30am-5.30pm Mon-Wed, Fri & Sat, 10.30am-8pm Thu) Easily recognised by the glumfest of Goths hovering outside the door, this place has been around for more than 20 years but remains a cult favourite for hippie and Goth clothes and Celtic jewellery.

Steensons (☎ 9024 8269; Bedford House, Bedford St; 10am-5.30pm Mon-Sat, to 7pm Thu) Showroom selling a range of stylish handmade jewellery in contemporary designs in silver, gold and platinum, from a workshop in Glenarm, County Antrim (p672).

Archive's Antique Centre (☎ 9023 2383; 88 Donegall Pass; ☻ 10.30am-5.30pm Mon-Fri, 10am-6pm Sat) This is a warren of curios and collectables spread over three floors, with Irish silver, brass, pub memorabilia, militaria, books and light fittings.

Tiso (☎ 9023 1230; 12-14 Cornmarket; ☻ 9.30am-5.30pm Mon, Tue, Fri & Sat, 10am-5.30pm Wed, 9.30am-8pm Thu, 1-5pm Sun) Make tracks to Tiso for hiking, climbing and camping gear and outdoor clothing.

Surf Mountain (☎ 9024 8877; 12 Brunswick St; ☻ 9am-5.30pm Mon-Sat) Yo dude – come and join the goatee-stroking, nad-scratching crew checking out Surf Mountain's skate and snowboard gear.

Black & Lizars (☎ 9032 1768; 8 Wellington Pl; ☻ 9am-5.30pm Mon-Sat) The place to go for all your photographic needs, both film and digital.

Matchetts Music (☎ 9026 8661; 6 Wellington Pl; ☻ 9am-5.30pm Mon-Sat) Stocks a range of acoustic instruments, from guitars and mandolins to penny whistles and bodhráns, as well as

books of lyrics and guitar chords for traditional Irish songs.

Phoenix Records (☎ 9023 9308; Haymarket Arcade, Royal Ave; 10am-5pm Mon-Sat) Owned by music producer Terry Hooley, the man who released *Teenage Kicks* by the Undertones on his Good Vibrations label back in 1978, this is Belfast's best alternative record shop and a source of tickets and info on the latest gigs.

Other good places to shop for Irish crafts and traditional Irish music include Cultúrlann MacAdam ÓFiaich (p588; open 9am to 5.30pm Monday to Friday, 10am to 5.30pm Saturday) and Conway Mill (p588; open 10am to 4pm Monday to Friday).

GETTING THERE & AWAY
Air
Flights from North America, continental Europe and several major UK airports land at **Belfast International Airport** (☎ 9448 4848; www.belfastairport.com; Aldergrove), 30km northwest of the city. For further information, see p716.

There are direct flights from Cork, Galway and most British cities to the convenient **George Best Belfast City Airport** (☎ 9093 9093; www.belfastcityairport.com; Airport Rd), just 6km northeast of the city centre.

Boat
The terminal for **Stena Line** (☎ 0870 570 7070; www.stenaline.co.uk) car ferries from Belfast to Stranraer in Scotland is 2km north of the city centre; head north along York St, and turn right into Dock St (just past the Yorkgate Centre). Other car ferries to and from Scotland dock at Larne, 30km north of Belfast (see p719).

Norfolkline (☎ 0870 600 4321; www.norfolkline-ferries.co.uk) ferries between Belfast and Liverpool dock at the Victoria terminal, 5km north of town. Take the M2 motorway north and turn right at junction No 1.

The **Steam Packet Company** (☎ 0871 222 1333; www.steam-packet.com) operates car ferries between Belfast and Isle of Man (two or three a week, April to September only). They dock at Donegall Quay, a short distance from the city centre.

For more information on ferry routes and prices, see p719.

Bus
Belfast has two bus stations. The main **Europa BusCentre** (☎ 9066 6630) is behind the Europa

Hotel and next door to Great Victoria St train station, reached via the Great Northern Mall beside the hotel. It's the main terminus for buses to Derry, Dublin and destinations in the west and south of Northern Ireland. The smaller **Laganside BusCentre** (☎ 9066 6630; Oxford St), near the river, is mainly for buses to County Antrim, eastern County Down and the Cookstown area.

There are **information desks** (7.45am-6.30pm Mon-Fri, 8am-6pm Sat) at both bus stations, where you can pick up regional bus timetables, and you can contact **Translink** (☎ 9066 6630; www.translink.co.uk) for timetable and fares information.

Typical one-way fares from Belfast:

Service	Fare (£)	Duration (hr)	Frequency
Armagh	7	1¼	hourly Mon-Fri, 8 Sat, 3 Sun
Ballycastle	8	2	3 daily Mon-Sat
Bangor	3	¾	half-hourly Mon-Sat, 8 Sun
Derry	9	1¾	half-hourly Mon-Sat, 11 Sun
Downpatrick	4.50	1	at least hourly Mon-Fri, 6 Sat, 4 Sun
Dublin	10	3	hourly Mon-Sun
Enniskillen	9	2¼	hourly Mon-Sat, 2 Sun
Newcastle	6	1¼	hourly Mon-Sat, 7 Sun

National Express (☎ 0870 580 8080; www.nationalexpress.com) runs a daily coach service between Belfast and London (£34, 14 hours) via the Stranraer ferry, Dumfries, Carlisle, Preston, Manchester and Birmingham. The ticket office is in the Europa BusCentre.

For information on bus fares, durations and frequencies in Ireland, see p721.

Train

Trains to Dublin and all destinations in Northern Ireland depart from Belfast's **Central Station** (East Bridge St), east of the city centre. Trains for Portadown, Lisburn, Bangor, Larne Harbour and Derry depart from **Great Victoria St Station** (Great Northern Mall), next to the Europa BusCentre.

For information on fares and timetables, contact **Translink** (☎ 9066 6630; www.translink.co.uk). The **NIR Travel Shop** (☎ 9023 0671; Great Victoria St Station; 9am-5pm Mon-Fri, to 12.30pm Sat) books train tickets, ferries and holiday packages.

If you arrive by train at Central Station, your rail ticket entitles you to a free bus ride into the city centre.

Typical train fares from Belfast:

Service	Fare (£)	Duration (hr)	Frequency
Bangor	4	½	half-hourly Mon-St, 8 Sun
Derry	10	2¼	7 or 8 daily Mon-Sat, 4 Sun
Dublin	24	2	8 daily Mon-Sat, 5 Sun
Larne Harbour	5	1	hourly
Newry	8	¾	10 daily Mon-Sat, 5 Sun
Portrush	8	1¾	7 or 8 daily Mon-Sat, 4 Sun

On Sundays you can buy a Sunday Day Tracker ticket (£5), which allows unlimited travel on all scheduled train services within Northern Ireland.

For more information on the train network in Ireland, see p725.

GETTING AROUND

Belfast possesses a rare but wonderful thing – an integrated public-transport system, with buses linking both airports to the central train and bus stations.

To/From the Airports

The Airport Express 300 bus runs from **Belfast International Airport** to the Europa BusCentre (one way/return £6/9, 30 minutes) every 10 or 15 minutes between 7am and 8pm, every 30 minutes from 8pm to 11pm, and hourly through the night; a return ticket is valid for one month. A taxi costs about £25.

The Airport Express 600 bus links **George Best Belfast City Airport** with the Europa BusCentre (one way/return £1.30/2.20, 15 minutes) every 15 or 20 minutes between 6am and 10pm. The taxi fare to the city centre is about £7.

For details of the Airporter bus linking both airports to Derry, see p653.

To/From the Ferry Terminals

You can walk from Donegall Quay to City Hall in about 15 minutes. Alternatively, Laganside BusCentre is only a five-minute walk away. There is no public transport to the Stena Line and Norfolk Line ferry terminals.

Trains to the ferry terminal at Larne Harbour depart from Great Victoria St Station.

Bicycle

National Cycle Network route 9 runs through central Belfast, mostly following the western bank of the River Lagan and the north shore of Belfast Lough.

You can hire bikes from **McConvey Cycles** (☎ 9033 0322; www.mcconveycycles.com; 183 Ormeau Rd; ☺ 9am-6pm Mon-Sat, to 8pm Thu) and Life Cycles (p593) from around £10 a day, or £40 a week.

Bus

Metro (☎ 9066 6630; www.translink.co.uk) operates the bus network in Belfast. An increasing number of buses are low-floor, 'kneeling' buses with space for one wheelchair.

Buy your ticket from the driver (change given); fares range from £1 to £1.60 depending on distance. The driver can also sell you a Metro Day Ticket (£3.50), giving unlimited bus travel within the City Zone all day Monday to Saturday. Cheaper versions allow travel any time after 10am Monday to Saturday (£2.50), or all day Sunday (£2.50).

Most city bus services depart from various stops on and around Donegall Sq, at City Hall. You can pick up a free bus map (and buy tickets) from the **Metro kiosk** (☺ 8am-5.30pm Mon-Fri) at the northwest corner of the square.

If you plan on using city buses a lot, it's worth buying a Smartlink Travel Card (available from the Metro kiosk, the Belfast Welcome Centre, and the Europa and Laganside Bus-Centres). The card costs an initial fee of £1.50, plus £5/10 per five/ten journeys – you can get it topped up as you want. Alternatively, you can get seven days' unlimited travel for £15.50. When you board the bus, you simply place the card on the ticket machine, and it automatically issues a ticket.

Car & Motorcycle

A car can be more of a hindrance than a help in Belfast, as parking is restricted in the city centre. For on-street parking between 8am and 6pm Monday to Saturday, you'll need to buy a ticket from a machine. For longer periods, head for one of the many multistorey car parks that are dotted around the city centre.

Major car hire agencies in Belfast:

Avis (www.avisworld.com) City (☎ 9024 0404; 69-71 Great Victoria St); George Best Belfast City Airport (☎ 0870 608 6317); Belfast International Airport (☎ 0870 608 6316)

Budget (www.budget-ireland.co.uk) City (☎ 9023 0700; 96-102 Great Victoria St); George Best Belfast City Airport (☎ 9045 1111); Belfast International Airport (☎ 9442 3332)

Europcar (www.europcar.com) George Best Belfast City Airport (☎ 9045 0904); Belfast International Airport (☎ 9442 3444)

Hertz (www.hertz.co.uk) George Best Belfast City Airport (☎ 9073 2451) Belfast International Airport (☎ 9442 2533)

PEOPLE'S TAXIS

The black taxis that cruise along the Falls and Shankill Rds in West Belfast have more in common with Turkey's 'dolmuş' minibuses than the black cabs of London. These are shared taxis that operate along fixed routes, departing only when full, then dropping off and picking up passengers as they go, more like buses than traditional taxis.

Indeed, the 'People's Taxis', as they became known, were introduced in the 1970s to replace local bus services that had been disrupted or cancelled as a result of street riots at the height of the Troubles. The drivers' associations that run the taxis are community-based ventures that provided much-needed employment during difficult times, and often gave jobs to ex-internees and prisoners who could not find work elsewhere. More than 30 years on, the black taxis are an accepted part of Belfast's public transport infrastructure. There is even a black taxi 'bus station' at Castle Junction.

Falls Rd taxis depart from Castle Junction at the corner of King and Castle Sts. During the day a sign in the windscreen shows their route; after 5.30pm the first person in the queue dictates the destination. You can hail a taxi anywhere; when you want to get out, knock on the window, and then pay the driver from the footpath.

Shankill Rd taxis depart from North St. You can hail them at bus stops; when you want to get out, say 'next stop' to the driver, and pay before you get out. Fares on both services are around £1 to £2 per person.

The Ireland-wide agency **Dooley Car Rentals** (☎ 9445 2522; www.dooleycarrentals.com; 175 Airport Rd, Belfast International Airport, Aldergrove) is reliable and offers good rates – around £130 a week for a compact car. You have to pay an extra £48 up front for a full tank of petrol, but if you return the car with an almost empty tank they're cheaper than the big names.

Taxi

For information on the black cabs that ply the Falls and Shankill Rds, see boxed text, p607. Regular black taxis have yellow plates back and front and can be hailed on the street.

Minicabs are cheaper but you have to order one by phone. Companies to call include **Fona Cab** (☎ 9023 3333) and **Value Cabs** (☎ 9080 9080).

Train

There are local trains every 20 or 30 minutes connecting Great Victoria St and Central Stations via City Hospital and Botanic Stations. There's a flat fare of £1 for journeys between any of these stops.

AROUND BELFAST

LISBURN & AROUND

The southwestern fringes of Belfast extend as far as Lisburn (Lios na gCearrbhach),

12km southwest of the city centre. Like Belfast, Lisburn grew rich on the proceeds of the linen industry in the 18th and 19th centuries. This history is celebrated in the excellent **Irish Linen Centre & Lisburn Museum** (☎ 9266 3377; Market Sq; admission free; ☻ 9.30am-5pm Mon-Sat), housed in the fine 17th-century Market House.

The museum on the ground floor has displays on the cultural and historic heritage of the region, while upstairs the award-winning 'Flax to Fabric' exhibition details the fascinating history of the linen industry in Northern Ireland – on the eve of WWI Ulster was the largest linen-producing region in the world, employing some 75,000 people.

There are plenty of audiovisual and hands-on exhibits – you can watch weavers working on Jacquard looms and even try your hand at spinning flax.

Lisburn Tourist Information Centre (☎ 9266 0038; Lisburn Sq; ☻ 9.30am-5pm Mon-Sat) is on the town's main square.

Buses 523, 530 and 532 from Belfast's Upper Queen St go to Lisburn (£2.30, 40 minutes, half-hourly Monday to Friday, hourly Saturday and Sunday), or catch the train (£3, 30 minutes, at least half-hourly Monday to Saturday, hourly Sunday) from either Belfast Central or Great Victoria St Stations.

ULSTER FOLK & TRANSPORT MUSEUMS

Two of Northern Ireland's finest **museums** (☎ 9042 8428; www.uftm.org.uk; Cultra, Holywood; per museum adult/child £5.50/3.50, combined ticket £7/4; ☻ 10am-6pm Mon-Sat, 11am-6pm Sun Jul-Sep, 10am-5pm Mon-Fri, 10am-6pm Sat, 11am-6pm Sun Mar-Jun, 10am-4pm Mon-Fri, 10am-5pm Sat, 11am-5pm Sun Oct-Feb) lie close to each other on either side of the A2.

On the south side is the Folk Museum, where farmhouses, forges, churches and mills, and a complete village have been reconstructed, with human and animal extras combining to give a strong impression of Irish life over the past few hundred years. From industrial times, there are red-brick terraces from 19th-century Belfast and Dromore. In summer, thatching and ploughing are demonstrated and there are characters dressed in period costume.

On the other side of the road is the Transport Museum, a sort of automotive zoo with displays of captive steam locomotives, rolling stock, motorcycles, trams, buses and cars.

Highlight of the car collection is the stainless steel–clad prototype of the ill-fated DeLorean DMC, made in Belfast in 1981. The car was a commercial disaster but achieved fame in the *Back to the Future* films.

Most popular is the RMS *Titanic* **display** (www.titanicinbelfast.com), which includes the original design drawings for the *Olympic* and *Titanic,* photographs of the ship's construction and reports of its sinking. Most poignant are the items of pre-sailing publicity, including an ad for the return trip that never was.

Buses to Bangor stop nearby. Cultra Station on the Belfast to Bangor train line is within a 10-minute walk.

Counties Down & Armagh

Seen from the hilltop viewpoint of Scrabo Tower, the treasures of County Down lie scattered around you like jewels on a table. The sparkling, island-fringed waters of Strangford Lough stretch to the south, with the bird-haunted mudflats of Castle Espie and Nendrum's ancient monastery on one shore, and the elegant country house of Mount Stewart and the picturesque Ards Peninsula on the other.

On a clear day you can see the Mourne Mountains in the distance, their velvet curves sweeping down to the sea, above the Victorian seaside resort of Newcastle. This compact range of granite and heather peaks offers the best hill-walking in the North, with expansive views of mountain, crag and sea. Nearby are Downpatrick and Lecale, the old stamping grounds of Ireland's patron saint.

Down is a region of lush fields and fertile farmland, a rich landscape in more ways than one – this is Belfast's wealthy hinterland, studded with expensive villas and endowed with more than its fair share of top golf courses and gourmet restaurants. It's easily reached from the capital, and at weekends you'll find city folks browsing the antique shops in Saintfield and Greyabbey, or slurping down fresh oysters in Dundrum and Portaferry.

Down's neighbour County Armagh is largely rural, from the low, rugged hills of the south to the lush apple orchards and strawberry fields of the north, with Ireland's ecclesiastical capital, the neat little city of Armagh, in the middle. With the army watch-towers gone, south Armagh is once again a peaceful backwater where you can wander back and forth across the border with the Republic without even noticing.

HIGHLIGHTS

- **Head for the Hills** The granite peaks of the Mourne Mountains (p627)
- **A Taste of Ulster** Top-notch restaurants in Hillsborough (opposite), Portaferry (p617) and Strangford (p624)
- **To the Manor Born** The stately halls and exquisite gardens of Mount Stewart House (p618)
- **Wildlife Encounter** Bird-watching at Castle Espie (p620) or seal-spotting near Portaferry (p617)
- **Rural Retreat** Off the beaten track in the back roads of South Armagh (p632)

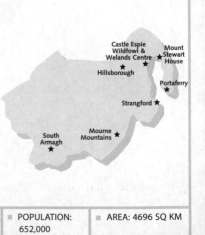

Castle Espie Wildfowl & Welands Centre ★

Mount Stewart House ★

Hillsborough ★

Portaferry ★

Strangford ★

Mourne Mountains ★

South Armagh ★

| ■ TELEPHONE AREA CODE: 028 FROM BRITAIN AND REST OF WORLD, 048 FROM REPUBLIC OF IRELAND | ■ POPULATION: 652,000 | ■ AREA: 4696 SQ KM |

COUNTY DOWN

CENTRAL COUNTY DOWN

Rich farmland spreads to the south of Belfast with only the rough moorland of Slieve Croob, southwest of Ballynahinch, breaking the flatness of the terrain. The attractive towns of Hillsborough and Banbridge lie on the main A1 road from Belfast to Newry.

Hillsborough

pop 2400

Hillsborough is a name familiar to British ears as the official residence of the Secretary of State for Northern Ireland – Hillsborough Castle is used to entertain visiting heads of state (US presidents George W Bush and Bill Clinton have both enjoyed its hospitality). It's also the Queen's official residence when she is in Northern Ireland.

The elegant little town of Hillsborough (Cromghlinn) was founded in the 1640s by Colonel Arthur Hill, who built a fort here to quell Irish insurgents. Fine Georgian architecture rings the square and lines Main St.

The **tourist information centre** (☎ 9268 9717; tic .hillsborough@lisburn.gov.uk; the Square; ☯ 9am-5.30pm Mon-Sat year-round, 2-6pm Sun Jul & Aug) is in the Georgian courthouse in the centre of the village.

SIGHTS & ACTIVITIES

The town's main attraction is **Hillsborough Castle** (☎ 9268 2244; Main St; guided tour adult/child £5/3.50, grounds only £2.50; ☯ 11am-4.30pm Sat May & Jun), a rambling, two-storey, late-Georgian mansion built in 1797 for Wills Hill, the first marquess of Downshire, and extensively remodelled in the 1830s and 1840s. The guided tour takes in the state drawing room and dining rooms, and the Lady Grey Room where UK Prime Minister Tony Blair and US President George W Bush had talks on Iraq in 2003.

Hillsborough Courthouse (☎ 9268 9717; tic.hills borough@lisburn.gov.uk; the Square; admission free; ☯ 9am-5.30pm Mon-Sat year-round, 2-6pm Sun Jul & Aug), a fine old Georgian building, houses various displays describing the working of the courts in the 18th and 19th centuries.

At the bottom of Main St is a statue of Arthur Hill, fourth marquess of Downshire, opposite a tree-lined avenue leading to **St Malachy's Parish Church** (Main St; admission free;

☯ 9am-5.30pm Mon-Sat), one of Ireland's most splendid 18th-century churches, with twin towers at the ends of the transepts and a graceful spire at the western end.

Close to the church is **Hillsborough Fort** (☎ 9268 3285; Main St; admission free; ☯ 10am-7pm Tue-Sat, 2-7pm Sun Apr-Sep, 10am-4pm Tue-Sat, 2-4pm Sun Oct-Mar). It was built as an artillery fort by Colonel Hill in 1650 and remodelled as a Gothic-style tower house in 1758.

FESTIVALS

Each year in late August/early September, around 10,000 people – plus 6000 oysters from Dundrum Bay – converge on the small village for a three-day **Oyster Festival** (www.hillsborough oysterfestival.com), a celebration of local food, drink and general good fun, which includes an international oyster-eating competition.

SLEEPING & EATING

Hillsborough is a bit of a culinary hot spot, with several excellent restaurants. These are popular places, so book a table at weekends to avoid disappointment.

Fortwilliam Country House (☎ 9268 2255; www .fortwilliamcountryhouse.com; 210 Ballynahinch Rd; s/d £40/65; P) The Fortwilliam offers B&B in four luxurious rooms stuffed with period furniture – our favourite is the Victorian room, with its rose wallpaper, huge antique mahogany wardrobe and view over the garden. Breakfast includes eggs from the chickens in the yard, with the smell of home-baked wheaten bread wafting from the Aga. Book well in advance.

Hillside Bar & Restaurant (☎ 9268 2765; 21 Main St; bar meals £7-11, 3-course dinner £28; ☯ bar meals noon-2.30pm & 4.30-9pm, restaurant 7.30-9.30pm Fri & Sat) This is a homely pub serving real ale (and mulled wine beside the fireplace in winter), with live jazz Sunday evenings and a dinky wee beer garden in a cobbled courtyard out the back. The upstairs restaurant offers formal dining, with crisp white table linen and sparkling crystal, and a menu offering dishes such as lobster tart, roast quail, venison and steak.

our pick **Plough Inn** (☎ 9268 2985; 3 the Square; mains bar £8-9, restaurant £13-17; ☯ bar lunches noon-2.30pm, restaurant 6-9.30pm) This fine old pub, with its maze of dark wood-panelled nooks and crannies, has been offering 'beer and banter' since 1758, and also offers fine dining in the restaurant around the back. Stone walls, low ceilings and a roaring fireplace make a cosy setting for an adventurous menu that ranges from sushi to steak.

GETTING THERE & AWAY
Goldline Express bus 238 from Belfast's Europa BusCentre to Newry stops at Hillsborough (£3, 25 minutes, at least hourly Monday to Saturday, eight Sunday).

Banbridge & Around
Banbridge (Droíchead na Banna) is another handsome 18th-century town, whose fortunes were founded on the linen trade.

The town's broad main drag, Bridge St, climbs a steep hill from the bridge across the River Bann (from which the town takes its name) to the unusual **Downshire Bridge** at the top of the hill. A cutting was made in the middle of the street in the 19th century to lower the crest of the hill and make the climb easier for the Royal Mail coaches, who had threatened to boycott the town because of the difficulty of scaling the incline.

On the opposite side of the river stands the **Crozier Monument**, which is adorned with four idiosyncratically sculpted polar bears. Captain Francis Crozier (1796–1848), a native of Banbridge, was commander of HMS *Terror* and froze to death in the Arctic during Sir John Franklin's ill-fated expedition in search of the Northwest Passage. Crozier lived in the fine blue and grey Georgian house across the road from the statue.

COUNTIES DOWN & ARMAGH

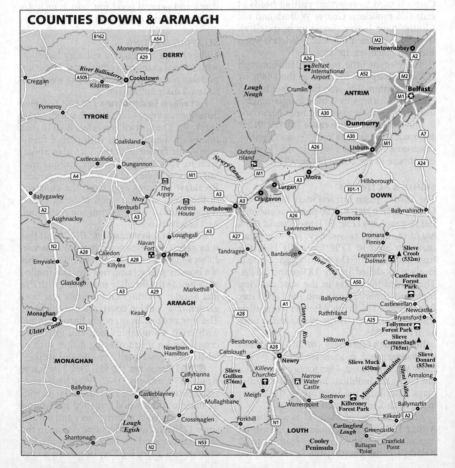

Banbridge is the starting point for the **Brontë Homeland Drive**, a signposted route along the Bann valley to Rathfriland, 16km to the southeast. Patrick Brontë, father of the famous literary sisters, was born and brought up here, and the locals like to think that her father's tales of the Mourne Mountains inspired the bleak setting for Emily's classic *Wuthering Heights*.

Milking this tenuous connection for all it's worth is the **Brontë Homeland Interpretive Centre** (☎ 4062 3322; Drumballyroney; adult/child £3/2; ☼ noon-4.30pm Fri-Sun Apr-Sep) in the former Drumballyroney School and Church, off the B10 road 13km southeast of Banbridge, where Patrick taught and preached. His birthplace is at

Emdale, 6km west of here, near the B3 road between Rathfriland and Loughbrickland.

Goldline Express bus 238 from Belfast's Europa BusCentre to Newry stops at Banbridge (£5, 45 minutes, at least hourly Monday to Saturday, eight Sunday).

Saintfield & Around

pop 3000

Saintfield is a pretty and prosperous little town, a popular weekend destination for visitors from Belfast who come to browse its dozen or so antique shops and tearooms.

Rowallane Garden (☎ 9751 0131; Crossgar Rd, Saintfield; adult/child £4.50/2; ☼ 10am-8pm mid Apr–mid Sep, to 4pm mid Sep–mid Apr, closed 24 Dec–1 Jan), 2km south of Saintfield, is renowned for its spectacular spring displays of rhododendrons and azaleas, which thrive behind a windbreak of Australian laurels, hollies, pines and beech trees. The walled gardens feature rare primulas, blue Himalayan poppies, plantain lilies, roses, magnolias and delicate autumn crocuses.

For lunch, try the **March Hare** (☎ 9751 9248; 2 Fairview; mains £3-5; ☼ 9am-5.30pm Mon-Sat) at the west end of the main street, a cosy little tearoom serving hearty, home-made soups, sandwiches and cakes.

Saintfield is 16km south of Belfast, and is a stop on the Goldline Express bus 215 service from Belfast to Downpatrick.

Legananny Dolmen

Ulster's most famous Stone Age monument is a strangely elegant tripod dolmen, looking as if some giant's hand has placed the capstone delicately atop the three slim uprights. Its elevated position on the western slopes of Slieve Croob (532m) gives it an impressive view to the Mourne Mountains.

Legananny is a challenge to find without the aid of a 1:50,000 scale map. Heading south from Ballynahinch along the B7 to Rathfriland, go through the hamlets of Dromara and Finnis, then look out for a minor road on the left (signposted Legananny Dolmen). Continue for a further 3km, through a crossroads, and look for another road on the left (a signpost is there, but difficult to spot). Continue over the hill for 2km, then turn left again at a farm. There's a parking place 50m along, and the dolmen is 50m uphill on the adjacent farm track.

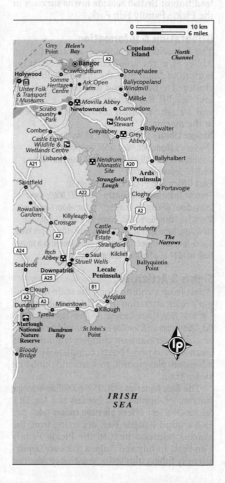

BELFAST TO BANGOR

The coastal region stretching east from Belfast to Bangor and beyond is commuter territory for the capital, and home to many of the North's wealthiest citizens – it's known locally as the 'Gold Coast'. The attractive **North Down Coastal Path** follows the shore from Holywood train station to Bangor Marina (15km), and continues east to Orlock Point.

For the Ulster Folk and Transport Museums, see p609.

Crawfordsburn

pop 500

The pretty little conservation village of Crawfordsburn lies just over 3km west of Bangor on the B20. The picturesque **our pick** **Old Inn** (☎ 9185 3255; www.theoldinn.com; 15 Main St, Crawfordsburn; r £85-130; **P**) here was once a resting place on the coach route between Belfast and Donaghadee (formerly the main ferry port for mainland Britain), and as a result has been patronised by many famous names, including the young Peter the Great (tsar of Russia), Dick Turpin (highwayman), former US president George Bush Sr, and a veritable roll call of literary figures including Swift, Tennyson, Thackeray, Dickens, Trollope and CS Lewis. Established in 1614, the Old Inn claims to be Ireland's oldest hotel, the original thatched cottage (now the bar) flanked by 18th-century additions. The atmosphere is cosy and welcoming, with log fires, low ceilings and wood panelling, and there's a lovely garden terrace at the back. The rooms, dressed up with Arts and Crafts–style wallpaper and mahogany woodwork, have bags of character, and the inn's oak-panelled **Restaurant 1614** (3-course dinner £30; ✆ 7-9.30pm Mon-Sat, 12.30-2.30pm Sun) is one of Northern Ireland's best.

The scenic glen behind the Old Inn runs through **Crawfordsburn Country Park** (☎ 9185 3621; South Bridge Rd, Helen's Bay; admission free; ✆ 9am-8pm Apr-Sep, to 4.45pm Oct-Mar) to reach the coast at one of County Down's best beaches; the park offers a number of good woodland and coastal walks. To the west lies **Grey Point Fort** (☎ 9185 3621; admission free; ✆ 2-5pm Wed-Mon Apr-Sep, 2-5pm Sat & Sun Oct-Mar), an early-20th-century gun emplacement with command post and lookout station. The 30-tonne six-inch coastal defence gun has been trained on Belfast Lough since 1904, though never fired in anger.

The B2 Belfast–Bangor bus stops at Crawfordsburn village (hourly); alternatively, you can take the train to Helen's Bay Station, a wonderful little Victorian halt dating from 1865 and built by the Marquess of Dufferin, who owned the surrounding estate.

BANGOR

pop 76,800

Bangor is to Belfast what Brighton is to London – a Victorian seaside resort that is undergoing a renaissance as an out-of-town base for city commuters. The Belfast–Bangor train line was built in the late 19th century to connect the capital with the then flourishing resort. The opening of a huge marina and a surge in property prices have boosted the town's fortunes in recent years, though the kitsch tradition of British seaside towns survives in the Pickie Family Fun Park.

Orientation & Information

The bus and train stations are together on Abbey St, at the uphill end of Main St. At the bottom of Main St is the marina with B&Bs clustered to the east and west on Queen's Pde and Seacliff Rd. Bangor has both a Main St and a High St, which converge on Bridge St at the marina.

Bangor Library (☎ 9127 0591; 80 Hamilton Rd; ✆ 9am-5.30pm Mon-Wed & Sat, to 9pm Thu & Fri) Internet access £1.50 for 30 minutes. Closed for building work till September 2008.

Post Office (☎ 9145 0150; 143 Main St)

Tourist Information Centre (☎ 9127 0069; www .northdown.gov.uk; 34 Quay St; ✆ 9am-6pm Mon, Tue, Thu & Fri, 10am-6pm Wed, 10am-5pm Sat & 1-5pm Sun Jul & Aug, 9am-5pm Mon, Tue, Thu & Fri, 10am-5pm Wed, 10am-4pm Sat, closed Sunday Sep-Jun) Housed in a tower built in 1637 as a fortified customs post.

Sights & Activities

Apart from strolling along the seafront, Bangor's main attraction is the **Pickie Family Fun Park** (☎ 9185 7030; Marine Gardens; ✆ 10am-10pm daily Easter-Oct, 10am-10pm Sat & Sun Nov-Easter), an old-fashioned seaside entertainment complex famous for its swan-shaped pedal boats, complete with kids adventure playground, go-karts and miniature steam train.

The **Blue Aquarius** (☎ 07779-600607; www.bangor boat.com; ✆ departures from 2pm daily Jul & Aug, Sat & Sun Apr-Jun & Sep) offers **pleasure cruises** (adult/child £5/2) around Bangor Bay, departing from the marina pontoon next to the Pickie Family Fun Park. In July and August there are family-friendly **fishing trips** (incl tackle and bait per adult/child

£12/10) departing at 9.30am and 7pm daily from the Eisenhower Pier (the right-hand side of the harbour, looking out to sea).

Housed in the converted laundry, stables and stores of Bangor Castle, the **North Down Heritage Centre** (☎ 9127 1200; Castle Park Ave; admission free; ⏱ 10am-4.30pm Tue-Sat, 2-4.30pm Sun year-round, 10am-4.30pm Mon Jul & Aug) displays, among other historical curiosities, a facsimile of *The Antiphonary of Bangor*, a small 7th-century prayer book and the oldest surviving Irish manuscript (the original is housed in Milan's Ambrosian Library). There's also an interesting section on the life of William Percy French (1854–1920), the famous entertainer and songwriter (Bangor is also home to the Percy French Society; http://www.percyfrench.org/pfindex.htm). The centre is in Castle Park, west of the train and bus stations.

The fishing village of Groomsport on the eastern edge of town has a picturesque harbour, overlooked by **Cockle Row Cottages** (☎ 9145 8882; admission free; ⏱ 11.30am-5.30pm Jun-Aug), one of which has been restored as a typical fisherman's home of 1910.

Sleeping

Ennislare House (☎ 9127 0858; www.ennislarehouse.com; 7-9 Princetown Rd; s/d £30/55; 🖳 🅿) Set in a lovely Victorian town house just 300m north of the train station, the Ennislare has big, bright rooms, stylish décor, and a friendly owner who can't do enough to make you feel welcome.

ourpick **Cairn Bay Lodge** (☎ 9146 7636; www.cairnbaylodge.com; 278 Seacliff Rd; s/d from £40/70; 🖳 🅿) This lovely seaside villa overlooking Ballyholme Bay, 1km east of the town centre, oozes Edwardian elegance with its oak-panelled lounge and dining room. There are five en-suite bedrooms that blend antique charm with contemporary style, beautiful gardens, gourmet breakfasts and sea views.

Bangor Bay Inn (☎ 9127 0696; www.bangorbayinn.com; 10-12 Seacliff Rd; s/d from £50/70; 🅿) This cosy 15-room hotel overlooking the marina combines business-class comfort with a homely atmosphere, a friendly bar and a good restaurant. The more expensive rooms have sunset views across the harbour.

Clandeboye Lodge Hotel (☎ 9185 2500; www.clandeboyelodge.com; 10 Estate Rd, Clandeboye; s/d from £85/95; 🖳 🅿) Looking a little like a modern, red-brick church set amid landscaped gardens on the southwest edge of town, the recently upgraded Clandeboye offers informal luxury –

big rooms, bathrobes, champagne and chocolates – plus a log fire in winter and a drinks terrace in summer.

Eating

Café Paul Rankin (☎ 9145 5400; 101 High St; mains £3-5; ⏱ 9am-5pm Mon-Sat, 10am-5pm Sun) This bright and funky café is seriously family friendly, with a kids menu, high-chairs, play area and free parking at the back. It serves breakfasts (from bagels to Ulster fries) till 11.30am, and has daily lunch specials.

ourpick **Jeffers by the Marina** (☎ 9185 9555; 7 Gray's Hill; mains £8-12; ⏱ 9am-4.30pm Mon, 9am-10pm Tue-Sat, 11am-8pm Sun) A chic little café-restaurant with a view of the harbour, Jeffers serves coffee, cakes and snacks all day but also has a fresh and interesting dinner menu that includes everything from a platter of hummus, feta and olive tapenade, to slow-cooked lamb with tomato, fennel and saffron rice.

Rioja (☎ 9147 0774; 119 High St; mains £9-13; ⏱ noon-2pm & 5-9pm Mon-Sat, to 9.30pm Fri & Sat, closed Mon Oct–mid Apr) Rioja is a relaxed bistro with terracotta tiles and candle-lit tables offering a range of Iberian, French and Italian dishes including *cataplana*, a Portuguese seafood casserole. It's unlicensed, so if you want a bottle of the eponymous wine, BYOB (corkage £1).

Coyle's Bistro (☎ 9127 0362; 44 High St; mains £13-17; ⏱ 5-9pm Tue-Sat, 5-8pm Sun) Despite being upstairs from a busy bar, this place is surprisingly intimate and inviting with wood panelling, mirrored walls and subdued lighting. The menu is resolutely modern with dishes such as cod tempura with wasabi, and shellfish and saffron risotto.

Entertainment

Jenny Watts (☎ 9127 0401; 41 High St) A traditional pub with a beer garden out back, Jenny's pulls in a mixed-age crowd, offering folk music on Tuesday nights, easy listening on Thursday, clubbing (upstairs) on Friday and Saturday, and jazz and blues on Sunday afternoon and evening. It also serves good pub grub, and kids are welcome at meal times.

Café Ceol (☎ 9146 8830; www.cafeceolbangor.com; 17-21 High St; admission free-£5; ⏱ 7pm-1am Wed-Fri, 7pm-1.45am Sat) Bangor's biggest and busiest nightclub has a sleek bar, an intimate lounge and a stylish club venue, Mint, which features student night on Wednesday, '80s music on Thursday and dance, house, funk and R&B on Saturday.

Getting There & Away

Ulsterbus (☎ 9066 6630; www.translink.co.uk) service B2 or 502 runs from Belfast's Laganside Bus-Centre to Bangor (£3, 50 minutes, every 30 minutes Monday to Saturday, eight Sunday). From Bangor, bus 3 goes to Donaghadee (£2.50, 25 minutes, hourly Monday to Saturday, four Sunday), and bus 6 goes to Newtownards (£2, 20 minutes, half-hourly).

There's also a regular train service from Belfast's Great Victoria St and Central stations to Bangor (£4, 30 minutes, half-hourly Monday to Saturday, hourly Sunday).

ARDS PENINSULA

The low-lying Ards Peninsula (An Aird) is the finger of land that encloses Strangford Lough, pinching against the thumb of the Lecale Peninsula at the Portaferry Narrows. The northern half of the peninsula has some of Ireland's most fertile farmland, with large expanses of wheat and barley, while the south is a landscape of neat fields, white cottages and narrow, winding roads. The eastern coast has some good sandy beaches.

Donaghadee

pop 6500

Donaghadee (Domhnach Daoi) was the main ferry port for Scotland until 1874, when the 34km sea crossing to Portpatrick was superseded by the Stranraer–Larne route. Now it's a pleasant harbour town that's fast becoming part of Belfast's commuter belt.

The town is home to **Grace Neill's**, which dates from 1611 and claims to be Ireland's oldest pub. Among its 17th-century guests was Peter the Great, tsar of Russia, who stopped for lunch in 1697 on his grand tour of Europe. In the 19th century, John Keats found the place 'charming and clean' but was 'treated to ridicule, scorn and violent abuse by the local people who objected to my mode of dress and thought I was some strange foreigner'.

From June to September **MV The Brothers** (☎ 9188 3403; www.nelsonsboats.co.uk) runs boat trips to Copeland Island (adult/child £3/2, departs 2pm daily, weather permitting), which was abandoned to the seabirds at the turn of the 20th century. There are also sea-angling trips (£7 per person, departures at 10am and 7pm), with all tackle and bait provided.

SLEEPING & EATING

Pier 36 (☎ 9188 4466; 36 the Parade; s/d £50/70; mains £8-18; �%︎ food 12.30-2.30pm & 5-9.30pm Wed-Sun) An excellent pub with a red-brick and terracotta-tiled restaurant at the back, dominated by a yellow Raeburn stove that turns out home-baked bread and the daily roast. The hearty menu includes soups, stews, sausage and champ, mussels, seafood, steaks and a good range of veggie dishes, and there are a couple of comfortable B&B rooms upstairs.

ourpick Grace Neill's (☎ 9188 4595; 33 High St; mains £8-15; �%︎ food noon-2.30pm & 5.30-9.30pm Mon-Sat, 12.30-8pm Sun) At the back of Ireland's oldest pub is one of the North's best modern bistros, its sea-green, khaki and red-brick walls decked with arty photos of old Donaghadee. The menu can best be described as upmarket comfort food, from beer-battered fish with chunky, hand-cut chips, and beef-and-Guinness pie, to wicked desserts such as Toblerone and Malteser cheesecake. There's live music on Sunday afternoons, too.

East Coast

The A2 runs along the east coast of the peninsula through the seaside villages and caravan parks of Millisle (Oileán an Mhuilinn), Ballywalter and Ballyhalbert, and the ugly fishing harbour of Portavogie. The best **beaches** are the Long Sand, immediately south of Ballywalter, and the seawater lagoon (enclosed by a stone dike for safe bathing) at Millisle.

Approximately 1.5km northwest of Millisle is **Ballycopeland Windmill** (☎ 9054 6552; Moss Rd; admission free; �%︎ 10am-6pm Tue-Sat & 2-6pm Sun Jul & Aug), a late-18th-century corn mill that remained in commercial use until 1915 and has been restored to full working order.

Portaferry

pop 3300

Portaferry (Port an Pheire), a neat huddle of streets around a medieval tower house, enjoys the most attractive setting on the Ards Peninsula, looking across the turbulent Narrows to a matching tower house in Strangford. A renowned marine biology station on the waterfront uses the lough as an outdoor laboratory, and you can investigate the local marine life yourself at the nearby Exploris aquarium. There are some good coastal walks, and in fine weather you can sit outside the pubs on the waterfront and watch the comings and goings of yachts and ferries.

The **tourist information centre** (☎ 4272 9882; tourism.portaferry@ards-council.gov.uk; Castle St; ☺ 10am-5pm Mon-Sat, 2-6pm Sun Easter-Sep) is in a restored stable near the tower house.

SIGHTS & ACTIVITIES

You can take a look around **Portaferry Castle** (admission free; ☺ 10am-5pm Mon-Sat, 2-6pm Sun Easter-Sep), a small 16th-century tower house beside the tourist information centre, which together with the tower house in Strangford used to control sea traffic through the Narrows.

Next to the tower house is the outstanding state-of-the-art aquarium, **Exploris** (☎ 4272 8062; www.exploris.org.uk; Castle St; adult/child £6.90/4; ☺ 10am-6pm Mon-Fri, 11am-6pm Sat, noon-6pm Sun Apr-Aug, 10am-5pm Mon-Fri, 11am-5pm Sat, 1-5pm Sun Sep-Mar), with displays of marine life from Strangford Lough and the Irish Sea. Touch tanks allow visitors to stroke and hold sea rays, starfish, sea anemones and other sea creatures. Exploris also has a seal sanctuary where orphaned, sick and injured seals are nursed back to health before being released into the wild.

Walk up to **Windmill Hill** above the town, topped by an old windmill tower, for a good view over the Narrows to Strangford. The Vikings named this stretch of water Strangfjörthr, meaning 'powerful fjord', because when the tide turns, as it does four times a day, 400,000 tonnes of water per minute churn through the gap at speeds of up to eight knots (15km/h). You get some idea of the tide's remarkable strength when you see the ferry being whipped sideways by the current.

There are pleasant **walks** on the minor roads along the shore, north for 2.5km to Ballyhenry Island (accessible at low tide), and south for 6km to the National Trust nature reserve of Ballyquintin Point, both good for bird-watching, seal-spotting, or just admiring the view of the Mourne Mountains.

From May to September **Des Rogers** (☎ 4272 8297) and **John Murray** (☎ 4272 8414) organise fishing and bird-watching trips, as well as pleasure cruises on the lough (per half-/full day around £75/150) for up to six people. Book in advance.

SLEEPING & EATING

Locally caught seafood is a feature of the menus at a handful of top restaurants clustered here and across the water in Strangford.

Barholm (☎ 4272 9598; www.barholmportaferry.co.uk; 11 the Strand; dm/s/d £13/18/35; ☺ year-round; Ⓟ) Barholm offers hostel-style and B&B accommodation in a Victorian villa in a superb seafront location opposite the ferry slipway, with a spacious kitchen, laundry facilities and a big, sunny conservatory for breakfast (£3.75 extra). It's popular with groups, so be sure to book ahead.

Adair's B&B (☎ 4272 8412; 22 the Square; s/d £20/38, f per person £19) Mrs Adair's friendly and good-value B&B is an anonymous-looking house right on the main square (there's no sign outside; look for No 22), with three spacious rooms – a single, a double, and a family room (for up to four people).

Fiddler's Green (☎ 4272 8393; www.fiddlersgreenportaferry.com; 10-12 Church St; s/d £30/50; Ⓟ) This popular pub and restaurant provides B&B in four homely rooms – one has a four-poster bed (per night £75) – neatly decorated with pine furniture and paintings, and serves up a stonking cooked breakfast. The pub has traditional music sessions every Friday, Saturday and Sunday night.

our pick **Narrows** (☎ 4272 8148; www.narrows.co.uk; 8 Shore Rd; s/d £70/100; Ⓟ) One of our favourite places to stay in the whole of Northern Ireland, the Narrows has stylish but unfussy, not-quite-minimalist bedrooms, all sunny and west-facing and every one of them with a sea view. The restaurant (lunch mains £7 to £11, dinner £14 to £17; open noon to 8.30pm Sunday to Thursday, to 9pm Friday and Saturday) is as relaxed and informal as the accommodation, with top-quality, simply prepared, local produce, home-baked bread and a good wine list. Dishes include seafood chowder, Strangford Lough mussels with a champagne-and-chive sauce, and seared scallops with Clonakilty black pudding.

Portaferry Hotel (☎ 4272 8231; www.portaferryhotel.com; 10 the Strand; s/d from £75/110; Ⓟ) Converted from a row of 18th-century terrace houses, this charming seafront hotel has an elegant, Georgian look to its rooms – ask for one with a sea view (£10 extra) – and has a good, family-friendly restaurant with a French-influenced menu.

GETTING THERE & AWAY

Ulsterbus buses 9, 509, 10 and 510 travel from Belfast to Portaferry (£6, 1¼ hours, 12 daily Monday to Saturday, four Sunday) via Newtownards, Mount Stewart and Greyabbey. More frequent services begin from Newtownards (some buses go via Carrowdore and don't stop at Mount Stewart and Greyabbey; check first).

The **ferry** (☎ 4488 1637) between Portaferry and Strangford sails every half-hour between 7.30am and 10.30pm Monday to Friday, 8am to 11pm Saturday and 9.30am to 10.30pm Sunday; the journey time is about 10 minutes. The one-way/same-day return fares are £5.30/8.50 for a car and driver; £3.40/5.30 for motorcyclists and their bikes; and £1.10/1.80 for car passengers and pedestrians.

Greyabbey
pop 1000

The village of Greyabbey is home to the splendid ruins of **Grey Abbey** (☎ 9054 6552; Church Rd; admission free; ⏰ 10am-7pm Tue-Sat, 2-7pm Sun Apr-Sep, 10am-4pm Sat, 2-4pm Sun Oct-Mar). The Cistercian abbey was founded in 1193 by Affreca, wife of the Norman aristocrat John de Courcy (the builder of Carrickfergus Castle), in thanks for surviving a stormy sea-crossing from the Isle of Man. The small visitor centre explains Cistercian life with paintings and panels.

The abbey church, which remained in use as late as the 18th century, was the first in Ireland to be built in the Gothic style. At the east end is a carved tomb possibly depicting Affreca; the effigy in the north transept may be her husband. The grounds, overlooked by 18th-century Rosemount House, are awash with trees and flowers on spreading lawns, making this an ideal picnic spot.

Hoops Courtyard, off Main St in the village centre, has a cluster of 18 little shops selling antiques and collectables; opening times vary, but all are open on Wednesday, Friday and Saturday afternoons. **Hoops Coffee Shop** (☎ 4278 8541; Hoops Courtyard, Main St; mains £4-5; ⏰ 10am-5pm Wed, Fri & Sat year-round, daily in Jul & Aug) is a traditional tearoom, with outdoor tables in the courtyard in fine weather, serving good lunches and wicked cream teas.

Mount Stewart House & Gardens

The magnificent 18th-century **Mount Stewart** (☎ 4278 8387; house tour & gardens adult/child £6.50/3, gardens only £5/2; ⏰ house noon-6pm daily Jul & Aug, noon-6pm Wed-Mon Sep, 1-6pm Mon & Wed-Fri, noon-6pm Sat & Sun May & Jun, noon-6pm Sat, Sun & public hols mid-Mar–Apr & Oct) is one of Northern Ireland's grandest stately homes. It was built for the marquess of Londonderry and is decorated with lavish plasterwork, marble nudes and priceless artworks – the portrait of the racehorse Hamble-

tonian by George Stubbs is one of the most important paintings in Ireland.

Much of the landscaping of the beautiful **gardens** (⏰ 10am-8pm May-Sep, to 6pm Apr & Oct, to 4pm mid Mar–Apr; ♿) was supervised in the early 20th century by Lady Edith, wife of the seventh marquess, for the benefit of her children – the Dodo Terrace at the front of the house is populated with unusual creatures from history (dinosaurs and dodos) and myth (griffins and mermaids), accompanied by giant frogs and duck-billed platypuses. The 18th-century **Temple of the Winds** (⏰ 2-5pm Sun Apr-Oct) is a folly in the classical Greek style built on a high point above the lough.

Mount Stewart is on the A20, 3km northwest of Greyabbey and 8km southeast of Newtownards. Buses from Belfast and Newtownards to Portaferry stop at the gate. The ground floor of the house and most of the gardens are wheelchair accessible. Last admission one hour before closing time.

NEWTOWNARDS & AROUND
pop 27,800

Founded in the 17th century on the site of the 6th-century Movilla monastery, Newtownards (Baile Nua na hArda) today is a busy but unexceptional commercial centre. The **tourist information centre** (☎ 9182 6846; tourism@ards-council.gov.uk; 31 Regent St; ⏰ 9.15am-5pm Mon-Fri, 9.30am-5pm Sat) is next to the bus station.

There's some fine 18th- and 19th-century architecture in the town, especially along Church St. Most striking of all is the 18th-century **Market House**, which once housed the town's prison – you can ask to see an original cell – and is now home to the **Ards Arts Centre** (☎ 9181 0803; Conway Sq; admission free; ⏰ 9am-5pm Mon-Thu, 9am-4.30pm Fri, 10am-4pm Sat), which hosts changing art exhibitions. The square in front of the Market House hosts a lively **market** every Saturday, and a traditional harvest fair in September.

The remains of **Movilla Abbey** and its 13th-century church have been almost swallowed up by the forest of gravestones in Movilla Cemetery (on Old Movilla Rd, on the B172 towards Millisle). There are some interesting 12th- and 13th-century grave slabs (thought by some to be those of Knights Templar) amid the abbey ruins.

The bus station is on Regent St, near the tourist office. Bus 5 goes to Belfast (£2.30,

35 minutes, around hourly Monday to Saturday, two Sunday).

Scrabo Country Park

Newtownards is overlooked by the prominent landmark of Scrabo Hill, located 2km southwest of town. It was once the site of extensive prehistoric earthworks, which were largely removed during construction of the 41m **1857 Memorial Tower** (☎ 9181 1491; admission free; ✆ 10.30am-6pm Sat-Thu Apr-Sep) in honour of the third marquess of Londonderry. Inside there's a slide show on Strangford Lough and a 122-step climb to the superb viewpoint at the top of the tower – on a clear day you can see Scotland, the Isle of Man, and even Snowdon in Wales. The disused sandstone quarries nearby provided material for many famous buildings, including Belfast's Albert Memorial Clock Tower.

Somme Heritage Centre

The grimly fascinating **Somme Heritage Centre** (☎ 9182 3202; www.irishsoldier.org; 233 Bangor Rd; adult/child £3.75/2.75; ✆ 10am-5pm Mon-Fri, noon-5pm Sat & Sun Jul & Aug, 10am-4pm Mon-Thu, noon-4pm Sat

Apr-Jun & Sep, 10am-4pm Mon-Thu, noon-4pm 1st Sat of month Oct-Mar) vividly illustrates the horrors of the WWI Somme campaign of 1916 from the perspective of men of the 10th (Irish), 16th (Irish) and 36th (Ulster) divisions. It's a high-tech show with short films and nothing celebratory about the exhibits, intended as a memorial to the men and women who died. A photographic display commemorates the suffragette movement and the part that women played in WWI.

The centre is 3km north of Newtownards on the A21 towards Bangor. The No 6 Bangor to Newtownards bus passes the entrance every half-hour or so.

Ark Open Farm

Opposite the Somme Heritage Centre, on the other side of the dual carriageway, is the **Ark Open Farm** (☎ 9182 0445; www.thearkopen farm.co.uk; 296 Bangor Rd; adult/child £3.90/3.20; ✆ 10am-6pm Mon-Sat, 2-6pm Sun, closes 5pm daily Oct-Feb). Hugely popular with families, the farm has displays of rare breeds of sheep, cattle, poultry, llamas and donkeys. Kids get to stroke and hand-feed the lambs, piglets and ducklings.

LORD CASTLEREAGH

As you wander around Mount Stewart, spare a thought for Robert Stewart, Lord Castlereagh (1769–1822), who spent his childhood here. Despite going down in history as one of Britain's most accomplished foreign secretaries, during his lifetime he was enormously unpopular with the public who saw him as the spokesman for a violently repressive government. He was savagely attacked in print by liberal reformers, including Daniel O'Connell – who denounced him as 'the assassin of his country' – and the poets Percy Bysshe Shelley and Lord Byron. The latter's notorious *Epitaph for Lord Castlereagh* could hardly be bettered for withering contempt:

> Posterity will ne'er survey
> A nobler scene than this:
> Here lie the bones of Castlereagh;
> Stop, traveller, and piss!

Castlereagh's father, the first marquess of Londonderry, primed his son's political career in 1790 by buying him a place in the Irish parliament as member for County Down. The campaign cost a cool £60,000, leaving the marquess unable to afford various planned improvements to Mount Stewart.

As Chief Secretary for Ireland in the government of William Pitt, Castlereagh was responsible for quelling the 1798 Rising and for passing the 1801 Act of Union. Later he served as foreign secretary during the Napoleonic wars, and represented Britain at the Congress of Vienna in 1815 (the 22 chairs on which European leaders sat during the congress are on show in Mount Stewart House). Political success did not bring happiness however; while still in office, Castlereagh succumbed to paranoia and depression, and committed suicide by slitting his own throat with a letter knife.

COUNTIES DOWN & ARMAGH

STRANGFORD LOUGH

Almost landlocked, Strangford Lough (Loch Cuan; www.strangfordlough.org) is connected to the open sea only by a 700m-wide strait (the Narrows) at Portaferry. Its western shore is fringed by humpbacked islands – half-drowned mounds of boulder clay (called drumlins) left behind by ice sheets at the end of the last Ice Age. On the eastern shore, the drumlins have been broken down by the waves into heaps of boulders that form shallow tidal reefs (known locally as 'pladdies').

Large colonies of grey seals frequent the lough, especially at the southern tip of the Ards Peninsula where the exit channel opens out into the sea. Birds abound on the shores and tidal mudflats, including brent geese wintering from Arctic Canada, eider ducks and many species of wader. Strangford Lough oysters are a local delicacy.

Castle Espie Wildfowl & Wetlands Centre

About 2km southeast of Comber, off the Downpatrick road (A22), is the **Castle Espie Wildfowl & Wetlands Centre** (☎ 9187 4146; www .wwt.org.uk; Ballydrain Rd, Comber; adult/child £5.50/2.75; ⏰ 10.30am-5pm Mon-Fri, 11am-5.30pm Sat & Sun Mar-Oct, 11am-4pm Mon-Fri, 11am-4.30pm Sat & Sun Nov-Feb). It's a haven for large gatherings of geese, ducks and swans – around 75% of the world's population of light-bellied brent geese spend the winter here – and a paradise for fledgling ornithologists. The best time to visit is in May and June, when the grounds are overrun with goslings, ducklings and cygnets.

SLEEPING & EATING

ourpick Anna's House B&B (☎ 9754 1566; www.annas house.com; Tullynagee, 35 Lisbarnett Rd, Lisbane; s/d from £45/70; P) Just west of Lisbane, Anna's is an ecofriendly country house set in a superb garden with views over a little lake (free angling for residents). The hospitality is second to none, the food is almost all organic and the bread is home-baked, with a breakfast menu that ranges from an Ulster fry through smoked salmon omelette to fresh fruit salad.

Old Schoolhouse Inn (☎ 9754 1182; www.the oldschoolhouseinn.com; Ballydrain Rd, Comber; s/d £50/70; P) Just south of Castle Espie on the road to Nendrum, the characterful Old Schoolhouse has 12 luxurious, modern rooms, each named for a former US president. The former classroom, now swathed in shades of deep claret and decorated with old musical instru-

ments, houses an award-winning restaurant (three-course dinner £22; open 7pm to 10pm Monday to Saturday and noon to 3pm Sunday) serving local produce cooked in French country-kitchen style.

Old Post Office Tearoom (☎ 9754 3335; 191 Killinchy Rd, Lisbane; mains £3-5; ⏰ 9.30am-5pm Mon-Sat) The thatched cottage that once housed the village post office has been lovingly converted into a tearoom and art gallery with walls of cream plaster and bare stone, pine furniture and a wood-burning stove. It serves great coffee and home-baked scones.

Nendrum Monastic Site

The Celtic monastic community of **Nendrum** (admission free; ⏰ 24hr) was built in the 5th century under the guidance of St Mochaoi (St Mahee). It is much older than the Norman monastery at Grey Abbey on the opposite shore and couldn't be more different. The scant remains provide a clear outline of its early plan with the foundations of a number of churches, a round tower, beehive cells and other buildings, as well as three concentric stone ramparts and a monks' cemetery, all in a wonderful island setting. A particularly interesting relic is the stone sundial that has been reconstructed using some of the original pieces. The minor road to Mahee Island from the lough's western shore crosses a causeway to Reagh Island and then a bridge guarded by the ruined tower of 15th-century Mahee Castle.

The small **visitor centre** (☎ 9754 2547; admission free; ⏰ 10am-7pm Tue-Sat & 2-7pm Sun Apr-Sep, 10am-4pm Sat & 2-4pm Sun Oct-Mar) screens an excellent video comparing Nendrum to Grey Abbey, and there's some interesting material about the concept of time and how we measure it, presented in a child-friendly fashion.

The site is signposted from Lisbane, on the A20 5km south of Comber.

Killyleagh

pop 2200

Killyleagh (Cill O Laoch) is a former fishing village dominated by the impressive **castle** (closed to the public) of the Hamilton family. Built originally by John de Courcy in the 12th century, the Scottish Baronial-style reconstruction of 1850 sits on the original Norman motte and bailey. Outside the gatehouse, a plaque commemorates Sir Hans Sloane, the naturalist born in Killyleagh in 1660, whose collection was the basis for the founding of the British Museum (London's Sloane Square is named after him). The parish church houses the tombs of members of the Blackwood family (marquesses of Dufferin), who married into the Hamiltons in the 18th century.

SLEEPING & EATING

Killyleagh Castle Towers (☎ 4482 8261; polly@killyleagh .plus.com; High St; 4-person apt per weekend/week £210/429; **P**) If you ever fancied staying in a castle, Killyleagh's three gatehouse towers (complete with spiral staircases and roof terraces) are available for weekly rental, including use of the castle gardens, swimming pool and tennis court. The two smaller towers sleep four and the largest sleeps five.

our pick **Dufferin Coaching Inn** (☎ 4482 8229; www .dufferincoachinginn.com; 35 High St; s/d £45/70) The comfortable lounge in this lovely Georgian house, complete with coal-fired stove and free Sunday papers, was once the village bank – the manager's office in the corner now houses a little library. The six plush rooms have crisp linen and fluffy towels, and some have four-poster beds; unusually, the smallest double has the bath *in* the bedroom, charmingly hidden behind a curtain. The excellent breakfasts include freshly squeezed orange juice, good coffee and scrambled eggs with smoked salmon.

Dufferin Arms (☎ 4482 1182; www.dufferinarms.co.uk; 35 High St; mains £7-15; ☙ noon-3pm & 5.30-9pm Mon-Wed, noon-9.30pm Thu-Sat, 12.30-7.30pm Sun) This comfortably old-fashioned pub, and the larger Stables Bar downstairs, serves decent pub grub, while the cosy, candle-lit Kitchen Restaurant offers a more intimate atmosphere. Bands play on Friday and Saturday nights from 9pm, with traditional sessions on Saturday afternoons.

GETTING THERE & AWAY

Ulsterbus buses 11 and 511 run from Belfast to Killyleagh (£4, one hour, eight daily Monday to Friday, five Saturday, two Sunday) via Comber. Bus 14 continues from Killyleagh to Downpatrick (£3, 20 minutes, eight daily Monday to Friday, four Saturday).

DOWNPATRICK

pop 10,300

St Patrick's mission to spread Christianity to Ireland began and ended at Downpatrick. Ireland's patron saint is associated with numerous places in this corner of Down – he made his first convert at nearby Saul, and is buried at Down Cathedral – and on St Patrick's Day (17 March) the town is crammed with crowds of pilgrims and revellers.

Downpatrick – now County Down's administrative centre – was settled long before the saint's arrival. His first church here was constructed inside the earthwork *dún* (fort) of Rath Celtchair, still visible to the southwest of the cathedral. The place later became known as Dún Pádraig (Patrick's Fort), anglicised to Downpatrick in the 17th century.

In 1176 the Norman John de Courcy is said to have brought the relics of St Colmcille and St Brigid to Downpatrick to rest with the remains of St Patrick, hence the local saying, 'In Down, three saints one grave do fill, Patrick, Brigid and Colmcille'. Later the town declined along with the cathedral until the 17th and 18th centuries, when the Southwell family developed the old town centre you see today. The best of its Georgian architecture is centred on English St and the Mall, which lead up to the cathedral.

Orientation & Information

The bus station is on Market St (the main A25 road south towards Newcastle), on the southern edge of the town centre.

The **tourist information centre** (☎ 4461 2233; www.visitdownpatrick.com; 53A Market St; ☙ 9.30am-6pm Mon-Sat & 2-6pm Sun Jul & Aug, 10am-5pm Mon-Sat Sep-Jun) is in the St Patrick Centre, just north of the bus station.

Sights

The **Mall** is the most attractive street in Downpatrick, with some lovely 18th-century architecture, including Soundwell School, built in 1733, and a courthouse with a finely decorated pediment.

SAINT PATRICK CENTRE

This centre houses a multimedia exhibition called **Ego Patricius** (☎ 4461 9000; www.saintpatrick

centre.com; 53A Market St; adult/child £4.90/2.50; 9.30am-6pm Mon-Sat & 10am-6pm Sun Jun-Aug, 9.30am-5.30pm Mon-Sat & 1-5.30pm Sun Apr, May & Sep, 10am-5pm Mon-Sat Oct-Mar, 9.30am-7pm St Patrick's Day), charting the life and legacy of Ireland's patron saint. Occasionally filled with parties of school kids, the exhibition uses audio and video presentations to tell St Patrick's story, often in his own words (taken from his *Confession*, written in Latin around the year AD 450, which begins with the words 'Ego Patricius', meaning 'I am Patrick'). At the end is a spectacular widescreen film that takes the audience on a swooping, low-level helicopter ride over the landscapes of Ireland.

DOWN CATHEDRAL

According to legend St Patrick died in Saul, where angels told his followers to place his body on a cart drawn by two untamed oxen, and that wherever the oxen halted, was where the saint should be buried. They supposedly stopped at the church on the hill of Down, now the site of the Church of Ireland's **Down Cathedral** (4461 4922; admission free; 9.30am-4.30pm Mon-Sat, 2-5pm Sun).

The cathedral is a testimony to 1600 years of building and rebuilding. Viking attacks wiped away all trace of the earliest churches, and the subsequent Norman cathedral and monasteries were destroyed by Scottish raiders in 1316. The rubble was used in a 15th-century church finished in 1512, but after the Dissolution of the Monasteries it was razed to the ground in 1541. Today's building dates largely from the 18th and 19th centuries, with a completely new interior installed in the 1980s.

In the churchyard immediately south of the cathedral is a slab of Mourne granite with the inscription 'Patric', placed there by the Belfast Naturalists' Field Club in 1900, marking the traditional site of **St Patrick's grave**.

To reach the cathedral, go up the stairs to the right of the Saint Patrick Centre and turn left at the top, opposite Down County Museum.

DOWN COUNTY MUSEUM

Downhill from the cathedral is **Down County Museum** (4461 5218; www.downcountymuseum.com; the Mall; admission free; 10am-5pm Mon-Fri, 1-5pm Sat & Sun), housed in the town's restored 18th-century jail. In a former cell block at the back are models of some of the prisoners once incarcerated there, and details of their sad sto-

ries. Displays cover the story of the Norman conquest of Down, but the biggest exhibit of all is outside – a short signposted trail leads to the **Mound of Down**, a good example of a Norman motte and bailey.

INCH ABBEY

Built by de Courcy for the Cistercians in 1180 on an earlier Irish monastic site, **Inch Abbey** (9054 6552; admission free; 24hr) is visible across the river from the cathedral. The English Cistercians had a strict policy of non-admittance to Irishmen and maintained this until the end in 1541. Most of the ruins are just foundations and low walls; the neatly groomed setting beside the marshes of the River Quoile is its most attractive feature.

To get there, head out of town on the A7 Belfast road for about 1.5km, then take the first left after crossing the river.

DOWNPATRICK & COUNTY DOWN RAILWAY

From mid-June to mid-September, plus December, St Patrick's Day, Easter, May Day and Halloween, this working **railway museum** (4461 5779; www.downrail.co.uk; Market St; adult/child £4.70/3.70; 2-5pm Sat & Sun) runs steam-hauled trains over a restored section of the former Belfast–Newcastle line. There is a western terminus at Ballydugan, and a northern one close to Inch Abbey, plus a halt next to the grave of King Magnus Barefoot, a Norwegian king who died in battle on this spot in 1103. The ticket price includes a return journey on the train and a tour around the engine shed and signal cabin.

QUOILE COUNTRYSIDE CENTRE

A tidal barrier was built at Hare Island, 3km downstream from Downpatrick, in 1957 to control flooding. The waters enclosed by the barrier now form the Quoile Pondage Nature Reserve, whose ecology is explained at the **Quoile Countryside Centre** (4461 5520; 5 Quay Rd; admission free; reserve 24hr, visitor centre 11am-5pm daily Apr-Aug, 1-5pm Sat & Sun Sep-Mar). The centre is housed in a little cottage beside the ruins of **Quoile Castle**, a 17th-century tower house. There's a **bird-watching hide** (10am-4pm;) on Castle Island, downstream from the centre.

Sleeping & Eating

Denvir's Hotel & Pub (4461 2012; www.denvirs hotel.com; 14 English St; s/d £38/60; P) Denvir's is an old coaching inn dating back to 1642, offering B&B in six characterful rooms with pine floorboards, Georgian windows and period fireplaces. The elegant, candle-lit restaurant (mains £8 to £12; open noon to 2.30pm and 5pm to 9pm) has an enormous, original stone fireplace and exposed timber roofbeams, and serves quality local produce in dishes such as smoked trout and Cashel blue cheese tart, and slow roast leg of lamb with minted organic vegetables.

Mill at Ballydugan (☎ 4461 3654; www.ballydugan mill.com; Drumcullen Rd, Ballydugan; s/d/f £55/75/85; P) This giant, eight-storey, 18th-century mill building overlooking Ballydugan Lake has been restored as a hotel and restaurant, housing 11 atmospheric rooms with lots of exposed stone and timber. It's 3km southwest of Downpatrick, off the A25.

Getting There & Away

Downpatrick is 32km southeast of Belfast. Buses 15, 15A and 515 depart from the Europa BusCentre in Belfast for Downpatrick (£5, one hour, at least hourly Monday to Friday, six Saturday, four Sunday). There's also the Goldline Express bus 215 (50 minutes, hourly Monday to Saturday).

Goldline Express bus 240 runs from Downpatrick to Newry (£5, 1¼ hour, six daily Monday to Saturday, two Sunday) via Dundrum, Newcastle, Castlewellan and Hilltown.

AROUND DOWNPATRICK

According to popular tradition the young St Patrick was kidnapped from Britain by Irish pirates and spent six years as a slave tending sheep (possibly on Slemish, p675) before escaping back home to his family. After religious training, he returned to Ireland to spread the faith and is said to have landed on the shores of Strangford Lough near Saul, northeast of Downpatrick. He preached his first sermon in a nearby barn, and eventually retired to Saul after some 30 years of evangelising.

Saul

On landing near this spot in AD 432, St Patrick made his first convert: Díchú, the local chieftain, who gave the holy man a sheep barn (*sabhal* in Gaelic, pronounced 'sawl') in which to preach. West of Saul village is the supposed site of the *sabhal*, with a replica 10th-century **church and round tower** built in 1932 to mark the 1500th anniversary of his arrival.

GUITAR-MAKER TO THE GREATS

Belfast-born George Lowden has been creating guitars in Northern Ireland since the 1970s, and his hand-built instruments have gained a world-wide reputation for excellence – satisfied Lowden owners include Eric Clapton, Van Morrison, Richard Thompson, Mark Knopfler and the Edge. If you're interested in buying one, you can get a tour of the workshop at **Lowden Guitars** (☎ 4461 9161; www.george lowden.com; 34 Down Business Park, Belfast Rd, Downpatrick; ☯ by prior arrangement Mon-Fri). However, be prepared to shell out upwards of £4000.

East of the village is the small hill of **Slieve Patrick** (120m), with stations of the cross along the path to the top and a massive 10m-high statue of St Patrick, also dating from 1932, on the summit. The hill is the object of a popular pilgrimage on St Patrick's Day.

Saul is 3km northeast of Downpatrick off the A2 Strangford road.

Struell Wells

These supposedly curative spring waters are traditionally associated with St Patrick – it is said he scourged himself here, spending 'a great part of the night, stark naked and singing psalms' immersed in what is now the **Drinking Well**. He must have been a hardy soul – the well-preserved but chilly 17th-century **bathhouses** here look more likely to induce ill health than cure it! The site has been venerated for centuries, although the buildings are all post-1600. Between the bathhouses and the ruined chapel stands the **Eye Well**, whose waters are said to cure eye ailments.

The wells are in a scenic, secluded glen 2km east of Downpatrick. Take the B1 road towards Ardglass, and turn left after passing the hospital.

LECALE PENINSULA

The low-lying Lecale Peninsula is situated east of Downpatrick, isolated by the sea and Strangford Lough to the north, south and east, and the marshes of the Quoile and Blackstaff Rivers to the west. In Irish it is Leath Chathail (pronounced lay-cahal), meaning 'the territory of Cathal' (an 8th-century prince), a region of fertile farmland that is fringed by fishing harbours, rocky bluffs and sandy beaches.

Lecale is a place of pilgrimage for Van Morrison fans – Coney Island, immortalised in his song of the same name, is between Ardglass and Killough in the south of the peninsula.

Strangford
pop 550

The picturesque fishing village of Strangford (Baile Loch Cuan) is dominated by **Strangford Castle** (☎ 9023 5000; Castle St; admission free), a 16th-century tower house that faces its counterpart across the Narrows in Portaferry. To get inside, ask for the keys from Mr Seed across the road at 39 Castle St (10am to 4pm). At the end of Castle St is a footpath called the **Squeeze Gut** that leads over the hill behind the village, with a fine view of the lough, before looping back to Strangford via tree-lined Dufferin Ave (1.5km), or continuing around the shoreline to Castle Ward Estate (4.5km).

Strangford is 16km northeast of Downpatrick. See p618 for details of the car ferry between Strangford and Portaferry.

SLEEPING & EATING

Castle Ward Estate Camp Site (☎ 4488 1680; 19 Castle Ward Rd; camp/caravan sites £7/12; ☒ mid-Mar–Sep) The entrance to this wooded, lough-shore National Trust site is separate from the main estate entrance (closer to Strangford village).

Cuan (☎ 4488 1222; www.thecuan.com; the Square; s/d £53/85, mains £8-15; ☒ food noon-9pm Mon-Thu, noon-9.30pm Fri & Sat, noon-8.30pm Sun; ℗) You can't miss the Cuan's duck-egg-green façade, just around the corner from the ferry slip. The atmospheric, wood-panelled restaurant here is the main attraction, serving giant portions of local seafood, lamb and beef, but there are also nine neat, comfortable and well-equipped rooms if you want to stay the night.

our pick Lobster Pot (☎ 4488 1288; 9-11 the Square; bar meals £6-11, restaurant mains £10-17; ☒ noon-9.30pm Mon-Sat, noon-9pm Sun) This charmingly old-fashioned pub overlooking the harbour has a smart, modern bistro at the back, with green marble tables and linen napkins, serving excellent seafood – the house speciality is, of course, local lobster, with a separate Lobster Menu available all day.

Castle Ward Estate

Castle Ward house enjoys a superb setting overlooking the bay to the west of Strangford,

but has something of a split personality. It was built in the 1760s for Lord and Lady Bangor – Bernard Ward and his wife, Anne – who were a bit of an odd couple. Their widely differing tastes in architecture resulted in an eccentric country residence – and a subsequent divorce. Bernard favoured the neoclassical style seen in the front façade and the main staircase, while Anne leant towards the Strawberry Hill Gothic of the rear façade, which reaches a peak in the incredible fan vaulting of her Gothic boudoir.

The house is now part of the National Trust's **Castle Ward Estate** (☎ 4488 1204; Park Rd; house & grounds adult/child £6.50/3, grounds only £4.30/2; ☒ house 1-6pm daily Easter Week, Jul & Aug, 1-6pm Sat, Sun & public hols Apr-Jun & Sep; grounds 10am-8pm daily Apr-Sep, 10am-4pm daily Oct-Mar). In the grounds you can visit a Victorian laundry museum, the Strangford Lough Wildlife Centre, Old Castle Ward (a fine 16th-century Plantation tower) and Castle Audley (a 15th-century tower house).

Kilclief Castle

Square-jawed and thick-set, **Kilclief Castle** (☎ 9023 5000; Kilclief; admission free; ☒ 10am-6pm Tue-Fri, 2-6pm Sat & Sun Jul & Aug) sprouts incongruously from a rural farmyard, framed between house and rickety barn. This is the oldest tower house in the county, built between 1413 and 1441 to guard the seaward entrance to the Narrows. It has some elaborate details and is thought to have been the prototype for Ardglass, Strangford and other castles in Lecale.

Kilclief Castle is on the A2, 4km south of Strangford.

Ardglass
pop 2900

Ardglass (Ard Ghlais) today is a small village with a busy fishing harbour, but in medieval times it was a major port and an important trading centre. The legacy of its heyday is the seven tower houses, dating from the 14th to the 16th centuries, that punctuate the hillside above the harbour.

The only one open to the public is **Jordan's Castle** (☎ 9181 1491; Low Rd; admission free; ☒ 10am-1pm Tue, Fri & Sat, 2-6pm Wed & Thu Jul & Aug), a four-storey tower near the harbour, built by a wealthy 15th-century merchant at the dawn of Ulster's economic development. The castle now houses a local museum and a collection of antiques accumulated by its last owner.

Ardglass is on the A2, 13km south of Strangford. Ulsterbus 16A runs from Downpatrick to Ardglass (20 minutes, hourly Monday to Friday, seven on Saturday, two on Sunday).

SLEEPING & EATING

Margaret's Cottage (☎ 4484 1080; www.margarets cottage.com; 9 Castle Pl; s/d £30/50; P) A dinky little flower-bedecked 18th-century cottage (with a modern upper floor), Margaret's is squeezed between Aldo's Restaurant and the ruins of Margaret's Castle and offers luxurious B&B accommodation, with four cosy rooms and an open fire in the lounge.

Aldo's Restaurant (☎ 4484 1315; 7 Castle Pl; mains £9-12; ☯ 5-10pm daily Jun-Aug, 5-10pm Thu-Sun, plus 12.30-2pm Sun year-round) A local institution, this cosy Italian restaurant serves excellent seafood, pasta and vegetarian dishes.

Curran's Bar (☎ 4484 1332; 83 Strangford Rd, Chapeltown; mains £8-18; ☯ food 12.30-9pm) This popular pub, 2.5km north of Ardglass on the A2 towards Strangford, has an atmospheric restaurant with worn wooden floors, a crackling open fire and old family photographs. It specialises in local seafood (try smoked haddock with braised leeks and dill butter) and prime Irish beef accompanied with potatoes and vegetables fresh from farmer Doyle along the road.

SOUTH DOWN & THE MOURNE MOUNTAINS
Newcastle
pop 7500

In the last couple of years the Victorian seaside resort of Newcastle (An Caisleán Nua) has undergone a multimillion-pound makeover, and now sports a snazzy new promenade stretching for more than a kilometre along the seafront, complete with modern sculptures and an elegant footbridge over the Shimna River. The facelift makes the most of Newcastle's superb setting on a 5km strand of golden sand at the foot of the Mourne Mountains, and there are hopes that it will transform the town's fortunes from fading bucket-and-spade resort to outdoor activities capital and gateway to the proposed Mourne National Park.

One short stretch of main street is still a gauntlet of amusement arcades and fast-food takeaways, which can get a bit raucous on Friday and Saturday nights, but the town is still a good base for exploring Murlough National

Nature Reserve and the Mourne Mountains – accessible from here on foot, by car or by public transport – while golfers from around the globe flock to the Royal County Down golf course, voted the 'best in the world outside the US' by the magazine Planet Golf in 2007.

ORIENTATION

As you exit the bus station, Main St stretches ahead towards the mountains, becoming Central Promenade (with the tourist office on the left) and then South Promenade. Turning left out of the bus station leads to a mini-roundabout; straight ahead is the beach, to the right is Downs Rd and the youth hostel, and to the left is the Slieve Donard Hotel.

INFORMATION

Coffee-Net (☎ 4372 7388; 5-7 Railway St; per 15 min £1; ☯ 9am-6pm Mon-Sat) Internet access in the coffee shop in the bus station.

Mourne Heritage Trust (☎ 4372 4059; www.mourne live.com; 87 Central Promenade; ☯ 9am-5pm Mon-Fri) Books, maps and brochures on the Mourne region, plus information on walking in the Mournes.

Post office (☎ 4372 2651; 6 Railway St) Opposite the bus station.

Tourist information centre (☎ 4372 2222; newcastle .tic@downdc.gov.uk; 10-14 Central Promenade; ☯ 9.30am-7pm Mon-Sat, 1-7pm Sun Jul & Aug, 10am-5pm Mon-Sat, 2-5pm Sun Sep-Jun) Sells local-interest books and maps, and a range of traditional and contemporary crafts.

SIGHTS & ACTIVITIES

Newcastle's main attraction is the **beach**, which stretches 5km northeast to **Murlough National Nature Reserve** (admission free, car park £3 May-Sep; ☯ 24hr), where footpaths and boardwalks meander among the grassy dunes, with great views back towards the Mournes.

Back in town, **Tropicana** (☎ 4372 5034; Central Promenade; adult/child £3/2.50; ☯ 11am-7pm Mon & Wed-Fri, 11am-5pm Tue & Sat, 1-5.30pm Sun Jul & Aug) is a family entertainment centre with outdoor heated fun pools, giant water slides, and paddling pools for toddlers.

At the south end of the seafront is the **Rock Pool** (☎ 4372 5034; South Promenade; adult/child £1.50/1.30; ☯ 10am-6pm Mon-Sat & 2-6pm Sun Jul & Aug), an outdoor seawater swimming pool that dates from the 1930s. If it's too cold for outdoor bathing, you can simmer away in a hot seaweed bath at nearby **Soak** (☎ 4372 6002; www .soakseaweedbaths.co.uk; 5A South Promenade; ☯ noon-8pm daily Jun-Sep, 2-8pm Mon, Thu & Fri, noon-8pm Sat & Sun Oct-May), where a one-hour session costs £20.

The little **harbour** at the south end of town once served the 'stone boats' that exported Mourne granite from the quarries of Slieve Donard. The **Granite Trail**, which begins across the road from the harbour, is a waymarked footpath that leads up a disused funicular railway line that once carried granite blocks to the harbour. The view from the top is worth the steep, 200m climb.

Stretching north of town is the **Royal County Down Golf Course** (☎ 4372 3314; www.royalcountydown .org; green fees weekday/weekend £135/150 May-Oct, £65/70 Oct-Mar). The challenging Championship Links – venue for the 2007 Walker Cup – is full of blind tee-shots and monster rough, and is regularly voted one of the world's top 10 golf courses. It's open to visitors on Monday, Tuesday, Thursday, Friday and Sunday.

SLEEPING

Tollymore Forest Park (☎ 4372 2428; 176 Tullybranigan Rd; camp/caravan sites £9-13) Many of Newcastle's 'camping sites' are caravans only – the nearest place where you can pitch a tent is 3km northwest of the town centre, amid the attractive scenery of Tollymore Forest Park. You can hike here (along Bryansford Ave and Bryansford Rd) in 45 minutes.

Newcastle Youth Hostel (☎ 4372 2133; www.hini .org.uk; 30 Downs Rd; dm £13; ☺ daily Mar-Oct, Fri & Sat nights only Nov & Dec, closed Jan & Feb) This hostel is only a few minutes' walk from the bus station, housed in an attractive 19th-century villa with sea views. It has 37 beds, mostly in six-bed dorms, a kitchen, a laundry and a TV room.

our pick Briers Country House (☎ 4372 4347; www .thebriers.co.uk; 39 Middle Tollymore Rd; s/d £38/55; **P**) A peaceful farmhouse B&B with a country setting and views of the Mournes, Briers is just 1.5km northwest of the town centre (signposted off the road between Newcastle and Bryansford). Huge breakfasts – vegetarian if you like – are served with a view over the garden, and evening meals are available by prior arrangement.

Harbour House Inn (☎ 4372 3445; www.stone boatrestaurant.com; 4 South Promenade; s/d £40/60; **P**) The Harbour House is a family-friendly pub and restaurant with four rooms upstairs that are a little tattered round the edges but clean and comfortable. It's next to the old harbour, almost 2km south of the bus station, a perfect base for climbing Slieve Donard.

Beach House (☎ 4372 2345; myrtle.macauley@tesco .net; 22 Downs Rd; s/d £40/70; **P**) Enjoy a sea view with your breakfast at the Beach House, an elegant Victorian B&B with three rooms (two with private bathroom) and a balcony (open to all guests) overlooking the beach.

Slieve Donard Resort & Spa (☎ 4372 3681; www .hastingshotels.com; Downs Rd; s/d from £120/150; **P** ☺) Established in 1897, the Slieve Donard is a magnificent, Victorian red-brick pile overlooking the beach, recently refurbished and equipped with a luxurious spa. This is where golf legends Tom Watson, Jack Nicklaus and Tiger Woods stay when they're in town.

EATING

Maud's (☎ 4372 6184; 106 Main St; mains £3-6; ☺ 9am-9.30pm) Maud's is a bright, modern café with picture windows framing a stunning view across the river to the Mournes. It serves breakfast, good coffee, a range of tempting scones and sticky buns, plus salads, crêpes, pizzas and pastas; there's a kids menu too.

Strand Restaurant & Bakery (☎ 4372 3472; 53-55 Central Promenade; mains £5-9; ☺ 8.30am-11pm Jun-Aug, 9am-6pm Sep-May) The Strand has been around since 1930, and dishes up great home-made ice cream and cakes, as well as serving all-day breakfast (£2 to £5), lunch and dinner in its traditional, seaside, chips-with-everything restaurant.

Percy French Bar & Restaurant (☎ 4372 3175; Downs Rd; mains £7-12; ☺ food served noon-2.30pm & 5.30-9pm) Themed after local composer William Percy French, this is an appealing, low-raftered barn of a place, with sea views in summer and a roaring log fire in winter. The menu includes steaks, salads, and Mexican and Italian dishes, with the choice of bar meals or a sit-down restaurant.

Campers can stock up on provisions at the **Lidl Supermarket** (3 Railway St; ☺ 9am-7pm Mon-Wed & Fri, 9am-9pm Thu, 9am-6pm Sat, 1-6pm Sun) in the red-brick former train station beside the bus station.

SHOPPING

Hill Trekker (☎ 4372 3842; 115 Central Promenade; ☺ 10am-5.30pm Tue-Sun), at the far south end of town, sells hiking, climbing and camping equipment.

GETTING THERE & AROUND

The bus station is on Railway St. Ulsterbus 20 runs to Newcastle from Belfast's Europa

BusCentre (£6, 1¼ hours, hourly Monday to Saturday, seven Sunday) via Dundrum. Bus 37 continues along the coast road from Newcastle to Annalong and Kilkeel (£3, 40 minutes, hourly Monday to Saturday, six Sunday).

Goldline Express bus 240 takes the inland route from Newry to Newcastle (£5, 50 minutes, six daily Monday to Saturday, two Sunday) via Hilltown and on to Downpatrick. You can also get to Newry along the coast road, changing buses at Kilkeel.

Wiki Wiki Wheels (☎ 4372 3973; 10B Donard St; ☷ 9am-6pm Mon-Sat, 2-6pm Sun) and **Ross Cycles** (☎ 4372 5525; Unit 9, Slieve Donard Shopping Centre, Railway St; ☷ 9.30am-6pm Mon-Sat, 2-5pm Sun), both near the bus station, hire out bikes for around £10/50 per day/week.

Around Newcastle
DUNDRUM
Second only to Carrickfergus as Northern Ireland's finest Norman fortress is **Dundrum Castle** (☎ 9181 1491; Dundrum; admission free; ☷ 10am-7pm Tue-Sat, 2-7pm Sun Apr-Sep, 10am-4pm Sat, 2-4pm Sun Oct-Mar), founded in 1177 by John de Courcy of Carrickfergus. The castle overlooks the sheltered waters of Dundrum Bay, famous for its oysters and mussels.

OURPICK **Mourne Seafood Bar** (☎ 4375 1377; 10 Main St; mains £7-16, 2-course lunch £9; ☷ noon-9.30pm daily Apr-Oct, closed Mon & Tue Nov-Mar) is a friendly and informal fishmonger-cum-restaurant set in a wood-panelled Victorian house with local art brightening the walls. As well as a choice of oysters served five different ways, the menu includes seafood chowder, crab, langoustines and daily fish specials.

Dundrum is 5km north of Newcastle. Bus 17 from Newcastle to Downpatrick stops in Dundrum (£2, 12 minutes, eight daily Monday to Friday, three Saturday, two Sunday).

TOLLYMORE FOREST PARK
This scenic **forest park** (☎ 4372 2428; Bryansford; car/pedestrian £4/2; ☷ 10am-dusk), 3km west of Newcastle, has lengthy walks along the Shimna River and across the northern slopes of the Mournes. The **visitor centre** (☷ noon-5pm daily Jun-Aug, noon-5pm Sat & Sun Sep-May), in 18th-century Clanbrassil Barn (it looks more like a church), has information on the flora, fauna and history of the park. Note: mountain-biking is not allowed in the park.

CASTLEWELLAN
A less rugged outdoor experience is offered by **Castlewellan Forest Park** (☎ 4377 8664; Main St, Castlewellan; car/pedestrian £4/2; ☷ 10am-dusk), with gentle walks around the castle grounds and **trout fishing** in its lovely lake (a daily permit costs £5).

Castlewellan village is the focus of the **Celtic Fusion Festival** (www.celticfusion.co.uk), a 10-day celebration of Celtic music, art, drama and dance at venues around County Down, including Castlewellan, Newcastle and Downpatrick.

Mourne Mountains
The hump-backed granite hills of the Mourne Mountains dominate the horizon as you head south from Belfast towards Newcastle. This is one of the most beautiful corners of Northern Ireland, a distinctive landscape of yellow gorse, grey granite and whitewashed cottages, the lower slopes of the hills latticed with a neat patchwork of dry-stone walls cobbled together from huge, rounded granite boulders.

The hills were made famous in a popular song penned by Irish songwriter William Percy French in 1896, whose chorus, 'Where the Mountains of Mourne sweep down to the sea', captures perfectly their scenic blend of ocean, sky and hillside. At the time of writing the government was looking at proposals to create **Mourne National Park** (www.mourneworkingparty.org).

The Mournes offer some of the best hill-walking and rock-climbing in the North. Specialist guidebooks include *The Mournes: Walks* by Paddy Dillon and *A Rock-Climbing Guide to the Mourne Mountains* by Robert Bankhead. You'll also need an Ordnance Survey map, either the 1:50,000 Discoverer Series (Sheet No 29: *The Mournes*), or the 1:25,000 Activity Series (*The Mournes*). You can buy maps at the tourist information centre in Newcastle.

HISTORY
The crescent of low-lying land on the southern side of the mountains is known as the Kingdom of Mourne. Cut off for centuries by its difficult approaches (the main overland route passed north of the hills), it developed a distinctive landscape and culture. Neither St Patrick nor the Normans (their nearest strongholds were at Greencastle and Dundrum) ventured here, and until the coast road was built in the early 19th century, the only access was on foot or by sea.

Smuggling provided a source of income in the 18th century. Boats carrying French spirits would land at night and packhorses would carry the casks through the hills to the inland road, avoiding the excise men at Newcastle. The Brandy Pad, an ex- smugglers' path from Bloody Bridge to Tollymore, is today a popular walking route.

Apart from farming and fishing, the main industry was the quarrying of Mourne granite. The quarried stone was carried down from the hills on carts to harbours at Newcastle, Annalong and Kilkeel where 'stone boats' shipped it out; kerbstones of Mourne granite are found in Belfast, Liverpool, London, Manchester and Birmingham. There are still several working quarries today, and Mourne granite has been used in the 9/11 British Memorial Garden in New York.

SIGHTS

At the heart of the Mournes is the beautiful **Silent Valley Reservoir** (☎ 9074 6581; car/motorcycle £3/2, plus per pedestrian adult/child £1.50/0.50; ☒ 10am-6.30pm Apr-Sep, 10am-4pm Oct-Mar), where the Kilkeel River was dammed in 1933. There are scenic, waymarked walks around the grounds, a **coffee shop** (☒ 11am-6.30pm daily Jun-Aug, 11am-6.30pm Sat &

Sun Apr, May & Sep) and an interesting exhibition on the building of the dam. From the car park a shuttle bus (adult/child return £1.20/0.90) will take you another 4km up the valley to the Crom Dam. It runs daily in July and August, weekends only in May, June and September.

The dry-stone **Mourne Wall** was built between 1904 and 1922 to keep livestock out of the catchment area of the Kilkeel and Annalong Rivers, which were to be dammed to provide a water supply for Belfast. (Poor geological conditions meant the Annalong could not be dammed, and its waters were diverted to the Silent Valley Reservoir via a 3.6km-long tunnel beneath Slieve Binnian.) The spectacular wall, 2m high, 1m thick and over 35km long, marches across the summits of 15 of the surrounding peaks including the highest, Slieve Donard (853m).

ACTIVITIES

If you fancy a shot at hill walking, rock-climbing, canoeing or a range of outdoor activities, **Bluelough Mountain & Water Sports Centre** (☎ 4377 0714; www.mountainandwater.com; Grange Courtyard, Castlewellan Forest Park) offers one-day, have-a-go sessions for individuals, couples and families (around £50 to £90 per person), and Sunday

---

WALK: SLIEVE DONARD

The rounded form of Slieve Donard (853m), the highest hill in Northern Ireland, looms above Newcastle like a slumbering giant. You can hike to the summit from various starting points in and around Newcastle, but remember – it's a stiff climb, and you shouldn't attempt it without proper walking boots, waterproofs and a map and compass.

On a good day the view from the top extends to the hills of Donegal, the Wicklow Mountains, the coast of Scotland, the Isle of Man and even the hills of Snowdonia in Wales. Two cairns near the summit were long believed to have been cells of St Donard, who retreated here to pray in early Christian times.

From Newcastle (9km, three hours)

This is the shortest but least interesting route. Begin at Donard Park car park, at the edge of town 1km south of the bus station. At the far end of the car park, turn right through the gate and head into the woods, with the river on your left. A gravel path leads up the Glen River valley to the saddle between Slieve Donard and Slieve Commedagh. From here, turn left and follow the Mourne Wall to the summit (see above for more on the Mourne Wall). Return by the same route.

From Bloody Bridge (10km, 3½ hours)

Start from the car park at Bloody Bridge on the A2 coast road 5km south of Newcastle (any bus to Kilkeel will drop you there). From here, an old smugglers' path called the Brandy Pad (see boxed text, p630) leads up the valley of the Bloody Bridge River past old granite workings to the saddle south of Slieve Donard. Turn right and follow the Mourne Wall to the summit; cross the wall first, as the best views are to your left. Return by the same route, or descend the Glen River to Newcastle.

afternoon taster sessions. They also rent canoes for £15/40 per hour/day.

If the weather is wet, you can still go rock-climbing at **hot rock** (☎ 4372 5354; www.hotrockwall .com; adult/child £4.50/2.50; ☒ 10am-5pm Sat-Mon, to 10pm Tue-Fri), the indoor climbing wall at Tollymore Mountain Centre. The entrance is on the B180, 2km west of the Tollymore Forest Park exit gate. You can hire rock boots and harness for £3.50.

Surfin' Dirt (☎ 07739-210119; Tullyree Rd, Bryansford; ☒ 10am-6pm Tue-Sun Jul & Aug, 11am-6pm Sat & Sun Apr-Jun & Sep-Nov) is a mountain-boarding track off the B180 3km west of Bryansford village. A three-hour beginner's session, including board, safety gear and instruction, costs £15.

More sedate outdoor activities are offered by the **Mount Pleasant Pony Trekking & Horse Riding Centre** (☎ 4377 8651; www.mountpleasantcentre.com; Bannonstown Rd, Castlewellan; per hr £12-15), which caters for both experienced riders and beginners, and offers various guided treks into the park. Short rides, beach rides and pony trekking can also be arranged.

Mourne Cycle Tours (☎ 4372 4348; www.mournecycle tours.com; 13 Spelga Ave, Newcastle) provide mountain and touring bike hire (from £10/15/80 per half-day/full day/week) and can arrange self-guided tours and family cycling weekends, including accommodation.

FESTIVALS

The Mournes are the venue for various hiking festivals, including the **Mourne International Walking Festival** (www.mournewalking.co.uk) in late June, and the Down District Walking Festival in early August.

SLEEPING

Meelmore Lodge (☎ 4372 6657; www.meelmorelodge .co.uk; 52 Trassey Rd, Bryansford; camping per adult/child £4/2.50, dm/tw £15/44; P) Set on the northern slopes of the Mournes, 5km west of Bryansford village, Meelmore has hostel accommodation with cosy lounge and kitchen, a family camp site and a coffee shop.

Cnocnafeola Centre (☎ 4176 5859; www.mourne hostel.com; Bog Rd, Atticall; dm/tw/f £14/36/55; P) This modern, purpose-built hostel is in the village of Atticall 6km north of Kilkeel, off the B27 Hilltown road, and 3km west of the entrance to Silent Valley. As well as a self-catering kitchen, there's a restaurant that serves breakfast (from £4), lunch and dinner.

GETTING THERE & AWAY

In July and August only, the Ulsterbus 405 Mourne Rambler service runs a circular route from Newcastle, calling at a dozen stops around the Mournes, including Bryansford (8 minutes), Meelmore (17 minutes), Silent Valley (40 minutes), Carrick Little (45 minutes) and Bloody Bridge (one hour). There are six buses daily – the first leaves at 9.30am, the last at 4.30pm; a £4 all-day ticket allows you to get on and off as many times as you like.

Bus 34A (July and August only) runs from Newcastle to the Silent Valley car park (30 minutes, four daily Monday to Friday, three Saturday, two Sunday), calling at Donard Park (five minutes) and Bloody Bridge (10 minutes).

Mournes Coast Road

The scenic drive south along the A2 coast road from Newcastle to Newry is the most memorable journey in Down. Annalong, Kilkeel and Rostrevor offer convenient stopping points from which you can detour into the mountains.

ANNALONG

The harbour at the fishing village of Annalong (Áth na Long) desperately wants to be picturesque, with an early 19th-century **Corn Mill** (☎ 4376 8736; Marine Park; adult/child £2/1.10; ☒ 2-6pm Wed-Mon Apr-Oct, 3-5pm Wed-Mon Nov-Mar) overlooking the river mouth on one side. The effect is spoiled a bit by graffiti and ugly buildings on the other side.

You can overnight at the family-oriented **Cornmill Quay Hostel** (☎ 4376 8269; www.cornmillquay .com; Marine Park; dm adult/child £15/10, d £40; P), set in a pretty little cottage courtyard above the harbour. There are also four self-catering cottages (from £350 a week in high season).

The attractive **Harbour Inn** (☎ 4376 8678; 6 Harbour Dr; mains £5-9; ☒ food 12.30-2.30pm, 5-8pm Sun-Fri, 12.30-9pm Sat) has an attractive lounge bar with sofas arranged along the picture windows beside the harbour, and an upstairs restaurant with a great view of the Mournes.

KILKEEL

Kilkeel (Cill Chaoil, meaning 'church of the narrow place') takes its name from the 14th-century **Church of St Colman**, whose ruins stand in the graveyard across the street from the tourist office. The town has a busy commercial fishing harbour and a quayside fish

WALK: THE BRANDY PAD

The Brandy Pad is an ancient smugglers' trail across the Mourne Mountains that was used in the 18th century to carry brandy, wine, tobacco and coffee to Hilltown, avoiding the excise officer at Newcastle. The trail begins at Bloody Bridge, 5km south of Newcastle.

The first part of the path follows the route up Slieve Donard from Bloody Bridge (see boxed text, p628) as far as the Mourne Wall (3.5km). On the far side of the wall a wide path contours north (to your right) across the lower slopes of Slieve Donard, then continues traversing west below the Castles, a huddle of weathered granite pinnacles. Beyond the peaty col beneath Slieve Commedagh, the path descends slightly into the valley of the Kilkeel River (or Silent Valley), and continues traversing with Ben Crom reservoir down to your left, to reach Hare's Gap and a reunion with the Mourne Wall.

Go through the gap in the wall and descend to the northwest, steeply at first then more easily on a broad and stony trail known as the Trassey Track which leads down to a minor road and the Trassey Bridge car park near Meelmore Lodge (12km from Bloody Bridge; allow three to five hours).

From here you can return to Newcastle on foot through Tollymore Forest Park, along the trail that begins immediately above the car park (8km; allow two to three hours), or (July and August only) you can catch the Mourne Rambler bus from either the car park or Meelmore Lodge.

market supplied by Northern Ireland's largest fishing fleet.

The **tourist information centre** (☎ 4176 2525; kdakilkeel@hotmail.com; Rooney Rd; ✆ 9am-1pm & 2-5.30pm Mon-Fri, also Sat Easter-Oct) is in the Nautilus Centre next to the harbour.

ROSTREVOR

Rostrevor (Caislean Ruairi) is a pretty Victorian seaside resort famed for its lively pubs. Each year in late July, folk musicians converge on the village for the **Fiddler's Green International Festival** (☎ 4173 9819; www.fiddlersgreenfestival.co.uk).

The town is noted for its many pubs, most of which have regular live music. The best ones to eat in are the **Kilbroney** (☎ 4173 8390; 31 Church St) and the **Celtic Fjord** (☎ 4173 8005; 8 Mary St).

To the east is **Kilbroney Forest Park** (☎ 4173 8134; Shore Rd; admission free; ✆ 9am-10pm Jun-Aug, to 5pm Sep-May). From the car park at the top of the forest drive, a 10-minute hike leads up to the **Cloughmore Stone**, a 30-tonne granite boulder inscribed with Victorian graffiti, and a superb view over the lough to Carlingford Mountain.

Warrenpoint

pop 7000

Warrenpoint (An Pointe) is a Victorian resort at the head of Carlingford Lough, its seaside appeal somewhat diminished by the large industrial harbour at the west end of town. Its broad streets, main square and recently renovated prom are pleasant enough,

though, and it has better sleeping and eating options than either Newry or Rostrevor.

The **tourist information centre** (☎ 4175 2256; Church St; ✆ 9am-1pm & 2-5pm Mon-Fri Oct-May, also Sat & Sun Jun-Sep) is in the town hall.

About 2km northwest of the town centre is **Narrow Water Castle** (☎ 9181 1491; admission free; ✆ 10am-1pm Tue, Fri & Sat, 2-6pm Wed & Thu Jul & Aug), a fine Elizabethan tower house built in 1568 to command the entrance to the Newry River.

SLEEPING & EATING

our pick **Whistledown & Finns** (☎ 4175 4174; www.whistledown.co.uk; 6 Seaview; s/d £40/70) This waterfront guesthouse offers country-style accommodation in five rooms (ask for No 2, with its pine four-poster bed and bay window overlooking the sea), and a stylish bar and restaurant (mains £9 to £14; open noon to 5pm & 7.30pm to 10pm Monday to Saturday, plus 12.30pm to 3.30pm Sunday).

Boathouse Inn (☎ 4175 3743; www.boathouseinn.com; 3 Marine Pde; s/d £45/70; P) The Boathouse offers two top-notch dining options: the Boathouse Restaurant (mains £11 to £17; open 7pm to 10pm), a chilled out, candle-lit bistro with a modern fusion menu, and the Vecchia Roma (mains £6 to £15; open noon to 2.30pm and 6pm to 11pm), a traditional, checked-tablecloth-and-candle-in-a-chianti-bottle Italian restaurant. It also has 12 comfortable but unremarkable rooms.

GETTING THERE & AWAY

Bus 39 runs between Newry and Warrenpoint (£2, 20 minutes, at least hourly Monday to Saturday, 10 on Sunday), with some services continuing to Kilkeel (one hour).

Newry

pop 22,975

Newry has long been a frontier town, guarding the land route from Dublin to Ulster through the 'Gap of the North', the pass between Slieve Gullion and the Carlingford hills, still followed by the main Dublin–Belfast road and railway. Its name derives from a yew tree (An tIúr) supposedly planted here by St Patrick.

The opening of the Newry Canal in 1742, linking the town with the River Bann at Portadown, made Newry into a busy trading port, exporting coal from Coalisland on Lough Neagh as well as linen and butter from the surrounding area.

Newry today is a major shopping centre, with a busy market on Thursday and Saturday, and makes a good base for exploring the Mourne Mountains, South Armagh and the Cooley Peninsula in County Louth.

INFORMATION

Coffee-Net (☎ 3026 3531; Newry BusCentre, the Mall; per 15min £1; ☷ 8.30am-6pm Mon-Fri, 9am-6pm Sat, 5-8pm Sun) Internet access.

Tourist information centre (☎ 3031 3170; Bagenal's Castle, Castle St; ☷ 9am-5pm Mon-Fri year-round, to 7pm Tue-Fri mid Jun–Sep, also 10am-4pm Sat Apr-Sep)

SIGHTS

So fierce was the rivalry between counties Down and Armagh in the 19th century, that when the new red-brick **town hall** was built in 1893 it was erected right on the border – on a three-arched bridge across the Newry River. The cannon outside was captured during the Crimean War (1853–56) and given to the town in memory of local volunteers who fought in the war.

Bagenal's Castle is the town's oldest surviving building, a 16th-century tower house built for Nicholas Bagenal, grand marshal of the English army in Ireland. Recently rediscovered, having been incorporated into more recent buildings, the castle has been restored and now houses the **Newry and Mourne Museum** (☎ 3031 3178; www.bagenalscastle.com; Castle St; admission free; ☷ 10am-4.30pm Mon-Sat & 1-4.30pm Sun),

with exhibits on the Newry Canal and local archaeology, culture and folklore.

The **Newry Canal** runs parallel to the river through the town centre, and is a focus for the city's redevelopment. A cycle path runs 30km north to Portadown, following the route of the canal. **Newry Ship Canal** runs 6km south towards Carlingford Lough, where the Victoria Lock has been restored to working order as part of a long-term project to reopen the whole canal to leisure traffic. Designed by Sir John Rennie, the civil engineer who designed Waterloo, Southwark and London Bridges in London, the ship canal allowed large, sea-going vessels to reach Albert Basin in the centre of Newry.

SLEEPING

Marymount (☎ 3026 1099; patricia.ohare2@btinternet.com; Windsor Ave; s/d £32/54; P) A modern bungalow in a quiet location up a hill off the A1 Belfast road, Marymount is only a 10-minute walk from the town centre. Only one of the three rooms comes with private bathroom.

Canal Court Hotel (☎ 3025 1234; www.canalcourt hotel.com; Merchants Quay; s/d from £80/130; P) You can't miss this huge, yellow building opposite the bus station. Although it's a modern hotel, it affects a deliberately old-fashioned atmosphere with leather sofas dotted around the vast wood-panelled lobby and a restaurant that veers dangerously close to chintzy.

EATING & DRINKING

Café Krem (☎ 3026 6233; 14 Hill St; mains £2-3; ☷ 8.30am-6pm Mon-Sat) A friendly, community atmosphere and the best coffee in town make Café Krem stand out from the crowd. There's also wicked hot chocolate, tasty *panini* (a type of Italian sandwich) and a couple of big, soft sofas to sink into.

Brass Monkey (☎ 3026 3176; 1-4 Sandy St; mains £7-12; ☷ food 12.30-2.30pm & 5-8pm) Newry's most popular pub, with Victorian brass, brick and timber décor, serves good bar meals ranging from lasagne and burgers to seafood and steaks.

Cobbles (☎ 3083 3333; 15 the Mall; mains £5-12; ☷ food 10am-9.30pm) This stylish lounge-bar is decked out in dark parquet flooring and blonde wood with leather chairs and banquettes in burgundy and cream. It dishes up big breakfasts (till noon), chunky lunches and delicious dinners from a fancy pub-grub menu that ranges from soup and a sandwich to home-made burgers and pizza.

GETTING THERE & AWAY

Newry BusCentre is on the Mall, opposite the Canal Court Hotel. Goldline Express bus 238 runs regularly to Newry from Belfast's Europa BusCentre (£7, 1¼ hours, at least hourly Monday to Saturday, eight Sunday) via Hillsborough and Banbridge.

Bus 44 runs from Newry to Armagh (£5, 1¼ hours, twice daily Monday to Friday, three on Saturday), and Goldline Express bus 295 goes from Newry to Enniskillen (£9, 2¾ hours, twice daily Monday to Saturday, July and August only) via Armagh and Monaghan. Bus 39 departs for Warrenpoint (20 minutes, at least hourly Monday to Saturday, 10 on Sunday) and Rostrevor (30 minutes), with 10 a day continuing to Kilkeel (£4, one hour).

The train station is 2.5km northwest of the centre, on the A25; bus 341 (free for train passengers) goes there hourly from the bus station. Newry is a stop on the service between Dublin (£16, 1¼ hours) and Belfast (£8, 50 minutes, 10 daily Monday to Saturday, five Sunday).

COUNTY ARMAGH

SOUTH ARMAGH

Rural and staunchly republican, South Armagh is known to its inhabitants as 'God's Country'. But to the British soldiers stationed there in the 1970s it had another, more sinister nickname – 'Bandit Country'. With the Republic only a few miles away,

South Armagh was a favourite venue for IRA cross-border attacks and bombings. For more than 30 years, British soldiers on foot patrol in village streets and the constant clatter of army helicopters were a part of everyday life.

The peace process has probably had more visible effect here than anywhere else in Northern Ireland. As part of the UK government's 'normalisation process' the army pulled out in 2007 – the hilltop watchtowers have all been removed (their former location marked here and there by a defiant Irish tricolour) and the huge barracks at Bessbrook Mill and Crossmaglen have been closed down.

Hopefully, a part of Ireland that was once notorious for its violence will once again be known for its historic sites, enchanting rural scenery and traditional music.

Bessbrook

pop 3150

Bessbrook (An Sruthán) was founded in the mid-19th century by Quaker linen manufacturer John Grubb Richardson as a 'model village' to house the workers at his flax mill. Rows of pretty terraced houses made from local granite line the two main squares, Charlemont and College, each with a green in the middle, and are complemented by a town hall, school, bathhouse and dispensary. It is said that Bessbrook was the inspiration for Bournville (near Birmingham in England), the model village built by the Cadbury family for their chocolate factory.

At the centre of the village is the massive **Bessbrook Mill**. Requisitioned by the British Army in 1970, it served as a military base for more than 30 years – the helipad on top was reputedly the busiest in Europe – until the troops moved out in 2007. There are plans to convert the mill building into apartments, and the new complex may house an art gallery and café.

Just south of Bessbrook is **Derrymore House** (☎ 8778 4753; ⊙ gardens 10am-7pm May-Sep, to 4pm Oct-Apr), an elegant thatched cottage built in 1776 for Isaac Corry, the Irish MP for Newry for 30 years; the Act of Union was drafted in the drawing room here in 1800. At the time of research the house was closed to the public, but the surrounding parkland – laid out by John Sutherland (1745–1826), one of the most celebrated disciples of English landscape gardener Capability Brown –

TOP 10 RESTAURANTS IN NORTHERN IRELAND (OUTSIDE BELFAST)

- 55 Degrees North (p660)
- Brown's Restaurant (p651)
- Grace Neill's (p616)
- Lime Tree (p655)
- Lobster Pot (p624)
- Mourne Seafood Bar (p627)
- Narrows (p617)
- Oscar's (p681)
- Plough Inn (p611)
- Uluru Bistro (p637)

offers scenic trails with views to the Ring of Gullion.

Bessbrook is 5km northwest of Newry. Bus 41 runs from Newry to Bessbrook (15 minutes, hourly Monday to Saturday), while buses 42 (to Crossmaglen) and 44 (to Armagh) pass the entrance to Derrymore House on the A25 Camlough road.

Ring of Gullion

The Ring of Gullion is a magical region steeped in Celtic legend, centred on Slieve Gullion (Sliabh gCuilinn; 576m) where the Celtic warrior Cúchulainn is said to have taken his name after killing the dog (*cú*) belonging to the smith Culainn. The 'ring' is a necklace of rugged hills strung between Newry and Forkhill, 15km to the southwest, encircling the central whaleback ridge of Slieve Gullion. This unusual concentric formation is a geological structure known as a ring-dyke.

KILLEVY CHURCHES

Surrounded by beech trees, these ruined, conjoined **churches** (admission free; ⊗ 24hr) were constructed on the site of a 5th-century nunnery that was founded by St Moninna. The eastern church dates from the 15th century, and shares a gable wall with the 12th-century western one. The west door, with a massive lintel and granite jambs, may be 200 years older still. At the side of the churchyard a footpath leads uphill to a white cross that marks St Moninna's holy well.

The churches are 6km south of Camlough, on a minor road to Meigh. Look out for a crossroads with a sign pointing west to the churches and east to Bernish Rock Viewpoint.

SLIEVE GULLION FOREST PARK

A 13km scenic drive through this **forest park** (admission free; ⊗ 8am-dusk) provides picturesque views over the surrounding hills. From the parking and picnic area at the top of the drive you can hike to the summit of Slieve Gullion, the highest point in County Armagh, topped by two early–Bronze Age cairns and a tiny lake (1.5km round trip). The park entrance is 10km southwest of Newry on the B113 road to Forkhill.

MULLAGHBANE & FORKHILL

In the village of Mullaghbane (Mullach Bán), just west of Slieve Gullion, is **Tí Chu-**

lainn (☎ 3088 8828; www.tichulainn.com; admission free; ⊗ 9am-5pm Mon-Fri, 11am-12.30pm Sat), a cultural activities centre that promotes the Irish language, local folklore, traditional music and storytelling. The centre houses an exhibition, craft shop and café. It also offers hostel-type accommodation (£40 for a room sleeping up to three people).

The pubs in nearby Forkhill hold traditional music sessions on Tuesday nights and alternate Saturdays, and a folk music festival in October.

Crossmaglen

pop 1600

Crossmaglen (Crois Mhic Lionnáin), arranged around one of Ireland's biggest market squares, is a strongly republican village just 4km inside the border. At the height of the Troubles the barracks at 'Cross' (or XMG, as it was known) was the most feared posting in the British Army.

Now the army has gone, and for today's visitors Crossmaglen is a friendly place with a reputation for Gaelic football (Crossmaglen Rangers were the All-Ireland Club Champions in 2007), horse breeding and lively pubs known for their excellent music sessions.

You can get tourist information at **RoSA** (☎ 3086 8900; 25-26 O'Fiaich Sq; ⊗ 9am-5pm Mon-Fri), and **Twisted Briar Tours** (☎ 3026 0488; twistedbriar tours@ireland.com) can provide customised tours of the area for around £70 per half day.

Murtagh's Bar (☎ 3086 1378; aidanmurtagh@hotmail .com; 13 North St; s/d £25/50) offers good craic, traditional music, bar meals and B&B, while the brand new **Cross Square Hotel** (☎ 3086 0505; www .crosssquarehotel.com; 4-5 O'Fiaich Sq; s/d £50/80; mains £7-10; ⊗ food served 9.30am-9pm) serves bar meals all day and an à la carte menu at lunch and dinner. There's live music on Friday, Saturday and Sunday nights.

Bus 42 runs from Newry to Crossmaglen (£4, 50 minutes, six daily Monday to Friday, four Saturday) via Camlough and Mullaghbane.

ARMAGH CITY

pop 14,600

The little cathedral city of Armagh (Ard Macha) has been an important religious centre since the 5th century, and today it remains the ecclesiastical capital of Ireland, the seat of both the Anglican and Roman Catholic archbishops of Armagh, and

COUNTIES DOWN & ARMAGH

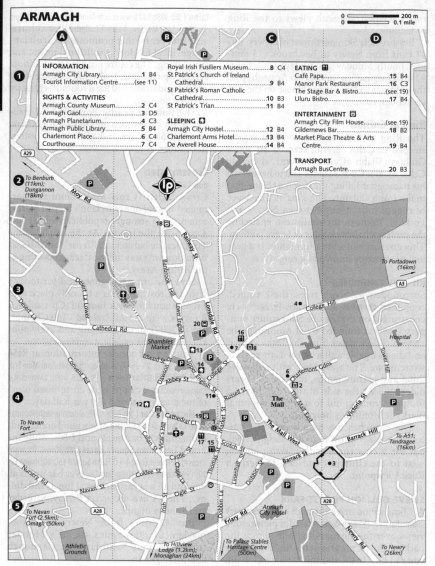

ARMAGH

INFORMATION	
Armagh City Library	1 B4
Tourist Information Centre	(see 11)

SIGHTS & ACTIVITIES	
Armagh County Museum	2 C4
Armagh Gaol	3 D5
Armagh Planetarium	4 C3
Armagh Public Library	5 B4
Charlemont Place	6 C4
Courthouse	7 C4

Royal Irish Fusiliers Museum	8 C4
St Patrick's Church of Ireland Cathedral	9 B4
St Patrick's Roman Catholic Cathedral	10 B3
St Patrick's Trian	11 B4

SLEEPING	
Armagh City Hostel	12 B4
Charlemont Arms Hotel	13 B4
De Averell House	14 B4

EATING	
Café Papa	15 B4
Manor Park Restaurant	16 C3
The Stage Bar & Bistro	(see 19)
Uluru Bistro	17 B4

ENTERTAINMENT	
Armagh City Film House	(see 19)
Gildernews Bar	18 B2
Market Place Theatre & Arts Centre	19 B4

TRANSPORT	
Armagh BusCentre	20 B3

primates of all Ireland. Their two cathedrals, both named for St Patrick, stare each other out from their respective hilltops.

Despite having a number of attractive Georgian buildings, the town has a bit of a dreary, run-down feel to it, with gap sites, wasteland and boarded-up windows spoiling the streetscape, but it's worth a visit for the fascinating Armagh Public Library and nearby Navan Fort.

History

When St Patrick began his mission to spread Christianity throughout Ireland, he chose a site close to Emain Macha (Navan Fort), the nerve centre of pagan Ulster, for his power base. In AD 445 he built Ireland's first stone church on a hill nearby (now home to the Church of Ireland cathedral), and later decreed that Armagh should have pre-eminence over all the churches in Ireland.

By the 8th century Armagh was one of Europe's best-known centres of religion, learning and craftwork. The city was divided into three districts (called *trians*), centred around English, Scottish and Irish streets. Armagh's fame was its undoing, however, as the Vikings plundered the city 10 times between AD 831 and 1013.

The city gained a new prosperity from the linen trade in the 18th century, a period whose legacy includes a Royal School, an astronomical observatory, a renowned public library and a fine crop of Georgian architecture.

Armagh is associated with some prominent historical figures. James Ussher (1580–1655), Archbishop of Armagh, was an avid scholar who is best known for pinning down the day of the Creation to Sunday, 23 October 4004 BC by adding up the generations quoted in the Bible, a date which was accepted as fact until the late 19th century. His extensive library became the nucleus of the great library at Trinity College, Dublin. Jonathan Swift (1667–1745), Dean of St Patrick's Cathedral, Dublin, and author of *Gulliver's Travels*, was a frequent visitor to Armagh, while the architect Francis Johnston (1760–1829), responsible for many of Dublin's finest Georgian streetscapes, was born in the city.

Information

Armagh City Library (☎ 3752 4072; Market St; ☽ 9.30am-5.30pm Mon, Wed & Fri, to 8pm Tue & Thu, to 5pm Sat) Internet access for £1.50 per 30 minutes.

Tourist information centre (☎ 3752 1800; www .visitarmagh.com; 40 English St; ☽ 9am-5pm Mon-Sat year-round, also noon-5.30pm Sun Jul & Aug, 2-5pm Sun Sep-Jun) Part of the St Patrick's Trian complex.

Sights

ST PATRICK'S TRIAN

The old Presbyterian church behind the tourist office has been turned into a heritage centre and visitor complex known as **St Patrick's Trian** (☎ 3752 1801; 40 English St; adult/child £4.75/3; ☽ 10am-5pm Mon-Sat year-round, noon-5pm Sun Jul & Aug, 2-5pm Sun Sep-Jun). There are three exhibitions: the Armagh Story explores the history of Armagh from pagan prehistory to

the present day; Patrick's Testament takes an interactive look at the ancient *Book of Armagh*; and for the kids there's the Land of Lilliput where Gulliver's adventures in Lilliput are recounted by a gigantic model of Jonathan Swift's famous creation.

ST PATRICK'S CHURCH OF IRELAND CATHEDRAL

The city's **Anglican cathedral** (☎ 3752 3142; Cathedral Close; admission £1; ☽ 10am-5pm Apr-Oct, 10am-4pm Nov-Mar, guided tours 11.30am-2.30pm Mon-Sat Jun-Aug) occupies the site of St Patrick's original stone church. The present cathedral's ground plan is 13th century but the building itself is a Gothic restoration dating from 1834 to 1840. A stone slab on the exterior wall of the north transept marks the burial place of Brian Ború, the High King of Ireland, who died near Dublin during the last great battle against the Vikings in 1014.

Within the church are the remains of an 11th-century **Celtic Cross** that once stood nearby, and the **Tandragee Idol**, a curious granite figure dating back to the Iron Age. In the south aisle is a **memorial to Archbishop Richard Robinson** (1709–94), who founded Armagh's observatory and public library. Guided tours, which should be booked in advance, cost £2 per person.

ARMAGH PUBLIC LIBRARY

The Greek inscription above the main entrance to **Armagh Public Library** (☎ 3752 3142; www.armaghrobinsonlibrary.org; 43 Abbey St; admission free, guided tour £2; ☽ 10am-1pm & 2-4pm Mon-Fri), founded in 1771 by Archbishop Robinson, means 'the medicine shop of the soul'. Step inside and you'd swear that the archbishop had just swept out of the door, leaving you to browse among his personal collection of 17th- and 18th-century books, maps and engravings.

The library's most prized possession is a first edition of *Gulliver's Travels*, published in 1726 and annotated by none other than Swift himself. It was stolen in an armed robbery in 1999, but was recovered, undamaged, in Dublin 20 months later.

Other treasures of the library include Sir Walter Raleigh's 1614 *History of the World*, the *Claims of the Innocents* (pleas to Oliver Cromwell) and a large collection of engravings by Hogarth and others.

ST PATRICK'S ROMAN CATHOLIC CATHEDRAL

The other **St Patrick's Cathedral** (☎ 3752 2802; Cathedral Rd; admission free; 🕙 9am-6pm Mon-Fri, 9am-8pm Sat, 8am-6.30pm Sun) was built between 1838 and 1873 in Gothic Revival style with huge twin towers dominating the approach up flight after flight of steps. Inside it seems almost Byzantine, with every piece of wall and ceiling covered in brilliantly coloured mosaics. The sanctuary was modernised in 1981 and has a very distinctive tabernacle holder and crucifix that seem out of place among the mosaics and statues of the rest of the church. Mass is said at 10am Monday to Friday, and at 9am, 11am and 5.30pm on Sunday.

THE MALL

The Mall, to the east of the town centre, was a venue for horse racing, cock fighting and bull baiting until the 18th century when Archbishop Robinson decided all that was a tad vulgar for a city of learning, and transformed it into an elegant Georgian park.

At its northern end stands the **courthouse**, rebuilt after being destroyed by a huge IRA bomb in 1993. It originally dates from 1809, designed by local man Francis Johnston, who later became one of Ireland's most famous architects. At the southern end, directly opposite the courthouse, is the forbidding **Armagh Gaol**. Built in 1780 to the design of Thomas Cooley, it remained in use until 1988.

The east side of the park is lined with handsome Georgian terraces. **Charlemont Place** is another creation of Francis Johnston, as is the portico fronting **Armagh County Museum** (☎ 3752 3070; the Mall East; admission free; 🕙 10am-5pm Mon-Fri, 10am-1pm & 2-5pm Sat). The museum displays prehistoric axe heads, items found in bogs, corn dollies and straw-boy outfits, and military costumes and equipment. Don't miss the gruesome cast-iron skull that once graced the top of the Armagh gallows.

The nearby **Royal Irish Fusiliers Museum** (☎ 3752 2911; the Mall East; admission free; 🕙 10am-12.30pm & 1.30-4pm Mon-Fri) tells the story of the 'Eagle Takers', the first regiment to capture one of Bonaparte's imperial eagle standards in 1811.

ARMAGH PLANETARIUM

The Armagh Observatory was founded by Archbishop Robinson in 1790 and is still Ireland's leading astronomical research institute. Aimed mainly at educating young people, the nearby **Armagh Planetarium** (☎ 3752 3689; www.armaghplanet.com; College Hill; admission to exhibition area per person £2, shows per adult/child £6/5; 🕙 1-5pm Tue-Fri, 11.30am-5pm Sat & Sun) has an interactive exhibition on space exploration, and a digital theatre that screens a range of spectacular half-hour shows on its domed ceiling (check website for show times).

PALACE STABLES HERITAGE CENTRE

The Primate's Palace, overlooking the ruins of a 13th-century Franciscan friary on the southern edge of town, was built for Archbishop Robinson when he was appointed primate of Ireland in 1769. The bishop's stables are now home to the **Palace Stables Heritage Centre** (☎ 3752 9629; Palace demesne; adult/child £4.75/3; 🕙 10am-5pm Mon-Sat & noon-5pm Sun Jun-Aug, 10am-5pm Mon-Sat & noon-5pm Sun Apr, May & Sep), a set of tableaux staffed by costumed guides illustrating how the archbishop's guests were entertained in the 18th century.

Sleeping

Armagh City Hostel (☎ 3751 1800; www.hini.org.uk; 39 Abbey St; dm/tw £15/32; 🕙 open daily Mar-Oct, Fri & Sat only Nov-Feb, closed 23 Dec-2 Jan; P) This modern, purpose-built hostel near the Church of Ireland Cathedral is more like a small hotel – there are six comfortable twin rooms with private bathrooms, TV and tea-and-coffee facilities, as well as 12 small dorms, a well-equipped kitchen, a laundry, a lounge and a reading room.

Hillview Lodge (☎ 3752 2000; www.hillviewlodge.com; 33 Newtownhamilton Rd; s/d £38/50; P) Just 1.5km south of Armagh, Hillview is a welcoming, family-run guesthouse with a self-contained accommodation block containing six appealing rooms with great countryside views. And there's a driving range next door if you feel like improving your golf swing.

De Averell House (☎ 3751 1213; www.deaverellhouse.net; 47 Upper English St; s/d £40/70; P) A converted Georgian town house with four spacious rooms and a self-catering apartment, the De Averell is run by a friendly landlord who can't do enough to help. Rooms at the front can be noisy; the twin at the back are the quietest.

Charlemont Arms Hotel (☎ 3752 2028; www.charlemontarmshotel.com; 57-65 English St; s/d £50/80; P) This hotel dates from the 19th century, but has been renovated in charming period décor – oak-panelled dining room, Victorian fireplaces, flagstone-floored cellar restaurant. The bedrooms, in contrast, are modern and stylish.

Eating

Café Papa (☎ 3751 1205; 15 Thomas St; mains £4-8; ☺ 9am-5.30pm Mon-Sat, 6-9pm Fri & Sat) This deli-cum-café serves good coffee, cakes, home-baked bread and gourmet sandwiches, and does bistro dinners on Friday and Saturday evenings when you can bring your own wine.

our pick Uluru Bistro (☎ 3751 8051; 16-18 Market St; mains £5-12; ☺ noon-2.30pm & 6-9.30pm Tue-Fri, noon-10pm Sat) The Aussie chef at Uluru brings a bit of antipodean flair to Armagh, with a fusion menu that ranges from Thai-style hot-and-sour chicken broth to marinated, char-grilled kangaroo, plus some local favourites such as beer-battered fish and chips.

Stage Bar & Bistro (☎ 3751828; Market Sq; mains £9-15; ☺ food noon-4pm Mon-Sat, 12.30-6pm Sun, 5-9pm Thu-Sat, café menu from 9.30am Mon-Sat, from noon Sun) This stylish little place is a chilled-out haven of coffee- and cream-coloured sofas and chairs in the theatre lobby, with a menu that offers some tasty vegetarian dishes – try vegetable tempura with teriyaki dip – as well as pork chops with cabbage and bacon, and fillet of salmon with cheese and herb sauce.

Manor Park Restaurant (☎ 3751 5353; 2 College Hill, the Mall; mains £19-25; ☺ noon-2.30pm daily, 5.30-9.30pm Mon-Thu, 5.30-10pm Fri & Sat) Crisp white linen and silver candlesticks complement a cosy olde-worlde décor of red-brick walls, parquet floors and Persian rugs in this atmospheric French restaurant. The menu runs the gastronomic gamut from frogs legs fricassee to local pollan and eel, with a wine list as long as the Loire. There's a two-course set menu for £21, available midweek only.

Entertainment

Market Place Theatre & Arts Centre (☎ 3752 1821; www.marketplacearmagh.com; Market St; ☺ box office 9.30am-4.30pm Mon-Sat) Armagh's main cultural venue hosts a 400-seat theatre, exhibition galleries, a restaurant, a café and the Stage Bar, which has live bands on Saturday nights.

Armagh City Film House (☎ 3751 1033; www.armaghfilmhouse.com; Market St; adult/child £4/3) Next door to the arts centre.

Gildernews Bar (☎ 3752 7315; 100 Railway St) Formerly Hughes' Bar, Gildernews has traditional music sessions every Tuesday at 10pm, and DJs on Friday and Saturday.

You may be lucky enough to catch a game of **road bowling** (www.irishroadbowling.ie), a traditional Irish game now played mostly in Armagh and Cork. Contestants hurl small metal bowls weighing 750g along quiet country lanes to see who can make it to the finishing line with the least number of throws. Games usually take place on Sunday afternoons in summer, with the Ulster Finals held at Armagh in late June. Ask for details at the tourist information centre.

Getting There & Away

Buses stop at Armagh BusCentre on Lonsdale Rd, north of the town centre.

Goldline Express bus 251 runs from Belfast's Europa BusCentre (£7, one to 1½ hours, hourly Monday to Friday, eight Saturday, three Sunday) to Armagh. Bus 44 runs from Armagh to Newry (£5, 1¼ hours, twice daily Monday to Friday, three on Saturday), and Goldline Express 295 runs to Enniskillen (£7, two hours, twice daily Monday to Saturday, July and August only) via Monaghan.

There are no direct services from Armagh to Derry – the fastest route (three hours) is via Dungannon (buses 72 and 273).

Armagh is a stop on the once-daily (except Saturday) bus 278 from Coleraine to Monaghan (change here for Dublin) and the once-daily bus 270 from Belfast to Galway.

AROUND ARMAGH CITY
Navan Fort

Perched atop a drumlin a little over 3km west of Armagh is Navan Fort (Emain Macha), the most important archaeological site in Ulster. It was probably a prehistoric provincial capital and ritual site, on a par with Tara in County Meath.

The Irish name Emain Macha means 'the twins of Macha', Macha being the same mythical queen or goddess after whom Armagh itself is named (from Ard Macha, 'heights of Macha'). The site is linked in legend with the tales of Cúchulainn and named as capital of Ulster and the seat of the legendary Knights of the Red Branch.

It was an important centre from around 1150 BC until the coming of Christianity; the discovery of the skull of a Barbary ape on the site indicates trading links with North Africa. The main circular earthwork enclosure is no less than 240m in diameter, and encloses a smaller circular structure and an Iron Age burial mound. The circular structure has intrigued archaeologists – it appears to be some sort of temple, whose roof was supported by concentric rows of wooden posts, and whose interior was filled with a vast pile of stones. Stranger still, the whole thing was set on fire soon after its construction around 95 BC, possibly for ritual purposes.

The nearby **Navan Centre** (☎ 3752 1800; 81 Killylea Rd, Armagh; adult/child £4.75/3; ☯ 10am-5pm Mon-Sat & noon-5pm Sun Jun-Aug, 10am-5pm Sat & noon-5pm Sun Apr, May & Sep) has exhibitions placing the fort in its historical context, and a re-creation of an Iron Age settlement.

You can walk to the site from Armagh (45 minutes), or you can take bus 73 to Navan village (10 minutes, seven daily Monday to Friday).

NORTH ARMAGH

North Armagh, 'the orchard of Ireland', is the island's main fruit-growing region, famed for its apples and strawberries. In May the countryside is awash with pink apple blossoms.

Ardress House

Starting life as a farmhouse, **Ardress House** (☎ 3885 1236; 64 Ardress Rd; adult/child £4/2; ☯ 2-6pm Sat, Sun & public hols mid-Mar–Sep) was extended and converted to a manor house in 1760. Much of the original neoclassical interior remains, including a table made in 1799 on which King George V signed the Constitution of Northern Ireland in 1921, and the farmyard houses a vast collection of machinery, along with a piggery and a smithy. The walled garden has been planted with a selection of the old apple varieties for which north Armagh's orchards are famous, and there are pleasant walks around the wooded grounds.

Ardress House is 15km northeast of Armagh, on the B28 halfway between Moy and Portadown.

Argory

A fine country house above the River Blackwater, the **Argory** (☎ 8778 4753; Derrycaw Rd; adult/child grounds & tour £5/2.50, grounds only per car £3; ☯ house 1-6pm daily Easter week & Jun-Aug, 1-6pm Sat, Sun & public hols mid-Mar–May & Sep–mid-Oct) retains most of its original 1824 fittings; some rooms are still lit by acetylene gas from the house's private plant. There are two formal gardens featuring roses, Victorian clipped-yew arbours and a lime walk by the river.

The Argory is 3.5km northeast of Moy on the Derrycaw road (off the B28), and 5km northwest of Ardress.

Oxford Island

Oxford Island National Nature Reserve protects a range of habitats – woodland, wildflower meadows, reedy shoreline and shallow lake margins – on the southern edge of Lough Neagh (see boxed text, below), and is criss-crossed with walking trails, information boards and bird-watching hides.

The **Lough Neagh Discovery Centre** (☎ 3832 2205; www.oxfordisland.com; Oxford Island, Lurgan; admission free; ☯ 9am-5pm Mon-Fri, 10am-5pm Sat & Sun, 6pm daily Jul & Aug), set in the middle of a reed-fringed pond inhabited by waterfowl, has a tourist information desk, a gift shop and a great little **café** (☯ 10am-4.30pm year-round, to 5.30pm Easter-Sep) with lake-shore views.

One-hour **boat trips** (☎ 3832 7573; adult/child £4/2; ☯ 1.30-6.30pm Sat & Sun Apr-Oct) on the lough depart from nearby Kinnego Marina, aboard the 12-seater cabin cruiser *Master McGra*.

Oxford Island is just north of Lurgan, signposted from Junction 10 on the M1 motorway.

LOUGH NEAGH

Lough Neagh (pronounced 'nay') is the largest freshwater lake in all of Britain and Ireland, big enough to swallow the city of Birmingham (West Midlands, UK, or Alabama, USA – either one would fit). Though vast (around 32km long and 16km wide), the lough is relatively shallow – never more than 9m deep – and is an important habitat for waterfowl. Its waters are home to the pollan, a freshwater herring found only in Ireland, and the dollaghan, a subspecies of trout, unique to Lough Neagh. Connected to the sea by the River Bann, the lough has been an important waterway and food source since prehistoric times, and still has an eel fishery that employs around 200 people.

The main points of access to the lough include Antrim Town (p674) on the eastern shore, Oxford Island (above) in the south, and Ballyronan and Ardboe (p692) in the west. The **Lough-shore Trail** (www.loughshoretrail.com) is a 180-km cycle route that encircles the lough. For most of its length it follows quiet country roads set back from the shore; the best sections for actually seeing the lough itself are west of Oxford Island and south from Antrim town.

Counties Derry & Antrim

The north coast of Northern Ireland, from Carrickfergus to Coleraine, is like a giant geology classroom. Here the patient workmanship of the ocean has laid bare the black basalt and white chalk that underlie much of County Antrim, and dissected the rocks into a scenic extravaganza of sea stacks and pinnacles, cliffs and caves, bordered by broad, sandy beaches swept by Atlantic surf. This rugged seaboard has some of the most beautiful coastal scenery in Ireland, but bring your boots as well as your camera – it's also an outdoor adventure playground that offers challenging coastal walks and extreme rock-climbing on the 100m-high crags of Fair Head. It's also home to the North's best surfing breaks.

Tourists flock to the surreal geological centrepiece of the Giant's Causeway, its popularity challenged only by the test-your-nerve tightrope of the Carrick-a-Rede rope bridge nearby, but you can escape the crowds amid the more sedate scenery of the Glens of Antrim, where the picturesque villages of Cushendun, Cushendall and Carnlough lie beneath lush green valleys and foaming waterfalls. To the west, County Derry's chief attraction is the historic city of Derry, nestled in a broad sweep of the River Foyle. It is the only surviving walled city in Ireland, and a walk around it is one of the highlights of a visit to Northern Ireland. Derry's other draws include the powerful political murals in the Bogside district and the lively music scene in its many pubs.

Northeast along the coast there are vast sandy beaches at Magilligan Point, Portstewart and Portrush, and from the basalt escarpment of Binevenagh, which overlooks the coast here, superb views across Lough Foyle beckon you towards the blue-hazed hills of County Donegal.

HIGHLIGHTS

- **City Lights** Ancient walls, modern murals and live music in the historic city of Derry (p640)
- **Catch A Wave** Surfing or body-boarding the Atlantic breakers at the beaches around Portrush (p659)
- **Coastal Challenge** A 16.5km hike along the spectacular Causeway Coast from Carrick-a-Rede to the Giant's Causeway (p666)
- **Test Your Nerve** The slender, swaying Carrick-a-Rede Rope Bridge (p664) near Ballycastle
- **Away From It All** Seabirds and seals at the remote western end of Rathlin Island (p668)

Rathlin Island ★
Causeway Coast ★   ★ Carrick-a-Rede Rope Bridge
★ Portrush
★ Derry

- TELEPHONE AREA CODE: 028 FROM BRITAIN AND REST OF WORLD, 048 FROM REPUBLIC OF IRELAND
- POPULATION: 532,000
- AREA: 4696 SQ KM

COUNTY DERRY

DERRY/LONDONDERRY
pop 83,700

Northern Ireland's second city comes as a pleasant surprise to many visitors. Derry (or Londonderry – see the boxed text, p644) may not be the prettiest of cities, and it certainly lags behind Belfast in terms of investment and redevelopment, but it has a great riverside setting, several fascinating historical sights and a determined air of can-do optimism that has made it the powerhouse of the North's cultural revival.

There's lots of history to absorb, from the Siege of Derry to the Battle of the Bogside – a stroll around the 17th-century city walls is a must, as is a tour of the Bogside murals – and the city's lively pubs are home to a burgeoning live music scene. But perhaps the biggest attraction is the people themselves: warm, witty and welcoming.

History

The defining moment of Derry's history was the Siege of Derry in 1688–89, an event whose echoes reverberate around the city's walls to this day. King James I granted the city a royal charter in 1613, and gave to the London livery companies (trade guilds) the task of fortifying Derry and planting the county of Coleraine

COUNTIES DERRY & ANTRIM

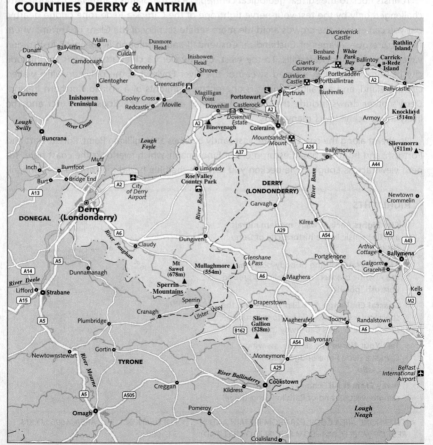

(soon to be renamed County Londonderry) with Protestant settlers.

In Britain, the Glorious Revolution of 1688 saw the Catholic King James II ousted in favour of the Protestant Dutch prince, William of Orange. Derry was the only garrison in Ireland that was not held by forces loyal to King James, and so, in December 1688, Catholic forces led by the earl of Antrim arrived on the east bank of the River Foyle, ready to seize the city.

They sent emissaries to discuss terms of surrender, but in the meantime troops were being ferried across the river in preparation for an assault. On seeing this, 13 apprentice boys barred the city gates with a cry of 'There'll be no surrender!'

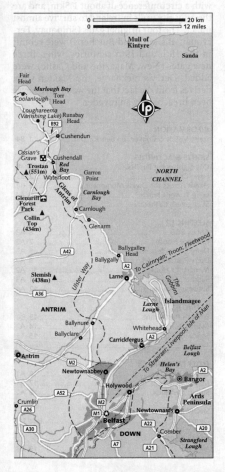

And so, on 7 December 1688, the Siege of Derry began. For 105 days the Protestant citizens of Derry withstood bombardment, disease and starvation (the condition of the besieging forces was not much better). By the time a relief ship burst through and broke the siege, an estimated half of the city's inhabitants had died. In the 20th century the Siege of Derry became a symbol of Ulster Protestants' resistance to rule by a Catholic Irish Republic, and 'No surrender!' remains to this day a loyalist battle-cry.

In the 19th century Derry was one of the main ports of emigration to the USA, a fact commemorated by the sculptures of an emigrant family standing in Waterloo Pl. It also played a vital role in the transatlantic trade in linen shirts: supposedly, local factories provided uniforms for both sides in the American Civil War. To this day Derry still supplies the US president with 12 free shirts every year.

Orientation
The centre of old Derry is the walled city on the western bank of the River Foyle. The bus station is just outside the walls at its north end; the modern city centre stretches north from here along Strand Rd. The train station is on the east bank of the River Foyle, across Craigavon Bridge, in a district known as the Waterside. The Bogside lies to the west of the walled city.

Information
BOOKSHOPS
Bookworm (Map p645; ☎ 7128 2727; 18-20 Bishop St Within; ⏰ 9.30am-5.30pm Mon-Sat) Good for books on Derry, the Troubles and Ireland generally. Also has an in-store café.

Eason (Map p645; ☎ 7137 7133; Foyleside Shopping Centre, Foyle St; ⏰ 9am-6pm Mon & Tue, 9am-9pm Wed-Fri, 9am-7pm Sat, 1-6pm Sun) The city's biggest bookshop, on level 3 of the shopping centre.

Foyle Books (Map p645; ☎ 7137 2530; 12A Magazine St; ⏰ 11am-5.15pm Mon-Fri, 10am-5pm Sat) Stocks a good selection of second-hand books.

INTERNET ACCESS
Café Calm (Map p645; ☎ 7126 8228; 4 Shipquay St; per 15min £1; ⏰ 8.30am-5pm Mon-Sat) Net access and excellent coffee.

Central Library (Map p645; ☎ 7127 2310; 35 Foyle St; per 30min £1.50; ⏰ 9.15am-8pm Mon & Thu, to 5.30pm Tue, Wed & Fri, to 5pm Sat).

COUNTIES DERRY & ANTRIM

COUNTIES DERRY & ANTRIM

MONEY

Bank of Ireland (Map p645; ☎ 7126 4992; 12 Shipquay St)

First Trust Bank (Map p645; ☎ 7136 3921; 15-17 Shipquay St)

Thomas Cook (Map p645; ☎ 7185 2552; 34 Ferryquay St)

POST

Post office (☉ 8.30am-5.30pm Mon, 9am-5.30pm Tue-Fri, 9am-12.30pm Sat); Main post office (Map p645; Custom House St) Bishop St Within (Map p645)

TOURIST INFORMATION

Derry Visitor & Convention Bureau (Map p642; ☎ 7126 7284; www.derryvisitor.com; 44 Foyle St; ☉ 9am-7pm Mon-Fri, 10am-6pm Sat, 10am-5pm Sun Jul-Sep, 9am-5pm Mon-Fri & 10am-5pm Sat Mar-Jun &

Oct, 9am-5pm Mon-Fri Nov-Feb) Covers all of Northern Ireland and the Republic as well as Derry. Sells books and maps, can book accommodation throughout Ireland and has a bureau de change.

Sights

Derry's walled city is Ireland's earliest example of town planning. It is thought to have been modelled on the French Renaissance town of Vitry-le-François, designed in 1545 by Italian engineer Hieronimo Marino; both are based on the grid plan of a Roman military camp, with two main streets at right angles to each other, and four city gates, one at the end of each street.

Completed in 1619, Derry's **city walls** (www .derryswalls.com) are about 8m high and 9m thick, with a circumference of about 1.5km, and are the only city walls in Ireland to survive almost intact. The four original gates (Shipquay, Ferryquay, Bishop's and Butcher's) were rebuilt in the 18th and 19th centuries, when three new gates (New, Magazine and Castle) were added. Derry's nickname, the Maiden City, derives from the fact that the walls have never been breached by an invader.

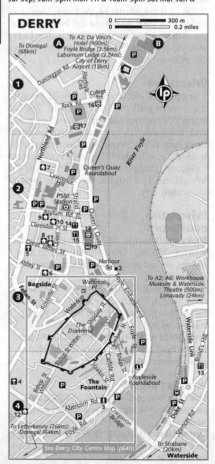

The walls were built under the supervision of the Honourable The Irish Society, an organisation created in 1613 by King James and the London livery companies to fund and oversee the fortification of Derry and the plantation of surrounding county with Protestant settlers. The society still exists today, though now its activities are mainly charitable, and it still owns Derry's city walls.

See p647) for a self-guided walk around the walls.

WALLED CITY

Inside the Magazine Gate is the award-winning **Tower Museum** (Map p645; ☎ 7137 2411; Union Hall Pl; adult/child £4/2; ☯ 10am-5pm Mon-Sat & 2-5pm Sun Jul & Aug, 10am-5pm Tue-Sat & bank holidays Mon Sep-Jun), housed in a replica 16th-century tower house. Head straight to the fifth floor for a view from the top of the tower, then work your way down through the excellent **Armada Shipwreck** exhibition, which tells the story of *La Trinidad Valenciera* – a ship of the Spanish Armada which was wrecked at Kinnagoe Bay in Donegal in 1588. It was discovered by the City of Derry Sub-Aqua Club in 1971 and excavated by marine archaeologists. On display are bronze guns, pewter tableware and personal items – a wooden comb, an olive jar, a shoe sole – recovered from the site, including a 2.5-tonne siege gun bearing the arms of Phillip II of Spain showing him as king of England.

The museum's other exhibition is the **Story of Derry**, where well-thought-out exhibits and audiovisuals lead you through the history of the city from the founding of the monastery of St Colmcille (Columba) in the 6th century to the Battle of the Bogside in the late 1960s. Allow a good two hours to do the museum justice.

Built between 1628 and 1633 from the same grey-green schist as the city walls, **St Columb's Cathedral** (Map p645; ☎ 7126 7313; London St; admission £2; ☯ 9am-5pm Mon-Sat Easter-Oct, 9am-1pm & 2-4pm Mon-Sat Nov-Easter) was the first post-Reformation church to be built in Britain and Ireland, and is Derry's oldest surviving building.

In the **porch** (under the spire, by the St Columb's Court entrance) you can see the original foundation stone of 1633 that records the cathedral's completion, inscribed:

> If stones could speake
> Then London's prayse
> Should sounde who
> Built this church and
> Cittie from the grounde

The smaller stone inset, inscribed '*In Templo Verus Deus Est Vereo Colendus*' (The True God is in His Temple and is to be truly worshipped), comes from the original church built here in 1164 and dedicated to the city's patron saint, Colmcille.

Also in the porch is a hollow mortar shell fired into the churchyard during the Great Siege of 1688–89; inside the shell were the terms of surrender. The neighbouring **chapter house** contains more historical artefacts, including paintings, old photos and the four huge padlocks used to secure the city gates in the 17th century.

The **nave**, built in a squat, solid style known as Planter's Gothic, shares the austerity of many Church of Ireland cathedrals, with thick walls, small windows, and an open-timbered roof (from 1823) resting on corbels depicting the heads of past bishops and deans. The bishop's throne, at the far end of the nave, is an 18th-century mahogany chair in ornate, Chinese Chippendale style.

The **chancel**, and the stained-glass east window depicting the Ascension, date from 1887. The flags on either side of the window were captured from the French during the Great Siege; although the yellow silk has been renewed several times since, the poles and gold wirework are original.

OUTSIDE THE WALLS

Standing just outside the city walls opposite the Tower Museum, the neo-Gothic **Guildhall** (Map p645; ☎ 7137 7335; Guildhall Sq; admission free; ☯ 9am-5pm Mon-Fri) was originally built in 1890, then rebuilt after a fire in 1908. As the seat of the old Londonderry Corporation, which institutionalised the policy of discriminating against Catholics over housing and jobs, it incurred the wrath of nationalists and was bombed twice by the Irish Republican Army (IRA) in 1972. From 2000 to 2005 it was the seat of the Bloody Sunday Inquiry (see boxed text, p646). The Guildhall is noted for its fine stained-glass windows, presented by the London Livery Companies. Guided tours are available in July and August.

The small, old-fashioned **Harbour Museum** (Map p645; ☎ 7137 7331; Harbour Sq; admission free; ☯ 10am-1pm & 2-4.30pm Mon-Fri), with models of ships, a replica of a *currach* – an early sailing boat of the type that carried St Colmcille to Iona – and the bosomy figurehead of the Minnehaha, is housed in the old Harbour Commissioner's Building next to the Guildhall.

COUNTIES DERRY & ANTRIM

As you enter the city across Craigavon Bridge, the first thing you see is the **Hands Across the Divide** monument. This striking bronze sculpture of two men reaching out to each other symbolises the spirit of reconciliation and hope for the future; it was unveiled in 1992, 20 years after Bloody Sunday.

Outside the city walls to the southwest is **Long Tower Church** (Map p642; ☎ 7126 2301; Long Tower St; admission free; ⊙ 9am-8.30pm Mon-Sat, 7.30am-7pm Sun), Derry's first post-Reformation Catholic church. Built in 1784 in neo-Renaissance style, it stands on the site of the medieval Teampall Mór (Great Church), built in 1164, whose stones were used to help build the city walls in 1609. Long Tower was built with the support of the Anglican bishop of the time, Frederick Augustus Harvey, who presented the capitals for the four Corinthian columns framing the ornate high altar.

The Roman Catholic **St Eugene's Cathedral** (Map p642; ☎ 7126 2894; Great James St; admission free; ⊙ 9am-8.30pm) was begun in 1851 as a response to the end of the Great Famine, and dedicated to St Eugene in 1873 by Bishop Kelly; the handsome east window (1891) is a memorial to the bishop. The bells of St Eugene's still ring every night at 9pm as a reminder of the Penal Laws (in force from 1691 until the early 19th century) which forbade Catholics to attend mass and subjected them to a 9pm curfew.

BOGSIDE

The Bogside district, to the west of the walled city, developed in the 19th and early 20th centuries as a working-class, predominantly Catholic, residential area. By the 1960s, its serried ranks of small, terraced houses had become an overcrowded ghetto of poverty and unemployment, a focus for the emerging civil rights movement and a hotbed of nationalist discontent.

In August 1969 the three-day 'Battle of the Bogside' – a running street battle between local youths and the Royal Ulster Constabulary (RUC) – prompted the UK government

---

DERRY-STROKE-LONDONDERRY

Derry/Londonderry is a town with two names. The settlement was originally named Doíre Calgaigh (Oak Grove of Calgach), after a pagan warrior-hero, then in the 10th century it was renamed Doíre Colmcille (Oak Grove of Columba), in honour of the 6th-century saint who established the first monastic settlement here.

In the following centuries the name was shortened and anglicised to Derrie or Derry. Then in 1613, in recognition of the Corporation of London's role in the 'plantation' of northwest Ulster with Protestant settlers, Derry was granted a royal charter and both town and county were renamed Londonderry. However, generally people continued to call it Derry in everyday speech.

When nationalists gained a majority on the city council in 1984, they voted to change its name from Londonderry City Council to Derry City Council. This infuriated unionists, and the name remains a touchstone for people's political views. Nationalists always use Derry, and vandals often deface the 'London' part of the name on road signs. Staunch unionists insist on Londonderry, which is still the city's (and county's) official name, used in government publications, Ordnance Survey maps, rail and bus timetables and Northern Ireland Tourist Board (NITB) literature.

On radio and TV, to avoid giving offence to either side, some announcers use both names together – 'Derry-stroke-Londonderry' – while the BBC uses Londonderry at its first mention in a report, and Derry thereafter (the local radio station avoids the dilemma by calling itself BBC Radio Foyle). Road signs in Northern Ireland point to Londonderry, those in the Republic point to Derry (or Doíre in Irish), and some tourism industry promotional material covers all bases, using Derry-Londonderry-Doíre.

In 2006 Derry City Council asked for a judicial review in the High Court of Belfast, claiming that the renaming of the council in 1984 effectively amended the charter of 1613, but in January 2007 the judge rejected the claim, saying that only new legislation or royal prerogative could change the city's name.

Luckily, not everyone takes the Derry/Londonderry controversy too seriously. One local radio presenter opted instead for the simpler 'Stroke City'! In fact, the majority of people in Northern Ireland, no matter what their political persuasion, still use 'Derry' in everyday speech, which is why we use the shorter version in this book.

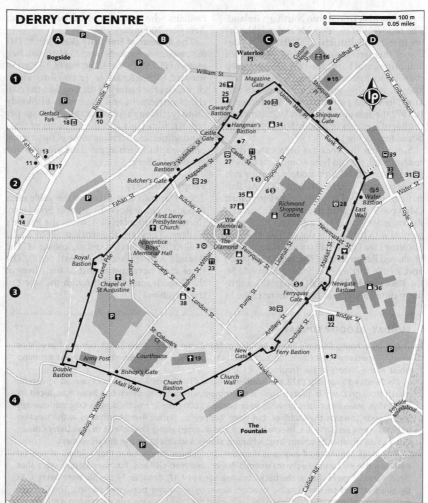

DERRY CITY CENTRE

INFORMATION		
Bank of Ireland	**1**	C2
Bookworm	**2**	B3
Branch Post Office	**3**	B3
Café Calm	**4**	D1
Central Library	**5**	D2
Eason	(see 36)	
First Trust Bank	**6**	C2
Foyle Books	**7**	C2
Main Post Office	**8**	C1
Thomas Cook	**9**	C3

SIGHTS & ACTIVITIES		
Bloody Sunday Memorial	**10**	A1
Bogside Artists Studio	**11**	A2
City Tours	**12**	D4
Death of Innocence Mural	**13**	A2
Foyle Cruise Line Ticket Office	(see 16)	
Free Derry Corner	**14**	A2

Guildhall	**15**	D1
Harbour Museum	**16**	C1
Hunger Strikers' Memorial	**17**	A2
Museum of Free Derry	**18**	A1
St Columb's Cathedral	**19**	B4
Tower Museum	**20**	C1

EATING		
Boston Tea Party	**21**	C2
Café Artisan	(see 2)	
Encore Brasserie	(see 28)	
Fitzroy's	**22**	D3
Sandwich Co	**23**	B3

DRINKING		
Badger's Bar	**24**	D3
Gweedore Bar	**25**	C1
Peadar O'Donnell's	**26**	C1

ENTERTAINMENT		
Mason's Bar	**27**	C2
Millennium Forum	**28**	D2
Nerve Centre	**29**	B2
Playhouse	**30**	C3
Sandino's Café-Bar	**31**	D2

SHOPPING		
Austins	**32**	C3
Cool Discs Music	**33**	D2
Craft Village	**34**	C1
Donegal Shop	**35**	C2
Foyleside Shopping Centre	**36**	D3
McGilloway Gallery	**37**	C2
Whatnot	**38**	B3

TRANSPORT		
Bus Station	**39**	D2

to send British troops into Northern Ireland. The residents of the Bogside and neighbouring Brandywell districts – 33,000 of them – declared themselves independent of the civil authorities, and barricaded the streets to keep the security forces out. 'Free Derry', as it was known, was a no-go area for the police and army, its streets patrolled by IRA volunteers. In 1972 the area around Rossville St witnessed the horrific events of Bloody Sunday (see the boxed text, below).

Since then the area has been extensively redeveloped, the old houses and flats demolished and replaced with modern housing and the population is now down to 8000. All that remains of the old Bogside is **Free Derry Corner** (Map p645) at the intersection of Fahan and Rossville Sts, where the gable end of a house painted with the famous slogan 'You Are Now Entering Free Derry' still stands. Nearby is the H-shaped **Hunger Strikers' Memorial** (Map p645) and, a little further north along Rossville St, the **Bloody Sunday Memorial** (Map p645), a simple granite obelisk that commemorates the 14

civilians who were shot dead by the British Army on 30 January 1972.

The **Museum of Free Derry** (Map p645; ☎ 7136 0880; www.museumoffreederry.org; 55-61 Glenfada Park; adult/child £3/1.50; ☻ 9am-4.30pm Mon-Fri, 1-4.30pm Sat year-round, 1-4.30pm Sun Jun-Sep), just off Rossville St, chronicles the history of the Bogside, the civil rights movement and the events of Bloody Sunday through photographs, newspaper reports, film clips and the accounts of first-hand witnesses, including some of the original photographs which inspired the murals of the People's Gallery.

People's Gallery

The 11 murals that decorate the gable ends of houses along Rossville St, near Free Derry Corner, are popularly known as the People's Gallery. They are the work of Tom Kelly, Will Kelly and Kevin Hasson, known as 'The Bogside Artists' (see boxed text, p648). The three men have spent most of their lives in the Bogside, and lived through the worst of the Troubles.

SUNDAY, BLOODY SUNDAY

Tragically echoing Dublin's Bloody Sunday of November 1920, when British security forces shot dead 14 spectators at a Gaelic football match in Croke Park, Derry's Bloody Sunday was a turning point in the history of the Troubles.

On Sunday 30 January 1972, the Northern Ireland Civil Rights Association organised a peaceful march through Derry in protest against internment without trial, which had been introduced by the British government the previous year. Some 15,000 people marched from Creggan through the Bogside towards the Guildhall, but were stopped by British Army barricades at the junction of William and Rossville Sts. The main march was diverted along Rossville St to Free Derry Corner, but a small number of youths began hurling stones and insults at the British soldiers.

The exact sequence of events is disputed, but it now seems clear that soldiers of the 1st Battalion the Parachute Regiment opened fire on unarmed civilians. Fourteen people were shot dead, some of them shot in the back; six were aged just 17. Another 14 people were injured, 12 by gunshots and two from being knocked down by armoured personnel carriers. The Catholic population of Derry, who had originally welcomed the British troops as a neutral force protecting them from Protestant violence and persecution, now saw the army as enemy and occupier. The ranks of the Provisional Irish Republican Army (IRA) swelled with a fresh surge of volunteers.

The Widgery Commission, set up to in 1972 to investigate the affair, failed to find anyone responsible. None of the soldiers who fired the 108 bullets, nor the officers in charge, were brought to trial or even disciplined; records disappeared and weapons were destroyed.

Long-standing public dissatisfaction with the Widgery investigation led to the massive **Bloody Sunday Inquiry** (www.bloody-sunday-inquiry.org.uk), headed by Lord Saville, which sat from March 2000 till December 2004. The inquiry heard from 900 witnesses, received 2500 witness statements, and allegedly cost the British taxpayer £400 million; its final report was due to be published in summer 2007.

The events of Bloody Sunday inspired rock band U2's most overtly political song, 'Sunday Bloody Sunday' (1983), and are commemorated in the Museum of Free Derry, the People's Gallery and the Bloody Sunday Monument, all in the Bogside (p644).

Their murals, mostly painted between 1997 and 2001, commemorate key events in the Troubles, including the Battle of the Bogside, Bloody Sunday, Operation Motorman (the British Army's operation to re-take IRA-controlled no-go areas in Derry and Belfast in July 1972) and the 1981 hunger strike. The most powerful images are those painted largely in monochrome, consciously evoking journalistic imagery – *Operation Motorman,* showing a British soldier breaking down a door with a sledgehammer; *Bloody Sunday,* with a group of men led by local priest Father Daly carrying the body of Jackie Duddy (the first fatality on that day); and *Petrol Bomber,* a young boy wearing a gas mask and holding a petrol bomb.

The most moving image is *The Death of Innocence,* which shows the radiant figure of 14-year-old schoolgirl Annette McGavigan, killed in crossfire between the IRA and the British Army on 6 September 1971, the 100th victim of the Troubles. She stands against the brooding chaos of a bombed-out building, the roof-beams forming a crucifix in the top right-hand corner. At the left, a downward-pointing rifle, broken in the middle, stands for the failure of violence, while the butterfly symbolises resurrection and the hope embodied in the peace process.

The final mural in the sequence, completed in 2004, is the *Peace Mural,* a swirling image of a dove of peace, rising out of the blood and sadness of the past towards the sunny yellow hope of a peaceful future.

The murals can be seen at www.cain.ulst.ac.uk/bogsideartists, and in the book *The People's Gallery* (available in Derry bookshops and through www.bogsideartists.com). The **Bogside Artists Studio** (☎ 7137 3842; Unit 7, Meenan Sq; tours per person £5) is tucked behind the Bogside Inn; tours are available for groups if booked in advance.

THE WATERSIDE

Across the river from the walled city lies the largely Protestant Waterside district. At the height of the Troubles, many Protestants living in and around the Bogside moved across the river to escape the worst of the violence.

Here you'll find the **Workhouse Museum** (☎ 7131 8328; 23 Glendermott Rd; admission free; 10am-4.30pm Mon-Thu & Sat) housed in Derry's original 1840–1946 workhouse. Daily life at the workhouse for the 800 inmates was designed to encourage them to leave as soon as possible, alive or dead. One of the exhibits is the grisly horse-drawn hearse used to carry away the corpses.

Other displays cover the Potato Famine, while the excellent Atlantic Memorial exhibition tells the story of the WWII Battle of the Atlantic and the major role that Derry played.

Walking Tour

You can make a complete circuit of Derry's walled city, walking along the top of the walls, in around 30 minutes. There are frequent sets of steps where you can get on and off.

This walk starts from the diamond, Derry's central square, dominated by the **war memorial** (1).

From the diamond, head along Butcher St to **Butcher's Gate** (2). At the height of the Troubles the gate reverted to its original, 17th-century role, serving as a security checkpoint controlling entry to the city centre from the Bogside. Turn right before the gate and climb the steps up onto the top of the city walls.

Stroll downhill across **Castle Gate** (3), added in 1865, to **Magazine Gate** (4), named for the powder magazine that used to be close by.

WALK FACTS

Start The diamond
Finish The diamond
Distance 2km
Duration 30 to 40 minutes

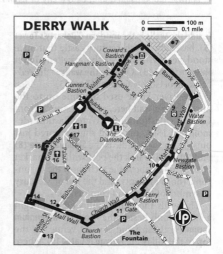

DERRY WALK

VOICES: THE BOGSIDE ARTISTS

The Bogside Artists – brothers Will and Tom Kelly, and friend Kevin Hasson – are famous as the creators of the murals that make up the People's Gallery. Tom and Kevin were 10 and 11 years old when the Troubles broke out in 1969, Will in his early 20s.

What was it like growing up in Derry during the Troubles? Kevin: 'One minute nobody knows about us or Derry or even Northern Ireland; the next thing, we are all over the international news. You could watch the daily riot later on TV in your own front room. As kids, you must understand we were still on fantasy island, as most kids are. Soldiers were, to us, aliens from another planet. We painted the soldier as such on our Bloody Sunday mural depicting the death of Jackie Duddy for that reason. That was our perception at the time and kids tend to see things bereft of all historical or other considerations. All in all, our growing up in Derry at that time could be described as very intense and very bitter-sweet.'

Will: 'We felt that our destiny had come. We were well clued-up on Marxist doctrine and, what with the riots in Paris and the struggle of the black population in America for democratic rights, we truly believed we were part of a global working-class revolution. A new world order was coming into being and we were in the front line. As a young man, the unfolding events faced one with questions of ultimate concern at a time when, in other circumstances, we would likely have been thinking of finding a secure job and starting a family. Individualistic pursuits had to be shelved in the face of imminent threats to oneself and one's family. In retrospect, the whole experience was very hyper-real. During the Hunger Strikes of 1980–81 it became surreal.'

Whose art do you admire? Will: 'Those old masters like Raphael, Mantegna, the Tiepolos and Michelangelo cannot be equalled when it comes to mural art. Diego Rivera was summoned from Paris 20 years or so *after* the revolution, so we are not as impressed by his work as those who have bought into the myth of Rivera as a contemporary freedom fighter. Incidentally, he did not portray Mexico's history as it was. What he did was offer a Marxist *interpretation* of that history. Not that we compare ourselves to Rivera. His body of work far exceeds our own. But we do recall one lady who came to our studio and told us that she had just returned from Mexico and considered our murals to be better than his! Go figure, as they say.'

Which of the Bogside murals means the most to you? Tom: 'The Death of Innocence, for me, is the one that stands out, both the pictorial content of it and the fact that it is a peace and antiwar mural painted long before any of us in Derry thought peace was even possible.'

Inside the walls is the modern **O'Doherty's Tower** (5), based on a 16th-century castle that once stood nearby. It houses the excellent **Tower Museum** (6; p643). Outside the walls is the red-brick, neo-Gothic **Guildhall** (7; p643).

The River Foyle used to come up to the northeastern wall here, and the stretch from Coward's Bastion to the Water Bastion (demolished 1844) once had ships moored just outside. In the middle is the **Shipquay Gate** (8) built in 1805 to link the port with the market area. Symbols above the arch show the cornucopia (horn of plenty) and the rod of Mercury (a symbol of trade and commerce).

The walls then turn southwest and begin a steep climb beside the modern **Millennium Forum** (9) theatre and concert venue. At the top of the hill is the **Ferryquay Gate** (10), where the apprentice boys barred the gate at the start of the Great Siege of 1688–89. In those days there would have been a drawbridge as well as a padlock on the gate. Both padlock and key can be seen in the chapter house of St Columb's Cathedral.

Above the gate is the image of the Reverend George Walker. Below in the arches to either side are metal rings; these were used to tether horses, which were not allowed into the inner city on market days.

The stretch of wall beyond overlooks the **Fountain housing estate** (11), the last significant Protestant community on the western bank of the Foyle (the vast majority of Derry's Protestants have moved across the river to the Waterside area or further afield). The round, brick-paved area on the ground out-

Kevin: 'Our *Peace Mural* means most to me, as we decided to do that 10 years before we were actually able to get around to realising it. Also, it had a strong community input where both Catholic and Protestant kids worked together to help design it. The dove, in fact, is not just a cliché – it refers to our city's patron saint, St Columba, whose Latin name Columbanus means 'dove'.'

Will: 'They're like our children – it's unfair to single any one out at the expense of the others. That said, it would be dishonest not to admit that our first-born, *The Petrol Bomber*, is a wee bit special.'

What is Derry like to visit? Will: 'We all agree that Derry is a very special city that is fast becoming the cultural focus of not only the North of Ireland but Ireland as a whole. It is a big city with the ambience and character of a village. The sense of freedom of the people, young and old, is truly infectious. You could pick any Derryman or woman and put them on stage for their wit alone. In short, Derry is fun. The girls here are very pretty too!

Above all, get to meet the locals, whom you will likely find enjoying a Guinness or two in the pubs. Have they got stories to tell! There's also a great view of the city and the lough from the hill of Creggan.'

Tom: 'Peadar O'Donnell's is the best place for traditional Irish music. The Craft Village I would recommend for lunch or a quiet drink.'

Kevin: 'For older visitors the Tower Hotel has good Irish music sessions that are very popular.'

Will: 'A short trip over the border to Buncrana will present you with more options, as well as a neat little beach where you can nurse your hangover the next morning.'

How do you see the future of Derry over the next 10 years? Will: 'There is a covert rivalry going on between Derry and Belfast with regards to the creative arts, that is reminiscent of the rivalry between Rome and Florence during the High Renaissance. It is a healthy rivalry that will bring out the very best in both cities. Alas, Dublin has sacrificed its old-world charm to commercialism, to the extent that neither Joyce, Beckett nor Behan would be able to recognise it if they came back. Dublin has painted itself out of the picture, frankly. It is fast becoming another Blackpool.'

Tom: 'With massive investment from Britain and America, the rapid growth of tourism and stronger economic relations between North and South, things can only get better for the people of Derry, especially for those of us who have lived through over 30 years of conflict. When you know how bad it can really get, you become grateful for what you have. Thankfully, we have plenty here to enjoy.'

side New Gate is where a 10m-high bonfire is lit on the night before the annual Apprentice Boys' march.

Bishop's Gate (12), which bisects the southern flank of the wall, was rebuilt in 1789 for the 100th anniversary of the Great Siege. Bishop Harvey, a keen antiquarian, had a hand in the reconstruction and requested a triumphal arch in honour of King William I. During the Great Siege, it was here that King James II demanded the surrender of the city.

Outside the gate on Bishop St Without is the one remaining turret of the 1791 **Old Gaol (13)**. Theobald Wolfe Tone, founder of the United Irishmen, spent some time in prison here following the failed rebellion of 1798.

The **Double Bastion (14)** at the southwestern corner of the walls is dominated by an army observation tower, bristling with listening and watching devices and splashed with paint bombs hurled from below the walls. Here you'll find Roaring Meg, the most famous of the cannons used during the Siege of Derry; the noise it made was said to be more terrifying than any physical damage it managed to inflict.

The next section of wall is known as the Grand Parade, and offers an excellent view over the Bogside estate. The prominent murals on the houses below were painted by the Bogside Artists (see boxed text, opposite).

An empty plinth on **Royal Bastion (15)** marks the former site of a monument to the Reverend George Walker, joint governor of the city during the Great Siege. The 27m-tall column, erected in 1826 and seen by local nationalists as a symbol of unionist domination, was blown up by the IRA in 1973. The restored statue of Walker now stands in a memorial garden next to the Apprentice Boys' Memorial Hall.

Behind the Royal Bastion is the 1872 Church of Ireland **Chapel of St Augustine** (**16**), built on the site of St Colmcille's 6th-century monastery. A little further along is the **Apprentice Boys' Memorial Hall** (**17**), its windows protected by steel grilles and, like the army observation tower, splashed with paint bombs. Behind it is the grand Corinthian temple of the **First Derry Presbyterian Church** (**18**).

Just past the church is the Butcher's Gate, from where you can return to the diamond, head down Magazine St to the Tower Museum, or descend Fahan St to the Bogside (p644) and the People's Gallery (p646).

Tours

City Sightseeing Bus Tours (Map p642; ☎ 9062 6888; www.city-sightseeing.com; adult/child £8/5; ⏲ 10am-4pm Mar-Oct) Runs open-top bus tours of the city departing hourly from the Derry Visitor & Convention Bureau, and also picking up passengers at the Guildhall.

City Tours (Map p645; ☎ 7127 1996; www.irishtour guides.com; Carlisle Stores, 11 Carlisle Rd) Runs one-hour Historic Derry walking tours starting from Carlisle Stores at 10am, noon and 2pm year-round and costing £4/2 per adult/child. There are also tours of the Bogside and of Derry's murals.

Derry Visitor & Convention Bureau (Map p642; ☎ 7126 7284; 44 Foyle St) Offers 1½-hour guided walking tours of the walled city for £6/4 per adult/child, starting from the bureau at 11.15am and 3.15pm Monday to Friday in July and August, and at 2.30pm Monday to Friday November to June. The price includes admission to St Columb's Cathedral.

Foyle Cruise Line (Map p642; ☎ 7136 2857; www .foylecruiseline.com; Harbour Museum, Harbour Sq) Operates daily cruises on the Foyle estuary. Trips to Culmore Bay (1¼ hours) cost £6/4.50 per adult/child and depart at 2pm; four-hour evening cruises to Greencastle with bar and entertainment cost £12/8 per adult/child, and depart at 8pm.

Festivals & Events

City of Derry Jazz Festival (☎ 7137 6545; www .cityofderryjazzfestival.com; early May) Four days of jazz at various venues.

Foyle Regatta (☎ 7137 5055; www.cruisenorth west.com; early Jul) River-based festival with tall ships, yacht races, boat trips, live music and shore-side street entertainment.

Gasyard Wall Féile (☎ 7126 2812; www.freederry .org/gasyard.html; early Aug) A major cultural festival that features live music, street performers, carnival, theatre and Irish-language events.

City of Derry Guitar Festival (☎ 7137 5550; www .cityofderryguitarfestival.com; late Aug) The grounds of University of Ulster host performances and master classes from guitar great around the world, including classical, acoustic, electric, flamenco and bass.

Halloween Carnival (☎ 7137 6545; www.derrycity .gov.uk/halloween; 27-31 Oct) Ireland's biggest street party has the entire city dressing up and dancing in the streets.

Foyle Film Festival (☎ 7126 7432; www.foylefilm festival.com; Nov) This week-long event is the North's biggest film festival.

Sleeping

It's best to book accommodation in advance during festival events.

BUDGET

OUR PICK Derry City Independent Hostel (Map p642; ☎ 7137 7989; www.derry-hostel.co.uk; 44 Great James St; dm/d from £11/36; 🖳) Run by experienced backpackers and decorated with souvenirs of their travels around the world, this small, friendly hostel is set in a Georgian town house, just a short walk northwest of the bus station. They have an annexe nearby called Dolce Vita, with stylishly decorated double rooms aimed at couples travelling together.

Derry Palace Hostel (Map p645; ☎ 7130 9051; www .paddyspalace.com; 1 Woodleigh Tce, Asylum Rd; dm from £11; 🖳 🅿) Part of the Ireland-wide Paddy's Palace chain, this hostel is central, comfortable and as friendly as they come. There's a sunny garden, a good party atmosphere and the staff regularly organise nights out at local pubs with traditional music.

MIDRANGE

Laburnum Lodge (☎ 7135 4221; www.laburnumlodge .com; 9 Rockfield, Madam's Bank Rd; s/d £30/45; 🖳 🅿) Readers recommended this suburban villa on a quiet street on the northern edge of town, impressed by the friendly welcome, spacious bedrooms and hearty breakfasts. If you don't have your own transport, the owner can pick you up from the train or bus station.

Sunbeam House (Map p642; ☎ 7126 3606; www.sun beamhouse.activehotels.com; 147 Sunbeam Tce, Bishop St; s/d £35/48) This attractive red-brick terraced house is a five-minute walk southwest of the walled city. The four cheerfully decorated rooms are a bit on the small side, but there's nothing cramped about the hospitality. Or the size of the breakfasts!

COUNTIES DERRY & ANTRIM

our pick **Merchant's House** (Map p642; ☎ 7126 9691; www.thesaddlershouse.com; 16 Queen St; s/d £35/50) Run by the same couple as the Saddler's House, this historic, Georgian-style town house is a gem of a B&B. It has an elegant lounge and dining room with marble fireplaces and antique furniture, TV and coffee-making facilities in all rooms, and home-made marmalade at breakfast. There are even bathrobes in the rooms. Call at the Saddler's House first to pick up a key.

Saddler's House (Map p642; ☎ 7126 9691; www .thesaddlershouse.com; 36 Great James St; s/d £35/50) Centrally located within a five-minute walk of the walled city, this friendly B&B is set in a lovely, Victorian town house. All seven rooms have private bathrooms, and you get to enjoy a huge breakfast in the family kitchen.

Abbey B&B (Map p642; ☎ 7127 9000; www.abbey accommodation.com; 4 Abbey St; s/d £35/50; ♿) There's a warm welcome waiting at this family-run B&B just a short walk from the walled city, on the edge of the Bogside. The six rooms are stylishly decorated and include family rooms with up to four beds.

Clarence House (Map p642; ☎ 7126 5342; www .guesthouseireland.co.uk; 15 Northland Rd; s/d £35/60; 🖳) A grand, red-brick Victorian town house, this place opened as Derry's first-ever B&B back in 1962. The Clarence's comfortably old-fashioned rooms are crammed with everything from trouser presses to hair dryers, the choice of breakfast stretches from porridge to fruit salad to full fry-up, and there's a bar in the lounge where your host, in true Irish fashion, can talk the hind legs off a Donegal donkey.

Da Vinci's Hotel (☎ 7127 9111; www.davincishotel .com; 15 Culmore Rd; r £50-85, ste from £120; 🖳 🅿) This sleek boutique hotel on the west bank of the Foyle is the accommodation of choice for visiting celebrities, business people and politicians, offering spacious, stylish rooms and a hip cocktail bar and restaurant. It's located 1.5km north of the city centre.

Eating

BUDGET

Boston Tea Party (Map p645; 15 Craft Village; snacks £2-4; ⊙ 9am-5.30pm Mon-Sat) Home-made soups, hot lunches, freshly baked cakes, friendly service and the best apple pie in town – what more could you want from a café?

Café Artisan (Map p645; ☎ 7128 2727; 18-20 Bishop St Within; mains £2-5; ⊙ 9.30am-5.30pm Mon-Sat) This cool little café is tucked away at the back of the Bookworm bookshop and serves delicious home-made soups, deli sandwiches, *panini* (type of Italian sandwich) and excellent cappuccinos.

Sandwich Co (sandwiches & salads £3-4; ⊙ 9am-5pm Mon-Sat); the Diamond (Map p645; ☎ 7137 2500); Strand Rd (Map p642; 61 Strand Rd) White bread, brown bread, baguettes, *panini*, ciabatta – this place offers good-value, choose-your-own sandwiches and salads.

MIDRANGE

Encore Brasserie (Map p645; ☎ 7137 2492; Millennium Forum, Newmarket St; mains lunch £6, dinner £10-13; ⊙ noon-4pm & 5-9pm) Set in the lobby of the city's main cultural venue, the Encore is a stylish little place with friendly, efficient service and a crowd-pleasing menu of perennial favourites from home-made lasagne to slow-braised lamb shanks served with honey-glazed carrots.

Fitzroy's (Map p645; ☎ 7126 6211; 2-4 Bridge St; mains £8-13; ⊙ 11am-10pm Mon-Sat, noon-8pm Sun) Informal Fitzroy's does café-style, burger-and-chips lunches till 5.30pm, and then bistro-style dinners, including Moroccan-style lamb kebab, baked cod with leek risotto, and Thai vegetable stir-fry. The set two-/three-course dinner for £12/15 (available from 8pm Monday to Thursday) is good value. There's a second entrance on Carlisle Rd.

Brown's Restaurant (Map p642; ☎ 7134 5180; 1 Bond's Hill, Waterside; mains £10-15; ⊙ noon-2.15pm Tue-Fri, 5.30-10pm Tue-Sat) From the outside, Brown's may not have the most promising location, but step inside and you're in a cool little enclave of brandy-coloured banquettes, chrome and mesh chairs, zebra-striped drapes and squiggly metal light fittings, with the odd Rothko print adorning the walls. The ever-changing menu is a gastronome's delight, making creative use of fresh local produce in dishes such as collops of monkfish in a sherry, roast pepper and chorizo cream sauce.

Mange 2 (Map p642; ☎ 7136 1222; 2 Clarendon St; mains £10-18; ⊙ noon-2.45pm & 5-10pm) Tea-lights flickering in pierced pottery bowls lend a bit of atmosphere to this Georgian-style dining room, an elegant venue for a bit of a splurge. The French fusion menu includes lots of Irish ingredients – try plump Strangford Lough mussels á la Basquaise (in a thick broth of roasted red pepper, garlic, wine and cream) – and a handful of good vegetarian dishes, and there's an 'early bird' three-course dinner (£32 for two including a bottle of wine, 5.30pm to 7pm Monday to Thursday).

SELF-CATERING

Tesco (Map p642; ☎ 0845 677 9639; Quayside Shopping Centre, Strand Rd; ⏱ 9am-9pm Mon-Thu, 8.30am-9pm Fri, 8.30am-8pm Sat, 1-6pm Sun) Self-caterers can stock up at this big supermarket, just north of the walled city.

Drinking

Whatever you do in Derry, don't miss an evening in the city's lively pubs – for the craic rather than the beer, which is nothing to write home about. They're friendly and atmospheric, mostly open until 1am, and are within easy walking distance of each other – there are six within dancing distance along Waterloo St.

Peadar O'Donnell's (Map p645; ☎ 7137 2138; 63 Waterloo St) A backpackers' favourite, Peadar's goes for traditional music sessions every night and often on weekend afternoons as well. It's done up as a typical Irish pub-cum-grocer down to shelves of grocery items, with a pig's head and hams hanging off the ceiling.

Badgers Bar (Map p645; ☎ 7136 0763; 16-18 Orchard St) A fine polished-brass and stained-glass Victorian pub crammed with wood-panelled nooks and crannies, Badgers overflows at lunchtime with shoppers enjoying quality pub grub, and offers a quiet haven in the evenings when it attracts a crowd of more mature drinkers.

Entertainment

CLUBS & LIVE MUSIC

Sandino's Café-Bar (Map p645; ☎ 7130 9297; www .sandinos.com; 1 Water St; admission free; ⏱ 11.30am-1am Mon-Sat, 1pm-midnight Sun) From the posters of Ché to the Free Palestine flag to the Fairtrade coffee, this relaxed café-bar exudes a liberal, left-wing vibe. There are live bands on Friday at 9.30pm, and occasionally midweek, and DJ sessions on Saturdays. On Sundays there's a traditional Irish music session at 3pm, and live jazz/soul or DJs from 9.30pm, plus regular theme nights, fundraising nights and political events. Check the website for details.

Mason's Bar (Map p645; ☎ 7136 0177; 10 Magazine St; admission free) The city that spawned the Undertones is still turning out raw, rumbustious live music and Mason's Friday night sessions, kicking off at 6pm, are the place to catch the latest offerings from local talent. There are three or four acts each week, as well as open-mic sessions on Monday and occasional live bands on Saturdays at 10pm; check out what's on at www.myspace.com/masons629.

Earth@Café Roc (Map p642; ☎ 7136 0556; 129-135 Strand Rd; admission free-£5) Derry's main night-club and bar complex, close to the university, has a student night on Tuesday, chart hits and dance anthems on Friday, and guest DJs on Saturday.

Gweedore Bar (Map p645; ☎ 7126 3513; 59-61 Waterloo St) Next door to Peadar O'Donnell's and part of the same complex, the Gweedore Bar hosts live rock bands most nights, with a DJ bar upstairs.

CONCERTS, THEATRE & CINEMA

Millennium Forum (Map p645; ☎ 7126 4455; www .millenniumforum.co.uk; Newmarket St) Ireland's biggest theatre auditorium is a major venue for dance, drama, concerts, opera and musicals.

Nerve Centre (Map p645; ☎ 7126 0562; www.nerve centre.org.uk; 7-8 Magazine St) The Nerve Centre was set up in 1990 as a multimedia arts centre to encourage young, local talent in the fields of music and film. The centre has a performance area, a theatre, a cinema (with an art-house programme), a bar and a café.

Playhouse (Map p645; ☎ 7126 8027; www.derryplay house.co.uk; 5-7 Artillery St; ⏱ box office 10am-5pm Mon-Fri) This community arts centre stages dance and theatre performances. It also houses the Context Gallery, which hosts exhibitions by local artists.

Waterside Theatre (☎ 7131 4000; www.water sidetheatre.com; Ebrington Centre, Glendermott Rd; ⏱ box office 9am-4.30pm Mon-Fri) Housed in a former factory 500m east of the River Foyle, this theatre stages drama, dance, comedy, children's theatre and live music.

Magee College (Map p642; ☎ 7137 5679; www .ulster.ac.uk/culture; University of Ulster, Northland Rd) The college hosts a variety of arts, theatre and classical-concert performances throughout the year.

Strand Multiplex (Map p642; ☎ 7137 3900; www .cineplex.ie; Quayside Shopping Centre, Strand Rd) This seven-screen multiplex is the place for mainstream movies.

Shopping

Ogmiós (Map p642; ☎ 7126 4132; 34 Great James St) Housed in the An Gaeláras Gaelic language centre, this craft shop stocks a good range of Irish-language books, traditional music CDs, musical instruments, pottery, prints and jewellery.

Donegal Shop (Map p645; ☎ 7126 6928; 8 Shipquay St) A long-established craft shop, the Donegal is crammed with Irish knitwear, Celtic jewellery, Donegal tweeds, Irish linen and souvenirs.

McGilloway Gallery (Map p645; ☎ 7136 6011; 6 Shipquay St) A commercial gallery that provides a showcase for the best of contemporary Irish art, the McGilloway sells work by local artists and stages around half a dozen exhibitions each year.

Whatnot (Map p645; ☎ 7128 8333; 22 Bishop St Within) The Whatnot is an interesting little antique shop crammed with jewellery, militaria, bric-a-brac and collectables.

Cool Discs Music (Map p645; ☎ 7126 0770; 6/7 Lesley House, Foyle St) One of Northern Ireland's best independent record shops, Cool Discs has a wide selection of music by Irish artists old and new.

Austins (Map p645; ☎ 7126 1817; 2 the Diamond) The world's oldest independent department store (established 1830), Austins is a good place to shop for Irish linen (they can ship your purchases overseas).

Foyleside Shopping Centre (Map p645; ☎ 7137 7575; Orchard St; ☺ 9am-6pm Mon & Tue, 9am-9pm Wed-Fri, 9am-7pm Sat, 1-6pm Sun) This is a huge, four-level mall just outside the eastern city walls, which contains a Marks & Spencer, Virgin Megastore, Dixons and other high-street chain stores.

The little courtyard of Craft Village (Map p645) is home to a handful of craft shops selling Derry crystal, hand-woven cloth, ceramics, jewellery and other local craft items. Enter from Shipquay St, Magazine St or Tower Museum.

Getting There & Away
AIR
City of Derry Airport (☎ 7181 0784; www.cityofderryairport.com) is about 13km east of Derry along the A2 towards Limavady. There are direct flights daily to Dublin and Glasgow International (British Airways), London Stansted, Liverpool, Nottingham East Midlands and Glasgow Prestwick (Ryanair).

BUS
The **bus station** (Map p645; ☎ 7126 2261) is on Foyle St, just northeast of the walled city.

Bus 212, the *Maiden City Flyer,* is a fast and frequent service between Derry and Belfast (£9, 1¾ hours, every 30 minutes Monday to Saturday, 11 on Sunday), calling at Dungiven. Goldline Express 274 goes from Derry to Dublin (£14, four hours, every two hours daily).

Other useful Ulsterbus services include the 273 to Omagh (£7, 1¼ hours, hourly Monday to Saturday, six Sunday) and the 234 to Limavady and Coleraine (£6, one hour, five daily Monday to Friday, two Sunday), continuing to Portstewart and Portrush twice daily.

Lough Swilly Bus Company (☎ 7126 2017) has an office upstairs at the bus station, and runs buses to Buncrana, Carndonagh, Dungloe, Letterkenny (£5, 30 to 45 minutes, nine daily Monday to Friday, five on Saturday) and Greencastle (one hour, three daily Monday to Saturday) in County Donegal. There's also a bus from Derry to Malin Head (£6, 1¼ hours, two daily) via Carndonagh on Monday, Wednesday, Friday and Saturday – a very scenic trip.

Bus Éireann (in Donegal ☎ 353-742 1309) service 64 runs from Derry to Galway (£13, 5¼ hours, two daily) via Letterkenny, Donegal and Sligo; another four a day terminate at Sligo.

The **Airporter** (Map p642; ☎ 7126 9996; www.airporter.co.uk; Quayside Shopping Centre, Strand Rd) bus service runs direct from Derry to Belfast International (one-way/return £15/25, 1½ hours) and George Best Belfast City (same fare, two hours) airports. Buses depart hourly Monday to Friday, every two hours on Saturday and Sunday.

TRAIN
Derry's train station (referred to as Londonderry in Northern Ireland timetables) is on the eastern side of the River Foyle; a free Rail Link bus connects it with the bus station on Foyle St. Trains to Belfast (£10, 2¼ hours, seven or eight daily Monday to Saturday, four on Sunday) are slower but more comfortable than the bus, and the section of line between Derry and Coleraine is very scenic. There are also frequent trains to Coleraine (£7, 45 minutes, seven daily), with connections to Portrush (£8, 1¼ hours).

Getting Around
Bus 143A to Limavady stops at City of Derry airport (30 minutes, five daily Monday to Fri-

day, three Saturday); otherwise a taxi costs about £10.

The local Ulsterbus Foyle buses leave from Foyle St, outside the bus station, with 13 routes leading to the suburbs and surrounding villages; a day ticket giving unlimited travel on these buses costs £1.20.

The **Derry Taxi Association** (☎ 7126 0247) and **Foyle Delta Cabs** (☎ 7126 3905) operate from the city centre to all areas.

The Foyle Valley cycle route runs through Derry, along the west bank of the river, on the way to Strabane.

LIMAVADY & AROUND

pop 12,000

Enchanted by a folk tune played by a blind fiddler outside her window in 1851, Limavady resident Jane Ross (1810–79) jotted down the melody – then known as O'Cahan's Lament, and later as the Londonderry Air. She had written down for the first time the tune that came to be known around the world as 'Danny Boy' – probably the most famous Irish song of all time.

Limavady was granted to Sir Thomas Phillips, the organiser of the Plantation of County Londonderry, by James I in 1612, after the last ruling chief, Sir Donnell Ballagh O'Cahan, was found guilty of rebellion (see p41 for more on the Plantation). Its original Gaelic name Léim an Mhadaidh means 'The Dog's Leap' and commemorates one of the O'Cahans' dogs that jumped a gorge across the River Roe to bring warning of an unexpected enemy attack.

The **tourist office** (☎ 7776 0307; 7 Connell St; ☉ 9am-5pm Mon-Fri year-round, to 5.45pm Jul & Aug, also 9.30am-5.30pm Sat May-Sep) is northeast of the town centre in the Limavady Borough Council Offices.

TOP FIVE B&BS IN NORTHERN IRELAND

- Anna's House B&B (County Down; p620)
- Briers Country House (County Down; p626)
- Fortwilliam Country House (County Down; p611)
- Merchant's House (County Derry; p651)
- Whitepark House B&B (County Antrim; p665)

Sights & Activities

Today Limavady is a quiet and prosperous small town. There's not much to see except the **blue plaque** on the wall at 51 Main St, opposite the Alexander Arms, commemorating the home of Jane Ross. The town hosts a **jazz and blues festival** (www.limavadyjazzandblues.com) in early June.

The lovely **Roe Valley Country Park**, about 3km south of Limavady, has riverside walks stretching for 5km either side of the River Roe. The area is associated with the O'Cahans, who ruled the valley until the Plantation. The 17th-century settlers saw the flax-growing potential of the damp river valley and the area became an important linen-manufacturing centre.

The **Dogleap Centre** (☎ 7772 2074; Roe Valley Country Park, 41 Dogleap Rd; admission free; ☉ 9am-6pm daily Apr-Sep, to 5pm Oct-Mar) houses a visitor centre and tearoom. Next door is Ulster's first domestic **hydroelectric power station**, opened in 1896; it opens on request at the visitor centre. The nearby **Weaving Shed Museum** (admission free; ☉ 1-5pm daily Jul & Aug, 1-5pm Sat & Sun May & Jun) contains old photographs and relics of the valley's flax industry. The scutch mill, where the flax was pounded, is a 20-minute walk away, along the river, past two watchtowers built to guard the linen when it was spread out in the fields for bleaching.

The River Roe is famous for its **trout and salmon fishing** (www.roeangling.com). Day tickets cost £15, and are available from **SJ Mitchell & Co** (☎ 7772 2128; Main St, Limavady), the Dogleap Centre and the Alexander Arms Hotel. The season runs from the third week in May until 20 October.

The park is signposted off the B192 road between Limavady and Dungiven. Bus 146 from Limavady to Dungiven will drop you at the turn-off; the park is about a 30-minute walk from the main road.

Sleeping & Eating

Alexander Arms Hotel (☎ 7776 3443; 34 Main St; s/d £28/45; Ⓟ) A long-established hotel and pub dating from 1875, the centrally located Alexander Arms is now a friendly, family-run place that offers B&B and serves pub grub and restaurant meals.

Hunter's Bakery & Oven Door Café (☎ 7772 2411; 5 Market St; mains £3-6; ☉ 9am-5.30pm Mon-Sat) If you fancy a quick snack, this homely bakery has a comfy cafeteria at the back, serving good coffee, cakes and light meals. It's a local institution, patronised by a cross-section of the community, with a pleasantly old-fashioned feel.

our pick **Lime Tree** (☎ 7776 4300; 60 Catherine St; mains £14-17; ◷ 6-9pm Tue-Fri, 6-9.30pm Sat) Unfussy décor in shades of burgundy and beige, softened by flickering tea-lights, makes for a relaxing atmosphere in Limavady's top eatery. The menu promotes local produce – from succulent Malin Head crab cakes, and seafood thermidor made with Donegal fish, to fillet steak from award-winning butcher Hunter's of Limavady, served with red wine and tarragon sauce – and includes vegetarian dishes that are a cut above the usual, such as spiced chickpea cakes with roast red pepper dressing. There's also a three-course set menu (£22), and an early-bird menu (two/three courses £12.50/15) available before 7pm Tuesday to Friday.

Getting There & Away

Bus 143 runs between Derry and Limavady hourly (four daily on Sunday). There's no direct bus to Belfast from Limavady but connections can be made at Coleraine or Dungiven. Bus 146 goes from Limavady to Dungiven (40 minutes, five daily Monday to Friday).

DUNGIVEN

pop 3000

As the main road from Belfast to Derry sweeps down from the bleak moors of the Glenshane Pass it sweeps right through the small market town of Dungiven (Dún Geimhin), 14km south of Limavady. The traffic-choked main street is almost as bleak as the moors, but it's worth stopping to take a look at the old priory.

You can get **tourist information** (☎ 7774 2428) from the reception desk in Dungiven Castle.

Sights

The remains of the Augustinian **Dungiven Priory**, off the A6 on the eastern edge of town, date back to the 12th century when it replaced a pre-Norman monastery.

In the chancel of the church is the magnificent **tomb of Cooey-na-Gal**, a chieftain of the O'Cahans, who died in 1385. It's difficult to see in the dark of the blocked-off chancel (bring a torch if you're really keen), but the tomb bears figures of six kilted *gallowglasses*, Scottish mercenaries hired by

Cooey O'Cahan as minders – they earned him the nickname 'na-Gal' ('of the Foreigners'). It's topped by a beautifully sculpted canopy of Gothic tracery.

Near the entrance to the churchyard is a **bullaun**, a mossy, hollowed stone originally used by the monks for grinding grain, but now collecting rainwater and used as a site of pilgrimage and prayer by people seeking cures for illnesses. A nearby tree is covered in prayer rags left by visiting pilgrims.

Sleeping

Flax Mill Hostel (☎ 7774 2655; www.flaxmill-textiles.com; Mill Lane, Derrylane; dm £6; ◷ Mar-Oct; **P**) The owners of this converted 18th-century flax mill grow their own organic veggies and generate their own electricity, but their main business is creating hand-woven textiles. There's basic hostel accommodation too. The mill is 5km north of Dungiven, signposted off the B192 road to Limavady.

Getting There & Away

The hourly Maiden City Flyer bus 212 between Derry and Belfast stops in Dungiven, as does the 246 from Limavady (£3, 25 minutes, six daily Monday to Friday, four Saturday, two Sunday).

COASTAL COUNTY DERRY
Magilligan Point

The huge triangular spit of land that almost closes off the mouth of Lough Foyle is mostly taken up by a military firing range, and is home to a once-notorious prison. Still, it's worth a visit for its vast sandy beaches – **Magilligan Strand** to the west, and the 9km sweep of **Benone Strand** to the northeast. On the point itself, watching over the entrance to Lough Foyle, stands a **Martello tower**, built during the Napoleonic Wars in 1812 to guard against French invasion.

Benone Tourist Complex (☎ 7775 0555; 59 Benone Ave; camp sites £9, caravans £13-15; ◷ 9am-10pm Jul & Aug, to dusk Apr-Jun & Sep, to 5pm Oct-Mar), adjacent to Benone Strand, has an outdoor heated pool, a children's pool, tennis courts and a putting green. Note that dogs are not allowed on the beach from May to September.

The **Lough Foyle Ferry** (in the Republic ☎ 074-938 1901; www.loughfoyleferry.com; car/motorcycle/pedestrian £7/3.50/2) runs between Magilligan Point and Greencastle in County Donegal all year round. The trip takes 10 minutes and runs every 15 minutes from 7.20am Monday to Friday and 9am Saturday and Sunday. The last ferry is at 9.50pm every day April to September and 7.50pm every day October to March.

Downhill

In 1774 the eccentric Bishop of Derry and fourth Earl of Bristol, Frederick Augustus Hervey, built himself a palatial home, Downhill, on the coast west of Castlerock. It burnt down in 1851, was rebuilt in 1876, and was finally abandoned after WWII. The ruins of the house now stand forlornly on a cliff top.

The original demesne covered some 160 hectares, which is now part of the National Trust's **Downhill Estate** (☎ 2073 1582; admission free; ☼ dawn-dusk). The beautiful landscaped gardens below the ruins of the house are the work of celebrated gardener Jan Eccles, who became custodian of Downhill at the age of 60 and created the garden over a period of 30 years. She died in 1997 aged 94.

The main attraction here is the little **Mussenden Temple** (admission free; parking at Lion's Gate £3 per car; ☼ 11am-6pm Sat, Sun & hols Mar-May & Sep, 11am-6pm daily Jun, 11am-7.30pm daily Jul & Aug, 11am-5pm Sat & Sun Oct), built by the bishop to house either his library or his mistress – opinions differ! The randy old clergyman continued an affair with the mistress of Frederick William II of Prussia well into his old age.

It's a pleasant, 20-minute walk to the temple from Castlerock, with fine views west to the beach at Benone and Donegal, and east to Portstewart and the shadowy outlines of the Scottish hills. Begin at the path along the seaward side of the caravan park; halfway there, you have to descend into a steep-sided valley and climb the steps on the far side of the little lake. On the beach below the temple, the bishop used to challenge his own clergy to horseback races, rewarding the winners with lucrative parishes.

On the main road 1km west of the temple, opposite the Downhill Hostel, the scenic **Bishop's Road** climbs steeply up through a ravine and heads over the hills to Limavady. There are spectacular views over Lough Foyle, Donegal and the Sperrin Mountains from the **Gortmore** picnic area, and from the cliff top at **Binevenagh Lake**.

ourpick Downhill Hostel (☎ 7084 9077; www.down hillhostel.com; 12 Mussenden Rd; dm/d from £10/30, f from £35 plus £5 per child; P) is a beautifully restored late-19th-century house, tucked beneath the sea cliffs and overlooking the beach, which offers very comfortable accommodation in six-bed dorms, doubles and family rooms. There's a big lounge with an open fire and a view of the sea, and you can hire wetsuits and body boards when the surf's up. You can even paint your own mugs, plates and bowls in the neighbouring pottery. There are no shops in Downhill so bring supplies with you.

Bus 134 between Limavady and Coleraine (20 minutes, 12 daily Monday to Friday, seven Saturday) stops at Downhill, as does the 234 between Derry and Coleraine.

Castlerock

Castlerock is a small seaside resort with a decent beach. At the turn-off from the main coast road towards Castlerock is the late-17th-century **Hezlett House** (☎ 2073 1582; guided tour adult/child £3/2; ☼ 1-6pm Wed-Mon Jul & Aug, 1-6pm Sat & Sun Jun), a thatched cottage noted for its cruck-truss roof gables of stone and turf strengthened with wooden crucks, or crutches. The interior decoration is Victorian.

Bus 134 between Limavady and Coleraine (20 minutes, 12 daily Monday to Friday, seven Saturday) stops at Castlerock, as does the 234 between Derry and Coleraine.

There are nine trains a day from Castlerock to Coleraine (£2, 10 minutes) and Derry (£7, 35 minutes) Monday to Saturday, and four on Sunday.

COLERAINE

pop 25,300

Coleraine (Cúil Raithin), on the banks of the River Bann, is an important transport hub and shopping centre. It was one of the original Plantation towns of County Londonderry, founded in 1613. The University of Ulster was established here in 1968 much to the chagrin of Derry, which had lobbied hard to win it.

Orientation & Information

The mostly pedestrianised town centre is on the east bank of the River Bann. From the combined train and bus station turn left along Railway Rd to find the **tourist information centre** (☎ 7034 4723; colerainetic@btconnect.com; Railway Rd; ☼ 9am-5pm Mon-Sat) then turn right at King's Gate St for the main shopping area and Coleraine Library (☎ 7034 2561; Queen St; ☼ 9.30am-8pm Mon-Thu, 9.30am-5pm Fri & Sat), which has public internet access for £1.50 per 30 minutes.

Sights & Activities

The tourist office has a *Heritage Trail* leaflet that will guide you around what little remains of the original Plantation town, including **St Patrick's Church**, parts of which date from 1613, and fragments of the town walls.

On the second Saturday of each month the **Causeway Speciality Market** (☼ 9am-2.30pm) is held in the Diamond, selling a range of local crafts and organic produce from hand-turned wooden bowls and home-made candles to farmhouse jam from Ballywalter and sheep-milk cheese from County Derry.

Just 1.5km south of the town centre, on the east bank of the river, is **Mountsandel Mount**, a massive and mysterious earthwork that may have been an early Christian stronghold or a later Anglo-Norman fortification. From the Mountsandel Forest parking area on Mountsandel Rd, a 2.5km circular walk leads high above the River Bann to the mount, where you descend steeply down to the riverbank and return upstream past the Victorian lock and weir at Cutts.

You can take a 1½-hour river cruise on the **Lady Sandel** (☎ 07798 786955; www.riverbanncruises .com; adult/child £8/5) from the jetty on Strand Rd (across the river from the town centre) up-stream to Macfinn via the lock at Cutts, or downstream to the river mouth. Boats depart at 3pm Saturday and Sunday from Easter to September, plus 11am and 2pm Monday to Friday from June to August.

Sleeping & Eating

There's not much accommodation in the town centre; most B&Bs are on the fringes.

Lodge Hotel & Travelstop (☎ 7034 4848; www .thelodgehotel.com; Lodge Rd; s/d from £63/78; P) The Lodge offers a choice of rooms with all mod cons in the main hotel, or slightly more basic rooms in the motel-style annexe (family rooms that sleep two adults and two kids from £63 per room without breakfast). It's fairly central too – less than 1km southeast of the town centre.

Camus Country House (☎ 7034 2982; 27 Curragh Rd, Castleroe; s/d £30/50; P) This lovely, ivy-clad, 17th-century house with views over the River Bann occupies the site of an 8th-century monastery, with an old Celtic cross in the adjacent cemetery. The owner can organise fishing trips on the river. It's on the A54, 5km south of town.

Ground (☎ 7032 8664; 25 Kings Gate St; mains £2-4; ☼ 9am-5.30pm Mon-Sat) This cheerful and child-friendly coffee shop serves excellent Fairtrade coffee and tasty organic grub, including soups, sandwiches, *panini* and home-baked cakes, as well as offering organic baby food, bibs, wipes and a nappy-changing room.

Getting There & Away

Goldline Express bus 218 links Coleraine to Belfast (£8, 1¾ hours, hourly Monday to Friday, seven on Saturday, three on Sunday), while bus 234 goes to Derry (£5.90, one hour, six to nine daily Monday to Saturday, two Sunday) via Limavady. See also Getting There & Away, p659.

There are regular trains from Coleraine to Belfast (£8, two hours, seven or eight daily Monday to Saturday, four on Sunday) and Derry (£7, 45 minutes, same frequency). A branch line links Coleraine to Portrush (£1.60, 12 minutes, hourly Monday to Saturday, 10 on Sunday).

PORTSTEWART
pop 7800

Ever since Victorian times, when English novelist William Thackeray described it as having an 'air of comfort and neatness', the seaside and golfing resort of Portstewart has cultivated a sedate, upmarket atmosphere that distinguishes it from populist Portrush, 6km further east. However, there's also a sizable student community from the University of Ulster in Coleraine.

The fantastic beach is the main attraction, along with a couple of world-class golf courses, a combination that has created the North's highest property prices and a large demand for holiday homes, which has led to concerns about overdevelopment.

Orientation & Information

Central Portstewart consists of a west-facing promenade with a harbour at the north end. A coastal walk, paralleled by Strand Rd, runs south for 1.5km to the beach of Portstewart Strand.

The **tourist information office** (☎ 7083 2286; Town Hall, the Crescent; ☼ 10am-1pm & 2-4.30pm Mon-Sat Jul & Aug) is in the library in the red-brick town hall at the south end of the promenade.

COUNTIES DERRY & ANTRIM

Sights & Activities

The broad, 2.5km beach of **Portstewart Strand** is a 20-minute walk south of the centre, or a short bus ride along Strand Rd. Parking is allowed on the firm sand, which can accommodate over 1000 cars (open all year round, £5 per car from Easter to October).

The **Port Path** is a 10.5km coastal footpath (part of the Causeway Coast Way) that stretches from Portstewart Strand to White Rocks, 3km east of Portrush.

Portstewart is within a few kilometres of three of Northern Ireland's top **golf courses** – the championship links at Portstewart Golf Club (green fees weekday/weekend £70/90), Royal Portrush (£110/125) and Castlerock (£60/75).

In early May the **North-West 200 motorcycle race** (www.northwest200.org) is run on a road circuit taking in Portrush, Portstewart and Coleraine. This classic race – Ireland's biggest outdoor sporting event – is one of the last to be run on closed public roads anywhere in Europe, and attracts up to 150,000 spectators; if you're not one of them, it's best to avoid the area on the race weekend.

Sleeping

Don't even think about turning up without a booking during the North-West 200 weekend in May.

BUDGET

Causeway Coast Independent Hostel (☎ 7083 3789; rick@causewaycoasthostel.fsnet.co.uk; 4 Victoria Tce; dm/tw from £10/30) This neat terraced house just northeast of the harbour has spacious four-, six- and eight-bed dorms plus three twin rooms, and good power showers. It has its own kitchen, laundry and welcoming open fire in winter.

Portstewart Holiday Park (☎ 7083 3308; 80 Mill Rd; camp & caravan sites £14) This is the nearest place to the promenade (a 15-minute walk away) that

you can pitch a tent. Coming from Coleraine on the A2, turn right at the Mill Rd/Strand Rd roundabout.

MIDRANGE

Cul-Erg B&B (☎ 7083 6610; www.culerg.co.uk; 9 Hillside; s/d £35/70; 🖳) This family-run B&B is in a modern, flower-bedecked terraced house just a couple of minutes' walk from the promenade. Warm and welcoming, it's set in a quiet cul-de-sac; the rooms at the back have a view of the sea.

Anchorage Inn (☎ 7083 2003; www.theanchorbar .com; 87-89 the Promenade; s/d from £45/75; Ⓟ) Part of a pub and restaurant complex, the Anchorage has 20 bright and cheerful rooms, some with sea views, just a one-minute walk from the promenade.

Cromore Halt Inn (☎ 7083 6888; www.cromore.com; 158 Station Rd; s/d £55/80; 🖳 Ⓟ ♿) About 1km east of the harbour, on the corner of Station Rd and Mill Rd, the motel-style Cromore has a dozen modern, businesslike rooms with wi-fi and modem connections, and a good restaurant.

Eating & Drinking

Morelli's (☎ 7083 2150; 53 the Promenade; mains £3-7; ☷ 9am-11pm, food to 8pm) Morelli's is a local institution, founded by Italian immigrants and famous for its mouth-watering ice cream since 1911. The menu includes pasta, pizza, sandwiches, omelettes, and fish and chips, as well as good coffee and cakes, and there's a great view across the bay to Mussenden Temple, Benone Strand and Donegal.

Harbour Café (☎ 7083 4103; 18 the Promenade; mains £4-8; ☷ 9am-7pm Mon-Fri, 9am-8pm Sat) This 'greasy spoon' is a favourite with locals, serving all-day breakfast (including veggie fry-ups), soups, sandwiches, *panini*, fish and chips and daily specials such as pepper steak. It's table service, but pay at the till as you leave.

Anchor Bar & Skippers (☎ 7083 2003; 87-89 Promenade; mains £7-14; ☷ food noon-9pm) The liveliest of Portstewart's traditional pubs, famed for its Guinness and hugely popular with students from the University of Ulster, the Anchor serves decent pub grub, opens till 1am and has DJ nights on Tuesday, Friday, Saturday and Sunday. There's also Skippers Wine Bar, which serves more sophisticated dishes such as chilli steak, Thai green curry and monkfish wrapped in Parma ham with pesto cream sauce.

TOP FIVE VIEWPOINTS IN NORTHERN IRELAND

- Binevenagh Lake (p656)
- Fair Head (p669)
- Cliffs of Magho (p686)
- Scrabo Hill (p619)
- Slieve Donard (p628)

Getting There & Away

Bus 140 plies between Coleraine and Portstewart (£2, 17 minutes) roughly every half-hour (fewer on Sunday). Also see Getting There & Around, below.

COUNTY ANTRIM

Getting There & Around

Translink (☎ 9066 6630; www.translink.co.uk) operates several bus services specially designed for tourists visiting the popular Antrim coast and Giant's Causeway areas.

The Antrim Coaster (bus 252) links Coleraine with Larne (£8, three hours, two daily Monday to Saturday) via Portstewart, Portrush, Bushmills, the Giant's Causeway, Ballycastle and the Glens of Antrim. One bus a day continues to/from Belfast's Europa Bus Centre (£8, four hours), departing Belfast at 9am and Larne at 10.05am and 3pm. Southbound buses leave Coleraine at 9.50am and 3.40pm. A Sunday service operates from July to September only.

From July to mid-September the Causeway Rambler (bus 402) links Bushmills Distillery and Carrick-a-Rede (£4, 25 minutes, seven daily) via the Giant's Causeway, White Park Bay and Ballintoy. The ticket allows unlimited travel in both directions for one day.

In July and August only, the Bushmills Bus 177, an open-topped (weather permitting) double-decker, runs from Coleraine to the Giant's Causeway (one way/day return £3/4.50, one hour, four daily) via Portstewart, Portrush, Dunluce Castle, Portballintrae and Bushmills Distillery.

PORTRUSH

pop 6300

The bustling seaside resort of Portrush (Port Rois) is bursting at the seams with holiday-makers in high season and, not surprisingly, many of its attractions are focused unashamedly on good, old-fashioned family fun. However, it is also one of Ireland's top surfing spots, and is home to the North's hottest nightclub.

The **tourist information centre** (☎ 7082 3333; Dunluce Centre, 10 Sandhill Dr; ☺ 9am-7pm daily mid-Jun-Aug, 9am-5pm Mon-Fri, noon-5pm Sat & Sun Apr–mid-Jun & Sep, noon-5pm Sat & Sun Mar & Oct) books accommodation and has a bureau de change.

Sights & Activities

Portrush's main attraction is the beautiful sandy beach of **Curran Strand** that stretches for 3km to the east of the town, ending at the scenic chalk cliffs of White Rocks.

The town is also famous for **Barry's** (☎ 7082 2340; www.barrysamusements.com; 16 Eglinton St; admission free, 50p-£2 per ride; ☺ 1-10.30pm daily Jul & Aug, 1-6pm Mon-Fri, 1-10.30pm Sat & 1-9.30pm Sun Jun, 1-10.30pm Sat & 1-9.30pm Sun Apr & May), Ireland's biggest amusement park filled with classic, family-friendly rides including a carousel, ghost train and dodgems.

There's more family-oriented fun at the **Dunluce Centre** (☎ 7082 4444; www.dunlucecentre.co.uk; 10 Sandhill Dr; admission £3.50-4.50; ☺ 10.30am-6.30pm daily Jul & Aug, noon-5pm Mon-Fri, noon-6pm Sat & Sun May & Jun, noon-6pm Sat & Sun Apr, noon-5pm Sat & Sun Sep & Oct), a hi-tech, indoor adventure playground especially for kids, with interactive games, a computerised treasure hunt and a 'turbo-tour' motion-simulator ride.

Waterworld (☎ 7082 2001; the Harbour; ☺ 10am-8pm Mon-Sat, noon-8pm Sun Jul & Aug, 10am-3pm Mon-Fri, 10am-6pm Sat & noon-6pm Sun Jun, 10am-6pm Sat & noon-6pm Sun May & Sep), by the harbour, has indoor swimming pools, waterslides and spa baths for children to play in (adult/child under eight years £4.50/2.50, family tickets for three/four/five persons £11.75/15.60/19.50), and ten-pin bowling (from £7.50 per land; open till 10pm).

You'll find even more activities for kids at **Portrush Countryside Centre** (☎ 7082 3600; Bath Rd; admission free; ☺ 10am-5pm Jul-Sep), including marine-life exhibits, a touch pool, rock-pool rambles and fossil hunts.

In summer, boats depart regularly for **cruises** or **fishing trips**; the tourist office has a list of operators. For horse riding contact the **Maddybenny Riding Centre** (☎ 7082 3394; Maddybenny Farm, Atlantic Rd; lessons & hacking per hr £12); beginners are welcome.

Portrush is the centre of Northern Ireland's **surfing** scene. From April to November the friendly **Troggs Surf Shop** (☎ 7082 5476; www.troggssurfshop.co.uk; 88 Main St; ☺ 10am-6pm) offers bodyboard/surfboard hire (per day £5/10) and wetsuit hire (per day £7), surf reports and general advice. A two-hour lesson including equipment hire costs £25.

Sleeping

Places fill up quickly during summer so it's advisable to book in advance.

BUDGET

Activity Breaks Portrush (☎ 07834-450893; 1 Hopefield Grange; dm/d from £12/36; 🖳 Ⓟ) Despite being rather incongruously set in a modern red-brick villa in a housing development 1km south of the town centre, this new hostel has excellent facilities including a spa bath, games room, smart kitchen, garden barbecue and free pick-up from the train or bus.

Carrick Dhu Caravan Park (☎ 7082 3712; 12 Ballyreagh Rd; camp & caravan sites from £14 🕑 Apr-Oct) This is a small site 1.5km west of Portrush on the A2 towards Portstewart. Facilities include a children's playground and restaurant.

A Pier View (☎ 7082 3234; www.apierview.co.uk; 53 Kerr St; s/d £25/50; Ⓟ) Any closer to the harbour and you'd be in it! This cosy B&B has three snug rooms, and great views over the harbour and beach from the luxurious lounge and conservatory-style breakfast room.

MIDRANGE

our pick Clarmont (☎ 7082 2397; www.clarmont.com; 10 Landsdowne Cres; s/d from £30/60) Our favourite among several guesthouses on Landsdowne Cres, the Clarmont has great views and, from polished pine floors to period fireplaces, has a décor that tastefully mixes Victorian and modern. Ask for a room with a bay window overlooking the sea.

Albany Lodge Guest House (☎ 7082 3492; www .albanylodgeni.co.uk; 2 Eglinton St; s/d from £60/90; Ⓟ) This elegant, four-storey Victorian villa has a great location close to the beach, with spectacular views along the coast. The rooms are spacious and welcoming, with pine furniture and warm colours, and the owners are friendly without being in your face. It's worth shelling out a few extra quid for the four-poster suite on the top floor, where you can soak up the view while reclining on your chaise-lounge.

Eating

BUDGET

Café 55 (☎ 7082 2811; 1 Causeway St; mains £2-5; 🕑 10am-10pm Tue-Sun) Tucked beneath 55 Degrees North, this licensed café serves good coffee and breakfast bagels and also has daily lunch specials such as fish pie.

Coast (☎ 7082 3311; the Harbour; mains £5-9; 🕑 12.30-2.30pm & 5-10pm Mon & Wed-Fri, 12.30-10.30pm Sat, 12.30-10pm Sun, closed Tue) Coast is another harbour-side choice, offering stone-baked pizzas, pasta dishes and a range of steak, chicken and fish dishes.

Harbour Bistro (☎ 7082 2430; the Harbour; mains £8-11; 🕑 12.15-2.15pm & 5-10pm Mon-Sat, 12.30-3pm & 5-9pm Sun) Quality grub – juicy steaks, home-made burgers, spicy chicken, oriental dishes and vegetarian meals – a family-friendly atmosphere (there's a kids menu) and a harbour-side location make the Harbour one of Portrush's most popular eating places.

MIDRANGE

our pick 55 Degrees North (☎ 7082 2811; 1 Causeway St; mains £9-14; 🕑 5.30-9pm Tue-Sun) One of the north coast's most stylish restaurants, 55 Degrees North boasts a wall of floor-to-ceiling windows allowing diners to soak up a spectacular panorama of sand and sea. The food is excellent, concentrating on clean, simple flavours and unfussy presentation, with dishes such as sea bass steamed with ginger and spring onion, and roast butternut squash with asparagus risotto. There's an early-bird menu (mains £5 to £9) available before 6.45pm weekdays.

Entertainment

Kelly's Complex (☎ 7082 6633; www.kellysportrush.co.uk; 1 Bushmills Rd) The North's top clubbing venue regularly features DJs from London and Manchester, and attracts clubbers from as far afield as Belfast and Dublin. Plain and small-looking from the outside, the TARDIS effect takes over as you enter a wonderland of seven bars and three dance floors, with décor ranging from old-world wood panelling and antiques to ultramodern brushed steel and mirrors. It's been around since 1996, but Lush!@Kellys (admission £10, open 9pm to 2am Saturday) is still one of the best club nights in Ireland. The highlight of the year is the **Beach Party** (www .thebeachparty.co.uk) on the East Strand at the end of June, which has attracted headline acts such as Fatboy Slim and Basement Jaxx.

The complex is on the A2 just east of Portrush, beside the Golf Links Holiday Park.

Getting There & Around

The bus terminal is near the Dunluce Centre. Bus 140 links Portrush with Coleraine (£2, 20 minutes) and Portstewart (£2, 17 minutes) every 20 minutes or so. Also see Getting There & Around, p659.

The train station is just south of the harbour. Portrush is served by trains from Coleraine (£2, 12 minutes, hourly Monday to Saturday, 10 on Sunday), where there are connections to Belfast or Derry.

For taxis call **Andy Brown's** (☎ 7082 2223) or **North West Taxis** (☎ 7082 4446). Both are near the town hall. A taxi to Kelly's is around £5, and it's £10 to the Giant's Causeway.

DUNLUCE CASTLE

Views along the Causeway Coast between Portrush and Portballintrae are dominated by the ruins of **Dunluce Castle** (☎ 2073 1938; 87 Dunluce Rd; adult/child £2/1; ☉ 10am-6pm Apr-Sep, 10am-5pm Oct-Mar, last admission 30 min before closing), perched atop a dramatic basalt crag. In the 16th and 17th centuries it was the seat of the MacDonnell family (the earls of Antrim from 1620), who built a Renaissance-style manor house within the walls. Part of the castle, including the kitchen, collapsed into the sea in 1639, taking seven servants and that night's dinner with it.

The landward wall has cannons salvaged from the *Girona*, a Spanish Armada vessel that foundered nearby (see boxed text, below). Below, a path leads down from the gatehouse to the Mermaid's Cave beneath the castle crag.

Dunluce is 5km east of Portrush, a one-hour walk away along the coastal path. All the buses that run along the coast stop at Dunluce Castle; see p659.

PORTBALLINTRAE

pop 750

During WWI Portballintrae was the only place in the UK to be shelled by a German submarine. And that's pretty much its only claim to fame. A once-pretty village set around a sand-fringed, horseshoe bay with a tiny harbour, today it suffers from rampant over-development, with new holiday apartments sprouting everywhere (fewer than half of the houses are permanently occupied). The village is an easy 2km walk from Bushmills, and 2.5km from the Giant's Causeway. The fine sandy beach of Bushfoot Strand stretches for 1.5km to the northeast.

Sweeney's Wine Bar (☎ 2073 2405; 6B Seaport Ave; mains £9-12; ☉ food served noon-3pm & 5-9pm), set in a converted 17th-century stable block, combines traditional pub décor – wood panelling, stained glass, old armchairs in front of an open fire – with a stylish two-storey conservatory, and serves good pub grub including steaks, chicken skewers with peanut dip and roast chilli ribs.

BUSHMILLS

pop 1350

The small town of Bushmills has long been a place of pilgrimage for connoisseurs of Irish whiskey. A good youth hostel and a restored rail link with the Giant's Causeway have also made it an attractive stop for hikers exploring the Causeway Coast.

Sights

Bushmills Distillery (☎ 2073 3218; www.bushmills.com; Distillery Rd; adult/child £5/2.50; ☉ 9.30am-5.30pm Mon-Sat, noon-5.30pm Sun) is the world's oldest legal distillery, having been granted a licence by King James I in 1608. Bushmills whiskey is made with Irish barley and water from St Columb's Rill, a tributary of the River Bush, and matured in oak barrels. During ageing, the alcohol content drops from around 60% to 40%; the spirit lost through evaporation is known,

---

WRECK OF THE GIRONA

The little bay 1km to the northeast of the Giant's Causeway is called Port na Spaniagh – Bay of the Spaniards. It was here, in October 1588, that the *Girona* – a ship of the Spanish Armada – was driven onto the rocks by a storm.

The *Girona* had escaped the famous confrontation with Sir Walter Raleigh's fleet in the English Channel, but along with many other fleeing Spanish ships had been driven north around Scotland and Ireland by bad weather. Though designed for a crew of 500, when she struck the rocks she was loaded with 1300 people – mostly survivors gathered from other shipwrecks – including the cream of the Spanish aristocracy. Barely a dozen survived.

Somhairle Buidhe (Sorley Boy) MacDonnell (1505–90), the constable of nearby Dunluce Castle, salvaged gold and cannons from the wreck, and used the money to extend and modernise his fortress – cannons from the ship can still be seen on the castle's landward wall. But it was not until 1968 that the wreck site was excavated by a team of archaeological divers. They recovered a magnificent treasure of gold, silver and precious stones, as well as everyday sailors' possessions, which are now on display in Belfast's Ulster Museum (p587).

COUNTIES DERRY & ANTRIM

rather sweetly, as 'the angels' share'. After a tour of the distillery you're rewarded with a free sample (or a soft drink), and four lucky volunteers get a whiskey-tasting session to compare Bushmills with other brands. Tours begin every 30 minutes (last tour 4pm) from April to October; from November to March there are six tours daily Monday to Friday, and four daily Saturday and Sunday.

The **Giant's Causeway & Bushmills Railway** (☎ 2073 2844; www.freewebs.com/giantscausewayrailway; adult/child return £5/2.50) follows the route of a 19th-century tourist tramway for 3km from Bushmills to below the Giant's Causeway visitor centre. The narrow-gauge line and locomotives (two steam and one diesel) were brought from a private line on the shores of Lough Neagh. Trains run hourly between 11am and 5.30pm, departing on the hour from the Causeway, on the half-hour from Bushmills, daily in July and August, weekends only from Easter to June, September and October.

Sleeping & Eating

Mill Rest Youth Hostel (☎ 2073 1222; www.hini.org.uk; 49 Main St; dm £14-15, d £35; ☼ closed 11am-2pm Jul & Aug, 11am-5pm Mar-Jun, Sep & Oct; ☐ ☐) This modern, purpose-built and child-friendly hostel is just off the diamond in the centre of town. Accommodation is mostly in four- to six-bed dorms with one twin room with private bathroom. There's also a kitchen, a restaurant, a laundry and a bike shed. The hostel is open daily March to October, Friday and Saturday nights only November to February.

Ballyness Caravan Park & B&B (☎ 2073 2393; www.ballynesscaravanpark.com; 40 Castlecatt Rd; camp & caravan sites £17; ☼ mid-Mar–Oct; ☐) This ecofriendly caravan park is about 1km south of Bushmills town centre on the B66.

our pick Bushmills Inn (☎ 2073 2339; www.bushmillsinn.com; 9 Dunluce Rd; s/d from £68/98; ☐) One of Northern Ireland's most atmospheric hotels, the Bushmills is an old coaching inn complete with peat fires, gas lamps and a round tower with a secret library. In our opinion, the cheapest rooms, in the old part of the inn, are the best – quirky and cosy – but there are larger, more luxurious ones in the neighbouring Mill House (double from £128). The inn's excellent restaurant (lunch mains £10 to £11, dinner mains £13 to £19; open noon to 9.30pm Monday to Saturday and 12.30pm to 9pm Sunday), with intimate wooden booths set in the old

17th-century stables, serves everything from sandwiches to full á la carte dinners.

Copper Kettle (☎ 2073 2560; 61 Main St; mains £3-5; ☼ 8.30am-5pm Mon-Sat, 10am-5pm Sun) This rustic tea-room serves breakfast fry-ups till 11.30am, and has daily lunch specials as well as good tea, coffee, cakes and scones.

Getting There & Away
See Getting There & Around, p659.

GIANT'S CAUSEWAY
When you first see it you'll understand why the ancients thought the causeway was not a natural feature. The vast expanse of regular, closely packed, hexagonal stone columns dipping gently beneath the waves looks for all the world like the handiwork of giants.

This spectacular rock formation – a national nature reserve and Northern Ireland's only Unesco World Heritage site – is one of Ireland's most impressive and atmospheric landscape features, but it is all too often swamped by visitors. If you can, try to visit midweek or out of season to experience it at its most evocative. Sunset in spring and autumn is the best time for photographs.

Orientation & Information
Visiting the Giant's Causeway itself is free of charge but the overcrowded, council-run car park charges £5/2 per car/motorcycle. It's an easy 1km walk from the car park down to the Causeway; minibuses with wheelchair access ply the route every 15 minutes (adult/child £1.60/80p return). Guided tours of the site (June to August only) cost £2.50/1 per adult/child.

Although a design for a new, world-class visitor centre for the Giant's Causeway was chosen in 2005, at the time of research there was no sign of it appearing. Meanwhile, a 'temporary' **visitor centre** (☎ 2073 1855; www.giantscausewaycentre.com; admission free, audiovisual show £1; ☼ 10am-6pm Jul & Aug, 10am-5pm Sep-Jun), which has been around since 2000, is housed in a wooden building beside the National Trust's gift shop and tearoom.

Sights & Activities
From the car park it's an easy 10- to 15-minute walk downhill on a tarmac road (wheelchair accessible) to the Giant's causeway itself. However, a much more interesting approach is to follow the cliff-top path northeast for

2km to the **Chimney Tops** headland, which has an excellent view of the Causeway and the coastline to the west, including Inishowen and Malin Head.

This pinnacled promontory was bombarded by ships of the Spanish Armada in 1588, who thought it was Dunluce Castle, and the wreck of the Spanish galleon *Girona* (see the boxed text, p661) lies just off the tip of the headland. Return towards the car park and about halfway back descend the Shepherd's Steps (signposted) to a lower-level footpath that leads down to the Causeway. Allow 1½ hours for the round trip.

Alternatively, you can visit the Causeway first, then follow the lower coastal path as far as Port Reostan, passing impressive rock formations such as the **Organ** (a stack of vertical basalt columns resembling organ pipes), the **Harp** (a fan of columns) and the **Giant's Eyes** (a pair of rust-red sockets where huge boulders have fallen out of the rock face), and return by climbing the Shepherd's Steps.

You can also follow the cliff-top path east as far as Dunseverick or beyond (see boxed text, p666).

Sleeping & Eating

Causeway Hotel (☎ 2073 1226; www.giants-causeway -hotel.com; 40 Causeway Rd; s/d £50/70; P) You can't beat it for location – the National Trust's Causeway Hotel is within a stone's-throw of the Causeway, a useful base if you want to explore the Causeway early or late in the day when the crowds are not around. Rooms 28 to 32 are the best, with outdoor terraces that enjoy sunset views over the Atlantic.

National Trust tearoom (☎ 2073 1582; snacks £2-4; 10am-5.30pm Jul & Aug, 10am-4.30pm Sep-Jun) Serves tea, coffee and light meals.

Getting There & Away

Bus 172 from Coleraine and Bushmills to Ballycastle passes the site year round. Also see Getting There & Around, p659.

GIANT'S CAUSEWAY TO BALLYCASTLE

Between the Giant's Causeway and Ballycastle lies the most scenic stretch of the Causeway Coast, with sea cliffs of contrasting black basalt and white chalk, rocky islands, picturesque little harbours and broad sweeps of sandy beach. It's best enjoyed on foot, following the 16.5km of waymarked **Causeway Coast Way** between the Carrick-a-Rede car park and the Giant's Causeway (see boxed text, p666), although the main attractions can also be reached by car or bus.

About 8km east of the Giant's Causeway is the meagre ruin of 16th-century **Dunseverick**

THE MAKING OF THE CAUSEWAY

The Mythology

The story goes that the Irish giant, Finn MacCool, built the Causeway so he could cross the sea to fight the Scottish giant Benandonner. When he got there he found his rival asleep and, seeing that the Scot was far bigger than he, fled back to Ireland. Soon, Finn's wife heard the angry Benandonner come running across the Causeway, so she dressed Finn in a baby's shawl and bonnet and put him in a crib. When the Scottish giant came hammering at Finn's door, Mrs MacCool warned him not to wake Finn's baby. Taking a glance at the cot, Benandonner decided that if this huge baby was Finn's child, then MacCool himself must be immense, and fled in turn back to Scotland, ripping up the causeway as he went. All that remains are its ends – the Giant's Causeway in Ireland, and the island of Staffa in Scotland (which has similar rock formations).

The Geology

The more prosaic scientific explanation is that the causeway rocks were formed 60 million years ago, when a thick layer of molten basaltic lava flowed along a valley in the existing chalk beds. As the lava flow cooled and hardened – from the top and bottom surfaces inward – it contracted, creating a pattern of hexagonal cracks at right angles to the cooling surfaces (think of mud contracting and cracking in a hexagonal pattern as a lake bed dries out). As solidification progressed towards the centre of the flow, the cracks spread down from the top, and up from the bottom, until the lava was completely solid. Erosion has cut into the lava flow, and the basalt has split along the contraction cracks, creating the hexagonal columns.

Castle, spectacularly sited on a grassy bluff. Another 1.5km on is the tiny seaside hamlet of **Portbradden**, with half a dozen harbourside houses and the tiny, blue-and-white **St Gobban's Church**, said to be the smallest in Ireland. Visible from Portbradden and accessible via the next junction off the A2 is the spectacular **White Park Bay** with its wide, sweeping sandy beach.

A few kilometres further on is **Ballintoy** (Baile an Tuaighe), another pretty village tumbling down the hillside to a picture-postcard harbour. The restored limekiln on the quayside once made quicklime using stone from the chalk cliffs and coal from Ballymoney.

The main attraction here is the famous (or notorious, depending on your head for heights) **Carrick-a-Rede Rope Bridge** (☎ 2076 9839; Ballintoy; adult/child £3.30/1.80; ☼ 10am-7pm Jun-Aug, to 6pm Mar-May, Sep & Oct). The 20m-long, 1m-wide bridge of wire rope spans the chasm between the sea cliffs and the little island of Carrick-a-Rede, swaying gently 30m above the rock-strewn water.

The island has sustained a salmon fishery for centuries; fishermen stretch their nets out

from the tip of the island to intercept the passage of the salmon migrating along the coast to their home rivers. The fishermen put the bridge up every spring as they have done for the last 200 years – though it's not, of course, the original bridge.

Crossing the bridge is perfectly safe, but it can be frightening if you don't have a head for heights, especially if it's breezy (in high winds the bridge is closed). Once on the island there are good views of Rathlin Island and Fair Head to the east. There's a small National Trust information centre and café at the car park.

Sleeping & Eating

Whitepark Bay Hostel (☎ 2073 1745; www.hini.org.uk; 157 White Park Rd, Ballintoy; dm/tw £15/35; ☼ Apr-Oct; Ⓟ) This modern, purpose-built hostel, near the west end of White Park Bay, has mostly four-bed dorms, plus twin rooms with TV, all with private bathroom. There is a common room positioned to soak up the view, and the beach is just a few minutes walk through the dunes.

Sheep Island View Hostel (☎ 2076 9391; www.sheepislandview.com; 42A Main St, Ballintoy; camp sites/dm

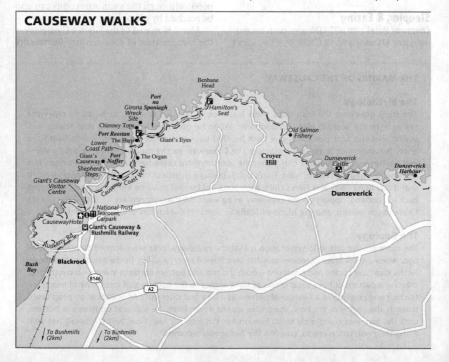

CAUSEWAY WALKS

£5/from £12; ☐ Ⓟ) This excellent independent hostel offers dorm beds, basic shared accommodation in the camping barn, or a place to pitch a tent. There's a kitchen and laundry, a village store nearby, and a free pick-up service from the Giant's Causeway, Bushmills and Ballycastle. It's on the main coast road near the turn-off to Ballintoy harbour, and makes an ideal overnight stop if you're hiking between Bushmills and Ballycastle.

our pick Whitepark House B&B (☎ 2073 1482; www.whiteparkhouse.com; Whitepark Rd, Ballintoy; s/d £50/90; Ⓟ) A beautifully restored 18th-century house overlooking White Park Bay, this B&B has traditional features such as antique furniture and a peat fire complemented by Asian artefacts gathered during the welcoming owners' oriental travels. There are three rooms – ask for one with a sea view.

Roark's Kitchen (☎ 2076 3632; Ballintoy Harbour; mains £2-5; 11am-7pm daily Jun-Aug, Sat & Sun only May & Sep) This cute little chalk-built tearoom on the quayside at Ballintoy serves teas, coffees, ice cream, home-baked apple tart and lunch dishes such as Irish stew or chicken and ham pie.

Getting There & Away

Bus 172 between Ballycastle, Bushmills and Coleraine (six daily Monday to Friday, one on Saturday, three Sunday) is the main, year-round service along this coast, stopping at the Giant's Causeway, Ballintoy and Carrick-a-Rede. Also see Getting There & Around, p659.

BALLYCASTLE
pop 4000

The harbour town and holiday resort of Ballycastle (Baile an Chaisil) marks the eastern end of the Causeway Coast. It's a pretty town with a good bucket-and-spade beach, but apart from that, there's not a lot to see. It's also the port for ferries to Rathlin Island.

The **tourist information office** (☎ 2076 2024; tourism@moyle-council.org; 7 Mary St; 9.30am-7pm Mon-Fri Jul & Aug, 9.30am-5pm Mon-Fri Sep-Jun) is in the district council building at the east end of town. There are a couple of banks with ATMs on Ann St, near the diamond.

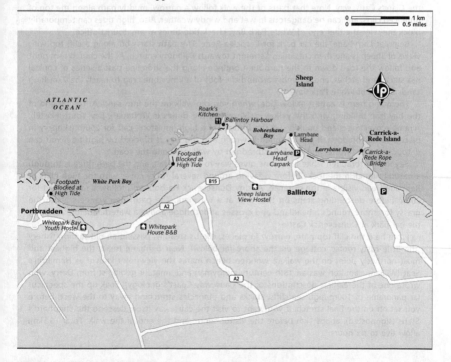

Sights & Activities

The town has a family-friendly **promenade**, with a giant sandpit for kids overlooking the marina. A footbridge leads east across the mouth of the Glenshesk River to a good sandy **beach**.

The tiny **Ballycastle Museum** (☎ 2076 2942; 61A Castle St; admission free; ☾ noon-6pm Mon-Sat Jul & Aug), in the town's 18th-century courthouse, has a collection of Irish arts and crafts works.

In the harbour car park is the **Marconi Memorial**, a plaque at the foot of a rock pinnacle. Guglielmo Marconi's assistants contacted Rathlin Island by radio from Ballycastle in 1898 to prove to Lloyds of London that wireless communication was a viable proposition. The idea was to send notice to London or Liverpool of ships arriving safely after a transatlantic crossing – most vessels on this route would have to pass through the channel north of Rathlin.

Just east of town are the ruins of **Bonamargy Friary**, founded in 1485. It's an attractive site to explore, but sadly the vault – which contains the tombs of MacDonnell chieftains, including Sorley Boy MacDonnell of Dunluce Castle – is not open to the public.

Sea Treks Ireland (☎ 2076 2372; www.seatreks -ireland.com) offer a range of high-speed boat trips out of Ballycastle harbour, including cruises along the coast to Carrick-a-Rede and tours around Rathlin Island from £25 per person.

You can go sea-angling with **Ballycastle Charters** (☎ 07751-345791); three-hour trips depart at 11am and 7pm Monday to Saturday,

---

WALK: CAUSEWAY COAST WAY

The official **Causeway Coast Way** (www.walkni.com) stretches for 53km from Portstewart to Ballycastle, but the most scenic section – the 16.5km between Carrick-a-Rede and the Giant's Causeway – can be done in a day and offers one of the finest coastal walks in Ireland.

There are cafés and public toilets at Larrybane, Ballintoy Harbour and the Giant's Causeway, and bus stops at Larrybane, Ballintoy village, Whitepark Bay Youth Hostel, Dunseverick Castle and the Giant's Causeway. Note that parts of the walk follow a narrow, muddy path along the top of unfenced cliffs, and can be dangerous in wet and windy weather. Also, high tides can temporarily block the way at either end of White Park Bay; check tide times at any tourist office.

Begin at Larrybane, the car park for Carrick-a-Rede. The path starts off along a cliff top with views of Sheep Island then cuts inland straight towards Ballintoy church. At the church turn right and follow the road down to the harbour. Continue along the shoreline past a series of conical sea stacks and arches, and scramble around the foot of a limestone crag to reach the 2km-long sandy sweep of White Park Bay.

The going here is easiest at low tide, when you can walk on the firm sand. At the far end of the bay (the building with the yellow gable above the dunes is Whitepark Bay Youth Hostel), scramble over rocks and boulders at the bottom of a high limestone cliff for 250m (slippery in places) to Portbradden. If you've timed it wrong and the way is blocked by high tide, you can detour up to the hostel and reach Portbradden by walking along the road.

Beyond Portbradden white limestone gives way to black basalt, and the path threads through a natural tunnel in the rocks before weaving around several rocky coves with the high cliffs of Benbane Head visible in the distance. At tiny Dunseverick Harbour you follow a minor road for 200m before descending steps on the right at a waymark. The path then wanders along the grassy foreshore, rounds a headland and crosses a footbridge above a waterfall before reaching the car park at Dunseverick Castle.

From here the cliff-top path, narrow in places, climbs steadily, passing an old salmon fishery (the little rusty-roofed cottage on the shore far below). Near Benbane Head, the highest and most northerly point on the walk, a wooden bench marks the viewpoint known as Hamilton's Seat (William Hamilton was an 18th-century clergyman and amateur geologist from Derry, who wrote one of the earliest descriptions of the Causeway Coast's geology). Soak up the spectacular panorama of 100m-high sea cliffs, stacks and pinnacles stretching away to the west, before you set off on the final stretch. If you want to visit the causeway itself, descend the Shepherd's Steps (signposted), about 1km before the visitor centre and the end of the walk. Total 16.5km; allow five to six hours.

and cost £15/10 per adult/child including tackle and bait.

Festivals

Ballycastle's **Ould Lammas Fair**, held on the last Monday and Tuesday of August, dates back to 1606. Thousands of people descend on the town for the market stalls and fairground rides, and to sample 'yellowman' and dulse. Yellowman is a hard chewy toffee that's available from a few months before the fair. Dulse is dried edible seaweed. The fruit shop on the diamond often stocks both delicacies.

Sleeping

BUDGET

Watertop Open Farm (☎ 2076 2576; www.watertop farm.co.uk; 188 Cushendall Rd; camp/caravan sites from £8/12; ☽ Easter-Oct) About 10km east of Ballycastle on the road to Cushendun, child-friendly Watertop is based in a working farm and activity centre, offering pony trekking, sheepshearing and farm tours.

Glenmore Caravan & Camping Park (☎ 2076 3584; www.glenmore.biz; 94 White Park Rd; camp/caravan sites from £9/11; ☽ Apr-Oct) Glenmore is a small and peaceful camping ground with its own trout-stocked fishing lough, about 4.5km west of Ballycastle on the B15 road to Whitepark Bay.

Castle Hostel (☎ 2076 2337; www.castlehostel.com; 62 Quay Rd; dm/d from £9/24) Set in a large, bay-windowed Victorian house with a welcoming fire in the common room, the Castle is just a few minutes walk from the bus stop and the beach. It has a bit of an old-fashioned feel, but in a pleasant, homely way, and the owner will point you to the best pubs for traditional music.

Ballycastle Backpackers (☎ 2076 3612; www.bally castlebackpackers.net; 4 North St; dm/tw £12.50/30; ⌨) This is a small and homely hostel set in a terraced house overlooking the harbour, with one six-bed dorm, a family room and a couple of twin and double rooms. There's also a cosy self-catering cottage in the backyard, with two twin rooms with private bathroom (£20 per person per night, also available for rental by the week).

MIDRANGE

Glenluce Guesthouse (☎ 2076 2914; www.glenluceguest house.com; 42 Quay Rd; s/d from £35/50; P) A large Victorian villa with 12 beautifully decorated rooms, Glenluce has a luxurious lounge, its own tea shop, and a veritable art gallery of local watercolours. It's only a few minutes' walk from the beach.

Corratavey B&B (☎ 2076 2845; www.corratavey .co.uk; 40 Quay Rd; d/f £50/63; P) Brass bedknobs, polished wood and warm colours lend a cosy feel to the rooms in this Victorian town house close to the beach. The owners are outdoor enthusiasts, and can recommend good walks in the area; they also speak Polish plus a little French and German.

Eating

Pantry (☎ 2076 9993; 41A Castle St; mains £2-4; ☽ 9am-5pm Mon-Sat) Housed in a former printer's shop with a lovely original black-and-white mosaic floor, this brisk and cheerful café serves a wide range of sandwiches, from pitta to *panini* and bagels to baguettes, as well as cappuccino and home-made cakes. It's uphill from the diamond.

Wysner's (☎ 2076 2372; 16 Ann St; mains £5-12; ☽ 8am-9pm Mon-Sat Jul & Aug, 8am-5pm Mon, Tue & Thu-Sat, 7-9pm Fri & Sat Sep-Jun) Popular with locals and visitors alike, Wysner's has a café at street level serving hearty lunches such as sausages with bacon-and-leek mash and onion gravy, and a restaurant upstairs with more sophisticated fare – steak, salmon or scallops – in the evenings.

our pick **Cellar Restaurant** (☎ 2076 3037; the diamond; mains £9-13; ☽ noon-10pm Mon-Sat, 5-10pm Sun Jun-Aug, 5-10pm daily Sep-May) This cosy little basement restaurant with intimate wooden booths and a big fireplace is the place to try local seafood – lobster grilled with garlic butter and Carrick-a-Rede salmon are both on the menu. There are also good vegetarian dishes such as roast vegetable foccacia and vegetable fajitas.

Getting There & Away

The bus station is on Station Rd, just east of the diamond. Ulsterbus Express 217 links Ballycastle with Ballymena, where you change to Goldline Express 218 for Belfast (£8, two hours, three daily Monday to Saturday).

Bus 172 goes along the coast to Coleraine (£4, one hour, six daily Monday to Friday, one on Saturday, three Sunday) via Ballintoy, the Giant's Causeway and Bushmills. Also see Getting There & Around, p659.

The ticket office for the Rathlin Island Ferry is beside the harbour.

RATHLIN ISLAND

pop 110

In spring and summer, rugged Rathlin Island (Reachlainn), 6km offshore from Ballycastle, is home to hundreds of seals and thousands of nesting seabirds. The island has a pub and restaurant, two shops and a handful of accommodation options.

The island was raided by Vikings in AD 795 and suffered again in 1575 when Sorley Boy MacDonnell sent his family here for safety only to have them massacred by the English, along with most of the inhabitants. The island's most illustrious visitor was Scottish hero Robert the Bruce, who spent some time in 1306 in a cave on the northeastern point learning a lesson in perseverance. Watching a spider's resoluteness in repeatedly trying to spin a web gave him the courage to have another go at the English, whom he subsequently defeated at Bannockburn.

The chief attraction is the coastal scenery and bird life of **Kebble National Nature Reserve** at the western end of the island. **RSPB West Light Viewpoint** (☎ 2076 3948; admission free; ◷ 11am-3pm Apr–mid Sep) provides stunning views of the neighbouring sea stacks, thick with guillemots, kittiwakes, razorbills and puffins in spring and early summer. During the summer a minibus service runs there from the harbour.

If you don't have time to visit Kebble, the best short walk on the island is through the National Trust's Ballyconagan Nature Reserve to the **Old Coastguard Lookout** on the north coast, with great views along the sea cliffs and across to the Scottish islands of Islay and Jura.

The **Boathouse Visitor Centre** (☎ 2076 3951; admission free; ◷ 10.30am-4pm May-Aug), south of the harbour, details the history, culture and ecology of the island, and can give advice on walks and wildlife.

Sleeping & Eating

You can camp for free on the eastern side of Church Bay in a field not far from the harbour. It is essential to book your accommodation in advance.

Kinramer Camping Barn (☎ 2076 3948; Kinramer; dm £5) This is a basic bunkhouse located on an organic farm, 5km (a one-hour walk) west from the harbour, where you bring your own food and bedding; book in advance. You might be able to get a lift there on one of the island minibuses.

Soerneog View Hostel (☎ 2076 3954; www.n-ireland holidays.co.uk/rathlin; Ouig; s/d £12.50/20; ◷ Apr-Sep) A private house, a 10-minute walk south of the harbour, Soerneog offers basic hostel-style accommodation in one double and two twin rooms.

Coolnagrock B&B (☎ 2076 3983; Coolnagrock; s/d £25/40; ◷ closed Dec) This well-appointed guesthouse is in the eastern part of the island, with great views across the sea to Kintyre. It's a 15-minute walk from the ferry, but you can arrange for the owner to pick you up.

Manor House (☎ 2076 3964; www.rathlinmanorhouse .co.uk; Church Quarter; s/d from £30/60) Restored and run by the National Trust, the 18th-century Manor House, on the north side of the harbour, is the island's biggest (12 rooms) and most pleasant place to stay. Evening meals are available by arrangement.

The Brockley Tearoom at the Manor House serves soups, sandwiches, cakes and scones, and you can get pub grub at **McCuaig's Bar** (☎ 2076 3974), just east of the harbour. There's a tiny grocery shop a few paces to the west of the ferry berth (turn left as you come off the pier).

Getting There & Around

A **ferry** (☎ 2076 9299; www.calmac.co.uk) operates daily (adult/child/bicycle return £10/5/1.30, 45 minutes) from Ballycastle; advance booking is recommended in spring and summer.

From April to September ferries depart Ballycastle at 10am, noon, 4.30pm and 6.30pm, and leave Rathlin at 8.30am, 11am, 3.30pm and 5.30pm. In winter boats leave Ballycastle at 10.30am and 4pm (4.30pm on Friday) and from Rathlin at 9am and 3pm.

You can't take your car to Rathlin, but nowhere on the island is more than 6km (about 1½ hours' walk) from the ferry pier. You can hire a bicycle (£8 per day) from Soerneog View Hostel, or take a minibus tour with **McGinn's** (☎ 2076 3451), who also shuttle visitors between the ferry and Kebble Nature Reserve from April to August.

GLENS OF ANTRIM

The northeastern corner of Antrim is a high plateau of black basalt lava overlying beds of white chalk. Along the coast, between Cushendun and Glenarm, the plateau has been dissected by a series of scenic, glacier-gouged valleys known as the Glens of Antrim.

WALK: FAIR HEAD

From the National Trust car park at Coolanlough, a waymarked path leads north past a small lake dotted with tiny islands, one of which is a *crannóg* (Neolithic island settlement). After 1.5km you arrive at the top of the impressive 180m-high basalt cliffs that mark Fair Head. The cliffs, one of Ireland's most important rock-climbing areas, are split here by a spectacular gully bridged by a fallen rock, known as the Grey Man's Path. The panorama of sea and islands extends from Rathlin Island in the west (to your left), with the Scottish island of Islay to its right, followed by the three pointed hills of Jura, the dark mass of the Mull of Kintyre and the tiny island of Sanda. To the east is the squat cone of Ailsa Craig with the coast of Ayrshire far beyond.

Turn right and follow the faint trail south along the cliff tops for 1.5km until you reach the upper car park on the Murlough Bay road. From here, another faint path, marked by yellow paint marks, strikes west for 1km back to Coolanlough. (Total 4km. Allow one to two hours.)

Two waymarked footpaths traverse the region: the Ulster Way (p700) sticks close to the sea, passing through all the coastal villages, while the 32km Moyle Way runs inland from Glenariff Forest Park to Ballycastle.

Torr Head Scenic Road

A few kilometres east of Ballycastle, a minor road signposted Scenic Route branches north off the A2. This alternative route to Cushendun is not for the faint-hearted driver (nor for caravans), as it clings, precarious and narrow, to steep slopes high above the sea. Side roads lead off to the main points of interest – Fair Head, Murlough Bay and Torr Head. On a clear day, there are superb views across the sea to Scotland, from the Mull of Kintyre to the peaks of Arran.

The first turn-off ends at the National Trust car park at Coolanlough, the starting point for a hike to Fair Head (see boxed text, above). The second turn-off leads steeply down to **Murlough Bay**. From the parking area at the end of this road, you can walk north along the shoreline to some ruined miners' cottages (10 minutes); coal and chalk were once mined in the cliffs above, and burned in a limekiln (south of the car park) to make quicklime.

The third turn-off leads you past some ruined coastguard houses to the rocky headland of **Torr Head**, crowned with a 19th-century coastguard station (abandoned in the 1920s). This is Ireland's closest point to Scotland – the Mull of Kintyre is a mere 19km away across the North Channel. In late spring and summer, a salmon fishery like the one at Carrick-a-Rede operates here, with a net strung out from the headland. The ancient ice house beside the approach road was once used to store the catch.

Cushendun

pop 350

The pretty seaside village of Cushendun is famous for its distinctive, Cornish-style cottages. Built between 1912 and 1925 at the behest of the local landowner, Lord Cushendun, they were designed by Clough Williams-Ellis, the architect of Portmeirion in north Wales. Much of Cushendun is now owned by the National Trust. There's a nice sandy beach, various short coastal walks (outlined on an information board beside the car park), and some impressive **caves** cut into the overhanging conglomerate sea cliffs south of the village (follow the trail around the far end of the holiday apartments south of the river mouth).

Another natural curiosity lies 6km north of the village on the A2 road to Ballycastle – **Loughareema**, also known as the Vanishing Lake. Three streams flow in but none flow out. The lough fills up to a respectable size (400m long and 6m deep) after heavy rain, but then the water gradually drains away through fissures in the underlying limestone, leaving a dry lake bed.

SLEEPING

Cushendun Caravan Park (☎ 2176 1254; 14 Glendun Rd; camp/caravan sites from £8/16; ✹ Easter-Sep) The local council-run camping ground enjoys a pleasant woodland setting just north of the village and a mere five-minute walk from the beach.

Cloneymore House (☎ 2176 1443; ann.cloneymore@ btinternet.com; 103 Knocknacarry Rd; s/d £35/45; P &) A traditional family B&B on the B92 road 500m southwest of Cushendun, Cloneymore has four spacious and spotless rooms named after Irish and Scottish islands – Aran is the biggest. There are wheelchair ramps and a stairlift, and all rooms are equipped for visitors with limited mobility.

Drumkeerin (☎ 2176 1554; www.drumkeeringuesthouse.com; 201A Torr Rd; s/d from £30/50; **P**) Drumkeerin is a comfortable modern bungalow 1km north of the village, owned by retired art teachers who offer courses in painting and drawing. Excellent breakfasts, including home-baked bread and scones, are served in a dining room with great views over beautiful gardens down to Cushendun Bay.

Mullarts Apartments (☎ 2176 1221; anne@mullarts.fsnet.co.uk; 114 Tromra Rd; d per weekend/week £150/400; **P**) An unusual alternative, Mullarts offers two luxury, self-catering apartments housed in a converted 19th-century church, 2.5km south of the village. Each apartment can sleep two to five people.

EATING & DRINKING

Cushendun Tearoom (☎ 2176 1506; 1 Main St; mains £3-9; ⏰ 11am-7pm daily Mar-Sep, 11am-7pm Mon-Fri Oct-Feb) The cosy village tearoom beside the bridge offers tea and cakes, sandwiches and salads, and hot lunch dishes such as fish and chips, grilled chicken and vegetable tortilla wraps.

Mary McBride's Pub (☎ 2176 1511; 2 Main St; mains £5-7; ⏰ food noon-9pm Apr-Sep, noon-8pm Oct-Mar) The original bar here (on the left as you go in) is the smallest in Ireland (2.7m by 1.5m) but there's plenty of elbow-bending room in the rest of the pub. It has lost some of its charm in recent years, and the food – standard pub grub – is not as good as it used to be, but it's the only place in the village for an evening meal.

GETTING THERE & AWAY

Bus 162 travels from Larne to Cushendun (£6, 1½ hours, one daily Monday to Friday), stopping at Glenarm and Carnlough; there are frequent trains and buses from Belfast to Larne. Bus 162A runs to Ballycastle (40 minutes, one daily Monday to Friday during school terms), departing from Cushendall at 9.25am and Cushendun at 9.36am; the return service leaves Ballycastle at 2.40pm. Also see Getting There & Around, p659.

Cushendall
pop 1250

Cushendall is a holiday centre (and traffic bottleneck) at the foot of Glenballyeamon, overlooked by the prominent flat-topped hill of Lurigethan. The beach is small and shingly,

though; there are better ones at Waterfoot and Cushendun.

The **tourist office** (☎ 2177 1180; 24 Mill St; ⏰ 10am-1pm & 2-5.30pm Mon-Fri, 10am-1pm Sat Jul-Sep, 10am-1pm Tue-Sat Oct-Jun) is run by the Glens of Antrim Historical Society, which also offers public internet access.

SIGHTS

The unusual red sandstone **Curfew Tower** at the central crossroads was built in 1817, based on a building the landowner had seen in China. It was originally a prison 'for the confinement of idlers and rioters'.

From the car park beside the beach, a coastal path leads 1km north to the picturesque ruins of **Layde Old Church**, with views across to Ailsa Craig (a prominent conical island also known as 'Paddy's Milestone') and the Scottish coast. Founded by the Franciscans, it was used as a parish church from the early 14th century until 1790. The graveyard contains several grand MacDonnell memorials. Near the gate stands an ancient, weathered ring-cross (with the arms missing), much older than the 19th-century inscription on its shaft.

In Glenaan, 4km northwest of Cushendall, is **Ossian's Grave**, a Neolithic court tomb romantically, but inaccurately, named after the legendary 3rd-century warrior-poet. The site is signposted off the A2; you can park at the farm and walk up.

SLEEPING & EATING

Cushendall Caravan Park (☎ 2177 1699; 62 Coast Rd; camp/caravan sites from £8/16; ⏰ Easter-Sep) This camping ground overlooks the sea, just over 1km south of the town centre.

Mountain View (☎ 2177 1246; 1 Kilnadore Rd; s/d £25/40; ⏰ Apr-Sep; **P**) The smell of home-baked bread wafts from the kitchen as you enter this good-value Victorian B&B with grand views, only a five-minute walk uphill from the village centre.

Cullentra House (☎ 2177 1762; www.cullentrahouse.com; 16 Cloughs Rd; s/d £25/40; **P**) This modern bungalow sits high above the village at the end of Cloughs Rd, offering good views of the craggy Antrim coast. The three rooms are spacious and comfy, and the breakfasts are as big as the owners' hospitality.

Harry's Restaurant (☎ 2177 2022; 10 Mill St; mains £9-13; ⏰ 12.30-9.30pm) With a cosy country-house feel, Harry's is the village's top eating place,

WALK: THE GLENARIFF CIRCUIT

This varied 7.5km hike, which ranges from the mossy depths of a waterfall-filled ravine to the edge of the high Antrim Plateau, is one of the best forest-park walks in Northern Ireland. Begin at the Laragh Lodge restaurant, and follow the boardwalk upstream (admission £1.50 Easter-Oct) along the Glenariff River to the foaming cascade of Ess-na-Larach, then continue steeply up the zigzags beyond. There's a junction at a wooden bench – the path to the left leads down to the forest park visitor centre (signposted), but go right on the trail heading upstream with the river down to your right.

At the next junction, turn right and cross a bridge (signposted Hermit's Fall), and follow this path uphill through another ravine with more waterfalls. At the top cross back over the river and bear right uphill for a few metres to a Tarmac road (there's a sign marked Scenic Trail pointing back the way you came). Cross the road and, a few metres further on, cross a second road and follow the obvious path up through the forest. You eventually emerge from the trees to get your first open view along Glenariff. Beyond, the path slowly curves around the right (south; there are more Scenic Trail waymarks, but you are following them in reverse). As you near the head of the next valley (that's the Inver River down below), the path forks near a wooden shelter, the left branch descending steeply; keep right here and continue right to the top of the glen.

The trail then curves left and crosses the three streams that feed the Inver River, then switch-backs up the far side and into thick pine forest, only to emerge into a clearing on a cliff top with a stunning view down Glenariff – the valley floor is slung like a green hammock between steep, black basalt crags. A short distance further on there's a very steep zigzag descent, followed by a level traverse to the left. When you reach a forest road turn right. After 1km it descends steeply leftwards down to a gate; take the path on the left and cross a footbridge over the river. Turn right, then right again and you'll find yourself back at your starting point. (Total 7.5km. Allow three to four hours.)

serving pub grub through the day, and an á la carte dinner from 6pm. There's a three-course Sunday lunch for £13/6.50 per adult/child.

Arthur's Tea & Coffee Warehouse (☎ 2177 1627; 1 Shore St; mains £2-4; ☺ 10am-5pm) This lively café serves good breakfasts, cakes and coffee, and home-made soups and snacks.

GETTING THERE & AWAY

Buses serving Cushendun (opposite) also serve Cushendall.

Glenariff

About 2km south of Cushendall is the village of **Waterfoot**, with a 2km-long sandy beach, the best on Antrim's east coast. From here the A43 Ballymena road runs inland along Glenariff, the loveliest of Antrim's glens. Views of the valley led the writer Thackeray to exclaim that it was a 'Switzerland in miniature', a claim that makes you wonder if he'd ever been to Switzerland.

At the head of the valley is **Glenariff Forest Park** (☎ 2175 8232; car/motorcycle/pedestrian £4/2/1.50; ☺ 10am-dusk) where the main attraction is **Ess-na-Larach Waterfall**, an 800m walk from the visitor centre. You can also walk to the waterfall

from Laragh Lodge, 600m downstream. There are various good walks in the park; the longest is a 10km circular trail.

There's hostel accommodation for hikers at **Ballyeamon Camping Barn** (☎ 2175 8451; www.bally eamonbarn.com; 127 Ballyeamon Rd; dm £10; ▯), 8km southwest of Cushendall on the B14 (1km north of its junction with the A43), and about 1.5km walk from the main entrance to the forest park.

Laragh Lodge (☎ 2175 8221; 120 Glen Rd; mains £8, 2-/3-course Sun lunch £10/12; ☺ 10.30am-11pm, food noon-9.30pm) is a restaurant and bar on a side road off the A43, 3km northeast of the park entrance. The cottage-style restaurant, draped with bric-a-brac, serves hearty meat-and-two-veg meals (no vegetarian options), and does a roast lunch on Sunday.

You can reach Glenariff Forest Park from Cushendun (£4, 30 minutes, four daily Monday to Friday, two Saturday) and Ballymena (£4, 40 minutes) on Ulsterbus 150.

Carnlough

pop 1500

Carnlough is an attractive little town with a pretty harbour and a historic hotel. Many of the buildings, made of local limestone, were commissioned by the marquess of Londonderry in 1854. The limestone quarries were in use until the early 1960s – the white stone bridge across the main street once carried a railway line that brought stone down to the harbour. The line is now a walkway that leads to the local beauty spot, Cranny Falls.

The **tourist information centre** (☎ 2888 5236; 14 Harbour Rd; ☼ 10am-10pm daily Easter-Sep, to 8pm Mon-Sat Oct-Easter) is in McKillop's general store, next to the Londonderry Arms Hotel.

SLEEPING & EATING

Londonderry Arms Hotel (☎ 2888 5255; www.glensof antrim.com; 20 Harbour Rd; s/d from £55/90; **P**) Dating from 1848, this atmospheric coaching inn was briefly owned by Winston Churchill, who sold it in 1921 (he once stayed in room 114). It has a wonderfully crusty, old-fashioned atmosphere, with various bits of antique furniture, wing-back armchairs and lots of polished mahogany, spoiled a little by 1970s avocado bathroom suites. The restaurant (mains £14 to £18) serves local lamb and seafood, while the wood-panelled bar is a shrine to the famous Irish racehorse Arkle.

Harbour Lights (☎ 2888 5950; 11 Harbour Rd; mains £7-12; ☼ noon-9pm Wed-Sun) This pleasant little café-cum-restaurant is set in a 19th-century house beside the former railway bridge, with an outdoor terrace overlooking the harbour.

GETTING THERE & AWAY

Bus 162 runs from Larne to Glenarm and Carnlough (£3, 40 minutes, five or six daily Monday to Saturday); one bus a day on weekdays continues north to Cushendall and Cushendun. Bus 128 goes to Ballymena (£3, one hour, four daily Monday to Saturday). Also see Getting There & Around, p659.

Glenarm

pop 600

Since 1750 Glenarm (Gleann Arma), the oldest village in the glens, has been the family seat of the MacDonnell family; the present 14th earl of Antrim lives in **Glenarm Castle** (☎ 2884 1203; www.glenarmcastle.com), on a private estate hidden behind the impressive wall that runs along the main road north of the bridge. The castle itself is closed to the public, except for two days in July when a Highland Games competition is held, but you can visit the lovely **Walled Garden** (adult/child £4/2; ☼ 11am-5pm Wed-Sun May-Sep).

The **tourist office** (☎ 2884 1705; 2 the Bridge; glenarm@nacn.org; ☼ 9.30am-5pm Mon-Fri, 2-6pm Sun) is beside the bridge on the main road. It has internet access for £2 per 30 minutes.

Take a stroll into the old village of neat Georgian houses (off the main road, immediately south of the river). Where the street opens into the broad expanse of Altmore St, look right to see the **Barbican Gate** (1682), the entrance to Glenarm Castle grounds. On the left is **Steensons** (☎ 2884 1445; Toberwine St; ☼ 9.30am-5.15pm Mon-Sat year-round, 1-5.30pm Sun Easter-Sep), a designer jewellery workshop and visitor centre where you can watch craftspeople at work.

Turn left here and climb steeply up Vennel St, then left again immediately after the last house along the Layde Path to the viewpoint, which has a grand view of the village and the coast.

Riverside House B&B (☎ 2884 1474; faith.pa@ btopenworld.com; 13 Toberwine St; s/d £30/45) is a nicely restored Georgian house in the heart of the old village. The two double rooms have chunky pine furniture and views over the river to Glenarm Castle.

See Carnlough section (left) for details of bus services.

LARNE

pop 17,600

As a major port for ferries from Scotland, Larne (Lutharna) is one of Northern Ireland's main points of arrival. However, with its concrete overpasses and the huge chimneys of Ballylumford power station opposite the harbour, poor old Larne is a little lacking in the charm department. After a visit to the excellent tourist information centre, there's no real reason to linger.

Larne Harbour train station is in the ferry terminal. It's a short bus ride or a 15-minute walk from here to the town centre – turn right on Fleet St and right again on Curran Rd, then left on Circular Rd. At the big roundabout, Larne Town train station is to your left, the **tourist information centre** (☎ 2826 0088; larnetourism@btconnect.com; Narrow Gauge Rd; ☼ 9am-5pm Mon-Sat Easter-Sep, 9am-5pm Mon-Fri Oct-Easter) is to the right, and the bus station is ahead (beneath the road bridge).

Getting There & Away
BOAT

For information on ferries from Larne to Scotland and England, see p719.

BUS

Bus 256 provides a direct service between the town centre and Belfast (£4, one hour, hourly Monday to Friday, six Saturday, plus three on Sunday July to September only).

Heading north to the Glens of Antrim, take bus 162 (see opposite) or the Antrim Coaster (see p659).

TRAIN

Larne has two train stations, Larne Town and Larne Harbour. Trains from Larne Town to Belfast Central (£5, one hour) depart at least hourly; those from the harbour are timed to connect with ferries. From Belfast Central you can continue to Botanic, City Hospital and Great Victoria St stations.

ISLANDMAGEE

Islandmagee (Oileán Mhic Aodha) is the finger of land that encloses Larne Lough to the east. There's a popular sandy beach at **Brown's Bay** at the northern end of the peninsula. Nearby is the picturesque little harbour of **Portmuck** and, just 300m offshore, the North's second-largest seabird nesting colony on **Muck Island**.

On the east coast lie the rugged basalt sea cliffs known as the **Gobbins**. The cliffs were developed as a tourist attraction in 1902, when a railway company engineer built a spectacular footpath along the coast from Whitehead, complete with steps, iron bridges and tunnels cut from the rock. By WWII the path had fallen into disrepair, and was closed for safety reasons. You can see photographs of the walkway in its heyday at the Ulster Museum (p587) in Belfast.

There's a good coastal walk from the car park at the north end of the promenade in **Whitehead**. It follows a walkway around the sea cliffs beneath Black Head lighthouse, past several deep caves, then climbs a steep flight of stairs to the lighthouse itself. From here you can descend a zigzag path to rejoin the shoreline trail back to the car park (3.5km in total).

From May to December the high-speed launch *North Irish Diver II* offers two-hour **boat trips** (☎ 9338 2246) from Whitehead harbour to the Gobbins and Muck Island (adult/child £20/15, minimum six people). It also offers a sea-taxi service to Bangor, a 15-minute trip, from £10 return.

There are also boat trips to the Gobbins from Bangor.

CARRICKFERGUS

pop 28,000

Northern Ireland's most impressive medieval fortress commands the entrance to Belfast Lough from the rocky promontory of Carrickfergus (Carraig Fhearghais). The old town centre opposite the castle has some attractive 18th-century houses and you can still trace a good part of the 17th-century city walls.

The **tourist information centre** (☎ 9335 8000; www.carrickfergus.org; Heritage Plaza, Antrim St; ☺ 10am-6pm Mon-Sat & 1-6pm Sun Apr-Sep, 10am-5pm Mon-Sat & 1-5pm Sun Oct-Mar) has a bureau de change and books accommodation.

Sights

The central keep of Ireland's first and finest Norman fortress, **Carrickfergus Castle** (☎ 9335 1273; Marine Hwy; adult/child £3/1.50; ☺ 10am-6pm Mon-Sat, noon-6pm Sun Jun-Aug, 10am-6pm Mon-Sat, 2-6pm Sun Apr, May & Sep, 10am-4pm Mon-Sat, 2-4pm Sun Oct-Mar), was built by John de Courcy soon after his 1177 invasion of Ulster. The massive walls of the outer ward were completed in 1242, while the red-brick gun ports were added in the 16th century. The keep houses a museum and the site is dotted with life-size figures illustrating the castle's history.

The castle overlooks the harbour where **William of Orange** landed on 14 June 1690, on his way to the Battle of the Boyne; a blue plaque on the old harbour wall marks the site where he stepped ashore, and a bronze statue of the man himself stands on the shore nearby.

The glass-fronted Heritage Plaza on Antrim St houses **Carrickfergus Museum** (☎ 9335 8049; 11 Antrim St; admission free; ☺ 10am-6pm Mon-Sat & 1-6pm Sun Apr-Sep, 10am-5pm Mon-Sat & 1-5pm Sun Oct-Mar), which has a small collection of artefacts relating to the town's history, and a pleasant coffee shop.

The parents of the seventh US president left Carrickfergus in the second half of the 18th century. His ancestral home was demolished in 1860, but the **Andrew Jackson Centre** (☎ 9336 6455; Boneybefore; admission free; ☺ 10am-1pm & 2-6pm Mon-Fri, 2-6pm Sat & Sun Jun-Sep, 10am-1pm & 2-4pm Mon-Fri, 2-4pm Sat & Sun Apr, May & Oct) is housed in a replica thatched cottage complete with fireside crane and earthen floor. It has displays on the life of Jackson, the Jackson family in Ulster and Ulster's connection with the USA. Next door is the **US Rangers Centre**, with a small exhibition on the first US rangers, who were trained during WWII in Carrickfergus before heading for Europe. The centre is on the coast, 2km north of the castle.

Sleeping & Eating

Keep Guesthouse (☎ 9336 7007; www.thekeepguest housecarrickfergus.co.uk; 93 Irish Quarter S; s/d £30/45) Just across the main road from the marina, and close to the town centre, the Keep has four rooms with attractive, modern décor and original art on the walls; go for the spacious double/family room on the first floor if possible.

Dobbin's Inn Hotel (☎ 9335 1905; www.dobbinsinn hotel.co.uk; 6-8 High St; s/d £48/68; mains £6-13; ☺ food 9am-9pm; ☑) In the centre of the old town, Dobbin's is a friendly and informal place with 15 small and creaky-floored but comfortable rooms. The building has been around for over three centuries, and has a priest's hole and an original 16th-century fireplace to prove it.

Courtyard Coffee House (☎ 9335 1881; 38 Scottish Quarter; snacks £2-4; ☺ 9am-4.45pm Mon-Sat) This café serves tasty home-made soups and light lunches as well as coffee and cakes, and has a second branch inside Carrickfergus Castle.

our pick **Wind Rose** (☎ 9335 1164; Rodgers Quay; mains £8-12; ☺ food noon-9pm) This stylish, modern bar-bistro, with a more formal restaurant upstairs (open Friday and Saturday evening only), serves a range of dishes from pasta and pizza to steaks and stir-fries. The outdoor terrace overlooking the forest of yacht masts in the marina is a real sun-trap on a summer afternoon.

Getting There & Away

There's an hourly train service between Carrickfergus and Belfast (£3, 30 minutes).

INLAND COUNTY ANTRIM

To the west of the high moorland plateau above the Glens of Antrim, the hills slope down to the agricultural lowlands of Lough Neagh and the broad valley of the River Bann. This region is rarely visited by tourists, who either take the coast road or speed through on the way from Belfast to Derry, but there are a few places worth seeking out if you have time to spare.

Antrim Town

pop 19,800

The town of Antrim (Aontroim) straddles the River Sixmilewater, close to an attractive bay on the shores of Lough Neagh. During the 1798 Rising, the United Irishmen fought a pitched battle along the length of the town's High St.

The **tourist information centre** (☎ 9442 8331; info@antrim.gov.uk; 16 High St; ☺ 9am-5.30pm Mon-Fri, 10am-3pm Sat Jul & Aug, 9am-5pm Mon-Fri, 10am-1pm Sat May, Jun & Sep, 9am-5pm Mon-Fri Oct-Apr) provides a free, self-guided heritage trail leaflet, and has internet access for £1.50 per 30 minutes.

The town centre is dominated by a bleakly modern shopping mall, but a few older buildings survive including the fine **courthouse**, which dates back to 1762. Beyond the courthouse is the **Barbican Gate** (1818) and a portion of the old castle walls.

Pass through the gate and the underpass beyond to reach **Antrim Castle Gardens** (admission free; ☺ 9.30am-dusk Mon-Fri, 10am-5pm Sat, 2-5pm Sun). The castle burned down many years ago, but the grounds remain as one of the few surviving examples of a 17th-century ornamental garden.

Lough Rd leads west from the town centre to **Antrim Lough Shore Park**, where the vast size of Lough Neagh (see boxed text, p638) is apparent. There are picnic tables and lakeside walking trails.

Goldline Express 219 from Belfast to Ballymena stops in Antrim (£4, 40 minutes, hourly Monday to Friday, seven on Saturday). There are also frequent trains from Belfast to Antrim (£4, 25 minutes, 10 daily Monday to Saturday, five on Sunday) continuing to Derry.

Ballymena

pop 29,200

Ballymena (An Baile Meánach) is the home turf of Ian Paisley, the founder and leader of the Free Presbyterian Church and the stridently antinationalist and anti-Catholic Democratic Unionist Party (DUP) and, since May 2007, First Minister of Northern Ireland. The town council was the first to be controlled by the DUP in 1977 and voted unanimously to remove all mention of Darwin's theory of evolution from religious education in Ballymena's schools. The town is also the birthplace of the actor Liam Neeson, of *Schindler's List* and *Star Wars* fame.

The **Ecos Environmental Centre** (☎ 2566 4400; www.ecoscentre.com; Broughshane Rd; admission free; ☺ 9am-5pm Mon-Fri, 10.30am-5pm Sat, noon-5pm Sun Jul & Aug, 9am-5pm Mon-Fri Sep-Jun), on the eastern edge of town, is a visitor centre dedicated

---

DETOUR: GALGORM

About 6km west of Ballymena is the **Galgorm Resort & Spa** (☎ 2588 0080; www.galgorm.com; 136 Fenaghy Rd, Galgorm; r from £130; P), a 19th-century manor house in a lovely setting on the bank of the River Maine. Recently taken over by the owners of Belfast's boutique hotel Ten Square (p595), the Galgorm has been redeveloped and extended to create one of Ireland's top country-house hotels.

The rustic atmosphere of the original **Gillie's Bar** (mains £7-16; ♥ food served 7am-10pm), set in the former stables, has been retained with bare stone walls, huge timber beams, a log fire and cosy sofas, but it has been extended into a spectacular, new, high-roofed barn with a huge, central free-standing chimney and a monumental staircase framed by crouching sphinxes – all in all, a pretty jaw-dropping setting for some of the fanciest pub grub in Ireland.

---

to alternative energy sources and sustainable technology – the centre's waste water is filtered through reed beds, and used to irrigate nearby willow coppices which provide fuel for heating and electricity, supplemented by solar panels. There are lots of hands-on exhibits to keep the kids amused, plus a picnic and play area, a pond with ducks to feed, and radio-controlled boats to play with.

Goldline Express 219 goes to Ballymena from Belfast (£6, one hour, hourly Monday to Friday, seven Saturday). Bus 128 goes to Carnlough on the coast (£3, one hour, four daily Monday to Saturday).

Trains from Belfast run more frequently (£6, 10 daily Monday to Saturday, five on Sunday); Ballymena is on the Derry–Belfast train line.

Slemish

The skyline to the east of Ballymena is dominated by the distinctive craggy peak of Slemish (438m). The hill is one of many sites in the North associated with Ireland's patron saint – the young St Patrick is said to have tended goats on its slopes. On St Patrick's Day, thousands of people make a pilgrimage to its summit; the rest of the year it's a pleasant climb, though steep and slippery in wet weather, rewarded with a fine view (allow one hour return from the parking area).

Arthur Cottage

The ancestors of Chester Alan Arthur (1830–86), 21st president of the USA, lived in an 18th-century thatched **cottage** (☎ 2588 0781; Dreen, Cullybackey; adult/child £2/1; ♥ 10.30am-5pm Mon-Fri, to 4pm Sat Easter-Sep) in Cullybackey, about 6km northwest of Ballymena. Staff in traditional costume give demonstrations of bread-making and other crafts on Tuesday, Friday and Saturday at 1.30pm throughout June, July (except on the 12th) and August.

Cullybackey is a stop on the Belfast–Derry railway line.

Counties Fermanagh & Tyrone

The ancient landscape of Fermanagh is shaped by ice and water, with rugged hills rising above quilted plains of half-drowned drumlins and shimmering, reed-fringed lakes. A glance at the map shows the county is around one-third water – as the locals will tell you, the lakes are in Fermanagh for six months of the year; for the other six, Fermanagh is in the lakes.

This watery maze is a natural playground for anglers – the loughs and rivers are stuffed with trout and pike – and for boaters. You can hire a motor cruiser and spend a week or two navigating the scenic waterways of Lough Erne and the River Shannon, which together form a 750km network of rivers, lakes and canals. If you prefer your boats without engines, the 50km Lough Erne Canoe Trail is a paddler's paradise.

The limestone ridges to the south of Lough Erne are riddled with caves – at Marble Arch you can explore an underground river; the higher hills are swathed with blanket bog, a rare and endangered habitat. This is all grand walking country, but there are also rainy-day attractions, such as the contrasting stately homes of Florence Court and Castle Coole, and the world-famous pottery at Belleek.

County Tyrone – from Tír Eoghain (Land of Owen, a legendary chieftain) – is the homeland of the O'Neill clan, and is dominated by the tweed-tinted moorlands of the Sperrin Mountains, whose southern flanks are dotted with prehistoric sites. Apart from the hiking opportunities offered by these heather-clad hills, the county's main attraction is the Ulster American Folk Park, a fascinating outdoor museum celebrating Ulster's historic links with the USA.

HIGHLIGHTS

- **Climb to the Lost World** Hike over rare blanket bog to the remote summit of Cuilcagh Mountain (p688)
- **Faces from the Past** Ponder the meaning of the strange stone figures on White Island (p684) and Boa Island (p685)
- **River of Adventure** Follow the course of an underground river as it flows through the Marble Arch Caves (p688)
- **Blazing Paddles** Hire a canoe and explore the reed-fringed backwaters of Lough Erne (p687)
- **The American Connection** Learn about the historical links between Ireland and the USA at the Ulster American Folk Park (p690)

- POPULATION: 227,000
- AREA: 5274 SQ KM

COUNTY FERMANAGH

ENNISKILLEN

pop 11,500

Perched amid the web of waterways that link Upper and Lower Lough Erne, Enniskillen (Inis Ceithleann, meaning Caitlin's Island) is an appealing town with a mile-long main street that rides the roller-coaster spine of the island's drumlin. (The locals say you're only a true Enniskilliner if you were born 'between the bridges'; that is, on the town's central island.) Its attractive waterside setting, bustling with boats in summer, plus a range of lively pubs and restaurants, make Enniskillen a good base for exploring Upper and Lower Lough Erne, Florencecourt and the Marble Arch Caves.

Though neither was born here, both Oscar Wilde and Samuel Beckett were pupils at Enniskillen's Portora Royal School (Wilde from 1864 to 1871, Beckett from 1919 to 1923); it was here that Beckett first studied French, a language he would later write in. The town's name is also prominent in the history of the Troubles – on Poppy Day (11 November) in 1987 an IRA bomb killed 11 innocent people during a service at Enniskillen's war memorial.

Orientation

The main street changes name half a dozen times between the bridges at either end; the prominent clock tower marks the town centre. The other principal street is Wellington Rd, south of and parallel to the main street, where you'll find the bus station, tourist office and car parking. If you're driving, try to avoid rush hour – the bridge at the west end is a traffic bottleneck.

Information

Bank of Ireland (☎ 6632 2136; 7 Townhall St)
Eason (☎ 6632 4341; 10 High St; ☺ 9am-5.30pm Mon-Sat) Local-interest books and maps.
Enniskillen Library (☎ 6632 2886; Hall's Lane; ☺ 9.15am-5.15pm Mon, Wed & Fri, 9.15am-7.30pm Tue & Thu, 9.15am-1pm & 2-5pm Sat) Internet access £1.50 per 30min.
Post office (3 High St) In Dolan's Centra grocery store.
Tourist Information Centre (☎ 6632 3110; www .fermanagh.gov.uk; Wellington Rd; ☺ 9am-7pm Mon-Fri, 10am-6pm Sat, 11am-5pm Sun Jul & Aug, 9am-5.30pm

Mon-Fri, 10am-6pm Sat, 11am-5pm Sun Easter-Jun & Sep, 9am-5.30pm Mon-Fri & 10am-2pm Sat & Sun Oct, 9am-5.30pm Mon-Fri Nov-Easter) Books accommodation, changes money, sells fishing licences and provides a postal and fax service.
Ulster Bank (☎ 6632 4034; 16 Darling St)

Sights

Enniskillen Castle (☎ 6632 5000; www.enniskillencastle .co.uk; Castle Barracks; adult/child £2.95/1.95; ☺ 2-5pm Mon & 10am-5pm Tue-Fri year-round, also 2-5pm Sat May-Sep & 2-5pm Sun Jul & Aug; ☺), a former stronghold of the 16th-century Maguire chieftains, guards the western end of the town's central island, its twin-turreted **Watergate** looming over passing fleets of cabin cruisers. Within the walls you'll find the **Fermanagh County Museum**, which has displays on the county's history, archaeology, landscape and wildlife. The 15th-century Keep contains the Royal Inniskilling Fusiliers Regimental Museum, full of guns, uniforms and medals – including eight Victoria Crosses awarded in WWI – and is dedicated to the regiment which was raised at the castle in 1689 to support the army of William I.

In Forthill Park, at the eastern end of town, stands **Cole's Monument** (adult/child £1/50p; ☺ 1.30-3pm mid-Apr–Sep). It commemorates Sir Galbraith Lowry–Cole (1772-1842), who was one of Wellington's generals and the son of the first earl of Enniskillen. Climb the 108 steps inside the column for a good view of the surrounding area (tickets on sale at the Enniskillen Tourist Information Centre).

Activities

The **Kingfisher Trail** is a waymarked, long-distance cycling trail that starts in Enniskillen and wends its way through the back roads of counties Fermanagh, Leitrim, Cavan and Monaghan. The full route is around 370km long, but a shorter loop, starting and finishing in Enniskillen, and travelling via Kesh, Belleek, Garrison, Belcoo and the village of Florencecourt, is only 115km – easily done in two days with an overnight stay at Belleek. You can get a trail map from the Enniskillen Tourist Information Centre.

You can hire bikes from the **Lakeland Canoe Centre** (☎ 6632 4250; www.arkoutdooradventure.com; Castle Island; half-/full-day £10/15). They also rent out two-person canoes (£20 for two hours).

You can buy **fishing** permits and licences from the tourist information office, or Home, Field and Stream (p681).

See p683 and p686 for boat-hire options, and boxed text, p687 for information on **cruising** the lakes.

Tours

Blue Badge Tours (☎ 6962 1430; breegemccusker@ btopenworld.com) offers guided tours of Enniskillen and the Lough Erne area with local historian Breege McCusker, who is a registered tourist guide. Special interest tours include prehistoric sites, monastic sites, carved stones and plantation castles.

Erne Tours (☎ 6632 2882; Round 'O' Quay, The Brook; adult/child £9/6; ⏱ 10.30am, 12.15pm, 2.15pm & 4.15pm daily Jul & Aug, 2.15pm daily Jun, 2.15pm daily Tue, Sat & Sun May, Sept & Oct) operates 1¾-hour cruises on Lower Lough Erne aboard the 56-seat water-

bus, MV *Kestrel*, calling at Devenish Island along the way. It departs from the Round 'O' Quay, just west of the town centre on the A46 to Belleek. There are also Saturday **evening cruises** (adult/child £30/15; ⏱ 6pm May-Sept) that include a three-course dinner at the Killyhevlin Hotel.

Sleeping

BUDGET

Bridges Youth Hostel (☎ 6634 0110; www.hini.org.uk; Belmore St; dm/s/tw £15/20/32; P &) This modern, purpose-built hostel has a great location overlooking a river in the centre of town. It has mostly four-bed dorms, each with an en suite, plus six twin rooms, a kitchen, a restaurant, a laundry and a bike shed.

COUNTIES FERMANAGH & TYRONE

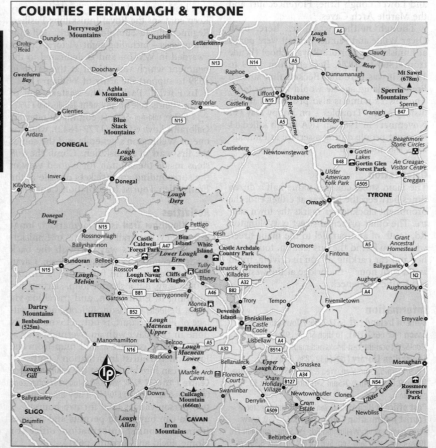

Rossole Guesthouse (☎ 6632 3462; 85 Sligo Rd; s/d £30/45) A modern Georgian-style house with a sunny conservatory overlooking a small lake, the five-room Rossole is an angler's delight – you can fish in the lake, and there are rowing boats for guests at the bottom of the garden. It's 1km southwest of the town centre on the A4 Sligo road.

Greenwood Lodge (☎ 6632 5636; www.greenwood lodge.co.uk; 17 Killivilly Ct, Tempo Rd; s/d £28/46; P) The owners of this spacious and modern villa, set on a quiet side street 3km northeast of town off the B80, go out of their way to make you feel welcome. The three homely bedrooms all have en suites, the breakfasts are freshly prepared, and there is secure storage available for bikes.

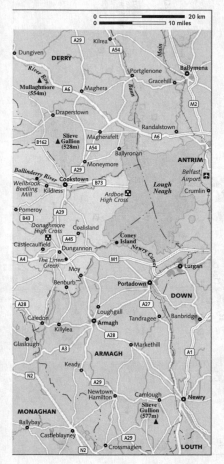

MIDRANGE

Railway Hotel (☎ 6632 2084; www.railwayhotel enniskillen.com; 34 Forthill St; s/d £37.50/75) Railway memorabilia dots the walls of this welcoming 130-year-old hotel, a reminder of Enniskillen's now-vanished railway line. The 19 rooms offer rather bijou B&B accommodation close to the centre of town; rooms at the front can be a bit noisy.

Mountview Guesthouse (☎ 6632 3147; www .mountviewguests.com; 61 Irvinestown Rd; s/d £40/60; P) Indulge in a spot of country-house comfort in this large, ivy-clad Victorian villa set in wooded grounds. There are three en-suite bedrooms, a luxurious lounge and even a snooker room with a full-size table. The Mountview looks out over Race Course Lough, just a 10-minute (800m) walk, north of the town centre.

Belmore Court Motel (☎ 6632 6633; www.motel .co.uk; Tempo Rd; d £55, apt £75-100; P ▯) Set in a converted row of terrace houses just east of the town centre, the Belmore has family 'mini-apartments' with cooking facilities, as well as four ordinary double rooms. Rates don't include breakfast.

TOP END

Killyhevlin Hotel (☎ 6632 3481; www.killyhevlin.com; Killyhevlin; s/d from £98/135; P ▯ ⅌) Enniskillen's top hotel is 1.5km south of town on the A4 Maguiresbridge road, in an idyllic setting overlooking Upper Lough Erne. Many of its 43 rooms have lakeside views; there are also 13 two-bedroom lakeside chalets (£250 per weekend April to June, £195 per weekend November to March; £575 per week July to October).

Eating
BUDGET

Johnston's Jolly Sandwich Bar (☎ 6632 2277; 3 Darling St; sandwiches £2-4; ☷ 8am-4pm Mon-Fri, 8.30am-4pm Sat) A traditional bakery selling excellent pick-and-mix sandwiches, soup, pies and cakes to take away or eat in.

Rebecca's Place (☎ 6632 4499; Buttermarket; snacks £2-5; ☷ 9.30am-5.30pm Mon-Sat) A more traditional café with pine tables and chairs, Rebecca's is set in a craft shop (see p681) and serves good sandwiches, salads and pastries.

Ruby's Coffee & Sandwich Bar (☎ 6632 9399; 10 High St; snacks £2-5; ☷ 9am-5.30pm Mon-Sat) Tucked upstairs in Eason's bookshop is this comfy nook furnished with sofas and armchairs, offering breakfast bagels and croissants, sandwiches

ENNISKILLEN

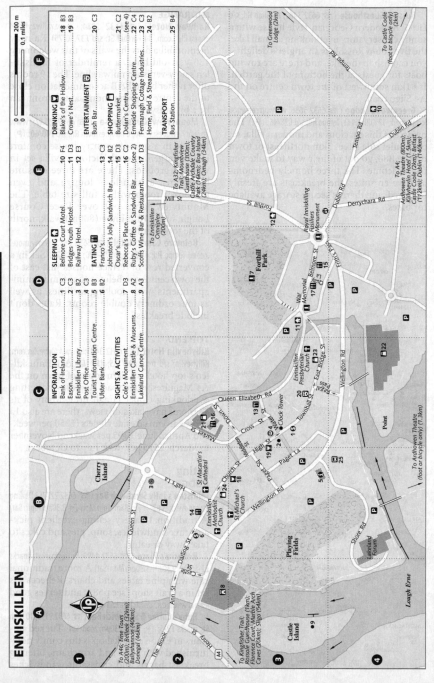

COUNTIES FERMANAGH & TYRONE

and salads, soups and baked potatoes. Free newspapers, too.

MIDRANGE

Franco's (☎ 6632 4424; Queen Elizabeth Rd; mains £8-18; ☻ noon-11pm) An atmospheric warren of wood-panelled, candlelit nooks set in a former blacksmith's forge, Franco's is always bustling and noisy, and serves a range of Italian, Asian and seafood dishes as well as filling pizzas and pasta dishes.

Scoffs Wine Bar & Restaurant (☎ 6634 2622; 17 Belmore St; mains £12-18; ☻ 5pm-late daily, 12.30-2.30pm Sun) This busy restaurant has a modern vibe with shades of chocolate-brown and burgundy, dark wood and dim candlelight, and an adventurous international menu that includes seared tuna steak with potato salad and aioli, and creamy leek-and-mushroom bake with hazelnut crumble, as well as more exotic offerings such as roast ostrich on black pudding and apple mash. The downstairs wine bar offers lighter meals.

ourpick Oscar's (☎ 6632 7037; 29 Belmore St; pizzas £8-12, mains £12-18; ☻ 5-10pm) Following a facelift and a change of management, this Enniskillen institution now sports a casual Tuscan-style restaurant upstairs, complete with a wood-fired pizza oven, and a more formal, Victorian dining room downstairs. The menu ranges from pizza and pasta through to flame-grilled steaks and seafood, with gourmet specials such as tartlet of goat's cheese with Clonakilty black pudding, and prawn ravioli with smoked cheddar and basil cream sauce. The kitchen can cater for various special diets if you warn them when booking.

Drinking

ourpick Blake's of the Hollow (William Blake; ☎ 6632 2143; 6 Church St) Ulster's best pint of Guinness awaits you in this traditional Victorian pub, almost unchanged since 1887, complete with marble-topped bar, four huge sherry casks, antique silver lamp holders and ancient wood panelling kippered by a century of cigarette smoke. There's traditional music from 9pm on Fridays.

Crowe's Nest (☎ 6632 5252; 12 High St) A lively bar with a conservatory and patio out the back for those sunny summer afternoons, the Nest has live music nightly from 10.30pm in the back bar and traditional music sessions on Monday nights during summer.

Entertainment

Bush Bar (☎ 6632 5210; 26 Townhall St) The nearest Enniskillen comes to a nightclub, with leather chairs and banquettes in various shades of coffee from dark roast to café au lait, a reasonable cocktail menu, and an upstairs dance floor that hosts DJs and live bands.

Ardhowen Theatre (☎ 6632 5440; www.ardhowentheatre.com; Dublin Rd; ☻ box office 11am-4.30pm Mon-Fri, 10am-7pm before a performance, 11am-1pm, 2-5pm & 6-7pm Sat) The programme includes concerts, local amateur and professional drama and musical productions, pantomimes and films. The theatre is about 2km southeast of the town centre on the A4, in an impressive glass-fronted building overlooking a lake.

Enniskillen Omniplex (☎ 6632 4777; www.omniplex.ie; Factory Rd) A seven-screen cinema, 700m north of the town centre on Race Course Lough.

Shopping

Buttermarket (☎ 6632 4499; Down St) The refurbished buildings in the old marketplace house a variety of craft shops and studios selling paintings, ceramics, jewellery and even fishing flies.

Erneside Shopping Centre (☎ 6632 5705; The Point; ☻ 9am-5.30pm Mon-Wed, Fri & Sat, 9am-9pm Thu, 1-5pm Sun) A modern complex of shops, cafés and a supermarket. The Millets store stocks camping and outdoor equipment.

Fermanagh Cottage Industries (☎ 6632 2260; 14 East Bridge St) A craft shop selling linen, lace and tweed.

Home, Field & Stream (☎ 6632 2114; 18 Church St) Has a wide range of fishing tackle and also sells fishing licences and permits.

Dolan's Centra (3 High St; ☻ 7.30am-9pm Mon-Sat, 9am-9pm Sun) A handy, late-opening minimarket and post-office counter; also sells Sunday newspapers.

Getting There & Away

Ulsterbus service 261 runs from Enniskillen to Belfast (£9, 2¼ hours, hourly Monday to Saturday, two Sunday) via Dungannon. Bus 296 runs to Omagh (£5, one hour, one daily Monday to Saturday) and, in the other direction, to Cork (8¼ hours; change at Longford) via Athlone (3½ hours). Bus 99 goes from Enniskillen to Bundoran (£6, 1¼ hours, four daily Monday to Saturday, two on Sundays) via Belleek (45 minutes).

Bus Éireann's 66 service runs to Sligo (£7, 1½ hours, five daily Monday to Saturday, two on Sundays) via Belcoo, and bus 30 between Dublin (£12, 2½ hours, seven daily Monday to Saturday, four Sunday) and Donegal (one hour) also stops in at Enniskillen and Belleek.

AROUND ENNISKILLEN
Castle Coole

When King George IV visited Ireland in 1821, the second earl of Belmore had a state bedroom specially prepared at Castle Coole in anticipation of a visit from the monarch. The king, however, was more interested in dallying with his mistress at Slane Castle, and never turned up. The bedroom, draped in red silk and decorated with paintings depicting *The Rake's Progress* (the earl's sniffy riposte to the king's extramarital shenanigans), is one of the highlights of the one-hour guided tour around **Castle Coole** (☎ 6632 2690; Dublin Rd, Enniskillen; adult/child £5/2.20; ☒ noon-6pm daily Jul & Aug, 1-6pm Fri-Wed Jun, 1-6pm Sat, Sun & public hols Apr, May & Sep).

Designed by James Wyatt, this Palladian mansion was built between 1789 and 1795 for Armar Lowry-Corry, the first earl of Belmore, and is probably the purest expression of late-18th-century neoclassical architecture in Ireland. It is built of silvery-white Portland stone, which was brought in at great expense from southern England – by ship to Ballyshannon, then overland to Lough Erne, by boat again to Enniskillen, and finally by bullock cart for the last 3km.

Building costs of £70,000 nearly bankrupted the first earl, but that didn't stop his son Somerset Lowry-Corry, the second earl, spending another £35,000 on exuberant Regency furnishings and decoration, best seen in the opulent, oval saloon where the family and friends would gather before dinner. The seventh earl of Belmore, John Armar Lowry-Corry, reserves part of the house for his private use, but most of the building is under the care of the National Trust.

The 600 hectares of landscaped **grounds** (car/pedestrian £2/free; ☒ 10am-8pm Apr-Sep, 10am-4pm Oct-Mar) contain a lake that is home to the UK's only nonmigratory colony of greylag geese. It is said that if the geese ever leave, the earls of Belmore will lose Castle Coole.

Castle Coole is on the A4 Dublin road, 2.5km southeast of Enniskillen. You can easily walk there from Enniskillen town centre in 30 minutes – fork left beyond Dunnes Stores and keep straight on along Castlecoole Rd.

Sheelin Irish Lace Museum

This **museum** (☎ 6634 8052; www.irishlacemuseum.com; Bellanaleck; adult/child £3/1.50; ☒ 10am-1pm & 2-6pm Mon-Sat Apr-Oct) houses a collection of beautiful Irish lace dating from 1850 to 1900. Lace making was an important cottage industry in the region both before and after the Famine – prior to WWI there were at least 10 lace schools in County Fermanagh. The museum is just over 6km southwest of Enniskillen in the village of Bellanaleck.

UPPER LOUGH ERNE

About 80km long, Lough Erne is made up of two sections: the Upper Lough to the south of Enniskillen, and the Lower Lough to the north. The two are connected by the River Erne, which begins its journey in County Cavan and meets the sea at Donegal Bay west of Ballyshannon.

Upper Lough Erne is not so much a lake as a watery maze of islands (more than 150 of them), inlets, reedy bays and meandering backwaters. Bird life is abundant, with flocks of whooper swan and goldeneye overwintering here, great crested grebes nesting in the spring, and Ireland's biggest heronry in a 400-year-old oak grove on the island of Inishfendra, just south of Crom Estate.

Lisnaskea is the main town, with shops, pubs, ATMs and a post office. An island at the north end of the lough, near Lisbellaw, is home to the **Belle Isle School of Cookery** (☎ 6638 7231; www.irish-cookery-school.com) which offers a range of cookery and wine courses lasting from one day to four weeks, with luxurious accommodation in Belle Isle Castle and its estate cottages. One-day courses cost £100, not including accommodation.

Crom Estate

Home to the largest area of natural woodland in Northern Ireland, the National Trust's beautiful **Crom Estate** (☎ 6773 8118; Newtownbutler; car/pedestrian £5.50/free; ☒ grounds 10am-7pm Jun-Aug, to 6pm mid-Mar–May & Sep; visitor centre 10am-6pm Easter Week & May-mid–Sep, to 6pm Sat & Sun mid-Mar–Apr & late Sep; ☒) is a haven for pine martens, rare bats and many species of bird.

You can walk from the visitor centre to the ruins of old Crom Castle, with its old walled garden, abandoned bowling green and ancient yew trees, and views over the reed-fringed lough to an island folly. There are rowing boats for hire (£5 per hour), and camping facilities (£10 per tent per night).

Check the **National Trust website** (www.ntni .org.uk) for details on bat-watching and other wildlife events.

The estate is on the eastern shore of the Upper Lough, 5km west of Newtownbutler.

Tours

The **Inishcruiser** (☎ 6772 2122; adult/child/family £7/5/20; ⏱ 2.30pm Sun & public hols Easter-Sep; ☒) offers 1½- to two-hour cruises on the lough leaving from the Share Holiday Village 5km southwest of Lisnaskea.

Activities

Day boats can be hired for fishing or exploring from **Knockninny Marina** (☎ 6774 8590; near Derrylin) on the west shore of the lough; rates are £40/60 per half-/full-day for a six-seater motor boat with cabin. The marina also rents bikes for £4.50/10 a half-/full-day. It is signposted from the main road just north of Derrylin.

Guests at the **Share Holiday Village** (☎ 6772 2122; www.sharevillage.org) near Lisnaskea can take part in canoeing, windsurfing, dinghy sailing, archery, orienteering and other activities for £10 per person per 2½-hour session.

Sleeping & Eating

Lisnaskea Caravan Park (☎ 6772 1040; Gola Rd, Mullynascarty; camp/caravan sites £8/12; ⏱ Apr-Oct) This local council-run site enjoys a beautiful wooded setting on the banks of the Colebrooke River about 2km northwest of Lisnaskea, on the B514 road towards Enniskillen.

Share Holiday Village (☎ 6772 2122; www.share village.org; Smiths Strand, Lisnaskea; camp/caravan sites £9.50/13.50; ⏱ Easter-Sep) Share is a charity that works towards the integration of people with and without disabilities through a range of activities and courses. The holiday village is mostly occupied by groups, but it also has a touring site with space for 13 caravans and 10 tents. Booking is strongly recommended. The village is 5km southwest of Lisnaskea, off the B127.

Donn Carragh Hotel (☎ 6772 1206; www.donn carraghhotel.com; Main St, Lisnaskea; s/d £40/70; ℗) There's not too much in the way of hotel or B&B accommodation around Upper Lough Erne; this pleasant but unexceptional 18-room hotel in the middle of Lisnaskea is the best of what there is.

Knockninny House (☎ 6774 8590; www.knockninny marina.com; near Derrylin; apt from £75/250/400 a night/ weekend/week; mains £3-7; ⏱ cafe 10am-5.30pm; ℗) A Victorian villa and Lough Erne's first hotel, Knockninny House, built in the 1870s, enjoys an idyllic lakeside setting, and now offers accommodation in two luxurious self-catering apartments (one sleeps five, the other seven), available by the night (weekdays only), weekend or week. There's also a café-patisserie with an outdoor terrace overlooking the marina, and a tiny sandy beach.

Kissin Crust (☎ 6772 2678; 125 Main St, Lisnaskea; mains £2-5; ⏱ 8.30am-5pm) Very popular with local people, this friendly coffee shop is stacked with home-baked apple pie, lemon meringue pie, quiches and scones, and serves up a lunch menu of home-made soup, freshly made sandwiches and a hot dish of the day.

Getting There & Away

From Enniskillen, Ulsterbus service 95 runs along the east side of the lough to Lisnaskea (£3, 25 minutes, five daily Monday to Friday, three on Saturdays, plus one on Sundays in July and August only), while bus 58 goes down the west side to Derrylin (£3, 40 minutes, six daily Monday to Friday, four on Saturdays), and continues to Belturbet in County Cavan.

LOWER LOUGH ERNE

Lower Lough Erne is a much more open expanse of water than the Upper Lough, with its 90-odd islands clustered mainly in the southern reaches. In early Christian times, when overland travel was difficult, Lough Erne was an important highway between the Donegal coast and inland Leitrim, and there are many ancient religious sites and other antiquities dotted around its shores. In medieval times the lough was part of an important pilgrimage route to Station Island in Lough Derg, County Donegal.

The following sights are described travelling anticlockwise around the lough from Enniskillen.

Devenish Island

Devenish Island (Daimh Inis, meaning Ox Island) is the biggest of several 'holy islands' in Lough Erne. The remains of an **Augustinian monastery**, founded here in the 6th century by St Molaise, include a superb 12th-century **round tower** in near perfect condition, the ruins of St Molaise's Church and St Mary's Abbey, an unusual 15th-century high cross, and many fascinating old gravestones. Four ladders allow you to climb to the top of the round tower for a cramped view out of the five tiny windows.

A speedboat **ferry** (☎ 6862 1588; adult/child return £3/2; ☺ 10am, 1pm, 3pm & 5pm daily Apr-Sep) crosses to Devenish Island from Trory Point landing. From Enniskillen, take the A32 towards Irvinestown and after 5km look for the sign on the left, just after a service station and immediately before the junction where the B82 and A32 part company. At the foot of the hill by the lough, turn left for the jetty.

You can also visit as part of a cruise with Erne Tours (p678) from Enniskillen.

Killadeas

The churchyard at Killadeas, 11km north of Enniskillen on the B82, contains several unusual carved stones. Most famous is the 1m-high **Bishop's Stone**, dating from between the 7th and 9th centuries, which has a Celtic head reminiscent of the White Island figures carved on its narrow western edge, and an engraving of a bishop with bell and crozier on the side. Located nearby is a slab set on edge, with several deep cup-marks (possibly bullauns) on one side, and a cross within a circle on the other. You will also find a broken phallic column and a large, perforated stone.

TOURS

The **Lady of the Lake** (☎ 6862 2200; www.ladyofthelaketours.com), based at the Erne Palace restaurant 2km north of the Manor House, offers cruises on the lough on Saturday and Sunday.

SLEEPING & EATING

The **Manor House Country Hotel** (☎ 6862 2211; www.manor-house-hotel.com; Killadeas; s/d from £100/125; ℗) A grand, 19th-century country house overlooking Lough Erne. It has had a thorough makeover in neoclassical style, complete with Greek temple-style lobby, Romanesque pool and Jacuzzis with a view over the lough. The public areas are impressive but the rooms, though luxurious, are a bit on the bland side. The hotel's **Watergate Bar** serves decent pub grub (mains £8 to £12), and has live music at weekends.

Castle Archdale Country Park

This **park** (☎ 6862 1588; Lisnarick; admission free; ℗ 9am-dusk), has pleasant woodland and lakeshore walks and cycle tracks in the former estate of 18th-century Archdale Manor. The island-filled bay was used in WWII as a base for Catalina flying boats, a history explained in the **visitor centre** (admission free; ℗ 11am-7pm Tue-Sun Jul & Aug, noon-6pm Sun Easter-Jun).

You can hire bikes for £4/8/12 per hour/half-day/day, or swap two wheels for four legs – the park offers pony trekking (£15 per hour) and short rides (£5 per 15 minutes) for beginners. There are also boats for hire (£30/45/60 per two hours/half-day/day), and you can also rent fishing rods (£5 a day including bait).

The park is 16km northwest of Enniskillen on the B82, near Lisnarick.

SLEEPING & EATING

Castle Archdale Caravan Park (☎ 6862 1333; www.castlearchdale.com; Castle Archdale Country Park; camp sites £10-15, caravan sites £15; ℗ Easter-Oct) This attractive, tree-sheltered site is dominated by onsite caravans, but has good facilities, including a shop, launderette, playground and restaurant.

ourpick Cedars Guesthouse (☎ 6862 1493; www.cedarsguesthouse.com; Drummal, Castle Archdale; s/d from £40/60; ℗) Set in a former rectory just south of the park entrance, this peaceful 10-room guesthouse goes for a Victorian country house feel, with rose-patterned bedspreads and antique-style furniture.

Rectory Bistro (mains £11-15; ℗ 6-9pm Wed-Sat, 12.30-3pm & 5-9pm Sun) Adjoining the Cedars Guesthouse, this bistro has a welcoming open fireplace, lots of golden pine lit by chunky candles and a sprinkling of Gothic motifs, with an aspirational menu that ranges from seafood chowder to monkfish fried with black pepper and ginger.

White Island

White Island, in the bay to the north of Castle Archdale Country Park, is the most haunting of Lough Erne's monastic sites. At the eastern tip of the island are the ruins of a small 12th-century church with a beautiful Romanesque door on its southern side. Inside are six extraordinary Celtic stone figures, thought to date from the 9th century, lined up along the wall like miniature Easter Island statues.

This line-up is a modern arrangement; most of them were discovered buried in the walls of the church in the 19th century, where the medieval masons had used them as ordinary building stones. The six main figures, all created by the same hand, are flanked on the left by a sheila-na-gig, which is probably contemporary with the church, and flanked on the right by a scowling stone face. The age and interpretation of these figures has been the subject of much debate; it has been suggested that the two central pairs, of equal height, were pillars that once supported a pulpit, and that they represent either saints or aspects of the life of Christ.

The first figure is holding a book (Christ the Evangelist?) and the second holds a bishop's crozier and bell (Christ as Bishop?). The third has been identified as the young King David, author of the Psalms. The fourth is holding the necks of two griffins (symbols of Christ's dual nature as both human and divine?). The fifth bears a sword and shield (Christ's Second Coming?) and the sixth is unfinished.

A **ferry** (☎ 6862 1892; adult/child £3/2; ☼ 11am-6pm daily Jul & Aug, 11am-5pm Sat & Sun Apr-Jun & Sep) crosses to the island hourly, on the hour (except for 1pm) from the marina in Castle Archdale Country Park; buy your ticket from the Billieve Boat Hire office. The crossing takes 15 minutes, and allows you around half an hour on the island.

Boa Island

Boa Island, at the northern end of Lower Lough Erne, is connected to the mainland at both ends – the main A47 road runs along its length. Spooky, moss-grown Caldragh graveyard, towards the western end of the island, contains the famous **Janus Stone**. Perhaps 2000 years old, this pagan figure is carved with two grotesque human heads, back to back. Nearby is a smaller figure called the **Lusty Man**, brought here from Lusty More island. Their origin and meaning have been lost in the mists of time.

There's a small sign indicating the graveyard, about 1.5km from the bridge at the western tip of the island.

SLEEPING & EATING

Lusty Beg Island (☎ 6863 3300; www.lustybeg.co.uk; Boa Island, Kesh; s/d £65/90; **P** **⊛**) This private island retreat, reached by ferry from a jetty halfway along Boa Island, has self-catering chalets to let (£435 to £740 a week in July and August, sleeping four to six people) but also offers B&B in its rustic 18-room Courtyard Motel. There's a tennis court, nature trail and canoeing on the lough for residents

The informal **Island Lodge Restaurant** (☎ 6863 1342; bar meals £7-12, 4-course dinner £25; ☼ 1-9pm Jul & Aug) on the island is open to all,

and serves everything from baked potatoes to smoked Irish salmon. You can summon the ferry from a telephone in the blockhouse on the slipway.

Castle Caldwell Forest Park

Castle Caldwell, built between 1610 and 1619, is nothing but a ruin, but the **park** (admission free; ☼ 24hr), about halfway between Boa Island and Belleek, has a nature reserve full of bird life, and is a major breeding ground for the common scoter.

At the entrance to the park is the **Fiddle Stone** (in the shape of a fiddle). The inscription, now too worn to read, commemorated a favourite musician who fell out of a boat while drunk:

On firm land only exercise your skill; there you may play and safely drink your fill. To the memory of Denis McCabe, Fiddler, who fell out of the St Patrick Barge belonging to Sir James Caldwell Bart. and Count of Milan and was drowned off this point August ye 13 1770.

Belleek

pop 550

Belleek's (Beal Leice) village street of colourful, flower-bedecked houses slopes up from a bridge across the River Erne, where it flows out of the Lower Lough towards Ballyshannon and the sea. The village is right on the border – the road south across the bridge passes through a finger of the Republic's territory for about 200m before leaving again – and shops accept both sterling and euros.

The imposing Georgian-style building beside the bridge houses the world-famous **Belleek Pottery** (☎ 6865 9300; www.belleek.ie; Main St; ☼ 9am-6pm Mon-Fri, 10am-6pm Sat, noon-6pm Sun Mar-Oct, 9am-5.30pm Mon-Fri & 10am-5.30pm Sat Nov & Dec, 9am-5.30pm Mon-Fri Jan & Feb), founded in 1857 to provide local employment in the wake of the Potato Famine. It has been producing fine Parian china ever since, and is especially noted for its delicate basketware. The visitor centre houses a small museum, showroom and restaurant, and there are **guided tours** (adult/child £4/free) of the pottery every half-hour from 9.30am to 12.15pm and 1.45pm to 4pm (till 3pm on Friday) Monday to Friday year round.

COUNTIES FERMANAGH & TYRONE

SLEEPING & EATING

Moohan's Fiddlestone (☎ 6665 8008; 15-17 Main St; s/d £35/50; P) This is a traditional Irish pub offering B&B in five en-suite rooms upstairs. The lively bar downstairs is a popular venue for impromptu music sessions, so don't expect peace and quiet in the evenings.

Hotel Carlton (☎ 6865 8282; www.hotelcarlton .co.uk; Main St; s/d £60/90; P) Though the rooms are plush and luxurious, the family-friendly Carlton has a welcoming and informal feel to it, and a lovely setting on the banks of the River Erne. There are frequent live music sessions in Potters Bar at the hotel.

Thatch Coffee Shop (☎ 6865 8181; 20 Main St; mains £4-5; ☺ 9am-5pm Mon-Sat) This cute little thatched cottage may be Belleek's oldest building (late 18th century), but it serves a thoroughly modern cup of coffee plus a range of home-made cakes and scones, soup and sandwiches.

Black Cat Cove (☎ 6865 8942; 28 Main St; mains £6-10; ☺ noon-9pm) This friendly, family-run pub with antique furniture and an open fire, that serves excellent bar meals. It also has music on Tuesday, Wednesday and Thursday nights from May to September.

Activities

FISHING

The lakes of Fermanagh are renowned for both coarse and game fishing. The Lough Erne trout-fishing season runs from the beginning of March to the end of September. Salmon fishing begins in June and also continues to the end of September. The mayfly season usually lasts a month from the second week in May. There's no closed season for coarse fish.

You'll need both a licence (issued by the Fisheries Conservancy Board) and a permit (from the owner of the fishery). Licences and permits can be purchased from the tourist information centre (p677) and Home, Field & Stream (p681), both in Enniskillen, and from the marina in Castle Archdale Country Park (p684), which also hires out fishing rods. A combined licence and permit for game fishing on Lough Erne costs £8.50/23 for three/14 days.

The **Belleek Angling Centre** in the Thatch Coffee Shop (left) in Belleek sells fishing tackle and can arrange boat hire for anglers, and you can get expert instruction in fly-casting from **Michael Shortt** (☎ 6638 8184; fish.teach@virgin.net).

Enniskillen's tourist information centre also provides a free guide to angling in Fermanagh and South Tyrone, which has full details of lakes and rivers, fish species, seasons and permit requirements.

BOAT HIRE

A number of companies hire out day boats at Enniskillen, Killadeas, Castle Archdale Country Park, Kesh and Belleek. Rates are about

---

WALK: THE CLIFFS OF MAGHO

The Cliffs of Magho – a 250m-high and 9km-long limestone escarpment – dominate the western end of Lough Erne, rising above a fringe of native woodland on the south shore. The view from the cliff top is one of the finest in Ireland, especially towards sunset, looking out over the shimmering expanse of lough and river to the Blue Stack Mountains, the sparkling waters of Donegal Bay and the sea cliffs of Slieve League. The hike to the top is strenuous, but not too long (2.5km round trip; allow one to two hours); the path is rough, and crumbling in places, so you'll need good hiking boots.

Begin at the Lough Navar Forest Park car park on the A46 road, 13km east of Belleek. Head straight uphill on a gravel track and the woodland path beyond. As the slope increases, the path begins to zigzag steeply up through broad-leaved woodland; the ground is bright with primroses in springtime. At the top, as the angle eases, the path cuts back right; where it forks, keep right. As you emerge from the trees the view bursts upon you unexpectedly, a fine reward for your efforts. You can follow the path along the cliff top for another 500m, with a choice of prime spots to sit down and enjoy a picnic.

Note: you can also reach the Magho viewpoint by car. The vehicle entrance to Lough Navar Forest Park (car £3; ☺ 10am-dusk) is on the minor Glennasheevar road between Garrison and Derrygonnelly, 20km southeast of Belleek (take the B52 towards Garrison, and fork left after 2.5km). Not as satisfying as the hike, though.

£10 to £15 per hour for an open rowing boat with outboard motor, to £50/75 per half-/full-day for a six-seater with cabin and engine. The tourist information centre in Enniskillen has a full list of companies and costs.

CANOEING
The **Lough Erne Canoe Trail** (www.nicanoeing.com) highlights the attractions along the 50km of lough and river between Belleek and Belturbet. The wide open expanses of the Lower Lough can build up big waves in a strong breeze, and is best left to experts, but the sheltered backwaters of the Upper Lough are ideal for beginners and families.

You can pick up a map and guide (£1.50), showing public access points, camping sites and other facilities along the trail from the tourist information office in Enniskillen (p677). Canoe hire is available from the Lakeland Canoe Centre (p677), also in Enniskillen, and Ultimate Watersports (see below).

WATERSPORTS
Working out of Castle Archdale marina and Lusty Beg island, **Ultimate Watersports** (☎ 07808-736818 or 07863-344172; www.ultimatewatersports.co.uk) offer equipment hire and instruction in waterskiing, wakeboarding, jet-skiing, canoeing, dinghy sailing and power-boating.

Getting There & Away
On the eastern side of the lough, Ulsterbus service 194 from Enniskillen to Pettigo via Irvinestown (four or five daily Monday to Saturday) stops near Castle Archdale Country Park (35 minutes) and Kesh (one hour). Bus

99 goes from Enniskillen to Belleek (£4, 45 minutes, four daily Monday to Saturday, two on Sundays) along the western shoreline via Blaney, Tully Castle and the Cliffs of Magho car park, terminating at Bundoran.

Bus 64 travels from Enniskillen to Belcoo (£2, 25 minutes, seven or eight daily Monday to Friday, three on Saturdays, one on Sundays); the Sunday bus and two of the Thursday buses continue to Garrison, Belleek and Bundoran.

WEST OF LOUGH ERNE
Florence Court
Part of the motivation for the first earl of Belmore to build Castle Coole (near Enniskillen; p682) was keeping up with the Joneses – in the 1770s his aristocratic neighbour William Willoughby Cole, the first earl of Enniskillen, had overseen the addition of grand, Palladian wings to the beautiful, baroque country house called Florence Court, named after his Cornish grandmother Florence Wrey.

Set in lovely wooded grounds in the shadow of Cuilcagh Mountain, **Florence Court** (☎ 6634 8249; Swanlinbar Rd, Florencecourt; adult/child £5/2.20; ☒ noon-6pm daily Easter Week, Jul & Aug, 1-6pm Wed-Mon Jun, 1-6pm Sat, Sun & public hols Apr, May & Sep) is famous for its rococo plasterwork and antique Irish furniture. The house was badly damaged by a fire in 1955 and much of what you see on the one-hour guided tour is the result of meticulous restoration, but the magnificent plasterwork on the ceiling of the dining room is original.

Florence Court feels more homely and lived-in than the rather cold and austere Castle Coole, especially since the family

---

CRUISING HOLIDAYS ON LOUGH ERNE

If you fancy exploring Lough Erne as captain of your own motor cruiser, well, you can – and without any previous experience or qualification. Several companies in Fermanagh hire out self-drive, live-aboard cabin cruisers by the week, offering a crash course (not literally, you hope) in boat-handling and navigation at the start of your holiday. Weekly rates in high season (July and August) range from about £600 for a two-berth to £1000 for a four-berth and £1600 for an eight-berth boat. Low- and mid-season rates are around 70% to 90% of the high-season rates.

The main cruiser hire companies in Fermanagh are:

Aghinver Boat Company (☎ 6863 1400; www.abcboats.com; Lisnarick, Lower Lough Erne)

Carrick Craft (☎ 3834 4993; www.cruise-ireland.com; Tully Bay, Lower Lough Erne)

Carrybridge Boat Company (☎ 6638 7034; Carrybridge, Lisbellaw, Upper Lough Erne)

Corraquill Cruising Holidays (☎ 6774 8712; www.corraquill.co.uk; Drumetta, Aghalane, Derrylin, Upper Lough Erne)

Manor House Marine (☎ 6862 8100; www.manormarine.com; Killadeas, Lower Lough Erne)

belongings of the sixth earl were returned. (The earl had a falling out with the National Trust in 1974 and stomped off to Scotland with all his stuff; it was returned after the death of his widow in 1998.) The library, in particular, feels as if the last earl has just nipped out for a stroll and could return at any minute.

In the **grounds** (car/pedestrian £3.50/free; ☉ 10am-8pm May-Sep, 10am-4pm Oct-Apr) you can explore the walled garden and, on the edge of Cottage Wood, southeast of the house, admire an ancient Irish yew tree. It's said that every Irish yew around the world is descended from this one.

The house is 12km southwest of Enniskillen. Take the A4 Sligo road and fork left onto the A32 to Swanlinbar. Ulsterbus service 192 from Enniskillen to Swanlinbar can drop you at Creamery Cross, about 2km from the house.

Marble Arch Caves

To the south of Lower Lough Erne lies a limestone plateau, where Fermanagh's abundant rainwater has carved out a network of subterranean caverns. The largest of these is **Marble Arch Caves** (☎ 6634 8855; www.marblearchcaves.net; Marlbank Scenic Loop, Florencecourt; adult/child £8/5; ☉ 10am-5pm Jul & Aug, to 4.30pm Easter-Jun & Sep), first explored by the French caving pioneer Edouard Martel in 1895, but not opened to the public until 1985.

The 1¼-hour tour of the caves begins with a short boat trip along the peaty, foam-flecked waters of the underground River Cladagh to Junction Jetty, where three subterranean streams – the Owenbrean, the Aghinrawn and the Sluh Croppa, which drain the northern slopes of Cuilcagh Mountain – meet up. You then continue on foot past the Grand Gallery and Pool Chamber,

COUNTIES FERMANAGH & TYRONE

WALK: CUILCAGH MOUNTAIN VIA THE LEGNABROCKY TRAIL

Rising above Marble Arch and Florence Court like a miniature Mount Roraima, Cuilcagh (pronounced cull-kay) Mountain (666m) is the highest point in Counties Fermanagh and Cavan, its summit right on the border between Northern Ireland and the Republic.

The mountain is a geological layer cake, with a cave-riddled limestone base, shale and sandstone flanks draped with a shaggy tweed skirt of blanket bog, and a high gritstone plateau ringed by steep, craggy slopes, all part of the Marble Arch Caves European Geopark (www.europeangeoparks.org).

Hidden among the sphagnum moss, bog cotton and heather of the blanket bog, you can find the sticky-fingered sundew, an insect-eating plant, while the crags echo to the 'krok-krok-krok' of ravens and the mewing of peregrine falcons. The otherworldly summit plateau, strewn with boulders and riven by deep fissures in the gritstone bedrock, is a breeding ground for golden plover and is rich in rare plants such as alpine clubmoss.

The hike to the summit is a 15km round trip (allow five or six hours); the first part is on an easy gravel track, but you'll need good boots to negotiate the boggy ground and steep slopes further on. Start at the Cuilcagh Mountain Park car park, 300m west of the entrance to Marble Arch Caves visitor centre (grid reference 121335; you'll need the Ordnance Survey 1:50,000 Discovery series map, sheet 26). Right next to the car park is the Monastir sink hole, a deep depression ringed by limestone cliffs where the Aghinrawn River disappears underground for its journey through the Marble Arch Caves system. (Note that the OS map has wrongly labelled this river the Owenbrean.)

Climb the stile beside the gate and set out along the Legnabrocky Trail, a 4WD track that winds through rich green limestone meadows before climbing across the blanket bog on a 'floating' bed of gravel and geotextiles – boardwalks off to one side offer a closer look at bog regeneration areas. The gravel track comes to an end at a gate about 4.5km from the start. From here you follow a line of waymarked wooden posts, squelching your way across spongy bog (don't stray from the route – there are deep bog holes where you can get stuck) before climbing steeply up to the summit ridge, with great views west to the crags above little Lough Atona. The waymarkers come to an end here, so you're on your own for the final kilometre across the plateau, aiming for the prominent cairn on the summit (a map and compass are essential in poor visibility).

The summit cairn is actually a Neolithic burial chamber; about 100m south of the summit you will find two rings of boulders, the foundations of prehistoric huts. On a clear day the view extends from the Blue Stack Mountains of Donegal to Croagh Patrick, and from the Atlantic Ocean to the Irish Sea. Return the way you came.

regaled all the time with food-related jokes from your guide. A man-made tunnel leads into the New Chamber (pioneering cave explorers originally wriggled through a natural tunnel high above here), from which the route follows the underground Owenbrean River, through the Moses Walk (a pathway sunk waist-deep into the river) to the Calcite Cradle, where the most picturesque formations are to be found. The caves are very popular, so it's wise to phone ahead and book a tour, especially if you're in a group of four or more. (The listed closing time is the starting time of the last tour.)

The caves take their name from a natural limestone arch that spans the River Cladagh where it emerges from the caves; you can reach it via a short walk along a signposted footpath from the visitor centre.

Unexpected serious flooding of the caves in the 1990s was found to have been caused by mechanised peat-cutting in the blanket bog – one of Ireland's biggest – on the slopes of Cuilcagh Mountain, whose rivers feed the caves. **Cuilcagh Mountain Park** was then established to restore and preserve the bog environment, and in 2001 the entire area was designated a Unesco Geopark. The park's geology and ecology are explained in the caves' visitor centre.

The Marble Arch Caves are 16km southwest of Enniskillen, and some 4km from Florence Court (an hour's walk), reached via the A4 Sligo road and the A32.

Loughs Melvin & Macnean

Lough Melvin and Lough Macnean are situated along the border with the Republic, on the B52 road from Belcoo to Belleek. Lough Melvin is famous for its salmon and trout fishing, and is home to two unusual trout species – the sonaghan, with its distinctive black spots, and the crimson-spotted gillaroo – that are unique to the lough, as well as brown trout, ferox trout and char.

The lakeside **Lough Melvin Holiday Centre** (☎ 6865 8142; www.melvinholidaycentre.com; Garrison; camp sites £9, caravan sites £13.50, dm £17-20, d from £30) offers caving, canoeing, walking and fishing holidays, and also has a camp site, dorm accommodation, en-suite rooms, and a restaurant and a coffee shop.

Corralea Activity Centre (☎ 6638 6668; www.activity ireland.com; Belcoo), based on Upper Lough Macnean, hires out bicycles (£10/15 per half-/

full-day) and two-person canoes (half-/full-day £15/20). It also offers instruction in activities such as caving, canoeing, climbing, windsurfing and archery from £22 per day.

The **Customs House Country Inn** (☎ 6638 6285; www.customshouseinn.com; Main St, Belcoo; s/d from £40/60; 2-/3-course dinner £18/21; **P**) is a welcoming pub decked out in acres of waxed oak and pine, with a cosy, candlelit restaurant and nine en-suite bedrooms, many with good views of Lough Macnean.

There is also gourmet dining a few hundred metres across the border in Blacklion, County Cavan (p483).

COUNTY TYRONE

OMAGH

pop 20,000

Situated at the confluence of the Rivers Camowen and Drumragh, which join to form the River Strule, Omagh is a busy market town that serves as a useful base for exploring the surrounding area by car.

Sadly, for a long time to come Omagh (An Óghmagh) will be remembered for the devastating car bomb in 1998 that killed 29 people and injured 200. Planted by the breakaway group Real IRA, the bomb was the worst single atrocity in the 30-year history of the Troubles. A memorial garden on Drumragh Avenue, 200m east of the bus station, remembers the dead.

The **tourist information centre** (☎ 8224 7831; tourism@omagh.gov.uk; Strule Arts Centre, Town Hall Sq, Bridge St; ☿ 9am-5pm Mon-Sat Apr-Sep, Mon-Fri Oct-Mar) is in the new arts centre, just across the river from the bus station. It has a Town Trail leaflet that guides you around Omagh's remaining historic buildings.

Sleeping & Eating

Omagh Independent Hostel (☎ 8224 1973; www.omagh hostel.co.uk; 9a Waterworks Rd; dm/tw from £10/24, camp sites £12; ☿ Mar-Oct) This peaceful, family-friendly and eco-friendly hostel is 4km northeast of town, tucked away on a back road off the B48 to Gortin. The lovely, rural setting is awash with flowers in summer; if you prefer, you can pitch a tent outside. If you ring from the bus station someone will come and pick you up.

our pick **Mullaghmore House** (☎ 8224 2314; www .mullaghmorehouse.com; Old Mountfield Rd; s £34-42, d £78;

🖥 P) Offering affordable country-house luxury, this beautifully restored Georgian villa boasts a gleaming mahogany-panelled library, billiards room and marble-lined steam room. The bedrooms have period cast-iron fireplaces and antique furniture, and the owners run courses on antique restoration and traditional crafts. It's 1.5km northeast of the town centre.

Riverfront Coffee Shop (☎ 8225 0011; 38 Market St; sandwiches £2-4; �9am-5.30pm Mon-Sat) This lively little eatery serves up excellent coffee, cakes, quiche, home-made soup, and mix-your-own sandwiches on baguettes, *panini* or ciabatta rolls, and also provides vegetarian, coeliac-friendly and low-carb options.

Grant's of Omagh (☎ 8225 0900; 29 George's St; mains £7-15; � 4-10pm Mon-Fri, noon-10pm Sat & Sun) Grant's – as in US president Ulysses S Grant – bathes in a golden glow of Irish emigrant nostalgia, from the fiddle and bodhrán on the wall above the smoke-blackened fireplace in the front bar to the American-themed restaurant in the back, with a menu that ranges from steak, burgers and lasagne to Cajun chicken and spicy enchiladas.

Getting There & Away
The bus station is on Mountjoy Rd, just north of the town centre along Bridge St.

Goldline Express bus 273 goes from Belfast to Omagh (£9, 1¾ hours, hourly Monday to Saturday, six on Sundays) via Dungannon and on to Derry (£7, 1¼ hours). Bus 94 goes to Enniskillen (£6, one hour, five or six daily Monday to Friday, three on Saturdays, one on Sundays) where you can change for Donegal, Bundoran or Sligo. Goldline Express bus 274 runs from Derry to Omagh (£7, one hour, every two hours), and continues to Dublin (£11, three hours) via Monaghan.

AROUND OMAGH
Ulster American Folk Park
In the 18th and 19th centuries thousands of Ulster people left their homes to forge a new life across the Atlantic; 200,000 emigrated in the 18th century alone. Their story is told here at one of Ireland's best museums, the **Ulster American Folk Park** (☎ 8224 3292; www.folkpark.com; Mellon Rd; adult/child £4.50/2.50; � 10.30am-6pm Mon-Sat, 11am-6.30pm Sun & public holidays Apr-Sep, 10.30am-5pm Mon-Fri Oct-Mar). Last admission is 1½ hours before closing.

The Exhibition Hall explains the close connections between Ulster and the USA – the American Declaration of Independence was signed by several Ulstermen – and includes a genuine Calistoga wagon. But the real appeal of the folk park is the outdoor museum where the 'living history' exhibits are split into Old World and New World areas, cleverly linked by passing through a mock-up of an emigrant ship. Original buildings from various parts of Ulster have been dismantled and re-erected here, including a blacksmith's forge, a weaver's thatched cottage, a Presbyterian meeting house and a schoolhouse. In the 'American' section of the park you can visit a genuine 18th-century settler's stone cottage and a log house, both shipped across the Atlantic from Pennsylvania.

Costumed guides and artisans are on hand to explain the arts of spinning, weaving, candle making and so on, and various events are held throughout the year, including re-enactments of American Civil War battles, a festival of traditional Irish music in May, American Independence Day celebrations in July, and the Appalachian and Bluegrass Music Festival in September. There's almost too much to absorb in one visit and at least half a day is needed to do the place justice.

The park is 8km northwest of Omagh on the A5. Bus 97 to Strabane stops outside the park (15 minutes). Buses depart from Omagh at 7.55am and 1.25pm Monday to Friday, and return at 3.20pm and 4.50pm. On Saturdays there are buses at 7.25am and 2.25pm, returning at 4.45pm (check times at the tourist office; p689).

SPERRIN MOUNTAINS
When representatives of the London guilds visited Ulster in 1609 the Lord Deputy of Ireland made sure they were kept well away from the Sperrin Mountains, fearing that the sight of these bleak, moorland hills would put them off the idea of planting settlers here. And when it rains there's no denying that the Sperrins can be dismal, but on a sunny spring day, when the russet bogs and yellow gorse stand out against a clear blue sky, they can offer some grand walking. The area is also dotted with thousands of standing stones and prehistoric tombs.

The main ridge of the Sperrins stretches for 30km along the border with County Derry. The highest summit is Mt Sawel (678m), rising above the B47 road from Plumbridge to Draperstown, a right little roller-coaster of a road that undulates across the southern slopes of the Sperrins. Halfway along it you'll find the **Sperrin Heritage Centre** (☎ 8164 8142; 274 Glenelly Rd, Cranagh; adult/child £2.70/1.65; ☯ 11.30am-5.30pm Mon-Fri, 11.30am-6pm Sat, 2-6pm Sun Easter-Oct) which offers an insight into the culture, natural history and geology of the region. Gold has been found in the Sperrins, and for an extra 85/45p you can try your luck at panning for gold in a nearby stream.

If you're thinking of walking up Mt Sawel, enquire at the Sperrin Heritage Centre about the best route. The climb is easy enough in good weather, but some farmers are not as accommodating as others about hikers crossing their land.

Gortin

The village of Gortin, about 15km north of Omagh, lies at the foot of Mullaghcarn (542m), the southernmost of the Sperrin summits (unfortunately capped by two prominent radio masts). Hundreds of hikers converge for a mass ascent of the hill on **Cairn Sunday** (the last Sunday in July), a revival of an ancient pilgrimage that first petered out in the 19th century. There are several good walks around the village, and a scenic drive to **Gortin Lakes**, with views north to the main Sperrin ridge.

A few kilometres south of Gortin, towards Omagh, is **Gortin Glen Forest Park** (☎ 8167 0666; Gortin Rd; car/pedestrian £3/free; ☯ 10am-dusk), whose dense conifer woodland is home to a herd of Japanese sika deer. An 8km scenic drive offers the chance to enjoy the views without breaking into a sweat.

There is hostel accommodation at the **Gortin Accommodation Suite** (☎ 8164 8346; www.gortin .net; 62 Main St; dm/f £10/50), a modern outdoor activity centre in the middle of Gortin village; it also has en-suite family rooms with one double and two single beds.

Creggan

About halfway along the A505 between Omagh and Cookstown (20km east of Omagh) is **An Creagán Visitor Centre** (☎ 8076 1112; www.an-creagan .com; Creggan; admission free; ☯ 11am-6.30pm Apr-Sep, 11am-4.30pm Oct-Mar), with an exhibition covering the ecology of the surrounding bogs and the archaeology of the region. There's also a restaurant and gift shop.

There are 44 prehistoric monuments within 8km of the centre, including the **Beaghmore Stone Circles**. What this site lacks in stature – the stones are all less than 1m tall –

TOP FIVE TRADITIONAL PUBS IN NORTHERN IRELAND

- Bittle's Bar (p601)
- Blake's of the Hollow (p681)
- Grace Neill's (p616)
- Dufferin Arms (p621)
- Peadar O'Donnell's (p652)

it makes up for in complexity, with seven stone circles (one filled with smaller stones, nicknamed 'dragon's teeth') and a dozen or so alignments and cairns. The stones are signposted about 8km east of Creggan, and 4km north of the A505.

Getting Around

Ulsterbus service 403, known as the *Sperrin Rambler,* runs twice daily Monday to Saturday between Omagh and Magherafelt, stopping at Gortin, the Sperrin Heritage Centre and Draperstown (in County Derry). The morning bus leaves Omagh at 10.05am, arriving at the Sperrin Heritage Centre at 11am; the return bus leaves the centre at 2.40pm.

COOKSTOWN & AROUND

Cookstown boasts the longest (2km) and widest (40m) street in Ireland, the legacy of an over-ambitious 18th-century town planner, but apart from that there's not much to see in town. The main sights here are in the surrounding countryside.

The **tourist information centre** (☎ 8676 9949; www.cookstown.gov.uk; Burn Rd, Cookstown; ☯ 9am-5pm Mon-Sat year round, 2-4pm Sun Jul & Aug) is in the Burnavon Arts and Cultural Centre, west of the main street.

Wellbrook Beetling Mill

Beetling, the final stage of linen making, involved pounding the cloth with wooden hammers, or beetles, to give it a smooth sheen. Restored to working order by the National Trust, 18th-century **Wellbrook Beetling Mill** (☎ 8674 8210; 20 Wellbrook Rd, Corkhill; adult/child £3.50/2; ☯ 2-6pm daily Easter Week, Jul & Aug, 2-6pm Sat, Sun & public hols mid-Mar–Jun & Sep) still has its original machinery, and stages demonstrations of the linen-making process led by guides in period costume. The mill is on a pretty

COUNTIES FERMANAGH & TYRONE

stretch of the Ballinderry River, 7km west of Cookstown, just off the A505 Omagh road.

Ballyronan Marina

Tucked in the northwest corner of Lough Neagh (see boxed text, p638), 16km northeast of Cookstown, Ballyronan Marina is the home port of the recently restored **Maid of Antrim** (☎ 2582 2159; www.maidofantrim.com). Built on Scotland's River Clyde in 1963, this vintage boat offers a range of cruises on the lough in the summer months, including a two-hour trip to National Trust–owned **Coney Island** in the south (adult/child £12/8).

Ardboe High Cross

A 6th-century monastic site overlooking Lough Neagh is home to one of Ireland's best-preserved and most elaborately decorated Celtic stone crosses. The 10th-century **Ardboe high cross** stands 5.5m tall, with 22 carved panels depicting biblical scenes. The western side (facing the road) has New Testament scenes: (from the bottom up) the Adoration of the Magi; the Miracle at Cana; the miracle of the loaves and fishes; Christ's entry into Jerusalem; the arrest (or mocking) of Christ; and, at the intersection of the cross, the Crucifixion.

The more weathered eastern face (towards the lough) shows Old Testament scenes: Adam and Eve; the Sacrifice of Isaac; Daniel in the Lions' Den; the Three Hebrews in the Fiery Furnace. The panels above may show the Last Judgement, and/or Christ in Glory. There are further scenes on the narrow north and south faces of the shaft.

Ardboe is 16km east of Cookstown. Take the B73 through Coagh and ignore the first (white) road sign for Ardboe. Keep straight on until you find the brown sign (on the right) for Ardboe High Cross.

Sleeping & Eating

Drum Manor Forest Park (☎ 8676 2774; Drum Rd, Oaklands; camp & caravan sites £9.50-11; ☉ Easter-Sep) This is a pleasant site 4km west of Cookstown on the A505, with lakes, forest trails, a butterfly farm and an arboretum.

Avondale B&B (☎ 8676 4013; www.avondalebb.co.uk; 31 Killycolp Rd; r per person £25; **P**) Set in a spacious Edwardian house with a large garden, patio and sun lounge, Avondale offers B&B in two en-suite family rooms (one double and one single bed in each). It's 3km south of Cookstown, just off the A29 Dungannon road.

ourpick Tullylagan Country House (☎ 8676 5100; www.tullylagan.com; 40b Tullylagan Rd; s/d £55/75; **P**) Set amid beautiful riverside gardens 4km south of Cookstown (just off the A29), the ivy-clad Tullylagan goes for the Victorian country manor feel, with shabby-chic sofas, gilt-framed mirrors on deep red walls, and marble-effect bathrooms with period taps. The **restaurant** (mains £10-15, ☉ noon-3pm & 6.30-9pm Mon-Sat, 12.30-2.30pm & 4-9pm Sun) specialises in fresh seafood and steaks.

Getting There & Away

The bus station is on Molesworth St, east of the main street. Bus 210 connects Cookstown with Belfast's Europa BusCentre (£7, 1¾ hours, four daily Monday to Saturday, two Sunday). Bus 80 shuttles between Cookstown and Dungannon (£3, 45 minutes, hourly Monday to Friday, eight Saturday).

DUNGANNON & AROUND

Dungannon is a pleasant enough market town halfway between Cookstown and Armagh, worth a brief stop in passing if you want to do a spot of shopping.

Killymaddy Tourist Information Centre (☎ 8776 7259; www.flavouroftyrone.com; 190 Ballygawley Rd; ☉ 9am-5pm Mon-Fri, 10am-4pm Sat & Sun) is at a caravan site 10km west of Dungannon on the A4 road towards Enniskillen.

Tyrone Crystal

Ireland's first crystal factory was established in Dungannon in 1771 by Benjamin Edwards from Bristol. It closed down in 1870, but in 1968 Tyrone's crystal industry was revived by a local priest, Father Austin Eustace, who raised funding to establish a new factory to help relieve local unemployment.

Today, **Tyrone Crystal** (☎ 8772 5335; www.tyrone crystal.com; Coalisland Rd, Killybrackey; tours adult/child £5/free; ☉ 9am-5pm Mon-Sat) continues to produce high-quality lead crystal. The factory offers guided tours of the manufacturing process, from the furnace where molten glass is prepared, through hand-blowing and moulding, to cutting and polishing. Admission to the showroom is free, and the tour price is reimbursed if you buy something.

The factory is 2.5km northeast of Dungannon on the A45 towards Coalisland – it's clearly signposted. Bus 80 to Cookstown stops nearby.

Linen Green

Housed in the former Moygashel Linen Mills, the **Linen Green** (☎ 8775 3761; www.thelinengreen.com; Moygashel; ☻ 10am-5pm Mon-Sat) complex includes a range of designer shops and factory outlets, plus a visitor centre with an exhibition covering the history of the local linen industry. It's a good place to shop for bargain men's and women's fashion, shoes, accessories and linen goods or to stop for lunch at the Deli on the Green (see right).

Donaghmore High Cross

The village of Donaghmore, 8km northwest of Dungannon on the B43 road to Pomeroy, is famed for its 10th-century Celtic high cross. It was cobbled together from two different crosses in the 18th century (note the obvious join halfway up the shaft) and now stands outside the churchyard. The carved biblical scenes are similar to those on the Ardboe cross (see opposite). The nearby **heritage centre** (☎ 8776 7039; Pomeroy Rd; admission free; ☻ 9am-5pm Mon-Fri) is based in a converted 19th-century school.

Grant Ancestral Homestead

Ulysses Simpson Grant (1822-85) led Union forces to victory in the American Civil War and later served as the USA's 18th president for two terms from 1869 to 1877. His maternal grandfather, John Simpson, emigrated from County Tyrone to Pennsylvania in 1760, but the farm he left behind at Dergenah has now been restored in the style of a typical Ulster smallholding, as it would have been during the time of Grant's presidency.

The furnishings in the **Grant Ancestral Homestead** (Dergina, Ballygawley; admission free; ☻ 9am-5pm Mon-Sat) are not authentic, but the original field plan of the farm survives together with various old farming implements. There's also an exhibition on the American Civil War, a picnic area and children's playground. Check opening times by calling the Killymaddy tourist information centre (opposite).

The site is 20km west of Dungannon, south of the A4; look out for the signpost 5.5km west of Killymaddy tourist information centre.

Sleeping & Eating

Dungannon Park (☎ 8772 7327; dpreception@dungannon .gov.uk; Moy Rd; camp/caravan sites £8/12; ☻ Mar-Oct) This small (20 pitches) council-run camp site is in a quiet, wooded location complete with its own trout-fishing lake, 2.5km south of Dungannon on the A29 towards Moy and Armagh.

Grange Lodge (☎ 8778 4212; www.grangelodge countryhouse.com; 7 Grange Rd; s/d from £55/79, 4-course dinner £28; ℗) The five-room Grange is a period gem set in its own 20-acre grounds. Parts of the house, which is packed with antiques, date from 1698, though most is Georgian with Victorian additions. The landlady is an award-winning cook, and the Grange runs cookery courses. Dinner is available as long as you book at least 24 hours in advance. It's 5km southeast of Dungannon, signposted off the A29 Moy road.

our pick **Deli on the Green** (☎ 8775 1775; 2 Linen Green, Moygashel; mains £5-7; ☻ 10am-5pm Mon-Sat) Take a break from browsing the designer goodies in the Linen Green shops to relax over lunch in this stylish little bistro. As well as the sandwiches and salads on offer at the deli counter, there are succulent home-made steakburgers, seared salmon fillet with champ, Thai chicken curry and pasta with roast pepper, tomato, rocket and goat's cheese sauce.

Viscounts Restaurant (☎ 8775 3800; 10 Northland Row, Dungannon; mains £9-15; ☻ noon-9.30pm Mon-Fri, 12.30-9.30pm Sat & Sun) Set in a converted church, child-friendly Viscounts offers carvery lunches, snacks and á la carte dinners. You can feast on steaks, pasta, stir-fries and vegetarian dishes in a mock medieval setting of knights' armour, swords and jousting banners. Booking is advisable at weekends.

Getting There & Away

Dungannon's bus station is just southwest of the town centre; turn right, cross the bridge and follow Scotch St to reach the main square. Bus 261 runs from Belfast's Europa BusCentre to Dungannon (£7, one hour, hourly Monday to Saturday, two on Sundays) and continues to Enniskillen (£7, 1½ hours). Bus 273 travels from Belfast to Derry via Dungannon and Omagh (hourly Monday to Saturday, six on Sundays).

Bus 80 shuttles between Cookstown and Dungannon (£3, 45 minutes, hourly Monday to Friday, eight on Saturdays). Bus 278 runs from Coleraine to Dungannon (£7, 1½ hours, two a day Monday to Friday, one daily on Saturdays and Sundays) and continues to Armagh (£4, 30 minutes), Monaghan and Dublin.

DIRECTORY

Directory

CONTENTS

ACCOMMODATION

Sleeping entries are categorised by price and then preference, with our favourites first. Our favourites are selected because they have a little something – or in some cases, a lot of something – that makes that bit more memorable, but we've also endeavoured, where possible, to highlight properties that walk the green walk and are committed to eco-responsibility.

Rates are per *room* per night, unless otherwise stated: budget (under €60/£40), midrange (€60-150/£40-100) and top end (over €150/£100), and high-season rates are given throughout. Where a range of prices is given,

PRACTICALITIES

- Use the metric system for weights, measures, speed limits and most sign-posting, except for the old-style black-on-white ones, which still use miles.
- Use the PAL system for video recorders and players.
- Plug appliances into the three flat pin sockets for (220V, 50Hz AC) power supply.
- Get an insight into Irish life with one of the world's best newspapers the *Irish Times* or Ireland's biggest-selling *Irish Independent*.
- Relish Irish political satire in the fortnightly magazine *Phoenix*, or brush up on current affairs in *Magill* magazine.
- Check both sides of Northern Irish current affairs with loyalist tabloid *News Letter* or the pro-republican *Irish News*.
- TV addicts should tune into *Questions and Answers* (RTE 1), a hard-hitting current affairs programme on Monday nights; or catch a great documentary on TG4, the national Irish-language station (subtitles are available).
- Tune into RTE Radio One (88-90 FM or 567/729 MW) for culture and politics; Lyric FM (96-99 FM) for nonstop classical music; or Newstalk 106-108 (106-108 FM) for commercial daytime current affairs and chitchat.

it refers to rates for different rooms during high season. Prices tend to be cheaper off-peak. Room prices in Dublin are disproportionately high and can be double what you would pay elsewhere in the country.

The majority of accommodation providers increase their rates by up to 10% on 'special' weekends, ie bank holidays or during major sporting events. Hotels will often offer packages, especially in low season, for more than one night's stay including dinner, and it's also worth asking for a discount from the quoted rack rate (tourist board-approved rate) from Monday to Thursday. Ironically, in city hotels cheaper rates may apply at weekends, when their main corporate clients disappear.

In low season (November to March) you can simply call in or ring ahead in rural areas. In peak season it's best to book ahead. Fáilte Ireland (Irish Tourist Board) or the Northern Ireland Tourist Board (NITB) will book serviced accommodation for a fee of €4 (£2), or self-catering for €7 (£2). Make telephone bookings through their booking system **Gulliver Ireland** (in Ireland ☎ 1850 61 61 61, in UK ☎ 0800 096 8644, in USA ☎ 1 888 827 3028, from everywhere else insert freephone prefix before ☎ 6686 6866).

Much of the accommodation closes during Christmas and New Year, especially in rural areas, and most charge a supplement.

B&Bs

The ubiquitous bed and breakfasts are small, family-run houses, farmhouses and period country houses with fewer than five bedrooms. Standards vary enormously, but most have some bedrooms with bathroom

at a cost of roughly €35 to €40 (£20 to £25) per person per night. In luxurious B&Bs, expect to pay €55 (£38) or more per person. Facilities in budget-end B&Bs may be very limited: TVs, telephones, kettles and the like are the trappings of midrange to top-end establishments. Remember, outside big cities most B&Bs only accept cash.

Camping & Caravan Parks

Camping and caravan parks aren't as common in Ireland as they are in Britain or on the continent. Some hostels have camping space for tents and also offer house facilities, which makes them better value than the main camping grounds. At commercial parks the cost is typically somewhere between €12 and €20 (£7 and £10) for a tent and two people. Prices for camp sites in this book are for two people unless stated otherwise. Caravan sites cost around €15 to €25 (£11 to £15). Most parks only open from Easter to the end of September or October.

Guesthouses

Essentially, guesthouses are much like upmarket B&Bs. The difference lies in their size, with guesthouses having between six and 30 bedrooms. Prices vary enormously according to the standard but the minimum you can expect to shell out is €35 (£22) per person (€40 in Dublin), and up to about €100 (£35) in upmarket places. Unlike hotels, the majority of guesthouses are unlicensed but many have restaurants and good facilities, and can take credit-card payment.

WEBSITE ACCOMMODATION RESOURCES

www.allgohere.com This website lists accommodation suitable for travellers with (and without) a disability to Northern Ireland.

www.corkkerry.ie A useful resource for accommodation and information throughout the southwest.

www.daft.ie Online classified paper for short- and long-term rentals.

www.discovernorthernireland.com NITB's accommodation-booking site.

www.elegant.ie Specialises in self-catering castles, period houses and unique properties.

www.familyhomes.ie Lists, you guessed it, family-run guesthouses and self-catering properties.

www.gulliver.ie Fáilte Ireland and the Northern Ireland Tourist Board's (NITB) web-based accommodation reservation system.

www.hostelworld.com A useful website for comparing hostels and booking beds.

www.ireland.travel.ie Fáilte Ireland's accommodation-booking site.

www.irishlandmark.com Not-for-profit conservation group that rents self-catering properties of historical and cultural significance such as castles, gate lodges and lighthouses.

www.stayinireland.com Lists guesthouses and self-catering options.

SOMETHING DIFFERENT

An alternative to normal caravanning is to hire a horse-drawn caravan with which to wander the countryside. In high season you can hire one for around €800 a week. Search www.ireland.ie for a list of operators, or see www.irishhorsedrawncaravans.com.

Another unhurried and pleasurable way to see the countryside (with slightly less maintenance) is by barge on one of the country's canal systems. As above, contact Fáilte Ireland for a list of rental companies.

Another option is to hire a boat, which you can live aboard while cruising Ireland's inland waterways. One company offering boats for hire on the Shannon-Erne Waterway is **Emerald Star** (☎ 071-962 0234; www .emeraldstar.ie).

Hostels

The prices quoted in this book for hostel accommodation are for those aged over 18. A dorm bed in high season generally costs €13 to €25 (£8 to £14).

An Óige and Hostelling International Northern Ireland (HINI) are the two associations that belong to Hostelling International (HI). About half of the hostels have family and smaller rooms. An Óige has 23 hostels scattered around the Republic and HINI has six in the North.

An Óige (☎ 01-830 4555; www.irelandyha.org; 61 Mountjoy St, Dublin 7; ⏰ 9.30am-5.30pm Mon-Fri)

HINI (☎ 028-9032 4733, area code 048 if calling from Republic; www.hini.org.uk; 22-32 Donegall Rd, Belfast BT12 5JN; ⏰ 24hr)

Ireland also has a large number of independent hostels, some excellent, but many high on character and low on facilities. The following associations, with hostels in the Republic and in the North, do their best to offer reliable accommodation:

Independent Holiday Hostels of Ireland (IHH; ☎ 01-836 4700; www.hostels-ireland.com; 57 Lower Gardiner St, Dublin 1)

Independent Hostel Owners of Ireland (IHO; ☎ 074-973 0130; www.holidayhound.com/ihi; Dooey Hostel, Glencolumbcille, Co Donegal)

Hotels

Hotels range from the local pub to medieval castles, and prices fluctuate accordingly. It's often possible to negotiate better deals than the published rates, especially out of season and online. Payment usually includes breakfast, and most hotels have TV, and tea- and coffee-making facilities and phones. You may find that some offer better rates than guesthouses.

House Swapping

House swapping has become a popular and affordable way to visit a country and enjoy a real home away from home. There are several agencies in Ireland that, for an annual fee, facilitate international swaps. The fee pays for access to a website and a book giving house descriptions, photographs and the owner's details. After that, it's up to you to make arrangements. Sometimes use of the family car is included.

Homelink International House Exchange (☎ 01-846 2598; www.homelink.ie; 95 Bracken Dr, Portmarnock, Co Dublin)

Intervac International Holiday Service (☎ 041-983 7969; www.intervac.com; Drogheda, Co Dublin; ⏰ 7-9pm Mon-Fri)

Rental Accommodation

Self-catering accommodation is often rented on a weekly basis and usually means an apartment or house where you look after yourself. The rates vary from one region and season to another. Fáilte Ireland publishes a guide for registered self-catering accommodation or you can check the website (www.ireland .travel.ie).

ACTIVITIES

Activities open up Ireland in a way that can be both cheap and relaxing, and offer a unique experience of the country. See also p565.

Bird-Watching

The variety and size of the flocks that visit or breed in Ireland make it of particular interest to bird-watchers. It's also home to some rare and endangered species. For a description of some birds found in Ireland, see p72.

There are more than 70 reserves and sanctuaries in Ireland, but some aren't open to visitors and others are privately owned, so you'll need permission from the proprietors before entering.

More information can be obtained from the tourist boards and from the following organisations:

Birds of Ireland News Service (☎ 01-830 7364; www
.birdsireland.com; 36 Claremont Ct, Glasnevin, Dublin 11)
BirdWatch Ireland (☎ 01-281 9878; www.bird
watchireland.ie; Rockingham Hs, Newcastle, Co Wicklow)
Runs bird-watching field courses, all of which take place on
Cape Clear in County Cork.
National Parks & Wildlife Service (☎ 01-888 2000;
www.npws.ie; 7 Ely Pl, Dublin 2)
Royal Society for the Protection of Birds (RSPB;
☎ 028-9049 1547; www.rspb.org.uk; Belvoir Park Forest,
Belfast, BT8 4QT)

Some useful publications on bird-watching are
Dominic Couzens' *Collins Birds of Britain and
Ireland* and the slightly out-of-date *Where to
Watch Birds in Ireland* by Clive Hutchinson.

Cycling

The tourist boards can supply you with a list
of operators who organise cycling holidays.
For more on the practicalities of travelling
round Ireland with a bike, see p720.

Both **Irish Cycling Safaris** (☎ 01-260 0749; www
.cyclingsafaris.com; Belfield Bike Shop, UCD, Dublin 4) and
Go Ireland (☎ 066-976 2094; www.goactivities.com; Old
Orchard House, Killorglin, Co Kerry) organise tours for
groups of cyclists in the southwest, southeast,
Clare, Connemara, Donegal and Antrim.

Fishing

Ireland is justly famous for its generally free
coarse fishing, covering bream, pike, perch,
roach, rudd, tench, carp and eel. Killing of
pike over 6.6lb (3kg) in weight is prohibited,
anglers are limited to one pike and killing
of coarse fish is frowned upon; anglers are
encouraged to return coarse fish alive. Freshwater game fish include salmon, sea trout and
brown trout. Some managed fisheries also
stock rainbow trout.

The enormous Shannon and Erne river
systems, stretching southwards from Leitrim
and Fermanagh, are prime angling spots, and
Cavan, the 'Lake County', is a favourite with
hardcore fishermen. In the west, the great
lakes of Corrib, Mask and Conn have plenty
of lakeshore B&Bs, good sturdy boats and
knowledgeable boatmen. These lakes can be
dangerous, as they tend to be littered with
hidden rocks and shoals.

While Ireland is a land of opportunity
for the angler, intensive agriculture and
the growth of towns have brought about a
general reduction in water quality in many
areas, markedly so in some. Fáilte Ireland

and the NITB produce several information
leaflets on fishing, accommodation, events
and licences required.

Licences in the Republic are available
from the local tackle shop or direct from
the **Central Fisheries Board** (☎ 01-884 2600; www
.cfb.ie; Unit 4, Swords Business Campus, Balheary Rd,
Swords, Dublin).

In the North, rod licences for coarse and
game fishing are obtainable from the **Foyle,
Carlingford & Irish Lights Commission** (☎ 028-7134
2100; www.loughs-agency.org; 22 Victoria Rd, Londonderry)
for the Foyle and Carlingford areas, and
from the **Fisheries Conservancy Board** (☎ 028-
3833 4666; www.fcbni.com; 1 Mahon Rd, Portadown, Co Armagh) for all other regions. You also require
a permit from the owner, which is usually
the **Department of Culture, Arts & Leisure, Inland
Waterways & Inland Fisheries Branch** (☎ 028-9025
8863; 3rd fl, Interpoint, 20-24 York St, Belfast BT15 1AQ).

Golf

Contact Fáilte Ireland, the NITB, the **Golfing
Union of Ireland** (☎ 01-505 4000; www.gui.ie; Unit 8
Block G, Maynooth Business Campus, Maynooth, Co Kildare),
or the **Irish Ladies Golf Union** (☎ 01-269 6244; www
.ilgu.ie; 1 Clonskeagh Sq, Clonskeagh Rd, Dublin 14) for
information on golfing holidays.

Green fees, usually based on a per-day
basis, start from around €25 (£15) on weekdays, but top-notch places charge up to €300
(£180). Courses are tested for their level of
difficulty; many are playable year round,
especially links.

Hang-gliding & Paragliding

Some of the finest hang-gliding and pa-
ragliding in the country is found at Mount
Leinster (p183) in Carlow, Great Sugarloaf
Mountain in Wicklow, Benone and Magil-
ligan Beaches (p655) in Derry and Achill
Island (p454) in Mayo. Check the **Irish Hang
Gliding & Paragliding Association** (www.ihpa.ie) and
Ulster Hang Gliding & Paragliding Club's (www.uhpc
.co.uk) websites for local pilots.

Horse Riding

Unsurprisingly, considering the Irish passion
for horses, riding is a popular pastime. There
are dozens of centres throughout Ireland,
offering possibilities ranging from hiring a
horse for an hour (from €25/£15) to fully
packaged, residential equestrian holidays.

Recommended outfits are Canadian-based
Hidden Trails (www.hiddentrails.com) and **Ballycumisk**

DIRECTORY

Riding School (☎ 028-37246, 087 961 6969; Ballycumisk, Schull, Co Cork)

Walking

There are many superb walks in Ireland, including 31 'waymarked ways' or designated long-distance paths of varying lengths. There are, however, some issues that have made what should be some of the best walking in Europe a frustrating or even disappointing experience. Some trails run through miles and miles of tedious forestry tracks and bitumen roads. The ways are marked with signposts showing the standard yellow arrow and hiker – in theory at least: waymarking is often variable and in some cases totally nonexistent.

Ireland has a tradition of relatively free access to open country but the growth in the number of walkers and the carelessness of a few have made some farmers less obliging. Unfortunately it's not uncommon to find unofficial signs on gateways barring access, or physical barriers blocking ways. If you come across this problem, refer to the local tourist office.

Another problem is with accommodation, which isn't always easily accessible, and some completely bypass the best local scenery.

The maintenance and development of the ways is administered in the Republic by the **National Waymarked Ways Advisory Committee** (NWWAC; ☎ 01-860 8823; www.walkireland.ie; Irish Sports Council, Top fl, Block A Westend Office Park, Blanchardstown, Dublin 15) and in the North by **Countryside Access & Activities Network** (CAAN; ☎ 028-9030 3930; The Stableyard, Barnett's Demesne, Belfast).

Some useful guides are Lonely Planet's *Walking in Ireland*, Michael Fewer's *Irish Long-Distance Walks* or *Best Irish Walks* by Joss Lynam.

EastWest Mapping (☎ /fax 054-77835; eastwest@eircom.net) has good maps of long-distance walks in the Republic and the North.

Tim Robinson of **Folding Landscapes** (☎ 095-35886; tandmfl@iol.ie) produces superbly detailed maps of the Burren, the Aran Islands and Connemara. His and Joss Lynam's *Mountains of Connemara: A Hill Walker's Guide* contains a useful detailed map.

For mountain rescue call ☎ 999.

ORGANISED WALKS

If you don't have a travelling companion you could consider joining an organised walking group.

Go Ireland (☎ 066-976 2094; www.goactivities.com; Old Orchard House, Killorglin, Co Kerry) Offers walking tours of the west.

South West Walks Ireland (☎ 066-712 8733; www.southwestwalksireland.com; 6 Church St, Tralee, Co Kerry) Provides a series of guided and self-guided walking programmes around the southwest, northwest and Wicklow.

BEARA WAY

This moderately easy, 196km walk forms a loop around the delightful Beara Peninsula (p239) in West Cork. The peninsula is relatively unused to mass tourism and makes a pleasant contrast with the Iveragh Peninsula to the north.

Part of the walk, between Castletownbere and Glengarriff, follows the route taken by Donal O'Sullivan and his band after the English took his castle following an 11-day siege in 1602. At Glengarriff, O'Sullivan met up with other families and set out on a journey north, hoping to reunite with other remaining pockets of Gaelic resistance. Of the 1000 or so men who set out that winter, only 30 completed the trek.

The Beara Way mostly follows old roads and tracks and rarely rises above 340m. There's no official start or finish point and the route can be walked in either direction. It could easily be reduced to seven days by skipping Bere and Dursey Islands, and if you start at Castletownbere you could reach Kenmare in five days or less.

BURREN WAY

This 35km walk traverses the Burren (p388) limestone plateau in County Clare. It presents a strange, unique landscape to the walker. There's very little soil and few trees but a surprising abundance of flora. The way stretches between Ballyvaughan, on the northern coast of County Clare, and Liscannor to the southwest, taking in the village of Doolin, famous as a traditional-music centre. The trail south of Doolin to the dramatic Cliffs of Moher is a highlight of the route. From the cliffs a new path has been developed inland towards Liscannor (older maps may show a route, now closed, along the cliffs).

The best time for this walk is late spring or early summer. The route is pretty dry, but walking boots are useful as the limestone can be sharp.

CAVAN WAY

In the northwest of County Cavan the villages of Blacklion and Dowra are the ends of the 26km Cavan Way. The path runs northeast–southwest past a number of Stone Age monuments – court cairns, ring forts and tombs – through an area said to be one of the last strongholds of druidism. At the midpoint is the Shannon Pot, the official source of the River Shannon on the slopes of the Cuilcagh Mountains. From Blacklion it's mainly hill walking; from Shannon Pot to Dowra it's mainly road. The highest point on the walk is Giant's Grave (260m). You'll need OSNI map No 26 and the *Cavan Way* map guide. The route can be boggy, so take spare socks!

Dowra links up with the Leitrim Way, which runs between Manorhamilton and Drumshanbo.

DINGLE WAY

This 168km walk in County Kerry loops round one of the most beautiful peninsulas in the country (see p284). It takes eight days to complete, beginning and ending in Tralee, with an average daily distance of 21km. The first three days offer the easiest walk but the first day, from Tralee to Camp, is the least interesting; it could be skipped by taking the bus to Camp and starting from there.

EAST MUNSTER WAY

This 70km walk travels through forest and open moorland, along small country roads and a river towpath. It's clearly laid out with black markers bearing yellow arrows, and could be managed in three days, starting at Carrick-on-Suir (p318) in County Tipperary and finishing at Clogheen in County Waterford. The first day takes you to Clonmel, the second to Newcastle and the last to Clogheen. Look out for new signposts between Carrick and Killeshin, where part of the badly eroded path has recently been rerouted.

KERRY WAY

The 214km Kerry Way is the Republic's longest waymarked footpath and is usually walked anticlockwise. It starts and ends in Killarney (p328) and stáys inland for the first three days, winding through the spectacular Macgillycuddy's Reeks (p255) and past 1041m Mt Carrantuohil, Ireland's highest mountain, before continuing around the Ring of Kerry (p258) coast through

---

MORE WALKS IN IRELAND

- The Wicklow Way – Glendalough To Aughrim (p155), County Wicklow
- The Great Sugarloaf (p161), County Wicklow
- Mt Seefin (p239), County Cork
- Reeks Ridge (p257), County Kerry
- Mt Brandon (p292), County Kerry
- Tipperary Heritage Way (p314), County Tipperary
- South Leinster Way (p336), County Kilkenny
- Killary Harbour (p435), County Galway
- Inisheer (p423), County Galway
- Blue Stack Mountains (p509), County Donegal
- Slieve Donard (p628), County Down
- Fair Head (p669), County Antrim
- Causeway Coast (p666), County Antrim
- The Cliffs Of Magho (p686), County Fermanagh
- Cuilcagh Mountain via the Legnabrocky Trail (p688), County Fermanagh

---

Cahirciveen, Waterville, Caherdaniel, Sneem and Kenmare.

You could complete the walk in about 10 days, provided you're up to a good 20km per day. With less time it's worth walking the first three days, as far as Glenbeigh, from where a bus or a lift could return you to Killarney.

Accommodation isn't a problem, but you need to book in July and August. In contrast, places to eat aren't common, so consider carrying your own food.

MOURNE TRAIL

The Mourne Trail is actually the southeastern section of the Ulster Way, south of Belfast, and runs from Newry (p631), around the Mourne Mountains (p627), to the seaside resort of Newcastle (p625) and then on to Strangford (p624), where you can take a ferry across to Portaferry (p616) and continue north to Newtownards (p618). From Newry to Strangford is a distance of 106km, which could probably be managed in four or five days.

There's gorgeous mountain, forest and coastal scenery along the way and, once you've left Newry, not many built-up areas to spoil the views. Provided you're reasonably fit and well shod, this is not an especially difficult route to walk, although it does climb as high as 559m at Slievemoughanmore, the highest point on the Ulster Way.

SLIEVE BLOOM WAY

Close to the geographical centre of Ireland, the Slieve Bloom Way is a 77km trail through Counties Offaly and Laois. It does a complete circuit of the Slieve Bloom Mountains (p356) taking in most major points of interest. The trail follows tracks, forest firebreaks and old roads, and crosses the Mountrath–Kinnitty and Mountrath–Clonaslee roads. The trail's highest point is at Glendine Gap (460m). The recommended starting point is the car park at Glenbarrow, 5km from Rosenallis.

Camping in state forests is forbidden, but there's plenty of open space outside the forest for tents; otherwise, accommodation en route is almost nonexistent. There is no public transport to the area, although buses do stop in the nearby towns of Mountrath and Rosenallis.

SOUTH LEINSTER WAY

The tiny village of Kildavin in County Carlow, just southwest of Clonegal on the slopes of Mt Leinster, is the northern starting point of the 100km South Leinster Way, which winds through Counties Carlow and Kilkenny. It follows remote mountain roads and river towpaths through the medieval villages of Borris (p352), Graiguenamanagh (p336), Inistioge (p335), Mullinavat and Piltown to the finish post at Carrick-on-Suir (p318) just inside the Tipperary border. The southerly section is not as scenic as the rest, but the low hills have their own charm and on a sunny day they offer fine views south over the Suir Valley and Waterford Harbour.

The way leads in a generally southwestward direction but could easily be done the opposite way. It should take four or five days, depending on whether you stop over in Graiguenamanagh.

Much of it is above 500m and the weather can change quickly: good walking boots, outdoor gear and emergency supplies are essential.

ULSTER WAY: NORTHEASTERN SECTION

The Ulster Way makes a circuit around the six counties of Northern Ireland and Donegal. In total the footpath covers just more than 900km, so walking all of it might take five weeks. However, it can easily be broken down into smaller sections that could be attempted during a short stay. The scenery along the way varies enormously, encompassing dramatic coastal views, gentler lakeside country and the mountainous inland terrain of the Mourne Mountains.

Some of the most spectacular scenery lies along the 165km northeastern section, which begins unpromisingly in Belfast's western suburbs, then follows the Glens of Antrim (p668) and the glorious Causeway Coast (p666), a Unesco World Heritage site. It can be completed in six or seven days. The stretch of coast immediately surrounding the Giant's Causeway is likely to be busy, especially in high summer, when you should book accommodation well ahead.

Walking this stretch of coast shouldn't be beyond most averagely fit and sensibly equipped people, but rockfalls along the coast can occasionally obstruct stretches of it. While some stretches of this walk can seem wonderfully wild, you're never going to be that far from civilisation.

ULSTER WAY: DONEGAL SECTION

The main Ulster Way crosses into Donegal at the small pilgrimage town of Pettigo on Lough Erne, but then circles straight back to Rosscor in Northern Ireland. A spur – also confusingly called the Ulster Way – cuts north across the central moorlands of Donegal to Falcarragh on the northern coast. In all, if you follow the spur, this stretch of walk is 111km long, which means it can be walked in four or five days. Bear in mind, however, that much of central Donegal is bleak, boggy terrain where walking can be tough, especially if the weather's bad – which it often is! Although the walking-man symbol sometimes appears on markers, in general you'll be looking out for white-painted posts which simply tell you that you're heading in the right direction.

This stretch of the Ulster Way is intended for wilderness lovers. Some of the scenery en route is truly magnificent: you pass the Blue Stack (p509) and Derryveagh Mountains and the 752m Mt Errigal (p529), Donegal's highest peak. The route also skirts the glorious

Glenveagh National Park (p530), where you might want to break your journey. There are few dramatic historic remains to distract you, but plenty of minor prehistoric burial sites.

WICKLOW WAY

Opened in 1982, the popular 132km Wicklow Way (www.wicklowway.com) was Ireland's first long-distance trail. Despite its name, it actually starts in southern Dublin and ends in Clonegal in County Carlow, although for most of the way it travels through Wicklow. From its beginnings in Marlay Park, Rathfarnham, in southern Dublin, the trail quickly enters a mountain wilderness (the highest point is White Hill at 633m). A mixture of forest walks, sheep paths, bog roads and mountain passes join up to provide a spectacular walk that passes by Glencree (p150), Powerscourt Estate (p148), Djouce Mountain, Luggala, Glenmacnass (p151), Glendalough (p152), Glenmalure (p156) and Aghavannagh.

Some sections are desolate, especially south of Laragh, with much of the trail above 500m. The weather can change quickly, so good walking boots, outdoor gear and emergency supplies are essential. There are many worthwhile detours: up Glenmacnass to the waterfall or up to the summit of Lugnaquilla Mountain, for example.

It can be done in either direction, though most walkers start in Dublin. For the entire trail, allow eight to 10 days, plus time for diversions. Breaking the journey at Laragh, just under halfway, would let you visit the monastic site at Glendalough and do some local walks. Because of the way's popularity, walking outside the busy June to August period is advisable. Camping is possible along the route, but ask permission from local farmers. In peak season you should book accommodation in advance, and if you're hostelling you'll need to carry food with you.

Some parts of the route such as the Derrybawn Ridge are badly eroded, and the National Park Service asks walkers to avoid these areas to prevent further damage. **EastWest Mapping** (☎ /fax 054-77835; eastwest@eircom.net) produced a new edition of a map guide to the Wicklow Way in 2005, with all changes and updates to the route included.

Rock Climbing

Ireland's mountain ranges aren't high – Mt Carrantuohil in Kerry's Macgillycuddy's

Reeks is the tallest mountain in Ireland at only 1041m – but they're often beautiful and offer some excellent climbing possibilities (see p266). The highest mountains are in the southwest.

Adventure centres around the country run courses and organise climbing trips. For further information contact the **Mountaineering Council of Ireland** (☎ 01-625 1115; www.mountaineering .ie), which also publishes climbing guides and the quarterly magazine *Irish Mountain Log*, or check www.climbing.ie.

Water Sports

With a staggering 3100km of coastline, and numerous rivers and lakes, Ireland provides plenty of opportunities for water sports.

CANOEING

Ireland's indented coastline makes it ideal for exploring by canoe. The type of canoeing in Ireland and degree of difficulty varies from gentle paddling to white-water canoeing and canoe surfing. The best time for white water is winter, when the heavier rainfall swells the rivers.

Check out the **Irish Canoe Union** (☎ 01-625 1105; www.irishcanoeunion.com).

SAILING

There is a long history of sailing in Ireland and the country has more than 120 yacht and sailing clubs, including the **Royal Cork Yacht Club** (☎ 021-483 1023; office@royalcork.com) at Crosshaven, which was established in 1720 and is the world's oldest. The most popular areas for sailing are the southwestern coast, especially between Cork Harbour and the Dingle Peninsula; the Kerry coastline; the coast of Antrim; along the sheltered coast north and south of Dublin; and some of the larger lakes such as Loughs Derg, Erne and Gill.

The **Irish Association for Sail Training** (☎ 01-605 1621; www.irishmarinefederation.com) watches over professional schools, and the national governing body is the **Irish Sailing Association** (☎ 01-280 0239; www.sailing.ie). A recommended publication, available from most booksellers, is *Irish Cruising Club Sailing Directions*. It contains details of port facilities, harbour plans and coast and tidal information.

SCUBA DIVING

Ireland has some of the best scuba diving in Europe, almost entirely off the western coast among its offshore islands and rocks. The best period for diving is roughly March to October. Visibility averages more than 12m but can increase to 30m on good days. For more details about scuba diving in Ireland, contact Comhairle Fó-Thuinn (CFT), the **Irish Underwater Council** (☎ 01-284 4601; www.scubaireland .com), Ireland's diving regulatory body, which publishes the dive magazine *SubSea* (also available online).

Divecology (☎ 028-28943; www.divecology.com; Cooradarrigan, Schull, Co Cork) is a good dive school, with trips to local wrecks.

SWIMMING & SURFING
Ireland has some magnificent coastline and some great sandy beaches: the cleaner, safer ones have EU Blue Flag awards. Get a list from the government agency **An Taisce** (☎ 01-454 1786; www.antaisce.org; Tailors' Hall, Back Lane, Dublin 8) or online at www.blueflag.org.

Surfers should visit www.surfingireland .net or www.victorkilo.com for beach reports and forecasts. Women should check out **Surf Honeys** (www.surfhoneys.com), which runs all-girl surfing lessons in Sligo 'to put the girl in the curl'! **Donegal Adventure Centre** (☎ 074-984 2418; www.donegal-holidays.com; Bay View Ave, Bundoran, Co Donegal) is an excellent youth-oriented surf school and **Bundoran Surf Co** (☎ 984 1968; www.bundoransurf co.com; Bundoran, Co Donegal) conduct surf lessons, kite-surfing and power-kiting.

The best months for surfing in Ireland, when the swells are highest, are September (when the water is warmest because of the Gulf Stream) and October. Some of the best locations are on the south and southwest coasts, for example Tramore (p192) in Waterford, and there are also big surfing schools in Sligo (p441) and Donegal (p511), where you can also have a blast at kite-surfing.

See also p511.

WATER-SKIING
There are water-ski clubs all over Ireland offering tuition, equipment and boats. A full list is available from the **Irish Water Ski Federation** (www.iwsf.ie).

WINDSURFING
The windsurfer has plenty of locations to indulge in this popular sport – even on the Grand Canal in Dublin! The western coast is the most challenging and the least crowded. The bay at Rosslare (see p174) County Wexford is ideal for windsurfing, with equipment and tuition available in summer. The **Irish Sailing Association** (☎ 01-280 0239; www.sailing.ie) is the sport's governing authority and has details of centres.

BUSINESS HOURS
The standard business hours are generally the same for both the Republic and Northern Ireland and are shown below, with any variations noted:

Banks 10am to 4pm (to 5pm Thursday) Monday to Friday
Offices 9am to 5pm Monday to Friday
Post offices Northern Ireland 9am to 5.30pm Monday to Friday, 9am to 12.30pm Saturday; Republic 9am to 6pm Monday to Friday, 9am to 1pm Saturday. Smaller post offices may close at lunch and one day a week.
Pubs Northern Ireland 11.30am to 11pm Monday to Saturday, 12.30pm to 10pm Sunday. Pubs with late licences open until 1am Monday to Saturday, and midnight Sunday; Republic 10.30am to 11.30pm Monday to Thursday, 10.30am to 12.30am Friday and Saturday, noon to 11pm Sunday (30 min 'drinking up' time allowed). Pubs with bar extensions open to 2.30am Thursday to Saturday; closed Christmas Day and Good Friday.
Restaurants Noon to 10.30pm; many close one day of the week.
Shops 9am to 5.30pm or 6pm Monday to Saturday (until 8pm on Thursday and sometimes Friday), noon to 6pm Sunday in bigger towns only. Shops in rural towns may close at lunch and one day a week.
Tourist offices 9am to 5pm Monday to Friday, 9am to 1pm Saturday. Many extend their hours in summer, and open fewer hours/days or close October to April.

CHILDREN
Successful travel with young children requires effort, but can be done. Try not to overdo things and consider using some sort of self-catering accommodation. It's sometimes easier to eat in (or to at least have the option), rather than be restricted by the relatively confined space of a hotel or B&B room. On the whole you'll find that restaurants and hotels, especially in the countryside, will go out of their way to cater for you and your children – with the exception of a few places, generally in the capital, where children aren't allowed after 6pm. Children are allowed in pubs until 7pm.

Most attractions sell cheaper family tickets, and family passes are available on public transport. It's always a good idea to talk to fellow travellers with (happy) children and locals on the road for tips on where to go. For further general information see Lonely Planet's *Travel with Children* by Cathy Lanigan.

Practicalities

Most hotels will provide cots at no extra charge and restaurants will have high chairs. Car seats (around €50/£25 per week) are mandatory for children in hire cars between the ages of nine months and four years. Bring your own seat for infants under about nine months as only larger forward-facing child seats are generally available. Remember not to place baby seats in the front if the car has an airbag.

Remarkably, nappy-changing facilities are scarce, even in city centres.

Ireland has one of the lowest rates of breast-feeding in the world; nevertheless you should be able to feed your baby in all but a few public places without jaws dropping.

Two great websites are www.eumom.ie for pregnant women and parents with young children, and www.babygoes2.com, which is an excellent travel site about family-friendly accommodation worldwide.

CLIMATE CHARTS

Thanks to the moderating effect of the Atlantic Gulf Stream, Ireland's climate is relatively mild for its latitude, with a mean annual temperature of around 10°C. The temperature drops below freezing only intermittently during winter, and snow is scarce – perhaps one or two brief flurries a year. The coldest months are January and February, when daily temperatures range from 4° to 8°C, with 7°C the average. In summer, temperatures during the day are a comfortable 15° to 20°C. During the warmest months, July and August, the average is 16°C. A hot summer's day in Ireland is 22° to 24°C, although it can sometimes reach 30°C. There are about 18 hours of daylight daily during July and August and it's only truly dark after about 11pm.

One thing you can be sure of about Irish weather is how little you can be sure of. It may be shirtsleeves and sunglasses in February, but winter woollies in March and even during the summer.

And then there's the rain. Ireland receives a lot of rain, with certain areas getting a soaking as many as 270 days of the year. County Kerry is the worst affected. The southeast is the driest, enjoying a more continental climate.

See also p20 for information about when to go.

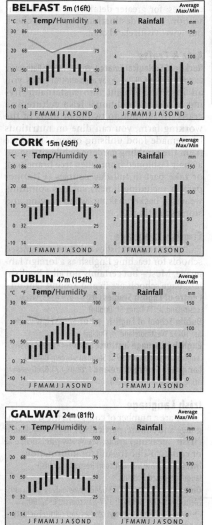

COURSES

There are a myriad of courses in Ireland, from archery classes to learning how to play the harp. Adventure Centres, where you can do everything from hill-walking to raft-building, are increasingly popular and we have listed them throughout the book. For cookery courses – an increasingly popular pastime – check out the Food & Drink chapter (p69). Below we have included only guidelines to courses; for greater details, see the relevant sections in the destination chapters or check out www.visitireland.com.

Arts & Crafts

Rockfield Ecological Estate (☎ 043-76025; Rathowen; tour €10, mains €20-25; ❤ by appointment) gives you an inspiring insight into sustainable living as well as traditional Irish culture and crafts. In addition to two-hour tours of the working farm, you can dine on nutritious homemade food utilising organic produce from the rambling gardens (while sitting on a chair fashioned from fallen tree branches); or take part in full-day courses (€100 per person including lunch) such as spinning, weaving, basket making, wood carving and stone sculpting.

English Language

Fáilte Ireland publishes a list of recognised schools for teaching English as a foreign language. Most – but certainly not all – English-language schools are in and around Dublin.

Centre of English Studies (☎ 01-671 4233; www .cesireland.ie; 31 Dame St, Dublin)
Dublin School of English (☎ 01-677 3322; www.dse .ie; 10-12 Westmoreland St, Dublin)
English Language Institute (☎ 01-475 2965; www .englishlanguage.com; 99 St Stephen's Green, Dublin)
Language Centre of Ireland (☎ 01-671 6266; www .lci.ie; 45 Kildare St, Dublin)

Irish Language

There are a number of courses in the Irish language and culture, particularly in the Gaeltacht (Irish-speaking) areas; see www.gaelsaoire.ie or contact Fáilte Ireland for information.

Intercelt (www.intercelt.com) Resource for Irish language-based holidays.
Oideas Gael (☎ 074-973 0248; www.oideas-gael.com; Glencolumbcille, Donegal; 3-/7-day courses €95/190; ❤ Mar-Sep) Irish language courses and cultural activity holidays.

Meditation

Jampa Ling Buddhist Centre (☎ 952 3448; www.jampa ling.org; Owendoon House, Bawnboy; dm/s/d incl meals €32/39/68) offers meditation courses. See p483 for details.

Music

In July and August, **Dingle Music School** (☎ 086-319 0438; Dykegate Lane, Kerry) offers beginners' workshops in bodhrán (from €12; noon Tues-day, Wednesday and Thursday, 11am on Saturday) and tin whistle (€25, 11am Monday). Bodhráns are supplied.

Harp workshops are conducted as part of the O'Carolan International Harp Festival & Summer School. See p491 for details.

CUSTOMS

Duty-free sales are not available when travelling within the EU. Goods for personal consumption bought in and exported within the EU incur no additional taxes, if duty has been paid somewhere in the EU. Over certain limits you may have to show that they are for personal use. The amounts that officially constitute personal use are 3200 cigarettes (or 400 cigarillos, 200 cigars or 3kg of tobacco) and either 10L of spirits, 20L of fortified wine, 60L of sparkling wine, 90L of still wine or 110L of beer. There's no customs inspection apart from those concerned with drugs and national security.

Travellers coming from outside the EU are allowed to import duty free 200 cigarettes, 1L of spirits or 2L of wine, 60ml of perfume and 250ml of *eau de toilette*.

Dogs and cats from anywhere outside Ireland and the UK are subject to strict quarantine laws. The EU Pet Travel Scheme, whereby animals are fitted with a microchip, vaccinated against rabies and blood tested six months *prior* to entry, is in force in the UK and the Republic of Ireland. No preparation or documentation is necessary for the movement of pets directly between the UK and the Republic. Contact the **Department of Agriculture, Food & Rural Development** (☎ 01-607 2000) in Dublin for further details.

DANGERS & ANNOYANCES

Ireland is safer than most countries in Europe, but normal precautions should be observed. In Dublin, drug-related crime is quite common and the city has its fair share of pickpockets and thieves (see p90).

Dublin is particularly notorious for car break-ins, and insurance policies often don't cover losses from cars.

Northern Ireland is as safe as anywhere else, but there are areas where the sectarian divide is bitterly pronounced, most notably in parts of Belfast. For the foreseeable future, it's probably best to ensure your visit to Northern Ireland doesn't coincide with the climax of the Orange marching season on 12 July; sectarian passions are usually inflamed and even many Northerners leave the province.

DISCOUNT CARDS
Heritage Discounts
Heritage Card (☎ 01-647 6587; www.heritageireland .com; Visitor Services, 51 St Stephen's Green, Dublin 2; adult/child & student/family €21/8/55) Entitles you to free access to over 75 sites for one year.

National Trust (☎ 0870 458 4000; www.national trust.org.uk; adult/under 25/family £43.50/19.50/77.50; Membership Dept, PO Box 39, Warrington WA5 7WD, UK) Entitles you to free admission to its 18 properties in Northern Ireland, but only really makes financial sense if you're touring its English sites too.

Senior Cards
Senior citizens are entitled to many discounts in Ireland on things such as public transport and museum admission fees, provided they show proof of age. The minimum qualifying age is usually 60 to 65 for men and 55 to 65 for women. In your home country, a lower age may already entitle you to travel packages and discounts (on car hire, for instance).

Car hire companies usually won't rent to drivers aged over 70 or 75.

Student & Youth Cards
The International Student Identity Card (ISIC; www.isiccard.com) gets discounts on transport, commercial goods and services, and admission to theatres, cinemas, museums and sights. The International Youth Travel Card (IYTC; www.isiccard.com) and European Youth Card (Euro<26 card; www .euro26.org) offer similar discounts for non-students under 26. All these cards are issued by hostelling organisations, student unions and student travel agencies.

EMBASSIES & CONSULATES
Irish Embassies & Consulates
Irish diplomatic offices overseas:

Australia Embassy (☎ 02-6273 3022; irishemb@cyberone.com.au; 20 Arkana St, Yarralumla, Canberra, ACT 2600)

Canada Embassy (☎ 613-233 6281; ottawaembassy@dfa .ie; 130 Albert St, Suite 1105, Ottawa, Ontario K1P 5G4)

France Embassy (☎ 01 44 17 67 00; paris@dfa.ie; 4 rue Rude, 75116 Paris)

Germany Embassy (☎ 030-220 720; Friedrichstrasse 200, 10117 Berlin)

Italy Embassy (☎ 06 697 9121; www.ambasciata-irlanda .it; Piazza di Campitelli 3, 00186 Rome)

Netherlands Embassy (☎ 070-363 09 93; www.irish embassy.nl; Dr Kuyperstraat 9, 2514 BA The Hague)

New Zealand Consulate (☎ 09-977 2256; consul@ireland.co.nz; Level 7, Citibank Bldg, 23 Customs Street East, Auckland)

UK Embassy (☎ 020-7235 2171; 17 Grosvenor Pl, London SW1X 7HR); Consulate (☎ 0131-226 7711; 16 Randolph Crescent, Edinburgh EH3 6TT); Consulate (☎ 029-2066 2000; Brunel House, 2 Fitzalan Rd, Cardiff CF24 0EB)

USA Embassy (☎ 202-462 3939; www.irelandemb.org; 2234 Massachusetts Ave, NW, Washington, DC 20008) There are also consulates in Boston, Chicago, New York and San Francisco.

United Kingdom (for Northern Ireland) diplomatic offices abroad:

Australia High Commission (☎ 02-6270 6666; www.britaus .net; Commonwealth Ave, Yarralumla, Canberra, ACT 2600)

Canada High Commission (☎ 613-237 1530; general enquiries@BritaininCanada.org; 80 Elgin St, Ottawa, Ontario K1P 5K7)

France Embassy (☎ 01 44 51 31 00; www.amb-grande-bretagne.fr; 35 rue du Faubourg St Honoré, 75383 Paris)

Germany Embassy (☎ 030-204 570; Wilhelmstrasse 70, 10117 Berlin)

Italy Embassy (☎ 06 4220 0001; www.britain.it; Via XX Settembre 80a, 00187 Rome)

Netherlands Embassy (☎ 070-427 04 27; www.britain .nl; Lange Voorhout 10, 2514 ED The Hague)

New Zealand High Commission (☎ 04-924 2888; www .britain.org.nz; 44 Hill St, Wellington)

USA Embassy (☎ 202-588 6500; www.britainusa.com; 3100 Massachusetts Ave NW, Washington, DC 20008)

Embassies & Consulates in Ireland
If you're even remotely responsible for any kind of trouble, your country's embassy won't be of any help to you – you're bound by Irish (and in the North, British) law. In genuine emergencies you might get some assistance: a free ticket is exceedingly unlikely but embassies might assist you with getting a new passport.

The following countries have embassies in Dublin:

Australia (☎ 01-664 5300; www.australianembassy.ie; 2nd fl, Fitzwilton House, Wilton Tce, Dublin 2)

Canada (☎ 01-417 4100; 4th fl, 65-68 St Stephen's Green, Dublin 2)

France (☎ 01-277 5000; chancellerie@ambafrance.ie; 36 Ailesbury Rd, Dublin 4)

Germany (☎ 01-269 3011; germany@indigo.ie; 31 Trimleston Ave, Booterstown, Blackrock, Co Dublin)

TRACING YOUR ANCESTORS

Many visitors come to Ireland purely to track down their Irish roots. Success in this activity is more likely if you have managed to obtain some basic facts about your Irish ancestors before leaving home. The names of your ancestors who left Ireland and their approximate dates of birth are essential, but it's also helpful to know the ancestors' counties and parishes of origin in Ireland, their religious denomination, and their parents' and spouses' names.

Good starting points for research in Ireland are the **National Library** (☎ 01-603 0200; www.nli .ie; Kildare St, Dublin 2); the **National Archives** (☎ 01-407 2300; www.nationalarchives.ie; Bishop St, Dublin 8); and the **Public Record Office of Northern Ireland** (Proni; ☎ 028-9025 5905; http://proni.nics.gov.uk; 66 Balmoral Ave, Belfast). Other helpful resources include the **General Register Office** (☎ 090-663 2900; www.groireland.ie; Government Offices, Convent Rd, Roscommon) and **General Register Office Northern Ireland** (☎ 028-9025 2000; www.groni.gov.uk; Oxford House, 49/55 Chichester St, Belfast). These agencies hold records of births, deaths and marriages in Ireland.

There are also numerous agencies and individuals that will do the research for you for a fee. For information on these, contact the **Association of Professional Genealogists in Ireland** (APGI; c/o The Honorary Secretary, 30 Harlech Cres, Clonskeagh, Dublin 14). In the North also contact the **Association of Ulster Genealogists & Record Agents** (Augra; c/o The Honorary Secretary, Glen Cottage, Glenmachan Rd, Belfast BT4 2NP).

Dozens of books are available on Irish genealogy. Tony McCarthy's *Irish Roots Guide* is a good introduction to the subject, and John Grenham's *Tracing Your Irish Ancestors* is an excellent comprehensive guide. North Americans in particular benefit from *A Genealogists Guide to Discovering Your Irish Ancestors* by Dwight Radford and Kyle Betit.

Italy (☎ 01-660 1744; info@italianembassy.ie; 63-65 Northumberland Rd, Ballsbridge, Dublin 4)
Netherlands (☎ 01-269 3444; info@netherlandsembassy.ie; 160 Merrion Rd, Ballsbridge, Dublin 4)
UK (☎ 01-205 3700; www.britishembassy.ie; 29 Merrion Rd, Ballsbridge, Dublin 4)
USA (☎ 01-668 8777; webmasterireland@state.gov; 42 Elgin Rd, Ballsbridge, Dublin 4)

The following countries have consular representation in Northern Ireland:
Germany (☎ 028-9024 4113; Chamber of Commerce House, 22 Great Victoria St, Belfast)
Netherlands (☎ 028-9077 9088; c/o All-Route Shipping Ltd, 14-16 West Bank Rd, Belfast)
USA (☎ 028-9038 6100; Danesfort House, 223 Stranmillis Rd, Belfast)

FESTIVALS & EVENTS

There are literally hundreds of festivals held throughout the year, but the summer months are the most popular; listed is a thumbnail sketch of the major events. Local tourist offices will have additional information. Also, the Association of Irish Festival Events (AOIFE) maintains a very useful website at www.aoifeonline.com; www.art.ie is worth perusing too. For regional festivals, see destination chapters.

FEBRUARY
Jameson Dublin International Film Festival
(☎ 872 1122; www.dubliniff.com) The island's biggest film festival, with local flicks, arty international films and advance releases of mainstream movies, runs during the last two weeks of the month.

MARCH
St Patrick's Day (17 March; ☎ 01-676 3205; www.st patricksday.ie) Ireland erupts into one giant celebration on 17 March. The biggest beano is in Dublin, where the streets reverberate to a cacophony of parades, fireworks and light shows for five days around 17 March. Over 250,000 attend. Cork, Armagh and Belfast also have parades; elsewhere festivities are less ostentatious.

APRIL
Irish Grand National (www.fairyhouseracecourse.ie) The showcase race in the national hunt season takes place at the County Meath racetrack on Easter Monday.
World Irish Dancing Championships (☎ 01-475 2220) About 4000 dancers from all over the globe compete in late March or early April. The location varies from year to year.

MAY
Cork International Choral Festival (☎ 021-421 5125; www.corkchoral.ie) One of Europe's premier choral festivals, with the winners going on to the Fleischmann International Trophy Competition; held over four days from the first Monday of May.

North West 200 (www.northwest200.org) Ireland's most famous road race is also the country's biggest outdoor sporting events; 150,000-plus line the triangular route to cheer on some of the biggest names in motorcycle racing. It is run in mid-May.

Irish Open Golf Championship (☎ 01-505 4000; www.irishopenatadaremanor.ie) Not as prestigious as the European Open, but still manages to attract its fair share of top European names. Played mid-May at Adare Manor, County Limerick, until 2010.

Fleadh Nua (☎ 01-280 0295; www.comhaltas.ie) Absorbing week of traditional music as Ennis, County Clare hosts one of the country's most important festivals during the third week of the month.

Cat Laughs (☎ 056-7763837; www.thecatlaughs.com) Kilkenny gets very, very funny from late May into early June for the country's best comedy festival, attracting the cream of local and international talent.

JUNE

Irish Derby (☎ 045-441205; www.curragh.ie) The best flat race in the country is run during the first week of the month at the County Kildare course; a great occasion for racing fans and people with fancy hats.

Bloomsday (☎ 878 8547; www.jamesjoyce.ie) Edwardian dress and breakfast of 'the inner organs of beast and fowl' are but two of the elements of the Dublin festival celebrating the day in which Joyce's *Ulysses* takes place; the real highlight is retracing Leopold Bloom's daily steps.

Wexford Opera Festival (☎ 053-912 2400; www.wexfordopera.com) Ireland's premier festival of classical music and opera runs for two weeks in early June in Johnstown Castle.

JULY

All-Ireland Open Dance Championships (☎ 091-632338; www.allirelanddancing.ie) From foxtrots to tangos, the best of Irish formal dancing in Gort, County Galway, over the first weekend of the month.

Willie Clancy Summer School (☎ 065-708 4281; www.setdancingnews.net/wcss/) Six days of intense traditional music workshops, gigs and pub sessions in Milltown Malbay, County Clare; the best players in the world generally show up.

Oxegen (www.mcd.ie) Two-day super-gig in mid-July at Punchestown Racecourse in County Kildare with heavy-weight headline acts.

Galway Film Fleadh (☎ 091-751655; www.galwayfilmfleadh.com) Irish and international releases make up the programme at one of the country's premier film festivals, held in early July.

Galway Arts Festival (☎ 091-509700; www.galwayartsfestival.ie) The most important arts festival in the country sees Galway City go mental for the last two weeks of the month, with lots of music and drama to go with the merriment.

O'Carolan International Harp Festival & Summer School (☎ 071- 964 7204; www.keadue.harp.net) Week-long festival in the Central North celebrating the blind composer of the tune to 'The Star-Spangled Banner'. Late July to Early August. See p491 for details.

AUGUST

Electric Picnic (☎ 01-478 9093; www.electricpicnic.ie) A boutique festival of alternative music in the grounds of Stradbally Hall, County Laois, in late August. Comedy, art, & a strong eco-friendly buzz complement the terrific music.

Féile An Phobail West Belfast (☎ 048-9031 3440; www.feilebelfast.com) Europe's largest community arts festival takes place on the Falls Rd in West Belfast over two weeks.

Fleadh Cheoil nah Éireann (☎ 01-280 0295; www.comhaltas.ie) The mother of all Irish music festivals attracts in excess of 250,000 to whatever town is playing host; it usually takes place over a week toward the end of the month.

Galway Races (☎ 091-753870; www.galwayraces.com) The biggest horse racing festival west of the Shannon draws massive crowds for the Irish equivalent of the Cheltenham Festival; it is held the first week of the month.

Mary from Dungloe (☎ 074-952 1254; www.maryfromdungloe.com) Ireland's second-most important beauty pageant takes place in Dungloe, County Donegal at the beginning of the month – it's really an excuse for a giant party but the girls really do want to be crowned the year's 'Mary.'

Puck Fair (☎ 066-976 2366; www.puckfair.ie) Three days of what must be one of the quirkiest festivals in Europe, as Killorglin, County Kerry, celebrates the crowning of a goat amidst plenty of mayhem in mid-August.

Rose of Tralee (www.roseoftralee.ie) The County Kerry town plays host to *the* Irish beauty pageant which attracts women with Irish links from all over the world. For everyone else, it's just an opportunity to drink, dance and have fun. It's held in the third week of the month.

SEPTEMBER

Lisdoonvarna Matchmaking Festival (☎ 065-707 4005; www.matchmakerireland.com) The County Clare town hosts this famous festival that attracts hopefuls from all over; it's all a bit of fun throughout the month.

Dublin Fringe Festival (☎ 01-872 9016; www.fringefest.com) Comedy and alternative fringe theatre precedes the main theatre festival and is often a hell of a lot more fun. It runs for two weeks from late September to early October.

Ballinasloe Horse Fair (☎ 090-964 3453; www.ballinasloe.com) Europe's oldest horse fair in this Galway town comes with a 10-day family festival that is a highlight of the calendar.

OCTOBER

Dublin Theatre Festival (☎ 01-677 8439; www.dub lintheatrefestival.com) The cream of Irish theatre festivals sees all manner of theatrics at most venues in the capital.

Cork Film Festival (☎ 021-427 1711; www.corkfilm fest.org) With a strong emphasis on local and short films, this excellent festival is held in Cork's three cinemas in early October.

Cork Jazz Festival (www.corkjazzfestival.com) Over the last weekend of the month the city goes mad for all kinds of Jazz in what is one of the country's most popular festivals.

All-Ireland Finals (www.gaa.ie) The second and fourth Sundays of the month see the finals of the hurling and Gaelic football championships respectively, with 80,000-plus thronging into Dublin's Croke Park for the biggest sporting days of the year.

OCTOBER-NOVEMBER

Belfast Festival at Queens (in UK ☎ 020-9097 1197; www.belfastfestival.com) Northern Ireland's top arts festival attracts performers from all over the world; on offer is everything from visual arts to dance.

DECEMBER

Christmas This is a quiet affair in the countryside, though on 26 December the ancient practice of Wren Boys is re-enacted, most notably in Dingle, County Kerry, when groups of children dress up and go about singing hymns.

FOOD

Our café and restaurant listings appear in order of price with the cheapest appearing first. We've used the following price ranges: budget (under €10/£10), midrange (€10 to €20/£10 to £20) and top end (above €20/£20). Please note that our hierarchies of favourite places aren't written in stone. As authors, we can crave for caviar on a Monday, and cod and chips on a Friday!

For explanations of peculiarities of Irish menus and further reading on Irish food and drink, see the Food & Drink chapter (p65), and the Irish Kitchen (p269).

GAY & LESBIAN TRAVELLERS

Although Irish laws on homosexuality are among the most liberal in Europe, attitudes toward homosexuals remain fairly intolerant outside of the gay and lesbian scenes in Dublin and to a lesser extent Galway, Cork and Belfast, forcing most to maintain a pretty low profile. There is a common age of consent of 17 (generally the Irish couldn't care less what you do behind closed doors), and neither gays nor lesbians (in the Republic) are excluded

from the armed forces, which is laudable in theory but doesn't mean that openly gay soldiers wouldn't be made to suffer. Although Pope Benedict XVI has seen fit to remind the world that being gay is a crime against God, the Catholic Church here maintains an air of discreet silence on gay and lesbian issues.

The monthly *Gay Community News* (www .gcn.ie), found online and in clubs and bars, is a free publication of the **National Lesbian & Gay Federation** (NLGF; ☎ 01-671 9076; 2 Scarlett Row, Temple Bar, Dublin).

Check out the following online resources for the gay and lesbian community:

Channel Queer (www.channelqueer.com)

Gaire (www.gaire.com)

Gay & Lesbian Youth Northern Ireland (www.glyni .org.uk)

Gay Ireland (www.gay.ie)

Useful organisations:

Northern Ireland Gay Rights Association (Nigra; nigra@dnet.co.uk; ☎ 028-9066 5257; PO Box 44, Belfast)

Outhouse (☎ 01-873 4932; www.outhouse.ie; 105 Capel St, Dublin 1) A gay, lesbian and transgender community centre.

The following helplines can be called from anywhere in Ireland:

Gay Men's Health Project (☎ 01-660 2189) Practical advice on men's health issues.

Gay Switchboard Dublin (☎ 01-872 1055; 🕙 7.30am-9.30pm Mon-Fri, 3.30-6pm Sat)

Lesbian Line Belfast (☎ 028-9023 8668; 🕙 7.30-10pm Thu)

Lesbian Line Dublin (☎ 01-872 9911; 🕙 7-9pm Thu)

Mensline Belfast (☎ 028-9032 2023; 🕙 7.30-10pm Mon-Wed)

HOLIDAYS

Public holidays can cause road chaos, as everyone tries to get somewhere else for the break. It's also wise to book accommodation in advance.

Public Holidays

Public holidays in the Republic, Northern Ireland or both:

New Year's Day 1 January

St Patrick's Day 17 March

Easter (Good Friday to Easter Monday inclusive) March/April

May Holiday 1st Monday in May

Christmas Day 25 December

St Stephen's Day (Boxing Day) 26 December

NORTHERN IRELAND
Spring Bank Holiday Last Monday in May
Orangeman's Day 12 July
August Holiday Last Monday in August

REPUBLIC
June Holiday 1st Monday in June
August Holiday 1st Monday in August
October Holiday Last Monday in October

St Patrick's Day and St Stephen's Day holidays are taken on the following Monday should they fall on a weekend. In the Republic, nearly everywhere closes on Good Friday even though it isn't an official public holiday. In the North, most shops open on Good Friday but close the following Tuesday.

School Holidays
In the Republic, standardised primary and secondary school holidays for 2007–08 are as follows:
Mid term break 29 October to 2 November
Christmas/New Year 21 December to 7 January
Mid term break 11 to 15 February
Easter 14 to 31 March
Summer July and August (June also for secondary schools)

In the North, holidays for primary and secondary schools vary. Visit www.deni.gov.uk/schools/index.htm then click on school holidays for a comprehensive rundown.

INSURANCE
Insurance is important: it covers you for everything from medical expenses and luggage loss to cancellations or delays in your travel arrangements, depending on your policy.

If you're an EU citizen, a European Health Insurance Card (EHIC; available from health centres, or from post offices in the UK) covers you for most medical care. Other countries, such as Australia, also have reciprocal agreements with Ireland and Britain, but many countries do not.

If you do need health insurance, remember that some policies offer lower and higher medical-expense options, but the higher one is chiefly for countries such as the USA that have extremely high medical costs. Everyone should be covered for the worst possible case, such as an accident requiring an ambulance, hospital treatment or an emergency flight home. You may prefer a policy that pays health-care providers directly rather than you having to pay on the spot and claim later. See p726 for health insurance details.

All cars on public roads must be insured. If you are bringing your own vehicle check that your insurance will cover you in Ireland.

INTERNET ACCESS
If you plan to carry your notebook or palmtop computer with you, remember that the power-supply voltage in Ireland may vary from that at home. To avoid frying your electronics, the best investment is a universal AC adaptor and a plug adaptor, which will enable you to plug in anywhere. Also worth purchasing is a 'global' or 'world' modem, as your PC-card modem may not work outside your home country. For comprehensive advice on travelling with portable computers, visit the World Wide Phone Guide at www.kropla.com. **Teleadapt** (www.teleadapt.com) sells all the gizmos and gubbins you'll need.

Major internet service providers (ISPs) such as **AOL** (www.aol.com), **CompuServe** (www.compuserve.com) and **AT&T** (www.att.com) have dial-in nodes in Ireland. If you access your internet email account at home through a smaller ISP, your best option is either to open an account with a global ISP, like those mentioned above, or to rely on internet cafés. Armed with your incoming (POP or IMAP) mail-server name, your account name and your password, you should be able to access your internet email account from any Net-connected machine in the world. However, the easiest solution is to open a free Web-based email account such as those provided by **Hotmail** (www.hotmail.com) or **Yahoo!** (mail.yahoo.com).

You'll find internet cafés in most major towns in Ireland. You can log on for €4 to €10 per hour in the Republic, or about £4 per hour in the North. Most public libraries have free internet access but it may only be available (to a queue of people) at certain hours when connections may be slow.

LEGAL MATTERS
If you need legal assistance contact the **Legal Aid Board** (☎ 066-947 1000; www.legalaidboard.ie). It has a number of local law centres listed in the phone book.

The possession of small quantities of marijuana attracts a fine or warning, but harder

DIRECTORY

drugs are treated more seriously. Public drunkenness is illegal but commonplace. Be aware that you will undoubtedly attract police attention if you're any way out of hand. Fighting is treated more harshly – you could easily end up in a cell for the night or worse.

MAPS

Many publishers produce some good-quality maps of Ireland. Michelin's 1:400,000-scale Ireland map (No 923) is a decent single sheet map, with clear cartography and most of the island's scenic roads marked. The four maps – North, South, East and West – that make up the Ordnance Survey Holiday map series at 1:250,000-scale are useful if you want more detail. Collins also publishes a range of maps covering Ireland.

For greater detail, map aficionados and walkers should look out for the Ordnance Survey Discovery series, which covers the whole island in 89 maps at a scale of 1:50,000. They're available at the **National Map Centre** (☎ 01-476 0471; www.mapcentre.ie; 34 Aungier St, Dublin 2), through www .osi.ie and many bookshops around Ireland.

Lonely Planet's *Dublin City Map* has a complete index of all streets and sights, a Dublin Area Rapid Transport (DART) and suburban rail plan and a unique walking tour of the city.

MONEY

To get a general idea of food and accommodation costs in Ireland, see p20 and p694 respectively. Tips of around 10% in metered cabs and in restaurants where the service charge isn't included are expected.

ATMs & Credit Cards

Credit cards make the perfect travelling companions: they're ideal for major purchases and let you withdraw cash from selected banks and ATMs. ATMs are usually linked to international money systems such as Cirrus, Maestro or Plus. Bear in mind, though, that each transaction incurs a currency conversion fee and credit cards can incur immediate and exorbitant cash advance interest rate charges.

Charge cards such as Amex and Diners Club don't have credit limits, but may not be accepted in smaller establishments. Visa and MasterCard are more widely accepted, though many B&Bs and some smaller or remote petrol stations take cash only.

FOR THE RECORD:

- The legal age to vote in Ireland is 18
- You can leave school when you're 16
- The legal drinking age is 18
- Smoking is legal at 16
- The heterosexual and homosexual age of consent is 17
- You can ride a moped when you're 16
- You can drive a car when you're 17

Remember to keep a note of the emergency telephone number to ring if your card is lost or stolen.

Cash & Travellers Cheques

Nothing beats cash for convenience – or risk. It's still a good idea, though, to arrive with some cash in the local currency (both euros and sterling, if travelling to the North) to tide you over.

Amex and Thomas Cook travellers cheques are widely recognised and they don't charge commission for cashing their own cheques. Eurocheques can also be cashed in Ireland. Travellers cheques are rarely accepted outside banks or used for everyday transactions (as they are in the USA).

Take most cheques in large denominations. It's only towards the end of a stay that you may want to change a small cheque to make sure you don't get left with too much local currency.

Currency

The Republic of Ireland adopted the euro in 2002. The euro (€) is divided into 100 cents. The reverse side of coins have a design particular to their country of issue (a Celtic harp in Ireland's case), but are legal tender in all countries that accept the euro (Austria, Belgium, Finland, France, Germany, Greece, Italy, Luxembourg, the Netherlands, Portugal and Spain). Remember that the UK is not a participant, so if you're travelling to Northern Ireland you'll have to change euros into UK pounds.

The British pound sterling (£) is used in Northern Ireland, where it is known as the Northern Irish pound. Northern Ireland notes, while equivalent in value to British pound notes, are not readily accepted in Britain, but British banks will swap them for you.

The best exchange rates are obtained at banks. Bureaus de change and other exchange facilities usually open for longer hours but the rate and/or commission will be worse. Many post offices operate a currency-exchange facility and open on Saturday morning. Exchange rates at the time of writing are on the inside front cover of this book.

International Transfers

The most practical way to receive money from overseas is by telegraphic transfer. There are two ways to do this. The first can take up to eight days through the banking system. Your bank sends money to an Irish bank nominated by you. You will need identification, most likely a passport, before the money is paid to you in euros, minus the transfer commission.

The quickest way to receive cash from home is to transfer it through Amex, Thomas Cook or Western Union.

It is not practical to receive money by bank draft. Irish banks are notorious sticklers about drafts and won't allow you to cash them unless you first open a bank account, a small bureaucratic nightmare. Even then, it can take three weeks to clear. If you're not planning a long stay, stick to telegraphic transfers.

Taxes & Refunds

Value-added tax (VAT) is a sales tax of 21% that applies to most luxury goods in Ireland, excluding books, children's footwear and second-hand clothing. Visitors from non-EU countries can claim back most of the VAT on purchases that are subsequently exported from the EU within three months of purchase.

Most shops in the Republic and Northern Ireland operate a taxback scheme – the most popular are Cashback and Ireland Tax Free – which operate roughly as follows: if you're a resident of a country outside the EU and buy something from a store displaying a Cashback or Ireland Tax Free sticker, you'll be given a relevant voucher with your purchase which can be refunded directly on to your credit card or in US, Canadian or Australian dollars, British pounds or euros at Dublin or Shannon airport; one advantage of Ireland Tax Free is that you can reclaim your tax at the nearest Travelex office, usually Thomas Cook.

If you reclaim more than €250 on any of your vouchers you'll need to get the voucher stamped at the customs booth in the arrivals hall at Dublin or Shannon airport before you can get your refund from the Cashback desk.

In Northern Ireland, shops participating in the Tax-Free Shopping refund scheme will give you a form or invoice on request to be presented to customs when you leave. After customs have certified the form, it will be returned to the shop for a refund.

PHOTOGRAPHY & VIDEO

Natural light in Ireland can be very dull, so to capture the sombre atmosphere use faster film, such as 400ASA; but 200ASA should do in most situations. Lonely Planet's full-colour *Travel Photography: A Guide to Taking Better Pictures,* written by internationally renowned travel photographer Richard I'Anson, is full of handy hints and is designed to take on the road.

In regard to taking photos in Northern Ireland, if you want to take photos of fortified police stations, army posts or other military or quasi-military paraphernalia, get permission first to be on the safe side. In the Protestant and Catholic strongholds of West Belfast it's best not to photograph people without permission: always ask first and be prepared to accept a refusal.

POST

Post offices in the Republic are operated by An Post, the Irish Postal Service, and in the North by Royal Mail.

In the Republic, postcards and small airmail letters weighing up to 50g cost €0.48 within Ireland, economy/priority €0.50/0.60 to Britain, and €0.55/0.65 to continental Europe and the rest of the world.

In the North, letters sent by 1st-/2nd-class mail to Britain cost £0.30/0.21 as long as they weigh less than 60g. Airmail letters under 20g cost £0.42 to continental Europe and £0.68 to the rest of the world (under 10g to the rest of the world for £0.47).

For post office opening hours see p702.

SOLO TRAVELLERS

Travelling alone in Ireland is easy. People are extremely sociable, especially in the countryside, and will be more than keen to chat with you in pubs or public places – whether you like it or not! Hostels and internet cafés are always good stomping grounds to meet fellow travellers, or you might consider combining independent travel with a short course or activity where you have more chance of meeting people. One disadvantage of solo travel is the extra cost of accommodation: many places charge per room, or if they charge per person, they also slap a single supplementary charge (up to 30%) on to the room rate.

TELEPHONE

Eircom is Ireland's largest telephone service provider, although deregulation of the telephone industry has seen the arrival of a number of other providers. In the North most public phones are owned by British Telecom (BT).

Peak per-minute charges for international calls from Ireland to selected countries:

To	Republic	North
Australia	€0.86	£0.22
Canada	€0.19	£0.15
France	€0.24	£0.17
Germany	€0.24	£0.17
Italy	€0.39	£0.20
Netherlands	€0.24	£0.17
New Zealand	€0.86	£0.29
UK	€0.15	£0.05
USA	€0.19	£0.14

Prices are lower in the evening and at the weekend. The above prices are for calls placed from land-line phones to other landline phones; international calls to mobiles can cost significantly more. Phone calls from hotel rooms cost at least double the standard rate. You can send and receive faxes from post offices (up to €2/£1 per page locally) or most hotels.

Rather than placing reverse-charge calls through the operator in Ireland, you can dial direct to your home-country operator and then reverse the charges or charge the call to a local phone credit card. To use the home-direct service dial the codes in the table below then the area code and, in most cases, the number you want. Your home-country operator will come on the line before the call goes through.

To call home from Ireland, dial the numbers outlined in the table (right).

Local telephone calls from a public phone in the Republic cost €0.25 for around three minutes (around €0.50 to a mobile), regardless of when you call. In Northern Ireland a local call costs a minimum of £0.20.

Pre-paid phonecards by Eircom or private operators, available in newsagencies and post offices, work from all pay phones and dispense with the need for coins.

Mobile Phones

With a penetration rate in excess of 96% and more than four million users, the Irish seem glued to their mobile phones and therefore always on hand to tell their friends that they're on their way. SMS is a national obsession, especially with young people, who communic8 mostly by txt.

Ireland uses GSM 900/1800, which is compatible with the rest of Europe and Australia but not with North American GSM 1900 (though some specially equipped North American phones do work here) or the totally different system in Japan. There are four service providers in Ireland. Vodafone is the most popular, followed by O2 Ireland, Meteor and 3. There are three mobile codes – 085, 086 and 087 – but Mobile Number Portability (MNP) allows customers to hold on to their codes whilst switching between providers.

All four service providers are linked with most international GSM providers, which will allow you to roam onto a local service once you arrive in Ireland. This means you can use your mobile phone to make local calls, but will be charged at the highest possible rate for all calls.

For around €50 you will get a Ready-to-Go pre-paid phone, your own number and anywhere up to €25 worth of airtime. As you use up your airtime, you simply buy a top-up card (€10 to €35) at a newsagency or petrol station. The other service providers have variations on this scheme. Similar schemes exist in Northern Ireland.

Phone Codes

When calling the Republic of Ireland from abroad, dial your international access code, followed by 353, followed by the domestic number minus the initial '0'. When calling Northern Ireland from abroad, dial your international access code, then 44 28, and then the local number. To call Northern Ireland from Britain, simply dial 028, then the local number. This changes to 048 when calling from the Republic. The area code for the whole of Northern Ireland is 028, so domestic callers need only dial the eight-digit local number.

To call UK numbers from the Republic dial 00 44, then the area code minus the initial '0', then the local number. Do the same for international calls, replacing 44 with the country code. To call Britain from Northern Ireland dial the area code followed by the local number. To place an international call or to call the Republic from Northern Ireland, dial 00 followed by the country code, then the area code (dropping any leading '0') and the local number.

To	From the Republic	From the North
Australia	☎ 1800 550 061 + number	☎ 0800 890 061 + number
France	☎ 1800 551 033 + number	☎ 0800 890 033 + number
Italy	☎ 1800 550 039 + number	☎ 0800 890 039 + number
New Zealand	☎ 1800 550 064 + number	☎ 0800 890 064 + number
Spain	☎ 1800 550 034 + number	☎ 0800 890 034 + number
UK – BT	☎ 1800 550 044 + number	n/a
USA – AT&T	☎ 1800 550 000 + number	☎ 0800 890 011 + number
USA – MCI	☎ 1800 551 001 + number	☎ 0800 890222 + number
USA – Sprint	☎ 1800 552 001 + number	☎ 0800 890 877 + number

TIME

In winter, Ireland is on Greenwich Mean Time (GMT), also known as Universal Time Coordinated (UTC), the same as Britain. In summer, the clock shifts to GMT plus one hour, so when it's noon in Dublin and London, it is 3am in Los Angeles and Vancouver, 7am in New York and Toronto, 1pm in Paris, 8pm in Singapore, and 10pm in Sydney. See p762 for World Time Zones.

TOILETS

Public toilets – often marked with the Irish *Fir* (Men) and *Mná* (Women) – are rarely seen outside the bigger towns, and even then they're usually only seen in shopping centres. That annoying 'Toilets are for customer use only' sign is fairly common in restaurants and pubs but if you ask politely and don't look like you're going to use the toilet to shoot up, most publicans are fairly easy-going. If the pub is crowded, who'll ever know you're not a customer?

TOURIST INFORMATION

Fáilte Ireland (in the Republic ☎ 1850 230 330, in the UK 0800 039 7000; www.discoverireland.ie) and the **Northern Irish Tourist Board** (NITB; head office ☎ 028-9023 1221; www.discovernorthernireland.com; 59 North St, Belfast) are mines of information.

Both websites include an accommodation booking service, or telephone reservations can be made via the tourist boards' system **Gulliver** (in the Republic ☎ 1800 668 668, in the UK 0800 783 5740, in the USA & Canada ☎ 800 398 4376).

Fáilte Ireland has an office in **Belfast** (☎ 028-9032 7888; 53 Castle St, Belfast) and NITB has an office in **Dublin** (within the Republic ☎ 01-679 1977, 1850 230 230; 16 Nassau St, Dublin).

In the Republic and the North there's a tourist office in almost every big town; most can offer a variety of services including accommodation and attraction reservations, bureau de change services, map and guidebook sales, and free publications. Fáilte Ireland also has six regional offices, which can give more in-depth information on specific areas.

Main Regional Tourist Offices in the Republic

Cork Kerry (☎ 021-425 5100; www.corkkerry.ie; Cork Kerry Tourism, Áras Discover, Grand Pde, Cork)

Dublin (www.visitdublin.com; Dublin Tourism Centre, St Andrew's Church, 2 Suffolk St, Dublin)

East Coast & Midlands (☎ 044-48761; www.east coastmidlands.com; East Coast & Midlands Tourism, Dublin Rd, Mullingar) For Kildare, Laois, Longford, Louth, Meath, North Offaly, Westmeath, Wicklow.

Ireland North-West & Lakelands (☎ 071-916 1201; www.irelandnorthwest.ie; Temple St, Sligo) For Cavan, Donegal, Leitrim, Monaghan, Sligo.

Ireland West (☎ 091-537 700; www.irelandwest.ie; Ireland West Tourism, Aras Failte, Forster St, Galway) For Galway, Roscommon, Mayo.

Shannon Region (☎ 061-361 555; www.shannon regiontourism.ie; Shannon Development, Shannon, Clare) For Clare, Limerick, North Tipperary, South Offaly.

South East (☎ 051-875 823; www.southeastireland .com; South East Tourism, 41 The Quay, Waterford) For Carlow, Kilkenny, Tipperary, Wexford.

Tourist Offices Abroad

Outside Ireland, Fáilte Ireland and the NITB unite under the banner Tourism Ireland, with offices in the following countries:

DIRECTORY

Australia (☎ 02-9299 6177; info@tourismireland.com
.au; 5th level, 36 Carrington St, Sydney, NSW 2000)
Canada (☎ 1800 223 6470; info.ca@tourismireland.com;
2 Bloor St West, Suite 1501, Toronto, Ontario M4W 3E2)
France (☎ 01 53 43 12 35; info.fr@tourismireland.com;
Tourisme Irlandais, 33 rue de Miromesnil, 75008 Paris)
Germany (☎ 069-9231 8500; info.de@tourismireland
.com; Gutleutstrasse 32, 60329 Frankfurt-am-Main)
Italy (☎ 02 5817 7311; Piazzale Cantore 4, 20123 Milan)
Netherlands (☎ 020-530 6050; info@ierland.nl; Iers
Nationaal Bureau voor Toerisme, Spuistraat 104, 1012 VA
Amsterdam)
New Zealand (☎ 09-379 3708; info@tourismireland
.co.nz; Dingwall Bldg, 2nd fl, 87 Queen St, Auckland)
UK (☎ 0800 039 7000; info.gb@tourismireland.com;
Nations House,103 Wigmore St, London, W1U 1QS)
USA (☎ 212-1418 0800; info.us@tourismireland.com;
17th fl, 345 Park Ave, New York, NY 10154)

TRAVELLERS WITH DISABILITIES

Travelling in Ireland with a disability can be
a frustrating experience, as facilities and access are quite poor by European standards.
Improvements are being made, but progress is
quite slow in some areas. If you have a physical disability, get in touch with your national
support organisation (preferably the travel
officer if there is one) before you go. It often
has libraries devoted to travel and can put you
in touch with agencies that specialise in tours
for the travellers with disabilities.

Guesthouses, hotels and sights in Ireland
are gradually being adapted for people with
disabilities. Fáilte Ireland and NITB's accommodation guides indicate which places are
wheelchair accessible.

Public transportation can be a bit-hit-and-
miss. In the big cities, most buses now have
low-floor access and priority space on board,
but the number of kneeling coaches on regional routes is still relatively small.

Trains are accessible with help. In theory, if
you call ahead, an employee of Iarnród Éireann (Irish Rail) will arrange to accompany
you to the train. Newer trains have audio
and visual information systems for visually
impaired and hearing-impaired passengers.

The **Citizens' Information Board** (☎ 01-605 9000;
www.citizensinformationboard.ie) in the Republic and
Disability Action (☎ 028-9066 1252; www.disability
action.org) in Northern Ireland can give some
advice, although most of their information
concerns disabled Irish citizens' rights. Travellers to Northern Ireland can check out the
website www.allgohere.com.

VISAS

UK nationals don't need a passport to visit
the Republic, but are advised to carry one
(or some other form of photo identification)
to prove that they *are* a UK national. It's also
necessary to have a passport or photo ID when
changing travellers cheques or hiring a car.
European Economic Area (EEA) citizens (that
is, citizens of EU states, plus Iceland, Liech-
tenstein and Norway) can enter Ireland with
either a passport or a national ID card.

Visitors from outside the EEA will need
a passport, which should remain valid for at
least six months after their intended arrival.

For EEA nationals and citizens of most
Western countries, including Australia, Canada, New Zealand and the USA, no visa is
required to visit either the Republic or Northern Ireland, but citizens of India, China and
many African countries do need a visa for the
Republic. Full visa requirements for visiting
the Republic are available online at www.dfa
.ie; for Northern Ireland's visa requirements
see www.ukvisas.gov.uk.

EEA nationals can stay for as long as they
like, but other visitors can usually remain for
up to three months in the Republic and up
to six months in the North. To stay longer in
the Republic, contact the local garda (police)
station or the **Garda National Immigration Bureau**
(☎ 01-666 9100; www.garda.ie/angarda/gnib.html; 13-14
Burgh Quay, Dublin 2). To stay longer in Northern
Ireland contact the **Home Office** (☎ 0870-606 7766;
www.homeoffice.gov.uk; Immigration & Nationality Directo-
rate, Lunar House, 40 Wellesley Rd, Croydon CR9 2BY, UK).

Citizens of member states of the EEA do
not need a work visa to work in the Republic.
Non-EEA nationals are allowed to work for
up to one year in the Republic, if they have a
specific job to come to and their employer has
obtained permission from the Department of
Enterprise, Trade and Employment (see opposite for Commonwealth exceptions).

Although you don't need an onward or
return ticket to enter Ireland, it could help
if there's any doubt that you have sufficient
funds to support yourself in Ireland.

VOLUNTEERING

Prosperous Western democracies don't afford the same volunteering opportunities as
you'd find elsewhere, but that doesn't mean
there aren't projects where you can lend a
volunteering hand. From painting walls in
Wicklow to helping out in hospitals in Gal-

way and guiding visitors in Dublin museums, your time and effort will be put to good use. Check out www.volunteeringireland.ie for all relevant information, including how to sign up and where to go.

WOMEN TRAVELLERS

Except for the occasional wolf whistle from a building site or the ham-fisted attempt at a chat-up by some drunken punter, women will probably find travelling a blissfully relaxing experience. Walking alone at night, especially in certain parts of Dublin, and hitching are probably unwise. Should you have serious problems, be sure to report them to the local tourist authorities.

There's little need to worry about what you wear in Ireland, and the climate is hardly conducive to topless sunbathing. Finding contraception is not the problem it once was, although anyone on the pill should bring adequate supplies.

The phone number for the Rape Crisis Centre is ☎ 1800 77 88 88.

WORK

Low-paid seasonal work is available in the tourist industry, usually in restaurants and pubs. Sometimes volunteer work is available in return for bed and board, for example from the **Burren Conservation Trust** (☎ 065-707 6105; jdmn@iol.ie; Admiral's Rest Seafood Restaurant, Fanore).

Citizens of other EU countries can work legally in Ireland. If you don't come from an EU country but have an Irish parent or grandparent, it's fairly easy to obtain Irish

citizenship without necessarily renouncing your own nationality, and this opens the door to employment throughout the EU. Obtaining citizenship isn't an overnight procedure, so enquire at an Irish embassy or consulate in your own country.

To work in the North, citizens of Commonwealth countries aged 17 to 27 can apply for a Working Holiday Entry Certificate that allows them to spend two years in the UK and to take work that's 'incidental' to a holiday. You need to apply for the certificate, before you travel, to the British consulate or high commission in your country. In the Republic, a similar system entitled the Working Holiday Authorisation allows citizens of Australia, New Zealand and Canada to work casually so they can take an extended holiday, and again you must be apply while still in your own country.

Commonwealth citizens with a UK-born parent may be eligible for a Certificate of Entitlement to the Right of Abode, which entitles them to live and work in the UK free of immigration control. Commonwealth citizens with a UK-born grandparent, or a grandparent born before 31 March 1922 in what's now the Republic, may qualify for a UK Ancestry Employment Certificate, allowing them to work full time for up to four years in the UK.

Visiting full-time US students aged 18 and over can get a four-month work permit for Ireland through **CIEE** (☎ 617 247 0350; www.ciee .org; 3 Copley Pl, 2nd fl, Boston, MA 02116).

Nixers (www.nixers.com) is a useful noticeboard site for those in search of casual labour.

Transport

CONTENTS

GETTING THERE & AWAY

ENTERING THE COUNTRY

An increase in the number of foreign nationals seeking asylum during the last decade has meant a far more rigorous questioning for those from African and Asian countries or from certain parts of Eastern Europe. The border between the Republic and Northern Ireland still exists as a political reality, but there are few if any checkpoints left; for non-EU nationals it is assumed the screening process occurred upon entry to the UK. For information on visa requirements turn to p714.

THINGS CHANGE...

The information in this chapter is particularly vulnerable to change. Check directly with the airline or a travel agency to make sure you understand how a fare (and ticket you may buy) works and be aware of the security requirements for international travel. Shop carefully. The details given in this chapter should be regarded as pointers and are not a substitute for your own careful, up-to-date research.

FARE GO

Travel costs throughout this book are for single (one-way) adult fares, unless otherwise stated.

Passport

EU citizens can travel freely to and from Ireland if bearing official photo ID. Those from outside the EU, however, must have a passport that remains valid for six months after entry.

AIR

Airports & Airlines

There are scheduled nonstop flights from Britain, continental Europe and North America to Dublin and Shannon, and good nonstop connections from Britain and continental Europe to Cork.

Cork (ORK; ☎ 021-431 3131; www.corkairport.com)
Dublin (DUB; ☎ 01-814 1111; www.dublinairport.com)
Shannon (SNN; ☎ 061-712 000; www.shannon airport.com)

Other airports in the Republic with scheduled services from Britain:
Donegal (CFN; ☎ 074-954 8284; www.donegalairport .ie; Carrickfinn)
Kerry (KIR; ☎ 066-976 4644; www.kerryairport.ie; Farranfore)
Knock (NOC; ☎ 094-67222; www.knockairport.com)
Waterford (WAT; ☎ 051-875 589; www.flywater ford.com)

In Northern Ireland there are flights to **Belfast International** (BFS; ☎ 028-9448 4848; www.belfast airport.com) from Britain, continental Europe and the USA.

Other airports in Northern Ireland that operate scheduled services from Britain:
Belfast City (BHD; ☎ 028-9093 9093; www.belfastcity airport.com)
Derry (LDY; ☎ 028-7181 0784; www.cityofderry airport.com)

The main Irish airlines:
Aer Árann (☎ 1890 462 726; www.aerarann.ie) A small carrier that operates flights within Ireland and also to Britain.

Aer Lingus (☎ 01-886 8888; www.aerlingus.com) The Irish national airline, with direct flights to Britain, continental Europe and the USA.
Ryanair (☎ 01-609 7800; www.ryanair.com) Ireland's no-frills carrier with inexpensive services to Britain and continental Europe.

Nearly all international airlines use Dublin as their hub. Airlines flying into and out of Ireland:

Aer Árann (☎ 1890 462 726; www.aerarann.ie)
Aer Lingus (☎ 01-886 8888; www.aerlingus.com)
Aeroflot (☎ 01-844 6166; www.aeroflot.com)
Air Canada (☎ 1800 709 900; www.aircanada.ca)
Air France (☎ 01-605 0383; www.airfrance.com)
Air Malta (☎ 1800 397 400; www.airmalta.com)
Air Wales (☎ 1800 465 193; www.airwales.com)
Alitalia (☎ 01-844 6035; www.alitalia.com)
American Airlines (☎ 01-602 0550; www.aa.com)
Belavia (☎ 061-474 082; www.belaviashannon.com; Shannon)
BMI British Midland (☎ 01-407 3036; www.flybmi.com)
British Airways (☎ 1800 626 747; www.britishairways .com)
City Jet (☎ 01-8700 300; www.cityjet.com)
Continental (☎ 1890 925 252; www.continental.com)
CSA Czech Airlines (☎ 01-814 4626; www.csa.cz)
Delta Airlines (☎ 1800 768 080; www.delta.com)
EasyJet (☎ 048-9448 4929; www.easyjet.com; Knock)
Finnair (☎ 01-844 6565; www.finnair.com)
Iberia (☎ 01-407 3017; www.iberia.com)
KLM (☎ 01-663 6900; www.klm.com)
Lufthansa (☎ 01-844 5544; www.lufthansa.com)
Malev Hungarian Airlines (☎ 01-844 4303; www .malev.com)
Ryanair (☎ 01-609 7800; www.ryanair.com)
Scandinavian Airlines (☎ 01-8445440; www .scandinavian.net)

Tickets

The dogfight on European routes between full-service and no-frills airlines has generally resulted in an all-round lowering of fares, which makes cheap tickets much easier to get than ever before. You can get your ticket from a travel agency (in person or online) or direct from the airline, where the best deals are usually available online. Whatever you do, shop around. Internet travel agencies work well if you're doing a straightforward trip, but more complicated travel arrangements are best handled by a real live travel agent, who knows the system, the options and the best deals. Be sure to check the terms and conditions of the cheapest fares before purchasing.

ONLINE BOOKING AGENCIES
Best Fares (www.bestfares.com) American site offering discounted airfares and hotel rooms.
Cheap Flights (www.cheapflights.com) American- and British-based site that lists discounted flights and packages.
ebookers (www.ebookers.com) Irish, web-based internet travel agency.
Expedia (www.expedia.co.uk) Microsoft's travel site.
Opodo (www.opodo.com) Joint booking service for nine European airlines.
Priceline (www.priceline.com) American, web-based travel agency.
STA Travel (www.statravel.com) International student travel agency.
Travelocity (www.travelocity.com) American, web-based travel agency.

Australia & New Zealand

There are no nonstop scheduled air services from Australia or New Zealand to Ireland; generally it's cheapest to fly to London or Amsterdam and continue from there. Most fares to European destinations can have a return flight to Dublin tagged on at little or no extra cost. Round-the-world (RTW) tickets are another good bet and are often better value than standard return fares.

The Saturday travel sections of the *Sydney Morning Herald* and Melbourne *Age* newspapers advertise cheap fares; in New Zealand, check the *New Zealand Herald* travel section.

Recommended agencies:

AUSTRALIA
Flight Centre (☎ 133 133; www.flightcentre.com.au)
Shamrock Travel (☎ 03-9602 3700; www.irishtravel .com.au)
STA Travel (☎ 1300 733 035; www.statravel.com.au)

NEW ZEALAND
Flight Centre (☎ 0800-243 544; www.flightcentre .co.nz)
STA Travel (☎ 0508-782 872; www.statravel.co.nz)

Canada

Air Canada is the only carrier flying directly to Ireland, from Toronto to both Dublin and Shannon. Your best bet for cheaper fares may be to connect to transatlantic gateways in the USA or to fly to London and continue on to Ireland from there. Check the travel sections of the *Globe & Mail*, *Toronto Star*, *Montreal Gazette* or *Vancouver Sun* for the latest offers.

Recommended agencies:

Canadian Affair (☎ 1604-678 6868; www.canadian -affair.com) Cheap one-way fares to British cities.

Flight Centre (☎ 1888-967 5355; www.flight centre.ca)

Travel CUTS (☎ 866-246 9762; www.travelcuts.com)

Continental Europe

Price wars have made flights to Ireland from continental Europe more affordable than ever. As far as European connections are concerned, **Aer Lingus** (www.aerlingus.com) is now a no-frills airline in all but name, with highly competitive fares to over 40 European cities. **Ryanair** (www.ryanair.com), which kicked off the price wars, is still very much in the fight, but it has the disadvantage of having to use secondary airports in or around the major cities, which can make for rather expensive and time-consuming transfers. There are also some excellent connections with Belfast. Check before you book.

UK

There is a mind-boggling array of flights between Britain and Ireland. The best deals are usually available online, and it's not unusual for airport taxes to exceed the base price of the ticket on the lowest fares (generally for early morning or late-night flights midweek).

Most regional airports in Britain have flights to Dublin and Belfast and some also provide services to Shannon, Cork, Kerry, Knock and Waterford.

USA

In the USA, discount travel agencies (consolidators) sell cut-price tickets on scheduled carriers. Aer Lingus is the chief carrier between the USA and Ireland, with flights from New York, Boston, Baltimore, Chicago and Los Angeles to Shannon, Dublin and Belfast. Heavy competition on transatlantic routes into London might make it cheaper to fly there and then continue on to Ireland. The Sunday travel sections of the *New York Times, San Francisco Chronicle-Examiner, Los Angeles Times* or *Chicago Tribune* list cheap fares.

Some of the more popular travel agencies:

Ireland Consolidated (☎ 212-661 1999; www .irelandair.com)

STA Travel (☎ 800-781 4040; www.statravel.com)

CLIMATE CHANGE & TRAVEL

Climate change is a serious threat to the ecosystems that humans rely upon, and air travel is the fastest growing contributor to the problem. Lonely Planet regards travel, overall, as a global benefit, but believes we all have a responsibility to limit our personal impact on global warming.

Flying & climate change

Pretty much every form of motorised travel generates carbon dioxide (the main cause of human-induced climate change) but planes are far and away the worst offenders, not just because of the sheer distances they allow us to travel, but because they release greenhouse gases high into the atmosphere. The statistics are frightening: two people taking a return flight between Europe and the US will contribute as much to climate change as an average household's gas and electricity consumption over a whole year.

Carbon offset schemes

Climatecare.org and other websites use 'carbon calculators' that allow travellers to offset the level of greenhouse gases they are responsible for with financial contributions to sustainable travel schemes that reduce global warming – including projects in India, Honduras, Kazakhstan and Uganda.

Lonely Planet, together with Rough Guides and other concerned partners in the travel industry, support the carbon offset scheme run by climatecare.org. Lonely Planet offsets all of its staff and author travel.

For more information check out our website: www.lonelyplanet.com.

LAND

Eurolines (www.eurolines.com) has a three-times-daily coach and ferry service from London's Victoria Station to Dublin Busáras. For information on border crossings see p721.

SEA

There are many ferry and fast-boat services from Britain and France to Ireland. Prices quoted throughout this section are one-way fares for a single adult on foot/up to two adults with a car, during peak season.

UK & Ireland
FERRY & FAST BOAT

There are numerous services between Britain and Ireland but it's definitely wise to plan ahead as fares can vary considerably, depending on the season, day, time and length of stay. Often, some return fares don't cost that much more than one-way fares and it's worth keeping an eye out for special offers. International Student Identity Card (ISIC) holders and Hostelling International (HI) members get a reduction on the normal fares.

These shipping lines operate between Britain and Ireland:

Irish Ferries (☎ 0870-517 1717; www.irishferries.com) For ferry and fast-boat services from Holyhead to Dublin, and ferry services from Pembroke to Rosslare.

Isle of Man Steam Packet Company/Sea Cat (☎ 1800 805 055; www.steam-packet.com) Ferry and fast-boat services from Liverpool to Dublin or Belfast via Douglas (on the Isle of Man), and from Troon to Belfast.

Norfolkline (in the UK ☎ 0870-600 4321, in the Republic ☎ 01-819 2999; www.norfolkline.com) Ferry services from Liverpool to Belfast and Dublin.

P&O Irish Sea (in the UK ☎ 0870-242 4777, in the Republic ☎ 01-407 3434; www.poirishsea.com) Ferry and fast-boat services from Larne to Cairnryan and Troon, and ferry services from Liverpool to Dublin.

Stena Line (☎ 0870-570 7070; www.stenaline.com) Ferry services from Holyhead to Dun Laoghaire, Fleetwood to Larne and Stranraer to Belfast, and fast-boat services from Holyhead to Dublin, Fishguard to Rosslare, and Stranraer to Belfast.

Swansea Cork Ferries (in the UK ☎ 01792-456 116, in the Republic ☎ 01-427 1166; www.swansea-cork.ie) Ferry services from Swansea to Cork.

The main routes from the UK to the Republic include:

Fishguard & Pembroke to Rosslare These popular, short ferry crossings take 3½ hours (from Fishguard) or four hours (from Pembroke) and cost around £24/114; the

FERRY ROUTES

cost drops significantly outside peak season. The fast boat crossing from Fishguard takes just under two hours and costs around £30/130.

Holyhead to Dublin & Dun Laoghaire The ferry crossing takes just over three hours and costs around £24/124. The fast-boat service from Holyhead to Dun Laoghaire takes a little over 1½ hours and costs £30/139.

Liverpool to Dublin The ferry service takes 8½ hours from Liverpool and costs £22/160. Cabins on overnight sailings cost more. The fast-boat service takes four hours and costs up to £35/240.

Swansea to Cork The 10-hour crossing costs around £30/160 but only operates from mid-March to early November.

The main routes from mainland Britain to the North:

Cairnryan to Larne The fast boat takes one hour and costs £19/175. The ferry takes 1¾ hours and costs £14/115.

Fleetwood to Larne The six-hour crossing costs £119; no foot passengers are carried.

Liverpool to Belfast The 8½-hour crossing costs £40/155 (incl meals) during the day and £30/235 (incl cabin and meals) at night.

TRANSPORT

Stranraer to Belfast The fast boat takes 1¾ hours and costs £20/130. The ferry takes 3¼ hours and costs £16/85.

It's possible to combine bus and ferry tickets from major UK centres to all Irish towns on the bus network, but with the availability of cheap flights it's hardly worth the hassle. The journey between London and Dublin takes about 12 hours and can cost as little as £15 one way. The London to Belfast trip takes 13 to 16 hours and costs £44 one way. For details in London contact **Eurolines** (☎ 0870-514 3219; www.eurolines.com).

France

FERRY

Brittany Ferries (in the Republic ☎ 021-427 7801, in France ☎ 02 98 29 28 00; www.brittany-ferries.com) Weekly service from Roscoff to Cork from early April to late September. The crossing takes 14 hours and costs up to €79/430 without accommodation.

Irish Ferries (in Rosslare ☎ 053-33158, in Cherbourg ☎ 02 33 23 44 44, in Roscoff ☎ 02 98 61 17 17; www.irishferries.com) One to three times a week from Roscoff to Rosslare from late April to late September; the crossing time is 17½ hours. Ferries from Cherbourg to Rosslare sail two to four times per week year round, except in late January and all of February; crossing time is 20½ hours. Both services cost up to €130/575 without accommodation.

GETTING AROUND

Travelling around Ireland is short, simple and sweet – or maddeningly long and infuriatingly complicated. Distances are relatively short and there's a good network of roads, but public transportation can be infrequent, expensive or both and – especially with trains – not reach many of the more interesting places.

Your own transport is a major advantage and it's worth considering car hire for at least part of your trip. Irish roads are markedly better than they used to be. There's a small but growing network of motorways to supplement the huge network of secondary and tertiary roads, although it is still true that smaller, rural roads can make for difficult driving conditions.

If you opt not to drive, a mixture of buses, the occasional taxi, plenty of time, walking and sometimes hiring a bicycle will get you just about anywhere.

AIR

Airlines in Ireland

Ireland's size makes domestic flying unnecessary unless you're in a hurry, but there are flights between Dublin and Belfast, Cork, Derry, Donegal, Galway, Kerry, Shannon and Sligo, as well as a Belfast–Cork service. Most flights within Ireland take around 30 to 50 minutes.

The only domestic carriers are:

Aer Árann (☎ 1890-462 726, in Dublin ☎ 01-814 5240, in Galway ☎ 091-593 034, in Cork ☎ 021-814 1058; www.aerarann.ie) Operates flights from Dublin to Belfast, Cork, Derry, Donegal, Galway, Kerry, Knock and Sligo; flights to the Aran Islands from Galway and a Belfast to Cork route.

Aer Lingus (information & bookings ☎ 01-886 8844, flight information ☎ 01-705 6705, in Belfast ☎ 028-9442 2888; www.aerlingus.ie) The main domestic airline.

BICYCLE

Ireland is a great place for bicycle touring, despite bad road surfaces in places and inclement weather. If you intend to cycle in the west, the prevailing winds mean it's easier to cycle from south to north. Both **Irish Cycling Safaris** (☎ 01-260 0749; www.cycling safaris.com; Belfield Bike Shop, UCD, Dublin 4) and **Go Ireland** (☎ 066-976 2094; www.goactivities.com; Old Orchard House, Killorglin, Co Kerry) organise tours for groups of cyclists in the southwest, the southeast, Clare, Connemara, Donegal and Antrim.

Bicycles can be transported by bus if there's enough room; the charge varies. By train the cost varies from €3 to €10 for a one-way journey, but bikes are not allowed on certain train routes, including the Dublin Area Rapid Transit (DART); check with **Iarnród Éireann** (☎ 01-836 3333).

Typical bicycle hire costs are €15 to €25 per day or €60 to €100 per week plus a deposit of around €100. There are many local independent outlets, but several dealers have outlets around the country:

Irish Cycle Hire (☎ 041-685 3772; www.irishcyclehire .com; Unit 6, Enterprise Centre, Ardee, Co Louth)

Raleigh Ireland (☎ 01-626 1333; www.raleigh.ie; Raleigh House, Kylemore Rd, Dublin) Ireland's biggest rental dealer.

Rent-a-Bike Ireland (☎ 061-416983; www.irelandrentabike.com; 1 Patrick St, Limerick, Co Limerick)

BOAT
Ferry

There are many boat services to islands lying off the coast, including to the Aran and Skellig Islands to the west, the Saltee Islands to the southeast, and Tory and Rathlin Islands to the north. Ferries also operate across rivers, inlets and loughs, providing useful shortcuts, particularly for cyclists.

Cruises are very popular on the 258km-long Shannon–Erne Waterway and on a variety of other lakes and loughs. The tourist offices only recommend operators that are registered with them. Details of non-tourist-board-affiliated boat trips are given under the relevant sections throughout this book.

BORDER CROSSINGS

Security has been progressively scaled down in Northern Ireland in recent years and all border crossings with the Republic are now open and generally unstaffed. Permanent checkpoints have been removed and ramps levelled. On major routes your only indication that you have crossed the border will be a change in road signs and the colour of number plates and postboxes.

BUS

Bus Éireann (☎ 01-836 6111; www.buseireann.ie; Busáras, Store St, Dublin) is the Republic's bus line and offers an extensive network throughout the south. Private buses compete – often very favourably – with Bus Éireann in the Republic and also run where the national buses are irregular or absent.

The larger bus companies will usually carry bikes for free but you should always check in advance to avoid surprises. **Ulsterbus** (☎ 028-9066 6600; www.ulsterbus.co.uk; Milewater Rd, Belfast) is the only bus service in Northern Ireland.

Bus Passes

Details of special deals and passes are given in the boxed text on p723.

Costs

Bus travel is much cheaper than train travel, and private buses often charge less than Bus Éireann. Generally, return fares cost little more than a one-way fare.

Some sample one-way (single) bus fares include the following:

Service	Cost	Duration (hrs)	Frequency (Mon-Sat)
Belfast-Dublin	£10	3	7
Derry-Belfast	£9	1¾	10+
Derry-Galway	£20	5¼	4
Dublin-Cork	€10.50	4½	6
Dublin-Donegal	€17.50	4	5
Dublin-Rosslare	€16	3	12
Dublin-Tralee	€22.50	6	12
Dublin-Waterford	€11.50	2¾	7
Killarney-Cork	€12.60	2	12
Killarney-Waterford	€17.60	4½	12

Reservations

Bus Éireann bookings can be made online but you can't reserve a seat for a particular service.

CAR & MOTORCYCLE

Ireland's new-found affluence means there are far more cars on the road, and the building of new roads and the upgrading of existing ones just cannot keep pace. Be prepared for delays, especially at holiday weekends. **AA Roadwatch** (☎ 1550 131 811; www.aaroadwatch.ie) provides traffic information in the Republic.

In the Republic, speed-limit and distance signs are in kilometres (although the occasional older white sign shows distances in miles); in the North, speed-limit and distance signs are in miles.

You'll need a good road map and sense of humour to deal with the severe lack of signposts in the Republic, and on minor roads be prepared for lots of potholes.

Petrol is considerably cheaper in the Republic than in the North. Most service stations accept payment by credit card, but some small, remote ones may take cash only.

All cars on public roads must be insured. If you are bringing your own vehicle in to the country, check that your insurance will cover you in Ireland.

Bring Your Own Vehicle

It's easy to take your own vehicle to Ireland and there are no specific procedures involved, but you should carry a vehicle registration document as proof that it's yours.

Automobile Association members should ask for a Card of Introduction entitling you to services offered by sister organisations (including maps, information, breakdown assistance, legal advice etc), usually free of charge.

TRANSPORT

ROAD DISTANCES (KM)

	Athlone	Belfast	Cork	Derry	Donegal	Dublin	Galway	Kilkenny	Killarney	Limerick	Rosslare Harbour	Shannon Airport	Sligo	Waterford	Wexford
Athlone	---														
Belfast	227	---													
Cork	219	424	---												
Derry	209	117	428	---											
Donegal	183	180	402	69	---										
Dublin	127	167	256	237	233	---									
Galway	93	306	209	272	204	212	---								
Kilkenny	116	284	148	335	309	114	172	---							
Killarney	232	436	87	441	407	304	193	198	---						
Limerick	121	323	105	328	296	193	104	113	111	---					
Rosslare Harbour	201	330	208	397	391	153	274	98	275	211	---				
Shannon Airport	133	346	128	351	282	218	93	135	135	25	234	---			
Sligo	117	206	336	135	66	214	138	245	343	232	325	218	---		
Waterford	164	333	126	383	357	163	220	48	193	129	82	152	293	---	
Wexford	184	309	187	378	372	135	253	80	254	190	19	213	307	61	---

Automobile Association (AA; www.aaireland.ie)
Northern Ireland (☎ 0870-950 0600, breakdown assistance 0800-667 788); Republic (Dublin ☎ 01-617 9999, Cork 021-425 2444, breakdown assistance 1800-667 788)
Royal Automobile Club (RAC; www.rac.ie) Northern Ireland (☎ 0800-029 029, breakdown assistance 0800-828 282); Republic (☎ 1890 483 483)

Driving Licence

Unless you have an EU licence, which is treated like an Irish one, your driving licence is valid for 12 months from the date of entry to Ireland, but you should have held it for two years prior to that. If you don't hold an EU licence it's a good idea to obtain an International Driving Permit (IDP) from your home automobile association before you leave. Your home-country licence is usually enough to hire a car for three months.

You must carry your driving licence at all times.

Hire

Car hire in Ireland is expensive, so you're often better off making arrangements in your home country with some sort of package deal. In July

and August it's wise to book well ahead. Most cars are manual; automatic cars are available but they're more expensive to hire.

The international hire companies and the major local operators have offices all over Ireland. **Nova Car Hire** (www.rentacar-ireland.com) acts as an agent for Alamo, Budget, European and National, and offers greatly discounted rates. In the Republic typical weekly high-season hire rates with Nova are around €150 for a small car, €185 for a medium-sized car, and €320 for a five-seater people carrier. In the North, similar cars are marginally more expensive.

When hiring a car be sure to check if the price includes collision-damage waiver (CDW), insurance (eg for car theft and windscreen damage), value-added tax (VAT) and unlimited mileage.

If you're travelling from the Republic into Northern Ireland it's important to be sure that your insurance covers journeys to the North. People aged under 21 aren't allowed to hire a car; for the majority of hire companies you have to be aged at least 23 and have had a valid driving licence for a minimum of one year. Some companies in the Republic won't

FERRY, BUS & TRAIN DISCOUNT DEALS

For Travel Across Europe

Eurail (www.eurail.com) passes are for non-Europeans who have been in Europe for less than six months. They are valid on trains in the Republic, but not in Northern Ireland, and offer discounts on Irish Ferries crossings to France. Passes are cheaper when bought outside Europe. In the USA and Canada phone ☎ 1888-667 9734. In London contact **Rail Europe** (☎ 0870-584 8848; 179 Piccadilly).

InterRail (www.interrail.com) passes give you a 50% reduction on train travel within Ireland and discounts on Irish Ferries and Stena Line services. Passes can be bought at most major train stations and student travel outlets.

For Travel Within Ireland

Travelsave stamps (€10 in the South, £7 in the North) entitle International Student Identity Card (ISIC) holders to a 50% discount on Irish trains and 15% off Bus Éireann services. Holders of an EYC (or EuroFairstamp) can get a 40% discount on trains with a Travelsave stamp. The stamps are available from Usit offices (www.usit.ie).

Iarnród Éireann's Faircard (€10) gives up to 50% reductions on any intercity journey to people aged under 26, while the Weekender (€7) gives up to 30% off (Friday to Tuesday) to people aged 26 and over.

Unlimited-Travel Tickets For Buses & Trains

Irish Rambler tickets cover bus-only travel within the Republic. They cost €53 (for three days' travel out of eight consecutive days), €116 (eight days out of 15) or €168 (15 days out of 30).

Irish Rover tickets combine services on Bus Éireann and Ulsterbus. They cost €73 (for three days' travel out of eight consecutive days), €165 (eight days out of 15) and €245 (15 days out of 30).

Iarnród Éireann Explorer tickets cover train travel in the Republic. They cost €138 (for five days travel out of 15 consecutive days) or €171 to include Northern Ireland.

Irish Explorer rail and bus tickets (€210) allow eight days' travel out of 15 consecutive days on trains and buses within the Republic.

Freedom of Northern Ireland passes allow unlimited travel on NIR, Ulsterbus and Citybus services for £14 for one day, £34 for three out of eight consecutive days, or £50 for seven consecutive days.

Emerald Card gives you unlimited travel throughout Ireland on all Iarnród Éireann, NIR, Bus Éireann, Dublin Bus, Ulsterbus and Citybus services. The card costs €236 (for eight days out of 15) or €406 (for 15 days out of 30).

Children aged under 16 pay half price for all these passes and for all normal tickets. Children aged under three travel for free on public transport. You can buy the above passes at most major train and bus stations in Ireland. Although they're good value, many of them make economic sense only if you're planning to travel around Ireland at the speed of light.

---

rent to you if you're aged 74 or over; there's no upper age limit in the North.

You can't hire motorbikes and mopeds.

Parking

Ireland is tiny and the Irish love their cars; the numbers just don't add up and parking is an expensive and difficult nightmare. Parking in towns and cities is either by meter, 'pay and display' tickets or disc parking (discs, which rotate to display the time you park your car, are available from newsagencies).

Purchase

It's more expensive to buy a car in Ireland than most other European countries. If you do buy a car (or intend to import one from another country) you must pay vehicle registration tax and motor tax, and take out insurance.

Road Rules

A copy of Ireland's road rules is available from tourist offices. Here are some of the most basic rules

TRANSPORT

- Drive on the left, overtake to the right.
- Safety belts must be worn by the driver and all passengers.
- Children aged under 12 aren't allowed to sit on the front seats.
- Motorcyclists and their passengers must wear helmets.
- When entering a roundabout, give way to the right.
- Speed limits are 120km/h on motorways, 100km/h on national roads, 80km/h on regional and local roads and 50km/h or as signposted in towns.
- The legal alcohol limit is 80mg of alcohol per 100ml of blood or 35mg on the breath (roughly two pints of beer an hour for a man, one for a woman). Note:

three pints (1½ for a woman) will put you over the limit.

HITCHING

Hitching is becoming increasingly less popular in Ireland, even though it's still pretty easy compared to other European countries. Travellers who decide to hitch should understand that they are taking a small but potentially serious risk, and we don't recommend it. If you do plan to travel by thumb, remember it's illegal to hitch on motorways.

LOCAL TRANSPORT

There are comprehensive local bus networks in Dublin (Dublin Bus), Belfast (Citybus) and some other larger towns. The Dublin Area

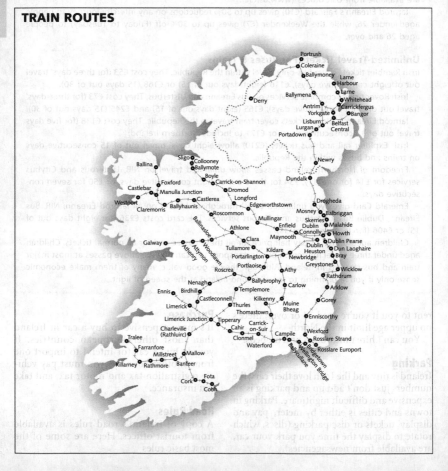

TRAIN ROUTES

Rapid Transport (DART) line in Dublin runs roughly the length of the city's coastline, while the brand new Luas tram system has two very popular lines. Taxis tend to be expensive.

TOURS

If your time is limited it might be worth considering an organised tour, though it's cheaper to see things independently, and Ireland is small enough for you to get to even the most remote places within a few hours. Tours can be booked through travel agencies, tourist offices in the major cities, or directly through the tour companies themselves.

Bus Éireann (☎ 01-836 6111; www.buseireann.ie; 59 Upper O'Connell St, Dublin) Runs day tours to various parts of the Republic and the North.

CIE Tours International (☎ 01-703 1888; www.cietours .ie; 35 Lower Abbey St, Dublin) Runs four- to 11-day coach tours of the Republic and the North, including accommodation and meals. The Taste of Ireland tour (five days) takes in Blarney, Ring of Kerry, Killarney, Cliffs of Moher and region around the River Shannon (€680 in high season).

Grayline Tours (☎ 01-872 9010; www.irishcitytours .com; 33 Bachelor's Walk, Dublin) Located in Dublin and offers half- and full-day tours (€22) from Dublin to Newgrange, Glendalough and north Dublin, and three- and four-day trips to the Ring of Kerry (€295 to €400).

Over the Top & Into the West Tours (☎ 01-869 0769; www.overthetoptours.com) Daily historical and heritage tours of Wicklow (€26), the Boyne Valley (€28), three-day tours of the west of Ireland (€255) and a five-day tour of Kerry and Cork (€370).

Paddywagon Tours (☎ 01-672 6007; www.paddy wagontours.com) Activity-filled three- and six-day tours all over Ireland with friendly tour guides. Accommodation is in IHH hostels.

Ulsterbus Tours (☎ 028-9033 7004; www.ulsterbus .co.uk) Runs a large number of day trips throughout the North and the Republic.

It's worth checking **GoIreland.com** (☎ 1800 668 668; www.goireland.com) for holiday packages.

For train enthusiasts, **Railtours Ireland** (☎ 01-856 0045; www.railtours.ie; 58 Lower Gardiner St, Dublin 1)

organises a series of one- and two-day train trips in association with Iarnród Éireann. A three-day trip from Dublin to Cork, Blarney Castle and Kerry costs €219.

TRAIN

Iarnród Éireann (Irish Rail; ☎ 01-836 2222; www.irishrail .ie; 35 Lower Abbey St, Dublin) operates trains in the Republic on routes that fan out from Dublin. The system is limited though: there's no north–south route along the western coast, no network in Donegal, and no direct connections from Waterford to Cork or Killarney.

Northern Ireland Railways (NIR; ☎ 028-9089 9411; Belfast Central Station) runs four routes from Belfast. One links with the system in the Republic via Newry to Dublin; the other three go east to Bangor, northeast to Larne and northwest to Derry via Coleraine (see map opposite).

Costs

Train travel is more expensive than bus travel and one-way fares are particularly poor value – a midweek return ticket is often about the same as a one-way fare. First-class tickets cost around €5 to €10 more than the standard fare for a single journey.

Some sample one-way fares:

Service	Cost	Duration (hr)	Frequency (Mon-Sat)
Belfast-Dublin	£24	2	half-hourly
Dublin-Cork	€56.50	3¼	8
Dublin-alway	€42	3¼	5
Dublin-Limerick	€43	2½	13
Dublin-Sligo	€26	3	3
Dublin-Tralee	€57	4½	8
Dublin-Waterford	€24	2½	7

Reservations

Iarnród Éireann takes reservations for all its train services. You need to fax your details (name, number of passengers, date and time of service, credit-card number and expiry date) to ☎ 01-703 4136.

Health

CONTENTS

BEFORE YOU GO

While Ireland has excellent health care, prevention is the key to staying healthy while abroad. A little planning before departure, particularly for pre-existing illnesses, will save trouble later. Bring medications in their original, clearly labelled, containers. A signed and dated letter from your physician describing your medical conditions and medications, including generic names, is also a good idea. If carrying syringes or needles, be sure to have a physician's letter documenting their medical necessity. Carry a spare pair of contact lenses and glasses, and take your optical prescription with you.

INSURANCE

If you're an EU citizen, a European Health Insurance Card (EHIC), available from health centres or, in the UK, post offices, covers you for most medical care. The EHIC won't cover you for non-emergencies, or emergency repatriation home. Citizens from other countries should find out if there is a reciprocal arrangement for free medical care between their country and Ireland. If you do need health insurance, make sure you get a policy that covers you for the worst possible case, such as an accident requiring an emergency flight home. Find out in advance if your insurance plan will make payments directly to providers, or reimburse you later for overseas health expenditures.

RECOMMENDED VACCINATIONS

No jabs are required to travel to Ireland. The World Health Organization, however, recommends that all travellers should be covered for diphtheria, tetanus, measles, mumps, rubella, polio and hepatitis B, regardless of their destination.

IN TRANSIT

DEEP VEIN THROMBOSIS (DVT)

Blood clots may form in the legs during plane flights, chiefly because of prolonged immobility. The longer the flight, the greater the risk. The chief symptom of deep vein thrombosis is swelling or pain of the foot, ankle, or calf, often on just one side. When a blood clot travels to the lungs, it may cause chest pain and difficulty breathing. Travellers with any of these symptoms should immediately seek medical attention.

To prevent the development of DVT on long flights you should walk about the cabin, contract the leg muscles while sitting, drink plenty of fluids and avoid alcohol and tobacco.

JET LAG & MOTION SICKNESS

To avoid jet lag (quite common when crossing more than five time zones) try drinking plenty of nonalcoholic fluids and eating light meals. Upon arrival, get exposure to natural sunlight and readjust your schedule (for meals, sleep etc) as soon as possible.

Antihistamines such as dimenhydrinate (Dramamine) or meclizine (Antivert, Bonine) are quite often the first choice for treating motion sickness. A herbal alternative is ginger.

IN IRELAND

AVAILABILITY & COST OF HEALTH CARE

Excellent health care is readily available and for minor self-limiting illnesses pharmacists can give valuable advice and sell over-the-counter medication. They can also advise when more specialised help is required and point you in the right direction.

TRAVELLERS' DIARRHOEA

If you develop diarrhoea, be sure to drink plenty of fluids, preferably in the form of an oral rehydration solution such as dioralyte. If diarrhoea is bloody, persists for more than 72 hours or is accompanied by fever, shaking, chills or severe abdominal pain you will need to seek urgent medical attention.

ENVIRONMENTAL HAZARDS
Heatstroke

Heat exhaustion (yes, even in Ireland it can still happen!) occurs following excessive fluid loss with insufficient replacement of fluids and salt. Symptoms include headache, dizziness and tiredness. Dehydration is already happening by the time you feel thirsty – aim to drink sufficient water to produce pale, diluted urine. To treat heat exhaustion drink water and/or fruit juice, and cool the body with cold water and fans.

Hypothermia

Hypothermia occurs when the body loses heat faster than it can produce it. As ever, proper preparation will reduce the risks of getting it. Even on a hot day in the mountains the weather can change rapidly, so carry waterproof garments, warm layers and a hat, and inform others of your route.

Hypothermia starts with shivering, loss of judgment and clumsiness. Without re-warming, the sufferer deteriorates into apathy, confusion and coma. Prevent further heat loss by seeking shelter, warm dry clothing, hot sweet drinks and shared body warmth.

Language

CONTENTS

In 2003 the government introduced the Official Languages Act whereby all official documents, street signs and official titles must be either in Gaeilge or bilingual. While Gaeilge (Irish) is the official language, it's only spoken in isolated pockets of rural Ireland known as Gaeltacht areas, the main ones being Cork *(Chorcaí)*, Donegal *(Dhún na nGall)*, Galway *(Gaillimhe)*, Kerry *(Chiarraí)* and Mayo *(Mhaigh Eo)*.

Irish is a compulsory subject in schools for those aged six to fifteen, but Gaeilge classes have traditionally been thoroughly academic and unimaginative, leading most kids to resent it as a waste of time. Ask people outside the Gaeltacht areas if they can speak Irish and nine out of 10 of them will probably reply, *'ahhh, cupla focal'* ('a couple of words') and they generally mean it. It's a pity that the treatment of Irish in schools has been so heavy-handed because many adults say they regret not having a greater grasp of it. At long last, and for the first time since the formation of the state, a new Gaeilge curriculum has recently been introduced that will cut the hours devoted to the subject but make the lessons more fun, practical and celebratory.

If you'd like a witty insight into the quirks of language in Ireland, get a copy of Lonely Planet's pocket-sized *Irish Language & Culture*.

PRONUNCIATION

Irish has three main dialects: Connaught Irish (Galway and northern Mayo), Munster Irish (Cork, Kerry and Waterford) and Ulster Irish (Donegal). The pronunciation guidelines given here are an anglicised version of modern standard Irish, which is essentially an amalgam of the three.

Vowels

Irish divides vowels into long (those with an accent) and short (those without) and, more importantly, broad (**a**, **á**, **o**, **ó**, **u** and **ú**) and slender (**e**, **é**, **i** and **í**), which can affect the pronunciation of preceding consonants.

a	as in 'cat'
á	as in 'saw'
e	as in 'bet'
é	as in 'hey'
i	as in 'sit'
í	as in 'marine'
o	as in 'son'
ó	as in 'low'
u	as in 'put'
ú	as in 'rule'

Consonants

Other than odd-looking clusters like **mh** and **bhf**, consonants are generally pronounced as they are in English.

bh	as the 'v' in 'voice'
bhf	as the 'w' in 'well'
c	always hard, as in 'cat'
ch	as the 'ch' in Scottish *loch*
d	as in 'do' when followed by a broad vowel; as the 'j' in 'jug' when followed by a slender vowel
dh	as the 'g' in 'gap' when followed by a broad vowel; as the 'y' in 'year' when followed by a slender vowel
mh	as the 'w' in 'well'
s	as in 'said' when before a broad vowel; as the 'sh' in ship when before a slender vowel and at the end of a word
t	as the 't' in 'toast' when before a broad vowel; as the 'ch' in 'church' before a slender vowel
th	as the 'h' in 'house'; as the 't' in 'mat' or silent at the end of a word

MAKING CONVERSATION

Hello.
> *Dia duit.*   dee·a gwit
> (lit: God be with you)

Hello. (reply)
> *Dia is Muire duit.*   dee·as moyra gwit
> (lit: God and Mary be with you)

CUPLA FOCAL

Here are a few cheeky phrases *os Gaeilge* (in Irish), which can help you impress the locals:

amadáin – fool
Dún do chlab! – Shut your mouth!
Ní ólfaidh mé go brách arís! (knee ohl-hee mey gu brawkh u-reeshch) – I'm never ever drinking again!
Póg ma thóin! – Kiss my arse!
Slainte! (slawn-cha) – Your health! (cheers)
Táim go maith! (thawm go mah) – I'm good!

Good morning.
Maidin mhaith.   maw-jin wah
Good night.
Oíche mhaith.   eek·heh wah
Goodbye.
Slán leat.   slawn lyat
(said by person leaving)
Goodbye.
Slán agat.   slawn agut
(said by person staying)
Welcome.
Ceád míle fáilte.   kade meela fawlcha
(lit: 100,000 welcomes)
Thank you (very) much.
Go raibh (míle)   goh rev (meela)
maith agat.   mah agut
..., (if you) please.
..., más é do thoil é.   ... maws ay do hall ay
Excuse me.
Gabh mo leithscéal.   gamoh lesh scale
How are you?
Conas a tá tú?   kunas aw taw too
(I'm) fine/good/OK.
(Tá mé) go maith.   (taw may) goh mah
What's your name?
Cad is ainm duit?   kod is anim dwit?

Also available from Lonely Planet:
Irish Language & Culture

My name is (Sean Frayne).
(Sean Frayne) is   (shawn frain) is
ainm dom.   anim dohm
Yes/It is.
Tá/Sea.   taw/sheh
No/It isn't.
Níl/Ní hea.   neel/nee heh
another/one more
ceann eile   kyawn ella
nice
go deas   goh dyass

BASIC WORDS & PHRASES

What is this/that?
Cad é seo/sin?   kod ay shoh/shin
I don't understand.
Ní thuigim.   nee higgim
I'd like to go to ...
Ba mhaith liom   baw wah lohm
dul go dtí ...   dull go dee ...
I'd like to buy ...
Ba mhaith liom ...   bah wah lohm ...
a cheannach   a kyanunkh

SIGNS

Leithreas	*lehrass*	Toilet
Fir	*fear*	Men
Mna	*m'naw*	Women
Gardaí	*gardee*	Police
Oifig An Phoist	*iffig ohn fwisht*	Post Office

DAYS & MONTHS

Monday	*Dé Luáin*	day loon
Tuesday	*Dé Máirt*	day maart
Wednesday	*Dé Ceádaoin*	day kaydeen
Thursday	*Déardaoin*	daredeen
Friday	*Dé hAoine*	day heeneh
Saturday	*Dé Sathairn*	day sahern
Sunday	*Dé Domhnaigh*	day downick

NUMBERS

1	*haon*	hayin
2	*dó*	doe
3	*trí*	tree
4	*ceathaír*	kahirr
5	*cúig*	koo·ig
6	*sé*	shay
7	*seacht*	shocked
8	*hocht*	hukt
9	*naoi*	nay
10	*deich*	jeh
11	*haon déag*	hayin jague
12	*dó dhéag*	doe yague
20	*fiche*	feekhe

LANGUAGE

Glossary

12th of July – the day the Orange Order marches to celebrate King William III's victory over the Catholic King James II at the Battle of the Boyne in 1690

An Óige – literally 'The Youth'; Republic of Ireland Youth Hostel Association
An Taisce – National Trust for the Republic of Ireland
Anglo-Norman – Norman, English and Welsh peoples who invaded Ireland in the 12th century
Apprentice Boys – loyalist organisation founded in 1814 to commemorate the Great Siege of Derry in August every year
ard – literally 'high'; Irish place name
ard rí – Irish 'high king'
Ascendancy – refers to the Protestant aristocracy descended from the Anglo-Normans and those who were installed here during the Plantations.

bailey – outer wall of a castle
bawn – area surrounded by walls outside the main castle, acting as a defence and as a place to keep cattle in times of trouble
beehive hut – see clochán
Black and Tans – British recruits to the Royal Irish Constabulary shortly after WWI, noted for their brutality
Blarney Stone – sacred stone perched on top of Blarney Castle; bending over backwards to kiss the stone is said to bestow the gift of the gab
bodhrán – hand-held goatskin drum
Bord Na Móna – the Irish turf board, charged with harvesting peat for use in power plants
boreen – small lane or roadway
Bronze Age – earliest metal-using period, around 2500 BC to 300 BC in Ireland; after the Stone Age and before the Iron Age
B-specials – Northern Irish auxiliary police force, disbanded in 1971
bullaun – stone with a depression, probably used as a mortar for grinding medicine or food and often found on monastic sites

CAC IRA – Continuity Army Council of the IRA, a breakaway group
caher – circular area enclosed by stone walls
cairn – mound of stones heaped over a prehistoric grave
cashel – stone-walled circular fort; see also *ráth*
cath – literally 'battle'; Irish place name
céilidh – session of traditional music and dancing; also called ceili
Celtic Tiger – nickname of the Irish economy during the growth years from 1990 to about 2002

Celts – Iron-Age warrior tribes that arrived in Ireland around 300 BC and controlled the country for 1000 years
ceol – music
cha – slang term for tea, as in a 'cup of cha'
champ – a dish of mashed potatoes with spring onions or leeks
chancel – eastern end of a church, where the altar is situated, reserved for the clergy and choir
chipper – slang term for fish 'n' chips fast-food restaurant
cill – literally 'church'; Irish place name; also known as kill
cillín – literally 'little cell'; a hermitage, or sometimes a small, isolated burial ground for unbaptised children and other 'undesirables'
Claddagh ring – ring worn in much of Connaught since the mid-18th century, with a crowned heart nestling between two hands; if the heart points towards the hand then the wearer is taken or married, towards the fingertip means he or she is looking for a mate
clochán – circular stone building, shaped like an old-fashioned beehivem, from the early Christian period
Connaught – one of the four ancient provinces of Ireland, made up of counties Galway, Leitrim, Mayo, Roscommon and Sligo; sometimes spelt Connacht.
Continuity IRA – anti-Agreement splinter republican group, opposed to any deal not based on a united Ireland
control zone – area of a town centre (usually the main street) where parked cars must not, for security reasons, be left unattended
craic – conversation, gossip, fun, good times; also known as crack
crannóg – artificial island made in a lake to provide habitation in a good defensive position
crios – multicoloured woven woollen belt traditionally worn in the Aran Islands
cromlech – see *dolmen*
cú – dog
culchie – derogatory nickname used by Dubliners for anyone not from the capital
currach – rowing boat made of a framework of laths covered with tarred canvas; also known as cúrach

Dáil – lower house of the Republic of Ireland Parliament
dairtheach – oratory, a small room set aside for private prayer
DART – Dublin Area Rapid Transport train line
delft – glazed blue-and-white earthenware from Holland; in Ireland the word refers to any kind of dishware
demesne – landed property close to a house or castle
diamond – town square

dolmen – tomb chamber or portal tomb made of vertical stones topped by a huge capstone; from around 2000 BC
draoícht – enchantment
drumlin – rounded hill formed by retreating glaciers
Dúchas – government department in charge of parks, monuments and gardens in the Republic; formerly known as the Office of Public Works
dún – fort, usually constructed of stone
DUP – Democratic Unionist Party; founded principally by Ian Paisley in 1971 in hard-line opposition to unionist policies as held by the UUP

Éire – Irish name for the Republic of Ireland
esker – gravel ridge

Fáilte Ireland – literally 'Welcome Board'; Irish Tourist Board
Fianna – mythical band of warriors who feature in many tales of ancient Ireland
Fianna Fáil – literally 'Warriors of Ireland'; a major political party in the Republic of Ireland, originating from the Sinn Féin faction opposed to the 1921 treaty with Britain
Fine Gael – literally 'Tribe of the Gael'; a major political party in the Republic, originating from the Sinn Féin faction that favoured the 1921 treaty with Britain; formed the first government of independent Ireland
fir – men (singular fear); sign on men's toilets
fleadh – festival
fulacht fiadh – Bronze-Age cooking place

Gaeltacht – Irish-speaking
gallery grave – tunnel-shaped burial chamber
gallóglí – mercenary soldiers of the 14th to 15th century; anglicised to gallowglasses
garda – Irish Republic police; plural gardaí
ghillie – fishing or hunting guide; also known as ghilly
gob – mouth; from Irish word gob, meaning bird's beak or bill
gort – literally 'field'; Irish place name
grá – love

Hibernia – literally 'Land of Winter'; Roman name for Ireland (the Romans had confused Ireland with Iceland)
hill fort – a hilltop fortified with ramparts and ditches, usually dating from the Iron Age
HINI – Hostelling International of Northern Ireland
húicéir – traditional Galway vessel; also known as a hooker
hurling – Irish sport similar to hockey
Hunger, the – how the Irish sometimes refer to the Great Famine of 1845–49

Iarnród Éireann – Republic of Ireland Railways
INLA – Irish National Liberation Association; formed in 1975 as an IRA splinter group unhappy at the cease-fire; it has maintained its own cease-fire since 1998

IRA – Irish Republican Army; the largest republican paramilitary organisation, founded 80 years ago with the aim to fight for a united Ireland; in 1969 the IRA split into the Official IRA and the Provisional IRA; the Official IRA is no longer active and the PIRA has become the IRA
IRB – Irish Republican Brotherhood; a secret society founded in 1858 and revived in the early 20th century; believed in independence, through violence if necessary, and was a precursor to the IRA; also known as the Fenians
Iron Age – in Ireland this lasted from the end of the Bronze Age, around 300 BC (the arrival of the Celts), to the arrival of Christianity, around the 5th century AD

jackeen – derogatory nickname used to describe anyone from Dublin; originally used to describe Dubliners who waved Union Jacks during Queen Victoria's visit in 1901
jarvey – driver of a jaunting car
jaunting car – Killarney's traditional horse-drawn transport

knackered – slang for tired or worn out

Leinster – one of the four ancient provinces of Ireland, made up of counties Carlow, Dublin, Kildare, Kilkenny, Laois, Longford, Louth, Meath, Offaly, West Meath, Wexford and Wicklow
leithreas – toilets
leprechaun – mischievous elf or sprite from Irish folklore
lough – lake, long narrow bay or arm of the sea
loyalist – person, usually a Northern Irish Protestant, insisting on the continuation of Northern Ireland's links with Britain
loyalist orders – consists mainly of the Orange Order and the Apprentice Boys committed to the union with the UK
Luas – Light Rail Transit system in Dublin; Irish for 'speed'
LVF – Loyalist Volunteer Force; an extreme loyalist paramilitary group opposed to the current peace process. It has been on cease-fire since 1998

marching season – Orange Order parades, which take place from Easter and throughout summer to celebrate the victory by Protestant King William III of Orange over Catholic James II in the Battle of the Boyne on 12 July 1690, and the union with Britain
Mesolithic – also known as the Middle Stone Age; time of the first human settlers in Ireland, about 8000 BC to 4000 BC
midden – refuse heap left by a prehistoric settlement
mná – women; sign on women's toilets
motte – early Norman fortification consisting of a raised, flattened mound with a keep on top; when attached to a bailey it is known as a motte-and-bailey fort, many of which were built in Ireland until the early 13th century
Munster – one of the four ancient provinces of Ireland, made up of counties Clare, Cork, Kerry, Limerick, Tipperary and Waterford

naomh – holy or saint

nationalism – belief in a reunited Ireland

nationalist – proponent of a united Ireland

Neolithic – also known as the New Stone Age; a period characterised by settled agriculture lasting from around 4000 BC to 2500 BC in Ireland; followed by the Bronze Age

NIR – Northern Ireland Railways

NITB – Northern Ireland Tourist Board

NNR – National Nature Reserves

NUI – National University of Ireland; made up of branches in Dublin, Cork, Galway and Limerick

North, the – political entity of Northern Ireland, not the northernmost geographic part of Ireland

Ogham stone – Ogham was the earliest form of writing in Ireland, using a variety of notched strokes placed above, below or across a keyline, usually on stone

Oireachtas – Parliament of the Republic, consisting of a lower and upper house, the Dáil and Senate

Orange Order – founded in 1795, the Orange Order is the largest Protestant organisation in Northern Ireland with a membership of up to 100,000; name commemorates the victory of King William of Orange in the Battle of the Boyne

Orangemen – members of the Orange Order; must be male

óstán – hotel

Palladian – style of architecture developed by Andrea Palladio (1508-80) based on ancient Roman architecture

paramilitaries – armed illegal organisations, either loyalist or republican, usually associated with the use of violence and crime for political and economic gain

Partition – division of Ireland in 1921

passage grave – Celtic tomb with a chamber reached by a narrow passage, typically buried in a mound

penal laws – laws passed in the 18th century forbidding Catholics from buying land and holding public office

Plantation – settlement of Protestant migrants (sometimes known as Planters) in Ireland in the 17th century

PSNI – Police Service of Northern Ireland

poteen – illegally brewed potato-based firewater

Prod – slang for Northern Irish Protestant

provisionals – Provisional IRA, formed after a break with the official IRA who are now largely inconsequential; named after the provisional government declared in 1916, they have been the main force combating the British army in the North; also known as provos

PUP – Progressive Unionist Party; a small unionist party seen as a political front for the UVF, it is pro the Good Friday Agreement

rashers – Irish bacon

ráth – circular fort with earth banks around a timber wall

Real IRA – splinter movement of the IRA and opposed to Sinn Féin's support of the Good Friday Agreement; the

Real IRA was responsible for the Omagh bombing in 1998 in which 29 people died; subsequently called a cease-fire but has been responsible for bombs in Britain and other acts of violence

Red Hand Commandos – illegal loyalist paramilitary group

Red Hand Defenders – breakaway loyalist paramilitary group formed in 1998 by dissident UFF and LVF members

Republic of Ireland – the 26 counties of the South

republican – supporter of a united Ireland

republicanism – belief in a united Ireland, sometimes referred to as militant nationalism

rí – petty kings

ring fort – circular habitation area surrounded by banks and ditches, used from the Bronze Age right through to the Middle Ages, particularly in the early Christian period

RTE – Radio Telefís Éireann; the national broadcasting service of the Republic of Ireland, with two TV and four radio stations

RUC – Royal Ulster Constabulary, the former name for the armed Police Service of Northern Ireland (PSNI)

sassenach – Irish word for Saxon, used to refer to anyone from England

SDLP – Social Democratic and Labour Party; the largest nationalist party in the Northern Ireland Assembly, instrumental in achieving the Good Friday Agreement; its goal is a united Ireland through nonviolent means; mostly Catholic

seisún – music session

sept – clan

shamrock – three-leafed plant said to have been used by St Patrick to illustrate the Holy Trinity

shebeen – from the Irish *síbín*; illicit drinking place or speakeasy

sheila-na-gig – literally 'Sheila of the teats'; female figure with exaggerated genitalia, carved in stone on the exteriors of some churches and castles; various explanations have been offered for the iconography, ranging from male clerics warning against the perils of sex to the idea that they represent Celtic war goddesses

shillelagh – stout club or cudgel, especially one made of oak or blackthorn

shinners – mildly derogatory nickname of members of Sinn Féin

Sinn Féin – literally 'We Ourselves'; a republican party with the long-term aim of a united Ireland; seen as the political wing of the IRA but it maintains that both organisations are completely separate

slí – hiking trail or way

snug – partitioned-off drinking area in a pub

souterrain – underground chamber usually associated with ring and hill forts; probably provided a hiding place or escape route in times of trouble and/or storage space for goods

South, the – Republic of Ireland
standing stone – upright stone set in the ground, common across Ireland and dating from a variety of periods; some are burial markers

tánaiste – Republic of Ireland deputy prime minister
taoiseach – Republic of Ireland prime minister
TD – *teachta Dála;* member of the Republic of Ireland Parliament
teampall – church
Tinkers – derogatory term used to describe Irish gypsies, communities that roam the country; see also *Travellers*
trá – beach or strand
Travellers – the politically correct term used today to describe Ireland's itinerant communities
Treaty – Anglo-Irish Treaty of 1921, which divided Ireland and gave relative independence to the South; cause of the 1922–23 Civil War
trian – district
Tricolour – green, white and orange Irish flag designed to symbolise the hoped-for union of the green Catholic Southern Irish with the orange Protestant Northern Irish
turlough – from the Irish *turlach;* a small lake that often disappears in dry summers

UDA – Ulster Defence Association; the largest loyalist paramilitary group; it has observed a cease-fire since 1994
UDP – Ulster Democratic Party; a small fringe unionist party with links to the banned loyalist UFF

UFF – Ulster Freedom Fighters, aka the Ulster Defence Association; this group is pro the Good Friday Agreement and has been on cease-fire since 1994
uillean pipes – Irish bagpipes with a bellow strapped to the arm; uillean is Irish for 'elbow'
Ulster – one of the four ancient provinces of Ireland; a term sometimes used to describe the six counties of the North, despite the fact that Ulster also includes counties Cavan, Monaghan and Donegal in the Republic
unionism – belief in the political union with Britain
unionist – person who wants to retain Northern Ireland's links with Britain
United Irishmen – organisation founded in 1791 aiming to reduce British power in Ireland; it led a series of unsuccessful risings and invasions
UUP – Ulster Unionist Party; the largest unionist party in Northern Ireland and the majority party in the Assembly, founded by Edward Carson; once the monolithic unionist organisation but now under threat from the *DUP*
UVF – Ulster Volunteer Force; an illegal loyalist Northern Irish paramilitary organisation

Volunteers – offshoot of the IRB that came to be known as the IRA

whisht – hush, keep quiet

yoke – general term for 'thing', as in 'would you give me that yoke?'

The Authors

FIONN DAVENPORT
Coordinating Author

Fionn ran away from Ireland at every opportunity, but could never stay away long. Paris was a pleasant distraction, New York kept him busy for awhile, but after each time he would land at Dublin, jump out of the rain into a taxi, stare at the grey mess of landscape between the airport and the city and ask himself what the hell he was doing. The answer has changed over the years: nowadays it has less to do with better squats and more to do with quality of life. For this edition, Fionn wrote Destination Ireland, Getting Started, Itineraries, History, Culture, Dublin, County Wicklow, Directory, Transport and Health.

JAMES BAINBRIDGE
Counties Wexford & Waterford, Kerry

James' first encounter with Ireland was a teenage jaunt to a music festival held in Tipperary and nicknamed 'Trip to Tip'. It was there that he learnt the ways of the trad session…and those of peach schnapps, unfortunately. Nonetheless, he's been a regular visitor to Ireland ever since, covering all the important spots: Dublin, Belfast and Ballycastle, County Antrim. Having researched some far-flung destinations for Lonely Planet, this time the Shropshire lad happily took a shorter trip to a land closer to his English home. He was well prepared for a month among the blarney-prone Celts by four years at the University of Glasgow, where most of his friends hailed from County Tyrone.

AMANDA CANNING
Food & Drink, Irish Kitchen, County Cork

Amanda has been hopping between her native England and Ireland since the media hype surrounding Dublin first lured her over in the 1990s. Since then she's fallen over at the Giants' Causeway, wished she'd gone to college in Belfast, eaten the finest cheese known to mankind in Cork and furtively swigged *poitín* in county Cavan. One day she hopes that the opening of a small, independent whiskey distillery will be the reason for her visit. While Amanda has commissioned the Ireland book from Lonely Planet's London office, this is her first time researching and writing it.

LONELY PLANET AUTHORS

Why is our travel information the best in the world? It's simple: our authors are independent, dedicated travellers. They don't research using just the internet or phone, and they don't take freebies in exchange for positive coverage. They travel widely, to all the popular spots and off the beaten track. They personally visit thousands of hotels, restaurants, cafés, bars, galleries, palaces, museums and more – and they take pride in getting all the details right, and telling it how it is. Think you can do it? Find out how at lonelyplanet.com.

TOM DOWNS
Environment, Ireland Outdoors, Counties Mayo & Sligo, Donegal

Tom's a Yank with some Irish in him. His great grandparents and some great uncles and aunts migrated from County West Meath in the 1890s and they settled in Iowa. Fortunately for Tom, his grandfather wasn't cut out for farming and moved to San Francisco. Tom makes regular visits to Ireland to have a few decent pints with the locals. Once, he spotted a highway sign in County West Meath that said 'Downs 10km'. He followed a winding road twice that distance but saw nothing but empty pastures. Counties Donegal and Mayo are his favourite parts of Ireland.

CATHERINE LE NEVEZ
Central North, County Galway

Catherine's wanderlust kicked in when she road-tripped Europe aged four, and she's been hitting the road at every opportunity since, completing her Doctorate of Creative Arts in Writing; Masters in Professional Writing; and post-grad qualifications in Editing and Publishing along the way.

Catherine's Celtic connections include Irish and Breton heritage as well as Irish mates who forewarned her that Ireland would be a grand country if it had a roof; and that the Guinness tastes better than anywhere else on earth. Catherine's since crisscrossed Ireland for several Lonely Planet gigs, discovering that the Guinness tastes so much better it more than makes up for the rain.

RYAN VER BERKMOES
Central South, Counties Limerick & Tipperary, Kilkenny, Clare, Meath & Louth

From Clare to Louth, with plenty of delights in between, Ryan Ver Berkmoes begs to differ with the Irish tourism official (of all people!) who called his territory 'the hole in the donut'. If you're sick of twee green crap in gift shops and want to experience the often-elusive 'real Ireland', he'd recommend his 10 counties in less time than it takes to pour a pint. Much less time. He's been doing this since he first roamed the hinterlands almost 25 years ago. From lost rural pubs to lost memory, he's revelled in a place where his first name brings a smile and his surname brings a 'huh?'

NEIL WILSON
Belfast, Counties Down & Armagh, Derry & Antrim, Fermanagh & Tyrone

Neil's first visit to Northern Ireland was in 1994, during the first flush of post-ceasefire optimism, and his interest in the history and politics of the place intensified a few years later when he found out that most of his mum's ancestors were from Ulster. Working on recent editions of Lonely Planet's *Ireland* guidebook has allowed him to witness first-hand the progress being made towards a lasting peace, and he was amazed to see Ian Paisley and Martin McGuinness sitting down together in Stormont in 2007. Neil is a full-time travel writer based in Edinburgh, Scotland, and has written more than 40 guidebooks for half a dozen publishers.

Behind the Scenes

THIS BOOK

Back in 1994, the first edition of *Ireland* was written by Jon Murray, Sean Sheehan and Tony Wheeler. The last (7th) edition was written by Fionn Davenport, Charlotte Beech, Tom Downs, Des Hannigan, Fran Parnell and Neil Wilson. This 8th edition was coordinated by Fionn (his fifth time on the book; second as coordinating author), with Neil and Tom joining us again too; the team was rounded out by James Bainbridge, Amanda Canning, Catherine Le Nevez and Ryan Ver Berkmoes.

This guidebook was commissioned in Lonely Planet's London office, and produced by the following:

Commissioning Editors Fiona Buchan, Janine Eberle
Coordinating Editor Dianne Schallmeiner
Coordinating Cartographer Valentina Kremenchutskaya

Coordinating Layout Designer Jacqui Saunders
Managing Editors Katie Lynch, Suzannah Shwer
Managing Cartographer Mark Griffiths
Managing Layout Designer Celia Wood
Assisting Editors Susie Ashworth, Yvonne Byron, Gennifer Ciavarra, Chris Girdler, Annelies Mertens, Averil Robertson, Laura Stansfeld, Louisa Syme, Phillip Tang, Fionnuala Twomey, Helen Yeates
Assisting Cartographers Hunor Csutoros, Corey Hutchison, Kusnandar, Jacqueline Nguyen, Andy Rojas, Amanda Sierp
Cover Designer Jane Hart
Colour Layout Designer Yvonne Bischofberger
Project Manager Craig Kilburn
Language Content Coordinator Quentin Frayne

Thanks to Jennifer Garrett, Mark Germanchis, Liz Heynes, Adam McCrow, Darren O'Connoll, Trent Paton, Jane Rawson, Lyahna Spencer, Simon Tillema

---

LONELY PLANET: TRAVEL WIDELY, TREAD LIGHTLY, GIVE SUSTAINABLY

The Lonely Planet Story

The story begins with a classic travel adventure: Tony and Maureen Wheeler's 1972 journey across Europe and Asia to Australia. There was no useful information about the overland trail then, so Tony and Maureen published the first Lonely Planet guidebook to meet a growing need.

From a kitchen table, Lonely Planet has grown to become the largest independent travel publisher in the world, with offices in Melbourne (Australia), Oakland (USA) and London (UK). Today Lonely Planet guidebooks cover the globe. There is an ever-growing list of books and information in a variety of media. Some things haven't changed. The main aim is still to make it possible for adventurous individuals to get out there – to explore and better understand the world.

The Lonely Planet Foundation

The Lonely Planet Foundation proudly supports nimble nonprofit institutions working for change in the world. Each year the foundation donates 5% of Lonely Planet company profits to projects selected by staff and authors. Our partners range from Kabissa, which provides small nonprofits across Africa with access to technology, to the Foundation for Developing Cambodian Orphans, which supports girls at risk of falling victim to sex traffickers.

Our nonprofit partners are linked by a grass-roots approach to the areas of health, education or sustainable tourism. Many projects we support – such as one with BaAka (Pygmy) children in the forested areas of Central African Republic – choose to focus on women and children as one of the most effective ways to support the whole community.

Sometimes foundation assistance is as simple as helping to preserve a local ruin like the Minaret of Jam in Afghanistan; this incredible monument now draws intrepid tourists to the area and its restoration has greatly improved options for local people.

Just as travel is often about learning to see with new eyes, so many of the groups we work with aim to change the way people see themselves and the future for their children and communities.

THANKS
JAMES BAINBRIDGE
Slainte to the following: the Edwardses in Annestown, Chris in Wexford, Allan Jones and Ballymaloe Cookery School, Arthur at Hotel Naomh Seosamh, Billy Colfer and all at Hook Head, the Kennedy Homestead, MacMurrough Farm Hostel; Johnny Maguire, Richard Clancy and Neptune's in Killarney, Miffy in Kenmare, Nora and Jim in Listowel, Michael and Sue in Killorglin, the tourist office, Gráinne and Martin in Dingle, Tralee tourist office, Garry and Ryle at Baily's Corner; Janine, Fionn and the other members of the 'LP Blarney Stone'; Kieron, Jamie and Carl for orchestral interpretations of Aphex Twin, scarlet fever and mobile phone credit.

AMANDA CANNING
Thanks, particularly, to Darina Allen, Frank Hederman, Veronica Steele, Seamus O'Hara and Peter Lyall for giving up their time and imparting their enthusiasm for the best of Cork's food and drink. Thanks also to all those incredibly helpful souls at tourist offices across the county. Finally, high-fives to all those people who dished out directions and cups of tea as I circled, hopelessly lost, round those confusing Cork roads. If it weren't for them, I'd still be sat, frowning and slightly tearful, somewhere between the R629 and R632 right now.

TOM DOWNS
In Ireland, thanks must go to Brendan Rohan, Angelique Rohan, Desmond Donnellan, Peter Byrne, Neil D Grant, Liam of Buncrana, Michael Quirke, Karen McGlinchey, Mary Kearney, Margaret Collins, Gerry Collins, Pat Geagan and a hitchhiker named Johnny Donaghue, who let himself into my car near Belmullet and chatted my ear off for about an hour. I'd also like to tip my hat to the knowledgeable gents who were digging the ditch in Achill, one of whom identified himself as 'king of the island'. Hope your concert in Cleveland was a huge success. At Lonely Planet, I'd like to thank my good friends Fiona Buchan, Janine Eberle, Mark Griffiths, Dianne Schallmeiner and Fionnuala Twomey.

CATHERINE LE NEVEZ
Sláinte to all who provided insights and inspiration: Declan Sharkey, Cormac and Diarmaid O'Culain, Helen O'Grady, Tony Tracy, Ronan Brennan, Aidan Murphy and family, Ciara O'Mahony, Lorraine and PJ on Inishmór, the kind locals who warmed me up with coffee on Inisheer and Inishmaan, Aoife Ní Thuairisg, Louise in Carrickmacross, Gerry Greensmyth, Jim Tierney, David Kelly, Vincent Queenan,

and Damien for the pint-pouring lessons (and the pints!). Cheers too to Regan and Janine for great contacts. At Lonely Planet, major thanks to Fiona Buchan, Janine Eberle, Mark Griffiths, and Fionn and the Ireland team. As ever, *merci surtout* to my family.

RYAN VER BERKMOES
Shamrocks aplenty to the many who made this such a delightful project. In Ireland, Emma Gorman, Tracey Coughlin et al were helpful and a special shout-out to the librarians of Nenagh who, like their colleagues everywhere, offered enthusiastic advice that was invaluable. I also enjoyed more companionship than usual: Ian Posthumous, who learned the real meaning of attitude and authority over pints in Kilkenny; Paula Fentiman, who put the wild in goose; Alevtina Chernorukova, whose stones had blarney; Paul McGinn and clan, who have been friends forever; Janine Eberle who put the head in my pint; and Erin Corrigan, my Irish honey. Also, Helena Kallianiotes, the Portland-based Shins, and Decemberists all provided needed diversion.

NEIL WILSON
Thanks to the friendly and helpful tourist office staff all over Northern Ireland, to black cab tour guide Ken Harper, to the Bogside Artists, to Stepanie Sim-Doran of the RSPB, and to Carol Downie, as ever, for support and company on the road.

OUR READERS
Many thanks to the travellers who used the last edition and wrote to us with helpful hints, useful advice and interesting anecdotes:

Timo Agema, Bernard Allan, Mary Annett, Carolina Baker, Lella Baker, Lisa Barrell, Felicity Barrow, Jeff Bedsole, Laurence Belgrave, Jim Bleasdale, Cathy Bolger, Jeanette Bolliger, Samuel Borrego, Anthony Butler, Shelley Chick-Gravel, Dean Clark, Cherry Cormack-Loyd, John Crofton, Johanna Cullen, Neil Cullen, John Cunningham, Elodie Darmani, Payal Doctor, Geoff Doran, Timothy Douglas, Adam Dowden, Maureen Downes, Steve Draper, Kevin Duff, Kate Duffy, Pauline Emberson, Matthew English, Hilary Ewell, Paul Fatt, Heike Fehrholz, Chiara Ferrari, Stephan Flake, Nicole Fornasier, Geer Furtjes, Keith Garrett, Hana Geha, Danny Gibson, Richard Gill, Jean Ginot, Letja De Goede, Rui Gonçalves, Frieda Goovaerts, Brian Gosling, Paul Green, Laura Griffin, I Hamiltan, Harry Hauber, Susan Hickey, Shirley Hooijinga, Kim Hornix, Niall Hughes, Jordan Ingram, Tamara Jackson, Casey Johnson, C Jordan, Pauliina Kankainen, Alistair King, Brand King, Esther Kleine, Cornelia Knopp, Sophia Koch, Eva Koehler, Esther Lee, Richard Lilly, Urban Lindell, Lois Lindley, Christoph Luhn, David Lynch, Dugald Macfarlane, Peter Marshall, Sonja Maurus, Adrian

SEND US YOUR FEEDBACK

We love to hear from travellers – your comments keep us on our toes and help make our books better. Our well-travelled team reads every word on what you loved or loathed about this book. Although we cannot reply individually to postal submissions, we always guarantee that your feedback goes straight to the appropriate authors, in time for the next edition. Each person who sends us information is thanked in the next edition – and the most useful submissions are rewarded with a free book. See the Behind the Scenes section.

To send us your updates – and find out about Lonely Planet events, newsletters and travel news – visit our award-winning website: **www.lonelyplanet.com/contact**.

Note: we may edit, reproduce and incorporate your comments in Lonely Planet products such as guidebooks, websites and digital products, so let us know if you don't want your comments reproduced or your name acknowledged. For a copy of our privacy policy, go to www.lonelyplanet .com/privacy.

McCarthy, Fiona Mclean, Deborah McQuaid, Karin Meister, Adrien de Mello, Brenda Millar, Heather Monell, Vicky Montcalm, Fabio Moscati, Breandán Murray, Ryan Mykita, Ruth Nevin, Paula New, Marina Nichelson, Hugh O'Beirne, Annicke O'Gara, Anne O'Shea, Penny Oakley, Jaime Odonovan, Anke Osterkamp, Phanis Pashos, Claudia Pfalzer, Mario Pichler, Karen Piotrowski, Anna Ptaszynska, Kathy Ramsey, Stacey Reherman, Gaylene Reisima, John Richards, Roger Robinson, Emily Rondel, Ashley Roof, Amanda Root, Belinda Roy, Catherine Savage, Alexandra Scheelke, Dieter Schwab, Tim & Jacqui Sherman, Matt Simington, Melanie Singleton, Gael Smits, Mick Speight, Eileen Stevens, Liam Stirrat, Danny Sullivan, Kerry

Sullivan, Sharon Sullivan, Rachel Thompson, Michelle Thorpe, Andrea & Mirka Torreggiani, Joanna Tracey, E van Power, Andy van Stokkum, Els Veldkamp, Jacinta Walpole, Pam Weber, Joshua Welbaum, Ellie Wendell, Ken Westmoreland, Stefan Wimmer, Inga Wolfgramm, Erika Zarate

ACKNOWLEDGMENTS

Many thanks to the following for the use of their content:

Globe on title page ©Mountain High Maps 1993 Digital Wisdom, Inc.

Index

000 Map pages
000 Photograph pages

INDEX

INDEX

INDEX

000 Map pages
000 Photograph pages

Rothe House 327
Russborough House 157-8
Strokestown Park House 488
Westport House & Country Park 447
Steam Museum & Lodge Park Walled
  Garden 343
Steele, Veronica 244, 272-3
Stone of Destiny 550
Stonyford 335
Stormont 591
stout 102
Stradbally 355-6
Stradbally Steam Museum 355
Straffan 343-4
Straffan Butterfly Farm 343
Strandhill 469-70
Strangford 624
Strangford Lough 620-1
Streedagh 474
Strokestown 488-9
Strokestown Park House 488
Struell Wells 623
surfing 511, 569-70, 702
  Achill Island 454
  Ballinskelligs 264
  Bundoran 510-11, **569**
  Castlegregory 290-1
  Clonakilty 224
  Donegal 511
  Dungloe 519
  Easky 471
  Enniscrone 471
  Inch 293
  Kilkee 383
  Lahinch 386
  Lough Gartan 529
  Portrush 659
  Rossnowlagh 509
  Strandhill 469-70
  Tramore 192
sustainable travel 21-3
  accommodation 22
  GreenDex 759-61
  internet resources 22, 75
  itinerary 29, **29**
swimming 702
  Culdaff 537
  Dublin 112
  Mullingar 497
  Tramore 192
Swiss Cottage 314-15

000 Map pages
000 Photograph pages

T
Taafe's Castle 574
Talbot Castle 553-4
Tara 549-51
Tara Brooch 96
Tarbert 284
taxis 607
  black-taxi tours 593-4
T-Bay 192
telephone services 712-13
Temple Bar 94, **84**
Termonfeckin 573
theatre 63-4
Thomas, Dylan 387
Thomastown 334-5
Thoor Ballylee 438
Thuairisg, Aoife ní 426
Thurles 319-20
Timahoe 356
time 713, **762-3**
Tintern Abbey 177
Tipperary, County 307-21, **308**
Tipperary Heritage Way 314
Tipperary town 307-9
Titanic Quarter 586
Titanic, the 586, 609
toilets 713
Tollymore Forest Park 627
Tomb of Cooey-na-Gal 655
tombs 61
Tone, Theobald Wolfe 36-9
Torr Head 669
Tory Island 521-3
tourist information 713-14
tours 725, *see also* walking tours
  Belfast 593-4
  black taxi 593-4
  Cobh 214
  Cork 205
  Derry 650
  Dingle Peninsula 284-5
  Dublin 114-15
  Enniskillen 678
  Galway city 408-9
  Glendalough 154-5, **153**, 8
  Kilkenny 328
  Killarney National Park 256
  Powerscourt 149
  Skellig Islands 264
  Tara 551
  Viking 500
  Waterford 188
Tower Museum 643
Trá Mhóir 430
Trá na Rossan 531

train travel 725
Tralee 278-81, **279**
Tramore 191-3
Tramore Beach 517
trekking, *see* walking
Tremayne, Peter 312
Trim 551-5, **552**
Trim Castle 553-4
Trinity College 90-3, **91**
Troubles, the 44-5, 646
  movies 47
Tubbercurry 471
Tullamore 365-6
Tullamore Dew Heritage Centre 365
Tullynally Castle 499
Turlough Round Tower 461
Turoe Stone 439
TV 54-5, 694
Twelve Bens 429
Tyrone, County 689-93, **678-9**
Tyrone Crystal 692

U
U2 59
UFOs 489
Ulster American Folk Park 690
Ulster Folk Museum 609
Ulster Museum 587
Ulster Plantation 478
Ulster Transport Museum 609
Ulster Way: Donegal Section 700-1
Ulster Way: Northeastern Section 700
Union Hall 227

V
vacations 708-9
Vale of Avoca 164-5
Valentia Island 262
Vandeleur Walled Garden 381
vegetarian travellers 68
Ventry 294
video 694, 711
Vikings 170, 184-5, 337-8
  tours 500
Vinegar Hill 181-2
Virginia 482
visas 714, *see also* passports
visual arts 63
volunteering 714-15

W
walking 566-8, 698-701
  Achill Island 454
  Baltimore 229
  Beara Way 244, 698, **566**

INDEX

GreenDex

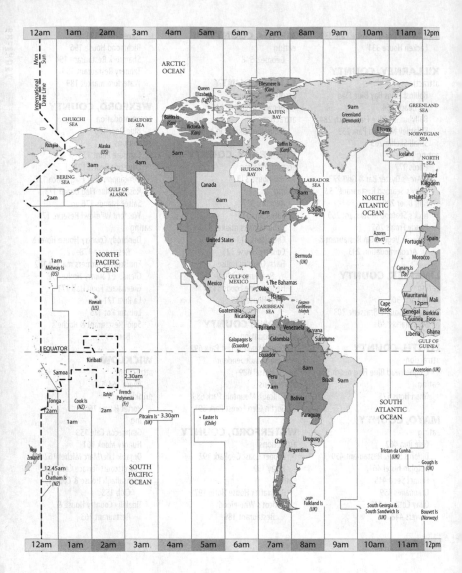

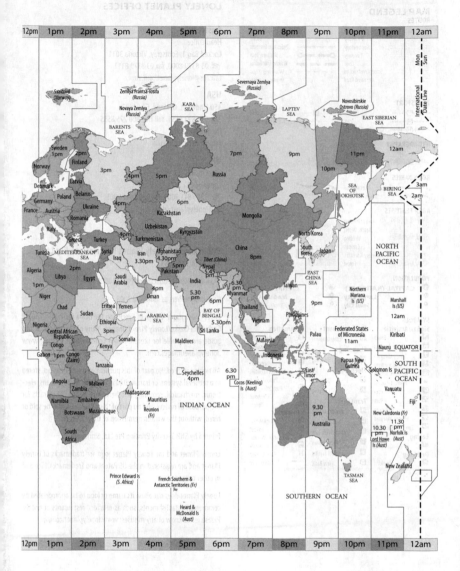

MAP LEGEND
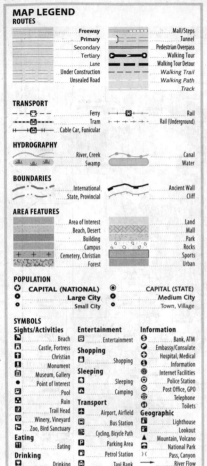

ROUTES

Freeway	Mall/Steps
Primary	Tunnel
Secondary	Pedestrian Overpass
Tertiary	Walking Tour
Lane	Walking Tour Detour
Under Construction	Walking Trail
Unsealed Road	Walking Path
	Track

TRANSPORT

Ferry	Rail
Tram	Rail (Underground)
Cable Car, Funicular	

HYDROGRAPHY

River, Creek	Canal
Swamp	Water

BOUNDARIES

International	Ancient Wall
State, Provincial	Cliff

AREA FEATURES

Area of Interest	Land
Beach, Desert	Mall
Building	Park
Campus	Rocks
Cemetery, Christian	Sports
Forest	Urban

POPULATION

○ CAPITAL (NATIONAL)	⊙ CAPITAL (STATE)
● Large City	⊙ Medium City
○ Small City	○ Town, Village

SYMBOLS

Sights/Activities	Entertainment	Information
Beach	Entertainment	Bank, ATM
Castle, Fortress	**Shopping**	Embassy/Consulate
Christian	Shopping	Hospital, Medical
Monument	**Sleeping**	Information
Museum, Gallery	Sleeping	Internet Facilities
Point of Interest	Camping	Police Station
Pool		Post Office, GPO
Ruin	**Transport**	Telephone
Trail Head	Airport, Airfield	Toilets
Winery, Vineyard	Bus Station	**Geographic**
Zoo, Bird Sanctuary	Cycling, Bicycle Path	Lighthouse
Eating	Parking Area	Lookout
Eating	Petrol Station	Mountain, Volcano
Drinking	Taxi Rank	National Park
Drinking		Pass, Canyon
		River Flow

LONELY PLANET OFFICES

Australia
Head Office
Locked Bag 1, Footscray, Victoria 3011
☎ 03 8379 8000, fax 03 8379 8111
talk2us@lonelyplanet.com.au

USA
150 Linden St, Oakland, CA 94607
☎ 510 893 8555, toll free 800 275 8555
fax 510 893 8572
info@lonelyplanet.com

UK
186 City Rd,
London EC1V 2QQ
☎ 020 7841 9000, fax 020 7841 9001
go@lonelyplanet.co.uk

Published by Lonely Planet Publications Pty Ltd
ABN 36 005 607 983

© Lonely Planet Publications Pty Ltd 2008

© photographers as indicated 2008

Cover photograph: Village of Eyeries on the Beara Peninsula, County Cork, Eoin Clarke/Lonely Planet Images. Many of the images in this guide are available for licensing from Lonely Planet Images: www .lonelyplanetimages.com.

Printed by SNP Security Printing Pte Ltd, Singapore

Although the authors and Lonely Planet have taken all reasonable care in preparing this book, we make no warranty about the accuracy or completeness of its content and, to the maximum extent permitted, disclaim all liability arising from its use.